The
Unfinished
Nation

A CONCISE HISTORY
OF THE AMERICAN PEOPLE

The
Unfinished
Nation

A CONCISE HISTORY
OF THE AMERICAN PEOPLE

Alan Brinkley

Columbia University

OVERTURE
BOOKS

McGraw-Hill, Inc.

New York   St. Louis   San Francisco   Auckland   Bogotá   Caracas
Lisbon   London   Madrid   Mexico   Milan   Montreal   New Delhi
Paris   San Juan   Singapore   Sydney   Tokyo   Toronto

THE UNFINISHED NATION: A Concise History of the American People

Adapted from *American History: A Survey*, by Brinkley, Current, Freidel, and Williams.

1 2 3 4 5 6 7 8 9 0 DOC DOC 9 0 9 8 7 6 5 4 3 2

ISBN 0-07-015033-8

This book was set in Janson by Black Dot, Inc.
R. R. Donnelley & Sons Company was printer and binder.
Maps were prepared by David Lindroth Inc.

Publisher: Roth Wilkofsky
Sponsoring Editor: Peter Labella
Associate Editor: Niels Aaboe
Editing Supervisor: Larry Goldberg
Designer: Wanda Siedlecka
Production Supervisor: Kathryn Porzio
Photo Editor: Elyse Rieder

Library of Congress Cataloging-in-Publication Data

Brinkley, Alan.
    The unfinished nation: a concise history of the American people /
    Alan Brinkley.
        p.   cm.
    Includes bibliographical references and index.
    ISBN 0-07-015033-8
    1. United States—History.   I. Title.
E178.1.B827   1993
973—dc20   92-26666

Contents

AMERICAN VOICES

DEBATING THE PAST

APPENDICES

List of Illustrations

List of Maps

Preface

The story of the American past, which is the subject of this book, is as contested today as it has been at any moment in its history. As the population of the United States becomes ever more diverse and as groups that once stood outside the view of scholarship thrust themselves into its center, historians are revealing the immense and, until recently, inadequately understood complexity of their country's past. The result has been the slow emergence of a richer and fuller history of the United States, but also a more fragmented and contentious one. That history offers a picture of a highly diverse people. It also provides a picture of a great nation.

Threading one's way through the many, conflicting demands of contemporary scholars and contemporary readers is no easy task. But I have tried in this book to find an acceptable middle ground between the claims of diversity and the claims of unity. The United States is, indeed, a nation of many cultures. We cannot understand its history without understanding the experiences of all the different groups that have shaped American society, without understanding the particular worlds that have developed within it based on race, gender, ethnicity, religion, class, or region.

But the United States is more than just a collection of different cultures. It is also a nation. And as important as understanding its diversity is understanding the forces that have drawn it together and allowed it to survive and flourish despite division. The United States has constructed a remarkably stable and enduring political system that touches the lives of all Americans. It has developed an immense, highly productive national economy that affects the working and consuming lives of virtually everyone. It has created a mass popular culture that colors the experiences and assumptions of almost all the American people, and the people of much of the rest of the world as well. One can admire these unifying forces for their contributions to America's considerable success as a nation, or condemn them for the ways they have contributed to inequality, injustice, and failure. But no one proposing to understand the history of the United States can afford to ignore them.

In the great historical narratives of the nineteenth and early twentieth centuries, the story of America moved smoothly and triumphantly from one clearly defined era to another, focusing on great events and great men and tracing the rise of national institutions. The late twentieth century has produced a different narrative, with frequent, sometimes jarring, changes of focus and direction. It devotes attention to private as well as public events, to failure as well as success, to difference as well as to unity. And yet it remains, in the end, a narrative, a story—newly complicated, perhaps, by our understanding of the many worlds of historical experience that once eluded us—but no less remarkable and compelling for those complications.

This book is an effort to tell this newer story of America for students of history and for general readers in a single, reasonably concise volume. It has its origins in a considerably larger book by Alan Brinkley, Richard N. Current, Frank Freidel, and T. Harry Williams, *American History: A Survey*, now in its eighth edition. But it is not simply an abridgment of that longer work. I have tried here to craft a new, more thematic, and more selective narrative that preserves the central elements of the larger text but presents a clearer and more readily accessible story. In addition to the central narrative (and the maps and illustrations that accompany it), readers will also find a collection of essays examining major interpretive debates among scholars; and they will find a series of excerpts from important or emblematic American autobiographies, journals, memoirs, and other works. Together, I hope, these elements will serve to introduce readers to enough different approaches to and areas of American history to make them aware of its extraordinary richness and diversity. I hope they will also give readers some sense of the shared experiences of Americans.

The title of this book, *The Unfinished Nation*, is meant to suggest several things. It is a reminder of America's exceptional diversity: of the degree to which, despite all the many efforts to build a single, uniform definition of the meaning of American nationhood, that meaning remains contested and diverse. It is a reference to the centrality of change in American history: to the way in which the nation has continually transformed itself and to how it continues to do so in our own time. And it is a description of the writing of American history itself, of the way historians are engaged in a continuing, ever unfinished, process of asking new questions of the past.

Many people contributed to this book: Chris Rogers, David Follmer, Niels Aaboe, Larry Goldberg, Roth Wilkofsky, and Peter Labella at McGraw-Hill; Ashbel Green at Knopf; Yanek Mieczkowski, my research assistant at Columbia; and several anonymous scholars who read and commented on the manuscript and saved me from many errors and inelegancies. I am grateful to them all. I will also be grateful to any readers who wish to offer comments, criticisms, and corrections as I prepare future editions. Suggestions can be sent to me in care of the Department of History, Columbia University, New York, NY 10027; I will respond to them as fully and constructively as I can.

ALAN BRINKLEY

The
Unfinished
Nation

A CONCISE HISTORY
OF THE AMERICAN PEOPLE

CHAPTER ONE

The Meeting of Cultures

America Before Columbus ~ *Europe Looks Westward*
The Arrival of the English

T HE DISCOVERY OF America did not begin with Christopher Columbus. It started many thousands of years earlier when human beings
first crossed an ancient land bridge over the Bering Strait into what is now
Alaska and—almost certainly without realizing it—began to people a new
continent.

AMERICA BEFORE COLUMBUS

No one is certain when these migrations began; recent estimates suggest
that they started between 14,000 and 16,000 years ago. They were probably
a result of the development of new stone-tipped spears and other hunting
implements that made it possible for humans to pursue the large animals
that regularly crossed between Asia and North America. Year after year, a
few at a time, these nomadic peoples—apparently drawn from a Mongolian
stock similar to that of modern-day eastern Siberia—entered the new
continent and moved deeper into its heart. Perhaps as early as 8000 B.C., the
migrations reached the southern tip of South America. By the end of the
fifteenth century A.D., when the first important contact with Europeans
occurred, America was the home of many millions of men and women.
Scholars estimate that well over 10 million people lived in South America
by 1500 and that perhaps 4 million lived in the territory that now constitutes
the United States.

The Civilizations of the South

The most elaborate of these societies emerged in South and Central America and in Mexico. In Peru, the Incas created a powerful empire of perhaps 6 million people. They developed a complex political system and a large network of paved roads that welded together the populations of many tribes under a single government. In Central America and on the Yucatan peninsula of Mexico, the Mayas built a sophisticated culture with a written language, a numerical system similar to the Arabic, an accurate calendar, and an advanced agricultural system. They were succeeded by the Aztecs, a once-nomadic warrior tribe from the north. In the late thirteenth century, the Aztecs established a precarious rule over much of central and southern Mexico and built elaborate administrative, educational, and medical systems comparable to the most advanced in Europe at the time. The Aztecs also developed a harsh religion that required human sacrifice. Their Spanish conquerors discovered the skulls of 100,000 victims in one location when they arrived in 1519.

The economies of these societies were based primarily on agriculture, but there were also substantial cities. Tenochtitlán, the Aztec capital built on the site of present-day Mexico City, had a population of over 100,000 in 1500, which was comparable to some of the largest European cities of the time. The Mayas (at Mayapan and elsewhere) and the Incas (in such cities as Cuzco and Machu Picchu) produced elaborate settlements with striking religious and ceremonial structures. These civilizations accomplished all this without some of the important technologies that Asian and European civilizations possessed. As late as the sixteenth century, no American society had yet developed wheeled vehicles.

The Civilizations of the North

The peoples north of Mexico—in the lands that became the United States and Canada—developed less elaborate but still substantial civilizations and political systems. Inhabitants of the northern regions of the continent subsisted on hunting, gathering, fishing, or some combination of the three. They included the Eskimos of the Arctic Circle, who fished and hunted seals and whose civilization spanned thousands of miles of largely frozen land; the big-game hunters of the northern forests, who led nomadic lives based on pursuit of moose and caribou; the tribes of the Pacific Northwest, whose principal occupation was salmon fishing and who created substantial permanent settlements along the coast; and a group of tribes spread through relatively arid regions of the Far West who developed successful communities, many of them quite wealthy and densely populated, based on fishing, hunting small game, and gathering edible seeds, roots, and other plant materials.

Other societies in North America were primarily agricultural. Among the most developed were those in the Southwest. The people of that arid region built large irrigation systems, and they constructed substantial towns of stone and adobe structures. In the Great Plains region, too, most tribes were engaged in sedentary farming (corn and other grains) and lived in large permanent settlements, although there were some small nomadic tribes that subsisted by hunting buffalo.

The Eastern third of what is now the United States—much of it covered with forests and inhabited by the Woodland Indians—had the greatest food resources of any area of the continent. The many tribes of the region engaged in farming, hunting, gathering, and fishing simultaneously. In the South there were substantial permanent settlements and large trading networks based on the corn and other grains grown in the rich lands of the Mississippi River valley. The city of Cahokia (near present-day St. Louis), was a large trading center. At its peak in A.D. 1200 it had a population of 40,000.

The agricultural societies of the Northeast were less stationary. Farming techniques there were designed to exploit the land quickly rather than to develop permanent settlements. Many of the tribes living east of the Mississippi River were linked together loosely by common linguistic roots. The largest of these language groups consisted of the Algonquin tribes, which lived along the Atlantic seaboard from Canada to Virginia; the Iroquois Confederation, which was centered in what is now upstate New York; and the Muskogean, which consisted of the tribes in the southernmost region of the Eastern seaboard. Alliances among the various Indian societies (even among those with common languages) were fragile, since the peoples of the Americas did not think of themselves as members of a single civilization. When Europeans arrived and began to threaten their way of life, tribes only rarely were able to unite in opposition to white encroachments.

In the last centuries before the arrival of Europeans, native Americans—like peoples in other areas of the world—were experiencing an agricultural revolution. In all areas of what is now the United States (if in varying degrees from place to place), tribes were becoming more sedentary and were developing new sources of food, clothing, and shelter. Most regions were experiencing significant population growth. And virtually all were developing the sorts of elaborate social customs and rituals that only relatively stationary societies can produce. Religion was as important to Indian society

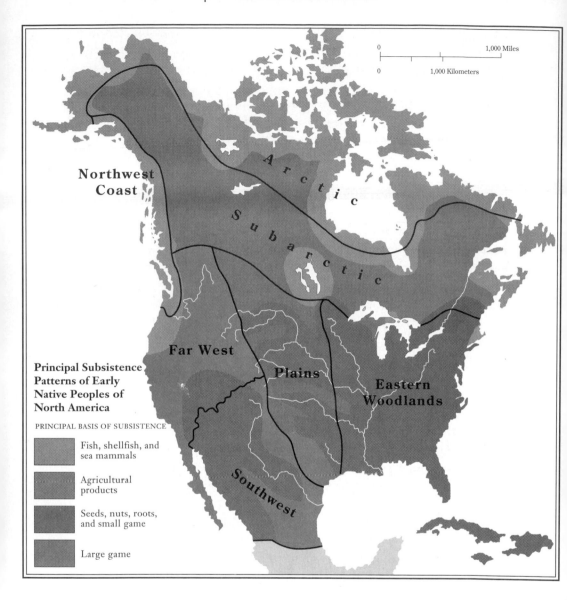

Principal Subsistence Patterns of Early Native Peoples of North America

PRINCIPAL BASIS OF SUBSISTENCE

Fish, shellfish, and sea mammals

Agricultural products

Seeds, nuts, roots, and small game

Large game

as it was to most other cultures and was usually closely bound up with the natural world on which the tribes depended. Native Americans worshiped many gods, whom they associated variously with crops, game, forests, rivers, and other elements of nature.

All tribes assigned women the jobs of caring for children, preparing meals, and gathering certain foods. But the allocation of other tasks varied from one society to another. Some tribal groups (notably the Pueblos of the

Southwest) reserved farming tasks almost entirely for men. Among others (including the Algonquins, the Iroquois, and the Muskogean), women tended the fields, while men engaged in hunting, warfare, or clearing land. Iroquois women and children were often left alone for extended periods while men were away hunting or fighting battles. As a result, women tended to control the social and economic organization of the settlements and played powerful roles within families.

EUROPE LOOKS WESTWARD

Europeans were almost entirely unaware of the existence of the Americas before the fifteenth century. A few early wanderers—Leif Ericson, an eleventh-century Norse seaman, and perhaps others—had glimpsed parts of the New World on their voyages. But even if their discoveries had become common knowledge (and they did not), there would have been little incentive for others to follow, for Europe in the Middle Ages (roughly A.D. 500–1500) was so divided and decentralized, so limited in its commerce, and

INDIANS OF NEW FRANCE The drawing is by the cartographer Charles Bécard de Granville, who was employed by the French government to make maps of their territories in North America. This depiction of Indian hunters traveling by river dates from approximately 1701.

so lacking in powerful political leaders that interest in great ventures remained limited. By the end of the fifteenth century, however, conditions in Europe had changed, and the incentive for overseas exploration had grown.

Commerce and Nationalism

Two changes in particular helped produce incentives for Europeans to look toward new lands. One was a result of the significant growth in Europe's population in the fifteenth century. The Black Death, a catastrophic epidemic of the bubonic plague that began in Constantinople in 1347, had killed (according to some estimates) as many as half the people of the Continent. But a century and a half later, the population had rebounded. With that growth came a reawakening of commerce and a general increase in prosperity. A new merchant class was emerging to meet the rising demand for goods from abroad. As trade increased, and as advances in navigation and shipbuilding made long-distance sea travel more feasible, interest in expanding trade even further grew quickly.

At the same time, new governments were emerging that were more united and powerful than the feeble political entities of the feudal past. In the western areas of Europe in particular, strong new monarchs were emerging, creating centralized nation-states, and growing eager to enhance the commercial growth of their nations.

Ever since the early fourteenth century, when Marco Polo and other adventurers had returned from the Orient bearing exotic goods (spices, cloths, dyes) and even more exotic tales, Europeans who craved commercial glory had dreamed above all of trade with the East. For two centuries, that trade had been limited by the difficulties of the long overland journey to the Asian courts. But in the fourteenth century, as the maritime talents of several western European societies increased, there began to be talk of finding a faster, safer route to the Orient by sea. In the late fifteenth century, some of the new monarchs were ready to finance daring voyages of exploration.

The first to do so were the Portuguese. Their maritime preeminence in the fifteenth century was in large part the work of Prince Henry the Navigator, who devoted much of his life to the promotion of exploration. Some of Henry's mariners went as far south as Cape Verde, on Africa's west coast. After his death in 1460, Portuguese explorers advanced farther still. In 1486, Bartholomeu Díaz rounded the southern tip of Africa (the Cape of Good Hope); and in 1497–1498 Vasco da Gama proceeded all the way around the cape to India. In 1500, the next Portuguese fleet bound for India, under the command of Pedro Cabral, was blown off course and happened upon the coast of Brazil. But by then, another man, in the service of another country, had already encountered the "New World".

Christopher Columbus

Christopher Columbus was born and reared in Genoa, Italy, and spent his early seafaring years in the service of the Portuguese. As a young man, he became interested in trying to reach the Orient by going west, across the Atlantic, rather than east, around Africa. Columbus's optimism rested on several basic misconceptions. He thought the world was far smaller than it actually is. He also believed that the Asian continent extended farther eastward than it actually does. Most important, he did not realize that anything lay to the west between Europe and the lands of Asia.

Columbus failed to convince the leaders of Portugal of the value of his plan, so he turned instead to Spain. Although the Spaniards were not yet as advanced a maritime people as the Portuguese, they were just as energetic and ambitious. And in the fifteenth century they were establishing a strong nation-state. The marriage of Spain's two most powerful regional rulers, Ferdinand of Aragon and Isabella of Castile, had produced the strongest monarchy in Europe, one that was eager to demonstrate its strength by sponsoring new commercial ventures.

Columbus appealed to Queen Isabella for support for his proposed westward voyage, and in 1492, after consolidating her position at home, she agreed. Commanding ninety men and three ships—the *Niña*, the *Pinta*, and the *Santa Maria*—Columbus left Spain in August 1492 and sailed west into the Atlantic. Ten weeks later, he sighted land and assumed he had reached an island off Asia. In fact, he had landed on an island in the Bahamas. When he pushed on and encountered Cuba, he assumed he had reached China. He returned to Spain, bringing with him several captured natives as evidence of his achievement. (He called the natives "Indians" because he believed they were from the East Indies in the Pacific.)

Columbus did not, however, bring back news of the great khan's court in China or any samples of the fabled wealth of the Indies. And so a year later, he tried again, this time with a much larger expedition. As before, he headed into the Caribbean, discovering several other islands and leaving a small and short-lived colony on Hispaniola. On a third voyage, in 1498, he finally reached the mainland and cruised along the northern coast of South America. He then realized, for the first time, that he had encountered not a part of Asia but a separate continent. Still, he remained convinced that Asia was only a short distance away.

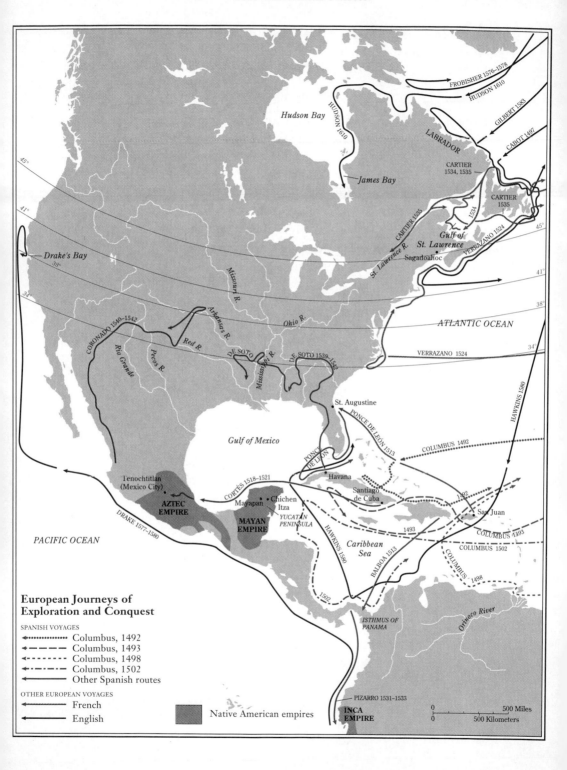

European Journeys of Exploration and Conquest

SPANISH VOYAGES
- ••••••••• Columbus, 1492
- ◄--------- Columbus, 1493
- ◄- - - - - - Columbus, 1498
- ◄-·-·-·- Columbus, 1502
- ◄———— Other Spanish routes

OTHER EUROPEAN VOYAGES
- ◄———— French
- ◄———— English

Native American empires

Columbus's celebrated accomplishments made him a popular hero for a time, but he ended his life in obscurity. Ultimately he was even unable to give his name to the land he had revealed to the Europeans. That distinction went instead to a Florentine merchant, Amerigo Vespucci, a passenger on a later Portuguese expedition to the New World, who wrote a series of vivid (if largely fictitious) descriptions of the lands he visited.

Partly as a result of Columbus's initiative, Spain began to devote greater resources and energy to maritime exploration and gradually replaced Portugal as the foremost seafaring nation. In 1513 the Spaniard Vasco de Balboa fought his way across the Isthmus of Panama and became the first European to gaze westward upon the great ocean that separated America from China. Seeking access to that ocean, Ferdinand Magellan, a Portuguese in Spanish employ, found the strait that now bears his name at the southern end of South America, struggled through the stormy narrows and into the ocean (so calm by contrast that he christened it the Pacific), and then proceeded to the Philippines. There Magellan died in a conflict with the natives, but his expedition went on to complete the first known circumnavigation of the globe (1519–1522). By 1550, Spaniards had explored the coasts of North America as far north as Oregon in the west and Labrador in the east.

The Spanish Empire

In time, Spanish explorers in the New World stopped thinking of America simply as an obstacle to their search for a route to the East and began instead to consider it a possible source of wealth in itself. The Spanish claimed for themselves the whole of the New World, except for a piece of it (today's Brazil) that was reserved by a papal decree for the Portuguese; and by the mid-sixteenth century, they were establishing a substantial American empire.

The early Spanish colonists, beginning with those Columbus brought on his second voyage, settled on the islands of the Caribbean. But then, in 1518, Hernando Cortés, who had been an unsuccessful Spanish government official in Cuba for fourteen years, decided to lead a small military expedition (about 600 men) against the Aztecs in Mexico and their powerful emperor, Montezuma, after hearing stories of great treasures there. His first assault on Tenochtitlán, the Aztec capital, failed. But Cortés and his army had, unknowingly, unleashed an assault on the Aztecs far more devastating than military attack: they had exposed the natives to smallpox. An epidemic of that disease decimated the Aztec population and made it possible for the Spanish to triumph in their second attempt at conquest. Through his ruthless suppression of the surviving natives, Cortés established himself as the most brutal of the Spanish *conquistadores* (conquerors). Twenty years later, Francisco Pizarro conquered Peru, revealed to the world the wealth of the Incas, and opened the way for other advances into South America.

The story of the Spanish warriors is one of great military daring and achievement. It is also a story of remarkable brutality and greed. The conquistadores subjugated and, in some areas, virtually exterminated the native populations. In this horrible way, they made possible the creation of a vast Spanish Empire in the New World.

Although the conquistadores had cleared the way for Spanish colonization of America, the task of creating settlements remained difficult. Spaniards who wished to launch expeditions to the New World had to get licenses

CORTÉS IN THE NEW WORLD An Aztec artist created this image of Hernando Cortés in Mexico. Cortés is visible at upper left, on horseback, wielding a sword. Other images suggest the destruction his arrival produced among the Aztecs. One of the most brutal and successful of the Spanish *conquistadores*, Cortés burned his ships upon landing at Vera Cruz (where he founded a city) in 1519 to prevent his men from turning back. In 1521, he captured the Aztec capital, Tenochtitlán, after a long siege.

from the crown and pay the monarch a fifth of any wealth gathered in the new colonies. Colonizers then had to equip and finance their expeditions without help from the government and assume the full risk of loss or ruin. They might succeed and make a fortune; they might fail and lose everything, including their lives.

The first Spanish settlers in America were interested only in exploiting the American stores of gold and silver, and they were fabulously successful. For 300 years, beginning in the sixteenth century, the mines in Spanish America yielded more than ten times as much gold and silver as the rest of the world's mines together. These riches made Spain for a time the wealthiest and most powerful nation on earth.

After the first wave of conquest, however, most Spanish settlers in America traveled to the New World for other reasons. Many went in hopes of creating a profitable agricultural economy in America, and they helped establish elements of European civilization permanently in America. Other Spaniards went to America to spread the Christian religion; after the 1840s priests or friars accompanied all colonizing ventures. Through the work of zealous missionaries, the influence of the Catholic church ultimately extended throughout South and Central America and Mexico.

By the end of the sixteenth century, the Spanish Empire had become one of the largest in the history of the world. It included the Caribbean islands, Mexico, and southern North America, where a second wave of European colonizers had established outposts. The Spanish fort established in 1565 at St. Augustine, Florida, became the first permanent European settlement in the present-day United States. The Spanish Empire also spread into South America and included what is now Chile, Argentina, and Peru. In 1580, when the Spanish and Portuguese monarchies temporarily united, Brazil came under Spanish jurisdiction as well.

It was, however, a colonial empire very different from the one the English would later establish in North America. The earliest Spanish ventures in the New World had operated largely independently of the throne, but by the end of the sixteenth century the monarchy had extended its authority directly into the governance of local communities, leaving colonists few opportunities to establish political institutions independent of the crown. The Spanish were far more successful than the British would be in extracting great surface wealth—gold and silver—from their American colonies. But they concentrated relatively less energy on making agriculture and commerce profitable in their colonies. The strict and inflexible commercial policies of the Spanish government made the problem worse. The

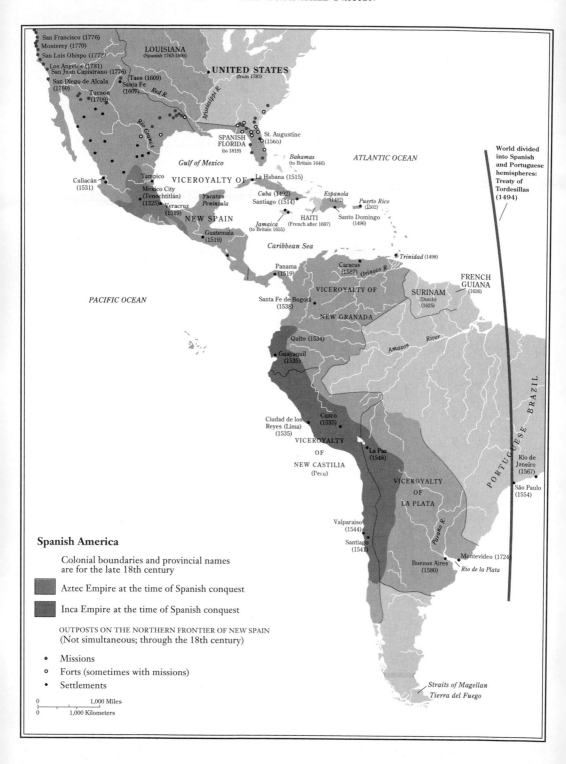

San Francisco (1776)
Monterey (1770)
San Luis Obispo (1772)
Los Angeles (1781)
San Juan Capistrano (1776)
San Diego de Alcala (1769)
Tucson (1709)
Taos (1609)
Santa Fe (1609)

LOUISIANA
(Spanish 1763–1800)

UNITED STATES
(from 1783)

Red R.

Mississippi R.

SPANISH FLORIDA
(to 1819)

St. Augustine
(1565)

Gulf of Mexico

Bahamas
(to Britain 1646)

ATLANTIC OCEAN

World divided into Spanish and Portuguese hemispheres: Treaty of Tordesillas (1494)

Culiacán
(1531)

Tampico

VICEROYALTY OF

La Habana (1515)

Mexico City
(Tenochtitlán)
(1325)

Veracruz
(1519)

Yucatan
Peninsula

Cuba (1492)
Santiago (1514)

Espanola
(1492)

Puerto Rico
(1502)

NEW SPAIN

Jamaica
(to Britain 1655)

HAITI
(French after 1697)

Santo Domingo
(1496)

Guatemala
(1519)

Caribbean Sea

Trinidad (1498)

Panama
(1519)

Caracas
(1567)

Orinoco R.

FRENCH GUIANA
(1626)

VICEROYALTY OF

Santa Fe de Bogotá
(1538)

SURINAM
(Dutch)
(1625)

PACIFIC OCEAN

NEW GRANADA

Quito (1534)

Amazon

River

Guayaquil
(1535)

Ciudad de los
Reyes (Lima)
(1535)

Cuzco
(1535)

VICEROYALTY
OF
NEW CASTILIA
(Peru)

La Paz
(1548)

Rio de
Janeiro
(1567)

São Paulo
(1554)

VICEROYALTY
OF
LA PLATA

Valparaiso
(1544)

Santiago
(1541)

Paraná R.

Montevideo (1724)

Buenos Aires
(1580)

Rio de la Plata

Straits of Magellan

Tierra del Fuego

Spanish America

Colonial boundaries and provincial names
are for the late 18th century

Aztec Empire at the time of Spanish conquest

Inca Empire at the time of Spanish conquest

OUTPOSTS ON THE NORTHERN FRONTIER OF NEW SPAIN
(Not simultaneous; through the 18th century)

• Missions

o Forts (sometimes with missions)

• Settlements

0   1,000 Miles

0   1,000 Kilometers

Spanish emphasis on surface riches ultimately had a stifling impact on Spain itself too. The supply of easy wealth from America weakened the incentive to promote domestic economic growth. That was one reason why Spain remained less developed than its northern European rivals and why its power declined so quickly in the seventeenth century.

But the biggest difference between the Spanish Empire and the later European colonization of North America was in the characters of the populations. The societies of English, French, and Dutch America were centered on farming and permanent settlement and emphasized family life. Hence, the Europeans in North America reproduced themselves rapidly after their first difficult years and in time came to outnumber the natives. The Spanish, by contrast, ruled their empire but did not people it. The number of European settlers in Spanish America always remained relatively small, and despite disease and war, the vast majority of the population continued to consist of natives. The Spanish Empire, therefore, was the product of a collision between and then a commingling of two cultures that had been developing for centuries along completely different lines.

Cultural Exchanges

European and native cultures never entirely merged in the Spanish Empire. Indeed, significant differences remain today between European and Indian cultures throughout South and Central America. Nevertheless, the arrival of whites launched a process of interaction between different peoples that left no one unchanged.

That Europeans were exploring the Americas at all was a result of their early contacts with the natives, from whom they had learned of the rich deposits of gold and silver. From then on, the history of the Americas became one of increasing levels of exchanges—some beneficial, some catastrophic— among different peoples and cultures. The first and perhaps most profound result of this exchange was the importation of European diseases to the New World. It would be difficult to exaggerate the consequences of the exposure of native Americans to such illnesses as influenza, measles, typhus, and above all smallpox—diseases to which Europeans had over time developed at least a partial immunity but to which Americans were tragically vulnerable. Millions died. In some areas, native populations were virtually wiped out within a few decades of their first contact with whites. On Hispaniola— where the Dominican Republic and Haiti are today and where Columbus landed and established a small, short-lived colony in the 1490s—the native population quickly declined from approximately 1 million to about 500. In the Mayan areas of Mexico, as much as 95 percent of the population perished within a few years of the natives' first contact with the Spanish. Some groups fared better than others; many (although not all) of the tribes north of Mexico, whose contact with European settlers came later and was often less intimate, were spared the worst of the epidemics. But for other areas of the New World, this was a catastrophe at least as grave as, and in some places far worse than, the Black Death that had killed as much as half the population of Europe two centuries before.

The decimation of native populations in the southern regions of the Americas was not, however, purely a result of exposure to infection. It was also a result of the conquistadores' quite deliberate policy of subjugation and extermination. Their brutality was in part a reflection of the ruthlessness with which Europeans waged war in all parts of the world. It was also a result of their conviction that the natives were "savages"—uncivilized peoples who could be treated as somehow not fully human. Ironically, it was also a consequence of the high level of development of some native societies. Had the natives truly been as primitive and disorganized as Europeans wanted to believe, there would have been little need to destroy them. But organized into substantial empires, they posed a serious threat to the conquistadores' ambitions. That, more than anything else, accounts for the thoroughness with which the Spanish set about obliterating native cultures. They razed cities and dismantled temples and monuments. They destroyed records and documents. They systematically killed Indian warriors, leaders, priests, and organized elites. By the 1540s, the combined effects of European diseases and European military brutality had all but destroyed the empires of Mexico and South America and allowed the Spanish to exert their authority with few organized challenges from the natives.

Not all aspects of the exchange were so disastrous to the Indians. The Europeans introduced to America important new crops (among them sugar and bananas), domestic livestock (cattle, pigs, and sheep), and perhaps most significantly the horse. Indians soon learned to cultivate the new crops, and European livestock spread widely among tribes that in the past had possessed virtually no domesticated animals other than dogs. The horse, in particular, became central to the lives of many natives and transformed their societies.

The exchange was at least as important (and more beneficial) to the Europeans. In both North and South America, the arriving white peoples learned from the natives new agricultural techniques appropriate to the demands of the new land. They discovered new crops, above all maize (corn), which Columbus took back to Europe from his first trip to America and which became an important staple in Europe itself as well as among European settlers in the New World. Such foods as squash, pumpkins, beans, sweet potatoes, tomatoes, peppers, and potatoes all found their way into European diets by way of native Americans. These and other American crops revolutionized European agriculture, enabling farmers to feed more people with more nutritious foods. That, in turn, facilitated the growth of the European population and the transformation of the European economy. Agricultural discoveries ultimately proved more important to Europe than the gold and silver the conquistadores valued so highly.

In South America, Central America, and Mexico, a society emerged in which Europeans and natives lived in intimate, if unequal, contact with one another. As a result, Indians adopted many features of European civilization, although seldom did those features survive the transfer to America unchanged. Many natives gradually came to speak Spanish or Portuguese, but they created a range of dialects fusing the European languages with elements of their own. Gradually, European missionaries—through a combination of persuasion and coercion—spread Catholicism through most areas of the Spanish Empire. But native Christians combined the new religion with features of their old ones.

Colonial officials were expected to take their wives with them to America, but among the ordinary settlers—the majority—European men outnumbered European women by at least ten to one. As a result, male Spanish immigrants had substantial sexual contact with native women. Intermarriage—sometimes forcible, sometimes with the agreement of native women responding to the shortage of native men—became frequent. Before long, the population of the colonies came to be dominated (numerically, at least) by people of mixed race, or *mestizos.*

Virtually all the enterprises of the Spanish and Portuguese colonists depended on an Indian work force. In some places, Indians were sold into slavery. More often, colonists used a coercive wage system by which Indians worked in the mines and on the plantations under duress for fixed periods, unable to leave without the consent of their employers. These indentured work forces survived in some areas of the South American mainland for many centuries. Yet even that was not, in the end, enough to meet the labor needs of the colonists—particularly since the native population had declined (and in some places virtually vanished) because of disease and war. As early as 1502, therefore, European settlers began importing slaves from Africa.

Africa and America

Over half of all the immigrants to the New World between 1500 and 1800 were Africans, virtually all of them sent to America against their will. Most came from a large region in west Africa below the Sahara Desert, known as Guinea.

Europeans and white Americans came to portray African society as primitive and uncivilized (in part to justify the enslavement of Africa's people). But most Africans were, in fact, civilized peoples with well-developed economies and political systems. The residents of upper Guinea had substantial commercial contact with the Mediterranean world—trading ivory, gold, and slaves for finished goods—and, largely as a result, became early converts to Islam. After the collapse of the ancient kingdom of Ghana around A.D. 1100, they created the even larger empire of Mali, which survived into the fifteenth century and whose trading center at Timbuktu became fabled as a meeting place of the peoples of many lands and a center of education.

Farther south, Africans were more isolated from Europe and the Mediterranean and were more politically fragmented. The central social unit was the village, which usually consisted of members of an extended family group. Some groups of villages united in small kingdoms. But no large empires emerged in the south comparable to the Ghana and Mali kingdoms farther north. Nevertheless, these southern societies developed extensive trade—in woven fabrics, ceramics, wooden and iron goods, as well as crops and livestock—both among themselves and, to a lesser degree, with the outside world.

African civilizations naturally developed economies that reflected the climates and resources of their lands. In upper Guinea, fishing and rice cultivation, supplemented by the extensive trade with Mediterranean lands, were the foundation of the economy. Farther south, Africans grew wheat and other food crops, raised livestock, and fished. There were some more nomadic tribes in the interior, who subsisted largely on hunting and gathering and developed less elaborate social systems. But most Africans were sedentary, farming people.

As in many Indian societies in America, but in contrast to the European tradition, African families tended to be matrilineal. That means that people traced their heredity through and inherited property from their mothers. Women played a major role, often the dominant role, in trade; in many areas, they were the principal farmers (while the men hunted, fished, and raised livestock); and everywhere, they managed child care and food preparation. Most tribes also divided political power by gender, with men choosing leaders and systems for managing male affairs and women choosing parallel leaders to handle female matters.

In those areas of west Africa where indigenous religions had survived the spread of Islam (which included most of the lands south of the empire of Mali), people worshiped many gods, whom they associated with various aspects of the natural world and whose spirits they believed lived in trees, rocks, forests, and streams. Most Africans also developed forms of ancestor worship and took great care in tracing family lineage; the most revered priests were generally the oldest people.

Small elites of priests and nobles stood at the top of African societies. Most people belonged to a large middle group of farmers, traders, crafts workers, and others. At the bottom of society were slaves—men and women who were put into bondage after being captured in wars, because of criminal behavior, or as a result of unpaid debts. Slavery was not usually permanent; people were generally in bondage for a fixed term, and in the meantime retained certain legal protections (including the right to marry). Children did not inherit their parents' condition of bondage. The slavery that Africans would experience at the hands of the Europeans was to be very different.

The African slave trade long preceded European settlement in the New World. As early as the eighth century, west Africans began selling slaves to traders from the Mediterranean. When Portuguese sailors began exploring the coast of Africa in the fifteenth century, they too bought slaves and took them back to Portugal, where there was a small but steady demand. In the sixteenth century, however, the market for slaves grew dramatically as a result of the growing European demand for sugar cane. The small areas of sugar cultivation in the Mediterranean were proving inadequate, and production soon moved to new areas: to the island of Madeira off the African coast, which became a Portuguese colony, and not long thereafter (still in the sixteenth century) to the Caribbean islands and Brazil. Sugar was a labor-intensive crop, and the demand for African workers in these new areas of cultivation was high. At first the slave traders were overwhelmingly Portuguese and, to a lesser extent, Spanish. By the seventeenth century, the Dutch had won control of most of the market. In the eighteenth century, the English dominated it; by then, slavery had spread well beyond its original locations in the Caribbean and South America and into the English colonies to the north.

THE ARRIVAL OF THE ENGLISH

England's first documented contact with the New World came only five years after Spain's. In 1497, John Cabot (like Columbus, a native of Genoa) sailed to the northeastern coast of North America on an expedition sponsored by King Henry VII. Other English navigators, continuing Cabot's unsuccessful search for a northwest passage through the New World to the Orient, explored other areas of North America during the sixteenth century. But nearly a century passed before the English made any serious efforts to establish colonies there. Like other European nations, England had to experience an internal transformation before it could begin settling new lands.

Incentives for Colonization

Interest in colonization grew in part as a response to the social and economic problems of sixteenth-century England. The English people suffered from frequent and costly European wars, and they suffered from almost constant religious strife within their own land. They suffered too from a harsh economic transformation of the countryside. Because the worldwide demand for wool was growing rapidly, many landowners were converting their land from fields for crops to pastures for sheep. The result was a significant growth in the wool trade—and a reduction in the amount of land available for growing food. Many of the displaced farmers became beggars or criminals. And England's food supply declined at the same time that the English population was growing—from 3 million in 1485 to 4 million in 1603. To some of the English, the New World began to seem attractive because it offered something that was growing scarce in England: land.

At the same time, new merchant capitalists were prospering from the expansion of foreign trade, particularly once merchants helped create a domestic cloth industry that allowed them to begin marketing finished goods. At first, most exporters did business almost entirely as individuals. In time, however, merchants developed more collective enterprises and formed enterprises that operated on the basis of charters from the monarch giving companies monopolies for trading in particular regions. Some were joint-stock companies, similar in some respects to modern corporations, with stockholders sharing risk and profit either on single ventures or, increasingly, on a permanent basis. These investors often made fantastic profits, and they were eager to continue the expansion of their profitable trade.

Central to this drive was the emergence of a new concept of economic life known as mercantilism. Mercantilism rested on the belief that the world's wealth was finite, that one person or nation could grow rich only at the expense of another, and that a nation's economic health depended, therefore, on extracting as much wealth as possible from foreign lands and exporting as little wealth as possible from home. The principles of mercantilism guided the economic policies of virtually all the great nation-states that were emerging in Europe in the sixteenth and seventeenth centuries and increased the competition among nations. Every European state was trying to find markets for its exports while trying to limit its imports. One result was the increased attractiveness of acquiring colonies, which could become the source of goods that a country might otherwise have to buy from other nations and could become a market for goods produced by the colonizing power.

In England, the mercantilistic program thrived at first on the basis of the flourishing wool trade with the European continent, and particularly with the great cloth market in Antwerp. In the 1550s, however, that glutted market began to collapse, and English merchants had to look elsewhere for overseas trade. The establishment of colonies seemed to be an answer to their problems. Some English also believed colonies would help alleviate poverty and unemployment by siphoning off the surplus population. Perhaps most important, colonial commerce would allow England to acquire products for which the nation had previously been dependent on foreigners—products such as lumber, naval stores, and silver and gold.

There were also religious motives for colonization. The Protestant Reformation began in Germany in 1517, when Martin Luther challenged some of the basic practices and beliefs of the Roman Catholic church—until then, the supreme religious authority. Luther quickly won a wide following among ordinary men and women in northern Europe. When the pope excommunicated him in 1520, Luther began leading his followers out of the Catholic church entirely.

As the spirit of the Reformation spread rapidly throughout Europe, other dissidents began offering other alternatives to Catholicism. The Swiss theologian John Calvin went even further than Luther had in rejecting the Catholic belief that human behavior or the church itself could affect an individual's prospects for salvation. Calvin introduced the doctrine of predestination. God "elected" some people to be saved and condemned others to damnation; each person's destiny was determined before birth, and no one could change that predetermined fate. But those who accepted Calvin's teachings came to believe that the way they led their lives might reveal to them their chances of salvation. A wicked or useless existence would be a sign of damnation; saintliness, diligence, and success could be signs of grace. Calvinism created anxieties among its followers, but it also produced a strong incentive to lead virtuous, productive lives. The new creed spread rapidly throughout northern Europe and produced (among other groups) the Huguenots in France and the Puritans in England.

At first, however, the English Reformation was less a result of these doctrinal revolts than of a political dispute between the king and the pope. In 1529 King Henry VIII, angered by the refusal of the pope to grant him a divorce from his Spanish wife (who had failed to bear him the son he desperately wanted), broke England's ties with the Catholic church and established himself as the head of the Christian faith in his country. After Henry's death, his Catholic daughter, Queen Mary, restored England's allegiance to Rome and persecuted those who resisted. But when Mary died in 1558, her half-sister, Elizabeth I, became England's sovereign and once again severed the nation's connection with the Catholic church, this time for good.

To many English people, however, the new Church of England—which differed little at first from the Catholic church—was not reformed enough. Some had been affected by the teachings of the European Reformation, and they complained that theirs was a church that had abandoned Rome without abandoning Rome's offensive beliefs and practices. They clamored for reforms that would "purify" the church, and thus they became known as "Puritans."

The most radical Puritans, known as Separatists, were determined to worship as they pleased in their own independent congregations, despite English laws that required all subjects to attend regular Anglican services. But most Puritans did not wish to leave the Church of England. They wanted, rather, to simplify Anglican forms of worship; reduce the power of the crown-appointed bishops, who were sometimes corrupt and extravagant; and reform the clergy, many of whom were uneducated men with little interest in or knowledge of theology. Like the Separatists, they grew increasingly frustrated by the refusal of either political or ecclesiastical authorities to respond to their demands.

Puritan discontent grew rapidly after the death of Elizabeth, the last of the Tudors, and the accession of James I, the first of the Stuarts, in 1603. Convinced that kings ruled by divine right, James quickly antagonized the Puritans, a group that included most of the rising businessmen, by resorting to illegal and arbitrary taxation, by favoring English Catholics in the granting of charters and other favors, and by supporting "high-church" forms of ceremony. By the early seventeenth century, some religious nonconformists were beginning to look for places of refuge outside the kingdom.

Many factors, therefore, combined to increase the interest of the English in peopling distant lands—social and economic instability, religious discontent, personal ambition, commercial greed. England's first experience with colonization, however, came not in the New World but in neighboring Ireland. The English had long laid claim to the island, but only in the late sixteenth century did serious efforts at colonization begin. The long, brutal process by which the English attempted (never entirely successfully) to subdue the Irish led to an important assumption about colonization that the English would take with them to America: the belief that settlements in foreign lands must retain a rigid separation from the native populations. Unlike the Spanish in America, the English in Ireland tried to build a separate society of their own, peopled with emigrants from England itself. They would take that concept with them to the New World.

The French and the Dutch in America

English settlers in North America were to encounter not only natives but also other Europeans who were, like them, driven by mercantilist ideas. There were scattered North American outposts of the Spanish Empire, whose residents looked on the English as intruders. More important, there were French and Dutch settlers.

France founded its first permanent settlement in America at Quebec in 1608, less than a year after the English started their first at Jamestown. The colony's population grew very slowly, but the French exercised an influence in the New World disproportionate to their numbers, because of their relationships with native Americans. Unlike the early English settlers, who hugged the coastline and traded with the Indians of the interior through intermediaries, the French forged close ties with natives deep inside the continent. French Jesuit missionaries established some of the first contacts between the two peoples. More important were the *coureurs de bois*—adventurous fur traders and trappers—who also penetrated far into the wilderness and developed an extensive trade that became one of the underpinnings of the French colonial economy. The French traders formed partnerships with the Indians and often became virtually a part of native society, living among the natives and at times marrying Indian women. The fur trade helped open the way for French agricultural estates (or *seigneuries*) along the St. Lawrence River and for the development of trade and military centers at Quebec and Montreal.

The English also faced competition from the Dutch in North America. Holland in the early seventeenth century was one of the leading trading nations of the world. In 1609 an English explorer in the employ of the Dutch, Henry Hudson, sailed up the river that was to be named for him in what is now New York State; and his explorations led to a Dutch claim on that territory and to the establishment of a permanent Dutch presence in the New World. In 1624, not long after the first two permanent English colonies took root in Jamestown and Plymouth, the Dutch created a wedge between them when the Dutch West India Company established a series of permanent trading posts on the Hudson, Delaware, and Connecticut rivers. The company actively encouraged settlement of the region, and the result was the colony of New Netherland and its principal town, New Amsterdam, on Manhattan Island. But the Dutch population remained relatively small.

The First English Settlements

The first permanent English settlement in the New World was established at Jamestown, in Virginia, in 1607. But for nearly thirty years before that, English merchants and adventurers had been engaged in a series of failed efforts to create colonies in America.

Through much of the sixteenth century, the English had harbored mixed feelings about the New World. They were intrigued by its possibilities, but they were also leery of Spain, which remained the dominant force in America and the dominant naval power in Europe. In 1588, however, King Philip II of Spain sent one of the largest military fleets in the history of warfare—the Spanish Armada—across the English Channel to attack England itself. The invasion failed. The smaller English fleet, taking advantage of its greater maneuverability, dispersed the Armada and, in a single stroke, ended Spain's domination of the Atlantic. The most important inhibition the English had retained about establishing themselves in the New World was now removed.

The pioneers of English colonization were Sir Humphrey Gilbert and his half-brother Sir Walter Raleigh—both friends of Queen Elizabeth, and both veterans of earlier colonial efforts in Ireland. In 1578 Gilbert obtained from Elizabeth a six-year patent granting him the exclusive right "to inhabit and possess any remote and heathen lands not already in the possession of any Christian prince." Five years later, after several setbacks, he led an expedition to Newfoundland and proceeded south looking for a good place to build a profitable colony. But a storm sank his ship, and he was lost at sea.

ROANOKE A drawing by one of the English colonists in the ill-fated Roanoke expedition of 1585 became the basis for this engraving by Theodore DeBry, published in England in 1590. A small European ship carrying settlers approaches the island of Roanoke, at left. The wreckage of several larger vessels farther out to sea and the presence of Indian settlements on the mainland and on Roanoke itself suggest some of the perils the settlers encountered.

Sir Walter Raleigh was undeterred. The next year, he secured his own six-year grant from the queen and sent a small group of men on an expedition to explore the North American coast. When they returned, Raleigh named the region they had explored Virginia, in honor of Elizabeth, who was unmarried and was known as the "Virgin Queen."

In 1585 Raleigh recruited his cousin, Sir Richard Grenville, to lead a group of men to the island of Roanoke, off the coast of what is now North Carolina, to establish a colony. Grenville deposited the settlers on the island, antagonized the natives by destroying an Indian village as retaliation for a minor theft, and returned to England. The following spring, with expected supplies and reinforcements from England long overdue, Sir Francis Drake unexpectedly arrived in Roanoke. The colonists boarded his ships and left.

Raleigh tried again in 1587, sending an expedition to Roanoke carrying ninety-one men, seventeen women (two of them pregnant), and nine children. The settlers attempted to take up where the first group of colonists had left off. (Shortly after arriving, one of the women—the daughter of the commander of the expedition, John White—gave birth to a daughter, Virginia Dare, the first American-born child of English parents.) White returned to England after several weeks, leaving his daughter and granddaughter behind, in search of supplies and additional settlers. Because of a war with Spain, he was unable to return to Roanoke for three years. When he did, in 1590, he found the island utterly deserted, with no clue to the fate of the settlers other than the cryptic inscription "Croatoan" carved on a post. No solution to the mystery of the "Lost Colony" has ever been found.

The Roanoke disaster marked the end of Sir Walter Raleigh's involvement in English colonization of the New World, and no later colonizer would receive grants of land in the New World as vast or undefined as those Raleigh and Gilbert had acquired. But despite the discouraging example of these first experiences, the colonizing impulse remained very much alive. In the early years of the seventeenth century, a group of London merchants to whom Raleigh had assigned his charter rights decided to renew the attempt at colonization in Virginia. A rival group of merchants, from the area around Plymouth, was also interested in American ventures and was sponsoring voyages of exploration farther north. In 1606 James I issued a new charter, which divided America between the two groups. The London group got the exclusive right to colonize in the south, and the Plymouth merchants received the same right in the north. Through the efforts of these and other companies, the first enduring English colonies would be established in America.

CHAPTER TWO

The English "Transplantations"

The Early Chesapeake ~ The Growth of New England
The Restoration Colonies ~ The Development of Empire

T HE ROANOKE FIASCO dampened enthusiasm for colonization in England for a time. But the lures of the New World—the presumably vast riches, the abundant land, the promise of religious freedom, the chance to begin anew—were too strong to be suppressed for very long. By the early seventeenth century, the effort to establish permanent English colonies in the New World resumed.

The new efforts were much like the earlier, failed ones: private ventures, with little planning or direction from the English government; small, fragile enterprises led by people unprepared for the hardships they were to face. Unlike the Roanoke experiment, they survived, but not before experiencing a series of disastrous setbacks.

Three conditions in particular shaped the character of these English settlements. First, the colonies were business enterprises, and one of their principal concerns was to produce a profit for their corporate sponsors. Second, the English colonies, unlike the Spanish, were designed to be "transplantations" of societies from the Old World to the New. As in Ireland, there were few efforts to blend English society with the society of the natives. And third, because the colonies were tied only indirectly to the crown, they began from the start to develop their own political and social institutions.

THE EARLY CHESAPEAKE

Once James I had issued his 1606 charters to the London and Plymouth Companies, the Plymouth group floundered and largely abandoned its efforts at settling the northern regions of British America. But the London

Company moved quickly and decisively to launch a colonizing expedition headed for Virginia—a party of 144 men aboard three ships, the *Godspeed*, the *Discovery*, and the *Susan Constant*, which set sail for America early in 1607.

The Founding of Jamestown

Only 104 men survived the journey. They reached the American coast in the spring of 1607, sailed into Chesapeake Bay and up a river they named the James, and established their colony on a peninsula. They called it Jamestown.

RECRUITING FOR THE COLONIES, 1609 This is the title page for a pamphlet that describes the attractions of settlement in the New World. Most accounts of the "excellent fruites" of life in Virginia were, like this one, written by people who had never seen America but who shared the excitement that the colonies inspired among the early-seventeenth-century English.

They chose an inland setting that they believed would offer them security from the natives. But they chose poorly. The site was low and swampy and subject to outbreaks of malaria. It was surrounded by thick woods, which were difficult to clear for cultivation. And it bordered the territories of powerful local Indians. The result could hardly have been more disastrous. For seventeen years, one wave of settlers after another attempted to make Jamestown a habitable and profitable colony. Every effort failed. The town became instead a place of misery and death, and the London Company found itself saddled with endless losses. All that could be said of Jamestown at the end of this first period of its existence was that it had survived.

The initial colonists ran into serious difficulties from the moment they landed. They had no prior exposure to the infections of the new land and were highly vulnerable to local diseases, particularly malaria. The promoters in London demanded a quick return on their investment and diverted the colonists' energies into futile searches for gold and only slightly more successful efforts to pile up lumber, tar, pitch, and iron for export. These energies would have been better spent on growing food. The promoters also had little interest in creating a family-centered community, and they sent virtually no women to Jamestown. Hence settlers could not establish real households and had difficulty feeling any sense of a permanent stake in the community.

By January 1608, when ships appeared with additional men and supplies, all but 38 of the first 104 colonists were dead. Jamestown, now facing extinction, survived largely as a result of the efforts of Captain John Smith, who at age twenty-seven was already a famous world traveler. Leadership in the colony had been bitterly divided until the fall of 1608, when Smith took control. He imposed work and order on the community. He also organized raids on neighboring Indian villages to steal food and kidnap natives. During the colony's second winter, fewer than a dozen (in a population of about 200) died. By the summer of 1609, when Smith returned to England, the colony was showing promise of survival. But Jamestown's ordeal was not over yet.

Reorganization and Expansion

As Jamestown struggled to survive, the London Company (now renamed the Virginia Company) was already dreaming of bigger things. In 1609, it obtained a new charter from the king, which increased its power and enlarged its territory. It raised money by selling additional stock. It offered stock in the company to planters who were willing to migrate at their own expense. And it provided free passage to Virginia for poorer people who would agree to serve the company for seven years. In the spring of 1609, confident that it was now poised to transform Jamestown into a successful venture, the company dispatched a fleet of nine vessels with about 600 people (including some women and children) to Virginia.

Disaster followed. One of the Virginia-bound ships was lost at sea in a hurricane. Another ran aground off Bermuda and was unable to free itself for months. Many of those who reached Jamestown, still weak from their long and stormy voyage, succumbed to fevers before winter came. The winter of 1609–1610 became known as the "starving time," a period worse than anything before. The local Indians, antagonized by the hostile actions of the early English settlers, killed off the livestock in the woods and kept the colonists barricaded within their palisade. The Europeans lived on what they could find: "dogs, cats, rats, snakes, toadstools, horsehides," and even the "corpses of dead men," as one survivor recalled. When the migrants who had run aground on Bermuda finally arrived in Jamestown the following May, they found about 60 emaciated people (out of 500 residents the previous summer) still alive. The new arrivals took the survivors onto their ship, abandoned the settlement, and set sail downriver for home. But as the refugees proceeded down the James, they met an English ship coming up the river—part of a fleet bringing supplies and the colony's first governor, Lord De La Warr. The departing settlers agreed to return to Jamestown. New relief expeditions with hundreds of colonists soon began to arrive, and the effort to turn a profit in Jamestown resumed.

Under the leadership of the first governors, Virginia survived and even expanded. New settlements began lining the river above and below Jamestown. That was partly because of the order and discipline the governors at times managed to impose and partly because of military assaults by the English on local Indian tribes to protect the new settlements. But it was also because the colonists had at last discovered a marketable crop—tobacco.

Europeans had become aware of tobacco soon after Columbus first returned from the West Indies, where he had seen the Cuban natives smoking small cigars (*tabacos*), which they inserted in the nostril. By the early seventeenth century, tobacco from the Spanish colonies was already in wide use in Europe. Then, in 1612, the Jamestown planter John Rolfe, noting that local Indians were growing a strain of tobacco, began trying to cultivate the crop in Virginia with seeds obtained from the Spanish colonies. Tobacco planting quickly spread up and down the James.

Almost immediately, tobacco cultivation created great pressure for territorial expansion. Tobacco growers needed large tracts of land to grow

Growth of the Chesapeake, 1607–1750

Map legend:
- Virginia Colony
- Fairfax Proprietary
- To Lord Baltimore, 1632
- Granville Proprietary
- (1649) Date settlement founded

Map labels: Boundary claimed by Lord Baltimore, 1632; PENNSYLVANIA; Boundary settlement, 1750; Wilmington (Fort Christina) (1638); WEST JERSEY; Frederick (1744); Baltimore (1729); MARYLAND; Dover (1717); Potomac R.; Providence (Annapolis) (c. 1648); LOWER COUNTIES OF DELAWARE; Fredericksburg (1671); Rappahannock R.; St. Marys (1634); Chesapeake Bay; VIRGINIA; Fort Royal; Fort Charles; Richmond (1645); Williamsburg (Middle Plantation) (1633); James R.; Fort Henry; Jamestown (1607); Yorktown (1631); ATLANTIC OCEAN; Newport News (1621); Norfolk (1682); Fort Christianna; NORTH CAROLINA; Elizabeth City (1634); Albemarle Sound; 0 50 Miles; 0 50 Kilometers

profitable crops; and because tobacco exhausted the soil very quickly, the demand for land increased even more. As a result, English farmers began establishing plantations deeper and deeper in the interior, isolating themselves from the center of European settlement at Jamestown and penetrating farther into the territory of the native tribes.

The tobacco economy also created a heavy demand for labor. To entice new workers to the colony, the Virginia Company established what it called the "headright" system. Headrights were fifty-acre grants of land. Those who already lived in the colony received two headrights (100 acres) apiece. Each new settler received a single headright for himself or herself. This system encouraged family groups to migrate together, since the more family members traveled to America, the more land the family would receive. In addition, anyone who paid for the passage of immigrants to Virginia would receive an extra headright for each arrival, an encouragement to the prosperous to import new laborers. As a result, some colonists were able to assemble large plantations.

The company also transported ironworkers and other skilled craftsmen to Virginia to diversify the economy. In 1619, it sent 100 Englishwomen to the colony (which was still overwhelmingly male) to become the wives of male colonists. It promised the male colonists the full rights of Englishmen (as provided in the original charter of 1606), an end to strict and arbitrary rule, and even a share in self-government. On July 30, 1619, delegates from the various communities met as the House of Burgesses. It was the first meeting of an elected legislature within what was to become the United States.

A month later, Virginia established another important precedent. As John Rolfe recorded, "about the latter end of August" a Dutch ship brought in "20 and odd Negroes." There is some reason to believe that the colonists did not consider these first Africans in Virginia slaves, that they thought of them rather as servants to be held for a term of years and then freed, like the white servants with whom the planters were already familiar. For a time, moreover, the use of black labor remained limited. Although Africans continued to trickle steadily into the colony, planters continued to prefer European indentured servants until at least the 1670s, when white servants began to become scarce and expensive. But the small group of blacks who arrived in 1619 marked the first step toward the enslavement of Africans within what was to be the American republic.

The European settlers in Virginia built their society not only on the coerced labor of imported Africans but also on the effective suppression of the local Indians. For two years, Sir Thomas Dale led unrelenting assaults against the Powhatan Indians and in the process kidnapped the great chief Powhatan's daughter Pocahontas. When Powhatan refused to ransom her, she converted to Christianity and in 1614 married John Rolfe. At that point, Powhatan ceased his attacks on the English in the face of overwhelming odds. But after his death several years later, his brother, Opechancanough, revived the effort to defend tribal lands and began secretly to plan the elimination of the English intruders. On a March morning in 1622, tribesmen called on the white settlements as if to offer goods for sale, and then suddenly attacked. Not until 347 whites of both sexes and all ages (including John Rolfe) lay dead were the Indian warriors finally forced to retreat. And not until over twenty years later were the Powhatans finally defeated.

By then, however, the Virginia Company in London was defunct. The company had poured virtually all its funds into its profitless Jamestown venture and in the aftermath of the 1622 Indian uprising faced imminent bankruptcy. In 1624, James I revoked the company's charter, and the colony at last came under the control of the crown. So it would remain until 1776.

With the stabilization of Virginia's English sponsorship, the suppression of the Indian threat, and the development of a profitable cash crop, the colony finally seemed secure. But this success had come at a terrible cost. In Virginia's first seventeen years, more than 8,500 white settlers had arrived in the colony. In 1624, the white population stood at 1,300. More than 80 percent had abandoned the colony or died.

Maryland and the Calverts

The Maryland colony ultimately came to look much like Virginia, but its origins were very different from those of its southern neighbor. George Calvert, the first Lord Baltimore, was a recent convert to Catholicism and a shrewd businessman, and he envisioned establishing a colony in America both as a great speculative venture in real estate and as a retreat for English Catholics oppressed by the Anglican establishment at home. Calvert died while still negotiating with the king for a charter to establish a colony in the Chesapeake region. But in 1632 his son Cecilius, the second Lord Baltimore, finally received the charter.

The Maryland charter was remarkable not only for the extent of the territory it granted to Calvert—an area that encompassed parts of what is now Pennsylvania, Delaware, and Virginia, in addition to present-day Maryland—but for the powers it bestowed on him. He and his heirs were to hold their province as "true and absolute lords and proprietaries." Their only obligation to the king was paying an annual fee to the crown.

Lord Baltimore named his brother, Leonard Calvert, as governor of the colony. In March 1634, two ships—the *Ark* and the *Dove*—bearing Calvert along with 200 or 300 other colonists, entered the Potomac River, turned into one of its eastern tributaries, and established the village of St. Mary's on a high, dry bluff. Neighboring Indians befriended the settlers and provided them with temporary shelter and with stocks of corn. The early Marylanders experienced no Indian assaults, no plagues, no starving time.

The Calverts needed to attract thousands of settlers to Maryland if their expensive colonial venture was to pay. As a result, they had to encourage the immigration of Protestants as well as their fellow English Catholics. The Calverts soon realized that Catholics would always be a minority in the colony, and so they adopted a policy of religious toleration, embodied in the 1649 "Act Concerning Religion," which assured freedom of worship to all Christians. Nevertheless, politics in Maryland remained plagued for years by tensions, and at times violence, between the Catholic minority and the Protestant majority.

The government in Maryland gradually came to resemble that of other English colonies in America in many ways. At the insistence of the first settlers, the Calverts agreed in 1635 to the calling of a representative assembly—the House of Delegates—whose proceedings were based on the rules of Parliament. But the proprietor retained absolute authority to distribute land as he wished; and since Lord Baltimore granted large estates to his relatives and to other English aristocrats, a distinct upper class soon established itself. By 1640, a severe labor shortage forced a modification of the land-grant procedure; and Maryland, like Virginia, adopted a headright system—a grant of 100 acres to each male settler, another 100 for his wife and each servant, and 50 for each of his children. But the great landlords of the colony's earliest years remained powerful even as the population grew larger and more diverse. Like Virginia, Maryland became a center of tobacco cultivation; and as in Virginia, planters worked their land with the aid, first, of indentured servants imported from England and then, beginning late in the seventeenth century, of slaves imported from Africa.

Turbulent Virginia

By the mid-seventeenth century, the Virginia colony had survived its early disasters. Its population was growing, and its economy was becoming more complex and profitable. Soon, factions began to emerge within the colony to compete for influence within the government, and particularly for influence over policies toward the natives.

For more than thirty years, one man—Sir William Berkeley, the royal governor of Virginia—dominated the politics of the colony. He took office in 1642 at the age of thirty-six and with but one interruption remained in control of the government until the 1670s. In his first years as governor, he helped open up the interior of Virginia by sending explorers across the Blue Ridge Mountains and crushing a 1644 Indian uprising. The defeated Indians agreed to a treaty ceding to England most of the territory east of the mountains and establishing a boundary west of which white settlement would be prohibited. But the rapid growth of the Virginia population made this agreement difficult to sustain. By 1650, Virginia's population of 16,000 was twice what it had been ten years before; by 1660, it had more than doubled again, to 40,000. By 1652, English settlers had established three counties in the territory set aside by the treaty for the Indians. Unsurprisingly, there were frequent clashes between natives and whites.

In the meantime, Berkeley was expanding his powers and making himself virtually an autocrat. By 1670, the vote for delegates to the House of Burgesses, once open to all white men, was restricted to landowners. Elections were rare, and the same burgesses, representing the established planters of the Eastern (or tidewater) region of the colony and subservient to the governor, remained in office year after year. The more recent settlers on the frontier were underrepresented in the assembly or not represented at all.

Resentment of the power of the governor and the tidewater aristocrats grew steadily in the newly settled lands of the west (often known as the "back country"). In 1676, this resentment helped create a major conflict, led by Nathaniel Bacon, a young, handsome aristocrat who had arrived in Virginia in 1673. Bacon had a good farm in the west and a seat on the governor's council. But like other members of the new back-country gentry, he was at odds in crucial ways with the governor and his tidewater allies, particularly over Indian policy. The frontier elite was in constant danger of attack from the tribes on whose lands they were encroaching, and they chafed at the governor's attempts to hold the line of settlement steady so as to avoid antagonizing the Indians. Bacon's rift with Berkeley was also a result of resentment that he was not part of the inner circle of the governor's council and that Berkeley refused to allow him a piece of the Indian fur trade, which the governor himself controlled.

Bloody events thrust Bacon into the role of leader of an anti-Berkeley faction. In 1675, a major conflict erupted in the west between whites and natives. As the fighting escalated, Bacon and other concerned landholders demanded that the governor send the militia. Berkeley, however, simply ordered the construction of several new forts along the western border. Bacon responded by offering to organize a volunteer army of back-country men who would do their own fighting. Berkeley, who saw Bacon as a potential rival and feared a needless slaughter of the natives, rejected the offer. Bacon ignored him and launched a series of vicious but unsuccessful pursuits of the Indian challengers.

When Berkeley heard of the unauthorized military effort, he dismissed Bacon from the governor's council and proclaimed him and his men to be rebels. Bacon now turned his army against the governor and, in what became known as Bacon's Rebellion, twice led his troops east to Jamestown. The first time he won a temporary pardon from the governor; the second time, after the governor reneged on the agreement, Bacon burned the city and drove the governor into exile. But then Bacon died suddenly of dysentery; and Berkeley, his position bolstered by the arrival of British troops, soon regained control. In 1677, the Indians (aware of their inability to defeat the white forces militarily) reluctantly signed a new treaty that opened new lands to white settlement.

Bacon's Rebellion was significant for several reasons. It was evidence of the continuing struggle to define the Indian and white spheres of influence in Virginia. It revealed the bitterness of the competition among rival elites and between easterners and westerners in particular. But it also demonstrated the potential for instability in the colony's large population of free, landless men. These men—most of them former indentured servants without property or prospects—had formed the bulk of Bacon's constituency during the rebellion. Their hatred of Indians drew them to Bacon, but they also harbored a deep animosity toward the landed gentry (of which Bacon himself was a part). One result was that landed elites in both eastern and western Virginia began to recognize a common interest in quelling social unrest from below. That was one of several reasons for their turning increasingly to the African slave trade to fulfill their need for labor. African slaves, unlike white indentured servants, did not need to be released after a fixed term and hence did not threaten to become an unstable, landless class.

THE GROWTH OF NEW ENGLAND

The northern regions of British North America were slower to attract settlers, in part because the Plymouth Company was never able to mount a successful colonizing expedition after receiving its charter in 1606. It did, however, sponsor exploration of the region. Captain John Smith, after his return from Jamestown, made an exploratory journey for the Plymouth merchants, wrote an enthusiastic pamphlet about the lands he had seen, and called them New England.

Plymouth Plantation

A discontented congregation of Puritan Separatists in England, not the Plymouth Company, established the first enduring European settlement in New England. In 1608, after years of persecution for attempting to practice their own religion, a congregation of Separatists from the hamlet of Scrooby began emigrating quietly (and illegally), a few at a time, to Leyden, Holland, where they could enjoy freedom of worship. But as foreigners in Holland, they could not join the Dutch guilds of craftsmen, and so they had to work at unskilled and poorly paid jobs. They also watched with alarm

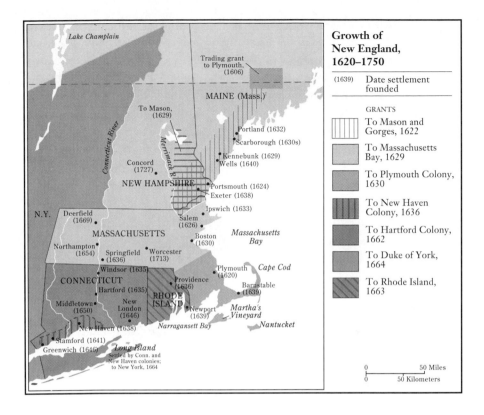

Growth of New England, 1620–1750

(1639) Date settlement founded

GRANTS

To Mason and Gorges, 1622

To Massachusetts Bay, 1629

To Plymouth Colony, 1630

To New Haven Colony, 1636

To Hartford Colony, 1662

To Duke of York, 1664

To Rhode Island, 1663

0   50 Miles
0   50 Kilometers

as their children began to speak Dutch, marry into Dutch families, and drift away from their church. Finally some of the Separatists decided to move again, across the Atlantic, where they hoped to create a stable, protected community and where they could spread "the gospel of the Kingdom of Christ in those remote parts of the world."

In 1620, leaders of the Scrooby group obtained permission from the Virginia Company to settle in Virginia and received informal assurances from the king that he would "not molest them, provided they carried themselves peaceably." Several English merchants advanced the necessary funds for the venture on the condition that the merchants share in the profits at the end of seven years. The "Pilgrims," as they saw themselves, sailed from Plymouth, England, in September 1620 aboard the *Mayflower*, with thirty-five "saints" (Puritan Separatists) and sixty-seven "strangers" (people who were not part of the congregation) aboard. In November, after a long and difficult voyage, they sighted land—the shore of what is now Cape Cod. That had not been their destination, but it was too late in the year to sail farther. So the Pilgrims chose a site for their settlement in the area just north of the cape, a place John Smith had labeled "Plymouth" on a map he had drawn during an earlier exploration of New England. Because Plymouth lay outside the London Company's territory, the settlers were not bound by the company's rules. So while still aboard ship, the "saints" in the group drew up an agreement, the Mayflower Compact, which established a civil government. Then, on December 21, 1620, they stepped ashore at Plymouth Rock.

The Pilgrims' first winter was a difficult one. Half the colonists perished from malnutrition, disease, and exposure. But the colony survived, in large part because of crucial assistance from local Indians, who showed them how to gather seafood and cultivate corn. After the first autumn harvest, the settlers invited the natives to join them in a festival, the original Thanksgiving. The Pilgrims could not create rich farms on the sandy and marshy soil around Plymouth, but they developed a profitable trade in fish and furs. New colonists arrived from England, and in a decade the population reached the modest total of 300.

The people of Plymouth Plantation chose as their governor the remarkable William Bradford, who in 1621 won them title to their land from the Council for New England (the successor to the old Plymouth Company, which had charter rights to the territory). He never succeeded in his efforts to obtain a royal charter giving the Pilgrims clear rights of self-government, but Bradford governed successfully for many years without any real interference from London.

The Pilgrims were always a poor community. As late as the 1640s, they had only one plow among them. But they were, on the whole, content to be left alone to live their lives in what they considered godly ways. At times, they spoke of serving as a model for other Christians. But the Pilgrims were less concerned about how they were viewed by others than were the Puritans who settled the larger and more ambitious English colonies to their north.

The Massachusetts Bay Experiment

Turbulent events in England in the 1620s generated a strong interest in colonization among other groups of Puritans. James I had been creating tensions for years by his effort to assert the divine right of kings and by his harsh, repressive policies toward Puritans. The situation grew worse when he was succeeded in 1625 by his son, Charles I, who was even more aggressively autocratic than his father. The new king tried to restore Roman Catholicism to England and to destroy religious nonconformity. The Puritans were particular targets of Charles's policies; many of them were impris-

A M E R I C A N   V O I C E S

WILLIAM BRADFORD

Safe Arrival of the Pilgrims at Cape Cod

BEING THUS ARRIVED in a good harbor, and brought safe to land, they fell upon their knees and blessed the God of Heaven who had brought them over the vast and furious ocean, and delivered them from all the perils and miseries thereof, again to set their feet on the firm and stable earth, their proper element. . . .

But here I cannot but stay and make a pause, and stand half amazed at this poor people's present condition; . . . they had now no friends to welcome them nor inns to entertain or refresh their weatherbeaten bodies; no houses or much less towns to repair to, to seek for succour. It is recorded in Scripture as a mercy to the Apostle and his shipwrecked company, that the barbarians showed them no small kindness in refreshing them, but these savage barbarians, when they met with them . . . were readier to fill their sides full of arrows than otherwise. . . . Besides, what could they see but a hideous and desolate wilderness, full of wild beasts and wild men—and what multitudes there might be of them they knew not. . . . Which way soever they turned their eyes (save upward to the heavens) they could have little solace or content in respect of any outward objects. For summer being done, all things stand upon them with a weatherbeaten face, and the whole country, full of woods and thickets, represented a wild and savage hue.

SOURCE: William Bradford, *Of Plymouth Plantation: 1620–1647*, ed. Samuel Eliot Morison, pp. 61–62. Copyright 1952 Samuel Eliot Morison. Reprinted by permission of Alfred A. Knopf, Inc.

oned for their beliefs. The king dissolved Parliament in 1629 (it was not to be recalled until 1640), ensuring that there would be no political redress.

In the midst of this turmoil, a group of Puritan merchants began organizing a new enterprise to take advantage of opportunities in America. At first, their interest was largely an economic one. They obtained a grant of land in New England for most of the area now comprising Massachusetts and New Hampshire; and they acquired a charter from the king (who was evidently unaware of their religious inclinations) allowing them to create the Massachusetts Bay Company and to establish a colony in the New World. In 1629, they were ready to dispatch a substantial group of settlers to New England.

Some members of the Massachusetts Bay Company, however, saw the enterprise as something more than a business venture. They decided to emigrate themselves and try to create in New England a refuge for Puritans. After buying out the interests of the company members who preferred to stay in England, the new owners elected a governor, John Winthrop, who commanded the expedition that sailed for New England in 1630: seventeen ships and 1,000 people, mostly family groups. It was the largest single migration of its kind in the seventeenth century. Winthrop carried with him the charter of the Massachusetts Bay Company, which meant that the colonists would be responsible to no company officials in England.

The Massachusetts migration quickly produced several settlements. The port of Boston, at the mouth of the Charles River, became the capital, but in the course of the next decade colonists established several other towns in eastern Massachusetts: Charlestown, Newtown (later renamed Cambridge), Roxbury, Dorchester, Watertown, Ipswich, Concord, Sudbury, and others. The Massachusetts Bay Company soon transformed itself into the Massachusetts colonial government. According to the terms of the original company charter, the "freemen" (the eight stockholders) formed the governing body (or "general court") of the colony. But the colonists redefined "freemen" to include all male citizens. John Winthrop continued to dominate the politics of Massachusetts Bay, but after 1634 he and most other officers of the colony had to face election each year.

Unlike the Separatist founders of Plymouth, the Puritan founders of Massachusetts had come to America with no intention of breaking away from the Church of England. Yet if they continued to feel any real attachment to the Anglican establishment, they gave little sign of it in their behavior. In every town, the community church had (in the words of the prominent minister John Cotton) "complete liberty to stand alone," without connection to Anglican hierarchy or ritual. Each congregation chose its own minister and regulated its own affairs. The result was what became the Congregational church, a church controlled by its own congregation.

The Massachusetts Puritans were not grim or joyless, as many critics would later come to believe, but they were serious and pious. They strove to lead useful, conscientious lives of thrift and hard work, and they honored material success as evidence of God's favor. Winthrop and the other founders of Massachusetts believed they were founding a holy commonwealth, a model—a "city upon a hill"—for the corrupt world to see and emulate. But if Massachusetts was to become a beacon to others, it had first to maintain its own purity and "holiness." And to that end, the ministers and the officers of the government worked closely together. Massachusetts dissidents had no more freedom of worship than the Puritans themselves had had in England.

Like other new settlements, the Massachusetts Bay colony had early difficulties. During the first winter (1629–1630), nearly 200 died and many others decided to leave. But more rapidly than Jamestown, the colony grew and prospered. The nearby Pilgrims and neighboring Indians helped with food and advice. Incoming settlers, many of them affluent, brought needed tools and other goods. The dominance of families in the colony (a sharp contrast to the early years at Jamestown) helped ensure a feeling of commitment to the community and a sense of order among the settlers, and it also ensured that the population would reproduce itself.

Spreading Settlement

It did not take long for English settlement to begin moving outward from Massachusetts Bay to other parts of New England and beyond. Some people migrated in search of more productive soil than the stony land around Boston provided. Others left because of the oppressiveness of the church-dominated government of Massachusetts. Tolerance for those who were not practicing Puritans was limited, and most had little choice but to conform or leave.

The Connecticut River valley, about 100 miles west of Boston, began attracting English families as early as the 1630s, despite the presence of powerful native tribes and despite claims to those lands by the Dutch. The Connecticut settlers were attracted by the valley's fertile lands and by its isolation from the religious character of Massachusetts Bay. In 1635, Thomas Hooker, a minister of Newtown (Cambridge), defied the Massachusetts government, led his congregation west, and established the town of Hartford. Four years later, the people of Hartford and of two other newly founded towns nearby established a colonial government of their own and adopted a constitution known as the Fundamental Orders of Connecticut. This created a government similar to that of Massachusetts Bay but gave a larger proportion of the men the right to vote and hold office. (Women were barred from voting virtually everywhere.) Another Connecticut colony grew up around New Haven on the Connecticut coast. Unlike Hartford, it reflected unhappiness with what its founders considered the increasing religious laxity in Boston. The Fundamental Articles of New Haven (1639) established a Bible-based government even stricter than that of Massachusetts Bay. New Haven remained independent until 1662, when a royal charter officially gave the Hartford colony jurisdiction over the New Haven settlements.

European settlement in what is now Rhode Island was a result of the religious and political dissent of Roger Williams, an engaging but controversial young minister who lived for a time in Salem, Massachusetts. Williams was a confirmed Separatist who argued that the Massachusetts church should abandon even its nominal allegiance to the Church of England. He was also friendly with the neighboring Indians and proclaimed that the land the colonists were occupying belonged to the natives and not to the king or to the Massachusetts Bay Company. The colonial government considered Williams dangerous and voted to deport him, but he escaped before they could do so. During the bitter winter of 1635–1636, he took refuge with Narragansett tribesmen; and the following spring he bought a tract of land from them, and with a few followers, created the town of Providence on it. Williams considered himself the proprietor of the region and he called for complete freedom of worship. In 1644, after obtaining a charter from Parliament, he established a government for Providence and the surrounding settlements—a government that was based on the Massachusetts pattern but that did not restrict the vote to church members or tax the people for church support. For a time, Rhode Island was the only colony in which all faiths (including Judaism) could worship without interference.

Another challenge to the established religious order in Massachusetts Bay came from Anne Hutchinson, an intelligent and charismatic woman from a substantial Boston family. Hutchinson argued that the faithful could communicate directly with God (as she claimed she herself had done) and gain from Him assurance of grace and salvation. Such teachings (known as the Antinomian heresy) were a serious threat to the spiritual authority of the established clergy. The belief that an individual could receive a revelation directly from God carried with it an implication that ministers were not essential to the task of discovering one's chance of salvation. Hutchinson also affronted prevailing assumptions about the proper role of women in

Puritan society. She was not a retiring, deferential wife and mother, but a powerful religious figure in her own right.

As Hutchinson's influence grew, and as she began to deliver open attacks on members of the clergy, the Massachusetts hierarchy mobilized to stop her. In 1638, she was convicted of heresy and sedition and banished. With her family and some of her followers, she moved to a point on Narragansett Bay not far from Providence. Later she moved south into New York, where in 1643 she and her family died during an Indian uprising.

METACOMET, OR KING PHILIP This eighteenth-century engraving by Paul Revere shows the Indian chieftain Metacomet, known to the English as King Philip of Mount Hope (the site of his tribe's principal stronghold). Metacomet, son of Massasoit, became chief of the Wampanoags in 1662 and inherited his tribe's resentment at having been forced from their lands along Narragansett Bay by European settlers.

The Hutchinson affair had an important impact on the settlement of the areas north of Massachusetts Bay. New Hampshire and Maine were established in 1629 by two English proprietors. But despite lavish promotional efforts, few settlers moved into these northern regions until the religious disruptions in Massachusetts Bay. In 1639, John Wheelwright, a disciple of Anne Hutchinson, led some of his fellow dissenters to Exeter, New Hampshire. Other groups—of both dissenting and orthodox Puritans—soon followed. The Massachusetts Bay Company tried to extend its authority over this entire northern territory, with partial success. New Hampshire became a separate colony in 1679, but Maine remained a part of Massachusetts until 1820.

Settlers and Natives

The first white settlers in New England generally maintained amicable relations with the natives and learned much from them. Indians taught whites how to grow vital food crops such as corn, beans, pumpkins, and potatoes; they also taught them crucial agricultural techniques, such as annual burning for fertilization and planting beans to replenish exhausted soil. European farmers also benefited from the extensive lands Indians had already cleared (and either abandoned or sold). White traders used Indians as partners in some of their most important trading activities (and particularly in the creation of the thriving North American fur trade). Indeed, commerce with the Indians was responsible for the creation of some of the first great fortunes in British North America. Other white settlers attempted to educate the Indians in European religion and culture. Protestant missionaries converted some natives to Christianity, and a few Indians became at least partially assimilated into white society.

But as in other areas of white settlement, tensions soon developed in New England between Europeans and natives—primarily as a result of the white colonists' insatiable appetite for land and their steady encroachments into Indian territory. The particular character of those conflicts—and the brutality with which whites assaulted their Indian foes—emerged as well out of Puritan attitudes toward the natives. The religious leaders of New England came to consider the tribes a threat to their hopes of creating a godly community in the New World, particularly once dissenters such as Roger Williams began forming close relationships with the tribes. Gradually, the image of Indians as helpful neighbors came to be replaced by the image of Indians as "heathens" and barbarians.

In 1637, hostilities broke out between English settlers in the Connecticut Valley and the Pequot Indians of the region, a conflict (known as the Pequot War) that ended disastrously for the natives. The Pequot tribe was almost wiped out. But the bloodiest and most prolonged encounter between whites and Indians in the seventeenth century began in 1675, a conflict that whites called King Philip's War. As in the Pequot War, an Indian tribe—the Wampanoags, under the leadership of a chieftain known to the white settlers as King Philip and among his own people as Metacomet—rose up to resist English encroachment on its lands and the efforts of the colonial government to impose English law on the natives. (A court in Plymouth had recently tried and hanged several Wampanoags for murdering a member of their own tribe.)

For three years, the natives inflicted terror on a string of Massachusetts towns, killing over a thousand people (including at least one-sixteenth of the white males in the colony). But the white settlers gradually prevailed, beginning in 1676. Massachusetts leaders recruited guides and spies from rival tribes, including a group of Mohawks who ambushed Metacomet, shot and killed him, and then bore his severed head to Boston to present to the colonial leaders. Without Metacomet, the fragile alliance among the tribes collapsed, and the white settlers were soon able to crush the uprising.

Yet these victories by the white colonists did not end the danger to their settlements. This was in part because other Indians in other tribes were still capable of launching wars. It was also because the New England settlers faced competition not only from the natives but also from the Dutch and the French, who claimed the territory on which some of the outlying settlements were established. The French, in particular, would pose a constant threat to the English through their alliance with the Algonquins. In later years, they would support hostile Indians in their attacks on the New England frontier.

THE RESTORATION COLONIES

By the end of the 1630s, then, English settlers had established the beginnings of what would eventually become six of the thirteen original states of the American republic: Virginia, Massachusetts, Maryland, Connecticut, Rhode Island, and New Hampshire. But for nearly thirty years after Lord Baltimore received the charter for Maryland in 1632, no new English colonies were established in America. England was preoccupied with troubles of its own at home.

The English Civil War

The unpopular James I had attracted widespread opposition in England before he died in 1625, but he never came into open conflict with Parliament. His son, Charles I, was not so fortunate. After he dissolved Parliament in 1629 and began ruling as an absolute monarch, he steadily alienated a growing number of his subjects—and the members of the powerful Puritan community above all. Finally, desperately in need of money, Charles called Parliament back into session in 1640 and asked it to levy new taxes. But he antagonized the members by dismissing them twice in two years; and in 1642, they organized a military force, thus beginning the English Civil War.

The conflict between the Cavaliers (the supporters of the king) and the Roundheads (the forces of Parliament, who were largely Puritans) lasted seven years. In 1649, the Roundheads defeated the king's forces, captured Charles himself, and beheaded the monarch. The stern Roundhead leader Oliver Cromwell replaced the king and assumed the position of "protector." But when Cromwell died in 1658, his son and heir proved unable to maintain his authority, and two years later, King Charles II, son of the beheaded monarch, returned from exile and seized the throne, thus completing what became known as the Stuart Restoration.

Among the results of the Restoration was the resumption of colonization in America. Charles II rewarded faithful courtiers with grants of land in the New World and in the twenty-five years of his reign issued charters for four additional colonies: Carolina, New York, New Jersey, and Pennsylvania. The new colonies were all proprietary ventures (modeled on Maryland rather than on Virginia and Massachusetts), in large part because private companies were no longer taking an interest in launching colonies, having finally realized that there were no quick profits to be had in the New World. The new colonies had different aims: not so much quick commercial success as permanent settlements that would provide proprietors with land and power.

The Carolinas

Carolina (a name derived from the Latin word for "Charles") was, like Maryland, carved in part from the original Virginia grant. In successive charters issued in 1663 and 1665, Charles II awarded eight proprietors joint title to a vast territory stretching south to the Florida peninsula and west to the Pacific Ocean. Like Lord Baltimore, they received almost kingly powers over their grant. They reserved tremendous estates for themselves and distributed the rest through a headright system similar to those in Virginia and Maryland, after which they collected annual payments from the settlers. Although committed Anglicans themselves, they welcomed settlers of all Christian faiths and guaranteed them religious freedom in the colonial charter. The proprietors also allowed a measure of political freedom, creating a representative assembly to make laws. They hoped to attract settlers from the existing American colonies and to avoid the expense of financing expeditions from England.

But their initial efforts to profit from settlement in Carolina failed dismally. A few early colonizing ventures were quickly abandoned, and most of the original proprietors soon concluded that the Carolina venture could not succeed. One man, however, persisted—Anthony Ashley Cooper. Cooper convinced the other proprietors to give up on attracting settlers from other colonies and to finance expeditions to Carolina from England, the first of which set sail with 300 people in the spring of 1670. Only 100 people survived the difficult voyage; those who did established a settlement at Port Royal on the Carolina coast. Ten years later they founded a city at the junction of the Ashley and Cooper rivers, which in 1690 became the colonial capital. They called it Charles Town (it was later renamed Charleston).

With the aid of the English philosopher John Locke, Cooper (now the Earl of Shaftesbury) drew up the Fundamental Constitution for Carolina in 1669 in an attempt to create a highly ordered society. It divided the colony into counties of equal size and divided each county into equal parcels. The largest number of parcels would be distributed among the proprietors themselves (who were to be known as "seigneurs"); a local aristocracy (consisting of lesser nobles known as "landgraves" or "caciques") would receive fewer parcels; and ordinary settlers ("leet-men") would receive less land still. At the bottom of this stratified society would be poor whites, who had no political rights, and African slaves, whose subjection would be complete. Proprietors, nobles, and other landholders would have a voice in the colonial parliament in proportion to the size of their landholdings.

In fact, however, Carolina developed along lines quite different from the carefully ordered vision of Shaftesbury and Locke. For one thing, the colony was never really united in anything more than name. The northern and southern regions of settlement were widely separated and socially and economically distinct from one another. The northern settlers were mainly backwoods farmers, scratching out a meager existence at subsistence agriculture. They developed no important aristocracy and for many years imported virtually no black slaves. In the south, fertile lands and the good harbor at Charles Town promoted a far more prosperous economy and a far more stratified, aristocratic society. Settlements grew up rapidly along the

Ashley and Cooper rivers, and colonists established a flourishing trade, particularly (beginning in the 1660s) in rice—which was to become the colony's principal commercial crop.

Southern Carolina very early developed close commercial ties to the large (and overpopulated) European colony on the Caribbean island of Barbados. During the first ten years of settlement, most of the new residents in Carolina were Barbadians, some of whom arrived with large groups of black workers and established themselves as substantial landlords. African slavery had taken root on Barbados earlier than in any of the mainland colonies; and the white Caribbean migrants—tough, uncompromising profit seekers—established a similar slave-based plantation society in Carolina.

For several decades, Carolina remained one of the most factious of all the English colonies in America. There were tensions between the small farmers of the Albemarle region in the north and the wealthy planters in the south. And there were conflicts between the rich Barbadians in southern Carolina and the smaller landowners around them. After Lord Shaftesbury's death, the proprietors proved unable to establish order. In 1719, the colonists seized control of the colony from them. Ten years later, the king divided the region into two royal colonies, North and South Carolina.

New Netherland and New York

In 1664, Charles II granted his brother James, the Duke of York, all the territory lying between the Connecticut and Delaware rivers. But the grant faced major challenges. The Massachusetts Bay Company claimed some of the territory, and, more importantly, the Dutch claimed the entire area and controlled settlements at New Amsterdam and other strategic points.

England and the Netherlands were already commercial rivals in Europe, and that rivalry now extended to America, where the Dutch served as a wedge between the northern and southern English colonies. In 1664, vessels of the English navy, under the command of Richard Nicolls, put in at New Amsterdam and extracted a surrender from the arbitrary and unpopular Dutch governor, Peter Stuyvesant. Several years later, in 1673, the Dutch reconquered and briefly held their old provincial capital. But they lost it again, this time for good, in 1674.

The Duke of York, now firmly in possession of his territory, renamed it New York and set out to govern the diverse region. New York contained not only Dutch and English but Scandinavians, Germans, French, a large number of Africans (imported as slaves by the Dutch West India Company), as well as members of several different Indian tribes. James wisely made no effort to impose his own Roman Catholicism on the colony. He delegated powers to a governor and a council but made no provision for representative assemblies.

Property holding and political power remained highly divided and highly unequal in New York. In addition to confirming the great Dutch "patroonships" already in existence, James granted large estates to some of his own political supporters in order to create a class of influential land-owners loyal to him. Power in the colony thus remained widely dispersed— among wealthy English landlords, Dutch patroons, fur traders, and the duke's political appointees. By 1685, when the Duke of York ascended the English throne as James II, New York contained about four times as many people (around 30,000) as when he had taken power over it twenty years before, and it was one of the most factious colonies in America.

Shortly after James received his charter, he gave a large part of the land south of New York to a pair of political allies, both Carolina proprietors, Sir John Berkeley and Sir George Carteret. Carteret named the territory New Jersey, after the island in the English Channel on which he had been born. But the venture in New Jersey generated few profits, and in 1674, Berkeley sold his half interest. The colony was divided into two jurisdictions, East and West Jersey, which squabbled with one another until 1702, when the two halves of the colony were again joined and became a single royal colony.

New Jersey, like New York (from which much of the population had come), was a colony of enormous ethnic and religious diversity, and the weak colonial government made few efforts to impose strict control over the fragmented society. But unlike New York, New Jersey developed no impor-tant class of large landowners; most of its residents remained small farmers. Nor did New Jersey (which, unlike New York, had no natural harbor) produce any single important city.

The Quaker Colonies

Pennsylvania was born out of the efforts of a dissenting English Protestant sect, the Society of Friends, to find a home for their own distinctive social order. The society began in the mid-seventeenth century under the leader-ship of George Fox, a Nottingham shoemaker, and Margaret Fell. Their followers came to be known as Quakers (from Fox's instruction to them to "tremble at the name of the Lord"). Unlike the Puritans, Quakers rejected the concept of predestination and original sin. All people, they believed, had divinity within themselves and need only learn to cultivate it; all could attain salvation. Also unlike the Puritans, Quakers granted women a position within the church generally equal to that of men.

The Quakers had no formal church government and no traditional church buildings, only meetinghouses. They had no paid clergy, and in their worship they spoke up one by one as the spirit moved them. Disregarding distinctions of gender and class, they addressed one another with the terms "thee" and "thou," words commonly used in other parts of English society only in speaking to servants and social inferiors. As confirmed pacifists, they would not take part in wars. Unpopular in England both with the government and with members of other religious orders (whose services Quakers occasionally disrupted), the Quakers began looking to America for asylum. A few migrated to New England or Carolina, but most Quakers wanted a colony of their own. As members of a despised sect, however, they could not get the necessary royal grant without the aid of someone influential at the court.

Fortunately for the Quaker cause, a number of wealthy and prominent men had converted to the faith. One of them was William Penn, whose father, Sir William Penn, was an admiral in the Royal Navy and a landlord of valuable Irish estates. Over his father's objections, the younger Penn converted to Quakerism, took up evangelism, and was sent repeatedly to prison. He soon began working with George Fox to create a Quaker colony in America.

Penn looked first to New Jersey, half of which (after 1674) belonged to two fellow Quakers. But in 1681, after the death of his father, he received from the king an even more valuable grant of lands. Penn had inherited his father's claim to a large debt from the king. Charles II paid the debt with an enormous grant of territory between New York and Maryland, which Penn was to control as both landlord and ruler. At the king's insistence, the territory was to be named Pennsylvania, after Penn's late father.

Through his informative and honest advertising, Penn soon made Pennsylvania the best-known and most cosmopolitan of all the English colonies in America, a place to which settlers flocked from England and the Continent. More than any other English colony, Pennsylvania prospered from the outset, because of Penn's successful recruiting, his thoughtful planning, and the region's mild climate and fertile soil. But the colony never became a great source of profit for Penn or his descendants. Indeed, Penn himself, near the end of his life, was imprisoned in England for debt and died in poverty in 1718.

But Penn was much more than a mere real-estate promoter, and he undertook in Pennsylvania what he called a "holy experiment." He personally sailed to Pennsylvania in 1682 to oversee the laying out, between the Delaware and the Schuylkill rivers, of the city he named Philadelphia ("Brotherly Love"), which with its rectangular streets helped set the pattern for most later cities in America. Penn recognized Indian claims to the land in the province, and he was scrupulous about reimbursing them for it. The Indians respected Penn, and during his lifetime the colony had no major battles with the natives.

But the colony was not without conflict. By the late 1690s, some residents of Pennsylvania were beginning to chafe at the nearly absolute power of the proprietor. Residents of the southern areas of the colony, in particular, complained that the government in Philadelphia was unresponsive to their needs. Pressure from these groups grew to the point that in 1701, shortly before he departed for England for the last time, Penn agreed to a Charter of Liberties for the colony. The charter established a representative assembly (consisting, alone among the English colonies, of only one house), which greatly limited the authority of the proprietor. The charter also permitted "the lower counties" of the colony to establish their own representative assembly. The three counties did so in 1703 and as a result became, in effect, a separate colony—Delaware—although until the Revolution it continued to have the same governor as Pennsylvania.

The Founding of Georgia

Not until 1733, decades after the founding of the Restoration colonies, did another new English settlement emerge in America: Georgia, the last English colony to be established in what would become the United States. Georgia was unlike any other colony. It was founded neither by a corporation nor by a wealthy proprietor. Its guiding purpose was neither the pursuit of profit nor the desire for a religious refuge. The founders of Georgia, led by General James Oglethorpe, were driven primarily by military and philanthropic motives. They wanted to erect a military barrier against the Spanish lands on the southern border of English America; and they wanted to provide a refuge for the impoverished, a place where English men and women without prospects at home could begin a new life.

The need for a military buffer between South Carolina and the Spanish settlements in Florida was growing urgent in the first years of the eighteenth century. There had been tensions between the Spanish and the English in

North America ever since the founding of Jamestown. And when hostilities broke out in Europe between Spain and England in 1701 (known in England as Queen Anne's War and on the Continent as the War of the Spanish Succession), fighting renewed in America as well. That war ended in 1713, but another European conflict with repercussions for the New World was continually expected.

Oglethorpe, a hero of Queen Anne's War, was very much aware of the military advantages of an English colony south of the Carolinas. Yet his interest in the settlement was primarily philanthropic. As head of a parliamentary committee investigating English prisons, he was moved by the plight of honest debtors rotting in confinement. Such prisoners, and other poor people in danger of succumbing to a similar fate, could, he believed, become the farmer-soldiers of the new colony in America.

A 1732 charter from King George II transferred the land between the Savannah and Altamaha rivers to Oglethorpe and his fellow trustees. Oglethorpe himself led the first colonial expedition to Georgia, which built a fortified town at the mouth of the Savannah River in 1733 and later constructed additional forts south of the Altamaha. The trustees organized the colony in part to make it militarily defensible. They limited the size of landholdings to make the settlement compact and easily defended against Spanish and Indian attacks. Blacks—free or slave—were excluded; rum was prohibited; Roman Catholics were excluded; and trade with the Indians was strictly regulated—all to limit the possibility of wartime insurrection or collusion with future enemies. In the end, only a few debtors were released from jail and sent to Georgia; but the trustees brought hundreds of needy tradesmen and artisans from England and Scotland and many religious refugees from Switzerland and Germany.

The strict rules governing life in the new colony helped stifle its development and create dissent in its early years. Settlers in Georgia needed a work force, and almost from the start they began demanding the right to buy slaves. Some opposed the restrictions on the size of individual property holdings. Many resented the nearly absolute political power of Oglethorpe and the trustees. As a result, newcomers to the region generally preferred to settle in South Carolina, where there were fewer restrictive laws. Eventually the trustees removed the limitation on individual landholding and later the ban on slavery and the prohibition of rum. In 1751, they returned control of the colony to the king, who immediately permitted the election of a representative assembly. Georgia continued to grow more slowly than the other southern colonies, but it now developed along lines roughly similar to those of South Carolina.

THE DEVELOPMENT OF EMPIRE

The English colonies in America had originated as quite separate projects, and for the most part they grew up independent of one another and subject to little more than nominal control from London. Yet by the mid-seventeenth century, the growing commercial success of the colonial ventures was producing pressure in England for a more rational, uniform structure to the empire.

The Drive for Reorganization

Reorganization, its advocates claimed, was necessary to ensure the success of the mercantile system, the foundation of the English economy. For the new possessions truly to promote mercantilist goals, England decided it would have to exclude foreigners (as Spain had done) from its colonial trade. But in that decision were the seeds of conflict, because many American colonists had developed a profitable trade with the Spanish, Dutch, and French and were likely to resist interference with it.

The English government began trying to regulate colonial trade in the 1650s, when Parliament passed laws to keep Dutch ships out of the English colonies. Later Parliament passed three important Navigation Acts. The first of them, in 1660, closed the colonies to all trade except that carried in by English ships and required that tobacco and other items be exported from the colonies only to England or to an English possession. The second act, in 1663, required that all goods sent from Europe to the colonies pass through England on the way, where they would be subject to English taxation. The third act, in 1673, imposed duties on the coastal trade among the English colonies, and it provided for the appointment of customs officials to enforce the Navigation Acts. These acts, with later amendments and additions, formed the legal basis of England's mercantile system in America for a century.

The Dominion of New England

Before the Navigation Acts, all the colonial governments (except that of Virginia, a "royal colony" with a governor appointed by the king) had operated largely independently of the crown, with governors chosen by the proprietors or by the colonists themselves and with powerful representative assemblies. Officials in London recognized that to increase their control over their colonies they would have to create an instrument separate from the independent-minded colonial governments, which were unlikely to enforce the new laws.

In 1675, the king created a new body, the Lords of Trade, to make recommendations for imperial reform. Following their advice, he moved in 1679 to increase his control over Massachusetts, the most defiant of the colonies. He stripped it of its authority over New Hampshire and chartered a separate, royal colony there whose governor he would himself appoint. He also began seeking legal grounds for revoking the colony's corporate charter and making Massachusetts itself a royal colony. He soon became convinced that he had found such grounds in the defiance of the Navigation Acts and the Lords of Trade by the Massachusetts General Court, which insisted that Parliament had no power to legislate for the colony. In 1684, the king finally succeeded in revoking the Massachusetts charter.

Charles II's brother, James II, who succeeded him to the throne in 1685, went further. He created a single Dominion of New England, which combined the government of Massachusetts with the governments of the rest of the New England colonies and later with those of New York and New Jersey as well. He eliminated the existing assemblies within the new Dominion and appointed a single governor, Sir Edmund Andros, to supervise the entire region from Boston. Andros's rigid enforcement of the Navigation Acts and his brusque dismissal of the colonists' claims to the "rights of Englishmen" made him quickly and thoroughly unpopular.

The "Glorious Revolution"

James II was not only losing friends in America; he was making powerful enemies in England by attempting to exercise autocratic control over Parliament and the courts and by appointing his fellow Catholics to high office. By 1688, his popular support had all but vanished, and Parliament invited his Protestant daughter Mary and her husband, William of Orange, ruler of the Netherlands, to assume the throne. James II (perhaps remembering what had happened to his father, Charles I) offered no resistance and fled to France. As a result of this bloodless coup, which the English called "the Glorious Revolution," William and Mary became joint sovereigns.

When Bostonians heard of the overthrow of James II, they moved quickly to unseat his unpopular viceroy in New England. Andros was arrested and imprisoned. The new sovereigns in England accepted the toppling of Andros, quickly abolished the Dominion of New England, and restored separate colonial governments. They did not, however, re-create them as they had been. In 1691, they combined Massachusetts with Plymouth and made it a royal colony. The new charter restored the General Court, but it gave the crown the right to appoint the governor. It also replaced church membership with property ownership as the basis for voting and officeholding.

Andros had been governing New York through a lieutenant governor, Captain Francis Nicholson, who enjoyed the support of the wealthy merchants and fur traders of the province. Other, less favored colonists—farmers, mechanics, small traders, and shopkeepers—had a long accumulation of grievances against Nicholson and his allies. The leadership of the New York dissidents fell to Jacob Leisler, a German immigrant and a prosperous merchant. He had married into a prominent Dutch family but had never won acceptance as one of the colony's ruling class. In May 1689, when news of the Glorious Revolution in England and the fall of Andros in Boston reached New York, Leisler raised a militia, captured the city fort, drove Nicholson into exile, and proclaimed himself the new head of government in New York. For two years, he tried in vain to stabilize his power in the colony amid fierce factional rivalry. In 1691, when William and Mary appointed a new governor, Leisler briefly resisted. He soon yielded, but his hesitation allowed his many political enemies to charge him with treason. He was convicted and executed. Fierce rivalry between what became known as the "Leislerians" and the "anti-Leislerians" dominated the politics of the factious colony for many years thereafter.

In Maryland, many people erroneously assumed when they heard news of the Glorious Revolution that their proprietor, the Catholic Lord Baltimore who was living in England, had sided with the Catholic James II and opposed William and Mary. So in 1689, an old opponent of the proprietor's government, the Protestant John Coode, led a revolt that drove out Lord Baltimore's officials and petitioned the crown for a charter as a royal colony. In 1691, William and Mary complied, stripping the proprietor of his authority. The colonial assembly established the Church of England as the colony's official religion and excluded Catholics from public office. Maryland became a proprietary colony again in 1715, but only after the fifth Lord Baltimore joined the Anglican church.

Thus the Glorious Revolution of 1688 in England touched off revolutions, mostly bloodless ones, in several colonies. Under the new king and queen, the representative assemblies that had been abolished were revived, and the scheme for colonial unification from above was abandoned. But the Glorious Revolution in America was not, as many Americans later came to believe, a clear demonstration of American resolve to govern itself or a clear victory for colonial self-rule. In New York and Maryland, in particular, the uprisings had more to do with local factional and religious divisions than with any larger vision of the nature of the empire. And while the insurgencies did succeed in eliminating the short-lived Dominion of New England, their ultimate results were governments that actually increased the crown's potential authority. As the first century of English settlement in America came to its end, the colonists were becoming more a part of the imperial system than ever before.

CHAPTER THREE

Life in Provincial America

The Colonial Population ~ *The Colonial Economy*
Patterns of Society ~ *The Colonial Mind*

A̲s THE EXTENT of settlement in North America grew, and as the economies of the colonies began to flourish, several distinctive ways of life emerged. The new American societies differed considerably from the society that most had attempted to re-create in the New World— the society of England. They differed as well from one another. Indeed, the pattern of society in some areas of North America seemed to resemble that of others scarcely at all. Americans would eventually decide that they had enough in common to enable them to join together and form a single nation. But regional differences would continue to shape their society throughout their history.

THE COLONIAL POPULATION

After uncertain beginnings at Jamestown and Plymouth, the non-Indian population of English North America grew rapidly and substantially, through continued immigration and through natural increase, until by the late seventeenth century European and African immigrants outnumbered the natives along the Atlantic coast.

A few of the early settlers were members of the English upper classes, but for the most part the early colonial population was decidedly unaristocratic. It included some members of the emerging English middle class, businessmen who migrated to America for religious or commercial reasons or both. But the dominant element was English laborers. Some came independently, such as the religious dissenters in early New England, who came as families, paid their own way, and settled on their own land. But in the Chesapeake, at least three-fourths of the immigrants in the seventeenth century arrived as indentured servants.

Indentured Servitude

The system of temporary servitude developed out of practices in England. Young men and women bound themselves to masters for fixed terms of servitude (usually four to five years) in exchange for passage to America, food, and shelter. Upon completion of their service, male indentures were supposed to receive clothing, tools, and occasionally land; in reality, however, many left service with nothing. Roughly one-fourth of the indentures in the Chesapeake were women, most of whom worked as domestic servants and could expect to marry when their terms of servitude expired, since men greatly outnumbered women in the region.

Most indentured servants came to the colonies voluntarily, but some did not. Beginning as early as 1617, the English government occasionally dumped shiploads of convicts in America to be sold into servitude. The government also transported prisoners taken in battles with the Scots and the Irish in the 1650s, as well as orphans, vagrants, and paupers. Other involuntary immigrants were victims of kidnapping, or "impressment," by unscrupulous investors and promoters.

By the late seventeenth century, the indentured servant population had become one of the largest elements of the population and was creating serious social problems. Some former indentures managed to establish themselves successfully as farmers, tradespeople, or artisans. Some women married propertied men. Others (mostly males) found themselves without land, without employment, without families, and without prospects; and there grew up in some areas, particularly the Chesapeake, a large floating population of young single men—such as those who supported Bacon's Rebellion—who served as a potential (and at times actual) source of social unrest. Even those free laborers who did find employment or land for themselves and settled down with families often did not stay put for very long. Many families simply pulled up stakes and moved to other, more promising locations every few years.

Beginning in the 1670s, a decrease in the birth rate and an improvement in economic conditions in England reduced the pressures on laboring men and women to emigrate, and the flow of indentured servants declined. Those who did travel to America as indentured servants generally avoided the Southern colonies, where working conditions were arduous and prospects for advancement were slim. In the Chesapeake, therefore, landowners were

AMERICAN VOICES

GOTTLIEB MITTLEBERGER

An Indentured Servant's Voyage from Germany to America

BOTH IN ROTTERDAM and in Amsterdam the people are packed densely, like herrings so to say, in the large sea-vessels. . . . During the voyage there is on board these ships terrible misery, stench, fumes, horror, vomiting, many kinds of sea-sickness, fever, dysentery, headache, heat, constipation, boils, scurvy, cancer, mouthrot, and the like, all of which come from old and sharply salted food and meat, also from very bad and foul water, so that many die miserably. . . . Many sigh and cry, "Oh, that I were at home again, and if I had to lie in my pigsty!" . . . Many hundred people necessarily die and perish in such misery, and must be cast into the sea, which drives their relatives . . . to such despair that it is almost impossible to pacify and console them. . . .

When the ships have landed at Philadelphia after their long voyage, no one is permitted to leave them except those who pay for their passage or can give good security; the others, who cannot pay, must remain on board the ships till they are purchased, and are released from the ships by their purchasers. The sick always fare the worst, for the healthy are naturally preferred and purchased first; and so the sick and wretched must often remain on board in front of the city for 2 or 3 weeks, and frequently die. . . . Many parents must sell and trade away their children like so many head of cattle. . . . It often happens that such parents and children, after leaving the ship, do not see each other again for many years, perhaps no more in their lives.

beginning to rely much more heavily on African slavery as their principal source of labor.

Birth and Death

Although immigration remained for a time the greatest source of population increase, the most important long-range factor in the growth of the colonial population was its ability to reproduce itself. Marked improvement in the reproduction rate began in New England and the mid-Atlantic colonies in the second half of the seventeenth century, and after the 1650s natural increase became the most important source of population growth in those areas. The New England population more than quadrupled through reproduction alone in the second half of the seventeenth century. That was not just because families were having large numbers of children. It was also because life expectancy in New England was unusually high, both in comparison to that of other colonies and in comparison to that of England.

Conditions improved much more slowly in the South. The high mortality rates in the Chesapeake region did not begin to decline to the levels of those elsewhere until the mid-eighteenth century. Throughout the seventeenth century, the average life expectancy for men in the region was just over forty years, and for women slightly less. (In New England, life expectancy was up to thirty years longer.) One in four children died in infancy, and half died before the age of twenty. Children who survived infancy often lost one or both of their parents before reaching maturity. Widows, widowers, and orphans thus formed a substantial proportion of the Chesapeake population. Only after settlers developed immunity to local diseases (particularly malaria) did life expectancy increase significantly. Population growth was substantial in the region, but it was largely a result of immigration.

The natural increases in the population in the seventeenth century were in large part a result of a steady improvement in the balance between men and women in the colonies. In the early years of settlement, more than three-quarters of the white population of the Chesapeake consisted of men. And even in New England, which from the beginning had attracted more families (and thus more women) than the Southern colonies, 60 percent of the inhabitants were male in 1650. Gradually, however, more women began to arrive in the colonies; and increasing birth rates, which of course produced roughly equal numbers of males and females, contributed to shifting the sex ratio as well. By the late seventeenth century, the proportion of males to females in all the colonies was becoming more balanced.

Women and Families in the Colonies

The importance of reproduction in the labor-scarce society of seventeenth-century America had significant effects on both the status and the life cycles of women. The high sex ratio meant that few women remained unmarried for long. The average European woman in America married for the first time at twenty or twenty-one years of age, considerably earlier than in England.

In the Chesapeake, the extraordinarily high mortality rate made the traditional patriarchal family structure of England—by which husbands and fathers exercised firm, even dictatorial control over the lives of their wives and children—difficult to maintain. Because so few families remained intact for long, rigid patterns of familial authority were constantly undermined and sexual mores grew more flexible than in England or other parts of America.

Because of the large numbers of indentured servants who were forbidden to marry until their terms of service expired, premarital sexual relationships were frequent. Over a third of Chesapeake marriages occurred with the bride already pregnant. Bastard children were usually taken from their mothers and bound out as indentured servants at a young age.

Women in the Chesapeake could anticipate a life consumed with childbearing. The average wife experienced pregnancies every two years. Those who lived long enough bore an average of eight children apiece (up to five of whom typically died in infancy or early childhood). Since childbirth was one of the most frequent causes of female death, relatively few women survived to see all their children grow to maturity.

But Southern white women did enjoy certain advantages. Because men were plentiful and women scarce, females had considerable latitude in choosing husbands. Because women generally married at a much younger age than men, they also tended to outlive their husbands. Widows were generally left with several children and with responsibility for managing a farm or plantation, a circumstance of enormous hardship but one that also gave them significant economic power. Widows seldom remained unmarried for long, however. And since many widows married men who were themselves widowers, complex combinations of households were frequent.

By the early eighteenth century, the demographic character of the Chesapeake was beginning to change, and with it the nature and structure of the typical family. Life expectancy was increasing, and indentured servitude was in decline. Natural reproduction was becoming the principal source of white population growth. The sex ratio was becoming more equal. One result of these changes was that life for white people in the region became less perilous and less arduous. Another result was that women lost some of the power that their small numbers had once given them. As families grew more stable, traditional patterns of male authority revived. By the mid-eighteenth century, Southern families were becoming highly patriarchal.

In New England, where many more immigrants arrived with family members and where death rates declined far more quickly, family structure was much more stable than in the Chesapeake and hence much more traditional. Because the sex ratio was less imbalanced, most men could expect to marry. But women remained in the minority. As in the Chesapeake, they married young, began producing children early, and continued to do so well into their thirties. In contrast to the situation in the South, however, Northern children were more likely to survive (the average family raised six to eight children to maturity), and their families were more likely to remain intact. Fewer New England women became widows, and those who did generally lost their husbands later in life. Hence women were less often cast in roles independent of their husbands. Young women, moreover, had less control over the conditions of marriage, both because there were fewer unmarried men vying for them and because their fathers were more likely to be alive and able to exercise control over their choices.

The longer lives in New England meant that parents continued to influence their children's lives far longer than did parents in the South. They did not often actually "arrange" marriages for their children, but few sons and daughters could choose a spouse entirely independently of their parents' wishes. Men tended to rely on their fathers for land to cultivate—generally a prerequisite for beginning families of their own. Women needed dowries from their parents if they were to hope to attract desirable husbands. Stricter parental supervision of children meant, too, that fewer women became pregnant before marriage than was the case in the South (although even in Puritan New England, the premarital pregnancy rate was as high as 20 percent in some communities).

Puritanism placed a high value on the family, which was not only the principal economic unit but the principal religious unit within every community. In one sense, then, women played important roles within the family because the position of wife and mother was highly valued in Puritan culture. At the same time, however, Puritanism served to reinforce the idea of nearly absolute male authority and the assumption of female weakness and inferiority. Women were expected to be modest and submissive. A wife was expected to devote herself almost entirely to serving the needs of her husband. Yet however subservient they may have been, women were vital to the family economy. They were continuously engaged in tasks crucial to the functioning of the farm—gardening, raising poultry, tending cattle, spinning, and weaving, as well as cooking, cleaning, and washing.

Family life in the Chesapeake colonies grew more patriarchal in the late seventeenth and early eighteenth centuries. New England families were growing somewhat less so. As settlement spread beyond the early Puritan centers, as the authority of the church began gradually to decline, and as sons began increasingly to chafe under the control of their fathers, family life became somewhat more fluid, and the rigid division of authority between generations and between the sexes that had characterized seventeenth-century communities became less universal.

The Beginnings of Slavery in English North America

The demand for black servants to supplement the scarce Southern labor supply existed almost from the first moments of settlement. The supply of African laborers, however, remained relatively restricted during much of the seventeenth century because the Atlantic slave trade did not serve the English colonies in America then. Gradually, however, a substantial commerce in slaves grew up within the Americas, particularly between the Caribbean islands and the Southern colonies of English America. By the late seventeenth century, the supply of black workers in North America was becoming plentiful.

As the commerce in slaves grew more extensive and more sophisticated, it also grew more horrible. Before it ended in the nineteenth century, it was responsible for the forced immigration of as many as 11 million Africans to North and South America and the Caribbean. Indeed, until the late eighteenth century, the number of African immigrants to the Americas was higher than that of Europeans. In the flourishing slave marts on the African coast, native chieftains made large numbers of blacks available by capturing members of enemy tribes in battle and bringing them out of the forests and to the ports. The terrified victims were then packed into the dark, filthy holds of ships for the horrors of the "middle passage"—the long journey to America, during which the black prisoners were kept chained in the bowels of the slave ships and supplied with only minimal food and water. Women were often victims of rape and other sexual abuse. Those who died en route, and many did, were simply thrown overboard. Slave traders tried to cram as many Africans as possible into their ships to ensure that enough would survive to yield a profit at journey's end. Upon arrival in the New World,

AFRICANS BOUND FOR AMERICA Shown here are the below-deck slave quarters of a Spanish vessel en route to the West Indies. A British warship captured the slaver, and a young English naval officer (Lt. Francis Meynell) made this watercolor sketch on the spot. The Africans seen in this picture appear somewhat more comfortable than prisoners on other slave ships, some of whom were chained and packed together so tightly that they had no room to stand or even sit.

slaves were auctioned off to white landowners and transported, frightened and bewildered, to their new homes.

North America was a less important destination for African slaves than were such other parts of the New World as the islands of the Caribbean and Brazil; fewer than 5 percent of the Africans imported to the Americas arrived first in the English colonies. At first, those blacks who were transported to what became the United States came not directly from Africa but from the West Indies. Not until the 1670s did traders start importing blacks directly from Africa to North America. Even then the flow remained small for a time, mainly because a single group, the Royal African Company of England, monopolized the trade and kept prices high and supplies low.

A turning point in the history of the black population in North America was 1697, the year the Royal African Company's monopoly was broken. With the trade now open to competition, prices fell and the number of blacks greatly increased. By 1700, about 25,000 black slaves lived in English North America. That was only 10 percent of the total non-Indian population. But because blacks were so heavily concentrated in a few Southern colonies, they were already beginning to outnumber whites in some areas. There were perhaps twice as many black men as black women in most areas, but in some places the African-American population grew by natural increase nevertheless. In the Chesapeake more new slaves were being born than were being imported from Africa. In South Carolina, by contrast, the arduous conditions of rice cultivation ensured that the black population would barely be able to sustain itself through natural increase until much later.

By 1760, the number of Africans in the colonies had increased to approximately a quarter of a million. A few (16,000 in 1763) lived in New England; slightly more (29,000) lived in the middle colonies. The vast majority, however, continued to live in the South. By then blacks had almost wholly replaced white indentured servants as the basis of the Southern work force.

For a time, the legal and social status of the African laborers remained somewhat fluid. In some areas—South Carolina, for example, where the number of black arrivals swelled more quickly than anywhere else—whites and blacks worked together at first on terms of relative equality. Some blacks were treated much like white hired servants, and some were freed after a fixed term of servitude. A few blacks themselves became landowners, and some apparently owned slaves of their own. By the late seventeenth century, however, a rigid distinction was emerging between blacks and whites. White workers could not be bound to a master indefinitely, but there was no legal requirement that masters free black workers after a term of service. Gradually, the assumption spread that blacks would remain in service permanently and that black children would inherit their parents' bondage. White beliefs about the inferiority of the black race reinforced the growing rigidity of the system. That slavery was developing in a society that was already multiracial also had an impact on its evolution. Whites had long ago defined themselves as a superior race in their relations with the native Indian population; the idea of subordinating an inferior race was, therefore, already part of European thinking by the time substantial numbers of Africans appeared in their midst.

The system of permanent servitude—American slavery—became legal in the early eighteenth century when colonial assemblies began to pass "slave codes" granting almost absolute authority to white masters over their slaves. One factor only determined whether a person was subject to the slave codes:

color. In the colonial societies of Spanish America, people of mixed race were granted a different (and higher) status than pure Africans. English America recognized no such distinctions. Any African ancestry was enough to classify a person as black.

Later Immigration

The most distinctive and enduring feature of the American population was that it brought together peoples of many different races, ethnic groups, and nationalities. North America was home to a substantial population of natives, to a growing number of English immigrants, to forcibly imported Africans, and to substantial non-English groups from Europe. When the flow of immigrants from England began to decline in the early eighteenth century, large numbers of whites continued to immigrate to North America from France, Germany, Switzerland, Ireland, Scotland, and Scandinavia.

The earliest of these non-English European immigrants were the French Calvinists, or Huguenots, escaping religious persecution in Roman Catholic France. A total of about 300,000 left France, a few of them for the English colonies of North America, after the Edict of Nantes, which had guaranteed them substantial liberties, was revoked in 1695. Many German Protestants suffered similarly from the arbitrary religious policies of their rulers, and all Germans suffered from the frequent wars between their principalities and France. Because of its proximity to France, the Rhineland of southwestern Germany, known as the Palatinate, was exposed to frequent invasion, which sent more than 12,000 Germans fleeing to England early in the eighteenth century; approximately 3,000 of them found their way to America. Most settled in Pennsylvania, where they ultimately became known to English settlers as the "Pennsylvania Dutch," (a corruption of the German term for their nationality, *Deutsch*). Other, later German immigrants headed to Pennsylvania as well, among them the Moravians and Mennonites, whose religious views were similar to those of the Quakers.

The most numerous of the newcomers were the so-called Scotch-Irish—Scotch Presbyterians who had settled in northern Ireland (in the county of Ulster) in the early seventeenth century. Most of the Scotch-Irish in America pushed out to the edges of European settlement and occupied land without much regard for who actually claimed to own it, whether absentee whites, Indians, or the colonial governments. They were as ruthless in their displacement and suppression of the Indians as they had been with the native Irish Catholics in Ireland.

There were also immigrants from Scotland itself and from southern

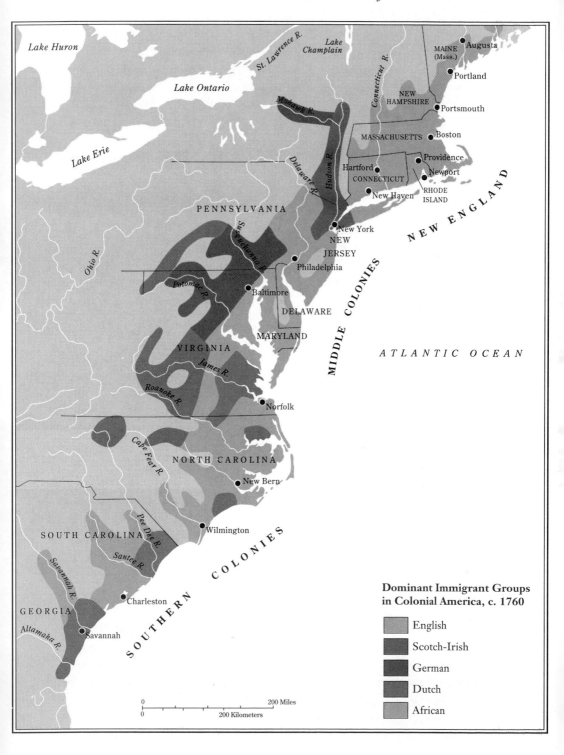

Lake Huron

St. Lawrence R.

Lake Champlain

MAINE (Mass.) Augusta

Connecticut R.

Portland

Lake Ontario

NEW HAMPSHIRE

Portsmouth

Mohawk R.

MASSACHUSETTS Boston

Lake Erie

Delaware R.

Hudson R.

Providence

Hartford Newport

CONNECTICUT

New Haven RHODE ISLAND

NEW ENGLAND

PENNSYLVANIA

Susquehanna R.

New York

NEW JERSEY

Ohio R.

Philadelphia

MIDDLE COLONIES

Potomac R.

Baltimore

DELAWARE

MARYLAND

ATLANTIC OCEAN

VIRGINIA

James R.

Roanoke R.

Norfolk

NORTH CAROLINA

Cape Fear R.

New Bern

Pee Dee R.

Wilmington

SOUTH CAROLINA

Santee R.

SOUTHERN COLONIES

Savannah R.

Charleston

GEORGIA

Altamaha R.

Savannah

Dominant Immigrant Groups in Colonial America, c. 1760

English

Scotch-Irish

German

Dutch

African

0   200 Miles

0   200 Kilometers

66 ~ THE UNFINISHED NATION

Ireland. Scottish Highlanders, some of them Roman Catholics, immigrated to North Carolina above all. Scottish Presbyterian Lowlanders, fleeing high rents and unemployment, left for America in large numbers shortly before the American Revolution. The Irish migrated steadily over a long period and by the time of the Revolution were almost as numerous as the Scots. Many of them had by then abandoned their Roman Catholic religion and much of their ethnic identity.

By 1775, the non-Indian population of the colonies was over 2 million—a nearly tenfold increase since the beginning of the century. Throughout the colonial period, the population nearly doubled every twenty-five years. Its continuing and increasing ethnic diversity became one of many factors dividing colonial society from the society of England.

THE COLONIAL ECONOMY

Farming dominated almost all areas of European and African settlement in North America throughout the seventeenth and eighteenth centuries. Even so, the economies of the different regions varied markedly from one another.

The Southern Economy

A strong European demand for tobacco enabled some planters in the Chesapeake (Maryland and Virginia) to grow enormously wealthy and at times allowed the region as a whole to prosper. But throughout the seventeenth and eighteenth centuries, production of tobacco frequently exceeded demand, and as a result the price of the crop could suffer severe declines. The result was a boom-and-bust cycle in the Chesapeake economy, with the first major bust occurring in 1640.

Most of the Chesapeake planters believed that the way to protect themselves from the instability of the market was to grow more tobacco. That only made the overproduction problem worse. It also encouraged those planters who could afford to do so to expand their landholdings, enlarge their fields, and acquire additional laborers. After 1700, tobacco plantations employing several dozen slaves or more were common.

South Carolina and Georgia relied on rice production, since the low-lying coastline with its many tidal rivers made it possible to build rice paddies that could be flooded and drained. Rice cultivation was arduous work—performed standing knee deep in malarial swamps—a task so difficult and unhealthy that white laborers generally refused to perform it. Hence planters in South Carolina and Georgia were far more dependent on slaves than were their Northern counterparts. African workers were adept at rice cultivation, in part because some of them had come from rice-producing regions of west Africa and in part because they were generally more accustomed to the hot and humid climate than were the Europeans.

Because of their dependence on large-scale cash crops, the Southern colonies developed less of a commercial or industrial economy than the colonies of the North. The trading in tobacco and rice was handled largely by merchants based in London and, later, in the Northern colonies. Few cities of more than modest size developed in the South. A pattern was established that would characterize the Southern economy, and differentiate it from that of other regions, for more than two centuries.

SELLING TOBACCO This late-seventeenth-century label was used in the sale of American tobacco in England. The drawing depicts Virginia as a land of bright sunshine, energetic slaves, and prosperous, pipe-smoking planters.

The Northern Economy

In the North, as in the South, agriculture continued to dominate, but it was agriculture of a more diverse kind. In addition to farming, there gradually emerged an important commercial sector of the economy.

One reason that agriculture did not remain the exclusive economic pursuit of the North was that conditions for farming were less favorable than in the South. In northern New England, in particular, colder weather and hard, rocky soil made it difficult for colonists to develop the kind of large-scale commercial farming system that Southerners were creating. Most New Englanders did not produce a staple crop that could become a major export item; they planted largely to meet the needs of their own families. Conditions for agriculture were better in southern New England and the middle colonies, where the soil was fertile and the weather more temperate. New York, Pennsylvania, and the Connecticut River valley were the chief suppliers of wheat to much of New England and to parts of the South.

Beginning with a failed effort to establish an ironworks in Saugus, Massachusetts, in the mid-seventeenth century, colonists in New England and the middle colonies embarked on industrial ventures as well. Almost every colonist engaged in a certain amount of industry at home. Occasionally these home industries provided families with goods they could trade or sell. Beyond these domestic efforts, craftsmen and artisans established themselves in colonial towns as cobblers, blacksmiths, riflemakers, cabinetmakers, silversmiths, and printers. In some areas, entrepreneurs harnessed water power to run small mills for grinding grain, processing cloth, or milling lumber. And in several places, large-scale shipbuilding operations began to flourish.

The largest industrial enterprise anywhere in English North America was the ironworks of the German ironmaster Peter Hasenclever in northern New Jersey. Founded in 1764 with British capital, it employed several hundred laborers, many of them imported from ironworks in Germany. There were other, smaller ironmaking enterprises in every northern colony (with particular concentrations in Massachusetts, New Jersey, and Pennsylvania), and there were ironworks as well in several of the southern colonies. But these and other growing industries did not become the basis for the kind of explosive industrial growth that Great Britain experienced in the late eighteenth century—in part because parliamentary regulations such as the Iron Act of 1750 restricted colonists from engaging in metal processing and stifled the development of a steel industry in America. Similar prohibitions reduced the manufacture of woolens, hats, and other goods. But the most important obstacles to industrialization in America were an inadequate labor supply, a small domestic market, and inadequate transportation facilities and energy supplies.

More important than manufacturing to the economy of the Northern colonies were extractive industries, which exploited the natural resources of the continent. By the mid-seventeenth century, the flourishing fur trade of earlier years was in decline; the supply of fur-bearing animals along the Atlantic seaboard had been nearly exhausted, and the interior fur trade was largely in the hands of the Algonquins and their French allies. More important now were lumbering, mining, and fishing, particularly in the waters off the New England coast. These industries provided commodities that could be exported to England in exchange for manufactured goods. And they helped, therefore, to produce the most distinctive feature of the Northern economy—a thriving commercial class.

The Rise of Commerce

Perhaps the most remarkable feature of colonial commerce in the seventeenth century was that it was able to survive at all. American merchants faced such bewildering and intimidating obstacles, and lacked so many of the basic institutions of trade, that they managed to stay afloat only with great difficulty. There was no commonly accepted money. The colonies had almost no gold or silver, and their paper currency was not acceptable as payment for goods from abroad. For many years, colonial merchants had to rely on barter or on money substitutes such as beaver skins.

A second obstacle was lack of information about supply and demand. Traders had no way of knowing what they would find in foreign ports; vessels sometimes stayed at sea for years, journeying from one port to another, trading one commodity for another, attempting to find some way to turn a profit. There were, moreover, an enormous number of small, fiercely competitive companies, which made the problem of rationalizing the system even more acute.

Nevertheless, commerce in the colonies survived and grew. There was an elaborate coastal trade, through which the colonies did business with one another and with the West Indies. The mainland colonies traded rum, agricultural products, meat, and fish. The islands offered sugar, molasses, and at times slaves in return. There was also trade with England, continental Europe, and the west coast of Africa. This commerce has often been described, somewhat inaccurately, as the "triangular trade," suggesting a neat process by which merchants carried rum and other goods from New

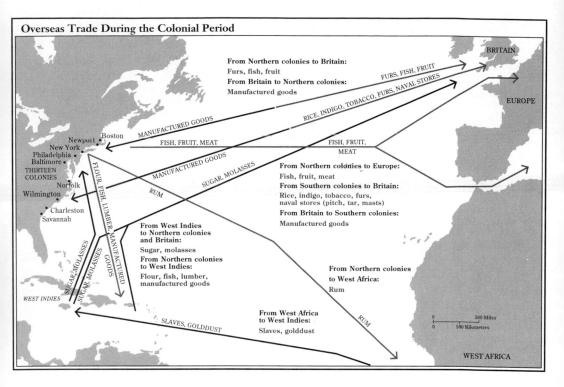

Overseas Trade During the Colonial Period

BRITAIN

EUROPE

From Northern colonies to Britain:
Furs, fish, fruit
From Britain to Northern colonies:
Manufactured goods

FURS, FISH, FRUIT

RICE, INDIGO, TOBACCO, FURS, NAVAL STORES

MANUFACTURED GOODS

FISH, FRUIT, MEAT

FISH, FRUIT, MEAT

Newport · Boston
New York
Philadelphia ·
Baltimore ·
THIRTEEN
COLONIES
Norfolk
Wilmington
Charleston
Savannah

FLOUR, FISH, LUMBER, MANUFACTURED

MANUFACTURED GOODS

SUGAR, MOLASSES

RUM

From Northern colonies to Europe:
Fish, fruit, meat
From Southern colonies to Britain:
Rice, indigo, tobacco, furs,
naval stores (pitch, tar, masts)
From Britain to Southern colonies:
Manufactured goods

From West Indies
to Northern colonies
and Britain:
Sugar, molasses
From Northern colonies
to West Indies:
Flour, fish, lumber,
manufactured goods

SUGAR, MOLASSES

SUGAR, MOLASSES

MANUFACTURED GOODS

WEST INDIES

From Northern colonies
to West Africa:
Rum

SLAVES, GOLDDUST

From West Africa
to West Indies:
Slaves, golddust

RUM

0   500 Miles
0   500 Kilometers

WEST AFRICA

England to Africa, exchanged their merchandise for slaves, whom they then transported to the West Indies (hence the term "middle passage" for the dread journey—it was the second of the three legs of the voyage), and then exchanged the slaves for sugar and molasses, which they shipped back to New England to be distilled into rum. In fact, the so-called "triangular" trade in rum, slaves, and sugar was a maze of highly diverse trade routes.

Out of this risky trade emerged a group of adventurous entrepreneurs who by the mid-eighteenth century were beginning to constitute a distinct merchant class concentrated in the port cities of the North. The British Navigation Acts protected them from foreign competition in the colonies. They had ready access to the market in England for such colonial products as furs, timber, and American-built ships. But they also developed markets illegally outside the British Empire—in the French, Spanish, and Dutch West Indies, where prices were often higher than in the British colonies.

During the eighteenth century, the colonial commercial system began to stabilize. But the trading sector of the American economy remained open to newcomers, largely because it—and the society on which it was based—was expanding so rapidly.

PATTERNS OF SOCIETY

Although there were sharp social distinctions in the colonies, the well-defined and deeply entrenched class system of England failed to reproduce itself in America. In England, land was scarce and the population large, and the relatively few landowners had enormous power over the landless. In America, in contrast, land was abundant and people were scarce. Aristocracies emerged there, to be sure; but they tended to rely less on landownership than on control of a substantial work force, and they were generally less secure and less powerful than their English counterparts. More than in England, there were opportunities in America for social mobility—both up and down. There were also new forms of community in America, and they varied greatly from one region to another.

The Plantation

The plantation system of the American South illustrated clearly the way in which colonial communities evolved in response to local conditions. The first plantations emerged in the tobacco-growing areas of Virginia and Maryland. Some of the early planters hoped to re-create in America the entrenched, landholding aristocracy of England, and in a few cases—notably in the great Maryland estates granted by Lord Baltimore to his relatives and friends—a semblance of such an aristocracy did emerge. On the whole, however, seventeenth-century colonial plantations were rough and relatively small estates. In the early days in Virginia, they were little more than crude clearings where landowners and indentured servants worked side by side in conditions so harsh that death was an everyday occurrence. Even in later years, when the death rate declined and the landholdings became more established, plantation work forces seldom exceeded thirty people. Most landowners lived in rough cabins or houses, with their servants or slaves nearby.

The economy of the plantation was a precarious one. Planters could not control their markets, so even the largest of them were constantly at risk. When prices fell—as tobacco prices did, for example, in the 1660s—they faced the prospect of ruin. The plantation economy created many new wealthy landowners, but it also destroyed many.

Because plantations were often far from cities and towns, they tended to become self-contained communities. Wealthier planters often created something approaching a full town on their plantations. Smaller planters lived more modestly, but still in a relatively self-sufficient world. On the larger estates, plantation mistresses, unlike the wives of small farmers, had servants to perform ordinary household chores, thus freeing up time they could devote to their husbands and children. But many also had to tolerate sexual liaisons between their husbands or sons and black women of the slave community.

Even though the fortunes of planters could rise and fall quickly, there were always particularly wealthy landowners who exercised great social and economic influence. A great landowner controlled not only the lives of those who worked his own plantation but the livelihood of poorer neighbors who could not compete with him and thus depended on him to market their crops and supply them with credit. Some whites were unable to own their land and rented their farms from wealthy planters. Such independent farmers, working with few or no slaves to help them, formed the majority of the Southern agrarian population; but the planters dominated the Southern agrarian economy.

The enslaved African-Americans, of course, lived very differently. On the smaller farms with only a handful of slaves, it was not always possible for a rigid separation to develop between whites and blacks. But over three-fourths of all blacks lived on plantations of at least ten slaves; nearly half lived in communities of fifty slaves or more. And in these places they began to develop a society and culture of their own. Although whites seldom encouraged formal marriages among slaves, blacks themselves developed a strong and elaborate family structure. Slaves attempted to construct nuclear families, and they managed at times to build stable households. But families were always precarious, because any member could be sold at any time to another planter, even to one in another colony. As a result, blacks placed special emphasis on extended kinship networks and created surrogate "relatives" for people separated entirely from their own families. There was also a distinctive slave religion, which blended Christianity with African folklore and which became a central element in the emergence of an independent black culture.

Nevertheless, black society was subject to constant intrusions from and interaction with white society. Black house servants, for example, were isolated from their own community and were under constant surveillance from whites. Black women were subject to the usually unwanted sexual advances from owners and overseers and hence to bearing mulatto children, who were rarely recognized by their white fathers but were generally accepted as members of the slave community. On some plantations, black workers were treated with kindness and sometimes responded with genuine devotion. On others, they encountered physical brutality and occasionally even sadism, against which they were virtually powerless.

There were several slave rebellions during the colonial period. The most important was the Stono Rebellion in South Carolina in 1739, during which about 100 blacks rose up, seized weapons, killed several whites, and attempted to escape south to Florida. The uprising was quickly crushed, and most participants were executed. A more frequent form of resistance was simply running away, but that provided no real solution either. There was nowhere to go. And so for most slaves, resistance took the form of subtle, and often undetected, defiance or evasion of their masters' wishes.

Most slaves, male and female, worked as field hands (with the women shouldering the additional burdens of cooking and child rearing). But on the larger plantations that aspired to genuine self-sufficiency, some slaves learned trades and crafts: blacksmithing, carpentry, shoemaking, spinning, weaving, sewing, midwifery, and others. These skilled crafts workers were at times hired out to other planters. Some set up their own establishments in towns or cities and shared their profits with their owners. A few were able to buy their freedom. There was a small free black population living in Southern cities by the time of the Revolution.

The Puritan Community

The characteristic social unit in New England was not the isolated farm but the town. In the early years of colonization, each new settlement drew up a "covenant" binding all residents together in a religious and social unit. The structure of the towns reflected the spirit of the covenant. Colonists laid out a village, with houses and a meetinghouse arranged around a central pasture, or "common." Thus families generally lived with their neighbors close by, reinforcing the strong sense of community. They divided up the outlying fields and woodlands among the residents; the size and location of a family's field depended on the family's numbers, wealth, and social station.

Once a town was established, residents held a yearly "town meeting" to decide important questions and to choose a group of "selectmen," who ran the town's affairs. Participation in the meeting was generally restricted to adult males who were members of the church. Only those who could give evidence of grace, of being among the elect (the "visible saints") assured of salvation, were admitted to full membership, although other residents of the town were required to attend church services.

New Englanders did not adopt the English system of primogeniture—the passing of all property to the firstborn son. Instead, a father divided up his land among all his sons. His control of this inheritance gave him great power over the family. Often a son would reach his late twenties before his father would allow him to move into his own household and work his own land. Even then, sons would usually continue to live in close proximity to their fathers. Young women were generally more mobile than their brothers, since they did not stand to inherit land.

The early Puritan community was, in short, a tightly knit organism. The town as a whole was bound together by the initial covenant, by the centralized layout of the village, by the power of the church, and by the town meeting. The family was held together by the rigid patriarchal structure that limited opportunities for younger members (males in particular) to strike out on their own. Yet as the years passed and the communities grew, this communal structure experienced strains. This was partly because of the increasing commercialization of New England society, which introduced new forces and new tensions into the communities of the region. It was also partly because of population growth. As towns grew larger, residents tended to cultivate lands farther and farther from the community center and, by necessity, to live at increasing distances from the church. Often, groups of outlying residents would apply for permission to build a church of their own, usually the first step toward creation of a wholly new town. Such applications could cause bitter quarrels between the original townspeople and those who proposed to break away.

The control of land by fathers also created strains. In the first generations, fathers generally controlled enough land to satisfy the needs of all their sons. After several generations, however, when such lands were being subdivided for the third or fourth time, there was often too little to go around, particularly in communities surrounded by other towns, with no room to expand outward. The result was that in many communities, groups of younger residents broke off and moved elsewhere—at times far away—to form towns of their own.

But it was only against the strict standards of the first years of settlement, and the even stricter standards of Puritan expectations, that New England towns were unraveling. Measured against most contemporary communities in England or other parts of America, the Puritan town remained remarkably communal.

The tensions building in Puritan communities could produce bizarre and disastrous events. One example was the widespread hysteria in the 1680s and 1690s over accusations of witchcraft (the human exercise of Satanic powers) in New England. The most famous outbreak (although by no means the only one) was in Salem, Massachusetts, where adolescent girls began to exhibit strange behavior and leveled charges of witchcraft against several West Indian servants steeped in voodoo lore. Hysteria spread throughout the town, and hundreds of people (most of them women) were accused of witchcraft. Nineteen residents of Salem were put to death before the trials finally ended in 1692; the girls who had been the original accusers later recanted and admitted that their story had been fabricated.

The Salem experience was not unique. Accusations of witchcraft spread through many New England towns in the early 1690s (and indeed had emerged regularly in Puritan society for many years before). Research into the background of accused witches reveals that most were middle-aged women, often widowed, with few or no children. Accused witches were, moreover, generally of low social position, were often involved in domestic conflicts, had frequently been accused of other crimes, and were considered abrasive by their neighbors. Many "witches" were women who were not

ACCUSATION OF A WITCH This picture, created in the 1690s by an artist working with inlaid wood, conveys something of the terror that witchcraft accusations produced in New England communities in the seventeenth century.

securely lodged within a patriarchal family structure and who seemed to defy the passive norms Puritan society had created for them. That suggests that tensions over gender roles played a substantial role in generating the crisis. The witchcraft controversies were also a reflection of the highly religious character of New England societies. New Englanders believed in the power of Satan and his ability to assert his power in the world. Belief in witchcraft was not a marginal superstition, rejected by the mainstream. It was a common feature of Puritan religious conviction.

Cities

Even the largest colonial community was scarcely bigger than a modern small town. Yet by the standards of the eighteenth century, cities did exist in America. In the 1770s the two largest ports—Philadelphia and New York—had populations of 28,000 and 25,000, respectively, which made them larger than most English urban centers. Boston (16,000), Charles Town (later Charleston), South Carolina (12,000), and Newport, Rhode Island (11,000), were also substantial communities by the standards of the day.

Colonial cities served as trading centers for the farmers of their regions and as marts for international commerce. Their leaders were generally merchants who had acquired substantial estates. Sharp class divisions may not often have emerged in the cities, but more than in any other area of colonial life (except of course in the relationship between masters and slaves) social distinctions were real and visible in urban areas.

Cities were the centers of much of what industry there was in the colonies, such as the distilleries for turning imported molasses into exportable rum. They were the locations of the most advanced schools and sophisticated cultural activities and of shops where imported goods could be bought. In addition, they were communities with urban social problems: crime, vice, pollution, traffic. Unlike smaller towns, cities needed to set up constables' offices and fire departments and develop systems for supporting the urban poor, whose numbers became especially large in times of economic crisis—to which cities were particularly vulnerable.

Finally, cities became places where new ideas could circulate and be discussed. There were newspapers, books, and other publications from abroad, and hence new intellectual influences. The taverns and coffeehouses of cities provided forums in which people could gather and debate the issues of the day. That is one reason why the Revolutionary crisis, when it began to build in the 1760s and 1770s, manifested itself first in the cities.

THE COLONIAL MIND

Intellectual life in colonial America revolved around the conflict between the traditional outlook of the sixteenth and seventeenth centuries, with its emphasis on a personal God deeply involved in individual lives, and the new spirit of the Enlightenment, which was sweeping both Europe and America and which stressed the importance of science and human reason. The old views placed a high value on a stern moral code in which intellect was less important than faith. The Enlightenment suggested that people had substantial control over their own lives and societies.

The Pattern of Religions

Religious toleration flourished in America to a degree unmatched in any European nation, not because Americans deliberately sought to produce it, but because conditions virtually required it. Settlers in America brought with them so many different religious practices that it proved impossible to impose a single religious code on any large area.

The experience of the Church of England illustrated how difficult the establishment of a common religion would be in the colonies. By law, Anglicanism was established as the official faith in Virginia, Maryland, New York, the Carolinas, and Georgia. In these colonies everyone, regardless of belief or affiliation, was supposed to be taxed for the support of the church. Except in Virginia and Maryland, however, the laws establishing the Church of England as the official colonial religion were largely ignored. Missionaries of the Society for the Propagation of the Gospel, founded in 1701 to spread the Anglican faith, had some success in Massachusetts and Connecticut. But Anglicanism never succeeded in becoming a dominant religious force in America.

Even in New England, where the Puritans had originally believed that they were all part of a single faith, there was a growing tendency in the eighteenth century for different congregations to affiliate with different denominations, especially Congregationalism and Presbyterianism. In parts of New York and New Jersey, Dutch settlers had established their own Calvinist denomination, Dutch Reformed, which survived after the colonies became part of the British Empire. The American Baptists (of whom Roger Williams is considered the first) were also originally Calvinistic in their theology, but a great variety of Baptist sects emerged. They shared the belief that rebaptism, usually by total immersion, was necessary when believers reached maturity. But while some Baptists remained Calvinists, believers in predestination, others came to believe in salvation by free will.

Protestants extended toleration to one another more readily than they did to Roman Catholics. Many Protestants feared and hated the pope. New Englanders, in particular, viewed their Catholic neighbors in New France (Canada) not only as commercial and military rivals but as agents of Rome bent on frustrating their own divine mission. In most of the English colonies, however, Roman Catholics were too few to cause serious conflict. They were most numerous in Maryland, and even there they numbered no more than 3,000. Perhaps for that reason they suffered their worst persecution in that colony. After the overthrow of the original proprietors in 1691, Catholics in Maryland not only lost their political rights but were forbidden to hold religious services except in private houses.

Jews in provincial America totaled no more than about 2,000 at any time. The largest community lived in New York City. Smaller groups settled in Newport and Charleston, and there were scattered Jewish families in all the colonies. Nowhere could they vote or hold office. Only in Rhode Island could they practice their religion openly.

By the beginning of the eighteenth century, some Americans were growing troubled by the apparent decline in religious piety in their society. With so many diverse sects existing side by side, some people were tempted to doubt whether any particular denomination, even their own, possessed a monopoly of truth. The movement of the population westward and the wide scattering of settlements had caused many communities to lose touch with organized religion. The rise of commercial prosperity created a secular outlook in urban areas. The progress of science and free thought in Europe—and the importation of Enlightenment ideas to America—caused at least some colonists to doubt traditional religious belief.

Concerns about declining piety surfaced as early as the 1660s in New England, where the Puritan oligarchy warned of a deterioration in the power of the church. Sabbath after Sabbath, ministers preached sermons of despair (known as "jeremiads"), deploring the signs of waning piety. By the standards of other societies or other eras, the Puritan faith remained remarkably strong. But New Englanders measured their faith by their own standards, and to them the "declension" of religious piety seemed a serious problem.

The Great Awakening

By the early eighteenth century, similar concerns were emerging in other regions and among members of other faiths. Everywhere, colonists were coming to believe, religious piety was in decline and opportunities for spiritual regeneration were dwindling. The result was the first great American revival: the Great Awakening.

The Great Awakening began in earnest in the 1730s, reached its climax in the 1740s, and brought a new spirit of religious fervor that many believed was reversing the trend away from piety. The revival had particular appeal to women (who constituted the majority of converts) and to younger sons of the third or fourth generation of settlers—those who stood to inherit the least land and who faced the most uncertain futures. The rhetoric of the revival emphasized the potential for every person to break away from the constraints of the past and start anew in his or her relationship to God— which seemed to reflect the desire of many people to break away from their families or communities and start a new life in the world.

Powerful evangelists from England helped spread the revival. John and Charles Wesley, the founders of Methodism, visited Georgia and other colonies in the 1730s. George Whitefield, a powerful open-air preacher and for a time an associate of the Wesleys, made several evangelizing tours through the colonies and drew tremendous crowds. But the evangelizers from abroad were less important to American revivalism in the long run than the colonial ministers attempting to restore religious fervor in America. The outstanding preacher of the Great Awakening was the New England Congregationalist Jonathan Edwards—a deeply orthodox Puritan but a highly original theologian. From his pulpit in Northampton, Massachusetts, Edwards attacked the new doctrines of easy salvation for all. He preached anew the traditional Puritan ideas of the absolute sovereignty of God, predestination, and salvation by God's grace alone. His vivid descriptions of hell could terrify his listeners.

The Great Awakening led to the division of existing congregations (between "New Light" revivalists and traditionalists) and to the founding of new ones. It also affected areas of society outside the churches. Some of the revivalists denounced book learning as a hindrance to salvation, and some communities repudiated secular education altogether. But other evangelists saw education as a means of furthering religion, and they founded or led schools for the training of New Light ministers.

Education

Many colonists placed a high value on education, despite the difficulties they confronted in gaining access to it. Some families tried to teach their children to read and write at home, although the heavy burden of work in most agricultural households limited the time available for schooling. In Massachusetts, a 1647 law required that every town support a public school; and while many communities failed to comply, a modest network of institutions emerged as a result. The Quakers and other sects operated church schools; and in some communities, widows or unmarried women conducted "dame schools" by holding private classes in their homes. In cities, master craftsmen set up evening schools for their apprentices.

White male Americans, at least, achieved a high degree of literacy in the eighteenth century. By the time of the Revolution, well over half of all white men could read and write, a rate substantially higher than that in most European countries. The literacy rate for women lagged behind the rate for men until the nineteenth century; and while opportunities for education beyond the primary level were scarce for men, they were almost nonexistent for women. Nevertheless, the literacy rate for females was also substantially higher than that of their European counterparts.

African-Americans, most of whom were enslaved, had virtually no access to education. Occasionally a master or mistress would teach slave children to read and write; but as the slave system became more firmly

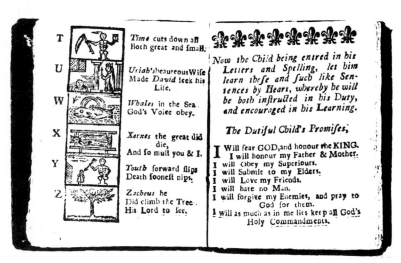

A "DAME SCHOOL" PRIMER More than the residents of any other region of North America (and far more than those of most of Europe), the New England colonists strove to educate their children and achieved perhaps the highest level of literacy in the world. Throughout the region, young children attended institutions known as "dame schools" (because the teachers were almost always women) and learned from primers such as this one.

entrenched, strong social (and ultimately legal) sanctions developed to discourage such efforts, lest literacy encourage slaves to question their stations. Indians, too, remained largely outside the white educational system—to a large degree by choice: most tribes preferred to educate their children in their own way. But some white missionaries and philanthropists established schools for Native Americans and helped create a small but significant population of Indians literate in spoken and written English.

Nowhere was the intermingling of traditional religiosity and the new spirit of the Enlightenment clearer than in the colleges and universities of colonial America. Of the six colleges in operation by 1763, all but two were founded by religious groups primarily for the training of preachers. Yet in almost all, the influences of the new scientific, rational approach to knowledge could be felt.

Harvard, the first American college, was established in 1636 by Puritan theologians who wanted to create a training center for ministers. (The college was named for a Charlestown minister, John Harvard, who had left his library and half his estate to the college). Decades later, in 1693, William and Mary College (named for the English king and queen) was established in Williamsburg, Virginia, by Anglicans; like Harvard, it was conceived as an academy to train clergymen. And in 1701, conservative Congregationalists, dissatisfied with the growing religious liberalism of Harvard, founded Yale (named for one of its first benefactors, Elihu Yale) in New Haven, Connecticut. Out of the Great Awakening emerged the College of New Jersey, founded in 1746 and known later as Princeton (after the town in which it was located); one of its first presidents was Jonathan Edwards. Despite the religious basis of these colleges, most of them offered curricula that included not only theology but logic, ethics, physics, geometry, astronomy, rhetoric, Latin, Hebrew, and Greek. King's College, founded in New York in 1754 and later renamed Columbia, was specifically devoted to the spread of secular knowledge; it had no theological faculty and was interdenominational from the start. The Academy and College of Philadelphia, which became the University of Pennsylvania, was from its birth in 1755 a completely secular institution, founded by a group of laymen under the inspiration of Benjamin Franklin.

After 1700, most colonial leaders received their entire education in America (rather than attending university in England, as had once been the case). But the advantages of higher education were not widely shared. Women, blacks, and Indians were excluded from all colleges and universities. And among white men, only those from relatively affluent families could afford to attend.

Concepts of Law and Politics

In law and politics, as in other parts of their lives, Americans in the seventeenth and eighteenth centuries believed that they were re-creating in the New World the practices and institutions of the Old. But as in other areas, they in fact created something very different.

Changes in the law in America resulted in part from the scarcity of English-trained lawyers, who were almost unknown in the colonies until after 1700. Although the American legal system adopted most of the essential elements of the English system, including such ancient rights as trial by jury, significant differences developed in court procedures, punishments, and the definition of crimes. In England, for example, a printed attack on a public official, whether true or false, was considered libelous. At the 1734 trial of the New York publisher John Peter Zenger, who was powerfully defended by the Philadelphia lawyer Andrew Hamilton, the courts ruled that criticisms of the government were not libelous if factually true—a verdict that removed some colonial restrictions on the freedom of the press.

More significant for the future of the relationship between the colonies and England were differences emerging between the American and British political systems. Because the royal government—in theory the ultimate authority over the colonies— was so far away, Americans created a group of institutions of their own that gave them a large measure of self-government. In most colonies, local communities grew accustomed to running their own affairs with minimal interference from higher authorities. The colonial assemblies came to exercise many of the powers that Parliament exercised in England. Provincial governors (appointed by the king after the 1690s) had broad powers on paper, but in fact their influence was sharply limited. Control over appointments and contracts resided largely in England or with local colonial leaders. A governor could be removed any time his patron in England lost favor. And in some cases, governors were not even familiar with the colonies they were meant to govern; most governors were Englishmen who came to the colonies for the first time to assume their offices.

The result of all this was that the focus of politics in the colonies became a local one, the provincial governments became accustomed to acting more or less independently of Parliament, and a set of assumptions and expectations about the rights of the colonists took hold in America that was not shared by policymakers in England. These differences caused few problems before the 1760s, because the British did little to exert the authority they believed they possessed. But when, beginning in 1763, the English government began attempting to tighten its control over the American colonies, a historic crisis resulted.

DEBATING THE PAST

The Origins of Slavery

THE DEBATE AMONG historians over how and why white Americans created a system of slave labor in the seventeenth century—and how and why they determined that African-Americans and no others should populate that system—has been an unusually lively one. At its center is a debate over whether slavery was a result of white racism, or whether racism was a result of slavery.

In 1950, Oscar and Mary Handlin published an influential article comparing slavery to other systems of "unfreedom" in the colonies. What separated slavery from other conditions of servitude, they argued, was that it was restricted to people of African descent, that it was permanent, and that it passed from one generation to the next. The unique characteristics of slavery, the Handlins argued, were part of an effort by colonial legislatures to increase the available labor force. White laborers needed an incentive to come to America; black laborers, forcibly imported from Africa, did not. The distinction between the conditions of white workers and the conditions of black workers was, therefore, based on legal and economic motives, not on racism.

Winthrop Jordan was one of a number of historians who later challenged the Handlins' thesis and argued that white racism, more than economic interests, produced African slavery. In *White Over Black* (1968), Jordan argued that Europeans had long viewed people of color—and black Africans in particular—as inferior beings appropriate for serving whites. Those attitudes migrated with white Europeans to the New World, and white racism shaped the treatment of Africans in America—and the nature of the slave labor system—from the beginning. Even without the economic

(continued on next page)

incentives the Hanlins described, in other words, whites would have been likely to oppress blacks in the New World.

Peter Wood's *Black Majority* (1974), a study of seventeenth-century South Carolina, was one of a number of works that moved the debate back towards social and economic conditions in the 1970s and after. Wood demonstrated that blacks and whites often worked together on relatively equal terms in the early years of settlement; that racism, in other words, did not inevitably shape the relationships between blacks and whites. But as rice cultivation expanded, it became more difficult to find white laborers willing to do the arduous work. The increase in the forcible importation of African workers, and the creation of a system of permanent bondage, was a response to this growing demand for labor. It was also a response to fears among whites that without slavery it would be difficult to control a labor force brought to America against its will. Edmund Morgan's *American Slavery, American Freedom* (1975) argued similarly that the southern labor system was at first relatively flexible and later grew more rigid. In colonial Virginia, he claimed, white settlers did not at first intend to create a system of permanent bondage for blacks or whites. But as the tobacco economy grew and created a high demand for cheap labor, white landowners began to feel uneasy about their dependence on a large group of dependent white workers. Such workers were difficult to recruit and control. Slavery, therefore, was less a result of racism than of the desire for whites to find a reliable and stable labor force.

In recent years, the debate over the origins of slavery has become part of a larger debate over the nature of racism in American (and world) history. Some scholars continue to argue, as Winthrop Jordan did in the 1960s, that racism is a powerful, autonomous part of white culture, which exists independent of other factors. Others argue that race as a category of distinction among human beings is itself meaningless; since there are no significant biological or genetic distinctions separating the races, the belief that there are important differences is always an invention, or "construction," designed to serve other needs. Just as historians have argued that eighteenth-century racism was a product and not a cause of slavery, so other scholars argue that racism in other times is an ideology created to justify systems of oppression that serve economic, political, or other needs.

CHAPTER FOUR

The Empire Under Strain

Origins of Resistance ~ *The Struggle for the Continent*
The New Imperialism ~ *Stirrings of Revolt* ~ *Cooperation and War*

A
S LATE AS the 1750s, few Americans objected to their membership in the British Empire. The imperial system had commercial and political benefits for the Americans. And it had few costs, because for the most part, the English government left the colonies alone. By the mid-1770s, however, the relationship between the American colonies and their British rulers had become so strained, so poisoned, so characterized by suspicion and resentment that the empire was on the verge of unraveling. And in the spring of 1775, the first shots were fired in a war that would ultimately win America its independence. How had it happened? And why so quickly?

ORIGINS OF RESISTANCE

In one sense, it had not happened quickly at all. Ever since the first days of English settlement in North America, the ideas and institutions of the colonies had been diverging from those in Britain in countless ways. In another sense, however, the Revolutionary crisis emerged in response to important and relatively sudden changes in the administration of the empire. Because in 1763, the English government began to enforce a series of policies toward its colonies that brought the differences between the two societies into sharp focus.

A Loosening of Ties

In the fifty years after the Glorious Revolution, the English Parliament (which became the British Parliament after the union of England and Scotland in 1707) established a growing supremacy over the king. During the reigns of George I (1714–1727) and George II (1727–1760), both of whom were German-born and unaccustomed to English ways, the prime minister and his cabinet became the nation's real executives. They held their positions not by the king's favor but by their ability to control a majority in Parliament.

These parliamentary leaders were less inclined than the seventeenth-century monarchs had been to try to tighten control over the empire. They depended politically on the great merchants and landholders, most of whom feared that any such efforts would reduce the profitability of the colonial trade. As a result, administration of colonial affairs remained decentralized and inefficient, with no single office or agency responsible for colonial affairs.

The character of the royal officials in America—the governors and other officers of the royal colonies and (in all the colonies) the naval officers and collectors of customs—contributed further to the looseness of the imperial system. Some of these officeholders were able and intelligent; most were not. Many, perhaps most, colonial officials had used bribery to obtain their offices; many, perhaps most, accepted bribes once they assumed their offices. Some appointees remained in England and hired substitutes to take their places in America.

Resistance to imperial authority centered in the colonial legislatures. By the 1750s the assemblies had become accustomed to levying taxes, making appropriations, approving appointments, and passing laws for their respective colonies. The assemblies came to look upon themselves as little parliaments, each practically as sovereign within its colony as Parliament itself was in England.

Intercolonial Disunity

Even so, the colonists continued to think of themselves as loyal English subjects. Many felt stronger ties to England than they did to one another, so great were the differences among the societies of the various colonies. Yet for all their differences, the colonies could not avoid forging connections with one another. As settlement became almost continuous along the seacoast, people of the different colonies came into closer contact. The gradual construction of roads, the rise of trade, and the creation of a colonial postal service also forged intercolonial ties.

Still, the colonists were reluctant to cooperate even when, in 1754, they faced a common threat from their old rivals, the French, and France's Indian allies. A conference of colonial leaders—with delegates from Pennsylvania, Maryland, New York, and New England—was meeting in Albany in that year to negotiate a treaty with the Iroquois. The delegates tentatively approved a plan offered by Benjamin Franklin to set up a "general government" in America to manage relations with the Indians on behalf of all the colonies. War with the French and Indians was already beginning when this Albany Plan was presented to the colonial assemblies. None approved it.

THE STRUGGLE FOR THE CONTINENT

The war that raged in North America through the late 1750s and early 1760s was part of a larger struggle between England and France for dominance in world trade and naval power. The British victory in that struggle, known in Europe as the Seven Years' War, confirmed England's commercial supremacy and cemented its control of the settled regions of North America.

In America, however, the conflict was also the final stage in a long struggle among the three principal powers in northeastern North America: the English, the French, and the Iroquois. For more than a century prior to the conflict—known in America as the French and Indian War—these three groups had maintained a precarious balance of power. The events of the 1750s upset that balance, produced a prolonged and open conflict, and established a precarious dominance for the English societies throughout the region. The war also brought English America into closer contact with British authority than ever before and raised to the surface some of the underlying tensions in the colonial relationship.

New France and the Iroquois Nation

The French and the English had coexisted relatively peacefully in North America for nearly a century. But by the 1750s, as both English and French settlements expanded, religious and commercial tensions began to produce new frictions and new conflicts.

By the end of the seventeenth century, the French Empire in America comprised a vast territory. In the 1680s, French explorers journeyed as far south as the delta of the Mississippi, claimed the surrounding country for France, and named it Louisiana in honor of King Louis XIV. Subsequent traders and missionaries wandered southwest as far as the Rio Grande and west to the Rocky Mountains. The French had by then revealed the outlines of, and laid claim to, the whole continental interior.

To secure their hold on these enormous claims, they founded a string of widely separated communities, strategically located fortresses, and far-flung missions and trading posts. Fort Louisbourg, on Cape Breton Island, guarded the approach to the Gulf of St. Lawrence. Would-be feudal lords established large estates *(seigneuries)* along the banks of the St. Lawrence River. And on a high bluff above the river stood the fortified city of Quebec, the center of the French Empire in America. Montreal to the south and Sault Sainte Marie and Detroit to the west marked the northern boundaries of French settlement. On the lower Mississippi emerged plantations much like those in the Southern colonies of English America, worked by black slaves and owned by "Creoles" (white immigrants of French descent). New Orleans, founded in 1718 to service the French plantation economy, was soon as big as some of the larger cities of the Atlantic seaboard; Biloxi and Mobile to the east completed the string of French settlement.

But the French, of course, shared the continental interior with a large and powerful Indian population. Both the French and the English were aware that the battle for control of North America would be determined in part by which group could best win the allegiance of native tribes—as trading partners and, at times, as military allies. The English—with their more advanced commercial economy—could usually offer the Indians better and more plentiful goods. But the French offered something that was often more important: tolerance. Unlike the English settlers, who strove constantly to impose their own social norms on the Indians they encountered, the French settlers in the interior generally adjusted their own behavior to Indian patterns. French fur traders frequently married Indian women and adopted tribal ways; Jesuit missionaries interacted comfortably with the natives and converted them to Catholicism by the thousands without challenging most of their social customs. By the mid-eighteenth century, therefore, the French had better and closer relations with most of the Indians of the interior than did the English.

The most powerful native group, however, had a different relationship with the French. The Iroquois Confederacy—five Indian nations (Mohawk, Seneca, Cayuga, Onondaga, and Oneida) that had formed a defensive alliance in the fifteenth century—had been the most powerful native presence in the Ohio Valley and a large surrounding region since the 1640s. For nearly a century, neither the French nor the English raised any serious challenge to Iroquois control of the region, and the Iroquois maintained their autonomy by avoiding too close a relationship with either group. They traded successfully with both the English and the French and astutely played the two groups off against each other. As a result, they maintained an uneasy balance of power in the Great Lakes region.

Anglo-French Conflicts

As long as England and France remained at peace and as long as the precarious balance in the North American interior survived, English and French colonists coexisted without serious difficulty. But after the Glorious Revolution in England, a series of Anglo-French wars erupted and continued intermittently in Europe for nearly eighty years.

The wars had important repercussions in America. King William's War (1689–1697) produced only a few, indecisive clashes between the English and the French in northern New England. Queen Anne's War, which began in 1701 and continued for nearly twelve years, generated more substantial conflicts: border fighting with the Spaniards in the south as well as with the French and their Indian allies in the north. The Treaty of Utrecht, which brought the conflict to a close in 1713, transferred substantial territory from the French to the English in North America, including Acadia (Nova Scotia) and Newfoundland.

Two decades later, disputes over British trading rights in the Spanish colonies produced a war between England and Spain that soon merged with a much larger European war, in which England and France lined up on opposite sides. The English colonists in America were soon drawn into the struggle, which they called King George's War, and between 1744 and 1748 they engaged in a series of conflicts with the French. New Englanders captured the French bastion at Louisbourg on Cape Breton Island; but the peace treaty that finally ended the conflict forced them to abandon it.

In the aftermath of King George's War, relations among the English, French, and Iroquois in North America quickly deteriorated. The Iroquois (in what appears to have been a major blunder) granted trading concessions in the interior to English merchants for the first time. The French, fearful (probably correctly) that the English were using the concessions as a first step toward expansion into French lands, began in 1749 to construct new fortresses in the Ohio Valley. The English interpreted the French activity as a threat to their western settlements, protested, and began making military preparations and building fortresses of their own. The balance of power that the Iroquois had carefully and successfully maintained for so long rapidly disintegrated.

For the next five years, tensions between the English and the French increased. In the summer of 1754 the governor of Virginia sent a militia force (under the command of an inexperienced young colonel, George Washington) into the Ohio Valley to challenge French expansion. Washington built a crude stockade (Fort Necessity) not far from Fort Duquesne, the larger outpost the French were building on the site of what is now Pittsburgh. After the Virginians staged an unsuccessful attack on a French detachment, the French countered with an assault on Fort Necessity, trapping Washington and his soldiers inside. After a third of them died in the fighting, Washington surrendered. The clash marked the beginning of the French and Indian War.

The Great War for the Empire

The French and Indian War lasted nearly nine years, and it moved through three distinct phases. During the first of these phases, from the Fort Necessity debacle in 1754 until the expansion of the war to Europe in 1756, it was primarily a local, North American conflict. The English colonists managed the war mainly on their own, and they focused largely on defending themselves against raids on their western settlements by the Indians of the Ohio Valley. Virtually all the tribes except the Iroquois were now allied with the French; they had interpreted the defeat of the Virginians at Fort Duquesne as evidence of British weakness. Even the Iroquois, who were nominally allied with the British, feared antagonizing the French. They remained largely passive in the conflict. By late 1755, many English settlers along the frontier had withdrawn to the east of the Allegheny Mountains to escape the hostilities.

The second phase of the struggle began in 1756, when the governments of France and England formally opened hostilities and a truly international conflict (the Seven Years' War) began. The fighting now spread to the West Indies, India, and Europe itself. But the principal struggle remained the one in North America, where so far England had suffered nothing but frustration and defeat. Beginning in 1757, William Pitt, the English secretary of state (and future prime minister), began to transform the war effort in America by bringing it for the first time fully under British control. Pitt himself planned military strategy, appointed commanders, and issued orders to the colonists. Military recruitment had slowed dramatically in America, and to replenish the army British commanders began forcibly enlisting colonists (a practice known as "impressment"). Officers also seized supplies from local farmers and tradesmen and compelled colonists to offer shelter to British troops—all generally without compensation. The Americans resented these new impositions and firmly resisted them—at times, as in a 1757 riot in New York City, violently. By early 1758, the friction between the British authorities and the colonists was threatening to bring the war effort to a halt.

Beginning in 1758, therefore, Pitt initiated the third and final phase of the war by relaxing many of the policies that Americans had found obnoxious.

He agreed to reimburse the colonists for all supplies requisitioned by the army. He returned control over recruitment to the colonial assemblies (which resulted in an immediate and dramatic increase in enlistments). And he dispatched large numbers of additional British troops to America. Finally, the tide of battle began to turn in England's favor. The French, who had always been outnumbered by the British colonists and who, after 1756, suffered from a series of poor harvests, were unable to sustain their early military successes. By mid-1758, the British regulars in America (who did the bulk of the actual fighting) and the colonial militias were seizing one French stronghold after another. Two brilliant English generals, Jeffrey Amherst and James Wolfe, captured the fortress at Louisbourg in July 1758; a few months later Fort Duquesne fell without a fight. The next year, at the end of a siege of Quebec, supposedly impregnable atop its towering cliff,

ALL thofe who prefer the Glory of bearing Arms to any fervile mean Employ, and have Spirit to ftand forth in Defence of their King and Country, againft the treacherous Defigns of *France* and *Spain*, in the

Suffex Light Dragoons,

Commanded by

Lt. Col. John Baker Holroyd,

Let them repair to

Where they fhall be handfomely Cloathed, moft compleatly Accoutred, mounted on noble Hunters. and treated with Kindnefs and Generofity.

RECRUITING FOR THE FRENCH AND INDIAN WAR The extravagant promises in this recruiting poster, distributed to colonists during the French and Indian War, suggests how difficult it sometimes was to persuade Americans to fight in the British army.

the army of General Wolfe struggled up a hidden ravine under cover of darkness, surprised the larger forces of the Marquis de Montcalm, and defeated them in a battle in which both commanders were slain. The dramatic fall of Quebec on September 13, 1759, marked the beginning of the end of the American phase of the war. A year later, in September 1760, the French army formally surrendered to Amherst in Montreal.

Peace finally came in 1763, with the Peace of Paris. Under its terms, the French ceded to Great Britain some of their West Indian islands, most of their colonies in India and Canada, and all other French territory in North America east of the Mississippi. They ceded New Orleans and their claims west of the Mississippi to Spain, thus surrendering all title to the mainland of North America.

The French and Indian War had profound effects on the British Empire and the American colonies. It greatly expanded England's territorial claims in the New World. At the same time, the cost of the war greatly enlarged Britain's debt and substantially increased British resentment of the Americans. English leaders were contemptuous of the colonists for what they considered American military ineptitude during the war; they were angry that the colonists had made so few financial contributions to a struggle waged largely for American benefit; they were particularly bitter that some colonial merchants had been selling food and other goods to the French in the West Indies throughout the conflict. All these factors combined to persuade many English leaders that a major reorganization of the empire, giving London increased authority over the colonies, would be necessary in the aftermath of the war.

The war had an equally profound but very different effect on the American colonists. It was an experience that forced them, for the first time, to act in concert against a common foe. And it seemed to establish certain precedents. The friction of 1756–1757 over British requisition and impressment policies and the 1758 return of authority to the colonial assemblies seemed to many Americans to confirm the illegitimacy of English interference in local affairs.

For the Indians of the Ohio Valley, the third major party in the French and Indian War, the British victory was disastrous. Those tribes that had allied themselves with the French had earned the enmity of the victorious English. The Iroquois Confederacy, which had allied itself with Britain, fared only slightly better. English officials saw the passivity of the Iroquois during the war (a result of their effort to hedge their bets and avoid antagonizing the French) as evidence of duplicity. In the aftermath of the peace settlement, the Iroquois alliance with the British quickly unraveled, and the Iroquois Confederacy itself began to crumble from within. The tribes would continue to contest the English for control of the Ohio Valley for another fifty years; but increasingly divided and increasingly outnumbered, they would seldom again be in a position to deal with their European rivals on terms of military or political equality.

THE NEW IMPERIALISM

With the treaty of 1763, England found itself truly at peace for the first time in more than fifty years. Undistracted by war, the British government could now turn its attention to the organization of its empire. And after the difficult experiences of the previous decade, many English leaders were convinced that the question of imperial organization could no longer be ignored. Saddled with enormous debts from the many years of fighting, England was desperately in need of new revenues from its empire. And responsible for vast new lands in the New World, the imperial government felt compelled to expand its involvement in its colonies.

Burdens of Empire

The experience of the French and Indian War, however, suggested that such increased involvement would not be easy to establish. Not only had the colonists proved so resistant to British control that Pitt had been forced to relax his policies in 1758, but the colonial assemblies had continued after that to respond to British needs slowly and grudgingly. Unwilling to be taxed by Parliament to support the war effort, the colonists were generally reluctant to tax themselves as well. Defiance of imperial trade regulations and other British demands continued.

With the territorial annexations of 1763, the area of the British Empire was suddenly twice as great as it had been, and the problems of governing it thus became many times more complex. Some English officials argued that the empire should restrain rapid settlement and development of the Western territories to avoid further costly conflicts with the Indians and perhaps even the French. Restricting settlement would also keep the land available for hunting and trapping. Others wanted to see the new territories opened for immediate development, but they disagreed among themselves about who should control the Western lands. The existing colonial governments made fervent, and often conflicting, claims of jurisdiction. Some officials in London wanted control to remain in England and wanted the territories to be considered entirely new colonies, unlinked to the existing settlements.

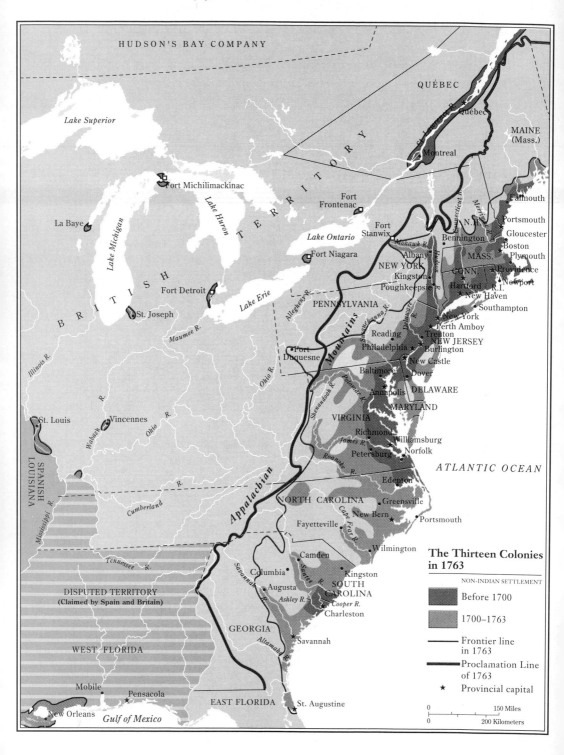

HUDSON'S BAY COMPANY

Lake Superior

QUÉBEC

MAINE
(Mass.)

La Baye

Lake Michigan

Lake Huron

Fort Michilimackinac

B R I T I S H   T E R R I T O R Y

Fort
Frontenac

Québec

Montreal

Falmouth

Portsmouth

N.H.

Gloucester

Fort
Stanwix

Bennington

Boston
Plymouth

Lake Ontario

Fort Niagara

Mohawk R.

Albany

MASS.

Fort Detroit

Lake Erie

NEW YORK

CONN.

Providence
Newport

Kingston

Hartford

R.I.

St. Joseph

Maumee R.

Allegheny R.

PENNSYLVANIA

Poughkeepsie

New Haven

Southampton

Susquehanna R.

Reading

New York
Perth Amboy

Delaware R.

Fort
Duquesne

Philadelphia

Trenton
NEW JERSEY
Burlington

Illinois R.

Ohio R.

Baltimore

New Castle
Dover

Wabash R.

Ohio R.

Appalachian Mountains

Shenandoah R.

Potomac R.

Annapolis

DELAWARE

MARYLAND

St. Louis

Vincennes

Ohio R.

VIRGINIA

Richmond
Williamsburg

James R.

Petersburg

Norfolk

SPANISH LOUISIANA

R.

Roanoke R.

ATLANTIC OCEAN

Mississippi R.

Cumberland R.

Edenton

NORTH CAROLINA

Greensville

Tennessee R.

Cape Fear R.

New Bern

Portsmouth

Fayetteville

DISPUTED TERRITORY
(Claimed by Spain and Britain)

Wilmington

Camden

Savannah R.

Columbia

Santee R.

Kingston
SOUTH
CAROLINA

Augusta

Ashley R.

Cooper R.

Charleston

WEST FLORIDA

GEORGIA

Altamaha R.

Savannah

Mobile

Pensacola

EAST FLORIDA

St. Augustine

New Orleans

Gulf of Mexico

**The Thirteen Colonies
in 1763**

NON-INDIAN SETTLEMENT

Before 1700

1700–1763

Frontier line
in 1763

Proclamation Line
of 1763

★ Provincial capital

0   150 Miles

0   200 Kilometers

At the same time, the government in London was running out of options in its effort to deal with its staggering war debt. Landlords and merchants in England itself were objecting strenuously to tax increases. And the reluctance of the colonial assemblies to pay for the war effort had suggested that England could not rely on any cooperation from them in its search for revenues. Only a system of taxation administered by London, the leaders of the empire believed, could effectively meet England's needs.

At this crucial moment in Anglo-American relations, with the imperial system in need of redefinition, the government of England was thrown into turmoil by the accession to the throne of a new king, George III, who assumed power in 1760. He brought two particularly unfortunate qualities to the office. First, he was determined, unlike his two predecessors, to reassert the authority of the monarchy. Pushed by his ambitious mother, he removed from power the relatively stable coalition of Whigs who had governed the empire for much of the century and replaced them with a new coalition of his own, assembled through patronage and bribes. The new ministries that emerged as a result of these changes were very unstable, each lasting in office an average of only about two years.

The king also had serious intellectual and psychological limitations. He suffered, apparently, from a rare mental disease that produced intermittent bouts of insanity. (Indeed, in the last years of his long reign he was, according to most accounts, a virtual lunatic, confined to the palace and unable to perform any official functions.) Yet even when George III was lucid and rational, which was most of the time in the 1760s and 1770s, he was painfully immature (he had been only twenty-two when he ascended the throne) and insecure. The king's personality, therefore, contributed both to the instability and to the intransigence of the British government during these critical years.

More directly responsible for the problems that soon emerged with the colonies, however, was George Grenville, whom the king made prime minister in 1763. Grenville, though a brother-in-law of William Pitt, did not share Pitt's sympathy with the American point of view. He agreed instead with the prevailing opinion within Britain that the colonists had been too long indulged and that they should be compelled to obey the laws and to pay a part of the cost of defending and administering the empire.

The British and the Tribes

With the defeat of the French, frontiersmen from the English colonies had begun immediately to move over the mountains and into tribal lands in the upper Ohio Valley. An alliance of Indian tribes, under the Ottawa chieftain

Pontiac, struck back. To prevent an escalation of the fighting that might threaten Western trade, the British government issued a ruling—the Proclamation of 1763—forbidding settlers to advance beyond the mountains that divided the Atlantic coast from the interior.

The Proclamation of 1763 gave London, rather than the provincial governments and their land-hungry constituents, power to control (and slow) the westward movement of the white population. Slower Western settlement would limit costly wars with the Indians. It would also slow the population exodus from the coastal colonies, where England's most important markets and investments were. And it would reserve opportunities for land speculation and fur trading for English rather than colonial entrepreneurs.

Although Native Americans had few illusions about the Proclamation, which required them to cede land east of the mountains to the white settlers, many Indian groups supported the agreement as the best bargain available to them. The Cherokee, in particular, worked actively to hasten the drawing of the boundary, hoping finally to put an end to white encroachments. Relations between the Western tribes and the British improved in at least some areas after the Proclamation, partly as a result of the work of the Indian superintendents the British appointed, who were sympathetic to tribal needs.

In the end, however, the Proclamation of 1763 failed to meet even the modest expectations of the Indians, because on the crucial point of the line of settlement, it was almost completely ineffective. White settlers continued to swarm across the boundary and continued to claim lands farther and farther into the Ohio Valley. The British authorities tried repeatedly to establish limits to the expansion. In 1768, new agreements with the Western tribes created a supposedly permanent boundary (which, as always, increased the area of white settlement at the expense of the Indians). But these treaties (signed respectively at Hard Labor Creek, South Carolina, and Fort Stanwix, New York) also failed to stop the white advance. Within a few years, the 1768 agreements were replaced with new ones, which pushed the line of settlement still farther west.

The Colonial Response

The Grenville ministry soon increased its authority in the colonies more directly. Regular British troops were stationed permanently in America; and under the Mutiny Act of 1765 the colonists were required to help provision and maintain the army. Ships of the British navy patroled American waters to search for smugglers. The customs service was reorganized and enlarged.

Royal officials were required to take up their colonial posts in person instead of sending substitutes. Colonial manufacturing was restricted, so that it would not compete with rapidly expanding industies in Great Britain.

The Sugar Act of 1764, designed in part to eliminate the illegal sugar trade between the continental colonies and the French and Spanish West Indies, established new vice-admiralty courts in America to try accused smugglers—thus cutting them off from sympathetic local juries. The Currency Act of 1764 required that the colonial assemblies stop issuing paper money. Most momentously, the Stamp Act of 1765 imposed a tax on every printed document in the colonies: newspapers, almanacs, pamphlets, deeds, wills, licenses. British officials were soon collecting more than ten times as much annual revenue in America as they had been before 1763. But the new policies created many more problems than they solved.

It was difficult for the colonists to resist these unpopular new laws. For one thing, Americans continued to harbor as many grievances against one another as they did against the authorities in London. In 1763, for example, a band of Pennsylvania frontiersmen known as the Paxton Boys descended on Philadelphia to demand tax relief and financial support for their defense against Indians; bloodshed was averted only by concessions frcm the colonial assembly. In 1771, a small-scale civil war broke out in North Carolina when the Regulators, farmers of the Carolina upcountry, organized and armed themselves to resist the high taxes that local sheriffs (appointed by the colonial governor) collected. An army of militiamen, most of them from the eastern counties, crushed the revolt in the Battle of Alamance. Nine on each side were killed and many others wounded. Afterward, six Regulators were hanged for treason.

Despite the conflicts, however, the new policies of the British government began after 1763 to create common grievances among virtually all colonists. For under the Grenville program, as Americans saw it, all people in all colonies would suffer. Northern merchants would suffer from restraints on their commerce, from the closing of the West to land speculation and fur trading, from the restriction of opportunities for manufacturing, and from the increased burden of taxation. Southern planters, in debt to English merchants, would now have to pay additional taxes and would be unable to ease their debts by speculating in Western land. Small farmers, the largest group in the colonies, would suffer from increased taxes and from the abolition of paper money, which had been the source of most of their loans. Workers in towns faced the prospect of narrowing opportunities, particularly because of the restraints on manufacturing and currency. The new restrictions came, moreover, at the beginning of a postwar economic depression.

The British government had poured money into the colonies to finance the war, but that flow stopped after 1763. Now the authorities in London proposed to aggravate the problem by taking money out of the colonies.

In reality, most Americans soon found ways to live with (or circumvent) the new British laws. The American economy was not being destroyed. But there was still a deep sense of unease, particularly in the cities—the places most directly affected by British policies. Periodic and increasingly frequent economic slumps, the frightening depression of the early 1760s, the growth of a large group of unemployed or semiemployed—all combined to produce great distress in some colonial cities, and particularly in Boston, the city suffering the worst economic problems.

Whatever the economic burdens of the imperial program, colonists considered the political burdens worse. Americans were accustomed (and deeply attached) to wide latitude in self-government. The key to it, they believed, was the right of the colonial assemblies to control appropriations for the costs of government within the colonies. By attempting to circumvent the colonial assemblies and raise extensive revenues directly from the public, the British government was challenging the basis of colonial political power.

STIRRINGS OF REVOLT

By the mid-1760s, therefore, a hardening of positions had begun in both England and America that would bring the colonies into increasing conflict with the mother country. The result was a progression of events that, more rapidly than anyone could have imagined, destroyed the English empire in America.

The Stamp Act Crisis

Grenville could not have devised a better method for antagonizing and unifying the colonies than the Stamp Act of 1765 if he had tried. Unlike the Sugar Act of a year earlier, which affected only a few New England merchants, the tax on printed documents fell on all Americans. The actual economic burdens of the Stamp Act were relatively light, but the precedent it seemed to set was ominous. In the past, taxes and duties on colonial trade had always been presented as measures to regulate commerce, not raise money. The Stamp Act, however, was a direct attempt by England to raise revenue in the colonies without the consent of the colonial assemblies. If

Americans accepted this new tax without resistance, the door would be open for more burdensome taxation in the future.

Few colonists believed that they could do anything more than grumble until the Virginia House of Burgesses sounded a "trumpet of sedition" that aroused Americans to action almost everywhere. Foremost among the Virginia malcontents was Patrick Henry, who made a dramatic speech to the House in May 1765, concluding with a vague prediction that if present policies were not revised, George III, like earlier tyrants, might lose his head. There were shocked cries of "Treason!" and, according to one witness, an immediate apology from Henry (although many years later he was quoted as having made the defiant reply: "If this be treason, make the most of it"). Henry introduced a set of resolutions declaring that Americans possessed the same rights as the English, especially the right to be taxed only by their own representatives; that Virginians should pay no taxes except those voted by the Virginia assembly; and that anyone advocating the right of Parliament to tax Virginians should be deemed an enemy of the colony. The House of Burgesses defeated some of Henry's resolutions, but all of them were printed and circulated as the "Virginia Resolves."

In Massachusetts at about the same time, James Otis persuaded his fellow members of the colonial assembly to call an intercolonial congress to take action against the new tax. And in October 1765, the Stamp Act Congress, as it was called, met in New York with delegates from nine colonies and petitioned the king and Parliament. Their petition denied that the colonies could rightfully be taxed except through their own provincial assemblies.

Meanwhile, in several colonial cities mobs began taking the law into their own hands. During the summer of 1765 serious riots broke out up and down the coast, the largest of them in Boston. Men belonging to the newly organized Sons of Liberty terrorized stamp agents and burned stamps. The agents, themselves Americans, hastily resigned. In Boston, the mob also attacked such pro-British "aristocrats" as the lieutenant governor, Thomas Hutchinson (who had privately opposed passage of the Stamp Act but who felt obliged to support it once it became law). Hutchinson's elegant house was pillaged and virtually destroyed.

At last the crisis subsided, largely because England backed down. The authorities in London were less affected by the political protests than by economic pressure. Many New Englanders had stopped buying English goods to protest the Sugar Act of 1764. Now the colonial boycott spread, and the Sons of Liberty intimidated reluctant colonists to participate in it.

The merchants of England, feeling the loss of much of their colonial market, begged Parliament to repeal the unpopular law. On March 18, 1766, the Stamp Act was repealed at the urging of the new prime minister, the Marquis of Rockingham. To satisfy his strong and vociferous opponents, Rockingham also pushed through the Declaratory Act, which confirmed parliamentary authority over the colonies "in all cases whatsoever." In their rejoicing over the repeal, most Americans paid little attention to this sweeping declaration of Parliament's power, but the Declaratory Act was clear evidence of how large a gulf had emerged between the English and American views of the imperial relationship.

The Townshend Program

The Rockingham government's policy of appeasement met substantial opposition in England. English landlords, a powerful political force, feared that not taxing the colonies would result in imposing new taxes on them. The king finally bowed to their pressure, dismissed the Rockingham ministry, and replaced it with a new government led by the aging but still powerful William Pitt (now Lord Chatham). Chatham had been a critic of the Stamp Act and had a reputation in America as a friend of the colonists. Once in office, however, he was so hobbled by gout and at times so incapacitated by mental illness that the actual leadership of his administration fell to the chancellor of the exchequer, Charles Townshend (pronounced "Townsend").

Townshend had to deal with imperial problems and colonial grievances left over from the Grenville ministry. With the Stamp Act repealed, the greatest American grievance involved the Mutiny (or Quartering) Act of 1765, which required the colonists to provide quarters and supplies for the British troops in America. The colonists did not object to quartering or supplying the troops; but they resented that these contributions were now mandatory, and they considered them another form of taxation without their consent. The Massachusetts and New York assemblies refused to vote the mandated supplies to the troops.

To enforce the law and to try again to raise revenues in the colonies, Townshend steered two measures through Parliament in 1767. First, the New York Assembly was disbanded until the colonists agreed to obey the Mutiny Act. (By singling out New York, Townshend thought he would avoid Grenville's mistake of arousing all the colonies at once.) Second, new taxes (known as the Townshend Duties) were levied on various goods imported to the colonies from England—lead, paint, paper, and tea. Townshend reasoned that since these were taxes purely on "external" transactions (imports from overseas) as opposed to the internal transactions the Stamp Act had taxed, the colonists could not object.

But the distinction between external and internal taxation meant little to the colonists. The purpose of the new duties, they claimed, was the same as that of the Stamp Act: to raise revenue from the colonists without their consent. And the suspension of the New York Assembly aroused the resentment of all the colonies. They considered this assault on the rights of one provincial government a threat on all of them.

The Massachusetts Assembly took the lead in opposing the new measures by circulating a letter to all the colonial governments urging them to stand up against every tax imposed by Parliament. At first, the document evoked little response outside Massachusetts. Then Lord Hillsborough, secretary of state for the colonies in London, warned that assemblies endorsing the Massachusetts letter would be dissolved. Massachusetts defiantly reaffirmed its support for the circular, and the other colonies supported Massachusetts.

Besides persuading Parliament to levy import duties and suspend the New York Assembly, Townshend took steps to enforce commercial regulations in the colonies more effectively. The most important of these steps was the establishment of a board of customs commissioners in America to stop the rampant corruption in the colonial customs houses. To some extent the plan worked. The new commissioners virtually ended smuggling in Boston, where they established their headquarters, although smugglers continued to carry on a busy trade in other colonial seaports.

The Boston merchants—accustomed to loose enforcement of the Navigation Acts and aggrieved now that the new commission was diverting the lucrative smuggling trade elsewhere—took the lead in organizing another boycott. Merchants in Philadelphia and New York joined them in a nonimportation agreement in 1768, and later some Southern merchants and planters also agreed to cooperate. The colonists boycotted British goods that were subject to the Townshend Duties; and throughout the colonies, American homespun and other domestic products became suddenly fashionable, while English luxuries fell from favor.

Late in 1767, Charles Townshend died—before the consequences of his ill-conceived program had become fully apparent. In March 1770, the new prime minister, Lord North, hoping to break the nonimportation agreement and divide the colonists, repealed all the Townshend Duties except the tea tax.

The Boston Massacre

Before news of the repeal reached America, an event in Massachusetts had electrified colonial opinion. The harassment of the new customs commissioners in Boston had grown so intense that the British government had placed four regiments of regular troops in the city—a constant affront to the colonists' sense of independence. Everywhere they went, Bostonians encountered British "redcoats," some of whom were arrogant, coarse, or provocative. Many poorly paid British soldiers wanted jobs in their off-duty hours, and they thus competed with local workers in an already tight market. Clashes between them were frequent.

On the night of March 5, 1770, a few days after a particularly intense skirmish between workers at a ship-rigging factory and British soldiers who were trying to find jobs there, a mob of dockworkers, "liberty boys," and others began pelting the sentries at the customs house with rocks and

THE BOSTON MASSACRE (1770), **BY PAUL REVERE** This is one of many engravings, by Revere and others, of the conflict between British troops and Boston laborers that became important as propaganda for the Patriot cause in the 1770s. Among the victims of the massacre listed by Revere was Crispus Attucks, probably the first black man to die in the struggle for American independence.

snowballs. Hastily, Captain Thomas Preston of the British regiment lined up several of his men in front of the building to protect it. There was some scuffling; one of the soldiers was knocked down; and in the midst of it all, apparently, several British soldiers fired into the crowd, killing five people (among them a mulatto sailor, Crispus Attucks).

This murky incident, almost certainly the result of panic and confusion, was quickly transformed by local resistance leaders into the "Boston Massacre"—a graphic symbol of British oppression and brutality. The victims became popular martyrs; the event became the subject of such lurid (and inaccurate) accounts as the widely circulated pamphlet *Innocent Blood Crying to God from the Streets of Boston*. A famous engraving by Paul Revere portrayed the massacre as a carefully organized, calculated assault on a peaceful crowd. The British soldiers, tried before a jury of Bostonians, were found guilty only of manslaughter and given token punishment. But colonial pamphlets and newspapers convinced many Americans that the soldiers were guilty of official murder. Year after year, resistance leaders marked the anniversary of the massacre with demonstrations and speeches.

The leading figure in fomenting public outrage over the Boston Massacre was Samuel Adams, the most effective radical in the colonies. He spoke frequently at Boston town meetings; and as one unpopular English policy followed another, his message attracted increasing support. England, he argued, had become a morass of sin and corruption; only in America did public virtue survive. In 1772, he proposed the creation of a "committee of correspondence" in Boston to publicize the grievances against England throughout the colony, and he became its first head. Other colonies followed Massachusetts's lead, and a loose inter-colonial network of political organizations was soon established that kept the spirit of dissent alive through the 1770s.

The Philosophy of Revolt

Although a superficial calm settled on the colonies for approximately three years after the Boston Massacre, the crises of the 1760s had helped arouse enduring ideological excitement and had produced instruments for publicizing colonial grievances. Gradually a political outlook took hold in America that would ultimately serve to justify revolt.

The ideas that would support the Revolution emerged from many sources. Some were indigenous to America, drawn from religious (particularly Puritan) sources or from the political experiences of the colonies. But these native ideas were enriched and enlarged by the importation of powerful arguments from abroad. Of most importance, perhaps, were the "radical" ideas of those in Great Britain who stood in opposition to their government. Some were Scots, who viewed the English state as tyrannical. Others were embittered "country Whigs," who felt excluded from power and considered the existing system corrupt and oppressive. Drawing from some of the great philosophical minds of earlier generations—most notably John Locke—these English dissidents framed a powerful argument against their government.

Central to this emerging ideology was a new concept of what government should be. Because humans were inherently corrupt and selfish, government was necessary to protect individuals from the evil in one another. But because any government was run by corruptible people, it needed safeguards against abuses of power. In the eyes of most English and American people, the English constitution was the best system ever devised to meet these necessities. By distributing power among the three elements of society—the monarchy, the aristocracy, and the common people—the English political system ensured that no individual or group could exercise authority unchecked by another. Yet by the mid-seventeenth century, dissidents in both England and America had become convinced that the constitution was in danger. A single center of power—the king and his ministers—was emerging, and the system was becoming a corrupt and dangerous tyranny.

Such arguments found little sympathy in most of England. The English constitution was not a written document; nor was it a fixed set of unchangeable rules. It was a general sense of the "way things are done," and most people in England were willing to accept evolutionary changes in it. Americans, by contrast, drew from their experience with colonial charters, in which the shape and powers of government were permanently inscribed on paper. They resisted the idea of a flexible, changing set of basic principles. Many colonists argued that the English constitution should itself be written down, to prevent fallible politicians from tampering with its essence.

Part of that essence, Americans believed, was their right to be taxed only with their own consent. When Townshend levied his external duties, the Philadelphia lawyer John Dickinson published a widely circulated pamphlet, *Letters of a Pennsylvania Farmer*, which argued that even external taxation was legal only when designed to regulate trade and not to raise a revenue. Gradually, most Americans ceased to accept even that distinction, and they finally took an unqualified stand: "No taxation without representation." Whatever the nature of a tax—whether internal or external, whether designed to raise revenue or to control trade—it could not be levied without the consent of the colonists themselves.

This clamor about "representation" made little sense to the English. According to the prevailing English theory, members of Parliament did not represent individuals or particular geographical areas. Instead, each member represented the interests of the whole nation and indeed the whole empire, no matter where the member happened to come from. The many unenfranchised boroughs of England, the whole of Ireland, and the colonies thousands of miles away—all were thus represented in the Parliament at London, even though they elected no representatives of their own. This was the theory of "virtual" representation. But Americans, drawing from their experiences with their town meetings and their colonial assemblies, believed in "actual" representation. Every community was entitled to its own representative, elected by the people of that community and directly responsible to them. Since they had none of their own representatives in Parliament, it followed that they were not represented there. According to the emerging American view of the empire, the colonial assemblies played the same role within the colonies—had the same powers, enjoyed the same rights—that Parliament did within England. The empire, the Americans argued, was a sort of federation of commonwealths, each with its own legislative body, all tied together by common loyalty to the king.

What may have made the conflict between England and America ultimately insoluble was a fundamental difference of opinion over the nature of sovereignty. By arguing that Parliament had the right to legislate for England and for the empire as a whole, but that only the provincial assemblies could legislate for the individual colonies, Americans were in effect arguing for a division of sovereignty. Parliament would be sovereign in some matters; the assemblies would be sovereign in others. To the British, such an argument was absurd. In any system of government there must be a single, ultimate authority. And since the empire was, in their view, a single, undivided unit, there could be only one authority within it: the English government of king and Parliament. Ultimately, that presented the colonists with a stark choice: between complete subordination to England and complete independence from it. Slowly, cautiously, they began moving toward independence.

The Tea Excitement

The apparent calm in America in the first years of the 1770s masked a growing sense of frustration and resentment in response to the continued and increasingly heavy-handed enforcement of the Navigation Acts. Popular anger was visible in occasional acts of rebellion. At one point, colonists seized a British revenue ship on the lower Delaware River. And in 1772, angry residents of Rhode Island boarded the British schooner *Gaspée*, set it afire, and sank it in Narragansett Bay.

What finally revived the Revolutionary fervor of the 1760s, however, was a new act of Parliament—one that the English government had expected to be relatively uncontroversial. It involved the business of selling tea. In 1773, Britain's East India Company (which possessed an official monopoly on trade with the Far East) was sitting on large stocks of tea that it could not sell in England. It was on the verge of bankruptcy. In an effort to save it, the government passed the Tea Act of 1773, which gave the company the right to export its merchandise directly to the colonies without paying any of the regular taxes that were imposed on the colonial merchants, who had traditionally served as the middlemen in such transactions. With these privileges, the company could undersell American merchants and monopolize the colonial tea trade.

The act proved inflammatory for several reasons. First, it angered influential colonial merchants, who feared being replaced and bankrupted by a powerful monopoly. More important, however, the Tea Act revived American passions about the issue of taxation without representation. The law provided no new tax on tea. But the original Townshend duty on the commodity—the only one of the original duties that had not been repealed—survived. It was the East India Company's exemption from that duty that put the colonial merchants at such a grave disadvantage in competition with the company. Lord North assumed that most colonists would welcome the new law because it would reduce the price of tea to consumers by removing the middlemen. But resistance leaders in America resented the monopolistic privileges of the company and, more important, argued that the law in effect represented an unconstitutional tax. The colonists responded by boycotting tea.

Unlike earlier protests, most of which had involved relatively small numbers of people, the tea boycott mobilized large segments of the population. It also helped link the colonies together in a common experience of mass popular protest. Particularly important to the movement were the activities of colonial women, who were among the principal consumers of tea and now became the leaders of the effort to boycott it. The Daughters of Liberty—a women's patriotic organization which, like the Sons of Liberty, was committed to agitating against British policies, proclaimed "that rather than Freedom, we'll part with our Tea."

In the last weeks of 1773, with strong popular support, leaders in various colonies made plans to prevent the East India Company from landing its cargoes in colonial ports. In Philadelphia and New York, determined colonists kept the tea from leaving the company's ships; and in Charleston, they stored it away in a public warehouse. In Boston, after failing to turn three ships away from the harbor, local patriots staged a spectacular drama. On the evening of December 16, 1773, three companies of fifty men each, masquerading as Mohawks, passed through a crowd of spectators, went aboard the three ships, broke open the tea chests, and heaved them into the harbor. As the electrifying news of the Boston "tea party" spread, other seaports staged similar acts of resistance of their own.

Parliament retaliated in four acts of 1774, closing the port of Boston, drastically reducing the powers of self-government in Massachusetts, permitting royal officers to be tried in other colonies or in England when accused of crimes, and providing for the quartering of troops by the colonists. These Coercive Acts—or, as they were more widely known in America, "Intolerable Acts"—were followed by the Quebec Act, which was unrelated to them but also provocative to English Americans. The law extended the boundaries of Quebec to include the French communities between the Ohio and Mississippi rivers. It also granted political rights to Roman Catholics and recognized the legality of the Roman Catholic church within the enlarged province. Many Americans feared that a plot was afoot in London to subject Americans to the authority of the pope. Those interested in Western lands, moreover, believed that the act would hinder westward expansion.

The Coercive Acts, far from isolating Massachusetts, made it a martyr in the eyes of residents of other colonies and sparked new resistance up and down the coast. Colonial legislatures passed a series of resolves supporting Massachusetts. Women's groups throughout the colonies mobilized to extend the boycotts of British goods and to create substitutes for the tea, textiles, and other commodities they were shunning. In Edenton, North Carolina, fifty-one women signed an agreement in October 1774 declaring their "sincere adherence" to the anti-British resolutions of their provincial assembly and proclaiming their duty to do "every thing as far as lies in our power" to support the "publick good."

COOPERATION AND WAR

Revolutions do not simply happen. They must be organized and led. Beginning in 1765, colonial leaders developed a variety of organizations for converting popular discontent into action—organizations that in time formed the basis for an independent government.

New Sources of Authority

The passage of authority from the royal government to the colonists themselves began on the local level. In colony after colony, local institutions responded to the resistance movement by simply seizing authority on their own. At times, entirely new institutions emerged and began to perform some of the functions of government.

The most effective of these new groups were the committees of correspondence that Adams had inaugurated in Massachusetts in 1772. Virginia later established the first intercolonial committees of correspondence, which made possible continuous cooperation among the colonies. And Virginia took the greatest step of all toward united action in 1774. After the royal governor dissolved the assembly, a rump session met in the Raleigh Tavern at Williamsburg, declared that the Intolerable Acts menaced the liberties of every colony, and issued a call for a Continental Congress.

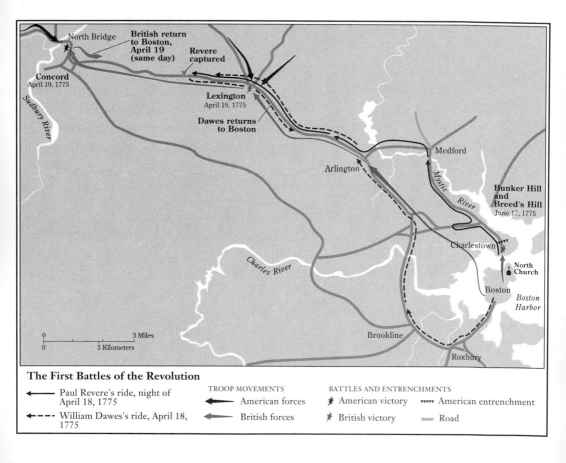

The First Battles of the Revolution

←——— Paul Revere's ride, night of April 18, 1775

◄- - - - William Dawes's ride, April 18, 1775

TROOP MOVEMENTS

◄——— American forces

◄——— British forces

BATTLES AND ENTRENCHMENTS

✸ American victory   ▵▵▵▵ American entrenchment

✸ British victory   ——— Road

Delegates from all thirteen colonies except Georgia were present when, in September 1774, the First Continental Congress convened in Philadelphia. They made five major decisions. First, in a close vote, they rejected a plan for a colonial union under British authority. Second, they endorsed a statement of grievances that reflected the influence of moderates by seeming to concede Parliament's right to regulate colonial trade and by addressing the king as "Most Gracious Sovereign," but it also included a more extreme demand for the repeal of all oppressive legislation passed since 1763. Third, they approved a series of resolutions from a Massachusetts convention recommending that military preparations be made for defense against possible attack by the British troops in Boston. Fourth, they agreed to a series of boycotts that they hoped would stop all trade with Great Britain, and they formed a "Continental Association" to see that these agreements were enforced. And fifth, the delegates agreed to meet again the following spring, indicating that they saw the Continental Congress as a continuing organization.

During the winter, the Parliament in London debated proposals for conciliating the colonists. Lord North finally won approval early in 1775 for a series of measures known as the Conciliatory Propositions. Parliament proposed that the colonies, instead of being taxed directly by Parliament, would tax themselves at Parliament's demand. With this offer, Lord North hoped to divide the American moderates, whom he believed represented the views of the majority, from the extremist minority. But his offer was too little and too late. It did not reach America until after the first shots of war had been fired.

Lexington and Concord

For months, the farmers and townspeople of Massachusetts had been gathering arms and ammunition and training as "minutemen," preparing to fight on a minute's notice. The Continental Congress had approved preparations for a defensive war, and the citizen-soldiers only waited for an aggressive move by the British regulars in Boston.

In Boston, General Thomas Gage, commanding the British garrison, considered his army too small to do anything without reinforcements. He resisted the advice of less cautious officers, who assured him that the Americans would never dare actually to fight, that they would back down quickly before any show of British force. When General Gage received orders to arrest the rebel leaders Sam Adams and John Hancock, known to be in the vicinity of Lexington, he still hesitated. But when he heard that the

THE BRITISH RETREAT FROM CONCORD, 1775 This American cartoon satirizes the retreat of British forces from Concord after the battle there on April 19, 1775. Patriot forces are lined up on the left, and the retreating British forces (portrayed with dog heads, perhaps because many of the soldiers were "wild" Irish) straggle off at right—some fleeing in panic, others gloating over the booty they have plundered from the burning homes above.

minutemen had stored a large supply of gunpowder in Concord (eighteen miles from Boston), he decided to act. On the night of April 18, 1775, he sent a detachment of about 1,000 men out from Boston on the road to Lexington and Concord. He hoped to surprise the colonials and seize the illegal supplies without bloodshed.

But patriots in Boston were watching the British movements closely; and during the night two horsemen, William Dawes and Paul Revere, were dispatched to warn the villages and farms. When the redcoats arrived in Lexington the next day, several dozen minutemen awaited them on the town common. Shots were fired and minutemen fell; eight of them were killed and ten more were wounded. Advancing to Concord, the British discovered that the Americans had hastily removed most of the powder supply, but the redcoats burned what was left of it. All along the road from Concord back to Boston, the British were harassed by the gunfire of farmers hiding behind trees, rocks, and stone walls. By the end of the day, the British had lost almost three times as many men as the Americans.

The first shots—the "shots heard round the world," as Americans later called them—had been fired. But who had fired them first? According to one of the minutemen at Lexington, the British commander, Major Thomas Pitcairn, had shouted to the colonists on his arrival, "Disperse, ye rebels!" When they ignored him, he ordered his troops to fire. British officers and soldiers claimed that the minutemen had fired first and that only after seeing the flash of American guns had they begun to shoot. Whatever the truth, the rebels succeeded in circulating their account well ahead of the British version, adorning it with tales of British atrocities. The effect was to rally to the rebel cause thousands of colonists, North and South, who previously had had little enthusiasm for it.

It was not immediately clear to the British, and even to many Americans, that the skirmishes at Lexington and Concord were the first battles of a war. But whether they recognized it at the time or not, the War for Independence had begun.

CHAPTER FIVE

The American Revolution

The States United ~ *The War for Independence* ~ *War and Society*
The Creation of State Governments ~ *The Search for a National Government*

WO STRUGGLES OCCURRED simultaneously during the seven years of war that began in April of 1775. One was the military conflict with Great Britain. The second was a political conflict within America.

The military conflict was, by the standards of later wars, a relatively modest one. Battle deaths on the American side totaled fewer than 5,000. By the standards of its own day, however, it was an unusually savage conflict, pitting not only army against army but the civilian population against a powerful external force. The shift of the war from a traditional, conventional struggle to a new kind of conflict—a revolutionary war for liberation—is what made it possible for the United States to defeat the more powerful British.

At the same time, Americans were wrestling with the great political questions that the conflict necessarily produced: first, whether to demand independence from Britain; then, how to structure the new nation they had proclaimed. Only the first of these questions had been resolved by the time of the British surrender at Yorktown in 1781.

THE STATES UNITED

Although many Americans had been expecting a military conflict with Britain for months, even years, the actual beginning of hostilities in 1775 found the colonies generally unprepared. A still-unformed nation faced the task of mobilizing for war against the world's greatest armed power. Americans faced that task deeply divided about what they were fighting for.

Defining American War Aims

Three weeks after the battles of Lexington and Concord, when the Second Continental Congress met in Philadelphia, delegates from every colony except Georgia (which was not represented until the following autumn) agreed to support the war. But they disagreed about its purpose. At one extreme was a group led by the Adams cousins (John and Samuel), Richard Henry Lee of Virginia, and others, who already favored independence; at the other extreme was a group led by such moderates as John Dickinson of Pennsylvania, who hoped for a quick reconciliation with Great Britain. Most of the delegates tried to find some middle ground between these positions. They voted for one last appeal to the king: the so-called Olive Branch Petition. Then, on July 6, 1775, they adopted a Declaration of the Causes and Necessity of Taking Up Arms. It proclaimed that the British government had left the American people with only two alternatives: "unconditional submission to the tyranny of irritated ministers or resistance by force."

Most Americans still believed they were fighting not for independence but for a redress of grievances within the British Empire. During the first year of fighting, however, many of them began to change their minds. The costs of the war—human and financial—were so high that the original war aims began to seem too modest to justify them. What lingering affection they retained for the mother country greatly diminished when the British began trying to recruit Indians, black slaves, and German mercenaries (the hated "Hessians") against them. When the British government rejected the Olive Branch Petition and instead enacted the Prohibitory Act, which closed the colonial ports (through a naval blockade) to all overseas trade and made no concessions to American demands except an offer to pardon repentant rebels, many colonists concluded that independence was the only remaining option.

An impassioned pamphlet crystallized these feelings in January 1776: *Common Sense*, by Thomas Paine, who had emigrated from England to America less than two years before. Paine wanted to persuade Americans that no reconciliation with Britain was possible. He wanted to turn the anger of Americans away from particular parliamentary measures and toward what he considered the root of the problem—the English constitution itself. It was simple common sense for Americans to break completely with a political system that could produce so corrupt a monarch as George III and could inflict such brutality on its own people.

Common Sense sold more than 100,000 copies in only a few months. To many of its readers it was a revelation. Although sentiment for independence was still far from unanimous, the first months of 1776 saw a rapid growth of support for the idea.

The Decision for Independence

In the meantime, the Continental Congress in Philadelphia was moving toward a complete break with England. It opened American ports to the ships of all nations except Great Britain, began negotiating with other nations, and recommended to the colonies that they establish governments independent of the empire, as in fact most already were doing.

At the beginning of the summer, finally, Congress appointed a committee to draft a formal declaration of independence. And on July 2, 1776, it adopted a resolution: "That these United Colonies are, and, of right, ought to be, free and independent states; that they are absolved from all allegiance to the British crown, and that all political connexion between them and the state of Great Britain is, and ought to be, totally dissolved." Two days later, on July 4, Congress approved the Declaration of Independence itself, which provided formal justifications for the actions the delegates had taken two days earlier.

The Declaration was largely the work of Thomas Jefferson, a thirty-three-year-old Virginian, although it was substantially revised by other delegates. (Among other changes, Congress struck out a passage condemning the slave trade to placate Southern slaveowners.) The final document was in two parts. In the first, Jefferson restated the familiar contract theory of John Locke: the theory that governments were formed to protect what Jefferson called "life, liberty and the pursuit of happiness." In the second part, he listed the alleged crimes of the king, who, with the backing of Parliament, had violated his contract with the colonists and thus had forfeited all claim to their loyalty. Little of what Jefferson wrote was new to the document's readers; the power of the Declaration lay in the eloquence with which it expressed beliefs already widespread in America.

Having asserted their independence, the individual colonies now began to call themselves states—a reflection of their belief that each province was now a sovereign entity. By 1781, most states had produced written constitutions for themselves that established republican governments. At the national level, however, the process was more uncertain and less immediately successful. For a time, Americans were not sure whether they even wanted a real national government; virtually everyone considered the individual colonies (now states) the real centers of authority. Yet fighting a war required a certain amount of central direction. In November 1777, finally, Congress adopted a plan for union. The document was known as the Articles of Confederation, and it confirmed the weak, decentralized system already in operation. (See pp. 136–137.)

Mobilizing for War

Organizing the war effort was a formidable task for the frail Congress and the new state governments. They had to find the money to pay for the war, and they had to raise and equip an army to fight it.

Financing the war was particularly difficult, because Congress lacked the authority and the states generally lacked the inclination to impose taxes on the public. Hard currency (gold and silver) had always been scarce in America. And when Congress requisitioned money from the state governments, none contributed more than a small part of its expected share. Congress had little success borrowing from the public, since few Americans could afford to buy bonds and those who could preferred to invest in more profitable ventures, such as privateering. So there was no alternative in the end but to issue paper money. Continental currency came from the printing presses in enormous batches, and the states printed currencies of their own. The result, predictably, was soaring inflation. Many American farmers and merchants began to prefer doing business with the British, who could pay for goods in gold or silver coin. (That was one reason why George Washington's troops suffered from food shortages at Valley Forge in the winter of 1777–1778; many Philadelphia merchants would not accept the paper money the army offered them.) Congress was unable to stop the inflation, and ultimately it was able to finance the war only by borrowing from other nations.

Raising and equipping the army was little easier. After the first surge of patriotism in 1775, only a small proportion of eligible men were willing to volunteer. States had to pay bounties or use a draft to recruit the needed men. At first, militiamen remained under the control of their respective states. But Congress recognized the need for a centralized military command, and it created a Continental army with a single commander in chief: George Washington. A forty-three-year-old Virginia planter-aristocrat who had commanded colonial forces during the French and Indian War, Washington had considerable military experience and was an early advocate of independence; he was admired, respected, and trusted by nearly all Patriots. He took command of the new army in June 1775.

Washington was not without shortcomings as a military commander.

Indeed, he lost more battles than he won. But whatever his faults and failures, he was indisputably a great war leader. With the aid of foreign military experts such as the Marquis de Lafayette from France and the Baron von Steuben from Prussia, he built a force that prevailed against the mightiest power in the world. Even more important, perhaps, Washington's steadiness, courage, and dedication to his cause provided the army—and the people—with a symbol of stability around which they could rally.

THE WAR FOR INDEPENDENCE

On the surface, all the advantages in the military struggle between America and Great Britain appeared to lie with the British. They had the greatest navy and the best-equipped army in the world. They had the resources of an empire. They had a coherent structure of command. The Americans, by contrast, were struggling to create an army and a government at the same time that they were trying to fight a war. Yet the United States had advantages too. Americans were fighting on their own ground. They were

REVOLUTIONARY SOLDIERS Jean Baptiste de Verger, a French officer serving in America during the Revolution, kept a journal of his experiences illustrated with watercolors. Here he portrays four American soldiers carrying different kinds of arms: a black infantryman with a light rifle, a musketman, a rifleman, and an artilleryman.

more committed to the conflict than the British. And beginning in 1777, they were receiving substantial aid from abroad.

But the American victory was not simply the result of these advantages, or even of the spirit and resourcefulness of the people and the army. It was a result, too, of a series of blunders and miscalculations by the British in the early stages of the fighting, when England could (and probably should) have won. And it was, finally, a result of the transformation of the war—through three distinct phases—into a new kind of conflict that the British military, for all its strength, was unable to win.

The First Phase: New England

For the first year of the conflict—from the spring of 1775 to the spring of 1776—the British were not entirely sure that they were fighting a war. Many English authorities thought that British forces were simply quelling pockets of rebellion in the contentious area around Boston.

American forces besieged the British army in Boston (under the command of General Thomas Gage) after the redcoats withdrew from Lexington and Concord. In the Battle of Bunker Hill (actually fought on Breed's Hill) on June 17, 1775, the Patriots suffered severe casualties and withdrew. But they inflicted even greater losses on the enemy (indeed, the heaviest casualties the British were to suffer in the entire war) and continued the siege. Early in 1776, the British decided that Boston was a poor place from which to fight. It was in the center of the most anti-British part of America, and it was also tactically indefensible, easily isolated and besieged. And so, on March 17, 1776, the redcoats left Boston for Halifax with hundreds of Loyalist refugees.

In the meantime, a band of Patriots to the south, at Moore's Creek Bridge in North Carolina, crushed an uprising of Loyalists (Americans still loyal to England and its king) on February 27, 1776, and discouraged a British plan to invade the Southern states. And to the north, the Americans began an invasion of Canada—hoping to remove the British threat and to win the Canadians to their cause. Generals Benedict Arnold and Richard Montgomery threatened Quebec in late 1775 and early 1776. Montgomery was killed in the assault on the city; and although a wounded Arnold kept up the siege for a time, the Quebec campaign ended in failure. Canada did not become the fourteenth state.

By the spring of 1776, it had become clear to the British that the conflict was not just a local phenomenon in the area around Boston. The American campaigns in Canada, the agitation in the South, and the growing evidence

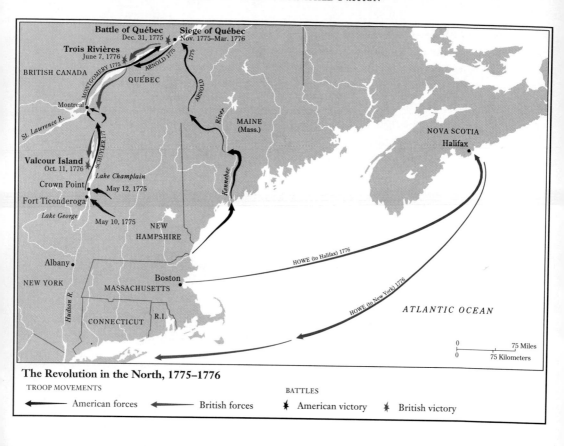

The Revolution in the North, 1775–1776

TROOP MOVEMENTS

⟵——— American forces   ⟵——— British forces

BATTLES

✳ American victory   ✳ British victory

of colonial unity all suggested that England must prepare to fight a much larger conflict.

The Second Phase: The Mid-Atlantic Region

It was during the next phase of the war, which lasted from 1776 until early 1778, that the British were in the best position to win. Indeed, had it not been for a series of blunders and misfortunes, they probably would have crushed the rebellion then.

The British regrouped quickly after their retreat from Boston. During the summer of 1776, in the weeks immediately following the Declaration of Independence, hundreds of British ships and 32,000 British soldiers arrived in New York, under the command of William Howe. Howe wanted to avoid an armed conflict with the Americans and hoped simply to awe them into submission. He offered Congress a choice between surrender with royal pardon and a battle against overwhelming odds.

A M E R I C A N V O I C E S

JOSEPH P. MARTIN

A Soldier's View of the Battle of Long Island

 [T]HE REGIMENT WAS ordered to Long Island, the British having landed in force there . . . I went to the top of the house where I had a full view of that part of the island . . . The horrors of battle there presented themselves to my mind in all their hideousness. . . . We were soon ordered to our regimental parade, from which, as soon as the regiment was formed, we were marched off for the ferry. At the lower end of the street were placed several casks of sea-bread . . . nearly hard enough for musket flints. As my good luck would have it, there was a momentary halt made; I improved the opportunity thus offered me, as every good soldier should upon all important occasions, to get as many of the biscuit as I possibly could. . . .

Our officers . . . pressed forward to the creek, where a large party of Americans and British were engaged. By the time we arrived, the enemy had driven our men into the creek . . . where such as could swim got across. Those that could not swim, and could not procure anything to buoy them up, sunk. . . . There was in this action a regiment of Maryland troops (volunteers), all young gentlemen. When they came out of the water and mud, looking like water rats, it was a truly pitiful sight. Many of them were killed in the pond, and more were drowned. Some of us went into the water . . . and took out a number of corpses and a great many arms that were sunk in the pond and creek.

To oppose Howe's great array, Washington could muster only about 19,000 inadequately armed and poorly trained soldiers, and no navy at all. Yet the Americans instantly rejected Howe's offer and chose continued war—which meant inevitably a succession of defeats. The British pushed the Patriot forces off Long Island, forced them to abandon Manhattan, and then drove them in slow retreat over the plains of New Jersey, across the Delaware River, and into Pennsylvania.

The British settled down for the winter in northern and central New Jersey, with an outpost of Hessians at Trenton on the Delaware River. But Washington did not sit still. On Christmas night 1776, he daringly recrossed the icy river, surprised and scattered the Hessians, and occupied Trenton. Then he advanced to Princeton and drove a force of redcoats from their base in the college there. But Washington was unable to hold either Princeton or Trenton and finally took refuge for the rest of the winter in the hills around Morristown. As the campaign of 1776 came to an end, the Americans could console themselves with the thought that they had won two minor victories, that their main army was still intact, and that the invaders were no nearer than before to the decisive triumph that Howe had so confidently antici- pated. But the British retained their heavy advantages in men and supplies.

For the campaigns of 1777 the British devised a strategy that, if Howe had stuck to it, might have cut the United States in two and prepared the way for final victory by Great Britain. Howe would move from New York up the Hudson to Albany, while another force would come down from Canada to meet him. John Burgoyne secured command of this northern force and prepared a two-pronged attack to the south along both the Mohawk and the upper Hudson approaches to Albany.

But after setting the plan in motion, Howe inexplicably abandoned his part of it. Instead of moving north to meet Burgoyne, he went south and attacked Philadelphia, in the hope that capturing the rebel capital would discourage the Patriots, rally the Loyalists, and bring the war to a speedy conclusion. He moved most of his forces by sea from New York to the head of the Chesapeake Bay, brushed Washington aside at the Battle of Brandy- wine Creek on September 11, and proceeded north to Philadelphia, which he took with little resistance. After launching an unsuccessful Patriot attack on October 4 at Germantown (just outside Philadelphia), Washington went into winter quarters at Valley Forge. The Continental Congress reassem- bled at York, Pennsylvania.

Howe's move to Philadelphia left Burgoyne to carry out the campaign in the north alone. Burgoyne sent Colonel Barry St. Leger up the St. Lawrence River toward Lake Ontario and the Mohawk, while he himself

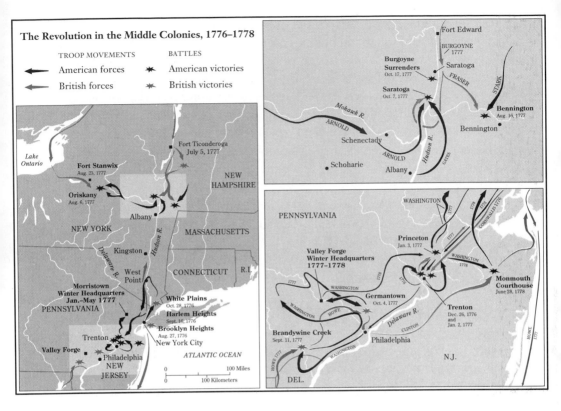

The Revolution in the Middle Colonies, 1776–1778

TROOP MOVEMENTS
American forces
British forces

BATTLES
American victories
British victories

advanced directly down the upper Hudson Valley. At first, all went well. Burgoyne easily seized Fort Ticonderoga and its large store of powder and supplies; Congress was so dismayed by the loss that it removed General Philip Schuyler from command of American forces in the north and replaced him with Horatio Gates.

By the time Gates took over, Burgoyne had already experienced two staggering defeats. In one of them—at Oriskany, New York, on August 6—Patriots held off a force of Indians and Tories commanded by St. Leger. That gave Benedict Arnold time to close off the Mohawk Valley to St. Leger's advance. In the other battle—at Bennington, Vermont, on August 16—New England militiamen mauled a detachment that Burgoyne had sent to seek supplies. Short of materials, with all help cut off, Burgoyne fought several costly engagements and then withdrew to Saratoga, where Gates surrounded him. On October 17, 1777, Burgoyne surrendered—an event that became a major turning point in the war.

The campaign in upstate New York was not just a British defeat. It was a setback for the ambitious efforts of several Iroquois leaders. Although the

Iroquois Confederacy had declared its neutrality in the Revolutionary War in 1776, not all of its members were content to remain passive. Among those who worked to expand the Indian role in the war were a Mohawk brother and sister, Joseph and Mary Brant. The Brants persuaded their own tribe to contribute to the British cause and attracted the support of the Seneca and Cayuga as well.

The alliance had unhappy consequences for the Iroquois. It further divided their already weakened Confederacy; only three of the Iroquois nations supported the British. Then, a year after their defeat at Oriskany, Indians joined British troops in a series of raids on outlying white settlements in upstate New York. Patriot forces under the command of General John Sullivan harshly retaliated, wreaking such destruction on Indian settlements that large groups of Iroquois fled north into Canada to seek refuge. Many never returned.

Securing Aid from Abroad

The leaders of the American effort knew that victory would not be likely without aid from abroad. And their most promising ally, they realized, was France, still smarting from its defeat by the British in 1763. The astute French foreign minister, the Count de Vergennes, understood that France had much to gain from seeing Britain lose a crucial part of its empire.

From the beginning, therefore, there was interest in an alliance on both the American and the French sides. At first, France provided the United States with badly needed supplies but remained reluctant to grant formal diplomatic recognition to the United States. After the Declaration of Independence, Benjamin Franklin himself went to France to lobby for aid and diplomatic recognition. Franklin and his cause became popular among the French, but Vergennes wanted some evidence that the Americans had a real chance of winning before he would agree to open French intervention. That evidence soon appeared in the form of reports of the British defeat at Saratoga.

That news arrived in London and Paris in early December 1777. In London, the news persuaded Lord North to make a new peace offer: complete home rule within the empire for Americans if they would quit the war. That worried Vergennes, who feared the Americans might accept the offer and thus destroy France's opportunity to weaken Britain. Prompted by Franklin, he decided that French assistance might persuade the Americans to continue the struggle. And on February 6, 1778, he reached agreement with American diplomats on formal recognition of the United States as a sovereign nation and on the groundwork for greatly expanded French assistance to the American war effort.

The entrance of France into the war made it an international conflict. In the course of the next two years, France, Spain, and the Netherlands all drifted into another general war with Great Britain in Europe. That contributed indirectly to the ultimate American victory by complicating England's task. All three nations contributed directly by offering financial and material assistance. But France was America's indispensable ally. It furnished the new nation with most of its money and munitions, and it provided a navy and an expeditionary force that were vital to the final, successful phase of the revolutionary conflict.

The Final Phase: The South

The failure of the British to crush the Continental army in the mid-Atlantic states, combined with the stunning American victory at Saratoga, transformed the war and ushered it into a new and final phase. This last phase of the military struggle in America was fundamentally different from either of the first two. After the defeat at Saratoga and the intervention of the French, the British government placed new limits on its commitment to the conflict. Instead of mounting a full-scale military struggle against the American army, the British tried to enlist the support of those elements of the American population—a majority, they continued to believe—who were still loyal to the crown; they worked, in other words, to undermine the Revolution from within. Since Loyalist sentiment was thought to be strongest in the South, and since the English also hoped slaves would rally to their cause, the main focus of the British effort shifted there.

The new strategy was a dismal failure. British forces spent three years (from 1778 to 1781) moving through the South, fighting small battles and large, and attempting to neutralize the territory through which they traveled. But they had badly overestimated the extent of Loyalist sentiment. Even where Loyalists were most numerous, they were often afraid to help the British because they feared reprisals from the Patriots around them. There were also logistical problems. Patriot forces could move at will throughout the region, living off the resources of the countryside, blending in with the civilian population, and leaving the British unable to distinguish friend from foe. The British, by contrast, suffered all the disadvantages of an army in hostile territory.

It was this phase of the conflict that made the war "revolutionary"—not only because it introduced a new kind of warfare, but because it had the effect of mobilizing and politicizing large groups of the population who had previously remained aloof from the struggle. With the war expanding into previously isolated communities, with many civilians forced to involve themselves whether they liked it or not, the political climate of the United States grew more heated than ever. And support for independence, far from being crushed as the British had hoped, greatly increased.

Against that backdrop occurred the important military encounters of the last years of the war. In the North, where significant numbers of British troops remained, the fighting settled into a stalemate. Sir Henry Clinton replaced the hapless William Howe in 1778 and moved what had been Howe's army from Philadelphia back to New York. There the British troops stayed for more than a year, with Washington and his army keeping watch around them. During that same winter, George Rogers Clark, on orders from the state of Virginia, led an expedition over the mountains that captured settlements in the Illinois country from the British and their Indian allies.

During this period of relative calm, the American forces were shocked by the exposure of treason on the part of General Benedict Arnold. Arnold had been one of the early heroes of the war; but now, convinced that the American cause was hopeless, he conspired with British agents to betray the Patriot stronghold at West Point on the Hudson River. When the scheme was exposed and foiled, Arnold fled to the safety of the British camp, where he spent the rest of the war.

The British did have some significant military successes during this period. On December 29, 1778, they captured Savannah, on the coast of Georgia. On May 12, 1780, they took the port of Charleston, South Carolina. And they inspired some Loyalists to take up arms and advance with them into the interior. But although the British were able to win conventional battles, they were constantly harassed as they moved through the countryside by Patriot guerrillas led by such resourceful fighters as Thomas Sumter, Andrew Pickens, and Francis Marion, the "Swamp Fox." Penetrating to Camden, South Carolina, Lord Cornwallis (Clinton's choice as British commander in the South) met and crushed a Patriot force under Horatio Gates on August 16, 1780. Congress recalled Gates, and Washington replaced him with Nathanael Greene, probably the ablest of all the American generals of the time next to Washington himself.

Even before Greene arrived in the war theater, the tide of battle had already begun to turn against Cornwallis. At King's Mountain (near the North Carolina–South Carolina border) on October 7, 1780, a band of Patriot riflemen from the backwoods killed, wounded, or captured an entire force of 1,100 New York and South Carolina Tories, upon whom Cornwallis

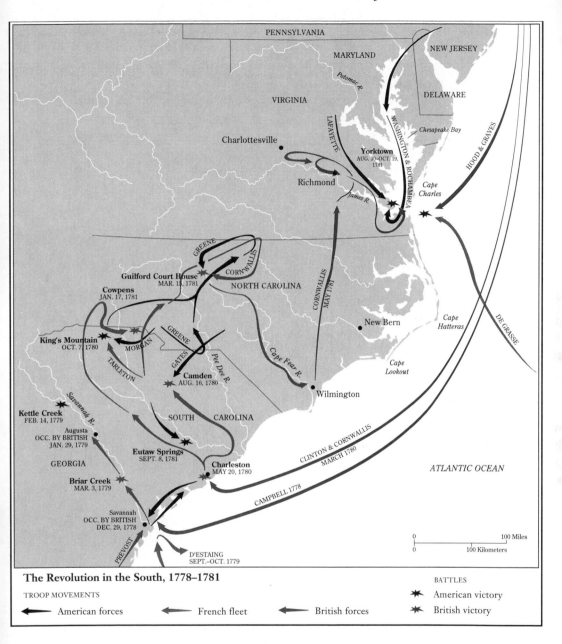

PENNSYLVANIA

MARYLAND

NEW JERSEY

DELAWARE

Potomac R.

VIRGINIA

Chesapeake Bay

LAFAYETTE

WASHINGTON & ROCHAMBEAU

HOOD & GRAVES

Charlottesville

Yorktown
AUG. 30–OCT. 19,
1781

Cape
Charles

Richmond

James R.

CORNWALLIS
MAY 1781

GREENE

Guilford Court House
MAR. 15, 1781

CORNWALLIS

NORTH CAROLINA

Cowpens
JAN. 17, 1781

New Bern

Cape
Hatteras

DE GRASSE

King's Mountain
OCT. 7, 1780

MORGAN

GREENE

TARLETON

GATES

Pee Dee R.

Cape Fear R.

Cape
Lookout

Camden
AUG. 16, 1780

Wilmington

Kettle Creek
FEB. 14, 1779

Savannah R.

SOUTH   CAROLINA

Augusta
OCC. BY BRITISH
JAN. 29, 1779

GEORGIA

Eutaw Springs
SEPT. 8, 1781

CLINTON & CORNWALLIS
MARCH 1780

ATLANTIC OCEAN

Briar Creek
MAR. 3, 1779

Charleston
MAY 20, 1780

Savannah
OCC. BY BRITISH
DEC. 29, 1778

CAMPBELL 1778

PREVOST

D'ESTAING
SEPT.–OCT. 1779

0   100 Miles

0   100 Kilometers

The Revolution in the South, 1778–1781

TROOP MOVEMENTS

BATTLES

⬅ American forces   ⬅ French fleet   ⬅ British forces

✸ American victory

✸ British victory

had depended as auxiliaries. Once Greene arrived, he confused and exasperated Cornwallis by dividing the American forces into fast-moving contingents while avoiding an open, conventional battle. One of the contingents inflicted what Cornwallis admitted was "a very unexpected and severe blow" at Cowpens on January 17, 1781. Finally, after receiving reinforcements,

Greene combined all his forces and maneuvered to meet the British at Guilford Court House, North Carolina. After a hard-fought battle there on March 15, 1781, Greene was driven from the field; but Cornwallis had lost so many men that he decided to abandon the Carolina campaign.

Cornwallis withdrew to the port town of Wilmington, North Carolina, to receive supplies. Later he moved north, hoping to carry on raids in the interior of Virginia. But Clinton, fearful that the southern army might be destroyed, ordered him to take up a defensive position on the peninsula between the York and James rivers and wait for transport to New York or Charleston. Cornwallis retreated to Yorktown and began to build fortifications there.

At that point, American and French forces descended on Yorktown in an effort to trap Cornwallis. Washington and the Count de Rochambeau marched a French-American army from New York to join the Marquis de Lafayette in Virginia, while Admiral de Grasse took a French fleet with additional troops up Chesapeake Bay to the York River. These joint operations caught Cornwallis between land and sea. After a few shows of resistance, he surrendered on October 17, 1781. Two days later, as a military band played the old tune "The World Turn'd Upside Down," he surrendered his whole army of more than 7,000.

Winning the Peace

Cornwallis's defeat provoked outcries in England against continuing the war. Lord North resigned as prime minister; Lord Shelburne emerged from the political wreckage to succeed him; and British emissaries appeared in France to talk informally with the American diplomats there, of whom the three principals were Benjamin Franklin, John Adams, and John Jay.

The Americans were under instructions to cooperate fully with France in their negotiations with England. But Vergennes, the French foreign minister, insisted that France could not agree to any settlement of the war with England until its ally Spain had achieved its principal war aim: winning back Gibraltar from the British. There was no real prospect of that happening soon, and the Americans began to fear that the alliance with France might keep them at war indefinitely. As a result, Franklin, Jay, and Adams began proceeding on their own, without informing Vergennes, and soon drew up a preliminary treaty with Great Britain, which was signed on November 30, 1782. Franklin, in the meantime, skillfully pacified Vergennes and avoided an immediate rift in the French-American alliance.

The final treaty was signed September 3, 1783, when both Spain and

France agreed to end hostilities. It was, on the whole, remarkably favorable to the United States in granting a clear-cut recognition of independence and a generous, though ambiguous, cession of territory—from the southern boundary of Canada to the northern boundary of Florida and from the Atlantic to the Mississippi. With good reason the American people celebrated as the last of the British occupation forces embarked from New York and General Washington, at the head of his troops, rode triumphantly into the city.

WAR AND SOCIETY

Historians have long debated whether the American Revolution was a social as well as a political revolution. But whatever the intentions or desires of those who produced and fought the War for Independence, the conflict had important effects on the nature of American society.

Loyalists and Minorities

Estimates differ as to how many Americans remained loyal to England during the Revolution, but it is clear that there were many—at least a fifth (and some estimate as much as a third) of the white population. Some were officeholders in the imperial government. Others were merchants whose trade was closely tied to the imperial system (although most merchants supported the Revolution). Still others were people who lived in relative isolation and had simply retained their traditional loyalties. There were also cultural and ethnic minorities who feared that an independent America would not offer them sufficient protection. And there were those who, expecting the British to win the war, were simply currying favor with the anticipated victors.

Hounded by Patriots in their communities, harassed by legislative and judicial actions, many of these Loyalists found themselves in an intolerable position during the war. Up to 100,000 fled the country. Those who could afford to—for example, the hated Tory governor of Massachusetts, Thomas Hutchinson—fled to England, where many lived in difficult and lonely exile. Others of more modest means moved to Canada, establishing the first English-speaking community in the province of Quebec. Some returned to America after the war and, as the early passions and resentments faded, managed to reenter the life of the nation. Others remained abroad for the rest of their lives.

The war had a significant effect on other minorities as well. No sect suffered more than the Anglicans, many of whose members were Loyalists and all of whom were widely identified with England. In Virginia and Maryland, the new Revolutionary regimes removed Anglicanism as the official religion and stopped funding it. In other states, Anglicans lost the economic aid they were accustomed to receiving from England. By the time the fighting ended, many Anglican parishes could no longer even afford clergymen. Anglicanism was permanently weakened from its losses during the Revolution. Also weakened were the Quakers in Pennsylvania and elsewhere, whose pacifism won them widespread unpopularity when they refused to support the war. The church was never to recover fully. Other Protestant denominations, however, grew stronger as a result of their enthusiastic support for the war. Presbyterian, Congregationalist, and Baptist churches successfully tied themselves to the Patriot cause.

Most American Catholics also supported the Patriots during the war and won increased popularity as a result. The church did not greatly increase its numbers as a result of the Revolution, but it did strengthen itself considerably as an institution. Shortly after the peace treaty was signed, the Vatican provided the United States with its own hierarchy and, in 1789, its first bishop. Hostility toward Catholics had not disappeared from American life, but the church had established a footing from which to withstand future assaults.

For the largest of America's minorities—the black population—the war had limited, but nevertheless significant, effects. For some, the Revolution meant freedom. Because so much of the fighting occurred in the South during the last years of the war, many slaves came into contact with the British army, which—in the interests of disrupting and weakening the American cause—emancipated thousands of them and took them out of the country. For other blacks, the Revolution meant exposure to the idea, although not the reality, of liberty. In towns and cities in particular, even blacks who could not read had exposure to the new ideas of liberty; and in some cases, they attempted to apply those ideas to themselves.

That was one reason why Revolutionary sentiment was more restrained in South Carolina and Georgia than in other colonies. Blacks constituted a majority in South Carolina and almost half the population in Georgia, and whites in both places feared that revolution would foment slave rebellions. The same fears discouraged English colonists in the Caribbean islands (who were even more greatly outnumbered by black slaves) from joining with the continental Americans in the revolt against Britain.

Native Americans and the Revolution

Indians viewed the American Revolution with considerable uncertainty. The American Patriots tried to persuade them to remain neutral in the conflict, which they insisted had nothing to do with the tribes. The British too generally sought to maintain Indian neutrality, fearing that native allies would prove unreliable and uncontrollable. Most tribes ultimately chose to stay out of the war.

But many Indians feared that the Revolution would replace a ruling group in which they had developed at least some measure of trust (the British) with one they considered generally hostile to them (the Patriots). The British had consistently sought to limit the expansion of white settlement into Indian land, even if unsuccessfully the Americans had spearheaded the encroachments. Thus some Indians, among them those Iroquois who participated in the Burgoyne campaign in upper New York, chose to join the English cause. Still others took advantage of the conflict to launch attacks of their own.

In the western Carolinas and Virginia, the Cherokee, led by Chief Dragging Canoe, launched a series of attacks on outlying white settlements in the summer of 1776. Patriot militias responded in great force, ravaging Cherokee lands and forcing the chief and many of his followers to flee west across the Tennessee River. Those Cherokee who remained behind agreed to a new treaty by which they gave up still more land. Some Iroquois, despite the setbacks at Oriskany, continued to wage war against Americans in the West and caused widespread destruction in large agricultural areas of New York and Pennsylvania—areas whose crops were of crucial importance to the Patriot cause. And although the retaliating American armies inflicted heavy losses on the Indians, the attacks continued throughout the war.

In the end, however, the Revolution generally weakened the position of Native Americans in several ways. The Patriot victory increased white demand for Western lands. Many whites resented the assistance such nations as the Mohawk had given the British and insisted on treating them as conquered people. Others derived from the Revolution a paternalistic view of the tribes that was only slightly less dangerous to the Native Americans than open hostility. Thomas Jefferson, for example, came to view the Indians as "noble savages," uncivilized in their present state but redeemable if they were willing to adapt to the norms of white society.

Among the Indians themselves, the Revolution increased the deep divisions that made it difficult for them to form a common front to resist the growing power of whites. In 1774, for example, the Shawnee Indians in western Virginia could attract no support from neighboring tribes when they attempted to lead a widespread uprising against white settlers moving into the lands that would later become Kentucky. They were defeated by the colonial militia and forced to cede still more land to white settlers. The Cherokee generated little support from surrounding tribes in their 1776 battles. The Iroquois, whose power had been eroding since the end of the French and Indian War, were unable to act in unison in the Revolution; and the nations that chose to support the British attracted little support from tribes outside the Confederacy (many of whom resented the long Iroquois domination of the interior).

Women's Rights and Women's Roles

The long Revolutionary War had a profound effect on American women. The departure of so many men to fight in the Patriot armies left wives, mothers, sisters, and daughters in charge of farms and businesses. Often, women handled these tasks with great success. But in many cases, inexperience, inflation, the unavailability of male labor, or the threat of enemy troops led to failure. Other women whose husbands or fathers were called away to war did not have even a farm or shop to fall back on. Cities and towns developed significant populations of impoverished women, who on occasion led protests against price increases or rioted and looted for food. On several other occasions (in New Jersey and Staten Island), women launched attacks on occupying British troops, whom they were required to house and feed at considerable expense.

Not all women stayed behind when the men went off to war. Sometimes by choice, more often by necessity, women flocked to the camps of the Patriot armies to join their male relatives. Despite the disapproval of many officers of these female "camp followers," the women were of significant value to the new army, which had not yet developed an adequate system of supply and auxiliary services; the women increased army morale and provided a ready source of volunteers to do cooking, laundry, nursing, and other necessary tasks. In the rough environment of the camps, traditional gender distinctions proved difficult to maintain. Considerable numbers of women became involved, at least intermittently, in combat—including the legendary "Molly Pitcher" (so named because she carried pitchers of water to soldiers on the battlefield), who watched her husband fall during one encounter and immediately took his place at a field gun. A few women even disguised themselves as men so as to be able to fight.

After the war, of course, the soldiers and the women who had accompanied them returned home. The experience of combat had little visible lasting impact on how society (or women themselves) defined female roles in peacetime. The Revolution did, however, call certain assumptions about women into question in other ways. The emphasis on liberty and the "rights of man" led some women to begin to question their position in society as well. "By the way," Abigail Adams wrote to her husband John Adams in 1776, "in the new code of laws which I suppose it will be necessary for you to make, I desire you would remember the ladies and be more generous and favorable to them than your ancestors. Do not put such unlimited power into the hands of the Husbands." Adams was calling for a relatively modest expansion of women's rights: for new protections against abusive and tyrannical men. A few women, however, went further. Judith Sargent Murray, one of the leading essayists of the late eighteenth century, wrote in 1779 that women's minds were as good as those of men and that girls as well as boys therefore deserved access to education.

Nevertheless few concrete reforms were enacted into law or translated into practice. Under English common law, an unmarried woman had certain legal rights, but a married woman had virtually no rights at all. Everything she owned and everything she earned belonged to her husband. She had no legal authority over her children. Because she had no property rights, she could not engage in any legal transactions on her own (buying or selling, suing or being sued, writing wills). She could not vote. Nor could she obtain a divorce; that too was a right reserved almost exclusively to men. The Revolution did little to change any of these legal customs. In some states, it did become easier for women to obtain divorces. And in New Jersey, women obtained the right to vote (although that right was repealed in 1807). Otherwise, there were few advances and some setbacks—including the loss of the right of widows to regain their dowries from their husbands' estates. The Revolution, in other words, did not really challenge the patriarchal legal system. In many ways, it actually confirmed and strengthened it.

But the Revolution did encourage people of both sexes to reevaluate the contribution of women to the family and society. Part of this change was a result of the participation of women in the Revolutionary struggle itself. And part was a result of the reevaluation of American life after the war. As the new republic searched for a cultural identity for itself, it attributed a higher value to the role of women as mothers. The new nation was, many Americans liked to believe, producing a new kind of citizen, steeped in the principles of liberty. Mothers had a particularly important task, therefore, in instructing their children in the virtues that the republican citizenry was expected now to possess. Wives were still far from equal partners in marriage, but their ideas and interests were receiving some respect.

The War Economy

The Revolution also produced important changes in the structure of the American economy. After more than a century of dependence on the British imperial system, American commerce suddenly found itself on its own. English ships no longer protected American vessels, but tried to drive them from the seas. British imperial ports—including those in England itself—were closed to American trade. But this disruption in traditional economic patterns served in the long run to strengthen the American economy. The end of imperial restrictions on American shipping opened up enormous new areas of trade to the nation. Colonial merchants had been violating British regulations for years, but the rules of empire had nevertheless served to inhibit American exploration of many markets. Now, enterprising merchants in New England and elsewhere began to develop new commerce in the Caribbean and South America. By the mid-1780s, American merchants were developing an important trade with the Orient. There was also a substantial increase in trade among the American states.

When English imports to America were cut off—first by the prewar boycott, then by the war itself—there were desperate efforts throughout the states to stimulate domestic manufacturing of certain necessities. No great industrial expansion resulted, but there was a modest increase in production and an even greater increase in expectations. Having broken politically with the British Empire, citizens of the new nation began to dream of breaking economically with it too—of developing a strong economy to rival that of the Old World.

THE CREATION OF STATE GOVERNMENTS

At the same time that Americans were struggling to win their independence on the battlefield, they were also struggling to create new institutions of government to replace the British system they had repudiated. That struggle continued for more than fifteen years, but its most important phase occurred during the war itself, at the state level.

The formation of state governments began early in 1776. At first, the new state constitutions reflected primarily the fear of bloated executive power that had done so much to produce the break with England. Gradually, however, Americans became equally concerned about the instability of a government too responsive to popular will. In a second phase of state constitution writing, therefore, they gave renewed attention to the idea of balance in government.

The Assumptions of Republicanism

If Americans agreed on nothing else when they began to build new governments for themselves, they agreed that those governments would be republican. To them, that meant a political system in which all power came from the people, rather than from some supreme authority (such as a king). The success of any government, therefore, depended on the nature of its citizenry. If the population consisted of sturdy, independent property owners imbued with civic virtue, then the republic could survive. If it consisted of a few powerful aristocrats and a great mass of dependent workers, then it would be in danger. From the beginning, therefore, the ideal of the small freeholder (the independent landowner) was basic to American political ideology.

Another crucial part of that ideology was the concept of equality. The Declaration of Independence had given voice to that idea in its most ringing phrase: "All men are created equal." It was a belief that stood in direct contrast to the old European assumption of an inherited aristocracy. The innate talents and energies of individuals, not their positions at birth, would determine their roles in society. Some people would inevitably be wealthier and more powerful than others. But all people would have to earn their success. There would be no equality of condition, but there would be equality of opportunity.

In reality, of course, the United States was never a nation in which all citizens were independent property holders. From the beginning, there was a sizable dependent labor force—the white members of which were allowed many of the privileges of citizenship, the black members of which were allowed virtually none. American women remained both politically and economically subordinate. Native Americans were systematically exploited and displaced. Nor was there ever full equality of opportunity. American society was more open and more fluid than that of most European nations, but wealth and privilege were often passed from one generation to another. The condition of a person's birth was almost always a crucial determinant of success.

Nevertheless, in embracing the assumptions of republicanism, Americans were adopting a powerful, even revolutionary ideology, and their experiment in statecraft became a model for many other countries. It made the United States for a time the most admired and studied nation on earth.

The First State Constitutions

Two states, Connecticut and Rhode Island, did not write new constitutions. They already had governments that were republican in all but name, and they simply deleted references to England and the king from their charters and adopted them as constitutions. The other eleven states, however, produced new documents.

The first and perhaps most basic decision was that the constitutions were to be written down. In England, the constitution was simply a vague understanding about the nature of government. Americans believed that the vagueness had produced corruption, so they insisted that the structures of their own governments be clearly recorded so no one could pervert them. The second decision was that the power of the executive, which Americans believed had grown bloated in England, must be limited. Pennsylvania eliminated the executive altogether. Most other states inserted provisions limiting the power of the governor over appointments, reducing or eliminating his right to veto bills, and preventing him from dismissing the legislature. Most important, every state forbade the governor or any other executive officer from holding a seat in the legislature, thus ensuring that, unlike in England, the two branches of government would remain wholly separate.

But the new constitutions did not move all the way toward direct popular rule. In Georgia and Pennsylvania, the legislature consisted of one popularly elected house. But in every other state, there was an upper and a lower chamber; and in most cases, the upper chamber was designed to represent the "higher orders" of society. There were property requirements for voters—some modest, some substantial—in all states.

The initial phase of constitution writing proceeded rapidly. Ten states completed the process before the end of 1776. Georgia and New York finished by the end of 1777. Massachusetts did not finally adopt a constitution until 1780, by which time the construction of state governments had moved into a new phase.

Revising State Governments

By the late 1770s, Americans were growing concerned about the apparent factiousness and instability of their new state governments, which were having trouble accomplishing anything at all. Many believed the problem was one of too much democracy. As a result, most of the states began to revise their constitutions to limit popular power. Massachusetts was the first to act on the new concerns. By waiting until 1780 to ratify its first constitution, Massachusetts allowed these changing ideas to shape its government; and the state produced a constitution that served as a model for others.

Two changes in particular characterized the Massachusetts and later constitutions. The first was a change in the process of constitution writing itself. Most of the first documents had been written by state legislatures and thus could easily be amended (or violated) by them. By 1780, sentiment was growing to find a way to protect the constitutions from those who had written them, to make it difficult to change the documents once they were approved. The solution was the constitutional convention: a special assembly of the people that would meet only for the purpose of writing the constitution and that would never (except under extraordinary circumstances) meet again. The constitution would be the product of the popular will; but once approved, it would be protected from the whims of public opinion and the political moods of the legislature.

The second change was a significant strengthening of the executive, a reaction to what many believed was the instability of the original state governments that had weak governors. The 1780 Massachusetts constitution made the governor one of the strongest in any state. He was to be elected directly by the people; he was to have a fixed salary (in other words, he would not be dependent on the good will of the legislature each year for his wages); he would have significant appointment powers and a veto over legislation. Other states followed. Those with weak or nonexistent upper houses strengthened or created them. Most increased the powers of the governor. Pennsylvania, which had had no executive at all at first, now produced a strong one. By the late 1780s, almost every state had either revised its constitution or drawn up an entirely new one in an effort to produce stability in government.

Toleration and Slavery

The new states moved far in the direction of complete religious freedom. Most Americans continued to believe that religion should play some role in government, but they did not wish to give special privileges to any particular denomination. The privileges that churches had once enjoyed were now largely stripped away. New York and the Southern states stopped subsidizing the Church of England, and the New England states stripped the Congregational church of many of its privileges. Boldest of all was Virginia. In 1786, it enacted a Statute of Religious Liberty, written by Thomas Jefferson, which called for the complete separation of church and state.

More difficult to resolve was the question of slavery. In areas where slavery was already weak—in New England, where there had never been many slaves, and in Pennsylvania, where the Quakers opposed slavery—it was abolished. Even in the South, there were some pressures to amend the institution; every state but South Carolina and Georgia prohibited further importation of slaves from abroad, and South Carolina banned the slave trade during the war. Virginia passed a law encouraging the freeing of slaves (manumission). Nevertheless, slavery survived in all the Southern and border states. There were several reasons: racist assumptions among whites about the inferiority of blacks; the enormous economic investments many white southerners had in their slaves; and the inability of even such men as Washington and Jefferson, who had deep moral misgivings about slavery, to envision any alternative to it. If slavery were abolished, what would happen to the black people in America? Few whites believed blacks could be integrated into American society as equals. In maintaining slavery, Jefferson once remarked, Americans were holding a "wolf by the ears." However unappealing it was to hold on to it, letting go would be even worse.

THE SEARCH FOR A NATIONAL GOVERNMENT

Americans were much quicker to agree on state institutions than they were on their national government. At first, most believed that the central government should remain a relatively weak and unimportant force and that each state would be virtually a sovereign nation. Such beliefs reflected the assumption that were a republican government to attempt to administer too large and diverse a nation, it would founder. It was in response to such ideas that the Articles of Confederation emerged.

The Confederation

The Articles of Confederation, which the Continental Congress had adopted in 1777, provided for a national government much like the one already in place. Congress would remain the central—indeed the only—institution of national authority. Its powers would expand to give it authority to conduct wars and foreign relations and to appropriate, borrow, and issue money. But it would not have power to regulate trade, draft troops, or levy taxes directly on the people. For troops and taxes it would have to make formal requests to the state legislatures, which could refuse them. There was to be no separate executive; the "president of the United States" would be merely the presiding officer at the sessions of Congress. Each state would have a single vote in Congress, and at least nine of the states would have to approve any important measure. All thirteen state legislatures would have to approve before the Articles could be ratified or amended.

The ratification process revealed broad disgreements over the plan. The small states had insisted on equal state representation, but the larger states wanted representation to be based on population. The smaller states prevailed on that issue. More important, the states claiming Western lands wished to keep them, but the rest of the states demanded that all such territory be turned over to the Confederation government. When New York and Virginia agreed to give up their Western claims, Maryland (the only state still holding out) approved the Articles of Confederation. They went into effect in 1781.

The Confederation, which existed from 1781 until 1789, was not the complete failure that subsequent accounts often describe. But it was far from a success. Lacking adequate powers to deal with interstate issues or to enforce its will on the states, and lacking sufficient stature in the eyes of the world to be able to negotiate effectively, it suffered a series of damaging setbacks.

Diplomatic Failures

Evidence of the low esteem in which the rest of the world held the Confederation was its difficulty in persuading Great Britain (and to a lesser extent Spain) to live up to the terms of the peace treaty of 1783.

The British had promised to evacuate American soil, but British forces continued to occupy a string of frontier posts along the Great Lakes within the United States. Nor did the British honor their agreement to make restitution to slaveowners whose slaves the British army had confiscated. There were also disputes over the Northeastern boundary of the new nation and over the border between the United States and Florida, which Britain had ceded back to Spain in the treaty. There were other diplomatic problems. American commerce, freed from imperial regulations, was expanding in new directions, but most American trade remained within the British Empire. Americans wanted full access to British markets; England, however, placed sharp postwar restrictions on that access.

In 1784, Congress sent John Adams as minister to London to resolve these differences, but Adams made no headway with the English, who could never be sure whether he represented a single nation or thirteen different ones. Throughout the 1780s, the British government refused even to return the courtesy of sending a minister to the American capital.

In dealing with the Spanish government, the Confederation demonstrated similar weakness. Its diplomats agreed to a treaty with Spain in 1786 that accepted the American interpretation of the Florida boundary in return for American recognition of Spanish possessions in North America and an agreement that the United States would limit its right to navigate the Mississippi for twenty years. But the Southern states, incensed at the idea of giving up their access to the Mississippi, blocked ratification.

The Confederation and the Northwest

The Confederation's most important accomplishment was its resolution of some of the controversies involving the Western lands—although even this was a partial and ambiguous achievement.

When the Revolution began, only a few thousand whites had lived west of the Appalachian divide; by 1790 their numbers had increased to 120,000. The Confederation had to find a way to include these new settlements in the political structure of the new nation. The Western settlers were already often in conflict with the established centers of the East over Indian policies, trade provisions, and taxes. And Congress faced the additional difficulty of competing with state governments for jurisdiction over the trans-Appalachian region. The landed states began to yield their claims to the Confederation in 1781, and by 1784 the states had ceded enough land to the Confederation to permit Congress to begin making policy for the national domain.

The Ordinance of 1784, based on a proposal by Thomas Jefferson, divided the Western territory into ten self-governing districts, each of which could petition Congress for statehood when its population equaled the number of free inhabitants of the smallest existing state. Then, in the Ordinance of 1785, Congress created a system for surveying and selling the Western lands. The territory north of the Ohio River was to be surveyed and marked off into neat rectangular townships. In every township four sections were to be set aside for the United States; the revenue from the sale of one of the others was to support creation of a public school. Sections were to be sold at auction for no less than one dollar an acre.

The original ordinances proved highly favorable to land speculators and less so to ordinary settlers, many of whom could not afford the price of the land. Congress compounded the problem by selling much of the best land to the Ohio and Scioto companies before making it available to anyone else. Criticism of these policies led to the passage in 1787 of another law governing Western settlement—legislation that became known as the "Northwest Ordinance." The 1787 Ordinance abandoned the ten districts established in

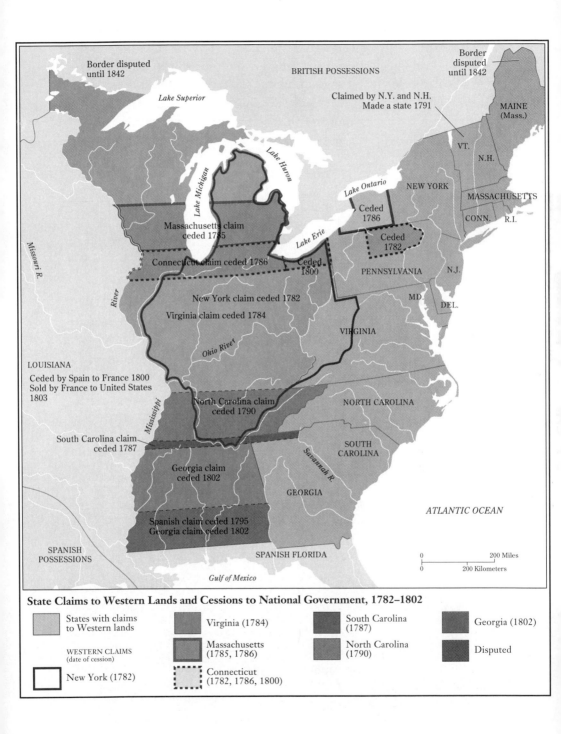

Border disputed until 1842

BRITISH POSSESSIONS

Border disputed until 1842

Lake Superior

Claimed by N.Y. and N.H.
Made a state 1791

MAINE
(Mass.)

Lake Michigan

Lake Huron

VT.

N.H.

Lake Ontario

NEW YORK

MASSACHUSETTS

Ceded 1786

Massachusetts claim
ceded 1785

Lake Erie

CONN.

R.I.

Connecticut claim ceded 1786

Ceded 1782

Ceded 1800

PENNSYLVANIA

N.J.

Missouri R.

New York claim ceded 1782

Virginia claim ceded 1784

MD.

DEL.

River

Ohio River

VIRGINIA

LOUISIANA
Ceded by Spain to France 1800
Sold by France to United States
1803

North Carolina claim
ceded 1790

NORTH CAROLINA

Mississippi

South Carolina claim
ceded 1787

SOUTH
CAROLINA

Savannah R.

Georgia claim
ceded 1802

GEORGIA

ATLANTIC OCEAN

Spanish claim ceded 1795
Georgia claim ceded 1802

SPANISH
POSSESSIONS

SPANISH FLORIDA

0   200 Miles

0   200 Kilometers

Gulf of Mexico

State Claims to Western Lands and Cessions to National Government, 1782–1802

States with claims
to Western lands

Virginia (1784)

South Carolina
(1787)

Georgia (1802)

WESTERN CLAIMS
(date of cession)

Massachusetts
(1785, 1786)

North Carolina
(1790)

Disputed

New York (1782)

Connecticut
(1782, 1786, 1800)

1784 and created a single Northwest Territory out of the lands north of the Ohio; the territory might subsequently be divided into between three and five territories. It also specified a population of 60,000 as a minimum for statehood, guaranteed freedom of religion and the right to trial by jury to residents of the Northwest, and prohibited slavery throughout the territory.

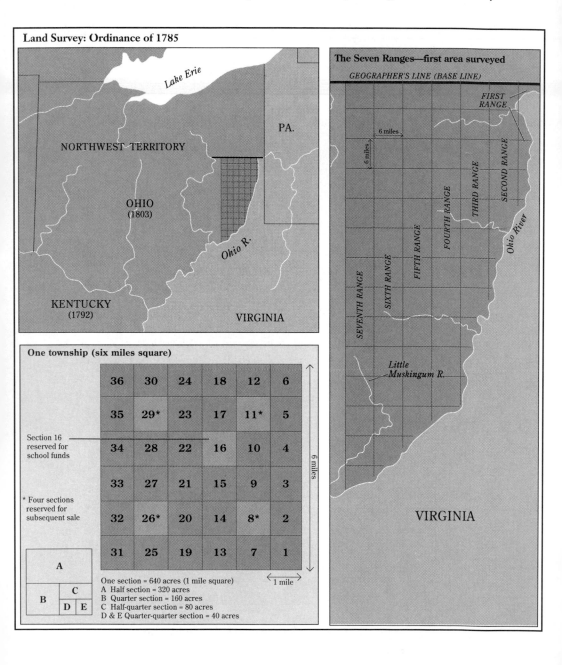

Land Survey: Ordinance of 1785

NORTHWEST TERRITORY

OHIO (1803)

KENTUCKY (1792)

Lake Erie

PA.

Ohio R.

VIRGINIA

The Seven Ranges—first area surveyed

GEOGRAPHER'S LINE (BASE LINE)

FIRST RANGE
SECOND RANGE
THIRD RANGE
FOURTH RANGE
FIFTH RANGE
SIXTH RANGE
SEVENTH RANGE

6 miles

Ohio River

Little Muskingum R.

VIRGINIA

One township (six miles square)

36	30	24	18	12	6
35	29*	23	17	11*	5
34	28	22	16	10	4
33	27	21	15	9	3
32	26*	20	14	8*	2
31	25	19	13	7	1

Section 16 reserved for school funds

* Four sections reserved for subsequent sale

6 miles

1 mile

A

B | C
D | E

One section = 640 acres (1 mile square)
A Half section = 320 acres
B Quarter section = 160 acres
C Half-quarter section = 80 acres
D & E Quarter-quarter section = 40 acres

The Western lands south of the Ohio River received less attention from Congress, and development was more chaotic there. The region that became Kentucky and Tennessee developed rapidly in the late 1770s, and in the 1780s speculators and settlers began setting up governments and asking for recognition as states. The Confederation Congress was never able successfully to resolve the conflicting claims in that region.

Indians and the Western Lands

On paper at least, the Western land policies of the Confederation created a system that brought order and stability to the process of white settlement in the Northwest. But in reality, order and stability came slowly and at great cost, because much of the land the Confederation was neatly subdividing and offering for sale consisted of territory claimed by the Indians of the region.

Congress tried to resolve that problem in 1784, 1785, and 1786 by persuading Iroquois, Choctaw, Chickasaw, and Cherokee leaders to sign treaties ceding substantial Western lands in the North and South to the United States. But those agreements proved ineffective. In 1786, the leadership of the Iroquois Confederacy repudiated the treaty it had signed two years earlier and threatened to attack white settlements in the disputed lands. Other tribes had never really accepted the treaties affecting them and continued to resist white movement into their lands.

Violence between whites and Indians on the Northwest frontier reached a crescendo in the early 1790s. In 1790 and again in 1791, the Miami, led by the famed warrior Little Turtle, defeated United States forces in two major battles near what is now the western border of Ohio; in the second of those battles, on November 4, 1791, 630 white Americans died in fighting at the Wabash River (the greatest military victory Indians had ever or would ever achieve in their battles with whites). Efforts to negotiate a settlement foundered on the Miami insistence that no treaty was possible unless it forbade white settlement west of the Ohio River. Negotiations did not resume until after General Anthony Wayne led 4,000 soldiers into the Ohio Valley in 1794 and defeated the Indians in the Battle of Fallen Timbers.

A year later, the Miami signed the Treaty of Greenville, ceding substantial new lands to the United States (which was now operating under the Constitution of 1789) in exchange for a formal acknowledgment of their claim to that portion of their territory they retained. This was the first time the new federal government recognized the sovereignty of Indian nations; in doing so, the United States was affirming that Indian lands could be ceded

LITTLE TURTLE Little Turtle led the Miami confederacy in its wars with the United States in what is now Ohio and Indiana in the early 1790s. For a time he seemed almost invincible, but in 1794 Little Turtle was defeated in the Battle of Fallen Timbers.

only by the tribes themselves. That hard-won assurance, however, proved a frail protection against the pressure for white expansion westward in later years.

Debts, Taxes, and Daniel Shays

The postwar depression, which lasted from 1784 to 1787, increased the perennial American problem of an inadequate money supply, a problem that bore particularly heavily on debtors. In dealing with the serious problem of debts, Congress most clearly demonstrated its weakness.

The Confederation itself had an enormous outstanding debt and few means with which to pay it. It had sold bonds during the war that were now due to be repaid; it owed money to its Revolutionary soldiers; it had substantial debts abroad. But it had no power to tax. It could only make requisitions of the states, and it received only about one-sixth of the money it requisitioned—barely enough to meet the government's ordinary operating expenses, too little to pay the debts. The fragile new nation was faced with the prospect of defaulting on its obligations.

This alarming prospect brought to the fore a group of leaders who would play a crucial role in the shaping of the republic for several decades. Committed nationalists, they sought ways to increase the powers of the central government and to permit it to meet its financial obligations. Robert Morris, the head of the Confederation's treasury; Alexander Hamilton, his young protégé; James Madison of Virginia; and others called for a "continental impost"—a 5 percent duty on imported goods, to be levied by Congress and used to fund the debt.

But the scheme met with substantial opposition. Many Americans feared that the impost plan would concentrate too much financial power in the hands of Morris and his allies in Philadelphia. Congress failed to approve the impost in 1781 and again in 1783. Angry and discouraged, the nationalists largely withdrew from any active involvement in the Confederation.

The states themselves generally relied on increased taxation to pay their own debts. But poor farmers, already burdened by debt and now burdened again by new taxes on their lands, considered such policies unfair, even tyrannical. They demanded that the state governments issue paper currency to increase the money supply and make it easier for them to meet their obligations. Resentment was especially high among farmers in New England, who felt that the states were squeezing them to enrich already wealthy bondholders in Boston and other towns. Debtors who failed to pay their taxes found their mortgages foreclosed and their property seized; sometimes they found themselves in jail.

Throughout the late 1780s, therefore, mobs of distressed farmers rioted periodically in various parts of New England. They caused the most serious trouble in Massachusetts. Dissidents in the Connecticut Valley and the Berkshire Hills, many of them Revolutionary veterans, rallied behind Daniel Shays, a former captain in the Continental army. Shays issued a set of demands that included paper money, tax relief, a moratorium on debts, the removal of the state capital from Boston to the interior, and the abolition of imprisonment for debt. During the summer of 1786, the Shaysites concentrated on preventing the collection of debts, private or public, and used force to keep courts from sitting and sheriffs from selling confiscated property. In Boston, members of the legislature, including Samuel Adams, denounced Shays and his men as rebels and traitors.

When winter came, the rebels advanced on Springfield hoping to seize weapons from the arsenal there. An army of state militiamen, financed by a loan from wealthy merchants who feared a new revolution, set out from Boston to confront them. In January 1787, this army met Shays's band and dispersed his ragged troops.

As a military enterprise, Shays's Rebellion was a failure. But it had important consequences for the future of the United States. In Massachusetts, it resulted in a few immediate gains for the discontented groups. Shays and his lieutenants, at first sentenced to death, were later pardoned; and Massachusetts offered the protesters some tax relief and a postponement of debt payments. More significantly, however, the rebellion added urgency to a movement already gathering support throughout the new nation—the movement to produce a new, national constitution.

DEBATING THE PAST

The American Revolution

THE LONGSTANDING DEBATE over the origins of the American Revolution has tended to reflect two broad schools of interpretation. One sees the Revolution largely as a political and intellectual event and argues that the revolt against Britain was part of a defense of ideals and principles. The other views the Revolution as a social and economic phenomenon and contends that material interests were at the heart of the rebellion.

The Revolutionary generation itself portrayed the conflict as a struggle over ideals, and this interpretation prevailed through most of the nineteenth century. But in the early twentieth century, historians influenced by the reform currents of the progressive era began to identify social and economic forces that they believed had contributed to the rebellion. Carl Becker, for example, wrote in a 1909 study of New York that two questions had shaped the Revolution: "The first was the question of home rule; the second was the question . . . of who should rule at home." The colonists were not only fighting the British; they were also engaged in a kind of civil war, a contest for power between radicals and conservatives that led to the "democratization of American politics and society."

Other "progressive" historians elaborated on Becker's thesis. J. Franklin Jameson, writing in 1926, argued, "Many economic desires, many social aspirations, were set free by the political struggle, many aspects of society profoundly altered by the forces thus let loose." Arthur M. Schlesinger maintained in a 1917 book that colonial merchants, motivated by their own interest in escaping the restrictive policies of British mercantilism, aroused American resistance in the 1760s and 1770s.

Beginning in the 1950s, a new generation of scholars began to reem-

(continued on next page)

phasize the role of ideology and de-emphasize the role of economic interests. Robert E. Brown (in 1955) and Edmund S. Morgan (in 1956) both argued that most eighteenth-century Americans shared common political principles and that the social and economic conflicts the progressives had identified were not severe. The rhetoric of the Revolution, they suggested, was not propaganda but a real reflection of the ideas of the colonists. Bernard Bailyn, in *The Ideological Origins of the American Revolution* (1967), demonstrated the complex roots of the ideas behind the Revolution and argued that this carefully constructed political stance was not a disguise for economic interests but a genuine ideology, rooted in deeply held convictions about rights and power, that itself motivated the colonists to act. The Revolution, he claimed, "was above all else an ideological, constitutional, political struggle and not primarily a controversy between social groups undertaken to force changes in the organization of the society or the economy."

By the late 1960s, however, a group of younger historians—many of them influenced by the New Left—were challenging the ideological interpretation again by illuminating social and economic tensions within colonial society that they claimed helped shape the Revolutionary struggle. Jesse Lemisch and Dirk Hoerder pointed to the actions of mobs in colonial cities as evidence of popular resentment of both American and British elites. They noted, for example, that Revolutionary crowds were likely to attack all symbols of wealth and power, whether British or American; that they displayed a range of class-based grievances not rooted in elite ideologies. Joseph Ernst reemphasized the significance of economic pressures on colonial merchants and tradesmen. Gary Nash, in *The Urban Crucible* (1979), emphasized the role of growing economic distress in colonial cities in creating a climate in which Revolutionary sentiment could flourish. Edward Countryman and Rhys Isaac both pointed to changes in the nature of colonial society and culture, and in the relationship between classes in eighteenth-century America, as a crucial prerequisite for the growth of the Revolutionary movement. Many of these newer social interpretations of the Revolution do not argue that the rebellion was a class conflict or that economic interests inevitably *determined* a person's stance toward the struggle. They argue, rather, that the relationship between interests and ideology must be a part of any workable explanation of the conflict.

CHAPTER SIX

The Constitution
and the New Republic

Toward a New Government ～ *Adoption and Adaptation*
Federalists and Republicans ～ *Asserting National Sovereignty*
The Downfall of the Federalists

B Y THE LATE 1780s, many Americans had grown dissatisfied with the Confederation. It was factious and unstable, unable to deal effectively with economic problems, and frighteningly powerless in the face of Shays's Rebellion. A decade earlier, Americans had deliberately avoided creating a genuine national government. Now they reconsidered. In 1787, in a burst of great political creativity, the nation created a new constitution and a new government consisting of three independent branches.

The American Constitution derived most of its principles from the state documents that had preceded it. But it was also a remarkable achievement in its own right. It created a system of government that has survived for more than two centuries as one of the stablest and most successful in the world. William Gladstone, the great nineteenth-century British statesman, once called the Constitution the "most wonderful work ever struck off at a given time by the brain and purpose of man." The American people generally agreed. Indeed, to many the Constitution took on some of the characteristics of a sacred document, an unassailable "fundamental law" from which all public policies and all political principles must spring.

Yet the adoption of the Constitution did not complete the creation of the republic. For while most Americans agreed that the Constitution was a nearly perfect document, they disagreed—at times fundamentally—on what that document meant. Out of those disagreements emerged the first great political battles of the new nation.

TOWARD A NEW GOVERNMENT

So unpopular and ineffectual had the Confederation Congress become by the mid-1780s that it began to lead an almost waiflike existence. In 1783, its members timidly withdrew from Philadelphia to escape army veterans demanding their back pay. They took refuge for a while in Princeton, New Jersey, then moved on to Annapolis, and in 1785 settled in New York. Through all of this, delegates were often scarce. Only with great difficulty could Congress produce a quorum to ratify the treaty with Great Britain ending the Revolutionary War. Only eight state delegations voted on the Confederation's most important piece of legislation, the Northwest Ordinance.

Advocates of Centralization

Weak and unpopular though the Confederation was, a great many citizens—probably a majority—remained wary of a strong central government. They had, they believed, fought the Revolutionary War to abolish remote and tyrannical authority; now they wanted to keep political power centered in the states, where it could be carefully and closely controlled. But some of the wealthiest and most powerful groups in the population were beginning to clamor in the 1780s for a more genuinely national government capable of dealing more effectively with the country's problems. By 1786, such demands had grown so intense that even defenders of the existing system reluctantly agreed that the government needed strengthening at its weakest point—its lack of power to tax.

The most resourceful advocate of centralization was Alexander Hamilton, the illegitimate son of a Scottish merchant in the West Indies, who had become a successful New York lawyer and had once served as an aide to George Washington. Hamilton had been unhappy with the Articles of Confederation, and the weak central government they had created, from the start. He now called for a national convention to overhaul the entire document.

He found an important ally in James Madison of Virginia, who persuaded the Virginia legislature to convene an interstate conference on commercial questions. Only five states sent delegates to the meeting, which was held at Annapolis, Maryland, in 1786; but the conference approved a proposal drafted by Hamilton (representing New York) for a convention of special delegates from all the states to meet in Philadelphia the next year and consider ways to "render the constitution of the Federal government adequate to the exigencies of the union."

At that point, in 1786, there seemed little reason to believe the Philadelphia convention would generate much wider interest than the Annapolis meeting had attracted. Only by winning the support of George Washington, the centralizers believed, could they hope to prevail. But Washington at first showed little interest in joining the cause. Then, early in 1787, the news of Shays's Rebellion spread throughout the nation. Thomas Jefferson, then the American minister in Paris, was not alarmed. "I hold," he confided in a letter to James Madison, "that a little rebellion, now and then, is a good thing, and as necessary in the political world as storms in the physical." But Washington took the news less calmly. "There are combustibles in every State which a spark might set fire to," he exclaimed. "I feel infinitely more than I can express for the disorders which have arisen. Good God!" He promptly made plans to travel to Philadelphia for the Constitutional Convention. His support gave the meeting wide credibility.

A Divided Convention

Fifty-five men, representing all the states except Rhode Island, attended one or more sessions of the convention that sat in the Philadelphia State House from May to September 1787. These "Founding Fathers," as they later became known, were relatively young men; the average age was forty-four, and only one delegate (Benjamin Franklin, then eighty-one) was genuinely aged. They were well educated by the standards of their time. Most represented the great property interests of the country, and many feared what one of them called the "turbulence and follies" of democracy. Yet all were also products of the American Revolution and retained the Revolutionary suspicion of concentrated power.

The convention unanimously chose Washington to preside over its sessions and then closed its business to the public and the press. (If James Madison had not kept a private diary chronicling the proceedings, historians might know little about what happened in Philadelphia.) It then ruled that each state delegation would have a single vote and that major decisions would require not unanimity, as they did in Congress, but a simple majority. Almost all the delegates agreed that the United States needed a stronger central government. But there agreement ended.

Virginia, the largest state in population, sent a well-prepared delegation to Philadelphia. James Madison (thirty-six years old) was its intellectual leader. He had devised in some detail a plan for a new "national" government; the Virginians used it to control the agenda of the convention from the start.

Edmund Randolph of Virginia opened the debate by proposing a central element of the Virginia Plan: that "a national government ought to be established, consisting of a supreme Legislative, Executive, and Judiciary." It was a drastic proposal, calling for a government fundamentally different from the existing Confederation. But so committed were the delegates to fundamental reform that they approved the resolution after only brief debate. Then Randolph introduced the details of Madison's Virginia Plan. It called for a national legislature of two houses. In the lower house, states would be represented in proportion to their population; thus the largest state (Virginia) would have about ten times as many representatives as the smallest (Delaware). Members of the upper house were to be elected by the lower house under no rigid system of representation; thus some of the smaller states might at times have no members at all in the upper house.

The proposal aroused immediate opposition among delegates from Delaware, New Jersey, and other small states. Some responded by arguing that the convention had authority to do no more than revise the existing Articles of Confederation. William Paterson of New Jersey offered an alternative (the New Jersey Plan) that would have retained the essence of the existing system. It preserved the existing one-house legislature of the Confederation, in which each state had equal representation; but it gave Congress expanded powers to tax and to regulate commerce. The majority of the delegates voted to table Paterson's proposal.

Supporters of the Virginia Plan now realized they would have to make concessions to the small states if the delegations were ever to agree. They conceded an important point by agreeing that the members of the upper house would be elected by the state legislatures, thereby ensuring that every state would be represented.

But many questions remained unresolved. Among the most important was the question of slavery. Would slaves be counted as part of the population in determining representation in Congress? Or would they be considered property, not entitled to representation? Delegates from the states with large slave populations wanted to have it both ways. They argued that slaves should be considered persons in determining representation but as property if the new government were to levy taxes on the states on the basis of population. Representatives from states where slavery had disappeared or was expected soon to disappear argued that slaves should be included in calculating taxation but not representation. No one argued seriously for giving slaves the right to vote or citizenship.

Compromise

The delegates bickered for weeks. By the end of June, as both temperature and tempers rose to uncomfortable heights, the convention seemed in danger of collapsing. But the delegates refused to give up (partly because of the patient urging of Benjamin Franklin). Finally, on July 2, the convention created a "grand committee," chaired by Franklin and with one delegate from each state, to resolve the remaining disagreements. The committee produced a proposal that became the basis of the "Great Compromise." Its most important achievement was resolving the difficult problem of representation. The proposal called for a legislature in which the states would be represented in the lower house on the basis of population; each slave would be counted as three-fifths of a free person in determining the basis for both representation and direct taxation. And the proposal called for an upper house in which the states would be represented equally with two members apiece. On July 16, 1787, the convention voted to accept the compromise.

In the next few weeks, the convention agreed to another important compromise on the explosive issue of slavery. The representatives of the Southern states feared that if the national government were granted power to regulate trade, it might interfere with slavery. The convention agreed to bar the new government from stopping the slave trade for twenty years. This was a large and difficult concession from the delegates who opposed slavery, but they agreed to it because they feared that without it the Constitution would fail.

Some important issues remained unaddressed. Most important was the absence of a list of individual rights, which would restrain the powers of the national government in the way that bills of rights restrained the state governments. Madison opposed the idea, arguing that specifying rights that were reserved to the people would, in effect, limit those rights. Others, however, feared that without such protections the national government might abuse its new authority.

The Constitution of 1787

Many people contributed to the creation of the American Constitution, but the most important person in the process was James Madison. Madison had devised the Virginia Plan, from which the final document ultimately emerged, and he did most of the drafting of the Constitution itself. Madison's most important achievement, however, was in helping resolve two important philosophical questions that had served as obstacles to the creation of an effective national government: the question of sovereignty and the question of limiting power.

The creation of the federal Constitution had required the resolution of difficult questions associated with sovereignty. How could a national government exercise sovereignty concurrently with state governments? Where did ultimate sovereignty lie? The answer, Madison and his contemporaries decided, was that all power, at all levels of government, flowed ultimately from the people. Thus neither the federal government nor the state governments were truly sovereign. All of them derived their authority from below. The opening phrase of the Constitution—"We the people of the United States of America"—is an expression of the belief of most of the framers that the new government derived its power not from the states but from the public at large.

The resolution of the problem of sovereignty made possible one of the distinctive features of the Constitution—its division of powers between the national and state governments. The Constitution and the government it created were to be the "supreme law" of the land; no state would have the authority to defy it. The federal government would have the power to tax, to regulate commerce, and to control the currency. At the same time, the Constitution left certain important powers in the hands of the states.

In addition to solving the question of sovereignty, the Constitution produced a distinctive solution to the problem of concentrated authority. Nothing so frightened the leaders of the new nation as the prospect of creating a tyrannical government. Indeed, that fear had been one of the chief obstacles to the creation of a national government at all. Drawing from the ideas of the French philosopher Baron de Montesquieu, most Americans had long believed that the best way to avoid tyranny was to keep government close to the people. A republic must remain confined to a relatively small area; a large nation would breed corruption and despotism because the rulers would be so distant from most of the people that there would be no way to control them. In the new American nation, these assumptions had led to the belief that the individual states must remain sovereign and that a strong national government would be dangerous.

Madison, however, helped break the grip of these assumptions by arguing that a large republic would be less, not more, likely to produce tyranny, because it would contain so many different factions that no single group would ever be able to dominate it. This idea of many centers of power "checking each other" and preventing any single, despotic authority from emerging also helped shape the internal structure of the federal government. The Constitution's most distinctive feature was its "separation of powers" within the government, its creation of "checks and balances" among the legislative, executive, and judicial branches. The forces within the government would constantly compete with (and often frustrate) one another. Congress would have two chambers, each checking the other, since both would have to agree before any law could be passed. The president would have the power to veto acts of Congress. The federal courts would be protected from both the executive and the legislature, because judges, once appointed by the president and confirmed by the Senate, would serve for life.

The "federal" structure of the government was designed to protect the United States from the kind of despotism that Americans believed had emerged in England. But it was also designed to protect the nation from another kind of despotism: the tyranny of the people. Shays's Rebellion, most of the founders believed, had been only one example of what could happen if a nation did not defend itself against the unchecked exercise of popular will. Thus in the new government, only the members of the House of Representatives would be elected directly by the people. Senators, the president, federal judges—all would be insulated in varying degrees from the public.

On September 17, 1787, thirty-nine delegates signed the Constitution, doubtless sharing the feelings that Benjamin Franklin expressed at the end: "Thus I consent, Sir, to this Constitution, *because I expect no better, and because I am not sure that it is not the best.*"

ADOPTION AND ADAPTATION

The delegates at Philadelphia had greatly exceeded their instructions from Congress and the states. Instead of making simple revisions in the Articles of Confederation, they had produced a plan for a completely different form of government. They feared, therefore, that the Constitution would not be ratified under the rules of the Articles of Confederation, which required unanimous approval by the state legislatures. So the convention changed the rules, proposing that the new government come into being when nine of the thirteen states ratified the Constitution and recommending that state conventions, not state legislatures, be called to ratify it.

Federalists and Antifederalists

The Congress in New York, demoralized and overshadowed by the events in Philadelphia, passively accepted the convention's work and submitted it to the states for approval. All the state legislatures except Rhode Island elected delegates to ratifying conventions, most of which had begun meeting by early 1788. Even before the ratifying conventions adjourned, however, a great national debate on the new Constitution had begun—in the state legislatures, in public meetings, in newspapers, and in ordinary conversations.

Supporters of the Constitution had a number of advantages. They were better organized. They had the support of the two most eminent men in America, Franklin and Washington. And they seized an appealing label for themselves: "Federalists"—a term that opponents of centralization had once used to describe themselves—thus implying that they were less committed to a "nationalist" government than in fact they were. The Federalists had the support of the ablest political philosophers of their time: Alexander Hamilton, James Madison, and John Jay. Those three men, under the joint pseudonym "Publius," wrote a series of essays—widely published in newspapers throughout the nation—explaining the meaning and virtues of the Constitution. The essays were later issued as a book, and they are known today as *The Federalist Papers*. They are among the greatest American contributions to political theory.

The Federalists called their critics "Antifederalists," which suggested that their rivals had nothing to offer except opposition. But the Antifederalists had serious and intelligent arguments of their own. They saw themselves as the defenders of the true principles of the Revolution. The Constitution, they believed, would betray those principles by establishing a strong, potentially tyrannical, center of power in the new national government. The new government, they claimed, would increase taxes, obliterate the states, wield dictatorial powers, favor the "well born" over the common people, and abolish individual liberty. But their biggest complaint was that the Constitution lacked a bill of rights, a concern that revealed one of the most important reasons for their opposition: their basic mistrust of human nature and of the capacity of human beings to wield power. The Antifederalists argued that any government that placed authority in the hands of a few powerful people would inevitably produce despotism. Their demand for a bill of rights was a product of this belief: no government could be trusted to protect the liberties of its citizens; only by enumerating the natural rights of the people could there be any certainty that those rights would be protected.

Despite the efforts of the Antifederalists, ratification proceeded quickly (although not without difficulty in several states) during the winter of 1787–1788. The Delaware convention was the first to act. It ratified the Constitution unanimously, as did New Jersey and Georgia. New Hampshire ratified the document in June 1788—the ninth state to do so. It was now theoretically possible for the Constitution to go into effect.

A new government could not hope to succeed, however, without Virginia and New York, whose conventions remained closely divided. But by the end of June, first Virginia and then New York had consented to the Constitution by narrow margins. The New York convention yielded to expediency—even some of the most staunchly Antifederalist delegates feared that the state's commercial interests would suffer if New York were to remain outside the new union. Massachusetts, Virginia, and New York all ratified on the assumption that a bill of rights would be added in the form of amendments to the Constitution. North Carolina's convention adjourned without taking action, waiting to see what happened to the amendments. Rhode Island did not even consider ratification.

Completing the Structure

The first elections under the Constitution were held in the early months of 1789. Almost all the newly elected members of Congress had favored ratification, and many had served as delegates to the Philadelphia convention. There was never any doubt about who would be the first president. George Washington had presided at the Constitutional Convention, and many who had favored ratification did so only because they expected him to preside over the new government as well. Washington received the votes of all the presidential electors. John Adams, a leading Federalist, became vice president. After a journey from his estate at Mount Vernon, Virginia, marked by elaborate celebrations along the way, Washington was inaugurated in New York on April 30, 1789.

The first Congress served in many ways almost as a continuation of the Constitutional Convention, because its principal responsibility was filling in the various gaps in the Constitution. Its most important task was drafting a bill of rights. By early 1789, even Madison had come to agree that some sort of bill of rights would be essential to legitimize the new government in the eyes of its opponents. On September 25, 1789, Congress approved twelve amendments, ten of which were ratified by the states by the end of 1791. What we know as the Bill of Rights is these first ten amendments to the Constitution. Nine of them placed limitations on Congress by forbidding it to infringe on certain fundamental rights: freedom of religion, speech, and the press; immunity from arbitrary arrest; trial by jury; and others. The Tenth Amendment reserved to the states all powers except those specifically withheld from them or delegated to the federal government.

THE INAUGURATION OF GEORGE WASHINGTON, APRIL
30, 1789 Washington took the oath of office as
the first president of the United States under the
new Constitution at Federal Hall in New York
City, which was then the nation's capital city.

On the subject of federal courts, the Constitution said only: "The
judicial power of the United States shall be vested in one Supreme Court,
and in such inferior courts as the Congress may from time to time ordain
and establish." It was left to Congress to determine the number of Supreme
Court judges to be appointed and the kinds of lower courts to be organized.
In the Judiciary Act of 1789, Congress provided for a Supreme Court of six
members and a system of lower district courts and courts of appeal. In the
same act, Congress gave the Supreme Court the power to make the final
decision in cases involving the constitutionality of state laws.

The Constitution referred indirectly to executive departments but did
not specify which ones or how many there should be. The first Congress
created three such departments—state, treasury, and war—and also estab-

lished the offices of the attorney general and postmaster general. To the office of secretary of the treasury Washington appointed Alexander Hamilton of New York, who at age thirty-two was an acknowledged expert in public finance. For secretary of war he chose a Massachusetts Federalist, General Henry Knox. As attorney general he named Edmund Randolph of Virginia, sponsor of the plan on which the Constitution had been based. As secretary of state he chose another Virginian, Thomas Jefferson.

FEDERALISTS AND REPUBLICANS

The resolution of these initial issues, however, did not resolve the disagreements about the nature of the new government. The framers of the Constitution had dealt with many controversies not by solving them but by papering them over with a series of vague compromises; as a result, the disagreements survived to plague the new government, and the first twelve years under the Constitution produced a politics of unusual acrimony.

At the heart of the controversies of the 1790s was the same basic difference in philosophy that had been at the heart of the debate over the Constitution. On one side stood a powerful group who believed that America required a strong, national government: that the country's mission was to become a genuine nation-state, with centralized authority, a complex commercial economy, and a proud standing in world affairs. On the other side stood another group—a minority at first, but one that gained strength during the decade—whose members envisioned a more modest central government. American society should not, this group believed, aspire to be highly commercial or urban. It should remain predominantly rural and agrarian. The centralizers became known as the Federalists and gravitated to the leadership of Alexander Hamilton. Their opponents acquired the name Republicans and gathered under the leadership of James Madison and Thomas Jefferson.

Hamilton and the Federalists

For twelve years, the Federalists retained firm control of the new government. That was in part because George Washington had always envisioned a strong national government and as president did little to stop those attempting to create one. But the president, Washington believed, should stand above political controversies, and so he avoided any personal involvement in the deliberations of Congress. As a result, the dominant figure in his administration became Alexander Hamilton, who exerted more influence than anyone else on domestic and foreign policy.

Of all the national leaders of his time, Hamilton was one of the most aristocratic in personal tastes and political philosophy; he believed that a stable and effective government required an elite ruling class. Thus the new government needed the support of the wealthy and powerful; and to get that, it needed to give elites a stake in its success. Hamilton proposed, therefore, that the existing public debt be "funded": that the various certificates of indebtedness that the old Congress had issued during and after the Revolution—many of them now in the possession of wealthy speculators—be called in and exchanged for interest-bearing bonds. He also recommended that the Revolutionary state debts be "assumed," taken over by the United States, to cause state as well as federal bondholders to look to the central government for eventual payment. Hamilton did not envision paying off and thus eliminating the debt; he wanted to create a large and permanent national debt, with new bonds being issued as old ones were paid off. The result, he believed, would be that the wealthy classes, who were the most likely to lend money to the government, would have a permanent stake in seeing the government survive.

Hamilton also wanted to create a national bank. It would provide loans and currency to businesses. It would give the government a safe place for the deposit of federal funds. It would facilitate the collection of taxes and the disbursement of the government's expenditures. And it would provide a stable center to the nation's small and feeble banking system. The bank would be chartered by the federal government and would have a monopoly of the government's own banking business, but much of its capital would come from private investors.

The funding and assumption of debts would require new sources of revenue for the national government. Hamilton recommended two kinds of taxes to complement the receipts anticipated from the sales of public land. One was an excise tax on alcoholic beverages, a tax that would be most burdensome to the whiskey distillers of the back country, especially those in Pennsylvania, Virginia, and North Carolina—small farmers who converted part of their corn and rye crop into whiskey. The other was a tariff on imports, which Hamilton saw not only as a way to raise money but as a way to protect domestic industries from foreign competition. In his famous "Report on Manufactures" of 1791, he outlined a plan for stimulating the growth of industry in the United States and spoke glowingly of the advantages to society of a healthy manufacturing sector.

The Federalists, in short, offered more than a vision of a stable new government. They offered a vision of the sort of nation America should become—a nation with a wealthy, enlightened ruling class, a vigorous, independent commercial economy, and a thriving industrial sector; a country able to play a prominent role in world economic affairs.

Enacting the Federalist Program

Few members of Congress objected to Hamilton's plan for funding the national debt; but many did oppose his proposal to fund the debt at par, that is, to exchange new bonds for old certificates of indebtedness on a dollar-for-dollar basis. The old certificates had been issued to merchants and farmers in payment for war supplies during the Revolution and to officers and soldiers of the Revolutionary army in payment for their services. Many of these holders had been forced to sell their bonds during the hard times of the 1780s to speculators, who had bought them at a fraction of their face value. James Madison, now a representative from Virginia, argued for a plan by which the new bonds would be divided between the original purchasers and the speculators. But Hamilton's allies insisted that such a plan was impracticable and that the honor of the government required a literal fulfillment of its earlier promises to pay. Congress finally passed the funding bill Hamilton wanted.

Hamilton's proposal that the federal government assume the state debts encountered greater difficulty. Its opponents argued that if the federal government took over the state debts, the states with few debts would have to pay taxes to service the states with large ones. Massachusetts, for example, owed much more money than did Virginia. Only by striking a bargain with the Virginians were Hamilton and his supporters able to win passage of the assumption bill.

The deal involved the location of the national capital. The Virginians wanted to create a new capital near them in the South. Hamilton met with Thomas Jefferson and agreed to provide Northern support for placing the capital in the South in exchange for Virginia's votes for the assumption bill. The bargain called for the construction of a new capital city on the banks of the Potomac River, which divided Maryland and Virginia, on land to be selected by George Washington. The government would move its operations by the beginning of the new century.

Hamilton's bank bill produced the most heated debates. Madison, Jefferson, Randolph, and others argued that because the Constitution made no provision for a national bank (or for Congress's issuing of articles of incorporation), Congress had no authority to create one. But Congress agreed to Hamilton's bill despite these objections, and Washington, despite some apparent reservations, signed it. The Bank of the United States began operations in 1791, under a twenty-year charter.

Hamilton also had his way with the excise tax, although protests from farmers later forced revisions to reduce the burden on the smaller distillers. He failed to win passage of a tariff as highly protective as he had hoped for, but the tariff law of 1792 did raise the rates somewhat.

Once enacted, Hamilton's program won the support of manufacturers, creditors, and other influential segments of the population, as he had hoped. But others found the Hamilton program less appealing. Small farmers, who formed the majority of the population, complained that they were being taxed excessively. They and others began to argue that the Federalist program served the interests not of the people but of small, wealthy elites. Out of this feeling an organized political opposition arose.

The Republican Opposition

The Constitution made no reference to political parties, and the omission was not an oversight. Most of the framers—and George Washington in particular—believed that organized parties were dangerous and to be avoided. Disagreement was inevitable on particular issues, but most of the founders believed that such disagreements need not and should not lead to the formation of permanent factions.

Yet not many years had passed after the ratification of the Constitution before Madison and others became convinced that Hamilton and his followers had become a dangerous, self-interested faction. Not only had the Federalists enacted a program that many of these leaders opposed, more ominously, Hamilton himself had, they believed, worked to establish a national network of influence that embodied all the worst features of a party. The Federalists had used the powers of their offices to reward their supporters and win additional allies. They had encouraged the formation of local associations—largely aristocratic in nature—to strengthen their standing in local communities. They were doing many of the same things, their opponents believed, that the corrupt British governments of the early eighteenth century had done.

Because the Federalists appeared to their critics to be creating such a menacing and tyrannical structure of power, there was no alternative but to organize a vigorous opposition. The result was the emergence of an alternative political organization, whose members called themselves "Republicans." (These first Republicans are not related to the modern Republican party, which was born in the 1850s.) By the late 1790s, the Republicans were going to even greater lengths than the Federalists to create an apparatus of partisan influence. In every state they had formed committees, societies, and caucuses; Republican groups were corresponding with one another across state lines; they were banding together to influence state and local elections. And they were justifying their actions by claiming, just as Hamilton and his supporters claimed, that they and they alone represented the true interests of the nation. Neither side was willing to admit that it was acting as a party; nor would either concede the right of the other to exist. This institutionalized factionalism is known to historians as the "first party system."

From the beginning, the preeminent figures among the Republicans were Thomas Jefferson and James Madison. Jefferson, the more politically magnetic of the two, became the most prominent spokesman for the cause. He promoted a vision of an agrarian republic, in which most citizens would farm their own land. Jefferson did not scorn commercial activity; farmers would, he assumed, market their crops through national and even international trade. Nor did he oppose industrial activity; Americans should, he believed, develop a certain amount of manufacturing capacity. But Jefferson did believe that the nation should be wary of too much urbanization and industrialization.

Although both parties had supporters in all parts of the country and among all classes, there were regional and economic differences. The Federalists were most numerous in the commercial centers of the Northeast and in such Southern seaports as Charleston; the Republicans were most numerous in the rural areas of the South and the West. The difference in their philosophies was visible in, among other things, their reactions to the progress of the French Revolution. As that revolution grew increasingly radical in the 1790s, with its attacks on organized religion, the overthrow of the monarchy, and eventually the execution of the king and queen, the Federalists expressed horror. But the Republicans applauded the democratic, antiaristocratic spirit they believed the French Revolution had displayed.

When the time came for the nation's second presidential election in 1792, both Jefferson and Hamilton urged Washington to run for a second term. The president reluctantly agreed. But while Washington had the respect of both factions, he was, in reality, more in sympathy with the Federalists than with the Republicans. And during his presidency, Hamilton remained the dominant figure in government.

ASSERTING NATIONAL SOVEREIGNTY

The Federalists consolidated their position—and attracted wide public support for the new national government—by acting effectively in two areas in which the old Confederation had been largely unsuccessful: the Western frontier and diplomacy.

Securing the West

Despite the Northwest Ordinance, the old Congress had largely failed to tie the outlying Western areas of the country firmly to the national government. Farmers in western Massachusetts had rebelled; settlers in Vermont, Kentucky, and Tennessee had flirted with seceding from the Union. At first, the new government under the Constitution faced similar problems.

In 1794, farmers in western Pennsylvania raised a major challenge to federal authority when they refused to pay the new whiskey excise tax and began terrorizing the tax collectors in the region. But the federal government did not leave settlement of the so-called Whiskey Rebellion to the authorities of Pennsylvania as Congress had left Shays's Rebellion to the authorities of Massachusetts. At Hamilton's urging, Washington called out the militias of three states and assembled an army of nearly 15,000, a larger force than he had commanded against the British during most of the Revolution; and he personally accompanied the troops into Pennsylvania. At the approach of the militiamen, the rebellion quickly collapsed.

The federal government won the allegiance of the whiskey rebels through intimidation. It won the loyalties of other Western people by accepting new states as members of the Union. The last of the original thirteen colonies joined the Union once the Bill of Rights had been appended to the Constitution—North Carolina in 1789 and Rhode Island in 1790. Vermont became the fourteenth state in 1791 after New York and New Hampshire agreed to give up their claims to it. Next came Kentucky, in 1792, when Virginia gave up its claim to that region. After North Carolina ceded its Western lands to the Union, Tennessee became a state in 1796.

The new government faced a greater challenge in more distant areas of the Northwest and the Southwest. The ordinances of 1784–1787, establishing the terms of white settlement in the West, had produced a series of border conflicts with Indian tribes resisting white settlement in their lands. The new government inherited these clashes, which continued with few interruptions for nearly a decade.

These clashes revealed another issue the Constitution had done little to

WASHINGTON IN COMMAND, 1794 When Pennsylvania farmers rose up in the Whiskey Rebellion in 1794, President Washington decided at once on a strong military response. This painting, credited to Frederick Kemmelmeyer, shows Washington reviewing troops in Cumberland, Maryland, as they prepare to march against the insurgents.

resolve: the place of the Indian nations within the new federal structure. The Constitution made almost no mention of Native Americans. It gave Congress power to "regulate Commerce . . . with the Indian tribes." And it bound the new government to respect treaties negotiated by the Confederation, most of which had been with the tribes. But none of this did very much to clarify the precise legal standing of Indians or Indian nations within the United States. The tribes received no direct representation in the new government. Above all, the Constitution did not address the major issue that would govern relations between whites and Indians: land. Indian nations lived within the boundaries of the United States, yet they claimed (and the white government at times agreed) that they had some measure of sovereignty over their own land. But neither the Constitution nor common law offered any clear guide to the rights of a "nation within a nation" or to the precise nature of tribal sovereignty, which ultimately depended on control of land. Thus, the relationship between the tribes and the United States remained to be determined by a series of treaties, agreements, and judicial decisions in a process that has continued for more than two centuries.

Maintaining Neutrality

Not until 1791 did Great Britain send a minister to the United States, and then only because Madison and the Republicans were threatening to place special trade restrictions on British ships. A new crisis in Anglo-American relations emerged in 1793 when the new French government established after the revolution of 1789 went to war with Great Britain. Both the president and Congress took steps to establish American neutrality in the conflict, but that neutrality was severely tested.

Early in 1794, the Royal Navy began seizing hundreds of American ships engaged in trade in the French West Indies, outraging public opinion in the United States. Anti-British sentiment rose still higher at the report that the governor general of Canada had delivered a warlike speech to the Indians on the Northwestern frontier. Hamilton was deeply concerned. War would mean an end to imports from England, and most of the revenue for maintaining his financial system came from duties on those imports.

Hamilton and the Federalists did not trust the State Department, now in the hands of the ardently pro-French Edmund Randolph, to find a solution to the crisis. So they persuaded Washington to name a special commissioner to go to England and negotiate a solution: the staunch New York Federalist and chief justice of the Supreme Court, John Jay. Jay was instructed to secure compensation for the recent British assaults on American shipping, to demand withdrawal of British forces from their posts on the frontier of the United States, and to negotiate a commercial treaty with Britain compatible with America's 1778 treaty with France.

The long and complex treaty Jay negotiated in 1794 failed to achieve these goals. But it was not without merit. It settled the conflict with Britain, avoiding a likely war. It provided for undisputed American sovereignty over the entire Northwest. It produced a reasonably satisfactory commercial relationship with a nation whose trade was important to the United States. Nevertheless, when the terms became known in America, criticism was intense and Jay was burned in effigy in some places. Opponents of the treaty—who included almost all the Republicans and even many Federalists—went to great lengths to defeat it in the Senate, cheered on by agents of France. But in the end the Senate ratified what was by then known as Jay's Treaty.

Jay's Treaty paved the way for a settlement of important American disputes with Spain. Under Pinckney's Treaty (negotiated by Thomas Pinckney and signed in 1795), Spain recognized the right of Americans to navigate the Mississippi to its mouth and to deposit goods at New Orleans for reloading on ocean-going ships; agreed to fix the northern boundary of Florida where Americans always had insisted it should be, along the 31st parallel; and commanded its authorities to prevent the Indians in Florida from launching raids north across the border.

THE DOWNFALL OF THE FEDERALISTS

Since almost everyone in the 1790s agreed that there was no place in a stable republic for organized parties, the emergence of the Republicans as a powerful and apparently permanent opposition seemed to the Federalists a grave threat to national stability. And so when major international perils

BURNING JOHN JAY IN EFFIGY Popular opposition to the treaty John Jay negotiated with Great Britain in 1794, which many considered more favorable to the English than the Americans, was eagerly exploited by Republicans in their effort to discredit the Federalists.

confronted the government in the 1790s, the temptation to move forcefully against this "illegitimate" opposition was strong. Facing what they believed was a stark choice between respecting individual liberties and preserving stability, the Federalists chose stability. Largely as a result of that decision, the Federalists never won another presidential election after 1796.

The Election of 1796

George Washington refused to run for a third term as president in 1796, thus removing the last impediment to open expression of the partisan rivalries that had been building over the previous eight years. Jefferson was the obvious candidate of the Republicans for president that year, but the Federalists faced a more difficult choice. Hamilton had created too many enemies to be a credible candidate. Vice President John Adams, directly associated with none of the controversial Federalist achievements, received the party's nomination for president at a caucus of the Federalists in Congress.

The Federalists were still clearly the dominant party. But without Washington to mediate, they fell victim to fierce factional rivalries that almost led to their undoing. Hamilton and many other Federalists (especially in the South) were not reconciled to Adams's candidacy and supported Thomas Pinckney. Adams defeated Jefferson by only three electoral votes and assumed the presidency as head of a divided party facing a powerful opposition. Jefferson became vice president as a result of finishing second. (Not until the adoption of the Twelfth Amendment in 1804 did electors vote separately for president and vice president.)

The Quasi War with France

American relations with Great Britain and Spain improved as a result of Jay's and Pinckney's treaties. But the nation's relations with revolutionary France quickly deteriorated. French vessels captured American ships on the high seas and at times imprisoned the crews. And when the South Carolina Federalist Charles Cotesworth Pinckney, brother of Thomas Pinckney, arrived in France, the government refused to receive him as the official representative of the United States.

In an effort to stabilize relations, Adams appointed a bipartisan commission to negotiate with France. When the Americans arrived in Paris in 1797, three agents of the French foreign minister, Prince Talleyrand, demanded a loan for France and a bribe for French officials before any negotiations could begin. Pinckney, now a member of the commission, responded succinctly and angrily: "No! No! Not a sixpence!"

When Adams heard of the incident, he sent a message to Congress denouncing the French insults and urging preparations for war. Before delivering the commissioners' report over to Congress, he deleted the names of the three French agents and designated them only as Messrs. X, Y, and Z. When the report was published, the "XYZ Affair," as it quickly became known, provoked an even greater reaction than Adams had expected. There was widespread popular outrage at France's actions and strong popular support for the Federalists' response. For nearly two years, 1798 and 1799, the United States found itself engaged in an undeclared war with France.

Adams persuaded Congress to cut off all trade with France, to abrogate the treaties of 1778, and to authorize American vessels to capture French armed ships on the high seas. In 1798, Congress created the Department of the Navy and appropriated money for the construction of new warships. The navy soon won a number of duels and captured a total of eighty-five French ships, including armed merchantmen. The United States also began cooperating so closely with the British as to be virtually a cobelligerent in England's war with France. The British provided the American navy with ammunition, furnished officers to help with the training and direction of American crews, and offered signaling information so that British and American ships could communicate readily with one another.

The French, taking note of all this, tried to conciliate the United States. Adams sent another commission to Paris in 1800, and the new French government (headed now by "first consul" Napoleon Bonaparte) agreed to a treaty with the United States that canceled the old agreements of 1778 and established new commercial arrangements. As a result, the "quasi war" came to a reasonably peaceful end, and the United States at last freed itself from the entanglements and embarrassments of its "perpetual" alliance with France.

Repression and Protest

The conflict with France helped the Federalists increase their majorities in Congress in 1798. Armed with this new strength they began to consider ways to silence the Republican opposition. The result was some of the most controversial legislation in American history: the Alien and Sedition Acts.

The Alien Act placed new obstacles in the way of foreigners who wished to become American citizens, and it strengthened the president's hand in dealing with aliens. The Sedition Act allowed the government to prosecute those who engaged in "sedition" against the government. In theory, only libelous or treasonous activities were subject to prosecution; but since such activities were defined in widely varying terms, the law in effect gave the government authority to stifle virtually any opposition. The Republicans interpreted the new laws as part of a Federalist campaign to destroy them and fought back.

President Adams signed the new laws but was cautious in implementing them. He did not deport any aliens, and he prevented the government from launching a broad crusade against the Republicans. But the legislation did have a significant repressive effect. The Alien Act discouraged immigration and encouraged some foreigners already in the country to leave. And the administration used the Sedition Act to arrest and convict ten men, most of them Republican newspaper editors whose only crime had been criticism of the Federalists in government.

Republican leaders pinned their hopes for a reversal of the Alien and Sedition Acts on the state legislatures. (The right of the Supreme Court to

CONGRESSIONAL PUGILISTS, 1798 This cartoon was inspired by the celebrated fight on the floor of the House of Representatives between Matthew
Lyon, a Republican representative from Vermont, and Roger Griswold, a
Federalist from Connecticut. Griswold (at right) attacks Lyon with his
cane, and Lyon retaliates with fire tongs. Other members of Congress seem
to be enjoying the battle.

nullify congressional legislation had not yet been established.) They laid out a theory for state action in two sets of resolutions in 1798–1799, one written (anonymously) by Jefferson and adopted by the Kentucky legislature and the other drafted by Madison and approved by the Virginia legislature. The Virginia and Kentucky Resolutions, as they were known, used the ideas of John Locke and the Tenth Amendment to the Constitution to argue that the federal government had been formed by a "compact" or contract among the states and possessed only certain delegated powers. Whenever a party to the contract, a state, decided that the central government had exceeded those powers, it had the right to "nullify" the appropriate laws.

The Republicans did not win wide support for the nullification idea; only Virginia and Kentucky declared the congressional statutes void. They did, however, succeed in elevating their dispute with the Federalists to the level of a national crisis. By the late 1790s, the entire nation was as deeply and bitterly politicized as at any time in its history. State legislatures at times resembled battlegrounds. Even the United States Congress was plagued with violent disagreements. In one celebrated incident in the chamber of the House of Representatives, Matthew Lyon, a Republican from Vermont, responded to an insult from Roger Griswold, a Federalist from Massachusetts, by spitting in Griswold's eye. Griswold attacked Lyon with his cane, Lyon fought back with a pair of fire tongs, and soon the two men were wrestling on the floor.

The "Revolution" of 1800

The 1800 presidential election was shaped by these bitter controversies. The presidential candidates were the same as four years earlier: Adams for the Federalists, Jefferson for the Republicans. But the campaign of 1800 was very different from the one preceding it. Indeed, it was probably the ugliest in American history. Adams and Jefferson themselves displayed reasonable dignity, but their supporters showed no such restraint. The Federalists accused Jefferson of being a dangerous radical and his followers of being wild men who, if they should come to power, would bring on a reign of terror comparable to that of the French Revolution. The Republicans portrayed Adams as a tyrant conspiring to become king, and they accused the Federalists of plotting to subvert human liberty and impose slavery on the people. There was considerable personal invective as well.

The election was close, and the crucial contest was in New York. There, Aaron Burr mobilized an organization of Revolutionary War veterans, the

Tammany Society, to serve as a Republican political machine. And through Tammany's efforts, the party carried the city by a large majority, and with it the state. Jefferson was, apparently, elected.

But an unexpected complication soon jeopardized the Republican victory. The Constitution called for each elector to "vote by ballot for two persons." The normal practice was that an elector would cast one vote for his party's presidential candidate and another for the vice presidential candidate. To avoid a tie, the Republicans had intended that one elector would refrain from voting for Burr. But the plan went awry. When the votes were counted, Jefferson and Burr each had 73. No candidate had a majority, and—in accordance with the Constitution—the House of Representatives had to choose between the two top candidates, Jefferson and Burr. Each state delegation would cast a single vote.

The new Congress, elected in 1800 with a Republican majority, was not to convene until after the inauguration of the president, so it was the Federalist Congress that had to decide the question. Some Federalists hoped to use the situation to salvage the election for their party; others wanted to strike a bargain with Burr and elect him. But after a long deadlock, several leading Federalists, most prominent among them Alexander Hamilton, concluded that Burr (whom many suspected of having engineered the deadlock in the first place) was too unreliable to trust with the presidency. On the thirty-sixth ballot, Jefferson was elected.

After the election of 1800, the only branch of the federal government left in Federalist hands was the judiciary. The Adams administration spent its last months in office taking steps to make the party's hold on the courts secure. By the Judiciary Act of 1801, passed by the lame duck Congress, the Federalists reduced the number of Supreme Court justiceships by one but greatly increased the number of federal judgeships as a whole. Adams quickly appointed Federalists to the newly created positions. Indeed, there were charges that he stayed up until midnight on his last day in office to finish signing the new judges' commissions. These officeholders became known as the "midnight appointments."

Even so, the Republicans viewed their victory as almost complete. The nation had, they believed, been saved from tyranny. A new era could now begin, one in which the true principles of America would once again govern the land. The exuberance with which the victors viewed the future—and the importance they ascribed to the defeat of the Federalists—was evident in the phrase Jefferson himself later used to describe his election. He called it the "Revolution of 1800." It remained to be seen how revolutionary it would really be.

CHAPTER SEVEN

The Jeffersonian Era

The Rise of Cultural Nationalism ~ *Stirrings of Industrialism*
Jefferson the President ~ *Doubling the National Domain*

THOMAS JEFFERSON AND his followers assumed control of the national government in 1801 as the champions of a distinctive vision of America. They favored a society of sturdy, independent farmers, happily free from the workshops, the industrial towns, and the city mobs of Europe. They celebrated localism and republican simplicity. Above all, they proposed a federal government of sharply limited power, with most public authority remaining at the level of the states.

Almost nothing worked out as they had planned, for during their years in power the young republic was developing in ways that made much of their vision obsolete. The American economy in the period of Republican ascendancy became steadily more diversified and complex, making the ideal of a simple, agrarian society impossible to maintain. American cultural life was dominated by a vigorous and ambitious nationalism reminiscent of (and often encouraged by) the Federalists. The Republicans did manage to translate some of their political ideals into reality. Jefferson dismantled much of the bureaucracy that the Federalists had erected in the 1790s and helped keep the federal government small and relatively weak. Yet at the same time, he frequently encountered situations that required him to exercise strong national authority.

The Republicans did not always like these nationalizing and modernizing trends, and on occasion they resisted them. For the most part, however, they had the sense to recognize what could not be changed. In adjusting to the new realities, they themselves began to become agents of the very transformation of American life they had once resisted.

THE RISE OF CULTURAL NATIONALISM

In many respects, American cultural life in the early nineteenth century reflected the Republican vision of the nation's future. Opportunities for education increased, the nation's literary and artistic life began to free itself from European influences, and American religion began to adjust to the spread of Enlightenment rationalism. In other respects, however, the new culture was posing a serious challenge to Republican ideals.

Educational and Literary Nationalism

Central to the Republican vision of America was the concept of a virtuous and enlightened citizenry. An ignorant electorate could not be trusted to preserve democracy; education was essential. Republicans believed, therefore, in the creation of a nationwide system of public schools, in which all male citizens would receive free education.

Such hopes were not fulfilled. No state actually created an effective system of free schools (although several endorsed the idea). In 1789, Massachusetts reaffirmed the colonial laws by which each town was obliged to support a school, but there was little enforcement. In Virginia, the state legislature ignored Jefferson's call for universal elementary education and for advanced education for the gifted. As late as 1815, not a single state had a comprehensive public school system.

Instead, schooling became primarily the responsibility of private institutions, most of which were open only to those who could afford to pay for them. In the South and in the mid-Atlantic states, most schools were run by religious groups. In New England, private academies were often more secular, many of them modeled on those founded by the Phillips family at Andover, Massachusetts, in 1778, and at Exeter, New Hampshire, three years later. By 1815, there were thirty such private secondary schools in Massachusetts, thirty-seven in New York, and several dozen more scattered throughout the country. Many were frankly aristocratic in outlook, training their students to become members of the nation's elite. There were a few educational institutions open to the poor, but not nearly enough to accommodate everyone; and the education they offered was usually clearly inferior to that provided for more prosperous students.

Private secondary schools such as those in New England generally accepted only male students; even many public schools excluded females from the classroom. Yet the late eighteenth and early nineteenth century did see some important advances in education for women. As Americans began to place a higher value on the importance of the "republican mother" who would help train the new generation, they had to ask how mothers could raise their children to be enlightened if they themselves were uneducated. Beginning as early as the 1770s and accelerating thereafter, such concerns helped speed the creation of female academies throughout the nation (usually for the daughters of affluent families). In 1789, Massachusetts required that its public schools serve females as well as males. Other states, although not all, soon followed.

Some women aspired to more. In 1784, Judith Sargent Murray published an essay defending the right of women to education, and defending it in terms very different from those used by most men. Men and women were equal in intellect and equal in potential, Murray argued. Women, therefore, should have precisely the same educational opportunities as men. What was more, they should have opportunities to earn their own livings and to establish a role for themselves in society apart from their husbands and families. Murray's ideas attracted relatively little support at the time.

Reformers who believed in the power of education to reform and redeem "backward" people spurred a growing interest in Indian education. Because Jefferson and his followers liked to think of Native Americans as "noble savages" (uncivilized but, unlike blacks, not necessarily innately inferior), they hoped that schooling the Indians in white culture would "uplift" the tribes. Although white governments did little to promote Indian education, missionaries and mission schools proliferated among the tribes. There were no comparable efforts to educate enslaved African-Americans, largely because their owners preferred that they remain ignorant and thus presumably less likely to rebel.

Higher education similarly diverged from Republican ideals. The number of colleges and universities in America grew substantially, from nine at the time of the Revolution to twenty-two in 1800, and the number increased steadily thereafter. None of the new schools, however, was truly public. Even universities established by state legislatures (in Georgia, North Carolina, Vermont, Ohio, and South Carolina, for example) relied on private contributions and tuition fees to survive. Scarcely more than one white man in a thousand (and virtually no women, blacks, or Indians) had access to any college education; and those few who did attend universities were almost without exception members of prosperous, propertied families.

Now that they had won their political independence, many Americans—Federalists and Republicans alike—aspired to a form of cultural independence. They dreamed of an American literary and artistic life that would rival the greatest achievements of Europe. A 1772 "Poem on the

Rising Glory of America" predicted that America was destined to become the "seat of empire" and the "final stage" of civilization, with "glorious works of high invention and of wond'rous art." The Connecticut schoolmaster and lawyer Noah Webster echoed such sentiments, arguing that the American schoolboy should be educated as a nationalist. "As soon as he opens his lips," Webster wrote, "he should rehearse the history of his own country; he should lisp the praise of liberty, and of those illustrious heroes and statesmen who have wrought a revolution in her favor."

Despite serious obstacles getting works by American writers published, a growing number of native authors began working to create a strong native literature. Among the most ambitious was the Philadelphia writer Charles Brockden Brown, who tried to use his novels to give voice to distinctively American themes, to convey the "soaring passions and intellectual energy" of his country. But his fascination with horror and deviance kept him from developing a popular audience. More successful was Washington Irving of New York, whose popular folk tales, recounting the adventures of such American rustics as Ichabod Crane and Rip Van Winkle, made him the widely acknowledged leader of American literary life in the early eighteenth century.

Religion and Revivalism

The American Revolution had weakened traditional forms of religious practice by detaching established churches from government and by elevating ideas of individual liberty and reason that challenged many ecclesiastical traditions. By the 1790s, only a small proportion of white Americans (perhaps as few as 10 percent) were members of formal churches, and ministers were complaining often about the "decay of vital piety."

Religious traditionalists were particularly alarmed about the emergence of new, "rational" religious doctrines—theologies that reflected modern, scientific attitudes and sharply de-emphasized the role of God in the world. "Deism," which had originated among Enlightenment philosophers in France, attracted such educated Americans as Jefferson and Franklin and by 1800 was reaching a moderately broad popular audience. Deists accepted the existence of God, but they considered Him a remote being who, after having created the universe, had withdrawn from direct involvement with the human race and its sins. Religious skepticism also produced the philosophies of "universalism" and "unitarianism," which emerged at first as dissenting views within the New England Congregational church. Disciples of these new ideas rejected the traditional Calvinist belief in predestination, arguing that salvation was available to all. They rejected, too, the idea of the Trinity. Jesus was only a great religious teacher, they claimed, not the son of God. So wide was the gulf between these dissenters and the Congregationalist establishment that a permanent schism finally occurred. The Universalist church was founded as a separate denomination in Gloucester, Massachusetts, in 1779, and the Unitarian church was established in Boston three years later.

Many Americans believed that the spread of rationalism foretold the end of traditional, evangelistic religion in the new nation. In reality, quite the contrary was true. Most Americans continued to hold strong religious beliefs; what had declined was their commitment to organized churches and denominations. Deism, Universalism, and Unitarianism appeared more powerful than they actually were, in part because those who clung to more traditional faiths were for a time confused and disorganized, unable to react effectively. Beginning in 1801, however, traditional religion staged a dramatic comeback in the form of a wave of revivalism known as the Second Great Awakening.

The origins of the awakening lay in the efforts of conservative theologians of the 1790s to fight the spread of religious rationalism and in the efforts of church establishments to revitalize their organizations. Presbyterians expanded their efforts on the Western fringes of white settlement, and conservatives became increasingly militant in response to dissenters. Methodism, founded in England by John Wesley, spread to America in the 1770s; authoritarian and hierarchical in structure, the Methodists sent itinerant preachers throughout the nation to win recruits for the new church, which soon became the fastest-growing denomination in America. Almost as successful were the Baptists, who were themselves relatively new to America; they found an especially fervent following in the South.

By 1800, the revivalist energies of all these denominations were combining to create the greatest surge of evangelical fervor since the first Great Awakening sixty years before. In only a few years, the revivalists mobilized a large proportion of the American people; and membership in those churches embracing revivalism—most prominently the Methodist, Baptist, and Presbyterian—was mushrooming. At Cane Ridge, Kentucky, in the summer of 1801, a group of evangelical ministers presided over the nation's first "camp meeting"—an extraordinary revival that lasted several days and impressed all who saw it with its size (some estimated that 25,000 people attended) and its fervor. Such events became common in subsequent years, as the Methodists in particular came to rely on them as a way to "harvest" new members.

The message of the Second Great Awakening was not entirely uniform, but its basic thrust was clear. Individuals must readmit God and Christ into their daily lives, must embrace a fervent, active piety, and must reject the skeptical rationalism that threatened traditional beliefs. Yet the wave of revivalism did not restore the religion of the past. Few denominations any longer accepted the idea of predestination; and the belief that a person could affect his or her own chances for salvation, rather than encouraging irreligion as many had feared, added intensity to the individual's search for salvation. The Awakening, in short, combined a more active piety with a belief in a God whose grace could be attained through faith and good works.

One of the striking features of the Awakening was the preponderance of women, particularly young women, within it. Female converts far outnumbered males. One reason for this was that women were more numerous in certain regions than men, who were more likely than women to strike out on their own and move west. Their marriage prospects thus diminished and their futures plagued with uncertainty, some women discovered in religion a foundation on which to build their lives. But even in areas where there was no shortage of men, women flocked to the revivals in enormous numbers,

THE CAMP MEETING Camp meetings became a popular feature of evangelical religion in America beginning in 1800. By the 1820s, there were about 1,000 such meetings a year, most of them in the South and the West. This lithograph, which dates from the 1830s, illustrates the central role of women in the religious revivals of the time.

which suggests that they may have been responding in part to changing economic roles as well. The movement of industrial work out of the home (where women had often contributed to the family economy through spinning and weaving) and into the factory—a process making rapid strides in the early nineteenth century—robbed women of one of their most important social roles. Religious enthusiasm helped compensate for the losses and adjustments these transitions produced; it also provided access to a new range of activities associated with the churches—charitable societies ministering to orphans and the poor, missionary organizations, and others—in which women came to play important roles.

Revivalism was not restricted to white society. In some areas of the country, revivals were open to people of all races. Many blacks not only attended the events but embraced the new religious fervor. Out of these revivals emerged a group of black preachers who became important figures within the slave community. Some of them translated the apparently egalitarian religious message of the Awakening—that salvation was available to all—into a similarly egalitarian message for blacks in the present world. Out of black revival meetings in Virginia, for example, arose an elaborate plan in 1800 (devised by Gabriel Prosser, the brother of a black preacher) for a slave rebellion and attack on Richmond. The plan was discovered and the rebellion forestalled by whites, but revivalism continued in subsequent years to create occasional racial unrest in the South.

The spirit of revivalism was particularly strong in these years among Native Americans, although its origins and the forms it took were very different from those in white or black society. The dislocations and military defeats Indians suffered in the aftermath of the American Revolution created a sense of crisis among many of the Eastern tribes in particular; as a result, the 1790s and early 1800s became an era of Indian religious fervor and prophecy. Presbyterian and Baptist missionaries were active among the Southern tribes and sparked a wave of conversions. But the most important revivalism came from the efforts of a great Indian prophet: Handsome Lake, a Seneca whose seemingly miraculous "rebirth" after years of alcoholism helped give him a special stature within his tribe. Handsome Lake, like the earlier Indian prophet Neolin, who had been active in the 1760s, called for a revival of traditional Indian ways. That meant repudiating the individualism of white society and restoring the communal quality of the Indian world. Handsome Lake's message spread through the scattered Iroquois communities that had survived the military and political setbacks of previous decades and inspired many Indians to give up whiskey, gambling, and other destructive customs derived from white society. But revivalism did not produce a restoration of traditional Iroquois culture. Handsome Lake encouraged Christian missionaries to become active within the tribes, and he urged Iroquois men to abandon their roles as hunters (partly because so much of their hunting land had been seized by whites) and become sedentary farmers instead. Iroquois women, who had traditionally done the farming, were to move into more domestic roles.

STIRRINGS OF INDUSTRIALISM

It was not only culturally and religiously that the nation was developing in ways unforeseen by Jefferson and his followers. Economically, the United States was taking the first, tentative steps toward a transformation that would ultimately shatter forever the vision of a simple, agrarian republic.

Technology and Transportation in America

While Americans were engaged in a revolution to win their independence, an even more important revolution was in progress in England: the emergence of modern industrialism. Power-driven machines were taking the place of hand-operated tools and were permitting manufacturing to become more rapid and extensive—with profound social and economic consequences. Not since the agrarian revolution thousands of years earlier, when humans had turned from hunting to farming for sustenance, had there been an economic change of a magnitude comparable to the industrial revolution. Centuries of traditions, of social patterns, of cultural and religious assumptions were challenged and often shattered.

Nothing even remotely comparable to the English industrial revolution occurred in America in the first two decades of the nineteenth century. Indeed, it was opposition to the kind of economic growth occurring in England that had helped the Republicans defeat the Federalists in 1800. Yet even while Jeffersonians warned of the dangers of rapid economic change, they were witnessing a series of technological advances that would ultimately help ensure that the United States too would be transformed.

Some of these technological advances were imported from England. Despite efforts by the British government to prevent the export of textile machinery or the emigration of skilled mechanics, a number of immigrants with advanced knowledge of English technology arrived in the United States eager to introduce the new machines to America. Samuel Slater, for example, used the knowledge he had acquired before leaving England to build a spinning mill in Pawtucket, Rhode Island, for the Quaker merchant Moses

Brown in 1790. It was generally recognized as the first modern factory in America.

More important than imported technology was that of purely domestic origin. America in the early nineteenth century produced several important inventors of its own. Among the most important was the Massachusetts-born, Yale-educated Eli Whitney. In 1793, Whitney, who was working as a tutor on a Georgia plantation, invented a machine that performed the arduous task of removing the seeds from short-staple cotton quickly and efficiently. It was dubbed the cotton gin ("gin" being a derivative of "engine"). With the device a single operator could clean as much cotton in a few hours as a group of workers had once needed a whole day to do. The results were profound. Soon cotton growing spread throughout the South. (Previously it had been restricted largely to the coast and the sea islands, the only places where "long-staple" cotton—easily cleaned without the cotton gin—could be grown.) Within a decade, the total cotton crop increased eightfold. African-American slavery, which with the decline of tobacco production had seemed for a time to be a dwindling institution, expanded and firmly fixed itself upon the South. The large supply of domestically produced fiber also served as a strong incentive to entrepreneurs in New England and elsewhere to develop a native textile industry.

One of the prerequisites for industrialization is a transportation system that allows the efficient movement of raw materials to factories and of finished goods to markets. The United States had no such system in the early years of the republic, and thus it had no domestic market extensive enough to justify large-scale production. But efforts were under way that would ultimately remove the transportation obstacle.

In river transportation, a new era began with the development of the steamboat. Oliver Evans's high-pressure engine, lighter and more efficient than the earlier steam engine created by James Watt in England in the 1760s, made steam more feasible for powering boats and, eventually, locomotives and mill machinery. The perfecting of the steamboat was chiefly the work of the inventor Robert Fulton and the promoter Robert R. Livingston. Their *Clermont*, equipped with paddle wheels and an English-built engine, sailed up the Hudson in the summer of 1807. In 1811, a partner of Livingston, Nicholas J. Roosevelt (a remote ancestor of Theodore Roosevelt), introduced the steamboat to the West by sending the *New Orleans* from Pittsburgh down the Ohio and Mississippi. The next year, the vessel began a profitable career of service between New Orleans and Natchez.

SLATER'S MILL Samuel Slater served as an apprentice in England in the 1780s to Richard Arkwright, an inventor of machinery for the new cotton mills that were driving the English industrial revolution. In 1790 Slater designed the first successful cotton-spinning mill in the United States at Pawtucket, Rhode Island. This drawing shows the Pawtucket bridge, falls, and mill as they appeared sometime between 1810 and 1819.

Meanwhile, what was to become known as the turnpike era had begun. In 1792, a corporation constructed a toll road running the sixty miles from Philadelphia to Lancaster, with a hard-packed surface of crushed rock. This venture proved so successful that similar turnpikes (so named for the kind of tollgate frequently used) were laid out from other cities to neighboring towns. But similar highways would not be extended over the mountains until governments began to participate in the financing of the projects.

Despite all the changes and all the advances, America remained in the early nineteenth century an overwhelmingly rural and agrarian nation. Only 3 percent of the population lived in towns of more than 8,000 in 1800. Ten percent of the non-Indian population lived west of the Appalachian Mountains, far from what urban centers there were. Even the nation's largest cities could not begin to compare, either in size or in cultural sophistication, with such European capitals as London and Paris (although Philadelphia, with 70,000 residents, New York, with 60,000, and others were becoming centers of commerce, learning, and urban culture comparable to many of the secondary cities of Europe).

It was still possible in the early nineteenth century to believe that this small, half-formed nation might not become a complex modern society. But forces were already at work that, in time, would lastingly transform the United States. And Thomas Jefferson, for all his commitment to the agrarian ideal, found himself, as president, obliged to confront and accommodate them.

JEFFERSON THE PRESIDENT

Privately, Thomas Jefferson may well have considered his victory over John Adams in 1800 to be what he later termed it: a revolution "as real . . . as that of 1776." Publicly, however, he was restrained and conciliatory, attempting to minimize the differences between the two parties and calm the passions that the bitter campaign had aroused. There was no complete repudiation of Federalist policies, no true "revolution." Indeed, at times Jefferson seemed to outdo the Federalists at their own work—most notably in overseeing a remarkable expansion of the territory of the United States.

In some respects, however, the Jefferson presidency did indeed represent a fundamental change in the direction of the federal government. The new administration oversaw a drastic reduction in the powers of some national institutions, and it forestalled the development of new powers in areas where the Federalists would certainly have attempted to expand them.

The Federal City and the "People's President"

The relative unimportance of the federal government during the era of Jefferson was symbolized by the character of the newly founded national capital, the city of Washington. John Adams had moved to the new seat of government during the last year of his administration. And there were many at that time who envisioned that the raw, uncompleted town would soon emerge as a great and majestic city, a focus for the growing nationalism that the Federalists were promoting. The French architect Pierre L'Enfant had designed the capital on a grand scale, with broad avenues radiating from the uncompleted Capitol building. Many Americans believed Washington would become the Paris of the United States.

In reality, throughout Jefferson's presidency—indeed, throughout most of the nineteenth century—Washington remained little more than a straggling, provincial village. Although the population increased steadily from the 3,200 counted in the 1800 census, it never rivaled that of New York, Philadelphia, and the other major cities of the nation. The city remained a raw, inhospitable community, with few public buildings of any consequence. Members of Congress viewed Washington not as a home but as a place to visit briefly during sessions of the legislature and leave as quickly as possible. Few owned houses there. Most lived in a cluster of simple boardinghouses in the vicinity of the Capitol. It was not unusual for a member of Congress to resign his seat in the midst of a session to return home if he had an opportunity to accept the more prestigious post of member of his state legislature.

As president, Jefferson acted in a spirit of democratic simplicity appropriate to the frontierlike character of the unfinished federal city. He was a wealthy and aristocratic planter by background, but he conveyed to the public an image of plain, almost crude disdain for pretension. He walked like an ordinary citizen to and from his inauguration at the Capitol, instead of riding in a coach at the head of a procession. In the presidential mansion, which had not yet acquired the name White House, he disregarded the courtly etiquette of his predecessors. He did not always bother to dress up, prompting the British ambassador to complain on one occasion of being received by the president in clothes that were "indicative of utter slovenliness and indifference to appearances."

Yet Jefferson managed nevertheless to impress most of those who knew him. He was a brilliant conversationalist, a gifted writer, and one of the nation's most intelligent and creative men, with a wider range of interests and accomplishments than any public figure in American history with the possible exception of Benjamin Franklin. In addition to politics and diplomacy, he was an active architect, educator, inventor, scientific farmer, and philosopher-scientist.

Jefferson was, above all, a shrewd and practical politician. He went to great lengths to eliminate the aura of majesty surrounding the presidency that he believed his predecessors had created. But he also worked hard to exert influence as the leader of his party, giving direction to Republicans in Congress by quiet and sometimes even devious means. Although the Republicans had objected strenuously to the efforts of their Federalist predecessors to build a network of influence through patronage, Jefferson used his powers of appointment as an effective political weapon. Like Washington before him, he believed that federal offices should be filled with men loyal to the principles and policies of the administration. By the end of his second term practically all federal jobs were held by loyal Republicans.

Jefferson was a popular president during his first term and had little difficulty winning reelection against the Federalist Charles C. Pinckney. The Republican ticket carried even the New England states (except Con-

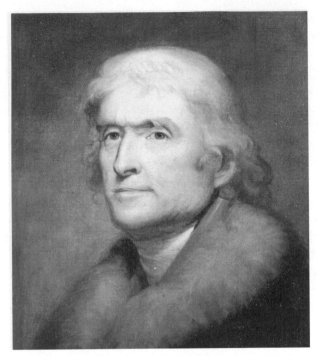

THOMAS JEFFERSON This 1805 portrait by the noted American painter Rembrandt Peale shows Jefferson at the beginning of his second term as president. It also conveys (through the simplicity of dress and the slightly unkempt hair) the image of democratic simplicity that Jefferson liked to project as the champion of the "common man."

necticut), and Jefferson won by the overwhelming electoral majority of 162 to 14. Republican membership of both houses of Congress increased.

Dollars and Ships

Under Washington and Adams, the Republicans believed, the government had been needlessly extravagant. Yearly federal expenditures had nearly tripled between 1793 and 1800. The public debt had also risen, as Hamilton had intended. And an extensive system of internal taxation, including the hated whiskey excise tax, had been erected.

The Jefferson administration moved deliberately to reverse these trends. In 1802, the president persuaded Congress to abolish all internal taxes, leaving customs duties and the sale of Western lands as the only source of revenue for the government. Meanwhile, Secretary of the Treasury Albert Gallatin drastically reduced government spending, cutting the already small staffs of the executive departments to minuscule levels. Although Jefferson was unable entirely to retire the national debt as he had hoped, he did cut it almost in half (from $83 million to $45 million).

Jefferson also scaled down the armed forces. He reduced the already tiny army of 4,000 men to 2,500. He pared down the navy from twenty-five ships in commission to seven, cutting the number of officers and sailors accordingly. Anything but the smallest of standing armies, he argued, might menace civil liberties and civilian control of government. And a large navy, he feared, might be misused to promote overseas commerce, which Jefferson believed should remain secondary to agriculture. Yet Jefferson was not a pacifist. At the same time that he was reducing the size of the army and navy, he helped establish the United States Military Academy at West Point, founded in 1802. And when trouble began brewing overseas, he began again to build up the fleet.

Such trouble appeared first in the Mediterranean, off the coast of northern Africa. For years the Barbary states of North Africa—Morocco, Algiers, Tunis, and Tripoli—had been demanding money from all nations whose ships sailed the Mediterranean as protection against piracy. Even Great Britain gave regular contributions to the pirates. During the 1780s and 1790s the United States too had agreed to treaties providing for annual tribute to the Barbary states, but Jefferson showed reluctance to continue this policy of appeasement.

In 1801, the pasha of Tripoli forced Jefferson's hand. Unhappy with American responses to his demands, he ordered the flagpole of the American consulate chopped down—a symbolic declaration of war. Jefferson responded cautiously and built up American naval forces in the area over the next several years. Finally, in 1805, he agreed to terms by which the United States ended the payment of tribute to Tripoli but paid a substantial (and humiliating) ransom for the release of American prisoners.

Conflict with the Courts

Having won control of the executive and legislative branches of government, the Republicans looked with suspicion on the judiciary, which remained largely in the hands of Federalist judges. Soon after Jefferson's first inauguration, his followers in Congress launched an attack on this last preserve of the opposition. Their first step was the repeal of the Judiciary

Act of 1801, thus eliminating the judgeships to which Adams had made his "midnight appointments."

The debate over the courts led to one of the most important judicial decisions in the history of the nation. Federalists had long maintained that the Supreme Court had the authority to nullify acts of Congress (although the Constitution said nothing specifically to support the claim), and the Court itself had actually exercised the power of judicial review in 1796 when it upheld the validity of a law passed by Congress. But the Court's authority in this area would not be secure, it was clear, until it actually declared a congressional act unconstitutional.

In 1803, in the case of *Marbury* v. *Madison*, it did so. William Marbury, one of Adams's "midnight appointments," had been named a justice of the peace in the District of Columbia. But his commission, although signed and sealed, had not been delivered to him before Adams left office. When Jefferson took office, his secretary of state, James Madison, refused to hand over the commission. Marbury asked the Supreme Court to direct Madison to perform his official duty. But the Court ruled that while Marbury had a right to his commission, the Court had no authority to order Madison to deliver it. On the surface, therefore, the decision was a victory for the administration. But of much greater importance than the relatively insignificant matter of Marbury's commission was the Court's reasoning in the decision.

The original Judiciary Act of 1789 had given the Court the power to compel executive officials to act in such matters as the delivery of commissions, and it was on that basis that Marbury had filed his suit. But the Court ruled that Congress had exceeded its authority, that the Constitution defined the powers of the judiciary, and that the legislature had no right to expand them. The relevant section of the 1789 act was, therefore, void. In seeming to deny its own authority, the Court was in fact radically enlarging it. The justices had repudiated a relatively minor power (the power to force the delivery of a commission) by asserting a vastly greater one (the power to nullify an act of Congress).

The chief justice of the United States at the time of the ruling (and until 1835) was John Marshall, one of the towering figures in the history of American law. A leading Federalist and prominent Virginia lawyer, he had served John Adams as secretary of state. (It was Marshall, ironically, who had neglected to deliver Marbury's commission in the closing hours of the administration.) In 1801, just before leaving office, Adams had appointed him chief justice; and almost immediately Marshall established himself as the dominant figure on the Court, shaping virtually all its most important rulings—including, of course, *Marbury* v. *Madison*. Through a succession of Republican presidents, he battled to give the federal government unity and strength. And in so doing, he established the judiciary as a coequal branch of government with the executive and the legislature—a position that the founders of the republic had never clearly indicated it should occupy.

DOUBLING THE NATIONAL DOMAIN

In the same year Jefferson was elected president of the United States, Napoleon Bonaparte made himself ruler of France with the title of first consul. In the year Jefferson was reelected, Napoleon named himself emperor. The two men had little in common. Yet for a time they were of great assistance to each other in international politics—until Napoleon's ambitions moved from Europe to America and created conflict and estrangement.

Jefferson and Napoleon

Having failed in a grandiose plan to seize India from the British Empire, Napoleon began to dream of restoring French power in the New World. The territory east of the Mississippi, which France had ceded to Great Britain in 1763, was now part of the United States and lost forever. But Napoleon hoped to regain the lands west of the Mississippi, which belonged to Spain. Under the secret Treaty of San Ildefonso of 1800, France regained title to Louisiana, which included almost the whole of the Mississippi Valley to the west of the river, plus New Orleans near the river's mouth. The Louisiana Territory would, Napoleon hoped, become the heart of a great French Empire in America.

Jefferson was unaware at first of Napoleon's imperial ambitions in America, and for a time he pursued a foreign policy that reflected his well-known admiration for France. But he began to reassess American relations with the French when he heard rumors of the secret transfer of Louisiana. Particularly troubling to Jefferson was French control of New Orleans, the outlet through which the produce of the fast-growing Western regions of the United States was shipped to the markets of the world. If France should actually take and hold New Orleans, Jefferson said, then "we must marry ourselves to the British fleet and nation."

Jefferson was even more alarmed when, in the fall of 1802, he learned that the Spanish intendant at New Orleans (who still governed the city, since the French had not yet taken formal possession of the region) had announced a disturbing new regulation. American ships sailing the Mississippi River had for many years been accustomed to depositing their cargoes in New Orleans for transfer to ocean-going vessels. The intendant now forbade the practice, even though Spain had guaranteed Americans that right in the Pinckney Treaty of 1795; the prohibition effectively closed the lower Mississippi to American shippers.

Westerners demanded that the federal government do something to reopen the river, and the president faced a dilemma. If he yielded to the frontier clamor and tried to change the policy by force, he would run the risk of a major war with France. If he ignored the Westerners' demands, he might lose political support. But Jefferson saw another solution. He instructed Robert Livingston, the American ambassador in Paris, to negotiate for the purchase of New Orleans. Livingston on his own authority proposed that the French sell the United States the rest of Louisiana as well.

In the meantime, Jefferson persuaded Congress to appropriate funds for an expansion of the army and the construction of a river fleet, and he hinted that American forces might soon descend on New Orleans and that the United States might form an alliance with Great Britain if the problems with France were not resolved. Perhaps in response, Napoleon suddenly decided to offer the United States the entire Louisiana Territory.

Napoleon had good reasons for the decision. His plans for an American empire had already gone seriously awry, partly because a yellow fever epidemic had wiped out much of the French army in the New World and partly because the expeditionary force he wished to send to reinforce the troops and take possession of Louisiana had been icebound in a Dutch harbor through the winter of 1802–1803. By the time the harbor thawed in the spring of 1803, Napoleon was preparing for a renewed war in Europe. He would not, he realized, have the resources to secure an American empire.

The Louisiana Purchase

Faced with Napoleon's startling proposal, Livingston and James Monroe, whom Jefferson had sent to Paris to assist in the negotiations, had to decide whether they should accept it even if they had no authorization from their government to do so. But fearful that Napoleon might withdraw the offer, they decided to proceed without further instructions from home. After some haggling over the price, Livingston and Monroe signed an agreement with Napoleon on April 30, 1803.

By the terms of the treaty, the United States was to pay a total of 80 million francs ($15 million) to the French government. The United States was also to grant certain exclusive commercial privileges to France in the port of New Orleans and was to incorporate the residents of Louisiana into the Union with the same rights and privileges as other citizens. The boundaries of the purchase were not clearly defined; the treaty simply specified that Louisiana would consist of the same territory France and Spain had claimed.

In Washington, the president was both pleased and embarrassed when he received the treaty. He was pleased with the terms of the bargain; but because he believed the Constitution should be strictly observed, he was uncertain about his authority to accept it, since the Constitution said nothing about the acquisition of new territory. But Jefferson's advisers persuaded him that his treaty-making power under the Constitution would justify the purchase of Louisiana; and Congress promptly approved the treaty and appropriated money to implement it. Finally, late in 1803, General James Wilkinson, the commissioner of the United States and the commander of a small occupation force, took formal control of the territory on behalf of the United States. In New Orleans, beneath a bright December sun, the French tricolor was lowered and the American flag raised.

Before long, the Louisiana Territory was organized on the general pattern of the Northwest Territory, with the assumption that it would be divided into states. The first of these was admitted to the Union as the state of Louisiana in 1812.

Exploring the West

Meanwhile, a series of explorations was revealing the geography of the far-flung new territory to white Americans. In 1803, even before Napoleon's offer to sell Louisiana, Jefferson helped plan an expedition that was to cross the continent to the Pacific Ocean, gather geographical facts, and investigate prospects for trade with the Indians. He named as its leader his private secretary and Virginia neighbor, the thirty-two-year-old Meriwether Lewis, a veteran of Indian wars who was skilled in the ways of the wilderness. Lewis chose as a colleague the twenty-eight-year-old William Clark, who—like George Rogers Clark, his older brother—was an experienced frontiersman and Indian fighter. In the spring of 1804, Lewis and Clark, with a company of four dozen men, started up the Missouri River from St. Louis. With the Shoshone woman Sacajawea as their interpreter, they eventually crossed the Rocky Mountains, descended the Snake and Columbia rivers, and in the late autumn of 1805 camped on the Pacific coast. In September 1806, they were back in St. Louis with elaborate records of the geography and the Indian civilizations they had observed along the way.

While Lewis and Clark were on their journey, Jefferson dispatched other explorers to other parts of the Louisiana Territory. Lieutenant Zebulon Montgomery Pike, twenty-six years old, led an expedition in the fall of 1805 from St. Louis into the upper Mississippi Valley. In the summer of 1806, he set out again, proceeding up the valley of the Arkansas River and into what later became Colorado, where he encountered, but failed in his attempt to climb, the peak that now bears his name. His account of his Western travels created an enduring (and inaccurate) impression among most Americans that the land between the Missouri and the Rockies was a desert that farmers could never cultivate and that ought to be left forever to the nomadic Indian tribes.

The Burr Conspiracy

Jefferson's triumphant reelection in 1804 suggested that most of the nation approved the new acquisition. But some New England Federalists raged against it. They realized that the more the West grew and the more new states joined the Union, the less power the Federalists and their region would retain. In Massachusetts, a group of the most extreme Federalists, known as the Essex Junto, concluded that the only recourse for New England was to secede from the Union and form a separate "Northern Confederacy." If a Northern Confederacy was to have any hope for lasting success as a separate nation, the Federalists believed, it would have to include New York and New Jersey as well as New England. But the leading Federalist in New York, Alexander Hamilton, refused to support the secessionist scheme.

Federalists in New York then turned to Hamilton's greatest political rival: Vice President Aaron Burr, a politician without prospects in his own party, because Jefferson had never forgiven him for the 1800 election deadlock. Burr accepted a Federalist proposal that he become their candidate for governor of New York in 1804, and there were rumors (unsupported by any evidence) that he had also agreed to support the Federalist plans for secession. Hamilton accused Burr of plotting treason and made numerous private remarks, widely reported in the press, about Burr's "despicable" character. When Burr lost the election, he blamed his defeat on Hamilton's malevolence and challenged him to a duel. Hamilton feared that refusing

A   M   E   R   I   C   A   N   V   O   I   C   E   S

LEWIS AND CLARK

Exploring the Louisiana Territory,
1804–1806

NOV. 7, 1805. A cloudy foggey morning. Some rain. We set out early, proceeded under the stard. [starboard] side under high ruged hills with steep assent, the shore boalt and rockey, the fog so thick we could not see across the river. Two canos of Indians met and returned with us to their village which is situated on the stard. side behind a cluster of marshey islands, on a narrow chanl. of the river through which we passed to the village of 4 houses. They gave us to eate some fish, and sold us fish, *wap pa to* roots, three dogs and 2 otter skins for which we gave fish hooks principally, of which they were verry fond. . . .

After delaying at this village one hour and a half we set out piloted by an Indian dressed in a salors dress, to the main chanel of the river. . . . A large marshey island near the middle of the river near which several canoes came allong side with skins, roots, fish &c. to sell, and had a temporey residence on this island. . . .

Great joy in camp. We are in view of the ocian (in the morning when the fog cleared off just below the last village, first on leaving this village, of Warkiacum) this great Pacific Ocean which we been so long anxious to see, and the roreing or noise made by the waves brakeing on the rockey shores (as I suppose) may be heard distinctly.

SOURCE: From *Original Journals of the Lewis and Clark Expedition.*

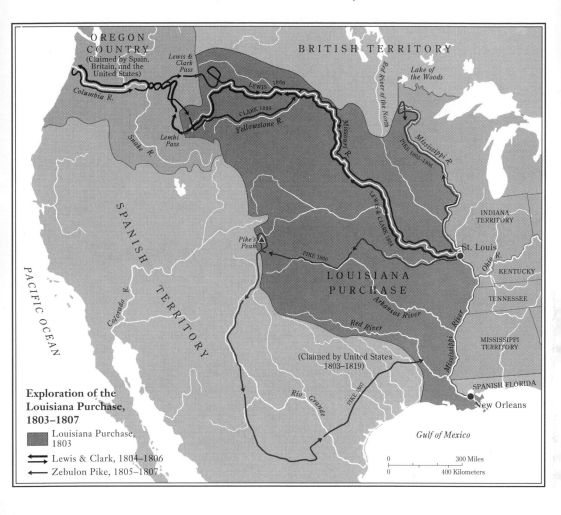

Exploration of the Louisiana Purchase, 1803–1807

- Louisiana Purchase, 1803
- Lewis & Clark, 1804–1806
- Zebulon Pike, 1805–1807

Burr's challenge would brand him a coward. And so, on a July morning in 1804, the two men met at Weehawken, New Jersey. Hamilton was mortally wounded; he died the next day.

The resourceful and charismatic Burr was now a political outcast, who had to flee New York to avoid an indictment for murder. He found new outlets for his ambitions in the West. Even before the duel, he had begun corresponding with prominent white settlers in the Southwest, especially with General James Wilkinson, now governor of the Louisiana Territory. Burr and Wilkinson, it seems clear, hoped to lead an expedition that would capture Mexico from the Spanish. But there were also rumors that they wanted to separate the Southwest from the Union and create a Western empire that Burr would rule. There is little evidence that these rumors were true.

Whether true or not, many of Burr's opponents chose to believe the rumors—including, ultimately, Jefferson himself. When Burr led a group of armed followers down the Ohio River by boat in 1806, disturbing reports flowed into Washington (the most alarming from Wilkinson, who had suddenly turned against Burr and who now informed the president that treason was afoot) that an attack on New Orleans was imminent. Jefferson ordered the arrest of Burr and his men as traitors. Burr was brought to Richmond for trial. Jefferson carefully managed the government's case from Washington. But Chief Justice Marshall, presiding over the case on circuit duty, limited the evidence the government could present and defined the charge in such a way that the jury had little choice but to acquit Burr.

The Burr conspiracy was in part the story of a single man's soaring ambitions and flamboyant personality. But it was also a symbol of the larger perils still facing the new nation. With a central government that remained deliberately weak, with vast tracts of land only nominally controlled by the United States, with ambitious political leaders willing, if necessary, to circumvent normal channels in their search for power, the legitimacy of the federal government—and indeed the existence of the United States as a stable and united nation—remained to be fully established.

CHAPTER EIGHT

War and Expansion

Causes of Conflict ~ *The War of 1812* ~ *Postwar Expansion*

WO VERY DIFFERENT conflicts took shape in the early nineteenth century that would, together, draw the United States into a difficult and frustrating war. One was the continuing tension in Europe, which in 1803 escalated once again into a full-scale conflict (the Napoleonic Wars). As fighting between the British and the French increased, each side took steps to prevent the United States from trading with (and thus assisting) the other.

The other conflict occurred in North America itself. It was a result of the ceaseless westward expansion of white settlement, which was now stretching to the Mississippi River and beyond, colliding again with a native population committed to protecting its lands from intruders. In both the North and the South, the threatened tribes mobilized to resist white encroachments. They began as well to forge connections with British forces in Canada and Spanish forces in Florida. The Indian conflict on land, therefore, became intertwined with the European conflict on the seas.

Together, the conflict on the seas and the conflict in the Western lands drew the United States into a war with Great Britain—the War of 1812, an unpopular struggle with ambiguous results. But the more important war, in the long run, was the conflict with the Indians. And in that, white America won a series of decisive victories.

CAUSES OF CONFLICT

Politicians at the time and historians since have argued over whether the conflict in the West or the conflict on the seas was the real cause of the War of 1812. In fact, the war cannot be understood without considering both.

Neutral Rights

The early nineteenth century saw a dramatic expansion of American shipping in the Atlantic. Britain retained significant naval superiority, but the British merchant marine was preoccupied with commerce in Europe and Asia and devoted little energy to trade with America. Thus the United States stepped effectively into the void and developed one of the most important merchant marines in the world, one that soon controlled a large proportion of the trade between Europe and the West Indies.

In 1805, at the Battle of Trafalgar, a British fleet virtually destroyed what was left of the French navy. Because France could no longer challenge the British at sea, Napoleon now chose to pressure England through economic rather than naval means. The result was what he called the Continental System, which was designed to close the European continent to British trade. Accordingly, he issued a series of decrees (one in Berlin in 1806 and another in Milan in 1807) barring British ships and neutral ships touching at British ports from landing their cargoes at any European port controlled by France or its allies. The British government replied to Napoleon's decrees by establishing—through a series of "orders in council"—a blockade of the European coast. The blockade required that any goods being shipped to Napoleon's Europe be carried either in British vessels or in neutral vessels stopping at British ports—precisely what Napoleon's policies forbade.

American ships were caught between Napoleon's Berlin and Milan decrees and Britain's orders in council. If they sailed directly for the European continent, they risked being captured by the British navy. If they sailed by way of a British port, they ran the risk of seizure by the French. Both of the warring powers were violating America's rights as a neutral nation. But most Americans considered the British, with their greater sea power, the worse offender. British ships pounced on Yankee merchantmen all over the ocean; the French could do so only in European ports. In particular, British vessels stopped American ships on the high seas and seized sailors off the decks, making them victims of "impressment."

Impressment

The British navy—with its floggings, its low pay, and its terrible shipboard conditions—was a "floating hell" to its sailors. Few volunteered. Most had had to be "impressed" (forced) into the service. At every opportunity they deserted. By 1807, many of these deserters had joined the American merchant marine or the American navy. To check this loss of vital manpower, the British claimed the right to stop and search American merchantmen (although not naval vessels) and reimpress deserters. They did not claim the right to take native-born Americans, but they did insist on the right to seize naturalized Americans born on British soil. In practice, the British navy often made no careful distinctions, impressing British deserters and native-born Americans alike into their service. Thousands of American sailors were thus kidnapped.

In the summer of 1807, the British went to more provocative extremes in an incident involving a vessel of the American navy. Sailing from Norfolk, with several alleged deserters from the British navy among the crew, the American naval frigate *Chesapeake* was hailed by the British ship *Leopard*. When the American commander, James Barron, refused to allow the British to search the *Chesapeake*, the *Leopard* opened fire. Barron was compelled to surrender, and a boarding party from the *Leopard* dragged four men off the American frigate.

When news of the *Chesapeake-Leopard* incident reached the American public, there was great popular clamor for revenge. If Congress had been in session, it might have declared war. But Jefferson and Madison tried to maintain the peace. Jefferson expelled all British warships from American waters to lessen the likelihood of future incidents. Then he sent instructions to his minister in England, James Monroe, to demand from the British government the complete renunciation of impressment. The British government disavowed the action of the officer responsible for the *Chesapeake-Leopard* affair and recalled him; it offered compensation for those killed and wounded in the incident; and it promised to return three of the captured sailors (one of the original four had been hanged). But the British cabinet refused to renounce impressment and instead reasserted its right to recover deserting seamen. The impressment issue therefore prevented any permanent settlement of Anglo-American differences.

"Peaceable Coercion"

In an effort to prevent future incidents that might bring the nation again to the brink of war, Jefferson presented a drastic measure to Congress when it reconvened late in 1807. The Republican legislators promptly enacted it into law. It was known as the Embargo, and it became one of the most controversial political issues of its time. The Embargo prohibited American ships from leaving the United States for any foreign port anywhere in the world. (If it had specified only British and French ports, Jefferson reasoned, it could have been evaded by means of false clearance papers.) Congress also passed a "force act" to give the government power to enforce the Embargo.

The law was widely evaded, but it was effective enough to create a serious depression through most of the nation. Hardest hit were the merchants and shipowners of the Northeast, most of them Federalists. Their once lucrative shipping business was at a virtual standstill, and they were losing money every day. They became convinced that Jefferson had acted unconstitutionally.

The election of 1808 came in the midst of the Embargo-induced depression. James Madison, Jefferson's secretary of state and political ally, was elected president; but the Federalist candidate, Charles Pinckney again, ran much more strongly than he had in 1804. The Federalists gained seats in Congress, although the Republicans still controlled both houses. The Embargo was clearly a growing political liability, and Jefferson decided to back down. A few days before leaving office, he approved a bill ending his experiment with what he called "peaceable coercion."

To replace the Embargo, Congress passed the Non-Intercourse Act just before Madison took office. It reopened trade with all nations but Great Britain and France. A year later, in 1810, the Non-Intercourse Act expired and was replaced by Macon's Bill No. 2, which reopened free commercial relations with Britain and France but authorized the president to prohibit commerce with either belligerent if it should continue violating neutral shipping after the other had stopped. Napoleon, in an effort to induce the United States to reimpose the Embargo against Britain, announced that France would no longer interfere with American shipping. Madison announced that an embargo against Great Britain alone would automatically go into effect early in 1811 unless Britain renounced its restrictions on American shipping.

In time, this new, limited embargo, although less well enforced than the earlier one, hurt the economy of England enough that the government repealed its blockade of Europe. But the repeal was too late to prevent war. In any case, naval policies were only part of the reason for tensions between Britain and the United States.

The "Indian Problem" and the British

Given the ruthlessness with which white settlers in North America had dislodged Indian tribes to make room for expanding settlement, it was hardly surprising that ever since the Revolution most Indians had continued to look to England—which had historically attempted to limit Western expansion—for protection. The British in Canada, for their part, had relied on the Indians as partners in the lucrative fur trade and as potential military allies. Even so, there had been relative peace in the Northwest for over a decade after Jay's Treaty and Anthony Wayne's victory over the tribes at Fallen Timbers in 1794. But the 1807 war crisis following the *Chesapeake-Leopard* incident revived the conflict between Indians and white settlers. Two important (and very different) leaders emerged to lead it: William Henry Harrison and Tecumseh.

The Virginia-born Harrison, already a veteran Indian fighter at age twenty-six, went to Washington as the congressional delegate from the Northwest Territory in 1799. He was a committed advocate of growth and development in the Western lands, and he was largely responsible for the passage in 1800 of the so-called Harrison Land Law, which enabled white settlers to acquire farms from the public domain on much easier terms than before.

In 1801, Jefferson appointed Harrison governor of Indiana Territory to administer the president's proposed solution to the "Indian problem." Jefferson offered the Indians a choice: they could convert themselves into settled farmers and become a part of white society, or they could migrate to the west of the Mississippi. In either case, they would have to give up their claims to their tribal lands in the Northwest.

Jefferson considered the assimilation policy a benign alternative to the continuing conflict between Indians and white settlers, a conflict he assumed the tribes were destined to lose. But to the tribes, the new policy seemed far from benign, especially given the bludgeonlike efficiency with which Harrison set out to implement it. He played off one tribe against another and used threats, bribes, trickery, and whatever other tactics he felt would help him conclude treaties. By 1807, the United States had extracted treaty rights from reluctant tribal leaders to eastern Michigan, southern Indiana, and most of Illinois. Meanwhile, in the Southwest, white Americans were taking millions of acres from other tribes in Georgia, Tennessee, and Mississippi. The Indians wanted desperately to resist, but the separate tribes were helpless by themselves against the power of the United States. They might have accepted their fate passively but for the emergence of two new factors.

One factor was the policy of the British authorities in Canada. After the *Chesapeake* incident and the surge of anti-British feeling throughout the United States, the British colonial authorities began to expect an American invasion of Canada and took desperate measures for their own defense. Among those measures were efforts to renew friendship with the Indians and provide them with increased supplies.

Tecumseh and the Prophet

The second, and more important, factor intensifying the border conflict was the rise of two remarkable native leaders. One was Tenskwatawa, a charismatic religious leader and orator known as the Prophet. He had experienced a mystical awakening in the process of recovering from alcoholism. Having freed himself from what he considered the evil effects of white culture, he began to speak to his people of the superior virtues of Indian civilization and the sinfulness and corruption of the white world. In the process, he inspired a religious revival that spread through numerous tribes and helped unite them. The Prophet's headquarters at the confluence of Tippecanoe Creek and the Wabash River (known as Prophetstown) became a sacred place for people of many tribes and attracted thousands of Indians from throughout the Midwest. Out of their common religious experiences, they began to consider joint political and military efforts as well.

The Prophet's brother Tecumseh—"the Shooting Star," chief of the Shawnees—emerged as the leader of these more secular efforts. Tecumseh understood, as few other Indian leaders had, that only through united action could the tribes hope to resist the steady advance of white civilization. Beginning in 1809, after tribes in Indiana had ceded vast lands to the United States, he set out to unite all the tribes of the Mississippi Valley, north and south. Together, he promised, they would halt white expansion, recover the whole Northwest, and make the Ohio River the boundary between the United States and Indian country. He maintained that Harrison and others, by negotiating treaties with individual tribes, had obtained no real title to land. The land belonged to all the tribes; none of them could rightfully cede any of it without the consent of the others. In 1811, Tecumseh left Prophetstown and traveled down the Mississippi to visit the tribes of the South and persuade them to join the alliance. During his absence, Governor Harrison saw a chance to destroy the growing influence of the two Indian leaders. With 1,000 soldiers he camped near Prophetstown, and on November 7, 1811, he provoked an armed conflict. Although the white forces suffered losses as heavy as those of the natives, Harrison drove off the Indians and burned the town. The Battle of Tippecanoe (named for the creek near which it was fought) disillusioned many of the Prophet's followers, who had believed that his magic would protect them; and Tecumseh returned to find the confederacy in disarray. But there were still warriors eager for combat, and by spring of 1812 they were active along the frontier, from Michigan to Mississippi, raiding white settlements and terrifying settlers.

The bloodshed along the Western borders was largely a result of the Indians' own initiative, but Britain's agents in Canada had encouraged and helped to supply the uprising. To Harrison and most white residents of the regions, there seemed only one way to make the West safe for Americans. That was to drive the British out of Canada and annex that province to the United States—a goal that many Westerners had long cherished for other reasons as well.

The Lure of Florida

While white "frontiersmen" in the North demanded the conquest of Canada, those in the South looked to the acquisition of Spanish Florida (a territory that included the present state of Florida and the southern areas of what is now Alabama, Mississippi, and Louisiana). The territory was a continuing threat to whites in the Southern United States. Slaves escaped across the Florida border; Indians in Florida launched frequent raids north into white settlements along the border. But white Southerners also coveted Florida because through it ran rivers that could provide residents of the Southwest access to valuable ports on the Gulf of Mexico.

In 1810, American settlers in West Florida (the area presently part of Mississippi and Louisiana) seized the Spanish fort at Baton Rouge and asked the federal government to annex the territory to the United States. President Madison happily agreed and then began scheming to get the rest of Florida too. The desire for Florida became yet another motivation for war with Britain. Spain was Britain's ally, and a war with England might provide an excuse for taking Spanish as well as British territory.

By 1812, therefore, war fever was raging on both the Northern and Southern borders of the United States. The white residents of these outlying regions made up a relatively small proportion of the national population and were represented in Congress by only a few, nonvoting territorial delegates. But their demands found substantial support in Washington among a group of determined young congressmen who soon earned the name of "War Hawks."

In the congressional elections of 1810, voters elected a large number of representatives of both parties eager for war with Britain. They represented a new generation, aggressive and impatient. The most influential of them came from the new states in the West or from the back country of the old states in the South. Two of their leaders, both recently elected to the House of Representatives, were Henry Clay of Kentucky and John C. Calhoun of

South Carolina, men of great intellect, magnetism, and ambition who would play a large role in national politics for nearly forty years. Both were supporters of war with Great Britain.

Clay was elected Speaker of the House in 1811, and he filled committees with those who shared his eagerness for war. He appointed Calhoun to the crucial Committee on Foreign Affairs. Both men began agitating for the conquest of Canada. Madison still preferred peace but was losing control of Congress. On June 18, 1812, he approved a declaration of war against Britain.

THE WAR OF 1812

Preoccupied with their struggle against Napoleon in Europe, the British were not eager for an open conflict with the United States. Even after the Americans declared war, Britain largely ignored them for a time. But in the fall of 1812, Napoleon launched a catastrophic campaign against Russia that left his army in disarray and his power in Europe diminished. By late 1813, with the French empire on its way to final defeat, Britain was able to turn its military attention to America.

The Course of Battle

Americans entered the War of 1812 with great enthusiasm, but events on the battlefield soon cooled their ardor. In the summer of 1812, American forces invaded Canada by way of Detroit, as part of a planned three-pronged attack. They were soon forced to retreat back to Detroit and in August surrendered the fort there. Other invasion efforts also failed. In the meantime, Fort Dearborn (Chicago) fell before an Indian attack.

Things went only slightly better for the United States on the seas. At first, American frigates won some spectacular victories over British warships, and American privateers destroyed or captured many British merchant ships, occasionally braving the coastal waters of the British Isles and burning vessels within sight of the shore. But by 1813, the British navy was counterattacking effectively, driving the American frigates to cover and imposing a blockade on the United States.

The United States did, however, achieve significant early military successes on the Great Lakes. First, the Americans took command of Lake Ontario; this permitted them to raid and burn York (now Toronto), the capital of Canada, before returning to their own lands across the lake.

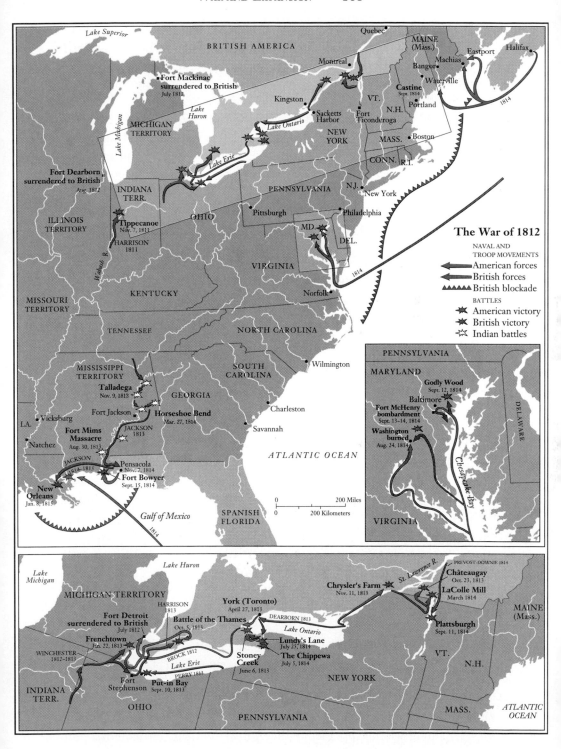

The War of 1812

NAVAL AND
TROOP MOVEMENTS

American forces
British forces
British blockade

BATTLES
★ American victory
★ British victory
☆ Indian battles

American forces then seized control of Lake Erie, mainly through the work of the youthful Oliver Hazard Perry, who engaged and dispersed a British fleet at Put-in Bay on September 10, 1813. This made possible, at last, an invasion of Canada by way of Detroit, which Americans could now reach easily by water. William Henry Harrison, the American commander in the West, pushed up the river Thames into upper Canada and on October 5, 1813, won a victory notable for the death of Tecumseh, who was serving as a brigadier general in the British army. The Battle of the Thames resulted in no lasting occupation of Canada, but it weakened and disheartened the Indians of the Northwest and greatly diminished their ability to defend their claims to the region.

In the meantime, another white military leader was striking an even harder blow at the Indians of the Southwest. The Creeks, aroused by Tecumseh on a Southern visit and supplied by the Spaniards in Florida, had been attacking white settlers near the Florida border. Andrew Jackson, a wealthy Tennessee planter and a general in the state militia, temporarily abandoned plans for an invasion of Florida and set off in pursuit of the Creeks. On March 27, 1814, in the Battle of Horseshoe Bend, Jackson's men took terrible revenge on the Indians—slaughtering women and children along with warriors—and broke the resistance of the Creeks. The tribe agreed to cede most of its lands to the United States and retreated westward, farther into the interior. The battle also won Jackson a commission as major general in the United States Army, and in that capacity he led his men farther south into Florida. On November 7, 1814, he seized the Spanish fort at Pensacola.

But the victories over the tribes were not enough to win the war. After the surrender of Napoleon in 1814, England began to transfer part of its European army to America and prepared to invade the United States from three approaches—Chesapeake Bay, Lake Champlain, and the mouth of the Mississippi. A British armada sailed up the Patuxent River from Chesapeake Bay and landed an army that marched to nearby Bladensburg, on the outskirts of Washington, where it dispersed a more numerous but poorly trained force of American militiamen. On August 24, 1814, the British troops entered Washington and put the government to flight. Then they set fire to several public buildings, including the White House, in retaliation for the earlier American burning of the Canadian capital at York. This was the low point of American fortunes in the war.

Leaving Washington in partial ruins, the invading army proceeded up the bay toward Baltimore. But Baltimore, guarded by Fort McHenry, was prepared. To block the approaching fleet, the American garrison had sunk several ships in the Patapsco River (the entry to Baltimore's harbor), thus forcing the British to bombard the fort from a distance. Through the night of September 13, Francis Scott Key (a Washington lawyer on board one of the British ships, where he was trying to secure the release of an American prisoner) watched the bombardment. The next morning, "by the dawn's early light," he could see the flag on the fort still flying; he recorded his pride in the moment by scribbling a poem—"The Star-Spangled Banner"—on the back of an envelope. The British withdrew from Baltimore. Key's words were soon set to the tune of an old English drinking song. (In 1931, "The Star-Spangled Banner" became the official national anthem.)

Meanwhile, American forces repelled another British invasion in northern New York; at the Battle of Plattsburgh, on September 11, 1814, they

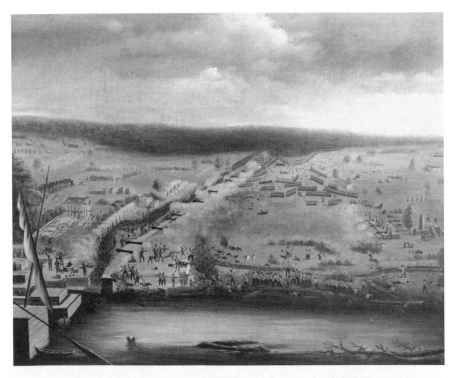

THE BATTLE OF NEW ORLEANS The Battle of New Orleans was the last major engagement and the greatest American victory on land of the War of 1812. General Andrew Jackson commanded about 4,500 troops and fended off superior British forces under the command of Sir Edward Pakenham (who was killed in the fighting). The artist Hyacinthe de Laclotte drew the sketch that became the basis of this painting while standing above the battlefield.

turned back a much more numerous British naval and land force and secured the Northern border of the United States. In the South, a formidable array of battle-hardened British veterans, fresh from the campaign against the French in Spain, landed below New Orleans and prepared to advance north up the Mississippi. Awaiting the British was Andrew Jackson with a motley collection of Tennesseans, Kentuckians, Creoles, blacks, pirates, and regular army troops drawn up behind earthen breastworks. On January 8, 1815, the redcoats advanced on the American fortifications, but the exposed British forces were no match for Jackson's well-protected men. After the Americans had repulsed several waves of attackers, the British finally retreated, leaving behind 700 dead (including their commander, Sir Edward Pakenham), 1,400 wounded, and 500 prisoners. Jackson's losses: 8 killed, 13 wounded. Only later did news reach North America that the United States and Britain had signed a peace treaty several weeks before the Battle of New Orleans. Even so, Americans long remembered the battle as a glorious victory, a sign of the rising power of the United States among the nations of the world.

The Revolt of New England

With a few notable exceptions, such as the battles of Put-in Bay and New Orleans, the military operations of the United States between 1812 and 1815 consisted of a series of humiliating failures. As a result, the American government faced increasing popular opposition as the contest dragged on. In New England, opposition both to the war and to the Republican government that was waging it was so extreme that some Federalists celebrated British victories. In Congress, in the meantime, the Republicans had continual trouble with the Federalist opposition, led by a young congressman from New Hampshire, Daniel Webster, who missed no opportunity to embarrass the administration.

By now the Federalists were very much in the minority in the country as a whole, but they were still the majority party in New England. Some of them began to dream of creating a separate nation in that region, which they could dominate and in which they could escape what they saw as the tyranny of slaveholders and backwoodsmen. Talk of secession revived and reached a climax in the winter of 1814–1815, when the republic appeared to be on the verge of ruin.

On December 15, 1814, delegates from the New England states met in Hartford, Connecticut, to discuss the grievances of their region against the Madison administration. The would-be seceders at the Hartford Convention were outnumbered by a comparatively moderate majority. But while the convention's report only hinted at secession, it reasserted the right of nullification and proposed seven amendments to the Constitution (presumably as the condition of New England's remaining in the Union)—amendments designed to protect New England from the growing influence of the South and the West.

Because the war was going badly and the government was becoming desperate, the New Englanders assumed that the Republicans would have to agree to their demands. Soon after the convention adjourned, however, the news of Jackson's smashing victory at New Orleans reached the cities of the Northeast. A day or two later, reports arrived from abroad of a treaty of peace. In the euphoria of this apparent triumph, the Hartford Convention and the Federalist party came to seem futile, irrelevant, even treasonable.

The Peace Settlement

Peace talks between the United States and Britain had begun even before the first battles of the War of 1812 were fought, but serious negotiations did not begin until August 1814, when American and British diplomats met in Ghent, Belgium. John Quincy Adams, Henry Clay, and Albert Gallatin led the American delegation.

Although both sides began with extravagant demands, the final treaty did very little except end the fighting itself. The Americans gave up their demand for a British renunciation of impressment and for the cession of Canada to the United States. The British abandoned their call for creation of an Indian buffer state in the Northwest and made other, minor territorial concessions. Other disputes were referred to arbitration. Hastily drawn up, the treaty was signed on Christmas Eve 1814.

Both sides had reason to accept this skimpy agreement. The British, exhausted and in debt from their prolonged conflict with Napoleon, were eager to settle the lesser dispute in North America. The Americans realized that with the defeat of Napoleon in Europe, the British would no longer have much incentive to interfere with American commerce. Indeed, by the end of 1815, impressment had all but ceased.

Other settlements followed the Treaty of Ghent and contributed to a long-term improvement in Anglo-American relations. A commercial treaty in 1815 gave Americans the right to trade freely with England and much of the British Empire. The Rush-Bagot agreement of 1817 provided for mutual disarmament on the Great Lakes; eventually (although not until 1872) the Canadian-American boundary became the longest "unguarded frontier" in the world.

For the other parties to the War of 1812, the Indian tribes east of the Mississippi, the Treaty of Ghent was of no lasting value. It required that the United States restore to the tribes lands seized by white Americans in the fighting, but those provisions were never enforced. Ultimately, the war was another disastrous blow to the capacity of Indians to resist white expansion. Tecumseh, their most important leader, was dead. The British, their most important allies, were gone from the Northwest. The inter-tribal alliance that Tecumseh and the Prophet had forged was in disarray. The end of the war served as a spur to white movement westward, and the Indians had lost much of their capacity to oppose the expansion.

No sooner did the war with England end in 1815 than Congress declared war again, this time against Algiers, which had taken advantage of the War of 1812 to resume sending its pirates out against American shipping in the Mediterranean. An American naval squadron under the command of Stephen Decatur sailed to the Mediterranean, captured a number of enemy ships, blockaded the coast of Algiers, and forced the dey (the Algerian ruler) to accept a treaty that not only ended the payment of tribute by the United States but required that Algiers pay reparations to America. Decatur then sailed on to Tunis and Tripoli and extracted similar concessions from them. This naval action in the Mediterranean did more to provide Americans with free access to the seas than the War of 1812 itself had done.

POSTWAR EXPANSION

In the aftermath of the war, American commerce revived and expanded, industry advanced rapidly, and westward expansion accelerated dramatically. It was a time of rapid economic growth—too rapid, as it turned out, for the boom was followed in 1819 by a disastrous bust. The collapse only temporarily slowed economic expansion, but it revealed clearly that the United States continued to lack some of the basic institutions necessary to sustain long-term growth.

Economic Growth and the Government

The aftermath of the war saw the emergence of political issues connected with national economic development: reestablishing the Bank of the United States (the first Bank's charter had not been renewed when it expired in 1811), protecting new industries, and building roads and waterways.

The wartime experience seemed to underline the need for another national bank. After the first Bank's charter expired, a large number of state banks sprang up and issued vast quantities of bank notes, often without a large enough reserve of gold or silver to support them. Soon there were many different kinds of notes, of widely varying value, in circulation at the same time, creating a confusion that made honest business difficult and counterfeiting easy.

Congress struck at the currency problem by chartering a second Bank of the United States in 1816. It was essentially the same institution as the one founded under Hamilton's leadership in 1791 except that it had more capital than its predecessor. The national bank could not prohibit state banks from issuing notes, but its size and power gave it the ability to dominate the state banks. It could compel them to issue only sound notes or risk being forced out of business.

American manufacturing had flourished during the war; with imports effectively blocked, native industry grew. Demand was so high that even with comparatively unskilled labor and poor management, new factories

THE UNITED STATES CAPITOL IN 1824 This slightly idealized view by the American artist Charles Burton shows the approach to the west front of the United States Capitol along Pennsylvania Avenue. The large, col-umned rotunda that today rises above the building was built in the 1860s to replace the simpler dome shown in this painting.

could make quick profits. The American textile industry had experienced particularly dramatic growth, spurred first by the Embargo of 1807 and then by the war. Between 1807 and 1815, the total number of cotton spindles increased more than fifteenfold, from 8,000 to 130,000. Until 1814, the textile factories—most of them in New England—produced only yarn and thread; the weaving of cloth was left to families operating handlooms at home. Then the Boston merchant Francis Cabot Lowell developed a power loom that was better than its English counterpart. In 1813, in Waltham, Massachusetts, Lowell founded the first mill in America to house spinning and weaving under a single roof. Lowell's company was an important step in revolutionizing American manufacturing.

As the War of 1812 came to an end, however, the prospects for American industry suddenly dimmed. British ships swarmed into American ports and unloaded cargoes of manufactured goods to be sold at prices much lower than those of domestic goods. The "infant industries" cried out for protection, arguing that they needed time to grow strong enough to withstand foreign competition. In 1816, protectionists in Congress won passage of a tariff law that effectively limited competition from abroad on cotton cloth and other items. There were objections from agricultural interests, who stood to pay higher prices for manufactured goods. But the nationalist dream of creating an important American industrial economy prevailed.

The nation's most pressing economic need in the aftermath of the war, however, was improvements in its transportation system that would provide manufacturers with access to raw materials and markets. An old debate resumed: Should the federal government help finance roads and other "internal improvements"? The idea of using government funds to finance road building was not a new one. When Ohio entered the Union in 1803, the federal government had allotted part of the proceeds from the sale of public lands there to building roads. In 1807, Congress enacted a law, proposed by the Jefferson administration, providing for construction of a national road, from the Potomac to the Ohio, financed partly by the Ohio land sales. The next year, it appropriated $20 million for another, more ambitious program of internal improvements. By 1818, the national road was completed to Wheeling, Virginia, on the Ohio River; and the Lancaster pike, funded in part by the state of Pennsylvania, extended west to Pittsburgh. The roads were heavily traveled and helped lower shipping rates across the mountains.

At the same time, on the rivers and the Great Lakes, steam-powered shipping was experiencing rapid expansion. By 1816, river steamers were beginning for the first time to journey up and down the Ohio River as far as Pittsburgh. Steamboats were soon carrying more cargo on the Mississippi than all the earlier forms of river transport combined. They stimulated the agricultural economy of the West and the South by providing access to markets at greatly reduced cost, and they enabled Eastern manufacturers to send their finished goods west much more readily.

But despite the progress with steamboats and turnpikes, there remained serious gaps in the nation's transportation network. In 1815, President Madison informed Congress of the "great importance of establishing throughout our country the roads and canals which can be best executed under the national authority." But when, shortly before Madison left office, Representative Calhoun steered to passage a bill that would have used the funds owed the government by the Bank of the United States to finance internal improvements, the president vetoed it. He supported the purpose of the bill, he explained, but he believed that Congress lacked authority to fund the improvements without a constitutional amendment. And so on the issue of internal improvements, at least, the nationalists fell short of their goals. For a time, the tremendous task of building the transportation network necessary for the growing American economy was left largely to state governments and private enterprise.

Westward Migration

One reason for the growing interest in internal improvements was the sudden and dramatic surge in westward expansion in the years following the War of 1812. By the time of the census of 1820, almost one of every four white Americans lived west of the Appalachians, compared with only one in seven a decade before.

The pressures driving Americans out of the East came in part from the continued growth of the population—both through natural increase and immigration. Between 1800 and 1820, the nation's population nearly doubled—from 5.3 million to 9.6 million. The growth of the nation's cities absorbed some of that increase; but most Americans were still farmers, and the agricultural lands of the East were by now largely occupied. In the South, the spread of the plantation system and its slave labor force limited opportunities for new white settlers.

Meanwhile, the West itself was becoming increasingly attractive to white settlers. The War of 1812 helped diminish one of the traditional inhibitions to Western expansion: fear of Indian opposition. In the aftermath

THE NATIONAL ROAD, 1827 This picture of heavy traffic along the National Turnpike suggests the rapid acceleration of commerce in the Eastern United States in the 1820s and the pressure that economic growth was placing on existing means of transportation. The painting also shows the Fair View Inn, which stood three miles from Baltimore, Maryland.

of the war, the federal government continued its policy of pushing the remaining tribes farther and farther west. A series of treaties in 1815 wrested still more land from the Indians.

The fertile lands now secure for white settlement drew migrants from throughout the East to what was then known as the Old Northwest (now part of the Midwest). Settlers traveled west by river and over land, established land claims, built lean-tos or cabins, and then hewed clearings out of the forests. Most grew corn to supplement the wild game they caught and the domestic animals they had brought with them. It was a rough existence, often plagued by loneliness, poverty, dirt, and disease. Men, women, and children worked side by side in the fields. Some had virtually no contact for weeks or months at a time with anyone outside their own families.

Life in the Northwest was not, however, always as solitary and individualistic as later myth suggested. Migrants often journeyed westward in groups, which at times became the basis of new communities where schools, churches, stores, and other shared institutions were built. The labor shortage in the interior meant that neighbors developed systems of mutual aid, gathering periodically to raise a barn, clear land, harvest crops, or make quilts. Gradually, white settlers built a thriving farm economy based largely on family units of modest size and committed to growing grain and raising livestock.

In the Southwest, the new agricultural economy emerged along different lines—just as the economy of the Old South had long been different from that of the Northeast. The principal attraction of the region was cotton, the market for which continued to grow. In the Southwest, around the end of the Appalachian range, stretched a broad zone within which cotton could thrive—including what was to become known as the Black Belt of central Alabama and Mississippi, a vast prairie with dark, productive soil.

The advance of the Southern frontier meant the spread not just of cotton but also of slavery. Usually the first arrivals were ordinary frontier people like those farther north, small farmers who made rough clearings in the forest. Then came wealthier planters, who bought up the cleared or partially cleared land, while the original settlers moved farther west and started over again. The large planters made the westward journey in a style quite different from that of the first settlers, traveling in great caravans with herds of livestock, wagonloads of household goods, long lines of slaves, and—at the rear—the planter's family riding in carriages. Success in the wilderness was by no means assured, even for the wealthiest settlers. But many planters soon expanded small clearings into vast fields of cotton and replaced the cabins of the pioneers with more sumptuous log dwellings and ultimately with imposing mansions that demonstrated the rise of a newly rich class.

The rapid growth of the West resulted in the admission of four new states to the Union in the immediate aftermath of the War of 1812: Indiana in 1816, Mississippi in 1817, Illinois in 1818, and Alabama in 1819.

The Far West

The Far Western areas of the continent remained largely unknown to most white Americans. Only New Englanders who were engaged in Pacific whaling or the China trade were familiar with the Oregon coast. Only fur traders and trappers had any knowledge of the land between the Missouri and the Pacific.

Before the War of 1812, John Jacob Astor's American Fur Company had established Astoria as a trading post at the mouth of the Columbia River in Oregon. When war came, Astor sold his interests to a British company and moved his own operations to the Great Lakes area, from which he eventually extended them westward to the Rockies. Other companies carried on operations up the Missouri and its tributaries and in the Rocky Mountains. At first, fur traders did most of their business by purchasing pelts from the Indians. But beginning with Andrew and William Ashley's Rocky Mountain Fur Company, founded in 1822, more and more traders dispatched white trappers into the wilderness to travel with the Indians in pursuit of furs.

The trappers (or "mountain men") explored the Far West and gained an intimate knowledge of the region and its people; but few wrote books or drew maps, so their knowledge did not spread widely. Public awareness of the region increased more as a result of the explorations of Major Stephen H. Long, who in 1819–1820 led nineteen soldiers on a journey through what is now Nebraska and eastern Colorado. Long wrote an influential report on his trip, assessing the region's potential for future settlement and development: "We do not hesitate in giving the opinion that it is almost wholly unfit for cultivation, and of course uninhabitable by a people depending upon agriculture for their subsistence." On the published map of his expedition, he labeled the Great Plains the "Great American Desert"—strengthening the mistaken belief, first advanced by Pike and others, that the land beyond the Missouri River was unfit for cultivation.

The "Era of Good Feelings"

The expansion of the economy, the growth of the West, the creation of new states—all reflected the rising spirit of nationalism that was permeating the United States in the years following the war. That spirit found reflection, for a time, in the course of American politics.

Ever since 1800, the presidency had remained in the hands of Virginians. After two terms in office Jefferson helped his secretary of state, James Madison, to succeed him; and after two more terms, Madison secured the presidential nomination for his own secretary of state, James Monroe. Many in the North were already expressing their impatience with the so-called Virginia Dynasty, but the Republicans had no difficulty electing their candidate in the listless campaign of 1816. Monroe received 183 ballots in the electoral college; his Federalist opponent, Rufus King of New York, only 34—from Massachusetts, Connecticut, and Delaware.

Monroe was sixty-one years old when he became president. In the course of his long and varied career, he had served as a soldier in the Revolution, as a diplomat, and most recently as a cabinet officer. He entered office under what seemed to be remarkably favorable circumstances. With the decline of the Federalists, his party faced no serious opposition. With the conclusion of the War of 1812, the nation faced no important international threats. American politicians had dreamed since the first days of the republic of a time in which partisan divisions and factional disputes might come to an end, a time in which the nation might achieve the harmony and virtue the founders had envisioned. In the postwar years, Monroe attempted to use his office to realize that dream.

He made that clear, above all, in the selection of his cabinet. For secretary of state, he chose the New Englander and former Federalist John Quincy Adams. Jefferson, Madison, and Monroe had all served as secretary of state before becoming president; Adams, therefore, immediately became the heir apparent, suggesting that the "Virginia Dynasty" would soon come to an end. Monroe asked Henry Clay to be secretary of war, but Clay chose to remain as Speaker of the House, so he named John C. Calhoun instead. In his other appointments, too, Monroe took pains to include both Northerners and Southerners, Easterners and Westerners, Federalists and Republicans—to harmonize the various interests and sections of the country in a government of national unity.

Soon after his inauguration, Monroe did what no president since Washington had done: he made a goodwill tour through the country. In New England, so recently the scene of rabid Federalist discontent, he was greeted everywhere with enthusiastic demonstrations. The *Columbian Centinel*, a Federalist newspaper in Boston, commenting on the "Presidential Jubilee" in that city, observed that an "era of good feelings" had arrived. This phrase became a popular label for the presidency of Monroe. On the surface, at least, the years of Monroe's presidency did appear to be an "era of good feelings." In 1820, Monroe was re-elected without opposition. For all practical purposes, the Federalist party had now ceased to exist.

John Quincy Adams and Florida

Like his father, the second president of the United States, John Quincy Adams had spent much of his life in diplomatic service. He had represented the United States in Britain, Russia, the Netherlands, and Prussia. He had helped negotiate the Treaty of Ghent. And he had demonstrated in all his assignments a calmness and firmness that made him one of the great diplomats in American history. He was also a committed nationalist; and when he assumed the office of secretary of state, he considered his most important task to be the promotion of American expansion.

CAPTURING THE SEMINOLES A contemporary woodcut illustrates
American troops under the command of Andrew Jackson taking two
Seminole chiefs into captivity in Florida in 1816.

His first challenge was Florida. The United States had already annexed
West Florida, but that claim was in dispute. Most Americans, moreover, still
believed the nation should gain possession of the entire peninsula. In 1817,
Adams began negotiations with the Spanish minister, Luis de Onís, in hopes
of resolving the dispute and gaining the entire territory for the United States.

In the meantime, however, events were taking their own course in
Florida itself. Andrew Jackson, now in command of American troops along
the Florida frontier, had orders from Secretary of War Calhoun to "adopt
the necessary measures" to stop the continuing raids on American territory
by Seminole Indians south of the Florida border. Jackson used those orders
as an excuse to invade Florida, seize the Spanish forts at St. Marks and
Pensacola, and order the hanging of two British subjects on the charge of
supplying and inciting the Indians.

Instead of condemning Jackson's raid, Adams urged the government to
assume responsibility for it, because he saw a chance to win an important
advantage in his negotiations with Spain. The United States, he told the
Spanish, had the right under international law to defend itself against threats
from across its borders. Since Spain was unwilling or unable to curb those

threats, America had simply done what was necessary. Jackson's raid had demonstrated to the Spanish that the United States could easily take Florida by force. Adams implied that the nation might consider doing so.

Onís realized, therefore, that he had little choice but to come to terms with the Americans. Under the provisions of the Adams-Onís Treaty of 1819, Spain ceded all of Florida to the United States and gave up its claim to territory north of the 42nd parallel in the Pacific Northwest. In return, the American government gave up its claims to Texas.

The Panic of 1819

But the Monroe administration had little time to revel in its diplomatic successes. At the same time Adams was negotiating with Onís, the nation was experiencing a serious economic crisis that helped revive many of the political disputes that the "era of good feelings" had presumably settled.

The Panic of 1819 followed a period of high foreign demand for American farm goods (a result of the disruption of European agriculture by the Napoleonic Wars) and thus of exceptionally high prices for American farmers. The rising prices for farm goods stimulated a land boom in the Western United States. Fueled by speculative investments, land prices soared well above the government-established minimum of $2 an acre; some land in the Black Belt of Alabama and Mississippi went for $100 an acre and more.

The availability of easy credit to settlers and speculators—from the government (under the land acts of 1800 and 1804); from state banks and wildcat banks; even for a time from the rechartered Bank of the United States—fueled the land boom. Beginning in 1819, however, new management at the national bank began tightening credit, calling in loans and foreclosing mortgages. The new governors also collected state bank notes and demanded payment in cash from the banks, many of which could not meet the demand and hence failed. These bank failures launched a financial panic, which many Americans, particularly those in the West, blamed on the Bank of the United States. Thus began a process that would eventually make the Bank's existence one of the nation's most burning political issues.

Six years of depression followed. Prices for both manufactured goods and agricultural produce fell rapidly. Manufacturers secured passage of a new tariff in 1824 to protect them from foreign competition. Indebted farmers won some relief through the land law of 1820 and the relief act of 1821, which lowered the price of land and reduced existing debts while extending their payment schedules.

Some Americans saw the Panic of 1819 and the widespread distress that followed as a warning that rapid economic growth and territorial expansion would destabilize the nation and threaten its survival. But most Americans by 1820 were irrevocably committed to such growth and expansion. Public debate in the future would revolve less around the question of whether such growth was good or bad than around the question of how it should be encouraged and controlled. That debate, which the Panic of 1819 did much to encourage, created new factional divisions within the Republican party and ultimately brought the era of nonpartisanship—the "era of good feelings"—to an acrimonious end.

CHAPTER NINE

A Resurgence of Nationalism

America's Economic Revolution ~ *Sectionalism and Nationalism*
The Revival of Opposition

IKE A "FIRE BELL IN THE NIGHT," as Thomas Jefferson put it, the issue of slavery arose after the War of 1812 to threaten the unity of the nation. The specific question was whether the territory of Missouri should be admitted to the Union as a free or as a slaveholding state. But the larger issue, one that would arise again and again to plague the republic, was the question of whether the vast new Western regions of the United States would ultimately be controlled by the North or by the South.

Yet the Missouri crisis, which was settled by a compromise in 1820, was significant at the time not only because it was a sign of the sectional crises to come but because it stood in such sharp contrast to the rising American nationalism of the 1820s. Whatever forces might be working to pull the nation apart, stronger ones were acting for the moment to draw it together. The American economy was experiencing remarkable growth. The federal government was acting in both domestic and foreign policy to assert a vigorous nationalism. Above all, perhaps, the United States was bound together by a set of shared sentiments and ideals: the memory of the Revolution, the veneration of the Constitution and its framers, the widely held sense that America had a special destiny in the world. Events would prove that the forces of nationalism were not, in the end, strong enough to overcome the emerging sectional differences. For the time being, however, they permitted the republic to enter an era of unprecedented expansion confident and united.

AMERICA'S ECONOMIC REVOLUTION

In the 1820s and 1830s, America began to experience the economic revolution that would, by the end of the century, almost entirely transform it. By the mid-1820s, the nation's economy was growing more rapidly than its population.

The American Population, 1820–1840

Three trends characterized the American population in the 1820s and 1830s, all of them contributing in various ways to economic growth: The population was increasing rapidly. Much of it was moving westward. And much of it was moving to towns and cities.

The American population had stood at only 4 million in 1790. By 1820, it had reached 10 million; by 1830, nearly 13 million; and by 1840, 17 million. The United States was growing much more rapidly in population

FOURTH OF JULY PICNIC AT WEYMOUTH LANDING (c. 1845), BY SUSAN MERRETT
Celebrations of Independence Day, like this one in eastern Massachusetts, became major festive events throughout the United States in the early nineteenth century, a sign of rising American nationalism.

than Britain or Europe. By 1860 it had a larger population than did the United Kingdom and had nearly overtaken Germany and France.

Public health efforts gradually improved, and the number and ferocity of epidemics (such as the great cholera plague of 1832) slowly declined, as did the mortality rate as a whole. But the population increase was also a result of a high birth rate. In 1840, the birth rate for white women stood at 6.14, a decline from the very high rates of the eighteenth century but still substantial enough to produce rapid population increases.

The African-American population increased more slowly than the white. After 1808, when the importation of slaves became illegal, the proportion of blacks to whites in the nation as a whole steadily declined. In 1820, there was one African-American to every four whites; in 1840, one to every five. The slower increase of the black population was a result of its comparatively high death rate. Slave mothers had large families, but life was shorter for both slaves and free blacks than for whites—a result of the enforced poverty in which virtually all African-Americans lived.

Immigration, choked off by wars in Europe and economic crises in America, contributed little to the American population in the first three decades of the nineteenth century. Of the total population of nearly 13 million in 1830, the foreign-born numbered fewer than 500,000. Soon, however, immigration began to grow once again. It reached a total of 60,000 in 1832 and nearly 80,000 in 1837. Reduced transportation costs and increasing economic opportunities in America helped stimulate the immigration boom, which also introduced new groups to the United States. In particular, the number of immigrants arriving from the southern (Catholic) counties of Ireland began to grow, reflecting the beginning of a tremendous influx of Irish Catholics that was to occur over the next two decades.

The Northwest and the Southwest continued to grow much more rapidly than did the rest of the country. By 1830, more than a fourth of the American people lived west of the Appalachians; by 1850, nearly half. As a result, some of the seaboard states found themselves with a depleted labor supply. Year after year such eastern states as Vermont, New Hampshire, and the Carolinas lost nearly as many people through migration as they gained by natural increase; their populations remained almost static.

Not all the Eastern migrants sought the unsettled West; some moved instead to the rapidly growing cities. In 1790, one person in thirty lived in a city (defined as a community of 8,000 or more); in 1820, one in twenty; and in 1840, one in twelve. The rise of New York City was particularly dramatic. By 1810 it was the largest city in the United States. That was partly

THE PORT OF NEW YORK, 1828 This view of South Street in Manhattan shows the East River lined with docks. Other docks, similarly busy, lined the Hudson River on the opposite side of the island. The population of New York City was approaching 150,000 by 1828.

a result of its superior natural harbor. It was partly a result of the Erie Canal (completed in 1825), which gave the city unrivaled access to the interior. And it was partly because of liberal state laws that made the city attractive for both foreign and domestic commerce.

The Canal Age

From 1790 until the 1820s, the so-called turnpike era, the United States had relied largely on roads for internal transportation. But roads alone were not adequate for the nation's expanding needs. And so, in the 1820s and 1830s, Americans began to construct other means of transportation as well.

The larger rivers, especially the Mississippi and the Ohio, became increasingly useful as steamboats grew in number and improved in design. New river boats carried to New Orleans the corn and other crops of Northwestern farmers and the cotton and tobacco of Southwestern planters. From New Orleans, ocean-going ships took the cargoes on to Eastern ports.

But neither the farmers of the West nor the merchants of the East were satisfied with this pattern of trade. Farmers would get better prices for their crops if they could ship them directly eastward to market, rather than by the roundabout river-sea route; and merchants could sell larger quantities of their manufactured goods if they could transport them more directly and economically to the West. New highways across the mountains provided a partial solution to the problem. But the costs of hauling goods overland, although lower than before the roads were built, were still too high for anything except the most compact and valuable merchandise. On a turnpike, four horses could haul one and a half tons eighteen miles in a day. But the same four horses could draw a boatload of a hundred tons twenty-four miles a day on a canal. Thus interest quickly grew in expanding the nation's water routes.

Canal building was too expensive for private enterprise, so the job of digging canals fell largely to the states. New York was the first to act. It had the natural advantage of a good route between the Hudson River and Lake Erie through the only break in the Appalachian chain. Yet the engineering tasks were still imposing. The distance was more than 350 miles, several times as long as any of the existing canals in America and interrupted by high ridges and a wilderness of woods. After a long public debate over whether the scheme was practical, canal advocates prevailed when De Witt Clinton, a late but ardent convert to the cause, became governor in 1817. Digging began on July 4, 1817.

The building of the Erie Canal was the greatest construction project Americans had ever undertaken. The canal itself was simple: basically a ditch, forty feet wide and four feet deep, with towpaths along the banks for the horses or mules that were to draw the canal boats. But it required hundreds of difficult cuts and fills, some of them enormous, to enable the canal to pass through hills and over valleys; stone aqueducts to carry it across streams; and eighty-eight locks, of heavy masonry with great wooden gates, to permit ascents and descents. The Erie Canal was not just an engineering triumph but an immediate financial success. It opened in October 1825, amid elaborate ceremonies and celebrations, and traffic was soon so heavy that, within about seven years, tolls had repaid the entire cost of construction. By providing access to the Great Lakes, the canal gave New York access to Chicago and the growing markets of the West.

The system of water transportation extended farther when the states of Ohio and Indiana, inspired by the success of the Erie Canal, provided water connections between Lake Erie and the Ohio River. These canals made it possible to ship goods by inland waterways all the way from New York to New Orleans, although it was still necessary to transfer cargoes several times among canal, lake, and river craft.

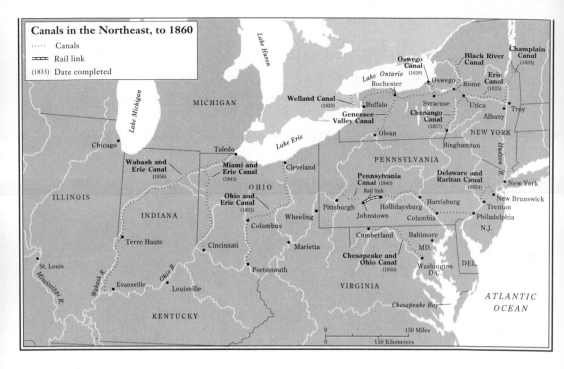

Canals in the Northeast, to 1860

..... Canals
≡≡≡ Rail link
(1833) Date completed

One of the immediate results of these new transportation routes was increased white settlement in the Northwest, because it had become easier for migrants to make the westward journey and to ship their produce back to markets. Although much of the Western produce continued to go downriver to New Orleans, an increasing proportion of it (including most of the wheat of the Northwest) went east to New York. And manufactured goods from throughout the East now moved in growing volume through New York and then by the new water routes to the West.

Rival cities along the Atlantic seaboard took alarm at the prospect of New York's acquiring so vast a hinterland, largely at their expense. But they had limited success in catching up. Boston, its way to the Hudson River blocked by the Berkshire Mountains, did not try to connect itself to the West by canal; its hinterland would remain confined largely to New England itself. Philadelphia and Baltimore had the still more formidable Allegheny Mountains to contend with. They made a serious effort at canal building, nevertheless, but with discouraging results. Pennsylvania's effort ended in an expensive failure. Maryland constructed part of the Chesapeake and Ohio Canal beginning in 1828, but only the stretch between Washington, D.C., and Cumberland, Maryland, was ever completed. In the South, Richmond and Charleston also aspired to build water routes to the Ohio Valley but never completed them.

For none of these rivals of New York did canals provide a satisfactory way to the West. Some cities, however, saw their opportunity in a different and newer means of transportation. Even before the canal age had reached its height, the era of the railroad was already beginning.

The Early Railroads

Railroads played no more than a secondary role in the nation's transportation system in the 1820s and 1830s; but railroad pioneers did lay the groundwork for the great surge of railroad building in midcentury that would link the nation together as never before. Railroads eventually became the primary transportation system for the United States and remained so until the construction of the interstate highway system in the mid-twentieth century.

Railroads emerged from a combination of technological and entrepreneurial innovations: the invention of tracks; the creation of steam-powered locomotives; and the development of trains as public carriers of passengers and freight. By 1804, both English and American inventors had experimented with steam engines for propelling land vehicles. In 1820, John Stevens ran a locomotive and cars around a circular track on his New Jersey estate. And in 1825, the Stockton and Darlington Railroad in England opened a short length of track and became the first line to carry general traffic.

American businessmen, especially in those seaboard cities that sought better communication with the West, quickly grew interested in the English experiment. The first company to begin actual operations was the Baltimore and Ohio, which opened a thirteen-mile stretch of track in 1830. In New York, the Mohawk and Hudson began running trains along the sixteen miles between Schenectady and Albany in 1831. By 1836, more than 1,000 miles of track had been laid in eleven states.

But there was not yet a true railroad system. Even the longest of the lines was comparatively short in the 1830s, and most of them served simply to connect water routes to one another, not to link one railroad to another. Even when two lines did connect, the tracks often differed in gauge (width), so cars from one line often could not fit onto the tracks of another. Schedules were erratic and wrecks were frequent. But railroads made some important advances in the 1830s and 1840s. Roadbeds were improved through the introduction of heavier iron rails. Steam locomotives became more flexible and powerful. Passenger cars were redesigned to be stabler, more comfortable, and larger.

Railroads and canals were soon competing bitterly with each other. For a time, the Chesapeake and Ohio Canal Company blocked the advance of the Baltimore and Ohio Railroad through the narrow gorge of the upper Potomac, which it controlled; and the state of New York prohibited railroads from hauling freight in competition with the Eric Canal and its branches. But railroads had so many advantages over canals that where free competition existed, they almost always prevailed.

The Expansion of Business

American business grew rapidly in the 1820s and 1830s, not only because of population growth and the transportation revolution but also because of the daring, imagination, and ruthlessness of a new generation of entrepreneurs.

One important change came in the retail distribution of goods, which was becoming increasingly systematic and efficient. In the larger cities, stores specializing in groceries, dry goods, hardware, and other lines appeared, although residents of smaller towns and villages still depended on the general store and did much of their business by barter. The organization of business was also changing. Most businesses continued to be operated by individuals or limited partnerships, and the dominating figures were still the great merchant capitalists, whose enterprises were generally owned by a

RACING ON THE RAILROAD Peter Cooper designed and built the first steam-powered locomotive in America in 1830 for the Baltimore and Ohio railroad. On August 28 of that year, he raced his locomotive (the "Tom Thumb") against a horse-drawn railroad car. This sketch depicts the moment when Cooper's engine overtook the horse-car.

single man. In some larger businesses, however, the individual merchant capitalist was giving way to the corporation. Corporations had the advantage of combining the resources of a large number of shareholders, and they began to develop particularly rapidly in the 1830s, when some legal obstacles to their formation were removed. Previously, a corporation could obtain a charter only by a special act of the state legislature—a cumbersome process that stifled corporate growth. By the 1830s, however, states were beginning to pass general incorporation laws, under which a group could secure a charter merely by paying a fee. The laws also established the privilege of limited liability, which meant that individual stockholders risked losing only the value of their own investment if a corporation should fail—they were not liable (as they had been in the past) for the corporation's larger losses. Corporations made possible the accumulation of much larger amounts of capital and hence the existence of much larger manufacturing and business enterprises.

But investment alone still provided too little capital to meet the demands of the most ambitious businesses. They relied on credit, which often created dangerous instability. Credit mechanisms remained very crude in the early nineteenth century. The government alone was permitted to issue currency, but the official currency was only gold and silver, not paper, and the amount was thus too small to support the demand for credit. Under pressure from corporate promoters, many banks issued large quantities of bank notes to provide capital for expanding business ventures. Many institutions issued notes far in excess of their own specie reserves. As a result, bank failures were frequent and bank deposits often insecure.

The Rise of the Factory

All of these changes—increasing population, improved transportation, and the expansion of business activity—contributed to perhaps the most profound economic development in mid-nineteenth-century America: the rise of the factory.

Before the War of 1812, most of what manufacturing there was in the United States took place within households or in small, individually operated workshops. Gradually, however, improved technology and increasing demand produced a fundamental change. It came first in the New England textile industry. There, beginning early in the nineteenth century, entrepreneurs were beginning to make use of new machines driven by waterpower that allowed them to bring textile operations together under a single roof. This factory system, as it came to be known, spread rapidly in the 1820s and began to make serious inroads into the old home-based system of spinning thread and weaving cloth. It also penetrated the shoe industry, concentrated in eastern Massachusetts. Shoemaking continued to be done largely by hand, but manufacturers were beginning to employ workers who specialized in one or another of the various tasks involved in production. Some factories began producing large numbers of identical shoes in ungraded sizes and without distinction as to rights and lefts. By the 1830s, factory production was spreading from textiles and shoes into other industries and from New England to other areas of the Northeast.

Machine technology advanced more rapidly in the United States in the mid-nineteenth century than in any other country in the world. Change was so rapid, in fact, that some manufacturers built their new machinery out of wood; by the time the wood wore out, they reasoned, improved technology would have made the machine obsolete. By the end of the 1830s, so advanced had American technology become—particularly in textile manufacturing—that industrialists in Britain and Europe were beginning to travel to the United States to learn new techniques, instead of the other way around.

Men and Women at Work

However advanced their technology, manufacturers still relied above all on a supply of labor. In later years, much of that supply would come from great waves of immigration from abroad. In the 1820s and 1830s, however, labor had to come primarily from the native population. Recruitment was not easy. City populations, although increasing, were still relatively small; 90 percent of the American people still lived and worked on farms. What produced the beginnings of an industrial labor supply was the transformation of American agriculture in the nineteenth century and a dramatic increase in food production. No longer did each region have to feed itself entirely from its own farms; it could import food from other regions—and particularly from the fertile lands of the newly settled West. As a result, the Northeastern agricultural economy slowly declined, and rural people began to look for work in the factories.

Two systems of recruitment emerged to bring this new labor supply to the expanding textile mills. One, common in the mid-Atlantic states and in parts of New England, brought whole families from the farm to the mill, where parents and children worked together tending the looms. The second system, common in Massachusetts, enlisted young women (mostly from farm families) in their late teens and early twenties. It was known as the Lowell or Waltham system, after the factory towns in which it first emerged.

A M E R I C A N   V O I C E S

MARY PAUL

Letter from the Lowell Mills, 1845

DEAR FATHER,

I received your letter on Thursday the 14th with much pleasure. I am well which is one comfort. My life and health are spared while others are cut off. Last Thursday one girl fell down and broke her neck, which caused instant death. She was going in or coming out of the mill and slipped down it being very icy. The same day a man was killed by the cars. Another had nearly all his ribs broken. Another was nearly killed by . . . having a bale of cotton fall on him. Last Tuesday we were paid. In all I had six dollars and sixty cents paid $4.68 for board. With the rest I got me a pair of rubbers and a pair of 50.cts shoes. Next payment I am to have a dollar a week beside my board. . . . Perhaps you would like something about our regulations about going in and coming out of the mill. At 5 o'clock in the morning the bell rings for the folks to get up and get breakfast. At half past six it rings for the girls to get up and at seven they are called into the mill. At half past 12 we have dinner are called back again at one and stay till half past seven. I get along very well with my work. I can doff as fast as any girl in our room. . . . I think that the factory is the best place for me and if any girl wants employment I advise them to come to Lowell.

SOURCE: Thomas Dublin, ed., *Farm to Factory: Women's Letters, 1830–1860* (New York: Columbia University Press, 1981), pp. 103–104.

THE ASSORTING ROOM Well-dressed young women work in the assorting room of a New England textile factory in the 1830s, while a young male supervisor oversees them. Eventually the relatively benign conditions portrayed in this drawing deteriorated considerably.

Most of these women worked in the factories for only a few years. Some saved their wages and returned home to marry and raise children. Others married men they met in the factories or in town and remained part of the industrial world, but even they often stopped working in the mills after marriage.

Labor conditions in these early years of the factory system were significantly better than those in English industry and better too than they would ultimately become in the United States. The employment of young children was a harsh practice, but usually less so than in Europe, since working children in American factories generally remained under the supervision of their parents.

Even more distinctive from the European labor system was the lot of working women in the mills in Lowell and factory towns like it. In England, woman workers in coal mines and other heavy industries were employed in unimaginably wretched conditions. English visitors to America considered the Lowell mills a female paradise by contrast. The Lowell workers lived in clean boardinghouses and dormitories maintained for them by the factory owners. They were well fed and closely supervised. Because many New Englanders considered the employment of women to be vaguely immoral, the factory owners were careful to guard the environment in which their employees lived, enforcing strict curfews and requiring regular church attendance. Wages for the Lowell workers were generous by the modest standards of the time. The women even found time to write and publish a monthly magazine, the *Lowell Offering*.

Yet even these relatively well-treated workers often found the transition from farm life to factory work difficult, even traumatic. They shared with men the shock of moving from a seasonal, relatively informal rural work schedule to the rigid, time-bound pattern of factory work. And female mill workers also suffered from a special disadvantage, since unlike men they had very few employment options. They had no access to construction work; they could not become sailors or dockworkers; only with great difficulty could they travel the country alone, as many men did, in search of opportunities.

The paternalistic factory system of Lowell and Waltham did not survive for long. In the highly competitive textile market that developed in the 1830s and 1840s—a market especially vulnerable to the booms and busts that afflicted the American economy as a whole—manufacturers were eager to reduce labor costs and hence reluctant to maintain the high living standards and reasonably attractive working conditions with which they had begun. Wages declined; the hours of work lengthened; the conditions of the boardinghouses deteriorated as the buildings decayed and overcrowding increased. In 1834, mill workers in Lowell organized a union—the Factory Girls Association—which staged a strike to protest a 25 percent wage cut. Two years later, the association struck again—against a rent increase in the boardinghouses. Both strikes failed, and a recession in 1837 virtually destroyed the organization. Eight years later, led by the militant Sarah Bagley, the Lowell women created the Female Labor Reform Association and began agitating for a ten-hour day and for improvements in conditions in the mills. By then, however, the character of the factory work force was changing again. Textile manufacturers were turning to a less rebellious labor supply: immigrants.

Immigrant workers had even less leverage than the women they at times displaced; thus they often encountered far worse working conditions. Construction gangs, made up increasingly of Irish immigrants, performed heavy, unskilled work on turnpikes, canals, and railroads under often terrible conditions. Because most of these workers had no marketable skills and because of native prejudice against them, they received wages so low—and received them so intermittently, since the work was seasonal and uncertain— that they generally did not earn enough to support their families in even minimal comfort.

By the 1840s, Irish workers predominated in the New England textile mills as well, and their arrival accelerated the deterioration of working conditions there. There was far less social pressure on owners to provide a decent environment for Irish workers than for native women. Employers began paying piece rates rather than a daily wage and employed other devices to speed up production and exploit the labor force more efficiently.

The factory system gradually displaced many of the skilled artisans who had once been the backbone of American manufacturing. In the face of competition from industrial capitalists, craftsmen began early in the nineteenth century to form organizations—the first American labor unions—to protect their endangered positions. In Philadelphia, Baltimore, Boston, New York, and other cities, the skilled workers of each craft formed societies for mutual aid. During the 1820s and 1830s, the craft societies began to combine on a citywide and then a national basis through organizations known as trade unions. In 1834, delegates from six cities founded the National Trades' Union; and in 1836, the printers and the cordwainers set up their own national craft unions. But this early labor movement soon collapsed in the face of hostile laws, hostile courts, and the Panic of 1837.

SECTIONALISM AND NATIONALISM

For a brief but alarming moment in 1819–1820, the increasing differences between the nation's two leading sections threatened the unity of the United States. But once a sectional crisis was averted with the Missouri Compromise, the forces of nationalism continued to assert themselves; and the federal government began to assume the role of promoter of economic growth.

The Missouri Compromise

When Missouri applied for admission to the Union as a state in 1819, slavery was already well established there. Even so, Representative James Tallmadge, Jr., of New York, proposed an amendment to the Missouri statehood bill that would prohibit the further introduction of slaves into Missouri and provide for the gradual emancipation of those already there. The Tallmadge Amendment provoked a controversy that was to rage for the next two years.

Since the beginning of the republic, partly by chance and partly by design, new states had come into the Union more or less in pairs, one from the North, another from the South. In 1819, there were eleven free states and eleven slave states; the admission of Missouri would upset that balance and establish a precedent that in the future might increase the political power of one section over another—hence the interest of both the North and the South in the question of slavery and freedom in Missouri.

The Missouri question was soon complicated by the application of Maine (previously the northern part of Massachusetts) for admission as a new state. Speaker of the House Henry Clay informed Northern members that if they blocked Missouri from entering the Union as a slave state, Southerners would block the admission of Maine. But Maine ultimately offered a way out of the impasse, as the Senate agreed to combine the Maine and Missouri proposals into a single bill. Maine would be admitted as a free state, Missouri as a slave state. Then Senator Jesse B. Thomas of Illinois proposed an amendment prohibiting slavery in the rest of the Louisiana Purchase territory north of the southern boundary of Missouri (the 36°30′

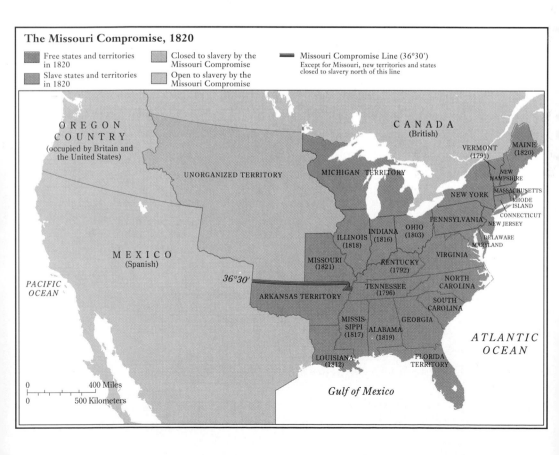

The Missouri Compromise, 1820

Free states and territories in 1820

Slave states and territories in 1820

Closed to slavery by the Missouri Compromise

Open to slavery by the Missouri Compromise

Missouri Compromise Line (36°30′)
Except for Missouri, new territories and states closed to slavery north of this line

parallel). The Senate adopted the Thomas Amendment, and Speaker Clay, although with great difficulty, guided the amended Maine-Missouri bill through the House.

Nationalists in both North and South hailed the Missouri Compromise as a happy resolution of a danger to the Union. But the debate over it had revealed a strong undercurrent of sectionalism that was competing with—although at the moment failing to derail—the powerful tides of nationalism.

Marshall and the Court

John Marshall served as chief justice of the United States for almost thirty-five years, from 1801 to 1835, and dominated the Court as no one

JOHN MARSHALL Marshall became Chief Justice of the United States Supreme Court in 1801 after establishing himself as one of the leaders of the Federalist party. He served as Chief Justice for thirty-five years, longer than anyone else in American history.

else before or since. Republican presidents filled vacancies with one after another Republican justice, but so influential was Marshall with his colleagues that he continued to carry a majority with him in most of the Court's decisions. More than anyone but the framers themselves, he molded the development of the Constitution itself: strengthening the judicial branch at the expense of the executive and legislature; increasing the power of the federal government at the expense of the states; and advancing the interests of the propertied and commercial classes.

Committed to promoting commerce, the Marshall Court firmly strengthened the inviolability of contracts as a cornerstone of American law. In *Fletcher* v. *Peck* (1810), which arose out of the notorious Yazoo land frauds, the Court had to decide whether the Georgia legislature of 1796 could rightfully repeal the act of the previous legislature granting lands under shady circumstances to the Yazoo Land Companies. In a unanimous decision, Marshall held that a land grant was a valid contract and could not be repealed even if corruption was involved. *Dartmouth College* v. *Woodward* (1819) expanded further the meaning of the contract clause of the Constitution. Having gained control of the New Hampshire state government, Republicans tried to revise Dartmouth's charter (granted by King George III in 1769) to convert the private college into a state university. The trustees (represented before the Court by Daniel Webster, a Dartmouth graduate) ruled that the legislature had unconstitutionally violated the college's contract. By proclaiming that corporation charters were contracts and that contracts were inviolable, the decision also placed important restrictions on the ability of state governments to control corporations.

In overturning not only the act of the legislature but the decisions of New Hampshire courts, the *Dartmouth College* case seemed to establish the right of the Supreme Court to override the decisions of state courts. But some advocates of states' rights, notably in the South, continued to challenge its right to do so. In *Cohens* v. *Virginia* (1821), Marshall explicitly affirmed the constitutionality of federal review of state court decisions. The states had given up part of their sovereignty in ratifying the Constitution, he explained, and their courts must submit to federal jurisdiction; otherwise, the federal government would be prostrated "at the feet of every state in the Union."

Meanwhile, in *McCulloch* v. *Maryland* (1819), Marshall confirmed the "implied powers" of Congress by upholding the constitutionality of the Bank of the United States. The Bank had become so unpopular in the South and the West that several of the states tried to drive branches out of business by outright prohibition or by prohibitory taxes. This case presented two constitutional questions to the Supreme Court: Could Congress charter a bank? And if so, could individual states ban it or tax it? Daniel Webster, one of the Bank's attorneys, argued that establishing such an institution came within the "necessary and proper" clause of the Constitution, and he added that the power to tax involved a "power to destroy." If the states could tax the Bank at all, they could tax it to death. Marshall adopted Webster's words in deciding for the Bank.

In the case of *Gibbons* v. *Ogden* (1824), the Court strengthened Congress's power to regulate interstate commerce. The state of New York had granted Robert Fulton and Robert Livingston's steamboat company the exclusive right to carry passengers on the Hudson River to New York City. Fulton and Livingston then gave Aaron Ogden the business of carrying passengers across the river between New York and New Jersey. But Thomas Gibbons, with a license granted under an act of Congress, went into competition with Ogden, who brought suit against him and was sustained by the New York courts. When Gibbons appealed to the Supreme Court, the justices faced the twofold question of whether "commerce" included navigation and whether Congress alone or Congress and the states together could regulate interstate commerce. Marshall replied that "commerce" was a broad term embracing navigation as well as the buying and selling of goods and asserted that the power of Congress to regulate such commerce was "complete in itself" and might be "exercised to its utmost extent." The state-granted monopoly, therefore, was void.

The lasting significance of *Gibbons* v. *Ogden* was that it freed transportation systems from restraints by the states and helped pave the way for unfettered capitalist growth. But its more immediate effect was that it headed off a movement to weaken the Supreme Court. Influential Republicans, mostly from the South and the West, were arguing that the Marshall Court was not merely interpreting the Constitution but illegitimately changing it. In Congress, they proposed measures to curb the Court's power. One senator suggested making the Senate, not the Court, the agency for deciding the constitutionality of state laws and settling interstate disputes. Other members introduced bills proposing to increase the size of the Court (from seven to ten justices) and to require more than a simple majority to declare a state law unconstitutional. Still others argued for "codification": for making legislative statutes the basis of the law, rather than the common-law precedents that judges used. Such a reform, codifiers argued, would limit the power of the judiciary and prevent "judge-made" law. The Court reformers failed to pass any of their measures; and after *Gibbons* v. *Ogden*, with its popular stand against monopoly power, hostility to the judicial branch of the government gradually died down.

The decisions of the Marshall Court established the primacy of the federal government over the states in regulating the economy and opened the way for an increased federal role in promoting economic growth. They protected corporations and other private economic institutions from local government interference. They were, in short, highly nationalistic decisions, designed to promote the growth of a strong, unified, and economically developed United States.

The Court and the Tribes

The nationalist inclinations of the Marshall Court were visible as well in a series of decisions concerning the legal status of Indian tribes within the United States. But these decisions not only affirmed the supremacy of the United States; they carved out a distinctive position for Native Americans within the constitutional structure.

The first of the crucial Indian decisions was in the case of *Johnson* v. *McIntosh* (1823). Leaders of the Illinois and Pinakeshaw tribes had sold parcels of their land to a group of white settlers (including Johnson), but they later signed a treaty with the federal government ceding to the United States territory that included those same parcels. The government proceeded to grant settlement rights to new white residents of the area (among them McIntosh) on the land claimed by Johnson. The Court was asked to decide which claim had precedence. Marshall's ruling, not surprisingly, favored the United States. But in explaining it, he offered a preliminary definition of the place of Indians within the nation. The tribes had a basic right to their tribal lands, he said, that preceded all other American law. Individual American citizens could not buy or take land from the tribes; only the federal government could do that.

Eight years later, in *Cherokee Nation* v. *Georgia*, the Marshall Court refused to hear a case filed by the Cherokees against a Georgia law abolishing their tribal legislature and courts. The Cherokee argued that because the tribe was a "foreign nation," the Supreme Court (which had constitutional responsibility for mediating disputes between the states and foreign nations) had jurisdiction. Marshall disagreed. The tribes were not foreign nations, he said. They did, however, have a special status within the nation. "Their relation to the United States resembles that of a ward to his guardian," he wrote. This was the origin of what became known as the "trust relationship," by which the United States claimed broad powers over the tribes but accepted substantial responsibility for protecting their welfare.

Most important was the Court's 1832 decision in *Worcester v. Georgia*. The Georgia state government had passed a law requiring that any United States citizen desiring to enter Cherokee territory obtain permission from the governor. Two missionaries (one of them named Worcester) sued, claiming the state was encroaching on the federal government's constitutionally mandated role to regulate trade with the tribes. Marshall invalidated the Georgia law, another important step in consolidating federal authority over the states. In doing so, he defined further the nature of the Indian nations. The tribes, he explained, were sovereign entities in much the same way Georgia was a sovereign entity, "distinct political communities, having territorial boundaries within which their authority is exclusive." In defending the power of the federal government, he was also affirming, indeed expanding, tribal authority.

The Marshall decisions, therefore, did what the Constitution itself had not done: they defined a place for Indian tribes within the American political system. The tribes had basic property rights. They were sovereign entities not subject to the authority of state governments. But the federal government, like a "guardian" governing its "ward," had ultimate authority over tribal affairs—even if that authority was, according to the Court, limited by the government's obligation to protect Indian welfare. These provisions were seldom enough to defend Indians from the steady westward march of white civilization. But they formed the basis of what legal protections the Indians have had.

The Latin American Revolution and the Monroe Doctrine

Just as the Supreme Court was asserting American nationalism in the shaping of the country's economic life, so the Monroe administration was asserting nationalism in foreign policy. As always, American diplomacy was principally concerned with Europe. But in dealing with Europe, Americans were forced in the 1820s to develop a policy toward Latin America, which was suddenly winning its independence.

Americans looking southward in the years following the War of 1812 beheld a gigantic spectacle: the Spanish Empire in its death throes, a whole continent in revolt, new nations in the making. Already the United States had developed a profitable commerce with Latin America and was rivaling Great Britain as the principal trading nation there. Many believed the success of the anti-Spanish revolutions would further strengthen America's position in the region.

In 1815, the United States proclaimed neutrality in the wars between Spain and its rebellious colonies, a position which implied a partial recognition of the rebels' status as nations. Moreover, the United States sold ships and supplies to the revolutionaries, clearly indicating that it was not genuinely neutral but was trying to help the insurgents. But Secretary of State John Quincy Adams and President James Monroe hesitated at first to take the risky step of formally recognizing the new governments unless Great Britain agreed to do so at the same time. The British declined. Finally, in 1822, nationalist impulses in the United States prevailed, and President Monroe decided to proceed alone. In defiance of the rest of the world, he established diplomatic relations with five new nations—La Plata (later Argentina), Chile, Peru, Colombia, and Mexico—making the United States the first country to recognize them.

In 1823, Monroe went further and announced a policy that would ultimately be known (beginning some thirty years later) as the "Monroe Doctrine." "The American continents," Monroe declared, ". . . are henceforth not to be considered as subjects for future colonization by any European powers." The United States would consider any foreign challenge to the sovereignty of existing American nations as an unfriendly act. At the same time, he proclaimed, "Our policy in regard to Europe . . . is not to interfere in the internal concerns of any of its powers."

The Monroe Doctrine emerged directly out of America's relations with Europe in the 1820s. After Napoleon's defeat, the nations of Europe combined in a "concert" to prevent future challenges to the "legitimacy" of established governments. Great Britain soon withdrew from the concert, leaving Russia and France the strongest of its four remaining members. In 1823, the four allies authorized France to intervene in Spain to restore the Bourbon dynasty, which a revolution had toppled. Some in England and the Americas feared that the allies might next support a French effort to retake the lost Spanish Empire in America.

To most Americans, and certainly to the secretary of state, an even greater threat was Great Britain, which Adams suspected had designs on Cuba. Adams feared the transfer of Cuba from Spain, a weak power, to Britain. He thought Cuba eventually should belong to the United States and wanted to keep it in Spanish hands until it fell to the United States. For a time, Monroe and Adams considered making their pronouncements about Latin America part of a joint statement with Great Britain. But Adams soon came to believe that the American government should act alone instead of following along like a "cock-boat in the wake of a British man-of-war." When the British lost interest in a joint statement, they only strengthened an already growing inclination within the administration to make its own pronouncement.

Monroe and Adams hoped the message would rally the people of Latin America to resist foreign intervention. They also hoped that by appealing to national pride, the message would help arouse the United States from a business depression, divert it from sectional politics, and increase its interest in the otherwise lackluster administration of Monroe. It did neither. But the Monroe Doctrine was important nevertheless for several reasons. It was an expression of the growing spirit of nationalism in the United States in the 1820s. It was an expression of concern about the forces that were already gathering to threaten that spirit. And it established the idea of American hegemony in the Western Hemisphere that later United States governments would invoke at will to justify policies in Latin America.

THE REVIVAL OF OPPOSITION

After 1816, the Federalist party offered no presidential candidate and soon ceased to exist as a national political force. National politics was now conducted wholly within the Republican party, which considered itself not a party at all but an organization representing the whole of the population.

Yet the policies of the federal government continued to spark opposition, and by the late 1820s partisan divisions were emerging once again. In some respects, the division mirrored the schism that had produced the first party system in the 1790s. The Republicans had in many ways come to resemble the early Federalist regimes in their promotion of economic growth and centralization. And the opposition, like the opposition in the 1790s, stood opposed to the federal government's expanding role in the economy. There was, however, a crucial difference. At the beginning of the century, the opponents of centralization had also often been opponents of economic growth. Now, in the 1820s, the controversy involved not whether but how the nation should continue to expand.

The "Corrupt Bargain"

Until 1820, when the Federalist party ceased effective operations and James Monroe ran for reelection unopposed, presidential candidates were nominated by caucuses of the two parties in Congress. In 1824, had the caucus system prevailed, Republicans in Congress would have produced a candidate who would have run unopposed again.

But in 1824, "King Caucus" was overthrown. The Republican caucus did nominate a candidate: William H. Crawford of Georgia, the secretary of the treasury. But other candidates received nominations from state legislatures and endorsements from irregular mass meetings throughout the country. One of them was Secretary of State John Quincy Adams, who held the office that was the traditional stepping stone to the presidency but who had little popular appeal. Another contender was Henry Clay, the Speaker of the House, who had a devoted personal following and a definite and coherent program: the "American System," which proposed creating a great home market for factory and farm producers by raising the protective tariff, strengthening the national bank, and financing internal improvements. Andrew Jackson, the fourth major candidate, had no significant legislative record, but he was a military hero and had the help of shrewd political allies from his home state of Tennessee.

Jackson received a plurality, although not a majority, of both the popular and the electoral vote. In the electoral college, he had 99 votes to Adams's 84, Crawford's 41, and Clay's 37. The final decision was left to the House of Representatives, which was to choose among the candidates with the three highest electoral votes. Clay was out of the running, but he was in a strong position to influence the result, both because he had carried several states and because he was Speaker of the House.

Supporters of Jackson, Crawford, and Adams all wooed Clay as the congressional vote approached. But Clay's course was already set. Crawford was no longer a serious candidate, since he was suffering from a paralyzing disease. And Jackson was Clay's most dangerous political rival in the West and had not supported Clay's legislative program. Adams was no friend of Clay either; but alone among the candidates, he was an ardent nationalist and a likely supporter of the American System. Clay gave his support to Adams, and the House elected him.

The Jacksonians were enraged enough at this, but they became much angrier when the new president announced that Clay was to be secretary of state. The State Department was the well-established route to the presidency, and Adams thus appeared to be naming Clay as his own successor. To the Jacksonians, it seemed clear that Clay and Adams must have agreed to make each other president—Adams now, Clay next; and they expressed outrage at this "corrupt bargain." Very likely there had been some sort of understanding between Clay and Adams; and although there was nothing corrupt, or even unusual, about it, it proved to be politically costly for both men.

The Second President Adams

Throughout his term in the White House, Adams and his policies were thoroughly frustrated by the political bitterness arising from the "corrupt bargain." In his inaugural address and in his first message to Congress, Adams recommended "laws promoting the improvement of agriculture, commerce, and manufactures, the cultivation of the mechanic and of the elegant arts, the advancement of literature, and the progress of the sciences, ornamental and profound"—a nationalist program reminiscent of Clay's American System. But Jacksonians in Congress prevented him from securing appropriations for most of these goals. He did win several million dollars to improve rivers and harbors and to extend the National Road westward from Wheeling; this was more than Congress had appropriated for internal improvements under all his predecessors together, but it was far less than he and Clay had envisioned.

Adams also experienced diplomatic frustrations. He appointed delegates to an international conference that the Venezuelan liberator, Simón Bolívar, had called in Panama in 1826. But Southerners in Congress opposed the idea of white Americans mingling with black delegates from Haiti, which would be represented in Panama. And supporters of Jackson charged that Adams intended to sacrifice American interests and involve the nation in an entangling alliance. Congress delayed approving the Panama mission so long that the American delegation did not arrive until after the conference was over.

Adams also lost a contest with the state of Georgia, which wished to remove the remaining Creek and Cherokee Indians from the state to gain their land as additional soil for cotton planters. The United States government, in a 1791 treaty, had guaranteed that land to the Creeks; but in 1825, white Georgians had extracted a new treaty from William McIntosh, the leader of one faction in the tribe and a long-time advocate of Indian cooperation with the United States. In the new treaty, the Creeks ceded their tribal lands in Georgia and Alabama and agreed to move west. The president believed the new treaty had no legal force, since McIntosh clearly did not represent the wishes of the tribe. Adams refused to enforce the treaty, setting up a direct conflict between the president and the state. The governor of Georgia defied the president and went ahead with plans for Indian removal. In 1827, the Creeks succumbed to pressure from Georgia and agreed to still another treaty, in which they again yielded their land, thus undercutting Adams's position.

Even more damaging to the administration was its support for a new tariff on imported goods in 1828. This measure originated in the demands of Massachusetts and Rhode Island woolen manufacturers, who complained that the British were dumping textiles on the American market at prices with which the domestic mill owners could not compete. They won support from the middle and Western states, but at the cost of provisions that antagonized the original New England supporters of the bill. The Western provisions placed high duties not only on woolens, as the New Englanders had wanted, but also on items the West produced. That distressed New England manufacturers; the benefits of protecting their manufactured goods from foreign competition now had to be weighed against the prospects of having to pay more for raw materials. The bill presented Adams with a dilemma, for he would lose friends whether he signed or vetoed it. Adams signed it, earning the animosity of Southerners, who cursed it as the "tariff of abominations."

Jackson Triumphant

By the time of the 1828 presidential election, a new two-party system had begun to emerge as a result of the divisions among the Republicans. On one side stood the supporters of John Quincy Adams, who called themselves the National Republicans and who supported the economic nationalism of the preceding years. Opposing them were the followers of Andrew Jackson, who took the name Democratic Republicans and who called for an assault on privilege and a widening of opportunity. Adams attracted the support of most of the remaining Federalists; Jackson appealed to a broad coalition that opposed the "economic aristocracy." But issues seemed to count for little in the end, as the campaign degenerated into a war of personal invective.

Jackson's victory was decisive, if sectional. He won 56 percent of the popular vote and an electoral majority of 178 votes to 83. But Adams swept virtually all of New England, and he showed significant strength in the mid-Atlantic region. Nevertheless, the Jacksonians considered their victory as complete and as important as Jefferson's in 1800. Once again, they believed, the forces of privilege had been driven from Washington. Once again, a champion of democracy would occupy the White House and restore liberty to the society and the economy. America had entered, some Jacksonians claimed, the "era of the common man."

Jacksonian America

ANY AMERICANS WERE growing apprehensive about the future of their republic in the 1820s and 1830s, as the nation expanded both economically and territorially. Some feared that the rapid growth of the United States would produce social chaos; they insisted that the country's first priority must be to establish order and a clear system of authority. Others argued that the greatest danger facing the nation was the growth of inequality and privilege; they believed that society's goal should be to eliminate the favored status of powerful elites and make opportunity more widely available. Advocates of this latter vision seized control of the federal government in 1829 with the inauguration of Andrew Jackson.

Despite their enthusiasm for the idea of democracy, Jackson and his followers were imperfect democrats. They did nothing to challenge (and indeed much to support) the existence of slavery; they supervised one of the most vicious assaults on American Indians in the nation's history; and they readily accepted economic, social, and gender inequality. Jackson himself was a frontier aristocrat, and most of those who served him were people of wealth and standing. But the Jacksonians were not usually aristocrats by birth. Convinced that they had risen to prominence on the basis of their own talents and energies, their goal in public life was to ensure that others like themselves would have the opportunity to do the same.

THE ADVENT OF MASS POLITICS

On March 4, 1829, thousands of Americans from all regions of the country—including many farmers, laborers, and others of humble rank—crowded before the United States Capitol to watch the inauguration of

Andrew Jackson. After the ceremonies, the crowd poured into a public reception at the White House, where, in their eagerness to shake the new president's hand, the people filled the state rooms to overflowing, trampled one another, soiled the carpets, and ruined the upholstery. "It was a proud day for the people," wrote Amos Kendall, one of Jackson's closest political associates. But Supreme Court Justice Joseph Story, a friend and colleague of John Marshall, looked on the inaugural levee, as it was called, and remarked with disgust: "The reign of King 'Mob' seems triumphant."

In fact, the "age of Jackson" was less a triumph of the people than Kendall hoped and Story feared. But it did mark a transformation of American politics that extended power widely to new groups. Once restricted to a relatively small group of property owners, politics now became open to virtually all the nation's white male citizens. In a political sense at least, the era had at least some claim to the title the Jacksonians gave it: the "age of the common man."

The Expanding Electorate

Until the 1820s, relatively few Americans had been permitted to vote; most states restricted the franchise to white male property owners or taxpayers or both, effectively removing a great mass of the less affluent from the voting roles. But even before Jackson's election, the franchise began to expand. Change came first in Ohio and other new states of the West, which, on joining the Union, adopted constitutions that guaranteed all adult white males the right to vote and permitted all voters the right to hold public office. Older states, concerned about the loss of their population to the West, began to grant similar political rights to their citizens, dropping or reducing their property ownership or taxpaying requirements. Eventually, every state democratized its electorate to some degree, although some later and less fully than others.

The wave of state reforms was generally peaceful, but in Rhode Island democratization efforts created considerable instability. The Rhode Island constitution (which was still basically the old colonial charter) barred more than half the adult males in the state from voting in the 1830s. The conservative legislature, chosen by this restricted electorate, consistently blocked all efforts at reform. In 1840, the lawyer and activist Thomas L. Dorr and a group of his followers formed a "People's party," held a convention, drafted a new constitution, and submitted it to a popular vote. It was overwhelmingly approved. The existing legislature rejected the Dorr docu-

JACKSON'S INAUGURAL LEVEE, 1829 Even in the relatively rustic days of
the early republic, presidential inaugurations often took place amid almost monarchical grandeur. But when Andrew Jackson entered office in
1829, having won election as the champion of democratic simplicity, he
avoided formal trappings and threw the White House open to the public.

ment and submitted a new constitution of its own to the voters. It was
narrowly defeated. The Dorrites, in the meantime, had begun to set up a
new government, under their own constitution, with Dorr as governor; and
so, in 1842, two governments were laying claims to legitimacy in Rhode
Island. The old state government proclaimed that Dorr and his followers
were rebels and began to imprison them. The Dorrites, in the meantime,
made a brief and ineffectual effort to capture the state arsenal. The Dorr
Rebellion, as it was known, quickly failed, and Dorr himself surrendered
and was briefly imprisoned. But the episode helped spur the old guard to
draft a new constitution, which greatly expanded the suffrage.

The democratization process was far from complete. In much of the
South, election laws continued to favor the planters and politicians of the
older counties and to limit the influence of more newly settled Western
areas. Free blacks could not vote anywhere in the South and hardly anywhere
in the North. Pennsylvania, in fact, amended its state constitution in 1838
to strip blacks of the right to vote, which they had previously enjoyed. In no
state could women vote. Nowhere was the ballot secret, and often it was cast
as a spoken vote rather than a written one, which meant that voters could
be, and often were, bribed or intimidated.

Despite the persisting limitations, however, the number of voters increased at a much more rapid rate than did the population as a whole. Indeed, one of the most striking political trends of the early nineteenth century was the change in the method of choosing presidential electors and the dramatic increase in popular participation in the process. In 1800, the legislature had chosen the presidential electors in ten states, and the people in only six. By 1828, electors were chosen by popular vote in every state but South Carolina. In the presidential election of 1824, fewer than 27 percent of adult white males had voted. In the election of 1828, the figure was 58 percent; and in 1840, 80 percent.

The high level of voter participation was only in part the result of an expanded electorate. It was also the result of a growing popular interest in politics and a strengthening of party organization.

The Legitimation of Party

Although party competition was part of American politics almost from the beginning of the republic, acceptance of the *idea* of party was not. For more than thirty years, most Americans who had opinions about the nature of government considered parties evils to be avoided and thought the nation should seek a broad consensus in which permanent factional lines would not exist. But in the 1820s and 1830s, those assumptions gave way to a new view: that permanent, institutionalized parties were a desirable part of the political process, that indeed they were essential to democracy.

The elevation of the idea of party occurred first at the state level, most prominently in New York. There, Martin Van Buren led a dissident political faction (known as the "Bucktails" or the "Albany Regency"). In the years after the War of 1812 this group began to challenge the established political elite—led by the aristocratic governor, De Witt Clinton—that had dominated the state for years. Factional rivalries were not new, of course; what was new about this one was the way in which Van Buren and his followers posed their challenge. Refuting the traditional view of a political party as undemocratic, they argued that only an institutionalized party, based in the populace at large, could ensure genuine democracy. The alternative was the sort of closed elite that Clinton had created. In this new kind of party, ideological commitments would be less important than loyalty to the party itself. Above all, for a party to survive, it must have a permanent opposition. Competing parties would give each political faction a sense of purpose; they would force politicians to remain continually sensitive to the will of the people; and they would check and balance each other in much the same way that the different branches of government checked and balanced one another.

By the late 1820s, this new idea of party was spreading beyond New York. The election of Jackson in 1828, the result of a popular movement that stood apart from the usual political elites, seemed further to legitimize it. In the 1830s, finally, a fully formed two-party system began to operate at the national level, with each party committed to its own existence as an institution and willing to accept the legitimacy of its opposition. The anti-Jackson forces began to call themselves the Whigs. Jackson's followers called themselves Democrats, thus giving a permanent name to the nation's oldest political party.

President of the Common Man

The Democratic party may have had no single ideological position, but Andrew Jackson himself did embrace a distinct, if simple, theory of democracy. Government, he said, should offer "equal protection and equal benefits" to all its white male citizens and favor no one region or class over another. In practice, that meant an assault on what Jackson and his associates considered the citadels of the Eastern aristocracy and an effort to extend opportunities to the rising classes of the West and the South.

Jackson's first target was the entrenched officeholders in the federal government, many of whom had been in place for a generation or more. Jackson bitterly denounced what he considered a "class" of permanent officeholders. Offices, he said, belonged to the people, not to a self-serving bureaucracy. Equally important, a large turnover in the bureaucracy would give him enormous patronage; it would allow him to reward his own supporters with offices.

One of his henchmen, William L. Marcy of New York, once explained, "To the victors belong the spoils"; and the process of giving out jobs as political rewards became known as the "spoils system." In the end, during the eight years of his presidency Jackson removed no more than one-fifth of the federal officeholders. But by embracing the philosophy of the "spoils system," a system already well entrenched in a number of state governments, the Jackson administration helped fix it firmly upon American politics.

Jackson supporters also worked to transform the process by which presidential candidates were selected. They had long resented the congressional caucus, which Jackson himself had avoided in 1828. In 1832, the president's followers staged a national convention to renominate him. In later generations, some would come to see the party convention as the source of corruption and political exclusivity, but those who created it in the 1830s considered it a great triumph for democracy. Through the convention, they believed, power in the party would arise directly from the people rather than from such elite political institutions as the caucus.

The spoils system and the political convention did limit the power of two entrenched elites—permanent officeholders and the exclusive party caucus. Yet neither really transferred power to the common people. Appointments to office almost always went to prominent political allies of the president and his associates. Delegates to national conventions were less often common men than members of local party elites. Political opportunity within the party was expanding, but much less so than Jacksonian rhetoric suggested.

"OUR FEDERAL UNION"

Jackson's belief in extending power beyond entrenched elites led him to want to reduce the functions of the federal government. A concentration of power in Washington would, he believed, restrict opportunity to those favored few with political connections. But Jackson also believed in forceful presidential leadership and was strongly committed to the preservation of the Union. Thus at the same time that Jackson was promoting an economic program to reduce the power of the national government, he was asserting the supremacy of the Union in the face of a potent challenge. For no sooner had he entered office than his own vice president—John C. Calhoun—began to champion a controversial (and, Jackson believed, dangerous) constitutional theory: nullification.

Calhoun and Nullification

Calhoun was forty-six years old in 1828, with a distinguished past and an apparently promising future. Running for vice president with Andrew Jackson, he could, it seemed, look forward to the presidency itself.

But the smoldering issue of the tariff created a dilemma for him. Once he had been an outspoken protectionist, strongly supporting the tariff of 1816. But by the late 1820s, many South Carolinians had come to believe that the tariff was responsible for the stagnation of their state's economy. In fact, that stagnation was largely a result of the exhaustion of South Carolina's farmland, which could no longer compete effectively with the newly opened and fertile lands of the Southwest. But most Carolinians blamed the "tariff of abominations" of 1828. Some exasperated Carolinians were ready to consider a drastic remedy—secession.

Calhoun's future political hopes rested on how he met this challenge in his home state. He did so by developing a theory that he believed offered a more moderate alternative to secession: the theory of nullification. Drawing from the ideas of Madison and Jefferson and their Virginia and Kentucky Resolutions of 1798–1799 and citing the Tenth Amendment to the Constitution, Calhoun argued that since the federal government was a creation of the states, the states—not the courts or Congress—were the final arbiters of the constitutionality of federal laws. If a state concluded that Congress had passed an unconstitutional law, then it could hold a special convention and declare the federal law null and void within the state. The nullification doctrine—and the idea of using it to nullify the 1828 tariff—quickly attracted broad support in South Carolina.

Calhoun's real hope was that the nullification theory would never be put to the test but would simply pressure the federal government to reduce

JOHN C. CALHOUN John Wesley Jarvis painted this portrait of a relatively young John C. Calhoun—before his identification with Southern nationalism destroyed what had once seemed his bright prospects for election to the presidency.

tariff rates. But Calhoun did not, he soon discovered, have as much influence in the new administration as he had hoped. For he had a powerful rival in Martin Van Buren.

The Rise of Van Buren

Van Buren was about the same age as Calhoun and equally ambitious. As leader of the Democratic party organization of New York, he had helped carry the state for Jackson in 1828 while getting himself elected governor. Van Buren resigned the governorship and went to Washington in 1829 when Jackson called him to head the new cabinet as secretary of state.

Jackson relied for advice on an unofficial circle of political allies who came to be known as the "Kitchen Cabinet," which included such Democratic newspaper editors as Isaac Hill of New Hampshire and Amos Kendall and Francis P. Blair of Kentucky. Van Buren alone was a member of both the official cabinet and this unofficial circle; so his influence with the president was unmatched. The two men grew closer still through a curious quarrel over etiquette that drove a wedge between the president and Calhoun.

Peggy O'Neale was the attractive daughter of a Washington tavern keeper with whom both Andrew Jackson and his friend John H. Eaton had taken lodgings while serving as senators from Tennessee. O'Neale was married, but rumors circulated in Washington in the mid-1820s that she and Senator Eaton were having an affair. O'Neale's husband died in 1828, and she and Eaton were soon married. A few weeks later, Jackson named Eaton secretary of war and thus made the new Mrs. Eaton a cabinet wife. The rest of the administration wives, led by Mrs. Calhoun, refused to receive her. Jackson (remembering the effects of public slander directed against his own late wife) was furious and demanded that the members of the cabinet accept her into their social world. Calhoun, under pressure from his wife, refused. Van Buren, a widower, befriended the Eatons and thus ingratiated himself with Jackson.

By 1831, partly as a result of the Peggy Eaton affair, Jackson had chosen Van Buren to succeed him in the White House. Calhoun's dreams of the presidency had all but vanished.

The Webster-Hayne Debate

In January 1830, a great debate in the United States Senate dramatically revealed the degree to which sectional issues were intruding into national politics. The controversy grew out of a seemingly routine Senate discussion of federal policy toward the public lands in the West. In the midst of the debate, a senator from Connecticut suggested that all land sales and surveys be temporarily discontinued. Senator Thomas Hart Benton of Missouri, the Jacksonian leader in the Senate, attacked the proposal, charging that it would serve the economic needs of the Northeast at the expense of the West.

Robert Y. Hayne, a young senator from South Carolina, took up Benton's argument. He had no direct interest in the Western lands, but he and other Southerners saw the issue as a way to win Western support for their drive to lower the tariff. Hayne argued that the South and the West were both victims of the tyranny of the Northeast and hinted that the two regions might combine to defend themselves against that tyranny.

Daniel Webster, now a senator from Massachusetts, took the floor the day after Hayne's speech. Although once an advocate of states' rights and an opponent of the tariff, he had changed his own position as the sectional passions of his own region had ebbed. Now he attacked Hayne, and through him Calhoun, for what he considered their challenge to the integrity of the Union. He was, in effect, challenging Hayne to a debate not on public lands and the tariff but on the issue of states' rights versus national power. Hayne, coached by Calhoun, responded with a defense of the theory of nullification. Webster then spent two full afternoons delivering what became known as his "Second Reply to Hayne," a speech that Northerners quoted and revered for years to come. He concluded with the ringing appeal: "Liberty *and* Union, now and for ever, one and inseparable!"

Calhoun's followers believed Hayne had the better of the argument, but their main concern was what President Jackson thought. The answer became clear at the annual Democratic party banquet in honor of Thomas Jefferson. After dinner, guests delivered a series of toasts. The president arrived with a written text in which he had underscored certain words: "Our *Federal* Union—*It must be preserved.*" While he spoke, he looked directly at Calhoun. The diminutive Van Buren, who stood on his chair to see better, thought he saw Calhoun's hand shake and a trickle of wine run down his glass as he responded to the president's toast with his own: "The Union— next to our liberty most dear." Sharp lines had been drawn.

The Nullification Crisis

In 1832, finally, the controversy over nullification produced a crisis when South Carolinians responded angrily to a congressional tariff bill that offered them no relief from the 1828 "tariff of abominations." Some militant South Carolinians were ready to secede from the Union, but Calhoun persuaded them to turn to nullification instead. The supporters of nullification won a substantial victory in the state elections of 1832. Almost immediately, the newly elected legislature summoned a state convention, which voted to nullify the tariffs of 1828 and 1832 and to forbid the collection of duties within the state. At the same time, South Carolina elected Hayne to serve as governor and Calhoun (who resigned as vice president) to replace Hayne as senator.

Jackson insisted that nullification was treason and that its adherents were traitors. He strengthened the federal forts in South Carolina and ordered a warship and several revenue ships to Charleston. When Congress convened early in 1833, Jackson's followers won approval of a force bill authorizing the president to use the military to see that acts of Congress were obeyed. Violence seemed a real possibility early in 1833.

Calhoun faced a predicament as he took his place in the Senate. Not a single state had come to South Carolina's support. Even South Carolina itself was divided and could not hope to prevail in a showdown with the federal government. Calhoun was saved by the timely intervention of Henry Clay, newly elected to the Senate, who devised a compromise by which the tariff would be lowered gradually until in 1842 it would reach approximately the same level as in 1816. The compromise and the force bill were passed on the same day, March 1, 1833. Jackson signed them both.

In South Carolina, the convention reassembled and repealed its nullification of the tariffs. But unwilling to allow Congress to have the last word, the convention nullified the force act—a purely symbolic act, since the tariff toward which the force act was directed had already been repealed. Calhoun and his followers claimed a victory for nullification, which had, they insisted, forced the revision of the tariff. They had some justification for doing so. But the episode taught Calhoun and his allies an important lesson: No state could defy the federal government alone.

The Removal of the Indians

Jackson's presidency coincided with a new and decisive phase in the long struggle between white settlement and Indian rights in the lands east of the Mississippi River. Jackson approached the conflict with a deep antipathy toward the tribes. That was in part a result of his earlier experiences leading military attacks against them; but it was also a result of a now widely shared view of Indians somewhat different from the view many Americans had embraced in the past.

In the eighteenth century, many whites had shared Thomas Jefferson's view of the Indians as "noble savages," peoples without real civilization but with an inherent dignity that made civilization possible among them. By the first decades of the nineteenth century, this vaguely philanthropic attitude was fading, particularly among the whites in the West. They were coming to view Native Americans simply as "savages," not only uncivilized but uncivilizable. Hence one reason for the growing white commitment to removing the Indians from all the lands east of the Mississippi was the belief that whites should not be expected to live in close proximity to savages. White Westerners also favored removal to put an end to violence and conflict in the Western areas of white settlement. Most of all, however, they favored Indian removal because the tribes still possessed valuable acreage that whites wanted.

The federal government had already removed many Indians from the East before Jackson became president, but substantial tribal enclaves remained. In the Old Northwest, the long process of expelling the woodland Indians culminated in a last battle in 1831–1832. An alliance of Sauk (or Sac) and Fox Indians under the fabled and now aged warrior Black Hawk fought white settlers in Illinois in an effort to overturn a treaty ceding tribal lands in that state to the United States; Black Hawk and his followers considered the agreement, signed by a rival tribal faction, illegal. The Illinois state militia and federal troops defeated the Indians. The Black Hawk War was notable for the viciousness of the white military efforts. White forces attacked the Indians even when they attempted to surrender, pursued them as they retreated, and slaughtered many of them.

More troubling to the government in the 1830s were the remaining Indian tribes of the South. In western Georgia, Alabama, Mississippi, and Florida lived what were known as the "Five Civilized Tribes"—the Cherokee, Creek, Seminole, Chickasaw, and Choctaw—most of whom had established settled and productive agricultural societies. They were, therefore, even more closely tied to their lands than many of the more nomadic tribes to the north.

The federal government had worked steadily through the first decades of the nineteenth century to negotiate treaties with the Southern Indians that would remove them to the West and open their lands for white settlement. But the negotiating process did not proceed fast enough to satisfy the region's whites. In 1830, finally, Congress passed the Removal Act, which appropriated new funds for negotiating treaties with the Southern tribes and relocating them in the West. By then, several Southern state governments were taking measures of their own to speed the removal. Most

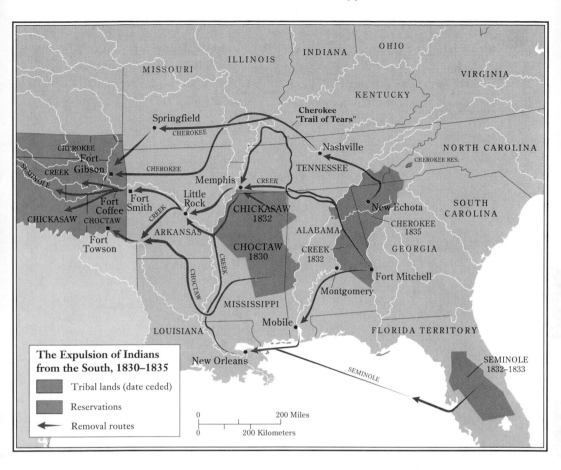

The Expulsion of Indians from the South, 1830–1835

Tribal lands (date ceded)

Reservations

Removal routes

0   200 Miles

0   200 Kilometers

tribes were too weak to resist white pressures and ceded their lands in return for only token payments. Some, however, resisted.

The Cherokees tried to stop the encroachments by the state of Georgia through an appeal in the Supreme Court, and the Court's decisions in *Cherokee Nation* v. *Georgia* and *Worcester* v. *Georgia* (see pp. 235–236) supported the tribe's contention that the state had no authority to negotiate with tribal representatives. But the Jackson administration refused to enforce the decisions.

In 1835, the United States government extracted a treaty from a minority faction of the Cherokees that ceded to Georgia the tribe's land in that state in return for $5 million and a reservation west of the Mississippi. The great majority of the 17,000 Cherokees did not recognize the treaty as legitimate and refused to leave their homes. But Jackson sent an army of 7,000 under General Winfield Scott to round them up and drive them westward. About 1,000 fled to North Carolina, where eventually the federal government provided them with a reservation in the Smoky Mountains that survives today. But most of the rest made a long, forced trek to Oklahoma beginning in the winter of 1838. Thousands, perhaps a quarter or more of the émigrés, perished before reaching their unwanted destination. In the harsh new reservations in which they were now forced to live, the survivors remembered the terrible journey as "The Trail Where They Cried," the Trail of Tears.

Between 1830 and 1838, virtually all the Five Civilized Tribes were expelled from the Southern states and forced to travel along their own Trail of Tears to "Indian Territory" (formally created by the Indian Intercourse Act of 1834), in what later became Oklahoma. The new territory seemed safely removed from existing white settlements and embraced land that most whites considered undesirable. It had the additional advantage, the government believed, of being bordered on the west by what explorers such as Edwin James and Stephen H. Long had christened the "Great American

THE TRAIL OF TEARS This twentieth-century painting by Robert Lindneux shows the forced evacuation of 18,000 Cherokee Indians from their ancestral lands in Georgia beginning in 1838. An epidemic of smallpox, along with starvation and exposure, cost thousands of Indians their lives. Here the Cherokees, guarded by soldiers carrying guns and bayonets, cross the Missouri River on their way to their new and unfamiliar homes in what is now Oklahoma.

Desert," land deemed unfit for habitation. Whites seemed unlikely ever to settle along the western borders of the Indian Territory, which meant that further conflict might be avoided. The Choctaws of Mississippi and western Alabama were the first to make the trek, beginning in 1830. The army moved out the Creeks of eastern Alabama and western Georgia in 1836. The Chickasaw in northern Mississippi began the long march westward a year later, and the Cherokees, finally, a year after that.

Only the Seminoles in Florida managed to resist the pressures, and even their success was limited. Like other tribes, the Seminoles had agreed under pressure to a settlement (the 1832–1833 treaties of Payne's Landing) by which they ceded their lands and agreed to move to Indian Territory within three years. Most did move west, but a substantial minority, under the leadership of the chieftain Osceola, balked and staged an uprising beginning in 1835 to defend their lands. (Joining the Indians in their struggle was a group of runaway black slaves, who had been living with the tribe.) The Seminole War dragged on for years. Jackson sent troops to Florida, but the Seminoles with their black associates were masters of guerrilla warfare in the jungle-like Everglades. Finally, in 1842, the government abandoned the war. By then, many of the Seminoles had been either killed or forced westward. But the relocation of the Seminoles, unlike the relocation of most of the other tribes, was never complete.

By the end of the 1830s, virtually all the important Indian societies east of the Mississippi (with a few exceptions such as the Seminoles and Cherokees) had been removed to the West. The tribes had ceded over 100 million acres of Eastern land to the federal government; they had received in return about $68 million and 32 million acres in the far less hospitable lands west of the Mississippi. There they lived, divided by tribe into a series of separate reservations, in a territory surrounded by a string of United States forts to keep them in (and to keep most whites out), in a region whose climate and topography bore little relation to anything they had known before. Eventually, even this forlorn enclave would face encroachments from white civilization.

JACKSON AND THE BANK WAR

Jackson was quite willing to use federal power against the Indian tribes. Where white Americans were concerned, however, he was consistently opposed to concentrating power either in the federal government or in elite institutions associated with it. An early example of that was his 1830 veto of a congressional measure providing a subsidy to the proposed Maysville Road in Kentucky. The bill was unconstitutional, Jackson argued, because the road in question lay entirely within Kentucky and was not, therefore, a part of "interstate commerce." But the bill was also unwise, because it committed the government to what Jackson considered extravagant expenditures. A similar resistance to federal power lay behind the most celebrated episode of Jackson's presidency: the war against the Bank of the United States.

Biddle's Institution

With its headquarters in Philadelphia and its branches in twenty-nine other cities, the Bank of the United States had a monopoly on the deposits of the federal government, which owned one-fifth of the Bank's stock; it also did a tremendous business in general banking. It provided credit to growing enterprises; it issued bank notes which served as a dependable medium of exchange throughout the country; and it exercised a restraining effect on the less well managed state banks. Nicholas Biddle, president of the Bank from 1823 on, had done much to put the institution on a sound and prosperous basis. Nevertheless, Andrew Jackson was determined to destroy it, convinced that it was a citadel of privilege that benefited Eastern elites and impeded the rise of aspiring capitalists in the West and elsewhere.

Opposition to the Bank came from two very different groups: the "soft-money" faction and the "hard-money" faction. Advocates of soft money consisted largely of state bankers and their allies. They objected to the Bank of the United States because it restrained the state banks from issuing notes freely. The hard-money people believed that coin was the only safe currency, and they condemned all banks that issued bank notes, including the Bank of the United States. The soft-money advocates were believers in rapid economic growth and speculation; the hard-money forces embraced older ideas of "public virtue" and looked with suspicion on expansion and speculation. Jackson himself supported the hard-money position, but he was also sensitive to the complaints of his many soft-money supporters in the West and the South. He made it clear that he would not favor renewing the charter of the Bank of the United States, which was due to expire in 1836.

Biddle was a Philadelphia aristocrat, unaccustomed to politics. But in his efforts to save the Bank, he began granting banking favors to influential men. In particular, he relied on Senators Clay and Webster, the latter of whom was connected with the Bank as legal counsel, director of the Boston branch, a frequent, heavy borrower, and Biddle's personal friend. Clay, Webster, and other advisers persuaded Biddle to apply to Congress for a recharter bill in 1832, four years ahead of the expiration date. Congress passed the recharter bill; Jackson vetoed it; and the Bank's supporters in Congress failed to override the veto. The Bank question then emerged as the paramount issue of the 1832 election, just as Clay had hoped.

In 1832, Clay ran for president as the unanimous choice of the National Republicans, who held a nominating convention in Baltimore late in 1831. But the "Bank War" failed to provide Clay with the winning issue for which he had hoped. Jackson, with Van Buren as his running mate, overwhelmingly defeated Clay (and several minor-party candidates) with 55 percent of the popular vote and 219 electoral votes (more than four times as many as Clay received). The results were a defeat not only for Clay but for Biddle.

The "Monster" Destroyed

Jackson was now more determined than ever to destroy the "monster." He could not legally abolish the institution before the expiration of its charter, but he could weaken it. He decided to remove the government's deposits from the Bank. His secretary of the treasury believed that such an action would destabilize the financial system and refused to give the order. Jackson removed him and appointed a replacement. When the new secretary similarly procrastinated, Jackson named a third: Roger B. Taney, the attorney general, a close friend and loyal ally of the president.

Taney began drawing on the government's deposits in the Bank of the United States and placing incoming receipts in a number of state banks (which Jackson's enemies called "pet banks"). When the administration began to transfer funds directly from the Bank of the United States to the pet banks (as opposed to the initial practice of simply depositing new funds in those banks), Biddle called in loans and raised interest rates, explaining that without the government deposits the Bank's resources were stretched too thin. He realized his actions were likely to cause financial distress, and he reasoned that a short recession would cause Congress to recharter the Bank.

As financial conditions worsened in the winter of 1833–1834, supporters of the Bank organized meetings around the country and sent petitions to Washington urging a rechartering of the Bank. But the Jacksonians blamed the recession on Biddle and refused to budge. The banker finally carried his contraction of credit too far and had to reverse himself to appease the business community. His hopes of winning a recharter of the Bank died in the process.

Jackson had won a considerable political victory. But when the Bank of the United States died in 1836, the country lost an important financial institution and was left with a fragmented and chronically unstable banking system that would plague the economy for many years.

The Taney Court

In the aftermath of the Bank War, Jackson moved against the most powerful institution of economic nationalism: the Supreme Court. In 1835, when John Marshall died, the president appointed as the new chief justice his trusted ally Roger B. Taney. Taney did not bring a sharp break in constitutional interpretation, but he did help modify Marshall's vigorous nationalism.

Perhaps the clearest indication of the new judicial mood was the celebrated case of *Charles River Bridge* v. *Warren Bridge* of 1837. The case involved a dispute between two Massachusetts companies over the right to build a bridge across the Charles River between Boston and Cambridge. One company had a longstanding charter from the state to operate a toll bridge, a charter that the firm claimed guaranteed it a monopoly of the bridge traffic. Another company had applied to the legislature for authorization to construct a second, competing bridge that would—since it would be toll-free—greatly reduce the value of the first company's charter. The first company contended that in granting the second charter, the legislature was engaging in a breach of contract; and it noted that the Marshall Court, in the *Dartmouth College* case and other decisions, had ruled that states had no right to abrogate contracts. But now Taney, speaking for the Democratic majority on the Court, supported the right of Massachusetts to award the second charter. The object of government, Taney maintained, was to promote the general happiness, an object that took precedence over the rights of property. A state, therefore, had the right to amend or abrogate a contract if such action was necessary to advance the well-being of the community. The decision reflected one of the cornerstones of the Jacksonian idea: that the key to democracy was an expansion of economic opportunity, which would not occur if older corporations could maintain monopolies and choke off competition from newer companies.

THE EMERGENCE
OF THE SECOND PARTY SYSTEM

Jackson's forceful—some claimed tyrannical—tactics in crushing first the nullification movement and then the Bank of the United States helped galvanize a growing opposition coalition that by the mid-1830s was ready to assert itself in national politics. It began as a gathering of national political leaders opposed to Jackson's use of power. Denouncing the president as "King Andrew I," they began to refer to themselves as Whigs, after the party in England that traditionally worked to limit the power of the king. As the new party began to develop as a national organization with constituencies in every state, its appeal became more diffuse. Nevertheless, both in its philosophy and in the nature of its membership, the Whig party was different from the party of Jackson.

With the emergence of the Whigs, the nation once again had two competing political parties. What scholars now call the "second party system" had begun what would turn out to be its relatively brief life.

The Two Parties

The philosophy of the Democratic party in the 1830s bore the stamp of Andrew Jackson, but it drew from many older traditions as well. Democrats envisioned a future of steadily expanding opportunities. The function of government, therefore, was to remove artificial obstacles to that expansion and to avoid creating new obstacles of its own. The federal government should be limited in power, except to the degree that it worked to eliminate social and economic arrangements that entrenched privilege and stifled opportunity. The rights of states should be protected except to the extent that state governments interfered with social and economic mobility. Jacksonian Democrats celebrated "honest workers," "simple farmers," and "forthright businessmen" and contrasted them to the corrupt, monopolistic, aristocratic forces of established wealth.

The Jacksonians were not hostile to wealth. Most Democrats believed in material progress, and many party leaders—including Jackson himself—were wealthy men. Yet Democrats tended to look with suspicion on government efforts to stimulate commercial and industrial growth. These efforts, they believed, generally produced such menacing institutions of power as the Bank of the United States. Democrats were less likely than Whigs to support chartered banks and corporations, state-supported internal improvements, even public schools. They were more likely than Whigs to support territorial expansion, which would, they believed, widen opportunities for aspiring Americans. Among the most radical members of the party—the so-called Locofocos, mainly workingmen and small businessmen and professionals in the Northeast—sentiment was strong for a vigorous, perhaps even violent, assault on monopoly and privilege far in advance of anything Jackson himself ever contemplated.

The political philosophy that became known as Whiggery favored expanding the power of the federal government, encouraging industrial and commercial development, and knitting the country together into a consolidated economic system. Whigs embraced material progress enthusiastically, but they were cautious about westward expansion, fearful that rapid territorial growth would produce instability. Their vision of America was of a nation embracing the industrial future and rising to world greatness as a commercial and manufacturing power. And although Whigs insisted that their vision would result in increasing opportunities for all Americans, they tended to attribute particular value to the elites they considered the enterprising, modernizing forces in society—the entrepreneurs and institutions that most effectively promoted economic growth. Thus while Democrats were inclined to oppose legislation establishing banks, corporations, and other modernizing institutions, Whigs generally favored such measures.

To some extent, the constituencies of the two major parties were reflections of these diffuse philosophies. The Whigs were strongest among the more substantial merchants and manufacturers of the Northeast; the wealthier planters of the South (those who favored commercial development and the strengthening of ties with the North); and the ambitious farmers and rising commercial class of the West—usually migrants from the Northeast—who advocated internal improvements, expanding trade, and rapid economic progress. The Democrats drew more support from smaller merchants and the workingmen of the Northeast; from Southern planters suspicious of industrial growth; and from Westerners—usually with Southern roots—who favored a predominantly agrarian economy and opposed the development of powerful economic institutions in their region. Whigs tended to be wealthier than Democrats, tended to have more aristocratic backgrounds, and tended to be more commercially ambitious.

But Whigs and Democrats alike were more interested in winning elections than in maintaining philosophical purity. And both parties made adjustments from region to region in order to attract the largest possible number of voters, often at the sacrifice of party philosophy. In New York, for example, the Whigs developed a popular following through a movement known as Anti-Masonry. The Anti-Mason party had emerged in the 1820s in response to widespread resentment against the secret and exclusive, hence supposedly undemocratic, Society of Freemasons. Such resentments increased in 1826 when a former Mason, William Morgan, mysteriously disappeared from his home in Batavia, New York, shortly before he was scheduled to publish a book purporting to expose the secrets of Freemasonry. The assumption was widespread that Morgan had been abducted and murdered by the vengeful Masons. Whigs seized on the Anti-Mason frenzy to launch spirited attacks on Jackson and Van Buren (both Freemasons), implying that the Democrats were connected with the antidemocratic conspiracy. By embracing Anti-Masonry, Whigs were portraying themselves as opponents of aristocracy and exclusivity. They were, in other words, attacking the Democrats with the Democrats' own issues. (Later, Anti-Masonry grew powerful enough to become the basis of a new political party.)

Religious and ethnic divisions also played an important role in determining the constituencies of the two parties. Irish and German Catholics, among the largest of the recent immigrant groups, tended to support the Democrats, who appeared to share their own vague aversion to commercial development and entrepreneurial progress and who seemed to respect and protect their cultural values and habits. Evangelical Protestants gravitated toward the Whigs because they associated the party with constant development and improvement, goals their own religion embraced. They envisioned a society progressing steadily toward unity and order, and they looked on the new immigrant communities as a threat to that progress—as groups that needed to be disciplined and taught "American" ways. In many communities, these and other local ethnic, religious, and cultural tensions were far more influential in determining party alignments than any concrete political or economic proposals.

The Whig party was more successful at defining its positions and attracting a constituency than it was in uniting behind a national leader. No one person was ever able to command the loyalties of the party in the way Jackson commanded the loyalties of the Democrats. Instead, Whigs tended to divide among three major figures: Henry Clay, Daniel Webster, and John Calhoun. Clay won support from many of those who favored internal improvements and economic development, what he called the American System; but his image as a devious political operator and his identification with the West proved an insuperable liability. He ran for president three times and never won. Daniel Webster, the greatest orator of his era, won broad support with his passionate speeches in defense of the Constitution and the Union; but his close connection with the Bank of the United States and the protective tariff, his reliance on rich men for financial support, and his excessive fondness for brandy prevented him from developing enough of a national constituency to win him the office he so desperately wanted. John C. Calhoun, the third member of what became known as the Great Triumvirate, never considered himself a true Whig, and his identification with the nullification controversy in effect disqualified him from national leadership in any case. Yet he sided with Clay and Webster on the issue of the national bank. And he shared with them a strong animosity toward Andrew Jackson.

The Whigs, in other words, were able to marshal an imposing array of national leaders, each with his own powerful constituency. Yet for many years they were unable to find a way to merge those constituencies into a single winning combination. The result was that while Whigs competed relatively evenly with the Democrats in congressional, state, and local races, they managed to win only two presidential elections in the more than twenty years of their history.

Their problems became particularly clear in 1836. The Democrats were united behind Andrew Jackson's personal choice for president, Martin Van Buren. The Whigs could not even agree on a single candidate. Instead, they ran several candidates, hoping to profit from the regional strength of each. Webster represented the party in New England; Hugh Lawson White of Tennessee ran in the South; and the former Indian fighter and hero of the War of 1812 from Ohio, William Henry Harrison, was the candidate in the middle states and the West. None of the three candidates could expect to get a majority in the electoral college, but party leaders hoped they might separately draw enough votes from Van Buren to prevent his getting a majority and throw the election to the House of Representatives, where the Whigs might be better able to elect one of their candidates. In the end, however, the three Whigs were no match for the one Democrat. Van Buren won easily, with 170 electoral votes to 124 for all his opponents.

POLITICS AFTER JACKSON

Andrew Jackson retired from public life in 1837, the most beloved political figure of his age. Martin Van Buren was very different from his predecessor and far less fortunate. He was never able to match Jackson's personal popularity; and his administration was plagued with economic difficulties that hurt the Democrats and helped the Whigs.

The Panic of 1837

Van Buren's success in the 1836 election was a result in part of a nationwide economic boom that was reaching its height in that year. Canal and railroad builders were at a peak of activity. Prices were rising, money was plentiful, and credit was easy as banks increased their loans and notes with little regard to their reserves of cash. The land business, in particular, was booming.

Between 1835 and 1837 nearly 40 million acres of public land were sold, nearly three-fourths of it to speculators, who purchased large tracts in hopes of reselling them at a profit. These land sales, along with revenues the government received from the tariff of 1833, created a series of substantial federal budget surpluses and made possible a steady reduction of the national debt (something Jackson had always advocated). From 1835 to 1837, the government for the first and only time in its history was out of debt, with a substantial surplus in the Treasury.

Congress and the administration now faced the question of what to do with the Treasury surplus. Reducing the tariff was not an option, since no one wanted to raise that touchy issue again. Instead, support began to build for returning the federal surplus to the states. An 1836 "distribution" act required that the federal government pay its surplus funds to the states each year in four quarterly installments as interest-free, unsecured loans. No one expected the "loans" to be repaid. The states spent the money quickly, mainly to encourage construction of highways, railroads, and canals. The distribution of the surplus thus gave further stimulus to the economic boom. At the same time, the withdrawal of federal funds strained the state (or "pet") banks in which they had been deposited by the government; they had to call in their own loans to make the transfer of funds to the state governments.

Congress did nothing to check the speculative fever, with which many congressmen themselves were badly infected. Webster, for one, was buying up thousands of acres in the West. But Jackson, always suspicious of paper currency, was unhappy that the government was selling good land and receiving in return various state bank notes worth no more than the credit of the issuing bank. In 1836, not long before leaving office, he issued a presidential order, the "specie circular," which stipulated that only gold or silver coins or currency backed by gold or silver could be accepted in payment for public lands. Jackson was right to fear the speculative fever but wrong in thinking the specie circular would cure it. On the contrary, it produced a financial panic that began in the first months of Van Buren's presidency. Hundreds of banks and hundreds of businesses failed. Unemployment grew. There were bread riots in some of the larger cities. Prices fell, especially the price of land. Many railroad and canal schemes were abandoned; several of the debt-burdened state governments ceased to pay interest on their bonds, and a few repudiated their debts, at least temporarily. It was the worst depression in American history to that point, and it lasted for five years. It was a political catastrophe for Van Buren and the Democrats.

Both parties bore some responsibility for the panic. The distribution of the Treasury surplus, which had weakened the state banks and helped cause the crash, had been a Whig measure. Jackson's specie circular, which had started a run on the banks as land buyers rushed to trade in their bank notes for specie, was also to blame. But the depression was only partly a result of federal policies. England and western Europe were facing panics of their own, which meant that European (and especially English) investors had been withdrawing funds from America, putting an added strain on American banks. A succession of crop failures on American farms reduced the purchasing power of farmers and required increased imports of food, which sent more money out of the country. Whatever its actual causes, the Panic of 1837 occurred during a Democratic administration. The Democrats paid the political price for it.

WHIG HEADQUARTERS The Whig Party managed in 1840 to disguise its relatively elitist roots by portraying its presidential candidate, the patrician General William Henry Harrison, as a product of a log cabin who enjoyed drinking hard cider from a jug. Pictures of log cabins abounded in Whig campaign posters, as seen in this drawing of a Harrison rally in Philadelphia.

The Van Buren Program

The Van Buren administration, which strongly opposed government intervention in the economy, did little to fight the depression. Some of the steps it took—borrowing money to pay government debts and accepting only specie for payment of taxes—may have made things worse. Other efforts failed in Congress: a "preemption" bill that would have given settlers the right to buy government land near them before it was opened for public sale, and another bill that would have lowered the price of land. Van Buren did succeed in establishing a ten-hour workday on all federal projects by issuing a presidential order, but he had few other legislative achievements.

The most important and controversial measure in the president's program was a proposal for a new financial system to replace the Bank of the United States. Under Van Buren's plan, known as the "independent treasury" or "subtreasury" system, government funds would be placed in an independent treasury at Washington and in subtreasuries in other cities. No private banks would have the government's money or name to use as a basis for speculation; the government and the banks would be "divorced." Van Buren called a special session of Congress in 1837 to consider the proposal, which failed in the House. In 1840, the administration finally succeeded in driving the measure through both houses of Congress. As a result, the American banking system remained highly decentralized, and almost entirely free of federal regulation, until the Federal Reserve Act of 1913.

The Log Cabin Campaign

As the campaign of 1840 approached, the Whigs realized that they would have to settle on one candidate for president. Accordingly, they held their first national nominating convention in Harrisburg, Pennsylvania, in December 1839. Passing over Henry Clay, who expected the nomination, the convention chose William Henry Harrison and, for vice president, John Tyler of Virginia. Harrison was a descendant of the Virginia aristocracy but had spent his adult life in the Northwest. He was a renowned soldier and a popular national figure. The Democrats nominated Van Buren. But because their party was, in some respects, no more united than the Whigs, they failed to nominate a vice presidential candidate, leaving the choice of that office to the electors.

The 1840 campaign illustrated how fully the ethos of party competition (the subordination of ideology to immediate political needs) had established itself in America. The Whigs—who had emerged as a party largely because of their opposition to Andrew Jackson's common-man democracy, who in most regions represented the more affluent elements of the population, who favored government policies that would aid business—presented themselves in 1840 as the party of the common people. So, of course, did the Democrats. Both parties used the same techniques of mass voter appeal, the same evocation of simple, rustic values. What mattered now was not the philosophical purity of the party but its ability to win votes. The Whig campaign was particularly effective in portraying William Henry Harrison, a wealthy man with a considerable estate, as a simple man of the people who loved log cabins and hard cider. Against such techniques and the effects of the depression the Democrats could not win. Harrison won the election with 234 electoral votes to 60 for Van Buren and with a popular majority of 53 percent.

The Frustration of the Whigs

Despite their decisive victory, the Whigs were to find the next four years frustrating and divisive ones. In large part, that was because their appealing new president, "Old Tippecanoe," William Henry Harrison, died of pneumonia one month after taking office. John Tyler now became the first vice president to succeed a fallen president. He moved quickly to establish a full claim to the office, despite objections from some that he should be considered no more than "acting president." Control of the administration had fallen to a man with whom the Whig party leadership had relatively weak ties. Harrison had generally deferred to Henry Clay and Daniel Webster, whom he named secretary of state. Under Tyler, things soon changed.

Tyler was a former Democrat who had left the party in reaction to what he considered Jackson's excessively egalitarian program and his imperious methods. But there were still signs of his Democratic past in his approach to public policy. The president did agree to bills abolishing the independent treasury system and raising tariff rates. But he refused to support Clay's attempt to recharter the Bank of the United States. And he vetoed several internal improvement bills sponsored by Clay and other congressional Whigs. Finally, a conference of congressional Whigs (many of whom referred scornfully to the new president as "His Accidency") read Tyler out of the party. Every cabinet member but Webster resigned; five former Democrats took their places. When Webster, too, left the cabinet, Tyler appointed Calhoun, who had rejoined the Democratic party, to replace him.

A new political alignment was taking shape. Tyler and a small band of conservative Southern Whigs were preparing to rejoin the Democrats. Into the common man's party of Jackson and Van Buren was arriving a faction with decidedly aristocratic political ideas, men who thought that government had an obligation to protect and even expand the institution of slavery and who believed in states' rights with almost fanatical devotion.

Whig Diplomacy

In the midst of these domestic controversies, a series of incidents brought Great Britain and the United States to the brink of war in the late 1830s.

Residents of the eastern provinces of Canada launched a rebellion against the British colonial government in 1837, and some of the rebels chartered an American steamship, the *Caroline*, to ship them supplies across the Niagara River from New York. British authorities in Canada seized the *Caroline* and burned it, killing one American in the process. The British government refused either to disavow the attack or to provide compensation for it, and resentment in the United States was high.

At the same time, tensions flared over the boundary between Canada and Maine, which had been in dispute since the treaty of 1783. In 1838, groups of Americans and Canadians, mostly lumberjacks, began moving into the Aroostook River region in the disputed area, precipitating a violent brawl between the two groups that became known as the "Aroostook War."

Several years later, there were yet more Anglo-American problems. In 1841, an American ship, the *Creole*, sailed from Virginia for New Orleans with more than 100 slaves aboard. En route the slaves mutinied, seized possession of the ship, and took it to the Bahamas. British officials there declared the slaves free, and the English government refused to overrule them. Many Americans, especially Southerners, were infuriated.

At this critical juncture a new government came to power in Great Britain; eager to reduce the tensions with the United States, it sent Lord Ashburton, an admirer of Americans, to negotiate an agreement on the Maine boundary and other matters. The result was the Webster-Ashburton Treaty of 1842, under which the United States received slightly more than half the disputed area and agreed to a revised Northern boundary as far west as the Rocky Mountains. Ashburton also eased the memory of the *Caroline* and *Creole* affairs by expressing regret and promising no future "officious interference" with American ships. The Webster-Ashburton Treaty was popular in America, and Anglo-American relations suddenly looked better than they had for many years.

During the Tyler administration, the United States established its first diplomatic relations with China as part of an effort to win a share in the newly emerging China trade. In the Treaty of Wang Hya, concluded in

1844, American diplomats secured the same trading privileges as the English. In the next ten years, American trade with China steadily increased.

In their diplomatic efforts, at least, the Whigs were able to secure some important successes. But by the end of the Tyler administration, the party could look back on few other victories. In the election of 1844, the Whigs lost the White House. They were to win only one more national election in their history before a great sectional crisis would arise that would shatter their party and, for a time, the Union.

DEBATING THE PAST

Jacksonian Democracy

T O MANY AMERICANS in the 1820s and 1830s, Andrew Jackson was a champion of democracy, a symbol of the spirit of antielitism and egalitarianism that was sweeping American life. Historians, however, have disagreed sharply not only in their assessments of Jackson himself but in their portrayal of American society in his era.

The "progressive" historians of the early twentieth century tended to see Jacksonian politics as a forebear of their own battles against economic privilege and political corruption. Frederick Jackson Turner encouraged scholars to see Jacksonianism as the product of the democratic West: a protest by the people of the frontier against the conservative aristocracy of the East, which they believed was restricting their own freedom and opportunity. Jackson represented those who wanted to make government responsive to the will of the people rather than to the power of special interests. The culmination of this progressive interpretation of Jacksonianism was the publication in 1945 of Arthur M. Schlesinger, Jr.'s *The Age of Jackson.* Schlesinger was less interested in the regional basis of Jacksonianism than the disciples of Turner had been. Jacksonian Democracy, he argued, was the effort "to control the power of the capitalist groups, mainly Eastern, for the benefit of non-capitalist groups, farmers and laboring men, East, West, and South." He portrayed Jacksonianism as an early version of modern reform efforts (in the progressive era and the New Deal) to "restrain the power of the business community."

Richard Hofstadter, in an influential 1948 essay, sharply disagreed. Jackson, he argued, was the spokesman of rising entrepreneurs—aspiring businessmen who saw the road to opportunity blocked by the monopolistic power of Eastern aristocrats. The Jacksonians opposed special privileges only to the extent that those privileges blocked their own road to success. They were less sympathetic to the aspirations of those below them. Bray Hammond, writing in 1957, argued similarly that the Jacksonian cause was "one of enterpriser against capitalist," of rising elites against entrenched

(continued on next page)

ones. Other historians, exploring the ideological origins of the movement, saw Jacksonianism less as a democratic reform movement than as a nostalgic effort to restore a lost (and largely imagined) past. Marvin Meyers's *The Jacksonian Persuasion* (1957) argued that Jackson and his followers looked with misgivings on the new industrial society emerging around them and yearned instead for a restoration of the agrarian, republican virtues of an earlier time.

Historians of the 1960s began examining Jacksonianism in entirely new ways: looking less at Jackson and his supporters and more at the nature of American society in the early nineteenth century—and the ways in which it challenged the rhetoric of the politics of the time. Lee Benson's *The Concept of Jacksonian Democracy* (1961) used new quantitative techniques to challenge those historians who tried to explain political alignments in the 1830s on the basis of region, class, occupation, or even ideology. Local and cultural factors—religion and ethnicity in particular—were, he argued, the crucial determinants of party divisions. If there was an egalitarian spirit alive in America in those years, he claimed, it extended well beyond the Democratic party and the followers of Jackson. Edward Pessen's *Jacksonian America* (1969) revealed that the democratic rhetoric of the age disguised the reality of an increasingly stratified society, in which inequality was growing more, not less, severe. Alan Dawley went further in 1977, arguing that the extension of political rights in the 1820s and 1830s not only failed to advance economic democracy, but undermined the ability of workers and other exploited groups to articulate and act upon their grievances.

Scholars in more recent years have continued to pay less attention to Jackson and the Democratic party than to the origins and character of democratic ideas generally. In *Chants Democratic* (1984), Sean Wilentz identified the rise in the 1820s of a powerful working-class identity, expressed through a set of ideas known as "republicanism" and stimulated (although not fundamentally shaped) by the democratic rhetoric of party politics at the time. Workers in New York, he showed, were attracted less to Jackson himself than to the idea that power in a republic should be widely dispersed. They were raising a genuinely radical challenge to the rise of laissez-faire capitalism and to an emerging wage-labor system that threatened to reduce once-independent artisans into factory laborers unable to control their own livelihoods.

CHAPTER ELEVEN

The North and the South: Diverging Societies

The Developing North ~ The Expanding South
The "Peculiar Institution"

A MERICANS IN THE first half of the nineteenth century were a highly nationalistic people. Yet in many respects the United States in those years was not truly a nation at all—at least not in the way nations would be defined in later times. It was, rather, a highly decentralized confederation of states, many of which had little in common with one another. Those states remained together in part because the union was so loose, and the central authority of the nation so weak, that the differences among them did not often have to be confronted. But when the United States began to move in the direction of greater national unity in the 1840s, it had to confront the reality of sharp sectional differences that threatened to tear the country apart.

There had been sectional differences among the American colonies as early as the seventeenth century. By the 1840s and 1850s, however, sectionalism had changed. Socially and economically, there were now four quite distinct regions: the Northeast, with a growing industrial and commercial economy based on free labor; the Northwest, a rapidly expanding agricultural region; the Southeast, with a settled, slave labor plantation system and (in some areas) declining economic fortunes; and the Southwest, a booming frontierlike region with an expanding cotton economy. Politically, however, many Americans soon came to view their nation as divided into two sections, each with a distinctive and relatively homogeneous culture: the North and the South.

THE DEVELOPING NORTH

The most conspicuous change in American life in the 1840s and 1850s was the rapid industrialization of the Northeast. Factories proliferated. Urban centers grew rapidly. New industrial capitalists and financiers accumulated great fortunes. The urban middle class grew in size and importance. And a rapidly expanding industrial labor force created a distinct working class. The Northeast, in partnership with its new economic ally the Northwest, was developing a complex, modern society, one that would greatly increase the differences that had always existed between that region and the South.

Northeastern Industry

Between 1840 and 1860, American industry experienced a steady and, in some fields, spectacular growth. In 1840, the total value of manufactured goods produced in the United States was $483 million; ten years later the figure had climbed to over $1 billion; and in 1860 it was almost $2 billion. The bulk of this growth occurred in New England and the mid-Atlantic states. Although the Northeast had only a little more than half the mills and factories of the nation, it produced more than two-thirds of the manufactured goods and employed more than two-thirds of the industrial workers.

Technological advances sped the growth of industry. The machine tools used in the factories of the Northeast were by the 1840s already better than those in European factories. The principle of interchangeable parts, first applied decades earlier in gun factories, was being introduced into many other industries. Coal was replacing wood as an industrial fuel and was being used to drive new steam engines, which were in turn replacing water power in northeastern factories. That made it possible to locate mills away from running streams and thus permitted industry to expand still more widely.

In an earlier period, the dominant economic figures in the Northeast had been the great merchant traders. They remained figures of substance in the 1840s, particularly those in New York, Philadelphia, and Boston who invested in the China trade and who dispatched the famous and beautiful clipper ships to Asia and Europe. But international trade was becoming relatively less important in these years than manufacturing; and the new economic leaders of the Northeast, therefore, were the factory owners, some of whom were merchant capitalists who had shifted their resources into manufacturing.

By the 1840s, the corporate form of organization was spreading rapidly to manufacturing, particularly in the textile industry. Ownership of American enterprise was moving away from individuals and families and toward its highly dispersed modern form: many stockholders, each owning a relatively small proportion of the total. The discovery of new and more flexible forms of financing was, along with the technological innovations of the era, a crucial factor in the advancement of industrialization.

Transportation and Communications

Transportation was essential to the new industrial economy, above all for forging ties between the industrial Northeast and the Northwest. In the 1830s, the Erie Canal had been the most important transportation route between the two regions. But after 1840, in the more populated areas east of the Mississippi, railroads gradually took over. In 1840, the total railroad trackage of the country was only 2,818 miles; by the end of the decade, the trackage figure had risen to 9,021 miles; and between 1850 and 1860, trackage tripled again. The Northeast had twice as much trackage per square mile as the Northwest and four times as much as the South. Railroads were even reaching west of the Mississippi, although no extensive system had yet emerged there.

In the South, such towns as Charleston, Atlanta, Savannah, Richmond, and Norfolk had rail connections with Memphis, and thus with the Mississippi River and the Northwest. Much of the South, however, remained unconnected to a national railroad system. Most lines in the region were short, local ones. In the North, by contrast, short lines were being consolidated into trunk lines; and extensive rail connections with the Northwest were already in place by the 1850s, when Chicago emerged as the rail center of the West. The great trunk lines diverted traffic from the Mississippi River, weakening further the connection between the Northwest and the South.

The construction of railroads was the single greatest economic project in American history to that point and required massive amounts of capital. Much of it came from private investors, but much of it also came from government. State and local governments contributed capital because they were eager to have railroad service. Even greater assistance came from the federal government. In 1850, Senator Stephen A. Douglas of Illinois and other railroad-minded politicians persuaded Congress to grant federal lands to Illinois to aid the Illinois Central Railroad, which was building toward the Gulf of Mexico. By 1860, Congress had allotted over 30 million acres to eleven states to subsidize other railroad lines.

Crucial to the operation of railroads, and important in other ways to the transformation of American life, was the telegraph, which burst into

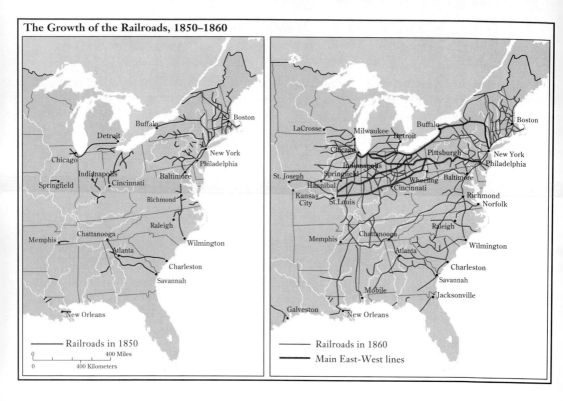

The Growth of the Railroads, 1850–1860

—— Railroads in 1850
—— Railroads in 1860
—— Main East-West lines

American life in 1844, when Samuel F. B. Morse, after several years of experimentation, succeeded in transmitting from Baltimore to Washington the news of James K. Polk's nomination for the presidency. By 1860, more than 50,000 miles of wire connected most parts of the country (although far more extensively in the North than in the South); and a year later, the Pacific telegraph, with 3,595 miles of wire, was operating between New York and San Francisco. By then, nearly all the independent lines had been absorbed into one organization, the Western Union Telegraph Company.

Cities and Immigrants

One of the most profound changes in the nature of Northeastern society in the antebellum period occurred in the character and distribution of the population, above all the growing size of cities. The populations of New York, Philadelphia, and Boston, for example, all nearly tripled between 1840 and 1860; New York's population was 1.2 million in 1860 if Brooklyn (then a separate municipality) is included. By 1860, 26 percent of the population of the free states was living in towns or cities (places of 2,500 people or more), a figure up from 14 percent in 1840. (In the South, by contrast, the increase of urban residents rose only from 6 percent in 1840 to 10 percent in 1860.)

The enlarged urban population was in part simply a reflection of the growth of the national population as a whole, which rose by more than a third—from 23 million to over 31 million—in the 1850s alone. But it was more directly a result of the flow of people into the cities from two sources: the native farmers of the Northeast, who were being forced off their lands by Western competition; and even more significantly by the 1850s, immigrants from Europe. Only 500,000 foreign immigrants had arrived in the United States in the 1830s (partly because of the serious depression in those years). But between 1840 and 1850, more than 1.5 million Europeans moved to America; in the 1850s, the number rose to 2.5 million. Almost half the population of New York City in the 1850s was foreign-born. In St. Louis, Chicago, and Milwaukee, the foreign born outnumbered the native born. Few immigrants settled in the South. Only 500,000 lived in the slave states in 1860, a third of them in Missouri.

The newcomers came from many different countries, but the overwhelming majority came from Ireland and Germany, where widespread poverty and political upheaval were driving many people out. By 1860, there were more than 1.5 million Irish-born and approximately 1 million German-born people in the United States. The great majority of the Irish remained in the Eastern cities where they landed and swelled the ranks of unskilled labor. Germans generally moved on to the Northwest, where they became farmers or went into business in the Western towns. The difference in settlement patterns was in part because Germans tended to arrive with at least some money, while the Irish generally arrived with none. But it was also because most German immigrants were members of family groups or were single men, for whom movement to the agricultural frontier was both possible and attractive, while the largest number of Irish immigrants consisted of single women, for whom movement west was much less plausible. Single women were more likely to stay in the Eastern cities, where factory and domestic work was available.

The Rise of Nativism

The new foreign-born population almost immediately became a major factor in American political life. Many politicians saw in the immigrant population a source of important potential support. They pushed state

LEAVING FOR AMERICA Irish emigrants bid friends and family goodbye as they board the mail coach from Cahirciveen in County Kerry, the first step in the long journey to the United States.

governments to liberalize their laws to allow unnaturalized immigrants to vote, and they eagerly courted the support of the new arrivals. Others, however, viewed the growing foreign population with alarm. Some argued that the immigrants were mentally and physically inferior and politically corrupt. Others complained that because the foreign born were willing to work for low wages, they were stealing jobs from the native work force. Protestants warned that the Catholic church was becoming a force in American government through the growing Irish population. Older-stock Americans feared that immigrants would become a radical force in politics. Out of these fears and prejudices emerged a number of secret societies to combat the "alien menace."

The first was the Native American Association, founded in 1837, which in 1845 was transformed into the Native American party. In 1850, nativist groups combined to form the Supreme Order of the Star-Spangled Banner, whose demands included banning Catholics or aliens from holding public office, enacting more restrictive naturalization laws, and establishing literacy tests for voting. The order adopted a strict code of secrecy, which included a secret password, used in lodges across the country: "I know nothing." Ultimately, members of the movement were labeled the "Know-Nothings."

After the 1852 elections, the Know-Nothings created a new political organization they called the American party. It scored an immediate and astonishing success in the elections of 1854. The Know-Nothings made a strong showing in Pennsylvania and New York and actually won control of the state government in Massachusetts. Outside the Northeast, however, their progress was more modest. And after 1854, the strength of the Know-Nothings declined. The party's most lasting impact was its contribution to the collapse of the second party system and the creation of new national political alignments.

Labor in the Northeast

In the early years of industrial growth, when mills were relatively few, the work force of the Northeastern factories had remained both small and for the most part impermanent. By the 1840s, however, the need for factory workers was such that a large, permanent laboring class was beginning to emerge, drawn from the new urban, immigrant population.

Working conditions quickly grew much worse than they had been for the Lowell and Waltham factory girls in the 1830s. Employers maintained no neat boardinghouses and dormitories for the new workers; they were left to find whatever accommodations they could in the squalid factory towns that were rapidly springing up. The factories themselves were becoming large, noisy, unsanitary, and often dangerous places to work; the average workday extended to twelve, often fourteen hours; and wages declined for all workers, but for women and children most of all.

Workers attempted at times to improve their lot. They tried, with little success, to persuade state legislatures to pass laws setting a maximum workday. Two states—New Hampshire in 1847 and Pennsylvania in 1848—actually passed laws barring employers from forcing employees to work more than ten hours without their consent; but the measures had little effect, since employers could require that workers agree to extended workdays as a condition of hiring. Three states—Massachusetts, New Hampshire, and Pennsylvania—passed laws regulating child labor. But the laws simply limited the workday to ten hours for children unless their parents agreed to something longer; again, employers had little difficulty persuading parents to consent to additional hours.

NEW ENGLAND TEXTILE WORKERS Women continued to constitute the majority of the work force in the cotton mills of New England even after the carefully monitored life of the "Lowell girls" became a thing of the past—as this 1868 engraving by Winslow Homer suggests.

Perhaps the greatest legal victory for industrial workers came when the Massachusetts supreme court ruled in 1842, in *Commonwealth* v. *Hunt*, that unions were lawful organizations and that the strike was a lawful weapon. Other state courts gradually followed suit. But the union movement of the 1840s and 1850s remained, on the whole, feeble and ineffective.

What organization there was among laborers usually occurred among limited groups of skilled workers. Their primary purpose was usually to protect the favored position of their members in the labor force by restricting admission to the skilled trades. Virtually all the early craft unions excluded women, even though female workers were numerous in almost every industry. As a result, women themselves created several women's protective unions in the 1850s, often with the support of middle-class female reformers. Like the male craft unions, however, the female protective unions had little power in dealing with employers.

Many factors combined to inhibit the growth of effective labor resistance in America, some of them the result of the growing number of immigrants in the work force. The newcomers were usually willing to work for lower wages than native workers; and because they were so numerous, manufacturers had little difficulty replacing disgruntled or striking native workers with eager immigrants. Ethnic divisions and tensions—both between natives and immigrants and among the various immigrant groups themselves—often caused working-class resentments to be channeled into internal bickering rather than into complaints against employers. Many immigrants expected to return to their original homes once they had earned enough money (and some actually did), which meant that they did not feel a strong stake in the long-term structure of the workplace. There was, finally, the sheer strength of the industrial capitalists, who had not only economic but political and social power and could usually triumph over even the most militant challenges.

Wealth and Mobility

The commercial and industrial growth of the United States greatly increased national wealth in the 1840s and 1850s and elevated the average income of the American people. But this increasing wealth was not widely or equally distributed. Some groups of the population, of course, shared hardly at all in the economic growth: enslaved African-Americans, Indians, landless farmers, and unskilled workers on the fringes of the manufacturing system. But even among the rest of the population, disparities of income were becoming ever more conspicuous. Wealth had always been unequally distributed in the United States, to be sure. But by the mid-nineteenth century, the concentration of wealth had become more pronounced than ever before. In 1860, 5 percent of the families in the United States possessed more than 50 percent of the wealth.

Why did this inequality not produce more resentment? There are several possible answers. First, however much the economic position of American workers was declining relative to that of other Americans, the absolute living standard of most laborers was improving. Factory workers generally ate better, were better clothed and housed, and had greater access to consumer goods than they had had on the farms or in the European societies from which they had migrated.

Second, there were opportunities for social mobility, for working one's way up the economic ladder, even if they were limited ones. A few workers managed to move from poverty to riches by dint of work, ingenuity, and luck—enough to support the dreams of those who watched them. A much larger number managed to move at least one notch up the ladder—for example, becoming in the course of a lifetime a skilled, rather than an unskilled, laborer. Such people could envision their children and grandchildren moving up even further.

Third, and more important than social mobility, was geographical mobility. Some workers saved their money and moved west to the new lands the government was opening; to some degree, the West became what the historian Frederick Jackson Turner later called a "safety valve" for discontent. Most workers, however, had neither the money nor the expertise to make such a move. Far more frequent was the migration of laborers, many of them victims of layoffs, from one industrial town to another looking for better opportunities. The rootlessness of this large segment of the work force—perhaps the most distressed segment—made effective organization and protest more difficult.

There was, finally, another "safety valve" for working-class discontent: politics. Economic opportunity may not have greatly expanded in the nineteenth century, but opportunities to participate in politics had. And to many working people, access to the ballot seemed to offer a way to help guide their society and to feel like a significant part of their communities.

Women and the "Cult of Domesticity"

Industrialization also produced profound changes in the nature and function of the American family. In the early decades of the nineteenth century (and for many years before that), the family itself had been the principal unit of economic activity. And among the farming population, which was still the majority, the family often remained a close-knit economic unit. But in the industrial economy of the rapidly growing cities, there was a marked erosion of the traditional economic function of the family. The urban household itself was seldom a center of production any longer. Instead, most income earners left home each day to work elsewhere. A sharp distinction began to emerge between the public world of the workplace— the world of commerce and industry—and the private world of the family— a world now dominated by housekeeping, child rearing, and other primarily domestic concerns.

The emerging distinction between the public and private worlds, between the workplace and the home, was accompanied by increasingly sharp distinctions between the social roles of men and women—distinctions that affected not just workers and farmers but the growing middle class as well. Traditional inequalities remained. Women had many fewer legal and political rights than did men, and within the family they remained under the virtually absolute authority of their husbands. Women were seldom encouraged—and in most cases were effectively barred—from pursuing education above the primary level. Not until 1837 did any college or university accept women students: Oberlin in Ohio, which educated both women and men; and Mt. Holyoke in Massachusetts, founded by Mary Lyon as an academy for women. Not until much later in the century were there more than a handful of others.

But however unequal the positions of men and women in the preindustrial era, those positions had generally been defined within the context of a household in which all members played important economic roles. In the middle-class family of the new industrial society, however, the husband was assumed to be the principal, usually the only, income producer. The wife was now expected to remain in the home and to engage in largely domestic activities. The image of women changed from one of contributors to the family economy to one of guardians of the "domestic virtues." Middle-class women, no longer producers, now became more important as consumers. They learned to place a higher value on keeping a clean, comfortable, and well-appointed home; on entertaining; on dressing elegantly and stylishly.

Within their own separate sphere, women began to develop a distinctive female culture. A "lady's" literature began to emerge to meet the demands of middle-class women. There were romantic novels (many of them by female writers), which focused on the private sphere that women now inhabited. There were women's magazines, which focused on fashions, shopping, homemaking, and other purely domestic concerns.

Most middle-class men—and many middle-class women—considered the new female sphere a vehicle for expressing special qualities that made women in some ways superior to men. Women were to be the custodians of morality and benevolence; they were to provide religious and moral instruction to their children and to counterbalance the acquisitive, secular impulses of their husbands. This "cult of domesticity," as some scholars have called it, gave many women greater material comfort than they had had in the past and placed a higher value on their "female virtues" and on their roles as wives and mothers. At the same time, it left women increasingly detached from the public world, with few outlets for their interests and energies.

Except for teaching and nursing—the favored occupations of unmarried middle-class women—work by women outside the household gradually came to be seen as a lower-class preserve. Working-class women continued to work in factories and mills, but under conditions far worse than those that the original, more "respectable" women workers of Lowell and Waltham had experienced. Domestic service became another frequent source of female employment. Now that production had moved outside the household, women who needed to earn money had to move outside their own homes to do so.

The Old Northwest

Agriculture was in steady decline in the states of the Northeast in the mid-nineteenth century. Some Eastern farmers continued to thrive by raising vegetables and fruits or producing dairy products to supply the growing urban population of the region. But the great staple crops became less and less important to the Northeastern economy—largely because of the dramatic agricultural growth in the states of what was then known as the Northwest (and is now called the Midwest).

There was more industry in this region than in the South; and in the two decades before the Civil War, the section experienced steady industrial growth, especially around Cleveland, Cincinnati, and Chicago. But for the white (and occasionally black) settlers who populated the lands that had by now been largely wrested from the natives, the Northwest was primarily an agricultural region.

The typical white citizen of the Northwest was not an industrial worker or a poor, marginal farmer, as was the case in the Northeast, but the owner of a reasonably prosperous family farm. The average size of Western farms was 200 acres, the great majority of them owned by the people who worked them; the farmers concentrated on corn, wheat, cattle, sheep, and hogs. Even relatively small farmers generally prospered, since the growing demand for farm products—both from the urban centers of the United States and from the industrial cities of Europe—resulted in steadily rising farm prices.

The growth of the agricultural economy of the Northwest had profound effects on sectional alignments in the United States. The Northwest sold most of its products to the residents of the Northeast. Eastern industry, in turn, found an important market for its products in the prospering West. Hence a strong economic relationship was emerging between the two regions that was profitable to both—and that was increasing the isolation of the South within the Union.

To meet the increasing demand for their products, farmers in the Northwest worked strenuously, and often frantically, to increase its productive capacities. One way they did so was by enlarging the area under cultivation during the 1840s. By 1850, the growing Western population had settled the prairie regions east of the Mississippi and was pushing beyond the river. But another way the Northwest increased production was by adopting more advanced (if at times wasteful and exploitive) agricultural techniques. New varieties of seed, notably Mediterranean wheat, which was hardier than the native type, were introduced in some areas. Better breeds of animals, such as hogs and sheep from England and Spain, were imported to take the place of native stock. More efficient grain drills, harrows, mowers, and hay rakes were developed and marketed. A steel plow, more durable than the older, iron ones, was introduced by John Deere in 1847.

Two new machines heralded a revolution in grain production. The most important was the automatic reaper, invented by Cyrus H. McCormick of Virginia, which replaced the hand-operated sickle and enabled small crews to harvest grain much more quickly than larger crews using sickles had been able to do. McCormick established a factory at Chicago, in the heart of the grain belt, in 1847. By 1860, more than 100,000 reapers were in use on Western farms. Almost as important to the grain grower was the thresher—a machine that separated the grain from the wheat stalks—which appeared in large numbers after 1840. Before then, grain was generally flailed by hand (seven bushels a day was a good average for a farm) or trodden by farm animals (twenty bushels a day on the average). A threshing machine could thresh twenty-five bushels or more in an hour.

Large portions of the Northwest—most of the upper third of the Great Lakes states—continued to be populated mainly by Indians until after the Civil War. In those areas, hunting and fishing, along with some sedentary agriculture, remained the principal economic activities. But the tribes never became fully integrated into the commercialized economy that was emerging elsewhere in the Northwest.

THE EXPANDING SOUTH

The South, like the North, experienced dramatic growth in the middle years of the nineteenth century. Southerners fanned out into the new territories of the Southwest and established new communities, new states, and new markets. The Southern agricultural economy grew increasingly productive and increasingly prosperous. Trade in such staples as sugar, rice, tobacco, and above all cotton made the South a major force in international commerce and created substantial wealth within the region.

Yet for all the expansion and change, the South experienced a much less fundamental transformation in these years than did the North. It had begun the nineteenth century as a primarily agricultural region; it remained overwhelmingly agrarian in 1860. It had begun the century with few important cities and little industry; and so it remained sixty years later. In 1800, the economy of the South had been dominated by a plantation system

Slavery and Cotton: The South in 1820 and 1860

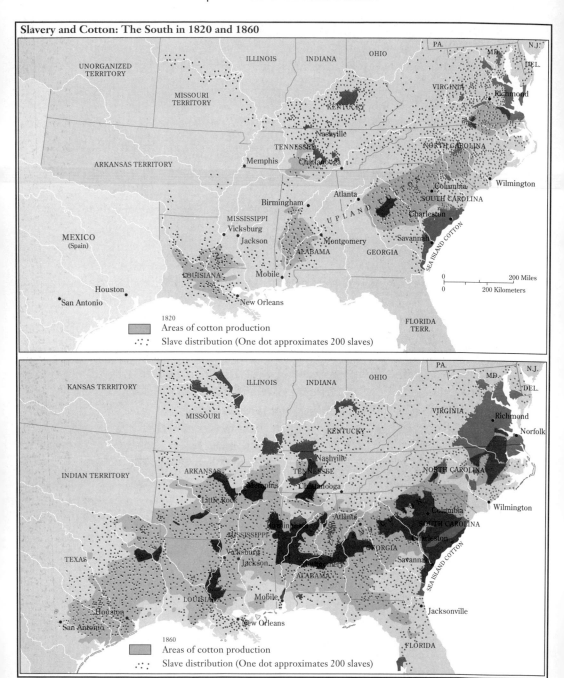

dependent on slave labor; by 1860, that system had only strengthened its grip on the region. As one historian has written, "The South grew, but it did not develop." As a result, it became increasingly unlike the North and increasingly sensitive to what it considered as threats to its distinctive way of life.

The Rise of King Cotton

The most important economic development in the South of the mid-nineteenth century was the shift of economic power from the "upper South"—such older and more developed states as Virginia, North Carolina, Maryland, and Kentucky—to the "lower South"—the expanding agricultural regions in the new states of the Southwest. That shift reflected above all the growing dominance of cotton in the Southern economy.

The decline of the tobacco economy in the upper South (a result of falling prices and soil exhaustion) and the natural limits of the sugar, rice, and long-staple cotton economies farther south might have forced the region to shift its attention to other, nonagricultural pursuits in the nineteenth century had it not been for the growing importance of a new product, which soon overshadowed all else: short-staple cotton. This hardier and coarser strain of cotton could be grown effectively in a variety of climates and in a variety of soils. It was more difficult to clean than the long-staple strain, but the invention of the cotton gin had largely solved that problem. By the 1820s, therefore, cotton production was spreading rapidly. From the western areas of South Carolina and Georgia, production moved into Alabama and Mississippi and then into northern Louisiana, Texas, and Arkansas. By the 1850s, cotton had come to be the linchpin of the Southern economy. By the time of the Civil War, it constituted nearly two-thirds of the total export trade of the United States and was bringing in nearly $200 million a year. The annual value of the rice crop, in contrast, was $2 million. It was little wonder that white Southerners now proclaimed: "Cotton is king!"

The prospect of tremendous profits from cotton quickly drew settlers by the thousands to the Southwest. Some were wealthy planters from the older states. Most were small slaveholders or slaveless farmers who hoped to become great planters. A similar shift occurred in the slave population. According to some estimates, 410,000 slaves moved from the upper South to the cotton states between 1840 and 1860—either accompanying masters who were themselves migrating to the Southwest or (more often) sold to planters already there. Indeed, the sale of slaves to the Southwest became an important economic activity in the upper South and helped the troubled planters of that region compensate for the declining value of tobacco and their other crops.

Southern Trade and Industry

In comparison to this booming agricultural expansion, other forms of economic activity developed slowly in the South. There was growing activity in flour milling and in textile and iron manufacturing, particularly in the upper South. The Tredegar Iron Works in Richmond, for example, compared favorably with the best iron mills in the Northeast. But industry remained an insignificant force relative to agriculture in the South, and it was even more insignificant when compared with the industry of the North.

To the degree that the South developed a nonfarm commercial sector, it was largely to serve the needs of the plantation economy. Brokers, or factors, marketed the planters' crops and provided planters with manufactured goods; they became figures of considerable influence in the region and established merchant communities in such towns as New Orleans, Charleston, Mobile, and Savannah. The South had only a very rudimentary financial system, and the factors often also served as bankers, providing planters with credit. There were also substantial groups of professional people in the South—lawyers, editors, doctors, and others; they too were closely tied to and dependent on the plantation economy.

These manufacturers, merchants, and professionals were, moreover, relatively insubstantial compared with the manufacturers, merchants, and professionals of the North, on whom Southerners were coming increasingly (and increasingly unhappily) to depend. Perceptive Southerners recognized the economic subordination of their region. As a result, there were calls for promoting Southern economic independence. Among the leading advocates was James B. D. De Bow of New Orleans, who published *De Bow's Review* from 1846 until 1860. The magazine warned constantly of the dangers of the "colonial" relationship between the sections. Yet *De Bow's Review* was itself evidence of the dependency of the South on the North. It was printed in New York, because no New Orleans printer had facilities adequate to the task; it was filled with advertisements from Northern manufacturing firms; and its circulation was always modest in comparison with those of Northern publications. In Charleston, for example, it sold an average of 173 copies per issue; *Harper's Magazine* of New York regularly sold 1,500 copies there.

Despite this awareness of the region's "colonial dependency," the South made few serious efforts to develop an economy that might challenge that dependency. An important question about antebellum Southern history, therefore, is why the region did so little to develop a larger industrial and commercial economy of its own.

One reason was the great profitability of the region's agricultural system, and particularly of cotton production. Another reason was that wealthy Southerners had so much capital invested in their land and in their slaves that they had little left for other investments. Some historians have suggested that the Southern climate—with its long, hot, steamy summers—was less suitable for industrial development than the climate of the North. Still others have gone so far as to claim that Southern work habits impeded industrialization; some white Southerners appeared—at least to many Northern observers—not to work very hard, to lack the strong work ethic that fueled Northern economic development.

But the Southern failure to create a flourishing commercial or industrial economy was also in part the result of a set of values distinctive to the South that discouraged the growth of cities and industry. White Southerners liked to think of themselves as representatives of a special way of life: one based on traditional values of chivalry, leisure, and elegance. Southerners were, some argued, "cavaliers," people happily free from the base, acquisitive instincts of Northerners and more concerned with creating a refined and gracious civilization than with rapid growth and development. But as appealing as the "cavalier" image was to Southern whites, it did not conform to the reality of most of Southern society.

Plantation Society

Only a small minority of Southern whites owned slaves. In 1850, when the total white population of the South was over 6 million, the number of slaveholders was only 347,525. Each slaveholder was normally the head of a family averaging five members. But even with all members of slaveowning families included in the figures, those owning slaves still amounted to perhaps no more than one-quarter of the white population. And of the minority of whites holding slaves, only a small proportion owned them in substantial numbers.

How, then, did the South come to be seen—both by the outside world and by many Southerners themselves—as a society dominated by great plantations and wealthy landowning planters? In large part, it was because the planter aristocracy—the cotton magnates, the sugar, rice, and tobacco nabobs, the whites who owned at least forty or fifty slaves and 800 or more acres—exercised power and influence far in excess of their numbers. They stood at the apex of society, determining the political, economic, and even social life of their region. Enriched by vast annual incomes, dwelling in palatial homes, surrounded by broad acres and many black servants, they became a class to which others paid deference.

Southerners liked to compare their planter class to the old upper classes of England and Europe: true aristocracies long entrenched. In fact, however, the Southern upper class was in most cases not at all similar to the landed aristocracies of the Old World. In the upper South—the tidewater region of Virginia, for example—some of the great aristocrats were people whose families had occupied positions of wealth and power for generations. In most of the South, however, there was no longstanding landed aristocracy. As late as the 1850s, most of the great landowners in the lower South were still first-generation settlers who had only relatively recently begun to live in anything like aristocratic style. Large areas of the "Old South" (as Americans later called the South of the pre–Civil War era) had been settled and cultivated for less than two decades at the time of the Civil War.

Nor was the world of the planter nearly as leisured and genteel as the "cavalier" myth would suggest. Growing staple crops was a business—often a big and highly profitable business; it was in its own way just as competitive and just as risky as the industrial enterprises of the North. Thus planters were, in many respects, as much capitalists as the industrialists of the North whose life styles they claimed to hold in contempt.

Wealthy Southern whites sustained their image of themselves as aristocrats in many ways. They adopted an elaborate code of "chivalry," which obligated white men to defend their "honor" (often through dueling). They avoided such "coarse" occupations as trade and commerce; those who did not become planters often gravitated toward the military, a "suitable" career for men raised in a culture in which medieval knights (as portrayed in the novels of Walter Scott) were a powerful and popular image. Above all, perhaps, the aristocratic ideal found reflection in the definition of a special role for Southern white women.

The "Southern Lady"

In some respects, affluent white women in the South occupied roles very similar to those occupied by middle-class white women in the North. Their lives were centered in the home, where they served as companions to (and hostesses for) their husbands and as nurturing mothers for their children. Seldom did "genteel" Southern white women engage in public activities or find income-producing employment.

But the life of the "Southern lady" was also in many ways very different from that of her Northern counterpart. For one thing, the cult of honor in the region meant that Southern white men attributed particular importance to the "defense" of women. In practice, this generally meant that white women were even more subordinate to men in Southern culture than they were in the North. George Fitzhugh, one of the South's most important social theorists, wrote in the 1850s: "Women, like children, have but one right, and that is the right to protection. The right to protection involves the obligation to obey."

The vast majority of females in the region lived on farms, relatively isolated from people outside their own families, with virtually no access to the "public world" and thus few opportunities to look beyond their roles as wives and mothers. For some white women, living on farms of modest size meant a fuller engagement in the economic life of the family than was becoming typical for middle-class women in the North. These women engaged in spinning, weaving, and other production; they participated in agricultural tasks; they helped supervise the slave work force. On the larger plantations, however, even these limited roles were often considered unsuitable for white women; and the "plantation mistress" became, in some cases, more an ornament for her husband than a meaningful part of the economy or the society.

Southern white women also had less access to education than their Northern counterparts. Nearly a quarter of all white women over twenty were completely illiterate; relatively few women had more than a rudimentary exposure to schooling. Even wealthy planters were not particularly interested in extensive schooling for their daughters. The few female "academies" in the South were designed largely to train women to be suitable wives.

Southern white women had other special burdens as well. The Southern white birth rate remained nearly 20 percent higher than that of the nation as a whole, and infant mortality in the region remained higher than elsewhere; nearly half the children born in the South in 1860 died before they reached five years of age. Male slaveowners had frequent sexual relationships with the female slaves on their plantations; the children of those unions became part of the plantation labor force and served as a constant reminder to white women of their husbands' infidelity. Black women (and men) were obviously the most important victims of such practices. But white women suffered too. However much they might resent their husbands' liaisons with slaves, the social code under which they lived generally prevented them from venting their anger (except toward slave women, whom plantation mistresses often treated very harshly), or even openly acknowledging that the relationships existed at all.

The "Plain Folk"

The typical white Southerner was not a great planter and slaveholder, but a modest yeoman farmer. Some owned a few slaves, with whom they worked and lived far more closely than did the larger planters. Most (in fact, two-thirds of all white families) owned no slaves at all. These "plain folk," most of whom owned their own land, devoted themselves largely to subsistence farming. There were occasional examples of poor farmers moving into the ranks of the planter class, but such cases were rare. Most yeomen knew they had little prospect of substantially bettering their lot.

One reason was the Southern educational system, which provided poor whites with few opportunities to learn and thus limited their chances of advancement. For the sons of wealthy planters, Southern colleges and universities were by 1860 enrolling more students than in any other region. But such institutions were open only to relatively wealthy people. And below the college level, where the white lower classes more often looked, the schools of the South were not only fewer but also inferior to those of the Northeast. The South had more than 500,000 white illiterates, over half the country's total.

In a few areas of the South, poor whites resented and set themselves apart from the plantation elite. These were mainly the Southern highlanders, the "hill people," who lived in the Appalachian ranges east of the Mississippi and in the Ozarks to the west of it. Of all Southern whites, they were the most isolated from the mainstream of the region's life. They practiced a crude form of subsistence agriculture, owned practically no slaves, and had a proud sense of seclusion. Such whites frequently expressed animosity toward the planter aristocracy of the other regions of the South and misgivings about (although seldom moral objections to) the system of slavery. The mountain region was the only part of the South to resist the movement toward secession when it developed. Even during the Civil War, many hill people refused to support the Confederacy; some fought for the Union.

But most nonslaveowning whites lived in the midst of the plantation system and did relatively little to oppose or resist it. Many, perhaps most of them, accepted that system because they were tied to it in important ways. Small farmers depended on the local plantation aristocracy for many things:

for access to cotton gins, for markets for their modest crops and their livestock, for financial assistance in time of need. In many areas, there were also extensive networks of kinship linking lower- and upper-class whites. The poorest resident of a county might easily be a cousin of the richest aristocrat.

There were other white Southerners, however, who did not share in the plantation economy in even these limited ways and yet continued to accept its premises. These were the members of that degraded class—numbering perhaps a half-million in 1850—known variously as "crackers," "sand hillers," or "poor white trash." Occupying the infertile lands of the pine barrens, the red hills, and the swamps, they lived in utter squalor. They often suffered from dietary deficiencies, resorted at times to eating clay, and were afflicted by pellagra, hookworm, and malaria. In some material respects, their plight was worse than that of the black slaves (who themselves often looked down on the poor whites).

Even among these Southerners—the true outcasts of white society in the region—there was no real opposition to the plantation system or slavery. In part, this was probably because these men and women were so benumbed by poverty that they had little strength to protest. But it resulted also from perhaps the single greatest unifying factor among the Southern white population—the one force most responsible for reducing tensions among the various classes. That force was race. However poor and miserable white Southerners might be, they could still consider themselves members of a ruling race; they could still look down on the black population of the region and feel a bond with their fellow whites born of a determination to maintain their racial supremacy. As Frederick Law Olmsted, a Northerner who visited the South and chronicled Southern society in the 1850s, wrote: "From childhood, the one thing in their condition which has made life valuable to the mass of whites has been that the niggers are yet their inferiors."

THE "PECULIAR INSTITUTION"

White Southerners often referred to slavery as the "peculiar institution." By that, they meant not that the institution was odd but that it was distinctive. And American slavery was distinctive indeed. The South in the mid-nineteenth century was the only area in the Western world except for Brazil and Cuba where slavery still existed; and Southern slavery differed even from its Caribbean and South American counterparts. Slavery, more than any other single factor, isolated the South from the rest of American society. And as that isolation increased, so did the commitment of Southerners to defend the institution.

Within the South itself, the institution of slavery had paradoxical results. On the one hand, it isolated blacks from whites, drawing a sharp and inviolable line between the races. As a result, blacks under slavery developed a distinct society and culture of their own. On the other hand, slavery created a unique bond between blacks and whites—masters and slaves—in the South. The two races may have maintained separate spheres, but each sphere was deeply influenced by, indeed dependent on, the other.

Varieties of Slavery

Slavery was an institution established and regulated in detail by law. The slave codes of the Southern states forbade slaves to hold property, to leave their masters' premises without permission, to be out after dark, to congregate with other slaves except at church, to carry firearms, or to strike a white person even in self-defense. The codes prohibited whites from teaching slaves to read or write, and they denied slaves the right to testify in court against white people. They contained no provisions to legalize slave marriages or divorces. If an owner killed a slave while punishing him, the act was generally not considered a crime. Slaves, however, faced the death penalty for killing or even resisting a white person or for inciting to revolt. The codes also contained extraordinarily rigid provisions for defining a person's race. Anyone with even a trace of African ancestry was considered black.

These and dozens of other regulations suggest that slaves lived under a uniformly harsh and dismal regime. In fact, however, the laws were unevenly applied. Sometimes slaves did acquire property, did learn to read and write, and did assemble with other slaves, in spite of laws to the contrary. There was, in short, considerable variety within the slave system. Some blacks lived in almost prisonlike conditions, rigidly and harshly controlled by their masters. Many (probably most) others enjoyed a certain flexibility and (at least in comparison to the regimen prescribed by law) a striking degree of autonomy.

Small farmers generally supervised their workers directly and often worked closely alongside them. On such farms, blacks and whites developed a form of intimacy unknown on larger plantations. The paternal relationship between such masters and their slaves could, like relationships between fathers and children, be warm and in some respects benevolent. It could also be tyrannical and cruel. In general, the evidence suggests, blacks themselves preferred to live on larger plantations, where they had more opportunities for privacy and for a social world of their own.

Although most slaveowners were small farmers, most slaves lived on plantations of medium or large size, with substantial African-American work forces. There the relationship between master and slave was not usually intimate. Substantial planters often hired overseers and even assistant over-seers to represent them. "Head drivers," trusted and responsible slaves often assisted by several subdrivers, acted under the overseer as foremen. On most plantations, slaves worked under the gang system, in which slaves were divided up into groups, each directed by a driver, and worked for as many hours as the overseer considered a reasonable workday.

Masters usually provided slaves with an adequate if rough diet, consisting mainly of corn meal, salt pork, and molasses. Many slaves were allowed to raise gardens for their own use and were issued fresh meat on special

RETURNING FROM THE COTTON FIELD In this photograph, South Carolina field workers return after a day of picking cotton, some of their harvest carried in bundles on their heads. A black slave driver leads the way.

occasions. They were given cheap clothing and shoes. They lived in rude cabins, called slave quarters, usually clustered together near the master's house. The plantation mistress or a doctor retained by the owner provided some medical care, but slave women themselves were the more important source.

Slaves worked hard, beginning with light tasks as children. Slave women worked particularly hard. They generally toiled in the fields with the men and then did traditional "women's chores"—cooking, cleaning, and child rearing—as well. Because slave families were often divided, with husbands and fathers living on neighboring plantations (or, at times, sold to plantation owners far away), many black women found themselves acting in effect as single parents. Black women thus acquired a higher measure of authority within their families than did most white women.

The conditions of American slavery were less severe than those of slavery in the Caribbean and South America. In those regions, the slave supply was constantly replenished well into the nineteenth century by the African slave trade, giving owners less incentive to protect their existing laborers. In the United States, newly imported slaves were in short supply, and thus there were strong economic incentives to maintain a healthy slave population. Some masters even hired Irish workers and other whites to do such dangerous or unhealthy tasks as clearing malarial swamps or handling cotton bales at the bottom of long chutes. Still, cruel or rash masters might forget their pocketbooks in the heat of anger. And slaves were often left to the discipline of overseers, who had no financial stake in their well-being; overseers were paid in proportion to the amount of work they could get out of the slaves they supervised.

Household servants had a somewhat easier life—physically at least—than did field hands. On large plantations, there was generally a domestic staff of nursemaids, housemaids, cooks, butlers, and coachmen. These people lived close to the master and his family, eating the leftovers from the family table and in some cases even sleeping in the "big house." Between the blacks and whites of such households affectionate, almost familial, relationships might develop. More often, however, house servants resented their isolation from their fellow slaves and the lack of privacy that came with living in such close proximity to the family of the master. Female household servants were especially vulnerable to sexual abuse by their masters. When emancipation came after the Civil War, it was often the house servants who were the first to leave the plantations of their former owners.

Slavery in the cities differed significantly from slavery in the country. On the relatively isolated plantations, slaves had little contact with free

A M E R I C A N   V O I C E S

JAMES L. BRADLEY

An African-American Describes
His Bondage, 1835

 I THINK I was between two and three years old when the soul-destroyers tore me from my mother's arms, some-where in Africa, far back from the sea. They carried me a long distance to a ship; all the way I looked back, and cried. The ship was full of men and women loaded with chains; but I was so small they let me run about on deck.

After many long days, they brought us into Charleston, South Carolina. A slaveholder bought me, and took me up into Pendleton County. I suppose that I staid with him about six months. He sold me to a Mr. Bradley, by whose name I have ever since been called. This man was considered a wonderfully kind master; and it is true that I was treated better than most of the slaves I knew. I never suffered for food, and never was flogged with the whip; but oh, my soul! I was tormented with kicks and knocks more than I can tell. . . .

I used to work very hard. I was always obliged to be in the field by sunrise, and I labored till dark stopping only at noon long enough to eat dinner. . . . My master had kept me ignorant of everything he could. . . . Yet from the time I was fourteen years old, I used to think a great deal about freedom. It was my heart's desire; I could not keep it out of my mind. Many a sleepless night I have spent in tears, because I was a slave. I looked back on all I had suffered—and when I looked ahead, all was dark and hopeless bondage.

SOURCE: John W. Blassingame, ed., *Slave Testimony* (Baton Rouge: Louisiana State University Press, 1977), pp. 687–688.

blacks and lower-class whites; a deep and seemingly unbridgeable chasm yawned between slavery and freedom. In the cities, however, masters could not supervise their slaves so closely if they hoped to use them profitably. Some—particularly skilled workers such as blacksmiths or carpenters— were hired out; after hours they often fended for themselves, neither their owners nor their employers bothering to supervise them. Thus urban slaves gained numerous opportunities to mingle with free blacks and with whites. In the cities, the line between slavery and freedom remained, but it grew less and less distinct.

Indeed, white Southerners generally considered slavery to be incompatible with city life; and as Southern cities grew, the relative number of slaves in them declined. Fearing conspiracies and insurrections, urban slaveowners sold off much of their male "property" to the countryside. The cities were left with an excess of black women while they continued to have an excess of white men (a situation that certainly helped to account for the birth of many mulattoes). While slavery in the cities declined, segregation of blacks, both free and slave, increased. Segregation was a means of social control intended to make up for the loosening of the discipline of slavery itself.

The Slave Trade

Although the importing of slaves from outside the United States largely ceased in 1808 (except for illegal smuggling), a flourishing slave trade continued through the 1850s. What sustained it was the great population movement from the upper South to the lower South and the great demand for slaves in the newly cultivated areas. Professional traders transported slaves from the tidewater region and the Carolinas over long distances to the Southwest, using trains and river or ocean steamers. On shorter journeys, the slaves moved on foot, trudging in coffles of hundreds along dusty highways. Eventually they arrived at such central markets as Natchez, New Orleans, Mobile, or Galveston, where purchasers collected to bid for them. At the auction, the bidders checked the slaves like livestock, watching them as they were made to walk or trot, inspecting their teeth, feeling their arms and legs, looking for signs of infirmity or age. Buyers were careful, because traders were known to deceive them by blacking gray hair, oiling withered skin, and concealing physical defects in other ways.

The domestic slave trade dehumanized all who were involved in it. It separated children from parents, and parents from each other. Even families kept together by scrupulous masters might be broken up in the division of the estate after the master's death. Planters who bought or sold slaves eased their consciences by holding the traders in contempt and assigning them a low social position.

Slave Resistance

Few issues have sparked as much debate among historians as the effects of slavery on the slaves themselves. Slaveowners, and many white Americans in later generations, liked to argue that the slaves were generally content, "happy with their lot." That may have been true in some cases. But it is clear that the vast majority of Southern blacks were not content with being slaves, that they yearned for freedom even though most realized there was little they could do to secure it. Evidence for that conclusion comes, if from nowhere else, from the reaction of slaves when emancipation finally came. Virtually all Southern blacks reacted to freedom with great joy, and relatively few chose to remain in the service of the whites who had owned them

HARRIET TUBMAN WITH ESCAPED SLAVES Harriet Tubman (c. 1820–1913) was born into slavery in Maryland. In 1849, when her master died, she escaped to Philadelphia to avoid being sold out of state. Over the next ten years, she assisted first members of her own family and then up to 300 other slaves to escape from Maryland to freedom. During the Civil War, she served alternately as a nurse and as a spy for Union forces in South Carolina. She is shown here, on the left, with some of the slaves she had helped to free.

before the Civil War (although most blacks, of course, remained for many years subservient to whites in one way or another).

The dominant response of African-Americans to slavery was a complex one: a combination of adaptation and resistance. At the extremes, slavery could produce two opposite reactions—each of which served as the basis for a powerful stereotype in white society. One extreme was what became known as the "Sambo"—the shuffling, grinning, head-scratching, deferential slave who acted out the role the white world expected. More often than not, the "Sambo" pattern of behavior was a charade, a façade assumed in the presence of whites. The other extreme was the slave rebel—the black who could not accommodate himself or herself to slavery. Rebellious slaves faced terrible consequences if they acted on their impulses, but many revolted, in large ways or small, nevertheless.

Actual slave revolts were extremely rare, but fear of them gripped white Southerners everywhere. In 1800, Gabriel Prosser gathered 1,000 rebellious slaves outside Richmond; but two blacks gave the plot away, and the Virginia militia was called out in time to head it off. Prosser and thirty-five others were executed. In 1822, the Charleston free black Denmark Vesey and his followers—rumored to total 9,000—made preparations for revolt; but again the word leaked out, and retribution followed. In 1831, Nat Turner, a slave preacher, led a band of blacks who armed themselves with guns and axes and, on a summer night, went from house to house in Southampton County, Virginia. They killed sixty white men, women, and children before being overpowered by state and federal troops. More than a hundred blacks were executed in the aftermath. Nat Turner's was the only actual slave insurrection in the nineteenth-century South.

Resistance to slavery usually took other, less drastic forms. In some cases, slaves worked "within the system" to free themselves from it—earning money with which they bought their own and their families' freedom. Some slaves were set free by their masters' wills, although state laws made it more and more difficult, and in some cases practically impossible, for owners to do that after the 1830s. By 1860, there were about 250,000 free blacks in the slaveholding states, more than half of them in Virginia and Maryland. A few (generally on the northern fringes of the slaveholding regions) bought land and prospered. Some owned slaves themselves, usually relatives whom they had bought in order to ensure their ultimate emancipation. Most, however, lived in urban areas in abject poverty. Law or custom closed many occupations to them, forbade them to assemble without white supervision, and placed numerous other restraints on them. Yet great as were the hardships of freedom, blacks usually preferred them to slavery.

Some blacks attempted to resist slavery by running away. A few escaped to the North or to Canada, especially after sympathetic whites began organizing the so-called underground railroad to assist them in flight. But the obstacles to a successful escape, particularly from the Deep South, were almost impossibly great. They included the hazards of distance, the slaves' ignorance of geography, and the white "slave patrols," which stopped wandering blacks on sight throughout the South demanding to see travel permits or pursued runaways through the woods using bloodhounds. Despite the obstacles, however, blacks continued to run away from their masters in large numbers. Some did so repeatedly, undeterred by the whippings and other penalties inflicted on them when captured.

But perhaps the most important method of slave resistance was simply a pattern of everyday behavior by which blacks defied their masters. That whites so often considered blacks to be lazy and shiftless suggests one means of resistance: refusal to work hard. Slaves might also steal from their masters or from neighboring whites. They might perform isolated acts of sabotage: losing or breaking tools (Southern planters gradually began to buy unusually heavy hoes because so many of the lighter ones got broken), performing tasks improperly, mistreating livestock, or faking illness. Some slaves deliberately maimed themselves. Others engaged in arson, which slaveowners feared almost as much as they feared insurrections.

Slave Religion and the Black Family

Resistance was only one aspect of the slave response to slavery. The other was an elaborate process of adaptation—a process that implied not contentment with bondage but recognition that there was no realistic alternative. One of the ways blacks adapted was by developing a rich and complex culture, one that enabled them to sustain a sense of racial pride and unity. In many areas, they retained a language of their own, sometimes incorporating African speech patterns into English. They developed a distinctive music, establishing in the process one of the greatest of all American musical traditions. The most important features of African-American culture, however, were embodied in the development of two powerful institutions: religion and the family.

A separate slave religion was not supposed to exist. Almost all blacks were Christians, and their masters expected them to worship under the supervision of white ministers—often in the same chapels as whites. Indeed, autonomous black churches were banned by law. Nevertheless, blacks throughout the South developed their own version of Christianity, at times incorporating such African practices as voodoo but more often simply bending religion to the special circumstances of bondage. Natural leaders emerging within the slave community rose to the rank of preacher; and when necessary, blacks would hold services in secret, often at night.

Black religion was more emotional than its white counterparts, and it reflected the influence of African customs and practices. Slave prayer meetings routinely involved fervent chanting, spontaneous exclamations from the congregation, and ecstatic conversion experiences. Black religion was also more joyful and affirming than that of many white denominations. And above all, black religion emphasized the dream of freedom and deliverance. In their prayers and songs and sermons, black Christians talked and sang of the day when the Lord would "call us home," "deliver us to freedom," "take us to the Promised Land." And while their white masters generally chose to interpret such language merely as the expression of hopes for life after death, blacks themselves used the images of Christian salvation to express their own dream of freedom in the present world.

The slave family was the other crucial institution of black culture in the South. The nuclear family was the dominant kinship model among African-Americans. But such families did not always operate according to white customs. Black women generally began bearing children at younger ages than most whites, often as early as age fourteen or fifteen. Slave communities did not condemn premarital pregnancy in the way white society did, and black couples would often begin living together before marrying. It was customary, however, for couples to marry soon after conceiving a child. Family ties were no less strong than those of whites, and many slave marriages lasted throughout the course of long lifetimes. When marriages did not survive, it was often because of circumstances over which blacks had no control. Up to a third of all black families were broken up by the slave trade.

The need for the black family to adapt itself to its own uncertain future accounted for some of its other distinctive characteristics. Networks of kinship—which grew to include not only spouses and their children but aunts, uncles, grandparents, even distant cousins—remained strong and important and often served to compensate for the breakup of nuclear families. A slave suddenly moved to a new area, far from his or her family, might create "fictional" kinship ties and become "adopted" by a family in the new community. Even so, the impulse to maintain contact with a spouse and children remained strong long after the breakup of a family. One of the most frequent causes of flight from the plantation was a slave's desire to find a husband, wife, or child who had been sent elsewhere.

In addition to establishing social and cultural institutions of their own, slaves adapted themselves to slavery by forming complex relationships with their masters. However much blacks resented their lack of freedom, they often found it difficult to maintain an entirely hostile attitude toward their owners. Not only were they dependent on whites for the material means of existence—food, clothing, and shelter; they also often derived from their masters a sense of security and protection. There was, in short, a paternal relationship between slave and master—sometimes harsh, sometimes kindly, but almost invariably important. That paternalism, in fact, became (even if not always consciously) a vital instrument of white control. By creating a sense of mutual dependence, whites helped reduce resistance to an institution that, in essence, was designed solely for the benefit of the ruling race.

DEBATING THE PAST

The Nature of Plantation Slavery

N O ISSUE IN American history has produced a richer literature or a more spirited debate than the nature of plantation slavery. The debate began even before the Civil War, when abolitionists strove to expose slavery to the world as a brutal, dehumanizing institution, while Southern defenders of slavery tried to depict it as a benevolent, paternalistic system. That same debate continued for a time after the Civil War; but by the late nineteenth century, with white Americans eager for sectional conciliation, most Northern and Southern chroniclers of slavery began to accept a romanticized and unthreatening picture of the Old South and its peculiar institution.

The first major scholarly examination of slavery was fully within this romantic tradition. Ulrich B. Phillips's *American Negro Slavery* (1918) portrayed slavery as an essentially benign institution in which kindly masters looked after submissive, childlike, and generally contented African-Americans. Phillips's apologia for slavery remained the authoritative work on the subject for nearly thirty years.

In the 1940s, as concern about racial injustice increasingly engaged the attention of white Americans, challenges to Phillips began to emerge. In 1941, for example, Melville J. Herskovits challenged Phillips's contention that black Americans retained little of their African cultural inheritance. In 1943, Herbert Aptheker published a chronicle of slave revolts as a way of challenging Phillips's claim that blacks were submissive and content.

A somewhat different challenge to Phillips emerged in the 1950s from historians who emphasized the brutality of the institution. Kenneth Stampp's *The Peculiar Institution* (1956) and, even more powerfully, Stanley Elkins's *Slavery* (1959) described a labor system that did serious physical and psychological damage to its victims. Stampp and Elkins portrayed slavery as something like a prison, in which men and women had virtually no space to develop their own social and cultural lives. Elkins compared the system to Nazi concentration camps during World War II and likened the childlike "Sambo" personality of slavery to the tragic distortions of character produced by the Holocaust.

In the early 1970s, an explosion of new scholarship on slavery shifted the emphasis away from the damage the system inflicted on African-Americans and toward the striking success of the slaves themselves in building a culture of their own despite their enslavement. John Blassingame in 1973, echoing Herskovits's claims of thirty years earlier, argued that "the most remarkable aspect of the whole process of enslavement is the extent to which the American-born slaves were able to retain their ancestors' culture." Herbert Gutman, in *The Black Family in Slavery and Freedom* (1976), challenged the prevailing belief that slavery had weakened and even destroyed the African-American family. On the contrary, he argued, the black family survived slavery with impressive strength, although with some significant differences from the prevailing form of the white family. Eugene Genovese's *Roll, Jordan, Roll* (1974) revealed how African-Americans manipulated the paternalist assumptions that lay at the heart of slavery to build a large cultural space of their own, within the system, where they could develop their own family life, social traditions, and religious patterns. That same year, Robert Fogel and Stanley Engerman published their controversial *Time on the Cross*, a highly quantitative study that supported some of the claims of Gutman and Genovese about black achievement but that went much further in portraying slavery as a successful and reasonably humane (if ultimately immoral) system. Slave workers, they argued, were better treated and lived in greater comfort than most Northern industrial workers of the same era. Their conclusions produced a storm of criticism.

Some of the most important recent scholarship on slavery has focused on the role of gender in shaping plantation society. Elizabeth Fox-Genovese, for example, argues in *Within the Plantation Household* (1988) that the world of black women was in many ways distinctive, defined by their dual roles as members of the plantation work force and anchors of the black family. She rejects the contention of some scholars that slave women formed special bonds, born of shared female experiences, with the plantation mistresses. But the role of gender, she argues, was nevertheless as important as the role of race in determining the nature of the "peculiar institution."

CHAPTER TWELVE

An Age of Reforms

The Romantic Impulse ~ *Remaking Society*
The Crusade Against Slavery

T HE UNITED STATES in the mid-nineteenth century was growing rapidly in geographical extent, in the size and diversity of its population, and in the dimensions and complexity of its economy. And like any people faced with such rapid and fundamental change, Americans reacted with ambiguity. On the one hand, they were excited by the new possibilities that economic growth was providing. On the other hand, they were painfully aware of the dislocations that it was creating: the challenges to traditional values and institutions, the social instability, the uncertainty about the future.

One result of these conflicting attitudes was the emergence of movements to "reform" the nation. Such movements were highly diverse, but most reflected one of two basic impulses, and at times elements of both. Some rested on an optimistic faith in human nature, a belief that within every individual resided a spirit that was basically good and that society should attempt to unleash. This assumption—which produced in both Europe and America a movement known as romanticism—stood in marked contrast to the traditional Calvinist assumption that human desires and instincts were sinful and needed to be repressed.

A second impulse was a desire for order and control. With their society changing so rapidly, with their traditional values and institutions being challenged and eroded, many Americans yearned above all for a restoration of stability and discipline to their nation. Often, this impulse embodied a conservative nostalgia for better, simpler times. But it also inspired efforts to create new institutions of social control, suited to the realities of the new age.

Reform efforts took many forms and could be found in every part of the nation. By the end of the 1840s, however, one issue—slavery—had come to overshadow all others. And one group of reformers—the abolitionists—had become the most influential of all. At that point, the reform impulse became another wedge between the North and the South.

THE ROMANTIC IMPULSE

"In the four quarters of the globe," wrote the English wit Sydney Smith in 1820, "who reads an American book? or goes to an American play? or looks at an American picture or statue?" The answer, he assumed, was obvious—no one.

American intellectuals were painfully aware of the low regard in which their culture was held by Europeans, and they tried in the middle decades of the century to create an American artistic life that would express their own nation's special virtues. At the same time, many of the nation's cultural leaders were striving for another kind of liberation, which was—ironically—largely an import from Europe: the spirit of romanticism. In literature, in philosophy, in art, even in politics and economics, American intellectuals were committing themselves to the liberation of the human spirit.

An American Literature

The effort to create a distinctively American literature, which Washington Irving and others had begun in the first decades of the century, made important advances in the 1820s through the work of the first great American novelist: James Fenimore Cooper. What most distinguished his work was its evocation of the American West. Cooper had a lifelong fascination with man's relationship to nature and with the challenges (and dangers) of America's expansion westward. His most important novels—among them *The Last of the Mohicans* (1826) and *The Deerslayer* (1841)—explored the experience of rugged white frontiersmen with Indians, pioneers, violence, and the law. Cooper not only celebrated the American spirit and landscape; he also evoked, through the character of Natty Bumppo, the ideal of the independent individual with a natural inner goodness—an ideal that many Americans feared was in jeopardy in the expanding, industrializing world of the East.

Another, slightly later group of American writers displayed more clearly the appeal of romanticism to the nation's artists and intellectuals. In 1855, Walt Whitman published his first book of poems, *Leaves of Grass*, and established himself as one of the nation's most important writers. These and later poems were celebrations of democracy, of the liberation of the individual spirit, and of the pleasures of the flesh. Whitman helped liberate verse from traditional, restrictive conventions; he also expressed a personal yearning for emotional and physical release and personal fulfillment—a yearning perhaps rooted in part in his personal experience as a homosexual living in a society profoundly intolerant of unconventional sexuality.

Less exuberant was Herman Melville, probably the greatest American writer of his era. The most important of his novels was *Moby Dick*, published in 1851—the story of Ahab, the powerful, driven captain of a whaling vessel, who was obsessed with his search for Moby Dick, the great white whale that had once maimed him. It was a story of courage and of the strength of human will. But it was also a tragedy of pride and revenge, and a metaphor for the harsh, individualistic, achievement-driven culture of nineteenth-century America.

The Transcendentalists

One of the outstanding expressions of the romantic impulse in America came from a group of New England writers and philosophers known as the transcendentalists. Borrowing heavily from German and English writers and philosophers, the transcendentalists embraced a theory of the individual that rested on a distinction between what they called "reason" and "understanding." Reason, as they defined it, was the highest human faculty; it was the individual's innate capacity to grasp beauty and truth by giving full expression to the instincts and emotions. Understanding, by contrast, was the use of intellect in the narrow, artificial ways imposed by society; it involved the repression of instinct and the victory of externally imposed learning. Every person's goal, therefore, should be liberation from the confines of "understanding" and cultivation of "reason." Each individual should strive to "transcend" the limits of the intellect and allow the emotions, the "soul," to create an "original relation to the Universe."

Transcendentalist philosophy emerged first among a small group of intellectuals centered in Concord, Massachusetts, and led by Ralph Waldo Emerson. A Unitarian minister in his youth, Emerson left the clergy in 1832 to devote himself to writing, teaching, and lecturing. In "Nature" (1836),

WALT WHITMAN This picture of the youthful, jaunty, bearded poet was the frontispiece for the first edition of *Leaves of Grass* (1855). It is an engraving from a painting by Francis B. Carpenter, one of the most successful portrait painters of the mid-nineteenth century.

Emerson wrote that in the quest for self-fulfillment, individuals should work for a communion with the natural world: "in the woods, we return to reason and faith. . . . Standing on the bare ground,—my head bathed by the blithe air, and uplifted into infinite space,—all mean egotism vanishes. . . . I am part and particle of God." In other essays, he was even more explicit in advocating a commitment of the individual to the full exploration of inner capacities. "Nothing is at last sacred," he wrote in "Self-Reliance" (1841), perhaps his most famous essay, "but the integrity of your own mind."

Almost as influential as Emerson was another Concord transcendentalist, Henry David Thoreau. Thoreau went even further than his friend Emerson in repudiating the repressive forces of society, which produced, he said, "lives of quiet desperation." Each individual should work for self-realization by resisting pressures to conform to society's expectations and responding instead to his or her own instincts. Thoreau's own effort to free himself—immortalized in *Walden* (1854)—led him to build a small cabin in the Concord woods on the edge of Walden Pond, where he lived alone for two years as simply as he could, attempting to liberate himself from repressive convention and from what he considered society's excessive interest in material comforts. "I went to the woods," he explained, "because I wished to live deliberately, to front only the essential facts of life, and see if I could not learn what it had to teach, and not, when I came to die, discover that I had not lived." Thoreau's rejection of what he considered the artificial constraints of society extended to his relationship with government. In 1846, he went to jail (briefly) rather than agree to pay a poll tax. He would not, he insisted, give financial support to a government that permitted the existence of slavery. In his 1849 essay "Resistance to Civil Government," he explained his refusal by arguing that a government which required an individual to violate his or her own morality had no legitimate authority. The proper response was "civil disobedience," or "passive resistance"—a public refusal to obey unjust laws.

Visions of Utopia

Although transcendentalism was at its heart an individualistic philosophy, it helped spawn the most famous of all nineteenth-century experiments in communal living: Brook Farm. The dream of the Boston transcendentalist George Ripley, Brook Farm was established in 1841 as an experimental community in West Roxbury, Massachusetts. There, according to Ripley, individuals would gather to create a new society that would permit every member to have full opportunity for self-realization. All residents would share equally in the labor of the community so that all could share too in the leisure, which was essential for cultivation of the self. (Ripley was one of the first Americans to attribute positive connotations to the idea of leisure; most of his contemporaries equated it with laziness and sloth.) The tension between the ideal of individual freedom and the demands of a communal society took their toll on Brook Farm. Many residents became disenchanted and left. When a fire destroyed the central building of the community in 1847, the experiment dissolved.

Among the original residents of Brook Farm was the writer Nathaniel Hawthorne, who expressed his disillusionment with the experiment and, to some extent, with transcendentalism in a series of novels voicing some of the same concerns that his contemporary Herman Melville was articulating. In *The Blithedale Romance* (1852), he wrote scathingly of Brook Farm itself. In other novels—most notably *The Scarlet Letter* (1850) and *The House of the*

Seven Gables (1851)—he wrote equally passionately about the price individuals pay for cutting themselves off from society. Egotism, he claimed (in an indirect challenge to the transcendentalist faith in the self), was the "serpent" that lay at the heart of human misery.

The failure of Brook Farm did not, however, prevent the formation of other experimental communities. The Scottish industrialist and philanthropist Robert Owen founded an experimental community in Indiana in 1825, which he named New Harmony. It was to be a "Village of Cooperation," in which every resident worked and lived in total equality. The community was an economic failure, but the vision that had inspired it continued to enchant Americans. Dozens of other "Owenite" experiments began in other locations in the ensuing years.

Redefining Gender Roles

Many of the new utopian communities (and many of the new social philosophies on which they rested) were centrally concerned with the relationship between men and women. Some experimented with a radical redefinition of gender roles.

Such a redefinition was central to one of the most enduring of the utopian colonies of the nineteenth century: the Oneida Community, established in 1848 in upstate New York by John Humphrey Noyes. The Oneida "Perfectionists," as residents of the community called themselves, rejected traditional notions of family and marriage. All residents, Noyes declared, were "married" to all other residents; there were to be no permanent conjugal ties. But Oneida was not, as horrified critics often claimed, an experiment in unrestrained "free love." It was a place where the community carefully monitored sexual behavior; where women were protected from unwanted childbearing; and where children were raised communally, often seeing little of their own parents. The Oneidans took pride in what they considered their liberation of women from the demands of male "lust" and from the traditional bonds of family.

The Shakers, too, made a redefinition of traditional gender roles central to their society. Founded by "Mother" Ann Lee in the 1770s, the society of the Shakers survived into the twentieth century. (Only a tiny remnant is left today.) But the Shakers attracted a particularly large following in the mid-nineteenth century and established more than twenty communities throughout the Northeast and Northwest in the 1840s. They derived their name from a unique religious ritual—a sort of dance, in which members of a congregation would "shake" themselves free of sin while performing a loud chant.

The most distinctive feature of Shakerism, however, was its commitment to complete celibacy—which meant, of course, that no one could be born to Shakerism; all Shakers had to choose the faith voluntarily. Shaker communities attracted about 6,000 members in the 1840s, more women than men. They lived in communities where contacts between men and women were strictly limited, and they endorsed the idea of sexual equality. Within Shaker society, women exercised the most power. Shakerism, one observer wrote in the 1840s, was a refuge from the "perversions of marriage" and "the gross abuses which drag it down."

The Shakers were not, however, motivated only by a desire to escape the burdens of traditional sexual roles. They were trying as well to create a society separated and protected from the chaos and disorder that they believed had come to characterize American life as a whole. In that, they were much like other dissenting religious sects and other utopian communities of their time.

The Mormons

Perhaps the most important effort to create a new and more ordered society within the old was that of the Church of Jesus Christ of Latter Day Saints, whose members are known as Mormons. Mormonism began in upstate New York as a result of the efforts of Joseph Smith, an energetic but economically unsuccessful man, who had spent most of his twenty-four years moving restlessly through New England and the Northeast. Then, in 1830, he published a remarkable document—the *Book of Mormon*—which he claimed was a translation of a set of golden tablets he had found in the hills of New York after a revelation by an angel of God. The *Book of Mormon* told the story of an ancient civilization in America, whose now vanished kingdom could become a model for a new holy community in the United States.

Gathering a small group of believers around him, Smith began in 1831 to seek a sanctuary for his new community of "saints," an effort that would continue, unhappily, for more than twenty years. Time and again, the Mormons attempted to establish their "New Jerusalem." Time and again, they met with persecution from surrounding communities suspicious of their radical religious doctrines—which included polygamy (the right of men to take several wives), a rigid form of social organization, and an intense secrecy that gave rise to wild rumors among their critics of conspiracy and depravity.

Driven from their original settlements in Independence, Missouri, and Kirtland, Ohio, the Mormons founded Nauvoo, Illinois, which in the early 1840s became an imposing and economically successful community. In 1844, however, Joseph Smith was arrested, charged with treason (for conspiring against the government to win foreign support for a new Mormon colony in the Southwest), and imprisoned in nearby Carthage, Illinois. There an angry mob attacked the jail, forced Smith from his cell, and shot and killed him. The Mormons now abandoned Nauvoo and, under the leadership of Smith's successor, Brigham Young, traveled across the desert—a society of 12,000 people, one of the largest group migrations in American history—and established a new settlement in Utah, the present Salt Lake City. There, at last, the Mormons were able to create a permanent settlement.

Like other experiments in social organization of the era, Mormonism reflected a belief in human perfectibility. God had once been a man, the church taught; and thus every man or woman could aspire to become, in effect, a god—as Joseph Smith had done. But the Mormons did not celebrate individual liberty. Instead, they created a highly organized, centrally directed, almost militarized social structure as a refuge against the disorder and uncertainty of the secular world. They placed particular emphasis on the structure of the family. The original Mormons were, for the most part, men and women who felt displaced in their rapidly changing society—economically marginal people left behind by the material growth and social progress of their era. In the new religion, they found security and order.

REMAKING SOCIETY

The reform impulse also helped create new movements to remake mainstream society—movements in which, to a striking degree, women formed both the rank and file and the leadership. By the 1830s, such movements had taken the form of organized reform societies. The new organizations worked on behalf of a wide range of goals: temperance; education; peace; the care of the poor, the handicapped, and the mentally ill; the treatment of criminals; the rights of women; and many more. Few eras in American history have witnessed as wide a range of reform efforts. And few eras have exposed more clearly the simultaneous attraction of Americans to the ideas of personal liberty and social order.

Revivalism, Morality, and Order

The philosophy of reform arose in part from the optimistic vision of those such as the transcendentalists who preached the divinity of the individual. But another, and in many respects more important, source was Protestant revivalism—the movement that had begun with the Second Great Awakening early in the century and had, by the 1820s, evolved into a powerful force for social reform.

The New Light evangelicals embraced the optimistic belief that every individual was capable of salvation through his or her own efforts. (Hence the term "Free Will Baptists," by which some described themselves.) Partly as a result, revivalism soon became not only a means of personal salvation but a mandate for the reform of the larger society. In particular, revivalism produced a crusade against personal immorality. "The church," said Charles Grandison Finney, the leading revivalist of his time, "must take right ground on the subject of Temperance, the Moral Reform, and all the subjects of practical morality which come up for decision from time to time."

THE DRUNKARD'S PROGRESS This 1846 lithograph by Nathaniel Currier shows what temperance advocates argued was the inevitable consequence of alcohol consumption. Beginning with an apparently innocent "glass with a friend," the young man rises step by step to the summit of drunken revelry, then declines to desperation and suicide while his abandoned wife and child grieve.

Evangelical Protestantism added major strength, therefore, to one of the most influential reform movements of the era: the crusade against drunkenness. No social vice, temperance advocates argued, was more responsible for crime, disorder, and poverty than the excessive use of alcohol. Women, who were particularly active in the temperance movement, complained that men spent money their families needed on alcohol and that drunken husbands often beat and abused their wives. Temperance also appealed to those who were alarmed by immigration; drunkenness, many nativists believed, was responsible for violence and disorder in immigrant communities and temperance was a way to discipline them. By 1840, temperance had become a major national movement, with powerful organizations and more than a million followers who had signed a formal pledge to forgo hard liquor.

As the movement gained in strength, it became divided in purpose. Some demanded legislation to restrict the sale and consumption of alcohol (Maine passed such a law in 1851); others insisted that temperance must rely on the conscience of the individual. Whatever their disagreements, however, most temperance advocates shared similar motives. By promoting abstinence, reformers were attempting to promote individual moral self-improvement. They were also trying to impose discipline on a disordered society.

Education and Rehabilitation

One of the most important reform movements of the mid-nineteenth century was the effort to produce a system of universal public education. As of 1830, no state had such a system, although some—such as Massachusetts—were supporting limited versions. Now, however, interest in public education grew rapidly.

The greatest of the educational reformers was Horace Mann, the first secretary of the Massachusetts Board of Education, which was established in 1837. To Mann and his followers, education was the only way to "counterwork this tendency to the domination of capital and the servility of labor." It was also the only way to protect democracy, for an educated electorate was essential to the workings of a free political system. Mann reorganized the Massachusetts school system, lengthened the academic year (to six months), doubled teachers' salaries (although he did not eliminate the large disparities between the salaries of male and female teachers), broadened the curriculum, and introduced new methods of professional training for teachers. Other states followed similar courses: building new schools, creating teachers' colleges, and offering many children access to education for the first time. By the 1850s, the principle (although not yet the reality) of tax-supported elementary schools was established in every state.

Yet the quality of public education continued to vary widely. In some places—Massachusetts, for example—educators were generally capable men and women, often highly trained, who had an emerging sense of themselves as career professionals. In other areas, however, teachers were often barely literate, and funding for education was severely limited. In much of the West, where the population was highly dispersed, many children had no access to schools at all. In the South, all African-Americans were barred from education (although approximately 10 percent of them managed to achieve literacy anyway), and only about a third of all white children of school age were actually enrolled in schools in 1860. In the North, 72 percent were enrolled; but even there, many students attended classes only briefly and casually.

The interest in education (and, implicitly, in the unleashing of individual talents that could result from it) was visible too in the growing movement to educate American Indians in the antebellum period. Some reformers, even many who considered black people inferior and unredeemable, believed that Indians could be "civilized" if only they could be taught the ways of the white world. Efforts by missionaries and others to educate Indians and encourage them to assimilate were particularly prominent in such areas of the Far West as Oregon, where substantial numbers of whites were beginning to settle in the 1840s and where conflicts with the natives had not yet become acute. Nevertheless, the great majority of Native Americans remained outside the reach of educational reform, either by choice or by circumstance or both.

Despite limitations and inequities, the achievements of the school reformers were impressive. By the beginning of the Civil War, the United States had one of the highest literacy rates of any nation of the world: 94 percent of the population of the North, 83 percent of the white population (and 58 percent of the total population) of the South.

The conflicting impulses that underlay the movement for school reform were visible in some of the different educational institutions that emerged. The belief in the potential of the individual sparked the creation of new institutions to help the handicapped, institutions that formed part of a great network of charitable activities known as the Benevolent Empire. Among them was the Perkins School for the Blind in Boston, the first such school in America. Nothing better exemplified the romantic spirit of the era than the belief of those who founded Perkins that even society's least-favored members—the unsighted and otherwise handicapped—could be helped to discover their own inner strength and wisdom.

More typical of educational reform, however, were efforts to use schools to impose a set of social values on children—values that reformers and others believed were appropriate for their new, industrializing society. These values included thrift, order, discipline, punctuality, and respect for authority. Horace Mann, for example, spoke of the role of public schools in extending democracy and expanding individual opportunity. But he spoke, too, of their role in creating social order: "The unrestrained passions of men are not only homicidal, but suicidal. . . . Train up a child in the way he should go, and when he is old he will not depart from it."

Similar impulses produced another powerful movement of reform: the creation of "asylums" for criminals and the mentally ill. In advocating prison and hospital reform, Americans were reacting against one of society's most glaring ills: antiquated jails and mental institutions whose inmates lived in almost inhuman conditions. Beginning in the 1820s, many states built new penitentiaries and mental asylums. New York built the first penitentiary at Auburn in 1821. In Massachusetts, the reformer Dorothea Dix began a national movement for new methods of treating the mentally ill.

But the creation of asylums for social deviants was not simply an effort to curb the abuses of the old system. It was also an attempt to reform and rehabilitate the inmates. New forms of prison discipline were designed to rid criminals of the "laxness" that had presumably led them astray. Solitary confinement and the imposition of silence on work crews (both instituted in Pennsylvania and New York in the 1820s) were meant to give prisoners opportunities to meditate on their wrongdoings and develop "penitence" (hence the name "penitentiary"). Some reformers argued that the discipline of the asylum could serve as a model for other potentially disordered environments—for example, factories and schools. Before long, however, penitentiaries and many mental hospitals fell victim to overcrowding, and the original reform ideal was gradually lost. Most prisons and many mental hospitals ultimately degenerated into little more than warehouses for inmates, with scant emphasis on rehabilitation.

Some of the same impulses that produced asylums underlay the emergence in the 1840s and 1850s of a new "reform" approach to the problems of Native Americans: the idea of the reservation. For several decades, the dominant thrust of the United States policy toward the Indians in areas of white settlement had been relocation. The principal motive behind relocation was simple: getting the tribes out of the way of white civilization. But among some whites there had also been another, if secondary, intent: to move the Indians to a place where they would be protected from whites and allowed to develop to a point at which assimilation might be possible. Even Andrew Jackson, whose animus toward Indians was legendary, once described the removals as part of the nation's "moral duty . . . to protect and if possible to preserve and perpetuate the scattered remnants of the Indian race."

It was a small step from the idea of relocation to the idea of the reservation, the notion of creating an enclosed region in which Indians would live in isolation from white society. Again, the reservations served white economic purposes above all, as they involved moving Native Americans out of good lands that white settlers wanted. But they also had a reform purpose. Just as prisons, asylums, and orphanages would provide society with an opportunity to train and uplift misfits and unfortunates within white society, so the reservations might provide a way to undertake what one official called "the great work of regenerating the Indian race."

The Rise of Feminism

The reform ferment of the antebellum period had a particular meaning for American women. As they played central roles in reform movements, women began to confront the problems they themselves faced in a male-dominated society. The result was the emergence of the first important American feminist movement.

Many of the women who became involved in reform movements in the 1820s and 1830s came to resent the social and legal restrictions that limited their participation. Some began to defy them. Sarah and Angelina Grimké, sisters born in South Carolina who had become active and outspoken abolitionists, ignored attacks by men who claimed that their activism was inappropriate to their gender. "Men and women were *CREATED EQUAL*," they argued. "They are both moral and accountable beings, and whatever is right for man to do, is right for women to do." Other reformers— Catharine Beecher, Harriet Beecher Stowe (her sister), Lucretia Mott, Elizabeth Cady Stanton, and Dorothea Dix—similarly pressed at the boundaries of "acceptable" female behavior, chafing at the restrictions placed on women by men.

In 1840, American female delegates arrived at a world antislavery convention in London, only to be turned away by the men who controlled the proceedings. Angered at the rejection, several of the delegates—notably Lucretia Mott and Elizabeth Cady Stanton—became convinced that their first duty as reformers should now be to elevate the status of women. Over the next several years, Mott, Stanton, and others began drawing pointed parallels between the plight of women and the plight of slaves; and in 1848, in Seneca Falls, New York, they organized a convention to discuss the question of women's rights. Out of the meeting came the "Declaration of Sentiments and Resolutions" (patterned on the Declaration of Independence), which stated that "all men and women are created equal," that women no less than men are endowed with certain inalienable rights. In demanding the right to vote, they launched a movement for woman suffrage that would survive until the battle was finally won in 1920. But the Seneca Falls document was at least equally important for its rejection of the whole notion that men and women should be assigned separate "spheres" in society.

Many of the women involved in these feminist efforts were Quakers. Quakerism had long embraced the ideal of sexual equality and had tolerated, indeed encouraged, the emergence of women as preachers and community leaders. Quakers had also been among the leaders of the antislavery movement, and Quaker women had played a leading role within those efforts. Not all Quakers went so far as to advocate full sexual equality in American society, but enough Quaker women coalesced around such demands to cause a schism in the yearly meeting of Friends in Genesee, New York, in 1848. That dissident faction formed the core of the group that organized the Seneca Falls convention. Of the women who drafted the Declaration of Sentiments there, all but Elizabeth Cady Stanton were Quakers. Stanton, joined two years later by Susan B. Anthony, led the movement to implement the Seneca Falls resolutions in the 1850s and beyond. Together, they ultimately transformed it into a powerful force for change.

Progress toward feminist goals was limited in the antebellum years, but certain individual women did manage to break the social barriers to advancement. Elizabeth Blackwell, born in England, gained acceptance and fame as a physician. Her sister-in-law Antoinette Brown Blackwell became the first ordained woman minister in the United States; and another sister-in-law, Lucy Stone, took the revolutionary step of retaining her maiden name after marriage. She became a successful and influential lecturer on women's rights. Emma Willard, founder of the Troy Female Seminary in 1821, and Catharine Beecher, who founded the Hartford Female Seminary in 1823, worked on behalf of women's education.

Feminists benefited greatly from their association with other reform movements, most notably abolitionism; but they also suffered as a result. The demands of women were usually assigned—even by some women themselves—a secondary position to what many considered the far greater issue of the rights of slaves.

THE CRUSADE AGAINST SLAVERY

The antislavery movement was not new to the mid-nineteenth century. But only in 1830 did it begin to gather the force that would ultimately enable it to overshadow virtually all other efforts at social reform.

Early Opposition to Slavery

In the early years of the nineteenth century, those who opposed slavery were, for the most part, a calm and genteel lot, expressing moral disapproval but doing little else. To the extent that there was an organized antislavery movement, it centered on the concept of colonization—the effort to resettle American blacks in Africa or the Caribbean. In 1817, a group of prominent white Virginians organized the American Colonization Society (ACS), which tried to challenge slavery without challenging property rights or Southern sensibilities. The ACS proposed a gradual freeing of slaves, with masters receiving compensation. The liberated blacks would then be transported out of the country and helped to establish a new society of their own. The ACS was not without impact. It received some funding from private donors, some from Congress, some from the legislatures of Virginia and Maryland. And it arranged to have several groups of blacks transported out of the United States, some of them to the west coast of Africa, where in 1830 they established the nation of Liberia. (In 1846, Liberia became an independent black republic, with its capital, Monrovia, named for the American president who had presided over the initial settlement.) But the ACS was in the end a negligible force. Neither private nor public funding was nearly enough to carry out the vast projects its supporters envisioned. In the space of a decade, they managed to "colonize" fewer slaves than were born in the United States in a month. Nothing, in fact, would have been enough; there were far too many blacks in America in the nineteenth century to be transported to Africa by any conceivable program. And the ACS met resistance, in any case, from blacks themselves, many of whom were now three or more generations removed from Africa and despite their loathing of slavery, had no wish to emigrate.

By 1830, colonization was failing rapidly, particularly since the cotton boom in the Deep South was increasing the commitment of planters to their labor system. Those opposed to slavery had reached what appeared to be a dead end.

Garrison and Abolitionism

At this crucial juncture, with the antislavery movement seemingly on the verge of collapse, a new figure emerged to transform it: William Lloyd Garrison. Born in Massachusetts in 1805, Garrison was in the 1820s an assistant to the New Jersey Quaker Benjamin Lundy, who published the leading antislavery newspaper of the time. Garrison grew impatient with his employer's moderate tone and mild proposals for reform. In 1831, therefore, he returned to Boston to found his own weekly newspaper, the *Liberator*.

Garrison's philosophy was so simple as to be genuinely revolutionary. Opponents of slavery, he said, should not, as earlier reformers had done, talk about the evil influence of slavery on white society; they should talk about the damage the system did to blacks. And they should, therefore, reject "gradualism" and demand the immediate, unconditional, universal abolition of slavery and the extension to blacks of all the rights of American citizenship. Garrison wrote in a relentless, uncompromising tone. "I am aware," he wrote in the very first issue of the *Liberator*, "that many object to the severity of my language; but is there not cause for severity? I will be as harsh as truth, and as uncompromising as justice. . . . I am in earnest—I will not equivocate—I will not excuse—I will not retreat a single inch—*and I will be heard.*"

Garrison soon attracted a large group of followers throughout the North, enough to enable him to found the New England Antislavery Society in 1832 and a year later, after a convention in Philadelphia, the American Antislavery Society. By 1835, there were more than 400 local societies; by 1838, there were 1,350, with more than 250,000 members.

Abolitionists were very much a part of the larger spirit of reform of their era. Like other reformers, they were calling for an unleashing of the individual human spirit, the elimination of artificial social barriers to fulfillment. Who, after all, was more in need of assistance in realizing individual potential than the enslaved blacks?

Black Abolitionists

Abolitionism had a particular appeal, perhaps needless to say, to the free black population of the North, which in 1850 numbered about 250,000, mostly concentrated in cities. These free blacks lived in conditions of poverty and oppression at times worse than those of their slave counterparts in the South. They were often the victims of mob violence; they had virtually no access to education; they could vote in only a few states; and they were barred from all but the most menial of occupations. Most worked either as domestic servants or as sailors in the American merchant marine, and their wages were so low that most lived in squalor. Some were kidnapped by whites and forced back into slavery.

For all their problems, however, Northern blacks were fiercely proud of their freedom and sensitive to the plight of those members of their race who remained in bondage; they were aware that their own position in society would remain precarious as long as slavery existed. Many in the 1830s came to support Garrison. But they also rallied to leaders of their own.

The greatest of the black abolitionists was Frederick Douglass, one of the most electrifying orators of his time. Born a slave in Maryland, Douglass

FREDERICK DOUGLASS Frederick Douglass was the most prominent African-American of the nineteenth century. Born in Maryland to an unknown white father and a slave mother, he escaped from slavery into the North in 1838. He quickly became a leader in the abolitionist movement.

escaped to Massachusetts in 1838, became an outspoken leader of antislavery sentiment, and spent two years lecturing in England, where he was lionized by members of that country's vigorous antislavery movement. On his return to the United States in 1847, Douglass purchased his freedom from his Maryland owner and founded an antislavery newspaper, the *North Star*, in Rochester, New York. He achieved wide renown as well for his autobiography, *Narrative of the Life of Frederick Douglass* (1845), in which he presented a damning picture of slavery. Douglass demanded not only freedom but full social and economic equality.

Antiabolitionism

The rise of abolitionism was a powerful force, but it provoked a powerful opposition as well. Almost all white Southerners, of course, were bitterly hostile to the movement. But even in the North, abolitionists were a small, dissenting minority whom most whites viewed as dangerous radicals. Some feared that abolitionism would produce a destructive war between the sections. Others feared that it would lead to a great influx of free blacks into the North.

The result of such fears was an escalating wave of violence directed against abolitionists in the 1830s. A mob in Philadelphia attacked the abolitionist headquarters there in 1834, burned it to the ground, and began a bloody race riot. Another mob seized Garrison on the streets of Boston in 1835 and threatened to hang him. He was saved from death only by being locked in jail. Elijah Lovejoy, the editor of an abolitionist newspaper in Alton, Illinois, was victimized repeatedly by mob violence and finally killed when he tried to defend his press from attack.

That so many men and women continued to embrace abolitionism in the face of such vicious opposition from within their own communities suggests that abolitionists were not people who made their political commitments lightly or casually. They were strong-willed, passionate crusaders who displayed not only enormous courage and moral strength but at times a fervency that many of their contemporaries (and some later historians) found disturbing. The mobs were only the most violent expression of a hostility to abolitionism that many, perhaps most, other white Americans shared.

Abolitionism Divided

By the mid-1830s, the abolitionist crusade had begun to experience serious internal strains and divisions. One reason was the violence of the antiabolitionists, which persuaded some members of the movement that a more moderate approach was necessary. Another reason was the growing radicalism of William Lloyd Garrison, who shocked even many of his own allies (including Frederick Douglass) by attacking not only slavery but the government itself. The Constitution, he said, was "a covenant with death and an agreement with hell." The nation's churches, he claimed, were bulwarks of slavery. In 1840, Garrison precipitated a formal division within the American Antislavery Society by insisting that women, who had always been central to the organization's work, be permitted to participate in the movement on terms of full equality. He continued after 1840 to arouse controversy with new and even more radical stands: an extreme pacifism that rejected even defensive wars; opposition to all forms of coercion—not just slavery but prisons and asylums; and finally, in 1843, a call for Northern disunion from the South. The nation could, he suggested, purge itself of the sin of slavery by expelling the slave states from the Union.

From 1840 on, therefore, abolitionism moved in many channels and spoke with many different voices. The Garrisonians, with their radical and uncompromising moral stance, remained influential. But others operated in more moderate ways, arguing that abolition could be accomplished only as the result of a long, patient, peaceful struggle—"immediate abolition gradually accomplished," as they called it. At first, they depended on "moral suasion." They appealed to the conscience of the slaveholders, attempting to convince them that their institution was sinful. When that produced no results, they turned to political action, seeking to induce the Northern states and the federal government to aid the cause. They joined the Garrisonians in helping runaway slaves find refuge in the North or in Canada through what became known as the underground railroad (although their efforts were never as highly organized as the name suggests). After the Supreme Court (in *Prigg* v. *Pennsylvania*, 1842) ruled that states need not aid in enforcing the 1793 law requiring the return of fugitive slaves to their owners, abolitionists won passage in several Northern states of "personal liberty laws," which forbade state officials to assist in the capture and return of runaways. And the antislavery societies petitioned Congress to abolish slavery in places where the federal government had jurisdiction—in the territories and in the District of Columbia—and to prohibit the interstate slave trade. But few members of the movement believed that Congress could constitutionally interfere with a "domestic" institution such as slavery within the individual states themselves.

Antislavery sentiment underlay the formation in 1840 of the Liberty party, which ran Kentucky antislavery leader James G. Birney for president.

But this party and its successors never campaigned for outright abolition (an illustration of the important fact that "antislavery" and "abolitionism" were not always the same thing). They stood instead for "free soil," for keeping slavery out of the territories. Some free-soilers were concerned about the welfare of blacks; others were people who cared nothing about slavery but simply wanted to keep the West a country for whites. Garrison dismissed free-soilism as "white-manism." But the free-soil position would ultimately do what abolitionism never could: attract the support of large numbers, even a majority, of the white population of the North.

The frustrations of political abolitionism drove some critics of slavery to embrace more drastic measures. A few began to advocate violence; it was a group of prominent abolitionists in New England, for example, who funneled money and arms to John Brown for his bloody uprisings in Kansas and Virginia. Others attempted to arouse public anger through propaganda. The most powerful of all abolitionist propaganda was Harriet

UNCLE TOM'S CABIN This poster (advertising, among other things, a German edition of Harriet Beecher Stowe's novel) did not exaggerate when it described *Uncle Tom's Cabin* as "The Greatest Book of the Age." There were, to be sure, greater literary accomplishments; but no American book of the nineteenth century had so profound a political impact.

Beecher Stowe's novel *Uncle Tom's Cabin*, published as a book in 1852. It rocked the nation. It sold more than 300,000 copies within a year of publication and was later issued again and again, becoming one of the most remarkable best sellers in American history. And it succeeded in bringing the message of abolitionism to an enormous new audience—not only those who read the book but those who watched dramatizations of its story by countless theater companies throughout the nation. Reviled throughout the South, Stowe became a hero to many in the North. And in both regions, her novel helped inflame sectional tensions to a new level of passion. Few books in American history have had so great an impact on the course of public events.

Even divided, therefore, abolitionism remained a powerful influence on the life of the nation. Only a relatively small number of people before the Civil War ever accepted the abolitionist position that slavery must be entirely eliminated in a single stroke. But the crusade that Garrison had launched, and that thousands of committed men and women kept alive for three decades, was a constant, visible reminder of how deeply the institution of slavery was dividing America.

CHAPTER THIRTEEN

The Impending Crisis

Expansion and War ~ A New Sectional Crisis
The Crises of the 1850s

U NTIL THE 1840s, the tensions between North and South remained relatively contained. Had no new sectional issues arisen, it is possible that the United States would have avoided a civil war, that the two sections might have resolved their differences peaceably over time. But new issues did arise, centered around the expansion of slavery. From the North came the strident and increasingly powerful abolitionist movement, which kept the issue alive in the public mind and increased sectional animosities. And from the West, more significantly, came a series of controversies that would ultimately destroy the fragile Union. For ironically, the vigorous nationalism that was in some ways helping to keep the United States together was also producing a desire for territorial expansion that would tear the nation apart.

EXPANSION AND WAR

More than a million square miles of new territory came under the control of the United States during the 1840s—the greatest wave of expansion since the Louisiana Purchase nearly forty years before. By the end of the decade, the nation possessed all the territory of the present-day United States except Alaska, Hawaii, and a few relatively small areas acquired later through border adjustments. Many factors accounted for this great new wave of expansion, but one of the most important was a set of ideas—an ideology known as "Manifest Destiny."

Manifest Destiny

Manifest Destiny reflected both the burgeoning pride that characterized American nationalism in the mid-nineteenth century and the idealistic vision of social perfection that fueled so much of the reform energy of the time. It rested on the idea that America was destined—by God and by history—to expand its boundaries over a vast area, an area that included, but was not necessarily restricted to, the continent of North America. American expansion was not selfish, its advocates insisted; it was an altruistic attempt to extend American liberty to new realms.

By the 1840s, the idea of Manifest Destiny had spread throughout the nation, publicized by the new "penny press," which made newspapers available to a far greater proportion of the population than ever before, and fanned by the rhetoric of nationalist politicians. Advocates of Manifest Destiny disagreed, however, about how far and by what means the nation should expand. Some had relatively limited territorial goals; others envisioned a vast new "empire of liberty" that would include Canada, Mexico, Caribbean and Pacific islands, and ultimately, a few dreamed, much of the rest of the world. Some believed that America should use force to achieve its expansionist goals, others that the nation should expand peacefully or not at all.

Not everyone embraced the idea of Manifest Destiny. Henry Clay and other prominent politicians feared, correctly as it turned out, that territorial expansion would reopen the painful controversy over slavery and threaten the stability of the Union. Their voices, however, were all but drowned out in the enthusiasm over expansion in the 1840s, which began with the issues of Texas and Oregon.

Texas and Oregon

The United States had once claimed Texas—which, as the 1830s began, was part of the republic of Mexico—as a part of the Louisiana Purchase, but it had renounced the claim in 1819. Twice thereafter, the United States had offered to buy Texas, only to meet with indignant Mexican refusals. But in the early 1820s, the Mexican government launched an ill-advised experiment. It began encouraging Americans to move into Texas in hopes of strengthening the economy of the territory and increasing its own tax revenues. Thousands of Americans, attracted by the rich soil in Texas, took advantage of Mexico's welcome. The great majority were white Southerners, and the slaves they brought with them. By 1835, approximately 35,000 Americans, white and black, were living in Texas.

Almost from the beginning, there was friction between the new settlers and the Mexicans. Finally the Mexican government, feeling threatened by the new settlers, tried to exert control. A new law increased the powers of the national government of Mexico at the expense of the state governments, a measure that Texans from the United States assumed was aimed specifically at them. In 1836, the American settlers defiantly proclaimed their independence from Mexico.

The Mexican dictator, Antonio de Santa Anna, advanced with a large army into Texas, where the American settlers were having difficulty organizing a resistance. Their garrison at the Alamo mission in San Antonio was annihilated after a famous, if futile, defense by a group of Texas "patriots," a group that included, among others, the renowned frontiersman Davy Crockett; another garrison at Goliad suffered substantially the same fate when the Mexicans murdered most of the force after it had surrendered. But General Sam Houston kept a small army together, and on April 23, 1836, at the Battle of San Jacinto (near present-day Houston), he defeated the Mexican army and took Santa Anna prisoner. Texas had effectively won its independence.

The new republic of Texas, through its first president, Sam Houston, immediately requested annexation by the United States. But many American Northerners opposed acquiring a large new slave territory, and others opposed increasing the Southern votes in Congress and in the electoral college. President Jackson feared annexation might cause an ugly sectional controversy and even a war with Mexico. He did not, therefore, support annexation, and he even delayed recognizing the new republic until 1837. Martin Van Buren also refrained from pressing the issue.

Spurned by the United States, Texas cast out on its own. Its leaders sought money and support from Europe. They dreamed of creating a vast southwestern nation, stretching to the Pacific, that would rival the United States—a dream that appealed to European nations eager to counter the growing power of the United States. England and France quickly recognized and concluded trade treaties with Texas. Observing this, President Tyler persuaded Texas to apply again for admission to the United States in 1844. But when Secretary of State Calhoun presented an annexation treaty to Congress as if its only purpose were to extend slavery, Northern senators rebelled and defeated it. The Texas question quickly became the central issue in the election of 1844.

Control of what was known as the Oregon Country, in the Pacific Northwest, was another major political issue in the 1840s. Its half-million square miles included the present states of Oregon, Washington, and Idaho, parts of Montana and Wyoming, and half of British Columbia. Both Britain and the United States claimed sovereignty in the region; and unable to resolve their claims diplomatically, they agreed in an 1818 treaty to allow citizens of each country equal access to the territory. This arrangement, known as "joint occupation," continued for twenty years, until it, too, broke down in the face of growing immigration.

The Westward Migration

Throughout the 1840s, 1850s, and 1860s, hundreds of thousands of white and black Americans moved to the Far Western regions of the continent, settling in areas that had previously been inhabited almost entirely by Indians and a few missionaries. Many were white planters from the Southern states, most of whom settled in Texas and brought slaves with them. But the largest number came from the Old Northwest (what we now know as the Midwest)—white men and women, and a few blacks, who undertook arduous journeys in search of new opportunities. Most traveled in family groups, until the early 1850s, when the great gold rush attracted many single men. Most were reasonably young people. Most had experienced earlier, if usually shorter, migrations in the past.

All were in search of a new life, but they harbored many different visions of what the new life would bring. Some (particularly after the discovery of gold in California in 1849) hoped for quick riches. Others wanted to acquire property for farming or speculation and planned to take advantage of the vast public lands the federal government was selling at modest prices. Still others hoped to establish themselves as merchants and serve the new white communities developing in the West. Some (among them the Mormons) were on religious missions or were attempting to escape hardships or oppression in the East.

Most migrants traveled west along the great overland trails. They generally gathered in one of several major depots in Iowa and Missouri (Independence, St. Joseph, or Council Bluffs), joined a wagon train led by hired guides, and set off with their belongings piled in covered wagons and their livestock trailing behind. The major route west was the 2,000-mile Oregon Trail, which stretched from Independence across the Great Plains and through the South Pass of the Rocky Mountains. From there, migrants

THE OREGON TRAIL Trappers and merchants had used the Oregon Trail to reach the Far West since early in the nineteenth century, but settlers traveling by wagon train dominated traffic along the trail beginning in the 1840s. This drawing by William Henry Jackson suggests both the ruggedness of the journey and the large dimensions of the migration.

moved north into Oregon or south (along the California Trail) to the northern California coast. Other migrations moved along the Santa Fe Trail, which extended southwest from Independence into New Mexico.

However they traveled, overland migrants faced great dangers and hardships. The mountain and desert terrain in the later portions of the trip were particularly difficult. Most journeys lasted five or six months (from May to November), and there was always pressure to get through the Rockies before the snows began, not always an easy task given the very slow pace of most wagon trains (about fifteen miles a day). There was also the danger of disease; many groups were decimated by cholera. And there were encounters with Indians.

In reality, Indians were usually more helpful than dangerous to the white migrants. They often served as guides through difficult terrain or aided travelers in crossing streams or herding livestock. They maintained an extensive trade with the white travelers in horses, clothing, and fresh food. But occasional Indian attacks on isolated travelers and small wagon trains frightened the white migrants into considering all Indians a threat. In the end, whites probably inflicted more violence on Indians during these overland journeys than the Indians did on whites. In any case, the number of deaths in such conflicts was relatively small in relation to the size of the migrations; fewer than 1,000 whites and Indians combined died in such conflicts between 1840 and 1860.

Even when migrants avoided disaster (as most did), the strains of the long journey caused significant changes in ordinary life. Conventional gender roles soon gave way to pressing necessities, and women began performing such traditionally "male tasks" as driving cattle and loading wagons. And despite the traditional image of westward migrants as rugged individualists, travelers found the journey an intensely collective experience. Indeed, one of the most frequent causes of disaster for travelers was the breakdown of the necessarily communal character of the migratory companies. Those who made the journey successfully generally learned the value of cooperation.

Polk and Expansion

By the mid-1840s, there were already substantial numbers of Americans living in settlements up and down the Pacific coast and more than 5,000 in Oregon. These new settlers (along with advocates of Manifest Destiny in the East) were urging the United States government to take possession of the disputed Oregon Territory. Such demands quickly became a factor in national politics.

The election of 1844 was widely expected to be a contest between two old foes: the Whig Henry Clay and the Democrat and former president Martin Van Buren. Both men tried to avoid taking a stand on the controversial issue of the annexation of Texas. Their separate statements on the question were so similar that many suspected they had collaborated in preparing them. Both favored annexation, but only with the consent of Mexico. Since such consent was unlikely, the statements meant virtually nothing.

Because sentiment for expansion was mild within the Whig party, Clay had no difficulty securing the nomination despite his noncommittal position. Among the Democrats, however, there were many supporters of annexation, particularly in the South; and they resented Van Buren's equivocal stand. The expansionists took control of the Democratic convention and nominated a strong supporter of annexation, James K. Polk—the first "dark horse" to win the presidential nomination of his party.

Polk was not as obscure as his Whig critics claimed, but neither was he a genuinely major figure within his party. Beginning in 1825, he had represented Tennessee in the House of Representatives for fourteen years, four of them as Speaker. Subsequently, he had been governor of Tennessee.

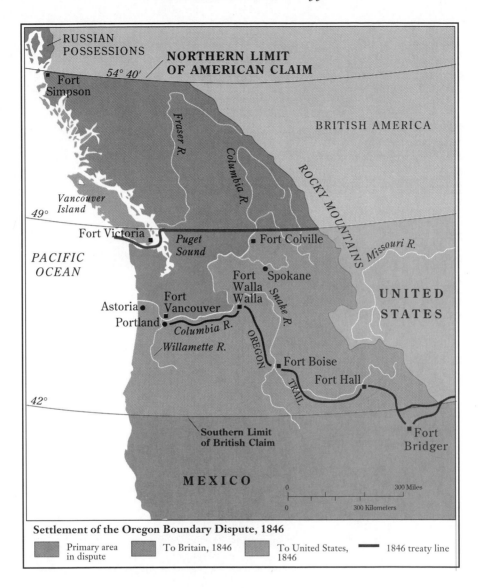

Settlement of the Oregon Boundary Dispute, 1846

Primary area in dispute

To Britain, 1846

To United States, 1846

1846 treaty line

But by 1844, he had been out of public office—and for the most part out of the public mind—for three years. What made his victory possible was the belief, expressed in the Democratic platform, "that the re-occupation of Oregon and the re-annexation of Texas at the earliest practicable period are great American measures." By combining the Oregon and Texas questions, the Democrats hoped to appeal to both Northern and Southern expansionists.

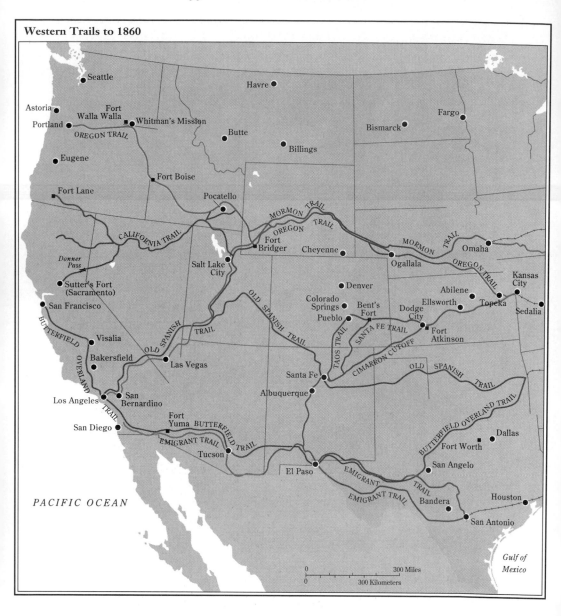

Western Trails to 1860

In a belated effort to catch up with public sentiment, Clay announced his qualified support for annexing Texas in midcampaign. But his tardy straddling probably cost him more votes than it gained. Polk carried the election by 170 electoral votes to 105, although his popular majority was less than 40,000. The Liberty party, running James G. Birney a second time, polled 62,000 votes (as compared with 7,000 in 1840), mainly from antislavery Whigs who had turned against Clay.

Polk may have been obscure, but he was intelligent and energetic; and he entered office with a clear set of goals and plans for attaining them. John Tyler accomplished the first of Polk's goals for him in the last days of his own presidency. Interpreting the election returns as a mandate for the annexation of Texas, the outgoing president won congressional approval for it in February 1845. Polk accepted the settlement Tyler had arranged, and in December 1845 Texas became a state.

Polk himself resolved the Oregon question, although not without difficulty and not without disappointing some of his supporters. Although publicly he seemed to support American title to all of the Oregon Territory, privately he was willing to compromise and set the boundary at the 49th parallel. But when the British minister in Washington rejected Polk's offer without even referring it to London, Polk again asserted the American claim to all of Oregon. There was loose talk of war on both sides of the Atlantic—talk that in the United States often took the form of the bellicose slogan "Fifty-four forty or fight!" (a reference to where the Americans hoped to draw the northern boundary of their part of Oregon). But neither country really wanted war. Finally, the British government offered to accept Polk's original proposal and divide the territory at the 49th parallel. The president, reluctant to alienate nationalists who wanted more, submitted the British proposal to the Senate without supporting it. No doubt to his relief, the Senate accepted the agreement; and on June 15, 1846, a treaty was signed fixing the boundary at the 49th parallel, where it remains today.

The Southwest and California

One of the reasons the Senate and the president had agreed so readily to the British proposal for settling the Oregon question was that new tensions were emerging in the Southwest—tensions that threatened to lead (and ultimately did lead) to a war with Mexico. As soon as the United States admitted Texas to statehood in 1845, the Mexican government broke diplomatic relations with Washington. To make matters worse, a dispute now developed over the boundary between Texas and Mexico. Texans claimed the Rio Grande as their western and southern border, a claim that would have added much of what is now New Mexico to Texas. Mexico still refused formally to concede the loss of Texas but argued nevertheless that the border had always been the Nueces River, to the north of the Rio Grande.

Polk recognized the Texas claim, and in the summer of 1845 he sent a small army under General Zachary Taylor to the Nueces line—to protect Texas, he claimed, against a possible Mexican invasion.

Only a few people lived in New Mexico, part of the area in dispute. Its trading center was the town of Santa Fe, 300 miles from the nearest settlements to the south and more than 1,000 miles from Mexico City and Vera Cruz. In the 1820s, the Mexican government had invited American traders into the region (just as it was inviting American settlers into Texas), hoping to speed development of the province. New Mexico, like Texas, soon began to become more American than Mexican. A flourishing commerce soon developed between Santa Fe and Independence, Missouri, with long caravans moving back and forth along the Santa Fe Trail, carrying manufactured goods west and bringing gold, silver, furs, and mules east in return. The Santa Fe trade, as it was called, further increased the American presence in New Mexico and signaled to advocates of expansion another direction for their efforts.

Americans were also increasing their interest in an even more distant province of Mexico: California. In this vast region lived members of several Western Indian tribes and perhaps 7,000 Mexicans, mostly descendants of Spanish colonists. Gradually, however, white Americans began to arrive: first maritime traders and captains of Pacific whaling ships, who stopped to barter goods or buy supplies; then merchants, who established stores, imported merchandise, and developed a profitable trade with the Mexicans and Indians; and finally pioneering farmers, who entered California from the east, by land, and settled in the Sacramento Valley. Some of these new settlers began to dream of bringing California into the United States.

President Polk soon came to share their dream and committed himself to acquiring both New Mexico and California for the United States. At the same time that he dispatched the troops under Taylor to the Nueces in Texas, he sent secret instructions to the commander of the Pacific naval squadron to seize the California ports if Mexico declared war. Representatives of the president quietly informed Americans in California that the United States would respond sympathetically to revolt against Mexican authority there.

Having appeared to prepare for war, Polk turned once more to diplomacy and dispatched a special minister, John Slidell, to try to buy off the Mexicans. But Mexican leaders rejected Slidell's offer to purchase the disputed territories. And on January 13, 1846, as soon as he heard the news, Polk ordered Taylor's army in Texas to move across the Nueces to the Rio Grande. For months, the Mexicans refused to fight. But finally, according to the accounts of American commanders, some Mexican troops crossed the Rio Grande and attacked a unit of American soldiers. Polk, who had been planning to request a declaration of war even without a military provocation, now told Congress: "War exists by the act of Mexico herself." On May 13, 1846, Congress declared war by votes of 40 to 2 in the Senate and 174 to 14 in the House.

The Mexican War

The war was not universally popular in the United States. Whig critics charged from the beginning that Polk had deliberately maneuvered the country into the conflict and that the border incident that had precipitated the declaration had been staged. Many argued that the hostilities with Mexico were draining resources and attention away from the more important issue of the Pacific Northwest; and when the United States finally reached its agreement with Britain on the Oregon question, opponents claimed that Polk had settled for less than he should have because he was preoccupied with Mexico. Opposition intensified as the war continued and as the public became aware of the casualties and expense.

American forces were generally successful in their campaigns against the Mexicans, but final victory did not come nearly as quickly as Polk had hoped. Through most of the war, the president himself planned the military strategy. He ordered Taylor to cross the Rio Grande and seize parts of northeastern Mexico, beginning with the city of Monterrey. Polk apparently thought Taylor could move south from Monterrey and, if necessary, threaten Mexico City itself. Taylor attacked Monterrey in September 1846 and, after a hard fight, captured it. But he let the Mexican garrison evacuate without pursuit. Polk now began to doubt the feasibility of his plan to move toward Mexico City. He feared that Taylor lacked the tactical skill for the campaign, and he became convinced that an advance south through the mountains would involve impossible supply problems. (He also feared Taylor's political ambitions, which extending the war might help advance.)

In the meantime, Polk ordered other offensives against New Mexico and California. In the summer of 1846, a small army under Colonel Stephen W. Kearny made the long march to Santa Fe and occupied the town with no opposition. Then he proceeded with a few hundred soldiers to California. There he joined a conflict already in progress that was being staged jointly by American settlers, a well-armed exploring party led by John C. Frémont, and the American navy: the so-called Bear Flag Revolution. Kearny brought

SCOTT'S ARMY IN MEXICO CITY General Winfield Scott leads an American army into the capital of Mexico in September 1847, marking final U.S. victory in the Mexican War. George W. Kendall of the New Orleans *Picayune* accompanied Scott throughout the assault on the city.

the disparate American forces together under his command, and by the autumn of 1846 he had completed the conquest of California.

The United States now controlled the two territories for which it had gone to war. But Mexico still refused to end the hostilities or cede the conquered territories. At this point, Polk and General Winfield Scott, the commanding general of the army and its finest soldier, devised a plan to force peace on the Mexicans—and, perhaps, gain even more new territory for the United States. Scott would assemble an army at Tampico, and the navy would transport it down the Mexican coast to Vera Cruz, where the Americans would establish a base. From Vera Cruz, Scott would move west along the National Highway to Mexico City. Scott conducted the campaign brilliantly. He took Vera Cruz and began moving inland. With an army that never numbered more than 14,000, he advanced 260 miles into enemy territory, kept casualties low by making flanking movements instead of frontal assaults, and finally achieved his objective without losing a battle. He inflicted a crushing defeat on the Mexican army at Cerro Gordo in the mountains and met no further resistance until he was within a few miles of Mexico City. After a hard fight on the outskirts of the capital, Americans occupied the city. A new Mexican government now took power and announced its willingness to negotiate a peace treaty.

President Polk was now growing thoroughly unclear about his objectives. He continued to encourage those who demanded that the United States annex much of Mexico itself. At the same time, concerned about the approaching presidential election, he was growing anxious to get the war finished quickly. Polk had sent to Mexico with the army a special presidential envoy who was authorized to negotiate a settlement. The agent, Nicholas Trist, concluded an agreement with the new Mexican government on February 2, 1848: the Treaty of Guadalupe Hidalgo. Mexico agreed to cede California and New Mexico to the United States and acknowledge the Rio Grande as the boundary of Texas. In return, the United States promised to assume the claims of its citizens against Mexico and pay the Mexicans $15 million. When the treaty reached Washington, Polk faced a dilemma. Trist had obtained most of Polk's original demands, but he had not satisfied the new, more expansive dreams of acquiring additional territory in Mexico itself. Polk angrily claimed that Trist had violated his instructions, but he soon realized that he had no choice but to accept the treaty. Some ardent expansionists were demanding that he hold out for annexation of—in a phrase widely bandied about at the time—"All Mexico!" Antislavery leaders, in the meantime, were charging that the demands for acquisition of Mexico were part of a Southern scheme to extend slavery to new realms. To silence this bitter and potentially destructive debate, Polk submitted the Trist treaty to the Senate, which approved it by a vote of 38 to 14. The war was over, and America had gained a vast new territory. But it had also acquired a new set of troubling and divisive issues.

A NEW SECTIONAL CRISIS

James Polk tried to be a president whose policies transcended sectional divisions. But conciliating the sections was becoming an ever more difficult task, and Polk gradually earned the enmity of Northerners and Westerners alike, who believed his policies (and particularly his enthusiasm for territorial expansion in the Southwest) favored the South at their expense.

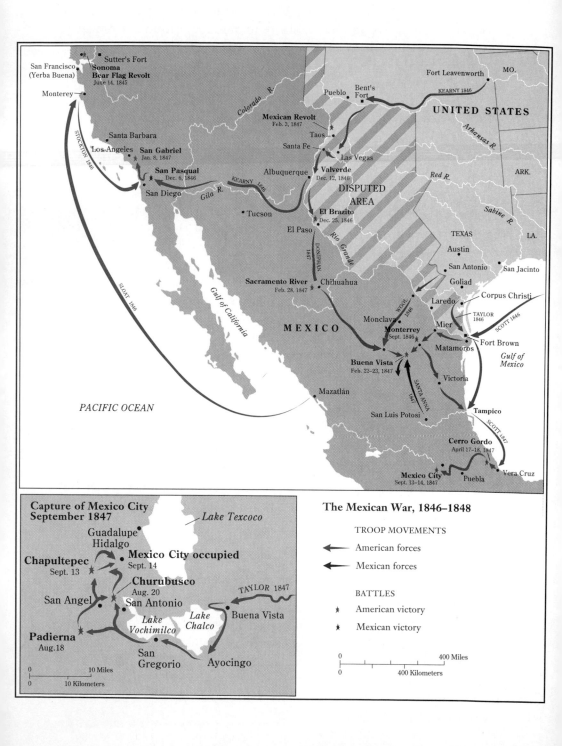

Sutter's Fort
San Francisco
(Yerba Buena)
Sonoma
Bear Flag Revolt
June 14, 1845
Monterey

Fort Leavenworth
MO.

Pueblo
Bent's
Fort
KEARNY 1846

UNITED STATES

Arkansas R.

STOCKTON 1846

Santa Barbara
Los Angeles
San Gabriel
Jan. 8, 1847

Mexican Revolt
Feb. 3, 1847
Taos
Santa Fe
Las Vegas
Albuquerque

Valverde
Dec. 12, 1846

ARK.

Red R.

Colorado R.

San Pasqual
Dec. 6, 1846
San Diego
KEARNY 1846
Gila R.

Tucson

**DISPUTED
AREA**

Sabine R.

El Brazito
Dec. 25, 1846

El Paso

DONIPHAN
1847

Rio Grande

TEXAS
Austin
San Antonio
San Jacinto

LA.

SLOAT 1846

Gulf of California

Sacramento River
Feb. 28, 1847
Chihuahua

MEXICO

Monclava
Monterrey
Monterrey
Sept. 1846

WOOL 1846

Laredo
Mier

Goliad

Corpus Christi

TAYLOR
1846

SCOTT 1846

Matamoros
Fort Brown

*Gulf of
Mexico*

PACIFIC OCEAN

Mazatlán

Buena Vista
Feb. 22-23, 1847

SANTA ANNA
1847

Victoria

San Luis Potosí

Tampico

SCOTT 1847

Cerro Gordo
April 17-18, 1847

Vera Cruz

Mexico City
Sept. 13-14, 1847
Puebla

**Capture of Mexico City
September 1847**

Lake Texcoco

Guadalupe
Hidalgo
Mexico City occupied
Sept. 14

Chapultepec
Sept. 13

Churubusco
Aug. 20
San Antonio

San Angel

TAYLOR 1847

San Angel
*Lake
Vochimilco*
*Lake
Chalco*
Buena Vista

Padierna
Aug.18

San
Gregorio
Ayocingo

0   10 Miles
0   10 Kilometers

The Mexican War, 1846–1848

TROOP MOVEMENTS

⬅ American forces

⬅ Mexican forces

BATTLES

✦ American victory

✦ Mexican victory

0   400 Miles
0   400 Kilometers

The Sectional Debate

In August 1846, while the Mexican War was still in progress, Polk asked Congress to appropriate $2 million for purchasing peace with Mexico. Representative David Wilmot of Pennsylvania, an antislavery Democrat, introduced an amendment to the appropriation bill prohibiting slavery in any territory acquired from Mexico. The so-called Wilmot Proviso passed the House but failed in the Senate. It would be called up, debated, and voted on repeatedly for years. Southern militants, in the meantime, had a plan of their own. They contended that since the territories belonged to the entire nation, all Americans had equal rights in them, including the right to move their slaves (which they considered property) into them.

President Polk supported a proposal to extend the Missouri Compromise (36°30′) through the new territories to the Pacific coast, banning slavery north of the line and permitting it south of the line. Others supported another compromise, originally called "squatter sovereignty" and later awarded the more dignified title of "popular sovereignty," which would allow the people of each territory (acting through their legislature) to decide the status of slavery there. The debate over these various proposals dragged on for many months. By the time Polk left office in 1849, nothing had been resolved.

The presidential campaign of 1848 dampened the controversy for a time as both Democrats and Whigs tried to avoid the slavery question. When Polk declined to run again, the Democrats nominated Lewis Cass of Michigan, a dull, aging party regular. The Whigs nominated a military hero with no political record, General Zachary Taylor of Louisiana. Opponents of slavery found the choice of candidates unsatisfying, and out of their discontent emerged the Free-Soil party, which drew from the existing Liberty party and the antislavery wings of the Whig and Democratic parties and which endorsed the Wilmot Proviso. Its candidate was former president Martin Van Buren.

Taylor won a narrow victory. But while Van Buren failed to carry a single state, he polled an impressive 291,000 votes (10 percent of the total), and the Free-Soilers elected ten members to Congress. Van Buren probably drew enough Democratic votes away from Cass, particularly in New York, to throw the election to Taylor.

Taylor and the Territories

Zachary Taylor was a Southerner and a slaveholder, but from his long years in the army he had acquired a national outlook. He recognized the impor-

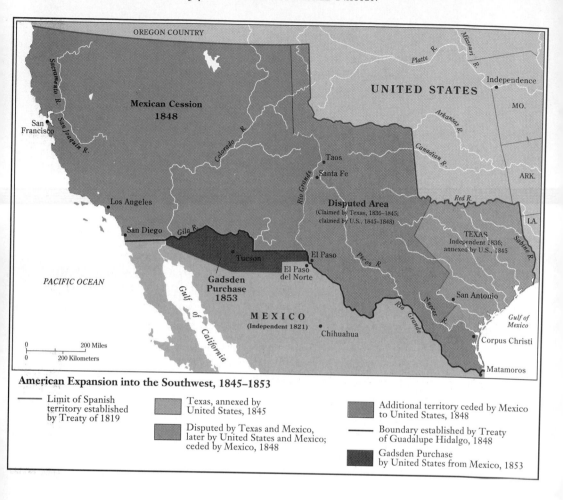

American Expansion into the Southwest, 1845–1853

—— Limit of Spanish
territory established
by Treaty of 1819

Texas, annexed by
United States, 1845

Disputed by Texas and Mexico,
later by United States and Mexico;
ceded by Mexico, 1848

Additional territory ceded by Mexico
to United States, 1848

—— Boundary established by Treaty
of Guadalupe Hidalgo, 1848

Gadsden Purchase
by United States from Mexico, 1853

tance of dealing with the problems of the newly acquired territories, which—in the absence of territorial governments—were still being administered by military officials. There was particular pressure to establish a new government in California, for that territory was experiencing a remarkable boom. In January 1848, gold was accidentally discovered in the Sacramento Valley. As word of the strike spread, thousands of Westerners, fired by dreams of quick riches, moved to the area to stake claims. By the end of the summer of 1848, news of the strike had reached the Eastern states and Europe and sparked an even greater gold rush. From all over the United States and from throughout the world, thousands of "forty-niners" poured into California—more than 80,000 in 1849 alone. By the end of that year, the territory had a population of roughly 100,000, enough to qualify it for statehood.

President Taylor believed statehood could become the solution to the issue of slavery in the territories. As long as the new lands were territories, the federal government was responsible for deciding the fate of slavery within them. But once they became states, their own governments would be able to settle the slavery question. Taylor ordered military officials in California and New Mexico to speed up the statehood movements. California promptly adopted a constitution that prohibited slavery, and in December 1849 Taylor asked Congress to admit California as a free state. New Mexico, he said, should be granted statehood when it was ready and should, like California, be permitted to decide for itself what it wanted to do about slavery. But Congress balked.

That was partly because of several other controversies concerning slavery that were complicating the debate over the territories. One was the effort of antislavery forces to abolish slavery in the District of Columbia, a movement bitterly resisted by Southerners. Another was the emergence of personal liberty laws in Northern states, which barred courts and police officers from helping to return runaway slaves to their owners. In response, Southerners demanded a stringent national fugitive slave law. Still another controversy involved a border dispute between Texas and New Mexico, as well as Texas's resentment at the failure of the federal government to take over the debts it had accumulated during its brief independence. But the biggest obstacle to the president's program was the white South's fear that two new free states would be added to the Northern majority. The number of free and slave states was equal in 1849—fifteen each. But the admission of California would upset the balance; and New Mexico, Oregon, and Utah might upset it further, leaving the South in a minority in the Senate, as it already was in the House.

Tempers were now rising to dangerous levels. Even many otherwise moderate Southern leaders were beginning to talk about secession from the Union. In the North, every state legislature but one adopted a resolution demanding the prohibition of slavery in the territories.

The Compromise of 1850

Faced with this unprecedented crisis, moderates and unionists spent the winter of 1849–1850 trying to frame a great compromise. The aging Henry Clay, who was spearheading the effort, believed that no compromise could last unless it settled all the issues in dispute between the sections. As a result, he took several measures which had been proposed separately, combined them into a single piece of legislation, and presented it to the Senate on January 29, 1850. The bill had five provisions. It proposed (1) that California be admitted as a free state; (2) that, in the rest of the lands acquired from Mexico, territorial governments be formed without restrictions on slavery; (3) that Texas yield in its boundary dispute with New Mexico and that the federal government compensate it by taking over its public debt; (4) that the slave trade, but not slavery itself, be abolished in the District of Columbia; and (5) that a new and more effective fugitive slave law be passed. These resolutions launched a debate that raged for seven months—both in Congress and throughout the nation. The debate occurred in two phases, the differences between which revealed much about how American politics was changing in the 1850s.

In the first phase of the debate, the dominant voices in Congress were those of old men—national leaders who still remembered Jefferson, Adams, and other founders—who argued for or against the compromise on the basis of broad ideals. Clay himself, seventy-three years old in 1850, was the most prominent of these spokesmen. He made a broad plea for sectional conciliation and appealed to shared sentiments of nationalism.

Early in March, another of the older leaders—John C. Calhoun, sixty-eight years old and so ill that he had to sit grimly in his seat while a colleague read his speech for him—joined the debate. Calhoun insisted that the North grant the South equal rights in the territories, that it agree to observe the laws concerning fugitive slaves, that it cease attacking slavery, and that it accept an amendment to the Constitution guaranteeing a balance of power between the sections. The amendment would provide for the election of dual presidents, one from the North and one from the South, each possessing a veto power. Calhoun was making radical demands that had no chance of passage. But he was expressing his belief in the importance of saving the Union; and like Clay, he was offering what he considered a comprehensive, permanent solution to the sectional problem—even if that solution would have required an abject surrender by the North.

After Calhoun came the third of the elder statesmen, the sixty-eight-year-old Daniel Webster. His "Seventh of March Address" was probably the greatest oratorical effort of his long career. Still nourishing presidential ambitions, he sought to calm angry passions and to rally Northern moderates to support Clay's compromise.

After six months of debate, however—six months dominated by ringing appeals to the memory of the founders, to nationalism, to idealism—the effort to win approval of the compromise failed. In July, Congress defeated the Clay proposal. And with that, the controversy moved into its second phase, in which a very different cast of characters would predominate. Clay, ill and tired, left Washington to spend the summer resting in the mountains. He would return, but never with his old vigor; he died in 1852. Calhoun had died even before the vote in July. And Webster in the course of the summer accepted a new appointment as secretary of state, thus removing himself from the Senate and from the debate.

In place of these leaders, a new, younger group now emerged. There was William H. Seward of New York, forty-nine years old, a wily political operator who staunchly opposed the proposed compromise. The ideals of Union were to him less important than the issue of eliminating slavery. There was Jefferson Davis of Mississippi, forty-two years old, a representative not of the old aristocratic South of Calhoun but of the new, cotton South—a hard, newly settled, and rapidly growing region. To him, the slavery issue was not only one of principles and ideals but also one of economic self-interest.

Most important of all, there was Stephen A. Douglas, a thirty-seven-year-old Democratic senator from Illinois. A Westerner from a rapidly growing state, he was an open spokesman for the economic needs of his section—and especially for the construction of railroads. His was a career devoted not to any broad national goals, as Clay's, Webster's, and even Calhoun's had often been, but devoted frankly to sectional gain and personal self-promotion.

The new leaders of the Senate were able, where the old leaders were not, to produce a compromise in 1850. In part, they were assisted by the great prosperity of the early 1850s, the result of expanding foreign trade, the flow of gold from California, and a boom in railroad construction. Conservative economic interests everywhere wanted to end the sectional dispute and concentrate on economic growth. Progress toward the compromise was also furthered by the disappearance of the most powerful obstacle to it: the president. President Taylor had been adamant that only after California and possibly New Mexico were admitted as states could other measures be discussed. He had threatened not only to veto any measure that diverged from this proposal but to use force against the South (even to lead the troops in person) if they attempted to secede. But on July 9, 1850, Taylor suddenly died—the victim of a violent stomach disorder following an attack of heat prostration. He was succeeded by Millard Fillmore of New York—a dull, handsome, dignified man who understood the political importance of

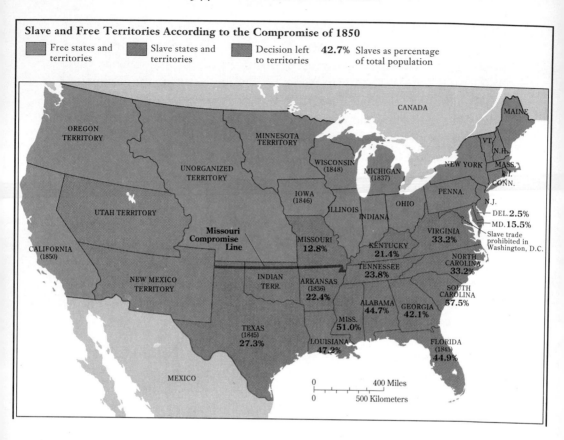

Slave and Free Territories According to the Compromise of 1850

Free states and territories • Slave states and territories • Decision left to territories • **42.7%** Slaves as percentage of total population

OREGON TERRITORY

MINNESOTA TERRITORY

CANADA

MAINE

VT.

N.H.

NEW YORK

MASS.

R.I.

CONN.

UNORGANIZED TERRITORY

WISCONSIN (1848)

MICHIGAN (1837)

PENNA.

N.J.

UTAH TERRITORY

IOWA (1846)

ILLINOIS

INDIANA

OHIO

DEL. **2.5%**

MD. **15.5%**

Slave trade prohibited in Washington, D.C.

Missouri Compromise Line

MISSOURI **12.8%**

KENTUCKY **21.4%**

VIRGINIA **33.2%**

CALIFORNIA (1850)

NEW MEXICO TERRITORY

INDIAN TERR.

ARKANSAS (1836) **22.4%**

TENNESSEE **23.8%**

NORTH CAROLINA **33.2%**

SOUTH CAROLINA **57.5%**

ALABAMA **44.7%**

GEORGIA **42.1%**

TEXAS (1845) **27.3%**

MISS. **51.0%**

LOUISIANA **47.2%**

FLORIDA (1845) **44.9%**

MEXICO

0   400 Miles

0   500 Kilometers

flexibility. He supported the compromise and used his powers of persuasion to swing Northern Whigs into line.

The new leaders also benefited, however, from their own pragmatic tactics. Douglas's first step, after the departure of Clay, was to break up the "omnibus bill" that Clay had envisioned as a great, comprehensive solution to the sectional crisis and introduce instead a series of separate measures to be voted on one by one. Thus representatives of different sections could support those elements of the compromise favorable to them and could abstain from voting on or could vote against those they opposed. Douglas also gained support by avoiding the grand appeals to patriotism of Clay and Webster and resorting instead to complicated backroom deals linking the compromise to such nonideological matters as the sale of government bonds and the construction of railroads. As a result of his efforts, by mid-September all the components of the compromise had been enacted by both houses of

Congress and signed by the president. The outcome was a great if clouded victory for Douglas and the forces of conciliation. The Compromise of 1850, unlike the Missouri Compromise thirty years before, was not a product of widespread agreement on common national ideals. It was, rather, a triumph of self-interest that had not resolved the underlying problems. Still, members of Congress hailed the measure as a triumph of statesmanship; and Millard Fillmore, signing it, called it a just settlement of the sectional problem, "in its character final and irrevocable."

THE CRISES OF THE 1850S

For a few years after the Compromise of 1850, the sectional conflict seemed briefly to be forgotten amid booming prosperity and growth. But the tensions between North and South remained, and the crisis continued to smolder until—in 1854—it once more burst into the open.

The Uneasy Truce

Both major parties endorsed the Compromise of 1850 in their platforms in 1852, and both parties nominated presidential candidates unlikely to arouse passionate opposition in either North or South. The Democrats chose the obscure New Hampshire politician Franklin Pierce and the Whigs the military hero General Winfield Scott, a man whose political views were so undefined that no one knew what he thought about the Compromise.

The gingerly way in which party leaders dealt with the sectional question could not prevent its divisive influence from intruding on the election. The Whigs were the principal victims. Already plagued by the defections of those antislavery Northerners who had formed the Free-Soil party in 1846, they alienated still more party members—the "Conscience" Whigs—by straddling the issue of slavery and refusing openly to condemn it. In the meantime, the Free-Soil party was gaining in numbers and influence in the North; its presidential candidate, John P. Hale, repudiated the Compromise of 1850. The divisions among the Whigs helped produce a victory for the Democrats in 1852.

Franklin Pierce, a charming, amiable man of no particular distinction, attempted to maintain party—and national—harmony by avoiding divisive issues, and particularly by avoiding the issue of slavery. But those issues arose despite him. They arose, in particular, because of Northern opposition to the Fugitive Slave Act, opposition which intensified after 1850 when Southerners began appearing occasionally in Northern states to pursue fugitives or to claim as slaves blacks who had been living for years in Northern communities. So fervently did many opponents of slavery resent such efforts that mobs formed in many cities to prevent enforcement of the law. Several Northern states also passed new personal liberty laws, which attempted to use state authority to interfere with the deportation of fugitive slaves. The supreme court of Wisconsin, in *Ableman* v. *Booth* (1857), even declared the federal Fugitive Slave Act void and ignored the United States Supreme Court when it overruled the Wisconsin ruling. White Southerners watched with growing anger and alarm as the one element of the Compromise of 1850 that they had considered a victory became virtually meaningless as a result of the extralegal device of mobs and through legal efforts of dubious constitutionality.

"Young America"

One of the ways Franklin Pierce hoped to dampen sectional controversy was through his support of a movement in the Democratic party known as "Young America." Its adherents saw the expansion of American democracy throughout the world as a diversion from what they considered the transitory issue of slavery. The great liberal and nationalist revolutions of 1848 in Europe stirred them to dream of a republican Europe with governments based on the model of the United States. They dreamed as well of expanding American commerce in the Pacific and acquiring new territories in the Western Hemisphere.

Few Americans in either section objected to displays of nationalism. But efforts to extend the nation's domain could not avoid becoming entangled with the sectional crisis. Pierce had been pursuing unsuccessful diplomatic attempts to buy Cuba from Spain (efforts begun in 1848 by Polk). But in 1854 a group of his envoys sent him a private document from Ostend, Belgium, making the case for seizing Cuba by force. When the Ostend Manifesto, as it became known, was leaked to the public, it enraged many antislavery Northerners, who charged the administration with conspiring to bring a new slave state into the Union.

The South, for its part, opposed all efforts to acquire new territory that would not support a slave system. The kingdom of Hawaii agreed to join the United States in 1854, but the treaty died in the Senate because it contained a clause prohibiting slavery in the islands. A powerful movement to annex Canada to the United States—a movement that had the support of many Canadians eager for access to American markets—similarly foundered, at least in part because of slavery.

The Kansas-Nebraska Controversy

What fully revived the sectional crisis, however, was the same issue that had produced it in the first place: slavery in the territories. By the 1850s, the line of white settlement had moved west to the great bend of the Missouri River. Beyond the boundaries of Missouri, Iowa, and what is now Minnesota stretched a great expanse of plains, which most white Americans had always believed was unfit for cultivation (it was widely known as the Great American Desert) and which the nation had therefore assigned to the Indian tribes it had dislodged from the more fertile lands to the east. Now it was becoming apparent that large sections of this region were, in fact, suitable for farming. In the states of the Old Northwest, therefore, prospective settlers urged the government to open the area to them, provide territorial governments, and—despite the solemn assurance the United States had earlier given the Indians of the sanctity of their reservations—dislodge the tribes so as to make room for white settlers. There was relatively little opposition from any segment of white society to the violation of Indian rights proposed by these demands. But the interest in further settlement raised two issues that did prove highly divisive and that gradually became entwined with each other: railroads and slavery.

As the nation expanded westward and as the problem of communication between the older states and the so-called trans-Mississippi West (the areas west of the Mississippi River) became more and more critical, broad support began to emerge for building a transcontinental railroad. The problem was where to place it—and in particular, where to locate the railroad's eastern terminus. Northerners favored Chicago, the rapidly growing capital of the free states of the Northwest. Southerners supported St. Louis, Memphis, or New Orleans—all located in slave states. The transcontinental railroad, in other words, was—like nearly everything else in the 1850s—becoming entangled in sectionalism. It had become a prize that both North and South were struggling to secure.

Pierce's secretary of war, Jefferson Davis of Mississippi, removed one obstacle to a Southern route. Surveys indicated that a road with a Southern terminus would have to pass through an area in Mexican territory. But Davis dispatched James Gadsden, a Southern railroad builder, to buy the region in question from Mexico. In 1853 Gadsden persuaded the Mexican government to accept $10 million in exchange for a strip of land that today comprises part of Arizona and New Mexico, the so-called Gadsden Purchase. But the acquisition simply intensified the sectional debate.

Stephen Douglas's strong interest in a transcontinental railroad led him to introduce in Congress a fateful legislative act that finally destroyed the Compromise of 1850. As a senator from Illinois, a resident of Chicago, and the acknowledged leader of Northwestern Democrats, Douglas naturally wanted the transcontinental railroad for his own city and section. He also realized the strength of the principal argument against the Northern route: that west of the Mississippi it would run mostly through country largely inhabited by Indians. As a result, he introduced a bill in January 1854 to organize (and thus open to white settlement) a huge new territory, known as Nebraska, west of Iowa and Missouri.

Douglas knew the South would oppose his bill because it would prepare the way for a new free state; the proposed territory was in the area of the Louisiana Purchase north of the Missouri Compromise line (36°30′) and hence closed to slavery. In an effort to make the measure acceptable to Southerners, Douglas inserted a provision that the status of slavery in the territory would be determined by the territorial legislature—that is, according to popular sovereignty. In theory, the region could choose to open itself to slavery (although few believed it actually would). When Southern Democrats demanded more, Douglas agreed to two changes in the bill: an additional clause explicitly repealing the antislavery provision of the Missouri Compromise (which the popular-sovereignty provision of his original bill had done implicitly), and a modification creating two territories, Nebraska and Kansas, instead of one, hence establishing a new territory (Kansas) that might become a slave state. In its final form the measure was known as the Kansas-Nebraska Act. President Pierce supported the bill; and after a strenuous debate, it became law in May 1854 with the unanimous support of the South and the partial support of Northern Democrats.

No piece of legislation in American history produced so many immediate, sweeping, and ominous changes. It destroyed the Whig party, which disappeared almost entirely by 1856, and along with it a conservative, nationalistic influence in American politics. It divided the Northern Democrats (many of whom were appalled at the repeal of the Missouri Compromise, which they considered an almost sacred part of the fabric of the Union) and drove many of them from the party.

Most important of all, it spurred the creation of a new party that was frankly sectional in composition and creed. People in both major parties who opposed Douglas's bill began to call themselves Anti-Nebraska Democrats and Anti-Nebraska Whigs. In 1854, they formed a new organization and named it the Republican party. In the elections of that year, the Republicans won enough seats in Congress to be able to organize the House of Representatives (with the help of the Know-Nothings) and won control of several Northern state governments.

"Bleeding Kansas"

Events in Kansas itself in the next two years increased the popular excitement in the North. White settlers from both the North and the South began moving into the territory almost immediately after the passage of the Kansas-Nebraska Act, and in the spring of 1855, elections were held for a territorial legislature. There were only about 1,500 legal voters in Kansas by then, but more than 6,000 people voted. That was because thousands of Missourians, some traveling in armed bands, had crossed into Kansas to vote. The result was that the proslavery forces elected a majority to the legislature, which proceeded immediately to enact a series of laws legalizing slavery. Outraged free-staters defied the legislature and elected delegates to a constitutional convention, which met at Topeka and adopted a constitution excluding slavery. They then chose their own governor and legislature and petitioned Congress for statehood. President Pierce denounced them as traitors and threw the full support of the federal government behind the proslavery territorial legislature.

A few months later a proslavery federal marshal assembled a large posse, consisting mostly of Missourians, to arrest the free-state leaders, who had set up their headquarters in Lawrence. The posse made the arrests and looted the town, killing several free-staters in the melee. Retribution came quickly. Among the most fervent opponents of slavery in Kansas was John Brown, a fiercely committed zealot who considered himself an instrument of God's will to destroy slavery. He gathered six followers and in one night murdered five proslavery settlers (as retribution for the five free-staters killed in Lawrence); he left their mutilated bodies to discourage other supporters of slavery from entering Kansas. The episode was known as the Pottawatomie Massacre; and its result was more civil strife in Kansas—irregular, guerrilla warfare conducted by armed bands, some of them more interested in land claims or loot than in ideologies. People in each section—Northerners and Southerners alike—came to believe that the events in

Kansas illustrated (and were caused by) the aggressive designs of the other section. Thus "Bleeding Kansas" became a symbol of the sectional controversy.

Another symbol soon appeared, in the United States Senate. In May 1856, Charles Sumner of Massachusetts rose to give a speech entitled "The Crime Against Kansas." Handsome, eloquent, humorless, and passionately doctrinaire, Sumner was a militant opponent of slavery. And in his speech, he gave particular attention to his colleague, Senator Andrew P. Butler of South Carolina, an outspoken defender of slavery. The South Carolinian was, Sumner claimed, the "Don Quixote" of slavery, having "chosen a mistress . . . who, though ugly to others, is always lovely to him, though polluted in the sight of the world, is chaste in his sight . . . the harlot slavery."

The pointedly sexual references and the general viciousness of the speech enraged Butler's nephew, Preston Brooks, a member of the House of Representatives from South Carolina, who resolved to deliver a public chastisement. Several days after the speech, Brooks approached Sumner at his desk in the Senate chamber during a recess, raised a heavy cane, and began beating him repeatedly on the head and shoulders. Sumner, trapped in his chair, rose in agony with such strength that he tore the desk from the bolts holding it to the floor; then he collapsed, bleeding and unconscious. So severe were his injuries that he was unable to return to the Senate for four years, during which time his state refused to replace him. He became a potent symbol throughout the North—a martyr to the barbarism of the South. Preston Brooks became a symbol too. Censured by the House, he resigned his seat, returned to South Carolina, and stood successfully for reelection. He had become a Southern hero. Like Sumner, he served as evidence of how strong the antagonism between North and South had become.

The Free-Soil Ideology

What had happened to produce such deep hostility between the two sections? There were, obviously, important social and economic differences between the North and the South and important disagreements, particularly over slavery in the territories. But neither the differences nor the disagreements would have been enough to disrupt the Union if they had not become tied up with other, larger concerns on both sides. As the nation expanded and political power grew more dispersed, the North and the South each became concerned with ensuring that its vision of America's future would be the dominant one. And those visions were becoming—partly as a result of internal developments within the sections themselves, partly because of each region's conceptions (and misconceptions) of what was happening outside it—increasingly distinct and increasingly rigid.

In the North, assumptions about the proper structure of society came to center on the belief in "free soil" and "free labor." The abolitionists generated some support for their argument that slavery was a moral evil and must be eliminated. Theirs, however, was never the dominant voice of the North. Instead, an increasing number of Northerners, gradually becoming a majority, came to believe that the existence of slavery was dangerous not because of what it did to blacks but because of what it threatened to do to whites. At the heart of American democracy, they argued, was the right of all citizens to own property, to control their own labor, and to have access to opportunities for advancement. The ideal society, in other words, was one of small-scale capitalism, in which everyone could aspire to a stake and to upward mobility. According to this vision, the South was the antithesis of democracy. It was a closed, static society, in which the slave system preserved an entrenched aristocracy and common whites had no opportunity to improve themselves. More than that, the South was a backward society—decadent, lazy, dilapidated. While the North was growing and prospering, displaying thrift, industry, and a commitment to progress, the South was stagnating, rejecting the Northern values of individualism and progress. The South was, Northern free-laborites further maintained, engaged in a conspiracy to extend slavery throughout the nation and thus to destroy the openness of Northern capitalism and replace it with the closed, aristocratic system of the South. This "slave power conspiracy," as it came to be known, threatened the future of every white laborer and property owner in the North. The only solution was to fight the spread of slavery and work for the day when the nation's democratic (i.e., free-labor) ideals would extend to all sections of the country—the day of the victory of what Northerners called "Freedom National."

This ideology lay at the heart of the new Republican party. There were abolitionists and others in the party who sincerely believed in the rights of blacks to freedom and citizenship. More important, however, were those who cared principally about the threat they believed slavery posed to white labor and to individual opportunity. This ideology also strengthened the commitment of Republicans to the Union. Since the idea of continued growth and progress was central to the free-labor vision, the prospect of dismemberment of the nation—a diminution of America's size and economic power—was unthinkable.

The Proslavery Argument

In the South, in the meantime, a very different ideology was emerging—one that was entirely incompatible with the free-labor ideology in the North. It emerged out of a rapid hardening of position among Southern whites on the issue of slavery.

As late as the early 1830s, a substantial number of Southern whites had harbored reservations about slavery. By the mid-1830s, however, this ambivalence about slavery was beginning to be replaced by a militant defense of the system. In part, the change was a result of events in the South. The Nat Turner uprising in 1831 terrified whites throughout the region, and they grew more determined than ever to make slavery secure. There was also an economic incentive to defend the system. With the expansion of the cotton economy into the Deep South, slavery—which had begun to seem unprofitable in many areas of the upper South—now became lucrative once again.

But the change was also a result of events in the North, and particularly of the growth of the Garrisonian abolitionist movement, with its strident attacks on Southern society. The popularity of Harriet Beecher Stowe's *Uncle Tom's Cabin* (see p. 324) was perhaps the most glaring evidence of the success of those attacks, but other abolitionist writings had been antagonizing white Southerners for years.

In response to these pressures, a number of white Southerners elaborated an intellectual defense of slavery. It began as early as 1832, when Professor Thomas R. Dew of the College of William and Mary outlined the case for slavery. It matured in 1852, when apologists for slavery summarized their views in an anthology that gave their ideology its name: *The Pro-Slavery Argument*. John C. Calhoun had stated the essence of their argument in 1837: Southerners should stop apologizing for slavery as a necessary evil and defend it as "a good—a positive good." It was good for the slaves, the Southern apologists argued, because, as inferior people, blacks needed the guidance of white masters; the slaves were, moreover, better off—better fed, clothed, and housed, and more secure—than Northern factory workers. Slavery was good for Southern society as a whole because it was the only way the two races could live together in peace. It was good for the entire country because the Southern economy, based on slavery, was the key to the prosperity of the nation.

Above all, Southern apologists argued, slavery was good because it served as the basis for the Southern way of life—a way of life superior to any other in the United States, perhaps in the world. White Southerners looking at the North saw a society that they believed was abandoning traditional American values and replacing them with a spirit of greed, debauchery, and destructiveness. "The masses of the North are venal, corrupt, covetous, mean and selfish," wrote one Southerner. Others wrote with horror of the factory system and the crowded, pestilential cities filled with unruly immigrants. The South, in contrast, was a stable, orderly society, operating at a slow and human pace. It had a labor system that avoided the feuds between capital and labor plaguing the North, a system that protected the welfare of its workers, a system that allowed the aristocracy to enjoy a refined and accomplished cultural life. It was, in short, as nearly perfect as any human civilization could become, an ideal social order in which all elements of the population were secure and content.

The defense of slavery rested, too, on increasingly elaborate arguments about the biological inferiority of African-Americans, who were, white Southerners argued, inherently unfit to take care of themselves, let alone exercise the rights of citizenship. And just as abolitionist arguments drew strength from Protestant theology in the North, the proslavery defense mobilized the Protestant clergy in the South to give the institution a religious and biblical justification.

By the 1850s, Southern leaders had not only committed themselves to a militant proslavery ideology. They had also become convinced that they must silence their opponents. Some Southern critics of slavery found it advisable to leave the region. Beginning in 1835 (when a Charleston mob destroyed sacks containing abolitionist literature in the city post office), Southern postmasters generally refused to deliver antislavery mail. Southern state legislatures passed resolutions demanding that Northern states suppress the "incendiary" agitation of the abolitionists. Southern representatives even managed for a time to impose a "gag rule" (adopted in 1836, repealed in 1844) on Congress, according to which all antislavery petitions would be tabled without being read. This growing intolerance of criticism of slavery further encouraged those Northerners who warned of the "slave power conspiracy" against their liberties.

Buchanan and Depression

It was in this unpromising climate—with the nation aroused by the Brooks assault and the continuing violence in Kansas, and with each section becoming increasingly militant in support of its own ideology—that the presidential campaign of 1856 began. Democratic party leaders wanted a candidate who had not made many enemies and who was not closely associated with the explosive question of "Bleeding Kansas." They chose James Buchanan of Pennsylvania, a reliable party stalwart who as minister to England had been safely out of the country during the recent controversies. The Republicans, participating in their first presidential contest, denounced the Kansas-Nebraska Act and the expansion of slavery but approved a program of internal improvements, thus combining the idealism of antislavery with the economic aspirations of the North. As eager as the Democrats to present a safe candidate, the Republicans nominated John C. Frémont, who had made a national reputation as an explorer of the Far West and who had no political record. In the meantime, the Native American, or Know-Nothing, party was beginning to break apart. At its convention, many Northern delegates withdrew because the platform was not sufficiently firm in opposing the expansion of slavery. The remaining delegates nominated former president Millard Fillmore. His candidacy was endorsed as well by a sad remnant of the Whig party, those who could not bring themselves to support either Buchanan or Frémont.

After a heated, even frenzied campaign, Buchanan won a narrow victory. He polled a plurality but not a majority of the popular votes: 1,833,000 to 1,340,000 for Frémont and 872,000 for Fillmore. A slight shift of votes in Pennsylvania and Illinois would have thrown those states into the Republican column and elected Frémont. More significant, perhaps, was that Frémont, who attracted virtually no votes at all in the South, received a third of all votes cast. In the North, he had outpolled all other candidates.

Buchanan had been in public life for more than forty years at the time of his inauguration; he was, at age sixty-five, the oldest president, except for William Henry Harrison, ever to have taken office. Whether because of age and physical infirmities or because of a more fundamental weakness of character, he became a painfully timid and indecisive president at a time when the nation cried out for strong, effective leadership.

In the year Buchanan took over, a financial panic struck the country, followed by a depression that lasted several years. European demand for American food had risen during the Crimean War of 1854–1856. When that demand fell off, agricultural prices declined. In the North, the depression strengthened the Republican party. Distressed manufacturers and farmers came to believe that the hard times were the result of the unsound policies of Southern-controlled Democratic administrations. They advocated a high protective tariff (the tariff had been lowered again in 1857), a homestead act, and internal improvements—all measures the South opposed. The frustrated economic interests of the North were being drawn into an alliance with antislavery elements and thus into the Republican party.

The Dred Scott *Decision*

The Supreme Court of the United States now projected itself into the sectional controversy with one of the most controversial decisions in its history—its ruling in the case of *Dred Scott* v. *Sanford*, handed down two days after Buchanan was inaugurated. Dred Scott was a Missouri slave, once owned by an army surgeon who had taken Scott with him to Illinois, a free state, and to a part of Wisconsin Territory where slavery was forbidden by the Missouri Compromise. Scott was persuaded by some abolitionists to bring suit in the Missouri courts for his freedom on the ground that residence in a free territory had made him a free man. The state supreme court decided against him. By then, the surgeon had died and ownership of Scott had been transferred to his widow's brother, J. F. A. Sanford, an abolitionist who lived in New York. Now Scott's lawyers could get the case into the federal courts on the ground that the suit lay between citizens of different states. Regardless of the final decision, Scott would be freed; his abolitionist owners would not keep him a slave. The case was intended not to determine Scott's future but to secure a federal decision on the status of slavery in the territories.

The Supreme Court was so divided that it was unable to issue a single ruling on the case. It released separate decisions on each of the major issues it had considered. Each of the justices, moreover, wrote a separate opinion. The thrust of the rulings, however, was a defeat for the antislavery movement and an affirmation of the South's argument that the Constitution guaranteed the existence of slavery. Chief Justice Roger Taney, who wrote one of the majority opinions, declared that Scott was not a citizen of Missouri or of the United States and hence could not bring a suit in the federal courts. According to Taney, no black could qualify as a citizen; indeed, blacks had virtually no rights at all under the Constitution. He went on to argue that Scott's sojourn in the North had not affected his status as a slave. Slaves were property, said Taney, and the Fifth Amendment prohibited Congress from taking property without "due process of law." Consequently, Congress possessed no authority to pass a law depriving persons of their slave property in the territories. The Missouri Compromise, therefore, had always been unconstitutional.

The ruling did nothing to challenge the right of an individual state to prohibit slavery within its borders, but the statement that the federal government was powerless to act on the issue was a drastic and startling one. Few judicial opinions have stirred as much popular excitement. Southern whites were elated: the highest tribunal in the land had sanctioned parts of the most extreme Southern argument. In the North, the decision produced widespread dismay. Republicans threatened that when they won control of the national government, they would reverse the decision—by "packing" the Court with new members.

Deadlock over Kansas

President Buchanan, who endorsed the *Dred Scott* decision, believed that the best solution to the controversy was to admit Kansas to the Union as a slave state. In response to his urgings, the proslavery territorial legislature called an election for delegates to a constitutional convention. The free-state residents refused to participate, claiming that the legislature had discriminated against them in drawing district lines. As a result, the proslavery forces won control of the convention, which met in 1857 at Lecompton, framed a constitution legalizing slavery, and refused to give voters a chance to reject it. When an election for a new territorial legislature was called, the antislavery groups turned out to vote and won a majority. The new legislature promptly submitted the Lecompton constitution to the voters, who rejected it by more than 10,000 votes.

Both sides had resorted to fraud and violence, but it was clear nevertheless that a majority of the people of Kansas opposed slavery. Buchanan, however, ignored the evidence and pressured Congress to admit Kansas under the Lecompton constitution. Stephen A. Douglas and other Western Democrats refused to support the president; and while Buchanan's proposal passed the Senate, Western Democrats helped block it in the House. Finally, in April 1858, Congress approved a compromise: the Lecompton constitution would be submitted to the voters of Kansas again. If the document won approval, Kansas would be admitted to the Union; if it was rejected, statehood would be postponed until the population of the territory reached the level required for a representative in Congress. Again, Kansas voters decisively rejected the Lecompton constitution. Not until the closing months of Buchanan's administration in 1861, when a number of Southern states had withdrawn from the Union, did Kansas enter the Union—as a free state.

The Emergence of Lincoln

Given the gravity of the sectional crisis, the congressional elections of 1858 took on a special importance. Of particular note was the United States Senate election in Illinois, which pitted Stephen A. Douglas, the most prominent Northern Democrat, against Abraham Lincoln, the most skillful politician in the Republican party.

THE LINCOLN-DOUGLAS DEBATES, ILLINOIS, 1858 The still clean-shaven Abraham Lincoln lost in his 1858 bid to replace Stephen Douglas as United States senator from Illinois, but he gained wide national recognition for his performance in the debates between the two candidates during the campaign.

Lincoln had been the leading Whig in Illinois and was now the state's leading Republican. But since he was not a national figure comparable to Douglas, he sought to increase his visibility by engaging Douglas in a series of debates. The Lincoln-Douglas debates attracted enormous crowds and received wide attention. By the time they ended, Lincoln had become nationally prominent.

The content of the debates revealed the deep disagreements between the two parties in the North. Douglas, defending popular sovereignty, accused the Republicans of promoting a war of sections, of wishing to interfere with slavery in the South, and of advocating social equality of the races. Lincoln denied these charges (properly, since neither he nor his party had ever advocated any of these things). He, in turn, accused the Democrats of conspiring to extend slavery into the territories and possibly into the free states as well (a charge that was equally unfounded).

At the heart of the debates, however, was a basic difference on the issue of slavery. Douglas appeared to have no moral position on the issue and, Lincoln claimed, did not care whether slavery was "voted up, or voted down." Lincoln's opposition to slavery was more fundamental. If the nation could accept that blacks were not entitled to basic human rights, he argued, then it could accept that other groups—immigrant laborers, for example—could be deprived of rights too. And if slavery were to extend into the Western territories, he argued, opportunities for poor white laborers to better their lots there might be lost. The nation's future, he argued (reflecting the central idea of the Republican party), rested on the spread of free labor.

Lincoln believed slavery was morally wrong, but he was not an abolitionist. That was in part because he could not envision an easy alternative to it in the areas where it already existed. He shared the prevailing view among Northern whites that the black race was not prepared (and perhaps never would be) to live on equal terms with whites. He and his party would "arrest the further spread" of slavery, that is, prevent its expansion into the territories; they would not directly challenge it where it already existed, but would trust that the institution would gradually die out there of its own accord.

Yet the implications of Lincoln's argument were more sweeping than this relatively moderate formula suggests, for both he and other Republicans believed that by restricting slavery to the South, they would be consigning slavery to its "ultimate extinction." As he said in the most famous speech of the campaign:

A house divided against itself cannot stand. I believe this government cannot endure permanently half slave and half free. I do not expect the

Union to be dissolved—I do not expect the house to fall—but I do expect it will cease to be divided. It will become all one thing, or all the other.

In the debate at Freeport, Lincoln asked Douglas if the people of a territory could exclude slavery prior to the formation of a state constitution. In other words, was popular sovereignty still workable despite the *Dred Scott* decision? Douglas replied that the people of a territory could legally exclude slavery before forming a state constitution simply by refusing to pass laws recognizing the right of slave ownership. Without such laws, he claimed, slavery could not exist. Douglas's reply became known as the Freeport Doctrine or, in the South, the Freeport Heresy. It satisfied his followers sufficiently to win him reelection to the Senate, but it aroused little enthusiasm and did nothing to enhance his national political ambitions.

Outside Illinois, the elections went heavily against the Democrats, who lost ground in almost every Northern state. The party retained control of the Senate but lost its majority in the House, with the result that the congressional sessions of 1858 and 1859 were bitterly deadlocked.

John Brown's Raid

The battles in Congress, however, were almost entirely overshadowed by a spectacular event that enraged and horrified the entire South and greatly hastened the rush toward disunion. In the fall of 1859, John Brown, the antislavery zealot whose bloody actions in Kansas had inflamed the crisis there, staged an even more dramatic episode, this time in the South itself. With private encouragement and financial aid from some prominent Eastern abolitionists (a group sometimes known as the "Secret Six"), he made elaborate plans to seize a mountain fortress in Virginia from which, he believed, he could foment a slave insurrection in the South. On October 16, he and a group of eighteen followers attacked and seized control of a United States arsenal in Harpers Ferry, Virginia. But the slave uprising Brown hoped to inspire did not occur, and he quickly found himself besieged in the arsenal by citizens, local militia companies, and before long United States troops under the command of Robert E. Lee. After ten of his men were killed, Brown surrendered. He was promptly tried in a Virginia court for treason against the state, found guilty, and sentenced to death. On December 2, 1859, he was hung. Six of his followers met a similar fate.

Probably no other single event did as much as the Harpers Ferry raid to convince white Southerners that they could not live safely in the Union. Despite their defiant defense of slavery, many were consumed with one great, if often secret, fear: the possibility of a general slave insurrection. And John Brown's raid, which many Southerners believed (incorrectly) had the support of the Republican party, suggested that the North was now committed to producing just such an insurrection. When abolitionists such as Wendell Phillips and Ralph Waldo Emerson began to glorify Brown as a new saint, and when his execution made him a martyr to thousands of Northerners, the white South reacted with shock and alarm (even though the great majority of Northerners denounced Brown and his actions).

The Election of Lincoln

The presidential election of 1860 had the most momentous consequences of any in American history. It was also among the most complex.

The Democratic party was torn apart by a battle between Southerners, who demanded a strong endorsement of slavery, and Westerners, who supported the idea of popular sovereignty. When the party convention met, in opportunely, in Charleston, South Carolina (a hotbed of secessionist

JOHN BROWN Even in this formal photographic portrait (taken in 1859, the last year of his life), John Brown conveys the fierce sense of righteousness that fueled his extraordinary activities in the fight against slavery.

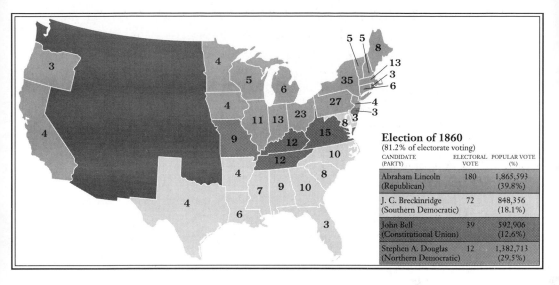

Election of 1860
(81.2% of electorate voting)

CANDIDATE (PARTY)	ELECTORAL VOTE	POPULAR VOTE (%)
Abraham Lincoln (Republican)	180	1,865,593 (39.8%)
J. C. Breckinridge (Southern Democratic)	72	848,356 (18.1%)
John Bell (Constitutional Union)	39	592,906 (12.6%)
Stephen A. Douglas (Northern Democratic)	12	1,382,713 (29.5%)

sentiment) in April, it endorsed the Western position. Delegates from eight states in the lower South walked out. The remaining delegates could not agree on a presidential candidate and finally adjourned the convention to meet again two months later in Baltimore. By the time the Democrats reconvened in June, some disenchanted Southerners had organized an alternative meeting in Richmond. The decimated convention at Baltimore nominated Stephen Douglas for president. The Southern Democrats in Richmond nominated John C. Breckinridge of Kentucky.

The Republican leaders, in the meantime, were working to broaden the base of their party. No longer content to present themselves simply as opponents of slavery, they tried now to appeal to every major interest group in the North that feared the South was blocking its economic aspirations. The platform endorsed such traditional Whig measures as a high tariff, internal improvements, a homestead bill, and a Pacific railroad to be built with federal financial assistance. It supported the right of each state to decide the status of slavery within its borders. But it also insisted that neither Congress nor territorial legislatures could legalize slavery in the territories. Passing over better known candidates, the Republican convention chose Abraham Lincoln as the party's presidential nominee. Lincoln was prominent enough to be respectable but obscure enough to have made few enemies. He was radical enough to please the antislavery faction in the party but conservative enough to satisfy the ex-Whigs.

But the Republicans were not yet conservative enough to satisfy all the former Whigs. In May, a group of them—mostly conservative elder statesmen—met in Baltimore and formed the Constitutional Union party in an effort to transcend sectional passions and create a truly national political movement. They nominated John Bell of Tennessee for president and Edward Everett of Massachusetts for vice president. They endorsed the Constitution and the Union and avoided taking a clear stand on the issue of slavery.

In the November election, Lincoln won the presidency with a majority of the electoral votes but only about two-fifths of the fragmented popular vote. The Republicans, moreover, failed to win a majority in Congress; and, of course, they did not control the Supreme Court. Even so, the election of Lincoln became the final signal to many white Southerners that their position in the Union was hopeless. And within a few weeks of Lincoln's victory, the process of disunion began—a process that would quickly lead to a prolonged and bloody war between two groups of Americans, both heirs to more than a century of struggling toward nationhood, each now convinced that it shared no common ground with the other.

CHAPTER FOURTEEN

The Civil War

The Secession Crisis ~ *The Mobilization of the North*
The Mobilization of the South ~ *Strategy and Diplomacy*
Campaigns and Battles

B Y THE END of 1860, the cords that had once bound the Union together seemed to have snapped. The almost mystical veneration of the Constitution and its framers was no longer working to unite the nation; residents of the North and South—particularly after the controversial *Dred Scott* decision—now differed fundamentally over what the Constitution said and what the framers had meant. The romantic vision of America's great national destiny had ceased to be a unifying force; the two sections now defined that destiny in different and apparently irreconcilable terms. The stable two-party system could not dampen sectional conflict any longer; that system had collapsed in the 1850s, to be replaced by a new one that accentuated rather than muted regional controversy. Above all, the federal government was no longer the remote, unthreatening presence it once had been; the need to resolve the status of the territories had made it necessary for Washington to deal with sectional issues in a direct and forceful way. And thus, beginning in 1860, the divisive forces that had always existed within the United States were no longer counterbalanced by unifying forces. As a result, the Union began to dissolve.

THE SECESSION CRISIS

Almost as soon as the news of Abraham Lincoln's election reached the South, the militant leaders of the region—the champions of the new concept of Southern "nationalism," men known both to their contemporar-

363

ies and to history as the "fire-eaters"—began to demand an end to the Union.

The Withdrawal of the South

South Carolina, long the hotbed of Southern separatism, went first. It called a special convention, at which the delegates voted unanimously on December 20, 1860, to withdraw the state from the Union. By the time Lincoln took office, six other Southern states—Mississippi (January 9, 1861), Florida (January 10), Alabama (January 11), Georgia (January 19), Louisiana (January 26), and Texas (February 1)—had seceded. In February 1861, representatives of the seven seceded states met at Montgomery, Alabama, and formed a new nation—the Confederate States of America. The re-

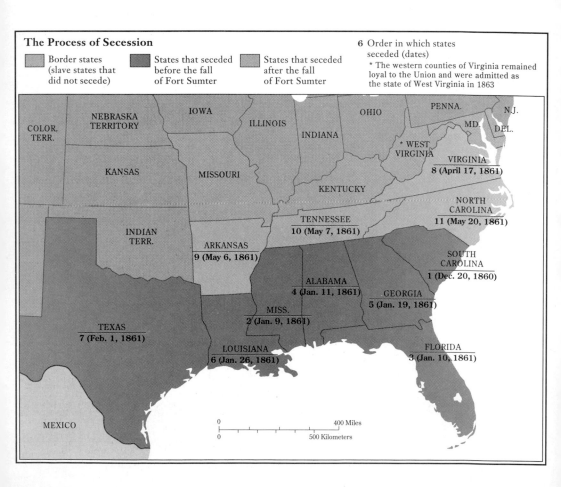

The Process of Secession

Border states (slave states that did not secede)

States that seceded before the fall of Fort Sumter

States that seceded after the fall of Fort Sumter

6 Order in which states seceded (dates)

* The western counties of Virginia remained loyal to the Union and were admitted as the state of West Virginia in 1863

COLOR. TERR.
NEBRASKA TERRITORY
IOWA
ILLINOIS
OHIO
PENNA.
N.J.
MD.
DEL.
INDIANA
KANSAS
MISSOURI
* WEST VIRGINIA
VIRGINIA
8 (April 17, 1861)
KENTUCKY
INDIAN TERR.
TENNESSEE
10 (May 7, 1861)
NORTH CAROLINA
11 (May 20, 1861)
ARKANSAS
9 (May 6, 1861)
SOUTH CAROLINA
1 (Dec. 20, 1860)
ALABAMA
4 (Jan. 11, 1861)
GEORGIA
5 (Jan. 19, 1861)
MISS.
2 (Jan. 9, 1861)
TEXAS
7 (Feb. 1, 1861)
LOUISIANA
6 (Jan. 26, 1861)
FLORIDA
3 (Jan. 10, 1861)
MEXICO

0   400 Miles
0   500 Kilometers

sponse from the North was confused and indecisive. President James Buchanan told Congress in December 1860 that no state had the right to secede from the Union, but he suggested that the federal government had no authority to stop a state if it did.

The seceding states immediately seized the federal property—forts, arsenals, government offices—within their boundaries. But they did not at first have sufficient military power to seize two fortified offshore military installations: Fort Sumter, on an island in the harbor of Charleston, South Carolina, garrisoned by a small force under Major Robert Anderson; and Fort Pickens, in the harbor of Pensacola, Florida. South Carolina sent commissioners to Washington to ask for the surrender of Sumter; but Buchanan, timid though he was, refused to yield it. Indeed, in January 1861, he ordered an unarmed merchant ship to proceed to Fort Sumter with additional troops and supplies. Confederate guns on shore fired at the vessel (the first shots between North and South) and turned it back. Still, neither section was yet ready to concede that war had begun. And in Washington, efforts began once more to forge a compromise.

The Failure of Compromise

Gradually, the compromise efforts came together around a proposal first submitted by Senator John J. Crittenden of Kentucky and known as the Crittenden Compromise. It called for several constitutional amendments, which would guarantee the permanent existence of slavery in the slave states and would satisfy Southern demands on such issues as fugitive slaves and slavery in the District of Columbia. But the heart of Crittenden's plan was a proposal to reestablish the Missouri Compromise line in all the present and future territory of the United States: slavery would be prohibited north of the line and permitted south of it. Southerners in the Senate seemed willing to accept the plan, but the Republicans were not. The compromise would have required that the Republicans abandon their most fundamental position: that slavery not be allowed to expand.

And so nothing had been resolved when Abraham Lincoln arrived in Washington for his inauguration—sneaking into the city in disguise on a night train to avoid assassination as he passed through the slave state of Maryland. In his eloquent inaugural address, Lincoln laid down several basic principles: Since the Union was older than the Constitution, no state could leave it. Acts of force or violence to support secession were insurrectionary. And the government would "hold, occupy, and possess" federal property in the seceded states—a clear reference to Fort Sumter.

Conditions at Fort Sumter were deteriorating quickly. Union forces there were running short of supplies; unless they received fresh provisions, the fort would have to be evacuated. Lincoln believed that if he surrendered Sumter, his commitment to maintaining the Union would no longer be credible. So he sent a relief expedition to the fort, carefully informing the South Carolina authorities that there would be no attempt to send troops or munitions unless the supply ships met with resistance. The new Confederate government now faced a dilemma. Permitting the expedition to land would seem to be a tame submission to federal authority. Firing on the ships or the fort would seem (to the North at least) to be aggression. Confederate leaders finally decided that to appear cowardly would be worse than to appear belligerent; they ordered General P. G. T. Beauregard, commander of Confederate forces at Charleston, to take the fort, by force if necessary. When Anderson refused to give up, the Confederates bombarded it for two days, April 12–13, 1861. On April 14, Anderson surrendered. The Civil War had begun.

Almost immediately, Lincoln began mobilizing the North for war. Equally promptly, four more slave states seceded from the Union and joined the Confederacy: Virginia (April 17, 1861), Arkansas (May 6), Tennessee (June 8), and North Carolina (May 20). The four remaining slave states, Maryland, Delaware, Kentucky, and Missouri, cast their lot with the Union (under heavy political and even military pressure from Washington).

The Opposing Sides

As the war began, only one thing was clear: all the important material advantages lay with the North. Its population was more than twice as large as that of the South (and more than four times as large as the nonslave population of the South), so the Union had a much greater manpower reserve both for its armies and its work force. The North had an advanced industrial system and was able by 1862 to manufacture almost all its own war materials. The South had almost no industry at all and had to rely on imports from Europe throughout the war.

In addition, the North had a much better transportation system than did the South, and in particular more and better railroads: twice as much trackage as the Confederacy had, and a much better integrated system of lines. In the course of the war, moreover, the already inferior Confederate railroad system steadily deteriorated, and by the beginning of 1864 it had almost collapsed.

At the start of the war, however, the material advantages of the North were not as decisive as they now appear to have been. The South was, for the most part, fighting a defensive war on its own land and thus had the advantage of local support and familiarity with the territory. The Northern armies, on the other hand, were fighting mostly within the South on unfamiliar ground, and amid hostile local populations; they had to maintain long lines of communications and had access only to the South's own inadequate transportation system. The commitment of the white population of the South to the war was, with limited exceptions, clear and firm. In the North, opinion about the war was more divided and support for it remained shaky until very near the end. A major Southern victory at any one of several crucial moments might have proved decisive by breaking the North's will to continue the struggle. Finally, many Southerners believed that the dependence of the English and French textile industries on American cotton would force them to intervene on the side of the Confederacy.

THE MOBILIZATION OF THE NORTH

In the North, the war produced considerable discord, frustration, and suffering. But it also produced prosperity and economic growth by giving a major stimulus to both industry and agriculture.

Economic Measures

With Southern forces now gone from Congress, the Republican party could exercise almost unchallenged supremacy. During the war, it enacted an aggressively nationalistic program to promote economic development.

The Homestead and Morrill Acts of 1862 promoted the rapid development of the West. The Homestead Act permitted any citizen or prospective citizen to claim 160 acres of public land and to purchase it for a small fee after living on it for five years. The Morrill Act transferred substantial public acreage to the state governments; they were to sell the land and use the proceeds to finance public education. This act led to the creation of many new state colleges and universities, the so-called land-grant institutions. Congress also passed a series of tariff bills that by the end of the war had raised duties to the highest level in the nation's history—a great boon to domestic industries eager for protection from foreign competition.

Congress also moved to complete the dream of a transcontinental railroad. It created two new federally chartered corporations: the Union Pacific Railroad Company, which was to build westward from Omaha, and the Central Pacific, which was to build eastward from California. The two projects were to meet in the middle and complete the link. The government provided free public lands and generous loans to the companies.

The National Bank Acts of 1863–1864 created a new national banking system. Existing or newly formed banks could join the system if they had enough capital and were willing to invest one-third of it in government securities. In return, they could issue United States Treasury notes as currency. The new system eliminated much of the chaos and uncertainty in the nation's currency and created a uniform system of national bank notes.

More difficult than promoting economic growth was financing the war itself. The government tried to do so in three ways: levying taxes, issuing paper currency, and borrowing. Congress levied new taxes on almost all goods and services; and in 1861 the government levied an income tax for the first time, with rates that eventually rose to 10 percent on incomes above $5,000. But taxation raised only a small proportion of the funds necessary for financing the war, and strong popular resistance prevented the government from raising the rates.

At least equally controversial was the printing of paper currency, or "greenbacks." The new currency was backed not by gold or silver but simply by the good faith and credit of the government (much like today's currency). The value of the greenbacks fluctuated according to the fortunes of the Northern armies. Early in 1864, with the war effort bogged down, a greenback dollar was worth only 39 percent of a gold dollar. Even at the close of the war, it was worth only 67 percent of a gold dollar. Because of the difficulty of making purchases with this uncertain currency, the government used greenbacks sparingly. The Treasury issued only $450 million worth of paper currency—a small proportion of the cost of the war but enough to produce serious inflation which raised prices by over 80 percent by the close of the war.

By far the largest source of financing for the war was loans. In previous wars, the government had sold bonds only to banks and to a few wealthy investors. Now, however, the Treasury persuaded ordinary citizens to buy over $400 million worth of bonds—the first example of mass financing of a war in American history. But public bond purchases constituted only a small part of the government's borrowing, which in the end totaled $2.6 billion, most of it from banks and large financial interests.

Raising the Union Armies

Over 2.1 million men served in the Union military forces during the course of the Civil War. But at the beginning of 1861, the regular army of the United States consisted of only 16,000 troops, many of them stationed in the West to protect white settlers from Indians. So the Union, like the Confederacy, had to raise its army mostly from scratch. Lincoln called for an increase of 23,000 in the regular army, but the bulk of the fighting, he knew, would have to be done by the volunteers in state militias. When Congress convened in July 1861, it authorized enlisting 500,000 volunteers for three-year terms (as opposed to the customary three-month terms).

But this voluntary system of recruitment produced adequate forces only briefly, during the first flush of enthusiasm for the war. By March 1863, Congress was forced to pass a national draft law. Virtually all young adult males were eligible to be drafted; but a man could escape service by hiring someone to go in his place or by paying the government a fee of $300. Although only about 46,000 men were ever actually conscripted, the draft greatly increased voluntary enlistments.

To a people accustomed to a remote and inactive national government, conscription was strange and threatening. Opposition to the law was widespread, particularly among laborers, immigrants, and Democrats opposed to the war (known as "Peace Democrats"). Occasionally it erupted into violence. Demonstrators against the draft rioted in New York City for four days in July 1863, killed over 100 people, mostly blacks (whom many opponents of the war blamed for the conflict), and burned down African-American homes, businesses, and even an orphanage. It was the bloodiest riot in American history. Only the arrival of federal troops halted the violence.

The Politics of Wartime

When Abraham Lincoln arrived in Washington early in 1861, many Republicans—noting his lack of national experience and his folksy, unpretentious manner—considered him a minor politician from the prairies, a man who would be easily controlled by the real leaders of his party. But the new president moved quickly to establish his own authority. He assembled a cabinet representing every faction of the Republican party and every segment of Northern opinion—men of exceptional prestige, influence, and in some cases arrogance, several of whom believed that they, not Lincoln, should be president. Lincoln moved boldly as well to use the war powers of the presidency, blithely ignoring inconvenient parts of the Constitution because, he said, it would be foolish to lose the whole by being afraid to disregard a part. He sent troops into battle without asking Congress for a declaration of war, arguing that the conflict was a domestic insurrection and that no congressional authorization was necessary. He increased the size of the regular army without receiving legislative authority to do so. He unilaterally proclaimed a naval blockade of the South.

Lincoln's greatest political problem was the widespread popular opposition to the war, mobilized by factions in the Democratic party. The Peace Democrats (or, as their enemies called them, "Copperheads") feared that agriculture and the Northwest were losing influence to industry and the East and that Republican nationalism was eroding states' rights. Lincoln used extraordinary methods to suppress them. He ordered military arrests of civilian dissenters and suspended the right of habeas corpus (the right of an arrested person to receive a speedy trial). At first, Lincoln used these methods only in sensitive areas such as the border states; but in 1862, he proclaimed that all persons who discouraged enlistments or engaged in disloyal practices were subject to martial law. In all, more than 13,000 persons were arrested and imprisoned for varying periods.

By the time of the presidential election of 1864, the North was rife with political dissension. The Republicans had suffered heavy losses in 1862, and in response leaders of the party tried to create a broad coalition of all the groups that supported the war. They called the new organization the Union party; but it was, in reality, little more than the Republican party and a small faction of War Democrats. The Union party nominated Lincoln for another term as president and Andrew Johnson of Tennessee, a War Democrat who had opposed his state's decision to secede, for the vice presidency.

The Democrats nominated George B. McClellan, a celebrated former Union general who had been relieved of his command by Lincoln, and adopted a platform denouncing the war and calling for a truce. McClellan repudiated that demand, but the Democrats were clearly the peace party in the campaign, trying to profit from growing war weariness and from the Union's discouraging military position in the summer of 1864.

At this crucial moment, however, several Northern military victories, particularly the capture of Atlanta, Georgia, early in September, rejuvenated Northern morale and boosted Republican prospects. Lincoln won reelection comfortably, with 212 electoral votes to McClellan's 21; the president carried every state except Kentucky, New Jersey, and Delaware. But Lincoln's lead in the popular vote was a more modest 10 percent. Had Union victories not occurred when they did, and had Lincoln not made special arrangements to allow Union troops to vote, the Democrats might have won.

The Politics of Emancipation

Despite their surface unity in 1864 and their general agreement on most economic matters, the Republicans disagreed sharply with one another on the issue of slavery. Radicals—led in Congress by such men as Representative Thaddeus Stevens of Pennsylvania and Senators Charles Sumner of Massachusetts and Benjamin Wade of Ohio—wanted to use the war to abolish slavery immediately and completely. Conservatives favored a slower, more gradual, and, they believed, less disruptive process for ending slavery. In the beginning, at least, they had the support of the president.

Despite the president's cautious view of emancipation, momentum began to gather behind it early in the war. In 1861, Congress passed the Confiscation Act, which declared that all slaves used for "insurrectionary" purposes (that is, in support of the Confederate military effort) would be considered freed. Subsequent laws in the spring of 1862 abolished slavery in the District of Columbia and in the Western territories and provided for the compensation of owners. In July 1862, the Radicals pushed through Congress the second Confiscation Act, which declared free the slaves of persons aiding and supporting the insurrection (whether or not the slaves themselves were doing so) and authorized the president to employ blacks, including freed slaves, as soldiers.

As the war progressed, the North seemed slowly to accept emancipation as a central war aim; nothing less, many believed, would justify the enormous sacrifices of the struggle. As a result, the Radicals gained increasing influence within the Republican party—a development that did not go unnoticed by the president, who decided to seize the leadership of the rising antislavery sentiment himself.

On September 22, 1862, after the Union victory at the Battle of Antietam, the president announced his intention to use his war powers to issue an executive order freeing all slaves in the Confederacy. And on January 1, 1863, he formally signed the Emancipation Proclamation, which declared forever free the slaves in all areas of the Confederacy except those already under Union control: Tennessee, western Virginia, and southern Louisiana. The proclamation did not apply to the border slave states, which had never seceded from the Union and which were not, therefore, subject to the president's war powers.

The immediate effect of the proclamation was limited, since it applied only to slaves still under Confederate control. But the document was of great importance nevertheless, because it clearly and irrevocably established that the war was being fought not only to preserve the Union but also to eliminate slavery. Eventually, as federal armies occupied much of the South, the proclamation became a practical reality and led directly to the freeing of thousands of slaves. About 186,000 of these emancipated blacks served as soldiers, sailors, and laborers for the Union forces. Even in areas not directly affected by the proclamation, the antislavery impulse gained strength. By the end of the war, slavery had been abolished in two Union slave states, Maryland and Missouri, and in three Confederate states occupied by Union forces: Tennessee, Arkansas, and Louisiana. The final step came in 1865, when Congress approved and the necessary states ratified the Thirteenth Amendment, which abolished slavery as an institution in all parts of the United States, not just the areas covered by the Emancipation Proclamation. After more than two centuries, legalized slavery finally ceased to exist in the United States.

The War and Society

The Civil War did not, as some historians used to claim, transform the North from an agrarian to an industrial society. Industrialization was already far advanced when the war began; and in some areas, the war actually retarded growth by diverting labor and resources to military purposes.

On the whole, however, the war sped the economic development of the North. That was in part a result of the political dominance of the Republican party and its promotion of nationalistic economic legislation. But it was also because the war itself required the expansion of certain sectors of the economy. Coal production increased by nearly 20 percent during the war. Railroad facilities improved—mainly through the adoption of a standard gauge (track width) on new lines. The loss of farm labor to the military forced many farmers to increase the mechanization of agriculture.

The war was a difficult experience for many American workers. Industrial laborers suffered a substantial loss of purchasing power, as prices in the North rose by more than 70 percent during the war while wages rose only about 40 percent. That was partly because liberalized immigration laws permitted a flood of new workers to enter the labor market and thus helped keep wages low. It was also because the increasing mechanization of production eliminated the jobs of many skilled workers. One result was a

THE U.S. SANITARY COMMISSION Matthew Brady took this photograph of female nurses and Union soldiers standing before an infirmary at Brandy Station, Virginia, near Petersburg, in 1864. The infirmary was run by the U.S. Sanitary Commission, the government-supported nursing corps that became indispensable to the medical care of wounded soldiers during the Civil War.

substantial increase in union membership in many industries and the creation of several national unions, for coal miners, railroad engineers, and others—organizations bitterly opposed and rigorously suppressed by employers.

Women found themselves, either by choice or by necessity, thrust into new and often unfamiliar roles. They took over positions vacated by men as teachers, retail salesclerks, office workers, and mill and factory hands. They were responding not only to the needs of employers for additional labor but to their own, often desperate, need for money. With husbands and fathers away in the army, many women were left destitute— particularly since military pay was small and erratic. Above all, women entered nursing, a field previously dominated by men. The United States Sanitary Commission, an organization of civilian volunteers led by Dorothea Dix, mobilized large numbers of female nurses to serve in field hospitals. By the end of the war, women were the dominant force in nursing; by the end of the century, nursing had become an almost entirely female profession.

THE MOBILIZATION OF THE SOUTH

Early in February 1861, representatives of the seven states that had seceded from the Union met at Montgomery, Alabama, to create a new Southern nation. When Virginia seceded several months later, the government of the Confederacy moved to Richmond—one of the few Southern cities large enough to house a government.

Southerners boasted loudly of the differences between their new nation and the nation they had left. Those differences were real. But there were also important similarities between the Union and the Confederacy, which became particularly clear as the two sides mobilized for war: similarities in their political systems, in the methods they used for financing the war and conscripting troops, and in the way they fought.

The Confederate Government

The Confederate constitution was almost identical to the Constitution of the United States, but with several significant exceptions. It explicitly acknowledged the sovereignty of the individual states (although not the right of secession). And it specifically sanctioned slavery and made its abolition (even by one of the states) practically impossible.

The constitutional convention at Montgomery named a provisional president and vice president: Jefferson Davis of Mississippi and Alexander H. Stephens of Georgia, who were later chosen by the general electorate, without opposition, for six-year terms. Davis had been a moderate, not an extreme, secessionist before the war. Stephens had argued against secession. The Confederate government, like the Union government, was dominated throughout the war by men of the center. It was also, like the Union government, dominated less by the old aristocracy of the East than by the newer aristocrats of the West, of whom Davis was the most prominent example.

Davis was, in the end, an unsuccessful president. He was a reasonably able administrator and the dominating figure in his government, encountering little interference from the generally tame members of his unstable cabinet and serving, in effect, as his own secretary of war. But he rarely provided genuinely national leadership. He spent too much time on routine items; and unlike Lincoln, he displayed a punctiliousness about legal and constitutional niceties inappropriate to the needs of a new nation at war. One shrewd Confederate official wrote: "All the revolutionary vigor is with the enemy. . . . With us timidity—hair splitting."

There were no formal political parties in the Confederacy, but its congressional and popular politics were badly divided nevertheless. Some white Southerners (and most blacks who were aware of the course of events) opposed secession and war altogether. Many white people in poorer "back-country" and "upcountry" regions, where slavery was limited, refused to recognize the new Confederate government or to serve in the Southern army; some worked or even fought for the Union. Most white Southerners supported the war, but as in the North many were openly critical of the government and the military, particularly as the tide of battle turned against the South and the Confederate economy decayed.

Money and Manpower

Financing the Confederate war effort was a monumental and ultimately impossible task. It involved creating a national revenue system in a society unaccustomed to large tax burdens. It depended on a small and unstable banking system that had little capital to lend. Because most wealth in the South was invested in slaves and land, liquid assets were scarce; and the Confederacy's only specie—seized from United States mints located in the South—was worth only about $1 million.

The Confederate Congress tried at first not to tax the people directly but to requisition funds from the individual states; but most of them were also unwilling to tax their citizens and paid their shares, when they paid them at all, with bonds or notes of dubious worth. In 1863, therefore, Congress enacted an income tax. But taxation never provided the Confederacy with very much revenue; it produced only about 1 percent of the government's total income. Borrowing was not much more successful. The Confederate government issued bonds in such vast amounts that the public lost faith in them and stopped buying them, and efforts to borrow money in Europe using cotton as collateral fared no better.

As a result, the Confederacy had to pay for the war through the least stable, most destructive form of financing: paper currency, which it began issuing in 1861. By 1864, the Confederacy had issued the staggering total of $1.5 billion in paper money, more than twice what the Union had produced. And unlike the Union, the Confederacy did not establish a uniform currency system; the national government, states, cities, and private banks all issued their own notes, producing widespread chaos and confusion. The result was a disastrous inflation—a 9,000 percent increase in prices in

CONFEDERATE VOLUNTEERS Smiling and apparently confident, young southern soldiers pose for a photograph in 1861, shortly before the first Battle of Bull Run. The Civil War was one of the first military conflicts extensively chronicled by photographers.

the course of the war (in contrast to 80 percent in the North)—with devastating effects on the new nation's morale.

Like the United States, the Confederacy first raised armies by calling for volunteers. And as in the North, by the end of 1861 voluntary enlistments were declining. In April 1862, therefore, Congress enacted a Conscription Act, which subjected all white males between the ages of eighteen and thirty-five to military service for three years. As in the North, a draftee could avoid service if he furnished a substitute. But since the price of substitutes was high, the provision aroused such opposition from poorer whites that it was repealed in 1863. Even more controversial were other exemptions that had no counterparts in the North, especially the exemption of one white man on each plantation with twenty or more slaves, a provision that caused smaller farmers to complain: "It's a rich man's war but a poor man's fight."

Even so, conscription worked for a time. At the end of 1862, about 500,000 soldiers were in the Confederate army. That number did not include the many slave men and women recruited by the military to perform such services as cooking, laundry, and manual labor, hence freeing additional white manpower for fighting. After 1862, however, conscription began producing fewer men, and the armed forces steadily decreased in size.

As 1864 opened, the government faced a critical manpower shortage. In a desperate move, Congress began trying to draft men as young as seventeen and as old as fifty. But in a nation suffering from intense war weariness, where many had concluded that defeat was inevitable, nothing could attract or retain an adequate army any longer. In 1864–1865, there were 100,000 desertions. In a frantic final attempt to raise men, Congress authorized the conscription of 300,000 slaves; but the war ended before this incongruous experiment could be attempted.

States' Rights Versus Centralization

The greatest source of division in the South, however, was not differences of opinion over the war, which most white Southerners generally supported, but the doctrine of states' rights. States' rights had become such a cult among many white Southerners that they resisted virtually all efforts to exert national authority, even those necessary to win the war. States' rights enthusiasts obstructed the conduct of the war in many ways. They restricted Davis's ability to impose martial law and suspend habeas corpus. They obstructed conscription. Recalcitrant governors such as Joseph Brown of Georgia and Zebulon M. Vance of North Carolina tried at times to keep their own troops apart from the Confederate forces and insisted on hoarding surplus supplies for their own states' militias.

The Confederate government still made substantial strides in centralizing power in the South; and by the end of the war, the Confederate bureaucracy was larger than its counterpart in Washington. The national government experimented, successfully for a time, with a "food draft"— which permitted soldiers to feed themselves by seizing crops from farms in their path. The government impressed slaves, often over the objections of their owners, to work as laborers on military projects. The Confederacy seized control of the railroads and shipping; it imposed regulations on industry; it limited corporate profits. States' rights sentiment was a significant handicap, but the South nevertheless took dramatic steps in the direction of centralization—becoming in the process increasingly like the region whose institutions it was fighting to escape.

Social Effects of the War

The war worked to transform Southern society in many of the same ways that it was changing the society of the North. It was particularly significant for Southern women. Because so many men left the farms and plantations to fight, the task of keeping families together and maintaining agricultural production fell increasingly to women. Slaveowners' wives often became responsible for managing large slave work forces; the wives of more modest farmers learned to plow fields and harvest crops. Substantial numbers of females worked in government agencies in Richmond. Even larger numbers chose nursing, both in hospitals and in temporary facilities set up to care for wounded soldiers. Others became schoolteachers.

The principal social effect of the war on the South, however, was widespread suffering and privation. Once the Northern naval blockade became effective, the South experienced massive shortages of almost everything. The region was overwhelmingly agricultural; but since it had concentrated so single-mindedly on producing cotton and other export crops, it did not grow enough food to meet its own needs. And despite the efforts of women to keep farms functioning, the departure of male workers seriously diminished the region's ability to keep up what food production there had been. Doctors were conscripted in large numbers to serve the needs of the military, leaving many communities without any medical care. Blacksmiths, carpenters, and other craftsmen were similarly in short supply.

As the war continued, the shortages, the inflation, and the suffering created increasing instability in Southern society. There were major food riots (some led by women) in cities in Georgia, North Carolina, and Alabama in 1863, as well as a large demonstration in Richmond that quickly turned violent. Resistance to conscription, food impressment, and taxation increased throughout the Confederacy.

STRATEGY AND DIPLOMACY

Militarily, the initiative in the Civil War lay mainly with the North, since it needed to defeat the Confederacy while the South needed only to avoid defeat. Diplomatically, however, the initiative lay with the South. It needed to enlist the recognition and support of foreign governments; the Union wanted only to preserve the status quo.

The Commanders

The most important Union military commander was Abraham Lincoln, whose previous military experience consisted only of brief service in his state militia. Lincoln was a successful commander in chief because he realized that numbers and resources were on his side and because he took advantage of the North's material advantages. He realized, too, that the proper objective of his armies was the destruction of the Confederate armies and not the occupation of Southern territory.

It was fortunate that Lincoln had a good grasp of strategy, because many of his generals did not. The problem of finding adequate commanders for the troops in the field plagued him throughout the first three years of the war.

From 1861 to 1864, Lincoln tried time and again to find a chief of staff capable of orchestrating the Union war effort. He turned first to General Winfield Scott, the aging hero of the Mexican War. But Scott was unprepared for the magnitude of the new conflict and retired on November 1, 1861. Lincoln then appointed the young George B. McClellan, who was the

ULYSSES S. GRANT One observer said of Grant (photographed here during the Wilderness campaign of 1864): "He habitually wears an expression as if he had determined to drive his head through a brick wall, and was about to do it." It was an apt metaphor for Grant's military philosophy, which relied on constant, unrelenting assault.

commander of the Union forces in the East, the Army of the Potomac; but the proud, arrogant McClellan had a wholly inadequate grasp of strategy and in any case returned to the field in March 1862. For most of the rest of the year, Lincoln had no chief of staff at all. And when he eventually appointed General Henry W. Halleck to the post, he found him an ineffectual strategist who left all substantive decision making to the president. Not until March 1864 did Lincoln finally find a general he trusted to command the war effort: Ulysses S. Grant, who shared Lincoln's belief in making enemy armies and resources, not enemy territory, the target of military efforts. Lincoln gave Grant a relatively free hand, but the general always submitted at least the broad outlines of his plans to the president for advance approval.

Lincoln's (and later Grant's) handling of the war effort faced constant scrutiny from the Committee on the Conduct of the War, a joint investigative committee of the two houses of Congress and the most powerful voice the legislative branch has ever had in formulating war policies. Established in December 1861 and chaired by Senator Benjamin F. Wade of Ohio, it complained constantly of the inadequate ruthlessness of Northern generals, which Radicals on the committee attributed (largely inaccurately) to a secret sympathy among the officers for slavery. The committee's efforts often seriously interfered with the conduct of the war.

Southern command arrangements centered on President Davis, who unlike Lincoln was a trained professional soldier but who, also unlike Lincoln, failed ever to create an effective central command system. Early in 1862, Davis named General Robert E. Lee as his principal military adviser. But in fact, Davis had no intention of sharing control of strategy with anyone. After a few months, Lee left Richmond to command forces in the field, and for the next two years Davis planned strategy alone. In February 1864, he named General Braxton Bragg as a military adviser, but Bragg never provided much more than technical advice. Not until February 1865 did the Confederate Congress create the formal position of general in chief. Davis named Lee to the post but made clear that he expected to continue to make all basic decisions. In any case, the war ended before the new command structure had time to take shape.

At lower levels of command, men of markedly similar backgrounds controlled the war in both the North and the South. Many of the professional officers on both sides were graduates of the United States Military Academy at West Point and the United States Naval Academy at Annapolis and thus had been trained in similar ways. Many were closely acquainted, even friendly, with their counterparts on the other side. Amateur officers played an important role in both armies as commanders of volunteer regiments. In both North and South, such men were usually economic or social leaders in their communities who appointed themselves officers and rounded up troops to lead. Although occasionally this system produced officers of real ability, more often it did not.

The Role of Sea Power

The Union had an overwhelming advantage in naval power, and it gave its navy two important roles in the war. One was enforcing a blockade of the Southern coast, which the president ordered on April 19, 1861. The other was assisting the Union armies in field operations.

The blockade of the South was never fully effective. The United States Navy could generally keep ocean-going ships out of Confederate ports, but for a time small blockade runners continued to slip through. Gradually, however, federal forces tightened the blockade by seizing the ports themselves. The last important port in Confederate hands—Wilmington, North Carolina—fell to the Union early in 1865.

The Confederates made bold attempts to break the blockade with new weapons. Foremost among them was an ironclad warship, constructed by plating with iron a former United States frigate, the *Merrimac*, which the Yankees had scuttled in Norfolk harbor when Virginia seceded. On March 8, 1862, the refitted *Merrimac*, renamed the *Virginia*, left Norfolk to attack a blockading squadron of wooden ships at nearby Hampton Roads. It destroyed two of the ships and scattered the rest. But the federal government had already built ironclads of its own. And one of them, the *Monitor*, arrived off the coast of Virginia only a few hours after the *Virginia's* dramatic foray. The next day, it met the *Virginia* in the first battle between ironclad ships. Neither vessel was able to sink the other, but the *Monitor* put an end to the *Virginia's* raids and preserved the blockade.

As a supporter of land operations, the Union navy was particularly important in the Western theater of war—the vast region between the Appalachian Mountains and the Mississippi River—where the larger rivers were navigable by large vessels. The navy transported supplies and troops and joined in attacking Confederate strong points. The South had no significant navy of its own and could defend against the Union gunboats only with fixed land fortifications, which proved no match for the mobile land-and-water forces of the Union.

Europe and the Disunited States

Judah P. Benjamin, the Confederate secretary of state for most of the war, was a clever and intelligent man, but he lacked strong convictions and confined most of his energy to routine administrative tasks. William Seward, his counterpart in Washington, gradually became one of the outstanding American secretaries of state. He had invaluable assistance from Charles Francis Adams, the American minister to London, who had inherited the considerable diplomatic talents of his father, John Quincy Adams, and his grandfather, John Adams.

At the beginning of the war, the sympathies of the ruling classes of England and France, the two nations whose support was most crucial to both sides, lay largely with the Confederacy. That was partly because the two nations imported much Southern cotton; but it was also because they were eager to weaken the United States, an increasingly powerful rival to them in world commerce, and because many admired the South's defense of aristocracy. But France was unwilling to take sides in the conflict unless England did so first. And in England, the government was reluctant to act

ROBERT E. LEE Lee provided a sharp contrast to his Northern counterpart, Ulysses S. Grant. Grant was slightly built, slouching, disheveled, and gruff. Lee was tall, dignified, and elegant in both dress and manner. He admired George Washington and attempted to emulate him in his conduct both of the war and of his life.

because there was powerful popular support for the Union. Important English liberals such as John Bright and Richard Cobden considered the war a struggle between free and slave labor and urged their followers to support the Union cause. The politically conscious but largely unenfranchised workers in Britain expressed their sympathy for the North frequently and unmistakably—in mass meetings, in resolutions, and through their champions in Parliament. After Lincoln issued the Emancipation Proclamation, these groups worked particularly avidly for the Union.

Southern leaders hoped to counter the strength of the British antislavery forces by arguing that access to Southern cotton was vital to the English and French textile industries. But this "King Cotton diplomacy," on which the Confederacy had staked so many of its hopes, was a failure. English manufacturers had a surplus of both raw cotton and finished goods on hand in 1861 and could withstand a temporary loss of access to American cotton. Later, as the supply of cotton began to diminish, both England and France managed to keep at least some of their mills open by importing cotton from Egypt, India, and other sources. Equally important, English workers, the people most seriously threatened by the cotton shortage, did not clamor to have the blockade broken. Even the 500,000 English textile workers thrown out of jobs as a result of mill closings continued to support the North. In the end, therefore, no European nation offered diplomatic recognition to the Confederacy or intervened in the war. No nation wanted to antagonize the United States unless the Confederacy seemed likely to win, and the South never came close enough to victory to convince its potential allies to support it.

Even so, there was considerable tension, and on occasion near hostilities, between the United States and Britain, beginning in the first days of the war. Great Britain declared itself neutral as soon as the fighting began; it was followed by France and other nations. The Union government was furious. Neutrality implied that the two sides to the conflict had equal stature, but Washington was insisting that the conflict was simply a domestic insurrection, not a war between two legitimate governments.

A more serious crisis, the so-called *Trent* affair, began in late 1861. Two Confederate diplomats, James M. Mason and John Slidell, had slipped through the then ineffective Union blockade to Havana, Cuba, where they boarded an English steamer, the *Trent*, for England. Waiting in Cuban waters was the American frigate *San Jacinto*, commanded by the impetuous Charles Wilkes. Acting without authorization, Wilkes stopped the British vessel, arrested the diplomats, and carried them in triumph to Boston. The British government demanded the release of the prisoners, reparations, and an apology. Lincoln and Seward, aware that Wilkes had violated maritime law and unwilling to risk war with England, spun out the negotiations until American public opinion had cooled off; then they released the diplomats with an indirect apology.

A second diplomatic crisis produced problems that lasted for years. Unable to construct large ships itself, the Confederacy bought six ships, known as commerce destroyers, from British shipyards. The best known of them were the *Alabama*, the *Florida*, and the *Shenandoah*. The United States protested that this sale of military equipment to a belligerent violated the laws of neutrality, and the protests became the basis, after the war, of damage claims by the United States against Great Britain.

CAMPAIGNS AND BATTLES

In the absence of direct intervention by the European powers, the two contestants in North America were left to resolve the conflict between themselves. They did so in four long years of bloody combat that produced more carnage than any war in American history, before or since. More than 618,000 Americans died in the course of the Civil War, far more than the 115,000 who perished in World War I or the 318,000 who died in World War II—more, indeed, than died in all other American wars through Vietnam combined. There were nearly 2,000 deaths for every 100,000 of population during the Civil War. In World War I, the comparable figure was only 109; in World War II, 241.

Despite the gruesome cost, the Civil War has become the most romanticized and the most intently studied of all American wars. In part, that is because the conflict produced—in addition to hideous fatalities—a series of military campaigns of classic strategic interest and a series of military leaders who displayed unusual brilliance and daring.

The Opening Clashes, 1861

The Union and the Confederacy fought their first major battle of the war in northern Virginia. A Union army of over 30,000 men under the command of General Irvin McDowell was stationed just outside Washington. About thirty miles away, at Manassas, was a slightly smaller Confederate army under P. G. T. Beauregard. If the Northern army could destroy the Southern one, Union leaders believed, the war might end at once. In mid-July, McDowell marched his inexperienced troops toward Manassas. Beauregard moved his troops behind Bull Run, a small stream north of Manassas, and called for reinforcements, which reached him the day before the battle. The two armies were now approximately the same size.

On July 21, in the First Battle of Bull Run, or First Battle of Manassas, McDowell almost succeeded in dispersing the Confederate forces. But the Southerners managed to stop a last strong Union assault and then began a savage counterattack. The Union troops, exhausted after hours of hot, hard fighting, suddenly panicked. They broke ranks and retreated chaotically. McDowell was unable to reorganize them, and he had to order a retreat to Washington—a disorderly withdrawal complicated by the presence along the route of many civilians, who had ridden down from the capital, picnic baskets in hand, to watch the battle from nearby hills. The Confederates, as disorganized by victory as the Union forces were by defeat, and short of supplies and transportation, did not pursue. The battle was a severe blow to Union morale and to the president's confidence in his officers. It also dispelled the illusion that the war would be a quick one.

Elsewhere, Union forces were achieving some small but significant victories in 1861. In Missouri, rebel forces gathered behind Governor Claiborne Jackson and other state officials who wanted to take the state out of the Union. Nathaniel Lyon, who commanded a small regular army force in St. Louis, moved his troops into southern Missouri to face the secessionists. On August 10, at the Battle of Wilson's Creek, he was defeated and killed—but not before he had seriously weakened the striking power of the Confederates. Union forces were subsequently able to hold most of the state.

Meanwhile, a Union force under George B. McClellan moved east from Ohio into western Virginia. By the end of 1861, it had "liberated" the antisecession mountain people of the region, who created their own state government loyal to the Union; the state was admitted to the Union as West Virginia in 1863. The occupation of western Virginia was of limited military value, since the mountains cut the area off from the rest of Virginia. It was, however, an important propaganda victory for the North.

The Western Theater

After the battle at Bull Run, military operations in the East settled into a long and frustrating stalemate. The first decisive operations in 1862 occurred, therefore, in the Western theater. Here the Union forces were trying to seize control of the southern part of the Mississippi River; this would divide the Confederacy and give the North easy transportation into the heart of the South. Northern soldiers advanced on the southern Mississippi from both the north and south, moving down the river from Kentucky and up from the Gulf of Mexico toward New Orleans.

In April, a Union squadron of ironclads and wooden vessels commanded by David G. Farragut gathered in the Gulf of Mexico, then smashed past weak Confederate forts near the mouth of the Mississippi, and from there sailed up to New Orleans. The city was virtually defenseless because

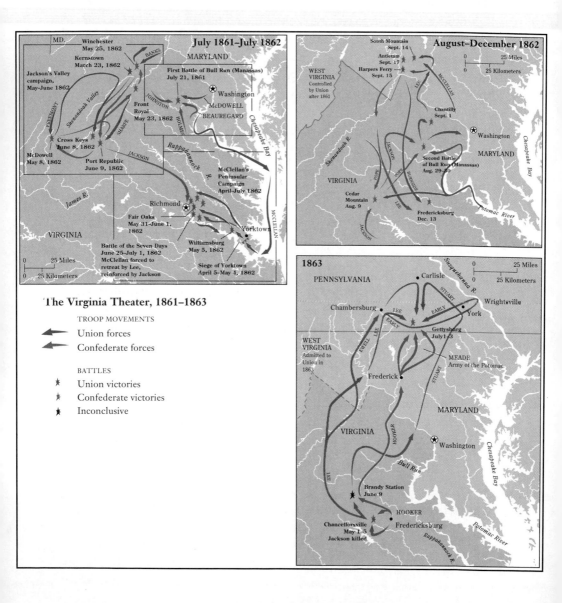

The Virginia Theater, 1861–1863

TROOP MOVEMENTS

Union forces

Confederate forces

BATTLES

* Union victories
* Confederate victories
* Inconclusive

the Confederate high command had expected the attack to come from the north. The surrender of New Orleans on April 25, 1862, was the first major Union victory and an important turning point in the war. From then on, the mouth of the Mississippi was closed to Confederate trade, and the South's largest city and most important banking center was in Union hands.

Farther north in the Western theater, Confederate troops under the command of Albert Sidney Johnston were stretched out in a long defensive line, whose center was at two forts in Tennessee, Fort Henry and Fort Donelson, on the Tennessee and Cumberland rivers respectively. But the forts were located well behind the main Southern flanks, a fatal weakness that Union commanders recognized and exploited. Early in 1862, Ulysses S. Grant attacked Fort Henry, whose defenders, awed by the ironclad river boats accompanying the Union army, surrendered with almost no resistance on February 6. Grant then moved both his naval and ground forces to Fort Donelson, where the Confederates put up a stronger fight but finally, on February 16, had to surrender. By cracking the Confederate center, Grant had gained control of river communications and forced Confederate forces out of Kentucky and half of Tennessee.

With about 40,000 men, Grant now advanced south along the Tennessee River to seize control of railroad lines vital to the Confederacy. From Pittsburg Landing, he marched to nearby Shiloh, Tennessee, where a force almost equal to his own and commanded by Albert Sidney Johnston and P. G. T. Beauregard caught him by surprise. The result was the Battle of Shiloh, April 6–7. In the first day's fighting (during which Johnston was killed), the Southerners drove Grant back to the river. But the next day, reinforced by 25,000 fresh troops, Grant recovered the lost ground and forced Beauregard to withdraw. After the narrow Union victory at Shiloh, Northern forces occupied Corinth, Mississippi, the hub of several important railroads, and took control of the Mississippi River as far south as Memphis.

Braxton Bragg, now in command of the Confederate army in the West, gathered his forces at Chattanooga, in eastern Tennessee, which the Confederacy still controlled. He hoped to win back the rest of the state and then move north into Kentucky. But first he had to face a Union army (commanded first by Don Carlos Buell and then by William S. Rosecrans), whose assignment was to capture Chattanooga. The two armies maneuvered for advantage inconclusively in northern Tennessee and southern Kentucky for several months until they finally met, on December 31–January 2, in the Battle of Murfreesboro, or Stone's River. Bragg was forced to withdraw to the south, his campaign a failure.

By the end of 1862, Union forces had made considerable progress in the West. But the major conflict remained in the East, and they were having much less success there.

The Virginia Front, 1862

Union operations were being directed in 1862 by George B. McClellan, commander of the Army of the Potomac and the most controversial general of the war. McClellan was a superb trainer of men, but he often seemed reluctant to commit his troops to battle. Opportunities for important engagements came and went, and McClellan seemed never to take advantage of them—claiming always that his preparations were not yet complete or that the moment was not right.

During the winter of 1861–1862, McClellan concentrated on training his army of 150,000 men near Washington. Finally, he designed a spring campaign whose purpose was to capture the Confederate capital at Richmond. But instead of heading overland directly toward Richmond, McClellan chose a complicated, roundabout route that he thought would circumvent the Confederate defenses. The navy would carry his troops down the Potomac to a peninsula east of Richmond, between the York and James rivers; the army would approach the city from there. The combined operations became known as the Peninsular campaign.

McClellan began the campaign with only part of his army. Approximately 100,000 men accompanied him down the Potomac. Another 30,000, under General Irvin McDowell, remained behind to protect Washington. McClellan insisted that Washington was safe as long as he was threatening Richmond, and he finally persuaded Lincoln to send him the additional men. But before the president could do so, a Confederate army under Thomas J. ("Stonewall") Jackson changed his plans. Jackson staged a rapid march north through the Shenandoah Valley, as if he were planning to cross the Potomac and attack Washington. Alarmed, Lincoln dispatched McDowell's corps to head off Jackson. In the brilliant Valley campaign of May 4–June 9, 1862, Jackson defeated two separate Union forces and slipped away before McDowell could catch him.

Meanwhile, Confederate troops under Joseph E. Johnston were attacking McClellan's advancing army outside Richmond. But in the two-day Battle of Fair Oaks, or Seven Pines (May 31–June 1), they could not repel the Union forces. Johnston, badly wounded, was replaced by Robert E. Lee, who then recalled Stonewall Jackson from the Shenandoah Valley. With a combined force of 85,000 to face McClellan's 100,000, Lee launched a new

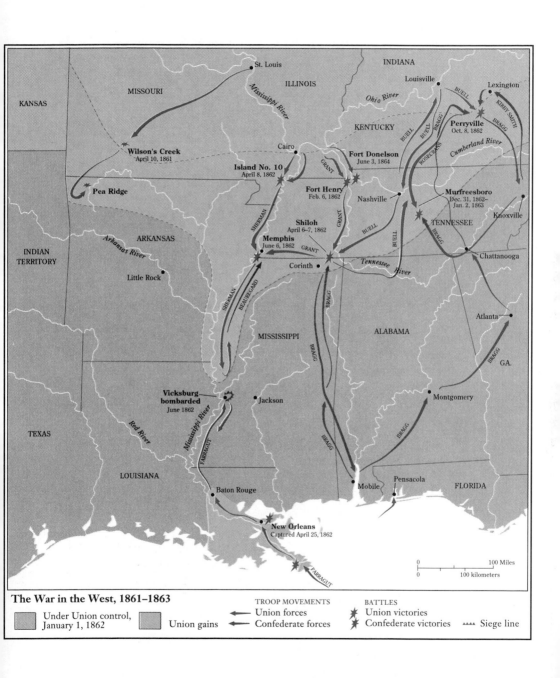

The War in the West, 1861–1863

Under Union control, January 1, 1862

Union gains

TROOP MOVEMENTS
Union forces
Confederate forces

BATTLES
Union victories
Confederate victories
Siege line

offensive, known as the Battle of the Seven Days (June 25–July 1). Lee wanted to cut McClellan off from his base on the York River and then destroy the isolated Union army. But McClellan fought his way across the peninsula and set up a new base on the James. There, with naval support, the Army of the Potomac was safe.

It was also only twenty-five miles from Richmond, with a secure line of water communications, and thus in a good position to renew the campaign. Time and again, however, McClellan found reasons for delay. Lincoln, instead of replacing McClellan with a more aggressive commander, finally ordered the army to move back to northern Virginia and join a smaller force under John Pope. The president hoped to begin a new offensive against Richmond on the direct overland route that he himself had always preferred.

As the Army of the Potomac left the peninsula by water, Lee moved north with the Army of Northern Virginia to strike Pope before McClellan could join him. Pope was as rash as McClellan was cautious, and he attacked the approaching Confederates without waiting for the arrival of all of McClellan's troops. In the ensuing Second Battle of Bull Run, or Second Battle of Manassas (August 29–30), Lee threw back the assault and routed Pope's army, which fled to Washington. With hopes for an overland campaign against Richmond now in disarray, Lincoln removed Pope from command and put McClellan in charge of all the federal forces in the region.

Lee soon went on the offensive again, heading north through western Maryland, and McClellan moved out to meet him. McClellan had the good luck to get a copy of Lee's orders, which revealed that a part of the Confederate army, under Stonewall Jackson, had separated from the rest to attack Harpers Ferry. But instead of attacking quickly before the Confederates could recombine, McClellan stalled and gave Lee time to pull most of his forces together behind Antietam Creek, near the town of Sharpsburg. There, on September 17, in the bloodiest engagement of the war, McClellan's 87,000-man army repeatedly attacked Lee's force of 50,000, with staggering casualties on both sides. In all, 6,000 men were killed, 17,000 wounded. Late in the day, just as the Confederate line seemed ready to break, the last of Jackson's troops arrived from Harpers Ferry to reinforce it. McClellan might have broken through with one more assault. Instead, he allowed Lee to retreat into Virginia. Technically, Antietam was a Union victory; but in reality, it was an opportunity squandered. In November, Lincoln finally removed McClellan from command for good.

McClellan's replacement, Ambrose E. Burnside, was a short-lived mediocrity. He tried to move toward Richmond by crossing the Rappahannock River at Fredericksburg, the strongest defensive point on the river. There, on December 13, he launched a series of attacks against Lee, all of them bloody, all of them hopeless. After losing a large part of his army, he withdrew to the north bank of the Rappahannock. He was relieved at his own request.

1863: Year of Decision

By the beginning of 1863, General Joseph Hooker was commanding the still formidable Army of the Potomac, whose 120,000 troops remained north of the Rappahannock, opposite Fredericksburg. But despite his formidable reputation (his popular nickname was "Fighting Joe"), Hooker showed little resolve as he launched his own campaign in the spring. Taking part of his army, Hooker crossed the river above Fredericksburg and moved toward the town and Lee's army. But at the last minute, he apparently lost his nerve and drew back to a defensive position in a desolate area of brush and scrub trees known as the Wilderness. Lee had only half as many men as Hooker had, but he boldly divided his forces for a dual assault on the Union army. In the Battle of Chancellorsville, May 1–5, Stonewall Jackson attacked the Union right and Lee himself charged the front. Hooker barely managed to escape with his army. Lee had frustrated Union objectives, but it was not an entirely happy victory. He had not destroyed the Union army. And his ablest officer, Jackson, was fatally wounded in the course of the battle.

While the Union forces were suffering repeated frustrations in the East, they were winning some important victories in the West. In the spring of 1863, Ulysses S. Grant was driving at Vicksburg, Mississippi, one of the Confederacy's two remaining strongholds on the southern Mississippi River. Vicksburg was well protected, surrounded by rough country on the north and low, marshy ground on the west, and had good artillery coverage of the river itself. But in May, Grant boldly moved men and supplies—over land and by water—to an area south of the city, where the terrain was better. He then attacked Vicksburg from the rear. Six weeks later, on July 4, Vicksburg—whose residents were by then literally starving as a result of a prolonged siege—surrendered. At almost the same time, the other Confederate strong point on the river, Port Hudson, Louisiana, also surrendered— to a Union force that had moved north from New Orleans. The Union had achieved one of its basic military aims: control of the whole length of the Mississippi. The Confederacy was split in two, with Louisiana, Arkansas, and Texas cut off from the other seceded states. The victories on the Mississippi were one of the great turning points of the war.

Early in the siege of Vicksburg, Lee proposed an invasion of Pennsylvania, which would, he argued, divert Union troops north and remove the pressure on the lower Mississippi. Further, he argued, if he could win a major victory on Northern soil, England and France might come to the Confederacy's aid. The war-weary North might even quit the war before Vicksburg fell.

In June 1863, Lee moved up the Shenandoah Valley into Maryland and then entered Pennsylvania. The Union Army of the Potomac, commanded first by Hooker and then by George C. Meade, moved north too, paralleling the Confederates' movement and staying between Lee and Washington. The two armies finally encountered one another at the small town of Gettysburg, Pennsylvania. There, on July 1–3, 1863, they fought the most celebrated battle of the war.

Meade's army established a strong, well-protected position on the hills south of the town. The confident and combative Lee attacked, even though his army of 75,000 was outnumbered by Meade's 90,000. His first assault on the Union forces on Cemetery Ridge failed. A day later, he ordered a second, larger effort. In what is remembered as Pickett's Charge, a force of 15,000 Confederate soldiers advanced for almost a mile across open country while being swept by Union fire. Only about 5,000 made it up the ridge, and this remnant finally had to surrender or retreat. By now, Lee had lost nearly a third of his army. On July 4, the same day as the surrender of Vicksburg, he withdrew from Gettysburg. The retreat was another major turning point in the war. Never again were the weakened Confederate forces able seriously to threaten Northern territory.

Before the end of the year, there was another important turning point, this one in Tennessee. After occupying Chattanooga on September 9, Union forces under William Rosecrans began an unwise pursuit of Bragg's retreating Confederate forces. Bragg was waiting for them just across the Georgia line, with reinforcements from Lee's army. The two armies engaged in the Battle of Chickamauga (September 19–20), one of the few battles in which the Confederates enjoyed a numerical superiority (70,000 to 56,000). Union forces could not break the Confederate lines and retreated back to Chattanooga.

Bragg now began a siege of Chattanooga itself, seizing the heights nearby and cutting off fresh supplies to the Union forces. Grant came to the rescue. In the Battle of Chattanooga (November 23–25), the reinforced Union army drove the Confederates back into Georgia. Northern troops then occupied most of eastern Tennessee. Union forces had now achieved a second important objective: control of the Tennessee River. Four of the

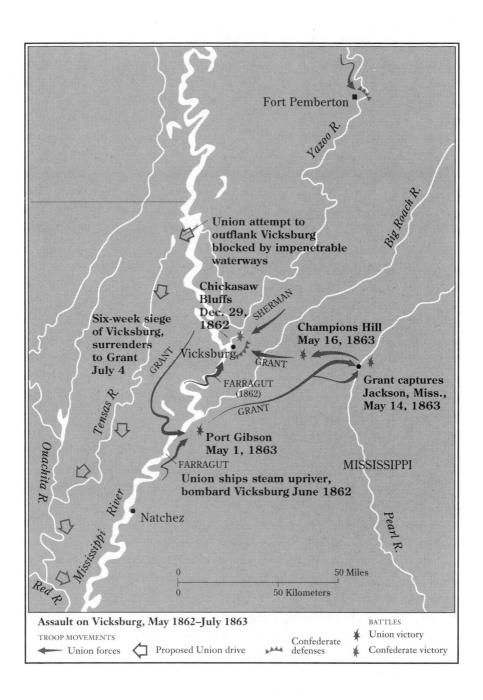

Fort Pemberton

Yazoo R.

Big Roach R.

Union attempt to outflank Vicksburg blocked by impenetrable waterways

Chickasaw Bluffs Dec. 29, 1862

SHERMAN

Champions Hill May 16, 1863

Six-week siege of Vicksburg, surrenders to Grant July 4

GRANT

Vicksburg

GRANT

Grant captures Jackson, Miss., May 14, 1863

FARRAGUT (1862)

Tensas R.

GRANT

MISSISSIPPI

Port Gibson May 1, 1863

FARRAGUT

Union ships steam upriver, bombard Vicksburg June 1862

Ouachita R.

Mississippi River

Natchez

Pearl R.

| 0 | | 50 Miles |
| 0 | | 50 Kilometers |

Red R.

Assault on Vicksburg, May 1862–July 1863

TROOP MOVEMENTS

◄─── Union forces ⬅ Proposed Union drive ▸▴▴▴ Confederate defenses

BATTLES

✳ Union victory

✳ Confederate victory

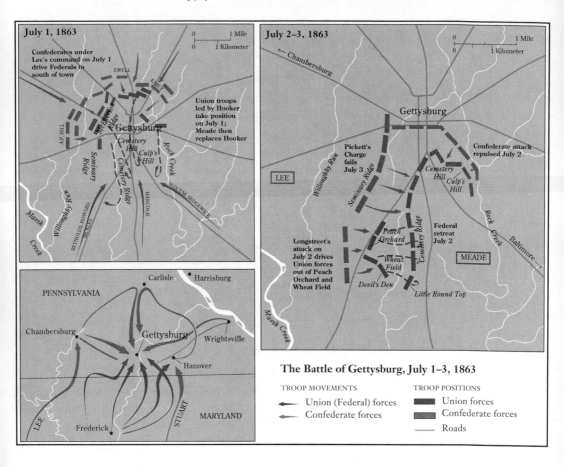

July 1, 1863

Confederates under Lee's command on July 1 drive Federals to south of town

EWELL

EWELL

A.P. HILL

Gettysburg

Cemetery Hill

Culp's Hill

Seminary Ridge

Cemetery Ridge

Rock Creek

SLOCUM, SEDGWICK

HANCOCK

REYNOLDS, HOWARD, SICKLES

Willoughby Run

Marsh Creek

Union troops led by Hooker take position on July 1; Meade then replaces Hooker

0 1 Mile
0 1 Kilometer

July 2–3, 1863

Chambersburg

Gettysburg

LEE

Willoughby Run

Seminary Ridge

Pickett's Charge fails July 3

Cemetery Hill

Culp's Hill

Cemetery Ridge

Confederate attack repulsed July 2

Federal retreat July 2

MEADE

Rock Creek

Baltimore

Longstreet's attack on July 2 drives Union forces out of Peach Orchard and Wheat Field

Peach Orchard

Wheat Field

Devil's Den

Little Round Top

Marsh Creek

0 1 Mile
0 1 Kilometer

PENNSYLVANIA

Carlisle • Harrisburg

Chambersburg

Gettysburg

Wrightsville

Hanover

LEE

STUART

Frederick

MARYLAND

The Battle of Gettysburg, July 1–3, 1863

TROOP MOVEMENTS
← Union (Federal) forces
← Confederate forces

TROOP POSITIONS
▬ Union forces
▬ Confederate forces
— Roads

eleven Confederate states were now effectively cut off from the Southern nation. No longer could the Confederacy hope to win independence through a decisive military victory. They could hope to win only by holding on and exhausting the Northern will to fight.

The Last Stage, 1864–1865

By the beginning of 1864, Ulysses S. Grant had become general in chief of all the Union armies. At long last, the president had found a general whom he could rely on to pursue the war doggedly and tenaciously. Grant was not a subtle strategic or tactical general; he simply believed in using the North's great advantage in troops and material resources to overwhelm the South. He was not afraid to absorb massive casualties as long as he was inflicting similar casualties on his opponents.

Grant planned two great offensives for 1864. In Virginia, the Army of the Potomac (technically under Meade's command, but really now under Grant's) would advance toward Richmond and force Lee into a decisive battle. In Georgia, the Western army, under William T. Sherman, would

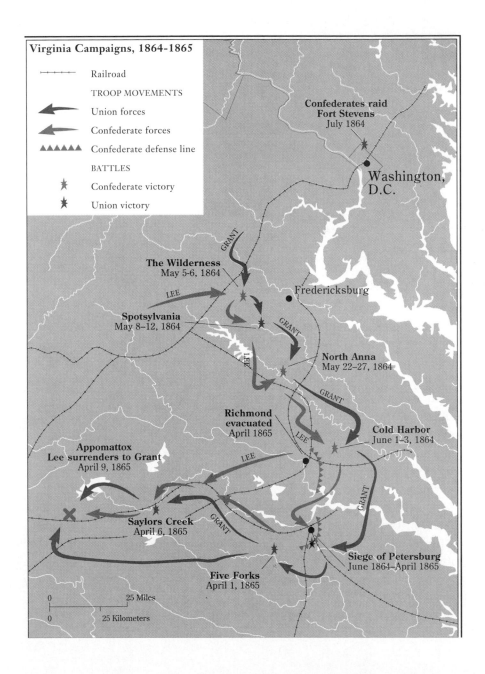

Virginia Campaigns, 1864-1865

+–+–+–+ Railroad

TROOP MOVEMENTS

⬅ Union forces

⬅ Confederate forces

▲▲▲▲▲▲ Confederate defense line

BATTLES

✳ Confederate victory

✱ Union victory

Confederates raid
Fort Stevens
July 1864

Washington, D.C.

GRANT

The Wilderness
May 5-6, 1864

LEE

Fredericksburg

Spotsylvania
May 8–12, 1864

GRANT

LEE

North Anna
May 22–27, 1864

GRANT

Richmond
evacuated
April 1865

LEE

Cold Harbor
June 1–3, 1864

Appomattox
Lee surrenders to Grant
April 9, 1865

LEE

GRANT

GRANT

Saylors Creek
April 6, 1865

Siege of Petersburg
June 1864–April 1865

Five Forks
April 1, 1865

0   25 Miles

0   25 Kilometers

advance east toward Atlanta and destroy the remaining Confederate force, which was now under the command of Joseph E. Johnston.

The northern campaign began when the Army of the Potomac, 115,000 strong, plunged into the rough, wooded Wilderness area of northwestern Virginia in pursuit of Lee's 75,000-man army. After avoiding an engagement for several weeks, Lee turned Grant back in the Battle of the Wilderness (May 5–7). But Grant was undeterred. Without stopping to rest or reorganize, he resumed his march toward Richmond. He met Lee again in the bloody, five-day Battle of Spotsylvania Court House, in which 12,000 Union troops and a large, but unknown, number of Confederates fell. Despite the enormous losses, Grant kept moving. But victory continued to elude him. Lee kept his army between Grant and the Confederate capital and on June 1–3 repulsed the Union forces again, just northeast of Richmond, at Cold Harbor. The month-long Wilderness campaign had cost Grant 55,000 men (killed, wounded, or captured) compared with Lee's 31,000. And Richmond still had not fallen.

Grant now changed his strategy. He moved his army east of Richmond, bypassing the capital altogether, and headed south toward the railroad center at Petersburg. If he could seize Petersburg, he could cut off the capital's communications with the rest of the Confederacy. But Petersburg had strong defenses; and once Lee came to the city's relief, the assault became a prolonged siege, which lasted nine months.

In Georgia, meanwhile, Sherman was facing a less ferocious resistance. With 90,000 men, he confronted Confederate forces of 60,000 under Johnston, who was unwilling to risk a direct engagement. As Sherman advanced, Johnston tried to delay him by maneuvering. The two armies fought only one real battle—Kennesaw Mountain, northwest of Atlanta, on June 27—where Johnston scored an impressive victory. Even so, he was unable to stop the Union advance toward Atlanta. Davis replaced Johnston with the combative John B. Hood, who twice daringly attacked Sherman's army but accomplished little except seriously weakening his own forces. Sherman took Atlanta on September 2. News of the victory electrified the North and helped unite the previously divided Republican party behind President Lincoln.

Hood now tried unsuccessfully to draw Sherman out of Atlanta by moving back up through Tennessee and threatening an invasion of the North. Sherman did not take the bait. But he did send Union troops to reinforce Nashville. In the Battle of Nashville on December 15–16, 1864, Northern forces practically destroyed what was left of Hood's army.

Meanwhile, Sherman had left Atlanta to begin his soon-to-be-famous "March to the Sea." Living off the land, destroying supplies it could not use, his army cut a sixty-mile-wide swath of desolation across Georgia. "War is all hell," Sherman had once said. By that he meant not that war is terrible, and to be avoided, but that it should be made as horrible and costly as possible for the opponent. He sought not only to deprive the Confederate army of war materials and railroad communications but also to break the will of the Southern people by burning towns and plantations along his route. By December 20, he had reached Savannah, which surrendered two days later. Sherman offered it to President Lincoln as a Christmas gift. Early in 1865, Sherman continued his destructive march, moving northward through South Carolina. He was virtually unopposed until he was well inside North Carolina, where a small force under Johnston could do no more than cause a brief delay.

In April 1865, Grant's Army of the Potomac—still engaged in the prolonged siege at Petersburg—finally captured a vital railroad junction southwest of the town. Without rail access to the South, cut off from other Confederate forces, plagued by heavy casualties and massive desertions, Lee

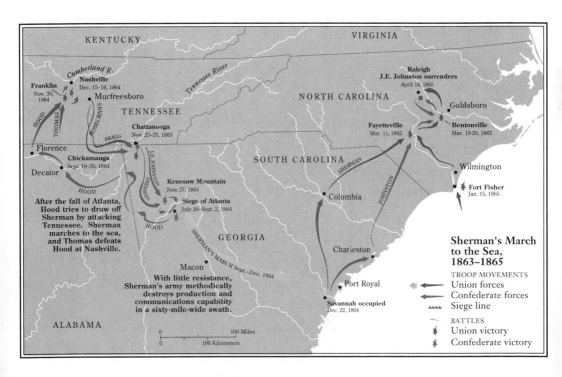

AMERICAN VOICES

J. J. HILL

The 29th Connecticut Colored Infantry Enters Richmond, April 1865

ALL WAS QUIET here until the 1st of April, when all was in readiness, and the order was given to strike tents and move on to Richmond. . . . On our march to Richmond, we captured 500 pieces of artillery, some of the largest kind, 6,000 stand of small arms, and the prisoners I was not able to number. The road was strewed with all kinds of obstacles, and men were lying all along the distance of seven miles. The main body of the army went up the New Market road. The 29th skirmished all the way, and arrived in the city at 7 a.m., and were the first infantry that entered the city. . . .

The 3rd [of April] President Lincoln visited the city. No triumphal march of a conqueror could have equalled in moral sublimity the humble manner in which he entered Richmond. I was standing on the bank of the James River viewing the scene of desolation when a boat, pulled by twelve sailors, came up the stream. It contained President Lincoln and his son. In some way the colored people on the bank of the river ascertained that the tall man wearing the black hat was President Lincoln. . . . As he approached, I said to a woman, "Madam, that is the man that made you free." . . . She gazed at him with clasped hands and said, "Glory to God, Give him the praise for his goodness," and she shouted till her voice failed her. . . . It was a man of the people among the people. It was a great deliverer among the delivered. No wonder tears came to his eyes. . . . After visiting Jeff Davis's Mansion, he proceeded to the rebel capital and from the steps delivered a short speech to the colored people as follows: ". . . God has made you free. Although you have been deprived of your God-given rights by your so-called masters, you are now as free as I am, and if those that claim to be your superiors do not know that you are free, take the sword and bayonet and teach them that you are—for God created all men free, giving to each the same rights of life, liberty, and the pursuit of happiness."

informed the Confederate government that he could no longer defend Richmond. Within hours, Jefferson Davis, his cabinet, and as much of the white population as could find transportation fled along with Lee's soldiers. That night, mobs roamed the city, setting devastating fires. And the next morning, Northern forces (led by an African-American infantry brigade) entered the Confederate capital. With them was Abraham Lincoln, who walked through the streets of the burned-out city surrounded by black men and women cheering him as the "Messiah" and "Father Abraham." In one particularly stirring moment, the president turned to a former slave kneeling on the street before him and said: "Don't kneel to me. . . . You must kneel to God only, and thank Him for the liberty you will enjoy hereafter."

With the remnant of his army, now about 25,000 men, Lee began moving west in the forlorn hope of finding a way around the Union forces so that he could move south and link up with Johnston in North Carolina. But the Union army pursued him and blocked his escape route. Lee finally recognized that further bloodshed was futile. He arranged to meet Grant at a private home in the small town of Appomattox Courthouse, Virginia, where on April 9 he surrendered what was left of his forces. Nine days later, near Durham, North Carolina, Johnston surrendered to Sherman.

In military terms, at least, the long war was now effectively over, even though Jefferson Davis refused to accept defeat. He moved south after leaving Richmond, hoping to reach Texas and continue the struggle from there. He was finally captured in Georgia. A few Southern diehards continued to fight, but even their resistance collapsed before long. And well before the last shot was fired, the difficult process of reuniting the shattered nation had begun.

D E B A T I N G T H E P A S T

The Causes of the Civil War

HE OUTLINES OF the scholarly debate over the causes of the Civil War became visible even before the war itself began. In 1858, Senator William H. Seward of New York took note of the two competing explanations of the sectional tensions that were then inflaming the nation. On one side, he said, stood those who believed the conflicts to be "accidental, unnecessary, the work of interested or fanatical agitators." Opposing them stood those (among them Seward himself) who believed there to be "an irrepressible conflict between opposing and enduring forces." Without realizing it, Seward had identified a division of opinion that would survive among historians for more than a century.

The irrepressible-conflict argument dominated historical discussion of the war from the 1860s to the 1920s. War was inevitable, some historians claimed, because there was no room for compromise on the central issue of slavery. Others de-emphasized slavery and pointed to the economic differences between the agrarian South and the industrializing North. Charles and Mary Beard, for example, wrote in 1927 of the "inherent antagonisms" between the interests of planters and those of industrialists. Each group was seeking to control the federal government to promote its own economic interests. Still others cited social and cultural differences between the two sections as the source of an irrepressible conflict. Slavery, the historian Allan Nevins argued, was only one factor in the cultural divergence that was making residents of the North and South "separate peoples." There were fundamental differences in "assumptions, tastes, and cultural aims" that made it virtually impossible for the two societies to live together in peace.

More recent proponents of "irrepressible-conflict" arguments similarly emphasize culture and ideology but define the concerns of the North and the South in different terms. Eric Foner, writing in 1970, argued that the moral concerns of abolitionists and the economic concerns of industrialists were less important in explaining Northern hostility to the South than was the broad-based "free-labor" ideology of the region. Northerners opposed slavery because they feared it might spread into their own region and threaten the position of free white laborers. Hence their insistence that it not be allowed to expand into the West.

Other historians have taken a very different view of the Civil War. Rather than arguing over what factors made the war inevitable, they have suggested that the differences between North and South were not so great as to require a conflict. The modern version of this position began to emerge in the 1920s, among a group known as the "revisionists." James G. Randall, for example, saw in the social and economic systems of the North and the South no differences so fundamental as to require a war. By the time the war began, he argued, slavery was already "crumbling in the presence of nineteenth century tendencies." The failures of a "blundering generation" of political leaders, not irrepressible differences, caused the Civil War. Avery Craven, writing in 1942, argued similarly that slavery was on the road to "ultimate extinction" and that skillful and responsible leaders could have produced a compromise solution that would have avoided war. David Donald, writing in 1960, agreed with Randall and Craven that compromise should have been possible. He was less critical than they of the political leaders of the 1850s; he argued, rather, that the rapid extension of democracy in both North and South had made it more difficult for "statesmen" to guard against popular passions. Michael Holt revived the "revisionist" argument in a 1978 book, in which he too emphasized the partisan ambitions of politicians who used sectional rivalries to advance their own aims. "Much of the story of the coming of the Civil War," he argued, "is the story of the successful efforts of Democratic politicians in the South and Republican politicians in the North to keep the sectional conflict at the center of the political debate."

Like the proponents of the "irrepressible conflict" interpretation, the "revisionists" have differed among themselves in important ways. But the explanation of the coming of the Civil War continues, more than a century later, to reflect the two schools of thought William Seward identified in 1858.

CHAPTER FIFTEEN

Reconstructing the Nation

The Problems of Peacemaking ～ *Radical Reconstruction*
The South in Reconstruction ～ *The Grant Administration*
The Abandonment of Reconstruction

EW PERIODS in the history of the United States have produced as much bitterness or created such enduring controversy as the era of Reconstruction—the years following the Civil War during which Americans attempted to reunite their shattered nation. Those who lived through the experience viewed it in sharply different ways. To many white Southerners, Reconstruction was a vicious and destructive experience—a period when vindictive Northerners inflicted humiliation and revenge on the prostrate South and unnecessarily delayed a genuine reunion of the sections. Northern defenders of Reconstruction, in contrast, argued that their policies were the only way to prevent unrepentant Confederates from restoring Southern society as it had been before the war; without forceful federal intervention, there would be no way to forestall the reemergence of a backward aristocracy and the continued subjugation of blacks—no way, in other words, to prevent the same sectional problems that had produced the Civil War in the first place.

To most black Americans at the time, and to many people of all races since, Reconstruction was notable for other reasons. Neither a vicious tyranny, as white Southerners charged, nor a drastic and necessary reform, as many Northerners claimed, it was, rather, an essentially moderate, even conservative program that fell far short of providing the newly freed slaves with the protection they needed. Reconstruction, in other words, was significant less for what it did than for what it failed to do. And when it came to an end, finally, in the late 1870s, black Americans found themselves once again abandoned.

CHARLESTON, 1865 Not until 1864 did substantial fighting and destruction begin to take place in the urban South. But in the last year of the war, several major cities (and many towns and smaller communities) experienced devastation at the hands of the Northern armies—among them Richmond, Atlanta, and (as seen here) Charleston.

THE PROBLEMS OF PEACEMAKING

In 1865, when the Confederacy finally surrendered to the North, no one in Washington knew quite what to do in response. Abraham Lincoln could not negotiate a treaty with the defeated government; he continued to insist that that government had no legal right to exist. Yet neither could he simply readmit the Southern states into the Union as if nothing had happened.

The Aftermath of War

The South after the Civil War was a desolate place. Towns had been gutted, plantations burned, fields neglected, bridges and railroads destroyed. Many white Southerners—stripped of their slaves through emancipation and stripped of the capital they had invested in now worthless Confederate bonds and currency—had no personal property. More than 258,000 Confederate soldiers had died in the war, and thousands more returned home wounded or sick. Many families had to rebuild their fortunes without the help of adult males. Many white Southerners faced starvation and homelessness.

If conditions were bad for Southern whites, they were far worse for Southern blacks—the 4 million men and women now emerging from bondage. As soon as the war ended, hundreds of thousands of them—young and old, many of them ill and feeble—left the plantations in search of a new life in freedom. But most had nowhere to go. They trudged to the nearest town or city or roamed the countryside, camping at night on the bare ground. Few had any possessions except the clothes they wore.

The response of many white Southerners to this desolation was an effort to restore their society to its antebellum form. Slavery had been abolished in some areas in 1863 by the Emancipation Proclamation and in all areas as of December 1865 by the Thirteenth Amendment. But many white planters wanted to continue slavery in an altered form by keeping black workers legally tied to the plantations. Blacks, of course, had a very different vision of the postwar South. They wanted, above all, to know and feel their freedom and to be assured that they were not again to lose it. They wanted to own land, to educate their children, and to gain the right to vote. The struggle between Southern blacks and whites over these competing visions was an unequal one, but for a time blacks had the benefit of at least some support from the federal government.

The government kept troops in the South to preserve order and protect the freedmen. And in March 1865, Congress established the Freedmen's Bureau, an agency of the army directed by General Oliver O. Howard. The Freedmen's Bureau distributed food to millions of former slaves. It established schools, staffed by missionaries and teachers who had been sent to the South by Freedmen's Aid Societies and other private and church groups in the North. It tried to settle blacks on lands of their own. (The bureau also offered considerable assistance to poor whites, many of whom were similarly destitute and homeless after the war.)

But the Freedmen's Bureau was not a permanent solution. It had authority to operate for only one year; and it was, in any case, far too small to deal effectively with the enormous problems facing Southern society. It remained up to the federal government to determine whether the hopes of Southern whites or those of Southern blacks would prevail.

Issues of Reconstruction

The terms by which the Southern states rejoined the Union had important implications for both major political parties. The Republican victories in 1860 and 1864 had been a result, in large part, of divisions within the Democratic party and, later, the removal of the South from the electorate. Leaders of both parties believed that readmitting the South would reunite the Democrats and weaken the Republicans. In addition, the Republican party had taken advantage of the absence of the South from Congress to pass a program of nationalistic economic legislation—railroad subsidies, protective tariffs, and other measures of benefit to Northern business leaders and industrialists. Should the Democratic party regain power with heavy Southern support, these programs would be in jeopardy. Complicating these practical questions were emotional concerns. Many Northerners believed the South should be punished for the suffering and sacrifice its rebellion had caused. And many Northerners believed, too, that the South should be transformed, made over in the North's urban-industrial image.

Even among the Republicans in Congress, there was considerable disagreement about the proper approach to Reconstruction—disagreement that reflected the same factional division (between the party's Conservatives and Radicals) that had created disputes during the war over emancipation. Conservatives insisted that the South accept the abolition of slavery, but they proposed few other conditions for the readmission of the seceded states. The Radicals, led by Representative Thaddeus Stevens of Pennsylvania and Senator Charles Sumner of Massachusetts, urged that the civil and military chieftains of the late Confederacy be punished, that large numbers of Southern whites be disenfranchised, that the legal rights of blacks be protected, and that the property of wealthy white Southerners who had aided the Confederacy be confiscated and distributed among the freedmen. Some Radicals favored granting suffrage to the former slaves. Others hesitated, since few Northern states permitted blacks to vote. Between the Radicals and the Conservatives stood a faction of uncommitted Republicans, the Moderates, who rejected the punitive goals of the Radicals but supported extracting at least some concessions from the South on black rights.

Plans for Reconstruction

President Lincoln's sympathies lay with the Moderates and Conservatives of his party. He believed that a lenient Reconstruction policy would encourage Southern Unionists and other former Whigs to join the Republican party and thus prevent the readmission of the South from strengthening the Democrats. More immediately, the Southern Unionists could become the nucleus of new, loyal state governments in the South. Lincoln was not uninterested in the fate of the freedmen, but he was willing to defer questions about race relations for the sake of rapid reunification.

Lincoln's Reconstruction plan, which he announced in December 1863, offered a general amnesty to those white Southerners—other than high officials of the Confederacy—who would pledge loyalty to the government and accept the elimination of slavery. When 10 percent of the number of voters in 1860 took the oath in any state, those loyal voters could set up a state government. Lincoln also hoped to extend suffrage to those blacks who were educated, owned property, and had served in the Union army. Three Southern states—Louisiana, Arkansas, and Tennessee, all under Union occupation—reestablished loyal governments under the Lincoln formula in 1864.

The Radical Republicans were astonished at the mildness of Lincoln's program. They persuaded Congress to deny seats to representatives from

ABRAHAM LINCOLN Lincoln was the subject of many photographic portraits, of which this one, by Matthew Brady, is one of the most famous.

the three "reconstructed" states and refused to count the electoral vote of those states in the election of 1864. But for the moment, the Radicals were uncertain about what form their own Reconstruction plan should take.

Their first effort to resolve that question was the Wade-Davis Bill, passed by Congress in July 1864. By its provisions, the president would appoint a provisional governor for each conquered state. When a majority (not Lincoln's ten percent) of the white males of the state pledged their allegiance to the Union, the governor could summon a state constitutional convention, whose delegates were to be elected by voters who had never borne arms against the United States (again, a major departure from Lincoln's plan). The new state constitutions would be required to abolish slavery, disenfranchise Confederate civil and military leaders, and repudiate debts accumulated by the state governments during the war. After these conditions were met, Congress would readmit the states to the Union. Like the president's proposal, the Wade-Davis Bill left up to the states the question of political rights for blacks.

Congress passed the bill a few days before it adjourned in 1864, and Lincoln disposed of it with a pocket veto. His action enraged the Radical leaders, and the pragmatic Lincoln realized he would have to accept at least some of the Radical demands. As a result, he began to move toward a new approach to Reconstruction.

The Death of Lincoln

What plan he might have produced no one can say. On the night of April 14, 1865, Lincoln and his wife attended a play at Ford's Theater in Washington. As they sat in the presidential box, John Wilkes Booth, an unsuccessful actor obsessed with aiding the Southern cause, entered the box from the rear and shot Lincoln in the head. Early the next morning, the president died.

The circumstances of Lincoln's death earned him immediate martyrdom. They also produced something close to hysteria throughout the North. There were accusations that Booth had acted as part of a great conspiracy—accusations that contained some truth. Booth did indeed have associates, one of whom shot and wounded Secretary of State William Seward the night of the assassination, another of whom abandoned at the last moment a scheme to murder Vice President Andrew Johnson. Booth himself escaped on horseback into the Maryland countryside, where, on April 26, he was cornered by Union troops and shot to death in a blazing barn. Eight other people were convicted by a military tribunal of participating in the conspiracy (at least two of them on the basis of virtually no evidence). Four were hanged.

To many Northerners, however, the murder of the president seemed evidence of an even greater conspiracy—one masterminded and directed by the unrepentant leaders of the defeated South. Militant Republicans exploited such suspicions relentlessly in the ensuing months, ensuring that Lincoln's death would help doom his plans for a relatively generous peace.

Johnson and "Restoration"

Leadership of the Moderates and Conservatives fell to Lincoln's successor, Andrew Johnson, who was not well suited, either by circumstance or personality, for the task. A Democrat until he had joined the Union ticket with Lincoln in 1864, he became president at a time of growing partisan passions. And Johnson himself was an intemperate and tactless man, filled with resentments and insecurities.

Johnson revealed his plan for Reconstruction—or "Restoration," as he preferred to call it—soon after he took office, and he implemented it during the summer of 1865 when Congress was in recess. Like Lincoln, he offered amnesty to those Southerners who would take an oath of allegiance. (High-ranking Confederate officials and all white Southerners with land worth $20,000 or more would have to apply to the president for individual pardons.) In most other respects, however, his plan resembled that of the Wade-Davis Bill. For each state, the president appointed a provisional governor, who would invite qualified voters to elect delegates to a constitutional convention. Johnson did not specify how many qualified voters were necessary, but he implied that he would require a majority (as had the Wade-Davis Bill). In order to win readmission to Congress, a state had to revoke its ordinance of secession, abolish slavery and ratify the Thirteenth Amendment, and repudiate Confederate and state war debts—essentially the same stipulations that had been laid down in Wade-Davis. The final procedure before restoration was that a state would elect a state government and send representatives to Congress.

By the end of 1865, all the seceded states had formed new governments—some under Lincoln's plan, some under Johnson's—and were ready to rejoin the Union, *if* Congress chose to recognize them when it met in December 1865. But Radicals in Congress vowed not to recognize the Johnson governments, just as they had previously refused to recognize the Lincoln regimes; for by now, Northern opinion had become more hostile toward the South than it had been a year earlier when Congress passed the

Wade-Davis Bill. Many Northerners were disturbed by the apparent reluctance of some delegates to the Southern conventions to abolish slavery and by the refusal of all the conventions to grant suffrage to any blacks. They were astounded that states claiming to be "loyal" should elect as state officials and representatives to Congress prominent leaders of the recent Confederacy. Particularly hard to accept was Georgia's choice of Alexander H. Stephens, former vice president of the Confederacy, as a United States senator.

RADICAL RECONSTRUCTION

Reconstruction under Johnson's plan—often known as "presidential Reconstruction"—continued only until Congress reconvened in December 1865. At that point, Congress refused to seat the senators and representatives of the states the president had "restored." Instead, it set up a new Joint Committee on Reconstruction to investigate conditions in the South and to advise Congress in devising a Reconstruction policy of its own. The period of "congressional" or "Radical" Reconstruction had begun.

The Black Codes

Meanwhile, events in the South were driving Northern opinion in even more radical directions. Throughout the South in 1865 and early 1866, state legislatures were enacting sets of laws known as the Black Codes, modeled in many ways on the codes that had regulated free blacks in the prewar South and designed to guarantee white supremacy. Although there were variations from state to state, all codes authorized local officials to apprehend unemployed blacks, fine them for vagrancy, and hire them out to private employers to satisfy the fine. Some of the codes forbade blacks to own or lease farms or to take any jobs other than as plantation workers or domestic servants. To the white South, the Black Codes were a realistic approach to a great social problem. To the North, and to most African-Americans, they represented a return to slavery in all but name.

Congress first responded to the Black Codes by passing an act extending the life of the Freedmen's Bureau and widening its powers. The bureau could now establish special courts for settling labor disputes; the courts could nullify work agreements forced on freedmen under the Black Codes. In April, Congress struck again at the Black Codes by passing the first Civil Rights Act, which declared blacks to be citizens of the United States and empowered the federal government to intervene in state affairs when necessary to protect the rights of citizens. Johnson vetoed both the Freedmen's Bureau and Civil Rights Acts, but Congress eventually overrode him.

The Fourteenth Amendment

In April 1866, the Radicals acted again. The Joint Committee on Reconstruction submitted a proposed Fourteenth Amendment to the Constitution, which Congress approved in early summer and sent to the states for ratification. Eventually, it became one of the most important of all the provisions in the Constitution.

The amendment offered the first constitutional definition of American citizenship. Everyone born in the United States, and everyone naturalized, was automatically a citizen and entitled to all the "privileges and immunities" guaranteed by the Constitution, including equal protection of the laws by both the state and national governments. There could be no other requirements. The amendment also imposed penalties—reduction of representation in Congress and in the electoral college—on states that denied suffrage to any adult male inhabitants. (This was the first time the Constitution had made reference to gender, and the wording clearly reflected the prevailing view in Congress and elsewhere that the franchise was properly restricted to men.) Finally, it prohibited those who had aided the Confederacy after having taken an oath to support the Constitution (that is, members of Congress and other federal officials) from holding any state or federal office unless two-thirds of Congress voted to pardon them.

Congressional Radicals made it clear that if Southern legislatures ratified the Fourteenth Amendment, their states would be readmitted to the Union. But of the former Confederate states, only Tennessee did so. The refusal of others to ratify, along with the refusal of Kentucky and Delaware, denied the amendment the necessary approval of three-fourths of the states and temporarily derailed it.

In the meantime, however, the Radicals were growing stronger, in part because of Northern anger at the South's and Johnson's recalcitrance. When bloody race riots broke out in New Orleans and other Southern cities—riots in which blacks were the principal victims—Radicals cited the incidents as evidence of the inadequacy of Johnson's policy. In the 1866 congressional elections, Johnson actively campaigned for Conservative candidates; but he did his own cause more harm than good with his intemperate speeches. The voters returned an overwhelming majority of Republicans, most of them Radicals, to Congress. In the Senate, there were now 42 Republicans to 11

Democrats; in the House, 143 Republicans to 49 Democrats. (The South remained largely unrepresented in both chambers.) Nothing now prevented the Republicans in Congress from devising a Reconstruction plan of their own.

The Congressional Plan

The Radicals passed three Reconstruction bills early in 1867. Johnson vetoed them all, but Congress overrode him. Finally, nearly two years after the end of the war, the federal government had established a coherent plan for Reconstruction.

That two-year delay had important effects on the way the South reacted to the program. In 1865, with the South reeling from its defeat and nearly prostrate, the federal government could probably have imposed almost any plan on the region without provoking much resistance. But by 1867, the South had already begun to reconstruct itself under the reasonably generous terms Lincoln and Johnson had extended. Measures that might once have seemed moderate now seemed radical, and the congressional Reconstruction plan created deep resentments and continuing resistance.

Under the congressional plan, Tennessee, which had ratified the Fourteenth Amendment, was promptly readmitted. But Congress rejected the Lincoln-Johnson governments of the other ten Confederate states and, instead, combined them into five military districts. Each was assigned a military commander who—in preparation for the readmission of the states—was to register qualifed voters, defined as all adult black males and those white males who had not participated in the rebellion. After the registration was completed, voters would elect a convention to prepare a new state constitution, which had to include provisions for black suffrage. Once voters ratified the new constitution, elections for a state government could be held. Finally, if Congress approved the constitution, if the state legislature ratified the Fourteenth Amendment, and if enough states ratified the amendment to make it part of the Constitution, then the state was to be restored to the Union.

By 1868, seven of the eleven former Confederate states (Arkansas, North Carolina, South Carolina, Louisiana, Alabama, Georgia, and Florida) had fulfilled these conditions (including ratification of the Fourteenth Amendment, which now became part of the Constitution) and were readmitted to the Union. Conservative whites held up the return of Virginia and Texas until 1869 and Mississippi until 1870. By then, Congress had added an additional requirement for readmission—ratification of another constitutional amendment, the Fifteenth, which forbade the states and the federal government to deny the suffrage to any citizen on account of "race, color, or previous condition of servitude." Several Northern and border states refused to approve the Fifteenth Amendment, and it was adopted only with the support of the four Southern states that had to ratify it in order to be readmitted to the Union.

To stop the president from interfering with their designs, the congressional Radicals passed two remarkable laws in 1867. One, the Tenure of Office Act, forbade the president to remove civil officials, including members of his cabinet, without the consent of the Senate. The principal purpose of the law was to protect the job of Secretary of War Edwin M. Stanton, who was the only Lincoln appointee still in Johnson's cabinet and who was cooperating with the Radicals. The other law, the Command of the Army Act, prohibited the president from issuing military orders except through the commanding general of the army (General Grant), whose headquarters were to be in Washington and who could not be relieved or assigned elsewhere without the consent of the Senate.

The congressional Radicals also took action to stop the Supreme Court from interfering with their plans. In 1866, the Court had declared in the case of *Ex parte Milligan* that military tribunals were unconstitutional in places where civil courts were functioning, a decision that seemed to threaten the system of military government the Radicals were planning for the South. Radicals in Congress immediately proposed legislation to require a two-thirds majority of the justices to overrule a law of Congress, to deny the Court jurisdiction in Reconstruction cases, to reduce its membership to three, and even to abolish it. The justices apparently took the hint. Over the next two years, the Court refused to accept jurisdiction in any cases involving Reconstruction.

The Impeachment of the President

Although President Johnson had long since ceased to be a serious obstacle to the passage of Radical legislation, he was still the official charged with administering the Reconstruction programs; and as such, the Radicals believed, he was a serious impediment to their plans. Early in 1867, they began looking for a way to get rid of him. According to the Constitution, only "high crimes or misdemeanors" in office were grounds for impeaching a president and removing him from office. Republicans could find nothing on which to base such charges until Johnson gave them what they considered a plausible reason for action. He deliberately violated the Tenure of

Office Act—in hopes of bringing a test case of the law before the courts. He dismissed Secretary of War Stanton even though the Senate had already refused to consent to the removal.

In the House of Representatives, elated Radicals impeached the president on eleven charges and sent the case to the Senate for trial. The first nine counts dealt with the violation of the Tenure of Office Act. The tenth and eleventh charged Johnson with slandering Congress and with not enforcing the Reconstruction Acts.

The trial before the Senate lasted throughout April and May 1868. The president's accusers argued that Johnson had defied Congress and was indeed guilty of high crimes and misdemeanors. His defenders claimed that he had acted properly in challenging what he considered an unconstitutional law. The Radicals put heavy pressure on all the Republican senators, but the Moderates (who were losing faith in the Radical program) vacillated. On the first three charges to come to a vote, seven Republicans joined the twelve Democrats to support acquittal. The vote was 35 to 19, one short of the constitutionally required two-thirds majority. After that, the Radicals dropped the impeachment campaign.

THE SOUTH IN RECONSTRUCTION

When white Southerners spoke bitterly in later years of the effects of Reconstruction, they referred most frequently to the governments Congress imposed on them—governments that were, they claimed, both incompetent and corrupt, that saddled the region with enormous debts, and that trampled on the rights of citizens. When black Southerners and their defenders condemned Reconstruction, in contrast, they spoke of its failure to guarantee to freedmen even the most elemental rights of citizenship—a failure that resulted in a new and cruel system of economic subordination. Both complaints had some justification, but most historians would now agree that the black criticisms of Reconstruction had a much stronger basis than the white ones.

The Reconstruction Governments

In the ten states of the South that were reorganized under the congressional plan, approximately one-fourth of the white males were at first excluded from voting or holding office, which produced black majorities among voters in South Carolina, Mississippi, and Louisiana (where blacks were also a majority of the population) and in Alabama and Florida (where they were not). But most suffrage restrictions were soon lifted so that nearly all white males could soon vote. After that, Republicans maintained control only with the support of many Southern whites.

Critics labeled these Southern white Republicans with the derogatory term "scalawags." Many were former Whigs who had never felt comfortable in the Democratic party. Some were wealthy (or once wealthy) planters or businessmen. Others were farmers who lived in remote areas where there had been little or no slavery and who hoped the Republican program of internal improvements would help end their economic isolation. White men from the North, known to their opponents as "carpetbaggers" (after the cheap suitcases some of them carried as they moved into the region), also served as Republican leaders in the South. Most of the carpetbaggers were veterans of the Union army who looked on the South as a new frontier, more

THE BURDENED SOUTH This Reconstruction-era cartoon expresses the South's sense of its oppression at the hands of Northern Republicans. President Grant rides in comfort in a carpetbag as the South staggers under the burden in chains.

promising than the West. They had settled there at war's end as hopeful planters, businessmen, or professionals.

The most numerous Republicans in the South were the black freedmen, most of whom had no previous experience in politics and tried, therefore, to build institutions through which they could learn to exercise their power. In several states, African-American voters held their own conventions to chart their future course. One such "colored convention," as Southern whites called it, assembled in Alabama in 1867 and announced: "We claim exactly the same rights, privileges and immunities as are enjoyed by white men—we ask nothing more and will be content with nothing less." Black churches also helped give unity and political self-confidence to the former slaves. After emancipation, most blacks withdrew from the white churches they had been compelled to attend on the plantations and formed their own—institutions based on the elaborate religious practices they had developed (occasionally surreptitiously) under slavery.

African-Americans played a significant role in the politics of the Reconstruction South. They served as delegates to the constitutional conventions. They held public offices of practically every kind. Between 1869 and 1901, twenty blacks served in the United States House of Representatives, two in the Senate. They served, too, in state legislatures and in various other state offices. Southern whites complained loudly (both at the time and for generations to come) about "Negro rule" during Reconstruction, but no such thing ever actually existed in any of the states. No black man was ever elected governor of a Southern state (although P. B. S. Pinchback, the African-American lieutenant governor of Louisiana, was acting governor briefly). Blacks never controlled any of the state legislatures (although African-Americans did once win a majority of seats in South Carolina's lower house). In the South as a whole, the percentage of black officeholders was far lower than the percentage of blacks in the population.

Expanding Budgets and Services

The record of the Reconstruction governments was mixed. Critics at the time and since have denounced them for corruption and financial extravagance, and there is some truth to both charges. Officeholders in many states enriched themselves through graft and other illicit activities. State budgets expanded to hitherto unknown totals, and state debts soared to previously undreamed-of heights. In South Carolina, for example, the public debt increased from $7 million to $29 million in eight years.

The corruption in the South, real as it was, was hardly unique to the

Reconstruction governments. Corruption was at least as rampant in the Northern states. The end of Reconstruction, moreover, did not end corruption in Southern state governments. In many states, in fact, corruption grew worse. And the state expenditures of the Reconstruction years were huge only in comparison with the meager budgets of the antebellum era. They represented an effort to provide the South with desperately needed services that antebellum governments had never offered: public education, public works programs, poor relief, and other costly new commitments. There were, to be sure, graft and extravagance in Reconstruction governments; there were also positive and permanent accomplishments.

Perhaps the most important of those accomplishments was a dramatic improvement in Southern education—an improvement that benefited both whites and blacks. In the first years of Reconstruction, much of the impetus for educational reform in the South came from outside groups—from the Freedmen's Bureau, from Northern private philanthropic organizations, from many Northern white women who traveled to the South to teach in freedmen's schools—and from African-Americans themselves. Over the opposition of many Southern whites, who feared that education would give blacks "false notions of equality," these reformers established a large network of schools for former slaves—4,000 schools by 1870, staffed by 9,000 teachers (half of them black), teaching 200,000 students (about 12 percent of the total school-age population of the freedmen). In the 1870s, Reconstruction governments began to build a comprehensive public school system in the South. By 1876, more than half of all white children and about 40 percent of all black children were attending schools in the South. Several black "academies," offering more advanced education, also began operating. Gradually, these academies grew into an important network of black colleges and universities.

Landownership

The most ambitious goal of the Freedmen's Bureau, and of some Republican Radicals in Congress, was to make Reconstruction the vehicle for a fundamental reform of landownership in the South. The effort failed. In the last years of the war and the first years of Reconstruction, the Freedmen's Bureau did oversee the redistribution of substantial amounts of land to freedmen in a few areas. By June 1865, the bureau had settled nearly 10,000 black families on their own land—most of it drawn from abandoned plantations. By the end of that year, however, the experiment was already collapsing. Southern plantation owners were returning and demanding the

AFTER SLAVERY Although many freed slaves remained agricultural laborers after Emancipation, a considerable number moved off the land
in search of new occupations and new homes. For many, that meant living for some time without stable employment or a permanent home.
This photograph from the late 1860s shows a group of former slaves at
a county almshouse in the South.

restoration of their property, and President Johnson was supporting their
demands. Despite the resistance of the Freedmen's Bureau, most of the
confiscated land was eventually returned to the original white owners.
Congress, moreover, never had much stomach for the idea of land redistribution. Very few Northern Republicans believed that the federal government had the right to confiscate property. Even so, the distribution of
landownership in the South changed considerably in the postwar years.
Among whites, there was a striking decline in landownership, from 80
percent before the war to 67 percent by the end of Reconstruction. Some
whites lost their land because of unpaid debt or increased taxes; some left
the marginal lands they had owned to move to more fertile areas, where
they rented. Among blacks, during the same period, the proportion who
owned land rose from virtually none to more than 20 percent.

Still, most blacks, and a growing minority of whites, did not own their
own land during Reconstruction; and some who acquired land in the 1860s
had lost it by the 1890s. Instead, they worked for others in one form or
another. Many black agricultural laborers—perhaps 25 percent of the to-

tal—simply worked for wages. Most, however, became tenants of white landowners—that is, they worked their own plots of land and paid their landlords either a fixed rent or a share of their crop (hence the term "sharecropping"). The new system represented a repudiation by blacks of the gang-labor system of the antebellum plantation, in which slaves had lived and worked together under the direction of a master. As tenants and sharecroppers, blacks enjoyed at least a physical independence from their landlords and had the sense of working their own land, even if in most cases they could never hope to buy it. But tenantry also benefited landlords in some ways, relieving them of the cost of purchasing slaves and of any responsibility for the physical well-being of their workers.

Incomes and Credit

In some respects, the postwar years were a period of remarkable economic progress for blacks. If the material benefits they had received under slavery are calculated as income, then prewar blacks had earned about a 22 percent share of the profits of the plantation system. By the end of Reconstruction, they were earning 56 percent. Measured another way, the per capita income of blacks rose 46 percent between 1857 and 1879, while the per capita income of whites declined 35 percent. This represented one of the most significant redistributions of income in American history.

But these figures are somewhat misleading. For one thing, while the black share of profits was increasing, the total profits of Southern agriculture were declining—a result of the dislocations of the war and a reduction in the world market for cotton. For another thing, while blacks were earning a greater return on their labor than they had under slavery, they were working less. Women and children were less likely to labor in the fields than in the past. Adult men tended to work shorter days. In all, the black labor force worked about one-third fewer hours during Reconstruction than it had been compelled to do under slavery—a reduction that brought the working schedule of blacks roughly into accord with that of white farm laborers. Nor did the income redistribution of the postwar years lift many blacks out of poverty. Black per capita income rose from about one-quarter of white per capita income to about one-half in the first few years after the war. After this initial increase, it rose hardly at all.

For blacks and poor whites alike, whatever gains there might have been as a result of land and income redistribution were often overshadowed by the ravages of the crop lien system. Few of the traditional institutions of credit in the South—the "factors" and banks—returned after the war. In their stead emerged a new system of credit, centered in large part on local country stores—some of them owned by planters, others owned by independent merchants. Blacks and whites, landowners and tenants—all depended on these stores for such necessities as food, clothing, seed, and farm implements. And since farmers do not have the same steady cash flow as other workers, customers usually had to rely on credit from these merchants in order to purchase what they needed. Most local stores had no competition (and went to great lengths to ensure that things stayed that way). As a result, they were able to set interest rates as high as 50 or 60 percent. Farmers had to give the merchants a lien (or claim) on their crops as collateral for the loans (thus the term "crop-lien system," generally used to describe Southern farming in this period). If a farmer suffered a few bad years in a row, as often happened, he could become trapped in a cycle of debt from which he could never escape.

This burdensome credit system had a number of effects on the region, almost all of them unhealthy. One was that some blacks who had acquired land during the early years of Reconstruction gradually lost it as they fell into debt. So, to a lesser extent, did white small landowners. Another was that Southern farmers became almost wholly dependent on cash crops—and most of all on cotton—because only such marketable commodities seemed to offer any possibility of escape from debt. Thus Southern agriculture, never sufficiently diversified even in the best of times, became more one-dimensional than ever. The relentless planting of cotton, moreover, was contributing to an exhaustion of the soil. The crop-lien system, in other words, was not only helping to impoverish small farmers; it was also contributing to a general decline in the Southern agricultural economy.

The African-American Family in Freedom

One of the most striking features of the black response to Reconstruction was the effort to build or rebuild family structures and to protect them from the interference they had experienced under slavery. A major reason for the rapid departure of so many blacks from plantations was the desire to find lost relatives and reunite families. Thousands of blacks wandered through the South looking for husbands, wives, children, or other relatives from whom they had been separated. Former slaves rushed to have their marriages, previously without legal standing, sanctified by church and law. Black families resisted living in the former slave quarters and moved instead to small cabins scattered widely across the countryside, where they could enjoy at least some privacy.

Within the black family, the definition of male and female roles quickly came to resemble that within white families. Many women and children ceased working in the fields. Such work, they believed, was a badge of slavery. Instead, many women restricted themselves largely to domestic tasks— cooking, cleaning, gardening, raising children, attending to the needs of their husbands. Still, economic necessity often compelled black women to engage in income-producing activities: working as domestic servants, taking in laundry, or helping their husbands in the field. By the end of Reconstruction, half of all black women over the age of sixteen were working for wages. And unlike white working women, most black female income earners were married.

THE GRANT ADMINISTRATION

Exhausted by the political turmoil of the Johnson administration, American voters in 1868 yearned for a strong, stable figure to guide them through the troubled years of Reconstruction. They did not find one. Instead, they turned trustingly to General Ulysses S. Grant, the hero of the war and, by 1868, a revered national idol. Grant was a disastrous president. During his two terms in office, he faced problems that would have taxed the abilities of a master of statecraft. Grant, however, was a dull and unimaginative man with few political skills and little vision.

The Soldier President

Grant could have had the nomination of either party in 1868. But believing that Republican Reconstruction policies were more attuned to public opinion than the Democratic alternatives, he accepted the Republican nomination. The Democrats nominated former governor Horatio Seymour of New York. The campaign was a bitter one, and Grant's triumph was surprisingly modest. He carried twenty-six states, Seymour eight. But Grant's popular majority was a scant 310,000 votes, a result of some 500,000 black votes in the reconstructed states of the South.

Grant entered the White House with no political experience of any kind, and his performance in office was clumsy and ineffectual from the start. Except for Hamilton Fish, whom Grant appointed secretary of state and who served for eight years with great distinction, most members of the cabinet were as dull and inept as the president. Grant relied chiefly, and increasingly, on the machine leaders in the party—the group most ardently devoted to the spoils system.

Grant used the spoils system even more blatantly than most of his predecessors. In doing so, he provoked the opposition of Senator Charles Sumner and other Republican leaders, who joined with reformers to agitate for a new civil-service system to limit the president's appointive powers. Nothing came of their efforts. Grant soon attracted the hostility of other Republicans as well. Many Northerners were growing disillusioned with Reconstruction. Disgusted by stories of corruption, extravagance, and incompetence in the South, they opposed Grant's continuing support of Radical programs there. Some Republicans suspected, too, that there was also corruption in the Grant administration itself. Still others criticized Grant because he did not support a tariff reduction.

By the end of Grant's first term, therefore, members of a substantial faction of the party—who referred to themselves as Liberal Republicans— had come to oppose what they called "Grantism." In 1872, hoping to prevent Grant's reelection, they bolted the party and nominated their own presidential candidate: Horace Greeley, veteran editor and publisher of the New York *Tribune*. The Democrats, somewhat reluctantly, named Greeley their candidate as well, hoping that the alliance with the Liberals would enable them to defeat Grant. But the effort was in vain. Grant won a substantial victory, polling 286 electoral votes and 3,597,000 popular votes to Greeley's 66 and 2,834,000. Greeley had carried only two Southern and four border states. Three weeks later, apparently crushed by his defeat, Greeley died.

The Grant Scandals

During the 1872 campaign, the first of a series of political scandals came to light that would plague Grant and the Republicans for the next eight years. It involved the French-owned Crédit Mobilier construction company, which had helped build the Union Pacific Railroad. The heads of Crédit Mobilier had used their positions as Union Pacific stockholders to steer large and fraudulent contracts to the construction company, thus bilking the Union Pacific (and the federal government, which provided large subsidies to the railroad) of millions. To prevent investigations, the directors had transferred some Crédit Mobilier stock to key members of Congress. But in 1872, Congress did conduct an investigation, which revealed that some highly placed Republicans—including Schuyler Colfax, now Grant's vice president—had accepted stock.

One dreary episode followed another in Grant's second term. Benjamin H. Bristow, Grant's third Treasury secretary, discovered that some of his officials and a group of distillers operating as a "whiskey ring" were cheating the government out of taxes by filing false reports. Then a House investigation revealed that William W. Belknap, secretary of war, had accepted bribes to retain an Indian-post trader in office (the so-called Indian ring). Other, lesser scandals added to the growing impression that "Grantism" had brought rampant corruption to government.

The Greenback Question

Compounding Grant's, and the nation's, problems was the financial crisis known as the Panic of 1873. It began with the failure of a leading investment banking firm, Jay Cooke and Company, which had invested too heavily in postwar railroad building. There had been panics before—in 1819, 1837, and 1857—but this was the worst one yet. The depression it produced lasted four years.

Debtors now pressured the government to inflate the value of their currency, which would have made it easier for them to pay their debts. More specifically, they urged the government to redeem its war bonds with greenbacks, paper currency of the sort printed during the Civil War, which would increase the amount of money in circulation. But Grant and most Republicans wanted a "sound" currency—based solidly on gold reserves—which would favor the interests of banks and other creditors.

The greenback question would not go away. There was, for one thing, the approximately $356 million in paper currency issued during the Civil War that was still in circulation. And in 1873, when the Supreme Court ruled in *Knox* v. *Lee* that greenbacks were legal, the Treasury issued more in response to the panic. The following year, Congress voted to raise the total further. But Grant, under pressure from Eastern financial interests, vetoed the measure.

In 1875, Republican leaders in Congress, in an effort to crush the greenback movement for good, passed the Specie Resumption Act. This law provided that after January 1, 1879, the greenback dollars, whose value constantly fluctuated, would be redeemed by the government and replaced with new certificates, firmly pegged to the price of gold. The law satisfied creditors, who had worried that debts would be repaid in debased paper currency. But "resumption" did little for debtors, because the gold-based money supply was never able to expand as much as they wanted.

In 1875, the "greenbackers," as the inflationists were called, formed their own political organization: the National Greenback party. Active in the next three presidential elections, it failed to gain widespread support. But it did keep the money issue alive. And in the 1880s, the greenback forces began to merge with another, more powerful group of currency reformers— those who favored silver as the basis of currency—to help produce a political movement that would ultimately attain enormous strength. The question of the proper composition of the currency was to remain one of the most controversial and enduring issues in late-nineteenth-century American politics.

Republican Diplomacy

The Johnson and Grant administrations achieved their greatest success in foreign affairs. The accomplishments were the work not of the presidents themselves, who displayed little aptitude for diplomacy, but of two out-standing secretaries of state: William H. Seward, who had served Lincoln and who remained in office until 1869; and Hamilton Fish, who served throughout the two terms of the Grant administration.

An ardent expansionist and advocate of a vigorous foreign policy, Seward acted with as much daring as the demands of Reconstruction politics and the Republican hatred of President Johnson would permit. Seward agreed to a Russian offer to sell Alaska to the United States for $7.2 million. Only with great difficulty was he able to persuade Congress to authorize the purchase, and he faced criticism from many who considered Alaska a useless frozen wasteland and derided it as "Seward's Folly" or "Seward's icebox." But Seward knew that Alaska was an important fishing center and a potential source of valuable resources such as gold. In 1867, Seward also engineered the American annexation of the tiny Midway Islands west of Hawaii.

In contrast with its often shambling course in domestic politics, the diplomatic performance of the Grant administration under Hamilton Fish was generally decisive and firm. Fish's first major challenge was resolving a burning controversy with England. Many Americans believed that the British government had violated the neutrality laws during the Civil War by permitting English shipyards to build ships (among them the *Alabama*) for the Confederacy. American demands that England pay for the damage these vessels had caused became known as the "Alabama claims."

Seward had tried to settle the Alabama claims through the Johnson-Clarendon Convention of 1869, which would have submitted the matter to arbitration. But the Senate rejected it because it contained no British apology. In 1871, Fish succeeded in forging a new agreement, the Treaty of Washington, which provided for international arbitration and in which Britain expressed regret for the escape of the *Alabama* from England.

THE ABANDONMENT OF RECONSTRUCTION

As the North grew increasingly preoccupied with its own political and economic problems, interest in Reconstruction began to wane. The Grant administration continued to protect Republican governments in the South, but less because of any interest in ensuring the position of freedmen than because of a desire to prevent the reemergence of a strong Democratic party in the region. But even the presence of federal troops was not enough to prevent white Southerners from overturning the Reconstruction regimes. By the time Grant left office, Democrats had taken back (or, as white Southerners liked to put it, "redeemed") seven of the governments of the former Confederate states.

For three other states—South Carolina, Louisiana, and Florida—the end of Reconstruction had to wait for the withdrawal of the last federal troops in 1877, a withdrawal that was the result of a long process of political bargaining and compromise at the national level.

The Southern States "Redeemed"

In the states where whites constituted a majority—the states of the upper South—overthrowing Republican control was relatively simple. By 1872, all but a handful of Southern whites had regained suffrage. Now a clear majority, they needed only to organize and elect their candidates.

In other states, where blacks were a majority or the populations of the two races were almost equal, whites used intimidation and violence to undermine the Reconstruction regimes. Secret societies—the Ku Klux Klan, the Knights of the White Camellia, and others—used terrorism to frighten or physically bar blacks from voting or otherwise exercising citizenship. Paramilitary organizations—the Red Shirts and White Leagues—armed themselves to "police" elections and worked to force all white males to join the Democratic party and to exclude all blacks from meaningful political activity. Strongest of all, however, was the simple weapon of economic pressure. Some planters refused to rent land to Republican blacks; storekeepers refused to extend them credit; employers refused to give them work.

In the meantime, Southern blacks were losing the support of many of their former advocates in the North. After the adoption of the Fifteenth Amendment in 1870, some reformers convinced themselves that their long campaign in behalf of black people was now over; that with the vote, blacks ought to be able to take care of themselves. Former Radical leaders such as Charles Sumner and Horace Greeley now began calling themselves Liberals, cooperating with the Democrats, and at times outdoing even the Democrats in denouncing what they viewed as black-and-carpetbag misgovernment. Within the South itself, many white Republicans joined the Liberals and moved into the Democratic party.

The Panic of 1873 further undermined support for Reconstruction. In the congressional elections of 1874, the Democrats won control of the House of Representatives for the first time since 1861. Grant took note of the changing temper of the North and stopped using military force to prop up the Republican regimes that were still standing in the South.

By the end of 1876, only three states were left in the hands of the Republicans—South Carolina, Louisiana, and Florida. In the state elections that year, Democrats (after using terrorist tactics) claimed victory in all three. But the Republicans claimed victory as well and were able to remain in office because of the presence of federal troops. If the troops were to be withdrawn, the last of the Republican regimes would fall.

The Compromise of 1877

Grant had hoped to run for another term in 1876, but most Republican leaders—shaken by recent Democratic successes, afraid of the scandals with which Grant was associated, and worried about the president's failing health—resisted. Instead, they sought a candidate not associated with the problems of the Grant years, one who might entice Liberals back and unite the party again. They settled on Rutherford B. Hayes, a former Union army officer and congressman, three times governor of Ohio, and a champion of civil-service reform. The Democrats united behind Samuel J. Tilden, the reform governor of New York, who had been instrumental in overthrowing the corrupt Tweed Ring of New York City's Tammany Hall.

Although the campaign was a bitter one, there were few differences of principle between the candidates, both of whom were conservatives committed to moderate reform. The November election produced an apparent Democratic victory. Tilden carried the South and several large Northern states, and his popular margin over Hayes was nearly 300,000 votes. But disputed returns from Louisiana, South Carolina, Florida, and Oregon, whose total electoral vote was 20, threw the election in doubt. Tilden had undisputed claim to 184 electoral votes, only one short of the majority. But Hayes could still win if he managed to receive all 20 disputed votes.

The Constitution had established no method to determine the validity of disputed returns. It was clear that the decision lay with Congress, but it was not clear with which house or through what method. (The Senate was Republican, and the House was Democratic.) Members of each party naturally supported a solution that would yield them the victory.

Finally, late in January 1877, Congress tried to break the deadlock by creating a special electoral commission to judge the disputed votes. The commission was to be composed of five senators, five representatives, and five justices of the Supreme Court. The congressional delegation would consist of five Republicans and five Democrats. The Court delegation would include two Republicans, two Democrats, and the only independent, Justice David Davis. But when the Illinois legislature elected Davis to the United States Senate, the justice resigned from the commission. His seat went instead to a Republican justice. The commission voted along straight party lines, 8 to 7, awarding every disputed vote to Hayes. Congress accepted the verdict on March 2. Two days later, Hayes was inaugurated.

Behind the resolution of the deadlock, however, lay a series of elaborate compromises among leaders of both parties. When a Democratic filibuster threatened to derail the commission's report, Republican Senate leaders met secretly with Southern Democratic leaders to work out terms by which the Democrats would support Hayes. According to traditional accounts, Republicans and Southern Democrats met at Washington's Wormley Hotel. In return for a Republican pledge that Hayes would withdraw the last federal troops from the South, thus permitting the overthrow of the last Republican governments there, the Southerners agreed to abandon the filibuster.

Actually, the story behind the "Compromise of 1877" is somewhat more complex. Hayes was already on record as favoring withdrawal of the troops. The real agreement, the one that won the Southern Democrats over, was reached before the Wormley meeting. As the price of their cooperation, the Southern Democrats (among them some former Whigs) exacted several pledges from the Republicans: the appointment of at least one Southerner to the Hayes cabinet, control of federal patronage in their areas, generous internal improvements, federal aid for the Texas and Pacific Railroad, and withdrawal of the troops. Many powerful Southern Democrats supported industrializing the region. They believed that Republican programs of federal support for business would aid their region more than the states' rights policies of the Democrats.

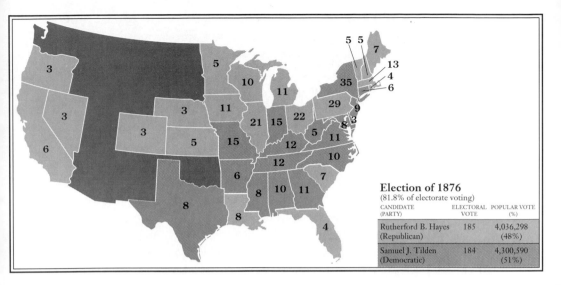

Election of 1876
(81.8% of electorate voting)

CANDIDATE (PARTY)	ELECTORAL VOTE	POPULAR VOTE (%)
Rutherford B. Hayes (Republican)	185	4,036,298 (48%)
Samuel J. Tilden (Democratic)	184	4,300,590 (51%)

In his inaugural address, Hayes announced that the South's most pressing need was the restoration of "wise, honest, and peaceful local self-government"—a signal that he planned to withdraw the troops and let white Democrats take over the state governments. The statement, and Hayes's subsequent actions, supported the widespread charges that he was paying off the South for acquiescing in his election and strengthened those who referred to him as "His Fraudulency." But the election had already created such bitterness that there was probably nothing Hayes could have done to mollify his critics, not even his promise to serve only one term.

The president and his party hoped to build up a "new Republican" organization in the South drawn from Whiggish conservative white groups and committed to modest support for black rights. But all such efforts failed. Although many white Southern leaders sympathized with Republican economic policies, resentment of Reconstruction was so deep that supporting the party was politically impossible. The "solid" Democratic South, which would survive until the mid-twentieth century, was taking shape. And the withdrawal of federal troops was a signal that the national government was giving up its attempt to control Southern politics and to improve the lot of blacks in Southern society.

The Legacy of Reconstruction

Reconstruction was not a complete failure in its effort to help African-Americans. There was a significant redistribution of income, from which blacks benefited. There was a more limited but not unimportant redistribution of landownership, which enabled some former slaves to acquire property. There was both a relative and an absolute improvement in the economic circumstances of most African-Americans.

Nor was Reconstruction as disastrous an experience for Southern whites as most believed at the time. The region had emerged from a prolonged and bloody war defeated and devastated; and yet within little more than a decade, the white South had regained control of its own institutions and, to a great extent, restored its traditional ruling class to power. Former Confederate leaders received no severe punishments. The federal government imposed no drastic economic reforms on the region and indeed few lasting political changes of any kind other than the abolition of slavery. Not many conquered peoples fare as well.

Yet for all that, Americans of the twentieth century cannot help but look back on Reconstruction as a tragic era. For in those years the United States failed in its first serious effort to resolve its oldest and deepest social problem—the problem of race. What was more, the experience so disappointed, disillusioned, and embittered white Americans that it would be nearly a century before they would try again in any serious way.

Why did this great assault on racial injustice end so badly? In part, it was because of the weaknesses and errors of the people who directed it. But in greater part, it was because attempts to produce solutions ran up against conservative obstacles so deeply embedded in the nation's life that they could not be dislodged. Veneration of the Constitution sharply limited the willingness of national leaders to infringe on the rights of states and individuals. A profound respect for private property and free enterprise prevented any real assault on economic privilege in the South. Above all, perhaps, a pervasive belief among many of even the most liberal whites that the black race was inherently inferior served as an obstacle to equality. Given the context within which Americans of the 1860s and 1870s were working, what is surprising, perhaps, is not that Reconstruction did so little but that it accomplished even as much as it did.

Given the odds confronting them, therefore, African-Americans had reason for pride in the limited gains they were able to make during Reconstruction. And future generations had reason for gratitude for two great charters of freedom—the Fourteenth and Fifteenth amendments to the Constitution—which, although largely ignored at the time, would one day serve as the basis for a "Second Reconstruction" that would renew the drive to bring freedom and equality to all Americans.

D E B A T I N G   T H E   P A S T

Reconstruction

D EBATE OVER THE nature of Reconstruction has been unusually intense, not only among historians but among much of the larger public as well. Indeed, few issues in American history have raised such deep and enduring passions.

Beginning in the late nineteenth century and continuing well into the twentieth, a relatively uniform and highly critical view of Reconstruction prevailed among historians—a reflection of a broad consensus among white Americans about the inferiority of blacks and of a yearning in both the North and the South for sectional reconciliation. William A. Dunning's *Reconstruction, Political and Economic* (1907) was the principal scholarly expression of this prevailing view. Dunning portrayed Reconstruction as a corrupt and oppressive outrage imposed on a prostrate South by a vindictive group of Northern Republican radicals. Unscrupulous carpetbaggers flooded the South and plundered the region. Ignorant African-Americans were thrust into political offices for which they were unfit. Reconstruction governments were awash in corruption and compiled enormous levels of debt. The Dunning interpretation dominated several generations of historical scholarship. It also helped shape such popular images of Reconstruction as those in the novel and film *Gone with the Wind*.

Among historians, at least, the Dunning interpretation gradually lost credibility in the face of a series of challenges. W. E. B. Du Bois, the great African-American scholar, offered one of the first alternative views in *Black Reconstruction* (1935). To Du Bois, Reconstruction was an effort by freed blacks (and their white allies) to create a more democratic society in the

(continued on next page)

South, and it was responsible for many valuable social innovations. In the early 1960s, John Hope Franklin and Kenneth Stampp, building on a generation of work by other scholars, published new histories of Reconstruction that replaced, and radically revised, the Dunning interpretation. Reconstruction, they argued, was a genuine, if flawed, effort to solve the problem of race in the South. The Reconstruction governments were not perfect, but they were bold experiments in interracial politics. Congressional radicals were not saints, but they were genuinely concerned with protecting the rights of former slaves. Reconstruction had brought important, if temporary, progress to the South and had created no more corruption there than governments were creating in the North at the same time. What was tragic about Reconstruction, the revisionists claimed, was not what it did to Southern whites but what it failed to do for Southern blacks. It was, in the end, too weak and too short-lived to guarantee African-Americans genuine equality.

In more recent years, some historians have begun to question the assessment of the first revisionists that, in the end, Reconstruction accomplished relatively little. Leon Litwack argued in *Been in the Storm So Long* (1979) that former slaves used the protections Reconstruction offered them to carve out a certain level of independence for themselves within southern society: strengthening churches, reuniting families, and resisting the efforts of white planters to revive the gang labor system.

Eric Foner's *Reconstruction: America's Unfinished Revolution* (1988) also emphasized how far African-Americans moved toward freedom and independence in a short time, how much of lasting value they were able to accomplish despite imposing obstacles, and how important they were in shaping the execution of Reconstruction policies. Reconstruction, he argues, "can only be judged a failure" as an effort to secure "blacks' rights as citizens and free laborers." But it "closed off even more oppressive alternatives. . . . The post-Reconstruction labor system embodied neither a return to the closely supervised gang labor of antebellum days, nor the complete dispossession and immobilization of the black labor force and coercive apprenticeship systems envisioned by white Southerners in 1865 and 1866. Nor were blacks, as in twentieth-century South Africa, barred from citizenship, herded into labor reserves, or prohibited by law from moving from one part of the country to another. . . . The doors of economic opportunity that had opened could never be completely closed."

CHAPTER SIXTEEN

The New South and the Far West

The South in Transition ~ *The Conquest of the Far West*
The Dispersal of the Tribes ~ *The Rise and Decline of the Western Farmer*

UCH OF THE United States in the years following Reconstruction was preoccupied with the expansion and development of an already advanced urban-industrial society. In two regions of America, however, the experience was quite different. In the South, the first region of the country to have been settled by English-speaking Europeans, and in the Far West, the last such region, the late nineteenth century was a time of new beginnings and important changes. For many residents of both regions, it was also a period of decline relative to the rest of the nation—a decline that would ultimately produce major social and political upheavals.

THE SOUTH IN TRANSITION

The Compromise of 1877—the agreement between Southern Democrats and Northern Republicans that helped settle the disputed election of 1876—was supposed to be the first step toward developing a stable, permanent Republican party in the South. In that respect, at least, it failed. In the years following the end of Reconstruction, white Southerners established the Democratic party as the only viable political organization for the region's whites.

By the end of 1877—after the last withdrawal of federal troops—every Southern state government had been "redeemed." That is, political power had been restored to white Democrats. Many white Southerners rejoiced at the restoration of what they liked to call "home rule." But in reality, political power in the region was soon more restricted than at any time since the Civil War. Once again, the South fell under the control of a powerful, conservative oligarchy, whose members were known variously as the "Redeemers" or the "Bourbons."

The "Redeemers"

In a few places, this post-Reconstruction ruling class was much the same as the ruling class of the antebellum period. In Alabama, for example, the old planter elite—despite challenges from new merchant and industrial forces—retained much of its former power and continued largely to dominate the state for decades. In most areas, however, the Redeemers constituted a genuinely new class. Merchants, industrialists, railroad developers, financiers—some of them former planters, some of them Northern immigrants who had become absorbed into the region's life, some of them ambitious, upwardly mobile white Southerners from the region's lower social tiers—combined a commitment to "home rule" and social conservatism with a commitment to economic development.

Whatever their differences, the various Bourbon governments of the New South behaved in many respects quite similarly. Conservatives had complained that the Reconstruction governments fostered widespread corruption, but the Redeemer regimes were, if anything, even more awash in fraud and waste. (In this, they were little different from governments in every region of the country.) Virtually all the new Democratic regimes, moreover, lowered taxes, reduced spending, and drastically diminished state services—including many of the most valuable accomplishments of Reconstruction. In one state after another, for example, state support for public school systems was reduced or eliminated.

By the late 1870s, dissenting groups were challenging the Bourbons: protesting the cuts in services and denouncing the commitment of the Redeemer governments to paying off the prewar and Reconstruction debts in full, at the original (usually high) rates of interest. There were demands as well for greenbacks, debt relief, and other economic reforms. (A few of the independent movements included significant numbers of blacks in their ranks, but all consisted primarily of lower-income whites.) By the mid-1880s, however, conservative Southerners—largely by exploiting racial prejudice—had effectively destroyed most of the dissenting movements.

Industrialization and "the New South"

Some Southern leaders in the post-Reconstruction era hoped to see their region become the home of a vigorous industrial economy. The South had lost the war, many argued, because its economy had been unable to compete with the modernized manufacturing capacity of the North. Now the region must "out-Yankee the Yankees" and build a "New South." Henry Grady, editor of the *Atlanta Constitution*, and other prominent spokesmen for a New South seldom challenged white supremacy. But they did advocate other important changes in Southern values. Above all, they promoted the virtues of thrift, industry, and progress—the same qualities that prewar Southerners had so often denounced in Northern society.

Partly as a result of their efforts, Southern industry expanded significantly in the years after Reconstruction and became a more important part of the region's economy than ever before. Most visible was the growth in textile manufacturing, which increased ninefold in the last twenty years of the century. In the past, Southern cotton had usually been shipped out of the region to manufacturers in the North or in Europe. Now textile factories appeared in the South itself—drawn to the region from New England by the abundance of water power, the ready supply of cheap labor, the low taxes, and the accommodating conservative governments. The tobacco processing industry, similarly, established an important foothold in the region, largely through the work of James B. Duke of North Carolina, whose American Tobacco Company established for a time a virtual monopoly over the processing of raw tobacco into marketable materials. In the lower South, and particularly in Birmingham, Alabama, the iron (and, later, steel) industry grew rapidly. By 1890, the Southern iron and steel industry represented nearly a fifth of the nation's total capacity.

Railroad development increased substantially in the post-Reconstruction years—at a rate far greater than that of the nation at large. Between 1880 and 1890, trackage in the South more than doubled. And the South took a giant step toward integrating its transportation system with that of the rest of the country when, in 1886, it changed the gauge (width) of its trackage to correspond with the standards of the North. No longer would it be necessary for cargoes heading into the South to be transferred from one train to another at the borders of the region.

Yet Southern industry developed within strict limits, and its effects on the region were never even remotely comparable to the effects of industrialization on the North. The Southern share of national manufacturing doubled in the last twenty years of the century, to 10 percent of the total. But that percentage was the same share the South had claimed in 1860; the region had, in other words, done no more than regain what it had lost during the war and its aftermath. The region's per capita income increased 21 percent in the same period. But at the end of the century, average income in the South was only 40 percent of that in the North; in 1860 it had been more than 60 percent. And even in those areas where development had been most rapid—textiles, iron, railroads—much of the capital had come from the North.

The growth of industry in the South required that the region recruit a substantial industrial work force for the first time. From the beginning, a high percentage of the factory workers (and an especially high percentage of textile workers) were women. Heavy male casualties in the Civil War had helped create a large population of unmarried women who desperately needed employment. Factories also hired entire families, many of whom were moving into towns from failed farms. Hours were long (often as much as twelve hours a day) and wages were far below the Northern equivalent; indeed, one of the greatest attractions of the South to industrialists was that employers were able to pay workers there as little as one-half what Northern workers received.

Life in most mill towns was rigidly controlled by the owners and managers of the factories. They rigorously suppressed attempts at protest or union organization. Company stores sold goods to workers at inflated prices and issued credit at exorbitant rates, and mill owners ensured that no competitors were able to establish themselves in the community. At the same time, however, the conditions of the mill town helped create a strong sense of community and solidarity among workers (even though they seldom translated such feelings into militancy).

Some industries, such as textiles, offered virtually no opportunities to black workers. Others—tobacco, iron, and lumber, for example—did provide blacks with some employment, usually the most menial and lowest-paid positions. Some mill towns, therefore, were places where black and white cultures came into close contact.

At times, industrialization proceeded on the basis of no wage-paying employment at all. Through the "convict-lease" system, Southern states leased gangs of convicted criminals to private interests as a cheap labor supply. The system exposed the convicts to brutal and at times fatal mistreatment. It paid them nothing (the leasing fees went to the states, not the workers). And it denied employment in railroad construction and other projects to the free labor force.

The Crop-Lien System

Despite significant growth in Southern industry, the region remained primarily agricultural. The most important economic reality in the post-Reconstruction South, therefore, was the impoverished state of agriculture. The 1870s and 1880s saw an acceleration of the process that had begun in the immediate postwar years: the imposition of systems of tenantry and debt peonage on much of the region; the reliance on a few cash crops rather than on a diversified agricultural system; and the increasing absentee ownership of valuable farmlands (many of them purchased by merchants and industrialists, who paid little attention to whether the land was being properly used). During Reconstruction, perhaps a third or more of the farmers in the South were tenants or sharecroppers; by 1900 the figure had increased to 70 percent.

At the center of the Southern agricultural system was the crop-lien system, which had emerged in the aftermath of the Civil War and had kept most small farmers (black and white) trapped in an endless cycle of debt. (See pp. 418–419.) Farmers who owned their own land often lost it as merchants seized it for payment of unpaid liens. Farmers who were already tenants or sharecroppers found themselves increasingly under the control of merchants and landlords, whom they had little hope of ever paying off completely.

The collapse of antebellum financial institutions and the increasing scarcity of banks and currency in the South meant that credit—always important to farmers, with their seasonal production—was very difficult to obtain. Control of credit often fell into the hands of "furnishing merchants": the owners of the local stores from which farmers bought their tools, seed, and other necessities. Few farmers ever had enough money to pay cash for what they needed, so they bought their supplies on credit, promising the merchant a share of their crop (or giving him a "lien" on it) when it was harvested.

Furnishing merchants (who were also often important landowners) seldom had competitors; indeed, they went to considerable lengths to ensure they retained a monopoly. So farmers had little choice but to pay the high prices and exorbitant interest the local merchants charged them. By the time farmers harvested their crops, they were often so deeply in debt that they had to turn over the entire harvest to the merchant. Even that was generally not enough. Thus year after year, their indebtedness grew.

The crop-lien system was one of several factors contributing to a social and economic transformation of the Southern back country, the piney woods and mountain regions where cotton and slavery had always been rare and where farmers lived ruggedly independent lives. Subsistence agriculture had long been the norm in these areas; but as indebtedness grew, many farmers now had to grow cash crops such as cotton, instead of the food crops they had traditionally cultivated, in order to make enough money to pay their debts. Opportunities for families to live largely self-sufficiently were declining; at the same time, opportunities for profiting within the market remained slim. The people of the back country would be among the most important constituents for the populist protests of the 1880s and 1890s.

The crop-lien system was particularly devastating to Southern blacks, few of whom owned their own land to begin with. Already dependent on landowners as tenants and sharecroppers, they were especially vulnerable to the economic tyranny of the furnishing merchant. These economic difficulties were compounded by social and legal discrimination, which in the post-Reconstruction era began to take new forms and to inspire new responses.

African-Americans and the New South

The "New South creed" was not the property of whites alone. Many African-Americans were attracted to the vision of progress and self-improvement as well. Some blacks succeeded in elevating themselves into a distinct middle class—one economically inferior to the white middle class, but nevertheless significant. A cardinal tenet of this rising group of blacks was that education was vital to the future of their race. With the support of Northern missionary societies and, to a far lesser extent, a few Southern state governments, they expanded the network of black colleges and institutes that had taken root during Reconstruction into an important educational system.

The chief spokesman for this commitment to education, and ultimately the major spokesman for his race as a whole, was Booker T. Washington, founder and president of the Tuskegee Institute in Alabama. Born into slavery, Washington had used his education (at Virginia's famous Hampton Institute) to pull himself out of poverty. He urged other blacks to follow the same road to self-improvement.

Washington's message was both cautious and hopeful. African-Americans should attend school, learn skills, and establish a solid footing in agriculture and the trades. Industrial, not classical, education should be their goal. Blacks should, moreover, refine their speech, improve their dress, and adopt habits of thrift and personal cleanliness; they should, in short, adopt the standards of the white middle class. Only thus, he claimed, could they win the respect of the white population, the prerequisite for any larger social gains. In a famous speech in Georgia in 1895, Washington outlined a philosophy of race relations that became widely known as the Atlanta Compromise. Blacks should forgo agitating for political rights, he said, and concentrate on self-improvement and preparation for equality.

Washington offered a powerful challenge to those whites who strove to discourage blacks from acquiring an education or winning any economic gains. But his message was also an implicit promise that blacks would not challenge the system of segregation that whites were then in the process of erecting. "In all things that are purely social," he once said, "we can be separate as the fingers yet one as the hand in things that relate to mutual progress."

The Birth of Jim Crow

Few white Southerners had ever accepted the idea of racial equality. That the former slaves acquired any legal and political rights at all after emancipation was in large part the result of federal support. That support all but vanished after 1877. Federal troops withdrew. Congress lost interest. And the Supreme Court effectively stripped the Fourteenth and Fifteenth amendments of much of their significance. In the so-called civil-rights cases of 1883, the Court interpreted the Fourteenth Amendment narrowly, ruling that it prohibited state governments from discriminating against people because of race but did not restrict private organizations or individuals from doing so. Thus railroads, hotels, theaters, and the like could legally practice segregation.

Eventually, the Court also validated state legislation that discriminated against blacks. In *Plessy* v. *Ferguson* (1896), a case involving a Louisiana law that required separate seating arrangements for the races on railroads, the Court held that separate accommodations did not deprive blacks of equal rights if the accommodations were equal, a decision that survived for years as part of the legal basis of segregated schools. In *Cumming* v. *County Board of Education* (1899), the Court ruled that laws establishing separate schools for whites were valid even if they provided no comparable schools for blacks.

Even before these decisions, white Southerners were working to strengthen white supremacy and to separate the races to the greatest extent possible. One illustration of this movement from subordination to segregation is black voting rights. In some states, disfranchisement had begun almost as soon as Reconstruction ended. But in other areas, black voting continued for some time after Reconstruction—largely because conservative whites believed they could control the black electorate and use it to beat back the attempts of poor white farmers to take control of the Democratic party.

In the 1890s, however, franchise restrictions became much more rigid. During those years, some small white farmers began to demand complete black disenfranchisement—both because of racial prejudice and because they objected to the black vote's being used against them by the Bourbons. Many members of the conservative elite, at the same time, began to fear that poor whites might unite politically with poor blacks to challenge them. They too began to support further franchise restrictions.

In devising laws to disenfranchise black males (black females, like white women, had never voted), the Southern states had to find ways to evade the Fifteenth Amendment, which prohibited states from denying anyone the right to vote because of race. Two devices emerged before 1900 to accomplish this goal. One was the poll tax or some form of property qualification; few blacks were prosperous enough to meet such requirements. Another was the "literacy" or "understanding" test, which required that voters demonstrate an ability to read and to interpret passages from the Constitution. Even those African-Americans who could read found it hard to pass the difficult tests white officials gave them.

Such restrictions affected poor white voters as well as blacks. By the late 1890s, the black vote had decreased by 62 percent, the white vote by 26 percent. One result was that some states passed so-called grandfather laws, which permitted men who could not meet the literacy and property qualifications to be enfranchised if their ancestors had voted before Reconstruction began, thus barring the descendants of slaves from the polls while allowing poor whites access to them. In many areas, however, ruling elites were quite content to see poor whites, a potential source of opposition to their power, barred from voting.

The Supreme Court proved as compliant in ruling on the disfranchising laws as it was in dealing with the civil-rights cases. The Court eventually voided the grandfather laws, but it validated the literacy tests (in the 1898 case of *Williams* v. *Mississippi*) and displayed a general willingness to let the Southern states define their own suffrage standards as long as evasions of the Fifteenth Amendment were not too glaring.

Laws restricting the franchise and segregating schools were only part of a network of state statutes—known as the "Jim Crow laws" (after a popular cartoon character of the day)—that by the first years of the twentieth century had institutionalized an elaborate system of segregation reaching into almost every area of Southern life. Blacks and whites could not ride together in the same railroad cars, sit in the same waiting rooms, use the same washrooms, eat in the same restaurants, or sit in the same theaters. Blacks were denied access to parks, beaches, and picnic areas; they were barred from many hospitals. Much of the new legal structure did no more than confirm what had already been widespread social practice in the South since well before the end of Reconstruction. But the Jim Crow laws also stripped blacks of many of the modest social, economic, and political gains they had made in the more fluid atmosphere of the late nineteenth century. They served, too, as a means for whites to retain control of social relations between the races in the newly growing cities and towns of the South, where traditional patterns of deference and subjugation were more difficult to preserve than in the countryside. What had been maintained by custom in the rural South was to be maintained by law in the urban South.

More than legal efforts were involved in this process. The 1890s witnessed a dramatic increase in white violence against blacks, which (along with the Jim Crow laws) served to inhibit black agitation for equal rights. The worst such violence—lynching of blacks by white mobs, either because the victims were accused of crimes or because they seemed somehow to have violated their proper station—reached appalling levels. In the nation as a whole in the 1890s, there was an average of 187 lynchings each year, more than 80 percent of them in the South. The vast majority of victims were black.

Those involved in lynchings often saw their actions as a legitimate form of law enforcement; and indeed, some victims of lynchings had in fact committed crimes. But lynchings were also a means by which whites controlled the black population through terror and intimidation. Thus, some lynch mobs killed blacks whose only "crime" had been presumptuousness. Others chose as victims outsiders in the community, whose presence threatened to disturb the normal pattern of race relations. Whatever the circumstances, the victims of lynch mobs were denied the protection of the laws and the opportunity to prove their innocence.

The rise of lynching shocked the conscience of many white Americans in a way that other forms of racial injustice did not. Almost from the start there was a substantial antilynching movement. Ida B. Wells, a committed black journalist, launched what became an international antilynching crusade with a series of impassioned articles in 1892 after the lynching of three of her friends in Memphis, Tennessee, her home. The movement gradually gathered strength in the first years of the twentieth century, attracting substantial support from whites (particularly white women) in both the North and the South. Its goal was a federal antilynching law, which would

LYNCH MOB, 1893 White Southerners sometimes traveled many miles to watch a lynching, such as this one of a black man accused of killing a three-year-old white girl. More common than these large public lynchings, however, were less conspicuous vigilante murders by small groups of whites.

allow the national government to do what state and local governments in the South were unwilling to do: punish those responsible for lynchings.

But the substantial white opposition to lynchings in the South stood as an exception to the general white support for suppression of the black race. Indeed, just as in the antebellum period, the shared commitment to white supremacy helped dilute class animosities between the poorer whites and the Bourbon oligarchies. Economic issues tended to take a subordinate role to race in Southern politics, distracting people from the glaring social inequalities that afflicted blacks and whites alike. The commitment to white supremacy, in short, was a burden for poor whites as well as for blacks.

The Origins of African-American Protest

Not all African-Americans were content with Booker T. Washington's cautious approach to racial progress. By the turn of the century a powerful challenge was emerging—to the philosophy of Washington and, more important, to the entire structure of race relations. The chief spokesman for this new approach was W. E. B. Du Bois.

Du Bois, unlike Washington, had never known slavery. Born in Massachusetts, he was educated at Fisk University in Atlanta and at Harvard, where he became the first African-American to earn a Ph.D. He grew to maturity with a far more expansive view than Washington of the goals of his race and the responsibilities of white society to eliminate prejudice and injustice. In *The Souls of Black Folk* (1903), he launched an open attack on the philosophy of the Atlanta Compromise, accusing Washington of encouraging white efforts to impose segregation and of unnecessarily limiting the aspirations of his race. Rather than content themselves with education at the trade and agricultural schools, Du Bois argued, qualified African-Americans (what he and others called the "talented tenth") should accept nothing less than a full university education. They should aspire to the professions. They should, above all, fight for the immediate restoration of their civil rights, not simply wait for them to be granted as a reward for patient striving.

In 1905, Du Bois and a group of his supporters met at Niagara Falls in Canada and launched what became known as the Niagara Movement. Four years later, after a race riot in Springfield, Illinois, they joined with white progressives sympathetic to their cause to form the National Association for the Advancement of Colored People (NAACP). Whites held most of the offices; but Du Bois, its director of publicity and research, was the guiding spirit.

Within less than a decade, the NAACP began to win some important victories in the federal courts in its drive to achieve equal rights. In *Guinn* v. *United States* (1915), the Supreme Court supported the association's position that the grandfather clause in an Oklahoma law was unconstitutional. (The statute denied the vote to citizens whose ancestors had not been enfranchised in 1860.) In *Buchanan* v. *Worley* (1917), the Court struck down a Louisville, Kentucky, law requiring residential segregation. The NAACP was not a radical, or even an egalitarian, organization. It relied, rather, on the efforts of the most intelligent and educated members of the black race, the "talented tenth" as Du Bois called them. Ultimately, its members believed, such efforts would benefit all blacks. By creating a trained elite, blacks would, in effect, be creating a leadership group capable of fighting for the rights of the race as a whole.

THE CONQUEST OF THE FAR WEST

By the time of the Civil War, the Western edge of English-speaking settlement in North America had already moved well beyond what it had been even twenty years before. White civilization had crossed the Mississippi and established a permanent foothold in the next tier of states—Minnesota, Iowa, Missouri, and Arkansas—as well as in the eastern parts of Nebraska, Kansas, and Texas. There had been a white settlement in Oregon since the early 1860s. And largely as a result of the great gold rush that began in 1849, there was a substantial English-speaking population (and a small but growing population of Chinese and other Asian immigrants) in California. But vast areas of the Far West remained free of any substantial numbers of English-speaking settlers. Living there was a significant population of Hispanics (some were immigrants from Mexico; others, long-standing residents who had lived in the region even before the United States acquired it). Above all, the lands were the homes of Indian tribes.

Delayed Settlement

Early white explorers had dubbed the Great Plains west of the Mississippi the "Great American Desert," and in the 1840s English-speaking migrants had hastened through it on their way to California and Oregon. By the 1860s, however, whites were beginning to move into the region in great numbers. They were attracted by gold and silver deposits, by the short-grass pasture for cattle and sheep, and by the sod and mountain meadowlands that seemed suited for farming or ranching. They were attracted, too, by the completion of the great transcontinental railroad lines and their feeders, which opened up the plains both to settlement and to commerce. The railroad companies themselves actively solicited new settlers (to create customers for their lines) by, among other things, selling company lands to them at low prices.

The federal government also encouraged settlement. The Homestead Act of 1862 permitted settlers to buy plots of 160 acres for small fees if they lived on them for five years. But 160 acres was too small for the grazing and grain farming of the arid Great Plains, so Congress eventually increased the allotments through a series of other measures passed between 1873 and 1878, which ultimately made it possible for settlers to acquire as much as 1,280 acres of land at little cost. Some got much more through the rampant fraud in the administration of the acts.

After Kansas became a state in 1861, the remaining Western territories of Washington, New Mexico, Utah, and Nebraska (all of which originally included much more territory than those states do today) were divided into smaller units. By the end of the 1860s, Nevada and Nebraska had become states; and white governments were operating in the new territories of Colorado, Dakota, Arizona, Idaho, Montana, and Wyoming. Colorado became a state in 1876; North and South Dakota, Montana, and Washington, in 1889; Wyoming and Idaho, in 1890. In 1896, Utah was admitted, after its Mormon leaders had convinced the government that polygamy (the practice by which men take several wives) had been abandoned. By 1900, only three territories—Arizona, New Mexico, and Oklahoma (formerly Indian Territory), in all of which nonwhites formed a majority of the populations—still awaited statehood.

The Arrival of the Miners

White settlement of the Far West moved in three distinct stages. The first was the development of mining, and hence the first part of the area to be extensively settled was the mineral-rich region of mountains and plateaus, where white settlers hoped to make quick fortunes by finding precious metals. The mining boom was brief. It began suddenly in about 1860, flourished until the 1890s, and then abruptly declined.

News of a gold or silver strike would spark several stages of settlement. First, individual prospectors would flock to the area to exploit the first ores largely by hand, with pan and placer mining. After the shallower deposits had been depleted by these methods, corporations moved in to engage in lode or quartz mining. Then, as those deposits dwindled, commercial mining either disappeared or contracted.

The first great mining boom began in 1858, when gold was discovered in the Pike's Peak district of what would soon be Colorado; the following year, 50,000 prospectors stormed into the region. Almost overnight Denver and other mining camps blossomed into instant "cities." A year later, miners from California began flocking to Nevada, where gold had been found in the Washoe district and silver in the great Comstock Lode. When the surface deposits dwindled, California investors bought up the claims of many prospectors and began quartz mining. From 1860 to 1880 the Nevada lodes yielded gold and silver bullion worth $306 million. More than a decade later, in 1874, gold was found in the Black Hills of southwestern Dakota Territory, sparking another, even briefer boom. With the inevitable fading of surface resources, corporations again took over from the miners, and the white population declined. Gold and silver created the most excitement, but the extraction of other, less glamorous minerals was more important to white development of the Far West in the long run: copper (launched in 1881 by the great Anaconda copper mine in Colorado), lead, tin, quartz, and zinc.

The mining communities were the home of people of many races and cultures. Indians, Mexicans, African-Americans, and Chinese lived along-

COLORADO BOOM TOWN After a prospector discovered silver nearby in 1890, miners flocked to the town of Creede, Colorado. For a time, 150 to 300 people arrived there daily. Like other such boom towns, however, Creede's prosperity was short-lived. In 1893 the price of silver collapsed, and Creede was soon almost deserted.

side whites, although seldom entirely harmoniously. White settlers tried to place boundaries on the acceptable social and economic behavior of non-whites, who generally had difficulty gaining ownership of land or finding any but menial jobs. Yet nonwhites were essential to the functioning of the mining economy as laborers in the mines and as providers of vital services in the towns.

Men greatly outnumbered women in the mining towns; and younger men, in particular, had difficulty finding female companions of comparable age. Those women who did gravitate to the new communities often came with their husbands, and their activities were generally (although not always) confined to the same kinds of domestic tasks that Eastern women per-formed. Single women, or women whose husbands were not earning enough money, sometimes worked for wages as cooks, laundresses, and tavern keepers. And in the sexually imbalanced mining communities, there was always a substantial market for prostitutes.

The Cattle Kingdom

Even while the mining empire was flourishing, the second stage of white settlement of the Far West was under way: the growth of cattle ranching. The open range—the unclaimed grasslands of the public domain—provided a huge area on the Great Plains where cattlemen could graze their herds free of charge and unimpeded by private farms. The railroads provided access to markets in the East.

The Western cattle industry was Mexican first. Long before citizens of the United States invaded the Southwest, Mexican ranchers had developed the techniques that the white cattlemen and cowboys of the Great Plains later employed: branding, roundups, roping, and others. They had also created the equipment of the herders—lariat, saddle, leather chaps, and spurs. Americans in Texas adopted the Mexican methods and carried them throughout the cattle kingdom. Texans also developed the largest herds and bred the horses—small, muscular broncos or mustangs—that enabled cowboys to control them.

At the end of the Civil War, an estimated 5 million cattle roamed the Texas ranges, and prices in Northern markets were rising. In 1866, some Texas cattle ranchers began driving their combined herds, some 260,000 head, north to Sedalia, Missouri, a market on the Missouri Pacific Railroad. Much of the total herd was lost along the way to outlaws and Indians. But the drive proved that cattle could be driven to distant markets and pastured along the trail, and that they would even gain weight during the journey. From that point on, the "long drive" became the basis of the cattle kingdom. Combined herds on the drives usually numbered from 2,000 to 5,000 head. Cowboys representing each of the major ranchers accompanied them. Many cowboys in the early years were veterans of the Confederate army. The next largest group consisted of blacks, followed by white Northerners, Mexicans, and others.

Abilene, Kansas, on the Kansas Pacific Railroad, was the first capital of the cattle kingdom. Between 1867 and 1871, cattlemen drove 1,460,000 head there along the Chisholm Trail. By the mid-1870s, however, farmers were beginning to occupy the open rangelands in western Kansas, impeding the drives, so new cattle centers developed farther west, in Nebraska, Wyoming, and Montana, as railroad lines moved out to meet them.

Open-range cattle ranching was risky business. "Texas fever"—a disease transmitted to cattle by ticks—could decimate a herd. Rustlers and Indians could seize livestock. And cattlemen faced increasing competition from other whites for use of the plains. Sheep ranchers from California and Oregon brought their flocks onto the range to compete for grass. Farmers ("nesters") from the East threw fences around their claims, blocking trails and breaking up the open range. A series of violent "range wars"—between sheepmen and cattlemen, between ranchers and farmers—erupted out of the tensions between these competing groups.

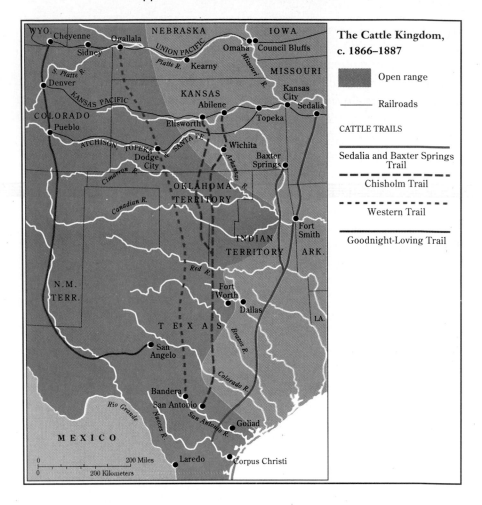

The Cattle Kingdom, c. 1866–1887

Open range

—————— Railroads

CATTLE TRAILS

Sedalia and Baxter Springs Trail

Chisholm Trail

Western Trail

Goodnight-Loving Trail

As the cattle industry became more profitable, it overexpanded. By the 1880s, there was no longer enough grass on the open range to support the enormous herds or sustain the long drives. Even nature turned hostile. Two severe winters, in 1885–1886 and 1886–1887, with a searing summer between them, devastated the plains, driving many ranchers out of business. The open-range industry and its long drives soon largely disappeared. But established cattle ranches—with fenced-in grazing land and stocks of hay for winter feed—survived and prospered.

Although the cattle industry was overwhelmingly male in its early years, there were always a few women involved in ranching and driving. As ranching became more sedentary, the presence of women greatly expanded.

By 1890, there were more than 250,000 women who owned ranches or farms in the Western States. Indeed, the region provided women with many opportunities that were closed to them in the East—including the opportunity to participate in politics. Wyoming was the first state in the Union to guarantee woman suffrage; and throughout the West, women established themselves as an important political presence (and occasionally as significant officeholders).

The Romance of the West

The West had always occupied a special place in the American imagination. But the vast regions of the Far West had a particularly strong romantic appeal. That was partly because the landscape, with its brilliant diversity and spectacular grandeur, was so different from anything white Americans had encountered before.

Even more appealing than the landscape, perhaps, was the rugged, free-spirited life style that many Americans associated with the West—a life style that stood in sharp contrast to the increasingly stable and ordered world of the East. Particular public interest attached to the figure of the cowboy, who was transformed remarkably quickly into a powerful and enduring figure of myth. Admiring Americans seldom thought about the dreariness of the cowboy's life: the tedium, the loneliness, the physical discomforts, the relatively few opportunities for advancement. Instead, in Western novels such as Owen Wister's *The Virginian* (1902), the cowboy became one of the most powerful symbols of what had long been an important ideal in the American mind—the ideal of the natural man.

But the Far West was particularly important to the nation's imagination because many Americans considered it the last frontier. One of the clearest and most influential statements of this vision of the West came from the historian Frederick Jackson Turner, of the University of Wisconsin. In 1893, at a meeting of the American Historical Association, the thirty-three-year-old Turner delivered a paper entitled "The Significance of the Frontier in American History." Westward expansion, he said, had stimulated individualism, nationalism, and democracy; it had defined American civilization. But now, Turner argued, the great unsettled lands were gone, "and with its going has closed the first period of American history."

In fact, Turner's concerns were both inaccurate and premature. A vast public domain still existed in the 1890s; during the forty years after Turner's address, the government was to give away many more acres than it had given as homesteads in the past. But if the "passing of the frontier" was largely a myth, it was a powerful one. And it kept the romantic image of the West alive for many decades to come.

THE DISPERSAL OF THE TRIBES

White Americans liked to think of the Far West as a vast unpeopled land awaiting settlement. In fact, the West already had a substantial population, mostly of Indians, before the white settlers arrived. Some were members of Eastern tribes—Cherokee, Creek, Winnebago, and others—who had been forcibly resettled west of the Mississippi in Indian Territory (later Oklahoma) before the Civil War. But most were members of tribes indigenous to the West.

The Western Tribes

The Western tribes had developed several different patterns of civilization. The Pueblo of the Southwest lived largely as farmers and had established permanent settlements. They continued to occupy lands guaranteed them by the Spanish before the annexation of the Western territories by the United States. They grew corn; they built towns and cities of adobe houses; they practiced elaborate forms of irrigation.

Other tribes in that region—the Navajo and Apache of western Texas and eastern New Mexico—lived less rooted lives and combined hunting with farming and sheep herding, moving their settlements from place to place. The most numerous Indian groups in the West, however, consisted of the plains Indians—the Sioux, the Blackfoot, the Cheyenne, the Kiowa, the Apache, the Comanche, the Crow, and others—who occupied large parts of what became Minnesota, the Dakotas, Nebraska, Idaho, and Montana. The plains Indians lived a largely nomadic life, because the semiarid, treeless plains encouraged a culture based on hunting. When a band halted, it constructed tepees as temporary dwellings; when it departed, it left the landscape almost completely undisturbed, a reflection of a reverence for nature central to Indian culture and religion.

The chief target of these Indian hunters was the buffalo, or bison—a huge grazing animal that provided the economic basis for the plains Indians' way of life. Its flesh was their principal source of food, and its skin supplied clothing, shoes, tepees, blankets, robes, and utensils. "Buffalo chips," dried manure, provided fuel; buffalo bones became knives and arrow tips; buffalo tendons formed the strings of bows.

Tribes (which sometimes numbered several thousand) were generally subdivided into "bands" of up to 500 men and women, often consisting of interrelated families. Each had its own governing council. Within each band, tasks were generally divided by gender. Women performed domestic and artistic roles: raising children, cooking, gathering roots and berries, preparing hides, and creating the artworks of tribal culture. They also tended fields and gardens in those places where bands settled long enough to raise crops. Men worked largely as hunters and traders and supervised the religious and military life of the band.

The plains Indians were proud and aggressive warriors, the most formidable foes white settlers had yet encountered. But they also suffered from several serious weaknesses that in the end made it impossible for them to prevail. Perhaps the most crippling was the inability of the various tribes (and often even of the bands within tribes) to unite against white aggression. Indeed the plains Indians were frequently distracted from their battles with whites by conflicts among the tribes themselves.

White Policies Toward the Tribes

The Western tribes were also victimized by the incompetence and duplicity of the white officials charged with protecting them. The policy of the federal government was to regard the tribes simultaneously as independent nations and as wards of the president in Washington, and to negotiate treaties with them that were solemnly ratified by the Senate. Seldom, however, did treaties or agreements with the tribes survive the pressure of white settlers eager for access to Indian lands. The history of relations between the United States and the Native Americans is, therefore, one of broken promises.

By the early 1850s, the idea of establishing one great territory in which all the tribes could live (the idea that had led to the creation of the Indian Territory in what is now Oklahoma) was in retreat. In the face of white demands for access to lands on the "One Big Reservation," the federal government created a new policy, known as "concentration." In 1851, each tribe was assigned its own reservation, confirmed by separate treaties (many of them illegitimately negotiated with unauthorized representatives, chosen by whites, known as "treaty chiefs"). The new arrangement had many benefits for whites and few for the Indians. It separated the tribes from one another and made them easier to defeat. It allowed the government to force tribes into scattered locations and to take over the most desirable lands for white settlement. But it did not survive as the basis of Indian policy for long.

In 1867, in the aftermath of a series of bloody conflicts, an Indian Peace Commission established by Congress recommended yet another "permanent" Indian policy. The commission recommended abandoning the policy of scattering the tribes and proposed relocating all the plains Indians in two large reservations—one in Indian Territory (Oklahoma), the other in the Dakotas. Government agents cajoled, bribed, and tricked the Arapaho, Cheyenne, Sioux, and other tribes into agreeing to treaties establishing the new reservations.

This policy worked no better than the previous ones. In part that was because the Bureau of Indian Affairs, the government agency responsible for administering the reservations, was appallingly incompetent and corrupt. Even the most honest and diligent of the Bureau's agents in the West were woefully unprepared for their jobs and had no understanding of tribal ways.

But the problem was also a result of the relentless slaughtering by whites of the buffalo herds that supported the tribes' way of life. Even in the 1850s, white migrants in the West had been killing buffalo to provide themselves with food and supplies. After the Civil War, white demand for buffalo hides became a national phenomenon—partly for economic reasons and partly as a fad. Professional hunters swarmed into the plains to gather hides they could sell in the East. Amateur hunters traveled to the plains to shoot buffalo for sport. Railroads organized large shooting expeditions to thin the herds, which were obstructions to traffic. The Southern herd was virtually exterminated by 1875, and within a few years the smaller Northern herd had met the same fate. In 1865, there had been at least 15 million buffalo; a decade later, fewer than a thousand of the great beasts survived. The army and the agents of the Bureau of Indian Affairs condoned and even encouraged the killing.

Indian Resistance

There was almost incessant fighting between whites and Indians on the frontier from the 1850s to the 1880s, as Indians struggled against the growing threats to their civilizations. Indian warriors, usually traveling in raiding parties of thirty to forty men, regularly attacked wagon trains, stagecoaches, and isolated ranches, often in retaliation for earlier attacks on them by whites. As the United States Army became more deeply involved in the fighting, the tribes began to focus more of their attacks on white soldiers.

At times, this small-scale fighting escalated into something resembling a war. During the Civil War, the eastern Sioux in Minnesota, cramped on an inadequate reservation and exploited by corrupt white agents, suddenly rebelled. Led by Little Crow, they killed more than 700 whites before being subdued by a force of regulars and militiamen. Thirty-eight of the Indians were hanged, and the tribe was exiled to the Dakotas.

At about the same time, the Arapaho and Cheyenne in eastern Colorado were in conflict with white miners settling in the region. Bands of Indians attacked stagecoach lines and settlements in an effort to regain territory they believed was theirs. In response to these incidents, whites called up a large territorial militia and the army issued dire threats. The governor urged all friendly Indians to congregate at army posts to protect themselves against retribution. One Arapaho and Cheyenne band under Black Kettle, apparently in response to the invitation, camped near Fort Lyon on Sand Creek in November 1864. Some members of the party were warriors, but Black Kettle believed he was under official protection and exhibited no hostile intention. Nevertheless, Colonel J. M. Chivington, apparently encouraged by the army commander of the district, led a volunteer militia force—much of it consisting of unemployed miners, many of whom were apparently drunk—to the unsuspecting camp and massacred perhaps 200 men, women, and children. Black Kettle and his Cheyennes escaped the Sand Creek massacre and moved south toward Texas. Four years later, a United States Army force under Colonel George A. Custer caught up with them near the border, killed Black Kettle, and slaughtered his people.

The treaties of 1867 brought a temporary lull in the conflicts. But in the early 1870s, more waves of white settlers, mostly miners, began to penetrate some of the lands in Dakota Territory supposedly guaranteed to the tribes in 1867. At the same time, the federal government, responding to the recommendations of another commission, decided that it would no longer recognize the tribes as independent entities or negotiate with tribal chiefs. It was a step intended to undermine the collective nature of Indian life and to force the Indians to assimilate into white culture—a goal cherished by many white reformers, who believed that only through assimilation could Indians thrive.

Indian resistance flared anew. In the Northern plains, the Sioux rose up in 1875 and left their reservation. When white officials ordered them to return, bands of warriors gathered in Montana and united under two great leaders: Crazy Horse and Sitting Bull. Three army columns set out to round

A M E R I C A N V O I C E S

Two Indian Leaders Face Conquest

Chief Joseph Surrenders, 1877

I am tired of fighting. The old men are all dead. [My brother] who led the young men is dead. It is cold, and we have no blankets. The little children are freezing to death. My people, some of them, have run away to the hills. No one knows where they are. I want to have some time to look for my children. Maybe I shall find them among the dead.

Hear me, my chiefs. From where the sun now stands, I will fight no more forever.

Sitting Bull Describes Life on the Sioux Reservation, 1883

Whatever you wanted of me I have obeyed. The Great Father sent me word that whatever he had against me in the past had been forgiven and thrown aside, and I accepted his promises and came in [the reservation]. And he told me not to step aside from the white man's path, and I am doing my best to travel in that path. I sit here and look around me now, and I see my people starving. We want cattle to butcher. That is the way you live, and we want to live the same way. When the Great Father told me to live like his people, I told him to send me six teams of mules, because that is the way the white people make a living. I asked for a horse and buggy for my children; I was advised to follow the ways of the white man, and that is why I asked for those things.

them up and force them back onto the reservation. With the expedition, as colonel of the famous Seventh Cavalry, was the dashing and reckless George A. Custer. At the Battle of the Little Bighorn in 1876—perhaps the most famous of all conflicts between whites and Indians—an unprecedented gathering of tribal warriors, estimated at more than 4,000, surprised Custer and part of his regiment in southern Montana, surrounded them, and killed them all.

But the Indians could not keep their troops united. The warriors soon drifted off in bands to elude pursuit or search for food, and the army ran them down singly and returned them to Dakota. The power of the Sioux was soon broken, and the proud leaders, Crazy Horse and Sitting Bull, finally gave up the fight and settled on reservations. Both were later killed by reservation police after being tricked or taunted into last shows of resistance.

Another dramatic example of Indian resistance occurred in Idaho in 1877. The Nez Percé, a small and relatively peaceful tribe, refused to accept white demands that they move to a smaller reservation. When United States troops converged on them, their able leader, Chief Joseph, attempted to lead the band into Canada. Most Nez Percé did not follow Joseph and instead moved west to Washington state. But those who did became a part of a remarkable chase. Pursued by four columns, Joseph and more than 500 men, women, and children, covered 1,321 miles in seventy-five days, repelling or evading the army time and again. Finally, however, the troops trapped the Indian band just short of the Canadian border. Chief Joseph surrendered. Like so many other defeated tribes, the Nez Percé were finally transported to Indian Territory in Oklahoma, where most of them soon died of disease and malnutrition (although Joseph himself lived until 1908).

The last Indians to sustain organized resistance against the whites were the Chiricahua Apaches, who fought intermittently from the 1860s to the late 1880s. The two ablest chiefs of this fierce tribe were Mangas Colorados and Cochise. Mangas was murdered during the Civil War by white soldiers who tricked him into surrendering, and in 1872 Cochise agreed to peace in exchange for a reservation that included some of the tribe's traditional land. But Cochise died in 1874, and his successor, Geronimo—unwilling to bow to white pressures to assimilate—fought on for more than a decade longer, establishing bases in the mountains of Arizona and Mexico and leading warriors in intermittent raids against white outposts. With each raid, however, the number of warring Apaches dwindled, as some warriors died and others drifted away to the reservation. By 1886, Geronimo's plight was hopeless. His band consisted of only about 30 people, including women and

THE SURRENDER OF GERONIMO The great Apache warrior Geronimo
(front row, third from right) sits with members of his diminished band
after surrendering to United States troops in 1886. The two men at
front row, left, are Geronimo's half brothers. The young boy at
front row, right, is his son.

children, while his white pursuers numbered perhaps 10,000. Geronimo
recognized the odds and surrendered, an event that marked the end of
formal warfare between Indians and whites.

But the end of the Apache wars was not the end of the violence. Another
tragic conflict between Indians and whites occurred in 1890 as a result of a
religious revival among the tribes. The Western Indians sensed that their
culture and their glories were irrevocably fading; some were also near
starvation because corrupt government agents had reduced their food
rations. As other tribes had done in trying times in the past, many of these
Indians turned to a prophet and joined a religious revival. This time the
prophet was Wovoka, a Paiute who inspired an ecstatic spiritual awakening
that began in Nevada and spread quickly to the plains. The new revival
emphasized the coming of a messiah, but its most conspicuous feature was
a mass, emotional "Ghost Dance," which apparently inspired mystical

visions among its participants. Among those visions were a retreat by white people from Indian lands and the restoration of the decimated buffalo herds. White agents on the Sioux reservation watched the dances in bewilderment and fear; some believed they might be the preliminary to hostilities and called for troops to stop the ceremonies.

Some of the Indian revivalists fled to the Badlands. When white troops caught up with them at Wounded Knee, South Dakota, fighting broke out in which about 40 white soldiers and more than 200 of the Indians, including women and children, died. What precipitated the conflict is a matter of dispute. But the battle soon turned into a one-sided massacre, as the white soldiers turned their new machine guns on the Indians and mowed them down in the snow.

The Dawes Act

Even before the Ghost Dance and the Wounded Knee tragedy, the federal government had launched new efforts to destroy the tribal structure of Indian life and culture. For nearly fifty years, its policy had been to create reservations in which the tribes would be isolated from white society. Now Congress—through the Dawes Severalty Act of 1887—abolished the practice by which tribes owned reservation lands communally. The reversal was an effort to force Indians to become landowners and farmers, abandon their traditional culture, and become part of white civilization.

The Bureau of Indian Affairs moved quickly and relentlessly to promote assimilation. Not only did they try to move Indian families onto their own plots of land; they also took Indian children away from their families and sent them to boarding schools run by whites, where they believed the young people could be educated to abandon tribal ways. Few Indians were prepared for this wrenching change from their traditional collective society to Western individualism. In any case, white administration of the program was so corrupt and inept, and Indian resistance so strong and enduring, that decades later the government simply abandoned it.

THE RISE AND DECLINE OF THE WESTERN FARMER

Farmers had begun moving into the plains region in the 1850s, challenging the ranchers and the Indians and occasionally coming into conflict with both. By the 1870s, farmers were pouring into the plains and beyond in great numbers, enclosing land that had once been hunting territory for Indians and grazing territory for open-range cattle, and establishing a new agricultural region.

Farming on the Plains

Many factors combined to produce this surge of Western settlement, but the most important was the railroads. Before the Civil War, the Great Plains had been accessible only through a difficult journey by wagon. But beginning in the 1860s, a great new network of railroad lines developed, spearheaded by the transcontinental routes Congress had authorized and subsidized in 1862. They made huge new areas of settlement accessible.

COMPLETING THE TRANSCONTINENTAL RAILROAD Officials of the Union Pacific and Central Pacific companies shake hands and exchange bottles of champagne at Promontory Point, Utah, on May 10, 1869, after the last spike has been driven to join the two lines and complete the nation's first transcontinental railroad.

The building of the transcontinental line was a dramatic and monumental achievement. Thousands of immigrant workers—mostly Irish on the Eastern route, Chinese on the Western—labored, in what were at times unimaginably difficult conditions, to penetrate mountain ranges, cross deserts, protect themselves against Indians, and—finally—connect the two lines at Promontory Point in northern Utah in the spring of 1869. But while this first transcontinental line captured the public imagination, the construction of subsidiary lines in the following years proved of greater importance to the West. State governments, imitating Washington, induced railroad development by offering direct financial aid, favorable loans, and more than 50 million acres of land (on top of the 130 million acres the federal government had already offered). Although operated by private corporations, the railroads were essentially government projects.

It was not only by making access to the Great Plains easier that the railroads helped spur agricultural settlement there. The railroad companies themselves actively promoted settlement—both to provide themselves with customers for their services and to increase the value of their vast landholdings. In addition, the companies set rates so low for settlers that almost anyone could afford the trip west. And they sold much of their land at very low prices and provided liberal credit to prospective settlers. Contributing further to the great surge of white agricultural expansion was a temporary change in the climate of the Great Plains. For several years in succession, beginning in the 1870s, rainfall in the plains states was well above average. White Americans now rejected the old idea that the region was the Great American Desert. Some even claimed that cultivation of the plains actually encouraged rainfall.

Even under the most favorable conditions, farming on the plains presented special problems. First was the problem of fencing. Farmers had to enclose their land, if for no other reason than to protect it from the herds of the open-range cattlemen. But traditional wood or stone fences were too expensive and were ineffective as barriers to cattle. In the mid-1870s, however, two Illinois farmers, Joseph H. Glidden and I. L. Ellwood, solved this problem by developing and marketing barbed wire, which became standard equipment on the plains and revolutionized fencing practices all over the country.

The second problem was water. Water was scarce even when rainfall was above average. After 1887, a series of dry seasons began. Lands that had been fertile now turned back into semidesert. Some farmers dealt with the problem by using deep wells pumped by steel windmills, or by turning to what was called dry-land farming (a system of tillage designed to conserve moisture in the soil by covering it with a dust blanket), or by planting drought-resistant crops. In many areas of the plains, however, only large-scale irrigation could save the endangered farms. But irrigation projects of the magnitude necessary required government assistance. And neither the state nor the federal government was prepared to fund the projects.

Most of the people who moved into the region had previously been farmers in the Midwest, the East, and Europe. In the booming years of the early 1880s, with land values rising, the new farmers had no problem obtaining extensive and easy credit and had every reason to believe they would soon be able to retire their debts. But the arid years of the late 1880s—during which crop prices were falling while production was becoming more expensive—changed that prospect. Tens of thousands of farmers could not pay their debts and were forced to abandon their farms. There was, in effect, a reverse migration: white settlers moving back to the East, sometimes turning once-flourishing communities into desolate ghost towns. Those who remained continued to suffer from falling prices (wheat, which had sold for $1.60 a bushel at the end of the Civil War, dropped to 49 cents in the 1890s) and persistent indebtedness.

Changes in Agriculture

American farming by the late nineteenth century no longer bore very much relation to the comforting image many Americans continued to embrace. The sturdy, independent farmer of popular myth was being replaced by the commercial farmer—a person attempting to do in the agricultural economy what industrialists were doing in the manufacturing economy.

Commercial farmers were not self-sufficient and made no effort to become so. They specialized in cash crops and sold them in national or world markets. They did not make their own household supplies or grow their own food but bought them instead at town or village stores. This kind of farming, when it was successful, raised the farmers' living standards. But it also made them dependent on bankers and interest rates, railroads and freight rates, national and European markets, world supply and demand. And unlike the capitalists of the industrial order, the farmers could not regulate their production or influence the prices of what they sold.

Between 1865 and 1900, agriculture became an international business. Farm output increased dramatically, not only in the United States but in Brazil, Argentina, Canada, Australia, New Zealand, Russia, and elsewhere.

At the same time, modern forms of communication and transportation—the telephone, the telegraph, steam navigation, railroads—were creating new markets around the world for agricultural goods. American commercial farmers, constantly opening new lands, produced much more than the domestic market could absorb; they relied on the world market to absorb their surplus, but in that market they faced major competition. Cotton farmers depended on export sales for 70 percent of their annual income, and wheat farmers for 30 to 40 percent; but the volatility of the international market put them at great risk.

Beginning in the 1880s, worldwide overproduction led to a drop in prices for most agricultural goods and hence to great economic distress for many of the more than 6 million American farm families. By the 1890s, 27 percent of the farms in the country were mortgaged; by 1910, 33 percent. In 1880, 25 percent of all farms were operated by tenants; by 1910, the proportion had grown to 37 percent. Commercial farming made some people fabulously wealthy. But the farm economy as a whole was suffering a significant decline relative to the rest of the nation.

The Farmers' Grievances

American farmers were painfully aware that something was wrong. But few yet understood the implications of national and world overproduction. Instead, they concentrated their attention and anger on more immediate, more comprehensible—and no less real—problems: inequitable freight rates, high interest charges, and an inadequate currency.

The farmers' first and most burning grievance was against the railroads. In many cases, the railroads charged higher rates for farm goods than for other kinds and higher rates in the South and West than in the Northeast. Railroads also controlled elevator and warehouse facilities in buying centers and charged arbitrary storage rates.

Farmers also resented the institutions controlling credit—banks, loan companies, insurance corporations. Since sources of credit in the West and South were few, farmers had to take loans on whatever terms they could get, often at interest rates of 10 to 25 percent. Many farmers had to pay these loans back in years when prices were dropping and currency was becoming scarce.

A third grievance concerned prices: both the prices farmers received for their products and the prices they paid for goods they bought. Farmers disposed of their products in a competitive world market over which they had no control and of which they had no advance knowledge. A farmer could plant a large crop at a moment when prices were high and find that by the time of the harvest the price had declined. Fortunes rose and fell in response to unpredictable forces. But many farmers became convinced (often with some reason) that "middlemen"—speculators, bankers, regional and local agents—were combining to fix prices so as to benefit themselves at the expense of the growers. Many farmers also came to believe (again, not entirely without reason) that manufacturers in the East were conspiring to keep the prices of farm goods low and the prices of industrial goods high. Farmers sold their crops in a competitive world market, but they bought manufactured goods in a domestic market protected by tariffs and dominated by trusts and corporations.

The Agrarian Malaise

These economic difficulties produced social, cultural, and ultimately political resentments. In part, this was a result of the isolation of farm life. Farm families in some parts of the country—particularly in the prairie and plains regions, where large farms were scattered over vast areas—were virtually cut off from the outside world and human companionship. During the winter months and spells of bad weather, the loneliness and boredom could become nearly unbearable. Many farmers lacked access to adequate education for their children, to proper medical facilities, to recreational or cultural activities, to virtually anything that might give them a sense of being members of a community. Older farmers felt the sting of watching their children leave the farm for the city. They felt the humiliation of being ridiculed as "hayseeds" by the new urban culture that was coming to dominate American life.

The result of this sense of isolation and obsolescence was a growing malaise among many farmers, a discontent that would help to create a great national political movement in the 1890s. The agrarian malaise also found reflection in the literature that emerged from rural America. Writers in the late nineteenth century might romanticize the rugged life of the cowboy and the Western miner. For the farmer, however, the image was different. Hamlin Garland, for example, reflected the growing disillusionment in a series of novels and short stories. In the past, Garland wrote in the introduction to his novel *Jason Edwards* (1891), the agrarian frontier had seemed to be "the Golden West, the land of wealth and freedom and happiness. All of the associations called up by the spoken word, the West, were fabulous, mythic, hopeful." Now, however, the bright promise had faded. The trials of rural life were crushing the human spirit. "So this is the reality of the dream!" a character in Jason Edwards exclaims. "A shanty on a barren plain, hot and lone as a desert. My God!" Once, sturdy yeoman farmers had viewed themselves as the backbone of American life. Now, they were becoming painfully aware that their position was declining in relation to the rising urban-industrial society to the east.

CHAPTER SEVENTEEN

Industrial Supremacy

Sources of Industrial Growth ~ *Capitalism and Its Critics*
The Ordeal of the Worker

ITH A STRIDE that astonished statisticians, the conquering hosts of business enterprise swept over the continent; twenty-five years after the death of Lincoln, America had become, in the quantity and value of her products, the first manufacturing nation of the world. What England had accomplished in a hundred years, the United States had achieved in half the time." So wrote the historians Charles and Mary Beard in the 1920s, expressing the amazement many Americans felt when they considered the remarkable expansion of their industrial economy in the late nineteenth century.

In fact, America's rise to industrial supremacy was not as sudden as such observers suggested. The nation had been building a manufacturing economy since early in the nineteenth century; industry was well established before the Civil War. But Americans were clearly correct in observing that the accomplishments of the last three decades of the nineteenth century overshadowed all the earlier progress. Those years witnessed nothing less than the transformation of the nation.

The remarkable growth did much to increase the wealth and improve the lives of many Americans. But such benefits were far from equally shared. While industrial titans and a growing middle class were enjoying a prosperity without precedent in the nation's history, workers, farmers, and others were experiencing an often painful ordeal that slowly edged the United States toward a great economic and political crisis.

SOURCES OF INDUSTRIAL GROWTH

Many factors contributed to the growth of American industry: abundant raw materials; a large and growing labor supply; a surge in technological innovation; the emergence of a talented, ambitious, and often ruthless group of entrepreneurs; a federal government eager to assist the growth of business; and a great and expanding domestic market for the products of manufacturing.

Industrial Technology

The rapid emergence of new technologies and the discovery of new materials and productive processes was one of the prerequisites to late-nineteenth-century industrial growth. In the entire history of the United States up to 1860, only 36,000 patents had been granted. For the period from 1860 to 1890, the figure was 440,000. Americans also benefited from comparable technological advances in Europe.

Some of the most important innovations were in communications. In 1866, Cyrus W. Field laid a transatlantic telegraph cable to Europe. During the next decade, Alexander Graham Bell developed the first commercially useful telephone; and by the 1890s, the American Telephone and Telegraph Company, which handled his interests, had installed nearly half a million telephones in American cities. Other inventions that speeded the pace of business organization were the typewriter (by Christopher L. Sholes in 1868), the cash register (by James Ritty in 1879), and the calculating or adding machine (by William S. Burroughs in 1891).

Among the most revolutionary innovations was the introduction in the 1870s of electricity as a source of light and power. Among the pioneers of electric lighting were Charles F. Brush, who devised the arc lamp for street illumination, and Thomas A. Edison, who invented the incandescent lamp (or light bulb), which could be used for both street and home lighting. Edison and others designed improved generators and built large power plants to furnish electricity to whole cities. By the turn of the century, electric power was becoming commonplace in street railway systems, in the elevators of urban skyscrapers, in factories, and increasingly in offices and homes.

A process by which iron could be transformed into steel—a much more durable and versatile material—had been discovered simultaneously in the 1850s by an Englishman, Henry Bessemer, and an American, William Kelly.

(The process consisted of blowing air through molten iron to burn out the impurities.) After the Civil War, the new process transformed the metal industry; and in 1868, the New Jersey ironmaster Abram S. Hewitt introduced from Europe another method of making steel—the open-hearth process. These techniques made possible the production of steel in great quantities and large dimensions, for use in the production of locomotives, steel rails, and girders for the construction of tall buildings.

The steel industry emerged first in western Pennsylvania and eastern Ohio, a region where iron ore and coal were abundant and where there was already a flourishing iron industry. Pittsburgh quickly became the center of the steel world. But the industry was growing so fast that new sources of ore were soon necessary. The upper peninsula of Michigan, the Mesabi range in Minnesota, and the area around Birmingham, Alabama, became important ore-producing centers by the end of the century, and new centers of steel production emerged near them: Cleveland, Detroit, Chicago, and Birmingham, among others. Most steel centers also had access to major waterways, permitting cheap transportation of goods to distant markets.

The oil industry emerged in the late nineteenth century largely in response to the steel industry's need for lubrication for its machines. (Not until later did oil become important primarily for its potential as a fuel.) The existence of petroleum reserves in western Pennsylvania, where oil often seeped to the surface of streams and springs, had been common knowledge for some time. At first, no one was quite sure what it was or what to do with it. In the 1850s, however, experiments commissioned by the Pennsylvania businessman George Bissell showed that the substance could be burned in lamps and that it could also yield such products as paraffin, naphtha, and lubricating oil. Bissell then raised money to begin drilling; and in 1859, Edwin L. Drake, one of Bissell's employees, established the first oil well near Titusville, Pennsylvania, which was soon producing 500 barrels of oil a month. Demand for petroleum grew quickly, and promoters soon developed other fields in Pennsylvania, Ohio, and West Virginia. By the 1870s, oil had advanced to fourth place among the nation's exports.

Other great innovations were emerging by the beginning of the twentieth century. The Italian inventor Guglielmo Marconi was taking the first steps toward the development of radio in the 1890s. The Wright brothers launched the first airplane flight at Kitty Hawk, North Carolina, in 1903. Perhaps most important, the automobile was in development. In the 1870s, designers in France, Germany, and Austria—inspired by the success of railroad engines—were already beginning to develop engines that might drive independently controlled vehicles. They achieved early successes with an "internal combustion engine," which used the expanding power of burning gas to drive pistons; and with this new engine, they created the first automobiles.

In the United States, the automobile industry developed rapidly. Charles and Frank Duryea built the first gasoline-driven motor vehicle in America in 1903. Three years later, Henry Ford produced the first of the famous cars that would bear his name. By 1910, the industry had become a major force in the economy, and the automobile was beginning to reshape American social and cultural life. In 1895, there were only four automobiles on the American highways. By 1917, there were nearly 5 million.

The Science of Production

Central to the growth of the automobile and other industries were changes in the techniques of production. By the turn of the century, many industrialists were embracing the new principles of "scientific management," often known as "Taylorism" because its leading theoretician was Frederick Winslow Taylor. Taylor's ideas were controversial during his lifetime, and they have remained controversial since. Taylor himself, and his many admirers, argued that scientific management was a way to manage human labor to make it compatible with the demands of the machine age. But scientific management was also a way to increase the employer's control of the workplace, to make working people less independent. Taylor urged employers to reorganize the production process by subdividing tasks. This would speed up production; it would also make workers more interchangeable (less skilled, less in need of training) and thus diminish a manager's dependence on any particular employee. If properly managed by trained experts, he claimed, workers using modern machines could perform simple tasks at much greater speed, greatly increasing productive efficiency.

The most important change in production technology in the industrial era was the emergence of mass production and, above all, of the moving assembly line, which Henry Ford introduced in his automobile plants in 1914. This revolutionary technique cut the time for assembling a chassis from twelve and a half hours to one and a half hours. It enabled Ford to raise the wages and reduce the hours of his workers while cutting the base price of his Model T from $950 in 1914 to $290 in 1929. It became a standard for many other industries.

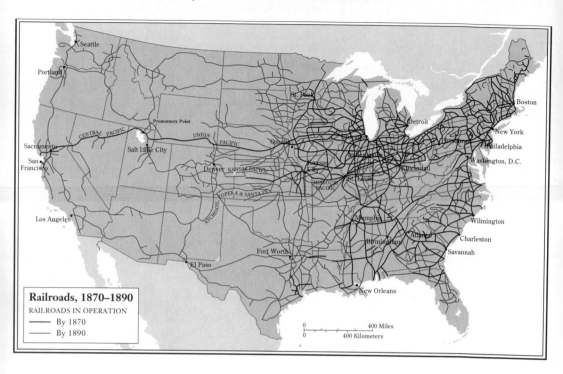

Railroads, 1870–1890

RAILROADS IN OPERATION
—— By 1870
—— By 1890

0   400 Miles
0   400 Kilometers

Railroad Expansion

The principal agent of industrial development in the late nineteenth century was the expansion of the railroads. Railroads promoted economic growth in many ways. They were the nation's principal method of transportation and gave industrialists access to distant markets and distant sources of raw materials. They were the nation's largest businesses and created new forms of corporate organization that served as models for other industries. And they were America's biggest investors, stimulating economic growth through their own enormous expenditures on construction and equipment.

In every decade in the late nineteenth century, total railroad trackage increased dramatically: from 30,000 miles in 1860, to 52,000 miles in 1870, to 93,000 in 1880, to 163,000 in 1890, and to 193,000 in 1900. Subsidies from federal, state, and local governments were (along with foreign loans and investments) vital to this expansion, which required far more capital than private entrepreneurs could raise by themselves. Equally important was the emergence of great railroad combinations that brought most of the nation's rails under the control of a few men. Through the last decades of the century, many railroad combinations continued to be dominated by one or two individuals. The achievements (and excesses) of these tycoons—Cornelius Vanderbilt, James J. Hill, Collis P. Huntington, and others—became symbols to much of the nation of great economic power concentrated in individual hands. But railroad development was less significant for the individual barons it created than for its contribution to the growth of a new institution: the modern corporation.

The Corporation

There had been various forms of corporations in America since colonial times, but the modern corporation emerged as a major force only after the Civil War. By then, railroad magnates and other industrialists realized that their great ventures could not be financed by any single person, no matter how wealthy, or even by any single group of partners.

Under the laws of incorporation passed in many states in the 1830s and 1840s, business organizations could raise money by selling stock to members of the public; after the Civil War, one industry after another began doing so. At the same time, affluent Americans began to consider the purchase of stock a good investment even if they were not themselves involved in the business whose stock they were purchasing. What made the practice appealing was that investors had only "limited liability"—that is, they risked only the amount of their investments; they were not liable for any debts the corporation might accumulate beyond that point. The ability to sell stock to a broad public made it possible for entrepreneurs to gather vast sums of capital and undertake great projects.

The Pennsylvania and other railroads were among the first to adopt the new corporate form of organization. But incorporation quickly spread beyond the railroad industry. In steel, the central figure was Andrew Carnegie, a Scottish immigrant who had worked his way up from modest beginnings and in 1873 opened his own steelworks in Pittsburgh. Soon he dominated the industry. His methods were much like those of other industrial titans. He cut costs and prices by striking deals with the railroads and then bought out rivals who could not compete with him. With his associate Henry Clay Frick, he bought up coal mines and leased part of the Mesabi iron range in Minnesota, operated a fleet of ore ships on the Great Lakes, and acquired railroads. Ultimately, he controlled the processing of his steel from mine to market. He financed his vast undertakings not only out of his own profits but out of the sale of stock. Then, in 1901, he sold out for $450 million to the banker J. Pierpont Morgan, who merged the Carnegie interests with others to create the giant United States Steel Corporation—a $1.4 billion enterprise that controlled almost two-thirds of the nation's steel production.

There were similar developments in other industries. Gustavus Swift developed a relatively small meat-packing company into a great national corporation. Isaac Singer patented a sewing machine in 1851 and created— in I. M. Singer and Company—one of the first modern manufacturing corporations.

Many of the corporate organizations developed a new approach to management. Large, national business enterprises needed more systematic administrative structures than the limited, local ventures of the past. As a

ANDREW CARNEGIE Carnegie was one of relatively small number of the great industrialists of the late nineteenth century who genuinely rose "from rags to riches." Born in Scotland, he came to the United States in 1848 and soon found work as a messenger in a Pittsburgh telegraph office. In 1873 he invested all his assets in the development of the first American steel mills. In 1901 he abruptly resigned from the industrial world and spent the remaining years of his life as a philanthropist. By the time of his death in 1919, he had given away some $350 million.

result, corporate leaders introduced a set of managerial techniques—the genesis of modern business administration—that relied on the division of responsibilities, a carefully designed hierarchy of control, modern cost-accounting procedures, and perhaps above all a new breed of business executive: the "middle manager," who formed a layer of command between workers and owners. Beginning in the railroad corporations, these new management techniques moved quickly into virtually every area of large-scale industry. Efficient administrative capabilities helped make possible another major feature of the modern corporation: consolidation.

Businessmen created large, consolidated organizations primarily through two methods. One was "horizontal integration"—the combining of a number of firms engaged in the same enterprise into a single corporation. The consolidation of many different railroad lines into one company was an example. Another method, which became popular in the 1890s, was "vertical integration"—the taking over of all the different businesses on which a company relied for its primary function. Carnegie Steel, which came to control not only steel mills but mines, railroads, and other enterprises, was an example of vertical integration.

The most celebrated corporate empire of the late nineteenth century was John D. Rockefeller's Standard Oil, a great combination created through both horizontal and vertical integration. Shortly after the Civil War, Rockefeller launched a refining company in Cleveland and immediately began trying to eliminate his competition. Allying himself with other wealthy capitalists, he proceeded methodically to buy out competing refineries. In 1870, he formed the Standard Oil Company of Ohio, which in a few years had acquired twenty of the twenty-five refineries in Cleveland, as well as plants in Pittsburgh, Philadelphia, New York, and Baltimore.

So far, Rockefeller had expanded only horizontally. But soon he began expanding vertically as well. He built his own barrel factories, terminal warehouses, and pipelines. Standard Oil owned its own freight cars and developed its own marketing organization. By the 1880s, Rockefeller had established such dominance within the petroleum industry that to much of the nation he served as the leading symbol of monopoly. He controlled access to 90 percent of the nation's refined oil.

Rockefeller and other industrialists saw consolidation as a way to cope with what they believed was the greatest curse of the modern economy: "cutthroat competition." Most businessmen claimed to believe in free enterprise and a competitive marketplace, but in fact they feared the existence of too many competing firms. They were convinced that substantial competition could spell instability and ruin for all. A successful enterprise, many capitalists believed (but did not say), was one that could eliminate or absorb its competitors.

As the movement toward combination accelerated, new vehicles emerged to facilitate it. The railroads began with so-called pool arrangements—informal agreements among various companies to stabilize rates and divide markets (arrangements that would, in later years, be known as cartels). But the pools did not work very well. If even a few firms in an industry were unwilling to cooperate (as was almost always the case), the pool arrangements collapsed.

The failure of the pools led to new techniques of consolidation resting less on cooperation than on centralized control. At first, the most successful such technique was the creation of the "trust"—pioneered by Standard Oil in the early 1880s and perfected by the banker J. P. Morgan. Over time, the word "trust" became a term for any great economic combination, but the trust was in fact a particular kind of organization. Under a trust agreement, stockholders in individual corporations transferred their stocks to a small group of trustees in exchange for shares in the trust itself. Owners of trust certificates often had no direct control over the decisions of the trustees; they simply received a share of the profits of the combination. The trustees themselves, on the other hand, might literally own only a few companies but could exercise effective control over many.

In 1889, the state of New Jersey helped produce a third form of consolidation by changing its laws of incorporation to permit companies to buy up other companies. Other states soon followed. That made the trust unnecessary and permitted actual corporate mergers. Rockefeller, for example, quickly relocated Standard Oil in New Jersey and created there what became known as a "holding company"—a central corporate body that would buy up the stock of various members of the Standard Oil trust and establish direct, formal ownership of the corporations in the trust.

By the end of the nineteenth century, as a result of corporate consolidation, 1 percent of the corporations in America were able to control more than 33 percent of the manufacturing. A system of economic organization was emerging that lodged enormous power in the hands of very few men—the great bankers of New York such as J. P. Morgan, industrial titans such as Rockefeller (who himself gained control of a major bank), and others.

Whether or not this ruthless concentration of economic power was the only way (or the best way) to promote industrial expansion, the industrial giants of the era were clearly reponsible for substantial economic growth.

They were integrating operations, cutting costs, creating a great industrial infrastructure, stimulating new markets, creating jobs for millions of unskilled workers, and opening the way to large-scale mass production. They were also creating the basis for some of the greatest public controversies of their era: a raging debate over concentrated economic and political power that continued well into the twentieth century.

CAPITALISM AND ITS CRITICS

The rise of big business was not without its critics. Farmers and workers saw in the growth of the new corporate power centers a threat to notions of a republican society in which wealth and authority were widely distributed. Middle-class critics pointed to the corruption that the new industrial titans seemed to produce in their own enterprises and in local, state, and national politics. The growing criticisms challenged the captains of industry to create a defense of the new corporate economy, one that would convince the public (and themselves) that such an economy was compatible with the ideology of individualism and equal opportunity that was so central to American life.

Survival of the Fittest

The new rationale for capitalism rested squarely on the older ideology of individualism. The new industrial economy, its defenders argued, was not shrinking opportunities for individual advancement. It was expanding those opportunities. It was providing every individual with a chance to succeed and attain great wealth.

There was an element of truth in such claims, but only a small element. Before the Civil War there had been few millionaires in America; by 1892 there were more than 4,000 of them. Some of them—Carnegie, Rockefeller, and a few others—were in fact what almost all millionaires claimed to be: "self-made men." But most of the new business tycoons had begun their careers from positions of comfort, privilege, and wealth. Nor was their rise to power and prominence always a result simply of hard work and ingenuity, as they liked to claim. It was also a result of ruthlessness and, at times, rampant corruption. Industrialists made large financial contributions to politicians, political parties, and government officials in exchange for assistance and support.

Nevertheless, most tycoons continued to claim that they had attained their wealth and power through hard work, acquisitiveness, and thrift—the traditional virtues of Protestant America. Those who succeeded, they argued, deserved their success, and those who failed had earned their failure—through their own laziness, stupidity, or carelessness. Such assumptions became the basis of a popular social theory of the late nineteenth century: Social Darwinism, the application to human society of Charles Darwin's laws of evolution and natural selection among species. Just as only the fittest survived in the process of evolution, the Social Darwinists argued, so in human society only the fittest individuals survived and flourished in the marketplace.

The English philosopher Herbert Spencer was the first and most important proponent of this theory. Society, he argued, benefited from the elimination of the unfit and the survival of the strong and talented. Spencer's books were popular in America in the 1870s and 1880s. And his teachings found prominent supporters among American intellectuals, most notably William Graham Sumner of Yale, who promoted similar ideas in lectures, articles, and a famous 1906 book, *Folkways*. Sumner did not agree with everything Spencer wrote, but he did share Spencer's belief that individuals must have absolute freedom to struggle, to compete, to succeed, or to fail.

Social Darwinism appealed to corporate leaders because it seemed to legitimize their success and confirm their virtues. It placed their activities within the context of traditional American ideas of freedom and individualism, and it justified their tactics. It was not, however, an ideology that had very much to do with the realities of the corporate economy. At the same time that businessmen were celebrating the virtues of competition and the free market, they were making active efforts to protect themselves from competition and to replace the natural workings of the marketplace with control by great combinations. Vicious competitive battle—the thing that Spencer and Sumner celebrated and called a source of healthy progress—was in fact the very thing that American businessmen most feared and tried to eliminate.

The Gospel of Wealth

Some businessmen attempted to temper the harsh philosophy of Social Darwinism with a gentler, if in some ways equally self-serving, idea: the "gospel of wealth." People of great wealth, advocates of this idea argued, had not only great power but great responsibilities. It was their duty to use their riches to advance social progress. Andrew Carnegie elaborated on the creed in his 1901 book, *The Gospel of Wealth*, in which he wrote that people of wealth should consider all revenues in excess of their own needs as "trust funds" to be used for the good of the community. Carnegie was only one of many great industrialists who devoted large parts of their fortunes to philanthropic works.

The notion of private wealth as a public blessing existed alongside another popular concept: the notion of great wealth as something available to all. Russell H. Conwell, a Baptist minister, became the most prominent spokesman for the idea by delivering one lecture, "Acres of Diamonds," more than 6,000 times between 1880 and 1900. Conwell told a series of stories, which he claimed were true, of individuals who had found opportunities for extraordinary wealth in their own back yards. (One such story involved a modest farmer who discovered a vast diamond mine in his own fields in the course of working his land.) Most of the millionaires in the country, Conwell claimed (inaccurately), had begun on the lowest rung of the economic ladder and had worked their way to success. Every industrious individual had the chance to do likewise.

Horatio Alger was the most famous promoter of the success story. Alger was originally a minister in a small town in Massachusetts but was driven from his pulpit as a result of a sexual scandal. He moved to New York, where he wrote his celebrated novels—*Ragged Dick*, *Tom the Bootblack*, *Sink or Swim*, and many others, more than 100 in all, which together sold more than 20 million copies. The titles and characters varied, but the story and message were invariably the same: a poor boy from a small town went to the big city to seek his fortune. By work, perseverance, and luck, he became rich.

Alternative Visions

Alongside the celebrations of competition, the justifications for great wealth, and the legitimation of the existing order stood a group of alternative philosophies, challenging the corporate ethos and at times capitalism itself.

One such philosophy emerged in the work of the sociologist Lester Frank Ward. Ward was a Darwinist, but he rejected the application of Darwinian laws to human society. In *Dynamic Sociology* (1883) and other books, he argued that civilization was not governed by natural selection but by human intelligence, which was capable of shaping society as it wished. In contrast to Sumner, who believed that state intervention to remodel the environment was futile, Ward thought that an active government engaged in positive planning was society's best hope. The people, through their government, could intervene in the economy and adjust it to serve their needs.

Other Americans skeptical of the laissez-faire ideas of the Social Darwinists adopted more drastic approaches to reform. Some dissenters found a home in the Socialist Labor party, founded in the 1870s and led for many years by Daniel De Leon, an immigrant from the West Indies. Although De Leon attracted a modest following in the industrial cities, the party never became a major political force and never polled more than 82,000 votes. De Leon's theoretical and dogmatic approach appealed to intellectuals more than to workers; and a dissident faction of his party, eager to forge ties with organized labor, broke away and in 1901 formed the more enduring American Socialist party.

Other radicals gained a wider following. One of the most influential was the California writer and activist Henry George. His angrily eloquent *Progress and Poverty*, published in 1879, became one of the best-selling nonfiction works in American publishing history. George tried to explain why poverty existed amidst the wealth created by modern industry. He blamed social problems on the ability of a few monopolists to grow wealthy as a result of rising land values. An increase in the value of land, he claimed, was a result not of any effort by the owner but of the growth of society around the land. It was an "unearned increment," and it was rightfully the property of the community. And so George proposed a "single tax," to replace all other taxes, which would return the increment to the people. The tax, he argued, would destroy monopolies, distribute wealth more equally, and eliminate poverty. Single-tax societies sprang up in many cities; and in 1886, George, with the support of labor and the socialists, narrowly missed being elected mayor of New York.

Rivaling George in popularity was Edward Bellamy, whose utopian novel *Looking Backward*, published in 1888, sold more than 1 million copies. It described the experiences of a young Bostonian who went into a hypnotic sleep in 1887 and awoke in the year 2000 to find a new social order in which want, politics, and vice were unknown. The new society had emerged from a peaceful, evolutionary process. The large trusts of the late nineteenth century had continued to grow in size and to combine with one another until ultimately they formed a single, great trust, controlled by the government, which distributed the abundance of the industrial economy equally among all the people. "Fraternal cooperation" had replaced competition. Class divisions had disappeared. Bellamy labeled the philosophy behind this vision "nationalism," and his work inspired the formation of more than 160 Nationalist Clubs to propagate his ideas.

The Problems of Monopoly

Relatively few Americans shared the views of those who questioned capitalism itself. But as time went on, a growing number of people were becoming deeply concerned about a particular, glaring aspect of capitalism: the growth of monopoly.

By the end of the century, a wide range of groups had begun to assail monopoly and economic concentration. Laborers, farmers, consumers, small manufacturers, conservative bankers and financiers, advocates of radical change—all joined the attack. They blamed monopoly for creating artificially high prices and for producing a highly unstable economy. Beginning in 1873, the economy fluctuated erratically, with severe recessions creating havoc every five or six years, each recession worse than the previous one, until finally, in 1893, the system seemed on the verge of total collapse.

Adding to the resentment of monopoly was the emergence of a new class of enormously and conspicuously wealthy people, whose life styles

"THE BOSSES OF THE SENATE" The magazine *Puck* conveyed through its savage cartoons the growing popular belief in the 1880s that the United States government had fallen under the control of corrupt "trusts." As bloated, reptilian plutocrats crowd the back of the U.S. Senate chamber, a sign in the gallery notes that the "People's Entrance" is "closed."

became an affront to those struggling to stay afloat in the erratic economy. According to one estimate early in the century, 1 percent of the families in the United States controlled nearly 88 percent of the nation's assets. Some of the wealthy—Andrew Carnegie, for example—lived relatively modestly and donated large sums to philanthropic causes. Others, however, lived in almost grotesque luxury. Observing their flagrant displays of wealth were the four-fifths of the American people who lived modestly, and at least 10 million people who lived below the commonly accepted poverty line. The standard of living was rising for everyone, but the gap between rich and poor was increasing dramatically. To those in difficult economic circumstances, the sense of relative deprivation could be as frustrating and embittering as poverty itself.

THE ORDEAL OF THE WORKER

The American working class was both a beneficiary and a victim of the growth of industrial capitalism. Most workers in the late nineteenth century experienced a real rise in their standard of living. But they did so at the cost of arduous and often dangerous working conditions, diminishing control over their own work, and a growing sense of powerlessness.

The Immigrant Work Force

The industrial work force expanded dramatically in the late nineteenth century as demand for factory labor grew. The source of that expansion was a massive migration into industrial cities—immigration of two sorts. The first was the continuing flow of rural Americans into factory towns and cities—people disillusioned with or bankrupted by life on the farm and eager for new economic and social opportunities. The second was the great wave of immigration from abroad (primarily from Europe, but also from Asia, Canada, and other areas) in the decades following the Civil War—an influx greater than that of any previous era. The 25 million immigrants who arrived in the United States between 1865 and 1915 were more than four times the number who had arrived in the fifty years before.

In the 1870s and 1880s, most of the immigrants came from the nation's traditional sources: England, Ireland, and northern Europe. By the end of the century, however, the major sources of immigrants had shifted, with large numbers of southern and eastern Europeans (Italians, Poles, Russians,

Greeks, Slavs, and others) moving into the country and into the industrial work force.

The new immigrants were coming to America in part to escape poverty and oppression in their homelands. But they were also lured to the United States by expectations of new opportunities. Some such expectations were realistic, but others were the result of false promises. Railroads tried to lure immigrants into their Western landholdings by distributing misleading advertisements overseas. Industrial employers actively recruited immigrant workers under the Labor Contract Law, which—until its repeal in 1885—permitted them to pay for the passage of workers in advance and deduct the amount later from their wages. Even after the repeal of the law, employers continued to encourage the immigration of unskilled laborers, often with the assistance of foreign-born labor brokers, such as the Greek and Italian *padrones* who recruited work gangs of their fellow nationals.

The arrival of these new groups introduced heightened ethnic tensions into the dynamics of the working class. Low-paid Poles, Greeks, and French Canadians began to displace higher-paid British and Irish workers in the textile factories of New England. Italians, Slavs, and Poles emerged as a major source of labor for the mining industry, traditionally dominated by native workers or northern European immigrants. Within industries, moreover, workers tended to cluster in particular occupations (and thus, often, at particular income levels) by ethnic group.

Wages and Working Conditions

The average standard of living for workers may have been rising in the years after the Civil War; but for many laborers, the return for their labor remained very small. At the turn of the century, the average income of the American worker was $400 to $500 a year—below the $600 figure that many believed was the minimum required to maintain a reasonable level of comfort. Nor did workers have much job security. All were vulnerable to the boom-and-bust cycle of the industrial economy, and some lost their jobs because of technological advances or because of the cyclical or seasonal nature of their work. Even those who kept their jobs could find their wages suddenly and substantially cut in hard times. Few workers, in other words, were ever very far from poverty.

American laborers faced a wide array of other hardships as well. For first-generation workers accustomed to the patterns of agrarian life, there was a difficult adjustment to the nature of modern industrial labor: the

CHILD LABOR Many working-class children of the early twentieth century found employment as "breaker boys," picking pieces of slate out of piles of coal. The coal dust was often so thick that they could hardly see one another, as this Lewis Hine photograph suggests.

performance of routine, repetitive tasks, often requiring little skill, on a strict and monotonous schedule. To skilled artisans whose once-valued tasks were now performed by machines, the new system was impersonal and demeaning. Factory laborers worked ten-hour days, six days a week; in the steel industry they worked twelve hours a day. Many worked in appallingly unsafe or unhealthy factories. Industrial accidents were frequent and severe. Compensation to the victims, either from their employers or from the government, was limited.

Women and Children at Work

The decreasing need for skilled work in factories induced many employers to increase the use of women and children, whom they could hire for lower wages than adult males. By 1900, 20 percent of all manufacturing workers were women; and 20 percent of all women (well over 5 million) were wage earners. Women worked in all areas of industry, even in some of the most arduous jobs. Most women, however, worked in a few industries where unskilled and semiskilled machine labor (as opposed to heavy manual labor) prevailed. The textile industry remained the largest single industrial employer of women. (Domestic service remained the most common female occupation overall.) Women worked for wages as low as $6 to $8 a week, well below the minimum necessary for survival (and well below the wages paid to men working the same jobs).

At least 1.7 million children under sixteen years of age were employed in factories and fields, more than twice the number of thirty years before; 10 percent of all girls aged ten to fifteen, and 20 percent of all boys, held jobs. Under the pressure of outraged public opinion, thirty-eight state legislatures passed child labor laws in the late nineteenth century; but these laws were of limited impact. Sixty percent of child workers were employed in agriculture, which was typically exempt from the laws. And even for children employed in factories, the laws merely set a minimum age of twelve years and a maximum workday of ten hours, standards that employers often ignored in any case.

Emerging Unionization

Laborers attempted to fight back against such conditions by adopting some of the same tactics their employers had used so effectively: creating large combinations—national unions. By the end of the century, however, their efforts had met with little success.

There had been craft unions in America, representing small groups of skilled workers, since well before the Civil War. Alone, however, individual unions could not hope to exert significant power in the economy. And during the recession years of the 1870s, unions faced the additional problem of widespread public hostility. When labor disputes with employers turned bitter and violent, as they occasionally did, much of the public instinctively blamed the workers (or the "radicals" and "anarchists" they believed were influencing the workers) for the trouble, rarely the employers. Particularly alarming to middle-class Americans was the emergence of the "Molly Maguires," in the anthracite coal region of western Pennsylvania. This militant labor organization occasionally used violence and even murder in its battle with coal operators. Much of the violence attributed to the Molly Maguires, however, was deliberately instigated by informers and agents employed by the mine owners, who wanted a pretext for ruthless measures suppressing unionization.

Excitement over the Molly Maguires paled beside the near hysteria that gripped the country during the railroad strike of 1877, which began when the Eastern railroads announced a 10 percent wage cut and which soon expanded into something approaching a class war. Strikers disrupted rail service from Baltimore to St. Louis, destroyed equipment, and rioted in the streets of Pittsburgh and other cities. State militias were called out, and in July President Hayes ordered federal troops to suppress the disorders in West Virginia. In Baltimore, eleven demonstrators died and forty were wounded in a conflict between workers and militiamen. In Philadelphia, the state militia killed twenty people when the troops opened fire on thousands of workers and their families who were attempting to block the railroad crossings. In all, over 100 people died before the strike finally collapsed several weeks after it had begun.

The great railroad strike was America's first major, national labor conflict, and it illustrated that disputes between labor and capital could no longer be localized in the increasingly national economy. It illustrated as well the depth of resentment among many American workers and the lengths to which they were prepared to go to express that resentment. And, finally, it indicated the serious problems afflicting the labor movement. The failure of the strike severely weakened the railroad unions and damaged the reputation of labor organizations in other industries as well.

The Knights of Labor

The first major effort to create a genuinely national labor organization was the founding in 1869 of the Noble Order of the Knights of Labor, under the leadership of Uriah S. Stephens. Membership was open to all who "toiled," a definition that included all workers, most business and professional people, and virtually all women—whether they worked in factories, as domestic servants, or in their own homes. The only excluded groups were lawyers, bankers, liquor dealers, and professional gamblers. The Knights of Labor was loosely organized, without much central direction. Its program was similarly vague. Although its leaders championed an eight-hour day and the abolition of child labor, they were more interested in long-range reform of the economy. The Knights hoped to replace the "wage system" with a new "cooperative system," in which workers would themselves control a large part of the economy.

For several years, the Knights remained a secret fraternal organization. But in the late 1870s, under the leadership of Terence V. Powderly, the order moved into the open and entered a spectacular period of expansion. By 1886, it claimed a total membership of over 700,000, including some militant elements that the moderate leadership could not always control. Local unions or assemblies associated with the Knights launched a series of railroad and other strikes in the 1880s in defiance of Powderly's wishes. Their failure helped discredit the organization. By 1890, the membership of the Knights had shrunk to 100,000. A few years later, the organization disappeared altogether.

The AFL

Even before the Knights began to decline, a rival association based on a very different organizational concept appeared. In 1881, representatives of a number of craft unions formed the Federation of Organized Trade and Labor Unions of the United States and Canada. Five years later, this body took the name it has borne ever since, the American Federation of Labor (AFL), and soon became the most important labor group in the country.

Rejecting the Knights' idea of one big union for everybody, the Federation was an association of essentially autonomous craft unions and represented mainly skilled workers. Samuel Gompers, the powerful leader of the AFL, accepted the basic premises of capitalism; his goal was simply to secure for the workers he represented a greater share of capitalism's material rewards. The AFL concentrated on labor's immediate objectives: wages, hours, and working conditions. While it hoped to attain its ends by collective bargaining, it was ready to use strikes if necessary. As one of its first objectives, the AFL demanded a national eight-hour day and called for a general strike if the goal was not achieved by May 1, 1886. On that day, strikes and demonstrations for a shorter workday took place all over the country, most of them staged by AFL unions but a few by more radical groups.

In Chicago, a center of labor and radical strength, a strike was already in progress at the McCormick Harvester Company. City police had been harassing the strikers, and labor and radical leaders called a protest meeting at Haymarket Square. When the police ordered the crowd to disperse, someone threw a bomb that killed seven policemen and injured sixty-seven others. The police, who had killed four strikers the day before, fired into the crowd and killed four more people. Conservative, property-conscious

Americans—frightened and outraged—demanded retribution, even though no one knew who had thrown the bomb. Chicago officials finally rounded up eight anarchists and charged them with murder, on the grounds that their statements had incited whoever had hurled the bomb. All eight scapegoats were found guilty after a remarkably injudicious trial. Seven were sentenced to death. One of them committed suicide, four were executed, and two had their sentences commuted to life imprisonment.

To most middle-class Americans, the Haymarket bombing was an alarming symbol of social chaos and radicalism. "Anarchism" now became in the public mind a code word for terrorism and violence, even though most anarchists were relatively peaceful visionaries dreaming of a new social order. For the next thirty years, the specter of anarchism remained one of the most frightening concepts in the American imagination. It was a constant obstacle to the goals of the AFL and other labor organizations, and it did particular damage to the Knights of Labor. However much they tried to distance themselves from radicals, labor leaders were always vulnerable to accusations of anarchism, as the violent strikes of the 1890s occasionally illustrated.

The Homestead Strike

The Amalgamated Association of Iron and Steel Workers, which was affiliated with the American Federation of Labor, was the most powerful trade union in the country. Its members were skilled workers, in great demand by employers and had thus long been able to exercise significant power in the workplace. In the mid-1880s, however, demand for skilled workers was in decline as new production methods and new, large-scale corporate organizations streamlined the steelmaking process. In the Carnegie system, which was coming to dominate the steel industry, the union was able to win a foothold in only one of the corporation's three major factories—the Homestead plant near Pittsburgh.

By 1890, Carnegie and his chief lieutenant, Henry Clay Frick, had decided that the Amalgamated "had to go" even at Homestead. Over the next two years, they repeatedly cut wages at Homestead. At first, the union acquiesced, aware that it was not strong enough to wage a successful strike. In 1892, however, the company stopped even discussing its decisions with the Amalgamated, in effect denying the union's right to negotiate at all. Finally, when Frick announced another wage cut at Homestead and gave the union two days to accept it, the Amalgamated called for a strike.

BREAKING THE HOMESTEAD STRIKE, 1892 State militiamen enter Homestead, Pennsylvania, to put an end to the Amalgamated union's violent strike by opening the Carnegie-owned steel plant to strikebreaking workers. This double photograph forms a "stereograph," which when viewed through a special lens (a "stereoscope") gave the impression of a three-dimensional scene.

Frick abruptly shut down the plant and called in 300 guards from the Pinkerton Detective Agency to enable the company to hire nonunion workers. The hated Pinkertons were well-known strikebreakers, and their mere presence was often enough to incite workers to violence. They approached the plant by river on barges on July 6, 1892. The strikers poured gasoline on the water, set it on fire, and then met the Pinkertons at the docks with guns and dynamite. A pitched battle broke out. After several hours of fighting, which brought death to three guards and ten strikers and injuries to many others, the Pinkertons surrendered and were escorted roughly out of town.

But the workers' victory was temporary. The governor of Pennsylvania, at the company's request, sent the state's entire National Guard contingent, some 8,000 troops, to Homestead. Production resumed, with strikebreakers now protected by troops. And public opinion turned against the strikers when a radical made an attempt to assassinate Frick. Slowly, workers drifted back to their jobs; and finally—four months after the strike began—the Amalgamated surrendered. By 1900, every major steel plant in the Northeast had broken with the Amalgamated, which now had virtually no power to resist. Its membership shrank from a high of 24,000 in 1891 (two-thirds of all eligible steelworkers) to fewer than 7,000 a decade later.

The Pullman Strike

A dispute of greater magnitude and equal bitterness, if less violence, was the Pullman strike in 1894. The Pullman Palace Car Company manufactured sleeping and parlor cars for railroads, which it built and repaired at a plant near Chicago. There the company built a 600-acre town, Pullman, and rented its trim, orderly houses to the employees. George M. Pullman, owner of the company, saw the town as a model solution of the industrial problem; he referred to the workers as his "children." But many residents chafed at the regimentation (and the high rents).

In the winter of 1893–1894, the Pullman Company slashed wages by about 25 percent, citing its own declining revenues in the depression. At the same time, Pullman refused to reduce rents in its model town, which were 20 to 25 percent higher than those for comparable accommodations in surrounding areas. Workers went on strike and persuaded the militant American Railway Union, led by Eugene V. Debs, to support them by refusing to handle Pullman cars and equipment. Within a few days thousands of railroad workers in twenty-seven states and territories were on strike, and transportation from Chicago to the Pacific coast was paralyzed.

Most state governors responded readily to appeals from strike-threatened businesses; but the governor of Illinois, John Peter Altgeld, was a man with demonstrated sympathies for workers and their grievances. Altgeld had criticized the trials of the Haymarket anarchists and had pardoned the convicted men who were still in prison when he took office. He refused to call out the militia to protect employers now. Bypassing Altgeld, railroad operators asked the federal government to send regular army troops to Illinois, using the pretext that the strike was preventing the movement of mail on the trains. President Grover Cleveland and Attorney General Richard Olney, a former railroad lawyer and a bitter foe of unions, complied. In July 1894, the president, over Altgeld's objections, ordered 2,000 troops to the Chicago area. A federal court issued an injunction forbidding the union to continue the strike. When Debs and his associates defied it, they were arrested and imprisoned. With federal troops protecting the hiring of new workers and with the union leaders in a federal jail, the strike quickly collapsed.

Sources of Labor Weakness

The last decades of the nineteenth century were years in which labor, despite its organizing efforts, made few real gains. Industrial wages rose hardly at all. Labor leaders won a few legislative victories—the abolition by Congress in 1885 of the Contract Labor Law; the establishment by Congress in 1868 of an eight-hour day on public works projects and in 1892 of the same workday for government employees; and state laws governing hours of labor and safety standards. But most such laws were not enforced. There were strikes and protests, but few real gains. The end of the century found most workers with less political power and less control of the workplace than they had had forty years before.

Workers failed to make greater gains for many reasons. The principal labor organizations represented only a small percentage of the industrial work force; the AFL, the most important, excluded unskilled workers, who were emerging as the core of the industrial work force, and along with them most women, blacks, and recent immigrants. Divisions within the work force contributed further to union weakness. Tensions among different ethnic and racial groups kept laborers divided.

Another source of labor weakness was the shifting nature of the work force. Many immigrant workers came to America intending to remain only briefly, to earn some money and return home. The assumption that they had no long-range future in the country eroded their willingness to organize. Other workers—natives and immigrants alike—were in constant motion, moving from one job to another, one town to another, seldom in one place long enough to establish any sort of institutional ties or exert any real power.

Above all, perhaps, workers made few gains in the late nineteenth century because of the strength of the forces arrayed against them. They faced corporate organizations of vast wealth and power, which were generally determined to crush any efforts by workers to challenge their prerogatives. And as the Homestead and Pullman strikes suggest, the corporations had the support of local, state, and federal authorities, who were willing to send in troops to "preserve order" and crush labor uprisings on demand.

Despite the creation of new labor unions, despite a wave of strikes and protests that in the 1880s and 1890s reached startling proportions, workers in the late nineteenth century failed on the whole to create successful organizations or to protect their interests in the way the large corporations managed to do. In the battle for power within the emerging industrial economy, almost all the advantages seemed to lie with capital.

CHAPTER EIGHTEEN

The Age of the City

The New Urban Growth ~ Society and Culture in Urbanizing America
High Culture in the Urban Age

T HE INDUSTRIALIZATION AND commercialization of America changed the face of society in countless ways. Nowhere, however, were the changes more profound than in the growth of cities and the creation of an urban society and culture. Having begun its life as a primarily agrarian republic, the United States in the late nineteenth century was becoming an urban nation.

THE NEW URBAN GROWTH

The great folk movement from the countryside to the city was not unique to the United States. It was occurring simultaneously throughout much of the Western world in response to industrialization and the factory system. But America, a society with little experience of great cities, found urbanization particularly jarring. The city attracted people because it offered conveniences, entertainments, and cultural experiences unavailable in rural communities. But it attracted people most of all because it offered more and better-paying jobs than were available in the countryside. Whatever the reasons, the urban population of America increased sevenfold in the half-century after the Civil War. And in 1920, the census revealed that for the first time, a majority of the American people lived in "urban" areas—defined as communities of 2,500 people or more.

Natural increase accounted for only a small part of the urban growth. Urban families experienced a high rate of infant mortality, a declining fertility rate, and a high death rate from disease. Without immigration, cities would have grown relatively slowly.

The Migrations

The late nineteenth century was an age of unprecedented geographical mobility, as Americans left the declining agricultural regions of the East at a dramatic rate. Some of those who left were moving to the newly developing farmlands of the West. But almost as many were moving to the cities of the East and the Midwest.

Among those leaving rural America for industrial cities in the 1880s were Southern blacks. That was a testament to the poverty, debt, violence, and oppression African-Americans encountered in the late-nineteenth-century South. The opportunities they found in cities were limited, but an improvement nevertheless over what they left behind. Factory jobs for blacks were rare and professional opportunities almost nonexistent. Urban blacks tended to work as cooks, janitors, and domestic servants, as well as in other service occupations. Since many such jobs were considered women's work, black women often outnumbered black men in the cities. By the end of the nineteenth century, there were substantial black communities (10,000 people or more) in over thirty cities.

The most important source of urban population growth in the late nineteenth century, however, was the arrival of great numbers of new immigrants from abroad. Some came from Canada, Latin America, and—particularly on the West Coast—China and Japan. But by far the greatest number came from Europe. After 1880, the flow of new arrivals began for the first time to include large numbers of people from southern and eastern Europe. By the 1890s, more than half of all immigrants came from these new regions, as opposed to fewer than 2 percent in the 1860s.

In earlier stages of immigration, most new immigrants from Europe (particularly Germans and Scandinavians) were at least modestly prosperous and educated. They had generally headed west—either to be farmers or to work as businessmen, professionals, or skilled laborers in Midwestern cities such as St. Louis, Cincinnati, and Milwaukee. Most of the new immigrants of the late nineteenth century lacked the capital to buy farmland and lacked the education to establish themselves in professions. So, like similarly poor Irish immigrants before the Civil War, they settled overwhelmingly in industrial cities, where they occupied largely unskilled jobs.

The Ethnic City

By 1890, most of the population of the major urban areas consisted of immigrants: 87 percent of the population in Chicago, 80 percent in New

York, 84 percent in Milwaukee and Detroit. (London, the largest industrial city in Europe, had by contrast a population that was 94 percent native.)

Equally striking was the diversity of the new immigrant populations. In other countries experiencing heavy immigration in this period, most of the new arrivals were coming from one or two sources. But in the United States, no single national group dominated. In the last four decades of the nineteenth century, substantial groups arrived from Italy, Germany, Scandinavia, Austria, Hungary, Russia, Great Britain, Ireland, Poland, Greece, Canada, Japan, China, Holland, Mexico, and other nations. In some towns, a dozen different ethnic groups might find themselves living in close proximity to one another.

Most of the new immigrants were rural people, and their adjustment to city life was often a painful one. To help ease the transition, many national groups formed close-knit ethnic communities within the cities: Italian, Polish, Jewish, Slavic, Chinese, French Canadian, Mexican, and other neighborhoods (often called "immigrant ghettoes") that attempted to re-create in the New World many of the features of the Old. Some ethnic neighborhoods consisted of people who had migrated to America from the same province, town, or village. Even when the population was more diverse, however, the community offered newcomers much that was familiar. They could find newspapers and theaters in their native languages, stores selling their native foods, church and fraternal organizations that provided links with their national pasts. Many immigrants also maintained close ties with their native countries. They stayed in touch with relatives who had remained behind. Some (perhaps as many as a third in the early years) returned to Europe after a relatively short time; others helped bring the rest of their families to America.

The cultural cohesiveness of the ethnic communities clearly eased the pain of separation from the immigrants' native lands. What role it played in helping immigrants become absorbed into the economic life of America is a more difficult question to answer. It is clear that some ethnic groups (Jews and Germans in particular) advanced economically more rapidly than others (for example, the Irish). One explanation is that, by huddling together in ethnic neighborhoods, immigrant groups tended to reinforce the cultural values of their previous societies. When those values were particularly well suited to economic advancement—as was, for example, the high value Jews placed on education—ethnic identification may have helped members of a group to improve their lots. When other values predominated—maintaining community solidarity, strengthening family ties, preserving order—progress could be less rapid.

Assimilation and Exclusion

Yet it would be easy to overstate the differences among the various immigrant communities, because virtually all groups had certain things in common. Most immigrants, of course, shared the experience of living in cities (and of adapting from a rural past to an urban present). Most were young; the majority of newcomers were between fifteen and forty-five years old. And in virtually all immigrant communities, the strength of ethnic ties had to compete against another powerful force: the desire for assimilation.

Many of the new arrivals had come to America with romantic visions of the New World. And however disillusioning they might find their first contact with the United States, they usually retained the dream of becoming true "Americans." Even some first-generation immigrants worked hard to rid themselves of all vestiges of their old cultures, to become thoroughly Americanized. Second-generation immigrants were even more likely to attempt to break with the old ways, to assimilate themselves completely into what they considered the real American culture. Some even looked with contempt on parents and grandparents who continued to defend traditional ethnic habits and values or who tried to maintain control of adult children. Young women, in particular, sometimes rebelled against parents who tried to arrange (or prevent) marriages, or who disapproved of women entering the workplace.

Assimilation was not, of course, entirely a matter of choice. Native-born Americans encouraged it, both deliberately and inadvertently, in countless ways. Public schools taught children in English, and employers often insisted that workers speak English on the job. Most stores sold mainly American products, forcing immigrants to adapt their diets, clothing, and life styles to American norms. Church leaders were often native-born Americans or more assimilated immigrants who encouraged their parishioners to adopt American ways. Some even reformed their theology and liturgy to make it more compatible with the norms of the new country. Reform Judaism, for example, was an effort by American Jewish leaders to make their faith less "foreign" to the dominant culture of a largely Christian nation.

The arrival of these vast numbers of new immigrants, and the way many of them clung to old ways and created culturally distinctive communities, provoked fear and resentment among some native-born Americans in much the same way earlier arrivals had done. Some people reacted against the immigrants out of generalized fears and prejudices, seeing in their "foreignness" the source of all the disorder and corruption of the urban world.

A M E R I C A N V O I C E S

ANZIA YEZIERSKA

A Jewish Immigrant Strains Against the Past

FOR SEVENTEEN YEARS I had stood [my father's] preaching and his bullying. But now all the hammering hell that I had to listen to since I was born cracked my brain. His heartlessness to Mother, his pitiless driving away Bessie's only chance to love, bargaining away Fania to a gambler and Mashah to a diamond-faker—when they each had the luck to win lovers of their own—all these tyrannies crashed over me. Should I let him crush me as he crushed them? No. This is America, where children are people. . . .

Blindly, I grabbed my things together into a bundle. I didn't care where I was going or what was to become of me. Only to break away from my black life. Only not to hear Father's preaching voice again. . . .

As I came through the door with my bundle, Father caught sight of me. "What's this?" he asked. "Where are you going?"

"I'm going back to work, in New York. . . . I've got to live my own life. It's enough that Mother and the others lived for you. . . . Thank God, I'm not living in olden times. Thank God I'm living in America! You made the lives of the other children. I'm going to make my own life!"

"You blasphemer!" His hand flung out and struck my cheek. "Denier of God! I'll teach you respect for the law!"

I leaped back and dashed for the door. The Old World had struck its last on me.

SOURCE: From the novel *Bread Givers* by Anzia Yezierska. Copyright © 1925 by Doubleday, copyright © 1952 by Anzia Yezierska, transferred to Louise Levitas Henriksen in 1970. Reprinted by permission of Persea Books, Inc.

Others had economic concerns. Native laborers were often incensed by the willingness of the immigrants to accept lower wages and to take over the jobs of strikers.

The rising nativism provoked political responses. In 1887, Henry Bowers, a self-educated lawyer obsessed with a hatred of Catholics and foreigners, founded the American Protective Association, a group committed to stopping immigration. By 1894, membership in the organization reportedly reached 500,000, with chapters throughout the Northeast and Midwest. That same year, a more genteel organization—the Immigration Restriction League—was founded in Boston by five Harvard alumni. It was dedicated to the belief that immigrants should be screened, through literacy tests and other standards designed to separate the "desirable" from the "undesirable."

Even before the rise of these new organizations, politicians were struggling to find answers to the "immigration question." In 1882 Congress responded to strong anti-Asian sentiment in California and elsewhere and excluded the Chinese, who had been arriving in large numbers on the West Coast and who, among other things, made up a significant portion of the work force building the Western railroads. In the same year, Congress denied entry to "undesirables"—convicts, paupers, the mentally incompetent—and placed a tax of 50 cents on each person admitted. Later legislation of the 1890s enlarged the list of those barred from immigrating and increased the tax.

But these laws kept out only a small number of aliens, and more ambitious restriction proposals made little progress in Congress. That was because many native-born Americans, far from fearing immigration, welcomed it and exerted strong political pressure against the restrictionists. Immigration was providing a cheap and plentiful labor supply to the rapidly growing economy; and many argued that America's industrial (and indeed agricultural) development would be impossible without it.

The Urban Landscape

The city was a place of remarkable contrasts. It had homes of almost unimaginable size and grandeur and hovels of indescribable squalor. It had conveniences unknown to earlier generations, and problems that seemed beyond the capacity of society to solve. Both the attractions and the problems were a result of the stunning pace with which cities were growing. The expansion of the urban population helped spur important new technological and industrial developments. But the rapid growth also produced mis-government, poverty, congestion, filth, epidemics, and great fires. The rate of growth was simply too fast for planning and building to keep pace.

One of the greatest problems was providing housing for the thousands of new residents who were pouring into the cities every day. For the prosperous, housing was seldom a worry. The availability of cheap labor and the increasing accessibility of tools and materials reduced the cost of building in the late nineteenth century and permitted anyone with even a moderate income to afford a house. Some of the richest urban residents lived in palatial mansions in the heart of the city. Many of the moderately well-to-do took advantage of less expensive land on the edges of the city and settled in new suburbs, linked to the downtowns by trains or streetcars.

Most urban residents, however, could not afford either to own a house in the city or to move to the suburbs. Instead, they stayed in the city centers and rented. And because demand was so high and space so scarce, they had little bargaining power. Landlords tried to squeeze as many rent-paying residents as possible into the smallest available space. In Manhattan, for example, the average population density in 1894 was 143 people per acre—a rate higher than that of the most crowded cities of Europe (Paris had 127 per acre, Berlin 101) and far higher than that of any other American city then or since. Landlords were also reluctant to invest much in immigrant housing; they were confident they could rent the dwellings they owned regardless of the conditions. In the cities of the South—Charleston, New Orleans, Richmond—poor blacks lived in crumbling former slave quarters. In Boston, immigrants moved into cheap three-story wooden houses ("triple deckers"), many of them decaying fire hazards. In Baltimore and Philadelphia, the new arrivals crowded into narrow brick row houses. And in New York and many other cities, they lived in tenements.

The word "tenement" had originally referred simply to a multiple-family rental building, but by the late nineteenth century it was used to describe slum dwellings only. The first tenements, built in 1850, had been hailed as a great improvement in housing for the poor. But most were, in fact, miserable places, with many windowless rooms, little or no plumbing or central heating, and perhaps a row of privies in the basement. Jacob Riis, a Danish immigrant and New York newspaper reporter and photographer, shocked many middle-class Americans with his sensational (and some would say sensationalized) descriptions and pictures of tenement life in his 1890 book, *How the Other Half Lives*. But the solution reformers often adopted was simply to raze slum dwellings without building any new housing to replace them.

A NEW YORK TENEMENT, 1910 This photograph of a woman and her children in a rear tenement bedroom was meant to illustrate the crowding and squalor of urban immigrant life. The photographer was Lewis Hine, who from 1907 to 1914 worked for a government committee investigating child labor and whose efforts to expose social conditions helped spur legislative action.

Urban growth posed monumental transportation challenges. Old downtown streets were often too narrow for the heavy traffic that was beginning to move over them. Most were without a hard, paved surface and resembled either a sea of mud or a cloud of dust, depending on the weather. But it was not simply the conditions of the streets that impeded urban transportation. It was the numbers of people who needed to move everyday from one part of the city to another, numbers that mandated the development of mass transportation. Streetcars drawn on tracks by horses had been introduced into some cities even before the Civil War. But the horsecars were not fast enough, so many communities developed new forms of mass transit. In 1870, New York opened its first elevated railway, whose noisy, filthy steam-powered trains moved rapidly above the city streets on massive iron structures. New York, Chicago, San Francisco, and other cities also experimented with cable cars, towed by continuously moving underground cables. Richmond, Virginia, introduced the first electric trolley line in 1888, and by 1895 such systems were operating in 850 towns and cities. Boston in 1897 opened the first American subway when it put some of its trolley lines underground. At the same time, cities were developing new techniques of road and bridge building. One of the great technological marvels of the 1880s was the completion of the Brooklyn Bridge in New York—a dramatic steel-cable suspension span designed by John A. Roebling.

Cities were growing upward as well as outward. In Chicago, the construction of the first modern "skyscraper"—by later standards a relatively modest building, ten stories high—launched a new era in urban architecture. Once builders perfected the technique of constructing tall buildings with cast iron and then steel beams, and once other inventors produced the electric elevator, no obstacle remained to even higher buildings.

Strains of Urban Life

The increasing congestion of the city and the absence of adequate public services produced serious hazards. One was fire. In one major city after another, fires destroyed large downtown areas. Chicago and Boston suffered "great fires" in 1871. Other cities—among them Baltimore and San Francisco, where a tremendous earthquake produced a catastrophic fire in 1906—experienced similar disasters. The great fires were terrible experiences, but they were also important events in the development of the cities involved. They encouraged the construction of fireproof buildings and the development of professional fire departments. They also forced cities to rebuild at a time when new technological and architectural innovations were available. Some of the modern, high-rise downtowns of American cities arose out of the rubble of great fires.

An even greater hazard than fire was disease, especially in poor neighborhoods with inadequate sanitation facilities. But an epidemic that began in a poor neighborhood could (and often did) spread easily into other neighborhoods as well. Few municipal officials recognized the relationship of improper sewage disposal and water contamination to such epidemic diseases as typhoid fever and cholera; and many cities lacked adequate systems for disposing of human waste until well into the twentieth century.

Above all, perhaps, the expansion of the city spawned widespread and often desperate poverty. Despite the rapid growth of urban economies, the sheer number of new residents ensured that many people would be unable to earn enough for a decent subsistence. Public agencies and private philanthropic organizations offered very limited relief. And they were generally dominated by middle-class people, who tended to believe that too much assistance would breed dependency and that poverty was the fault of the poor themselves. Some charitable societies—for example, the Salvation Army, which began operating in America in 1879, one year after it was founded in London—concentrated more on religious revivalism than on the relief of the homeless and hungry.

Poverty and crowding naturally bred crime and violence. Much of it was relatively petty, the work of pickpockets, con artists, swindlers, and petty thieves. But some was more dangerous. The American murder rate rose rapidly in the late nineteenth century (even as such rates were declining in Europe), from 25 murders for every million people in 1880 to over 100 by the end of the century. The rising crime rates encouraged many cities to develop larger and more professional police forces. But police forces themselves could spawn corruption and brutality, particularly since jobs on them were often filled through political patronage.

Americans and Europeans alike reacted to the city with marked ambivalence. It was a place of strong allure and great excitement. Yet it was also a place of alienating impersonality, of a new feeling of anonymity, of a different kind of work with which the individual could feel only limited identification. To some, it was also a place of degradation and exploitation. Theodore Dreiser's novel *Sister Carrie* (1900) exposed one troubling aspect of urban life: the plight of single women (like Dreiser's heroine, Carrie) who moved from the countryside into the city and found themselves without any means of support. Carrie first took an exhausting and ill-paying job in a Chicago shoe factory; then she drifted into a life of "sin," exploited by predatory men. Many women were experiencing in reality the dilemmas Carrie experienced in fiction. Living in conditions of extreme poverty and hardship, some moved into prostitution—which, degrading and dangerous as it was, produced a livelihood and a sense of community for desperate people.

The Machine and the Boss

Newly arrived immigrants, many of whom could not speak English, were much in need of institutions to help them adjust to American urban life. But they could expect little assistance from government or from middle-class philanthropic institutions. Some ethnic communities created their own self-help organizations. But for many residents of the inner cities, the principal source of assistance was the political "machine."

The urban machine was one of America's most distinctive political institutions. It owed its existence to the power vacuum that the chaotic growth of cities (and the very limited growth of governments) had created. It was also a product of the potential voting power of large immigrant communities. Any politician who could mobilize that power stood to gain enormous influence or public office. And so there emerged a group of "urban" bosses, themselves often of foreign birth or parentage. Many were Irish, because they spoke English and because some had previous political experience from the long Irish struggle against the English at home.

The principal function of the political boss was simple: to win votes for his organization. That meant winning the loyalty of his constituents. To do so, a boss might provide them with occasional relief—a basket of groceries or a bag of coal. He might step in to save those arrested for petty crimes from jail. When he could, he found work for the unemployed. Above all, he rewarded many of his followers with patronage: with jobs in city government or in such city agencies as the police (which the machine's elected officials often controlled); with jobs building or operating the new transit systems; and with opportunities to rise in the political organization itself.

Machines were also vehicles for making money. Politicians enriched themselves and their allies through various forms of graft and corruption. Some of it might be fairly open—what George Washington Plunkitt of New York's Tammany Hall called "honest graft." For example, a politician might discover in advance where a new road or streetcar line was to be built, buy an interest in the land near it, and profit when the city had to buy the land from him or when property values rose as a result of the construction. But there was also covert graft. Officials received kickbacks from contractors in exchange for contracts to build streets, sewers, public buildings, and other projects; and they sold franchises for the operation of such public utilities as street railways, waterworks, and electric light and power systems. The most famously corrupt city boss was William M. Tweed, boss of New York City's Tammany Hall in the 1860s and 1870s, whose extravagant use of public funds on projects that paid kickbacks to the organization finally landed him in jail in 1872. Middle-class critics cited corruption as the principal characteristic of the machine, but other things were at least as important. Political organizations were responsible for modernizing city infrastructures, for expanding the role of government, and for creating stability in a political and social climate that otherwise would have lacked a center.

Several factors made boss rule possible. One was the power of immigrant voters, who were less concerned with middle-class ideas of political morality than with obtaining the services that machines provided and reformers did not. Another was the link between the political organizations and many wealthy, prominent citizens who profited from their dealings with bosses and resisted efforts to overthrow them. Still others were the rising tax revenues in fast-growing cities and the enormous public expenditures on infrastructure projects, combined with the structural weakness of city governments, which had few established procedures for controlling the expenditures. Within the municipal government, no single official usually had decisive power or responsibility. Instead, authority was generally divided among many officeholders and was limited by the state legislature. The boss, by virtue of his control over his machine, formed an "invisible government" that provided an alternative to the inadequacy of the regular government.

The urban machine was not without competition. Reform groups frequently mobilized public outrage at the corruption of the bosses and often succeeded in driving machine politicians from office. Tammany, for example, saw its candidates for mayor and other high city offices lose almost as often as they won in the last decades of the nineteenth century. But the reform organizations typically lacked the permanence of the machine; and more often than not, their power faded after a few years. Thus, many critics of machines began to argue for more basic reforms: for structural changes in the nature of city government.

SOCIETY AND CULTURE IN URBANIZING AMERICA

For urban middle-class Americans, the last decades of the nineteenth century were a time of dramatic advances. Indeed, it was in those years that a distinctive middle-class culture began to exert a powerful influence over the whole of American life. Other groups in society advanced less rapidly, or not at all; but almost no one was unaffected by the rise of the new urban, consumer culture.

The Rise of Mass Consumption

The growth of American industry could not have occurred without the expansion of markets for the goods being produced. Much of the emerging mass market for industrial goods consisted of the increasingly wealthy middle class. But much of it also consisted of less affluent people who consumed more because mass production and mass distribution were making consumer goods less expensive.

Incomes were rising for almost everyone in the industrial era, although at highly uneven rates. The most conspicuous result of the new economy was the creation of vast fortunes, but perhaps the most important result for society as a whole was the growth and increasing prosperity of the middle class. The salaries of clerks, accountants, middle managers, and other "white-collar" workers rose by an average of a third between 1890 and 1910—and in some parts of the middle class, much higher. Doctors, lawyers, and other professionals, for example, experienced a particularly dramatic increase in both the prestige and the profitability of their professions. Working-class incomes rose too in those years, although from a much lower base and often more slowly. The iron and steel industries saw workers' hourly wages increase by a third between 1890 and 1910; but industries with large female work forces—shoes, textiles, and paper—saw more modest increases, as did almost all industries in the South.

Also important to the new mass market was the development of affordable products and the creation of new merchandising techniques, which made many consumer goods available to a mass market for the first time. A good example of such changes was the emergence of ready-made clothing. In the early nineteenth century, most Americans had made their own clothing—usually from cloth they bought from merchants, at times from fabrics they spun and wove themselves. The invention of the sewing machine and the spur that the Civil War (and its demand for uniforms) gave to the manufacture of clothing created an enormous industry devoted to producing ready-made garments. By the end of the century, virtually all Americans bought their clothing from stores. Partly as a result, much larger numbers of people became concerned with personal style. Interest in women's fashion, for example, had once been a luxury reserved for the relatively affluent. Now middle-class and even working-class women could strive to develop a distinctive style of dress.

Another example was the way Americans bought and prepared food. The development and mass production of tin cans in the 1880s created a large new industry devoted to packaging and selling canned food and

THE DEPARTMENT STORE, C. 1892 This detail from an advertisement shows an interior cross section of the Abraham and Straus department store in Brooklyn, New York. Early department stores boasted not just of the variety of their merchandise but also of the magical qualities of the consumer world they created.

condensed milk. Refrigerated railroad cars made it possible for perishables—meats, vegetables, dairy products, and other foodstuffs—to be transported over long distances without spoiling. The growth of artificially frozen ice made it possible for many more households to afford iceboxes. Among other things, the changes meant improved diets and better health. Life expectancy rose six years in the first two decades of the twentieth century.

Changes in marketing also altered the way Americans bought goods. Small local stores faced competition from new "chain stores." The Atlantic and Pacific Tea Company (the A & P) began a national network of grocery stores in the 1870s. F. W. Woolworth's built a chain of dry goods stores. Sears and Roebuck established a large market for its mail-order merchandise by distributing an enormous catalogue each year. Even people in remote rural areas could order its products.

In larger cities, the emergence of great department stores helped transform buying habits and turn shopping into a more alluring and glamorous activity. Marshall Field in Chicago created one of the first American department stores—a place deliberately designed to create a sense of wonder and excitement. Similar stores emerged in New York, Brooklyn, Boston, Philadelphia, and other cities.

The rise of mass consumption had particularly dramatic effects on American women, who were generally the primary consumers within families. Women's clothing styles changed much more rapidly and dramatically than those of men. Women generally bought and prepared food for their families, so the availability of new food products changed not only the way everyone ate but the way women shopped and cooked. Canning and refrigeration meant greater variety in the diet. It also meant that food did not always have to be purchased on the day it was eaten. The consumer economy also produced new employment opportunities for women as salesclerks in department stores and as waitresses in rapidly proliferating restaurants. And it spawned the creation of a new movement in which women were to play a vital role: the consumer protection movement. The National Consumers League, formed in the 1890s under the leadership of Florence Kelley, attempted to mobilize the power of women as consumers to force retailers and manufacturers to improve wages and working conditions.

Leisure and Sport

Closely related to the growth of consumption was a growing interest in leisure time, which for many people was increasing rapidly. Members of the urban middle and professional classes had large blocks of time in which they were not at work—evenings, weekends, even vacations. Working hours in many factories declined, from an average of nearly seventy hours a week in 1860 to under sixty in 1900. Even farmers found that the mechanization of agriculture gave them more free time. The lives of many Americans were becoming more compartmentalized, with clear distinctions between work and leisure that had not existed in the past. The change produced a search for new forms of recreation and entertainment.

Among the most important responses to this search was the rise of organized spectator sports, and especially baseball, which by the end of the century was well on its way to becoming the "national pastime." A game much like baseball—known as "rounders" and derived from cricket—had enjoyed limited popularity in Great Britain in the early nineteenth century. Versions of the game began to appear in America in the early 1830s, well before Abner Doubleday (who is erroneously believed to have invented baseball) laid out a diamond-shaped field in West Point, New York, in 1839 and attempted to standardize the rules.

By the end of the Civil War, interest in the game had grown rapidly. More than 200 amateur or semiprofessional teams or clubs existed, many of which joined a national association and proclaimed a set of standard rules. As the game grew in popularity, it offered opportunities for profit. The first salaried team, the Cincinnati Red Stockings, was formed in 1869. Other cities soon fielded professional teams, and in 1876 they banded together in the National League. A rival league, the American Association, soon appeared. It eventually collapsed, but in 1901 the American League emerged to replace it. And in 1903, the first modern World Series was played, in which the American League Boston Red Sox beat the National League Pittsburgh Pirates. By then, baseball had become an important business and a great national preoccupation (at least among men), attracting paying crowds at times as large as 50,000.

Baseball had great appeal to working-class males. The second most popular game, football, appealed at first to a more elite segment of the male population, in part because it originated in colleges and universities. The first intercollegiate football game in America occurred between Princeton and Rutgers in 1869, and soon the game began to become entrenched as part of collegiate life. Early intercollegiate football bore only an indirect relation to the modern game; it was more similar to what is now known as rugby. By the late 1870s, however, the game was becoming standardized and was taking on the outlines of its modern form. Basketball was invented in 1891 at Springfield, Massachusetts, by Dr. James A. Naismith, a Canadian working as athletic director for a local college. Boxing, which had long been a disreputable activity concentrated primarily among the urban lower classes, became by the 1880s a more popular and in some places more reputable sport.

The major spectator sports of the era were activities open almost exclusively to men. But a number of other sports were emerging in which women became important participants. Golf and tennis seldom attracted crowds in the late nineteenth century, but both experienced a rapid increase in participation among relatively wealthy men and women. Bicycling and croquet also enjoyed widespread popularity in the 1890s among women as well as men. Women's colleges were beginning to introduce their students to more strenuous sports as well—track, crew, swimming, and (beginning in the late 1890s) basketball—challenging the once-prevalent notion that vigorous exercise was dangerous to women.

Leisure and Popular Culture

Other forms of popular entertainment developed in the cities in response to the large potential markets there. Many ethnic communities maintained their own theaters, in which immigrants heard the music of their homelands and listened to comedians making light of their experiences in the New

World. Urban theaters also introduced some of the most distinctively American entertainment forms: the musical comedy, which evolved gradually from the comic operettas of European theater; and vaudeville, a form of theater adapted from French models, which remained the most popular urban entertainment in the first decades of the twentieth century. Even saloons and small community theaters could afford to offer their customers vaudeville, which consisted of a variety of acts (musicians, comedians, magicians, jugglers, and others) and was, at least in the beginning, inexpensive to produce. As the economic potential of vaudeville grew, some promoters—most prominently Florenz Ziegfeld of New York—staged much more elaborate spectacles.

Vaudeville was also one of the few entertainment media open to black performers. They brought to it elements of the minstrel shows they had earlier developed for black audiences in the late nineteenth century. Some minstrel singers (including the most famous, Al Jolson) were whites wearing heavy makeup (or "blackface"), but most were black. Entertainers of both races performed music based on the gospel and folk tunes of the plantation and on the jazz and ragtime of black urban communities. Performers of both

A NICKELODEON An early movie theater, with musicians providing a live accompaniment to a silent film. The first feature-length sound picture (or "talkie"), *The Jazz Singer*, appeared in 1927.

races also tailored their acts to prevailing white prejudices, ridiculing blacks by acting out demeaning stereotypes.

The most important form of mass entertainment (until the invention of radio and television), and the one that reached most widely across the nation, was the movies. Thomas Edison and others had created the technology of the motion picture in the 1880s. Soon after that, short films became available to individual viewers watching peepshows in pool halls, penny arcades, and amusement parks. Soon, larger projectors made it possible to project the images onto big screens, which permitted substantial audiences to see films in theaters. By 1900, Americans were becoming attracted in large numbers to these early movies—usually plotless films of trains or waterfalls or other spectacles designed mainly to show off the technology. The great D. W. Griffith carried the motion picture into a new era with his silent epics—*The Birth of a Nation* (1915), *Intolerance* (1916), and others—which introduced serious (if notoriously racist) plots and elaborate productions to filmmaking. Motion pictures were the first truly mass-entertainment medium—one that reached all areas of the country and almost all groups in the population.

Not all popular entertainment, however, involved public events. Many Americans amused themselves privately by reading novels and poetry. The so-called dime novels, cheaply bound and widely circulated, became popular after the Civil War, with tales of the Wild West, detective stories, sagas of scientific adventure (such as the Tom Swift stories), and novels of "moral uplift" (among them those of Horatio Alger). Publishers also distributed sentimental novels of romance, which developed a large audience among women, as did books about animals and about young children growing up. Louisa May Alcott's *Little Women*, most of whose readers were women, sold more than 2 million copies.

Mass Communications

Urban-industrial society required new vehicles for transmitting news and information. And so American publishing and journalism experienced an important change in the decades following the Civil War. Between 1870 and 1910, the circulation of daily newspapers increased nearly ninefold (from under 3 million to more than 24 million), a rate three times as great as the rate of population increase. And while standards varied widely from one paper to another, American journalism began to develop the beginnings of a professional identity. Salaries of reporters increased; many newspapers began separating the reporting of news from the expression of opinion; and newspapers themselves became important businesses.

One striking change was the emergence of national press services, which made use of the telegraph to supply papers throughout the country with news and features and which contributed, as a result, to the standardization of the product. By the turn of the century important newspaper chains had emerged as well. The most powerful was owned by William Randolph Hearst, who by 1914 controlled nine newspapers and two magazines. Hearst and rival publisher Joseph Pulitzer helped popularize what became known as "yellow journalism"—a deliberately sensational, even lurid, style of reporting presented in bold graphics, designed to reach a mass audience uninterested in the sober, detailed reporting of more traditional newspapers. Another major change occurred in the nature of American magazines. Beginning in the 1880s, a new kind of magazine appeared, designed to achieve a mass circulation. One of the pioneers in this field was Edward W. Bok, who took over the *Ladies' Home Journal* in 1899 and, by targeting a mass female audience, built the circulation of the journal to over 700,000.

HIGH CULTURE IN THE URBAN AGE

In addition to the important changes in popular culture that accompanied the rise of cities and industry, there were profound changes in the realm of "high culture"—in the ideas and activities of intellectuals and elites. Even the idea of a distinction between "highbrow" and "lowbrow" culture was new to the industrial era. In the early nineteenth century, most cultural activities attracted people of widely varying backgrounds and targeted people of all classes. By the late nineteenth century, however, elites were developing a cultural and intellectual life quite separate from the popular amusements of the urban masses.

The Literature of Urban America

Many foreign observers and even some Americans in the late nineteenth century viewed the culture of the United States with contempt. Critics claimed that American life, despite its glittering surface, was essentially acquisitive and corrupt, with little cultural depth. But whatever the quality of culture and society in late-nineteenth-century America, the growth of industry and the rise of the city were having profound effects on them. Some writers and artists—the local-color writers of the South, for example, and Mark Twain, in such novels as *Huckleberry Finn* and *Tom Sawyer*—responded to the new civilization by evoking an older, more natural world. But others grappled directly with the modern order.

One of the strongest impulses in late-nineteenth- and early-twentieth-century American literature was the effort to re-create urban social reality. This trend toward realism found an early voice in Stephen Crane, who—although best known for his novel of the Civil War, *The Red Badge of Courage* (1895)—was the author of an earlier, powerful indictment of the plight of the working class. Crane created a sensation in 1893 when he published *Maggie: A Girl of the Streets*, a grim picture of urban poverty and slum life. Theodore Dreiser, Frank Norris, and Upton Sinclair—whose 1906 novel, *The Jungle*, inspired federal legislation with its exposure of abuses in the meat-packing industry—were similarly drawn to social issues as themes. Kate Chopin, a Southern writer who explored the oppressive features of traditional marriage, encountered widespread public abuse (and in some places formal bans) after publication of her shocking novel *The Awakening* in 1899. It described a young wife and mother who abandoned her family in search of personal fulfillment. William Dean Howells, in *The Rise of Silas Lapham* and other works, described what he considered the shallowness and corruption in ordinary American life styles.

Other critics of American society responded to the new civilization not by attacking it but by withdrawing from it. The historian Henry Adams published an autobiography in 1906, *The Education of Henry Adams*, which portrayed a man disillusioned with and unable to relate to his society, even though he continued to live in it. The novelist Henry James lived the major part of his adult life in England and Europe and produced a series of coldly realistic novels—*The American* (1877), *Portrait of a Lady* (1881), *The Ambassadors* (1903), and others—that showed his ambivalence about the merits of both American and European civilization.

Art in the Age of the City

American art through most of the nineteenth century had been overshadowed by the art of Europe. By 1900, however, a number of American artists, although some continued to study and even live in Europe, broke from the Old World traditions and experimented with new styles. Winslow Homer was vigorously American in his paintings of New England maritime life and other native subjects. James McNeil Whistler was one of the first Western artists to appreciate the beauty of Japanese color prints and to introduce Oriental concepts into American and European art.

By the first years of the new century, some American artists were turning decisively away from the traditional academic style (a style perhaps best exemplified in America by the brilliant portraitist John Singer Sargent). Instead, many younger painters were exploring the same grim aspects of modern life that were becoming the subject of American literature. Members of the so-called Ashcan School produced work startling in its naturalism and stark in its portrayal of the social realities of the era. John Sloan portrayed the dreariness of American urban slums; George Bellows caught the vigor and violence of his time in paintings and drawings of prizefights; Edward Hopper explored the starkness and loneliness of the modern city. The Ashcan artists were also among the first Americans to appreciate expressionism and abstraction; and they showed their interest in new forms in 1913 when they helped stage the famous "Armory Show" in New York City, which displayed works of the French postimpressionists and of some American moderns.

The Impact of Darwinism

The single most profound intellectual development in the late nineteenth century was the widespread acceptance of the theory of evolution, associated most prominently with the English naturalist Charles Darwin. Darwinism argued that the human species had evolved from earlier forms of life (and most immediately from simian creatures similar to apes) through a process of "natural selection." It challenged almost every tenet of traditional religious faith. History, Darwinism suggested, was not the working out of a divine plan, as most Americans had always believed. It was a random process dominated by the fiercest or luckiest competitors.

The theory of evolution met widespread resistance at first from educators, theologians, and even many scientists. By the end of the century, however, the evolutionists had converted most members of the urban professional and educated classes. Even many middle-class Protestant religious leaders had accepted the doctrine, making significant alterations in theology to accommodate it. Evolution had become enshrined in schools and universities; virtually no serious scientist any longer questioned its basic validity. Unseen by most urban Americans at the time, however, the rise of Darwinism was contributing to a deep schism between the new, cosmopolitan culture of the city—which was receptive to new ideas such as evolution—and the more traditional, provincial culture of some rural areas—which remained wedded to fundamentalist religious beliefs and older values. Thus the late nineteenth century saw not only the rise of a liberal Protestantism in tune with new scientific discoveries. It also saw the beginning of an organized Protestant fundamentalism, which would make its presence felt politically in the 1920s and again in the 1980s.

Darwinism helped spawn other new intellectual currents. There was the Social Darwinism of William Graham Sumner and others, which industrialists used so enthusiastically to justify their favored position in American life. But there were also more sophisticated philosophies, among them a doctrine that became known as "pragmatism," which seemed peculiarly a product of America's changing material civilization. William James, a Harvard psychologist (and brother of the novelist Henry James), was the most prominent publicist of the new theory, although earlier intellectuals such as Charles S. Peirce and later ones such as John Dewey were also important to its development and dissemination. According to the pragmatists, modern society should rely for guidance not on inherited ideals and moral principles but on the test of scientific inquiry. No idea or institution (not even religious faith) was valid, they claimed, unless it worked, unless it stood the test of experience.

A similar concern for scientific inquiry was intruding into the social sciences and challenging traditional orthodoxies. Economists such as Richard T. Ely and Simon Patten argued for a more active and pragmatic use of the discipline. Sociologists such as Edward A. Ross and Lester Frank Ward urged applying the scientific method to the solution of social and political problems. Historians such as Frederick Jackson Turner and Charles Beard argued that economic factors more than spiritual ideals had been the governing force in historical development. John Dewey proposed a new approach to education that placed less emphasis on the rote learning of traditional knowledge and more on a flexible, democratic approach to schooling, one that enabled students to acquire knowledge that would help them deal with the realities of their society. The relativistic implications of Darwinism also promoted the growth of anthropology and encouraged some scholars to begin examining other cultures—most significantly, perhaps, the culture of American Indians—in new ways. Some white Americans began to look at Indian society as a coherent culture with its own norms and values that were worthy of respect and preservation, even though they were different from those of white society.

Toward Universal Schooling

A society that was coming to depend increasingly on specialized skills and scientific knowledge was, of course, a society with a high demand for education. The late nineteenth century, therefore, was a time of rapid expansion and reform of American schools and universities.

One example was the spread of free public primary and secondary education. In 1860, there were only 100 public high schools in the entire United States. By 1900, the number had reached 6,000 and by 1914 over 12,000. By 1900, compulsory school attendance laws were in effect in thirty-one states and territories. But education was still far from universal. Rural areas lagged far behind urban-industrial ones in funding public education. And in the South, blacks had very limited access to any schools at all.

Educational reformers sought to provide educational opportunities to the Indian tribes as well, in an effort to "civilize" them and help them adapt to white society. In the 1870s, reformers recruited small groups of Indians to attend Hampton Institute (a primarily black college). In 1879 they organized the Carlisle Indian Industrial School in Pennsylvania. Like many black colleges, Carlisle emphasized the kind of practical "industrial" education that Booker T. Washington had urged on blacks. Ultimately, however, these reform efforts failed, partly because of inadequate funding and commitment and partly because the venture itself—the effort to remove Indians from their traditional surroundings and transform them into members of white society—was unpopular with its intended beneficiaries.

Colleges and universities were also proliferating rapidly in the late nineteenth century. They benefited particularly from the Morrill Land Grant Act of the Civil War era, by which the federal government had donated land to states for the establishment of colleges. After 1865, states in the South and West took particular advantage of the law. In all, sixty-nine "land-grant" institutions were established in the last decades of the century—among them the state university systems of California, Illinois, Minnesota, and Wisconsin. Other universities benefited from millions of dollars contributed by business and financial tycoons. Rockefeller, Carnegie, and others gave generously to such schools as Columbia, Chicago, Harvard, Northwestern, Princeton, Syracuse, and Yale. Other philanthropists founded new universities or reorganized older ones and perpetuated their family names—Vanderbilt, Johns Hopkins, Cornell, Duke, Tulane, and Stanford.

Education for Women

The post–Civil War era saw, too, an important expansion of educational opportunities for women, although such opportunities continued to lag far behind those available to men and were almost without exception denied to black women.

Most public high schools accepted women readily, but opportunities for higher education were fewer. At the end of the Civil War, only three American colleges were coeducational. In the years after the war, many of the land-grant colleges and universities in the Midwest and such private universities as Cornell and Wesleyan began to admit women along with men. But coeducation was less crucial to women's education in this period than was the creation of a network of women's colleges. Mount Holyoke in central Massachusetts had begun its life in 1836 as a "seminary" for women;

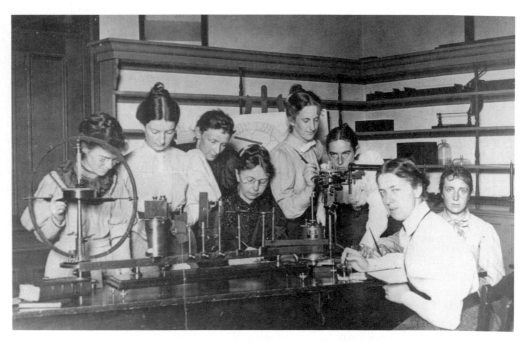

WELLESLEY COLLEGE STUDENTS IN PHYSICS CLASS Wellesley College, founded in 1870, was the first women's college in America to have scientific laboratories, including the physics lab shown here. Wellesley was one of a number of institutions founded shortly after the Civil War to give young women access to advanced education.

it became a full-fledged college in the 1880s, at about the same time that entirely new female institutions were emerging: Vassar, Wellesley, Smith, Bryn Mawr, Wells, and Goucher. A few of the larger private universities created separate colleges for women on their campuses (Barnard at Columbia and Radcliffe at Harvard, for example). Proponents of women's colleges saw the institutions as places where female students would not be treated as "second-class citizens" by predominantly male student bodies and faculties.

The female college was among the first examples of an important phenomenon in the history of modern American women: the emergence of a distinctive women's community. Most faculty members and many administrators were women (usually unmarried). And the life of the college produced a spirit of sorority and commitment among educated women that had important effects in later years, as women became the leaders of many reform activities. Most female college graduates ultimately married, but they married at a more advanced age than their noncollege counterparts. A significant minority, perhaps over 25 percent, did not marry at all, but devoted themselves to careers. The growth of female higher education clearly became for some women a liberating experience, persuading them that they had roles to perform in society other than as wives and mothers.

CHAPTER NINETEEN

From Stalemate to Crisis

The Politics of Equilibrium ～ *The Agrarian Revolt*
The Crisis of the 1890s

HE ENORMOUS CHANGES America was experiencing in the late nineteenth century strained not only the nation's traditional social arrangements but its political institutions as well. Economic growth brought both progress and disorder. And it was to government, gradually, that Americans began to look for leadership in their search for stability.

Yet American government during much of this period was ill equipped to deal with the new challenges confronting it. In the face of unprecedented dilemmas, it responded with apparent passivity and confusion. Its leaders, for the most part, seemed political mediocrities. The issues with which it was concerned generally had little to do with the nation's most important problems. Rather than taking active leadership of America's dramatic transformation, the American political system for nearly two decades after the end of Reconstruction (a period often called "the Gilded Age," a phrase used by Mark Twain) was locked in a rigid stalemate—watching the remarkable changes that were occurring in the nation and doing little to affect them. The result was a set of problems and grievances that festered and grew without any natural outlet. It was not surprising, under the circumstances, that in the 1890s the United States entered a period of national crisis.

THE POLITICS OF EQUILIBRIUM

To modern eyes, the nature of the American political system in the late nineteenth century appears in many ways paradoxical. The two political parties enjoyed a strength and stability during those years that neither was ever to know again. And yet the federal government, which the two parties were struggling to control, was doing little of importance. In fact, most Americans in those years engaged in political activity not because of an interest in particular issues but because of broad regional, ethnic, or religious sentiments. Party loyalty had less to do with positions on public policy than with the way Americans defined themselves culturally.

The Party System

The most striking feature of the late-nineteenth-century party system was its remarkable stability. From the end of Reconstruction until the late 1890s, the electorate was divided almost precisely evenly between the Republicans and the Democrats. Loyalties fluctuated almost not at all. Sixteen states were solidly and consistently Republican, and fourteen states (most of them in the South) were solidly and consistently Democratic. Only five states (the most important of them New York and Ohio) were usually in doubt; and it was in them that national elections were commonly decided, often on the basis of voter turnout. The Republican party captured the presidency in all but two of the elections of the era, but the party was not really as dominant as those victories suggest. In the five presidential elections beginning in 1876, the average popular-vote margin separating the Democratic and Republican candidates was 1.5 percent. The congressional balance was similarly stable. Between 1875 and 1895, the Republicans generally controlled the Senate and the Democrats generally controlled the House; in any given election, the number of seats that shifted from one party to the other was very small.

As striking as the balance between the parties was the intensity of public loyalty to them. In most of the country, Americans viewed their party affiliations with a passion and enthusiasm that is difficult for later generations to understand. Voter turnout in presidential elections between 1860 and 1900 averaged over 78 percent of all eligible voters (as compared with only slightly over 50 percent in the 1970s and 1980s). Even in nonpresidential years, from 60 to 80 percent of the voters turned out to cast ballots for congressional candidates. Large groups of potential voters were disfranchised in these years: women in most states; almost all blacks and many poor whites in the South. But for adult white males outside the South, there were few franchise restrictions. The remarkable turnout represented a genuinely mass-based politics.

Party politics in the late nineteenth century occupied a central position in American culture, comparable in some ways to the role that spectator sports and mass popular entertainment play today. Political campaigns were often the most important public events in the lives of communities. Political organizations served important social and cultural functions. Political identification was almost as important to most individuals as identification with a church or an ethnic group. Partisanship was an intense, emotional force, widely admired and often identified with patriotism.

What explains this remarkable loyalty to the two political parties? It was not, certainly, because the parties took distinct positions on important public issues. Party loyalties reflected other factors. Region was perhaps the most important. To white Southerners, loyalty to the Democratic party was a matter of unquestioned faith. It was the vehicle by which they had triumphed over Reconstruction, the vehicle by which they preserved white supremacy. To many old-stock Northerners, white and black, Republican loyalties were equally intense for the opposite reason. The party of Lincoln had freed the slaves and preserved the Union; it was a bulwark against slavery and treason.

Religious and ethnic differences also shaped party loyalties. The Democratic party attracted most of the Catholic voters, most of the recent immigrants, and most of the poorer workers; those three groups, of course, often overlapped. The Republican party appealed to Northern Protestants and citizens of old stock. Among the few substantive issues on which the parties took clearly different stands were matters concerning immigrants. The Republicans tended to be more nativist and to support measures restricting immigration. Republicans tended as well to favor temperance legislation. Catholics and immigrants viewed such proposals as an assault on their cultures and life styles and opposed them, and the Democratic party followed their lead.

Party identification, then, was usually more a reflection of cultural inclinations than a calculation of economic interest. Individuals might affiliate with a party because their parents had done so; or because it was the party of their region, their church, or their ethnic group. Most clung to their party loyalties with great persistence and passion.

Presidents and Patronage

One reason the two parties managed to avoid major conflicts over substantive issues was that the federal government (and for the most part state and local governments as well) did very little. There were few concrete policy issues over which to disagree. The leaders of both parties, therefore, were primarily concerned not with policy but with office—with winning elections and controlling patronage. Both parties were dominated by powerful bosses and machines chiefly concerned with controlling and dispensing jobs. The Democrats relied on the big city organizations (such as New York's Tammany Hall), which enabled them to mobilize the voting power of immigrants. The Republicans tended to depend on strong statewide organizations such as those of Roscoe Conkling in New York or Matt Quay of Pennsylvania.

The power of party bosses had an important effect on the power of the presidency. The office had great symbolic importance, but its occupants were unable to do very much except distribute government appointments. A new president had to make almost 100,000 appointments (most of them

PRESIDENT AND MRS. RUTHERFORD B. HAYES Hayes was one of a series of generally undistinguished late-nineteenth-century presidents whose subordination to the fiercely competitive party system left them with little room for independent leadership. This photograph captures the dignity and sobriety that Hayes and his wife sought to convey to the public.

in the post office, the only really large government agency); and to do that, he had to rely on a tiny staff working in a few rooms in the White House. Even in making appointments, presidents had limited latitude, since they had to avoid offending the various factions within their own parties.

Sometimes that proved impossible, as the presidency of Rutherford B. Hayes (1877–1881) demonstrated. By the end of his term, two groups—the Stalwarts, led by Roscoe Conkling of New York, and the Half-Breeds, captained by James G. Blaine of Maine—were competing for control of the Republican party and threatening to split it. The dispute between the Stalwarts and the Half-Breeds was characteristic of the political battles of the era. It had virtually no substantive foundation. Rhetorically, the Stalwarts favored traditional, professional machine politics, while the Half-Breeds favored reform. In fact, neither group was much interested in political change; each simply wanted a larger share of the patronage pie. Hayes tried to satisfy both and ended up satisfying neither.

The battle over patronage overshadowed all else during Hayes's unhappy presidency. His one important substantive initiative—an effort to create a civil-service system—attracted no support from either party. And his early announcement that he would not seek reelection only weakened him further. He had virtually no power in Congress. The Democrats controlled the House throughout his presidency and the Senate during the last two years of his term. And Senate Republicans, led by Roscoe Conkling, opposed his efforts to defy the machines in making appointments. (His popularity with politicians in Washington was not enhanced by the unwillingness of his wife, a temperance advocate widely known as "Lemonade Lucy," to permit alcoholic beverages to be served in the White House.) Hayes's presidency was a study in frustration.

The Republicans managed to retain the presidency in 1880 in part because of rising prosperity and in part because they managed to agree on a ticket that made it possible for the Stalwarts and the Half-Breeds briefly to paper over their differences. After a long convention deadlock, they nominated a "dark horse," James A. Garfield, a veteran congressman from Ohio and a Half-Breed; to conciliate the Stalwarts, the convention gave the vice presidential nomination to Chester A. Arthur of New York, a Conkling henchman. To oppose Garfield, the Democrats nominated General Winfield Scott Hancock, a minor Civil War commander with no national following. Benefiting from the end of the recession of 1879, Garfield won a decisive electoral victory, although his popular-vote margin was very thin. The Republicans also captured both houses of Congress.

Garfield began his presidency by trying to defy Conkling and the Stalwarts in his appointments and by showing support for civil-service reform. He soon found himself embroiled in an ugly public quarrel with both Conkling and Thomas Platt, the other senator from New York and another important Stalwart leader. But before it could be resolved, Garfield was victimized by the spoils system in a more terrible sense. On July 2, 1881, only four months after his inauguration, Garfield was shot twice while standing in the Washington railroad station by an apparently deranged gunman (and unsuccessful office seeker) who shouted, "I am a Stalwart and Arthur is president now!" Garfield lingered for nearly three months but finally died, a victim as much of bungled medical treatment as of the wounds themselves.

Chester A. Arthur, who succeeded Garfield, had spent a political lifetime as a devoted, skilled, and open spoilsman and a close ally of Roscoe Conkling. But on becoming president, he tried—like Hayes and Garfield before him—to follow an independent course and even to promote reform. He was undoubtedly influenced by the horrible circumstances that had brought him to the presidency and by his realization that the Garfield assassination had to some degree discredited the traditional spoils system.

The revelation of the "new" Arthur dismayed the party bosses. He kept most of Garfield's appointees in office. He also supported civil-service reform, aware that the legislation was likely to pass whether he supported it or not. In 1883, finally, Congress passed the first national civil-service measure, the Pendleton Act, which identified some federal jobs to be filled by competitive written examinations rather than by patronage. Relatively few offices fell under civil service at first, but its reach extended steadily so that by the mid-twentieth century most federal employees were civil servants.

The Return of the Democrats

The unsavory election of 1884 was typical of national political contests in the late nineteenth century for its emphasis on personalities rather than policies. The Republicans repudiated Arthur and chose instead their most popular and controversial figure, Senator James G. Blaine of Maine— known to his adoring admirers as "the Plumed Knight" but to thousands of other Americans as a symbol of seamy party politics. An independent reform faction, known derisively by their critics as the "mugwumps," announced they would bolt the party and support an honest Democrat.

Rising to the bait, the Democrats nominated Grover Cleveland, the "reform" governor of New York. He differed from Blaine on no substantive issues but had acquired a reputation as an enemy of corruption.

In a campaign filled with personal invective, what may have decided the election was the last-minute introduction of a religious controversy. Shortly before the election, a delegation of Protestant ministers called on Blaine in New York City; their spokesman, Dr. Samuel Burchard, referred to the Democrats as the party of "rum, Romanism, and rebellion." Blaine was slow to repudiate Burchard's indiscretion, and Democrats quickly spread the news that Blaine had tolerated a slander on the Catholic church. Cleveland's narrow victory was probably a result of an unusually heavy Catholic vote for the Democrats in New York. Cleveland won 219 electoral votes to Blaine's 182; his popular margin was only 23,000.

Grover Cleveland was respected, if not often liked, for his stern and righteous opposition to politicians, grafters, pressure groups, and Tammany Hall. He had become famous as the "veto governor," as an official who was not afraid to say no. He was the embodiment of an era in which few Americans believed the federal government could, or should, do very much. His administration was characterized from beginning to end by an unwavering commitment to economy in government.

Cleveland did grapple with one major economic issue. He had always doubted the wisdom of protective tariffs (taxes on imported goods designed to protect domestic producers). And he concluded finally that the existing high rates were responsible for the annual surplus in federal revenues, which was tempting Congress to pass the "reckless" and "extravagant" legislation he so frequently vetoed. In December 1887, therefore, he asked Congress to reduce the tariff rates. Democrats in the House approved a tariff reduction; but Senate Republicans defiantly passed a bill of their own actually raising the rates. The resulting deadlock made the tariff an issue in the election of 1888.

The Democrats renominated Cleveland and supported tariff reductions. The Republicans settled on former Senator Benjamin Harrison of Indiana, who was obscure but respectable (and the grandson of President William Henry Harrison); and they endorsed protection. The campaign was the first since the Civil War to involve a clear question of economic difference between the parties. It was also one of the most corrupt (and one of the closest) elections in American history. Harrison won an electoral majority of 233 to 168, but Cleveland's popular vote exceeded Harrison's by 100,000, making him, with Samuel Tilden, one of only two presidential candidates since the Civil War to win the popular vote and lose the election.

Emerging Issues

Benjamin Harrison's record as president was little more substantial than that of his grandfather, who had died a month after taking office. One reason for Harrison's failure was the intellectual drabness of the members of his administration—beginning with the president himself and extending through his cabinet. Another was Harrison's unwillingness to make any effort to influence Congress. And yet during Harrison's dreary administration, public opinion was beginning to force the government to confront some of the pressing social and economic issues of the day. Most notably, perhaps, sentiment was rising in favor of legislation to curb the power of trusts.

By the mid-1880s, fifteen Western and Southern states had adopted laws prohibiting combinations that restrained competition. But corporations found it easy to escape limitations by incorporating in states such as New Jersey and Delaware that offered them special privileges. If antitrust legislation was to be effective, it would have to come from the national government. Responding to growing popular demands, both houses of Congress passed the Sherman Antitrust Act in July 1890, almost without dissent. Most members of Congress saw the act as a largely symbolic measure, one that would help deflect public criticism but was not likely to have any real effect on corporate power.

For over a decade after its passage, the Sherman Act had virtually no impact. As of 1901, the Justice Department had instituted many antitrust suits against unions, but only fourteen against business combinations; there had been few convictions. The courts, meanwhile, weakened the bill considerably. In *United States* v. *E. C. Knight Co.* (1895), in which the government charged that a single trust controlled 98 percent of refined-sugar manufacturing in the country, the Supreme Court rejected the government's case. The sugar trust was engaged in manufacturing, not in interstate commerce, the Court declared; and so, despite its obviously monopolistic characteristics, it was not illegal—since the Sherman Act's only legal basis was the clause of the Constitution giving Congress the right to regulate interstate commerce.

The Republicans were more interested, however, in the issue they believed had won them the 1888 election: the tariff. Representative William McKinley of Ohio and Senator Nelson W. Aldrich of Rhode Island drafted the highest protective measure ever proposed to Congress. Known as the McKinley Act, it became law in October 1890. But Republican leaders apparently misinterpreted public sentiment, for the party suffered a stunning reversal in the 1890 congressional election. The Republicans' substantial Senate majority was slashed to 8; in the House, the party retained only 88 of the 323 seats. McKinley himself was among those who went down to defeat. Nor were the Republicans able to recover in the course of the next two years. In the presidential election of 1892, Benjamin Harrison once again supported protection; Grover Cleveland, renominated by the Democrats, once again opposed it. Only a new third party, the People's party, with James B. Weaver as its candidate, advocated any serious economic reform. Cleveland won 277 electoral votes to Harrison's 145 and had a popular margin of 380,000. Weaver ran far behind. For the first time since 1878, the Democrats won a majority of both houses of Congress.

The policies of Cleveland's second term were much like those of his first—devoted to minimal government and hostile to active state measures to deal with social or economic problems. But this time, a major economic crisis created popular demands for a more active government. For the most part, Cleveland resisted those pressures.

Again, he supported a tariff reduction, which the House approved but the Senate gutted. Cleveland denounced the result but allowed it to become law as the Wilson-Gorman Tariff. The bill threw one small crumb to agrarian interests: a small federal income tax (2 percent of incomes over $4,000). But the Supreme Court declared the new tax unconstitutional. Only after approval of the Sixteenth Amendment in 1913 was the federal government able to tax incomes. Public pressure was also growing in the 1880s for regulation of the railroads. Farm organizations in the Midwest (most notably the Grangers) had persuaded several state legislatures to pass regulatory legislation in the early 1870s. But in 1886, the Supreme Court—in *Wabash, St. Louis, and Pacific Railway Co.* v. *Illinois*, known as the *Wabash* case—ruled one of the Granger Laws in Illinois unconstitutional, holding that it was an attempt to control interstate commerce that infringed on the exclusive power of Congress. Later, the courts limited the powers of the states to regulate commerce even within their own boundaries.

Railroad regulation, it was now clear, could come only from the federal government. Congress grudgingly responded to public pressure in 1887 with the Interstate Commerce Act, which banned discrimination in rates between long and short hauls, required that railroads publish their rate schedules and file them with the government, and declared that all interstate rail rates must be "reasonable and just"—although the act did not define what that meant. A five-person agency, the Interstate Commerce Commission (ICC), was to administer the act. But it had to rely on the courts to enforce its rulings. For almost twenty years after its passage, the Interstate Commerce Act—haphazardly enforced and narrowly interpreted by the courts—was without practical effect.

The agitation over the tariff, the trusts, and the railroads was a sign that the dramatic changes in the American economy were creating problems that much of the public considered too important and dangerous to ignore. But the federal government's response to that agitation reflected the continuing weakness of the American state. The government still lacked institutions adequate to perform any significant role in American economic life. And American politics still lacked an ideology sufficient to justify any major expansion of government responsibilities. The effort to create such institutions and to produce such an ideology would occupy much of American public life in the coming decades. And it became visible first in a dramatic dissident movement that shattered the political equilibrium that the nation had experienced for the previous twenty years.

THE AGRARIAN REVOLT

No group watched the performance of the federal government in the 1880s with more dismay than American farmers. Isolated from the urban-industrial society that was beginning to dominate national life, suffering from a long, painful economic decline, afflicted with a sense of obsolescence, rural Americans were keenly aware of the problems of the modern economy and particularly eager for government assistance in dealing with them. The result was the emergence of one of the most powerful movements of political protest in American history: what became known as Populism.

The Grangers

Farmers had been making efforts to organize politically for several decades before the 1880s. The first major farm organization had its origins shortly after the Civil War in a tour through the South by a minor Agriculture Department official, Oliver H. Kelley, who became appalled by what he considered the isolation and drabness of rural life. In 1867 he left the government and helped found the National Grange of the Patrons of Husbandry, from which emerged a network of local organizations. At first, the Granges simply tried to teach new scientific agricultural techniques and attempted to create a feeling of community, to relieve the loneliness of rural life. But when the depression of 1873 caused a sharp decline in farm prices, membership rapidly increased and the direction of the organization changed. Granges in the Midwest began to organize marketing cooperatives, which would allow farmers to circumvent the hated middlemen. And they promoted political action to curb the monopolistic practices of the railroads and warehouses.

The Grangers succeeded for a time both in creating an impressive network of farm cooperatives and in putting effective pressure on state legislatures. At their peak, their supporters controlled the legislatures in most of the Midwestern states. The result was the Granger Laws of the early 1870s, by which many states imposed strict regulations on railroad rates and practices. But the destruction of the new regulations by the courts, combined with the political inexperience of many Grange leaders and the return

"THE GRANGE AWAKENING THE SLEEPERS" This 1873 cartoon suggests the way the Grange embraced many of the same concerns that the Farmers' Alliances and their People's party later expressed. A farmer is attempting to arouse passive citizens (lying in place of the "sleepers," or cross ties on railroad tracks).

of prosperity in the late 1870s, produced a dramatic decline in the power of the association by the end of the decade.

The Alliances

The successor to the Granges as the leading vehicle of agrarian protest began to emerge even before the Granger movement had faded. As early as 1875, farmers in parts of the South (most notably in Texas) were banding together in so-called Farmers' Alliances. By 1880, the Southern Alliance had more than 4 million members; and a comparable Northwestern Alliance was taking root in the plains states and the Midwest and developing ties with its Southern counterpart.

Like the Granges, the Alliances formed cooperatives and other marketing mechanisms. They established stores, banks, processing plants, and other facilities for their members—to free them from dependence on the hated "furnishing merchants" who kept so many farmers in debt. Some Alliance leaders, however, saw the movement in larger terms: as an effort to build a new society in which economic competition might give way to cooperation—not a rigid collectivism but a sense of mutual, neighborly responsibility that would enable farmers to resist oppressive outside forces. Alliance lecturers traveled throughout rural areas lambasting the concentration of power in the hands of a few great corporations and financial institutions.

Although the Alliances quickly became far more widespread than the Granges had ever been, they suffered from similar problems. Their cooperatives did not always work well, partly because the market forces operating against them were sometimes too strong to be overcome and partly because the cooperatives themselves were often mismanaged. These economic frustrations helped push the movement into a new phase at the end of the 1880s: the creation of a national political organization.

In 1889, the Southern and Northwestern Alliances, despite continuing differences between them, agreed to a loose merger. The next year the Alliances held a national convention at Ocala, Florida, and issued the so-called Ocala Demands, which were, in effect, a party platform. In the 1890 off-year elections, candidates supported by the Alliances won partial or complete control of the legislatures in twelve states. They also won six governorships, three seats in the Senate, and approximately fifty in the House of Representatives. Many of the successful Alliance candidates were simply Democrats who had benefited—often passively—from Alliance endorsements. But dissident farmers drew enough encouragement from the results to contemplate further political action, including forming a party of their own.

Plans for a third party were discussed at meetings in Cincinnati in May 1891 and St. Louis in February 1892—meetings attended by many Northern Alliance members, a smaller but still significant number of Southern Alliance leaders, and representatives of the fading Knights of Labor, whom some farm leaders hoped to bring into the coalition. Then, in July 1892, 1,300 exultant delegates poured into Omaha, Nebraska, to proclaim the creation of the new party, approve an official set of principles, and nominate candidates for the presidency and vice presidency. The new organization's official name was the People's party, but the movement was more commonly referred to as Populism.

The election of 1892 demonstrated the potential power of the new movement. The Populist presidential candidate—James B. Weaver of Iowa, a former Greenbacker—polled more than 1 million votes, 8.5 percent of the total, and carried six mountain and plains states for 22 electoral votes. Nearly 1,500 Populist candidates won election to state legislatures and local offices. The party elected three governors, five senators, and ten congressmen. It could also claim the support of many Republicans and Democrats in Congress who had been elected by appealing to Populist sentiment.

The Populist Constituency

Already, however, there were signs of the limits of Populist strength. Populism had great appeal to farmers, and particularly to small farmers with little long-range economic security—people whose operations were only minimally mechanized, if at all, who relied on one crop, and who had access only to limited and unsatisfactory mechanisms of credit. But Populism failed to move much beyond that group. There were energetic efforts to include labor within the coalition. Representatives of the Knights of Labor attended early organizational meetings; the new party added a labor plank to its platform—calling for shorter hours for workers and restrictions on immigration and denouncing the use of private detective agencies as strikebreakers in labor disputes. But Populism never attracted any substantial labor support, in part because the economic interests of labor and the interests of farmers were often at odds.

In the South in particular, white Populists struggled with the question of accepting African-Americans in the party, since their numbers and their poverty made them possibly valuable allies. And indeed there was an important black component to the movement—a network of "Colored Alliances" that by 1890 numbered over 1.25 million members. But most white Populists were willing to accept the assistance of blacks only as long as it was clear that whites would remain indisputably in control. When Southern conservatives began to attack the Populists for undermining white supremacy, the interracial character of the movement quickly faded.

Populist Ideas

The reform program of the Populists was spelled out first in the Ocala Demands of 1890 and then, even more clearly, in the Omaha platform of 1892. It proposed a system of "subtreasuries," which would replace and strengthen the cooperatives with which the Granges and Alliances had been experimenting for years. The government would establish a network of warehouses, where farmers could deposit their crops. Using those crops as collateral, growers could then borrow money from the government at low rates of interest and wait for the price of their goods to go up before selling them. In addition, the Populists called for the abolition of national banks, which they believed were dangerous institutions of concentrated power; the end of absentee ownership of land; the direct election of United States senators (which would weaken the power of conservative state legislatures); and other devices to improve the ability of the people to influence the political process. They called as well for regulation and (after 1892) government ownership of railroads, telephones, and telegraphs. And they demanded a system of government-operated postal savings banks, a graduated income tax, the inflation of the currency, and, later, the remonetization of silver.

Some Populists were openly anti-Semitic. Others were anti-intellectual, anti-Eastern, and antiurban. Yet the occasional bigotry of some Populists should not be allowed to dominate the image of Populism as a whole, which was a serious and usually responsible effort to find solutions to real problems. Populists emphatically rejected the laissez-faire orthodoxies of their time, the idea that the rights of ownership are absolute. They raised one of the most overt and powerful challenges of the era to the direction in which American industrial capitalism was moving. Populism was less a challenge to industrialization or to capitalism itself than a response to what the Populists considered the brutal and chaotic way in which the economy was developing. Progress and growth should continue, they urged, but it should be strictly defined by the needs of individuals and communities.

THE CRISIS OF THE 1890s

The agrarian protest was only one of many indications of the national political crisis emerging in the 1890s. There was a severe depression, which began in 1893. There was widespread labor unrest and violence, culminating in the tumultuous strikes of 1894. There was the continuing failure of either major party to respond to the growing distress. And there was the rigid conservatism of Grover Cleveland, who took office for the second time just at the moment that the economy collapsed. Out of this growing sense of crisis came some of the most heated political battles in American history, culminating in the dramatic campaign of 1896, on which, many Americans came to believe, the future of the nation hung.

The Panic of 1893

The Panic of 1893 precipitated the most severe depression the nation had ever experienced. It began in March 1893, when the Philadelphia and Reading Railroads declared bankruptcy, unable to meet demands for payment by British banks from whom they had borrowed large sums. Two months later, the National Cordage Company failed as well. Together, the two corporate failures triggered a collapse of the stock market. And since many of the major New York banks were heavy investors in the market, a wave of bank failures soon began. That caused a contraction of credit, which meant that many of the new, aggressive businesses that had recently begun operations soon went bankrupt because they were unable to secure the loans they needed. There were other, longer-range causes of the financial collapse. Depressed prices in agriculture since 1887 had weakened the purchasing power of farmers, the largest group in the population. Depression conditions that had begun earlier in Europe were resulting in a loss of American markets abroad and a withdrawal by foreign investors of gold invested in the United States. Railroads and other major industries had expanded far too rapidly, well beyond market demand.

The depression reflected, too, the degree to which all parts of the American economy were now interconnected, the degree to which failures in one area affected all other areas. And the depression showed how dependent the economy was on the health of the railroads, which remained the nation's most powerful corporate and financial institutions. When the railroads suffered, as they did beginning in 1893, everything suffered.

Once the panic began, its effects spread with startling speed. Within six months, more than 8,000 businesses, 156 railroads, and 400 banks failed. Already low agricultural prices tumbled further. Up to 1 million workers, 20 percent of the labor force, lost their jobs—the highest level of unemployment in American history to that point, a level comparable to that of the Great Depression of the 1930s. The depression was unprecedented not only in its severity but also in its persistence. Although there was slight improvement beginning in 1895, prosperity did not fully return until after 1898.

The suffering the depression caused naturally produced social unrest, not least among the enormous numbers of unemployed workers. In 1894, Jacob S. Coxey, an Ohio businessman and Populist, began advocating an inflation of the currency and a massive public works program to create jobs for the unemployed. When it became clear that his proposals were making no progress in Congress, Coxey organized a march of the unemployed (known as "Coxey's Army") to Washington to present his demands to the government. Congress took no action on the demands.

COXEY'S ARMY Jacob S. Coxey's "army" of the unemployed marches toward Washington in 1894 to demand relief from the federal government. Although several thousand people started out from various parts of the country to join the army, only about 400 actually reached the Capitol. The protest disbanded after Coxey and several others were arrested for "trespassing" on the grounds of the United States Capitol.

There were major labor upheavals as well during the decade—of which the Homestead and Pullman strikes were only the most prominent examples. (See pp. 482–485.) To many middle-class Americans, the worker unrest was a sign of a dangerous social instability, even perhaps a revolution. Labor radicalism—some of it real, much of it imagined by the frightened middle class—was seldom far from the public mind, heightening the general sense of crisis.

The Silver Question

The financial panic weakened the nation's monetary system, and in the minds of many conservatives, among them President Cleveland, the instability of the currency was the primary cause of the depression. The "money question" became the basis for some of the most dramatic political conflicts of the era.

The currency issue is a complicated and confusing one, and it has often been difficult for later generations to understand the enormous passions the controversy aroused. The heart of the debate was over what would form the basis of the dollar, what would lie behind it and give it value. Today, the value of the dollar rests on little more than public confidence in the government. But in the nineteenth century, currency was assumed to be worthless if there was not something concrete behind it—precious metal (specie), which holders of paper money could collect if they presented their currency to a bank or to the Treasury.

During most of its existence as a nation, the United States had recognized two metals—gold and silver—as a basis for the dollar, a formula known as "bimetallism." In the 1870s, however, that had changed. The official ratio of the value of silver to the value of gold for purposes of creating currency (the "mint ratio") was 16 to 1: sixteen ounces of silver equaled one ounce of gold. But the actual commercial value of silver (the "market ratio") was much higher than that. Owners of silver could get more by selling it for manufacture into jewelry and other objects than they could by taking it to the mint for conversion to coins. So they stopped taking it to the mint, and the mint stopped coining silver.

In 1873, Congress passed a law that seemed simply to recognize the existing situation by officially discontinuing silver coinage. Few objected at the time. But later in the 1870s, the market value of silver fell well below the official mint ratio of 16 to 1. (Sixteen ounces of silver, in other words, were now worth *less*, not more, than one ounce of gold.) Silver was suddenly available for coinage again, and it soon became clear that Congress had foreclosed a potential method of expanding the currency. Before long, many Americans concluded that a conspiracy of big bankers had been responsible for the "demonetization" of silver and referred to the law as the "Crime of '73."

Two groups of Americans were especially determined to undo the "Crime of '73." One consisted of the silver-mine owners, now understandably eager to have the government take their surplus silver and pay them much more than the market price. The other group consisted of discontented farmers, who wanted an increase in the quantity of money—an inflation of the currency—as a means of raising the prices of farm products and easing payment of the farmers' debts. The inflationists demanded that the government return at once to "free silver"—that is, to the "free and unlimited coinage of silver" at the old ratio of 16 to 1. But by the time the depression began in 1893, Congress had made no more than a token response to their demands.

At the same time, the nation's gold reserves were steadily dropping. And the Panic of 1893 intensified the demands on those reserves. President Cleveland believed that the chief cause of the weakening gold reserves was the Sherman Silver Purchase Act of 1893, which had required that the government purchase (but not coin) silver and pay for it in gold. Early in his second administration, therefore, a special session responded to his request and repealed the Sherman Act—although only after a bitter and divisive battle that helped create a permanent split in the Democratic party. The president's gold policy had aligned the Southern and Western Democrats in a solid phalanx against him and his Eastern followers.

By now, both sides had invested the currency question with great symbolic and emotional importance. Supporters of the gold standard considered its survival essential to the honor and stability of the nation. Because the supply of gold was limited, a gold-based currency would be assured of stable, long-term value. Supporters of free silver considered the gold standard an instrument of tyranny and silver an instrument of liberation. The issue aroused widespread passions rarely seen in American politics, culminating in the tumultuous presidential election of 1896.

"A Cross of Gold"

Republicans, watching the failure of Cleveland and the Democrats to deal effectively with the depression, were confident of success in 1896. Party leaders, led by the Ohio boss Marcus A. Hanna, settled on former Senator

William McKinley, author of the 1890 tariff act and now governor of Ohio, as the party's presidential candidate. The Republican platform opposed the free coinage of silver except by agreement with the leading commercial nations (which everyone realized was unlikely). Thirty-four delegates from the mountain and plains states walked out in protest and joined the Democratic party.

The Democratic convention of 1896 was the scene of unusual drama. Southern and Western delegates, eager to fight off the challenge of the People's party, were determined to seize control of the party from conservative Easterners and incorporate some Populist demands—among them free silver—into the Democratic platform. They wanted as well to nominate a prosilver candidate. The divided platform committee presented two reports to the convention. The majority report, the work of Westerners and Southerners, called for tariff reduction, an income tax, "stricter control" of trusts and railroads, and—most prominently—free silver. The minority report, the product of the party's Eastern wing, echoed the Republican platform by opposing the free coinage of silver except by international agreement. The debate over the two competing platforms dominated the convention.

Defenders of the gold standard seemed to prevail in the debate, until the final speech. Then William Jennings Bryan, a handsome, thirty-six-year-old congressman from Nebraska, already well known as an effective orator, mounted the podium to address the convention. His great voice echoed through the hall as he delivered a defense of free silver that became one of the most famous political speeches in American history. The closing passage sent his audience into something close to a frenzy: "If they dare to come out in the open and defend the gold standard as a good thing, we will fight them to the uttermost. Having behind us the producing masses of this nation and the world, supported by the commercial interests, the laboring interests and the toilers everywhere, we will answer their demand for a gold standard by saying to them: 'You shall not press down upon the brow of labor this crown of thorns; you shall not crucify mankind upon a cross of gold.'" It became known as the "Cross of Gold" speech.

The convention voted to adopt the prosilver platform. Perhaps more important, the agrarians had found a leader. The following day, Bryan (as he had eagerly, and not entirely secretly, hoped) was nominated for president on the fifth ballot. He remains the youngest man ever nominated for president by a major party.

The choice of Bryan and the nature of the Democratic platform created a quandary for the Populists. They had expected both major parties to adopt

WILLIAM JENNINGS BRYAN Bryan addresses a crowd late in his career,
displaying the flamboyant oratorical style that characterized his public
life from the beginning. The poster at the lower left of the platform
shows him as he appeared in the 1890s, when, as a young congressman
from Nebraska, he became known as the "Boy Orator of the Platte"
and the leader of the national free-silver movement.

conservative programs and nominate conservative candidates, leaving the
Populists to represent the growing forces of protest. But now the Democrats had stolen much of their thunder. The Populists faced the choice of
naming their own candidate and splitting the protest vote or endorsing
Bryan and losing their identity as a party. The Populists had embraced the
free-silver cause, but they supported it somewhat reluctantly, convinced
that other issues remained more important. Many Populists argued that
"fusion" with the Democrats—who had endorsed free silver but ignored the
other, more important Populist demands—would destroy their party. But
the majority concluded that there was no viable alternative. Amid considerable acrimony, the convention voted to support Bryan. In a feeble effort to
maintain their independence, the Populists repudiated the Democratic
nominee for vice president and chose their own, Tom Watson of Georgia.

The Conservative Victory

The campaign of 1896 produced desperation among conservatives. The
business and financial community, frightened beyond reason at the prospect
of a Bryan victory, contributed lavishly to the Republican campaign, which

may have spent as much as $7 million, as compared with the Democrats' $300,000. From his home at Canton, Ohio, McKinley conducted a dignified "front-porch" campaign before pilgrimages of the Republican faithful, customary behavior in an age when many Americans considered it undignified to campaign too openly for the presidency.

Bryan showed no such restraint. He became the first presidential candidate in American history to stump the country systematically, to appear in villages and hamlets—indeed, the first to say frankly to the voters that he wanted to be president. He traveled 18,000 miles (mostly in the West and South) and addressed an estimated 5 million people. But Bryan may have done himself more harm than good. His revivalistic, camp-meeting style pleased old-stock Protestants, but it alienated many of the immigrant Catholics and other ethnics who normally voted Democratic. Employers, meanwhile, warned workers that a Bryan victory would cost them their jobs, thus intimidating many traditional Democrats into supporting McKinley or not voting at all.

On election day, McKinley polled 271 electoral votes to Bryan's 176 and received 51.1 percent of the popular vote to Bryan's 47.7. Bryan carried only those areas of the South and West where miners or struggling staple farmers predominated. The Democratic program, like that of the Populists, had been too narrow to win a national election.

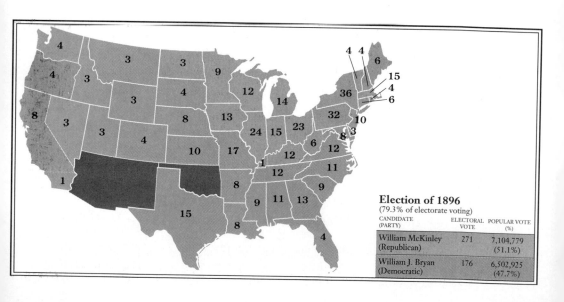

Election of 1896
(79.3% of electorate voting)

CANDIDATE (PARTY)	ELECTORAL VOTE	POPULAR VOTE (%)
William McKinley (Republican)	271	7,104,779 (51.1%)
William J. Bryan (Democratic)	176	6,502,925 (47.7%)

For the Populists and their allies, the election results were a disaster. They had gambled everything on their "fusion" with the Democratic party and lost. Within months of the election, the People's party began to dissolve. Never again would American farmers unite so militantly to demand economic reform. And never again would so large a group of Americans raise so forceful a protest against the nature of the industrial economy.

McKinley and Prosperity

The administration of William McKinley, which began in the aftermath of turmoil, saw a return to relative calm. One reason was the exhaustion of dissent. By 1897, when McKinley took office, the labor unrest that had so frightened many middle-class Americans and so excited working-class people had subsided. With the simultaneous decline of agrarian protest, two of the greatest destabilizing forces in the nation's politics were—temporarily at least—removed. Another reason was the character of the McKinley administration itself, which was politically shrewd and committed to a reassuring stability. Most important, however, was the gradual easing of the economic crisis, a change that undercut the appeal of many of those who were agitating for change.

McKinley and his allies committed themselves fully to only one issue, one on which they knew virtually all Republicans were agreed: the need for higher tariff rates. Within weeks of McKinley's inauguration, the administration won approval of the Dingley Tariff, raising duties to the highest point in American history. The administration dealt more gingerly with the explosive silver question (an issue McKinley himself had never considered very important in any case). McKinley sent a commission to Europe to explore the possibility of a silver agreement with Great Britain and France. As he and everyone else anticipated, the effort produced no agreement. The Republicans then enacted the Currency, or Gold Standard, Act of 1900, which confirmed the nation's commitment to the gold standard.

And so the "battle of the standards" ended in victory for the forces of conservatism. Economic developments at the time seemed to vindicate them. Prosperity returned beginning in 1898. Foreign crop failures sent U.S. farm prices surging upward, and American business entered another cycle of booming expansion. Prosperity and the gold standard, it seemed, were closely allied.

But while the free-silver movement had failed, it had raised an important question for the American economy. In the quarter-century before

1900, the countries of the Western world had experienced a spectacular growth in productive facilities and population. Yet the supply of money had not kept pace with economic progress, because the supply was tied to gold and the amount of gold had remained practically constant. Had it not been for a dramatic increase in the gold supply in the late 1890s (a result of new techniques for extracting gold from low-content ores and the discovery of huge new gold deposits in Alaska, South Africa, and Australia), Populist predictions of financial disaster might in fact have proved correct. In 1898, two and a half times as much gold was produced as in 1890, and the currency supply was soon inflated far beyond anything Bryan and the free-silver forces had proposed.

By then, however, Bryan—like many other Americans—was becoming engaged with another major issue: a growing United States presence in world affairs and the possibility of America becoming an imperialist nation.

DEBATING THE PAST

Populism

T HE SCHOLARLY DEBATES over the nature of Populism have tended to reflect a larger debate over the nature of popular mass movements. To some historians, mass uprisings seem dangerous and potentially antidemocratic; and to them, the Populist movement has usually appeared ominous. To others, such insurgency is evidence of a healthy democratic resistance to oppression; and to them, Populism has generally seemed more appealing.

The latter view shaped the first, and for many years the only, general history of Populism: John D. Hicks's *The Populist Revolt* (1931). Reflecting the influence of Frederick Jackson Turner, Hicks portrayed Populism as an expression of the healthy, democratic sentiments of the West. Populists were reacting rationally and constructively to the harsh impact of Eastern industrial growth on agrarian society, and they were proposing potentially valuable reforms to restrict the power of the new financial titans. Populism was, he wrote, "the last phase of a long and perhaps a losing struggle—the struggle to save agricultural America from the devouring jaws of industrial America."

In the early 1950s, scholars sensitive to the nature of European fascism and contemporary communism took a more suspicious view of mass popular politics and a more hostile view of Populism. The leading figure in this reinterpretation was Richard Hofstadter. In *The Age of Reform* (1955), he conceded that the Populists had genuine grievances and advanced some sensible reforms. But he concentrated on revealing what he called the "soft" and "dark" sides of the movement. Populism, Hofstadter claimed, rested on a romanticized and obsolete vision of the role of farmers in American society. And it was permeated with bigotry and ignorance.

Hofstadter's harsh portrait inspired a series of spirited challenges. Norman Pollack, beginning in 1962, argued that the agrarian revolt rested

(continued on next page)

not on nostalgic and romantic concepts but on a sophisticated and even radical vision of reform. A year later, Walter T. K. Nugent attempted to show that Populists were not bigoted, that they not only tolerated but welcomed Jews and other minorities into their party. And in 1976, Lawrence Goodwyn published *Democratic Promise*, the first full-scale history of the Populist movement since Hicks's study forty-five years earlier. Goodwyn described Populism as a "cooperative crusade," battling against the "coercive potential of the emerging corporate state." It was offering a genuine alternative to the inequities of modern, corporate capitalism; and it was promoting that alternative by developing an intensely democratic popular movement.

At the same time that historians were debating the meaning of Populism, they were also arguing over who the Populists were. Hicks, Hofstadter, and Goodwyn, for all their many disagreements, shared a belief that Populists were victims of economic distress—usually one-crop farmers in economically marginal regions victimized by drought and debt. Others, however, have suggested that this description is, if not wrong, at least inadequate. Sheldon Hackney maintained in 1969 that Populists in Alabama were not only economically troubled but socially rootless, "only tenuously connected to society by economic function, by personal relationships, by stable community membership, by political participation, or by psychological identification with the South's distinctive myths." Peter Argersinger, Stanley Parsons, James Turner, and others have similarly suggested that Populists tended to be people who were socially and even geographically isolated. Steven Hahn's 1983 study *The Roots of Southern Populism* described the poor farmers of "upcountry" Georgia who became Populists as people almost entirely unconnected to the modern capitalist economy. They were reacting not simply to the distress of being "left behind," but also to a real economic threat to their way of life from the intrusion into their world of a new commercial order of which they were not a part and from which they were unlikely to benefit.

There has, finally, been continuing disagreement over whether Populism has survived into the twentieth century—whether it is part of an enduring political language used by such later popular leaders as Huey Long, George Wallace, or even Ross Perot, or whether the idea of Populism has meaning only in reference to the insurgents of the 1890s.

CHAPTER TWENTY

The Imperial Republic

Stirrings of Imperialism ~ War with Spain
The Republic As Empire

HE AMERICAN REPUBLIC had been an expansionist nation since the earliest days of its existence. Throughout the first half of the nineteenth century, as the population of the United States grew and pressed westward, the government, through purchase or conquest, had continually acquired new lands: the trans-Appalachian West, the Louisiana Territory, Florida, Texas, Oregon, California, New Mexico, Alaska. It was the nation's "Manifest Destiny," many Americans believed, to expand into new realms.

In the last years of the nineteenth century, with little room left for territorial growth on the North American continent, expansionism moved into a new phase. In the past, the nation had generally annexed land adjacent to its existing boundaries; American citizens could move there relatively easily, and the new lands could ultimately become states of the Union. But the expansionism of the 1890s, the new Manifest Destiny, involved acquiring possessions separate from the continental United States: distant island territories, many thickly populated, most of which were unlikely to attract massive settlement from America, few of which were expected to become states of the Union. The United States was joining England, France, Germany, and others in the great imperial drive that was, by the end of the century, to bring much of the non-industrial world under the control of the industrial powers of the West.

STIRRINGS OF IMPERIALISM

For over two decades after the Civil War, the United States expanded geographically hardly at all. By the 1890s, however, some Americans were ready—indeed, eager—to resume the course of Manifest Destiny that had inspired their ancestors to wrest an empire from Mexico in the expansionist 1840s.

The New Manifest Destiny

Several developments helped shift American attention to lands across the seas. The experience of subjugating the Indian tribes had established a precedent for exerting colonial control over dependent peoples. The supposed "closing of the frontier," widely heralded by Frederick Jackson Turner and others in the 1890s, produced fears that natural resources would soon dwindle and that alternative sources must be found abroad. The depression that began in 1893 encouraged some businessmen to look for new markets abroad. The bitter social protests of the time—the Populist movement, the free-silver crusade, the bloody labor disputes—led some politicians to urge a more aggressive foreign policy as an outlet for frustrations that would otherwise destabilize domestic life.

Foreign trade was becoming increasingly important to the American economy in the late nineteenth century. The nation's exports had totaled about $392 million in 1870; by 1900, the figure had reached $1.4 billion. Many Americans began to consider the possibility of acquiring colonies that might expand overseas markets further. "Today," Senator Albert J. Beveridge of Indiana cried in 1899, "we are raising more than we can consume. Today, we are making more than we can use. Therefore, we must find new markets for our produce, new occupation for our capital, new work for our labor."

Americans were, moreover, well aware of the imperialist fever that was raging through Europe. It was leading the major powers to partition most of Africa among themselves and to turn covetous eyes on the Far East and the feeble Chinese Empire. Some Americans feared that their nation would soon be left out, that no territory would remain to be acquired.

Scholars and others found a philosophic justification for expansionism in Charles Darwin's theories. They contended that nations or "races," like biological species, struggled constantly for existence and that only the fittest could survive. For strong nations to dominate weak ones was, therefore, in accordance with the laws of nature. (This was an application to world affairs of the same strained reinterpretation of Darwinism that industrialists and others had long been applying to domestic economic affairs in the form of Social Darwinism.)

The ablest and most effective apostle of imperialism was Alfred Thayer Mahan, a captain and later admiral in the navy. Mahan's thesis—presented in *The Influence of Sea Power upon History* (1890) and other works—was simple: Countries with sea power were the great nations of history; the greatness of the United States, bounded by two oceans, would rest on naval power. Among other things, effective sea power required colonies. Mahan believed America should, at the least, acquire defensive bases in the Caribbean and the Pacific and take possession of Hawaii and other Pacific islands.

Mahan feared that the United States did not have a large enough navy to play the great role he envisioned. But during the 1870s and 1880s, the government launched a shipbuilding program that by 1898 had moved the United States to fifth place among the world's naval powers, and by 1900 to third.

Hemispheric Hegemony

James G. Blaine, who served as secretary of state in two Republican administrations in the 1880s, led the early efforts to expand American influence into Latin America, where, Blaine believed, the United States must look for markets for its surplus goods. In October 1889, he helped organize the first Pan-American Congress, which attracted delegates from nineteen nations. The delegates agreed to create the Pan-American Union, a weak international organization located in Washington that served as a clearinghouse for distributing information to the member nations. But they rejected Blaine's more substantive proposals: an inter-American customs union and arbitration procedures for hemispheric disputes.

The second Cleveland administration took a similarly lively interest in Latin America. In 1895, it supported Venezuela in a dispute with Great Britain over the boundary between Venezuela and British Guiana. When the British ignored American demands that the matter be submitted to arbitration, Secretary of State Richard Olney charged that Britain was violating the Monroe Doctrine. When Britain still did not act, Cleveland created a special commission to determine the boundary line; if Britain resisted the commission's decision, he insisted, the United States should be willing to go to war to enforce it. As war talk raged throughout the country, the British government finally realized that it had stumbled into a genuine diplomatic crisis and agreed to arbitration.

Hawaii and Samoa

The islands of Hawaii in the mid-Pacific had been an important way station for American ships in the China trade since the early nineteenth century. By the 1880s, officers of the expanding United States Navy were looking covetously at Pearl Harbor on the island of Oahu as a possible permanent base for American ships. Pressure for an increased American presence in

Hawaii was emerging from another source as well: the growing number of Americans who had settled on the islands and who had gradually come to dominate their economic and political life.

Commercial relations were inexorably pushing Hawaii into the orbit of the United States. An 1875 treaty permitted Hawaiian sugar to enter the United States duty-free and obliged the Hawaiian kingdom to make no territorial or economic concessions to other powers. In 1887, a new treaty granted the United States exclusive use of Pearl Harbor as a naval station. The McKinley Tariff of 1890 strengthened sentiment among Americans in Hawaii for union with the United States. The tariff gave domestic producers of sugar a bounty and deprived Hawaii of its privileged position in the American sugar market. Annexation would give Hawaiian planters the same bounty that American planters were receiving. It seemed the only alternative to economic disaster.

In 1891, in the midst of growing sentiment among white Hawaiians for union with the United States, the passive native king, Kalakaua, died and was succeeded by Queen Liliuokalani, a nationalist determined to eliminate American influence in the government. The American residents resisted. In 1893 they staged a revolution and called on the United States for protection. After the American minister ordered marines from a warship in Honolulu harbor to go ashore to aid the rebels, the queen yielded her authority. A provisional government, dominated by Americans, immediately sent a delegation to Washington to negotiate a treaty of annexation. President Harrison happily signed an annexation agreement in February 1893. But the Senate refused to ratify the treaty, and Grover Cleveland, the new president, refused to support it. Debate over the annexation of Hawaii continued until 1898, when the Republicans returned to power and approved the agreement.

The Samoan islands, 3,000 miles south of Hawaii, had also long served as a way station for American ships in the Pacific trade. As American commerce with Asia increased, business groups in the United States regarded Samoa with new interest, and the American navy began eyeing the Samoan harbor at Pago Pago. In 1878, the Hayes administration extracted a treaty from Samoan leaders that provided for an American naval station at Pago Pago. The treaty bound the United States to arbitrate any differences between Samoa and other nations. Clearly, the United States now expected to have a voice in Samoan affairs.

But Great Britain and Germany were also interested in the islands, and they too secured treaty rights from the native princes. For the next ten years the three powers jockeyed for dominance in Samoa, playing off one native ruler against another and coming dangerously close to war. Finally, the three powers agreed to create a tripartite protectorate over Samoa, with the native chiefs exercising only nominal authority. The three-way arrangement failed to halt the intrigues and rivalries of its members; and in 1899, the United States and Germany divided the islands between them, compensating Britain with territories elsewhere in the Pacific. The United States retained the harbor at Pago Pago.

WAR WITH SPAIN

Imperial ambitions had thus begun to stir within the United States well before the late 1890s. But a war with Spain in 1898 turned those stirrings into overt expansionism. The war transformed America's relationship to the rest of the world, and it left the nation with a far-flung overseas empire.

Controversy over Cuba

The Spanish-American War emerged out of events in Cuba, which along with Puerto Rico represented virtually all that remained of Spain's once-extensive American empire. Cubans had been resisting Spanish rule since at least 1868, when they began a long but ultimately unsuccessful fight for independence. Many Americans had sympathized with the Cubans during that ten-year struggle, but the United States did not intervene.

In 1895, the Cubans rose up again. (Although their goal was an end to Spanish misrule, the island's problems were now in part a result of the Wilson-Gorman Tariff of 1894, whose high duties on sugar had prostrated Cuba's important sugar economy by cutting off exports to the United States, the island's principal market.) This rebellion produced a ferocity on both sides that horrified Americans. The Cubans deliberately devastated the island to force the Spaniards to leave. The Spanish, commanded by General Valeriano Weyler (known in the American press as "Butcher" Weyler), confined civilians in certain areas to hastily prepared concentration camps, where they died by the thousands, victims of disease and malnutrition. The Spanish had used some of these same savage methods during the earlier struggle in Cuba without shocking American sensibilities. But the revolt of 1895 was reported more fully and floridly by American newspapers, and particularly by the new "yellow press" of William Randolph Hearst and Joseph Pulitzer, who were engaged in a ruthless circulation war with each other in New York City and elsewhere. In their effort to play to popular sentiment, they gave the impression that all the cruelties were being perpetrated by the Spaniards.

A growing population of Cuban émigrés in the United States—centered in Florida, New York, Philadelphia, and Trenton, New Jersey—gave extensive support to the Cuban Revolutionary party (whose headquarters was in New York) and helped publicize its leader, José Martí, who was killed in Cuba in 1895. Later, Cuban-Americans formed other clubs and associations to support the cause of *Cuba Libre* (Free Cuba). In some areas of the country, their efforts were as important as those of the yellow journalists in generating popular support for the revolution.

The mounting storm of indignation against Spain did not persuade President Cleveland to intervene in the conflict. He proclaimed American neutrality and tried to stop the agitation by Cuban refugees in New York City. But when McKinley became president in 1897, he took a stronger stand. He formally protested Spain's "uncivilized and inhuman" conduct, causing the Spanish government (fearful of American intervention) to recall Weyler, modify the concentration policy, and grant the island a qualified autonomy. At the end of 1897, with the insurrection losing ground, it seemed that American involvement in the war might be averted.

But whatever chances there were for a peaceful settlement vanished as a result of two dramatic incidents in February 1898. The first occurred when a Cuban agent in Havana stole a private letter written by Dupuy de Lôme, the Spanish minister in Washington, and turned it over to the American press. It described McKinley as a weak man and "a bidder for the admiration of the crowd." This was no more than what many Americans, including some Republicans, were saying about their president (Assistant Secretary of the Navy Theodore Roosevelt described McKinley as having "no more backbone than a chocolate eclair"). But coming from a foreigner, it created intense popular anger. Dupuy de Lôme promptly resigned.

While excitement over the de Lôme letter was still high, the American battleship *Maine* blew up in Havana harbor with a loss of more than 260 people. The ship had been ordered to Cuba in January to protect American lives and property against possible attacks by Spanish loyalists. Many Americans assumed that the Spanish had sunk the ship, particularly when a naval court of inquiry reported that an external explosion by a submarine mine had caused the disaster. (Later evidence suggested that the disaster was actually the result of an accidental explosion inside one of the engine rooms.) War hysteria swept the country, and Congress unanimously appropriated $50 million for military preparations. "Remember the *Maine*!" became a national chant for revenge.

THE YELLOW PRESS AND THE WRECK OF THE *MAINE* No evidence
was ever found tying the Spanish to the explosion in Havana
harbor that destroyed the American battleship *Maine* in
February 1898. Nevertheless, newspapers in the United States
ran sensational stories designed to arouse public sentiment in
support of a war against the Spanish. This front page from
Joseph Pulitzer's *New York World* is an example of the lurid
coverage the event received.

McKinley still hoped to avoid a conflict. But others in his administration (including Theodore Roosevelt) were clamoring for war. In March
1898, the president asked Spain to agree to an armistice, negotiations for a
permanent peace, and an end to the concentration camps. Spain agreed to
stop the fighting and eliminate the concentration camps, but it refused to
negotiate with the rebels and reserved the right to resume hostilities at its
discretion. That satisfied neither public opinion nor Congress. A few days
later, McKinley asked for and, on April 25, received a congressional declaration of war.

"A Splendid Little War"

Secretary of State John Hay called the Spanish-American conflict "a splendid little war," an opinion that most Americans—with the exception of
many of the enlisted men who fought in it—seemed to share. Declared in

April, it was over in August. That was in part because Cuban rebels had already greatly weakened the Spanish resistance, which made the American intervention in many respects little more than a "mopping up" exercise. Only 460 Americans were killed in battle or died of wounds, although some 5,200 perished of disease: malaria, dysentery, and typhoid, among others. Casualties among Cuban insurgents, who continued to bear the brunt of the struggle, were much higher.

Yet the American war effort was not without difficulties. United States soldiers faced serious supply problems: a shortage of modern rifles and ammunition, uniforms too heavy for the warm Caribbean weather, inadequate medical services, and skimpy, almost indigestible food. The regular army numbered only 28,000 troops and officers, most of whom had experience in quelling Indian outbreaks but none in larger-scale warfare. That meant that, as in the Civil War, the United States had to rely heavily on National Guard units, organized by local communities and commanded for the most part by local leaders without military experience. The entire mobilization process was conducted with remarkable inefficiency.

There were also racial conflicts. A significant proportion of the American invasion force consisted of black soldiers. Some were volunteer troops

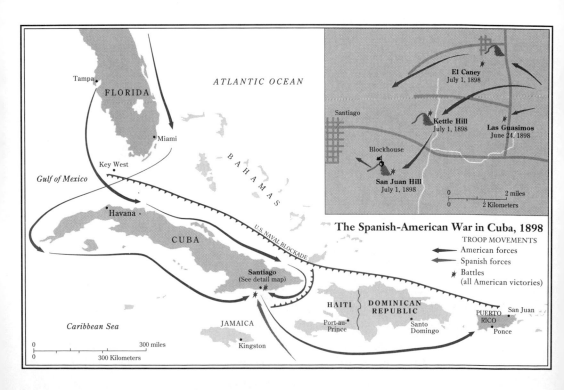

The Spanish-American War in Cuba, 1898

put together by black communities (although some governors refused to allow the formation of such units). Others were members of the four black regiments in the regular army, who had been stationed on the frontier to defend white settlements against Indians and were now transferred east to fight in Cuba. As the black soldiers traveled through the South toward the training camps, they chafed at the rigid segregation to which they were subjected and occasionally openly resisted the restrictions. Black soldiers in Georgia deliberately made use of a "whites only" park; in Florida, they beat a soda-fountain operator for refusing to serve them; in Tampa, white provocations and black retaliation led to a night-long riot that left thirty wounded.

Racial tensions continued in Cuba itself, where American blacks played crucial roles in some of the important battles of the war (including the famous charge at San Juan Hill) and won many medals. Nearly half the Cuban insurgents fighting with the Americans were black, and unlike their American counterparts they were fully integrated into the rebel army. (Indeed, two of the leading insurgent commanders, Antonio Maceo and Quintin Bandera, were black men.) The sight of black Cuban soldiers fighting alongside whites as equals gave African-Americans a stronger sense of the injustice of their own position.

Seizing the Philippines

No agency in the American military had clear authority over strategic planning. Only the navy had worked out an objective, but its objective had little to do with freeing Cuba. Assistant Secretary of the Navy Theodore Roosevelt was an ardent imperialist, an active proponent of war, and a man uninhibited by the fact that he was a relatively lowly figure in the military chain of command. Roosevelt unilaterally strengthened the navy's Pacific squadron and instructed its commander, Commodore George Dewey, to attack Spanish naval forces in the Philippines, a colony of Spain, in the event of war.

Immediately after war was declared, Dewey sailed for the Philippines. On May 1, 1898, he steamed into Manila Bay and completely destroyed the aging Spanish fleet there. Only one American sailor had died in the battle (of heatstroke), and George Dewey, immediately promoted to admiral, became the first hero of the war. Several months later, after the arrival of an American expeditionary force, the Spanish surrendered the city of Manila itself. In the rejoicing over Dewey's victory, few Americans paused to note that the character of the war was changing. What had begun as a war to free Cuba was becoming a war to strip Spain of its colonies.

The Battle for Cuba

Cuba, however, remained the principal focus of American military efforts. At first, the American commanders planned a long period of training before actually sending troops into combat. But when a Spanish fleet under Admiral Pascual Cervera slipped past the American navy into Santiago harbor, on the southern coast of Cuba, plans changed quickly. The American Atlantic fleet quickly bottled Cervera up in the harbor. And the army's commanding general, Nelson A. Miles, hastily altered his strategy. He ordered General William R. Shafter to leave Tampa in June with a force of 17,000 to attack Santiago. Both the departure from Florida and the landing in Cuba were scenes of fantastic incompetence. It took five days for the relatively small army to get ashore, and that was with the enemy offering no opposition.

Shafter moved toward Santiago, which he planned to surround and capture. On the way he met and defeated Spanish forces at Las Guasimas and, a week later, in two simultaneous battles, El Caney and San Juan Hill. At the center of the fighting (and on the front pages of the newspapers) during all these engagements was a cavalry unit known as the Rough Riders. Nominally commanded by General Leonard Wood, its real leader was Colonel Theodore Roosevelt, who had resigned from the Navy Department to get into the war and who had struggled with an almost desperate fury to ensure that his regiment made it to the front before the fighting ended. Roosevelt rapidly emerged as a hero of the conflict. His fame rested in large part on his role in leading a bold, if perhaps reckless, charge up Kettle Hill (a charge that was a minor part of the larger battle for the adjacent San Juan Hill) directly into the face of Spanish guns. Roosevelt himself emerged unscathed, but nearly a hundred of his soldiers were killed or wounded. He remembered the battle as "the great day of my life."

Although Shafter was now in position to assault Santiago, his army was so weakened by sickness that he feared he might have to abandon his position, particularly as the commander of the American naval force blockading Santiago refused to enter the harbor because of mines. Disaster seemed imminent. But unknown to the Americans, the Spanish government had by now decided that Santiago was lost and had ordered Cervera to evacuate. On July 3, even though he knew the effort was hopeless, Cervera

THE ROUGH RIDERS Theodore Roosevelt, center, poses with some of the Rough Riders after their famous charge in the Battle of San Juan Hill. The brigade had an unofficial anthem: "Rough, rough, we're the stuff. We want to fight, and we can't get enough."

tried to escape the harbor. The waiting American squadron destroyed his entire fleet. On July 16, the commander of the Spanish ground forces in Santiago surrendered. At about the same time, an American army landed in Puerto Rico and occupied it against virtually no opposition. On August 12, an armistice ended the war.

Decision for Imperialism

Under the terms of the armistice, Spain recognized the independence of Cuba. It ceded Puerto Rico (now occupied by American troops) and the Pacific island of Guam to the United States. And it accepted continued American occupation of Manila pending the final disposition of the Philippines.

The vagueness of the agreement on the Philippines reflected the American confusion over what to do with the islands. Although few Americans objected to annexing nearby Puerto Rico or the distant and seemingly insignificant Guam, annexation of the Philippines was intensely controversial. Supporters and opponents alike realized that acquiring so large and important a territory would mean a major change in America's position in the world.

McKinley claimed to be reluctant to support annexation. But, according to his own accounts, he emerged from an agonizing night of prayer convinced that there were no acceptable alternatives. Returning the Philippines to Spain would be "cowardly and dishonorable," he claimed. Turning the islands over to another imperialist power (France, Germany, or Britain) would be "bad business and discreditable." Granting them independence would be irresponsible; the Filipinos were "unfit for self government." The only solution was "to take them all and to educate the Filipinos, and uplift and Christianize them, and by God's grace do the very best we could by them." Growing popular support for annexation and the pressure of the imperialist leaders of his party undoubtedly helped him reach this decision of conscience.

The Treaty of Paris, signed in December 1898, brought a formal end to the war. It confirmed the terms of the armistice concerning Cuba, Puerto Rico, and Guam. But American negotiators startled the Spanish by demanding that they cede the Philippines to the United States. The Spanish objected briefly, but an American offer of $20 million for the islands softened their resistance. They accepted all the American terms.

In the United States Senate, however, resistance was fierce. During debate over ratification of the treaty, a powerful anti-imperialist movement arose throughout the country to oppose acquisition of the Philippines. Among the anti-imperialists were some of the nation's wealthiest and most powerful figures: Andrew Carnegie, Mark Twain, Samuel Gompers, Senator John Sherman, and others. Their motives were various. Some believed simply that imperialism was immoral, a repudiation of America's commitment to human freedom. Some feared "polluting" the American population by introducing "inferior" Asian races into it. Industrial workers feared being undercut by a flood of cheap laborers from the new colonies. Conservatives feared the large standing army and entangling foreign alliances that they thought imperialism would require and that they believed would threaten American liberties. Sugar growers and others feared unwelcome competition from the new territories. The Anti-Imperialist League, established by upper-class Bostonians, New Yorkers, and others late in 1898 to fight against annexation, attracted a widespread following in the Northeast and waged a vigorous campaign against ratification of the Paris treaty.

Favoring ratification was an equally varied group. There were the exuberant imperialists such as Theodore Roosevelt, who saw the acquisition of empire as a way to reinvigorate the nation, to keep alive what they considered the healthy, restorative influence of the war. Some businessmen saw opportunities in the Philippines and believed annexation would position the United States to dominate the Oriental trade. And most Republicans saw partisan advantages in acquiring valuable new territories through a war fought and won by a Republican administration. Perhaps the strongest argument in favor of annexation, however, was the apparent ease with which it could be accomplished. The United States, after all, already possessed the islands.

When anti-imperialists warned of the danger of acquiring heavily populated territories whose people might have to become citizens, the imperialists had a ready answer: The nation's longstanding policies toward Indians—treating them as dependents rather than as citizens—had created a precedent for annexing land without absorbing people. Senator Henry Cabot Lodge of Massachusetts, one of the leading imperialists in Congress, made the point explicitly:

> The other day . . . a great Democratic thinker announced that a Republic can have no subjects. He seems to have forgotten that this Republic not only has held subjects from the beginning, . . . but [that we have] acquired them by purchase. . . . [We] denied to the Indian tribes even the right to choose their allegiance, or to become citizens.

The fate of the treaty remained in doubt for weeks, until it received the unexpected support of William Jennings Bryan. Bryan was a fervent anti-imperialist who hoped to move the issue out of the Senate and make annexation the subject of a national referendum in 1900, when he expected to be the Democratic presidential candidate again. Bryan persuaded a number of anti-imperialist Democrats to support the treaty so as to set up the 1900 debate. The Senate ratified it finally on February 6, 1899.

But Bryan miscalculated. If the election of 1900 was in fact a referendum on the Philippines, as Bryan tried to make it, it proved beyond doubt that the nation had decided in favor of imperialism. Once again, Bryan ran against McKinley; and once again, McKinley won—even more decisively than in 1896. It was not only the issue of the colonies, however, that ensured McKinley's victory. The Republicans were the beneficiaries of growing national prosperity—and also of the colorful personality of their vice presidential candidate, Colonel Theodore Roosevelt, the hero of San Juan hill.

THE REPUBLIC AS EMPIRE

The new American empire was a small one by the standards of the great imperial powers of Europe. But it created large problems. It embroiled the United States in the politics of both Europe and the Far East in ways the nation had always tried to avoid in the past. It also drew Americans into a brutal war in the Philippines.

Governing the Colonies

Three of the new American dependencies—Hawaii, Alaska, and Puerto Rico—presented relatively few problems. They received territorial status (and their residents American citizenship) relatively quickly: Hawaii in 1900, Alaska in 1912, and Puerto Rico (in stages) by 1917. The navy took control of Guam and Tutuila. And some of the smallest, least populated Pacific islands the United States had acquired it simply left alone.

Cuba was a thornier problem. American military forces, commanded by General Leonard Wood, remained there until 1902 to prepare the island

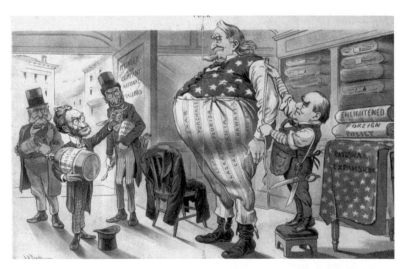

"MEASURING UNCLE SAM FOR A NEW SUIT," BY J. S. PUGHE, IN *PUCK* MAGA-
ZINE, 1900 President William McKinley is approvingly depicted here
as a tailor, measuring his client for a suit large enough to accommodate
the new possessions the United States obtained in the aftermath of the
Spanish-American War. The cartoon tries to link this expansion with
earlier, less controversial ones such as the Louisiana Purchase.

for independence. They built roads, schools, and hospitals; reorganized the legal, financial, and administrative systems; and introduced medical and sanitation reforms. But the United States was also laying the basis for years of American economic domination of the island. When Cuba drew up a constitution that made no reference to the United States, Congress responded by passing the Platt Amendment in 1901 and pressuring Cuba into incorporating the amendment's terms into its constitution. The Platt Amendment barred Cuba from making treaties with other nations (thus, in effect, giving the United States effective control of Cuban foreign policy); it gave the United States the right to intervene in Cuba to preserve independence, life, and property; and it required Cuba to permit American naval stations on its territory. The amendment left Cuba only nominally independent politically. And American capital, which quickly took over the island's economy, made the new nation an American economic appendage as well.

The Philippine War

Americans did not like to think of themselves as imperial rulers in the European mold. Yet like other imperial powers, the United States soon discovered—as it had discovered at home in its relations with the Indians—that subjugating another people required more than ideals; it also required strength and brutality. That, at least, was the lesson of the American experience in the Philippines, where American forces soon became engaged in a long and bloody war with insurgent forces fighting for independence.

The conflict in the Philippines is the least remembered of all American wars. It was also one of the longest (it lasted from 1898 to 1902) and one of the most vicious. It involved 200,000 American troops and resulted in 4,300 American deaths, nearly ten times the number who had died in combat in the Spanish-American War. The number of Filipinos killed in the conflict is still in dispute, but it seems likely that at least 50,000 natives (and perhaps many more) died. The American occupiers faced guerrilla tactics in the Philippines very similar to those the Spanish occupiers had faced prior to 1898 in Cuba. And they soon found themselves drawn into the same pattern of brutality that had outraged so many Americans when Weyler had used them in the Caribbean.

The Filipinos had been rebelling against Spanish rule even before 1898. And as soon as they realized the Americans had come to stay, they rebelled against them as well. Ably led by Emilio Aguinaldo, who claimed to head the legitimate government of the nation, Filipinos harried the American army of occupation from island to island for more than three years. At first,

American commanders believed the rebels had only a small popular follow-ing. But by early 1900, General Arthur MacArthur, an American com-mander in the islands (and the father of General Douglas MacArthur), was writing: "I have been reluctantly compelled to believe that the Filipino masses are loyal to Aguinaldo and the government which he heads."

To MacArthur and others, that realization was not a reason to moderate American tactics or conciliate the rebels. It was a reason to adopt more severe measures. Gradually, the American military effort became more systemati-cally vicious and brutal. Captured Filipino guerrillas were treated not as prisoners of war but as murderers. Most were summarily executed. On some islands, entire communities were evacuated—the residents forced into con-centration camps while American troops destroyed their villages, farms, crops, and livestock. A spirit of savagery grew among American soldiers, who came to view the Filipinos as almost subhuman and at times seemed to take pleasure in killing almost arbitrarily.

By 1902, reports of the brutality and of the American casualties had soured the American public on the war. But by then, the rebellion had largely exhausted itself and the occupiers had established control over most of the islands. The key to their victory was the March 1901 capture of Aguinaldo, who later signed a document in which he urged his followers to stop fighting and declared his own allegiance to the United States. (Aguinaldo then retired from public life and lived quietly until 1964.) Fighting continued in some places for another year, and the war revived intermittently until as late as 1906; but American possession of the Philippines was now secure.

In the summer of 1901, the military transferred authority over the islands to William Howard Taft, who became the first civilian governor. Taft announced that the American mission in the Philippines was to prepare the islands for independence, and he gave the Filipinos broad local autonomy. The Americans also built roads, schools, bridges, and sewers; instituted major administrative and financial reforms; and established a public health system. Filipino self-rule slowly increased. But not until July 4, 1946, did the islands finally gain their independence.

The Open Door

The acquisition of the Philippines greatly increased the already strong American interest in Asia. Americans were particularly concerned about the future of China, with which the United States already had an important trade and which was now so enfeebled that it provided a tempting target for exploitation by stronger countries. By 1900, England, France, Germany,

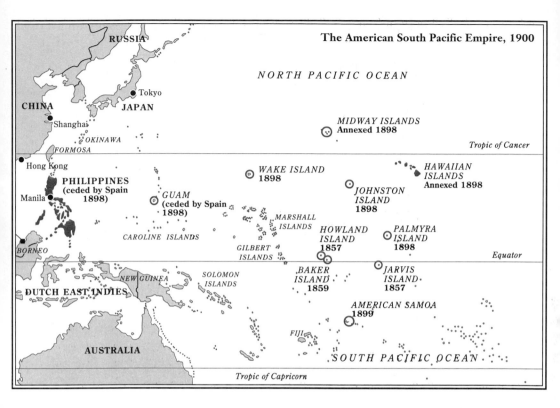

The American South Pacific Empire, 1900

Russia, and Japan were beginning to carve up China among themselves, pressuring the Chinese government for "concessions" that gave them effective economic control over various regions or, in some cases, simply seizing Chinese territory and claiming it as their own "spheres of influence." Many Americans feared the process would soon cut them out of the China trade altogether.

Eager for a way to protect American interests in China without risking war, McKinley issued a statement in September 1898 saying the United States wanted access to China, but no special advantages there: "Asking only the open door for ourselves, we are ready to accord the open door to others." Later, Secretary of State John Hay translated the president's words into policy when he addressed identical messages—which became known as the "Open Door notes"—to England, Germany, Russia, France, Japan, and Italy. He asked them to approve three principles: Each nation with a "sphere of influence" in China was to respect the rights and privileges of other nations in its sphere; Chinese officials were to continue to collect tariff duties in all spheres (the existing tariff favored the United States); and nations were not to discriminate against other nations in levying port dues and railroad rates within their own spheres. Together, these principles would allow the United States to trade freely with the Chinese without fear of interference and without having to become militarily involved in the region.

But the Open Door proposals were coolly received in Europe and Japan. Russia openly rejected them; each of the other powers claimed to accept them in principle but to be unable to act unless all the other powers agreed. Hay refused to consider this a rebuff. He announced that all the powers had accepted the principles of the Open Door and that the United States expected them to observe those principles. But unless the United States was willing to resort to war, it could not prevent any nation that wanted to violate the Open Door from doing so.

THE BOXER REBELLION American troops march through the grounds of the Temple of Agriculture in Beijing's Imperial City during the Boxer Rebellion in 1900. They were among 5,000 American soldiers summoned to China. In mid-August, they joined British, Russian, Japanese and French soldiers to rescue diplomats, foreigners, and Christians who had barricaded themselves in the city's diplomatic quarter in June to protect themselves from the Boxers.

No sooner had the diplomatic maneuvering over the Open Door ended than the Boxers, a secret Chinese martial-arts society, launched a revolt against foreigners in China. The climax of the Boxer Rebellion was a siege of the entire foreign diplomatic corps in the British embassy in Peking. The imperial powers (including the United States) sent an international expeditionary force into China to rescue the diplomats. In August 1900, it fought its way into Peking and broke the siege.

McKinley and Hay had agreed to American participation so as to secure a voice in the settlement of the uprising and to prevent the partition of China. Hay now won support for his Open Door approach from England and Germany and then induced the other participating powers to accept compensation from the Chinese for the damages the Boxer Rebellion had caused. Chinese territorial integrity survived at least in name, and the United States retained access to its lucrative trade.

A Modern Military System

The war with Spain had revealed glaring deficiencies in the American military system. The army had exhibited the greatest weaknesses, but the entire military organization had failed to coordinate its efforts. Had the United States been fighting a more powerful nation, disaster might have resulted. After the war, McKinley appointed Elihu Root, an able New York corporate lawyer, as secretary of war to supervise a major overhaul of the armed forces. (Root was one of the first of several generations of attorney-statesmen who moved easily between public and private roles and constituted what has often been called the American "foreign policy establishment.") Between 1900 and 1903, Root created a new military system.

The Root reforms enlarged the regular army from 25,000 to a maximum of 100,000. They established federal command of the National Guard, ensuring that never again would the nation fight a war with volunteer regiments over which the federal government had only limited control. They sparked the creation of a system of officer training schools, including the Army Staff College (later the Command and General Staff School) at Fort Leavenworth, Kansas, and the Army War College in Washington, D.C. And in 1903, they established a general staff (now known as the Joint Chiefs of Staff) to act as military advisers to the secretary of war. As a result of the new reforms, the United States entered the twentieth century with something resembling a modern military system. The country would make substantial use of it in the turbulent century to come.

CHAPTER TWENTY-ONE

The Rise
of Progressivism

The Progressive Impulse ~ *The Assault on the Parties*
Crusades for Order and Reform

ELL BEFORE THE turn of the century, many Americans had become convinced that the rapid industrialization and urbanization of their society had created intolerable problems—that the nation's most pressing need was to impose order on the growing chaos and to curb industrial society's most glaring injustices. In the early years of the new century, that outlook acquired a name: progressivism.

Not even those who called themselves progressives could always agree on what the word "progressive" really meant. Indeed, more than one historian has suggested that the word ultimately came to mean so many different things to so many different people that it ceased to mean anything at all. Yet if progressivism was a phenomenon of great scope and diversity, it was also one that rested on an identifiable set of central assumptions. It was, first, an optimistic vision. Progressives believed, as their name implies, in the idea of progress. They believed that society was capable of improvement, even of perfection, and that continued growth and advancement were the nation's destiny. But progressives believed, too, that growth and progress could not continue to occur recklessly, as they had in the late nineteenth century. The "natural laws" of the marketplace, and the doctrines of laissez faire and Social Darwinism that celebrated those laws, were not sufficient to create the order and stability that the growing society required. Purposeful human intervention was necessary to solve the nation's problems. Progressives did not always agree on the form that intervention should take, but most believed that government could play an important role in the process.

THE PROGRESSIVE IMPULSE

Beyond these central premises, progressivism flowed outward in a number of different directions. One powerful impulse was the spirit of "antimonopoly," the fear of concentrated power and the urge to limit and disperse authority and wealth. A second progressive impulse was a belief in the importance of social cohesion: the belief that individuals are not autonomous but part of a great web of social relationships, that the welfare of any single person is dependent on the welfare of society as a whole. And a third progressive impulse was a belief in organization and efficiency: the belief that social order was a result of intelligent social organization and rational procedures for guiding social and economic life. These varied reform impulses were not entirely incompatible with one another. Many progressives made use of all these ideas at times as they tried to restore order and stability to their turbulent society.

The Muckrakers and the Social Gospel

Among the first to articulate the new spirit of reform was a group of crusading journalists who began in the late nineteenth and early twentieth centuries to direct public attention toward social, economic, and political injustices. They became known as the "muckrakers" after Theodore Roosevelt accused one of them of raking up muck through his writings. They were committed to exposing scandal, corruption, and injustice to public view.

At first, their major targets were the trusts and particularly the railroads, which the muckrakers considered dangerously powerful and deeply corrupt. Exposés of the great corporate organizations began to appear as early as the 1860s, when Charles Francis Adams, Jr., and others uncovered corruption among the railroad barons. By the turn of the century, many muckrakers were turning their attention to government and particularly to the urban political machines. The most influential, perhaps, was Lincoln Steffens, a reporter for *McClure's* magazine. His portraits of "machine government" and "boss rule"; his exposures of "boodlers" in cities as diverse as St. Louis, Minneapolis, Cleveland, Cincinnati, Chicago, Philadelphia, and New York; his tone of studied moral outrage (as reflected in the title of his series and of the book that emerged from it, *The Shame of the Cities*)—all helped arouse sentiment for urban political reform. The muckrakers reached the peak of their influence in the first decade of the twentieth century. They investigated governments, labor unions, and corporations. They explored the problems of child labor, immigrant ghettoes, prostitution, and family disorganization. They denounced waste and destruction of natural resources, the subjugation of women, even occasionally the oppression of blacks.

The moralistic tone of the muckrakers' exposés reflected one important aspect of emerging progressive sentiment: a sense of outrage at social and economic injustice. That outrage, combined with a humanitarian sense of social responsibility, helped produce one of the central missions of many reformers: the pursuit of "social justice." A clear expression of that concern was the rise of what became known as the "Social Gospel." By the early twentieth century, it had become a powerful movement within American Protestantism (and, to a lesser extent, within American Catholicism and

MCCLURE'S MAGAZINE, MAY 1903 *McClure's* was the leading outlet for a form of journalism known as "muckraking," which exposed social and economic scandals in the hope of promoting reform. This issue contains articles by two of the leading muckrakers, Lincoln Steffens and Ida Tarbell.

Judaism) to redeem the nation's cities. The Salvation Army, which began in England but soon spread to the United States, was a Christian social welfare organization with a vaguely military structure. By 1900, it had recruited 3,000 "officers" and 20,000 "privates" and was offering both material aid and spiritual service to the urban poor. In addition, many ministers, priests, and rabbis left traditional parish work to serve in the troubled cities. Charles Sheldon's *In His Steps* (1898), the story of a young minister who abandoned a comfortable post to work among the needy, sold more than 15 million copies and established itself as the most successful novel of the era. The engagement of religion with reform helped bring to progressivism a powerful moral impulse and a concern for the plight of some of society's most impoverished and degraded people.

The Settlement House Movement

One of the strongest elements of progressive thought was the belief that the environment shaped individual development. Social Darwinists such as William Graham Sumner had argued that people's fortunes reflected their inherent "fitness" for survival. Most progressive theorists disagreed. Ignorance, poverty, even criminality, they argued, were not the result of inherent moral or genetic failings or of the workings of providence. They were, rather, the effects of an unhealthy environment. To elevate the distressed, therefore, required an improvement of the conditions in which the distressed lived.

Nothing produced more distress, many reformers believed, than the crowded immigrant neighborhoods of American cities. One response to the problems of such communities, borrowed from England, was the settlement house. The most famous, and one of the first, was Hull House, which opened in 1889 in Chicago as a result of the efforts of Jane Addams. It became a model for more than 400 similar institutions throughout the nation. Staffed by members of the educated middle class, settlement houses sought to help immigrant families adapt to the language and customs of their new country. Settlement houses avoided the condescension and moral disapproval of earlier philanthropic efforts. But they generally embodied a belief that middle-class Americans had a responsibility to impart their own values to immigrants and to teach them how to live middle-class life styles. Even the word "settlement" suggested as much: middle-class people "settling" in the inner city and bringing civilization to the urban frontier.

A M E R I C A N   V O I C E S

JANE ADDAMS

First Days at Hull House

FROM THE FIRST it seemed understood that we were ready to perform the humblest neighborhood services. We were asked to wash the newborn babies, and to prepare the dead for burial, to nurse the sick, and to "mind the children." Occasionally these neighborly offices unexpectedly uncovered ugly human traits. . . . a little Italian bride of fifteen sought shelter with us one November evening, to escape her husband who had beaten her every night for a week when he returned home from work, because she had lost her wedding ring; two of us officiated quite alone at the birth of an illegitimate child because the doctor was late in arriving, and none of the honest Irish matrons would "touch the likes of her." . . .

We were . . . early impressed with the curious isolation of many of the immigrants; an Italian woman once expressed her pleasure in the red roses that she saw at one of our receptions in surprise that they had been "brought so fresh all the way from Italy." She would not believe for an instant that they had been grown in America. . . . Her conception of America had been the untidy street in which she lived and had made her long struggle to adapt herself to American ways.

But in spite of some untoward experiences, we were constantly impressed with the uniform kindness and courtesy we received. Perhaps these first days laid the simple human foundations which are certainly essential for continuous living among the poor: . . . the conviction . . . that the things which make men alike are finer and better than the things that keep them apart, and that these basic likenesses, if they are properly accentuated, easily transcend the less essential differences of race, language, creed, and tradition.

SOURCE: Jane Addams, *Twenty Years at Hull House* (New York: The Macmillan Company, 1910), pp. 88–89.

Central to the settlement houses were the efforts of college women. Indeed, the movement became a training ground for many important female leaders of the twentieth century, including Eleanor Roosevelt. The settlement houses also helped spawn another important institution of reform: the profession of social work—a profession in which women were to play an important role. The professional social worker combined a compassion for the poor with a commitment to the values of bureaucratic progressivism: scientific study, efficient organization, reliance on experts.

The Allure of Expertise

As the emergence of the social work profession suggests, progressives involved in humanitarian efforts often placed high value on knowledge and expertise. Even nonscientific problems, they believed, could be analyzed and solved scientifically. Many reformers came to believe that only enlightened experts and well-designed bureaucracies could create the stability and order America needed.

This belief found expression in many ways, among them the writings of a new group of scholars and intellectuals. Unlike the Social Darwinists of the nineteenth century, these theorists were no longer content with merely justifying the existing industrial system. They spoke instead of the creation of a new civilization, one in which the expertise of scientists and engineers could be brought to bear on the problems of the economy and society. Among the most influential was the social scientist Thorstein Veblen. Harshly critical of the industrial tycoons of the late nineteenth century—the "leisure class," as he satirically described them in his first major work, *A Theory of the Leisure Class* (1899)—Veblen proposed instead a new economic system in which power would reside in the hands of highly trained engineers. Only they, he argued, could fully understand the "machine process" by which modern society must be governed.

In practical terms, the impulse toward expertise and organization helped produce the idea of scientific management, or "Taylorism." It encouraged the development of modern mass-production techniques and, above all, the assembly line. It inspired a revolution in American education and the creation of a new area of inquiry—social science, the use of scientific techniques in the study of society and its institutions. It produced a generation of bureaucratic reformers concerned with the structure of organizations and committed to building new political and economic institutions capable of managing a modern society. It also helped create a movement toward organization among the expanding new group of middle-class professionals.

The Professions

The late nineteenth century saw a dramatic expansion in the number of Americans engaged in administrative and professional tasks. Industries needed managers, technicians, and accountants as well as workers. Cities required commercial, medical, legal, and educational services. The new technology required scientists and engineers who, in turn, required institutions and instructors to train them. By the turn of the century, the people performing these services had come to constitute a distinct social group— what some have called a new middle class.

The new middle class placed a high value on education and individual accomplishment. By the early twentieth century, its millions of members were building organizations and establishing standards to secure their position in society. As their principal vehicle, they created the modern, organized professions. The idea of professionalism had been a frail one in America even as late as 1880. But as the demand for professional services increased, so did the pressures for reform.

Among the first to respond was the medical profession. Throughout the 1890s, doctors who considered themselves trained professionals began forming local associations and societies. In 1901, they reorganized the American Medical Association (AMA) into a national professional society. By 1920, nearly two-thirds of all American doctors were members. The AMA quickly called for strict, scientific standards for admission to the practice of medicine, with doctors themselves serving as protectors of the standards. State and local governments responded by passing new laws that required the licensing of all physicians and that restricted licenses to those practitioners approved by the profession.

There was similar movement in other professions. By 1916, lawyers in all forty-eight states had established professional bar associations, virtually all of which had succeeded in creating central examining boards, composed of lawyers, to regulate admission to the profession. Increasingly, aspiring lawyers found it necessary to enroll in graduate programs, and the nation's law schools accordingly expanded greatly, both in numbers and in the rigor of their curricula. Businessmen supported the creation of schools of business administration and created their own national organizations: the National Association of Manufacturers in 1895 and the United States Chamber of

Commerce in 1912. Even farmers, long the symbol of the romantic spirit of individualism, responded to the new order by forming, through the National Farm Bureau Federation, a network of agricultural organizations designed to spread scientific farming methods, teach sound marketing techniques, and lobby for the interests of their members.

Among the chief purposes of the new professionalism was guarding entry into the professions. This was only partly an effort to defend the professions from the untrained and incompetent. The admission requirements also protected those already in the professions from excessive competition and lent prestige and status to the professional label. Some professions used their entrance requirements to exclude blacks, women, immigrants, and other "undesirables" from their ranks. Others used them simply to keep the numbers down, to ensure that demand for the services of existing members would remain high.

Women and the Professions

American women found themselves excluded—both by custom and by active barriers of law and prejudice—from most of the emerging professions. But a substantial number of middle-class women—particularly those emerging from the new women's colleges and from the coeducational state universities—nevertheless entered professional careers.

A few women managed to establish themselves as physicians, lawyers, engineers, scientists, and corporate managers. Several leading medical schools admitted women, and about 5 percent of all American physicians were female in 1900 (a proportion that remained unchanged until the 1960s). Most, however, turned by necessity to those professions that society considered "suitable" for women. Settlement houses and social work provided two "appropriate" professional outlets for women. The most important, however, was teaching. Indeed, in the late nineteenth century, more than two-thirds of all grammar-school teachers were women, and perhaps 90 percent of all professional women were teachers. For educated black women, in particular, teaching was often the only professional opportunity they could hope to find. The existence of segregated black schools in the South created a substantial market for African-American teachers.

Women also dominated other professional activities. Nursing had become primarily a women's field when it was still considered a menial occupation, akin to domestic service. But by the early twentieth century, it too was adopting professional standards. Prospective nurses generally

SETTLEMENT HOUSE WORKERS Nurses from the Henry Street settlement in New York leave their headquarters to begin their visits to the homes of poor immigrants in lower Manhattan. This photograph dates from the early 1900s.

needed certification from schools of nursing and could not simply learn on the job. Women also found opportunities as librarians, another field beginning to define itself in professional terms. And many women entered academia—often receiving advanced degrees at such predominantly male institutions as the University of Chicago, MIT, and Columbia, and finding professional opportunities in the new and expanding women's colleges.

The "women's professions" had much in common with other professions: the value they placed on training and expertise, the creation of professional organizations and a professional "identity," the monitoring of admission to professional work. But they also had distinctive qualities. Careers such as teaching, nursing, and library work were "helping" professions. They involved working primarily with other women or with children.

Their activities occurred in places that seemed different from the offices that dominated the predominantly male business and professional worlds; such places as schools, hospitals, and libraries had a vaguely "domestic" or "feminine" image.

The Clubwomen

Many middle-class women who did not enter professional careers neverthe-less played an important role in the effort to remake society. In the vanguard of progressive social reforms was a large network of women's associations that proliferated rapidly beginning in the 1880s and 1890s. Large numbers of women gravitated to the growing temperance movement. Others turned to women's clubs.

The women's clubs began largely as cultural organizations to provide middle- and upper-class women with an outlet for their intellectual energies. In 1892, when women formed the General Federation of Womens Club's to coordinate the activities of local organizations, there were more than 100,000 members in nearly 500 clubs. Eight years later, there were 160,000 members; and by 1917, over 1 million.

By the early twentieth century, the clubs were becoming less concerned with cultural activities and more concerned with making a contribution to social betterment. Much of what they did was uncontroversial: planting trees; supporting schools, libraries, and settlement houses; building hospi-tals and parks. But clubwomen also supported such controversial measures as child labor laws, worker compensation, pure food and drug legislation, occupational safety, reforms in Indian policy, and—beginning in 1914—woman suffrage. Because many club members were from wealthy families, some organizations had substantial funds at their disposal to make their influence felt.

Black women occasionally joined clubs dominated by whites. But African-Americans also formed clubs of their own, some of which affiliated with the General Federation, but more of which became part of the independent National Association of Colored Women. They modeled themselves primarily on their white counterparts, but some black clubs also took positions on issues of particular concern to blacks. Some crusaded against lynching and called for congressional legislation to make lynching a federal crime. Others protested aspects of segregation.

The women's club movement raised few overt challenges to prevailing assumptions about the proper role of women in society. But it did represent an important effort by women to extend their influence beyond the traditional female sphere within the home and the family. Few clubwomen were willing to accept the arguments of such committed feminists as Charlotte Perkins Gilman, who in her 1898 book, *Women and Economics*, argued that the traditional definition of sexual roles was exploitive and obsolete. The club movement, rather, allowed women to define a space for themselves in the public world without openly challenging the existing, male-dominated order.

But the importance of the club movement did not lie simply in what it did for middle-class women. It lay also in what those women did for the working-class people they attempted to help. The women's club movement was an important force in winning passage of state (and ultimately federal) laws that regulated the conditions of woman and child labor, that established government inspection of workplaces, that regulated the food and drug industries, and that applied new standards to urban housing. In many of these efforts, the clubwomen formed alliances with such other women's groups as the Women's Trade Union League, founded in 1903 by female union members and upper-class reformers and committed to persuading women to join unions.

THE ASSAULT ON THE PARTIES

Sooner or later, most progressive goals required the involvement of government. Only government, reformers agreed, could effectively counter the powerful private interests that threatened the nation. But American government at the dawn of the new century was, progressives believed, poorly adapted to perform their ambitious tasks. At every level, political institutions were outmoded, inefficient, and corrupt. Before society could be effectively reformed, it would be necessary to reform government itself. In the beginning, at least, many progressives believed that such reform should start with an assault on the domination of government and politics by the political parties, which they thought had become corrupt, undemocratic, and reactionary.

Early Attacks

Attacks on party dominance had been frequent in the late nineteenth century. Greenbackism and Populism, for example, had been efforts to break the hammerlock with which the Republicans and Democrats controlled public life. The Independent Republicans (or mugwumps; see p. 517) had attempted to challenge the grip of partisanship; and former mugwumps became important supporters of progressive political reform activity in the 1890s and later.

The early assaults enjoyed some success. In the 1880s and 1890s, for example, most states adopted the secret ballot. Prior to that, the political parties themselves had printed ballots (or "tickets"), which they distributed to their supporters, who then simply went to the polls to deposit the tickets in the ballot box. The old system had made it possible for bosses to monitor the voting behavior of their constituents; it had also made it difficult for voters to "split" their tickets—to vote for candidates of different parties for different offices. The new secret ballot—printed by the government and distributed at the polls, where it was filled out and deposited in secret—helped chip away at the power of the parties over the voters. (It also excluded many illiterate and non-English speaking voters.)

By the late 1890s, critics of the parties were expanding their goals. Party rule could be broken, they believed, in one of two ways. It could be broken by increasing the power of the people, by permitting them to circumvent partisan institutions and express their will directly at the polls. Or it could be broken by placing more power in the hands of nonpartisan, nonelective officials, insulated from political life. Reformers promoted measures that moved along both those paths.

Municipal Reform

Many progressives believed the impact of party rule was most damaging in the cities. Municipal government, therefore, became the first target of those working for political reform. Muckraking journalists such as Lincoln Steffens were especially successful in arousing public outrage at corruption and incompetence in city politics.

The muckrakers struck a responsive chord among a powerful group of urban middle-class progressives. For several decades after the Civil War, "respectable" citizens of the nation's large cities had avoided participation in municipal government. Viewing politics as a debased and demeaning activity, they shrank from contact with the "vulgar" elements who were coming to dominate public life. By the end of the century, however, a new generation of activists—some of them members of old aristocratic families, others a part of the new middle class—were taking a renewed interest in government.

They faced a formidable array of opponents. In addition to challenging the powerful city bosses and their entrenched political organizations, they were attacking a large group of special interests: saloon owners, brothel keepers, and, perhaps most significantly, those businessmen who had established lucrative relationships with the urban machines and viewed reform as a threat to their profits. Allied with these interests were many influential newspapers, which ridiculed the reformers as naïve do-gooders. Finally, there was the great constituency of urban working people, many of them recent immigrants, for whom the machines were a source of needed jobs and services. Gradually, however, the reformers gained in political strength—in part because of their own growing numbers, in part because of the failures of the existing political leadership. And in the first years of the twentieth century, they began to score some important victories.

One of the first major successes came in Galveston, Texas, where the old city government proved completely unable to deal with the effects of a destructive tidal wave in 1900. Capitalizing on public dismay, reformers (many of them local businessmen) won approval of a new city charter. The mayor and council were replaced by an elected, nonpartisan commission. In 1907, Des Moines, Iowa, adopted its own version of the commission plan, and other cities soon followed.

Another approach to reform, similarly motivated by the desire to remove city government from the hands of the parties, was the city-manager plan (first adopted in Staunton, Virginia, in 1908), by which elected officials hired an outside expert—often a professionally trained business manager or engineer—to take charge of the government. The city manager would presumably remain untainted by the corrupting influence of politics. By the end of the progressive era, almost 400 cities were operating under commissions, and another 45 employed city managers.

In most urban areas, and in the larger cities in particular, the enemies of party had to settle for less absolute victories. Some cities made the election of mayors nonpartisan (so that the parties could not choose the candidates) or moved them to years when no presidential or congressional races were in progress (to reduce the influence of the large turnouts that party organizations produced on such occasions). Reformers tried to make city council members run at large so as to limit the influence of ward leaders and district bosses. They tried to strengthen the power of the mayor at the expense of the city council, on the assumption that reformers were more likely to get a sympathetic mayor elected than win control of the entire council.

Statehouse Progressivism

But the assault on boss rule in the cities often did not produce results satisfying to reformers. As a result, many progressives turned to state government as an agent for reform. These state-level progressives, like their municipal counterparts, considered existing state governments unfit to provide reform. They looked with particular scorn on state legislatures, whose ill-paid, relatively undistinguished members were, they believed, generally incompetent, often corrupt, and always controlled by party bosses. Many reformers began looking for ways to circumvent the legislatures (and the party bosses that controlled them) by increasing the power of the electorate.

Two of the most important changes were innovations first proposed by Populists in the 1890s: the initiative and the referendum. The initiative allowed reformers to circumvent state legislatures altogether by submitting legislation directly to the voters in general elections. The referendum provided a method by which actions of the legislature could be returned to the electorate for approval. By 1918, more than twenty states had enacted one or both of these reforms.

The direct primary and the recall were, similarly, efforts to limit the power of parties and improve the quality of elected officials. The primary election was an attempt to take the selection of candidates away from the bosses and give it to the people. (In the South, it was also a device for excluding African-Americans from voting.) The recall gave voters the right to remove a public official from office at a special election, which could be called after a sufficient number of citizens had signed a petition. By 1915 every state in the nation had instituted primary elections for at least some offices. The recall encountered more strenuous opposition, but some states adopted it as well.

Reform efforts proved most effective in states that elevated vigorous and committed politicians to positions of leadership. In New York, Governor Charles Evans Hughes exploited progressive sentiment to create a commission to regulate public utilities. In California, Governor Hiram Johnson promoted reforms to limit the political power of the Southern Pacific Railroad. In New Jersey, Woodrow Wilson, the Princeton University president who was elected governor in 1910, used executive leadership to win reforms designed to end New Jersey's widely denounced position as the "mother of trusts."

But the most celebrated state-level reformer was Robert M. La Follette of Wisconsin. Elected governor in 1900, he helped turn his state into what reformers across the nation described as a "laboratory of progressivism." The Wisconsin progressives won approval of direct primaries, initiatives, and referendums. They regulated railroads and utilities. They passed laws to regulate the workplace and provide compensation for laborers injured on the job. They instituted graduated taxes on inherited fortunes, and they nearly doubled state levies on railroads and other corporate interests. Ultimately, La Follette would find himself overshadowed by other national progressive leaders. In the early years of the century, however, few men were as effective in publicizing the message of reform. None was as successful in bending state government to that goal.

Parties and Interest Groups

The reformers did not, of course, eliminate party from American political life. But they did diminish the parties' centrality. Evidence of that came from, among other things, the decline in voter turnout. In the late nine-

ROBERT LA FOLLETTE CAMPAIGNING IN WISCONSIN After three terms as governor of Wisconsin, La Follette began a long career in the United States Senate in 1906 during which he worked uncompromisingly for advanced progressive reforms—so uncompromisingly, in fact, that he was often almost completely isolated.

teenth century, up to 81 percent of eligible voters routinely turned out for national elections. In the early twentieth century, while turnout remained very high by today's dismal standards, the figure declined markedly. In the presidential election of 1900, 73 percent of the electorate voted. By 1912, the figure had dropped to about 59 percent. Never again did voter turnout reach as high as 70 percent.

At the same time that parties were declining, another kind of power center was beginning to replace them: what have become known as "interest groups." Beginning late in the nineteenth century and accelerating rapidly in the twentieth, new organizations emerged, outside the party system, that were designed to pressure government to do the bidding of their members: professional organizations; trade associations, representing particular businesses and industries; labor organizations; farm lobbies; and many others. Social workers, the settlement house movement, women's clubs, and others learned to operate as interest groups to advance their demands. A new pattern of politics, in which many individual interests organized to influence government directly rather than operating through party structures, was emerging. It would become the characteristic form of American politics in the twentieth century.

Reform by Machine

One result of the assault on the parties was a change in the party organizations themselves, which attempted to adapt to the new realities so as to preserve their influence. Such efforts achieved considerable success. Some party machines emerged from the progressive era almost as powerful as they had entered it. In large part, this was because bosses themselves recognized that they must change in order to survive. Thus they sometimes allowed their machines to become vehicles of social reform. One example was New York's Tammany Hall, the nation's oldest and most notorious city machine. Its astute leader, Charles Francis Murphy, began in the early years of the century to fuse the techniques of boss rule with some of the concerns of social reformers. Murphy did nothing to challenge the fundamental workings of Tammany Hall. At the same time, however, Tammany began to take an increased interest in state and national politics, which it had traditionally scorned; and it used its political power on behalf of legislation to improve working conditions, protect child laborers, and eliminate the worst abuses of the industrial economy.

In 1911, a terrible fire swept through the factory of the Triangle Shirtwaist Company in New York; 146 workers, most of them women, died. Many of them had been trapped inside the burning building because management had locked the emergency exits to prevent malingering. For the next three years, a state commission studied not only the background of the fire but the general condition of the industrial workplace; and by 1914, it had issued a series of reports calling for major reforms in the conditions of modern labor.

The report itself was a classic progressive document, based on the testimony of experts, filled with statistics and technical data. Yet when its recommendations reached the New York legislature, its most effective supporters were not middle-class progressives but two Tammany Democrats: Senator Robert F. Wagner and Assemblyman Alfred E. Smith. With the support of Murphy and the backing of other Tammany legislators, they steered through a series of pioneering labor laws that imposed strict regulations on factory owners and established effective mechanisms for enforcement.

CRUSADES FOR ORDER AND REFORM

Reformers directed many of their energies at the political process. But they also crusaded on behalf of what they considered moral issues. There were campaigns to eliminate alcohol from national life, to curb prostitution, to regulate divorce. There were efforts to restrict immigration or curb the power of monopoly in the industrial economy. There were crusades to resolve what many considered longstanding injustices, of which the most prominent was the campaign for woman suffrage. Proponents of each of those reforms believed that success would help regenerate society as a whole.

The Temperance Crusade

Many progressives considered the elimination of alcohol from American life a necessary step in restoring order to society. Workers in settlement houses and social agencies abhorred the effects of drinking on working-class families: Scarce wages vanished as workers spent hours in saloons; drunkenness spawned violence, and occasionally murder, within urban families. Women, in particular, saw alcohol as a source of some of the greatest problems of working-class wives and mothers, and hoped through temperance to reform abusive or irresponsible male behavior and thus improve women's lives. Employers, too, regarded alcohol as an impediment to industrial efficiency; workers often missed time on the job because of drunkenness or, worse, came to the factory intoxicated and performed their tasks sloppily and dangerously. Critics of economic privilege denounced the liquor industry as one of the nation's most sinister trusts. And political reformers, who looked on the saloon (correctly) as one of the central institutions of the machine, saw an attack on drinking as part of an attack on the bosses. Out of such sentiments emerged the temperance movement.

Temperance had been a major reform movement before the Civil War, mobilizing large numbers of people (and particularly large numbers of women) in a crusade with strong evangelical overtones. Beginning in the 1870s, it experienced a major resurgence. As in the antebellum years, it was a movement led and supported primarily by women. In 1873, temperance advocates formed the Women's Christian Temperance Union (WCTU), led after 1879 by Frances Willard. By 1911, it had 245,000 members and had become the largest single women's organization in American history to that point. The WCTU publicized the evils of alcohol and the connection between drunkenness and family violence, unemployment, poverty, and disease. In 1893, the Anti-Saloon League joined the temperance movement and, along with the WCTU, began to press for a specific legislative solution: the legal abolition of saloons. Gradually, that demand grew to include the complete prohibition of the sale and manufacture of alcoholic beverages.

Despite substantial opposition from immigrant and working-class voters, pressure for prohibition grew steadily through the first decades of the new century. By 1916, nineteen states had passed prohibition laws. But since the consumption of alcohol was actually increasing in many unregulated areas, temperance supporters were beginning to advocate a national prohibition law. America's entry into World War I, and the moral fervor it unleashed, provided the last push to the advocates of prohibition. In 1917, with the support of rural fundamentalists who opposed alcohol on moral and religious grounds, progressive advocates of prohibition steered through Congress a constitutional amendment embodying their demands. Two years later, after ratification by every state in the nation except Connecticut and Rhode Island (bastions of Catholic immigrants), the Eighteenth Amendment became law, to take effect in January 1920.

Immigration Restriction

Virtually all reformers agreed that the growing immigrant population had created social problems, but there was wide disagreement on how best to respond. Some progressives believed that helping the new residents adapt to American society was the proper approach. Others argued that efforts at assimilation had failed and that the only solution was to limit the flow of new arrivals.

In the first decades of the century, therefore, pressure grew to close the nation's gates. New scholarly theories, appealing to the progressive respect for expertise, argued that the introduction of immigrants into American society was diluting the purity of the nation's racial stock. The spurious "science" of eugenics spread the belief that human inequalities were hereditary and that immigration was contributing to the multiplication of the unfit. A special federal commission of "experts," chaired by Senator William P. Dillingham of Vermont, issued an elaborate report filled with statistics and scholarly testimony. It argued that the newer immigrant groups—largely southern and eastern Europeans—had proved themselves less assimilable than earlier immigrants. Immigration, the report implied, should be restricted by nationality. Even many people who rejected racial arguments supported limiting immigration as a way to solve such urban problems as overcrowding, unemployment, strained social services, and social unrest.

The combination of these concerns gradually won for the nativists the support of some of the nation's leading progressives: Theodore Roosevelt, Senator Henry Cabot Lodge, and others. Powerful opponents—employers who saw immigration as a source of cheap labor, immigrants themselves, and the immigrants' political representatives—managed to block the restriction movement for a time. But by the beginning of World War I (which itself effectively blocked immigration temporarily), the nativist tide was clearly gaining strength.

Suffrage for Women

Perhaps the largest single reform movement of the progressive era, indeed one of the largest in American history, was the fight for woman suffrage—a movement that attracted support from both women and men.

It is sometimes difficult for today's Americans to understand why the suffrage (or right-to-vote) issue could have become the source of such enormous controversy in the early twentieth century. But at the time, suffrage seemed to many of its critics a very radical demand—in part because of the rationale some of its supporters used to advance it. Throughout the late nineteenth century, many suffrage advocates presented their views in terms of "natural rights," arguing that women deserved the same rights as men—including, first and foremost, the right to vote. Elizabeth Cady Stanton, for example, wrote in 1892 of woman as "the arbiter of her own destiny. . . . if we are to consider her as a citizen, as a member of a great nation, she must have the same rights as all other members." A woman's role as "mother, wife, sister, daughter" was "incidental" to her larger role as a part of society.

This was an argument that boldly challenged the views of many men (and even many women) who believed that society required a distinctive female "sphere" in which women would serve first and foremost as wives and mothers. And so a powerful antisuffrage movement emerged, which challenged this apparent threat to the existing social order.

SUFFRAGISTS Suffrage activists hang posters along the boardwalk in the beachfront town of Long Branch, New Jersey. Twenty-nine states had permitted women at least some access to the ballot before ratification of the Nineteenth Amendment in 1920. New Jersey was not one of them.

The suffrage movement began to overcome this opposition and to win some substantial victories in the first years of the twentieth century. That was in part because suffragists were becoming better organized and more politically sophisticated than their opponents. Under the leadership of Anna Howard Shaw, a Boston social worker, and Carrie Chapman Catt, a journalist from Iowa, the National American Woman Suffrage Association grew from a membership of about 13,000 in 1893 to over 2 million in 1917. The involvement of such well-known and widely admired women as Jane Addams gave added respectability to the cause.

But the movement also gained strength because many of its most prominent leaders began to justify suffrage in "safer," less threatening ways. Suffrage, some supporters began to argue, would not challenge the "separate sphere" in which women resided. It would allow women to bring their special and distinct virtues more widely to bear on society's problems. It was, they claimed, precisely because women occupied a distinct sphere—because as mothers and wives and homemakers they had special experiences and special sensitivities to bring to public life—that woman suffrage could make such an important contribution to politics. In particular, many suffragists argued that enfranchising women would help the temperance movement, by giving its largest group of supporters a political voice. Some suffrage advocates claimed that once women had the vote, war would become a thing of the past, since women would—by their calming, peaceful influence—help curb the belligerence of men. That was one reason why World War I gave the final, decisive push to the movement for suffrage.

Not all suffragists narrowed their arguments. Among working-class, immigrant, and black women in particular, suffrage continued to generate substantial support precisely because it seemed so radical, because it promised to reshape the role of women and reform the social order. But among members of the middle class, the separation of the suffrage movement from more radical feminist goals, and its association with other reform causes of concern to many Americans, helped it gain widespread support.

The principal triumphs of the suffrage movement began in 1910. That year, Washington became the first state in fourteen years to extend suffrage to women. California joined it a year later, and in 1912 four other Western states did the same. In 1913, Illinois became the first state east of the Mississippi to embrace woman suffrage. And in 1917 and 1918, New York and Michigan—two of the most populous states in the Union—gave women the vote. By 1919, thirty-nine states had granted women the right to vote in at least some elections; fifteen had allowed them full participation. In

1920, finally, suffragists won ratification of the Nineteenth Amendment, which guaranteed political rights to women throughout the nation.

To some feminists, however, the victory seemed less than complete. Alice Paul, the head of the militant National Woman's party (founded in 1916), never accepted the relatively conservative "separate sphere" justification for suffrage. She argued that the Nineteenth Amendment alone would not be sufficient to protect women's rights. Women needed more: a constitutional amendment that would provide clear, legal protection for their rights and would prohibit all discrimination on the basis of sex. But Alice Paul's argument found limited favor even among many of the most important leaders of the recently triumphant suffrage crusade.

The Dream of Socialism

At no time in the history of the United States to that point, and in few times after it, did radical critiques of the capitalist system attract more support than in the period between 1900 and 1914. Although never a force to rival, or even seriously threaten, the two major parties, the Socialist party of America grew during the progressive era into a force of considerable strength. In the election of 1900, it had attracted the support of fewer than 100,000 voters; in 1912, its durable leader and perennial presidential candidate, Eugene V. Debs, received nearly 1 million ballots. Strongest in urban immigrant communities (particularly among Germans and Jews), it attracted the loyalties, too, of a substantial number of Protestant farmers in the South and Midwest. Socialists won election to over 1,000 state and local offices. And they had the support at times of such intellectuals as Lincoln Steffens, the crusader against municipal corruption, and Walter Lippmann, the brilliant young journalist and social critic. Florence Kelley, Frances Willard, and other women reformers were attracted to socialism because of its support for pacifism and labor militancy.

Virtually all socialists agreed on the need for basic structural changes in the economy, but they differed widely on the extent of those changes and the tactics necessary to achieve them. Some endorsed the radical goals of European Marxists; others envisioned a more moderate reform that would allow small-scale private enterprise to survive but would nationalize the major industries. Militant groups within the party favored militant direct action. Most conspicuous was the radical labor union the Industrial Workers of the World (IWW), whose members were known to their opponents as the "Wobblies." Under the leadership of William ("Big Bill") Haywood, the IWW advocated a single union for all workers, making it one of the few labor organizations of its time committed to organizing the unskilled, and abolition of the "wage slave" system; it rejected political action in favor of strikes—especially the general strike. The Wobblies were widely believed to have been responsible for the dynamiting of railroad lines and power stations and other acts of terror, although evidence of their actual participation in such activities is slim.

More moderate socialists advocated peaceful change through political struggle, and it was they who dominated the party. They emphasized a gradual education of the public to the need for change and patient efforts within the system to enact it. But by the end of World War I, because the party had refused to support the war effort and because of a growing wave of antiradicalism that subjected the socialists to enormous harassment and persecution, socialism was in decline as a significant political force.

Decentralization and Regulation

Many reformers agreed with the socialists that the greatest threat to the nation's economy was excessive centralization and consolidation but retained a faith in the possibilities of reform within a capitalist system. Rather than nationalize basic industries, they hoped to restore the economy to a more human scale. Few envisioned a return to a society of small, local enterprises; some consolidation, they recognized, was inevitable. They did, however, argue that the federal government should work to break up the largest combinations and enforce a balance between the need for bigness and the need for competition. This viewpoint came to be identified particularly closely with Louis D. Brandeis, a brilliant lawyer and later justice of the Supreme Court, who spoke and wrote widely (most notably in his 1913 book, *Other People's Money*) about the "curse of bigness."

Other progressives were less enthusiastic about the virtues of competition. More important to them was efficiency, which they believed economic concentration encouraged. What government should do, they argued, was not fight "bigness" but guard against abuses of power by large institutions. It should distinguish between "good trusts" and "bad trusts," encouraging the good while disciplining the bad. Since economic consolidation was destined to remain a permanent feature of American society, continuing oversight by a strong, modernized government, led by a strong president, was essential. One of the most influential spokesmen for this emerging "nationalist" position was Herbert Croly, whose 1909 book, *The Promise of American Life*, became one of the most influential progressive documents.

Opinions varied widely on how that unity should be achieved. But increasingly, attention focused on some form of coordination of the industrial economy. To some, that meant businesses themselves should learn new ways of cooperation and self-regulation; some of the most energetic "progressive" reformers of the period, in fact, were businessmen searching for ways to bring order to their own troubled world. To others, the solution was for government to play a more active role in regulating and planning economic life. One of those who came to endorse that position (although not fully until after 1910) was Theodore Roosevelt, who became for a time the most powerful symbol of the reform impulse at the national level.

D E B A T I N G   T H E   P A S T

Progressivism

U NTIL THE EARLY 1950s, most historians seemed to agree on the central characteristics of early twentieth-century progressivism. It was just what the progressives themselves said it was: a movement by the "people" to curb the power of "special interests." More specifically, it was a protest by an aroused citizenry against the excessive power of urban bosses, corporate moguls, and corrupt elected officials.

In 1951, George Mowry began the process of challenging these assumptions by examining progressives in California and describing them as a small, privileged elite of business and professional figures: people who considered themselves the natural leaders of society and who were trying to recover their fading influence from the new capitalist institutions that had displaced them. Progressivism was not, in other words, a popular, democratic movement; it was the effort of a displaced elite to restore its authority. Richard Hofstadter expanded on this idea in *The Age of Reform* (1955) by describing reformers as people afflicted by "status anxiety," fading elites suffering not from economic but from psychological discontent.

The Mowry-Hofstadter argument soon encountered a range of challenges. In 1963, Gabriel Kolko published his influential study *The Triumph of Conservatism*, in which he rejected both the older "democratic" view of progressivism and the newer "status-anxiety" view. Progressive reform, he argued, was not an effort to protect the people from the corporations; it was, rather, a vehicle through which corporate leaders used the government to protect themselves from competition. Regulation, Kolko argued, was "invariably controlled by the leaders of the regulated industry and directed towards ends they deemed acceptable or desirable."

A more moderate reinterpretation came from historians embracing what would later be called the "organizational" approach to twentieth-century American history. First Samuel Hays, in *The Response to Industrial-*

ism (1957), and then Robert Wiebe, in *The Search for Order* (1967), portrayed progressivism as a broad effort by businessmen, professionals, and other middle-class people to bring order and efficiency to political and economic life. In the new industrial society, economic power was increasingly concentrated in large, national organizations, while social and political life remained centered primarily in local communities. Progressivism, Wiebe argued, was the effort of a "new middle class"—a class tied to the emerging national economy—to stabilize and enhance its position in society by bringing those two worlds together.

In the 1970s and 1980s, scholarship on progressivism moved in so many different directions that some historians came to despair of finding any consistent meaning in the term. Much of the new scholarship focused on discovering new groups among whom "progressive" ideas and efforts flourished. Historians found evidence of progressivism in the rising movement by consumers to define their interests; in the growth of reform movements among African-Americans; in the changing nature of urban political machines. Particularly influential was the effort to reveal the crucial role of women in promoting reform as a way of protecting their interests within a rapidly changing domestic sphere or of expanding their role in the public world.

Other scholars attempted to identify progressivism with broad changes in the structure and culture of politics. Richard McCormick, writing in 1981, argued that the crucial change in the "progressive era" was the decline of political parties and the corresponding rise of interest groups working for particular social and economic goals. Progressivism, he and others have suggested, was not so much a coherent "movement" as part of the broader process by which Americans adapted their political and social systems to the realities of the modern industrial age. At the same time, many historians were arguing that the role of women in progressive efforts helped determine the nature of early-twentieth-century reform, that women not only dominated many reform activities but shaped them to serve what they perceived to be the interests of their gender.

The search for the "essence" of progressivism will undoubtedly continue. But the scholarship of recent decades suggests that the real answer to the nature of progressive reform may be a recognition of its enormous diversity.

CHAPTER TWENTY-TWO

The Battle
for National Reform

Theodore Roosevelt and the Progressive Presidency
The Troubled Succession ~ Woodrow Wilson and the New Freedom
The "Big Stick": America and the World, 1901–1917

E fforts to reform the industrial economy encountered repeated frustrations at the state and local level. The great combinations were national in scope, and reformers gradually concluded that only national action could effectively control their power. Beginning early in the twentieth century, they began to look to the federal government.

But just as at the state and local levels, the national government—mired in partisan politics—seemed poorly suited to serve as an agent of reform. Progressives attempted to make it more responsive to their demands. Some reformers, for example, urged an end to the system by which state legislatures elected the members of the United States Senate; they proposed instead a direct popular election, which they believed would force the Senate to react more directly to public demands. The Seventeenth Amendment, passed by Congress in 1912 and ratified by the states in 1913, provided for that change.

But even a reformed Congress, progressives believed, could not be expected to provide the kind of coherent leadership their agenda required. Congress was too clumsy, too divided, too tied to local, parochial interests. If the federal government was truly to fulfill its mission, most reformers agreed, it would require leadership from one office capable of providing "modern," "efficient" leadership: the presidency.

THEODORE ROOSEVELT AND
THE PROGRESSIVE PRESIDENCY

To a generation of progressive reformers, Theodore Roosevelt was more than an admired public figure; he was an idol. No president before and few after attracted such attention and devotion. Yet for all his popularity among reformers, Roosevelt was in many respects decidedly conservative. He earned his extraordinary popularity less because of the extent of his reforms than because of his ebullient public personality and because he brought to his office a broad conception of its powers and invested the presidency with something of its modern status as the center of national political life.

The Accidental President

When President William McKinley suddenly died in September 1901, the victim of an assassination, Roosevelt (who had been elected vice president less than a year before) was only forty-two years old, the youngest man ever to assume the presidency. Already, however, he had achieved a reputation within the Republican party as something of a wild man. Party leaders sensed his independence and despaired of controlling him. Mark Hanna, who had warned McKinley against selecting Roosevelt as his running mate, exclaimed, "Now look, that damned cowboy is president of the United States!" But Roosevelt as president never openly rebelled against the leaders of his party. He became, rather, a champion of cautious, moderate change.

Roosevelt envisioned the federal government not as the agent of any particular interest but as a mediator of the public good, with the president at its center. This attitude found expression in Roosevelt's policies toward the great industrial combinations. He was not opposed to the principle of economic concentration, but he acknowledged that consolidation produced dangerous abuses of power. He allied himself, therefore, with those progressives who urged regulation (but not destruction) of the trusts.

At the heart of Roosevelt's policy was his desire to win for government the power to investigate the activities of corporations and publicize the results. The pressure of educated public opinion, he believed, would alone eliminate most corporate abuses. Government could legislate solutions for those that remained. Although Roosevelt was not a trust buster at heart, he engaged in a few highly publicized efforts to break up combinations. In 1902, he ordered the Justice Department to invoke the Sherman Antitrust Act against a great new railroad monopoly in the Northwest, the Northern

Securities Company. At the same time, however, he assured financial leaders that the suit did not signal a general campaign to dissolve trusts. Although he filed more than forty additional antitrust suits during the remainder of his presidency, Roosevelt made no serious effort to reverse the prevailing trend toward economic concentration.

A similar commitment to establishing the government as an impartial regulatory mechanism shaped Roosevelt's policy toward labor. In the past, federal intervention in industrial disputes had almost always meant action on behalf of employers. Roosevelt was willing to consider labor's position as well. When a bitter 1902 strike by the United Mine Workers against the anthracite coal industry dragged on long enough to endanger coal supplies for the coming winter, Roosevelt asked both the operators and the miners to accept impartial federal arbitration. When the mine owners balked, Roosevelt threatened to send federal troops to seize the mines and resume coal production. The operators finally relented. Arbitrators awarded the strikers a 10 percent wage increase and a nine-hour day but no recognition of their union—less than they had wanted but more than they would likely have won without Roosevelt's intervention. Despite such episodes, Roosevelt viewed himself as no more the champion of labor than of management. On several occasions, he ordered federal troops to intervene in strikes on behalf of employers.

Reform was not Roosevelt's main priority during his first years as president. He was principally concerned with winning the election in his own right, which meant not antagonizing the conservative Republican Old Guard. By early 1904, Roosevelt had all but neutralized his opposition within the party. He won its presidential nomination with ease. And in the general election, where he faced a pallid conservative Democrat, Alton B. Parker, he captured over 57 percent of the popular vote and lost no states outside the South. Now, relieved of immediate political concerns, he was free to display the extent (and the limits) of his commitment to reform.

The Square Deal

During the 1904 campaign, Roosevelt boasted that he had worked in the anthracite coal strike to provide everyone with a "square deal." In his second term, he tried to extend his square deal further. One of his first targets was the powerful railroad industry. The Interstate Commerce Act of 1887, establishing the Interstate Commerce Commission (ICC), had been an early effort to regulate the industry; but over the years, the courts had sharply limited its influence. The Hepburn Railroad Regulation Act of 1906 sought to restore some regulatory authority to the government by giving the ICC authority to inspect the books of railroad companies. But it was too cautious a bill to satisfy progressives.

Roosevelt also pressured Congress to enact the Pure Food and Drug Act, which, despite weaknesses in its enforcement mechanisms, restricted the sale of dangerous or ineffective medicines. When Upton Sinclair's powerful novel *The Jungle* appeared in 1906, featuring appalling descriptions of conditions in the meat-packing industry, Roosevelt insisted on passage of the Meat Inspection Act, which ultimately helped eliminate many diseases once transmitted in impure meat. Starting in 1907, he proposed even more stringent measures: an eight-hour day for workers, broader compensation for victims of industrial accidents, inheritance and income taxes, regulation of the stock market, and others. He also started openly to

MAKING SAUSAGES The shockingly unsanitary conditions by which meatpackers (such as those shown here in the Chicago stockyards) made sausages inspired Upton Sinclair's novel *The Jungle*, which in turn precipitated federal legislation, the Meat Inspection Act of 1906, establishing government inspection of meat products.

criticize conservatives in Congress and the judiciary, who were obstructing these programs. The result was not only a general stalemate in Roosevelt's reform agenda but a widening gulf between the president and the conservative wing of his party.

Roosevelt's aggressive policies on behalf of conservation contributed to that gulf. A lifelong sportsman and naturalist, he had long been concerned about the unchecked exploitation of America's natural resources and its remaining wilderness. Using executive powers, he limited private development on millions of acres of undeveloped government land by adding them to the previously modest national forest system. When conservatives in Congress restricted his authority over public lands in 1907, Roosevelt and his chief forester, Gifford Pinchot, worked furiously before the bill became law to seize all the forests and many of the water power sites still in the public domain.

Roosevelt was the first president to take an active interest in the new and struggling American conservation movement, and his policies had a lasting effect on national environmental policies. More than most public figures, he was sympathetic to the concerns of the naturalists—those within the movement committed to protecting the natural beauty of the land. But

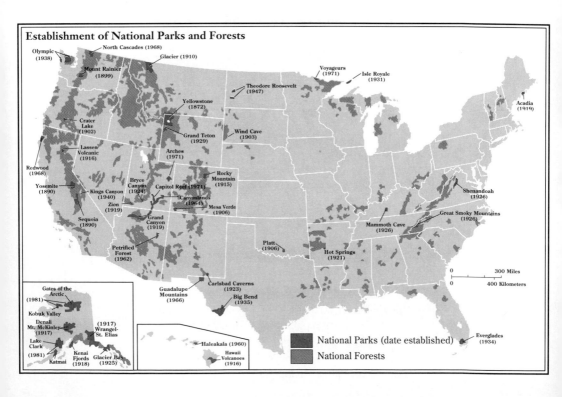

Establishment of National Parks and Forests

National Parks (date established)

National Forests

Roosevelt's policies tended to favor another faction within the conservation movement—those who believed in carefully managed development. That was in part a result of the influence of Pinchot, the first director of the National Forest Service, who supported rational and efficient human use of the wilderness.

The Old Guard may have opposed Roosevelt's efforts to extend government control over vast new lands. But they eagerly supported another important aspect of Roosevelt's natural resource policy: public reclamation and irrigation projects. In 1902, the president backed the Newlands Reclamation Act, which provided federal funds for the construction of dams, reservoirs, and canals in the West—projects to open new lands for cultivation and, years later, to provide cheap electric power. It was the beginning of many years of federal aid for irrigation and power development in the Western states.

Despite the flurry of reforms Roosevelt was able to enact, the government still had relatively little control over the industrial economy. That became clear in 1907, when a serious panic and recession began. Conservatives blamed Roosevelt's "mad" economic policies for the disaster. And while the president, naturally (and correctly), disagreed, he nevertheless acted quickly to reassure business leaders that he would not interfere with their private recovery efforts.

The great financier J. P. Morgan helped construct a pool of the assets of several important New York banks to prop up shaky financial institutions. The key to the arrangement, Morgan told the president, was the purchase by U.S. Steel of the shares of the Tennessee Coal and Iron Company, currently held by a threatened New York bank. He would, he insisted, need assurances that the purchase would not prompt antitrust action. Roosevelt tacitly agreed, and the Morgan plan proceeded. Whether or not as a result, the panic soon subsided.

Roosevelt loved being president, and many people assumed he would run for the office again in 1908 despite the longstanding tradition of presidents' serving no more than two terms. But the panic of 1907, combined with Roosevelt's growing "radicalism" during his second term, so alienated conservatives in his own party that he might have had difficulty winning the Republican nomination for another term despite his great popularity. In 1904, moreover, he had made a public promise to step down four years later. And so, after nearly eight energetic years in the White House, during which he had transformed the role of the presidency in American government, Theodore Roosevelt, fifty years old, retired from public life—briefly.

THE TROUBLED SUCCESSION

William Howard Taft, who assumed the presidency in 1909, had been Theodore Roosevelt's most trusted lieutenant and his hand-picked successor; progressive reformers believed him to be one of their own. But Taft had also been a restrained and moderate jurist, a man with a punctilious regard for legal process; conservatives expected him to abandon Roosevelt's aggressive use of presidential powers. By seeming acceptable to almost everyone, Taft won election to the White House in 1908 with almost ridiculous ease. He received his party's nomination virtually uncontested. His victory in the general election in November—over William Jennings Bryan, running forlornly for the Democrats for the third time—was a foregone conclusion. Taft entered the White House on a wave of good feeling.

Four years later, however, Taft would leave office the most decisively defeated president of the twentieth century, with his party deeply divided and the government in the hands of a Democratic administration for the first time in twenty years. Taft's failure was a result in part of his own character and style: his cautious, limited use of presidential powers; his failure to match Roosevelt's personal dynamism. (Contributing to Taft's image as a not very vigorous man was his enormous weight, which at times rose to 350 pounds.) More significant, however, was that having come into office as the darling of progressives and conservatives alike, he soon found that he could not please both groups. Gradually he found himself, without really intending it, pleasing the conservatives and alienating the progressives.

Taft and the Progressives

Taft's first problem arose in the opening months of the new administration, when he called Congress into special session to lower protective tariff rates, an old progressive demand. But the president made no effort to overcome the opposition of the congressional Old Guard, arguing that it would violate the constitutional doctrine of separation of powers if he were to intervene in legislative matters. The result was the feeble Payne-Aldrich Tariff, which reduced tariff rates scarcely at all and in some areas actually raised them. Progressives resented the president's passivity and were suspicious of his motives.

With Taft's standing among Republican progressives deteriorating and with the party growing more and more deeply divided, a sensational controversy broke out late in 1909 that helped destroy Taft's popularity with reformers for good. Many progressives had been unhappy when Taft replaced Roosevelt's secretary of the interior, James R. Garfield, an aggressive conservationist, with Richard A. Ballinger, a more conservative corporate lawyer. Suspicion of Ballinger grew when he attempted to invalidate Roosevelt's removal of nearly 1 million acres of forests and mineral reserves from the public lands available for private development.

In the midst of this mounting concern, Louis Glavis, an Interior Department investigator, charged the new secretary with having once connived to turn over valuable public coal lands in Alaska to a private syndicate for personal profit. Glavis took the evidence to Gifford Pinchot, still head of the Forest Service and a critic of Ballinger's policies. Pinchot took the charges to the president. Taft investigated them and decided they were groundless. But Pinchot was not satisfied, particularly after Taft fired Glavis for his part in the episode. He leaked the story to the press and asked Congress to investigate the scandal. The president discharged him for insubordination, and the congressional committee appointed to study the controversy, dominated by the Old Guard, exonerated Ballinger. But progressives throughout the country supported Pinchot. The controversy aroused as much public passion as any dispute of its time; and when it was over, Taft had alienated the supporters of Roosevelt completely and, it seemed, irrevocably.

The Return of Roosevelt

During most of these controversies, Theodore Roosevelt was far away: on a long hunting safari in Africa and an extended tour of Europe. To the American public, however, Roosevelt remained a formidable presence. And his return to New York in the spring of 1910 was a major public event.

Roosevelt insisted that he had no plans to return to active politics, but his resolve lasted less than a week. Politicians began flocking immediately to his home at Oyster Bay, Long Island, for conferences. Roosevelt took an active role in several New York political controversies; and within a month, he announced that he would embark on a national speaking tour before the end of the summer. Furious with Taft, he was becoming convinced that he alone was capable of reuniting the Republican party.

The real signal of Roosevelt's decision to assume leadership of Republican reformers came in a speech he gave on September 1, 1910, in Osawatomie, Kansas. In the speech, he outlined a set of principles, which he labeled the "New Nationalism," that made clear he had moved a consider-

ROOSEVELT AT OSAWATOMIE Roosevelt's famous speech at Osawatomie, Kansas, in 1910 was the most radical of his career and openly marked his break with the Taft administration and the Republican leadership.

able way from the cautious conservatism of the first years of his presidency. Influenced by Herbert Croly's writings, he argued that social justice was possible only through the vigorous efforts of a strong federal government whose executive acted as the "steward of the public welfare." Those who thought primarily of property rights and personal profit "must now give way to the advocate of human welfare, who rightly maintains that every man holds his property subject to the general right of the community to regulate its use to whatever degree the public welfare may require it." He supported graduated income and inheritance taxes, workers' compensation for industrial accidents, regulation of the labor of women and children, tariff revision, and firmer regulation of corporations.

Spreading Insurgency

The congressional elections of 1910 provided further evidence of how far the progressive revolt had spread. In primary elections, conservative Republicans suffered defeat after defeat while almost all the progressive incumbents were reelected. In the general election, the Democrats, who were now offering progressive candidates of their own, won control of the House of Representatives for the first time in sixteen years and gained strength in the Senate. Reform sentiment seemed clearly on the rise. But Roosevelt still denied any presidential ambitions and claimed that his real purpose was to pressure Taft to return to progressive policies. Two events, however, changed his mind.

The first was a 1911 antitrust decision by the Taft administration. Taft had been more active than Roosevelt in enforcing the provisions of the Sherman Antitrust Act and had launched dozens of suits against corporate combinations. On October 27, 1911, the administration announced a suit against U.S. Steel, charging, among other things, that the 1907 acquisition of the Tennessee Coal and Iron Company had been illegal. Roosevelt had approved that acquisition in the midst of the 1907 panic, and he was enraged by the implication that he had acted improperly.

But Roosevelt was reluctant at first to become a candidate for president, largely because Senator Robert La Follette had been working since 1911 to secure the presidential nomination for himself. But La Follette's candidacy stumbled in February 1912, when, exhausted and distraught over his daughter's illness, he appeared to suffer a nervous breakdown during a speech in Philadelphia. Roosevelt announced his candidacy on February 22.

TR Versus Taft

La Follette retained some diehard support. But for all practical purposes, the campaign for the Republican nomination had now become a battle between Roosevelt, the champion of the progressives, and Taft, the candidate of the conservatives. Roosevelt scored overwhelming victories in all thirteen presidential primaries and arrived at the convention convinced that he was the choice of the party rank and file. Taft, however, remained the choice of most party leaders, whose preference was decisive.

The battle for the nomination at the Chicago convention revolved around an unusually large number of contested delegates: 254 in all. Roosevelt needed fewer than half the disputed seats to clinch the nomination. But the Republican National Committee, controlled by the Old Guard, awarded all but 19 of them to Taft. At a rally the night before the convention opened, Roosevelt addressed 5,000 cheering supporters and announced that if the party refused to seat his delegates, he would continue his own candidacy outside the party. "We stand at Armageddon," he told the roaring crowd, "and we battle for the Lord." The next day, he led his supporters out of the convention, and out of the party. Taft was then quietly nominated on the first ballot.

Roosevelt summoned his supporters back to Chicago in August for another convention, this one to launch the new Progressive party and nominate himself as its presidential candidate. Roosevelt approached the battle feeling, as he put it, "fit as a bull moose" (thus giving his new party an enduring nickname). But by then, he was aware that his cause was virtually hopeless. That was partly because many of the insurgents who had supported him during the primaries refused to follow him out of the Republican party. It was also because of the man the Democrats had nominated for president.

WOODROW WILSON AND THE NEW FREEDOM

The 1912 presidential contest was not simply one between conservatives and reformers. It was also one between two brands of progressivism, that reflected two different views of America's future. And it was one that matched the two most important national leaders of the early twentieth century in unequal contest.

Woodrow Wilson

Reform sentiment had been gaining strength within the Democratic as well as the Republican party in the first years of the century. At the 1912 Democratic convention in Baltimore in June, Champ Clark, the conservative Speaker of the House, was unable to assemble the necessary two-thirds majority because of progressive opposition. Finally, on the forty-sixth ballot, Woodrow Wilson, the governor of New Jersey and the only genuinely progressive candidate in the race, emerged as the party's nominee.

Wilson had risen to political prominence by an unusual path. He had been a professor of political science at Princeton until 1902, when he was named president of the university. Elected governor of New Jersey in 1910, he demonstrated a commitment to reform that he had already displayed as a university president; and during his two years in the statehouse, he earned a national reputation for winning passage of progressive legislation.

As a presidential candidate in 1912, Wilson presented a progressive program that came to be called the "New Freedom." Wilson's New Freedom differed from Roosevelt's New Nationalism, most clearly in its approach to economic policy and the trusts. Roosevelt believed in accepting economic concentration and using government to regulate and control it. Wilson seemed to side with those who (like Brandeis) believed that bigness was both unjust and inefficient, that the proper response to monopoly was not to regulate it but to destroy it.

The 1912 presidential campaign was something of an anticlimax. William Howard Taft, resigned to defeat, delivered a few desultory, conservative speeches and then lapsed into silence. Roosevelt campaigned energetically (until a gunshot wound from a would-be assassin forced him to the sidelines during the last weeks before the election), but he failed to draw any significant numbers of Democratic progressives away from Wilson. In November, Roosevelt and Taft split the Republicans; Wilson held onto the Democratics and won. He polled only a plurality of the popular vote: 42 percent, compared with 27 percent for Roosevelt, 23 percent for Taft, and 6 percent for the socialist Eugene Debs. But in the electoral college, Wilson won 435 of the 531 votes. Roosevelt had carried only six states, Taft two, Debs none.

The Scholar as President

Wilson was a bold and forceful president. More than William Howard Taft, more even than Theodore Roosevelt, Wilson concentrated the powers of the executive branch in his own hands. He exerted firm control over his

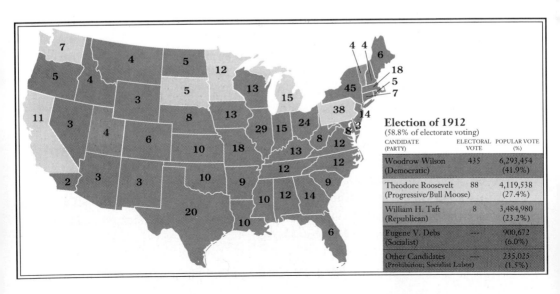

Election of 1912
(58.8% of electorate voting)

CANDIDATE (PARTY)	ELECTORAL VOTE	POPULAR VOTE (%)
Woodrow Wilson (Democratic)	435	6,293,454 (41.9%)
Theodore Roosevelt (Progressive/Bull Moose)	88	4,119,538 (27.4%)
William H. Taft (Republican)	8	3,484,980 (23.2%)
Eugene V. Debs (Socialist)	----	900,672 (6.0%)
Other Candidates (Prohibition; Socialist Labor)	----	235,025 (1.5%)

cabinet, and he delegated real authority only to those whose loyalty to him was beyond question. Perhaps the clearest indication of his style of leadership was the identity of the most powerful figure in his administration: Colonel Edward M. House, an intelligent and ambitious Texan who held no office and whose only claim to authority was his personal intimacy with the president.

In legislative matters, Wilson skillfully used his position as party leader and his appointive powers to weld together a coalition of Southern conservatives and Northern and Western progressives who would, he believed, support his program. Democratic majorities in both houses of Congress made his task easier, as did the realization of many Democrats that the party must enact a progressive program in order to maintain those majorities.

Wilson's first triumph as president was a substantial lowering of the protective tariff. The Underwood-Simmons Tariff, passed in a special session of Congress that Wilson summoned shortly after his inauguration, provided cuts substantial enough, progressives believed, to introduce real competition into American markets and thus to help break the power of trusts. It passed easily in the House; and despite Senate efforts to weaken its provisions, the bill survived more or less intact. Wilson had succeeded where Roosevelt and Taft had not. To make up for the loss of revenue under the new tariff, Congress approved a graduated income tax, which the recently adopted Sixteenth Amendment to the Constitution now permitted. This first modern income tax imposed a 1 percent tax on individuals and corporations earning over $4,000, with rates ranging up to 6 percent on incomes over $500,000.

Wilson held Congress in session through the summer to work on a major reform of the American banking system. Few argued that change was unnecessary, but there were many different opinions about how best to attack the problem. Some legislators, among them Representative Carter Glass of Virginia, wanted to decentralize control of the banking system so as to limit the power of the great Wall Street financiers without substantially increasing the power of government. Others, including William Jennings Bryan and fellow agrarians, wanted firm government control. Wilson endorsed a plan that divided power in the system. The government would have substantial control at the national level; the bankers would retain control at the local level. The Federal Reserve Act passed both houses of Congress and was signed by the president on December 23, 1913. It was the most important piece of domestic legislation of Wilson's administration.

The Federal Reserve Act created twelve regional banks, each to be owned and controlled by the individual banks of its district. The regional Federal Reserve banks would hold a certain percentage of the assets of their member banks in reserve; they would use those reserves to support loans to private banks at an interest (or "discount") rate that the Federal Reserve system would set; they would issue a new type of paper currency—Federal Reserve notes—which would become the nation's basic medium of trade and would be backed by the government. Most important, perhaps, they would serve as central institutions able to shift funds quickly to troubled areas—to meet increased demands for credit or to protect imperiled banks. Supervising and regulating the entire system was a national Federal Reserve Board, whose members were appointed by the president. All "national" banks were required to join the system; smaller banks were encouraged to do the same. Nearly half the nation's banking resources were represented in the system within a year, and 80 percent by the late 1920s.

The cornerstone of Wilson's campaign for the presidency had been his promise to attack economic concentration, most notably to destroy monopolistic trusts. By the beginning of his second year in office, however, his approach to the trusts appeared to have changed. He was moving away from his earlier insistence that government dismantle the combinations and toward a commitment to regulating them. On this issue, at least, the New Freedom was beginning to resemble the New Nationalism.

In 1914, he proposed two measures to deal with the problem of monopoly. There was a proposal to create a federal agency through which the government would help business police itself—in other words, a regulatory commission of the type Roosevelt had advocated in 1912. There were, in addition, proposals to strengthen the government's power to prosecute and dismantle the trusts—a decentralizing approach more characteristic of Wilson's campaign. The two measures took shape, ultimately, as the Federal Trade Commission Act and the Clayton Antitrust Act.

The Federal Trade Commission Act created a regulatory agency of the same name that would help businesses determine in advance whether their actions would be acceptable to the government. The agency would also have authority to launch prosecutions against "unfair trade practices," which the law did not define, and it would have wide power to investigate corporate behavior. The act, in short, increased the government's regulatory authority significantly. Wilson signed it happily. But he seemed to lose interest in the Clayton Antitrust Bill and did little to protect it from conservative assaults, which greatly weakened it. The vigorous legal pursuit of monopoly that Wilson had promised in 1912 never materialized. The future, he had apparently decided, lay with government supervision.

Retreat and Advance

By the fall of 1914, Wilson believed that the program of the New Freedom was essentially complete and that agitation for reform would now subside. He refused to support the movement for national woman suffrage. Deferring to Southern Democrats, and reflecting his own Southern background, he condoned the reimposition of segregation in the agencies of the federal government (in contrast to Theodore Roosevelt, who had ordered the elimination of many such barriers). When congressional progressives attempted to enlist his support for new reform legislation, he dismissed their proposals as unconstitutional or unnecessary.

The congressional elections of 1914, however, shattered the president's complacency. Democrats suffered major losses in the House of Representatives, and voters who in 1912 had supported the Progressive party began returning to the Republicans. Wilson would not be able to rely on a divided opposition when he ran for reelection in 1916. By the end of 1915, Wilson had begun to support a second flurry of reforms. In January 1916, he appointed Louis Brandeis to the Supreme Court, making him not only the first Jew but the most advanced progressive to serve there. Later, he supported a measure to make it easier for farmers to receive credit and one creating a system of workers' compensation for federal employees.

Much of this renewed effort at reform suggested that Wilson had moved even closer to the New Nationalism. He was sponsoring measures that expanded the role of the national government in important ways, giving it new instruments by which it could regulate the economy and help shape the nation's economic and social structure. In 1916, for example, Wilson supported the Keating-Owen Act, the first federal law regulating child labor. The measure prohibited the shipment of goods produced by underage children across state lines, thus giving an expanded importance to the constitutional clause assigning Congress the task of regulating interstate commerce. (It would be some years before the Supreme Court would uphold this interpretation of the clause; the Court invalidated the Keating-Owen Act in 1918.) The president similarly supported measures that used federal taxing authority as a vehicle for legislating social change. After the Court struck down Keating-Owen, a new law attempted to achieve the same goal by imposing a heavy tax on the products of child labor. (The Court later struck it down too.) And the Smith-Lever Act of 1914 demonstrated another way in which the federal government could influence local behavior; it used federal spending to change public behavior by offering matching federal grants to states that agreed to support agricultural extension education.

THE "BIG STICK": AMERICA AND THE WORLD, 1901–1917

American foreign policy during the progressive years reflected many of the same impulses that were motivating domestic reform. But more than that, it reflected the nation's new sense of itself as a world power with far-flung economic and political interests.

Roosevelt and "Civilization"

Theodore Roosevelt was well suited, both by temperament and by ideology, for an activist foreign policy. He believed in the value and importance of using American power in the world (a conviction he once described by citing the proverb, "Speak softly, but carry a big stick"). And he believed that an important distinction existed between the "civilized" and "uncivilized" nations of the world. "Civilized" nations, as he defined them, were predominantly white and Anglo-Saxon or Teutonic; "uncivilized" nations were generally non-white, Latin, or Slavic. But racism was only partly the basis of the distinction. At least as important was economic development. He believed, therefore, that Japan, a rapidly industrializing society, had earned admission to the ranks of the civilized.

Civilized nations were, by Roosevelt's definition, producers of industrial goods; uncivilized nations were suppliers of raw materials and markets. There was, he believed, an economic relationship between the two parts that was vital to both of them. A civilized society, therefore, had the right and duty to intervene in the affairs of a "backward" nation to preserve order and stability—for the sake of both nations. Accordingly, Roosevelt became an early champion of the development of American sea power. By 1906, Roosevelt's support had enabled the American navy to attain a size and strength surpassed only by that of Great Britain (although Germany was fast gaining ground).

Protecting the Open Door in Asia

Roosevelt considered the "Open Door" vital for maintaining American trade in the Pacific and for preventing any single nation from establishing dominance there. He looked with alarm, therefore, at the military rivalries involving Japan, Russia, Germany, and France in Asia.

In 1904 the Japanese staged a surprise attack on the Russian fleet at Port Arthur in southern Manchuria, a province of China that both Russia and Japan hoped to control. Roosevelt, hoping to prevent either nation from becoming dominant there, agreed to a Japanese request to mediate an end to the conflict. Russia, faring badly in the war, had no choice but to agree. At a peace conference in Portsmouth, New Hampshire, in 1905, Roosevelt extracted from the embattled Russians a recognition of Japan's territorial gains and from the Japanese an agreement to cease the fighting and expand no further. At the same time, he negotiated a secret agreement with the Japanese to ensure that the United States could continue to trade freely in the region. Roosevelt won the Nobel Peace Prize in 1906 for his work in ending the Russo-Japanese War. But in the years that followed, relations between the United States and Japan steadily deteriorated. Having destroyed the Russian fleet at Port Arthur, Japan now emerged as the preeminent naval power in the Pacific and soon began to exclude American trade from many of the territories it controlled.

It did not help matters that in 1906 the school board of San Francisco voted to segregate the city's Asian schoolchildren in separate schools; or that a year later, the California legislature attempted to pass legislation limiting the immigration of Japanese laborers into the state. Anti-Asian riots in California and inflammatory stories in the Hearst papers about the "Yellow Peril" further fanned resentment in Japan. The president persuaded the San Francisco school board to rescind its edict in return for a Japanese agreement to stop the flow of agricultural immigrants into California. Then, lest the Japanese government construe his actions as a sign of weakness, Roosevelt sent sixteen battleships of the new American navy (known as the "Great White Fleet") on an unprecedented voyage around the world that included a call on Japan—to remind the Japanese of the potential might of the United States.

The Iron-Fisted Neighbor

Roosevelt took a particular interest in events in what he (and most other Americans) considered the nation's special sphere of interest: Latin America. Unwilling to share trading rights, let alone military control, with any other nation, Roosevelt embarked on a series of ventures in the Caribbean and South America that established a pattern of American intervention in the region that would long survive his presidency.

Crucial to Roosevelt's thinking was an incident early in his administration. When the government of Venezuela began in 1902 to renege on debts to European bankers, naval forces of Britain, Italy, and Germany blockaded the Venezuelan coast. Then German ships began to bombard a Venezuelan port amid rumors that Germany planned to establish a permanent base in the region. Roosevelt used the threat of American naval power to pressure the German navy to withdraw.

The incident helped persuade Roosevelt that European intrusions into Latin America could result not only from aggression but from instability or irresponsibility (such as defaulting on debts) within the Latin American nations themselves. As a result, in 1904 he added a "Roosevelt Corollary" to the Monroe Doctrine. The United States, he claimed, had the right not only to oppose European intervention in the Western Hemisphere but to intervene itself in the domestic affairs of its neighbors if those neighbors proved unable to maintain order on their own.

The immediate motivation for the Roosevelt Corollary, and the first

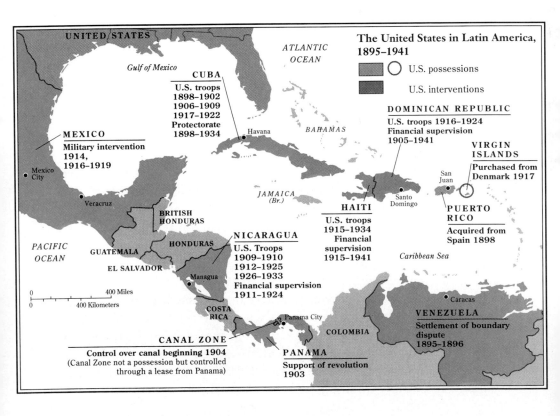

opportunity for using it, was a crisis in the Dominican Republic. A revolution had toppled its corrupt and bankrupt government in 1903, but the new regime proved no better able than the old to make good on the country's $22 million in debts to European nations. Using the Roosevelt Corollary rationale, Roosevelt established, in effect, an American receivership, assuming control of Dominican customs and distributing 45 percent of the revenues to the Dominicans and the rest to foreign creditors. This arrangement lasted, in one form or another, for more than three decades.

In 1902, the United States had granted political independence to Cuba, but only after the new government had agreed to the so-called Platt Amendment to its constitution, giving the United States the right to prevent any foreign power from intruding into the new nation. In 1906, when domestic uprisings seemed to threaten the internal stability of the island, Roosevelt reasoned that America must intervene to "protect" Cuba from disorder. American troops landed in Cuba, quelled the fighting, and remained there for three years.

The Panama Canal

The most celebrated accomplishment of Roosevelt's presidency was the construction of the Panama Canal. Linking the Atlantic and the Pacific by creating a channel through Central America had been an unfulfilled dream of many nations since the mid-nineteenth century. Roosevelt was determined to achieve it.

The first step was the 1901 Hay-Pauncefote Treaty between America and Britain, canceling an 1850 pact in which the two nations had agreed to construct any such canal together. The United States was now free to act alone. The next step was to choose a site for the canal. At first, Roosevelt and many others favored a route across Nicaragua, which would permit a sea-level canal requiring no locks. But they soon turned instead to the narrow Isthmus of Panama in Colombia, the site of an earlier, failed effort by a French company to construct a channel. Although the Panama route was not at sea level (and would thus require locks), it was shorter than the one in Nicaragua. And construction was already about 40 percent complete. When the French company lowered the price for its holdings from $109 million to $40 million, the United States chose Panama.

BUILDING THE PANAMA CANAL Construction proceeds at the Gatun Middle Locks, November 1910. Whatever its political implications, the Panama Canal was one of the great engineering feats of the early twentieth century.

Roosevelt dispatched John Hay, his secretary of state, to negotiate an agreement with Colombian diplomats in Washington that would allow construction to begin without delay. Under heavy American pressure, the Colombian chargé d'affaires, Tomas Herrán, unwisely signed an agreement giving the United States perpetual rights to a six-mile-wide "canal zone" across Colombia; in return, the United States would pay Colombia $10 million and an annual rental of $250,000. The treaty produced outrage in the Colombian senate, which refused to ratify it. Colombia then sent a new representative to Washington with instructions to demand at least $20 million from the Americans plus a share of the payment to the French.

Roosevelt was furious and began to look for ways to circumvent the Colombian government. Philippe Bunau-Varilla, chief engineer of the French canal project, was a ready ally. In November 1903, he helped organize and finance a revolution in Panama. There had been many previous revolts, all of them failures. But this one had the support of the United States. Roosevelt landed troops from the U.S.S. *Nashville* in Panama to "maintain order." Their presence prevented Colombian forces from suppressing the rebellion, and three days later Roosevelt recognized Panama as an independent nation. The new Panamanian government quickly agreed to the terms the Colombian senate had rejected. Work on the canal proceeded rapidly, and it opened in 1914.

Taft and "Dollar Diplomacy"

Like his predecessor, William Howard Taft worked to advance the nation's economic interests overseas. But he showed little interest in Roosevelt's larger vision of world stability. Taft's secretary of state, the corporate attorney Philander C. Knox, worked aggressively to extend American investments into less developed regions. Critics called his policies "Dollar Diplomacy."

The Taft-Knox foreign policy faced its severest test, and encountered its greatest failure, in the Far East. Ignoring Roosevelt's tacit 1905 agreement with Japan to limit American involvement in Manchuria, the new administration responded to pressure from American bankers and moved aggressively to increase America's economic influence in the region. In particular, Knox worked to include the United States in a consortium of Western powers formed to build railroads in China; and when the Europeans agreed, he went further and tried to exclude the Japanese from any role in Manchuria's railroads. When Japan responded by forming a loose alliance with Russia, the entire railroad project quickly collapsed.

In the Caribbean, the new administration continued and even expanded upon Roosevelt's policies of limiting European and expanding American influence in the region. That meant, Taft and Knox believed, not only preventing disorder but establishing a significant American economic presence there—replacing the investments of European nations with investments from the United States. But Dollar Diplomacy also had a more violent side. When a revolution broke out in Nicaragua in 1909, the administration quickly sided with the insurgents (who had been inspired to revolt by an American mining company) and sent American troops into the country to seize the customs houses. As soon as peace was restored, Knox encouraged American bankers to offer substantial loans to the new government, thus increasing Washington's financial leverage over the country. When the new pro-American government faced an insurrection less than two years later, Taft again landed American troops in Nicaragua, this time to protect the existing regime. The troops remained there for more than a decade.

Diplomacy and Morality

Woodrow Wilson entered the presidency with relatively little interest or experience in international affairs. Yet he faced international challenges of a scope and gravity unmatched by those of any president before him. Although the greatest test of Wilsonian diplomacy did not occur until after World War I, many of the qualities that he would bring to that ordeal were evident in his foreign policy from his first moments in office, and particularly in his dealings with Latin America.

Having already seized control of the finances of the Dominican Republic in 1905, the United States established a military government there in 1916 when the Dominicans refused to accept a treaty that would have made the country a virtual American protectorate. The military occupation lasted eight years. In Haiti, which shares the island of Hispaniola with the Dominican Republic, Wilson landed the marines in 1915 to quell a revolution in the course of which a mob had murdered an unpopular president. American military forces remained in the country until 1934, and American officers drafted the new Haitian constitution adopted in 1918. When Wilson began to fear that the Danish West Indies might be about to fall into the hands of Germany, he bought the colony from Denmark and renamed it the Virgin Islands. Concerned about the possibility of European influence in Nicaragua, he signed a treaty with that country's government ensuring that no other nation would build a canal there and winning for the United States the right to intervene in Nicaragua's internal affairs to protect American interests.

Wilson's view of America's role in the Western Hemisphere became clearest in his dealings with Mexico. For many years, under the friendly auspices of the corrupt dictator Porfirio Díaz, American businessmen had been establishing an enormous economic presence in Mexico. In 1910, however, Díaz had been overthrown by the popular leader Francisco Madero, who promised democratic reform but who also seemed hostile to American businesses in Mexico. With American approval, Madero was himself deposed early in 1913 by a reactionary general, Victoriano Huerta. The Taft administration, in its last weeks in office, prepared to recognize the new Huerta regime and welcome back a receptive environment for American investments in Mexico. Before it could do so, however, the new government murdered Madero, and Woodrow Wilson took office in Washington. The new president instantly announced that he would never recognize Huerta's "government of butchers."

The problem dragged on for years. At first, Wilson hoped that simply by refusing to recognize Huerta he could help topple the regime and bring to power the opposing Constitutionalists, led by Venustiano Carranza. But when Huerta, with the support of American business interests, established a full military dictatorship in October 1913, the president became more assertive. He pressured the British to stop supporting Huerta. Then he offered to send American troops to assist Carranza. Carranza, aware that such an open alliance with the United States would undermine his popular support in Mexico, declined the offer; but he did secure the right to buy arms in the United States.

In April 1914, a minor naval incident provided the president with an excuse for more open intervention. An officer in Huerta's army briefly arrested several American sailors from the U.S.S. *Dolphin* who had gone ashore in Tampico. The men were immediately released, but the American admiral—unsatisfied with the apology he received—demanded that the Huerta forces fire a twenty-one-gun salute to the American flag as a public display of penance. The Mexicans refused. Wilson used the trivial incident as a pretext for seizing the Mexican port of Veracruz.

Wilson had envisioned a bloodless action, but in a clash with Mexican troops in Veracruz, the Americans killed 126 of the defenders and suffered 19 casualties of their own. Now at the brink of war, Wilson began to look for a way out. His show of force, however, had helped strengthen the position of the Carranza faction, which captured Mexico City in August and forced Huerta to flee the country. At last, it seemed, the crisis might be over.

But Wilson was not yet satisfied. He reacted angrily when Carranza refused to accept American guidelines for the creation of a new government, and he briefly considered throwing his support to still another aspirant to leadership: Carranza's erstwhile lieutenant Pancho Villa, who was now leading a rebel army of his own. When Villa's military position deteriorated, however, Wilson abandoned him and finally, in October 1915, granted preliminary recognition to the Carranza government. But by now he had created yet another crisis. Villa, angry at what he considered an American betrayal, retaliated in January 1916 by taking sixteen American mining engineers from a train in northern Mexico and shooting them. Two months later, he led his soldiers (or "bandits," as the United States preferred to call them) across the border into Columbus, New Mexico, where they killed seventeen more Americans. His goal, apparently, was to destabilize relations

PANCHO VILLA AND HIS SOLDIERS In 1913, when this photograph was taken, Pancho Villa (second from left) was still on good terms with the government of Woodrow Wilson, which viewed him as a fighter for democracy in Mexico. Three years later, Wilson declared Villa a "bandit" and sent American troops into Mexico in a futile effort to capture him.

between Wilson and Carranza and provoke a war between them, which might provide him with an opportunity to improve his own declining fortunes.

With the permission of the Carranza government, Wilson ordered General John J. Pershing to lead an American expeditionary force across the Mexican border in pursuit of Villa. The American troops never found Villa, but they did engage in two ugly skirmishes with Carranza's army, in which forty Mexicans and twelve Americans died. Again, the United States and Mexico stood at the brink of war. But at the last minute, Wilson drew back. He quietly withdrew American troops from Mexico; and in March 1917, he at last granted formal recognition to the Carranza regime. By now, however, Wilson's attention was turning elsewhere—to the far greater international crisis engulfing the European continent and ultimately much of the world.

CHAPTER TWENTY-THREE

America and the Great War

The Road to War ～ *"War Without Stint"*
The Search for a New World Order ～ *A Society in Turmoil*

HE GREAT WAR, as it was known to a generation unaware that another, greater war would soon follow, began quietly in August 1914 when Austria-Hungary invaded the tiny Balkan nation of Serbia. Within weeks, however, it had grown into a widespread conflagration, engaging the armies of most of the major nations of Europe and shattering forever the delicate balance of power that had maintained a general peace on the Continent since the early nineteenth century. Americans looked on with horror as the war became the most savage in history, and as it dragged on, murderously and inconclusively, for two and a half years. But Americans also believed at first that the conflict had little to do with them. They were wrong. After nearly three years of attempting to affect the outcome of the conflict without becoming embroiled in it, the United States formally entered the war in April 1917.

THE ROAD TO WAR

The causes of the war in Europe have been the subject of continued debate for nearly eighty years. What is clear is that the European nations had by 1914 created an unusually precarious international system that careened into war very quickly on the basis of what most historians agree was a minor series of provocations.

The Collapse of the European Peace

The major powers of Europe were organized by 1914 in two great, competing alliances. The "Triple Entente" linked Britain, France, and Russia. The "Triple Alliance" united Germany, the Austro-Hungarian Empire, and Italy. The chief rivalry, however, was not between the two alliances but between the great powers that dominated them: Great Britain and Germany—the former long established as the world's most powerful colonial and commercial nation, the latter ambitious to expand its own empire and become at least Britian's equal.

The Anglo-German rivalry may have been the most important underlying source of the tensions that led to World War I, but it was not the immediate cause of its outbreak. The conflict emerged most directly out of a controversy involving nationalist movements within the Austro-Hungarian Empire. On June 28, 1914, the Archduke Franz Ferdinand, heir to the throne of the tottering empire, was assassinated while paying a state visit to Sarajevo. Sarajevo was the capital of Bosnia, a province of Austria-Hungary that Slavic nationalists wished to annex to neighboring Serbia; the archduke's assassin was a Serbian nationalist.

This local controversy quickly escalated through the workings of the system of alliances that the great powers had constructed. Germany supported Austria-Hungary's decision to launch a punitive assault on Serbia. The Serbians called on Russia to help with their defense. The Russians began mobilizing their army on July 30. Things quickly careened out of control. By August 3, Germany had declared war on both Russia and France and had invaded Belgium in preparation for a thrust across the French border. On August 4, Great Britain—ostensibly to honor its alliance with France, but more importantly to blunt the advance of its principal rival—declared war on Germany. Russia and the Austro-Hungarian Empire formally began hostilities on August 6. Italy, the Ottoman Empire (Turkey) and other, smaller nations all joined the fighting later in 1914 or 1915. By the end of the year, virtually the entire European continent (and part of Asia) was embroiled in a major war.

Wilson's Neutrality

Wilson called on his fellow citizens in 1914 to remain "impartial in thought as well as deed." But that was impossible, for several reasons. For one thing, many Americans were not, in fact, genuinely impartial. Some sympathized with the German cause (German-Americans, because of affection for Germany; Irish-Americans, because of hatred of Britain). Many more (including Wilson himself) sympathized with Britain. Lurid reports of German atrocities in Belgium and France, skillfully exaggerated by British propagandists, strengthened the hostility of many Americans toward Germany.

Economic realities also made it impossible for the United States to deal with the belligerents on equal terms. The British had imposed a naval blockade on Germany to prevent munitions and supplies from reaching the enemy. As a neutral, the United States had the right, in theory, to trade with Germany. A truly neutral response to the blockade would be either to defy it or to stop trading with Britain as well. But while the United States could survive an interruption of its relatively modest trade with the Central Powers (Germany, the Austro-Hungarian Empire, and the Ottoman Empire), it could not easily weather an embargo on its much more extensive trade with the Allies (Britain, France, Italy, and Russia), particularly when war orders from Britain and France soared after 1914, helping produce one of the greatest economic booms in the nation's history. So America tacitly ignored the blockade of Germany and continued trading with Britain. By 1915, the United States had gradually transformed itself from a neutral power into the arsenal of the Allies.

The Germans, in the meantime, were resorting to a new and, in American eyes, barbaric tactic: submarine warfare. Unable to challenge British domination on the ocean's surface, Germany began early in 1915 to use the newly improved submarine to try to stem the flow of supplies to England. Enemy vessels, the Germans announced, would be sunk on sight. Months later, on May 7, 1915, a German submarine sank the British passenger liner *Lusitania* without warning, causing the deaths of 1,198 people, 128 of them Americans. The ship was, it later became clear, carrying not only passengers but munitions; but most Americans considered the attack an unprovoked act.

Wilson angrily demanded that Germany promise not to repeat such outrages and that the Central Powers affirm their commitment to neutral rights (among which, he implausibly insisted, was the right of American citizens to travel on the nonmilitary vessels of belligerents). The Germans finally agreed to Wilson's demands, but tensions between the nations continued to grow. Early in 1916, in response to an announcement that the Allies were now arming merchant ships to sink submarines, Germany proclaimed that it would fire on such vessels without warning. A few weeks later, it attacked the unarmed French steamer *Sussex*, injuring several American passengers. Again, Wilson demanded that Germany abandon its "unlawful" tactics; again, the German government relented.

Preparedness Versus Pacifism

Despite the president's increasing bellicosity in 1916, he was still far from ready to commit the United States to war. One obstacle was American domestic politics. Facing a difficult battle for reelection, Wilson could not ignore the powerful factions that continued to oppose intervention.

The question of whether America should make military and economic preparations for war provided a preliminary issue over which pacifists and interventionists could debate. Wilson at first sided with the antipreparedness forces, denouncing the idea of an American military build-up as needless and provocative. As tensions between the United States and Germany grew, however, he changed his mind. In the fall of 1915, he endorsed an ambitious proposal by American military leaders for a large and rapid increase in the nation's armed forces. By midsummer 1916, armament for a possible conflict was well under way.

Still, the peace faction wielded considerable political strength, as became clear at the Democratic Convention in the summer of 1916. The convention became almost hysterically enthusiastic when the keynote speaker, enumerating Wilson's accomplishments, punctuated his list of the president's diplomatic achievements with the chant, "What did we do? What did we do? . . . We didn't go to war! We didn't go to war!" That speech helped produce one of the most prominent slogans of Wilson's reelection campaign: "He kept us out of war." During the campaign, Wilson did nothing to discourage those who argued that the Republican candidate, the progressive New York governor Charles Evans Hughes, was more likely than he to lead the nation into war. Wilson ultimately won reelection by one of the smallest margins for an incumbent in American history: fewer than 600,000 popular votes and only 23 electoral votes. The Democrats retained a precarious control over Congress.

A War for Democracy

The election was behind him, and tensions between the United States and Germany were unabated. But Wilson still required a justification for American intervention that would unite public opinion and satisfy his own sense of morality. In the end, he created that rationale himself. The United States, Wilson insisted, had no material aims in the conflict. The nation was, rather, committed to using the war as a vehicle for constructing a new world order, one based on the same progressive ideals that had motivated a generation of reform efforts in America. In a speech before a joint session of Congress in January 1917, he presented a plan for a postwar order in which the United States would help maintain peace through a permanent league of nations—a peace that would ensure self-determination for all nations, a "peace without victory." These were, Wilson believed, goals worth fighting for if there was sufficient provocation. That provocation came quickly.

In January, after months of bloody but inconclusive warfare in the trenches of France, the military leaders of Germany decided on one last dramatic gamble to achieve victory. They would launch a series of major assaults on the enemy's lines in France. At the same time, they would begin unrestricted submarine warfare (against American as well as Allied ships) to cut Britain off from vital supplies. Then, on February 25, the British gave Wilson an intercepted telegram from the German foreign minister, Arthur Zimmermann, to the government of Mexico, which was still awash in anti-American sentiment in the wake of Wilson's interventions there. It proposed that in the event of war between Germany and the United States, the Mexicans should join with Germany against the Americans. In return, they would regain their "lost provinces" in the north (Texas and much of the rest of the American Southwest) when the war was over. Widely publicized by British propagandists and in the American press, the Zimmermann telegram inflamed public opinion and helped build up popular sentiment for war. Wilson drew additional comfort from another event, in March 1917. A revolution in Russia toppled the reactionary czarist regime and replaced it with a new, republican government. The United States would now be spared the embarrassment of allying itself with a despotic monarchy. The war for a progressive world order could proceed untainted.

On the rainy evening of April 2, two weeks after German submarines had torpedoed three American ships, Wilson appeared before a joint session of Congress and asked for a declaration of war. Even then, opposition remained. For four days, pacifists in Congress carried on their futile struggle. When the declaration of war finally passed on April 6, fifty representatives and six senators had voted against it.

"WAR WITHOUT STINT"

Armies on both sides in Europe were decimated and exhausted by the time of Woodrow Wilson's declaration of war. The German offensives of early 1917 had failed to produce an end to the struggle, and French and British counteroffensives had accomplished little beyond adding to the appalling number of casualties. The Allies looked desperately to the United States for help. Wilson, who had called on the nation to wage war "without stint or limit," was eager to oblige.

The Military Struggle

American intervention had its most immediate effect on the conflict at sea. By the spring of 1917, Great Britain was suffering such vast losses from attacks by German submarines—one of every four ships setting sail from British ports never returned—that its ability to continue receiving vital supplies from across the Atlantic was in question. Within weeks of joining the war, the United States had begun to alter the balance. A fleet of American destroyers aided the British navy in its assault on the U-boats. Other American warships escorted merchant vessels across the Atlantic. Americans also helped plant antisubmarine mines in the North Sea. The results were dramatic. Sinkings of Allied ships had totaled nearly 900,000 tons in the month of April 1917; by December, the figure had dropped to 350,000; by October 1918, it had declined to 112,000.

Many Americans had hoped that providing naval assistance alone would be enough to turn the tide in the war, but it quickly became clear that a major commitment of American ground forces would be necessary as well to shore up the tottering Allies. Britain and France had few remaining reserves. By early 1918, Russia had withdrawn from the war altogether. After the Bolshevik Revolution in November 1917, the new communist government, led by V. I. Lenin, negotiated a hasty and costly peace with the Central Powers, thus freeing German troops to fight on the western front.

But the United States did not have a large enough standing army to provide the necessary ground forces in 1917. Some (including Theodore Roosevelt, who hoped to raise and lead a regiment himself, much as he had done in the Spanish-American War) urged a voluntary recruitment process. The president, however, decided that only a national draft could provide the needed men; and despite protests, he won passage of the Selective Service

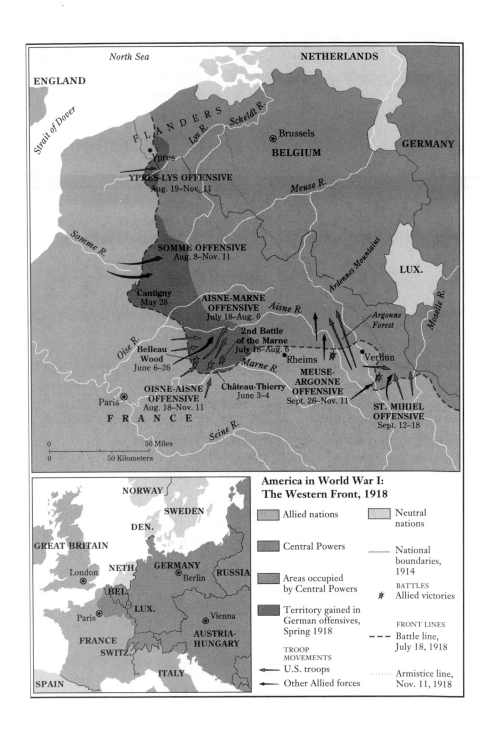

America in World War I:
The Western Front, 1918

Act in mid-May. The draft brought nearly 3 million men into the army; another 2 million joined various branches of the armed services voluntarily.

The engagement of these forces in combat was intense but brief. Not until the spring of 1918 were significant numbers of American troops available for battle. Eight months later, the war was over. Under the command of General John J. Pershing, the American troops joined the existing Allied forces in turning back a series of new German assaults. In early June, they assisted the French in repelling a bitter German offensive at Château-Thierry, near Paris. Six weeks later, the American Expeditionary Force (AEF) helped turn away another assault, at Rheims, farther south. By July 18, the German advance had been halted, and the Allies were beginning a successful offensive of their own. On September 26, an American fighting force of over 1 million soldiers advanced against the Germans in the Argonne Forest as part of a 200-mile attack that lasted nearly seven weeks. By the end of October, the force had helped push the Germans back toward their own border and had cut the enemy's major supply lines to the front.

Faced with an invasion of their own country, German military leaders now began to seek an armistice—an immediate cease-fire that would, they hoped, serve as a prelude to negotiations among the belligerents. Pershing wanted to drive on into Germany itself; but other Allied leaders, after first insisting on terms that made the agreement (in their eyes at least) little

LONGPONT, FRANCE, 1918 American soldiers lead German prisoners-of-war through the streets of a French town shortly before the end of World War I. The devastation was typical of many areas of France where heavy fighting occurred.

different from a surrender, accepted the German proposal. On November 11, 1918, the Great War shuddered to a close.

Organizing the Economy for War

By the time the war ended, the federal government had appropriated $32 billion for expenses directly related to the conflict. This was a staggering sum by the standards of the time. The entire federal budget had seldom exceeded $1 billion before 1915, and the nation's entire gross national product had been only $35 billion as recently as 1910. To raise the money, the government relied on two devices. First, it launched a major drive to solicit loans from the American people by selling "Liberty Bonds" to the public. By 1920, the sale of bonds, accompanied by elaborate patriotic appeals, had produced $23 billion. At the same time, new taxes were bringing in an additional sum of nearly $10 billion—some from levies on the "excess profits" of corporations, much from new, steeply graduated income and inheritance taxes that ultimately rose as high as 70 percent in some brackets.

An even greater challenge was organizing the economy to meet war needs. The administration tried two very different approaches. In 1916, Wilson established a Council of National Defense, composed of members of his cabinet, and a Civilian Advisory Commission, which set up local defense councils in every state and locality. Economic mobilization, according to this first plan, was to rest on a large-scale dispersal of power to local communities.

But this early administrative structure soon proved completely unworkable. Some members of the Council of National Defense, many of them disciples of the engineering gospel of Thorstein Veblen and the "scientific management" principles of Frederick Winslow Taylor, urged a more centralized approach. Instead of dividing the economy geographically, they proposed dividing it functionally by organizing a series of planning bodies, each to supervise a specific sector of the economy. Thus one agency would control transportation, another agriculture, another manufacturing. The administrative structure that slowly emerged from such proposals was dominated by a series of "war boards," one to oversee the railroads (led by Secretary of the Treasury William McAdoo), one to supervise fuel supplies (largely coal), another to handle food (a board that helped elevate to prominence the brilliant young engineer and business executive Herbert Hoover). The boards were not without weaknesses, but they generally succeeded in meeting essential war needs without paralyzing the domestic economy.

At the center of the effort to rationalize the economy was the War Industries Board (WIB), an agency created in July 1917 to coordinate government purchases of military supplies. Casually organized at first, it stumbled badly until March 1918, when Wilson restructured it and placed it under the control of the Wall Street financier Bernard Baruch. From then on, the board wielded powers greater (in theory at least) than any government agency had ever possessed. Baruch decided which factories would convert to the production of which war materials and set prices for the goods they produced. When materials were scarce, Baruch decided to whom they should go. When corporations were competing for government contracts, he chose among them. He was, it seemed, providing the centralized regulation of the economy that some progressives had long urged.

In reality, the vaunted efficiency of the WIB was something of a myth. The agency was, in fact, plagued by mismanagement and inefficiency and was less responsible for the nation's ability to meet its war needs than the

WOMEN WAR WORKERS With much of the male work force fighting overseas, women moved into occupations that in other times would have been considered "unsuitable" for them. One such occupation, pictured here, was delivering huge blocks of ice daily to households to be used (in this age before electric refrigeration) in wooden iceboxes.

sheer extent of American resources and productive capacities. Nor was the WIB in any real sense an example of state control of the economy. Baruch viewed himself, openly and explicitly, as a partner of business; and within the WIB, businessmen themselves—the so-called "dollar-a-year men," who took paid leave from their corporate jobs and worked for the government for a token salary—supervised the affairs of the private economy. Baruch ensured that manufacturers coordinating their efforts in accord with his goals would be exempt from antitrust laws. He helped major industries earn enormous profits from their efforts. Rather than working to restrict private power and limit corporate profits, as many progressives had urged, the government was working to enhance the private sector through a mutually beneficial alliance.

This growing link between the public and the private sectors extended, although in greatly different form, to labor. The National War Labor Board, established in April 1918, served as the final mediator of labor disputes. It pressured industry to grant important concessions to workers: an eight-hour day, the maintenance of minimal living standards, equal pay for women doing equal work, recognition of the right of unions to organize and bargain collectively. In return, it insisted that workers forgo all strikes and that employers not engage in lockouts. To the delight of Samuel Gompers, membership in labor unions increased by more than 1.5 million between 1917 and 1919.

The effort to organize the economy for war produced some spectacular accomplishments: Hoover's efficient organization of food supplies, McAdoo's success in establishing state control of the railroads, and others. In other areas, however, progress was so slow that the war was over before many of the supplies ordered for it were ready. Even so, many leaders of both government and industry emerged from the experience convinced of the advantages of a close, cooperative relationship between the public and the private sectors. Some hoped to continue and extend the wartime experiments in the peacetime world.

The Search for Social Unity

The idea of unity—not only in the direction of the economy but in the nation's social purpose—had been the dream of many progressives for decades. To them, the war seemed to offer an unmatched opportunity for the United States to close ranks behind a great common cause. In the process, they hoped, society could achieve a lasting sense of collective purpose. In fact, however, the search for unity produced considerable repression.

Government leaders were painfully aware that public sentiment about American involvement in the war had been divided before April 1917 and remained so even after the declaration of war. Many believed that a crucial prerequisite for victory was the uniting of public opinion behind the war effort. The government approached that task in several ways.

The most conspicuous of its efforts was a vast propaganda campaign aimed at drumming up enthusiasm for the conflict. It was orchestrated by the Committee on Public Information (CPI), under the direction of the Denver journalist George Creel. The CPI supervised the distribution of over 75 million pieces of printed material and controlled much of the information that was available for newspapers and magazines. Creel encouraged journalists to exercise "self-censorship" when reporting war news, and most journalists—fearful of more coercive measures—complied by covering the war largely as the government wished. The CPI attempted at first to distribute only the "facts," believing that the truth would speak for itself. As the war continued, however, the committee's tactics became increasingly crude. Government-promoted posters and films were by 1918 becoming lurid portrayals of the savagery of the Germans.

The government also soon began efforts to suppress dissent. CPI-financed advertisements in magazines appealed to citizens to report to the authorities any evidence among their neighbors of disloyalty, pessimism, or yearning for peace. The Espionage Act of 1917 gave the government new tools with which to combat spying, sabotage, or obstruction of the war effort (crimes that were often broadly defined). More repressive were two measures of 1918: the Sabotage Act of April 20 and the Sedition Act of May 16. These bills expanded the meaning of the Espionage Act to make illegal any public expression of opposition to the war; in practice, they allowed officials to prosecute anyone who criticized the president or the government.

The most frequent target of the new legislation (and one of the reasons for its enactment in the first place) were such anticapitalist groups as the Socialist party and the Industrial Workers of the World (IWW). Unlike their counterparts in Europe, American socialists had not dropped their opposition to the war after their country had decided to join it. Many Americans had favored the repression of socialists and radicals even before the war; the wartime policies now made it possible to move against them with full legal sanction. Eugene V. Debs, the humane leader of the Socialist party and an opponent of the war, was sentenced to ten years in prison in 1918. A pardon by President Warren G. Harding ultimately won his release in 1921. Big Bill Haywood and members of the IWW were especially energetically prosecuted. Only by fleeing to the Soviet Union did Haywood avoid a long imprisonment. In all, more than 1,500 people were arrested in 1918 for the crime of criticizing the government.

State and local governments, corporations, universities, and private citizens contributed as well to the climate of repression. Vigilante mobs sprang up to "discipline" those who dared challenge the war. A cluster of citizens' groups emerged to mobilize "respectable" members of their communities to root out disloyalty. The American Protective League, probably the largest of such groups, enlisted the services of 250,000 people, who served as "agents"—prying into the activities and thoughts of their neighbors, opening mail, tapping telephones, and in general attempting to impose unity of opinion on their communities. The most frequent victims of such activities were immigrants: Irish-Americans, because of their historic animosity toward the British and because some had, before 1917, expressed hopes for a German victory; Jews, because many had expressed opposition to the anti-Semitic policies of the Russian government, until 1917 one of the Allies; and others. Immigrant ghettoes were strictly policed by "loyalist" citizens' groups. Even some settlement house workers, many of whom had once championed ethnic diversity, contributed to such efforts.

The greatest target of abuse was the German-American community. Its members had unwittingly contributed to their plight. In the first years of the war in Europe, some had openly advocated American assistance to the Central Powers, and many had opposed United States intervention on behalf of the Allies. But while most German-Americans supported the American war effort once it began, public opinion turned bitterly hostile. A campaign to purge society of all things German quickly gathered speed, at times assuming ludicrous forms. Sauerkraut was renamed "liberty cabbage." Hamburger became "liberty sausage." Performances of German music were frequently banned. German books were removed from the shelves of libraries. Courses in the German language were removed from school curricula. Germans were routinely fired from jobs in war industries, lest they "sabotage" important tasks. Some were fired from positions entirely unrelated to the war, among them Karl Muck, the German-born conductor of the Boston Symphony Orchestra. Vigilante groups subjected Germans to harassment and beatings, including a lynching in southern Illinois in 1918. Relatively few Americans favored such extremes, but many came to agree with the belief of the eminent psychologist G. Stanley Hall that "there is something fundamentally wrong with the Teutonic soul."

THE SEARCH FOR A NEW WORLD ORDER

Woodrow Wilson had led the nation into war promising a more just and stable peace at its conclusion. Even before the armistice, he was preparing to lead the fight for what he considered a democratic postwar settlement— for a set of war aims resting on a vision of a new world order that became known as Wilsonian internationalism.

The Fourteen Points

On January 8, 1918, Wilson appeared before Congress to present the principles for which he claimed the nation was fighting. The war aims were listed under fourteen headings, widely known as the Fourteen Points; but they fell into three broad categories. First, Wilson's proposals contained a series of eight specific recommendations for adjusting postwar boundaries and for establishing new nations to replace the defunct Austro-Hungarian and Ottoman empires. Those recommendations reflected his belief in the right of all peoples to self-determination. Second, there was a set of five general principles to govern international conduct in the future: freedom of the seas, open covenants instead of secret treaties, reductions in armaments, free trade, and impartial mediation of colonial claims. Finally, there was a proposal for a "League of Nations" that would help implement these new principles and territorial adjustments and resolve future controversies.

There were serious flaws in Wilson's proposals. He provided no formula for deciding how to implement the "national self-determination" he prom- ised for subjugated peoples. He made no mention of the new Soviet leadership in Russia, even though its existence had frightened the Western governments (and had helped spur Wilson to announce his own war aims in an effort to undercut Lenin's appeal). He said little about economic rivalries and their effect on international relations, even though such eco- nomic tensions had been in large part responsible for the war. Nevertheless, Wilson's international vision quickly came to enchant not only much of his own generation (in both America and Europe) but members of generations to come. It reflected his belief, strongly rooted in the ideas of progressivism, that the world was as capable of just and efficient government as were individual nations—that once the international community accepted certain basic principles of conduct, and once it constructed modern institutions to implement them, the human race could live in peace.

Wilson was confident, as the war neared its end, that popular support would enable him to win Allied approval of his peace plan. There were, however, ominous signs both at home and abroad that his path might be more difficult than he expected. In Europe, leaders of the Allied powers were preparing to resist him even before the armistice was signed. Britain and France in particular, having suffered terrible losses and having developed great bitterness toward Germany as a result, were in no mood for a benign and generous peace. David Lloyd George, the British prime minister, had campaigned for reelection in 1918 by calling for the execution of Kaiser Wilhelm II.

At the same time, Wilson was encountering problems at home. In 1918, with the war almost over, Wilson unwisely appealed to the American voters to support his peace plans by electing Democrats to Congress in the November elections. Days later, the Republicans captured majorities in both houses. Domestic economic troubles, more than international issues, had been the most important factor in the voting; but because of the president's ill-timed appeal, the results damaged his ability to claim broad popular support for his peace plans.

The leaders of the Republican party, in the meantime, were developing their own reasons for opposing Wilson. Many were angry that he had tried to make the 1918 balloting a referendum on his war aims, especially since many Republicans had been supporting the Fourteen Points. Wilson further antagonized them when he refused to appoint any important Republicans to the negotiating team that would represent the United States at the peace conference in Paris.

But the president considered such matters unimportant. There would be only one member of the American negotiating team with any real authority: Wilson himself. And once he had produced a just and moral treaty, he believed, the weight of world and American opinion would compel his enemies to support him.

The Paris Peace Conference

Wilson arrived in Europe to a welcome such as few men in history have experienced. To the war-weary people of the Continent, he was nothing less than a savior, the man who would create a new and better world. When he entered Paris on December 13, 1918, he was greeted, some claimed, by the largest crowd in the history of France. The negotiations themselves, however, proved less satisfying.

The principal figures in the negotiations were the leaders of the victorious Allied nations: David Lloyd George, the prime minister of Great Britain; Georges Clemenceau, the president of France; Vittorio Orlando, the prime minister of Italy; and Wilson, who hoped to dominate them all. Some of Wilson's advisers had warned him that if agreement could not be reached at the "summit," there would be nowhere else to go and that it would be better to begin negotiations at a lower level. Wilson, however, was adamant; he alone would represent the United States.

From the beginning, the atmosphere of idealism Wilson had sought to create was competing with a spirit of national aggrandizement. There was, moreover, a pervasive sense of unease about the unstable situation in eastern Europe and the threat of communism. Russia, whose new Bolshevik government was still fighting "White" counterrevolutionaries, was unrepresented in Paris; but the radical threat it seemed to pose to Western governments was never far from the minds of the delegates. Wilson himself had sent American troops into Russia in 1918, allegedly to protect trapped Czech forces but really, many believed, to support the anti-Bolshevik forces in the civil war there.

In this tense and often vindictive atmosphere, Wilson was unable to win approval of many of the broad principles he had espoused: freedom of the seas, which the British refused even to discuss; free trade; "open covenants openly arrived at" (the Paris negotiations themselves were often conducted in secret). Despite his support for "impartial mediation" of colonial claims, he was forced to accept a transfer of German colonies in the Pacific to Japan, to which the British had promised them in exchange for Japanese assistance in the war. His pledge of "national self-determination" for all peoples suffered numerous assaults. Economic and strategic demands were constantly coming into conflict with the principle of cultural nationalism.

Where the treaty departed most conspicuously from Wilson's ideals was on the question of reparations. When the conference began, the president opposed demanding reparations from the defeated Central Powers. The other Allied leaders, however, were intransigent, and slowly Wilson gave way and accepted the principle of reparations, the specific sum to be set later by a commission. The final amount, established in 1921, was less than some earlier demands but far more than the crippled German economy could absorb.

Wilson did manage to win some important victories in Paris in setting boundaries and dealing with former colonies. But his most visible triumph, and the one of most importance to him, was the creation of a permanent international organization to oversee world affairs and prevent future wars. On January 25, 1919, the Allies voted to accept the "covenant" of the League of Nations; and with that, Wilson believed, the peace treaty was transformed from a disappointment into a success. Any mistakes and inequities that had emerged from the peace conference, he was convinced, could be corrected later by the League.

The covenant provided for an assembly of nations that would meet regularly to debate means of resolving disputes and protecting the peace. Authority to implement League decisions would rest with a nine-member Executive Council; the United States would be one of five permanent members of the council, along with Britain, France, Italy, and Japan. The covenant left many questions unanswered, most notably how the League would enforce its decisions. Wilson, however, was confident that once established, the new organization would find suitable answers.

The Ratification Battle

Wilson was well aware of the political obstacles awaiting him at home. Many Americans, accustomed to their nation's isolation from Europe, questioned the wisdom of this major new commitment to internationalism. Others had serious reservations about the specific features of the treaty and the covenant. After a brief trip to Washington in February 1919, during which he listened to harsh objections to the treaty from members of the Senate and others, he returned to Europe and insisted on certain modifications in the covenant (limiting America's obligations to the League) to satisfy his critics. The changes were not enough to mollify his opponents, but Wilson refused to go further.

Wilson presented the Treaty of Versailles (which took its name from the former royal palace outside Paris where the final negotiating sessions had taken place) to the Senate on July 10, 1919. In the weeks that followed, he refused to consider even the most innocuous compromise. But members of the Senate had many objections to the treaty. Some—the so-called "Irreconcilables," many of them Western isolationists—opposed the agreement on principle. But many other opponents, with less fervent convictions, were principally concerned with constructing a winning issue for the Republicans in 1920. Most notable of these was Senator Henry Cabot Lodge

THE BIG FOUR The principal negotiators of the Versailles Treaty—Vittorio Orlando, prime minister of Italy; Lloyd George, prime minister of Great Britain; Georges Clemenceau, president of France; and Woodrow Wilson—pose for a group portrait in the library of the Ritz Hotel in Paris.

of Massachusetts, the powerful chairman of the Foreign Relations Committee. Lodge loathed President Wilson. ("I never thought I could hate a man as I hate Wilson," Lodge once said.) He used every possible tactic to obstruct, delay, and amend the treaty.

Public sentiment clearly favored ratification, so at first Lodge could do little more than play for time. Gradually, however, Lodge's general opposition to the treaty crystallized into a series of "reservations"—amendments to the League covenant further limiting American obligations to the organization. Wilson might still have won approval at this point if he had agreed to some relatively minor changes in the language of the treaty. But the president refused to yield. The United States had a moral obligation, he claimed, to respect the terms of the agreement precisely as they stood. When he realized the Senate would not budge, he decided to appeal to the public.

What followed was a political disaster and a personal tragedy. Wilson embarked on a grueling, cross-country speaking tour to arouse public support for the treaty. For more than three weeks, he traveled over 8,000 miles by train, speaking as often as four times a day, resting hardly at all.

Finally, he reached the end of his strength. After speaking at Pueblo, Colorado, on September 25, 1919, he collapsed with severe headaches. Canceling the rest of his itinerary, he rushed back to Washington, where, a few days later, he suffered a major stroke. For two weeks, he was close to death; for six weeks more, he was so seriously ill that he could conduct virtually no public business. His wife and his doctor formed an almost impenetrable barrier around him, shielding the president from any official pressures that might impede his recovery and preventing the public from receiving any accurate information about the gravity of his condition.

Wilson ultimately recovered enough to resume a limited official schedule, but he was essentially an invalid for the remaining eighteen months of his presidency. His left side was partially paralyzed; more important, his mental and emotional state was unstable. His condition only intensified what had already been his strong tendency to view public issues in moral terms and to resist any attempts at compromise. When the Foreign Relations Committee finally sent the treaty to the Senate, recommending nearly fifty amendments and reservations, Wilson refused to consider any of them. When the full Senate voted in November to accept fourteen of the reservations, Wilson gave stern directions to his Democratic allies: they must vote only for a treaty with no changes whatsoever; any other version must be defeated. On November 19, 1919, forty-two Democrats, following the president's instructions, joined thirteen Republican "irreconcilables" to reject the amended treaty. When the Senate voted on the original version without any reservations, thirty-eight senators, all but one a Democrat, voted to approve it; fifty-five voted no.

There were sporadic efforts to revive the treaty over the next few months. But Wilson's opposition to anything but the precise settlement he had negotiated in Paris remained too formidable an obstacle to surmount. He was, moreover, becoming convinced that the 1920 national election would serve as a "solemn referendum" on the League. By now, however, public interest in the peace process had begun to fade—partly as a reaction against the tragic bitterness of the ratification fight, but more in response to a series of other crises.

A SOCIETY IN TURMOIL

Even during the Paris Peace Conference, many Americans were concerned less about international matters than about turbulent events at home. Some of this unease was a legacy of the almost hysterical social atmosphere of the war years; some of it was a response to issues that surfaced after the armistice.

The Troubled Economy

The war ended sooner than almost anyone had anticipated; and without warning, without planning, the nation was launched into the difficult task of economic reconversion. At first, the wartime boom continued. But the postwar prosperity rested largely on the lingering effects of the war (government deficit spending continued for some months after the armistice) and on sudden, temporary demands (a booming market for scarce consumer goods at home and a strong market for American products in the war-ravaged nations of Europe). The postwar boom was accompanied, moreover, by raging inflation, a result in part of the precipitous abandonment of wartime price controls. Through most of 1919 and 1920, prices rose at an average of more than 15 percent a year.

Finally, late in 1920, the economic bubble burst as many of the temporary forces that had created it disappeared and as inflation began killing the market for consumer goods. Between 1920 and 1921, the gross national product declined nearly 10 percent; 100,000 businesses went bankrupt; 453,000 farmers lost their land; and nearly 5 million Americans lost their jobs.

Well before the recession began, there was a dramatic increase in labor unrest. The raging inflation of 1919 wiped out the modest wage gains workers had achieved during the war; many laborers were worried about job security, as hundreds of thousands of veterans returned to the work force; arduous working conditions—such as the twelve-hour day in the steel industry—continued to be a source of discontent. Employers aggravated the resentment by using the end of the war (and the end of government controls) to rescind benefits they had been forced to concede to workers in 1917 and 1918—most notably recognition of unions. The year 1919, therefore, saw an unprecedented wave of strikes—more than 3,600 in all, involving over 4 million workers. In January, a walkout by shipyard workers in Seattle, Washington, evolved into a general strike that brought the entire city to a virtual standstill. In September, there was a strike by the Boston police force, which was demanding recognition of its union in the wake of substantial layoffs and wage cuts. Seattle had remained generally calm; but with its police off the job, Boston erupted in violence and looting.

THE GREAT STEEL STRIKE Striking steelworkers stand around uneasily as mounted police patrol the streets of a steel town near Pittsburgh, during the Great Steel Strike of 1919.

These and other strikes aroused widespread middle-class hostility to the unions, a hostility that played a part in defeating the greatest strike of 1919: a steel strike that began in September, when 350,000 steelworkers in several Midwestern cities demanded an eight-hour day and recognition of their union. The steel strike was long and bitter and climaxed in a riot in Gary, Indiana, in which eighteen strikers were killed. Steel executives managed to keep most plants running with nonunion labor, and public opinion was so hostile to the strikers that the AFL timidly repudiated them. By January, the strike had collapsed. It was a setback from which organized labor would not recover for more than a decade.

The Red Scare

To much of the public at the time, the industrial warfare appeared to be a frightening omen of instability and radicalism. This was in part because other evidence emerging at the same time seemed likewise to suggest the existence of a radical menace. The Russian Revolution of November 1917 indicated that communism was no longer simply a theory but now an important regime. Concerns about the communist threat grew in 1919 when the Soviet government announced the formation of the Communist International (or Comintern), whose purpose was to export revolution around the world.

In America, meanwhile, there was, in addition to the great number of imagined radicals, a modest number of real ones. These small groups of radicals were presumably responsible for a series of bombings in the spring of 1919 that produced great national alarm. In April, the post office intercepted several dozen parcels addressed to leading businessmen and politicians that were triggered to explode when opened. Two months later, eight bombs exploded in eight cities within minutes of one another, suggesting a nationwide conspiracy. One of them damaged the façade of United States Attorney General A. Mitchell Palmer's home in Washington.

In response to these and other provocations, what became known as the Red Scare began. Nearly thirty states enacted new peacetime sedition laws imposing harsh penalties on those who promoted revolution; some 300 people went to jail as a result. There were spontaneous acts of violence against supposed radicals in some communities, and more calculated efforts by universities and other institutions to expel radicals from their midst.

Perhaps the greatest contribution to the Red Scare came from the federal government. On New Year's Day, 1920, Attorney General A. Mitchell Palmer and his ambitious young assistant, J. Edgar Hoover, orchestrated a series of raids on alleged radical centers throughout the country and arrested more than 6,000 people. The Palmer Raids had been intended to uncover huge caches of weapons and explosives; they netted a total of three pistols and no dynamite. Most of those arrested were ultimately released, but about 500 who were not American citizens were summarily deported.

The ferocity of the Red Scare soon abated, but its effects lingered well into the 1920s, most notably in the celebrated case of Sacco and Vanzetti. In May of 1920, two Italian immigrants, Nicola Sacco and Bartolomeo Vanzetti, were charged with the murder of a paymaster in Braintree, Massachusetts. The case against them was questionable and suffused with nativist prejudices and fears; but because both men were confessed anarchists, they faced a widespread public presumption of guilt. They were convicted and sentenced to death. Over the next several years, public support for Sacco and Vanzetti grew to formidable proportions. But all requests for a new trial or a pardon were denied. On August 23, 1927, amid widespread protests around the world, Sacco and Vanzetti, still proclaiming their innocence, died in the electric chair.

Racial Unrest

No group suffered more from the inflamed climate of the postwar years than American blacks. Over 400,000 blacks served in the army, half of them in Europe and more than 40,000 of them in combat. They had endured numerous indignities during the conflict. They had been placed in segregated units, under the command of white officers who often held them in contempt. They had put up with these humiliations, however, in the belief that their service would earn them the gratitude of the nation when they returned.

For many other American blacks, the war raised expectations in other ways. Nearly half a million migrated from the rural South to industrial cities (often enticed by Northern "labor agents," who offered them free transportation) in search of the factory jobs the war was rapidly generating. This was the beginning of what became known as the "Great Migration." Within a few years, the nation's racial demographics were transformed; suddenly there were large black communities crowding into Northern cities, in some of which very few African-Americans had lived in the past. Just as black soldiers expected their military service to enhance their social status, so black factory workers regarded their move north as an escape from racial prejudice and an opportunity for economic gain.

By 1919, the racial climate had become savage and murderous. In the South, there was a sudden increase in lynchings: more than seventy blacks, some of them war veterans, died at the hands of white mobs in 1919 alone. In the North, black factory workers faced widespread layoffs as returning white veterans displaced them from their jobs. Black veterans were disillusioned when they returned to find a society still unwilling to grant them any significant opportunities for advancement. Rural black migrants to Northern cities encountered white communities unfamiliar with and generally hostile to them; and as whites became convinced that African-American workers with lower wage demands were hurting them economically, animosity grew. The result was a rash of urban disorders. As early as 1917, serious race riots had flared in Houston, Philadelphia, and East St. Louis (where forty-nine people, thirty-nine of them African-Americans, were killed). In Chicago in 1919, a black teen-ager swimming in Lake Michigan on a hot July day happened to drift toward a white beach. Whites on shore allegedly stoned him unconscious; he sank and drowned. The incident inflamed already severe racial tensions in the city, and for more than a week Chicago was virtually at war. In the end, 38 people died—15 whites and 23 blacks—and 537 were injured; over 1,000 people were left homeless. The

Chicago riot was the worst but not the only racial violence during the so-called "Red Summer" of 1919; in all, 120 people died in such racial outbreaks in the space of little more than three months.

The NAACP urged blacks to fight back, to defend themselves and demand government protection. At the same time, a black Jamaican, Marcus Garvey, began to attract a wide following in the United States with an ideology of black nationalism. Garvey encouraged American blacks to take pride in their own achievements and to develop an awareness of their African heritage—to reject assimilation into white society and develop pride in their own race. Garvey even urged supporters to leave America and return to Africa, where they could create a new society of their own. At the peak of his popularity, Garvey claimed a following of 4 million. In the end, however, most African-Americans had little choice but to acquiesce in the social and economic subjugation being forced on them.

The Retreat from Idealism

On August 26, 1920, the Nineteenth Amendment, guaranteeing women the right to vote, became part of the Constitution. To the woman suffrage movement, this was the culmination of nearly a century of struggle. To many progressives, who had seen the inclusion of women in the electorate as a way of bolstering their political strength, it seemed to promise new support for reform. Yet the passage of the Nineteenth Amendment marked not the beginning of an era of reform but the end of one.

The economic problems, the labor unrest, the fear of radicalism, the racial tensions—all combined in the years immediately following the war to produce a general sense of disillusionment. That became particularly apparent in the election of 1920. Woodrow Wilson wanted the campaign to be a referendum on the League of Nations, and the Democratic candidates, Governor James M. Cox of Ohio and Assistant Secretary of the Navy Franklin D. Roosevelt, dutifully tried to keep Wilson's ideals alive. The Republican presidential nominee, however, offered a different vision. He was Warren Gamaliel Harding, an obscure Ohio senator whom party leaders had chosen as their nominee confident that he would do their bidding once in office. Harding offered no ideals, only a vague promise of a return, as he later phrased it, to "normalcy." He won in a landslide. The Republican ticket received 61 percent of the popular vote and carried every state outside the South. The party made major gains in Congress as well. To many Americans it seemed that, for better or worse, a new era had begun.

CHAPTER TWENTY-FOUR

The New Era

The New Economy ~ *The New Culture*
A Conflict of Cultures ~ *Republican Government*

T HE 1920S ARE often remembered as an era of affluence, conservatism, and cultural frivolity: the Roaring Twenties, the age of what Warren G. Harding once called "normalcy." In reality, however, the decade was a time of significant, even dramatic social, economic, and political change. It was an era in which the American economy not only enjoyed spectacular growth but developed new forms of organization. It was a time in which American popular culture reshaped itself to reflect the increasingly urban, industrial, consumer-oriented society of the United States. And it was a decade in which American government, for all its conservatism, experimented with new approaches to public policy that helped pave the way for the important period of reform that was to follow. That was why contemporaries liked to refer to the 1920s as the "New Era"—an age in which America was becoming a modern nation.

At the same time, however, the decade saw the rise of a series of spirited and at times effective rebellions against the modern developments that were transforming American life. The intense cultural conflicts that characterized the 1920s were evidence of how much of American society remained unreconciled to the modernizing currents of the New Era.

THE NEW ECONOMY

After the recession of 1921–1922, the United States began a long period of almost uninterrupted prosperity and economic expansion. Less visible at the time, but equally significant, was the survival (and even the growth) of severe inequalities and imbalances.

Economic Growth and Organization

No one could deny the remarkable, some believed miraculous, feats of the American economy in the 1920s. The nation's manufacturing output rose by more than 60 percent during the decade. Per capita income grew by a third. Inflation was negligible. A mild recession in 1923 interrupted the pattern of growth; but when it subsided early in 1924, the economy expanded with even greater vigor than before.

The economic boom was a result of many things, but one of the most important causes was technology, and the great industrial expansion it made possible. The automobile industry, as a result of the development of the assembly line and other innovations, now became one of the most important industries in the nation. It stimulated growth in other, related industries as well. Auto manufacturers purchased the products of steel, rubber, glass, and tool companies. Auto owners bought gasoline from the oil corporations. Road construction in response to the proliferation of motor vehicles itself became an important industry. The increased mobility that the automobile made possible increased the demand for suburban housing, fueling a boom in the construction industry.

Other new industries benefiting from technological innovations contributed as well to the economic growth. Radio became a booming concern within a few years of its commercial debut in 1920. The motion picture industry expanded dramatically, especially after the introduction of sound in 1927. Aviation, electronics, home appliances, plastics, synthetic fibers, aluminum, magnesium, oil, electric power, and other industries fueled by technological advances—all grew dramatically and spurred the economic boom.

Large sectors of American business were accelerating their drive toward national organization and consolidation. Certain industries—notably those such as steel and automobiles, dependent on large-scale mass production—seemed naturally to move toward concentrating production in a few large firms. Others—industries less dependent on technology and less susceptible to great economies of scale—proved resistant to consolidation, despite the efforts of many businessmen to promote it.

Some industries less prone to domination by a few great corporations attempted to stabilize themselves not through consolidation but through cooperation. An important vehicle was the trade association—a national organization created by various members of an industry to encourage coordination in production and marketing techniques. But trade associations worked best in the mass-production industries that had already succeeded in limiting competition through consolidation. In more decentralized industries, such as cotton textiles, their effectiveness was limited.

The strenuous efforts by industrialists throughout the economy to find ways to curb competition through consolidation or cooperation reflected a strong fear of overcapacity. Even in the booming 1920s, industrialists remembered how too-rapid expansion and overproduction had helped produce recessions in 1893, 1907, and 1920. The great, unrealized dream of the New Era was to find a way to stabilize the economy so that such collapses would never occur again.

Workers in the Era of Capital

The remarkable economic growth was accompanied by a continuing, and in some areas even increasing, maldistribution of wealth and purchasing

THE STEAMFITTER Lewis Hine was among the first American photographers to recognize his craft as an art. In this carefully posed photograph from the mid-1920s, Hine made a point that many other artists were making in other media: The rise of the machine could serve human beings, but might also bend them to its own needs.

power. More than two-thirds of the American people in 1929 lived at no better than what one major study described as the "minimum comfort level." Half of those languished at or below the level of "subsistence and poverty." Large segments of society, unable to organize, were without power to protect their economic interests.

American labor experienced both the successes and the failures of the 1920s as much as any other group. On the one hand, most workers saw their standard of living rise during the decade; many enjoyed greatly improved working conditions and other benefits. Some employers in the 1920s, eager to avoid disruptive labor unrest and forestall the growth of unions, adopted paternalistic techniques that came to be known as "welfare capitalism." Henry Ford, for example, shortened the workweek, raised wages, and instituted paid vacations. By 1926, nearly 3 million industrial workers were eligible for pensions on retirement. When labor grievances surfaced despite these efforts, workers could voice them through the so-called company unions that were emerging in many industries—workers' councils and shop committees, organized by the corporations themselves. But welfare capitalism, in the end, gave workers no real control over their own fates. Company unions were feeble vehicles. And welfare capitalism survived only as long as industry prospered. After 1929, with the economy in crisis, the entire system collapsed.

Welfare capitalism affected only a relatively small number of workers in any case. Most laborers worked for employers interested primarily in keeping their labor costs to a minimum. Workers as a whole, therefore, received wage increases that were proportionately far below the increases in corporate profits. Unskilled workers, in particular, saw their wages increase very slowly—by only a little over 2 percent between 1920 and 1926. In the end, American workers remained in the 1920s a relatively impoverished and powerless group. Their wages rose; but the average annual income of a worker remained below $1,500 a year when $1,800 was considered necessary to maintain a minimally decent standard of living. Only by relying on the earnings of several family members at once could many working-class families make ends meet.

Some laborers continued to consider effective independent union movement their best hope. But the New Era was a bleak time for labor organization, in part because many unions themselves were relatively conservative and failed to adapt to the realities of the modern economy. The American Federation of Labor remained wedded to the concept of the craft union, in which workers were organized on the basis of particular skills. In the meantime, a huge new segment of the work force was emerging:

unskilled industrial workers, many of them recent immigrants from south-ern or eastern Europe. They received little attention from the craft unions and found themselves, as a result, with no organizations to join. William Green, who became president of the AFL in 1924, was committed to peaceful cooperation with employers and strident opposition to commu-nism and socialism. He frowned on strikes.

A growing proportion of the work force consisted of women, who were concentrated in what have since become known as "pink-collar" jobs—low-paying service occupations with many of the same problems as manufactur-ing employment. Large numbers of women worked as secretaries, sales-clerks, and telephone operators and in other nonmanual service capacities. Because such positions were not technically industrial jobs, the AFL and other labor organizations were uninterested in organizing these workers. Similarly, the half-million African-Americans who had migrated from the rural South into the cities during the Great Migration after 1914 had few opportunities for union representation. The skilled crafts represented in the AFL often worked actively to exclude blacks from their trades and organi-zations. Most blacks worked in jobs in which the AFL took no interest at all—as janitors, dishwashers, garbage collectors, domestics, and other ser-vice jobs. A. Philip Randolph's Brotherhood of Sleeping Car Porters was one of the few important unions dominated and led by African-Americans.

But whatever the weaknesses of the unions, the strength of the corpo-rations was the principal reason for the absence of effective labor organiza-tion. After the turmoil of 1919, corporate leaders worked hard to spread the doctrine that unionism was somehow subversive, that a crucial element of democratic capitalism was the protection of the "open shop" (a shop in which no worker could be required to join a union). The crusade for the open shop, euphemistically titled the "American Plan," received the en-dorsement of the National Association of Manufacturers in 1920 and became a pretext for a harsh campaign of union busting across the country. As a result, union membership fell from more than 5 million in 1920 to under 3 million in 1929.

The Plight of the Farmer

Like industry, American agriculture in the 1920s was embracing new tech-nologies for increasing production. The number of tractors on American farms, for example, quadrupled during the 1920s, helping to open 35 million new acres to cultivation. Agricultural production was increasing in other parts of the world as well. But unlike increased industrial production, increased agricultural production did not stimulate an increase in demand. The result was overproduction, a disastrous decline in food prices, and a severe drop in farmers' income beginning early in the 1920s. Farm income in 1920, had been 15 percent of the national total; by 1929, it was 9 percent. The average farmer made only about a quarter as much money each year in the 1920s as the average nonfarmer. More than 3 million people left agriculture altogether in the course of the decade. Of those who remained, many were forced into tenancy—losing ownership of their lands and having to rent instead from banks or other landlords.

In response, some farmers began to demand relief in the form of government price supports. Through organizations such as the Farm Bureau Federation, they put increasing pressure on Congress (where farmers continued to enjoy disproportionately high representation). One price-raising scheme in particular came to dominate agrarian demands: the idea of "parity." Parity referred to a price for an agricultural commodity based on the average price of the crop during the years 1909–1913 (a good time for farmers) as compared with the general average of all prices during the same period. Its purpose was to ensure that farmers would earn back at least their production costs no matter how the national or world agricultural market might fluctuate. Champions of parity urged high tariffs against foreign agricultural goods and a government commitment to buy surplus domestic crops at parity and sell them abroad at whatever the market would bring.

The legislative expression of the demand for parity was the McNary-Haugen Bill, named after its two principal sponsors in Congress and introduced repeatedly between 1924 and 1928. In 1926, Congress approved a bill requiring parity for grain, cotton, tobacco, and rice, but President Coolidge vetoed it. In 1928, it won congressional approval again, only to succumb to another presidential veto.

THE NEW CULTURE

The increasingly urban and consumer-oriented culture of the 1920s helped Americans in all regions live their lives and perceive their world in increasingly similar ways. That same culture exposed them to a new set of values that reflected the prosperity and complexity of the modern economy.

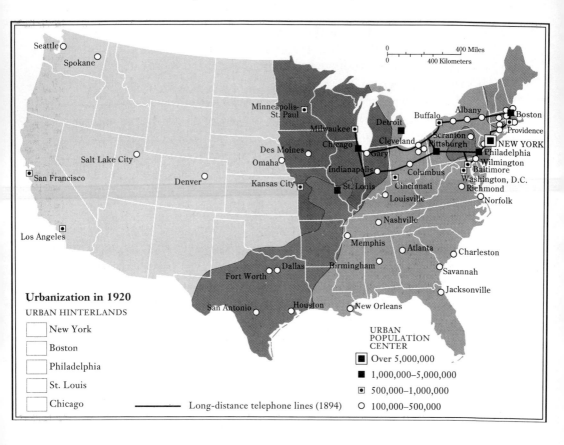

Urbanization in 1920

URBAN HINTERLANDS

- New York
- Boston
- Philadelphia
- St. Louis
- Chicago

———— Long-distance telephone lines (1894)

URBAN
POPULATION
CENTER

- Over 5,000,000
- 1,000,000–5,000,000
- 500,000–1,000,000
- 100,000–500,000

Consumerism and Communications

The United States of the 1920s was becoming a consumer society—a
society in which many men and women (although not, of course, all) could
afford not merely the means of subsistence but a considerable measure of
additional, discretionary goods and services; a society in which many people
could buy items not just because of need but for pleasure. Middle-class
families purchased new appliances such as electric refrigerators, washing
machines, and vacuum cleaners. Men and women wore wristwatches and
smoked cigarettes. Women purchased cosmetics and mass-produced fashions. Above all, Americans bought automobiles. By the end of the decade,
there were more than 30 million cars on American roads.

No group was more aware of the emergence of consumerism (or more
responsible for creating it) than the advertising industry. The first advertising and public relations firms (N. W. Ayer and J. Walter Thompson) had
appeared well before World War I; but in the 1920s, partly as a result of

techniques pioneered by wartime propaganda, advertising came of age. Publicists no longer simply conveyed information; they sought to identify products with a particular life style. They also encouraged the public to absorb the values of promotion and salesmanship and to admire those who were effective "boosters" and publicists. One of the most successful books of the 1920s was *The Man Nobody Knows*, by advertising executive Bruce Barton. It portrayed Jesus Christ as not only a religious prophet but also a "super salesman." Barton's message, a message apparently in tune with the new spirit of the consumer culture, was that Jesus had been a man concerned with living a full and rewarding life in this world; twentieth-century men and women should be concerned with doing the same.

The advertising industry could never have had the impact it did without the emergence of new vehicles of communication that made it possible to reach large audiences quickly and easily. Newspapers were being absorbed into national chains. Mass-circulation magazines—*Collier's, Ladies' Home Journal*, the *Saturday Evening Post*, and others—attracted broad, national audiences. The movies were becoming an ever more popular and powerful form of mass communication; over 100 million people saw films in 1930, as compared with 40 million in 1922.

The most important communications vehicle, however, was the only one truly new to the 1920s: radio. The first commercial radio station in America, KDKA in Pittsburgh, began broadcasting in 1920; and the first national radio network, the National Broadcasting Company, was formed in 1927. By 1923, there were more than 500 radio stations, covering virtually every area of the country; by 1929, more than 12 million families owned radio sets.

The influence of the consumer culture, and its increasing emphasis on immediate, personal fulfillment, was even visible in religion. Theological modernists—among them Harry Emerson Fosdick and A. C. McGiffert—taught their followers to abandon some of the traditional tenets of evangelical Christianity (literal interpretation of the Bible, belief in the Trinity, attribution of human traits to the deity) and to accept a faith that would help individuals to live more fulfilling lives in the present world.

The New Woman

College-educated women were no longer pioneers in the 1920s. There were now two and even three generations of graduates of women's or coeducational colleges and universities; and some were making their presence felt in professional areas that in the past women had rarely penetrated.

Still, professional opportunities for women remained limited by society's assumptions about what were suitable occupations for them. Although there were notable success stories about female business executives, journalists, doctors, and lawyers, most professional women remained confined to such traditionally "feminine" fields as fashion, education, social work, and nursing or to the lower levels of business management. The "new professional woman" was a vivid and widely publicized image in the 1920s. In reality, however, most employed women were nonprofessional, lower-class workers. Middle-class women, in the meantime, remained largely in the home.

Yet the 1920s constituted a new era for middle-class women nonetheless. In particular, the decade saw a redefinition of motherhood. Shortly after World War I, an influential group of psychologists—the "behaviorists," led by John B. Watson—began to challenge the long-held assumption that women had an instinctive capacity for motherhood. Maternal affection was not, they claimed, sufficient preparation for child rearing. Instead, mothers should rely on the advice and assistance of experts and professionals: doctors, nurses, and trained educators in nursery schools and kindergartens.

For many middle-class women, these changes devalued what had been an important and consuming activity. Many attempted to compensate by devoting new attention to their roles as wives and companions. A woman's relationship with her husband assumed a greatly enhanced importance. And many women now openly considered their sexual relationships with their husbands not simply a means of procreation, as earlier generations had been taught to do, but an important and pleasurable experience in its own right, as the culmination of romantic love.

One result was progress in birth control. The pioneer of the American birth-control movement, Margaret Sanger, began her career as a promoter of the diaphragm and other birth-control devices out of a concern for working-class women; she believed that large families were among the major causes of poverty and distress in poor communities. By the 1920s (partly because she had limited success in persuading working-class women to accept her teachings), she was becoming more concerned with persuading middle-class women of the benefits of birth control. Birth-control devices began to find a large market among middle-class women, even though some techniques remained illegal in many states (and abortion remained illegal nearly everywhere).

The new, more secular view of womanhood had effects on women beyond the middle class as well. Some women concluded that in the New Era it was no longer necessary to maintain a rigid, Victorian female "respectability." They could smoke, drink, dance, wear seductive clothes and makeup, and attend lively parties. Those assumptions became the basis of the "flapper"—the modern woman whose liberated life style found expression in dress, hair style, speech, and behavior. The flapper life style had a particular impact on lower-middle-class and working-class single women, who were flocking to new jobs in industry and the service sector. (The young, middle-class, "Bohemian" women most often associated with the flapper image were, in fact, imitating a style that emerged among this larger group.) At night, such women flocked to clubs and dance halls in search of excitement and companionship.

Despite all the changes, most women remained highly dependent on men—both in the workplace and in the home—and relatively powerless when men exploited that dependence. The realization that the "new woman" was as much myth as reality inspired some American feminists to continue their crusade for reform. The National Woman's party, under the leadership of Alice Paul, pressed on with its campaign for the Equal Rights Amendment, although it found little support in Congress (and met continued resistance from other feminist groups). Nevertheless, women's organizations and female political activities grew in many ways in the 1920s. Responding to the suffrage victory, women organized the League of Women Voters and the women's auxiliaries of both the Democratic and Republican parties. Female-dominated consumer groups grew rapidly and increased the range and energy of their efforts.

Women activists won an apparent triumph in 1921 when they helped secure passage of a measure in keeping with the traditional feminist goal of securing "protective" legislation for women: the Sheppard-Towner Act. It provided federal funds to states to establish prenatal and child health-care programs. From the start, however, it produced controversy. Alice Paul and her supporters opposed the measure, complaining that it classified all women as mothers. Margaret Sanger complained that the new programs would discourage birth-control efforts. More important, the American Medical Association fought Sheppard-Towner, warning that it would introduce untrained outsiders into the health-care field. In 1929, Congress terminated the program.

The Disenchanted

Many artists and intellectuals coming of age in the 1920s were experiencing a disenchantment with modern America so fundamental that they were often able to view it only with contempt. As a result, they adopted a role different from that of most intellectuals of earlier eras. Rather than trying to influence and reform their society, they isolated themselves from it and embarked on a restless search for personal fulfillment.

At the heart of their critique of modern society was a sense of personal alienation, a belief that contemporary America no longer provided the individual with avenues by which he or she could achieve personal fulfillment. This disillusionment had its roots in many things, but in nothing so deeply as the experience of World War I. To those who had fought in the conflict, and even to many who had not, the aftermath of the war was shattering. The repudiation of Wilsonian idealism, the restoration of "business as usual," and the growing emphasis on materialism and consumerism suggested that nothing had been gained. The war had been a fraud; the suffering and the dying had been in vain.

One result of this alienation was a series of savage critiques of modern society by a wide range of writers, some of whom were known as the "debunkers." Among them was the Baltimore journalist H. L. Mencken, who delighted in ridiculing everything Americans held dear: religion, politics, the arts, even democracy itself. When someone asked Mencken why he continued to live in a society he found so loathsome, he replied: "Why do people go to the zoo?" Echoing Mencken's contempt was the novelist Sinclair Lewis, the first American to win a Nobel Prize in literature. In a series of savage novels—*Main Street* (1920), *Babbitt* (1922), *Arrowsmith* (1925), and others—he lashed out at one aspect of modern bourgeois society after another. Intellectuals of the 1920s claimed to reject the "success ethic" that they believed dominated American life (even though many of them hoped for—and a few achieved—commercial and critical success on their own terms). The novelist F. Scott Fitzgerald, for example, ridiculed the American obsession with material success in *The Great Gatsby* (1925).

Some artists and intellectuals expressed their disillusionment by leaving America to live in France, making Paris for a time a center of American artistic life. Others moved to the Southwestern United States—to the art colonies at Taos and Santa Fe, New Mexico—attracted by the cultural and geographical distinctiveness of the region. Some adopted hedonistic life styles, involving alcohol, drugs, casual sex, and wild parties. Most of these young men and women, however, believed the only real refuge from the travails of modern society was art. Only art, they argued, could allow them full individual expression; only the act of creation could offer them fulfillment.

The result of this quest for fulfillment through art was not, for the most part, real personal satisfaction for the writers and artists themselves; many continued to lead restless, unhappy lives. They did, however, produce a body of work that made the decade one of the great eras of American literature. The roster of important American writers who did significant work in the 1920s may have no equal in any other period: Ernest Hemingway, Fitzgerald, Lewis, Thomas Wolfe, John Dos Passos, Ezra Pound, T. S. Eliot, Gertrude Stein, Edna Ferber, William Faulkner, and Eugene O'Neill.

Not all intellectuals of the 1920s, however, expressed alienation and despair. Some expressed reservations about their society not by withdrawing from it but by advocating reform. John Dewey, for example, kept alive the philosophical tradition of pragmatism and appealed for "practical" education and experimentation in social policy. Charles and Mary Beard, perhaps the most influential historians of their day, stressed economic factors, and the clash of competing economic interests, in tracing the development of modern society.

To another group of intellectuals, the solution to contemporary problems lay neither in escapism nor in progressivism but in an exploration of their own cultural or regional origins. In New York City, a new generation of black intellectuals created a flourishing African-American culture widely described as the "Harlem Renaissance." The Harlem poets, novelists, and artists drew heavily from their African roots in an effort to prove the richness of their own racial heritage (and not incidentally to demonstrate to whites that their race was worthy of respect). The poet Langston Hughes captured much of the spirit of the movement in a single sentence: "I am a Negro—and beautiful." Other black writers in Harlem and elsewhere—James Weldon Johnson, Countee Cullen, Zora Neale Hurston, Claude McKay, Alain Locke—as well as black artists and musicians helped to establish a thriving culture rooted in the historical legacy of their race.

A strangely similar effort was under way among an influential group of white Southern intellectuals. Known first as the "Fugitives" and later as the "Agrarians," these young poets, novelists, and critics sought to counter the depersonalization of industrial society by evoking the strong rural and, they argued, communitarian traditions of their own region. In their controversial manifesto *I'll Take My Stand* (1930), a collection of essays by twelve Southern intellectuals, they issued a simultaneously radical and conservative appeal for a rejection of the doctrine of "economic progress" and the spiritual debilitation that had accompanied it. The supposedly "backward" South, they argued, could serve as a model for a nation drunk with visions of limitless growth and modernization.

A M E R I C A N   V O I C E S

LANGSTON HUGHES

I, Too (1926)

I, too, sing America.

I am the darker brother.
They send me to eat in the kitchen
When company comes,
But I laugh,
And eat well,
And grow strong.

Tomorrow,
I'll be at the table
When company comes.
Nobody'll dare
Say to me,
'Eat in the kitchen,'
Then.

Besides,
They'll see how beautiful I am
And be ashamed—

I, too, am America.

SOURCE: From *Selected Poems* by Langston Hughes. Copyright 1926 by Alfred A. Knopf, Inc. and renewed 1954 by Langston Hughes. Reprinted by permission of the publisher.

A CONFLICT OF CULTURES

The modern, secular culture of the 1920s was not unchallenged. It grew up alongside an older, more traditional culture, with which it continually and often bitterly competed. The older culture expressed the outlook of generally less affluent, less urban, more provincial Americans—men and women who continued to revere traditional values and customs and who feared and resented modernist threats to their way of life. The result of their fears was a series of harsh cultural controversies.

Prohibition

When the prohibition of the sale and manufacture of alcohol went into effect in January 1920, it had the support of most members of the middle class and most of those who considered themselves progressives. Within a year, however, it had become clear that the "noble experiment," as its defenders called it, was not working well. Prohibition did substantially reduce drinking, at least in some regions of the country. But it also produced conspicuous and growing violations that made the law an almost immediate source of disillusionment and controversy.

The government hired only 1,500 agents to enforce prohibition, and in many places they received little help from local law enforcement agencies. Before long, it was almost as easy to acquire illegal alcohol in much of the country as it had once been to acquire legal alcohol. And since an enormous, lucrative industry was now barred to legitimate businessmen, organized-crime figures took it over.

Many middle-class progressives who had originally supported prohibition soon soured on the experiment. But an enormous constituency of provincial, largely rural, Protestant Americans continued vehemently to defend it. To them, prohibition had always meant more than drinking. It represented the effort of an older America to maintain its dominance in a society in which they were becoming relatively less powerful. Drinking, which they associated with the modern city and with Catholic immigrants, became a symbol of the new culture they believed was displacing them.

As the decade proceeded, opponents of prohibition (or "wets," as they came to be known) gained steadily in influence. Not until 1933, however, when the Great Depression added weight to their appeals, were they finally able effectively to challenge the "drys" and win repeal of the Eighteenth Amendment.

Nativism and the Klan

As with prohibition (itself in part a result of old-stock Americans trying to discipline the new immigrant population), agitation for a curb on foreign immigration to the United States had begun in the nineteenth century; and as with prohibition, it had gathered strength in the years before the war largely because of the support of middle-class progressives. Such concerns had not been sufficient in the first years of the century to win passage of curbs on immigration; but in the years immediately following the war, when immigration began to be associated with radicalism, popular sentiment on behalf of restriction grew rapidly.

In 1921, Congress passed an emergency immigration act, establishing a quota system by which annual immigration from any country could not exceed 3 percent of the number of persons of that nationality who had been in the United States in 1910. The new law cut immigration from 800,000 to 300,000 in any single year, but the nativists remained unsatisfied. The National Origins Act of 1924 banned immigration from east Asia entirely and reduced the quota for Europeans from 3 to 2 percent. The quota would be based, moreover, not on the 1910 census, but on the census of 1890, a

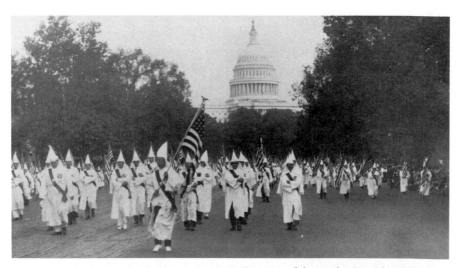

THE KU KLUX KLAN IN WASHINGTON, 1926 So powerful was the Ku Klux Klan in the mid-1920s that its members felt emboldened to march openly and defiantly down the streets of major cities—even down Pennsylvania Avenue in Washington, in the shadow of the Capitol of the United States.

year in which there had been far fewer southern and eastern Europeans in the country. What immigration there was, in other words, would heavily favor northwestern Europeans—people of "Nordic" or "Teutonic" stock. Five years later, a further restriction set a rigid limit of 150,000 immigrants a year. In the years that followed, immigration officials seldom permitted even half that number actually to enter the country.

But the nativism of the 1920s extended well beyond restricting immigration. To defenders of an older, more provincial America, the growth of large communities of foreign peoples, alien in their speech, their habits, and their values, came to seem a direct threat to their own embattled way of life. Among other things, this provincial nativism helped instigate the rebirth of the Ku Klux Klan as a major force in American society. The first Klan, founded during Reconstruction, had died in the 1870s. But in 1915, shortly after the premiere of the film *The Birth of a Nation*, which celebrated the early Klan, a new group of Southerners established a modern version of the society. At first the new Klan, like the old, was largely concerned with intimidating blacks. After World War I, however, concern about blacks gradually became secondary to concern about Catholics, Jews, and foreigners. At that point, membership in the Klan expanded rapidly and dramatically, not just in the small towns and rural areas of the South but in industrial cities in the North and Midwest. By 1924, there were reportedly 4 million members, and the largest state Klan was not in the South but in Indiana. Beginning in 1925, a series of scandals involving the organization's leaders precipitated a slow but steady decline in the Klan's influence.

Most Klan units (or "klaverns") tried to present their members as patriots and defenders of morality; and some did nothing more menacing than stage occasional parades and rallies. Often, however, the Klan also operated as a brutal, even violent, opponent of "alien" groups and as a defender of traditional, fundamentalist morality. Klansmen systematically terrorized blacks, Jews, Catholics, and foreigners. At times, they did so violently, through public whipping, tarring and feathering, arson, and lynching. What the Klan feared, however, was not simply "foreign" or "racially impure" groups; it was anyone who posed a challenge to traditional values. Klansmen persecuted not only immigrants and blacks but those white Protestants they considered guilty of irreligion, sexual promiscuity, or drunkenness. The Ku Klux Klan, in short, was fighting not just to preserve racial homogeneity but to defend its definition of traditional culture against the values and morals of modernity.

Religious Fundamentalism

Another cultural controversy of the 1920s was the result of a bitter conflict over the place of religion in contemporary society. By 1921, American Protestantism was already divided into two warring camps. On one side stood the modernists: mostly urban, middle-class people who had attempted to adapt religion to the teachings of modern science and to the realities of their modern, secular society. On the other side stood the fundamentalists: provincial, largely (although not exclusively) rural men and women fighting to preserve traditional faith and to maintain the centrality of religion in American life. The fundamentalists were outraged at the abandonment of traditional beliefs in the face of scientific discoveries. They insisted the Bible was to be interpreted literally. Above all, they opposed the teachings of Charles Darwin, who had openly challenged the biblical story of the Creation. Human beings had not evolved from lower orders of animals, the fundamentalists insisted. They had been created by God, as described in the Book of Genesis.

Fundamentalism was a highly evangelical movement, interested in spreading the doctrine to new groups. Evangelists, among them the celebrated former professional baseball player Billy Sunday, traveled from state to state (particularly in the South and parts of the West) attracting huge crowds to their revival meetings. Protestant modernists looked on much of this activity with condescension and amusement. But by the mid-1920s, to the great alarm of modernists, evangelical fundamentalism was gaining political strength in some states with its demands for legislation to forbid the teaching of evolution in the public schools. In Tennessee in March 1925, the legislature actually adopted a measure making it illegal for any public school teacher "to teach any theory that denies the story of the divine creation of man as taught in the Bible."

When the fledgling American Civil Liberties Union (ACLU) offered free counsel to any Tennessee educator willing to defy the law and become the defendant in a test case, a twenty-four-year-old biology teacher in the town of Dayton, John T. Scopes, agreed to have himself arrested. And when the ACLU decided to send the famous attorney Clarence Darrow to defend Scopes, the aging William Jennings Bryan (now an important fundamentalist spokesman) announced that he would travel to Dayton to assist the prosecution. Journalists from across the country, among them H. L. Mencken, flocked to Tennessee to cover the trial, which opened in an almost circus atmosphere. Scopes had, of course, clearly violated the law; and a verdict of guilty was a foregone conclusion, especially when the judge refused to permit "expert" testimony by evolution scholars. Scopes was fined $100, and the case was ultimately dismissed in a higher court because of a technicality. Nevertheless, Darrow scored an important victory for the modernists by calling Bryan himself to the stand to testify as an "expert on the Bible." In the course of the cross-examination, which was broadcast by radio to much of the nation, Darrow made Bryan's stubborn defense of biblical truths appear foolish and finally tricked him into admitting the possibility that not all religious dogma was subject to only one interpretation.

The Scopes trial did not resolve the conflict between fundamentalists and modernists. Four other states soon proceeded to pass antievolution laws of their own, and the issue continued to smolder for decades.

The Democrats' Ordeal

The anguish of provincial Americans attempting to defend an embattled way of life proved particularly troubling to the Democratic party, which was seriously debilitated during the 1920s as a result of tensions between its urban and rural factions. More than the Republicans, the Democrats consisted of a diverse coalition of interest groups, linked to the party more by local tradition than common commitment. Among those interest groups were prohibitionists, Klansmen, and fundamentalists on one side and Catholics, urban workers, and immigrants on the other.

In 1924, the tensions between them proved devastating. At the Democratic National Convention in New York that summer, a bitter conflict broke out over the platform when the party's urban wing attempted to win approval of planks calling for the repeal of prohibition and a denunciation of the Klan. Both planks narrowly failed. More serious was a deadlock in the balloting for a presidential candidate. Urban Democrats supported Alfred E. Smith, the Irish Catholic Tammanyite who had risen to become a progressive governor of New York; rural Democrats backed William McAdoo, Woodrow Wilson's Treasury secretary (and son-in-law), later to become a senator from California, who had skillfully positioned himself to win the support of Southern and Western delegates suspicious of Tammany Hall and modern urban life. For 103 ballots, the convention dragged on, until finally both Smith and McAdoo withdrew and the party settled on a compromise: the corporate lawyer John W. Davis.

A similar schism plagued the Democrats again in 1928, when Al Smith finally secured his party's nomination for president after another acrimonious but less prolonged battle. He was not, however, able to unite his divided party—in part because of widespread anti-Catholic sentiment, especially in the South; and in part because of Smith's own conspicuous New York provincialism. He was the first Democrat since the Civil War not to carry the entire South. Elsewhere, although he did well in large cities, he carried no states at all except Massachusetts and Rhode Island. Smith's opponent, and the victor in the presidential election, was a man who perhaps more than any other personified the modern, prosperous, middle-class society of the New Era: Herbert Hoover. The business civilization of the 1920s, with its new institutions, fashions, and values, continued to arouse the animosity of large portions of the population; but the majority of the American people appeared to have accepted and approved it. In 1928, at least, the New Era seemed to be permanently enshrined—as the success of the Republican party, its political embodiment, suggested.

REPUBLICAN GOVERNMENT

For twelve years, beginning in 1921, both the presidency and the Congress rested in the hands of the Republican party—a party in which the power of reformers had greatly dwindled. For most of those years, the federal government enjoyed a warm and supportive relationship with the American business community. Yet the government of the New Era was also more

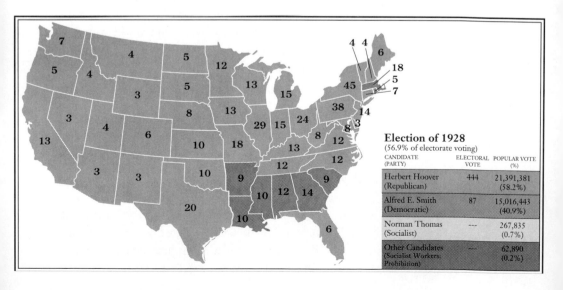

Election of 1928
(56.9% of electorate voting)

CANDIDATE (PARTY)	ELECTORAL VOTE	POPULAR VOTE (%)
Herbert Hoover (Republican)	444	21,391,381 (58.2%)
Alfred E. Smith (Democratic)	87	15,016,443 (40.9%)
Norman Thomas (Socialist)	---	267,835 (0.7%)
Other Candidates (Socialist Workers; Prohibition)	---	62,890 (0.2%)

than the passive, pliant instrument that critics often described. It attempted to serve in many respects as an active agent of economic change.

Harding and Coolidge

Nothing seemed more clearly to illustrate the unadventurous character of 1920s' politics than the characters of the two men who served as president during most of the decade: Warren G. Harding and Calvin Coolidge.

Harding was elected to the presidency in 1920, having spent many years in public life doing little of note. An undistinguished senator from Ohio, he had received the Republican presidential nomination as a result of an agreement among leaders of his party, who considered him, as one noted, a "good second-rater." Harding appointed capable men to the most important cabinet offices; he attempted to stabilize the nation's troubled foreign policy; and he displayed on occasion a vigorous humanity, as when he pardoned socialist Eugene V. Debs in 1921. But even as he attempted to rise to his office, he seemed baffled by his responsibilities, as if he recognized his own unfitness. "I am a man of limited talents from a small town," he reportedly told friends on one occasion. "I don't seem to grasp that I am President." Harding's intellectual limits were compounded by personal weaknesses: his penchant for gambling, illegal alcohol, and attractive women. Unsurprisingly, perhaps, Harding soon found himself delegating much of his authority to others: to members of his cabinet, to political cronies, to Congress, to party leaders.

Harding realized the importance of capable subordinates in an administration in which the president himself was reluctant to act. But he lacked the strength to abandon the party hacks who had helped create his political success. One of them, Harry Daugherty, the Ohio party boss principally responsible for his meteoric political ascent, he appointed attorney general. Another, New Mexico Senator Albert B. Fall, he made secretary of the interior. Members of the so-called Ohio Gang filled important offices throughout the administration.

Unknown to the public (and perhaps also to Harding), Daugherty, Fall, and others were engaged in fraud and corruption. The most spectacular scandal involved the rich naval oil reserves at Teapot Dome, Wyoming, and Elk Hills, California. At the urging of Fall, Harding transferred control of those reserves from the Navy Department to the Interior Department. Fall then secretly leased them to two wealthy businessmen and received in return nearly half a million dollars in "loans" to ease his private financial troubles.

Fall was ultimately convicted of bribery and sentenced to a year in prison; Harry Daugherty barely avoided a similar fate for his part in another scandal.

In the summer of 1923, only months before Senate investigations and press revelations brought the scandals to light, a tired and depressed Harding left Washington for a speaking tour in the West and a visit to Alaska. In Seattle late in July, he suffered severe pain, which his doctors wrongly diagnosed as food poisoning. A few days later, in San Francisco, he died. He had suffered two major heart attacks.

In many ways, Calvin Coolidge, who succeeded Harding in the presidency, was utterly different from his predecessor. Where Harding was genial, garrulous, and debauched, Coolidge was dour, silent, even puritanical. And while Harding was, if not perhaps personally corrupt, then at least tolerant of corruption in others, Coolidge seemed honest beyond reproach. In other ways, however, Harding and Coolidge were similar figures. Both took an essentially passive approach to their office.

Like Harding, Coolidge had risen to the presidency on the basis of few substantive accomplishments. Elected governor of Massachusetts in 1919,

CALVIN COOLIDGE President Coolidge opens the 1924 professional baseball season in characteristically dour form.

he had won national attention with his laconic response to the Boston police strike that year: "There is no right to strike against the public safety." That was enough to make him his party's vice presidential nominee in 1920. Three years later, after Harding's death, he took the oath of office by the light of a kerosene lamp, from his father, a justice of the peace.

If anything, Coolidge was even less active as president than Harding, partly as a result of his conviction that government should interfere as little as possible in the life of the nation and partly as a result of his own personal lassitude. ("No president of my time ever slept so much," the journalist William Allen White once said of Coolidge, whose penchant for long naps was well known.) He proposed no significant legislation and took little part in the running of the nation's foreign policy. In 1924, he received his party's presidential nomination virtually unopposed. Running against John W. Davis, he won a comfortable victory: 54 percent of the popular vote and 382 of the 531 electoral votes. Robert La Follette, the candidate of the reincarnated Progressive party, received 16 percent of the popular vote but carried only his home state of Wisconsin. Coolidge probably could have won renomination and reelection in 1928. Instead, in characteristically laconic fashion, he walked into a press room one day and handed each reporter a slip of paper containing a single sentence: "I do not choose to run for president in 1928."

Government and Business

The story of Harding and Coolidge themselves, however, is only a part—and by no means the most important part—of the story of their administrations. However inert the New Era presidents may have been, much of the federal government was working effectively and efficiently during the 1920s to adapt public policy to the widely accepted goal of the time: helping business and industry operate with maximum efficiency and productivity. The close relationship between the private sector and the federal government that had been forged during World War I continued.

Secretary of the Treasury Andrew Mellon, a wealthy steel and aluminum tycoon, devoted himself to working for substantial reductions in taxes on corporate profits and personal incomes and inheritances. Largely because of his efforts, Congress cut them all by more than half. Mellon also worked closely with President Coolidge after 1924 on a series of measures to trim dramatically the already modest federal budget. The administration even managed to retire half the nation's World War I debt.

The most prominent member of the cabinet was Commerce Secretary Herbert Hoover, who considered himself, and was considered by others, a notable progressive. During his eight years in the Commerce Department, Hoover constantly encouraged voluntary cooperation in the private sector as the best avenue to stability. But the idea of voluntarism did not require that the government remain passive; on the contrary, public institutions, Hoover believed, had a duty to play an active role in creating the new, cooperative order. Above all, Hoover became the champion of the concept of business "associationalism"—a concept that envisioned the creation of national organizations of businessmen in particular industries. Through these trade associations, private entrepreneurs could, Hoover believed, stabilize their industries and promote efficiency in production and marketing. Hoover resisted those who urged that the government sanction collusion among manufacturers to fix prices. He did, however, believe that shared information and limited cooperation would keep competition from becoming destructive and thus improve the strength of the economy as a whole.

The probusiness policies of the Republican administrations were not without their critics. In Congress, progressive reformers of the old school continued to criticize the monopolistic practices of big business, to attack government's alliance with the corporate community, and to decry social injustices. Occasionally, they were able to mobilize enough support to win congressional approval of progressive legislation, most notably the McNary-Haugen plan for farmers and an ambitious proposal to use federal funds to develop public electric power projects on the Tennessee River at Muscle Shoals. But the progressive reformers lacked the power to override the presidential vetoes that their bills almost always received.

Some progressives derived encouragement from the election of Herbert Hoover—widely regarded as the most progressive member of the Harding and Coolidge administrations—to the presidency in 1928. Hoover easily defeated Al Smith, the Democratic candidate. And he entered office promising bold new efforts to solve the nation's remaining economic problems. But Hoover had few opportunities to prove himself. Less than a year after his inauguration, the nation plunged into the severest and most prolonged economic crisis in its history—a crisis that brought many of the optimistic assumptions of the New Era crashing down and launched the nation into a period of unprecedented social innovation and reform.

CHAPTER TWENTY-FIVE

The Great Depression

The Coming of the Depression ~ *The American People in Hard Times*
The Ordeal of Herbert Hoover

E IN AMERICA today," Herbert Hoover had proclaimed in August 1928, not long before his election to the presidency, "are nearer to the final triumph over poverty than ever before in the history of any land. The poorhouse is vanishing from among us." Only fifteen months later, those words would return to haunt him, as the nation plunged into the severest and most prolonged economic depression in its history—a depression that continued in one form or another for a full decade, not only in the United States but throughout much of the rest of the world. The Depression was a traumatic experience for individual Americans, who faced unemployment, the loss of land and other property, and in some cases homelessness and starvation. It also placed great strains on the political and social fabric of the nation.

THE COMING OF THE DEPRESSION

The sudden financial collapse in 1929 came as an especially severe shock because it followed so closely a period in which the New Era seemed to be performing another series of economic miracles.

In February 1928, stock prices began a steady ascent that continued, with only a few temporary lapses, for a year and a half. Between May 1928 and September 1929, the average price of stocks rose over 40 percent. The stocks of the major industrials—the stocks that are used to determine the Dow Jones Industrial Average—doubled in value in that same period. Trading mushroomed from 2 or 3 million shares a day to over 5 million, and at times to as many as 10 or 12 million. There was, in short, a widespread speculative fever that grew steadily more intense, particularly once broker-age firms began encouraging the mania by offering absurdly easy credit to those buying stocks.

The Great Crash

In the autumn of 1929, the market began to fall apart. On October 21 and again on October 24, there were alarming declines in stock prices, in both cases followed by a temporary recovery. (The second recovery was engineered by J. P. Morgan and Company and other big bankers, who conspicuously bought up stocks to restore public confidence.) But on October 29, "Black Tuesday," all efforts to save the market failed. Sixteen million shares of stock were traded; the industrial index dropped 43 points, wiping out all the gains of the previous year; stocks in many companies became virtually worthless. Within a month stocks had lost half their September value, and they continued to decline for years after that. In July 1932, the industrial index—which had stood at 452 in September 1929—bottomed out at 58. The market remained deeply depressed for more than four years and did not fully recover for over a decade.

Popular folklore has established the stock market crash as the beginning, and even the cause, of the Great Depression. But although October 1929 might have been the first visible sign of the crisis, the Depression had earlier beginnings and more important causes.

Causes of the Depression

Economists, historians, and others have argued for decades about the causes of the Great Depression. But most agree on several things. They agree, first, that what is remarkable about the crisis is not that it occurred; periodic recessions are a normal feature of capitalist economies. What is remarkable is that it was so severe and that it lasted so long. The important question, therefore, is not so much why there was a depression but why it was such a bad one. Most observers agree, too, that a number of different factors account for the severity of the crisis, even if there is considerable disagreement about which was the most important.

One of those factors was a lack of diversification in the American economy in the 1920s. Prosperity had depended excessively on a few basic industries, notably construction and automobiles. In the late 1920s, those industries began to decline. Expenditures on construction fell from $11 billion to under $9 billion between 1926 and 1929. Automobile sales fell by more than a third in the first nine months of 1929. Newer industries were emerging to take up the slack—among them petroleum, chemicals, and plastics—but had not yet developed enough strength to compensate for the decline in other sectors.

A second important factor was the maldistribution of purchasing power and, as a result, a weakness in consumer demand. As industrial and agricultural production increased, the proportion of the profits going to farmers, workers, and other potential consumers was too small to create an adequate market for the goods the economy was producing. Even in 1929, after nearly a decade of economic growth, more than half the families in America lived on the edge of or below the minimum subsistence level—too poor to buy the goods the industrial economy was producing.

A third major problem was the credit structure of the economy. Farmers were deeply in debt—their land was mortgaged, and crop prices were too low to allow them to pay off what they owed. Small banks, especially those tied to the agricultural economy, were in constant trouble in the 1920s as their customers defaulted on loans; many of them failed. Large banks were in trouble too. Although most American bankers were very conservative, some of the nation's biggest banks were investing recklessly in the stock market or making unwise loans.

A fourth factor contributing to the coming of the Depression was America's position in international trade. Late in the 1920s, European demand for American goods began to decline. That was partly because European industry and agriculture were becoming more productive and partly because some European nations were having financial difficulties and could not afford to buy goods from overseas. But it was also because the European economy was being destabilized by the international debt structure that had emerged in the aftermath of World War I.

The international debt structure, therefore, was a fifth factor contributing to the Depression. When the war came to an end in 1918, all the European nations that had been allied with the United States owed large sums of money to American banks, sums much too large to be repaid out of their shattered economies. That was one reason why the Allies had insisted (over Woodrow Wilson's objections) on reparation payments from Germany and Austria. Reparations, they believed, would provide them with a way to pay off their own debts. But Germany and Austria were themselves in economic trouble after the war; they were no more able to pay the reparations than the Allies were able to pay their debts.

The American government refused to forgive or reduce the debts. Instead, American banks began making large loans to European governments with which they paid off their earlier loans. Thus debts (and reparations) were being paid only by piling up new and greater debts. In the late 1920s, and particularly after the American economy began to weaken in 1929, the European nations found it much more difficult to borrow money from the United States. At the same time, high American protective tariffs were making it difficult for them to sell their goods in American markets. Without any source of foreign exchange with which to repay their loans, they began to default. The collapse of the international credit structure was one of the reasons the Depression spread to Europe (and grew much worse in America) after 1931.

Progress of the Depression

The stock market crash of 1929 did not so much cause the Depression, then, as help trigger a chain of events that exposed longstanding weaknesses in the American economy. During the next three years, the crisis grew steadily worse.

The most serious problem was the collapse of much of the banking system. Over 9,000 American banks either went bankrupt or closed their doors to avoid bankruptcy between 1930 and 1933. Depositors lost over $2.5 billion in deposits. Partly as a result of these banking closures, the nation's money supply greatly decreased. The total money supply, according to some measurements, fell by more than a third between 1930 and 1933. The declining money supply meant a decline in purchasing power, and thus deflation. Manufacturers and merchants began reducing prices, cutting back on production, and laying off workers. Some economists argue that a severe depression could have been avoided if the Federal Reserve system had acted more responsibly. Late in 1931, in a misguided effort to build international confidence in the dollar, it raised interest rates, which contracted the money supply even further and hastened the demise of many banks and corporations.

The collapse was so rapid and so devastating that at the time it created only bewilderment among many of those who attempted to explain it. The American gross national product plummeted from over $104 billion in 1929 to $76.4 billion in 1932—a 25 percent decline in three years. In 1929, Americans had spent $16.2 billion to promote capital growth; in 1933, they invested only a third of a billion. The consumer price index declined 25 percent between 1929 and 1933; the wholesale price index, 32 percent.

SELLING APPLES, NEW YORK CITY In the fall of 1931 and again in the fall of 1932, large numbers of unemployed took to selling apples on the streets of major cities and became in the process a popular symbol of economic despair.

Gross farm income dropped from $12 billion to $5 billion in four years. By 1932, according to the relatively crude estimates of the time, 25 percent of the American work force was unemployed. (Some believe the figure was even higher.) For the rest of the decade, unemployment averaged nearly 20 percent, never dropping below 15 percent. Up to another one-third of the work force was "underemployed"—experiencing major reductions in wages, hours, or both.

THE AMERICAN PEOPLE
IN HARD TIMES

Someone asked the British economist John Maynard Keynes in the 1930s whether he was aware of any historical era comparable to the Great Depression. "Yes," Keynes replied. "It was called the Dark Ages, and it lasted 400 years." The Depression did not last 400 years. It did, however, bring unprecedented despair to the economies of the United States and much of the Western world. And it had far-reaching effects on American society and culture.

Unemployment and Relief

The suffering extended into every area of society. In the industrial Northeast and Midwest, cities were becoming virtually paralyzed by unemployment. Cleveland, Ohio, for example, had an unemployment rate of 50 percent in 1932; Akron, 60 percent; Toledo, 80 percent. Unemployed workers walked through the streets day after day looking for jobs that did not exist. An increasing number of families were turning to state and local public relief systems, just to be able to eat. But those systems, which in the 1920s had served only a small number of indigents, were totally unequipped to handle the new demands being placed on them. In many cities, therefore, relief simply collapsed. Private charities attempted to supplement the public relief efforts, but the problem was far beyond their capabilities as well. State governments felt pressure to expand their own assistance to the unemployed; but tax revenues were declining along with everything else, and state leaders balked at placing additional strains on already tight budgets.

In rural areas conditions were in many ways worse. Farm income declined by 60 percent between 1929 and 1932. A third of all American farmers lost their land. In addition, a large area of agricultural settlement in the Great Plains was suffering from a catastrophic natural disaster: one of

DOWN AND OUT, 1930 A "bread line" forms outside a rescue society. Evangelical missions such as this one, which was originally established to encourage Chinese immigrants to convert to Christianity, shifted their energies to offering assistance to the unemployed as the crisis of the Great Depression grew.

the worst droughts in the history of the nation. Beginning in 1930, the region, which came to be known as the "Dust Bowl" and which stretched north from Texas into the Dakotas, experienced a steady decline in rainfall and an accompanying increase in heat. The drought continued for a decade, turning what had once been fertile farm regions into virtual deserts. It is a measure of how productive American farmers were and how depressed the market for agricultural goods had become that even with these disastrous conditions, the farm economy continued through the 1930s to produce far more than American consumers could afford to buy.

Many farmers, like many urban unemployed, left their homes in search of work. In the South, in particular, many dispossessed farmers—black and white—simply wandered from town to town, hoping to find jobs or hand-outs. Hundreds of thousands of families from the Dust Bowl (often known as "Okies," since many came from Oklahoma) traveled to California and other states, where they found conditions little better than those they had left. Owning no land of their own, many worked as agricultural migrants, traveling from farm to farm picking fruit and other crops at starvation wages.

African-Americans and the Depression

Most African-Americans had not shared very much in the prosperity of the previous decade; they now experienced more unemployment, homeless-ness, malnutrition, and disease than they had in the past, and more than most whites experienced.

As the Depression began, over half of all black Americans still lived in the South. Most were farmers. The collapse of prices for cotton and other staple crops left some with no income at all. Many left the land altogether—either by choice or because they had been evicted by landlords who no longer found the sharecropping system profitable. Some migrated to South-ern cities. But there, unemployed whites believed they had first claim to what work there was, and some now began to take positions as janitors, street cleaners, and domestic servants, displacing the blacks who formerly occu-pied them. By 1932, over half the blacks in the South were without employ-ment. And what limited relief there was went almost invariably to whites first.

Unsurprisingly, therefore, many black Southerners—perhaps 400,000 in all—left the South in the 1930s and journeyed to the cities of the North. There they generally found less blatant discrimination. But conditions were in most respects little better than those in the South. In New York, black unemployment was nearly 50 percent. In other cities, it was higher. Two million African-Americans—half the total black population of the country—were on some form of relief by 1932.

Traditional patterns of segregation and disfranchisement in the South survived the Depression largely unchallenged. But a few particularly notorious examples of racism did attract the attention of the nation. The most celebrated was the Scottsboro case. In March 1931, nine black teen-agers were taken off a freight train in northern Alabama (in a small town near Scottsboro) and arrested for vagrancy and disorder. Later, two white women who had also been riding the train accused them of rape. In fact, there was overwhelming evidence, medical and otherwise, that the women had not been raped at all; they may have made their accusations out of fear of being arrested themselves. Nevertheless, an all-white jury in Alabama quickly convicted all nine of the "Scottsboro boys" (as they were known to both friends and foes) and sentenced eight of them to death.

The Supreme Court overturned the convictions in 1932, and a series of new trials began that gradually attracted national attention. The International Labor Defense, an organization associated with the Communist party, came to the aid of the accused youths and began to publicize the case. The trials continued throughout the 1930s. Although the white Southern juries who sat on the case never acquitted any of the defendants, all of them eventually gained their freedom—four because the charges were dropped, four because of early paroles, and one because he escaped. The last of the Scottsboro defendants did not leave prison until 1950.

The Depression was a time of important changes in the role and behavior of leading black organizations. The NAACP, for example, began to work diligently to win a position for blacks within the emerging labor movement, supporting the formation of the Congress of Industrial Organizations and helping break down racial barriers within labor unions. Partly as a result of such efforts, more than half a million blacks were able to join the labor movement. In the steelworkers union, for example, African-Americans constituted about 20 percent of the membership.

Hispanics in Depression America

Similar patterns of discrimination confronted many Mexicans and Mexican-Americans. The Hispanic population of the United States had been growing steadily since early in the century, largely in California and other areas of the Southwest through massive immigration from Mexico (which was specifically excluded from the immigration restriction laws of the

1920s). Chicanos (as Mexican-Americans are sometimes known) filled many of the same menial jobs there that blacks had traditionally filled in other regions. Some farmed small, marginal tracts. Some became agricultural migrants, traveling from region to region harvesting fruit, lettuce, and other crops. Even during the prosperous 1920s, it had been a precarious existence. The Depression made things significantly worse. As in the South, unemployed whites in the Southwest demanded jobs held by Hispanics, jobs that whites had previously considered beneath them. Thus Mexican unemployment rose quickly to levels far higher than those for whites. Some Mexicans were, in effect, forced to leave the country by officials who arbitrarily removed them from relief rolls or simply rounded them up and transported them across the border. Perhaps half a million Chicanos left the United States for Mexico, many involuntarily, in the first years of the Depression.

Those who remained faced persistent discrimination. Most relief programs excluded Mexicans from their rolls or offered them benefits far below those available to whites. Hispanics generally had limited access to American schools. Many hospitals refused them admission. Unlike American blacks, who had established certain educational and social facilities of their own in response to discrimination, Hispanics generally had nowhere to turn. Even many who possessed American citizenship found themselves treated like foreigners.

There were, occasionally, signs of organized resistance by Mexican-Americans themselves, most notably in California, where some formed a union of migrant farm workers. But harsh repression by local growers and the public authorities allied with them prevented such organizations from having much impact. Like African-American farm workers, many Hispanics began as a result to migrate to cities such as Los Angeles, where they lived in a poverty comparable to that of urban blacks in the South and Northeast.

Women and Families in the Great Depression

The economic crisis served in many ways to strengthen the widespread belief that a woman's proper place was in the home. Most men and many women believed that with employment so scarce, what work there was should go to men. There was a particularly strong belief that no woman whose husband was employed should accept a job. Indeed, from 1932 until 1937, it was illegal for more than one member of a family to hold a federal civil-service job.

But the widespread assumption that married women, at least, should not work outside the home did not stop them from doing so. Both single and married women worked in the 1930s, despite public condemnation of the practice, because they or their families needed the money. In fact, the largest new group of female workers consisted of precisely those people who, according to popular attitudes, were supposed to be leaving the labor market: wives and mothers. By the end of the Depression, 25 percent more women were working than had been doing so at the beginning.

This occurred despite considerable obstacles. Professional opportunities for women declined because unemployed men began moving into professions such as teaching and social work that had previously been considered women's fields. Female industrial workers were more likely to be laid off or to experience wage reductions than their male counterparts. But white women also had certain advantages in the workplace. The nonprofessional jobs that women traditionally held—as salesclerks and stenographers, and in other service positions—were less likely to disappear than the predominantly male jobs in heavy industry.

Black women, however, enjoyed few such advantages. In the South, in particular, they suffered massive unemployment because of a great reduction of domestic service jobs. As many as half of all black working women lost their jobs in the 1930s. Even so, at the end of the 1930s, 38 percent of black women were employed, as compared with 24 percent of white women. That was because black women—both married and unmarried—had always been more likely to work than white women, less out of preference than out of economic necessity.

For American feminists, the Depression years were, on the whole, a time of frustration. Although economic pressures pushed more women into the work force, those same pressures helped to erode the frail support feminists had won in the 1920s for the idea of women becoming economically and professionally independent. In the difficult years of the 1930s, such aspirations seemed to many to be less important than dealing with economic hardship. By the end of the 1930s, American feminism had reached its lowest ebb in nearly a century.

The economic hardships of the Depression years placed great strains on American families. Middle-class families that had become accustomed in the 1920s to a steadily rising standard of living now found themselves plunged suddenly into uncertainty, because of unemployment or the reduction of incomes among those who remained employed. Some working-class families too had achieved a precarious prosperity in the 1920s and saw their gains disappear in the 1930s.

A M E R I C A N   V O I C E S

A Pennsylvania Mother Responds to the Depression, December 1930

 NOW THAT OUR income is but $15.60 a week (their are five of us My husband Three little children and myself). My husband who is a world war Veteran . . . became desperate and applied for Compensation or a pension from the Government and was turned down and that started me thinking. [The government should provide] enough to pay all world war veterans a pension, dysabeled or not dysabeled and there by relieve a lot of suffering, and banish resentment that causes Rebellions and Bolshevism. Oh why is it that it is allways a bunch of overley rich, selfish, dumb, ignorant money hogs that persist in being Senitors, legislatures, representitives. Where would they and their possessions be if it were not for the Common Soldier, the common laborer that is compelled to work for a starvation wage. for I tell you again the hog of a Landlord gets his there is not enough left for the necessaries if a man has three or more children. . . . In the Public Schools our little children stand at salute and recite a "rig ma role" in which is mentioned "Justice to all" What a lie, what a naked lie, when honest, law abiding citizens, decendents of Revilutionary heros, Civil War heros, and World war heros are denied the priviledge of owning their own homes, that foundation of good citizenship, good morals, and the very foundation of good government the world over. . . . Oh for a few Statesmen, oh for but one statesman, as fearless as Abraham Lincoln, the amancipator who died for us.

SOURCE: Robert S. McElvaine, ed., *Down & Out in the Great Depression* (Chapel Hill: University of North Carolina Press, 1983), pp. 47–48.

Such circumstances forced many families to retreat from the consumer patterns they had developed in the 1920s. Women often returned to sewing clothes for themselves and their families and to preserving their own food rather than buying such products in stores. Others engaged in home businesses—taking in laundry, selling baked goods, accepting boarders. Many households expanded to include more distant relatives. Parents often moved in with their children and grandparents with their grandchildren, or vice versa.

But the Depression also worked to erode the strength of many family units. There was a decline in the divorce rate, but largely because divorce was now too expensive for some. More common was the informal breakup of families, particularly the desertion of families by unemployed men trying to escape the humiliation of being unable to earn a living. The marriage rate and the birth rate both declined for the first time since the early nineteenth century.

Values and Culture

Prosperity and industrial growth had done much to shape American values in the 1920s. Mainstream culture, at least, had celebrated affluence and consumerism and had stressed the importance of personal gratification through both. Many Americans assumed, therefore, that the experience of hard times would have profound effects on the nation's social values.

In general, however, American social values seemed to change relatively little in response to the Depression. Rather, many people responded to hard times by redoubling their commitment to familiar ideas and goals.

No assumption would seem to have been more vulnerable to erosion during the Depression than the belief that the individual was in control of his or her own fate, that anyone displaying sufficient talent and industry could become a success. And in some respects, the economic crisis did work to undermine the traditional "success ethic" in America. Many people began to look to government for assistance; many learned to blame corporate moguls, international bankers, "economic royalists," and others for their distress. Yet the Depression did not destroy the success ethic.

The survival of the ideals of work and individual advancement was evident in many ways, not least in the reactions of those most traumatized by the Depression: conscientious working people who suddenly found themselves without employment. Some expressed anger and struck out at the economic system. Many, however, seemed to blame themselves. That was one reason why the effects of the Depression were sometimes hard to see, because the unemployed tended to hide themselves, unwilling to display to the world what many of them considered their own personal failure.

At the same time, millions responded eagerly to reassurances that they could, through their own efforts, restore themselves to prosperity and success. Dale Carnegie's *How to Win Friends and Influence People* (1936), a self-help manual preaching individual initiative, was one of the best-selling books of the decade. Harry Emerson Fosdick, a Protestant theologian who similarly preached the virtues of positive thinking and individual initiative, attracted large audiences with his radio addresses.

Not all Americans, of course, responded to the crisis of the Depression so passively. Many men and women believed that the economic problems of their time were the fault of society, not of individuals, and that some collective social response was necessary. Such beliefs found expression in, among other places, American artistic and intellectual life.

Just as many progressives had become alarmed when, early in the twentieth century, they "discovered" the existence of widespread poverty in the cities, so many Americans were shocked during the 1930s at their discovery of debilitating rural poverty. Perhaps most effective in conveying the dimensions of rural poverty was a group of documentary photographers, many of them employed by the federal Farm Security Administration in the late 1930s, who traveled through the South recording the nature of agricultural life. Men such as Roy Stryker, Walker Evans, Arthur Rothstein, and Ben Shahn and women such as Margaret Bourke-White and Dorothea Lange produced memorable studies of farm families and their surroundings, studies designed to show the savage impact of a hostile environment on its victims.

Many writers, similarly, turned away from the personal concerns of the 1920s and devoted themselves to exposés of social injustice. Erskine Caldwell's *Tobacco Road* (1932), which later became a long-running play, was an exposé of poverty in the rural South. James Agee's *Let Us Now Praise Famous Men* (1941), with photographs by Walker Evans, was a careful, nonjudgmental description of the lives of three poor rural families in the South. Richard Wright, a major African-American novelist, exposed the plight of residents of the urban ghetto in *Native Son* (1940). John Steinbeck's *The Grapes of Wrath* (1939) portrayed the trials of a migrant family in California, concluding with an open call for collective social action against injustice. John Dos Passos's *U.S.A.* trilogy (1930) openly attacked modern capitalism. Playwright Clifford Odets provided an explicit demonstration of the appeal of political radicalism in *Waiting for Lefty* (1935).

But the cultural products of the 1930s that attracted the widest popular audiences were those that diverted attention away from the Depression. The two most powerful instruments of popular culture in the 1930s—radio and the movies—provided mostly light and diverting entertainment. Although radio stations occasionally carried socially and politically provocative programs, the staple of broadcasting was escapism: comedies such as *Amos 'n Andy*, adventures such as *Superman*, *Dick Tracy*, and *The Lone Ranger*, and other entertainment programs. Hollywood continued to exercise tight control over its products through its resilient censor Will Hays, who ensured that most movies carried only safe, conventional messages. A few films, such as the adaptation of *The Grapes of Wrath* (1940), did explore political themes. Director Frank Capra provided a muted social message in several of his comedies—*Mr. Deeds Goes to Town* (1936), *Mr. Smith Goes to Washington* (1939), and *Meet John Doe* (1941)—which celebrated the virtues of the small town and the decency of the common people in contrast to the selfish, corrupt values of the city and the urban rich. Gangster films and westerns celebrated violence and implicitly glamorized resistance to authority. Often, however, the commercial films of the 1930s were deliberately and explicitly escapist: lavish musicals and "wacky" comedies designed to divert audiences from their troubles and, very often, satisfy their fantasies about quick and easy wealth.

Popular literature, similarly, offered Americans an escape from the Depression. Two of the best-selling novels of the decade were romantic sagas set in bygone eras: Margaret Mitchell's *Gone with the Wind* (1936) and Hervey Allen's *Anthony Adverse* (1933). Leading magazines, and particularly such popular new photographic journals as *Life*, focused on fashions, stunts, and eye-catching scenery. Even the newsreels distributed to movie theaters across the country tended to give more attention to beauty contests and ship launchings than to the Depression itself.

The Allure of the Left

For a relatively small but important group of Americans—intellectuals, artists, workers, African-Americans, and others who became disenchanted for various reasons with the prevailing values of American life—the Depression produced a commitment, for a time at least, to radical politics.

The importance of the 1936 Spanish Civil War to many American intellectuals was a good example of how the left produced a sense of commitment and purpose in individual lives. The battle against the Spanish fascists of Francisco Franco (who was receiving support from Hitler and Mussolini) attracted a substantial group of young Americans, more than 3,000 in all, who formed the "Abraham Lincoln Brigade" and traveled to Spain to join in the fight. About a third of its members died in combat; but those who survived remembered the experience with pride, as one of the great moments of their lives.

Instrumental in creating the Lincoln brigade, and directing many of its activities, was the American Communist party. Its membership reached perhaps 100,000 at its peak in the mid-1930s. For several years beginning in 1935, the party dropped its insistence on working completely apart from other organizations and began to advocate a democratic alliance of all antifascist groups in the United States, a "Popular Front." It began to praise Franklin Roosevelt and John L. Lewis, a powerful (and strongly anticommunist) labor leader. It adopted the slogan "Communism is twentieth-century Americanism."

The party was active in organizing the unemployed in the early 1930s and staged a hunger march in Washington, D.C., in 1931. Party members were among the most effective union organizers in some industries. And the party was one of the few political organizations to take a firm stand in favor of racial justice; its active defense of the Scottsboro defendants was but one example of its efforts to ally itself with the aspirations of African-Americans. It also helped organize a union of black sharecroppers in Alabama, which resisted—in several instances violently—efforts of white landowners and authorities to displace them from their farms.

But despite its efforts to appear a patriotic organization, the American Communist party was always under the close and rigid supervision of the Soviet Union. Its leaders took their orders from the Comintern in Moscow. Most members obediently followed the "party line." The subordination of the party leadership to the Soviet Union was most clearly demonstrated in 1939, when Stalin signed a nonaggression pact with Nazi Germany. Moscow then sent orders to the American Communist party to abandon the Popular Front idea and return to its old stance of harsh criticism of American liberals; and the leaders in the United States immediately obeyed—although thousands of disillusioned members left the party as a result.

The Socialist party of America, now under the leadership of Norman Thomas, also cited the economic crisis as evidence of the failure of capitalism and sought vigorously to win public support for its own political program. Among other things, it attempted to mobilize support among the rural poor. The Southern Tenant Farmers Union (STFU), supported by the party, attempted to create a biracial coalition of sharecroppers, tenant farmers, and others to demand economic reform. Neither the STFU nor the party itself, however, made any real progress toward establishing socialism as a major force in American politics. By 1936, in fact, membership in the Socialist party had fallen below 20,000.

THE ORDEAL OF HERBERT HOOVER

Herbert Hoover began his presidency in March 1929 believing, like most Americans, that the nation faced a bright and prosperous future. For the first six months of his administration, he attempted to expand the policies he had advocated during his eight years as secretary of commerce, policies that would, he believed, complete a stable system of cooperative individualism and sustain a successful economy. The economic crisis that began before the year was out forced the president to deal with a new set of problems; but for most of the rest of his term, he continued to rely on the principles that had always governed his public life.

The Hoover Program

Hoover's first response to the Depression was to attempt to restore public confidence in the economy. "The fundamental business of this country, that is, production and distribution of commodities," he said in 1930, "is on a sound and prosperous basis." Subsequently, he summoned leaders of business, labor, and agriculture to the White House and urged upon them a program of voluntary cooperation for recovery. He implored businessmen not to cut production or lay off workers; he talked labor leaders into forgoing demands for higher wages or better hours. But by mid-1931, economic conditions had deteriorated so much that the structure of voluntary cooperation he had erected collapsed. Frightened industrialists soon began cutting production, laying off workers, and slashing wages.

Hoover also attempted to use government spending as a tool for fighting the Depression. The president proposed to Congress an increase of $423 million—a substantial sum by the standards of the time—in federal public works programs; and he exhorted state and local governments to fund public construction. But Hoover was not willing to spend enough money,

HERBERT HOOVER RECEIVING A LOAD OF POTATOES The Maine Potato Growers Association sent a team of oxen to Washington with a load of Maine potatoes in 1931. They presented them as a gift to President Hoover on the White House lawn on November 23, to remind him of the difficulties that faced the agricultural economy as the Great Depression worsened.

or to spend it for a long enough time, to do very much good. And when economic conditions worsened, he became less willing to increase government spending, worrying instead about maintaining federal solvency. In 1932, at the depth of the Depression, he proposed a tax increase to help the government avoid a deficit.

Even before the stock market crash, Hoover had begun to construct a program to assist the troubled agricultural economy. In April 1929, he proposed the Agricultural Marketing Act, which established for the first time a major government bureaucracy to help farmers maintain prices. A federally sponsored Farm Board would administer a budget of $500 million, from which it could make loans to national marketing cooperatives or establish corporations to buy surpluses and thus raise prices. At the same time, Hoover attempted to protect American farmers from international competition by raising agricultural tariffs. The Hawley-Smoot Tariff of 1930 contained protective increases on seventy-five farm products.

Neither the Agricultural Marketing Act nor the Hawley-Smoot Tariff ultimately helped American farmers significantly. The Marketing Act relied on voluntary cooperation among farmers and gave the government no authority to effect what the agricultural economy most badly needed: a limit on production. Prices continued to fall despite its efforts. The Hawley-Smoot Tariff provoked foreign governments to enact trade restrictions of their own in reprisal, further diminishing the market for American agricultural goods.

By the spring of 1931, Herbert Hoover's political position had deteriorated considerably. In the 1930 congressional elections, Democrats won control of the House and made substantial inroads in the Senate by promising increased government assistance to the economy. Many Americans held the president personally to blame for the crisis. Shantytowns established on the outskirts of cities were labeled "Hoovervilles." Democrats urged the president to support more vigorous programs of relief and public spending. Hoover, instead, seized on a slight improvement in economic conditions early in 1931 as proof that his policies were working.

The international financial panic of the spring of 1931 destroyed the illusion that the economic crisis was coming to an end. Throughout the 1920s, European nations had depended on loans from American banks to allow them to make payments on their debts. After 1929, when they could no longer get such loans, the financial fabric of several European nations began to unravel. In May 1931, the largest bank in Austria collapsed. Over the next several months, panic gripped the financial institutions of neighboring countries. The American economy rapidly declined to new lows.

By the time Congress convened in December 1931, conditions had grown so desperate that Hoover supported a series of measures designed to keep endangered banks afloat and protect homeowners from foreclosure on their mortgages. More important was a bill passed in January 1932 establishing the Reconstruction Finance Corporation (RFC), a government agency whose purpose was to provide federal loans to troubled banks, railroads, and other businesses. It even made funds available to local governments to support public works projects and assist relief efforts. Unlike some earlier Hoover programs, it operated on a large scale. In 1932, the RFC had a budget of $1.5 billion for public works alone.

Nevertheless, the new agency failed to deal directly or forcefully enough with the real problems of the economy to produce any significant recovery. Because the RFC was permitted to lend funds only to those financial institutions with sufficient collateral, much of its money went to large banks and corporations. And at Hoover's insistence, it helped finance only those public works projects that promised ultimately to pay for themselves (toll bridges, public housing, and others). Above all, the RFC did not have enough money to make any real impact on the Depression; and it did not even spend all the money it had. Of the $300 million available to support local relief efforts, the RFC lent out only $30 million in 1932. Of the $1.5 billion public works budget, it released only about 20 percent.

The Rise of Popular Protest

For the first several years of the Depression, most Americans were either too stunned or too confused to raise any effective protest. By the middle of 1932, however, dissident voices began to be heard.

In the Midwest, farmers called for legislation similar to the McNary-Haugen Bill of the 1920s by which the government would guarantee them a return on their crops at least equal to the cost of production. Lobbyists from the larger farm organizations pressured members of Congress to act, and some disgruntled farmers staged public protests in the capital. But neither the president nor Congress showed any signs of movement.

In the summer of 1932, a group of unhappy farm owners gathered in Des Moines, Iowa, to establish a new organization: the Farmers' Holiday Association, which endorsed the withholding of farm products from the market—in effect a farmers' strike. The strike began in August in western Iowa, spread briefly to a few neighboring areas, and succeeded in blockading several markets; but in the end it dissolved in failure. The scope of the effort was too modest to affect farm prices, and many farmers in the region refused to cooperate in any case. Nevertheless, the uprising created considerable consternation in state governments in the farm belt and even more in Washington, where the president and much of Congress were facing a national election.

A more celebrated protest movement emerged from a less likely quarter: American veterans. In 1924, Congress had approved the payment of a $1,000 bonus to all those who had served in World War I, the money to be paid beginning in 1945. By 1932, however, many veterans were demanding that the bonus be paid immediately. Hoover, concerned about balancing the budget, refused to comply. In June, more than 20,000 veterans, members of the self-proclaimed Bonus Expeditionary Force, or "Bonus Army," marched into Washington, built crude camps around the city, and promised to stay until Congress approved legislation to pay the bonus. A few of the veterans departed in July, after Congress had voted down their proposal. Most, however, remained where they were.

Their continued presence in Washington was an embarrassment to Herbert Hoover. Finally, in mid-July, he ordered police to clear the marchers out of several abandoned federal buildings in which they had been staying. A few marchers threw rocks at the police, and someone opened fire; two veterans fell dead. Hoover considered the incident evidence of dangerous radicalism. He ordered the United States Army to assist the police in clearing out the buildings.

General Douglas MacArthur, the army chief of staff, carried out the mission himself (with the assistance of his aide, Dwight D. Eisenhower) and greatly exceeded the president's orders. He led the Third Cavalry (under the command of George S. Patton), two infantry regiments, a machine-gun detachment, and six tanks down Pennsylvania Avenue in pursuit of the Bonus Army. The veterans fled in terror. MacArthur followed them across the Anacostia River, where he ordered the soldiers to burn their tent city to the ground. More than 100 marchers were injured. One baby died.

The incident served as perhaps the final blow to Hoover's already battered political standing. Hoover's own cold and gloomy personality did nothing to change the public image of him as aloof and unsympathetic to distressed people. The Great Engineer, the personification of the optimistic days of the 1920s, had become a symbol of the nation's failure to deal effectively with its startling reversal of fortune.

The Election of 1932

As the 1932 presidential election approached, few people doubted the outcome. The Republican party dutifully renominated Herbert Hoover for a second term in office, but the lugubrious atmosphere of their convention made it clear that few delegates believed he could win. The Democrats, in the meantime, gathered jubilantly in Chicago to nominate the governor of New York, Franklin Delano Roosevelt.

Roosevelt had been a well-known figure in the party for many years already. A Hudson Valley aristocrat, a distant cousin of Theodore Roosevelt (a connection strengthened by his marriage in 1904 to the president's niece,

Eleanor), and a handsome, charming young man, he progressed rapidly: from a seat in the New York State legislature to a position as assistant secretary of the navy under Woodrow Wilson during World War I to his party's vice presidential nomination in 1920 on the ill-fated ticket with James M. Cox. Less than a year later, he was stricken with polio. Although he was never again able to walk without the use of crutches and braces, he built up sufficient physical strength to return to politics in 1928. When Al Smith received the Democratic nomination for president that year, Roosevelt was elected to succeed him as governor. In 1930, he easily won reelection.

Roosevelt worked no miracles in New York, but he did initiate enough positive programs of government assistance to be able to present himself as a more energetic and imaginative leader than Hoover. Equally important, he avoided such divisive cultural issues as religion and prohibition; and by emphasizing the economic grievances that most Democrats shared, he assembled a coalition within the party that enabled him to win his party's nomination. In a dramatic break with tradition, he flew to Chicago to address the convention in person and accept the nomination.

In the course of his acceptance speech, Roosevelt aroused the delegates with his ringing promise: "I pledge you, I pledge myself, to a new deal for the American people," giving his program a name that would long endure. Neither then nor in the subsequent campaign, however, did Roosevelt give much indication of what that program would be. But Herbert Hoover's unpopularity virtually ensured Roosevelt's election.

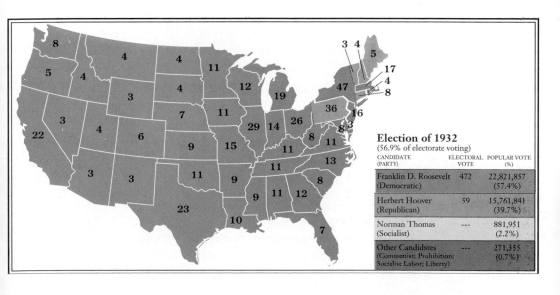

Election of 1932
(56.9% of electorate voting)

CANDIDATE (PARTY)	ELECTORAL VOTE	POPULAR VOTE (%)
Franklin D. Roosevelt (Democratic)	472	22,821,857 (57.4%)
Herbert Hoover (Republican)	59	15,761,841 (39.7%)
Norman Thomas (Socialist)	---	881,951 (2.2%)
Other Candidates (Communist; Prohibition; Socialist Labor; Liberty)	---	271,355 (0.7%)

In November, to the surprise of no one, Roosevelt won by a landslide. He received 57.4 percent of the popular vote to Hoover's 39.7. In the electoral college, the result was even more overwhelming. Hoover carried Pennsylvania, Connecticut, Vermont, New Hampshire, and Maine. Roosevelt won everything else. Democrats won majorities in both houses of Congress. It was a broad and convincing mandate, but it was not yet clear what Roosevelt intended to do with it.

THE CHANGING OF THE GUARD Well before the event actually occurred, Peter Arno of the *New Yorker* magazine drew this image
of Franklin D. Roosevelt and Herbert Hoover traveling together
to the Capitol for Roosevelt's inauguration. It predicted with remarkable accuracy the mood of the uncomfortable ride—Hoover
glum and uncommunicative, Roosevelt buoyant and smiling.
This was to have been the magazine's cover for the week of the
inauguration; but after an attempted assassination of the
president-elect several weeks earlier in Florida (in which the
mayor of Chicago was killed), the editors decided to substitute a
more subdued drawing.

The Interregnum

The period between the election and the inauguration (which in the early 1930s lasted more than four months) was a season of growing economic crisis. Presidents-elect traditionally do not involve themselves directly in government. But in a series of brittle exchanges with Roosevelt in the months following the election, Hoover tried to exact from the president-elect a pledge to maintain policies of economic orthodoxy. Roosevelt genially refused.

In February, only a month before the inauguration, a new crisis developed when the American banking system began to collapse. Public confidence in the banks was ebbing; depositors were withdrawing their money in panic; and one bank after another was closing its doors and declaring bankruptcy. In mid-February, the governor of Michigan, one of the states hardest hit by the panic, ordered all banks temporarily closed. Other states soon followed, and by the end of the month banking activity was restricted drastically in every state but one. Hoover again asked Roosevelt to give prompt public assurances that there would be no tinkering with the currency, no heavy borrowing, no unbalancing of the budget. Roosevelt again refused.

March 4, 1933, was, therefore, a day of both economic crisis and considerable personal bitterness. On that morning, Herbert Hoover, convinced that the United States was headed for disaster, rode glumly down Pennsylvania Avenue with a beaming, buoyant Franklin Roosevelt, who would shortly be sworn in as the thirty-second president of the United States.

CHAPTER TWENTY-SIX

The New Deal

Launching the New Deal ~ The New Deal in Transition
The New Deal in Disarray ~ Limits of the New Deal

RANKLIN ROOSEVELT SERVED longer as president than anyone else before or since, and during his twelve years in office he became more central to the life of the nation than any chief executive had ever been. Most important, his administration constructed a series of programs that permanently altered the federal government and its relationship to society.

By the end of the 1930s, the New Deal (as the Roosevelt administration was called) had created many of the broad outlines of the political world we know today. It had constructed the beginnings of a modern welfare system. It had extended federal regulation over new areas of the economy. It had presided over the birth of the modern labor movement. It had made the government a major force in the agricultural economy. It had created a powerful coalition within the Democratic party that would dominate American politics for most of the next thirty years. And it had produced the beginnings of a new liberal ideology that would govern reform efforts for several decades after the war. One thing the New Deal had not done, however, was end the Great Depression. It had helped stabilize the economy in 1933, and there had been a limited, if erratic, recovery after that. But by the end of 1939, many of the basic problems of the Depression remained unsolved.

LAUNCHING THE NEW DEAL

Roosevelt's first task upon taking office was to alleviate the panic that was threatening to create chaos in the financial system. He did so in part by force of personality and in part by constructing very rapidly an ambitious and diverse program of legislation.

THE ROOSEVELT SMILE The battered hat, the uptilted cigarette holder, the jaunty smile—all were hallmarks of Franklin Roosevelt's ebullient public personality. In part, at least, the president's hearty optimism was a deliberate pose, adopted to distract attention from the paralysis that had denied him the use of his legs since 1921.

Restoring Confidence

Much of Roosevelt's early success was a result of his ebullient personality. He was the first president to make regular use of the radio; and his friendly "fireside chats," during which he explained his programs and plans to the people, helped build public confidence in the administration. Roosevelt held frequent informal press conferences and won both the respect and the friendship of most reporters.

But Roosevelt could not rely on image alone. On March 6, two days after taking office, he issued a proclamation closing all American banks for four days until Congress could meet in special session to consider banking reform legislation. So great was the panic about bank failures that the "bank holiday," as the president euphemistically described it, created a general sense of relief and hope.

Three days later, Roosevelt sent to Congress the Emergency Banking Act, a generally conservative bill (much of it drafted by holdovers from the Hoover administration) designed primarily to protect the larger banks from being dragged down by the weakness of smaller ones. The bill provided for Treasury Department inspection of all banks before they would be allowed to reopen, for federal assistance to some troubled institutions, and for a thorough reorganization of those banks in the greatest difficulty. A confused and frightened Congress passed the bill within a few hours of its introduction. Whatever else the new law accomplished, it helped dispel the panic. Three-quarters of the banks in the Federal Reserve system reopened within the next three days, and $1 billion in hoarded currency and gold flowed back into them within a month. The immediate banking crisis was over.

On the morning after passage of the Emergency Banking Act, Roosevelt sent to Congress another measure—the Economy Act—designed to convince the public (and especially the business community) that the federal government was in safe, responsible hands. The act proposed to balance the federal budget by cutting the salaries of government employees and reducing pensions to veterans by as much as 15 percent. Otherwise, the president warned, the nation faced a $1 billion deficit. Like the banking bill, this one passed through Congress almost instantly—despite heated protests from some congressional progressives.

Roosevelt also moved in his first days in office to put to rest one of the divisive issues of the 1920s. He supported and then signed a bill to legalize the manufacture and sale of beer with a 3.2 percent alcohol content—an interim measure pending the repeal of prohibition, for which a constitutional amendment (the Twenty-first) was already in process. The amendment was ratified later in 1933.

Agricultural Adjustment

These initial actions were largely stopgaps, to buy time for more comprehensive programs. The first such program was the Agricultural Adjustment Act, which Congress passed in May 1933. Its most important feature was its provision for reducing crop production to end agricultural surpluses and halt the downward spiral of farm prices.

Under the "domestic allotment" system of the act, producers of seven basic commodities (wheat, cotton, corn, hogs, rice, tobacco, and dairy products) would decide on production limits for their crops. The government, through the Agricultural Adjustment Administration (AAA), would then tell individual farmers how much they should produce and would pay them subsidies for leaving some of their land idle. A tax on food processing (for example, the milling of wheat) would provide the funds for the new payments. Farm prices were to be subsidized up to the point of parity.

The results of the AAA efforts were in many ways heartening. Prices for farm commodities did indeed rise in the years after 1933, and gross farm income increased by half in the first three years of the New Deal. The agricultural economy as a whole emerged from the 1930s much more stable and prosperous than it had been in many years. The AAA did, however, tend to favor larger farmers over smaller ones, particularly since local administration of its programs often fell into the hands of the most powerful producers in a community. New Deal farm programs actually contributed to dispossessing some struggling farmers, even if unintentionally. By distributing payments to landowners, not those who worked the land, the government did little to discourage planters who were reducing their acreage from evicting tenants and sharecroppers and firing field hands.

In January 1936, the Supreme Court struck down the crucial provisions of the Agricultural Adjustment Act, arguing that the government had no constitutional authority to require that farmers limit production. But within a few weeks the administration had secured passage of new legislation (the Soil Conservation and Domestic Allotment Act), which permitted the government to pay farmers to reduce production so as to "conserve soil," prevent erosion, and accomplish other secondary goals. The new law apparently met the Court's objections.

It also attempted to correct one of the injustices of the original act: its failure to protect sharecroppers and tenant farmers. Now landlords were required to share the payments they received for cutting back production with those who worked their land. (The new requirements were, however, largely evaded.) The administration launched other efforts to assist poor farmers as well. The Resettlement Administration, established in 1935, and its successor, the Farm Security Administration, created in 1937, provided loans to help farmers cultivating submarginal soil to relocate on better lands. But the programs never moved more than a few thousand farmers. More effective was the Rural Electrification Administration, created in 1935, which worked to make electric power available for the first time to thousands of farmers through utility cooperatives.

Industrial Recovery

The challenge of rescuing the industrial economy from the spiraling deflation of the early 1930s was even more important to the administration. Ever since 1931, leaders of the United States Chamber of Commerce and many others had been urging the government to adopt an antideflation scheme that would permit trade associations to cooperate in stabilizing prices within their industries. Existing antitrust laws clearly forbade such practices, but businesspeople argued that the economic emergency justified a suspension of the restrictions. Herbert Hoover had refused to endorse suspension of the antitrust laws. But the Roosevelt administration was more receptive.

In exchange for relaxing antitrust provisions, however, New Dealers insisted on additional provisions that would deal with other economic problems. Businesspeople would have to make important concessions to labor—recognize the workers' right to bargain collectively through unions—to ensure that the incomes of workers would rise along with prices. And to ensure that consumer buying power would not lag behind, the administration added a major program of public works spending designed to pump needed funds into the economy. The result of these many impulses was the National Industrial Recovery Act, which Congress passed in June 1933.

At first, the new program appeared to work miracles. At its center was a new federal agency, the National Recovery Administration (NRA), under the direction of the flamboyant and energetic Hugh S. Johnson. Johnson approached the task of fighting deflation in two ways. First, he called on every business establishment in the nation to accept a temporary "blanket code": a minimum wage of between thirty and forty cents an hour, a maximum workweek of thirty-five to forty hours, and the abolition of child labor. The result, he claimed, would be to raise consumer purchasing power, increase employment, and eliminate the sweatshop. At the same time, Johnson was busy negotiating another, more specific set of codes with leaders of the nation's major industries. These industrial codes set floors below which no company would lower prices or wages in its search for a competitive advantage, and they included agreements on maintaining employment and production. He quickly won agreements from almost every major industry in the country.

From the beginning, however, the NRA encountered serious difficulties, and the entire effort ultimately dissolved in failure. The codes themselves were hastily and often poorly written. Administering them was beyond the capacities of federal officials with no prior experience in running so vast a program. Large producers consistently dominated the code-writing process and ensured that the new regulations would work to their advantage and to the disadvantage of smaller firms. And the codes at times did more than simply set floors under prices; they actively and artificially raised them—at times to levels higher than was necessary to ensure a profit and far higher than market forces would have dictated.

Attempts to increase consumer purchasing power did not progress as quickly as the efforts to raise prices. Section 7(a) of the National Industrial Recovery Act promised workers the right to form unions and engage in collective bargaining and encouraged many workers to join unions for the first time. But Section 7(a) contained no enforcement mechanisms. Hence recognition of unions by employers (and thus the significant wage increases the unions were committed to winning) did not follow. The Public Works Administration (PWA), established to administer the NIRA's spending programs, only gradually allowed the $3.3 billion in public works funds to trickle out. Not until 1938 was the PWA budget pumping an appreciable amount of money into the economy.

Perhaps the clearest evidence of the NRA's failure was that industrial production actually declined in the months after the agency's establishment—from an index of 101 in July 1933 to 71 in November—despite the rise in prices the codes had helped to create. By the spring of 1934, therefore, the NRA was besieged by criticism; and businessmen were flaunting its provisions. That fall, Roosevelt pressured Johnson to resign and established a new board of directors to oversee the NRA. Then in 1935, the Supreme Court intervened.

The constitutional basis for the NRA had been Congress's power to regulate commerce among the states, a power the administration had interpreted very broadly. In 1935, a case came before the Court involving alleged NRA code violations by the Schechter brothers, who operated a wholesale poultry business confined to Brooklyn, New York. The Court ruled unanimously that the Schechters were not engaged in interstate commerce and, further, that Congress had unconstitutionally delegated legislative power to the president to draft the NRA codes. The legislation establishing the agency, therefore, was declared void. Roosevelt denounced the justices for their "horse-and-buggy" interpretation of the interstate commerce clause. He was rightly concerned, for the reasoning in the *Schechter* case threatened many other New Deal programs as well. But the destruction of the NRA itself may have been a blessing for the New Deal, providing it with a convenient way to abolish the failed experiment.

Regional Planning

The AAA and the NRA largely reflected the beliefs of New Dealers who favored economic planning but wanted private interests (farmers or business leaders) to dominate the planning process. In some areas, however, other reformers—those who believed that the government itself should be the chief planning agent in the economy—managed to establish dominance. Their most conspicuous success, and one of the most celebrated accomplishments of the New Deal, was an unprecedented experiment in regional planning: the Tennessee Valley Authority (TVA).

The TVA had its roots in a political controversy of the 1920s. Progressive reformers had agitated for years for public development of the nation's water resources as a source of cheap electric power. In particular, they had urged completion of a great dam at Muscle Shoals on the Tennessee River in Alabama—a dam begun during World War I but left unfinished when the war ended. But opposition from the utilities companies had been too powerful to overcome.

In 1932, however, one of the great utility empires—that of the electricity magnate Samuel Insull—collapsed spectacularly, amid widely publicized exposés of corruption. Hostility to the utilities soon grew so intense that the companies were no longer able to block the public power movement. The result was legislation supported by the president and enacted by Congress in May 1933 creating the Tennessee Valley Authority. The TVA was intended not only to complete the dam at Muscle Shoals and build others in the region, and not only to generate and sell electricity from them to the public at reasonable rates. It was also to be the agent for a comprehensive redevelopment of the entire region: for stopping the disastrous flooding that had plagued the Tennessee Valley for centuries, for encouraging the development of local industries, for supervising a substantial program of reforestation, and for helping farmers improve productivity.

Opposition by conservatives within the administration ultimately blocked some of the ambitious social planning projects proposed by the more visionary TVA administrators, but the Authority revitalized the region in numerous ways. It built dams and waterways. It virtually eliminated flooding in the region. It provided electricity to thousands who had never before had it. Throughout the country, largely because of the "yardstick" provided by the TVA's cheap production of electricity, private power rates declined. Still, the Authority worked no miracles. The Tennessee Valley remained a generally impoverished region despite its efforts. And like many other New Deal programs, it made no serious effort to challenge local customs and racial prejudices.

Financial Reforms

A belief that the health of the economy rested above all on the nature of the currency had been a staple of American political thought for more than half a century. For a time, the New Deal too attempted to deal with the nation's problems with monetary reform.

Roosevelt was not an inflationist at heart, but he soon came to consider the gold standard a major obstacle to the restoration of adequate prices. On April 18, 1933, the president issued an executive order that officially ended the country's already weakened adherence to the gold standard. A few weeks later, Congress passed legislation confirming his decision. By itself, the repudiation of the gold standard meant relatively little. But both before and after the April decision, the administration experimented in various ways with manipulating the value of the dollar—by making substantial purchases of gold and silver and later by establishing a new, fixed standard for the dollar (reducing its gold content substantially from the 1932 amount). The resort to government-managed currency—that is, to a dollar whose value could be raised or lowered by government policy according to economic circumstances—created an important precedent for future federal policies and permanently altered the relationship between the public and the private sectors. It did not, however, have any immediate impact on the depressed American economy.

Through other legislation, the early New Deal increased federal authority over previously unregulated or weakly regulated areas of the economy. The Glass-Steagall Act of June 1933 gave the government authority to curb irresponsible speculation by banks. More important, perhaps, it established the Federal Deposit Insurance Corporation, which guaranteed all bank deposits up to $2,500. In other words, even should a bank fail, small depositors would be able to recover their money. Finally, in 1935, Congress passed a major banking act that transferred much of the authority once wielded by the regional Federal Reserve banks to the Federal Reserve Board in Washington.

To protect investors in the stock market, Congress passed the so-called Truth in Securities Act of 1933, requiring corporations issuing new securities to provide full and accurate information about them to the public. Another act, of June 1934, established the Securities and Exchange Commission (SEC) to police the stock market.

The Growth of Federal Relief

Millions of Americans were unemployed and in desperate need of assistance in 1933, and the relief efforts of private organizations and state and local governments were unable to meet the demand. The Roosevelt administration did not consider relief its most important task, but it recognized the necessity of doing something to help impoverished Americans survive until the government could revive the economy to the point where relief might not be necessary.

Among Roosevelt's first acts as president was the establishment of the Federal Emergency Relief Administration (FERA), which provided cash grants to states to prop up bankrupt relief agencies. To administer the program, he chose the director of the New York State relief agency, Harry Hopkins, who disbursed the FERA grants widely and rapidly. But both Hopkins and Roosevelt had misgivings about establishing a government "dole."

They felt somewhat more comfortable with another form of government assistance: work relief. Thus when it became clear that the FERA grants would not be sufficient to pull the country through the winter, the administration established a second program: the Civil Works Administration (CWA). Between November 1933 and April 1934, it put more than 4 million people to work on temporary projects. Some of them were of lasting value, such as the construction of roads, schools, and parks; others were little more than make-work. To Hopkins, however, the important thing was pumping money into an economy badly in need of it and providing assistance to people with nowhere else to turn.

Most of these early relief programs had short lives. Like the FERA, the CWA was intended to be only a temporary expedient. In the spring of 1934, the president began to dismantle the agency, and he ultimately disbanded it altogether. Most economists now agree that massive and sustained government spending would have been the quickest and most effective way to end the Depression. But few policymakers in the 1930s shared that belief.

Roosevelt's favorite relief project was the Civilian Conservation Corps (CCC). Established in the first weeks of the new administration, the CCC was designed to provide employment to the millions of urban young men who could find no jobs in the cities and who many feared might become a source of urban crime and violence. At the same time, it was intended to advance the work of conservation and reforestation—goals Roosevelt had long cherished. The CCC created a series of camps in national parks and forests and in other rural and wilderness settings. There young men (women

THE CIVILIAN CONSERVATION CORPS CCC workers in Wind River,
Washington, in 1933 uproot two-year-old fir trees, which they will
then ship to other locations for transplanting. The CCC's many
defenders, among them Franklin Roosevelt, believed that exposing
young urban men to work in the "great outdoors" was at least as
valuable to them as providing them with a salary.

were excluded from the program) worked in a semimilitary environment on
such projects as planting trees, building reservoirs, developing parks, and
improving agricultural irrigation. CCC camps were segregated by race,
with the vast majority restricted to whites and a few open to blacks,
Mexicans, and Indians.

Mortgage relief was a pressing need for millions of farm owners and
homeowners. The Farm Credit Administration, which within two years
refinanced one-fifth of all farm mortgages in the United States, was one
response to that problem. The Frazier-Lemke Farm Bankruptcy Act of 1933
was another. It enabled some farmers to regain their land even after the
foreclosure of their mortgages. Despite such efforts, however, 25 percent of
all American farm owners had lost their land by 1934. Homeowners were
similarly troubled, and in June 1933 the administration established the
Home Owners' Loan Corporation, which by 1936 had refinanced the

mortgages of more than 1 million householders. A year later, Congress established the Federal Housing Administration to insure mortgages for new construction and home repairs—a measure that combined an effort to provide relief with a program to stimulate lasting recovery of the construction industry.

The relief efforts of the first two years of the New Deal were intended to be limited and temporary. But they helped stimulate interest in other forms of social protection. Ultimately, the creation of a permanent welfare system would be one of the New Deal's most important and lasting accomplishments.

THE NEW DEAL IN TRANSITION

Seldom has an American president enjoyed such remarkable popularity as Franklin Roosevelt did during his first two years in office. But by early 1935, with no end to the Depression yet in sight, the New Deal was beginning to find itself the target of fierce public criticism. In the spring of 1935, partly in response to these growing attacks, Roosevelt launched an ambitious new program of legislation that has often been called the "Second New Deal."

Critics of the New Deal

Some of the most strident attacks on the New Deal came from critics on the right. Roosevelt had tried for a time to conciliate conservatives and business leaders. By the end of 1934, however, it was clear that the American right in general, and much of the corporate world in particular, had become irreconcilably hostile to the New Deal. In August 1934, a group of the most fervent (and wealthiest) Roosevelt opponents, led by members of the Du Pont family, formed the American Liberty League, designed specifically to arouse public opposition to the New Deal's "dictatorial" policies and its supposed attacks on free enterprise. The new organization generated wide publicity and caused some concern within the administration. In fact, however, it was never able to expand its constituency much beyond the Northern industrialists who had founded it. At its peak, membership in the organization numbered only about 125,000.

The real impact of the Liberty League and other conservative attacks on Roosevelt was not to undermine the president's political strength. It was, rather, to convince Roosevelt that his efforts to conciliate the business community had failed. By 1936, he no longer harbored any illusions about cooperation with conservatives. The forces of "organized money," he said near the end of his campaign for reelection, "are unanimous in their hate for me—and I welcome their hatred."

Roosevelt's critics on the far left also managed to produce alarm among some supporters of the administration; but like the conservatives, they proved to have only limited strength. The Communist party, the Socialist party, and other radical and semiradical organizations were at times harshly critical of the New Deal. But they too failed ever to attract genuine mass support.

More menacing to the New Deal than either the far right or the far left was a group of dissident political movements that defied easy ideological classification. Some were marginal "crackpot" organizations with little popular following. Others gained substantial public support within particular states and regions. Three men, however, succeeded in mobilizing genuinely national followings.

Dr. Francis E. Townsend, an elderly California physician, rose from obscurity to lead a movement of more than 5 million members with his plan for federal pensions for the elderly. According to the Townsend Plan, all Americans over the age of sixty would receive monthly government pensions of $200, provided they retired (thus freeing jobs for younger, unemployed Americans) and spent the money in full each month (which would pump needed funds into the economy). By 1935, the Townsend Plan had attracted the support of many older men and women. And while the plan itself made little progress in Congress, the public sentiment behind it helped build support for the Social Security system, which Congress did approve in 1935.

Father Charles E. Coughlin, a Catholic priest in the Detroit suburb of Royal Oak, Michigan, achieved even greater renown through his weekly sermons broadcast nationally over the radio. He proposed a series of monetary reforms—remonetization of silver, issuing of greenbacks, and nationalization of the banking system—that he insisted would restore prosperity and ensure economic justice. At first a warm supporter of Franklin Roosevelt, by late 1934 he had become disheartened by what he claimed was the president's failure to deal harshly enough with the "money powers." In the spring of 1935, he established his own political organization, the National Union for Social Justice. He was attracting public support throughout much of the nation—primarily from Catholics, but from others as well. He was widely believed to have one of the largest regular radio audiences of anyone in America.

HUEY LONG Few public speakers could arouse a crowd
more effectively than Huey Long of Louisiana, known to
many as "the Kingfish" (a nickname borrowed from the
popular radio show *Amos 'n Andy*). It was Long's effective
use of radio, however, that contributed most directly to his
spreading national popularity in the early 1930s.

Most alarming of all to the administration was the growing national
popularity of Senator Huey P. Long of Louisiana. Long had risen to power
in his home state through his strident attacks on the banks, oil companies,
and utilities and on the conservative political oligarchy allied with them.
Elected governor in 1928, he launched an assault on his opponents so
thorough and forceful that they were soon left with virtually no political
power whatever. Many claimed that he had, in effect, become a dictator.
(Friends and enemies alike called him the "Kingfish," a nickname borrowed
from the popular *Amos 'n Andy* radio show.) But he also maintained the
overwhelming support of the Louisiana electorate, in part because of his

flamboyant personality and in part because of his solid record of conventional progressive accomplishment: building roads, schools, and hospitals; revising the tax codes; distributing free textbooks; lowering utility rates. Barred by law from succeeding himself as governor, he ran in 1930 for a seat in the United States Senate, won easily, and left the state government in the hands of loyal, docile allies.

Long, like Coughlin, supported Franklin Roosevelt for president in 1932. But within six months of Roosevelt's inauguration he had broken with the president. As an alternative to the New Deal, he advocated a drastic program of wealth redistribution, a program he ultimately named the Share-Our-Wealth Plan. The government, he claimed, could end the Depression easily by using the tax system to confiscate the surplus riches of the wealthiest men and women in America, whose fortunes were, he claimed, so bloated that not enough wealth remained to satisfy the needs of the great mass of citizens. That surplus wealth would allow the government to guarantee every family a minimum "homestead" of $5,000 and an annual wage of $2,500.

Long made little effort to disguise his interest in running for president. In 1934, he established his own national organization: the Share-Our-Wealth Society, which soon attracted a large following—not only in Long's native South but in New York, Pennsylvania, parts of the Midwest, and above all California. A poll by the Democratic National Committee in the spring of 1935 disclosed that Long might attract more than 10 percent of the vote if he ran as a third-party candidate, enough to tip a close election to the Republicans.

Long, Coughlin, Townsend, and other dissidents had certain concerns in common. They spoke harshly of the "plutocrats," "international bankers," and other remote financial powers who were, they claimed, not only impoverishing the nation but exercising tyrannical power over individuals and communities. They spoke equally harshly, however, of the dangers of excessive government bureaucracy, attacking the New Deal for establishing a menacing, "dictatorial" state. They envisioned a society in which government would, through a series of simple economic reforms, guarantee prosperity to every American without exercising intrusive control over private and community activities.

To members of the Roosevelt administration, the dissident politics appeared in 1935 to have become a genuine threat to the president. An increasing number of advisers were warning Roosevelt that he would have to do something dramatic to counter their strength.

The "Second New Deal"

Roosevelt launched the so-called Second New Deal in the spring of 1935 in response both to the growing political pressures and to the continuing economic crisis. The new proposals represented, if not a new direction, at least a change in the emphasis of New Deal policy. Perhaps the most conspicuous change was in the administration's attitude toward big business. Symbolically at least, the president was now willing to attack corporate interests openly. In March, for example, he proposed to Congress an act designed to break up the great utility holding companies, and he spoke harshly of monopolistic control of their industry. Congress did indeed pass the Holding Company Act of 1935 (often known as the "death sentence" bill), but furious lobbying by the utilities resulted in amendments that sharply limited its effects.

Equally alarming to affluent Americans was a series of tax reforms proposed by the president in 1935, a program conservatives quickly labeled a "soak-the-rich" scheme. Apparently designed to undercut the appeal of Huey Long's Share-Our-Wealth Plan, the Roosevelt proposals called for establishing the highest and most progressive peacetime tax rates in history. Rates in the highest brackets reached 75 percent on income, 70 percent on inheritance, and 15 percent on corporate income. In fact, however, the actual impact of these taxes was far less radical than the president liked to claim (as Huey Long quickly pointed out).

The Supreme Court decision in 1935 to invalidate the National Industrial Recovery Act solved some problems for the administration, but it also created others. Section 7(a) of the now-defunct act had guaranteed workers the right to organize and bargain collectively. Supporters of labor, both in the administration and in Congress, advocated quick action to restore that protection. With the president himself slow to respond, a group of progressives in Congress led by Senator Robert F. Wagner of New York introduced what became the National Labor Relations Act of 1935. The new law, popularly known as the Wagner Act, provided workers with more federal protection than Section 7(a) of the National Industrial Recovery Act had offered. It created a crucial enforcement mechanism, the National Labor Relations Board (NLRB), which would have power to compel employers to recognize and bargain with legitimate unions. The president was not entirely happy with the bill, but he signed it anyway. That was in large part because American workers themselves had by 1935 become so important and vigorous a force that Roosevelt realized his own political future would depend in part on responding to their demands.

Labor Militancy

The emergence of a powerful trade union movement in the 1930s was one of the most important social and political developments of the decade. It occurred partly in response to government efforts to enhance the power of unions; but it was also a result of the increased militancy of American workers and their leaders.

During the 1920s, most workers had displayed relatively little militancy in challenging employers or demanding recognition of their unions. In the 1930s, however, many of the factors that had impeded militancy vanished or grew weaker. Business leaders and industrialists lost (at least temporarily) the ability to control government policies. Both Section 7(a) of the National Industrial Recovery Act of 1933 and the Wagner Act of 1935 were passed over the strong objections of most (although not all) corporate leaders. Equally important, new and more militant labor organizations emerged to challenge the established, conservative unions.

The growing militancy first became obvious in 1934, when newly organized workers (many of them inspired by the collective bargaining provisions of the National Industrial Recovery Act) demonstrated an assertiveness and at times radicalism seldom seen in recent years. Some became involved in violent confrontations with employers and local authorities. Despite the new militancy, however, it was clear that without stronger legal protection, most organizing drives would end in frustration. Once the Wagner Act became law, the search for more effective forms of organization rapidly gained strength in labor ranks.

The American Federation of Labor, under the leadership now of William Green, remained committed to the idea of the craft union: organizing workers on the basis of their skills. But that concept had little to offer unskilled laborers, who now constituted the bulk of the industrial work force. During the 1930s, therefore, a new concept of labor organization challenged the craft union ideal: industrial unionism. Advocates of this approach argued that all the workers in a particular industry should be organized in a single union, regardless of what functions the workers performed. All autoworkers should be in a single automobile union; all steelworkers should be in a single steel union. United in this way, workers would greatly increase their power.

Leaders of the AFL craft unions for the most part opposed the new concept. But industrial unionism found a number of important advocates, most prominent among them John L. Lewis, the talented, flamboyant, and eloquent leader of the United Mine Workers. At first, Lewis and his allies attempted to work within the AFL, but friction between the new industrial organizations Lewis was promoting and the older craft unions grew rapidly.

At the 1935 AFL convention, Lewis became embroiled in a series of angry confrontations (and one celebrated fistfight) with craft union leaders before finally walking out. A few weeks later, he created the Committee on Industrial Organization—a body officially within the AFL but unsanctioned by its leadership. After a series of bitter jurisdictional conflicts, the AFL finally expelled the new committee from its ranks, and along with it all the industrial unions it represented. In response, Lewis renamed the committee the Congress of Industrial Organizations (CIO), established it in 1936 as an organization directly rivaling the AFL, and became its first president. The schism clearly weakened the labor movement in many ways. But by freeing the advocates of industrial unionism from the restrictive rules of the AFL, it gave impetus to the creation of powerful new organizations.

The CIO also expanded the constituency of the labor movement. It was more receptive to women and to blacks than the AFL had been, in part because women and blacks were more likely to be relegated to unskilled jobs and in part because CIO organizing drives targeted previously unorganized industries (textiles, laundries, tobacco factories, and others) where women and minorities constituted much of the work force. The CIO was also a more militant organization than the AFL. By the time of the 1936 schism, it was already engaged in major organizing battles in the automobile and steel industries.

Organizing Battles

Out of several competing auto unions, the United Auto Workers (UAW) was gradually emerging preeminent in the early and mid-1930s. But although it was gaining recruits, it was making little progress in winning recognition from the corporations.

In December 1936, however, autoworkers employed a controversial and effective new technique for challenging corporate opposition: the sit-down strike. Employees in several General Motors plants in Detroit simply sat down inside the plants, refusing either to work or to leave, thus preventing the company from using strikebreakers. The tactic spread to other locations, and by February 1937 strikers had occupied seventeen GM plants. The strikers ignored court orders and local police efforts to force them to vacate the buildings. When Michigan's governor, Frank Murphy, a liberal Democrat, refused to call up the National Guard to clear out the strikers, and when the federal government also refused to intervene on behalf of employers, General Motors relented. In February 1937, it became the first major manufacturer to recognize the UAW; other automobile companies soon did the same. The sit-down strike proved effective for rubber workers and others as well, but it survived only briefly as a labor technique. Its apparent illegality aroused so much public opposition that labor leaders soon abandoned it.

In the steel industry, the battle for unionization was less easily won. In 1936, the Steel Workers' Organizing Committee (SWOC; later the United Steelworkers of America) began a major organizing drive involving thousands of workers and frequent, at times bitter strikes. These conflicts were notable not only for the militancy of the (predominantly male) steelworkers themselves but for the involvement of thousands of women (many of them wives or relatives of workers), who provided important logistical support for

THE MEMORIAL DAY MASSACRE A newsreel photographer captured the moment, May 30, 1937, when Chicago police using guns, tear gas, and clubs charged striking workers near the Republic Steel plant in South Chicago. Ten strikers died as a result of the melee, and many more were injured.

the strikers and who at times took direct action by creating a buffer between strikers and the police.

In March 1937, to the surprise of almost everyone, United States Steel, the giant of the industry, recognized the union rather than risk a costly strike at a time when it sensed itself on the verge of recovery from the Depression. But the smaller companies (known collectively as "Little Steel") were less accommodating. On Memorial Day 1937, a group of striking workers from Republic Steel gathered with their families for a picnic and demonstration in South Chicago. When they attempted to march peacefully (and legally) toward the steel plant, police opened fire on them. Ten demonstrators were killed; another ninety were wounded. Despite a public outcry against the "Memorial Day Massacre," the harsh tactics of Little Steel were successful. The 1937 strike failed.

But the victory of Little Steel was one of the last gasps of the kind of brutal strikebreaking that had proved so effective in the past. In 1937 alone, there were 4,720 strikes—over 80 percent of them settled in favor of the unions. By the end of the year, more than 8 million workers were members of unions recognized as official bargaining units by employers (as compared with 3 million in 1932). By 1941, that number had expanded to 10 million and included the workers of Little Steel, whose employers had finally recognized the SWOC.

Social Security

From the first moments of the New Deal, important members of the administration, most notably Secretary of Labor Frances Perkins, had been lobbying for a system of federally sponsored social insurance for the elderly and the unemployed. In 1935, Roosevelt gave public support to what became the Social Security Act, which Congress passed the same year. It established several distinct programs. For the elderly, there were two types of assistance. Those who were presently destitute could receive up to $15 a month in federal assistance. More important for the future, many Americans presently working were incorporated into a pension system, to which they and their employers would contribute by paying a payroll tax; it would provide them with an income on retirement. Pension payments would not begin until 1942 and even then would provide only $10 to $85 a month to recipients. And broad categories of workers (including domestic servants and agricultural laborers, among them blacks and women) were excluded from the program. But the act was a crucial first step in building the nation's most important social program for the elderly.

In addition, the Social Security Act created a system of unemployment insurance, which employers alone would finance and which made it possible for workers laid off from their jobs to receive government assistance for a limited period of time. It also established a system of federal aid to disabled people and a program of aid to dependent children.

The framers of the Social Security Act wanted to create a system of "insurance," not "welfare." And the largest programs (old-age pensions and unemployment insurance) were in many ways similar to private insurance programs, with contributions from participants and benefits available to all. But the act also provided considerable direct assistance based on need—to the elderly poor, to the disabled, to dependent children. These groups were widely perceived to be small and genuinely unable to support themselves. But in later generations those programs would expand until they assumed dimensions that the planners of Social Security had neither foreseen nor desired. Whatever one thinks of Social Security, however, it is clear that the 1935 act was the most important single piece of social welfare legislation in American history.

New Directions in Relief

Social Security was designed primarily to fulfill long-range goals. But millions of unemployed Americans had immediate needs. To help meet them, the administration established in 1935 the Works Progress Administration (WPA). Like the Civil Works Administration and other earlier efforts, the WPA established a system of work relief for the unemployed. But it was much bigger than the earlier agencies, both in the size of its budget ($5 billion at first) and in the energy and imagination of its operations.

Under the direction of Harry Hopkins, the WPA was responsible for building or renovating 110,000 public buildings (schools, post offices, government office buildings) and for constructing almost 600 airports, more than 500,000 miles of roads, and over 100,000 bridges. In the process, the WPA kept an average of 2.1 million workers employed and pumped needed money into the economy.

The WPA also displayed remarkable flexibility and imagination in offering assistance to those whose occupations did not fit into any traditional category of relief. The Federal Writers Project of the WPA, for example, gave unemployed writers a chance to do their work and receive a government salary. The Federal Arts Project, similarly, helped painters, sculptors, and others to continue their careers. The Federal Music Project and the Federal Theater Project oversaw the production of concerts and plays, creating work for unemployed musicians, actors, and directors.

Other relief agencies emerged alongside the WPA. The National Youth Administration (NYA) provided work and scholarship assistance to high-school and college-age men and women. The Emergency Housing Division of the Public Works Administration began federal sponsorship of public housing.

The hiring practices of the WPA, the NYA, and other work-relief programs revealed another important, if at the time largely unrecognized, feature of the New Deal welfare system. Men and women alike were in distress in the 1930s (as in all difficult times). But the new welfare system dealt with members of the two sexes in very different ways. For men, the government concentrated mainly on work relief—on such programs as the CCC, the CWA, and the WPA, all of which were overwhelmingly male. The principal government aid to women was not work relief but cash assistance—most notably through the Aid to Dependent Children program of Social Security, which was designed largely to assist single mothers. This disparity in treatment reflected a widespread assumption that men consti-tuted the bulk of the paid work force and that women needed to be treated within the context of the family. In fact, millions of women were already employed by the 1930s.

The 1936 "Referendum"

The presidential election of 1936, it was clear from the start, was to be a national referendum on Franklin Roosevelt and the New Deal. And while in 1935 there had been reason to question the president's political prospects, by the middle of 1936—with the economy visibly reviving—there could be little doubt that he would win a second term. The Republican party nominated the moderate governor of Kansas, Alf M. Landon, and produced a program that promised, in effect, to continue the programs of the New Deal—but "constitutionally," and without running a deficit. Republican conservatives seemed impotent even within their own party.

Roosevelt's dissident challengers now appeared similarly powerless. One reason was the violent death of their most effective leader, Huey Long, who was assassinated in Louisiana in September 1935. Another reason was the ill-fated alliance among several of the remaining dissident leaders in 1936. Father Coughlin, Dr. Townsend, and Gerald L. K. Smith (an intemperate henchman of Huey Long) joined forces that summer to establish a new political movement—the Union party, which nominated an undistinguished North Dakota congressman, William Lemke, for president.

The result was the greatest landslide in American history to that point. Roosevelt polled just under 61 percent of the vote to Landon's 36 percent. The Republican candidate carried only Maine and Vermont. The Democrats increased their already large majorities in both houses of Congress. The Union party received fewer than 900,000 votes.

The election results demonstrated the party realignment that the New Deal had produced. The Democrats now controlled a broad coalition of Western and Southern farmers, the urban working classes, the poor and unemployed, and the black communities of Northern cities, as well as traditional progressives and committed new liberals—a coalition that constituted a substantial majority of the electorate. It would be decades before the Republican party could again muster anything approaching a true majority coalition of its own.

THE NEW DEAL IN DISARRAY

Roosevelt emerged from the 1936 election at the zenith of his popularity. Within months, however, the New Deal was mired in serious new difficulties—a result of continuing opposition, of the president's own political errors, and of major economic setbacks.

The Court Fight and the "Purge"

The 1936 mandate, Franklin Roosevelt believed, made it possible for him to do something about the problem of the Supreme Court. No program of reform, he had become convinced, could long survive the obstructionist justices, who had already struck down the NRA and the AAA and threatened to invalidate even more legislation.

In February 1937, Roosevelt offered a solution. Without informing congressional leaders in advance, he sent a surprise message to Capitol Hill proposing a general overhaul of the federal court system; included among the many provisions was one to add up to six new justices to the Supreme Court. The courts were "overworked," he claimed, and needed additional manpower and younger blood to enable them to cope with their increasing burdens. But Roosevelt's real purpose was to give himself the opportunity to appoint new, liberal justices and change the ideological balance of the Court.

Conservatives were outraged at the "court-packing plan," and even many Roosevelt supporters were disturbed by what they considered evidence of the president's hunger for power. Still, Roosevelt might well have persuaded Congress to approve at least a compromise measure had not the Supreme Court itself intervened. Even before the court-packing fight began, the ideological balance of the Court had been precarious. Four justices consistently opposed the New Deal, and three generally supported it. Of the remaining two, Chief Justice Charles Evans Hughes often sided with the progressives and Associate Justice Owen J. Roberts usually voted with the conservatives.

On March 29, 1937, Roberts, Hughes, and the three progressive justices voted together to uphold a state minimum-wage law—in the case of *West Coast Hotel* v. *Parrish*—thus reversing a 5-to-4 decision of the previous year invalidating a similar law. Two weeks later, again by a 5-to-4 margin, the Court upheld the Wagner Act; and in May, it validated the Social Security Act. The Court had prudently moderated its position to make the court-packing bill unnecessary. Congress ultimately defeated it.

On one level, the affair was a significant victory for Franklin Roosevelt. The Court was no longer an obstacle to New Deal reforms, particularly after the older justices began to retire, to be replaced by Roosevelt appointees. But the court-packing episode did lasting damage to the administration. By giving members of his own party an excuse to oppose him, he had helped destroy his congressional coalition. From 1937 on, Southern Democrats and other conservatives voted against his measures much more often than in the past.

A year later, the president's political situation deteriorated further. Roosevelt was determined to regain the initiative in his legislative battles, and in several primary campaigns in spring 1938 he openly spoke against members of his own party who had opposed his programs. Not only was he unable to unseat any of the five Democratic senators against whom he campaigned, but his "purge" efforts drove an even deeper wedge between the administration and its conservative opponents.

Retrenchment and Recession

By the summer of 1937, the national income, which had dropped from $82 billion in 1929 to $40 billion in 1932, had risen to nearly $72 billion. Other economic indices showed similar advances. Roosevelt seized on these improvements as an excuse to try to balance the federal budget, convinced by Treasury secretary Henry Morgenthau and many economists that the real danger now was no longer depression but inflation. Between January and August 1937, for example, he cut the WPA in half, laying off 1.5 million relief workers. A few weeks later, the fragile boom collapsed. The index of industrial production dropped from 117 in August 1937 to 76 in May 1938. Four million additional workers lost their jobs. Economic conditions were soon almost as bad as the bleak days of 1932–1933.

The recession of 1937 was a result of many factors. But to many observers at the time (including, apparently, Roosevelt), it seemed to be a direct result of the administration's unwise decision to reduce spending. And so the new crisis forced a reevaluation of policies. The advocates of government spending as an antidote to the Depression stood vindicated, it seemed; and the notion of using government deficits to stimulate the economy established a timid foothold in American public policy. In April 1938, the president asked Congress for an emergency appropriation of $5 billion for public works and relief programs, and government funds soon began pouring into the economy once again. Within a few months, another tentative recovery seemed to be under way, and the advocates of spending pointed to it as proof of the validity of their approach.

At the same time, a group of younger liberals in the administration who saw the recession as the result of excessively concentrated corporate power were urging the president to launch a new assault on monopoly. In April 1938, Roosevelt sent a stinging message to Congress, vehemently denouncing what he called an "unjustifiable concentration of economic power" and asking for the creation of a commission to examine that concentration with an eye to major reforms in the antitrust laws. In response, Congress established the Temporary National Economic Committee (TNEC), whose members included representatives of both houses of Congress and officials from several executive agencies. At about the same time, Roosevelt appointed a new head of the antitrust division of the Justice Department: Thurman Arnold, a Yale Law School professor who soon proved to be the most vigorous director ever to serve in that office.

By the end of 1938, however, it was becoming clear that these ambitious new goals faced an uncertain future. For the New Deal had by then essentially come to an end. Congressional opposition now made it difficult for the president to enact any major new programs. But more important, perhaps, the threat of world crisis hung heavy in the political atmosphere, and Roosevelt was gradually growing more concerned with persuading a reluctant nation to prepare for war than with pursuing new avenues of reform.

LIMITS OF THE NEW DEAL

In the 1930s, Roosevelt's principal critics were conservatives, who accused him of abandoning the Constitution and establishing a menacing, even tyrannical state. In more recent years, the New Deal's most vocal critics have attacked it from the left, pointing to the major problems it did not solve and the important groups it failed to represent. A full understanding of the New Deal requires examining not just its achievements but also its limits.

African-Americans and the New Deal

One group the New Deal did relatively little to assist was African-Americans. The administration was not hostile to black aspirations. On the contrary, the New Deal was probably more sympathetic to them than any previous government of the twentieth century had been. Eleanor Roosevelt spoke throughout the 1930s on behalf of racial justice and put continuing pressure on her husband and others in the federal government to ease discrimination against blacks. The president himself appointed a number of blacks to significant second-level positions in his administration, creating an informal network of officeholders that became known as the "Black Cabinet." Eleanor Roosevelt, Interior Secretary Harold Ickes, and WPA director Harry Hopkins all made efforts to ensure that New Deal relief programs did not exclude blacks; and by 1935, an estimated 30 percent of all African-Americans were receiving some form of government assistance. One result was a historic change in black electoral behavior. As late as 1932,

ELEANOR ROOSEVELT AND MARY McLEOD BETHUNE Mrs. Roosevelt was a leading champion of racial equality within her husband's administration, and her commitment had an important impact on the behavior of the government even though she held no official post. She is seen here meeting in 1937 with Aubrey Williams, executive director of the National Youth Administration, and Mary McLeod Bethune, the agency's Director of Negro Affairs.

most American blacks were voting Republican, as they had been doing since the Civil War. By 1936, more than 90 percent of them were voting Democratic—the beginnings of a political alliance that would endure for many decades.

Blacks supported Franklin Roosevelt because they knew he was not their enemy. But they had few illusions that the New Deal represented a millennium in American race relations. The president was, for example, never willing to risk losing the support of Southern Democrats by supporting legislation to make lynching a federal crime or to ban the poll tax, one of the most potent tools by which white Southerners kept blacks from voting.

New Deal relief agencies did not challenge, and indeed reinforced, existing patterns of discrimination. The Civilian Conservation Corps established separate black camps. The NRA codes tolerated paying blacks less than whites doing the same jobs. African-Americans were largely excluded from employment in the TVA. The Federal Housing Administration refused to provide mortgages to blacks moving into white neighborhoods, and the first public housing projects financed by the federal government were racially segregated. The WPA routinely relegated black and Hispanic workers to the least skilled and lowest-paying jobs; when funding ebbed, African-Americans, like women, were among the first to be dismissed.

The New Deal was not hostile to black Americans, and it did much to help them advance. But it refused to make the issue of race a significant part of its agenda.

The New Deal and the "Indian Problem"

New Deal policy toward the Indian tribes marked a significant break from the approach in the years before Roosevelt, largely because of the efforts of the extraordinary commissioner of Indian affairs in the 1930s, John Collier. Collier was greatly influenced by the work of twentieth-century anthropologists who advanced the idea of cultural relativism—the theory that every culture should be accepted and respected on its own terms and that no culture is inherently superior to another. Cultural relativism was a challenge to the three-centuries-old assumption among white Americans that Indians were "savages" and that white society was inherently superior and more "civilized."

Collier favored legislation that would, he hoped, reverse the pressures on Native Americans to assimilate and allow them to remain Indians. Not all tribal leaders agreed with Collier. Indeed, his belief in the importance of preserving Indian culture would not find its greatest support among the tribes until the 1960s. Nevertheless, Collier effectively promoted legislation—which became the Indian Reorganization Act of 1934—to advance his goals. Among other things it restored to the tribes the right to own land collectively (reversing the allotment policy adopted in 1887, which encouraged the breaking up of tribal lands into individually owned plots) and to elect tribal governments. In the thirteen years after passage of the 1934 bill, tribal land increased by nearly 4 million acres, and Indian agricultural income increased dramatically (from under $2 million in 1934 to over $49 million in 1947).

Even with the redistribution of lands under the 1934 act, however, Indians continued to possess, for the most part, only territory whites did not want—much of it arid, some of it desert. And as a group, they continued to constitute the poorest segment of the population. The efforts of the 1930s did not solve, or even greatly alleviate, what some called the "Indian problem." They did, however, provide Indians with some tools for rebuilding the viability of the tribes.

Women and the New Deal

Symbolically, at least, the New Deal marked a breakthrough in the role of women in public life. Roosevelt appointed the first female member of the cabinet in the nation's history, Secretary of Labor Frances Perkins. He also named more than 100 other women to positions at lower levels of the federal bureaucracy. But New Deal support for women operated within limits. Even many of the women in the administration were concerned not so much about achieving gender equality as about obtaining special protections for women.

The New Deal generally supported the belief (not always matched by practice) that in hard times women should withdraw from the workplace to open up more jobs for men. Frances Perkins, for example, spoke out against what she called the "pin-money worker"—the married woman working to earn extra money for the household. New Deal relief agencies offered relatively little employment for women. The NRA sanctioned sexually discriminatory wage practices. The Social Security program excluded domestic servants, waitresses, and other predominantly female occupations.

As with African-Americans, so also with women: The New Deal was not actively hostile; in many ways, it was unprecedentedly supportive. It did, however, accept prevailing cultural norms. There was not yet sufficient political pressure from women themselves to persuade the administration to do otherwise.

The New Deal and the Economy

The most frequent criticisms of the New Deal involve its failure genuinely to revive or reform the American economy. New Dealers never fully recognized the value of government spending as a vehicle for recovery, and their efforts along other lines never succeeded in ending the Depression. The economic boom sparked by World War II, not the New Deal, finally ended the crisis. Nor did the New Deal substantially alter the distribution of power within American capitalism; and it had only a small impact on the distribution of wealth among the American people.

Nevertheless, the New Deal did have a number of important and lasting effects on both the behavior and the structure of the American economy. It helped elevate new groups—workers, farmers, and others—to positions from which they could at times effectively challenge the power of the corporations. It increased the regulatory functions of the federal government in ways that helped stabilize previously troubled areas of the economy: the stock market, the banking system, and others. And the administration helped establish the basis for new forms of federal fiscal policy, which in the postwar years would give the government tools for promoting and regulating economic growth.

The New Deal also created the rudiments of the American welfare state, through its many relief programs and above all through the Social Security system. The conservative inhibitions New Dealers brought to this task ensured that the welfare system that ultimately emerged would be limited in its impact (at least in comparison with those of other industrial nations), would reinforce some traditional patterns of gender and racial discrimination, and would be expensive and cumbersome to administer. But for all its limits, the new system marked a historic break with the nation's traditional reluctance to offer any public assistance whatever to its neediest citizens.

D E B A T I N G   T H E   P A S T

The New Deal

ONTEMPORARIES OF FRANKLIN ROOSEVELT debated the impact of the New Deal with ferocious intensity: conservatives complaining of a menacing tyranny of the state, liberals celebrating the New Deal's progressive achievements, people on the left charging that the reforms of the 1930s were largely cosmetic and left the nation's fundamental problems unsolved. Although the conservative critique of the New Deal has found relatively little scholarly expression since Roosevelt's death, the liberal and left positions continued for many years to shape the way historians described the Roosevelt administration.

The dominant view from the beginning was an approving liberal interpretation, and its most important early voice was that of Arthur M. Schlesinger, Jr. He argued in the three volumes of *The Age of Roosevelt* (1957–1960) that the New Deal marked a continuation of the long struggle between public power and private interests, a struggle Roosevelt had moved to a new level as the unconstrained influence of business elites finally encountered an effective challenge. What emerged from the New Deal was a system of reformed capitalism, with far more protection for workers, farmers, consumers, and others than they had enjoyed in the past.

At almost the same time, however, other historians were offering more qualified assessments of the New Deal, even if ones that remained securely within the liberal framework Schlesinger had used. Richard Hofstadter argued in 1955 that the New Deal was a "drastic new departure . . . different from anything that had yet happened in the United States"; that it gave American liberalism a "social-democratic tinge that had never before been present in American reform movements"; but that its highly pragmatic approach lacked a central, guiding philosophy. James MacGregor Burns argued in 1956 that Roosevelt's wily political methods often led him away from the proper goals of reform, that he had failed to make full use of his

(continued on next page)

potential as a leader and had accommodated himself unnecessarily to existing patterns of power.

William Leuchtenburg's *Franklin D. Roosevelt and the New Deal* (1963) was the first systematic "revisionist" interpretation. Leuchtenburg was a sympathetic critic, arguing that most of the limitations of the New Deal were the result of political and ideological constraints over which Roosevelt had little control. But he challenged the views of earlier scholars who had proclaimed the New Deal a "revolution" in social policy. Leuchtenburg could muster only enough enthusiasm to call it a "halfway revolution," one that helped some previously disadvantaged groups (most notably farmers and workers) but that did little or nothing for many others (blacks, sharecroppers, the urban poor).

Harsher criticisms soon emerged. Barton Bernstein in a 1968 essay compiled a dreary chronicle of missed opportunities and inadequate responses to problems and concluded that the New Deal had saved capitalism, but at the expense of the least powerful and least favored members of society. Ronald Radosh, Allen Matusow, Paul Conkin, Thomas Ferguson, and other scholars writing in a climate shaped by the New Left's attack on liberalism expanded on these criticisms; the New Deal, they contended, was part of the twentieth-century tradition of "corporate liberalism"—a tradition in which reform is closely wedded to the needs and interests of capitalism.

But the attack from the left did not develop very far beyond its preliminary statements. Instead, by the early 1980s, most scholars seemed to have accepted a revised liberal view: that the New Deal was a significant (and, most agree, valuable) reform effort, even if one that worked within rigid, occasionally crippling limits. The scholarship of the last decade, therefore, has paid less attention to arguing over whether or not the New Deal was a good thing, and more attention to the nature of the constraints it faced and to the way it fits into larger patterns of political development.

The phrase "New Deal liberalism" came in the postwar era to seem synonymous with a broad range of reform ideas, many of which had very little connection to the New Deal itself. In fact, the liberal accomplishments of the 1930s can be understood only in the context of their own time; later liberal efforts have drawn from that legacy but also altered it to fit the needs and assumptions of different eras.

CHAPTER TWENTY-SEVEN

The Global Crisis, 1921–1941

The Diplomacy of the New Era ~ *Isolationism and Internationalism*

ENRY CABOT LODGE of Massachusetts, chairman of the Senate
Foreign Relations Committee and one of the most powerful
figures in the Republican party, led the fight against ratification of the
Treaty of Versailles in 1918 and 1919. In part because of his efforts, the
treaty was defeated. The United States failed to join the League of Nations;
and American foreign policy embarked on an independent course that for
the next two decades would attempt, but ultimately fail, to expand American
influence and maintain international stability without committing the
United States to any lasting relationships with other nations.

Lodge was not an isolationist. He recognized that America had
emerged from World War I the most powerful nation in the world. He
believed the United States should exert its influence internationally. But he
believed, too, that America's expanded role in the world should reflect the
nation's own interests and its own special virtues; it should leave the United
States unfettered with obligations to anyone else. He said in 1919:

> We are a great moral asset of Christian civilization. . . . How did we get
> there? By our own efforts. Nobody led us, nobody guided us, nobody
> controlled us. . . . I would keep America as she has been—not isolated,
> not prevent her from joining other nations for . . . great purposes—but
> I wish her to be master of her own fate.

In the end, the limited American internationalism of the interwar years
proved insufficient to protect the interests of the United States, to create
global stability, or to keep the nation from becoming involved in the most
catastrophic war in human history.

THE DIPLOMACY OF THE NEW ERA

Critics of American foreign policy in the 1920s often described it with a single word: isolationism. But in reality, the United States played a more active role in world affairs in the 1920s than it had at almost any previous time in its history.

Replacing the League

By the time the Harding administration took office in 1921, American membership in the League of Nations was no longer a realistic possibility. But Secretary of State Charles Evans Hughes wanted to find something with which to replace the League as a guarantor of world peace and stability. He embarked on a series of efforts to build safeguards against future wars—safeguards, however, that would not hamper American freedom of action in the world.

The most important of such efforts was the Washington Conference of 1921—an attempt to prevent a destabilizing naval armaments race among the United States, Britain, and Japan. Hughes proposed a plan for dramatic reductions in the fleets of all three nations and a ten-year moratorium on the construction of large warships. To the surprise of almost everyone, the conference ultimately agreed to accept most of Hughes's terms. The Five-Power Pact of February 1922 established limits for total naval tonnage and a ratio of armaments among the signatories. For every 5 tons of American and British warships, Japan would maintain 3 and France and Italy 1.75 each.

The Washington Conference began the New Era effort to protect world peace (and the international economic interests of the United States) without accepting international obligations. The Kellogg-Briand Pact of 1928 concluded it. When the French foreign minister, Aristide Briand, asked the United States in 1927 to join an alliance against Germany, Secretary of State Frank Kellogg (who had replaced Hughes in 1925) proposed instead a multilateral treaty outlawing war as an instrument of national policy. Fourteen nations signed the agreement in Paris on August 27, 1928, amid great solemnity and wide international acclaim. Forty-eight other nations later joined the pact. It contained no instruments of enforcement.

Debts and Diplomacy

The first responsibility of diplomacy, Hughes, Kellogg, and others agreed, was to ensure that American overseas trade faced no obstacles. Preventing a dangerous and expensive armaments race and reducing the possibility of war were two steps to that end. So were new financial arrangements to deal with international debts. The Allied powers of Europe were struggling to repay $11 billion in loans they had contracted with the United States during and shortly after the war. At the same time, Germany was attempting to pay the reparations levied by the Allies. With the financial structure of Europe on the brink of collapse as a result, the United States stepped in with a solution.

Charles G. Dawes, an American banker, negotiated an agreement in 1924 among France, Britain, Germany, and the United States under which American banks would provide enormous loans to the Germans, enabling them to meet their reparations payments; in return, Britain and France would agree to reduce the amount of those payments. The Dawes Plan became the source of a troubling circular pattern in international finance. The United States would lend money to Germany, which would use that money to pay reparations to France and England, which would in turn use those funds (as well as large loans they themselves were receiving from American banks) to repay war debts to the United States. The flow was able to continue only by virtue of the enormous debts Germany and the other European nations were acquiring to American banks and corporations. Some in the American government warned that the reckless expansion of overseas loans and investments threatened disaster—that the United States was becoming too dependent on unstable European economies. Such warnings fell, for the most part, on deaf ears; and the American economic involvement in Europe continued to expand until the worldwide depression shattered the system in 1931.

The government felt even fewer reservations about assisting American economic expansion in Latin America. During the 1920s, American military forces maintained a presence in Nicaragua, Panama, and several other countries in the region, while United States investments in Latin America more than doubled. American banks were offering large loans to Latin American governments, just as they were in Europe; and just as in Europe, the Latin Americans were having difficulty earning the money to repay them in the face of the formidable United States tariff barrier.

Hoover and the World Crisis

After the relatively placid international climate of the 1920s, the diplomatic challenges facing the Hoover administration must have seemed bewildering. The world financial crisis that had begun in 1929 and greatly intensified after 1931 was producing a dangerous nationalism in Europe, toppling some existing political leaders and replacing them with powerful, belligerent governments committed to expansion as a solution to their economic problems. Hoover was confronted with the beginning of a process that would ultimately lead to war.

In Latin America, Hoover tried to repair some of the damage created by earlier American policies. He made a ten-week good-will tour through the region before his inauguration. Once in office, he generally abstained from intervening in the internal affairs of neighboring nations and moved to withdraw American troops from Nicaragua and Haiti. When economic distress led to the collapse of several Latin American regimes, Hoover

HITLER AND MUSSOLINI   The German and Italian dictators, shown here reviewing troops together in Berlin in the mid-1930s, acted publicly as if they were equals. Privately, however, Hitler viewed Mussolini with contempt, and the Italian dictator complained frequently of being treated as a junior partner by his ally.

announced a new policy: America would grant diplomatic recognition to any sitting government in the region without questioning the means it had used to obtain power. He even repudiated the Roosevelt Corollary to the Monroe Doctrine by refusing to permit American intervention when several Latin American countries defaulted on debt obligations to the United States in October 1931.

In Europe, the administration enjoyed few successes in its efforts to promote economic stability. When Hoover's proposed moratorium on debts in 1931 failed to attract broad support or produce financial stability, he refused to cancel all war debts to the United States as many economists advised him to do. Several European nations promptly went into default. American efforts to extend the disarmament agreements of the 1920s met with similar frustration. Efforts to extend the 1921 limits on naval construction fell victim to French and British fears of German and Japanese militarism. And the World Disarmament Conference in Geneva in 1932 similarly ended in frustration.

The ineffectiveness of American diplomacy in Europe was particularly troubling in light of the new governments on the Continent. Benito Mussolini's Fascist party had been in control of Italy since the early 1920s and had become increasingly nationalistic and militaristic. Still more ominous was the growing power of the National Socialist (or Nazi) party in Germany. By the late 1920s, the Weimar Republic, the nation's government since the end of World War I, had been largely discredited by, among other things, a ruinous inflation. Adolf Hitler, the leader of the Nazis, was growing rapidly in popular favor and would take power in 1933. Hitler believed in the genetic superiority of the Aryan (German) people and in extending German territory to provide *Lebensraum* (living space) for the German "master race." He also displayed a pathological anti-Semitism and a passionate militarism.

More immediately alarming to the Hoover administration was a major crisis in Asia—another early step toward World War II. The Japanese, suffering from an economic depression of their own, were concerned about the increasing power of the Soviet Union and of Chiang Kai-shek's nationalist China. In particular, they were alarmed at Chiang's insistence on expanding his government's power in Manchuria, which remained officially a part of China but over which the Japanese had maintained effective economic control since 1905. In 1931, Japan's military leaders staged what was, in effect, a coup and took control of the government in Tokyo. Weeks later, they launched an invasion of northern Manchuria. They had conquered the region by the end of the year. Hoover permitted Secretary of State Henry Stimson to issue stern warnings to the Japanese but barred him from cooperating with the League of Nations to impose economic sanctions against them. Early in 1932, Japan expanded its aggression farther into China, attacking the city of Shanghai and killing thousands of civilians.

By the time Hoover left office, early in 1933, the international system the United States had attempted to create in the 1920s—a system based on voluntary cooperation among nations and on an American refusal to commit itself to any collective obligations—had collapsed. The United States faced a choice. It could adopt a more energetic form of internationalism and enter into firmer and more meaningful associations with other nations. It could resort to nationalism and try to deal with international problems alone. Or it could ignore global problems altogether. For the next six years, it experimented with elements of all three approaches.

ISOLATIONISM AND INTERNATIONALISM

The administration of Franklin Roosevelt faced a dual challenge as it entered office in 1933. It had to deal with the worst economic crisis in the nation's history, and it had to deal as well with the effects of a decaying international structure.

Depression Diplomacy

Perhaps Roosevelt's sharpest break with the policies of his predecessor was on the question of American economic relations with Europe. Hoover had argued that only by resolving the question of war debts and reinforcing the gold standard could the American economy hope to recover. He had, therefore, agreed to participate in the World Economic Conference, to be held in London in June 1933, to attempt to resolve these issues. By the time the conference assembled, however, Roosevelt had already become convinced that the gold value of the dollar had to be allowed to fall in order for American goods to be able to compete in world markets. Shortly after the conference convened, he released what became known as the "bombshell message," repudiating the orthodox views of most of the delegates and rejecting any agreement on currency stabilization. The conference quickly dissolved without reaching agreement.

At the same time, Roosevelt abandoned the commitments of the Hoover administration to settle the issue of war debts through international agreement. In April 1934 he signed a bill that prohibited American banks from making loans to any nation in default on its debts. The result was to stop the old, circular system by which debt payments continued only by virtue of increasing American loans; within months, war-debt payments from every nation except Finland stopped for good.

The United States and Russia had viewed each other with mistrust and even hostility since the Bolshevik Revolution of 1917, and the American government still had not officially recognized the Soviet regime in 1933. But a growing number of influential Americans were urging a change in policy—largely because the Soviet Union appeared to be a possible source of trade. The Russians, for their part, were hoping for American cooperation in containing Japan. In November 1933, the United States and the Soviet Union agreed to open formal diplomatic relations.

Despite this promising beginning, however, relations with the Soviet Union soon soured once again. American trade failed to establish a foothold in Russia, disappointing hopes in the United States; and the American government did little to reassure the Soviets that it was interested in stopping Japanese expansion in Asia, dousing expectations in Russia. By the end of 1934, the Soviet Union and the United States were once again viewing each other with considerable mistrust. And the Soviet leader, Josef Stalin, was beginning to consider making agreements of his own with the fascist governments of Japan and Germany.

The Good Neighbor Policy

The United States succeeded during the 1930s in increasing both its exports to and its imports from Latin America by over 100 percent. At the same time, the Roosevelt administration was taking a new approach toward Latin America, an approach which became known as the "Good Neighbor Policy" and which expanded on the changes the Hoover administration had made. At an Inter-American Conference in Montevideo, Uruguay, in December 1933, Secretary of State Cordell Hull signed a formal convention declaring: "No state has the right to intervene in the internal or external affairs of another." By repudiating military intervention, Roosevelt, like Hoover, eased tensions between the United States and its neighbors considerably. But the Good Neighbor Policy did little to stem the growing American domination of the Latin American economy.

The Rise of Isolationism

With the international system of the 1920s now decayed beyond repair, the United States faced a choice between more active efforts to stabilize the world and more energetic attempts to isolate the nation from it. Most Americans unhesitatingly chose the latter. Support for isolationism emerged from many quarters. Some Wilsonian internationalists had grown disillusioned with the League of Nations and its inability to stop Japanese aggression in Asia. Other Americans were listening to the argument that powerful business interests—Wall Street, munitions makers, and others— had tricked the United States into participating in World War I. An investigation by a Senate committee chaired by Senator Gerald Nye of North Dakota claimed to reveal exorbitant profiteering and tax evasion by many corporations during the war, and it suggested that bankers had pressured Wilson to intervene in the war so as to protect their loans abroad. (Few historians now lend much credence to these charges.)

Roosevelt himself was sympathetic to some of the isolationist arguments. But he continued to hope for at least a modest American role in maintaining world peace. In 1935, he proposed to the Senate a treaty to make the United States a member of the World Court—a largely symbolic gesture. Nevertheless, isolationists such as Father Coughlin and William Randolph Hearst aroused popular opposition to the agreement, and the Senate voted it down. The president would not soon again attempt to challenge the isolationist tide.

In the summer of 1935, it became clear that Mussolini's Italy was preparing to invade Ethiopia. Fearing the invasion would provoke a new European war, American legislators began to design legal safeguards to prevent the United States from being dragged into the conflict. The result was the Neutrality Act of 1935, followed by additional acts in 1936 and 1937. The 1935 law established a mandatory arms embargo against both sides in any military conflict and directed the president to warn American citizens against traveling on the ships of warring nations. Thus, isolationists believed, the "protection of neutral rights" could not again become an excuse for American intervention in war. The 1936 Neutrality Act renewed these provisions, and the 1937 law added new ones, establishing the so-called "cash-and-carry" policy, by which belligerents could purchase only nonmilitary goods from the United States and could do so only by paying cash and shipping their purchases themselves.

Isolationist sentiment showed its strength again in 1936–1937 in response to the civil war in Spain. The Falangists of General Francisco Franco, a group much like the Italian fascists, revolted in July 1936 against the existing republican government. Hitler and Mussolini supported Franco, both vocally and with weapons and supplies. Some individual Americans traveled to Spain to assist the republican cause, but the United States government joined with Britain and France in an agreement to offer no assistance to either side.

Roosevelt, however, was slowly becoming convinced that the course of international events required some more forceful American response. Particularly disturbing was the deteriorating situation in Asia. In the summer of 1937, Japan intensified its six-year-old assault on Manchuria and attacked China's five northern provinces. Roosevelt responded in a speech in Chicago in October 1937. He warned of the dangers of the Japanese actions and argued that aggressors should be "quarantined" by the international community to prevent the contagion of war from spreading. He was deliberately vague about what such a "quarantine" would mean. Even so, public response to the speech was disturbingly hostile, and Roosevelt drew back. On December 12, 1937, Japanese aviators bombed and sank the United States gunboat *Panay*, almost certainly deliberately, as it sailed the Yangtze River in China. But so reluctant was the Roosevelt administration to antagonize the isolationists that the United States eagerly seized on Japanese claims that the bombing had been an accident, accepted Japan's apologies, and overlooked the attack.

The Failure of Munich

In 1936, Hitler had moved the revived German army into the Rhineland, rearming an area that France had, in effect, controlled since World War I. In March 1938, German forces marched into Austria; and Hitler proclaimed a union (or *Anschluss*) between Austria, his native land, and Germany, his adopted one. Neither in America nor in most of Europe was there much more than a murmur of opposition.

The Austrian invasion, however, soon created another crisis, for Germany had by now occupied territory surrounding three sides of western Czechoslovakia, a region Hitler dreamed of annexing. In September 1938, he demanded that Czechoslovakia cede him part of that region, the Sudetenland, an area in which many ethnic Germans lived. Although Czechoslovakia was prepared to fight to stop Hitler, it needed assistance from other nations. But most Western governments, including the United States, were willing to pay almost any price to settle the crisis peacefully. On September

29, Hitler met with the leaders of France and Great Britain at Munich in an effort to resolve the crisis. The French and British agreed to accept the German demands in Czechoslovakia in return for Hitler's promise to expand no farther.

The Munich accords, which Roosevelt applauded at the time, were the most prominent element of a policy that came to be known as "appeasement" and that came to be identified (not altogether fairly) largely with British Prime Minister Neville Chamberlain. Whoever was to blame, the policy was a failure. In March 1939, Hitler occupied the remaining areas of Czechoslovakia, violating the Munich agreement unashamedly. And in April, he began issuing threats against Poland.

At that point, both Britain and France gave assurances to the Polish government that they would come to its assistance in case of an invasion;

THE BLITZ, LONDON The German Luftwaffe terrorized London and other British cities in 1940–1941 and again late in the war by bombing civilian areas indiscriminately in an effort to break the spirit of the English people. The effort failed, and the fortitude of the British did much to arouse support for their cause in the United States.

they even tried, too late, to draw the Soviet Union into a mutual defense agreement. But Stalin, who had not even been invited to the Munich Conference, had already decided he could expect no protection from the West. He signed a nonaggression pact with Hitler in August 1939, freeing the Germans for the moment from the danger of a two-front war.

Shortly after that, Hitler staged an incident on the Polish border to allow him to claim that Germany had been attacked; and on September 1, 1939, he launched a full-scale invasion of Poland. Britain and France, true to their pledges, declared war on Germany two days later. World War II had begun.

Neutrality Tested

"This nation will remain a neutral nation," the president declared shortly after the hostilities began in Europe, "but I cannot ask that every American remain neutral in thought as well." There was never any question that both he and the majority of the American people favored Britain, France, and the other Allied nations in the contest. The question was how much the United States was prepared to do to assist them.

At the very least, Roosevelt believed, the United States should make armaments available to the Allied armies to help them counteract the German munitions industry. In September 1939, he asked Congress to revise the Neutrality Acts and lift the arms embargo against any nation engaged in war. Powerful isolationist opposition forced Congress to maintain the prohibition on American ships entering war zones. But the 1939 law did permit belligerents to purchase arms on the same cash-and-carry basis that the earlier Neutrality Acts had established for the sale of nonmilitary materials.

For a time, it was possible to believe that little more would be necessary. After the German armies quickly subdued Poland, the war in Europe settled into a long, quiet lull that lasted through the winter and spring—a "phony war," some called it. (In the meantime, the Soviet Union overran first the small Baltic republics of Latvia, Estonia, and Lithuania and then, in late November, established effective control over Finland. The United States responded with nothing more than an ineffective "moral embargo" on the shipment of armaments to Russia.)

Whatever illusions Americans had harbored about the war in western Europe were shattered in the spring of 1940 when Germany launched a massive invasion to the west—first attacking Denmark and Norway, sweeping next across the Netherlands and Belgium, and driving finally deep into the heart of France. Allied efforts proved futile against the Nazi *blitzkrieg*. One western European stronghold after another fell into German hands. On June 10, Mussolini invaded France from the south as Hitler was attacking from the north. On June 22, finally, France fell, and Nazi troops marched into Paris. A new collaborationist French regime assembled in Vichy; and in all Europe, only the shattered remnants of the British and French armies, rescued from the beaches of Dunkirk, remained to oppose the Axis forces.

On May 16, in the midst of the offensive, Roosevelt asked Congress for an additional $1 billion for defense and received it quickly. That was one day after Winston Churchill, the new British prime minister, had sent Roosevelt the first of many long lists of requests for armaments, without which, he insisted, England could not long survive. Some Americans (including the United States ambassador to London, Joseph P. Kennedy) argued that the British plight was already hopeless, that any aid to the English was a wasted effort. But the president was determined to make war materials available to Britain. He even circumvented the cash-and-carry provisions of the Neutrality Acts by giving England fifty American destroyers (most of them left over from World War I) in return for the right to build American bases on British territory in the Western Hemisphere; and he returned to the factories a number of new airplanes purchased by the American government so that the British could buy them instead.

Roosevelt was able to take such steps in part because of a major shift in American public opinion. By July 1940, more than 66 percent of the public (according to opinion polls) believed that Germany posed a direct threat to the United States. Congress was, therefore, more willing to permit expanded American assistance to the Allies. It was also becoming more concerned about the need for internal preparations for war, and in September it approved the Burke-Wadsworth Act, inaugurating the first peacetime military draft in American history.

But the isolationists were far from finished. A powerful new isolationist lobby entitled the America First Committee, whose members included such prominent Americans as Charles Lindbergh and Senators Gerald Nye and Burton Wheeler, joined the debate over American policy toward the war. The lobby had at least the indirect support of a large proportion of the Republican party. The debate was a bitter one. Through the summer and fall of 1940, moreover, it was complicated by a presidential campaign.

The biggest political question of 1940 was whether Franklin Roosevelt would break with tradition and run for an unprecedented third term. The president himself did not reveal his own wishes. But by refusing to withdraw from the contest, he made it impossible for any rival Democrat to establish a claim to the nomination. And when, just before the Democratic Convention in July, he let it be known that he would accept a "draft" from his party, the issue was virtually settled. The Democrats quickly renominated him and even reluctantly swallowed his choice for vice president: Agriculture Secretary Henry A. Wallace, a man too liberal and too controversial for the taste of many party leaders.

The Republicans, again uncertain how to oppose Roosevelt effectively, nominated for president a politically inexperienced Indiana businessman, Wendell Willkie, who benefited from a powerful grass-roots movement. Both the candidate and the party platform took positions little different from Roosevelt's: they would keep the country out of war but would extend generous assistance to the Allies. Willkie was an appealing figure and a vigorous campaigner, and he managed to evoke more public enthusiasm than any Republican candidate in decades. The election was closer than in either 1932 or 1936, but Roosevelt still won decisively. He received 55 percent of the popular vote to Willkie's 45 percent, and he won 449 electoral votes to Willkie's 82.

Neutrality Abandoned

In the last months of 1940, with the election behind him and with the situation in Europe deteriorating, Roosevelt began to make subtle but profound changes in the American role in the war. Great Britain was virtually bankrupt and could no longer meet the cash-and-carry requirements imposed by the Neutrality Acts. The president, therefore, proposed a new system for supplying Britain: "lend-lease." It would allow the government not only to sell but to lend or lease armaments to any nation deemed "vital to the defense of the United States." In other words, America could funnel weapons to England on the basis of no more than Britain's promise to return them when the war was over. Isolationists attacked the measure bitterly, but Congress enacted the bill by wide margins.

With lend-lease established, Roosevelt soon faced another serious problem. Attacks by German submarines had made shipping lanes in the Atlantic extremely dangerous. The British navy was losing ships more rapidly than it could replace them and was finding it difficult to transport materials across the Atlantic from America. Secretary of War Henry Stimson (who had been Hoover's secretary of state and who returned to the cabinet at Roosevelt's request in 1940) argued that the United States should itself convoy vessels to England; but Roosevelt took a more limited approach. He argued that the western Atlantic was a neutral zone and the responsibility of the American nations. By July 1941, therefore, American ships were patrolling the ocean as far east as Iceland.

At first, Germany did little to challenge these obviously hostile American actions. By September 1941, however, the situation had changed. Nazi forces had invaded the Soviet Union in June of that year. When the Soviets did not surrender, as many had predicted, Roosevelt persuaded Congress to extend lend-lease privileges to them. Now American industry was providing vital assistance to Hitler's foes on two fronts, and the American navy was protecting the flow of those goods to Europe. In September, Nazi submarines began a concerted campaign against American vessels. Roosevelt ordered American ships to fire on German submarines "on sight." In October, Nazi submarines hit two American destroyers and sank one of them, the *Reuben James*, killing many American sailors. Congress now voted to allow the United States to arm its merchant vessels and to sail all the way into belligerent ports. The United States had, in effect, launched a naval war against Germany.

In August 1941, Roosevelt met with Churchill aboard a British vessel off the coast of Newfoundland. The president made no military commitments, but he did join with the prime minister in releasing a document that became known as the Atlantic Charter, in which the two nations set out "certain common principles" on which to base "a better future for the world." It called openly for "the final destruction of the Nazi tyranny" and for a new world order in which every nation controlled its own destiny. It was, in effect, a statement of war aims.

The Road to Pearl Harbor

Japan, in the meantime, was taking advantage of events in Europe to extend its empire in the Pacific. In September 1940, the Japanese signed the Tripartite Pact, a loose defensive alliance with Germany and Italy (although in reality, the European Axis powers never developed a very strong relationship with Japan). In July 1941, imperial troops moved into Indochina and seized the capital of Vietnam, a colony of France. The United States, having broken Japanese codes, knew their next target would be the Dutch East Indies; and when Tokyo failed to respond to Roosevelt's stern warnings, the president froze all Japanese assets in the United States, severely limiting Japan's ability to purchase needed American supplies.

Tokyo now faced a choice. Either it would have to repair relations with the United States to restore the flow of supplies or it would have to find those supplies elsewhere, most notably by seizing British and Dutch possessions in the Pacific. At first, the Tokyo government seemed willing to negotiate. But in October, militants in Tokyo forced the moderate prime minister out of office and replaced him with the leader of the war party, General Hideki Tojo. There seemed little alternative now to war.

For several weeks, the Tojo government maintained a pretense of wanting to continue negotiations. But Tokyo had already decided it would not yield on the question of China, and Washington had made clear that it would accept nothing less than a reversal of that policy. By late November, the State Department had given up on the possibility of a peaceful settle-

THE JAPANESE ATTACK PEARL HARBOR, DECEMBER 7, 1941 The destroyer U.S.S. *Shaw*, immobilized in a floating drydock in Pearl Harbor in December 1941, survived the first wave of Japanese bombers unscathed. But in the second attack, the Japanese scored a direct hit, which blew off the ship's bow.

ment. American intelligence, meanwhile, had decoded Japanese messages that made clear a Japanese attack was imminent. But Washington did not know where the attack would take place. Most officials continued to believe that the Japanese would move first not against American territory but against British or Dutch possessions to the south. A combination of confusion and miscalculation caused the government to overlook indications that Japan intended a direct attack on American forces.

At 7:55 A.M. on Sunday, December 7, 1941, a wave of Japanese bombers attacked the United States naval base at Pearl Harbor in Hawaii. A second wave came an hour later. Within two hours, the United States lost 8 battleships, 3 cruisers, 4 other vessels, 188 airplanes, and several vital shore installations. More than 2,400 soldiers and sailors died, and another 1,000 were injured. The Japanese suffered only light losses.

American forces were now greatly diminished in the Pacific (although by a fortunate accident, no American aircraft carriers—the heart of the Pacific fleet—had been at Pearl Harbor on December 7). Nevertheless, the raid on Hawaii unified the American people behind war. On December 8, after a stirring speech by the president, the Senate voted unanimously and the House voted 388 to 1 to approve a declaration of war against Japan. Three days later, Germany and Italy, Japan's European allies, declared war on the United States; on the same day, December 11, Congress reciprocated without a dissenting vote.

CHAPTER TWENTY-EIGHT

America in a World at War

War on Two Fronts ~ *The American People in Wartime*
The Defeat of the Axis

THE ATTACK ON Pearl Harbor had thrust the United States into the greatest and most terrible war in the history of humanity. World War I had destroyed centuries-old European social and political institutions. But World War II created unprecedented carnage and horror, not only in Europe but around much of the rest of the globe. And in the end, it changed the world as profoundly as any event of the twentieth century, perhaps any century.

Less readily apparent is how profoundly the war changed America—its society, its politics, and its image of itself. Except for the combatants themselves, most Americans experienced the war at a remove of several thousand miles. They endured no bombing, no invasion, no massive dislocations, no serious material privations. Veterans returning home in 1945 and 1946 found a country that looked very much like the one they had left—something that clearly could not be said of veterans returning home to Britain, France, Germany, Russia, or Japan.

But World War II did transform the United States in profound, if not always readily visible, ways. As the poet Archibald MacLeish said in 1943, "The great majority of the American people understand very well that this war is not a war only, but an end and a beginning—an end to things known and a beginning of things unknown. We have smelled the wind in the streets that changes weather. We know that whatever the world will be when the war ends, the world will be different." The story of American involvement in the war, therefore, is not just the story of how the military forces and the industrial might of the United States contributed to the defeat of Germany, Italy, and Japan. It is also the story of the creation of a new world, both abroad and at home.

WAR ON TWO FRONTS

Whatever political disagreements and social tensions there may have been among the American people during World War II, there was striking unity of opinion about the conflict itself. But both unity and confidence were severely tested in the first, troubled months of 1942.

Containing the Japanese

Ten hours after the strike at Pearl Harbor, Japanese airplanes attacked the American airfields at Manila in the Philippines, destroying much of America's remaining air power in the Pacific. Three days later Guam, an American possession, fell to Japan; Wake Island and Hong Kong followed. The great British fortress of Singapore in Malaya surrendered in February 1942, the Dutch East Indies in March, Burma in April. In the Philippines, exhausted Filipino and American troops gave up their defense of the islands on May 6.

American strategists planned two broad offensives to turn the tide against the Japanese. One, under the command of General Douglas MacArthur, would move north from Australia, through New Guinea, and eventually to the Philippines. The other, under Admiral Chester Nimitz, would move west from Hawaii toward major Japanese island outposts in the central Pacific. Ultimately, the two offensives would come together to invade Japan itself.

The Allies achieved their first important victory in the Battle of the Coral Sea, just northwest of Australia, on May 7–8, 1942, when American forces turned back the previously unstoppable Japanese. A month later, there was an even more important turning point northwest of Hawaii. An enormous battle raged for four days, June 3–6, 1942, near the small American outpost at Midway Island, at the end of which the United States, despite great losses, was clearly victorious. The American navy destroyed four Japanese aircraft carriers and lost only one of its own; the action regained control of the central Pacific for the United States.

The Americans took the offensive for the first time several months later in the southern Solomon Islands, to the east of New Guinea. In August 1942, American forces assaulted three of the islands: Gavutu, Tulagi, and Guadalcanal. A struggle of terrible ferocity developed at Guadalcanal and continued for six months, inflicting heavy losses on both sides. In the end, however, the Japanese were forced to abandon the island—and with it their last chance of launching an effective offensive to the south.

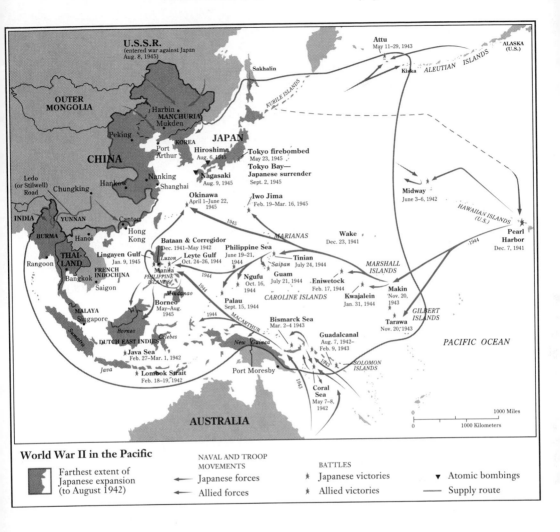

World War II in the Pacific

Farthest extent of Japanese expansion (to August 1942)

NAVAL AND TROOP MOVEMENTS
- ← Japanese forces
- ← Allied forces

BATTLES
- ✹ Japanese victories
- ✹ Allied victories

- ▼ Atomic bombings
- — Supply route

In both the southern and the central Pacific, therefore, the initiative had shifted to the United States by mid-1943. The Japanese advance had been halted. The Americans, with aid from the Australians and the New Zealanders, now began the slow, arduous process of moving toward the Philippines and Japan itself.

Holding Off the Germans

In the European war, the United States was fighting in cooperation with Britain and with the exiled "Free French" forces in the west; and it was trying also to conciliate its new ally, the Soviet Union, which was now fighting Hitler in the east. The army chief of staff, General George C. Marshall, supported a plan for a major Allied invasion of France across the English Channel in the spring of 1943; and he placed a hitherto little known general, Dwight D. Eisenhower, in charge of planning the operation. But the American plan faced challenges from the other Allies. The Soviet Union, which was absorbing the brunt of the German war effort (as it would throughout the conflict), wanted the Allied invasion to begin at the earliest possible moment. The British, on the other hand, wanted first to launch a series of Allied offensives around the edges of the Nazi empire—in northern Africa and southern Europe—before undertaking the major invasion of France.

Roosevelt was torn, but he ultimately decided to support the British plan—in part because he was eager to get American forces into combat quickly and feared that a cross-Channel invasion would take a long time to prepare. At the end of October 1942, the British opened a counteroffensive

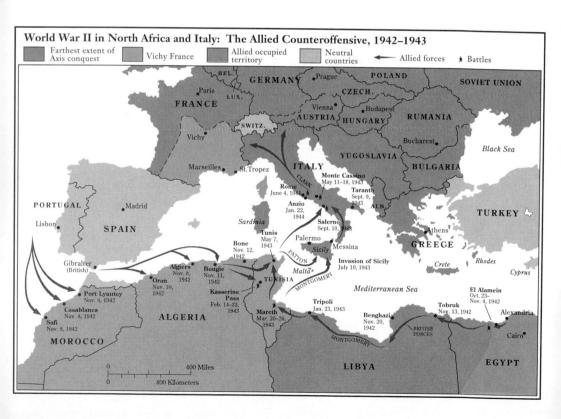

World War II in North Africa and Italy: The Allied Counteroffensive, 1942–1943

Farthest extent of Axis conquest | Vichy France | Allied occupied territory | Neutral countries | ← Allied forces | ★ Battles

against Nazi forces in North Africa under General Erwin Rommel, who was threatening the Suez Canal. In a major battle at El Alamein, they forced the Germans to retreat from Egypt. On November 8, Anglo-American forces landed at Oran and Algiers in Algeria and at Casablanca in Morocco—areas under the Nazi-controlled French government at Vichy—and began moving east toward Rommel. The Germans threw the full weight of their forces in Africa against the inexperienced Americans and inflicted a serious defeat on them at the Kasserine Pass in Tunisia. General George S. Patton, however, regrouped the American troops and began an effective counteroffensive. With the help of Allied air and naval power and of British forces attacking from the east under Field Marshall Bernard Montgomery (the hero of El Alamein), the American offensive finally drove the last Germans from Africa in May 1943.

The North African campaign had tied up so large a proportion of the Allied resources that the planned May 1943 cross-Channel invasion of France had to be postponed, despite angry complaints from the Soviet Union. By now, however, the threat of a Soviet collapse seemed much diminished, for during the winter of 1942–1943, the Red Army had successfully held off a major German assault at Stalingrad in southern Russia. Hitler had committed such enormous forces to the battle, and had suffered such appalling losses, that he could not continue his eastern offensive.

The Soviet successes persuaded Roosevelt to agree, in a January 1943 meeting with Churchill in Casablanca, to a British plan for an Allied invasion of Sicily. Churchill argued that the operation in Sicily might knock Italy out of the war and tie up German divisions that might otherwise be stationed in France. On the night of July 9, 1943, American and British armies landed in southeast Sicily; thirty-eight days later, they had conquered the island and were moving onto the Italian mainland. In the face of these setbacks, Mussolini's government collapsed and the dictator himself fled north toward Germany. Although Mussolini's successor, Pietro Badoglio, quickly committed Italy to the Allies, Germany moved eight divisions into the country and established a powerful defensive line south of Rome. The Allied offensive on the Italian peninsula, which began on September 3, 1943, soon bogged down. Not until May 1944 did the Allies resume their northward advance. On June 4, 1944, they captured Rome.

The invasion of Italy contributed to the Allied war effort in several important ways. But it postponed the invasion of France by as much as a year, deeply embittering the Soviet Union and giving the Soviets time to begin moving toward the countries of eastern Europe.

America and the Holocaust

In the midst of this intensive fighting, the leaders of the American government found themselves confronted with one of history's great tragedies: the Nazi campaign to exterminate the Jews of Europe—the Holocaust. As early as 1942, high officials in Washington had incontrovertible evidence that Hitler's forces were rounding up Jews and others (including Poles, homosexuals, and communists) from all over Europe, transporting them to concentration camps in eastern Germany and Poland, and systematically murdering them. (The death toll would ultimately reach 6 million Jews and at least 4 million others.) News of the atrocities was reaching the public as well, and pressure began to build for an Allied effort to end the killing or at least to rescue some of the surviving Jews.

The American government consistently resisted almost all such entreaties. Although Allied bombers were flying missions within a few miles of the most notorious death camp, at Auschwitz in Poland, pleas that the planes try to destroy the crematoria at the camp were rejected as militarily unfeasible. So were similar requests that the Allies try to destroy railroad lines leading to the camp. The United States also resisted pleas that it admit large numbers of the Jewish refugees attempting to escape Europe.

In fairness to American leaders, there was probably little they could have done to save most of Hitler's victims. But more forceful action by the United States (and Britain, which was even less amenable to Jewish requests for assistance) might well have saved at least some lives. Policymakers found it possible to justify abandoning the Jews to their fate by concentrating their attention solely on the larger goal of winning the war. Any diversion of energy and attention to other purposes, they apparently believed, would distract them from the overriding goal of victory.

THE AMERICAN PEOPLE IN WARTIME

Not since the Civil War had the United States been involved in so prolonged and consuming a military experience as World War II. American armed forces engaged in combat around the globe for nearly four years. American society, in the meantime, experienced changes that reached into virtually every corner of the nation.

Prosperity and the Rights of Labor

World War II had its most profound impact on American domestic life by ending the Great Depression at last. By the middle of 1941, the economic problems of the 1930s—unemployment, deflation, industrial sluggishness—had virtually vanished before the great wave of wartime industrial expansion.

The most important agent of the new prosperity was government spending, which after 1939 was pumping more money into the economy each year than all the New Deal relief agencies combined had done. In 1939, the federal budget had been $9 billion; by 1945, it had risen to $100 billion. Largely as a result, the gross national product soared: from $91 billion in 1939 to $166 billion in 1945. Personal incomes in some regions grew by as much as 100 percent or more. The demands of wartime production created a shortage of consumer goods, so many wage earners diverted much of their new affluence into savings, which would later help keep the economic boom alive in the postwar years.

Instead of the prolonged and debilitating unemployment that had been the most troubling feature of the Depression economy, the war created a serious labor shortage. The armed forces took over 15 million men and women out of the civilian work force at the same time that the demand for labor was rising rapidly. Nevertheless, the civilian work force increased by almost 20 percent during the war. The 7 million who had previously been unemployed accounted for some of the increase; the employment of many people previously considered inappropriate for the work force—the very young, the elderly, minorities, and, most important, several million women—accounted for the rest of it.

The war gave an enormous boost to union membership, which rose from about 10.5 million in 1941 to over 13 million in 1945. But it also created important new restrictions on the ability of unions to fight for their members' demands. The government was principally interested in keeping production moving without disruption and preventing inflation. It managed to win two important concessions from union leaders toward those ends. One was the "no-strike" pledge, by which unions agreed not to stop production in wartime. Another was the so-called Little Steel formula, which set a 15 percent limit on wage increases. In return, the government provided labor with a "maintenance-of-membership" agreement, which ensured that the thousands of new workers pouring into unionized defense plants would be automatically enrolled in the unions. The agreement guaranteed the continued health of the union organizations, but in return workers had to give up the right to demand major gains during the war.

Despite the no-strike pledge, there were nearly 15,000 work stoppages during the war, mostly wildcat strikes (strikes unauthorized by the union leadership), many protesting harsh working conditions and high levels of stress. When the United Mine Workers defied the government by striking in May 1943, Congress reacted by passing, over Roosevelt's veto, the Smith-Connally Act (War Labor Disputes Act), which required that unions wait thirty days before striking and which empowered the president to seize a struck war plant. In the meantime, public animosity toward labor rose rapidly, and many states passed laws to limit union power.

Stabilizing the Boom and Mobilizing Production

The fear of deflation, the central concern of the 1930s, gave way during the war to a fear of inflation, particularly after prices rose 25 percent in the two years before Pearl Harbor. In October 1942, Congress grudgingly responded to the president's request and passed the Anti-Inflation Act, which gave the administration authority to freeze agricultural prices, wages, salaries, and rents throughout the country. Enforcement of these provisions was the task of the Office of Price Administration (OPA), led first by Leon Henderson and then by Chester Bowles. In part because of its success, inflation was a much less serious problem during World War II than it had been during World War I.

Even so, the OPA was never popular. There was widespread resentment of its controls over wages and prices. And there was only grudging acquiescence to its complicated system of rationing scarce consumer goods: coffee, sugar, meat, butter, canned goods, shoes, tires, gasoline, and fuel oil. Black-marketing and overcharging grew in proportions far beyond OPA policing capacity.

From 1941 to 1945, the federal government spent a total of $321 billion—twice as much as it had spent in the entire 150 years of its existence to that point, and ten times as much as the cost of World War I. The national debt rose from $49 billion in 1941 to $259 billion in 1945. The government borrowed about half the revenues it needed by selling $100 billion worth of bonds. Much of the rest it raised by radically increasing income tax rates, through the Revenue Act of 1942. To simplify collection, Congress enacted a withholding system of payroll deductions in 1943.

The search for an effective mechanism to mobilize the economy for war began as early as 1939 and continued for nearly four years. One failed agency after another attempted to bring order to the mobilization effort. Finally, in January 1942, the president responded to widespread criticism by creating the War Production Board (WPB), under the direction of former Sears Roebuck executive Donald Nelson. In theory, the WPB was to be a "superagency," with broad powers over the economy. In fact, it never had as much authority as its World War I equivalent, the War Industries Board.

Throughout its troubled history, therefore, the WPB found itself constantly outmaneuvered and frustrated. It was never able to win complete control over military purchases; the army and navy often circumvented the board entirely in negotiating contracts with producers. It was never able to satisfy the complaints of small business, which charged (correctly) that most contracts were going to large corporations. Gradually, the president transferred much of the WPB's authority to a new office located within the White House: the Office of War Mobilization (OWM). But the OWM was only slightly more successful than the WPB.

Despite the administrative problems, however, the war economy managed to meet almost all of the nation's critical war needs. By the beginning of 1944, American factories were, in fact, producing more than the government needed. Their output was twice that of all the Axis countries combined.

African-Americans and the War

During World War I, many African-Americans had eagerly seized the chance to serve in the armed forces, believing that their patriotic efforts would win them an enhanced position in postwar society. They had been cruelly disappointed. As World War II approached, blacks were again determined to use the conflict to improve the position of their race—this time, however, not by currying favor but by making demands.

In the summer of 1941, A. Philip Randolph, president of the Brotherhood of Sleeping Car Porters, an important black union, began to insist that the government require companies receiving defense contracts to integrate their work forces. To mobilize support for the demand, Randolph planned a massive march on Washington. Roosevelt finally persuaded Randolph to cancel the march in return for a promise to establish the Fair Employment Practices Commission (FEPC) to investigate discrimination against blacks in war industries. The FEPC's enforcement powers, and thus its effectiveness, were limited, but its creation was a rare symbolic victory for African-American demands of the government.

TRAINING AFRICAN-AMERICAN FIGHTER PILOTS Black air corps cadets receive advanced training in Tuskegee, Alabama, during World War II. African-American pilots were generally restricted to flying supply and support missions, but many fought for—and some won—the right to fly in combat as well.

The need for labor in war plants greatly increased the migration of blacks from the rural areas of the South into industrial cities. The migration bettered the economic condition of many African-Americans, but it also created urban tensions and occasionally violence. The most serious conflict occurred in Detroit in 1943, when racial friction in the city produced a major riot in which thirty-four people died, twenty-five of them blacks.

Despite such tensions, the leading black organizations redoubled their efforts during the war to challenge the system of segregation. The Congress of Racial Equality (CORE), organized in 1942, mobilized mass popular resistance to discrimination in a way that the older, more conservative organizations had never done. Randolph, Bayard Rustin, James Farmer, and other, younger black leaders helped organize sit-ins and demonstrations in segregated theaters and restaurants. Their defiant public spirit would survive into the 1950s and help produce the civil-rights movement.

Pressure for change was also growing within the military. At first, the armed forces maintained their traditional practice of limiting blacks to the most menial assignments, keeping them in segregated training camps and units, and barring them entirely from the Marine Corps and the army air forces. Gradually, however, military leaders were forced to make adjustments—in part because of public and political pressures, but also because they recognized that these forms of segregation were wasting manpower. By the end of the war, the number of black servicemen had increased sevenfold, to 700,000; some training camps were being at least partially integrated; blacks were being allowed to serve on ships with white sailors; and more black units were being sent into combat. But tensions remained. In some of the partially integrated army bases—Fort Dix, New Jersey, for example—riots occasionally broke out when blacks protested having to serve in segregated divisions. Substantial discrimination survived in all the services until well after the war. But within the military, as within society at large, the traditional pattern of race relations was slowly eroding.

Indians and the War

Approximately 25,000 Indians performed military service during World War II. Many Native Americans served in combat. Others (mostly Navajos) became "code-talkers," working in military communications and speaking their own language (which enemy forces would be unlikely to understand) over the radio and the telephones. The war had important effects on the Indians who served in the military. It brought them into intimate contact (often for the first time) with white society, and it awakened among some of them a taste for the material benefits of life in capitalist America that they would retain after the war. Some never returned to the reservations, but chose to remain in the non-Indian world and assimilate to its ways.

The war had important effects, too, on those Native Americans who stayed on the reservations. Little war work reached the tribes. Government subsidies dwindled. Talented young people left the reservations to serve in the military or work in war production, creating manpower shortages in some tribes. The wartime emphasis on national unity undermined support for the revitalization of tribal autonomy that the Indian Reorganization Act of 1934 had launched. New pressures emerged to eliminate the reservation system and require the tribes to assimilate into white society—pressures so severe that John Collier, the energetic director of the Bureau of Indian Affairs who had done so much to promote the reinvigoration of the reservations, resigned in 1945.

Mexican-American War Workers

Large numbers of Mexican workers entered the United States during the war in response to labor shortages on the Pacific coast and in the Southwest. The American and Mexican governments agreed in 1942 to a program by which *braceros* (contract laborers) would be admitted to the United States for a limited time to work at specific jobs, and American employers in some parts of the Southwest began actively recruiting Hispanic workers. During the Depression, many Mexican farm workers had been deported to make room for desperate white workers. The wartime labor shortage caused farm owners to begin hiring them again. More important, however, Mexicans were able for the first time to find significant numbers of factory jobs. They formed the second-largest group of migrants (after blacks) to American cities in the 1940s. They were concentrated mainly in the West, but there were significant Mexican communities in Chicago, Detroit, and other industrial cities in the Midwest and East.

The sudden expansion of Mexican-American neighborhoods created tensions and occasionally conflict in some American cities. White residents of Los Angeles became alarmed at the activities of Mexican-American teen-agers, many of whom were joining street gangs (*pachucos*). They were particularly distinctive because of their style of dress, which whites considered outrageous. They wore long, loose jackets with padded shoulders, baggy pants tied at the ankles, long watch chains, broad-brimmed hats, and greased, ducktail hair styles. The outfit was known as a "zoot suit."

In June 1943, animosity toward the "zoot-suiters" produced a four-day riot in Los Angeles, during which white sailors stationed at a base in Long Beach invaded Mexican-American communities and attacked "zoot-suiters" (in response to alleged attacks by them on servicemen). The police did little to restrain the sailors, who grabbed Hispanic teen-agers, tore off and burned their clothes, cut off their ducktails, and beat them. When Hispanics tried to fight back, the police moved in and arrested them. In the aftermath of the "zoot suit riots," Los Angeles passed a law prohibiting the wearing of zoot suits.

Women and Children in Wartime

The war drew increasing numbers of women into roles from which they had previously been largely barred, either by custom or law. The number of women in the work force increased by nearly 60 percent, as many women took industrial jobs to replace male workers serving in the military. And these wage-earning women were more likely to be married and were on the whole older than most of those who had entered the work force in the past.

But while economic and military necessity eroded some of the popular objections to women in the workplace, obstacles remained. Many factory owners continued to categorize jobs by gender, reserving the most lucrative positions for men. (Female work, like male work, was also categorized by race: black women were usually assigned more menial tasks, and paid at a lower rate, than their white counterparts.) Still, women did make important inroads in industrial employment during the war. Women had been working in industry for over a century, but some began now to take on heavy industrial jobs that had long been considered "men's work." The famous wartime image of "Rosie the Riveter" symbolized the new importance of the female industrial worker. Women joined unions in substantial numbers, and they helped erode at least some of the prejudice, including the prejudice against mothers working, that had previously kept many of them from paid employment.

In the end, however, most women workers during the war were employed not in factories but in service-sector jobs. Above all, they worked for the government, whose bureaucratic needs expanded dramatically alongside its military and industrial needs. Even within the military, which enlisted substantial numbers of women as WAACs (army) and WAVEs (navy), most female work was clerical.

The new opportunities produced new problems. Many mothers whose husbands were in the military had to combine working with caring for their children. The scarcity of child-care facilities or other community services meant that some women had no choice but to leave young children—often known as "latch-key children" or "eight-hour orphans"—at home alone (or sometimes locked in cars in factory parking lots) while they worked.

Perhaps in part because of the family dislocations the war produced, juvenile crime rose markedly in the war years. Young boys were arrested at rapidly increasing rates for car theft and other burglary, vandalism, and vagrancy. The arrest rate for prostitutes, many of whom were teen-age girls, rose too, as did the incidence of venereal disease. For many children, however, the distinctive experience of the war years was not crime but work. More than a third of all teen-agers between the ages of fourteen and eighteen were employed late in the war, causing some reduction in high-school enrollments.

The return of prosperity helped increase the marriage rate and lower the age at which people married, but many marriages were unable to survive the pressures of wartime separation. The divorce rate rose rapidly. The rise

A M E R I C A N V O I C E S

SARAH KILLINGSWORTH

An African-American Woman Encounters the Wartime Industrial Boom

THE WAR STARTED and jobs kinda opened up for women that the men had. . . . They started takin' applications at Douglas, to work in a defense plant. I was hired.

I didn't want a job on the production line. I heard so many things about accidents. . . . I was frightened. All I wanted to do was get in the factory, because they were payin' more than what I'd been makin'. . . . I got the job workin' nights in the ladies' rest room, which wasn't hard. . . .

I do know one thing, this place was very segregated when I first come here. Oh, Los Angeles, you just couldn't go and sit down like you do now. You had certain places you went. You had to more or less stick to the restaurants and hotels where black people were. It wasn't until the war that it really opened up. 'Cause when I come out here it was awful, just like bein' in the South. . . .

For a person that grew up and knew nothin' but hard times to get out on my own at eighteen years old and make a decent livin' and still make a decent person outa myself, I really am proud of me. . . .

In ways it was too bad that so many lives were lost. But I think it was for a worthy cause, because it did make a way for us. And we were able to really get out.

SOURCE: Studs Terkel, *The Good War*, pp. 113–116. Copyright ©1984 by Studs Terkel. Reprinted by permission of Pantheon Books.

in the birth rate that accompanied the increase in marriages was the first sign of what would become the great postwar "baby boom."

The Internment of the Japanese-Americans

During World War I, popular prejudice against the German people—and against German-Americans—had run high. No such passions emerged against Germans, Italians, or Americans of German and Italian descent during World War II. The same could not be said, however, about the Japanese. After the attack on Pearl Harbor, government propaganda and popular culture combined to create an image of the Japanese as a devious, malign, and savage people.

Predictably, this racial animosity soon extended to Americans of Japanese descent. There were not many Japanese-Americans in the United States—only about 127,000, most of them concentrated in a few areas in

REGISTERING FOR INTERNMENT, 1942 Japanese-Americans, forcibly removed from their homes by military authorities on the West Coast, wait in line to sign up for an internment that would continue until the last days of World War II. Many were American citizens.

California. About a third of them were unnaturalized, first-generation immigrants (Issei); two-thirds were naturalized or native-born citizens of the United States (Nisei). Because they generally kept to themselves and preserved traditional Japanese cultural patterns, it was possible for others to imagine that the Japanese-Americans were engaged in conspiracies on behalf of their ancestral homeland. (There is no evidence to suggest that they actually were.) Public pressure to remove the "threat" grew steadily.

Finally, in February 1942, in response to pressure from military officials and political leaders on the West Coast and recommendations from the War Department, the president authorized the army to "intern" the Japanese-Americans. More than 100,000 people (Issei and Nisei alike) were rounded up, told to dispose of their property however they could (which often meant simply abandoning it), and taken to what the government euphemistically termed "relocation centers" in the "interior." In fact, they were facilities little different from prisons, many of them located in the Western mountains and desert. Conditions in the internment camps were not brutal, but they were harsh and uncomfortable. More important, loyal, hard-working Americans were forced to spend up to three years in grim, debilitating isolation, barred from lucrative employment, provided with only minimal medical care, and deprived of decent schools for their children. (In Hawaii, by contrast, residents of Japanese descent encountered little harassment, perhaps because they were more numerous and more crucial to the economy of the islands.) The Supreme Court upheld the evacuation in a 1944 decision; and although most of the Japanese-Americans were released later that year, they were largely unable to win any compensation for their losses until Congress finally acted to redress the wrongs in the late 1980s.

The Retreat from Reform

Late in 1943, Franklin Roosevelt publicly suggested that "Dr. New Deal," as he called it, had served its purpose and should now give way to "Dr. Win-the-War." The statement reflected the president's own genuine shift in concern: victory was now more important than reform. But it reflected, too, the political reality that had emerged during the first two years of war. Liberals in government were finding themselves unable to enact new programs. They were even finding it difficult to protect existing ones from conservative assault.

The greatest assault on New Deal reforms came from conservatives in Congress, who seized on the war as an excuse to do what many had wanted to do in peacetime: dismantle many of the achievements of the New Deal. They were assisted by the end of mass unemployment, which decreased the need for such relief programs as the Civilian Conservation Corps and the Works Progress Administration (both of which were abolished). They were assisted, too, by their own increasing numbers. In the congressional elections of 1942, Republicans gained 47 seats in the House and 10 in the Senate.

Republicans approached the 1944 election determined to exploit what they believed was resentment of wartime regimentation and unhappiness with Democratic reform. They nominated as their candidate the young and vigorous governor of New York, Thomas E. Dewey. Roosevelt was unopposed within his party; but Democratic leaders pressured him to abandon Vice President Henry Wallace, an advanced New Dealer and hero of the CIO, and replace him with a more moderate figure. Roosevelt reluctantly acquiesced in the selection of Senator Harry S. Truman of Missouri, who had won acclaim as chairman of the Senate War Investigating Committee (known as the Truman Committee), which had compiled an impressive record uncovering waste and corruption in wartime production.

The conduct of the war was not an issue in the campaign. Instead, the election revolved around domestic economic issues and, indirectly, the president's health. The president was, in fact, gravely ill, suffering from, among other things, arteriosclerosis. It is not too much to say that he was dying. But the campaign seemed momentarily to revive him. He made several strenuous public appearances late in October, which dispelled popular doubts about his health and ensured his reelection. He captured 53.5 percent of the popular vote to Dewey's 46 percent (the lowest percentage of his four campaigns); and he won 432 electoral votes to Dewey's 99. Democrats lost 1 seat in the Senate, gained 20 in the House, and maintained control of both.

THE DEFEAT OF THE AXIS

By the middle of 1943, America and its allies had succeeded in stopping the Axis advance both in Europe and in the Pacific. In the next two years, the Allies themselves seized the offensive and launched a series of powerful drives that rapidly led the way to victory.

The Liberation of France

By early 1944, American and British bombers were attacking German industrial installations and other targets almost around the clock, drastically cutting production and impeding transportation. Especially devastating was the massive bombing of such German cities as Leipzig, Dresden, and Berlin. A February 1945 incendiary raid on Dresden created a great

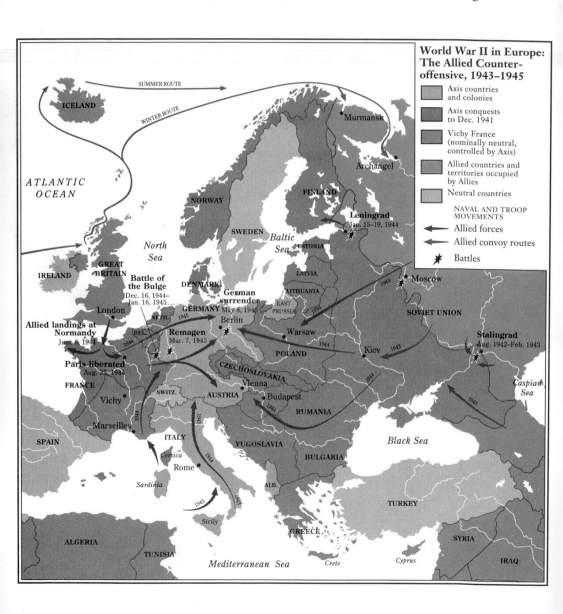

D-DAY, 1944 American infantry troops wade ashore along the beaches of Normandy, June 6, 1944, to begin the great Allied invasion of France— one of the principal turning points of the war in Europe.

firestorm that destroyed three-fourths of the previously undamaged city and killed approximately 135,000 people, almost all civilians. The morality of such attacks has been much debated in the years since the war; but at the time, few Americans questioned the claims of military leaders that the bombing cleared the way for the great Allied invasion of France in the late spring.

An enormous offensive force had been gathering in England for two years: almost 3 million troops, and perhaps the greatest array of naval vessels and armaments ever assembled in one place. On the morning of June 6, 1944, this vast invasion force moved into action. The landing came not at the narrowest part of the English Channel, where the Germans had expected and prepared for it, but along sixty miles of the Cotentin Peninsula on the coast of Normandy. While airplanes and battleships offshore bombarded the Nazi defenses, 4,000 vessels landed troops and supplies on the beaches. (Three divisions of paratroopers had been dropped behind the German lines the night before.) Fighting was intense along the beach, but the superior manpower and equipment of the Allied forces gradually prevailed. Within a week, the German forces had been dislodged from virtually the entire Normandy coast.

For the next month, further progress remained slow. But in late July in the Battle of Saint-Lô, General Omar Bradley's First Army smashed through the German lines. George S. Patton's Third Army, spearheaded by heavy tank attacks, then moved through the hole Bradley had created and began a drive into the heart of France. On August 25, Free French forces arrived in Paris and liberated the city from four years of German occupation. By mid-September the Allied armies had driven the Germans almost entirely out of France and Belgium.

The great Allied drive came to a halt, however, at the Rhine River against a firm line of Nazi defenses. In mid-December, German forces struck in desperation along fifty miles of front in the Ardennes Forest. In the Battle of the Bulge (named for a large bulge that appeared in the American lines as the Germans pressed forward), they drove fifty-five miles toward Antwerp before they were finally stopped at Bastogne. It was the last major battle on the western front.

While the Allies were fighting their way through France, Soviet forces were sweeping westward into central Europe and the Balkans. In late January 1945, the Russians launched a great offensive toward the Oder River inside Germany. By early spring, they were ready to launch a final assault against Berlin. General Omar Bradley, in the meantime, was pushing toward the Rhine from the west. Early in March, his forces captured the city of Cologne, on the river's west bank. The next day, he discovered and seized an undamaged bridge over the river at Remagen; Allied troops were soon pouring across the Rhine. In the following weeks the British commander, Montgomery, with a million troops, pushed into Germany in the north while Bradley's army, sweeping through central Germany, completed the encirclement of 300,000 German soldiers in the Ruhr.

The German resistance was now broken on both fronts. American forces were moving eastward faster than they had anticipated and could have beaten the Russians to Berlin and Prague. The American and British high commands decided, instead, to halt the advance along the Elbe River in central Germany to await the Russians. That decision enabled the Soviets to occupy eastern Germany and Czechoslovakia.

On April 30, with Soviet forces on the outskirts of Berlin, Adolf Hitler killed himself in his bunker in the capital. And on May 8, 1945, the remaining German forces surrendered unconditionally. V-E (Victory in Europe) Day prompted great celebrations in western Europe and in the United States, tempered by the knowledge of the continuing war against Japan.

The Pacific Offensive

In February 1944, American naval forces under Admiral Chester Nimitz won a series of victories in the Marshall Islands and cracked the outer perimeter of the Japanese Empire. Within a month, the navy had destroyed other vital Japanese bastions. American submarines, in the meantime, were decimating Japanese shipping and crippling Japan's domestic economy.

A more frustrating struggle was in progress in the meantime on the Asian mainland. In 1942, the Japanese had forced General Joseph H. Stilwell of the United States out of Burma and had moved their own troops as far west as the mountains bordering on India. For a time, Stilwell supplied the isolated Chinese forces still fighting Japan with an aerial ferry over the Himalayas. In 1943, finally, he led Chinese, Indian, and a few American troops back through northern Burma, constructing a road and pipeline across the mountains into China (the Burma Road, also known as the Ledo Road or Stilwell Road); the road opened in the fall of 1944.

By then, however, the Japanese had launched a major counteroffensive and had driven so deep into the Chinese interior that they threatened the terminus of the Burma Road and the center of Chinese government at Chungking. The Japanese offensive precipitated a long-simmering feud between General Stilwell and Premier Chiang Kai-shek of China. Stilwell was indignant because Chiang was using many of his troops to maintain an armed frontier against the Chinese communists and would not deploy those troops against the Japanese.

The decisive battles of the war against Japan, however, occurred in the Pacific. In mid-June 1944, an enormous American armada struck the heavily fortified Mariana Islands and, after some of the bloodiest operations of the war, captured Tinian, Guam, and Saipan, 1,350 miles from Tokyo. In September, American forces landed on the western Carolines. And on October 20, General MacArthur's troops landed on Leyte Island in the Philippines. The Japanese now employed virtually their entire fleet against the Allied invaders in three major encounters—which together constituted the decisive Battle of Leyte Gulf, the largest naval engagement in history. American forces held off the Japanese onslaught and sank four Japanese carriers, all but destroying Japan's capacity to continue a serious naval war.

Nevertheless, as American forces advanced closer to the Japanese mainland early in 1945, the imperial forces seemed only to increase their resistance. In February 1945, American marines seized the tiny volcanic island of Iwo Jima, only 750 miles from Tokyo, but only after the costliest battle in the history of the Marine Corps.

The battle for Okinawa, an island only 370 miles south of Japan, was further evidence of the strength of the Japanese resistance in these last desperate days. Week after week, the Japanese sent *Kamikaze* (suicide) planes against American and British ships, sacrificing 3,500 of them while inflicting great damage. Japanese troops on shore launched desperate nighttime attacks on the American lines. The United States and its allies suffered nearly 50,000 casualties before finally capturing Okinawa in late June 1945. Over 100,000 Japanese died in the siege.

It seemed that the same kind of bitter fighting would await the Americans when they invaded Japan. But there were signs early in 1945 that such an invasion might not be necessary. The Japanese had almost no ships or planes left with which to fight. The firebombing of Tokyo in May, in which American bombers dropped napalm on the city and created a firestorm in which over 80,000 people died, further weakened the Japanese will to resist. Moderate Japanese leaders, who had long since concluded the war was lost, were increasing their power within the government and were looking for ways to bring the fighting to an end, although they continued to face powerful opposition from military leaders. Whether the moderates could ultimately have prevailed is a question about which historians and others continue to disagree. In any case, their efforts became superfluous in mid-July 1945, when American scientists successfully tested the world's first atomic weapon.

The Manhattan Project and Atomic Warfare

Reports had reached the United States in 1939 that Nazi scientists had taken the first step toward the creation of an atomic bomb, a weapon more powerful than any ever previously devised. The United States and Britain immediately began a race to develop the weapon before the Germans did.

Over the next three years, the government secretly poured nearly $2 billion into the so-called Manhattan Project—a massive scientific effort conducted at hidden laboratories in Oak Ridge, Tennessee; Los Alamos, New Mexico; and other sites. (Its name had emerged earlier, when many of the atomic physicists had been working at Columbia University in New York.) The scientists pushed ahead much faster than anyone had predicted. Even so, the war in Europe ended before they were ready to test the first bomb. Just before dawn on July 16, 1945, in the desert near Alamogordo,

New Mexico, the scientists gathered to witness the first atomic explosion in history: a blinding flash of light brighter than any ever seen on earth, and a huge, billowing mushroom cloud.

News of the explosion reached President Harry S. Truman (who had taken office in April on the death of Roosevelt) in Potsdam, Germany, where he was attending a conference of Allied leaders. He issued an ultimatum to the Japanese (signed jointly by the British) demanding that they surrender by August 3 or face utter devastation. When the Japanese failed to meet the deadline, Truman ordered the air force to use the new atomic weapons against Japan.

Controversy has continued for decades over whether Truman's decision to use the bomb was justified and what his motives were. Some have argued that the atomic attack was unnecessary—that had the United States agreed to the survival of the emperor (which it ultimately did agree to in any case), or had it waited only a few more weeks, the Japanese would have surrendered. Others argue that nothing less than the atomic bombs could have persuaded the Japanese to surrender without a costly American invasion. Some critics of the decision, including some of the scientists involved in the

HIROSHIMA AFTER THE BOMB Where once a bustling city stood, only rubble remains. This photograph shows the center of Hiroshima shortly after it was devastated by the first of two atomic bombs the United States dropped on Japan in the last days of World War II.

Manhattan Project, have argued that whatever the Japanese intentions, the United States, as a matter of morality, should not have used the terrible new weapon.

The nation's military and political leaders, however, showed little concern about such matters. Truman, who had not even known of the existence of the Manhattan Project until he became president, was, apparently, making what he believed to be a simple military decision. A weapon was available that would end the war quickly; he could see no reason not to use it.

On August 6, 1945, an American B-29, the *Enola Gay*, dropped an atomic weapon on the Japanese industrial center at Hiroshima. With a single bomb, the United States completely incinerated a four-square-mile area at the center of the previously undamaged city. More than 80,000 civilians died, according to later American estimates. Many more survived to suffer the crippling effects of radioactive fallout or to pass those effects on to their children in the form of birth defects.

The Japanese government, stunned by the attack, was at first unable to agree on a response. Two days later, on August 8, the Soviet Union declared war on Japan. And the following day, another American plane dropped another atomic weapon—this time on the city of Nagasaki—inflicting 100,000 deaths and horrible damage on yet another unfortunate community. Finally, the emperor intervened to break the stalemate in the cabinet; and on August 14, the government announced that it was ready to give up. On September 2, 1945, on board the American battleship *Missouri*, anchored in Tokyo Bay, Japanese officials signed the articles of surrender.

The greatest war in the history of mankind had come to an end, and the United States had emerged from it not only victorious but in a position of unprecedented power, influence, and prestige. It was a victory, however, that few could greet with unambiguous joy. Fourteen million combatants had died in the struggle. Many more civilians had perished. The United States had suffered only light casualties in comparison with some other nations, but the cost had still been high: 322,000 dead, another 800,000 injured. And despite the sacrifices, the world continued to face an uncertain future, menaced by the threat of nuclear warfare and by an emerging antagonism between the world's two strongest nations—the United States and the Soviet Union—that would darken the peace for many decades to come.

CHAPTER TWENTY-NINE

America and the Cold War

VEN BEFORE World War II ended, there were signs of tension between the United States and the Soviet Union. Once the hostilities were over, those tensions quickly grew to create what became known as a "Cold War" between the two former allies that would cast its shadow over international affairs for decades. The Cold War also had profound effects on American domestic life, ultimately producing the most corrosive outbreak of antiradical hysteria of the century. America in the postwar years was both powerful and prosperous, but it was also for a time troubled and uncertain about its future.

ORIGINS OF THE COLD WAR

No issue in twentieth-century American history has aroused more debate than the question of the origins of the Cold War. Some have claimed that Soviet duplicity and expansionism created the international tensions, others that American provocations and imperial ambitions were at least equally to blame. Most historians agree, however, that wherever the preponderance of blame may lie, both the United States and the Soviet Union contributed to the atmosphere of hostility and suspicion that quickly clouded the peace.

Sources of Soviet-American Tension

The wartime alliance between the United States and the Soviet Union was an aberration from the normal tenor of Soviet-American relations, for the two nations had long viewed each other with deep mutual mistrust. At the heart of their differences in the 1940s, however, was a fundamental difference in the ways the great powers envisioned the postwar world. One vision was that of many people in the United States. First openly outlined in the Atlantic Charter in 1941, it was a vision of a world in which nations abandoned their traditional belief in military alliances and spheres of influence and governed their relations with one another through democratic processes, with an international organization serving as the arbiter of disputes and the protector of every nation's right of self-determination.

The other vision was that of the Soviet Union and to some extent, it gradually became clear, of Great Britain. Both Stalin and Churchill had signed the Atlantic Charter. But Britain had always been uneasy about the implications of the self-determination ideal for its own enormous empire. And the Soviet Union was determined to create a secure sphere for itself in Central and Eastern Europe as protection against possible future aggression from the West. Both Churchill and Stalin, therefore, tended to envision a postwar structure in which the great powers would control areas of strategic interest to them, in which something vaguely similar to the traditional European balance of power would reemerge.

By the end of the war Roosevelt was able to win at least the partial consent of Winston Churchill to his principles; but although he believed at times that Stalin would similarly relent, he never managed to steer the Soviets from their determination to control Central and Eastern Europe and from their vision of a postwar order in which each of the great powers would dominate its own sphere. Gradually, the differences between these two positions would turn the peacemaking process into a form of warfare.

Wartime Diplomacy

Serious strains began to develop in the alliance with the Soviet Union as early as 1942, a result of Stalin's irritation at delays in opening the second front and his resentment of the Anglo-American decision to invade North Africa before Europe. In this deteriorating atmosphere, Roosevelt and Churchill met in Casablanca, Morocco, in January 1943 to discuss Allied strategy. (Stalin had declined Roosevelt's invitation to attend.) The two leaders could not accept Stalin's most important demand—the immediate opening of a second front. But they tried to reassure Stalin by announcing that they would accept nothing less than the unconditional surrender of the Axis powers. It was a signal that the Americans and British would not negotiate a separate peace with Hitler and leave the Soviets to fight on alone.

In November 1943, Roosevelt and Churchill traveled to Teheran, Iran, for their first meeting with Stalin. By now, however, Roosevelt's most effective bargaining tool—Stalin's need for American assistance in his struggle against Germany—had been largely removed. The German advance against Russia had been halted; Soviet forces were now launching their own westward offensive. Meanwhile, new tensions had emerged in the alliance as a result of the refusal by the British and Americans to allow any Soviet participation in the creation of a new Italian government following the fall of Mussolini. To Stalin, at least, the American vision of an "open world" already seemed to be a double standard: America and Britain expected to have a voice in the future of Eastern Europe, but the Soviet Union was to have no voice in the future of the West.

Nevertheless, the Teheran Conference seemed in most respects a success. Roosevelt and Stalin established a cordial personal relationship. Stalin agreed to an American request that the Soviet Union enter the war in the Pacific soon after the end of hostilities in Europe. Roosevelt, in turn, promised that an Anglo-American second front would be established within six months. All three leaders agreed in principle to a postwar international organization and to efforts to prevent a resurgence of German expansionism.

On other matters, however, the origins of future disagreements were already visible. Most important was the question of the future of Poland. Roosevelt and Churchill were willing to agree to a movement of the Soviet border westward, allowing Stalin to annex some historically Polish territory. But on the nature of the postwar government in the portion of Poland that would remain independent, there were sharp differences. Roosevelt and Churchill supported the claims of the Polish government-in-exile that had been functioning in London since 1940; Stalin wished to install another, procommunist exiled government that had spent the war in Lublin, in the Soviet Union. The three leaders avoided a bitter conclusion to the Teheran Conference only by leaving the issue unresolved.

Yalta

For more than a year after Teheran, the Grand Alliance among the United States, Britain, and the Soviet Union alternated between high tension and warm amicability. In the fall of 1944, Churchill flew by himself to Moscow for a meeting with Stalin to resolve issues arising from a civil war in Greece. In return for a Soviet agreement to cease assisting Greek communists, who were challenging the British-supported monarchical government, Churchill consented to a proposal whereby control of Eastern Europe would be divided between Britain and the Soviet Union. To Roosevelt, however, the Moscow agreement was evidence of how little the Atlantic Charter principles seemed to mean to his two most important allies.

In February 1945, Roosevelt joined Churchill and Stalin for a great peace conference in the Soviet city of Yalta. On a number of issues, the Big Three reached mutually satisfactory agreements. In return for Stalin's renewed promise to enter the Pacific war, Roosevelt agreed that the Soviet Union should receive the Kurile Islands north of Japan; should regain southern Sakhalin Island and Port Arthur, both of which Russia had lost in the 1904 Russo-Japanese War; and could exercise some influence (along with the government of China) in Manchuria. The negotiators also agreed to accept a plan for a new international organization, a plan that had been hammered out the previous summer at a conference in Washington, D.C., at the Dumbarton Oaks estate. The new United Nations would contain a General Assembly, in which every member would be represented, and a Security Council, with permanent representatives of the five major powers (the United States, Britain, France, the Soviet Union, and China), each of which would have veto power, and temporary delegates from several other nations. These agreements became the basis of the United Nations charter, drafted at a conference of fifty nations beginning April 25, 1945, in San Francisco. The United States Senate ratified the charter in July by a vote of 80 to 2 (a striking contrast to the slow and painful defeat it had administered to the charter of the League of Nations twenty-five years before).

On other issues, however, the Yalta Conference either left fundamental differences unresolved or papered them over with weak and unstable compromises. Basic disagreement remained about the postwar Polish government. Stalin, whose armies now occupied Poland, had already installed a government composed of the procommunist "Lublin" Poles. Roosevelt and Churchill insisted that the pro-Western "London" Poles must be allowed a place in the Warsaw regime. Roosevelt envisioned a government based on free, democratic elections—which both he and Stalin recognized the pro-Western forces would win. Stalin agreed only to a vague compromise by which an unspecified number of pro-Western Poles would be granted a place in the government. He reluctantly consented to hold "free and unfettered elections" in Poland, but he made no commitment to a date for them. They did not take place for more than forty years.

Nor was there agreement about the future of Germany. Stalin wanted to impose $20 billion in reparations on the Germans, of which Russia would receive half. Roosevelt and Churchill agreed only to leave final settlement of the issue to a future reparations commission. A more important difference was in the way the leaders envisioned postwar German politics and society. Roosevelt seemed to want a reconstructed and reunited Germany—one that would be permitted to develop a prosperous, modern economy while remaining under the careful supervision of the Allies. Stalin wanted a permanent dismemberment of Germany. The final agreement was, like the Polish accord, vague and unstable. The United States, Great Britain, France, and the Soviet Union would each control its own "zone of occupation" in Germany—the zones to be determined by the position of troops at the end of the war. Berlin, the German capital, was already well inside the Soviet zone, but because of its symbolic importance it would itself be divided into four sectors, one for each nation to occupy. At an unspecified date, the nation would be reunited; but there was no agreement on how the reunification would occur. As for the rest of Europe, the conference produced a murky accord on the establishment of interim governments "broadly representative of all democratic elements." They would be replaced ultimately by permanent governments "responsible to the will of the people" and created through free elections. Once again, no specific provisions or timetables accompanied the agreements.

The Yalta accords, in other words, were less a settlement of postwar issues than a set of loose principles that sidestepped the most divisive issues. Roosevelt, Churchill, and Stalin returned home from the conference each apparently convinced that he had signed an important agreement. But the Soviet interpretation of the accords differed so sharply from the Anglo-American interpretation that the illusion endured only briefly. In the weeks following the Yalta Conference, Roosevelt watched with growing alarm as the Soviet Union moved systematically to establish procommunist governments in one Central and Eastern European nation after another and as Stalin refused to make the changes in Poland that the president believed he had promised.

But Roosevelt did not abandon hope. Still believing the differences could be settled, he left Washington early in the spring for a vacation at his retreat in Warm Springs, Georgia. There, on April 12, 1945, he suffered a sudden, massive stroke and died.

THE COLLAPSE OF THE PEACE

Harry S. Truman, who succeeded Roosevelt in the presidency, had almost no familiarity with international issues. Nor did he share Roosevelt's faith in the flexibility of the Soviet Union. Roosevelt had believed that Stalin was, essentially, a reasonable man with whom an ultimate accord could be reached. Truman, in contrast, sided with those in the government (and there were many) who considered the Soviet Union fundamentally untrustworthy and viewed Stalin himself with suspicion and even loathing.

The Failure of Potsdam

Truman had been in office only a few days before he decided to "get tough" with the Soviet Union. Stalin had made what the new president considered solemn agreements with the United States at Yalta. The United States would insist that he honor them. Dismissing the advice of Secretary of War Stimson that the Polish question was a lost cause and not worth a world crisis, Truman met on April 23 with Soviet Foreign Minister Molotov and sharply chastised him for violations of the Yalta accords.

In fact, Truman had only limited leverage by which to compel the Soviet Union to carry out its agreements. Russian forces already occupied Poland and much of the rest of Central and Eastern Europe. Germany was already divided among the conquering nations. The United States was still engaged in a war in the Pacific and was neither able nor willing to enter in a second conflict in Europe. Truman insisted that the United States should be able to get "85 percent" of what it wanted, but he was ultimately forced to settle for much less.

He conceded first on Poland. When Stalin made a few minor concessions to the pro-Western exiles, Truman recognized the Warsaw government, hoping that noncommunist forces might gradually expand their influence there. Until the 1980s, they did not. Other questions remained, above all the question of Germany. To settle them, Truman met in July at Potsdam, in Russian-occupied Germany, with Churchill (who was replaced as prime minister by Clement Attlee in the midst of the negotiations) and Stalin. Truman reluctantly accepted adjustments of the Polish-German border that Stalin had long demanded; he refused, however, to permit the Russians to claim any reparations from the American, French, and British zones of Germany. The result, in effect, was to confirm that

Germany would remain divided, with the western zones united into one nation, friendly to the United States, and the Russian zone surviving as another nation, with a pro-Soviet, communist government. Soon, the Soviet Union was siphoning between $1.5 and $3 billion a year out of its zone of occupation.

The China Problem

Central to American hopes for an open, peaceful world "policed" by the great powers was a strong, independent China. But even before the war ended, the American government was aware that those hopes faced a major, perhaps insurmountable obstacle: the Chinese government of Chiang Kai-shek. Chiang was generally friendly to the United States, but he had few other virtues. His government was corrupt and incompetent. His popular legitimacy was feeble. And Chiang himself lived in a world of almost surreal isolation, unable or unwilling to face the problems that were threatening to engulf him. Ever since 1927, the nationalist government he headed had been engaged in a prolonged and bitter rivalry with the communist armies of Mao Zedong. So successful had the communist challenge grown that Mao was in control of one-fourth of the population by 1945.

At Potsdam, Truman had managed to persuade Stalin to recognize Chiang as the legitimate ruler of China; but Chiang was rapidly losing his grip on his country. Some Americans urged the government to try to find a "third force" to support as an alternative to either Chiang or Mao. A few argued that America should try to reach some accommodation with Mao. Truman, however, decided reluctantly that he had no choice but to continue supporting Chiang. For the next several years, as the long struggle between the nationalists and the communists erupted into a full-scale civil war, the United States continued to pump money and weapons to Chiang, even as it was becoming clear his cause was lost. But Truman was not prepared to intervene militarily to save the nationalist regime.

Instead, the American government was beginning to consider an alternative to China as the strong, pro-Western force in Asia: a revived Japan. Abandoning the restrictive occupation policies of the first years after the war (when General Douglas MacArthur had governed the nation), the United States lifted all restrictions on industrial development and encouraged rapid economic growth in Japan. The vision of an open, united Asia had been replaced, as in Europe, with an acceptance of the necessity of developing a strong, pro-American sphere of influence.

The Containment Doctrine

By the end of 1945, the Grand Alliance was a shambles, and with it any realistic hope of a postwar world constructed according to the Atlantic Charter ideals Roosevelt and others had supported. Instead, a new American policy was slowly emerging. Rather than attempting to create a unified, "open" world, the West would work to "contain" the threat of further Soviet expansion. The United States would be the leading force in that effort.

The new doctrine emerged in part as a response to events in Europe in 1946. In Turkey, Stalin was trying to win some control over the vital sea lanes to the Mediterranean. In Greece, communist forces were again threatening the pro-Western government; the British had announced they could no longer provide assistance. Faced with these challenges, Truman decided to enunciate a firm new policy. In doing so, he drew from the ideas of the influential American diplomat George F. Kennan, who warned that in the Soviet Union the United States faced "a political force committed fanatically to the belief that with the U.S. there can be no permanent *modus vivendi*," and that the only answer was "a long-term, patient but firm and vigilant containment of Russian expansive tendencies." On March 12, 1947, Truman appeared before Congress and used Kennan's warnings as the basis of what became known as the Truman Doctrine. "I believe," he argued, "that it must be the policy of the United States to support free peoples who are resisting attempted subjugation by armed minorities or by outside pressures." In the same speech he requested $400 million—part of it to bolster the armed forces of Greece and Turkey, another part to provide economic assistance to Greece. Congress quickly approved the measure.

The American commitment ultimately helped ease Soviet pressure on Turkey and helped the Greek government defeat the communist insurgents. More important, it established a basis for American foreign policy that would survive for more than thirty years. On the one hand, the Truman Doctrine was a way of accommodating the status quo: it accepted that there was no immediate likelihood of overturning the communist governments Stalin had established in Eastern Europe. On the other hand, it was a strategy for the future: communism was an innately expansionist force, and it must be contained within its present boundaries.

The Marshall Plan

An integral part of the containment policy was a proposal to aid in the economic reconstruction of Western Europe. There were many motives:

humanitarian concern for the European people; a fear that Europe would remain an economic drain on the United States if it could not quickly rebuild and begin to feed itself; a desire for a strong European market for American goods. But above all, American policymakers believed that unless something could be done to strengthen the shaky pro-American governments in Western Europe, those governments might fall under the control of rapidly growing domestic communist parties.

In June 1947, therefore, Secretary of State George C. Marshall announced a plan to provide economic assistance to all European nations (including the Soviet Union) that would join in drafting a program for recovery. Although Russia and its Eastern satellites quickly and predictably rejected the plan, sixteen Western European nations eagerly participated. Whatever domestic opposition there was in the United States largely vanished after a sudden coup in Czechoslovakia in February 1948 that established a Soviet-dominated communist government there. In April, Congress approved the creation of the Economic Cooperation Administration, the agency that would administer the Marshall Plan, as it became known. And over the next three years, the Marshall Plan channeled over $12 billion of American aid into Europe, helping to spark a substantial economic revival. By the end of 1950, European industrial production had risen 64 percent, communist strength in the member nations was declining, and opportunities for American trade had revived.

Mobilization at Home

That the United States had fully accepted a continuing commitment to the containment policy became clear in 1947 and 1948 through a series of measures designed to maintain American military power at near wartime levels. In 1948, at the president's request, Congress approved a new military draft and revived the Selective Service System. In the meantime, the United States, having failed to reach agreement with the Soviet Union on international control of nuclear weapons, redoubled its own efforts in atomic research, elevating nuclear weaponry to a central place in its military arsenal. The Atomic Energy Commission, established in 1946, became the supervisory body charged with overseeing all nuclear research, civilian and military alike.

Particularly important was the National Security Act of 1947, which created several instruments of foreign policy. A new Department of Defense would oversee all branches of the armed services, combining functions previously performed by the War and Navy departments. A National Security Council (NSC), operating out of the White House, would govern foreign and military policy. A Central Intelligence Agency (CIA) would be responsible for collecting information through both open and covert methods and, as the Cold War continued, for engaging secretly in political and military operations on behalf of American goals. The National Security Act, in other words, gave the president expanded powers with which to pursue the nation's international goals. It centralized in the White House control that had once been widely dispersed; it enabled the president to take

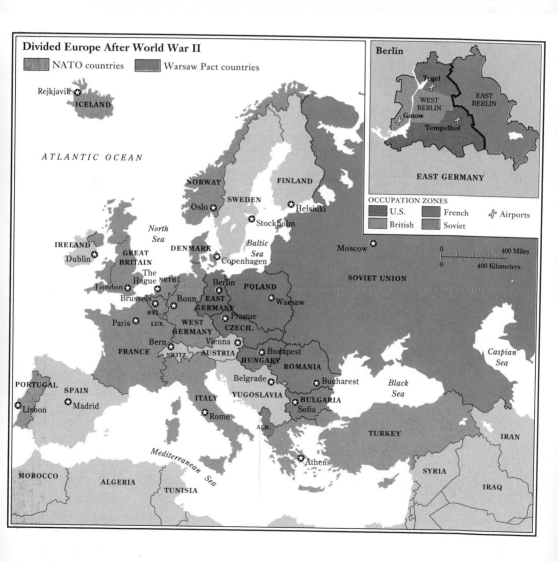

Divided Europe After World War II

NATO countries   Warsaw Pact countries

Berlin

Togel

WEST BERLIN   EAST BERLIN

Gatow

Tempelhof

EAST GERMANY

OCCUPATION ZONES

U.S.   French   ✠ Airports

British   Soviet

Rejkjavik

ICELAND

ATLANTIC OCEAN

NORWAY   FINLAND

SWEDEN

Oslo   Helsinki

Stockholm

North Sea

Baltic Sea

Moscow

IRELAND   DENMARK

Dublin   GREAT BRITAIN   Copenhagen

The Hague NETH.   SOVIET UNION

London   Berlin   POLAND

Brussels   Bonn   EAST GERMANY   Warsaw

BEL.   Prague

Paris   LUX.   WEST   CZECH.

GERMANY

Bern   Vienna

FRANCE   SWITZ.   AUSTRIA   Budapest

HUNGARY   ROMANIA

Belgrade   Bucharest   Black Sea

PORTUGAL   SPAIN   ITALY   YUGOSLAVIA   BULGARIA

Lisbon   Madrid   Rome   Sofia

ALB.   TURKEY   IRAN

Mediterranean Sea   Athens

MOROCCO   ALGERIA   TUNISIA   SYRIA   IRAQ

Caspian Sea

0   400 Miles

0   400 Kilometers

warlike actions without an open declaration of war; and it created vehicles by which the government could at times act politically and militarily overseas behind a veil of secrecy.

The Road to NATO

At about the same time, the United States was moving to strengthen the military capabilities of Western Europe. Convinced that a reconstructed Germany was essential to the hopes of the West, Truman reached an agreement with England and France to merge the three western zones of occupation into a new West German republic (which would include the American, British, and French sectors of Berlin, even though that city lay well within the Soviet zone). Stalin responded quickly. On June 24, 1948, he imposed a tight blockade around the western sectors of Berlin. If Germany was to be officially divided, he was implying, then the country's Western government would have to abandon its outpost in the heart of the Soviet-controlled eastern zone. Truman refused to do so. Unwilling to risk war through a military response to the blockade, he ordered a massive airlift to supply the city with food, fuel, and supplies. The airlift continued for more than ten months, transporting nearly 2.5 million tons of material, keeping a city of 2 million people alive, and transforming West Berlin into a symbol of the West's resolve to resist communist expansion. In the spring of 1949, Stalin lifted the now ineffective blockade. And in October, the division of Germany into two nations— the Federal Republic in the west and the Democratic Republic in the East—became official.

The crisis in Berlin accelerated the consolidation of what was already in effect an alliance among the United States and the countries of Western Europe. On April 4, 1949, twelve nations signed an agreement establishing the North Atlantic Treaty Organization (NATO) and declaring that an armed attack against one member would be considered an attack against all. The NATO countries would, moreover, maintain a standing military force in Europe to defend against what many believed was the threat of a Soviet invasion. The American Senate quickly ratified the treaty, which fused European nations that had been fighting one another for centuries into a strong and enduring alliance. The formation of NATO spurred the Soviet Union to create an alliance of its own with the communist governments in Eastern Europe—an alliance formalized in 1955 by the Warsaw Pact.

Survival Secrets for Atomic Attacks

ALWAYS PUT FIRST THINGS FIRST

Try to Get Shielded

If you have time, get down in a basement or subway. Should you unexpectedly be caught out-of-doors, seek shelter alongside a building, or jump in any handy ditch or gutter.

Drop Flat on Ground or Floor

To keep from being tossed about and to lessen the chances of being struck by falling and flying objects, flatten out at the base of a wall, or at the bottom of a bank.

Bury Your Face in Your Arms

When you drop flat, hide your eyes in the crook of your elbow. That will protect your face from flash burns, prevent temporary blindness and keep flying objects out of your eyes.

NEVER LOSE YOUR HEAD

SURVIVING NUCLEAR WAR Preoccupation with the possibility of a nuclear war reached a fever pitch in the early years of the atomic era. The Federal Civil Defense Agency, which in 1950 issued these simple rules for civilians to follow in dealing with an atomic attack, was one of many organizations attempting to convince the American public that a nuclear war was survivable.

The Enduring Crisis

For a time, Americans believed that these initial achievements had turned the tide of the battle against communism. But a series of events in 1949 eroded that confidence and propelled the Cold War in new directions. An announcement in September that the Soviet Union had successfully exploded its first atomic weapon, years earlier than predicted, shocked and frightened many Americans. So did the collapse of Chiang Kai-shek's nationalist government in China, which occurred with startling speed in the last months of 1949. Chiang fled with his political allies and the remnants of his army to the offshore island of Formosa (Taiwan), and the entire Chinese mainland came under the control of a communist government that many Americans believed to be an extension of the Soviet Union. Few policymakers shared the belief of the so-called China lobby that the United States should now commit itself to the rearming of Chiang Kai-shek. But neither would the United States recognize the new communist regime. The Chinese mainland would remain almost entirely closed to the West for a generation. The United States, in the meantime, would devote increased attention to the revitalization of Japan as a buffer against Asian communism, ending the American occupation in 1952.

In response to these and other setbacks, Truman called for a thorough review of American foreign policy. The result was a National Security Council report, commonly known as NSC-68, which outlined a shift in the American position. The first statements of the containment doctrine—the writings of George Kennan, the Truman Doctrine speech—made at least some distinctions between areas of vital interest to the United States and areas of less importance to the nation's foreign policy. They also had viewed containment as a commitment shared among the United States and its allies. But the April 1950 document argued that the United States could no longer rely on other nations to take the initiative in resisting communism. It must itself establish firm and active leadership of the noncommunist world. And it must move to stop communist expansion anywhere it occurred, regardless of the intrinsic strategic or economic value of the lands in question. Among other things, the report called for a major expansion of American military power, with a defense budget almost four times the previously projected figure.

AMERICA AFTER THE WAR

The crises overseas were not the only frustrations the American people encountered after the war. The nation also faced serious economic difficulties in adapting to the peace. The instability that resulted contributed to an increasingly heated political climate.

The Problems of Reconversion

Despite predictions that the end of the war would return America to Depression conditions, economic growth continued after 1945. Pent-up consumer demand from workers who had accumulated substantial savings during the war helped spur the boom. So did a $6 billion tax cut. The Servicemen's Readjustment Act of 1944, better known as the GI Bill of Rights, provided housing, education, and job training subsidies to veterans and increased spending even further.

This flood of consumer demand ensured that there would be no new depression, but it contributed to more than two years of serious inflation, during which prices rose at rates of 14 to 15 percent annually. In the summer of 1946, the president vetoed an extension of the authority of the wartime Office of Price Administration, thus eliminating price controls. (He was opposed not to the controls but to congressional amendments that had weakened the OPA.) Inflation soared to 25 percent before he relented a month later and signed a bill little different from the one he had rejected.

Compounding the economic difficulties was a sharp rise in labor unrest, driven in part by the impact of inflation. By the end of 1945, there had already been major strikes in the automobile, electrical, and steel industries. In April 1946, John L. Lewis led the United Mine Workers out on strike, shutting down the coal fields for forty days. Fears grew rapidly that without vital coal supplies, the entire nation might virtually grind to a halt. Truman finally forced coal production to resume by ordering government seizure of the mines. But in the process, he pressured mine owners to grant the union most of its demands, which he had earlier denounced as inflationary. Almost simultaneously, the nation's railroads suffered a total shutdown—the first in the nation's history—as two major unions walked out on strike. By threatening to use the army to run the trains, Truman pressured the strikers back to work after only a few days.

Reconversion was particularly difficult for the millions of women and minorities who had entered the work force during the war. With veterans returning home and looking for jobs in the industrial economy, employers tended to push women, blacks, Hispanics, and others out of the plants to make room for white males. Some of the war workers, particularly women, left the work force voluntarily, out of a desire to return to their former domestic lives. But as many as 80 percent of women workers, and virtually all black and Hispanic males, wanted to continue working. The postwar inflation, the pressure to meet the growing expectations of a high-consumption society, the rising divorce rate (which left many women responsible for their own economic well-being)—all combined to create a high demand for paid employment among women. As they found themselves excluded from industrial jobs, therefore, women workers moved increasingly into other areas of the economy (above all, the service sector).

The Fair Deal Rejected

Days after the Japanese surrender, Truman submitted to Congress a twenty-one-point domestic program outlining what he later termed the "Fair Deal." It called for expansion of Social Security benefits, the raising of the legal minimum wage from 40 to 65 cents an hour, a program to ensure full employment through aggressive use of federal spending and investment, a permanent Fair Employment Practices Act, public housing and slum clear-

HARRY AND BESS TRUMAN AT HOME Shortly before the 1944 Democratic National Convention, Senator Truman and his wife posed for photographers in the kitchen of their Washington apartment and conveyed the "common man" image that Truman retained throughout his public life. A few weeks later, Truman was a candidate for vice president; and less than a year after that, he and Mrs. Truman were living in the White House.

ance, long-range environmental and public works planning, and government promotion of scientific research. Weeks later he added other proposals: federal aid to education, government health insurance, prepaid medical care, funding for the St. Lawrence Seaway, and nationalization of atomic energy. The president was declaring an end to the wartime moratorium on liberal reform.

But the Fair Deal programs fell victim to the same public and congressional conservatism that had crippled the last years of the New Deal. Indeed, that conservatism seemed to be intensifying, as the November 1946 congressional elections suggested. Using the simple but devastating slogan "Had Enough?" the Republican party won control of both houses of Congress.

The new Republican Congress quickly moved to reduce government spending and chip away at New Deal reforms. Its most notable action, perhaps, was its assault on the Wagner Act of 1935. Conservatives had always resented the new powers the legislation had granted unions; and in response to the labor difficulties during and after the war, such resentments intensified sharply. The result was the Labor-Management Relations Act of 1947, better known as the Taft-Hartley Act. It made illegal the closed shop (a workplace in which no one can be hired without first being a member of a union). And although it continued to permit the creation of union shops (in which workers must join a union after being hired), it permitted states to pass "right-to-work" laws prohibiting even that. This provision, the controversial Section 14(b), remained a target of the labor movement for decades. The Taft-Hartley Act also empowered the president to call for a ten-week "cooling-off" period before a strike by issuing an injunction against any work stoppage that endangered national safety or health. Outraged workers and union leaders denounced the measure as a "slave labor bill." Truman vetoed it. But both houses easily overruled him the same day.

The Taft-Hartley Act did not destroy the labor movement, as many union leaders had predicted. But it did damage weaker unions in relatively lightly organized industries such as chemicals and textiles; and it made far more difficult the organizing of workers who had never been union members at all, especially in the South and West.

The Election of 1948

Truman and his advisers believed that the American public was not ready to abandon the achievements of the New Deal, despite the 1946 election results. As they planned strategy for the 1948 campaign, therefore, they placed their hopes in an appeal to enduring Democratic loyalties. Throughout 1948, Truman proposed one reform measure after another (including, on February 2, the first major civil-rights bill of the century). Congress ignored or defeated them all, but the president was building campaign issues for the fall.

There remained, however, the problem of Truman's personal unpopularity—the assumption among much of the electorate that he lacked stature and that his administration was weak and inept—and the deep divisions within the Democratic party. At the Democratic Convention that summer, two factions abandoned the party altogether. Southern conservatives were angered by Truman's proposed civil-rights bill and by the approval at the convention of a civil-rights plank in the platform (engineered by Hubert Humphrey, the reform mayor of Minneapolis). They walked out and formed the States' Rights (or "Dixiecrat") party, with Governor Strom Thurmond of South Carolina as its nominee. At the same time, some members of the party's left wing joined the new Progressive party, whose candidate was Henry A. Wallace. Wallace supporters objected to what they considered the slow and ineffective domestic policies of the Truman administration, but they resented even more the president's confrontational stance toward the Soviet Union.

In addition, many Democratic liberals unwilling to leave the party attempted to dump the president in 1948. The Americans for Democratic Action (ADA), a coalition of liberals, tried to entice Dwight D. Eisenhower, the popular war hero, to contest the nomination. Only after Eisenhower had refused did liberals bow to the inevitable and concede the nomination to Truman. The Republicans, in the meantime, had once again nominated Governor Thomas E. Dewey of New York, whose substantial reelection victory in 1946 had made him one of the nation's leading political figures. Austere, dignified, and competent, he seemed to offer an unbeatable alternative to the president.

Only Truman, it seemed, believed he could win. As the campaign gathered momentum, he became ever more aggressive, turning the fire away from himself and toward Dewey and the "do-nothing, good-for-nothing" Republican Congress, which was, he told the voters, responsible for fueling inflation and abandoning workers and common people. To dramatize his point, he called Congress into special session in July to give it a chance, he said, to enact the liberal measures the Republicans had recently written into their platform. Congress met for two weeks and, predictably, did almost nothing.

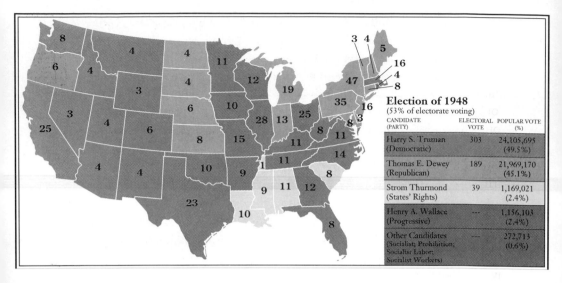

Election of 1948
(53% of electorate voting)

CANDIDATE (PARTY)	ELECTORAL VOTE	POPULAR VOTE (%)
Harry S. Truman (Democratic)	303	24,105,695 (49.5%)
Thomas E. Dewey (Republican)	189	21,969,170 (45.1%)
Strom Thurmond (States' Rights)	39	1,169,021 (2.4%)
Henry A. Wallace (Progressive)	---	1,156,103 (2.4%)
Other Candidates (Socialist; Prohibition; Socialist Labor; Socialist Workers)	---	272,713 (0.6%)

The president traveled nearly 32,000 miles and made 356 speeches, delivering blunt, extemporaneous attacks. He had told Alben Barkley, his running mate, "I'm going to fight hard. I'm going to give them hell." He called for repeal of the Taft-Hartley Act, increased price supports for farmers, and strong civil-rights protection for African-Americans. (He was the first president to campaign in Harlem since it had become a predominantly black community.) He sought, in short, to re-create much of Franklin Roosevelt's New Deal coalition. To the surprise of virtually everyone, he succeeded. On election night, he won a narrow but decisive victory: 49.5 percent of the popular vote to Dewey's 45.1 percent (with the two splinter parties dividing the small remainder evenly between them), and an electoral margin of 303 to 189. Democrats, in the meantime, had regained both houses of Congress by substantial margins. It was perhaps the most dramatic comeback in the history of presidential elections.

The Fair Deal Revived

Despite the Democratic victories, the Eighty-first Congress was no more hospitable to Truman's Fair Deal reform than its Republican predecessor had been. Truman did win some important victories, to be sure. Congress raised the legal minimum wage from 40 cents to 75 cents an hour. It approved an important expansion of the Social Security system, increasing benefits by 75 percent and extending them to 10 million additional people. And it passed the National Housing Act of 1949, which provided for the construction of 810,000 units of low-income housing accompanied by long-term rent subsidies. (Inadequate funding plagued the program for years, and the initial goal was reached only in 1972.)

But on other issues—national health insurance and aid to education among them—Truman made little progress. Nor was he able to persuade Congress to accept the civil-rights legislation he proposed in 1949, legislation that would have made lynching a federal crime, provided federal protection of black voting rights, abolished the poll tax, and established a new Fair Employment Practices Commission to curb discrimination in hiring. Southern Democrats filibustered to kill the bill.

Truman did proceed on his own to battle several forms of racial discrimination. He ordered an end to discrimination in the hiring of government employees. He began to dismantle segregation within the armed forces. And he allowed the Justice Department to become actively involved in court battles against discriminatory statutes. The Supreme Court, in the meantime, signaled its own growing awareness of the issue by ruling, in *Shelley* v. *Kraemer* (1948), that the courts could not be used to

KOREA, AUGUST 1950 American troops stand watch at a bridge they had demolished to slow down North Korean troop movements. Until MacArthur's surprise landing at Inchon on September 15, the United Nations forces (most of them American) played a largely defensive role, defending a small area in southeast Korea.

enforce private "covenants" meant to bar blacks from residential neighborhoods. The achievements of the Truman years made only minor dents in the structure of segregation, but they were the tentative beginnings of a federal commitment to confront the problem of race.

THE KOREAN WAR

On June 24, 1950, the armies of communist North Korea swept across their southern border in an invasion of the pro-Western half of the Korean peninsula to the south. Within days, they had occupied much of South Korea, including Seoul, its capital. Almost immediately, the United States committed itself to the conflict. It was the first American military engagement of the Cold War.

The Divided Peninsula

By the summer of 1945, both the United States and the Soviet Union had sent troops into Korea against the Japanese. When World War II ended, neither the Americans nor the Soviets were willing to leave. Instead, they divided the nation, supposedly temporarily, along the 38th parallel. The Russians finally departed in 1949, leaving behind a communist government in the north with a strong, Soviet-equipped army. The Americans left a few months later, handing control to the pro-Western government of Syngman Rhee, anticommunist but only nominally democratic. He had a relatively small military, which he used primarily to suppress internal opposition.

The relative weakness of the south offered a strong temptation to nationalists in the North Korean government who wanted to reunite the country. The temptation grew stronger when the American government implied that it did not consider South Korea within its own "defense perimeter." The role of the Soviet Union remains unclear; there is some reason to believe that the North Koreans acted without Stalin's approval. But the Soviets supported the offensive once it began.

The Truman administration responded quickly. On June 27, 1950, the president ordered limited American military assistance to South Korea, and on the same day he appealed to the United Nations to intervene. The Soviet Union was boycotting the Security Council at the time (to protest the council's refusal to recognize the new communist government of China) and was thus unable to exercise its veto power. As a result, American delegates

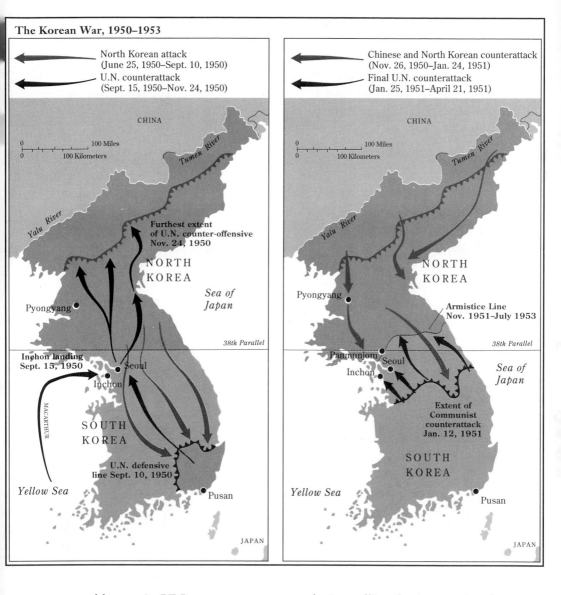

The Korean War, 1950–1953

North Korean attack
(June 25, 1950–Sept. 10, 1950)

U.N. counterattack
(Sept. 15, 1950–Nov. 24, 1950)

Chinese and North Korean counterattack
(Nov. 26, 1950–Jan. 24, 1951)

Final U.N. counterattack
(Jan. 25, 1951–April 21, 1951)

CHINA

100 Miles
100 Kilometers

Tumen River

Yalu River

Furthest extent
of U.N. counter-offensive
Nov. 24, 1950

NORTH
KOREA

Sea of
Japan

Pyongyang

38th Parallel

Inchon landing
Sept. 15, 1950

Seoul

Inchon

MACARTHUR

SOUTH
KOREA

U.N. defensive
line Sept. 10, 1950

Yellow Sea

Pusan

JAPAN

CHINA

100 Miles
100 Kilometers

Tumen River

Yalu River

NORTH
KOREA

Pyongyang

Armistice Line
Nov. 1951–July 1953

38th Parallel

Panmunjom

Seoul

Inchon

Sea of
Japan

Extent of
Communist
counterattack
Jan. 12, 1951

SOUTH
KOREA

Yellow Sea

Pusan

JAPAN

were able to win UN agreement to a resolution calling for international assistance to the Rhee government. On June 30, the United States ordered its own ground forces into Korea, and Truman appointed General Douglas MacArthur to command the UN operations there. (Several other nations provided assistance and troops, but the "UN" armies were, in fact, overwhelmingly American.)

The intervention in Korea was the first expression of the newly expansive American foreign policy outlined in NSC-68. But the administration quickly went beyond NSC-68. It decided that the war would be an effort not simply at containment but also at "liberation." After a surprise American invasion at Inchon in September had routed the North Korean forces from the south and sent them fleeing back across the 38th parallel, Truman gave MacArthur permission to pursue the communists into their own territory. His aim, as an American-sponsored UN resolution proclaimed in October, was to create "a unified, independent and democratic Korea."

From Invasion to Stalemate

For several weeks, MacArthur's invasion of North Korea proceeded smoothly. On October 19, the capital, Pyongyang, fell to the UN forces. Victory seemed near. By November 4, however, eight divisions of the Chinese army had entered the war. The UN offensive stalled and then collapsed. Through December 1950, outnumbered American forces fought a bitter, losing battle against the Chinese divisions, retreating at almost every juncture. Within weeks, communist forces had pushed the Americans back below the 38th parallel once again and had recaptured the South Korean capital of Seoul. By mid-January 1951 the rout had ceased; and by March the UN armies had managed to regain much of the territory they had recently lost, taking back Seoul and pushing the communists north of the 38th parallel for the second time. But with that, the war degenerated into a protracted stalemate.

From the start, Truman had been determined to avoid a direct conflict with China, which he feared might lead to a new world war. Once China entered the war, he began seeking a negotiated solution to the struggle; and for the next two years, he insisted that there be no wider war. But he faced a formidable opponent in General MacArthur, who resisted any limits on his military discretion. The United States was really fighting the Chinese, MacArthur argued. It should, therefore, attack China itself, if not through an actual invasion, then at least by bombing communist forces massing north of the Chinese border. In March 1951, he indicated his unhappiness in a public letter to House Republican leader Joseph W. Martin that concluded: "There is no substitute for victory." His position had wide popular support.

The Martin letter came after nine months during which MacArthur had resisted Truman's decisions. More than once, the president had warned the general to keep his objections to himself. The release of the Martin letter, therefore, struck the president as intolerable insubordination. On April 11, 1951, he relieved MacArthur of his command.

There was a storm of public outrage. Sixty-nine percent of the American people supported MacArthur, a Gallup poll reported. When the general returned to the United States later in 1951, he was greeted with wild enthusiasm. Public criticism of Truman finally abated somewhat when a number of prominent military figures, including General Omar Bradley, publicly supported the president's decision. But substantial hostility toward Truman remained.

In the meantime, the Korean stalemate continued. Negotiations between the opposing forces began at Panmunjom in July 1951, but the talks—and the war—dragged on until 1953.

Limited Mobilization

Just as the war in Korea produced only a limited American military commitment abroad, so it created only a limited economic mobilization at home. Still, the government did try to control the wartime economy in several important ways.

First, Truman set up the Office of Defense Mobilization to fight inflation by holding down prices and discouraging high union wage demands. When these cautious regulatory efforts failed, the president took more drastic action. Railroad workers walked off the job in 1951, and Truman, who considered the workers' demands inflationary, ordered the government to seize control of the railroads. That helped keep the trains running, but it had no effect on union demands. Workers ultimately got most of what they had demanded. In 1952, during a nationwide steel strike, Truman seized the steel mills, citing his powers as commander in chief. But in a 6-to-3 decision, the Supreme Court ruled that the president had exceeded his authority, and Truman was forced to relent. A long and costly strike followed, and the president's drastic actions appeared to many to have been both rash and ineffective.

The Korean War gave a significant boost to economic growth by pumping new government funds into the economy at a point when many believed it was about to decline. But the war had other, less welcome effects. It came at a time of rising insecurity about America's position in the world and intensified anxiety about communism. As the long stalemate continued, producing 140,000 American dead and wounded, frustration turned to anger. The United States, which had recently won the greatest war in history, seemed unable to conclude what many Americans considered a minor border skirmish in a small country. Many began to believe that

AMERICAN VOICES

WHITTAKER CHAMBERS

The Hiss Case

 I BELIEVED THAT I was not meant to be spared from testifying [against Alger Hiss]. I sensed, with a force greater than any fear or revulsion, that it was for this that my whole life had been lived. For this I had been a Communist, for this I had ceased to be a Communist. . . . This challenge was the terrible meaning of my whole life, of all that I had done that was evil, of all that I had sought that was good, of my weakness and my strength. . . .

For the moment had arrived when some man must be a witness. . . . The danger to the nation from Communism had now grown acute, both within its own house and abroad. Its existence was threatened. And the nation did not know it. For the first time, the [House Unamerican Activities] Committee's subpoena gave me an opportunity to tell what I knew about that danger. . . .

I did not wish to harm, more than was unavoidable, those whom I must testify against. . . . But I must testify that they had been concealed Communists and that an underground had existed in the Government. . . . They and I must stand up in face of the nation and confess what we had been that it might take alarm, throw off its apathy and skepticism, see that the enemy really was embedded in its midst, and be given time to act and save itself. That was the least that we could do in atonement.

SOURCE: Whittaker Chambers, *Witness*, pp. 533–534. Copyright ©1952 by Whittaker Chambers. Reprinted by permission of Random House.

something must be deeply wrong—not only in Korea but within the United States as well. Such fears contributed to the rise of the second major campaign of the century against domestic communism.

THE CRUSADE AGAINST SUBVERSION

Why did the American people develop a growing fear of internal communist subversion that by the early 1950s had reached the point of near hysteria? There are many possible answers, but no single definitive explanation.

One factor was obvious. Communism was not an imagined enemy in the 1950s. It had tangible shape, in Josef Stalin and the Soviet Union. Adding to the concern were the setbacks America had encountered in its battle against communism: the Korean stalemate, the "loss" of China, the Soviet development of an atomic bomb. Searching for someone to blame, many were attracted to the idea of a communist conspiracy within American borders. But there were other factors as well, rooted in events in American domestic politics.

HUAC and Alger Hiss

Much of the anticommunist furor emerged out of the search by the Republican party for an issue with which to attack the Democrats, and out of the efforts of the Democrats to take that issue away. Beginning in 1947, the House Un-American Activities Committee (HUAC) held widely publicized investigations to prove that, under Democratic rule, the government had tolerated (if not actually encouraged) communist subversion. The committee turned first to the movie industry, arguing that communists had infiltrated Hollywood and tainted American films with propaganda. Writers and producers, some of them former communists, were called to testify; and when some of them ("the Hollywood Ten") refused to answer questions about their own political beliefs and those of their colleagues, they were sent to jail for contempt. Others were barred from employment in the industry when Hollywood, attempting to protect its public image, adopted a "blacklist" of those of "suspicious loyalty."

More alarming to the public was HUAC's investigation into charges of disloyalty leveled against a former high-ranking member of the State Department: Alger Hiss. In 1948, Whittaker Chambers, a self-avowed former communist agent, now a conservative editor at *Time* magazine, told the committee that Hiss had passed classified State Department documents to him in 1937 and 1938. When Hiss sued him for slander, Chambers produced microfilms of the documents (called the "pumpkin papers," because Chambers had kept them hidden in a pumpkin in his vegetable garden). Hiss could not be tried for espionage because of the statute of limitations (a law that protects individuals from prosecution for most crimes after seven years have passed). But largely because of the relentless efforts of Richard M. Nixon, a freshman Republican congressman from California and a member of HUAC, Hiss was convicted of perjury and served several years in prison. The Hiss case not only discredited a prominent young diplomat; it cast suspicion on a generation of liberal Democrats and made it possible for the public to believe that communists had actually infiltrated the government. It also transformed Nixon into a national figure and helped him win a seat in the U.S. Senate in 1950.

The Federal Loyalty Program and the Rosenberg Case

Partly to protect itself against Republican attacks, partly to encourage support for the president's foreign policy initiatives, the Truman administration in 1947 initiated a widely publicized program to review the "loyalty" of federal employees. In August 1950, the president authorized sensitive agencies to fire people deemed no more than "bad security risks." By 1951, more than 2,000 government employees had resigned under pressure and 212 had been dismissed.

The employee loyalty program became a signal throughout the executive branch to launch a major assault on subversion. The attorney general established a widely cited list of supposedly subversive organizations. The director of the Federal Bureau of Investigation (FBI), J. Edgar Hoover, investigated and harassed alleged radicals. The anticommunist frenzy quickly grew so intense that even a Democratic Congress felt obliged to bow to it. In 1950, Congress passed the McCarran Internal Security Act, which, among other restrictions on "subversive" activity, required that all communist organizations register with the government and publish their records. Truman vetoed the bill. Congress easily overrode his veto.

The successful Soviet detonation of an atomic bomb in 1949, earlier than generally expected, suggested to some people that there had been a conspiracy to pass American atomic secrets to the Russians. In 1950, Klaus

Fuchs, a young British scientist, seemed to confirm those fears when he testified that he had delivered to the Russians details of the manufacture of the bomb. The case ultimately settled on an obscure New York couple, Julius and Ethel Rosenberg, members of the Communist party. The government claimed the Rosenbergs had received secret information from Ethel's brother, a machinist who had worked on the Manhattan Project in New Mexico, and had passed it on to the Soviet Union through other agents (including Fuchs). The Rosenbergs were convicted and, on April 5, 1951, sentenced to death. After two years of appeals and public protests, they died in the electric chair on June 19, 1953, proclaiming their innocence to the end.

All these factors—the HUAC investigations, the Hiss trial, the loyalty investigations, the McCarran Act, the Rosenberg case—combined with other concerns by the early 1950s to create a fear of communist subversion that seemed to grip the entire country. State and local governments, the judiciary, schools and universities, labor unions—all sought to purge themselves of real or imagined subversives. A pervasive fear settled on the country—not only the fear of communist infiltration but the fear of being suspected of communism. It was a climate that made possible the rise of an extraordinary public figure, whose behavior at any other time might have been dismissed as preposterous.

THE ROSENBERGS Julius and Ethel Rosenberg leave federal court in a police van after being convicted in March 1951 of transmitting atomic secrets to the Soviet Union. A week later, Judge Irving Kaufman sentenced them to death.

McCarthyism

Joseph McCarthy was an undistinguished, first-term Republican senator from Wisconsin when, in February 1950, he suddenly burst into national prominence. In the midst of a speech in Wheeling, West Virginia, he lifted a sheet of paper and claimed to "hold in my hand" a list of 205 known communists currently working in the American State Department. No person of comparable stature had ever made so bold a charge against the federal government; and in the weeks to come, as McCarthy repeated and expanded on his accusations, he emerged as the nation's most prominent leader of the crusade against domestic subversion.

Within weeks of his charges against the State Department, McCarthy was leveling accusations at other agencies. After 1952, with the Republicans in control of the Senate and McCarthy the chairman of a special subcommittee, he conducted highly publicized investigations of subversion in many areas of the government. McCarthy never produced conclusive evidence that any federal employee had communist ties. But a growing constituency adored him nevertheless for his coarse, "fearless" assaults on a government establishment that many considered arrogant, effete, even traitorous. Republicans, in particular, rallied to his claims that the Democrats had been responsible for "twenty years of treason" and that only a change of parties could rid the country of subversion. McCarthy, in short, provided his followers with an issue into which they could channel a wide range of resentments: fear of communism, animosity toward the country's "Eastern establishment," and frustrated partisan ambitions.

For a time, McCarthy intimidated all but a few people from opposing him. Even the highly popular Dwight D. Eisenhower, running for president in 1952, did not speak out against him, although he disliked McCarthy's tactics and was outraged at, among other things, McCarthy's attacks on General George Marshall.

The Republican Revival

Public frustration over the stalemate in Korea and popular fears of internal subversion combined to make 1952 a bad year for the Democratic party. Truman, whose own popularity had diminished almost to the vanishing point, wisely withdrew from the presidential contest. The party united instead behind Governor Adlai E. Stevenson of Illinois. Stevenson's dignity, wit, and eloquence made him a beloved figure to many liberals and intellectuals. But those same qualities seemed only to fuel Republican charges that

Stevenson lacked the strength or the will to combat communism sufficiently.

Stevenson's greatest problem, however, was the Republican candidate opposing him. Rejecting the efforts of conservatives to nominate Robert Taft or Douglas MacArthur, the Republicans turned to a man who had no previous identification with the party: General Dwight D. Eisenhower—military hero, commander of NATO, president of Columbia University in New York—who won nomination on the first ballot. He chose as his running mate the young California senator who had gained national prominence through his crusade against Alger Hiss: Richard M. Nixon.

In the fall campaign, Eisenhower attracted support through his geniality and his statesmanlike pledges to settle the Korean conflict. Nixon (after surviving early accusations of financial improprieties, which he effectively neutralized in a famous television address, the "Checkers speech") effectively exploited the issue of domestic anticommunism by attacking the Democrats for "cowardice" and "appeasement." The response at the polls was overwhelming. Eisenhower won both a popular and an electoral landslide: 55 percent of the popular vote to Stevenson's 44 percent, 442 electoral votes to Stevenson's 89. Republicans gained control of both houses of Congress for the first time since 1946. The election of 1952 ended twenty years of Democratic government. And while it might not have seemed so at the time, it also signaled the end of some of the worst turbulence of the postwar era.

D E B A T I N G   T H E   P A S T

The Cold War

F OR MORE THAN a decade after the beginning of the Cold War, few historians saw any reason to challenge the official American interpretation of its origins. The breakdown of relations between the United States and the Soviet Union was, most agreed, a direct result of Soviet expansionism and of Stalin's violation of the wartime agreements forged at Yalta and Potsdam. The Soviet imposition of communist regimes in Eastern Europe was part of a larger ideological design to spread communism throughout the world. American policy was the logical and necessary response.

Disillusionment with the official justifications for the Cold War began to find expression even in the late 1950s, when anticommunist sentiment in America remained strong and pervasive. William Appleman Williams's *The Tragedy of American Diplomacy* (1959) insisted that the Cold War was simply the most recent version of a consistent American effort in the twentieth century to preserve an "open door" for American trade in world markets. The confrontation with the Soviet Union, he argued, was less a response to Soviet aggressive designs than an expression of the American belief in the necessity of capitalist expansion.

As the Vietnam War grew larger and more unpopular in the 1960s, the scholarly critique of the Cold War quickly gained intensity. Walter LaFeber's *America, Russia, and the Cold War,* first published in 1967, maintained that America's supposedly idealistic internationalism at the close of the war was in reality an effort to ensure a postwar order shaped in the American image—with every nation open to American influence (and to American trade). That was why the United States was so eager to misinterpret Soviet policy, much of which reflected a perfectly reasonable concern to ensure the security of the Soviet Union itself, as part of a larger aggressive design. Important to many revisionist arguments has been the American decision to use atomic weapons against Japan in 1945. Gar Alperovitz's *Atomic Diplomacy* (1965) expanded on arguments that had begun to appear as early as 1948 and claimed that American decision makers used the bombs not to win the war (for Japan was already effectively defeated) but to impress and intimidate the Soviet Union so as to make it more "manageable" after the war.

The revisionist interpretations of the Cold War ultimately produced a reaction of their own: what has come to be known as "postrevisionist" scholarship. Some postrevisionists have done little more than revive the traditional, orthodox interpretations of the 1950s. But the most important works in this school have attempted to strike a balance between orthodoxy and revisionism and to identify areas of blame and patterns of misconception on both sides of the conflict. Thomas G. Patterson, John Lewis Gaddis, Melvin Leffler, and others have presented a picture of two nations—each with a highly inadequate understanding of the other—struggling to preserve a wartime alliance that had in fact temporarily disguised a basic difference in outlook and interests. "The United States and the Soviet Union were doomed to be antagonists," Ernest May wrote in 1984. "There probably was never any real possibility that the post-1945 relationship could be anything but hostility verging on conflict."

The collapse of Soviet communism and the dissolution of the Soviet empire will undoubtedly stimulate new interpretations of the Cold War and will (by facilitating the opening of Soviet archives) cast new light on many contested issues. For the moment, however, the dominant scholarly view is one that de-emphasizes the question of who is to blame and emphasizes the ways in which both sides learned to manage a conflict that neither could easily have avoided.

CHAPTER THIRTY

The Affluent Society

Abundance and Society ~ *The Rise of the Civil-Rights Movement*
Eisenhower Republicanism ~ *Eisenhower, Dulles, and the Cold War*

I F AMERICA EXPERIENCED a golden age in the 1950s and early 1960s, as many Americans believed at the time and many continue to believe today, it was largely a result of two developments. One was a booming national prosperity, which profoundly altered the social, economic, and even physical landscape of the United States, as well as the way many Americans thought about their lives and their world. The other was the continuing struggle against communism, a struggle that created considerable anxiety but that also encouraged Americans to look even more approvingly at their own society.

But if these powerful forces created a widespread sense of national purpose and self-satisfaction, they also helped blind many Americans to serious problems plaguing large groups of the population. More than 30 million Americans, according to some estimates, continued to live in poverty in the 1950s. And significant minorities—most prominently the 10 percent of the American people who were black—continued to suffer social, political, and economic discrimination. Ironically, perhaps, the very things that made America seem so successful in the 1950s also contributed, in the end, to making the nation's social problems more difficult to avoid.

ABUNDANCE AND SOCIETY

Perhaps the most striking feature of American society in the 1950s and early 1960s was the booming, almost miraculous economic growth that made even the heady 1920s seem pale by comparison. It was a better-balanced and more widely distributed prosperity than that of thirty years earlier. It was not, however, as universal as some Americans liked to believe.

Economic Growth

By 1949, despite the continuing problems of postwar reconversion, an economic expansion had begun that would continue with only brief interruptions for almost twenty years. Between 1945 and 1960, the gross national product grew by 250 percent, from $200 billion to over $500 billion. Unemployment, which during the Depression had averaged between 15 and 25 percent, remained at about 5 percent or lower throughout the 1950s and early 1960s. Inflation, in the meantime, hovered around 3 percent a year or less.

The causes of this growth were varied. Government spending, which had ended the Depression in the 1940s, continued to stimulate growth through public funding of schools, housing, veterans' benefits, welfare, and interstate highways. Above all, there was military spending. Economic growth was at its peak during the first half of the 1950s, when military spending was highest because of the Korean War. In the late 1950s, with spending on armaments in decline, the rate of growth declined by half.

The national birth rate reversed a long pattern of decline with the so-called baby boom, which had begun during the war and peaked in 1957. The nation's population rose almost 20 percent in the decade, from 150 million in 1950 to 179 million in 1960. The baby boom meant increased consumer demand and expanding economic growth.

The rapid expansion of suburbs—whose population grew 47 percent in the 1950s—helped stimulate growth in several important sectors of the economy. The number of privately owned cars (more essential for suburban than for urban living) more than doubled in a decade, sparking a great boom in the automobile industry. Demand for new homes helped sustain a vigorous housing industry. The construction of roads, which was both a cause and a result of the growth of suburbs, stimulated the economy as well.

Because of this unprecedented growth, the economy grew nearly ten times as fast as the population in the thirty years after the war. And while that growth was far from equally distributed, it affected most of society. The average American in 1960 had over 20 percent more purchasing power than in 1945, and more than twice as much as during the prosperous 1920s. The American people had achieved the highest standard of living of any society in the history of the world.

Capital and Labor

There were more than 4,000 corporate mergers in the 1950s; and more than ever before, a relatively small number of large-scale organizations controlled an enormous proportion of the nation's economic activity. By the end of the decade, half of the net corporate income in the nation was going to only slightly more than 500 firms, or one-tenth of 1 percent of the total number of corporations.

A similar consolidation was occurring in the agricultural economy. Increasing mechanization reduced the need for farm labor, and the agricultural work force declined by more than half in the two decades after the war. Mechanization also endangered one of the most cherished American institutions: the family farm. By the 1960s, relatively few individuals could any longer afford to buy and equip a modern farm; and much of the nation's most productive land had been purchased by financial institutions and corporations.

Corporations enjoying booming growth were reluctant to allow strikes to interfere with their operations; and since the most important labor unions were now so large and entrenched that they could not easily be suppressed or intimidated, business leaders made important concessions to them. As early as 1948, Walter Reuther, president of the United Automobile Workers, obtained a contract from General Motors that included a built-in "escalator clause"—an automatic cost-of-living increase pegged to the consumer price index. In 1955, Reuther received a guarantee from Ford Motor Company of continuing wages to autoworkers even during layoffs. A few months later, steelworkers in several corporations won a guaranteed annual salary. By the mid-1950s, factory wages in all industries had risen substantially, to an average of $80 per week.

The labor movement enjoyed significant success in winning better wages and benefits for workers already organized in strong unions. For the majority of laborers who were as yet unorganized, however, there were fewer advances. Total union membership remained relatively stable, at about 16 million, throughout the 1950s; and while this was in part a result of a shift in the work force from blue-collar to white-collar jobs, it was also a result of new obstacles to organization. The Taft-Hartley Act and the state right-to-work laws that the act spawned made it more difficult to create new unions powerful enough to demand recognition from employers.

The economic successes of the 1950s helped pave the way for a reunification of the labor movement. In December 1955, the American Federation of Labor and the Congress of Industrial Organizations ended their twenty-year rivalry and merged to create the AFL-CIO, under the leadership of George Meany.

But success also bred stagnation and corruption in some union bureaucracies. In 1957, the powerful Teamsters Union became the subject of a congressional investigation; and its president, David Beck, was charged with the misappropriation of union funds. Beck ultimately stepped down to be replaced by Jimmy Hoffa, whom government investigators pursued for nearly a decade before finally winning a conviction against him (for tax evasion) in 1967. The United Mine Workers, similarly, became tainted by violence and charges of corruption.

Consumerism and Suburbanization

Among the most striking social developments of the immediate postwar era was the rapid extension of a middle-class life style and outlook to an expanding portion of the population. The American middle class was becoming a larger, more powerful, and more self-conscious force than it had ever been before.

LEVITTOWN BEFORE THE TREES A section of the Levittown on Long Island in New York, photographed in July 1948 a few months after the first families moved in. The Levitt family pioneered techniques in constructing mass-produced housing that made possible the proliferation of similar inexpensive suburbs in many areas of the country.

At the center of middle-class culture in the 1950s was a growing absorption with consumer goods. That was a result of increased prosperity, of the increasing variety and availability of products, and of the adeptness of advertisers in creating a demand for those products. It was also a result of the growth of consumer credit, which increased by 800 percent between 1945 and 1957 through the development of credit cards, revolving charge accounts, and easy-payment plans. Prosperity fueled such longtime consumer crazes as the automobile, and Detroit responded to the boom with ever-flashier styling and accessories. Consumers also responded eagerly to the development of such new products as dishwashers, garbage disposals, television, and high-fidelity and stereo record players.

A third of the nation's population lived in suburbs by 1960. The growth of suburbs was a result not only of increased affluence but of important innovations in home building, which made single-family houses affordable to millions of new people. The most famous of the suburban developers, William Levitt, came to symbolize the new suburban growth with his use of mass-production techniques to construct a large housing development on Long Island, near New York City. The houses sold for under $10,000. Young couples—often newly married war veterans eager to start a family—rushed to purchase the inexpensive homes, not only in the Levittowns but in similar developments that soon began appearing throughout the country.

Why did so many Americans want to move to the suburbs? One reason was the enormous importance postwar Americans placed on family life after five years of war during which families had often been separated or otherwise disrupted. Suburbs provided families with larger homes than they could find (or afford) in the cities, and thus made it easier to raise larger numbers of children. They provided privacy. They also provided security from the noise and dangers of urban living. They offered space for the new consumer goods—the appliances, cars, boats, outdoor furniture, and other products—that middle-class Americans craved.

For many Americans, suburban life also helped provide a sense of community that was sometimes difficult to develop in large, crowded, impersonal urban areas. In later years, the suburbs would come under attack for their supposed conformity, homogeneity, and isolation. But in the 1950s, many people were attracted by the idea of living in a community populated largely by people of similar age and background, and they found it easier to form friendships and social circles there than in the city. Women in particular often valued the presence of other nonworking mothers living nearby to share the tasks of child raising.

Another factor motivating white Americans to move to the suburbs was race. Most suburbs were restricted to white inhabitants—both because relatively few blacks could afford to live in them and because of formal and informal barriers that kept even prosperous blacks out. In an era when the black population of most cities was rapidly growing, many white families fled to the suburbs to escape the integration of urban neighborhoods and schools.

Suburban neighborhoods were often very much alike. But they were not uniform. The Levittowns and inexpensive developments like them ultimately became the homes of mainly lower-middle-class people one step removed from the inner city. Other, more affluent suburbs became enclaves of wealthy families. Around virtually every city, a clear hierarchy emerged of upper-class suburban neighborhoods and more modest ones, just as such gradations had emerged years earlier among urban neighborhoods.

The Suburban Family

For professional men (who tended to work in the city, at some distance from their homes), suburban life generally meant a rigid division between their working and personal worlds. For many middle-class women, it meant an increased isolation from the workplace. The enormous cultural emphasis on family life in the 1950s strengthened popular prejudices against women entering the professions or occupying any paid job at all. Many middle-class husbands considered it demeaning for their wives to be employed. And many women themselves shied away from the workplace when they could afford to, in part because of prevailing ideas about motherhood (popularized by such widely consulted books as Dr. Benjamin Spock's *Baby and Child Care*, first published in 1946) that instructed women to stay at home with their children.

Affluent women, then, faced heavy pressures—both externally and internally imposed—to remain in the home and concentrate on raising their children. Some women, however, had to balance these pressures against other, contradictory ones. As expectations of material comfort rose, many middle-class families needed a second income to maintain the standard of living they desired. As a result, the number of married women working outside the home increased in the postwar years—even as the social pressure for them to stay out of the workplace grew. By 1960, nearly a third of all married women were part of the paid work force.

The Birth of Television

Television, perhaps the most powerful medium of mass communication in history, was central to the culture of the postwar era. Experiments in broadcasting pictures (along with sound) had begun as early as the 1920s, but commercial television began only shortly after World War II. It experienced a phenomenally rapid growth. In 1946, there were only 17,000 television sets in the country; by 1957, there were 40 million sets in use—almost as many sets as there were families. More people had television sets, according to one report, than had refrigerators.

The impact of television on American life was rapid, pervasive, and profound. By the late 1950s, television news had replaced newspapers, magazines, and radios as the nation's most important vehicle of information. Television advertising helped create a vast market for new fashions and products. Televised athletic events gradually made professional and college sports one of the important sources of entertainment (and one of the biggest businesses) in America. Television entertainment programming, almost all of it controlled by the three national networks (and their corporate sponsors), replaced movies and radio as the principal source of diversion for American families.

EISENHOWER AND DULLES Although President Eisenhower himself was a somewhat colorless television personality, his was the first administration to make extensive use of the new medium to promote its policies and dramatize its actions. The president's press conferences were frequently televised, and on several occasions Secretary of State John Foster Dulles reported to the president in front of the cameras.

Much of the programming of the 1950s and early 1960s created a relatively uniform image of American life—an image that was predominantly white, middle-class, and suburban, an image epitomized by such popular situation comedies as *Ozzie and Harriet* and *Leave It to Beaver*. But television also conveyed other images: the gritty, urban working-class families in Jackie Gleason's *The Honeymooners*; the childless show-business family of the early *I Love Lucy*; the unmarried professional women in *Our Miss Brooks* and *My Little Margie*. Television not only sought to create an idealized image of a homogeneous suburban America. It also sought to convey experiences at odds with that image, but to convey them in warm, unthreatening terms—taking social diversity and cultural conflict and domesticating them, turning them into something benign and even comic.

Yet television also, inadvertently, created conditions that could accentuate social conflict. Even those unable to share in the affluence of the era could, through television, acquire a vivid picture of how the rest of their society lived. At the same time that television was reinforcing the homogeneity of the white middle class, therefore, it was also contributing to the sense of alienation and powerlessness among groups excluded from the world it portrayed.

Science and Space

In 1961, *Time* magazine chose as its "man of the year" not a specific person but "the American Scientist." The choice was an indication of the widespread fascination with which Americans in the age of atomic weapons viewed science and technology. Major medical advances accounted for much of that fascination. Jonas Salk's vaccine to prevent polio was provided to the public free by the federal government beginning in 1955, and within a few years it had virtually eliminated the much feared polio from American life. Other dread diseases such as diphtheria and tuberculosis also all but vanished from society as new drugs and treatments were discovered. Infant mortality and the death rate among young children both declined significantly in the first twenty-five years after the war (although less than in Western Europe). Average life expectancy in that same period rose by five years, to seventy-one.

But Americans were at least equally attracted to other scientific and technological innovations: the jet plane, the computer, synthetics, new types of commercially prepared foods. And nothing better illustrated the nation's veneration of scientific expertise than the popular enthusiasm for the American space program.

The program began in large part because of the Cold War. When the Soviet Union announced in 1957 that it had launched a satellite—*Sputnik*—into outer space, the American government (and much of society) reacted with alarm, as if the Soviet achievement was also a massive American failure. Strenuous efforts began to improve scientific education in the schools, to develop more research laboratories, and, above all, to speed the development of America's own exploration of outer space. The centerpiece of that exploration was the manned space program, established in 1958 with the selection of the first American space pilots, or "astronauts," who quickly became the nation's most revered heroes. On May 5, 1961, Alan Shepard became the first American launched into space (several months after a Soviet "cosmonaut," Yuri Gagarin, had made a similar, if longer, flight). On February 2, 1962, John Glenn (later a United States senator) became the first American to orbit the globe (again, only after Gagarin had already done so).

Interest in the space program remained high in the summer of 1969, when Neil Armstrong and Edwin Aldrin became the first men to walk on the surface of the moon. Not long after that, however, the government began to cut the funding for future missions; and popular enthusiasm for the program began to wane.

Organized Society and Its Detractors

Large-scale organizations and bureaucracies increased their influence over American life in the postwar era, as they had been doing for many decades before. White-collar workers came to outnumber blue-collar laborers for the first time, and an increasing proportion of them worked in corporate settings with rigid hierarchical structures. Industrial workers also confronted large bureaucracies both in the workplace and in their own unions.

As in earlier eras, Americans reacted to these developments with ambivalence, often hostility. The debilitating impact of bureaucratic life on the individual slowly became one of the central themes of popular and scholarly debate. William H. Whyte, Jr., produced one of the most widely discussed books of the decade: *The Organization Man* (1956), which attempted to describe the special mentality of the worker in a large, bureaucratic setting. Self-reliance, Whyte claimed, was losing place to the ability to "get along" and "work as a team" as the most valuable trait in the modern character. Sociologist David Riesman made similar observations in *The Lonely Crowd* (1950), in which he argued that the traditional "inner-directed" man, who judged himself on the basis of his own values and the esteem of his family, was giving way to a new "other-directed" man, more concerned with winning the approval of the larger organization or community.

The most derisive critics of bureaucracy, and of middle-class society generally, were a group of young poets, writers, and artists generally known as the "beats" (or, by derisive critics, as "beatniks"). They wrote harsh critiques of what they considered the sterility and conformity of American life, the meaninglessness of American politics, and the banality of popular culture. Allen Ginsberg's dark, bitter poem *Howl* (1955) decried the "Robot apartments! invincible suburbs! skeleton treasuries! blind capitals! demonic industries!" of modern life. Jack Kerouac produced what may have been the central document of the Beat Generation in his novel *On the Road* (1957)— an account of a cross-country automobile trip that depicted the rootless, iconoclastic life style of Kerouac and his friends.

Other, less starkly alienated writers also used their work to express misgivings about the enormity and impersonality of modern society. Saul Bellow produced a series of novels—*The Adventures of Augie March* (1953), *Seize the Day* (1956), *Herzog* (1964), and others—that chronicled the difficulties of urban American Jews in finding fulfillment in modern urban America. J. D. Salinger wrote in *The Catcher in the Rye* (1951) of a prep-school student, Holden Caulfield, who was unable to find any area of society—school, family, friends, city—in which he could feel secure or committed.

The Other America

Despite the growing general prosperity of America in the 1950s and 1960s, much of the population continued to struggle on the fringes of the economic boom. In 1948, farmers had received 8.9 percent of the national income; in 1956, they received only 4.1 percent. In part, this decline reflected the steadily shrinking farm population. But it also reflected declining farm prices, which affected even those farmers who managed to survive.

Farmers, at least, were able to attract some public attention to their plight. Other, poorer groups languished in virtual obscurity. Inner-city ghettoes were expanding rapidly in the 1950s. In most places, that was a result of African-American farmers moving from country to city and of a significant growth in the black population as a whole. In New York, Los

Angeles, and many smaller cities in the Southwest, immigrants from Puerto Rico, Mexico, and other Spanish-speaking areas created significant poor Hispanic neighborhoods (or *barrios*) as well. Historic patterns of racial discrimination doomed large proportions of these communities to continuing, and in some cases increasing, poverty.

A similar predicament faced residents of several particularly destitute rural regions—most notably the Appalachian areas of the Southern and border states, where the decline of the coal industry was eroding the only significant economic support many communities had known. Lacking adequate schools, health care, and services, the residents of Appalachia, like the residents of the urban ghettoes, were almost entirely shut off from the mainstream of American economic life. Not until the 1960s, when such exposés as Michael Harrington's *The Other America* (1962) began drawing attention to the continuing existence of poverty in the nation, did the middle class begin to recognize the seriousness of the problem.

THE RISE OF THE CIVIL-RIGHTS MOVEMENT

After decades of skirmishes, an open battle began in the 1950s against racial segregation and discrimination, a battle that would prove to be one of the longest and most difficult of the century. White Americans played an important role in the civil-rights movement. But pressure from African-Americans themselves was the crucial element in raising the issue of race to prominence.

The Brown *Decision and "Massive Resistance"*

On May 17, 1954, the Supreme Court announced one of the most important decisions in its history in the case of *Brown v. Board of Education of Topeka*. In considering the legal segregation of a Kansas public school system, the Court rejected its own 1896 *Plessy v. Ferguson* decision, which had ruled that communities could provide blacks with separate facilities as long as the facilities were equal to those of whites. The Brown decision unequivocally declared the segregation of public schools on the basis of race unconstitutional.

The *Brown* decision was the culmination of many decades of effort by black opponents of segregation, and particularly by a group of talented NAACP lawyers, many of them trained at Howard University in Washington by the great legal educator Charles Houston. Thurgood Marshall, William Hastie, James Nabrit, and others spent years filing legal challenges to segregation in one state after another, nibbling at the edges of the system, and accumulating precedents to support their assault on the "separate but equal" doctrine itself. The same lawyers filed the suits against the school boards of Topeka, Kansas, and several other cities that became the basis for the *Brown* decision.

The Topeka suit involved the case of a black girl who had to travel several miles to a segregated public school every day even though she lived virtually next door to a white elementary school. When the case arrived before the Supreme Court, the justices concluded that school segregation inflicted unacceptable damage on those it affected, regardless of the relative quality of the separate schools. Chief Justice Earl Warren explained the unanimous opinion of his colleagues: "We conclude that in the field of public education the doctrine of 'separate but equal' has no place. Separate educational facilities are inherently unequal." The following year, the Court issued another decision (known as *"Brown* II") to provide rules for implementing the 1954 order. It ruled that communities must work to desegregate their schools "with all deliberate speed," but it set no timetable and left specific decisions up to lower courts.

In some communities, for example Washington, D.C., compliance came relatively quickly and quietly. More often, however, strong local opposition (what came to be known in the South as "massive resistance") produced long delays and bitter conflicts. Some school districts ignored the ruling altogether. Others attempted to circumvent it with purely token efforts to integrate. More than 100 Southern members of Congress signed a "manifesto" in 1956 denouncing the *Brown* decision and urging their constituents to defy it. Southern governors, mayors, local school boards, and nongovernmental pressure groups (including hundreds of White Citizens' Councils) all worked to obstruct desegregation. By the fall of 1957, only 684 of 3,000 affected school districts in the South had even begun to desegregate their schools. The *Brown* decision, far from ending segregation, had launched a prolonged battle between federal authority and state and local governments.

The Eisenhower administration was not eager to commit itself to that battle. But in September 1957, it faced a case of direct state defiance of federal authority and felt compelled to act. Federal courts had ordered the desegregation of Central High School in Little Rock, Arkansas. An angry white mob tried to block implementation of the order by blockading the entrances to the school, and Governor Orval Faubus refused to do anything to stop the obstruction. President Eisenhower finally responded by sending federal troops to Little Rock to keep the peace and ensure that the court orders would be obeyed. Only then did Central High School admit its first black students.

The Expanding Movement

The *Brown* decision helped spark a growing number of popular challenges to segregation in the South. On December 1, 1955, Rosa Parks, an African-American woman, was arrested in Montgomery, Alabama, when she refused to give up her seat on a Montgomery bus to a white passenger (as required by the Jim Crow laws that regulated race relations in the city and through-

ROSA PARKS IN THE FRONT OF THE BUS In December 1955 Rosa Parks was arrested in Montgomery, Alabama, for refusing to obey a law that required her to give up her seat to a white passenger and move to the back of the bus. Her defiance sparked an almost total boycott of Montgomery's transit system by black citizens. Just over a year later, the U.S. Supreme Court ruled that racial segregation of public transit systems was unconstitutional.

out most of the South). Parks, an active civil-rights leader in the community, had apparently decided spontaneously to resist the order to move. Her feet were tired, she later explained. The arrest of this admired woman produced outrage in the city's African-American community, which organized a successful boycott of the bus system to demand an end to segregated seating.

The bus boycott owed much of its success to the prior existence of well-organized black citizens' groups. A black women's political caucus had, in fact, been developing plans for some time for a boycott of the segregated buses. Local leaders seized on Rosa Parks as the vehicle for their plans, because she was so well suited to serve as a symbol of the movement. Once launched, the boycott was almost completely effective. It put economic pressure not only on the bus company (a private concern) but on many Montgomery merchants, because the bus boycotters found it difficult to get to downtown stores and tended to shop instead in their own neighborhoods. Even so, the boycott might well have failed had it not been for a Supreme Court decision late in 1956, inspired in part by the protest, that declared segregation in public transportation to be illegal. The buses in Montgomery abandoned their discriminatory seating policies, and the boycott came to a close.

The most important accomplishments of the Montgomery boycott were less its immediate victories than its success in establishing a new form of racial protest and in elevating to prominence a new figure in the movement for civil rights. The man chosen to lead the boycott movement once it was launched was a local Baptist pastor, Martin Luther King, Jr., son of a prominent Atlanta minister, a powerful orator, and a gifted leader. King was reluctant at first to assume the leadership of the movement. But once he accepted the role, he became consumed by it.

King's approach to black protest was based on the doctrine of nonviolence—that is, of passive resistance even in the face of direct attack. He drew from the teachings of Mahatma Gandhi, the Indian nationalist leader; from Henry David Thoreau and his doctrine of civil disobedience; and from Christian dogma. And he produced an approach to racial struggle that captured the moral high ground for his supporters. He urged African-Americans to engage in peaceful demonstrations; to allow themselves to be arrested, even beaten, if necessary; and to respond to hate with love. For the next thirteen years—as leader of the Southern Christian Leadership Conference (SCLC), an interracial group he founded shortly after the bus boycott—he was the most influential and most widely admired black leader in the country. The popular movement he came to represent soon spread throughout the South and throughout the country.

EISENHOWER REPUBLICANISM

Dwight D. Eisenhower was the least experienced politician to serve in the White House in the twentieth century. He was also among the most popular and politically successful presidents of the postwar era. At home, he pursued essentially moderate policies, avoiding most new initiatives but accepting the work of earlier reformers. Abroad, he continued and even intensified American commitments to oppose communism but brought to some of those commitments a measure of restraint that his successors did not always match.

"What's Good for General Motors . . ."

The first Republican administration in twenty years staffed itself with men drawn from the same quarter as those who had staffed Republican administrations in the 1920s: the business community. But many in the American business community had acquired a very different social and political outlook by the 1950s from that of their predecessors of earlier decades. Above all, many of the nation's leading businessmen and financiers had reconciled themselves to at least the broad outlines of the Keynesian welfare state the New Deal had launched. Indeed, many corporate leaders had come to see it as something that actually benefited them—by helping maintain social order, by increasing mass purchasing power, and by stabilizing labor relations.

To his cabinet, Eisenhower appointed wealthy corporate lawyers and business executives who were not apologetic about their backgrounds. Charles Wilson, president of General Motors, assured senators considering his nomination for secretary of defense that he foresaw no conflict of interest because he was certain that "What was good for our country was good for General Motors, and vice versa." But missing from most members of this business-oriented administration was the deep hostility to "government interference" that had so dominated corporate attitudes three decades before.

Eisenhower's leadership style, which stressed delegation of authority to subordinates, helped enhance the power of his cabinet officers and others. Secretary of State John Foster Dulles was widely believed to be running American foreign policy almost single-handedly (although it has since become clear that the president was far more deeply involved in international decisions than was often apparent at the time). The president's White House chief of staff, former New Hampshire governor Sherman Adams, exercised broad authority over relations with Congress and strictly controlled access to the president—until he left office in disgrace, near the end of Eisenhower's presidency, after he was discovered to have accepted gifts from a wealthy businessman.

Eisenhower's consistent inclination was to limit federal activities and encourage private enterprise. He supported the private rather than public development of natural resources (and once talked about selling the Tennessee Valley Authority to a private company). To the chagrin of farmers, he lowered federal support for farm prices. He also removed the last limited wage and price controls maintained by the Truman administration. He opposed the creation of new social service programs such as national health insurance. He strove constantly to reduce federal expenditures (even during the recession of 1958) and balance the budget. He ended 1960, his last full year in office, with a $1 billion surplus.

The president took few new initiatives in domestic policy, but he resisted pressure from the right wing of his party to dismantle those welfare policies of the New Deal that had survived the conservative assaults of the war years and after. Indeed, during his term, he agreed to extend the Social Security system to an additional 10 million people and unemployment compensation to an additional 4 million people; and he agreed to increase the minimum hourly wage from 75 cents to $1. Perhaps the most significant legislative accomplishment of the Eisenhower administration was the Federal Highway Act of 1956, which authorized $25 billion for a ten-year effort to construct over 40,000 miles of interstate highways. The program was to be funded through a highway "trust fund," whose revenues would come from new taxes on the purchase of fuel, automobiles, trucks, and tires.

In 1956, Eisenhower ran for a second term, even though he had suffered a serious heart attack the previous year. With Adlai Stevenson opposing him once again, he won by another, even greater landslide, receiving nearly 57 percent of the popular vote and 442 electoral votes to Stevenson's 89. Still, Democrats retained the control of both houses of Congress they had won back in 1954. And in 1958—during a serious recession—they increased that control by substantial margins.

The Decline of McCarthyism

The Eisenhower administration did little in its first years in office to discourage the anticommunist furor that had gripped the nation. Indeed, in many ways it helped sustain it. The president intensified the search for subversives in the government, which Truman had begun several years earlier. More than 2,220 federal employees resigned or were dismissed as a result of security investigations.

By 1954, such policies were beginning to produce significant popular opposition—an indication that the anticommunist passion of several years earlier was beginning to abate. The clearest signal of that change was the political demise of Senator Joseph McCarthy.

During the first year of the Eisenhower administration, McCarthy continued to operate with impunity. The president, who privately loathed him, nevertheless refused to speak out against him in public. Relatively few others—in the political world or in the press—were any more courageous. But McCarthy finally overreached himself in January 1954 when he attacked Secretary of the Army Robert Stevens and the armed services in general. At that point, the administration and influential members of Congress organized a special investigation of the charges, which became known as the Army-McCarthy hearings. They were among the first congressional hearings to be nationally televised.

The result was devastating to McCarthy. Watching McCarthy in action—bullying witnesses, hurling groundless (and often cruel) accusations, evading issues—much of the public began to see him as a villain, and even

THE ARMY-McCARTHY HEARINGS Senator Joseph McCarthy uses a map to show the supposed distribution of communists throughout the United States during the televised 1954 Senate hearings to mediate the dispute between McCarthy and the U.S. Army. Joseph Welch, chief counsel for the army, remains conspicuously unimpressed.

a buffoon. In December 1954, the Senate voted 67 to 22 to condemn him for "conduct unbecoming a senator." Three years later, with little public support left, he died—a victim, apparently, of complications arising from alcoholism.

EISENHOWER, DULLES, AND THE COLD WAR

The threat of nuclear war with the Soviet Union created a sense of high anxiety in international relations in the 1950s. But the nuclear threat had another effect as well. With the potential devastation of an atomic war so enormous, both superpowers began to edge away from direct confrontations. The attention of both the United States and the Soviet Union began to turn to the rapidly escalating instability in the nations of the Third World.

Dulles and "Massive Retaliation"

Eisenhower's secretary of state, and (except for the president himself) the dominant figure in the nation's foreign policy in the 1950s, was John Foster Dulles, an aristocratic corporate lawyer with a stern moral revulsion to communism. He entered office denouncing the containment policies of the Truman years as excessively passive, arguing that the United States should pursue an active program of "liberation," which would lead to a "rollback" of communist expansion. Once in power, however, he had to defer to the far more moderate views of the president himself, and he began to develop a new set of doctrines that reflected the impact of nuclear weapons on the world.

The most prominent of those doctrines was the policy of "massive retaliation," which Dulles announced early in 1954. The United States would, he explained, respond to communist threats to its allies not by using conventional forces in local conflicts (a policy that had led to so much frustration in Korea) but by relying on "the deterrent of massive retaliatory power" (by which he clearly meant nuclear weapons).

In part, the new doctrine reflected Dulles's inclination for tense confrontations, an approach he once defined as "brinksmanship"—pushing the Soviet Union to the brink of war in order to exact concessions. But the real force behind the massive retaliation policy was economics. With pressure growing both in and out of government for a reduction in American military expenditures, an increasing reliance on atomic weapons seemed to promise, as some advocates put it, "more bang for the buck."

At the same time, Dulles intensified the efforts of Truman and Acheson to "integrate" the entire noncommunist world into a system of mutual defense pacts modeled on NATO—although the new alliances were far weaker than the European pact. By the end of the decade, the United States had become a party to almost a dozen such treaties in all areas of the world.

France, America, and Vietnam

What had been the most troubling foreign policy concern of the Truman years—the war in Korea—plagued the Eisenhower administration only briefly. On July 27, 1953, negotiators at Panmunjom finally signed an agreement ending the hostilities. Each antagonist was to withdraw its troops a mile and a half from the existing battle line, which ran roughly along the 38th parallel, the prewar border between North and South Korea. A conference in Geneva was to consider means by which to reunite the nation peacefully—although in fact the 1954 meeting produced no agreement and left the cease-fire line as the apparently permanent border between the two countries.

Almost simultaneously, however, the United States was becoming drawn into a long, bitter struggle in Southeast Asia. Ever since the end of World War II, France had been attempting to restore its authority over Vietnam, its one-time colony, which it had had to abandon to the Japanese during World War II. Opposing the French, however, were the powerful nationalist forces of Ho Chi Minh, determined to win independence for their nation. Ho had hoped for American support in 1945, on the basis of the anticolonial rhetoric of the Atlantic Charter and Franklin Roosevelt's speeches, and also because he had received support from American intelligence forces during World War II while he was fighting the Japanese. But he was then, as he had been for many years, not only a committed nationalist but a committed communist. The Truman administration ignored him and supported the French, one of America's most important Cold War allies.

By 1954, Ho was receiving aid from communist China and the Soviet Union. America, in the meantime, was paying most of the costs of France's ineffective military campaign in Vietnam since 1950. Early in 1954, 12,000 French troops became surrounded in a disastrous siege at the city of Dienbienphu. Only American intervention, it was clear, could prevent the total collapse of the French military effort. Yet despite the urgings of Secretary of State Dulles, Vice President Nixon, and others, Eisenhower refused to permit direct American military intervention in Vietnam, claiming that neither Congress nor America's other allies would support such action.

Without American aid, the French defense of Dienbienphu finally collapsed on May 7, 1954; and France quickly agreed to a settlement of the conflict at the same conference in Geneva that summer that was considering the Korean settlement. The Geneva accords on Vietnam of July 1954, to which the United States was not a direct party, established a supposedly temporary division of Vietnam along the 17th parallel. The north would be governed by Ho Chi Minh, the south by a pro-Western regime. Democratic elections would be the basis for uniting the nation in 1956.

The agreement marked the end of the French commitment to Vietnam and the beginning of an expanded American presence there. The United States helped establish a pro-American government in the south, headed by Ngo Dinh Diem, a member of his country's Roman Catholic minority. Diem, it was clear, would not permit the 1956 elections, which he knew he would lose. He felt secure in his refusal because the United States had promised to provide him with ample military assistance against any attack from the north. (There is some evidence that the Soviet Union, eager to avoid a confrontation with the United States at this point, was at the same time pressuring Ho and his regime not to press for an election.)

Israel and the Crises of the Middle East

The establishment of a Jewish state in Palestine had been the dream of a powerful international Zionist movement for more than half a century before World War II. The plight of homeless Jews uprooted by the war, and the international horror at revelations of the Holocaust, gave new strength to Zionist demands in the late 1940s. So did the enormous immigration of European Jews into Palestine after 1945, despite the efforts of Britain (which had governed the region since World War I) to limit them.

Finally, Britain brought the problem to the United Nations, which responded by recommending the partition of Palestine into a Jewish and an Arab state. On May 14, 1948, British rule ended, and Jews proclaimed the existence of the nation of Israel. President Truman recognized the new government the following day. But the creation of Israel, while it resolved some conflicts, created others. Palestinian Arabs, unwilling to accept being displaced from what they considered their own country, fought determinedly against the new state in 1948—the first of several Arab-Israeli wars.

Committed as the American government was to Israel, it was also concerned about the stability and friendliness of the Arab regimes in the area. The reason was simple: The region contained the richest oil reserves in the world, reserves in which American companies had already invested heavily, reserves on which the health of the American (and world) economy would ultimately come to depend. Thus the United States reacted with alarm as it watched Mohammed Mossadegh, the nationalist prime minister of Iran, begin to resist the presence of Western corporations in his nation in the early 1950s. In 1953, the American CIA joined forces with conservative Iranian military leaders to engineer a coup that drove Mossadegh from office. To replace him, the CIA helped elevate the young Shah of Iran, Mohammed Reza Pahlevi, from his position as a token constitutional monarch to that of a virtually absolute ruler. The Shah remained closely tied to the United States for the next twenty-five years.

American policy was less effective in dealing with the nationalist government of Egypt, under the leadership of General Gamal Abdel Nasser, which began to develop a trade relationship with the Soviet Union in the early 1950s. In 1956, to punish Nasser for his friendliness toward the communists, Dulles withdrew American offers to assist in building the great Aswan Dam across the Nile. A week later, Nasser retaliated by seizing control of the Suez Canal from the British, saying that he would use the income from it to build the dam himself. The repercussions of that seizure were quick and profound.

On October 29, 1956, Israeli forces struck a preemptive blow against Egypt. The next day the British and French landed troops in the Suez to drive the Egyptians from the canal. Dulles and Eisenhower feared that the Suez crisis would drive the Arab states toward the Soviet Union and precipitate a new world war. By refusing to support the invasion, and by joining in a United Nations denunciation of it, the United States helped pressure the French and British to withdraw and helped persuade Israel to agree to a truce with Egypt.

Nasser's continuing flirtation with the Soviet Union strengthened American resolve to resist the growth of communist influence (which the United States increasingly associated with Arab nationalism) in the Middle East. In 1958, as pan-Arab forces loyal to Nasser challenged the government of Lebanon, Eisenhower ordered 5,000 American marines to land on the beaches of Beirut to protect the existing regime; British troops entered Jordan at about the same time to resist a similar threat there. The effect of the interventions was negligible. The governments of both countries managed to stabilize their positions on their own, and within months both the American and the British forces withdrew.

Latin America and "Yankee Imperialism"

World War II and the Cold War had eroded the limited initiatives of the Good Neighbor Policy toward Latin America, as American economic aid now flowed increasingly to Europe. Latin American animosity toward the United States grew steadily during the 1950s, as many people in the region began to regard the influence of American corporations in their countries as a form of imperialism. Such concerns deepened in 1954, when the Eisenhower administration ordered the CIA to help topple the new, leftist government of Jacobo Arbenz Guzmán in Guatemala, a regime that Dulles (responding to the entreaties of the United Fruit Company, a major investor in Guatemala fearful of Arbenz) argued was potentially communist. Four years later, the depths of anti-American sentiment became clear when Vice President Richard Nixon visited the region, to be greeted in city after city by angry, hostile, occasionally dangerous mobs.

No nation in the region had been more closely tied to America than Cuba. Its leader, Fulgencio Batista, had ruled as a military dictator since 1952, when with American assistance he had toppled a more moderate government. Cuba's relatively prosperous economy had become a virtual fiefdom of American corporations, which controlled almost all the island's natural resources and had cornered over half the vital sugar crop. American-organized crime syndicates controlled much of Havana's lucrative hotel and night-life business. Beginning in 1957, a popular movement of resistance to the Batista regime began to gather power under the leadership of Fidel Castro. By late 1958, the Batista forces were in almost total disarray. And on January 1, 1959, with Batista now in exile in Spain, Castro marched into Havana and established a new government.

At first, many Americans reacted warmly to Castro. But once Castro began implementing drastic policies of land reform and expropriating foreign-owned businesses and resources, Cuban-American relations rapidly deteriorated. Of particular concern to Eisenhower and Dulles was the Cuban regime's growing interest in communist ideas and tactics. When Castro began accepting assistance from the Soviet Union in 1960, the United States cut back the "quota" by which Cuba could export sugar to America at a favored price. Early in 1961, as one of its last acts, the

Eisenhower administration severed diplomatic relations with Castro. The American CIA had already begun secretly training Cuban expatriates for an invasion of the island to topple the new regime. Isolated by the United States, Castro soon cemented an alliance with the Soviet Union.

Europe and the Soviet Union

Although the problems of the Third World were moving slowly toward the center of American foreign policy, the direct relationship with the Soviet Union and the effort to resist communist expansion in Europe remained the principal concerns of the Eisenhower administration.

Even as the United States was strengthening NATO and rearming West Germany, however, many Americans continued to hope for negotiated solutions to some of the remaining problems dividing the superpowers. Such hopes grew after the death of Stalin in 1953, especially when the Soviet Union extended a peace overture to the rebellious Tito government in Yugoslavia, returned a military base to Finland, signed a peace treaty with Japan, and ended its long military occupation of Austria by allowing that nation to become an independent, neutral state. In 1955, Eisenhower and other NATO leaders met with the Soviet premier, Nikolai Bulganin, at a cordial summit conference in Geneva. But when a subsequent conference of foreign ministers met to try to resolve specific issues, they could find no basis for agreement.

Relations between the Soviet Union and the West soured further in 1956 in response to the Hungarian Revolution. Inspired by riots in Poland a year earlier, Hungarian dissidents had launched a popular uprising in November 1956 to demand democratic reforms. For several days, they had control of the Hungarian government. But before the month was out, Soviet tanks and troops entered Budapest to crush the uprising and restore an orthodox, pro-Soviet regime. The Eisenhower administration refused to intervene. But the suppression of the uprising convinced many American leaders that Soviet policies had not softened as much as the events of the previous two years had suggested.

The failure of conciliation brought renewed vigor to the Cold War and, among other things, greatly intensified the Soviet-American arms race. Both nations engaged in extensive nuclear testing. Both nations redoubled efforts to develop effective intercontinental ballistic missiles, which could deliver atomic warheads directly from one continent to another. The American military, in the meantime, developed a new breed of atomic-powered submarines, capable of launching missiles from under water anywhere in the world.

The arms race not only increased tensions between the United States and Russia; it increased tensions within each nation as well. In America, public concern about nuclear war was becoming a pervasive national nightmare, a preoccupation never far from popular thought. Movies, television programs, books, popular songs—all expressed the concern. Fear of communism, therefore, combined with fear of atomic war to create a persistent national anxiety.

The U-2 Crisis

In this tense and fearful atmosphere, the Soviet Union raised new challenges to the West in Berlin in 1958. The continuing existence of an anticommunist West Berlin inside communist East Germany remained an irritant and embarrassment to the Soviets. In November 1958, Nikita Khrushchev, who had succeeded Bulganin as Soviet premier and Communist party chief earlier that year, renewed the demands of his predecessors that the NATO powers abandon the city. The United States and its allies refused.

Khrushchev declined to force the issue. Instead, he suggested that he and Eisenhower discuss the issue personally, both in visits to each other's countries and at a summit meeting in Paris in 1960. The United States agreed. Khrushchev's 1959 visit to America produced a cool but polite public response. Plans proceeded for the summit conference and for Eisenhower's visit to Moscow shortly thereafter. Only days before the scheduled beginning of the Paris meeting, however, the Soviet Union announced that it had shot down an American U-2, a high-altitude spy plane, over Russian territory. Its pilot, Francis Gary Powers, was in captivity. The Eisenhower administration responded clumsily, at first denying the allegations and then, when confronted with proof of them, awkwardly admitting that they were true. Khrushchev lashed back angrily, breaking up the Paris summit almost before it could begin and withdrawing his invitation to Eisenhower to visit the Soviet Union. But the U-2 incident was probably only a pretext. By the spring of 1960, Khrushchev was under pressure from hard-liners in the Kremlin to toughen his stance toward the West, and he knew that no agreement was possible on the Berlin issue. The U-2 incident may simply have been an excuse to avoid what he believed would be fruitless negotiations.

The events of 1960 provided a somber backdrop for the end of the Eisenhower administration. After eight years in office, Eisenhower had failed to eliminate the tensions between the United States and the Soviet Union. He had failed to end the costly and dangerous armaments race. And he had presided over a transformation of the Cold War from a relatively limited confrontation with the Soviet Union in Europe to a global effort to resist communist subversion. Yet Eisenhower had brought to these matters his own sense of the limits of American power. He had resisted military intervention in Vietnam. And he had placed a measure of restraint on those who urged the creation of an enormous American military establishment. In his farewell address in January 1961, he warned of the "unwarranted influence" of a vast "military-industrial complex." His caution, in both domestic and international affairs, stood in marked contrast to the attitudes of his successors, who argued that the United States must act more boldly and aggressively on behalf of its goals at home and abroad.

CHAPTER THIRTY-ONE

The Ordeal of Liberalism

Expanding the Liberal State ～ The Battle for Racial Equality
From "Flexible Response" to Vietnam ～ The Traumas of 1968

B Y THE LATE 1950s, a growing restlessness was becoming visible beneath the apparently placid surface of American society. Anxiety about America's position in the world, growing pressures from African-Americans and other minorities, the increasing visibility of poverty, the rising frustrations of women, and other long-suppressed discontents were beginning to make themselves felt in the nation's public life. Ultimately, that restlessness would make the 1960s one of the most turbulent eras of the twentieth century. But at first, it contributed to a bold and confident effort by political leaders to attack social and international problems within the framework of conventional liberal politics.

EXPANDING THE LIBERAL STATE

Those who yearned for a more active government in the late 1950s and who accused the Eisenhower administration of allowing the nation to "drift" looked above all to the presidency for leadership. The two men who served in the White House through most of the 1960s—John Kennedy and Lyndon Johnson—seemed for a time to be the embodiment of these liberal hopes.

John Kennedy

The campaign of 1960 produced two young candidates who claimed to offer the nation active leadership. The Republican nomination went almost uncontested to Vice President Richard Nixon, who promised moderate reform. The Democrats, in the meantime, emerged from a spirited primary campaign united, somewhat uneasily, behind John Fitzgerald Kennedy, an attractive and articulate senator from Massachusetts who had narrowly missed being the party's vice presidential candidate in 1956.

John Kennedy grew up in a world of ease and privilege. He was the son of the wealthy, powerful, and highly controversial Joseph P. Kennedy, former American ambassador to Britain. Decorated for bravery during World War II, he returned to Massachusetts in 1946 and, making liberal use of both his own war record and his family's money, won a seat in Congress. Six years later, he was elected to the United States Senate, and in 1958 reelected by a record margin. Within days of his triumph, he was planning his campaign for the White House. He premised his campaign, he said, "on the single assumption that the American people are uneasy at the present drift in our national course." But his appealing public image was at least as important as his political positions in attracting popular support.

A vigorous effort on behalf of Nixon by President Eisenhower in the closing days of the campaign, combined with continuing doubts about Kennedy's youth (he turned forty-three in 1960) and religion (he was a Catholic), almost enabled the Republicans to close what had at one time been a substantial Democratic lead. But in the end, Kennedy held on to win a tiny plurality of the popular vote—49.9 percent to Nixon's 49.6 percent—and only a slightly more comfortable electoral majority—303 to 219.

Kennedy had campaigned promising a program of domestic legislation more ambitious than any since the New Deal, a program he described as

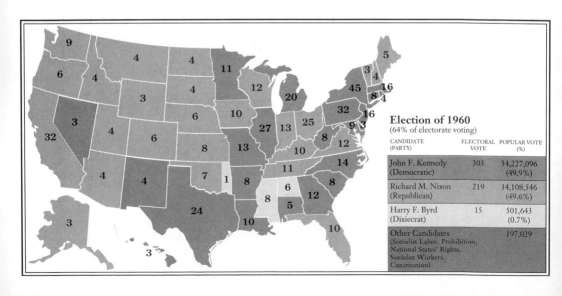

Election of 1960
(64% of electorate voting)

CANDIDATE (PARTY)	ELECTORAL VOTE	POPULAR VOTE (%)
John F. Kennedy (Democratic)	303	34,227,096 (49.9%)
Richard M. Nixon (Republican)	219	34,108,546 (49.6%)
Harry F. Byrd (Dixiecrat)	15	501,643 (0.7%)
Other Candidates (Socialist Labor, Prohibition, National States' Rights, Socialist Workers, Constitution)		197,029

the "New Frontier." But he had serious problems with Congress. Although Democrats remained in control of both houses, their majority included many conservatives from the South and elsewhere, who were far more likely to vote with the Republicans than with Kennedy. One after another of Kennedy's legislative proposals, therefore, found themselves hopelessly stalled.

As a result, the president had to look elsewhere for opportunities to display positive leadership. One area where he believed he could do that was the economy. Economic growth was sluggish in 1961 when Kennedy entered the White House, with unemployment hovering at about 6 percent of the work force. Kennedy initiated a series of tariff negotiations with foreign governments—the "Kennedy Round"—in an effort to stimulate American exports. He began to consider an expanded use of Keynesian fiscal and monetary tools—culminating in his 1962 proposal for a substantial federal tax cut to stimulate the economy.

He also used his personal prestige to battle inflation. In 1962, several steel companies, led by U.S. Steel, announced that they were raising their prices by $6 a ton, a move certain to trigger similar action by the rest of the industry. Kennedy put heavy pressure on U.S. Steel president Roger Blough and other steel executives to rescind the increase. The companies soon relented. But it was a fleeting victory. Kennedy's relationship with the corporate community was now permanently strained, and a few months later the steel companies quietly raised prices again. The president did not protest.

More than any other president of the century (except perhaps the two Roosevelts and, later, Ronald Reagan), Kennedy made his own personality an integral part of his presidency and a central focus of national attention. Nothing illustrated that more clearly than the popular reaction to the tragedy of November 22, 1963. Kennedy had traveled to Texas with his wife and Vice President Lyndon Johnson for a series of political appearances. While the presidential motorcade rode slowly through the streets of Dallas, shots rang out. Two bullets struck the president—one in the throat, the other in the head. He was sped to a nearby hospital, where minutes later he was pronounced dead. Lee Harvey Oswald, who appeared to be a confused and embittered Marxist, was arrested for the crime later that day, and then mysteriously murdered by a Dallas nightclub owner, Jack Ruby, two days later as he was being moved from one jail to another. (The popular assumption at the time was that both Oswald and Ruby had acted alone, assumptions endorsed by a federal commission, chaired by Chief Justice Earl Warren, that was appointed to investigate the assassination. In

JOHN F. KENNEDY AND HIS ADVISERS Kennedy meets in the White House with Robert McNamara and General Maxwell Taylor, two men who would play important roles in the process that would lead to full-scale American military intervention in Vietnam.

later years, however, many Americans—and in 1978 a congressional sub-committee—claimed that the Warren Commission report had not revealed the full story.)

The death of President Kennedy was one of several traumatic public episodes in national history that have left a permanent mark on all who experienced it. Millions of Americans suspended their normal activities for four days to watch the televised events surrounding the presidential funeral. Images of Kennedy's widow, his small children, his funeral procession, his grave site at Arlington Cemetery with its symbolic eternal flame—all became deeply embedded in the public mind. When in later times Americans would look back at the optimistic days of the 1950s and early 1960s and wonder how everything had subsequently seemed to unravel, many would think of November 22, 1963, as the beginning of the change.

Lyndon Johnson

At the time, however, much of the nation took comfort in the personality and performance of Kennedy's successor in the White House, Lyndon Baines Johnson. Johnson was a native of the poor "hill country" of west Texas and had risen to eminence by dint of extraordinary, even obsessive effort and ambition. He was elected to Congress in 1937 as a fervent supporter of Franklin Roosevelt, and he rose steadily in influence by cultivating the favor of party leaders. In 1948, he won election to the United States Senate; a few years later he became the Senate majority leader, a job in which he displayed a legendary ability to persuade and cajole his colleagues into following his lead. Having failed to win the Democratic nomination for president in 1960, he surprised many who knew him by agreeing to accept the second position on the ticket with Kennedy. The events in Dallas thrust him into the White House.

Johnson's rough-edged, even crude personality could hardly have been more different from Kennedy's. But like Kennedy, Johnson was a man who believed in the active use of power. And he proved, in the end, more effective than his predecessor in translating his goals into reality. Between 1963 and 1966, he compiled the most impressive legislative record of any president since Franklin Roosevelt. He was aided by the tidal wave of emotion that followed the death of President Kennedy, which helped win support for many New Frontier proposals. But Johnson also constructed a remarkable reform program of his own, one that he ultimately labeled the "Great Society." And he won approval of much of it through the same sort of skillful lobbying in Congress that had made him an effective majority leader.

Johnson envisioned himself, as well, as a great "coalition builder." He wanted the support of everyone, and for a time he very nearly got it. His first year in office was, by necessity, dominated by the campaign for reelection. There was little doubt that he would win—particularly after the Republican party fell under the sway of its right wing and nominated the conservative Senator Barry Goldwater of Arizona. Liberal Republicans abandoned Goldwater and openly supported Johnson. In the November election, the president received a larger plurality, over 61 percent, than any candidate before or since. Goldwater managed to carry only his home state of Arizona and five states in the Deep South. Record Democratic majorities in both houses of Congress, many of whose members had been swept into office only because of the margin of Johnson's victory, ensured that the president would be able to fulfill many of his goals. Johnson seemed well on his way to achieving his cherished aim: becoming the most successful reform president of the century.

The Assault on Poverty

The domestic programs of the Kennedy and Johnson administrations had two basic goals: maintaining the strength of the American economy and expanding the responsibilities of the federal government for social welfare.

For the first time since the 1930s, the federal government took steps in the 1960s to create important new social welfare programs. The most important of these, perhaps, was Medicare: a program to provide federal aid to the elderly for medical expenses. Its enactment in 1965 came at the end of a bitter, twenty-year debate between those who believed in the concept of national health assistance and those who denounced it as "socialized medicine." But the program as it went into effect removed many objections. For one thing, it avoided the stigma of "welfare" by making Medicare benefits available to all elderly Americans, regardless of need (just as Social Security had done with pensions). That created a large middle-class constituency for the program. The program also defused the opposition of the medical community by allowing doctors serving Medicare patients to practice privately and to charge their normal fees; Medicare simply shifted responsibility for paying those fees from the patient to the government. In 1966, Johnson steered to passage the Medicaid program, which extended federal medical assistance to welfare recipients of all ages. Criticism of the two programs grew in subsequent years, both from those who thought Medicare and Medicaid were inadequate and from those who thought they were too expensive. But broad public support ensured their survival.

Medicare and Medicaid were the first steps in a much larger assault on poverty—one that Kennedy had been contemplating in the last months of his life and that Johnson launched only weeks after taking office. The centerpiece of this "war on poverty," as Johnson called it, was the Office of Economic Opportunity (OEO), which created an array of new educational, employment, housing, and health-care programs. But the OEO was controversial from the start, in part because of its commitment to the idea of "community action."

Community action was an effort to involve members of poor communities themselves in the planning and administration of the programs designed to help them. It was an effort to promote what some of its advocates called "maximum feasible participation." The Community Action programs provided some important benefits. In particular, they provided jobs for many poor people and gave them valuable experience in administrative and political work. Many people who went on to significant careers in politics or community organizing, including many black and Hispanic politicians who would rise to prominence in the 1970s and 1980s, got their start in Community Action programs.

The programs were also important to American Indians. The Community Action approach allowed tribal leaders to design and run programs for themselves and to apply for funds from the federal government on an equal basis with state and municipal authorities. Administering these programs helped produce a new generation of tribal leaders who learned much about political and bureaucratic power from the experience.

But despite its achievements, the Community Action approach proved impossible to sustain. Many programs fell victim to mismanagement or to powerful opposition from the local governments with which they were at times competing. Some activists in Community Action agencies employed tactics that mainstream politicians considered frighteningly radical. The apparent excesses of a few agencies damaged the popular image of the Community Action program, and indeed the war on poverty, as a whole.

The OEO spent nearly $3 billion during its first two years of existence, and it helped reduce poverty significantly in certain areas. But it fell far short of eliminating poverty altogether. That was in part because of the weaknesses of the programs themselves and in part because funding for them, inadequate from the beginning, dwindled as the years passed and a costly war in Southeast Asia became the nation's first priority.

Cities, Schools, and Immigration

Closely tied to the antipoverty program were federal efforts to promote the revitalization of decaying cities and to strengthen the nation's schools. The Housing Act of 1961 offered $4.9 billion in federal grants to cities for the preservation of open spaces, the development of mass-transit systems, and the subsidization of middle-income housing. In 1966, Johnson established a new cabinet agency, the Department of Housing and Urban Development (whose first secretary, Robert Weaver, became the first African-American ever to serve in the cabinet). Johnson also inaugurated the Model Cities program, which offered federal subsidies for urban redevelopment.

Kennedy had long fought for federal aid to public education, but he had failed to overcome two important obstacles: Many Americans feared that aid to education was the first step toward federal control of the schools; and Catholics insisted that federal assistance must extend to parochial as well as public schools, a demand that raised serious constitutional issues and one that Kennedy refused to consider. Johnson managed to circumvent both objections with the Elementary and Secondary Education Act of 1965 and a series of subsequent measures. The bills extended aid to both private and parochial schools and based the aid on the economic conditions of the students, not on the needs of the schools themselves. Total federal expenditures for education and technical training rose from $5 billion to $12 billion between 1964 and 1967.

The Johnson administration also supported the Immigration Act of 1965, one of the most important pieces of legislation of the 1960s, even if largely unnoticed at the time. The law maintained a strict limit on the number of newcomers admitted to the country each year (170,000), but it eliminated the "national origins" system established in the 1920s, which gave preference to immigrants from northern Europe over those from other parts of the world. It continued to restrict immigration from some parts of Latin America, but it allowed people from all parts of Europe, Asia, and Africa to enter the United States on an equal basis. This meant that large new categories of immigrants—and especially large numbers of Asians— would begin entering the United States by the early 1970s and changing the character of the American population.

Legacies of the Great Society

The great surge of reform of the Kennedy-Johnson years reflected a new awareness of social problems in America. It also reflected the confident belief of liberals that America's resources were virtually limitless and that purposeful public effort could surmount any obstacle. By the time Johnson left office, legislation had been either enacted or initiated to deal with a remarkable number of social issues: poverty, health care, education, cities, transportation, the environment, consumer protection, agriculture, science, the arts.

Taken together, the Great Society reforms meant a significant increase in federal spending. For a time, rising tax revenues from the growing economy nearly compensated for the new expenditures. In 1964, Johnson managed to win passage of the $11.5 billion tax cut that Kennedy had first proposed in 1962. The cut increased the federal deficit, but it helped produce substantial economic growth over the next several years that made up for much of the revenue initially lost. As Great Society programs began to multiply, however, and particularly as they began to compete with the escalating costs of America's military ventures, the federal budget rapidly outpaced increases in revenues. In 1961, the federal government had spent $94.4 billion. By 1970, that sum had risen to $196.6 billion.

The high costs of the Great Society programs and the inability of the government to find the revenues to pay for them contributed to a growing disillusionment in later years with the idea of federal efforts to solve social problems. By the 1980s, many Americans had become convinced that the Great Society efforts had not worked and that, indeed, government programs to solve social problems could not work. Others, however, argued equally fervently that social programs had made important contributions both to the welfare of the groups they were designed to help and to the health of the economy as a whole. They pointed, in particular, to the reduction of hunger in America, the inclusion of poor people in health-care programs, and the increased services available to young children.

Whether because of economic growth or because of government antipoverty efforts—or, as seems most likely, because of both—the decade of the 1960s saw the most substantial decrease in poverty in the United States of any period in the nation's history. In 1959, according to the most widely accepted estimates, 21 percent of the American people lived below the officially established poverty line. By 1969, only 12 percent remained below that line. The improvements affected blacks and whites in about the same proportion: 56 percent of the black population had lived in poverty in 1959, while only 32 percent did so ten years later—a 42 percent reduction; 18 percent of all whites had been poor in 1959, but only 10 percent were poor a decade later—a 44 percent reduction.

THE BATTLE FOR RACIAL EQUALITY

The nation's most important domestic initiative in the 1960s was the effort to provide justice and equality to African-Americans. It was the most difficult commitment, the one that produced the severest strains on American society. But it was one that could not be avoided. African-Americans were themselves ensuring that the nation would have to deal with the problem of race.

A M E R I C A N   V O I C E S

MALCOLM X

The Angriest Negro in America

THEY CALLED ME "the angriest Negro in America." I wouldn't deny that charge. I spoke exactly as I felt. "I *believe* in anger. The Bible says there is a *time* for anger." They called me "a teacher, a fomentor of violence." I would say point blank, "That is a lie. I'm not for wanton violence, I'm for justice. I feel that if white people were attacked by Negroes—if the forces of law prove unable, or inadequate, or reluctant to protect those whites from those Negroes—then those white people should protect and defend themselves from those Negroes, using arms if necessary. And I feel that when the law fails to protect Negroes from whites' attack, then those Negroes should use arms, if necessary, to defend themselves." . . .

What was wrong with that? I'll tell you what was wrong. I was a black man talking about physical defense against the white man. The white man can lynch and burn and bomb and beat Negroes—that's all right: "Have patience" . . . "The customs are entrenched" . . . "Things are getting better."

Well, I believe it's a crime for anyone who is being brutalized to continue to accept that brutality without doing something to defend himself. . . . I don't go for non-violence if it also means a delayed solution. To me a delayed solution is a non-solution.

SOURCE: *The Autobiography of Malcolm X*, pp. 366–367. © 1964 by Alex Haley and Malcolm X, © 1965 by Malcolm X and Betty Shabazz. Reprinted by permission of Ballantine Books.

Expanding Protests

John Kennedy had long been sympathetic to the cause of racial justice, but he was hardly a committed crusader. Like many presidents before him, he feared alienating Southern Democratic voters and powerful Southern Democrats in Congress. His administration hoped to contain the racial problem by expanding enforcement of existing laws and supporting litigation to overturn existing segregation statutes.

But the pressure for change could not long be contained. In February 1960, black college students in Greensboro, North Carolina, staged a sit-in at a segregated Woolworth's lunch counter; and in the following months, such demonstrations spread throughout the South, forcing many merchants to integrate their facilities. In the fall of 1960, some of those who had participated in the sit-ins formed the Student Nonviolent Coordinating Committee (SNCC), which worked to keep the spirit of resistance alive.

In 1961, an interracial group of students, working with the Congress of Racial Equality (CORE), began what they called "freedom rides." Traveling by bus throughout the South, they tried to force the desegregation of bus stations. They were met in some places with such savage violence on the part of whites that the president finally dispatched federal marshals to help keep the peace and ordered the integration of all bus and train stations. In the meantime, SNCC workers began fanning out through black communities and even into remote rural areas to encourage blacks to challenge the obstacles to voting that white society had created. The SCLC created citizen education and other programs—many of them organized by the remarkable Ella Baker, one of the great grass-roots leaders of the movement—to mobilize black workers, farmers, housewives, and others to challenge segregation and discrimination.

Events in Alabama in 1963 helped bring the growing movement to something of a climax. In April, Martin Luther King, Jr., helped launch a series of nonviolent demonstrations in Birmingham, Alabama, a city unsurpassed in the strength of its commitment to segregation. Police Commissioner Eugene "Bull" Connor personally supervised a brutal effort to break up the peaceful marches, arresting hundreds of demonstrators and using attack dogs, tear gas, electric cattle prods, and fire hoses—at times even against small children—as much of the nation watched televised reports in horror. Two months later, Governor George Wallace stood in the doorway of a building at the University of Alabama to prevent the court-ordered enrollment of several black students. Only after the arrival of federal marshals did he give way. The same night, NAACP official Medgar Evers was murdered in Mississippi.

A National Commitment

The events in Alabama and Mississippi were a warning to the president that he could not any longer contain or avoid the issue of race. In an important television address the night of the University of Alabama confrontation, Kennedy spoke eloquently of the "moral issue" facing the nation. Days later, he introduced a series of new legislative proposals prohibiting segregation in "public accommodations" (stores, restaurants, theaters, hotels), barring discrimination in employment, and increasing the power of the government to file suits on behalf of school integration.

To generate support for the legislation, and to dramatize the power of the growing movement, more than 200,000 demonstrators marched down the Mall in Washington, D.C., in August 1963 and gathered before the Lincoln Memorial for the largest civil-rights demonstration in the nation's history. Martin Luther King, Jr., in one of the greatest speeches of his distinguished oratorical career, aroused the crowd with a litany of images prefaced again and again by the phrase "I have a dream." The march was the high-water mark of the peaceful, interracial civil-rights movement—and one of the last moments of real harmony within it.

The assassination of President Kennedy three months later gave new impetus to the battle for civil-rights legislation. The ambitious measure that Kennedy had proposed in June 1963 was stalled in the Senate after having passed through the House of Representatives with relative ease. Early in 1964, after Johnson had applied both public and private pressure, supporters of the measure finally mustered the two-thirds majority necessary to close debate and end a filibuster by Southern senators; and the Senate passed the most comprehensive civil-rights bill in the history of the nation.

The Battle for Voting Rights

Having won a significant victory in one area, the civil-rights movement shifted its focus to another: voting rights. During the summer of 1964, thousands of civil-rights workers, black and white, Northern and Southern, spread out through the South, but primarily in Mississippi, to work on behalf of black voter registration and participation. The campaign was known as "Freedom Summer," and it produced a violent response from some Southern whites. Three of the first freedom workers to arrive in the South—two whites, Andrew Goodman and Michael Schwerner, and one black, James Chaney—were murdered. Local law enforcement officials were involved in the crime.

The "Freedom Summer" also produced the Mississippi Freedom Democratic party (MFDP), an integrated alternative to the regular state party organization. Under the leadership of Fannie Lou Hamer and others, the MFDP challenged the regular party's right to its seats at the Democratic National Convention that summer. President Johnson, with King's help, managed to broker a compromise by which members of the MFDP could be seated as observers, with promises of party reforms later on, while the regular party retained its official standing. Both sides grudgingly accepted the agreement, but both were embittered by it.

KING MARCHES THROUGH SELMA Martin Luther King, Jr., and his wife, Coretta (right), lead demonstrators on a march through Selma, Alabama, during his turbulent campaign for black voting rights in 1965. Selma was one of the last of the great interracial crusades on behalf of civil rights.

A year later, in March 1965, King helped organize a major demonstration in Selma, Alabama, to press the demand for the right of blacks to register to vote. Selma sheriff Jim Clark led local police in a brutal attack on the demonstrators—which, as in Birmingham, was televised to a horrified nation. Two Northern whites participating in the Selma march were murdered in the course of the effort there—one, a minister, beaten to death in the streets of the town; the other, a Detroit housewife, shot as she drove along a highway at night. The national outrage that followed the events in Alabama helped push Lyndon Johnson to propose and win passage of the Civil Rights Act of 1965, which provided federal protection to blacks attempting to exercise their right to vote.

But important as such gains were, they failed to satisfy the rapidly rising expectations of American blacks, as the focus of the movement began to move from political to economic issues.

The Changing Movement

For decades, the nation's African-American population had been undergoing a major demographic shift; and by the 1960s, the problem of race was no longer a primarily Southern or rural one, as it had been earlier in the century. By 1966, 69 percent of American blacks were living in metropolitan areas and 45 percent outside the South. Although the economic condition of much of American society was improving, in the poor urban communities in which the black population was concentrated, things were getting significantly worse. More than half of all American nonwhites lived in poverty at the beginning of the 1960s; black unemployment was twice that of whites.

By the mid-1960s, therefore, the issue of race was moving out of the South and into the rest of the nation. The legal battle against school desegregation had moved beyond the initial assault on "de jure" segregation (segregation by law) to an attack on "de facto" segregation (segregation by practice, as through residential patterns), thus carrying the fight into Northern cities. Many African-American leaders (and their white supporters) were demanding, similarly, that the battle against job discrimination move to a new level. Employers should not only abandon negative measures to deny jobs to blacks; they should adopt positive measures to recruit minorities, thus compensating for past injustices. Lyndon Johnson gave his support to the concept of "affirmative action" in 1965. Over the next decade, affirmative action guidelines gradually extended to virtually all institutions doing business with or receiving funds from the federal government (including schools and universities)—and to many others as well.

A symbol of the movement's new direction, and of the problems it would cause, was a major campaign in the summer of 1966 in Chicago, in which King played a prominent role. Organizers of the Chicago campaign hoped to direct national attention to housing and employment discrimination in Northern industrial cities in much the same way similar campaigns had exposed legal racism in the South. But the Chicago campaign not only evoked vicious and at times violent opposition from white residents of that city; it failed to attract wide attention or arouse the national conscience in the way events in the South had done.

Urban Violence

Well before the Chicago campaign, the problem of urban poverty had thrust itself into national prominence when riots broke out in black neighborhoods in major cities, terrifying much of the nation's white population. There were a few scattered disturbances in the summer of 1964, most notably in New York City's Harlem. The first large race riot since the end of World War II occurred the following summer in the Watts section of Los Angeles. In the midst of a traffic arrest, a white police officer struck a protesting black bystander with his club. The incident triggered a storm of anger and a week of violence. Thirty-four people died during the uprising, which was eventually quelled by the National Guard; twenty-eight of them were black. In the summer of 1966, there were forty-three additional outbreaks, the most serious of them in Chicago and Cleveland. And in the summer of 1967, there were eight major riots, including the largest of them all—a racial clash in Detroit in which forty-three people (thirty-three of them black) died.

Televised reports of the violence alarmed millions of Americans and created both a new sense of urgency and a growing sense of doubt among those whites who had embraced the cause of racial justice only a few years before. A special Commission on Civil Disorders, created by the president in response to the riots, issued a celebrated report in the spring of 1968 recommending massive spending to eliminate the abysmal conditions of the ghettoes. To many white Americans, however, the lesson of the riots was the need for stern measures to stop violence and lawlessness.

Black Power

Disillusioned with the ideal of peaceful change in cooperation with whites, an increasing number of African-Americans were turning to a new approach to the racial issue: the philosophy of "black power." Black power could mean many different things. But in all its forms, it suggested a shift away from the goal of assimilation and toward increased awareness of racial distinctiveness.

Perhaps the enduring impact of the black-power ideology was a social and psychological one: instilling racial pride in African-Americans who had been taught by their nation's dominant culture to think of themselves as somehow inferior to whites. But black power had political manifestations as well, most notably in creating a deep schism within the civil-rights movement. Traditional black organizations that had emphasized cooperation with sympathetic whites—groups such as the NAACP, the Urban League, and King's Southern Christian Leadership Conference—now faced competition from more radical groups. The Student Nonviolent Coordinating Commit-

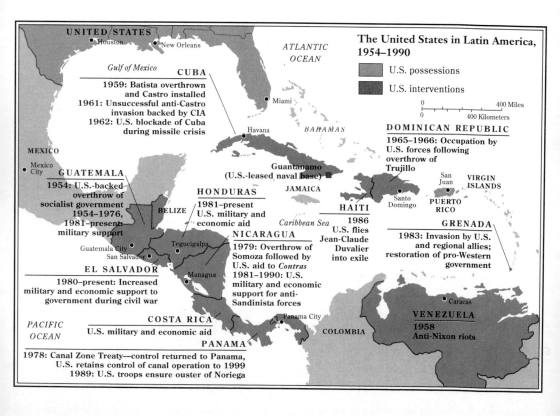

The United States in Latin America, 1954–1990

U.S. possessions

U.S. interventions

0 — 400 Miles
0 — 400 Kilometers

CUBA
1959: Batista overthrown and Castro installed
1961: Unsuccessful anti-Castro invasion backed by CIA
1962: U.S. blockade of Cuba during missile crisis

DOMINICAN REPUBLIC
1965–1966: Occupation by U.S. forces following overthrow of Trujillo

GUATEMALA
1954: U.S.-backed overthrow of socialist government
1954–1976, 1981–present: military support

HONDURAS
1981–present
U.S. military and economic aid

HAITI
1986
U.S. flies Jean-Claude Duvalier into exile

GRENADA
1983: Invasion by U.S. and regional allies; restoration of pro-Western government

NICARAGUA
1979: Overthrow of Somoza followed by U.S. aid to *Contras*
1981–1990: U.S. military and economic support for anti-Sandinista forces

EL SALVADOR
1980–present: Increased military and economic support to government during civil war

COSTA RICA
U.S. military and economic aid

VENEZUELA
1958
Anti-Nixon riots

PANAMA
1978: Canal Zone Treaty—control returned to Panama, U.S. retains control of canal operation to 1999
1989: U.S. troops ensure ouster of Noriega

Guantanamo (U.S.-leased naval base)

tee and the Congress of Racial Equality had both begun as relatively moderate, interracial organizations. SNCC, in fact, had been a student branch of the SCLC. By the mid-1960s, however, these and other groups were calling for more radical and occasionally even violent action against the racism of white society and were openly rejecting the approaches of older, more established black leaders.

Particularly alarming to whites were such overtly revolutionary organizations as the Black Panthers, based in Oakland, California, and the separatist group, the Nation of Islam, which denounced whites as "devils" and appealed to blacks to embrace the Islamic faith and work for complete racial separation. The most celebrated of the Black Muslims, as whites often termed them, was Malcolm Little, who had adopted the name Malcolm X ("X" to denote his lost African surname). He died in 1965 when black gunmen, presumably under orders from rivals within the Nation of Islam, assassinated him. But he remained a major figure in many black communities long after his death—as important and revered a symbol to many African-Americans as Martin Luther King, Jr.

FROM "FLEXIBLE RESPONSE" TO VIETNAM

In international affairs as much as in domestic reform, the optimistic liberalism of the Kennedy and Johnson administrations dictated a more active and aggressive approach to dealing with the nation's problems than in the past.

Diversifying Foreign Policy

The Kennedy administration entered office convinced that the United States needed to be able to counter communist aggression in more flexible ways than the atomic-weapons-oriented defense strategy of the Eisenhower years permitted. In particular, Kennedy was unsatisfied with the nation's ability to meet communist threats in "emerging areas" of the Third World—the areas in which, Kennedy believed, the real struggle against communism would be waged in the future. He gave enthusiastic support to the development of the Special Forces (or "Green Berets," as they were soon known)—soldiers trained specifically to fight guerrilla conflicts and other limited wars.

Kennedy also favored expanding American influence through peaceful means. To repair the badly deteriorating relationship with Latin America, he proposed an "Alliance for Progress": a series of projects undertaken cooperatively by the United States and Latin American governments for peaceful development and stabilization of the nations of that region. Its purpose was both to spur social and economic development and to inhibit the rise of Castro-like movements in other Central or South American countries. Kennedy also inaugurated the Agency for International Development (AID) to coordinate foreign aid. And he established what became one of his most popular innovations: the Peace Corps, which sent young American volunteers abroad to work in developing areas.

Among the first foreign policy ventures of the Kennedy administration was a disastrous assault on the Castro government in Cuba. The Eisenhower administration had launched the project; and by the time Kennedy took office, the CIA had been working for months to train a small army of anti-Castro Cuban exiles in Central America. On April 17, 1961, with the approval of the new president, 2,000 of the armed exiles landed at the Bay of Pigs in Cuba, expecting first American air support and then a spontaneous uprising by the Cuban people on their behalf. They received neither. At the last minute, as it became clear things were going badly, Kennedy withdrew the air support, fearful of involving the United States too directly in the invasion. The expected uprising did not occur. Instead, well-armed Castro forces easily crushed the invaders, and within two days the entire mission had collapsed.

Confrontations with the Soviet Union

In the grim aftermath of the Bay of Pigs, Kennedy traveled to Vienna in June 1961 for his first meeting with Soviet Premier Nikita Khrushchev. Their frosty exchange of views did little to reduce tensions between the two nations. Nor did Khrushchev's continuing irritation over the existence of a noncommunist West Berlin in the heart of East Germany.

Particularly embarrassing to the communists was the mass exodus of residents of East Germany to the West through the easily traversed border in the center of Berlin. Before dawn on August 13, 1961, the Soviet Union stopped the exodus by directing East Germany to construct a wall between East and West Berlin. Guards fired on those who continued to try to escape. For nearly thirty years, the Berlin Wall served as the most potent physical symbol of the conflict between the communist and noncommunist worlds.

The rising tensions culminated the following October in the most dangerous and dramatic crisis of the Cold War. During the summer of 1962,

American intelligence agencies had become aware of the arrival of a new wave of Soviet technicians and equipment in Cuba and of military construction in progress. On October 14, aerial reconaissance photos produced clear evidence that the Soviets were constructing sites on the island for offensive nuclear weapons. To the Soviets, placing missiles in Cuba probably seemed a reasonable—and relatively inexpensive—way to counter the presence of American missiles in Turkey (and a way to deter any future American invasion of Cuba). But to Kennedy and most other Americans, the missile sites represented an act of aggression by the Soviets toward the United States. Almost immediately, the president decided that the weapons could not be allowed to remain. On October 22, he ordered a naval and air blockade around Cuba, a "quarantine" against all offensive weapons. Preparations were under way for an American air attack on the missile sites when, late in the evening of October 26, Kennedy received a message from Khrushchev implying that the Soviet Union would remove the missile bases in exchange for an American pledge not to invade Cuba. Ignoring other, tougher Soviet messages, the president agreed. The crisis was over.

The Cuban missile crisis brought the world closer to nuclear war than at any time since World War II. And in the following months, both seemed ready to move toward a new accommodation. In June 1963, President Kennedy spoke at American University in Washington, D.C., and seemed for the first time to offer hope for a peaceful rapprochement with the Soviet Union. That same summer, the United States and the Soviet Union concluded years of negotiation by agreeing to a treaty to ban the testing of nuclear weapons in the atmosphere—the first step toward mutual arms reduction since the beginning of the Cold War.

Johnson and the World

Lyndon Johnson entered the presidency lacking even John Kennedy's limited prior experience with international affairs. He was eager, therefore, not only to continue the policies of his predecessor but to prove quickly that he too was a strong and forceful leader.

An internal rebellion in the Dominican Republic gave him an early opportunity to do so. A 1961 assassination had toppled the repressive dictatorship of General Rafael Trujillo, and for the next four years various factions in the country had struggled for dominance. In the spring of 1965, a conservative military regime began to collapse in the face of a revolt by a broad range of groups on behalf of the left-wing nationalist Juan Bosch.

Arguing (without any evidence) that Bosch planned to establish a pro-Castro, communist regime, Johnson dispatched 30,000 American troops to quell the disorder. Only after a conservative candidate defeated Bosch in a 1966 election were the forces withdrawn.

From Johnson's first moments in office, however, his foreign policy was almost totally dominated by the bitter civil war in Vietnam and by the expanding involvement of the United States there. In many respects, Johnson was simply the unfortunate legatee of commitments initiated by his predecessors. But the determination of the new president, and of others within his administration, to prove their resolve in the battle against communism helped produce the final, decisive steps toward a full-scale commitment.

Guns and Advisers

The American involvement in Vietnam had developed so slowly and imperceptibly that when it began spectacularly to expand, in 1964 and 1965, few could remember how it had originated. The first steps toward intervention had seemed at the time to be little more than minor events on the periphery of the larger Cold War. American aid to French forces in Indochina before 1954 had been limited and indirect; the nation's involvement with the Diem regime thereafter, while more substantial, seemed for several years no greater than its involvement with many other Third World governments. But as Diem began to face growing internal opposition, and as the threat from the communist regime to the north appeared to grow, the United States found itself drawn ever deeper into what would ultimately become widely known as the "quagmire."

Ngo Dinh Diem had been an unfortunate choice as the basis of American hopes for a noncommunist South Vietnam. Autocratic, aristocratic, and corrupt, he staunchly resisted any economic reforms that would weaken the position of the Vietnamese upper class and the power of his own family. A fervent Roman Catholic, he invited dissent through his efforts to suppress Buddhism, the religion of the majority of Vietnamese.

Diem's own limitations intensified problems that would have faced any South Vietnamese ruler, for North Vietnam had never accepted the partition of the country in 1954. When Diem began in the late 1950s to try to exterminate the communist cadres that were loyal to Ho Chi Minh but remained in the south, the North Vietnamese ordered a resumption of the war. Communists in the south organized the National Front for the Liberation of South Vietnam (NLF), known to many Americans as the Viet Cong. The communist government in Hanoi sent crucial assistance and, as the war continued, began introducing troops of its own into the south.

His political and military position steadily deteriorating, Diem appealed to the United States for assistance. The Eisenhower administration increased the flow of weapons and ammunition to South Vietnam during its last years in office and introduced the first few American military advisers to the area—about 650 in all. The Kennedy administration expanded that assistance considerably, despite misgivings about Diem, by increasing the flow of munitions into South Vietnam and raising the number of American military personnel to 15,500.

Even so, by 1963, the Diem regime stood on the brink of collapse. The military struggle against the Viet Cong was going badly. Diem's brutal tactics against Buddhist demonstrators in Saigon had produced a religious crisis as well. Several Buddhist monks burned themselves to death in the streets of the capital, arousing further popular resistance to the government and horrifying the American public, which witnessed the immolations on television. Early in November, after receiving tacit assurances of support from the United States, South Vietnamese military leaders staged a coup, during which Diem, his brother, and others were murdered. A few weeks later, John Kennedy too was dead.

From Aid to Intervention

Lyndon Johnson, therefore, inherited what was already a substantial American commitment to the survival of an anticommunist South Vietnam. During his first months in office, he expanded the American involvement in Vietnam only slightly, sending an additional 5,000 military advisers there and preparing to send 5,000 more. Then, early in August 1964, the president announced that American destroyers on patrol in international waters in the Gulf of Tonkin had been attacked by North Vietnamese torpedo boats. Later information raised serious doubts as to whether the administration reported the attacks accurately. At the time, however, virtually no one questioned Johnson's portrayal of the incident as a serious act of aggression or his insistence that the United States must respond. By a vote of 416 to 0 in the House and 88 to 2 in the Senate, Congress hurriedly passed the Gulf of Tonkin Resolution, which authorized the president to "take all necessary measures" to protect American forces and "prevent further aggression" in

CHINA

Lao Cai

Than Uyen

Yen Bay

Red River

NORTH VIETNAM

BURMA

Dienbienphu

Hanoi

Haiphong

Red River
Delta

Pak Seng

PLAIN
OF JARS

Ban Ban

Luang
Prabang

Gulf of Tonkin

Hainan

Vang Vieng

L A O S

Vientiane

Vinh

Udon Thani

Phanom

Mekong R.

Dong Hoi

Vinh Linh

DMZ (Demilitarized Zone)

QUANG TRI
PROVINCE

Khesanh

Hue

Phu Bai

Da Nang

South China Sea

THAILAND

Hoi An

Tamky

Takhli

Chulai

My Lai

Don Muang

Udon Ratchathani

Quang Ngai

Lop Buri

Ratchasima

Dak To

Kontum

PLATEAU
OF KONTUM

Ankhe

Pleiku

Quinhon

Bangkok

Battambang

Angkor Wat

PLATEAU
OF DARLAC

Sattahip

Tonle Sap

CAMBODIA

Ban Me Thout

Gulf of Thailand

Kompong
Chom

Da Lat

Nhatrang

Camranh Bay

Phnom
Penh

Prey
Veng

Bo Duc

1970:

Tay Ninh

Phanrang

**U.S. and South Vietnam
troops entered Viet Cong
strongholds inside Cambodia**

Ben Cat

SOUTH

Bienhua

VIETNAM

Sihanoukville

Tan Son Nhut
Airbase

Saigon

Vung Tau

**The War in Vietnam and
Indochina, 1964–1975**

Rach Gia

Cantho

MEKONG DELTA

□ U.S. bases

Quan Long

U.S. and South Vietnam
invasion of Cambodia

0   100 Miles

0   100 Kilometers

CA MAU
PENINSULA

Con Son

Ho Chi Minh Trail
(communist supply route)

FRIENDSHIP HIGHWAY

Southeast Asia. The resolution became, in Johnson's view at least, an open-ended legal authorization for escalation of the conflict.

With the South Vietnamese leadership still in disarray and the communist military pressure on the South growing stronger, more and more of the burden of opposition to the Viet Cong fell on the United States. In February 1965, seven marines died when communist forces attacked an American military base at Pleiku. Johnson retaliated by ordering American bombings of the north, in an attempt to destroy the depots and transportation lines responsible for the flow of North Vietnamese soldiers and supplies into South Vietnam. The bombing continued intermittently until 1972. A month later, in March 1965, two battalions of American marines landed at Da Nang in South Vietnam. There were now more than 100,000 American troops in Vietnam.

Four months later, the president finally admitted that the character of the war had changed. American soldiers would now, he announced, begin playing an active combat role in the conflict. By the end of the year, there were more than 180,000 American combat troops in Vietnam; in 1966, that number doubled; and by the end of 1967, there were over 500,000 American soldiers there. In the meantime, the air war had intensified until the tonnage of bombs dropped ultimately exceeded that in all theaters during World War II. And American casualties were mounting. By the spring of 1966, more than 4,000 Americans had been killed.

The Quagmire

For more than seven years, American combat forces remained bogged down in a war that the United States was never able either to win or fully to understand. Combating a foe whose strength lay less in weaponry than in its infiltration of the population, the United States responded with heavy-handed technological warfare designed for conventional battles against conventional armies. American forces succeeded in winning most of the major battles in which they became engaged. There were astounding (if not always reliable) casualty figures showing that far more communists than Americans were dying in combat. But if the war was not actually being lost, neither was it being won.

Central to the American war effort was the heralded "pacification" program, whose purpose was to push the Viet Cong from particular regions and then "pacify" those regions by winning the "hearts and minds" of the people. Routing the Viet Cong was often possible, but the subsequent pacification was more difficult. American forces were not adept at estab-

ON PATROL IN VIETNAM, JUNE 1965 Several weeks before President Johnson announced that American ground troops would enter the Vietnam War, United States soldiers were already engaged in combat. These marines, patrolling the area around the American base at Da Nang, were ambushed by communist guerrillas moments after this photograph was taken. One marine was killed and three were wounded.

lishing rapport with provincial Vietnamese; and the American military never gave that part of the program a very high priority in any case. Gradually, the pacification program gave way to the more heavy-handed relocation strategy, through which American troops uprooted villagers from their homes, sent them fleeing to refugee camps or into the cities (producing by 1967 more than 3 million refugees), and then destroyed the vacated villages and surrounding countryside.

As the war dragged on and victory remained elusive, some American officers and officials began to urge the president to expand the military efforts. Some argued for heavier bombing and increased troop strength; others insisted that the United States attack communist enclaves in surrounding countries; a few began to urge the use of nuclear weapons. The Johnson administration, however, resisted. Unwilling to abandon its commitment to South Vietnam for fear of destroying American "credibility" in the world, the government was also unwilling to expand the war too far, for fear of provoking direct intervention by the Chinese, the Soviets, or both. In the meantime, the president began to encounter additional obstacles and frustrations at home.

The War at Home

Few Americans, and even fewer influential ones, had protested the American involvement in Vietnam as late as the end of 1965. But as the war dragged on and its futility began to become apparent, political support for it began to erode. A series of "teach-ins" on university campuses, beginning at the University of Michigan in 1965, sparked a national debate over the war before such debate developed inside the government itself. By the end of 1967, American students opposed to the war had become a significant political force. Enormous peace marches in New York, Washington, D.C., and other cities drew broad public attention to the antiwar movement. In the meantime, a growing number of journalists, particularly reporters who had spent time in Vietnam, helped sustain the movement with their frank revelations about the brutality and apparent futility of the war.

The growing chorus of popular protest soon began to stimulate opposition to the war from within the government. Senator J. William Fulbright of Arkansas, chairman of the powerful Senate Foreign Relations Committee, turned against the war and in January 1966 began to stage highly publicized and occasionally televised congressional hearings to air criticisms of it. Other members of Congress joined Fulbright in opposing Johnson's policies—including, in 1967, Robert F. Kennedy, brother of the slain president, now a senator from New York. Even within the administration, the consensus seemed to be crumbling. Robert McNamara, who had done much to help extend the American involvement in Vietnam, quietly left the government, disillusioned, in 1968. His successor as secretary of defense, Clark Clifford, became a quiet but powerful voice within the administration on behalf of a cautious scaling down of the commitment.

In the meantime, the American economy was beginning to suffer. Johnson's commitment to fighting the war while continuing his Great Society reforms—his promise of "guns and butter"—proved impossible to maintain. The inflation rate, which had remained at 2 percent through most of the early 1960s, rose to 3 percent in 1967, 4 percent in 1968, and 6 percent in 1969. In August 1967, Johnson asked Congress for a tax increase—a 10 percent surcharge that was widely labeled a "war tax"—which he knew was necessary if the nation was to avoid even more ruinous inflation. In return, congressional conservatives demanded and received a $6 billion reduction in the funding for Great Society programs.

THE TRAUMAS OF 1968

By the end of 1967, the twin crises of the war in Vietnam and the deteriorating racial situation at home, crises that fed upon and inflamed each other, had produced profound social and political tensions. In the course of 1968, those tensions seemed suddenly to burst to the surface and threaten national chaos. Not since World War II had the United States experienced so profound a sense of crisis.

JOHNSON AND HUMPHREY, MARCH 27, 1968 Four days before announcing he would not run for reelection, a grim and tired Lyndon Johnson, accompanied by Vice President Hubert Humphrey, receives a briefing on the military situation in Vietnam.

The Tet Offensive

On January 31, 1968, the first day of the Vietnamese New Year (Tet), communist forces launched an enormous, concerted attack on American strongholds throughout South Vietnam. A few cities, most notably Hue, fell to the communists. Others suffered major disruptions. But what made the Tet offensive so shocking to the American people, who saw vivid reports of it on television, was the sight of communist forces in the heart of Saigon, setting off bombs, shooting down South Vietnamese officials and troops, and holding down fortified areas (including, briefly, the grounds of the American embassy). The Tet offensive also suggested to the American public something of the brutality of the fighting in Vietnam. In the midst of the fighting, television cameras recorded the sight of a South Vietnamese officer shooting a captured Viet Cong soldier in the head in the streets of Saigon.

American forces soon dislodged the Viet Cong from most of the positions they had seized, and the Tet offensive in the end cost the communists such appalling casualties that they were significantly weakened for months to come. Indeed, the Tet defeats permanently depleted the ranks of the NLF and forced North Vietnamese troops to take on a much larger share of the subsequent fighting. But all that had little impact on American opinion. Tet may have been a military victory for the United States; but it was a political defeat for the administration, a defeat from which it would never fully recover.

In the following weeks, opposition to the war grew substantially. Leading newspapers and magazines, television commentators, and mainstream politicians began taking public stands in favor of de-escalation of the conflict. Within weeks of the Tet offensive, public opposition to the war had almost doubled. And Johnson's personal popularity rating had slid to 35 percent, the lowest of any president since Harry Truman.

The Political Challenge

Beginning in the summer of 1967, dissident Democrats tried to mobilize support behind an antiwar candidate who would challenge Lyndon Johnson in the 1968 primaries. When Robert Kennedy turned them down, they recruited Senator Eugene McCarthy of Minnesota. A brilliantly orchestrated campaign by young volunteers in the New Hampshire primary produced a startling showing by McCarthy in March; he nearly defeated the president.

A few days later, Robert Kennedy finally entered the campaign, embittering many McCarthy supporters but bringing his own substantial strength among blacks, poor people, and workers to the antiwar cause. Polls showed the president trailing badly in the next scheduled primary, in Wisconsin. On March 31, Johnson went on television to announce a limited halt in the bombing of North Vietnam—his first major concession to the antiwar forces—and, much more surprising, his withdrawal from the presidential contest.

For a moment, it seemed as though the antiwar forces had won. Robert Kennedy quickly established himself as the champion of the Democratic primaries, winning one election after another. In the meantime, however, Vice President Hubert Humphrey, with the support of President Johnson, entered the contest and began to attract the support of party leaders and of the many delegations that were selected not by popular primaries but by state party organizations. He soon appeared to be the front runner in the race.

The King Assassination

In the midst of this bitter political battle, in which the war had been the dominant issue, the attention of the nation suddenly turned again to race in response to a shocking tragedy. On April 4, Martin Luther King, Jr., who had traveled to Memphis, Tennessee, to lend his support to striking black sanitation workers in the city, was shot and killed while standing on the balcony of his motel. The assassin, James Earl Ray, who was captured days later in London, had no apparent motive. Subsequent evidence suggested that he had been hired by others to do the killing, but he himself never revealed the identity of his employers.

King's tragic death produced an outpouring of grief matched in recent memory only by the reaction to the death of John Kennedy. Among American blacks, it also produced anger. In the days after the assassination, major riots broke out in more than sixty American cities. Forty-three people died; more than 3,000 suffered injuries; as many as 27,000 people were arrested.

The Kennedy Assassination and Chicago

Robert Kennedy continued his campaign for the presidential nomination. Late in the night of June 6, he appeared in the ballroom of a Los Angeles hotel to acknowledge his victory in that day's California primary. As he left the ballroom after his victory statement, Sirhan Sirhan, a young Palestinian apparently enraged by pro-Israeli remarks Kennedy had recently made, emerged from a crowd and shot him in the head. Early the next morning, Kennedy died.

The presidential campaign continued gloomily during the last weeks before the convention. Hubert Humphrey, who had seemed likely to win the nomination even before Robert Kennedy's death, now faced opposition only from McCarthy's weakened campaign. Humphrey's nomination seemed assured, despite the embittered claims of many Democrats that Humphrey would simply continue the policies of the Johnson administration. The approaching Democratic Convention, therefore, began to take on the appearance of an exercise in futility; and antiwar activists, despairing of winning any victories within the convention, began to plan major demonstrations outside it.

When the Democrats finally gathered in Chicago in August, even the most optimistic observers were predicting a turbulent convention. Inside the hall, delegates bitterly debated an antiwar plank in the party platform that both Kennedy and McCarthy supporters favored. Miles away, in a downtown park, thousands of antiwar protesters were staging demonstrations. On the third night of the convention, as the delegates were beginning their balloting on the now virtually inevitable nomination of Hubert Humphrey, demonstrators and police clashed in a bloody riot in the streets of Chicago. Hundreds of protesters were injured as police attempted to disperse them with tear gas and billy clubs. Aware that the violence was being televised to the nation, the demonstrators taunted the authorities with the chant, "The whole world is watching!" And Hubert Humphrey, who had spent years dreaming of becoming his party's candidate for president, received a nomination that night which appeared at the time to be almost worthless.

The Conservative Response

The turbulent events of 1968 persuaded many observers that American society was in the throes of revolutionary change. In fact, however, the prevailing response of the American people to the turmoil was a conservative one.

The most visible sign of the conservative backlash was the surprising success of the campaign of George Wallace for the presidency. Wallace had established himself in 1963 as one of the leading spokesmen for the defense

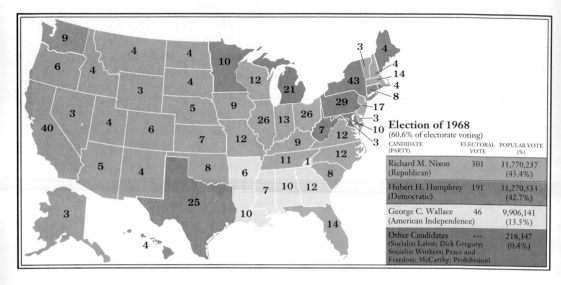

Election of 1968
(60.6% of electorate voting)

CANDIDATE (PARTY)	ELECTORAL VOTE	POPULAR VOTE (%)
Richard M. Nixon (Republican)	301	31,770,237 (43.4%)
Hubert H. Humphrey (Democratic)	191	31,270,533 (42.7%)
George C. Wallace (American Independence)	46	9,906,141 (13.5%)
Other Candidates (Socialist Labor; Dick Gregory; Socialist Workers; Peace and Freedom; McCarthy; Prohibition)	---	218,347 (0.4%)

of segregation when, as governor of Alabama, he had attempted to block the admission of black students to the University of Alabama. In 1968, he became a third-party candidate for president, basing his campaign on a host of conservative grievances. He denounced the forced busing of students, the proliferation of government regulations and social programs, and the permissiveness of authorities toward race riots and antiwar demonstrations. There was never any serious chance that Wallace would win the election; but his standing in the polls rose at times to over 20 percent.

A more effective effort to mobilize the "silent majority" in favor of order and stability was under way within the Republican party. Richard Nixon, whose political career had seemed at an end after his losses in the presidential race of 1960 and a California gubernatorial campaign two years later, reemerged as the preeminent spokesman for what he sometimes called "Middle America." Nixon recognized that many Americans were tired of hearing about their obligations to the poor, tired of hearing about the sacrifices necessary to achieve racial justice, tired of judicial reforms that seemed designed to help criminals. By offering a vision of stability, law and order, government retrenchment, and "peace with honor" in Vietnam, he easily captured the nomination of his party for the presidency. And after the spectacle of the Democratic Convention, he enjoyed a commanding lead in the polls as the November election approached.

That lead diminished greatly in the last weeks before the voting. Old doubts about Nixon's character continued to haunt the Republican candidate. A skillful last-minute surge by Hubert Humphrey, who managed to restore a tenuous unity to the Democratic party, narrowed the gap further. And the Wallace campaign appeared to be hurting the Republicans more than the Democrats. In the end, however, Nixon eked out a victory almost as narrow as his defeat in 1960. He received 43.4 percent of the popular vote to Humphrey's 42.7 percent (a margin of only about 500,000 votes), and 301 electoral votes to Humphrey's 191. George Wallace, who like most third-party candidates faded in the last weeks of the campaign, still managed to poll 13.5 percent of the popular vote and to carry five Southern states with a total of 46 electoral ballots. Nixon had hardly won a decisive personal mandate. But the election made clear that a majority of the American electorate was more interested in restoring stability than in promoting social change.

D E B A T I N G T H E P A S T

The Vietnam Commitment

HE DEBATE OVER why the United States became involved in the conflict in Vietnam (which is only one of many debates about the meaning of the war) has centered on two different, if related, questions. One is an effort to assess the broad objectives Americans believed they were pursuing in Vietnam. The other is an effort to explain how and why policymakers made the specific decisions that led the United States to a military commitment in Indochina.

Scholars and writers such as Norman Podhoretz, Guenter Lewy, and R. B. Smith, reflecting the official government explanation of American intervention in the war, have argued that the communist aggression in Vietnam was part of a Chinese and Soviet design to spread revolution throughout Asia. America, therefore, was not only protecting Vietnam, although that was an important part of its mission; it was also defending the rest of Asia, which would soon be threatened by communism if Vietnam fell. The intervention in Vietnam was a rational and even necessary expression of America's legitimate security interests and its belief in democracy.

Most scholars, however, have been more skeptical. Historians on the left argue that America's intervention in Vietnam was a form of imperialism—part of a larger effort by the United States after World War II to impose a particular political and economic order on the world. "The Vietnam War," Gabriel Kolko wrote in 1985, "was for the United States the culmination of its frustrating postwar effort to merge its arms and politics to halt and reverse the emergence of states and social systems opposed to the international order Washington sought to establish." Others argued that the United States fought in Vietnam to serve the domestic economic interests that had a stake in the region or in the arms production the war stimulated. Other, more moderate critics blame the Vietnam intervention on the myopia of a foreign policy elite unwilling to question its own unreflective commitment to containing communism everywhere and unable to distinguish between international aggression and domestic insurgency.

Those who have looked less at the nation's broad objectives than at the workings of the policymaking process have also produced competing explanations. David Halberstam's *The Best and the Brightest* (1972) argued that policymakers deluded themselves into thinking they could achieve their goals in Vietnam by ignoring, suppressing, or dismissing information that should have suggested that they were wrong; because of arrogance or ideological rigidity, they simply refused to consider that victory was beyond their grasp.

Larry Berman, writing in 1982, offered a rather different view. Neither Johnson nor his advisers were unaware of the obstacles to success in Vietnam. Almost everyone suspected that victory would be difficult, even impossible, to attain. The president was not misled or misinformed. But Johnson committed troops to the war anyway, because he feared that allowing Vietnam to fall would ruin him politically and destroy his hopes for building his "Great Society" at home. Leslie Gelb and Richard Betts made a related argument in 1979. Vietnam, they claimed, was the logical, perhaps inevitable result of a political and bureaucratic order shaped by the ideology of the Cold War. However costly the intervention in Vietnam, policymakers concluded, the costs of not intervening and allowing South Vietnam to fall always seemed higher. The war escalated in the 1960s not because American aims changed but because the situation in Vietnam deteriorated to the point where nothing short of intervention would prevent defeat. Only when the national and international political situation itself shifted in the late 1960s and early 1970s—only when it became clear that the political costs of staying in Vietnam were higher than the political costs of getting out—was it possible for the United States to begin disengaging.

CHAPTER THIRTY-TWO

The Crisis of Authority

The Turbulent Society ∽ The Mobilization of Minorities ∽ The New Feminism
Nixon, Kissinger, and the War ∽ Nixon, Kissinger, and the World
Politics and Economics in the Nixon Years ∽ The Watergate Crisis

THE ELECTION OF Richard Nixon in 1968 was the result of more than the unpopularity of Lyndon Johnson and the war. It was the result, too, of a broad public reaction against what many Americans considered a dangerous assault on the foundations of their society and culture. In Richard Nixon they found a man who seemed perfectly to match their mood. Himself a product of a hard-working, middle-class family, he projected an image of stern dedication to traditional values. Yet the presidency of Richard Nixon, far from returning calm and stability to American politics, coincided with, and helped to produce, more years of crisis.

THE TURBULENT SOCIETY

What was perhaps most alarming to conservative Americans in the 1960s and 1970s was a pattern of social and cultural protest by younger Americans, who were giving vent to two related impulses. One was the impulse, emerging from the political left, to create a great new community of "the people," which would rise up to break the power of elites and force the nation to end the war, pursue racial and economic justice, and transform its political life. The other, at least equally powerful impulse was related to, but not entirely compatible with, the first: the vision of personal "liberation." It found expression in part through the efforts of groups—African-Americans, Indians, Hispanics, women, gay people, and others—to define and assert themselves and make demands on the larger society. It also found expression through the efforts of individuals to create a new culture—one that would allow them to escape from what some considered the dehumanizing pressures of the modern "technocracy."

The New Left

Among the products of the racial crisis and the war in Vietnam was a radicalization of many American students, who in the course of the 1960s formed what became known as the New Left. The New Left emerged from many sources, but from nothing so much as the civil-rights movement, in which many idealistic young white Americans had become involved in the early 1960s. Within a few years, some white civil-rights activists were beginning to consider broader political commitments. In 1962, a group of students (most of them white) gathered in Michigan to form an organization to give voice to their demands: Students for a Democratic Society (SDS). Their declaration of beliefs, the Port Huron Statement, expressed their disillusionment with the society they had inherited and their determination to build a new politics. In the following years, SDS became the leading organization of student radicalism.

Since most members of the New Left were students, their radicalism centered for a time on issues related to the modern university. A 1964 dispute at the University of California at Berkeley over the rights of students to engage in political activities on campus—the Free Speech Movement—was the first outburst of what was to be nearly a decade of campus turmoil. Students at Berkeley and elsewhere protested the impersonal character of the modern university, and they denounced the role of educational institutions in sustaining what they considered corrupt or immoral public policies. The antiwar movement greatly inflamed and expanded the challenge to the universities; and beginning in 1968, campus demonstrations, riots, and building seizures became almost commonplace. At Columbia University in New York, students seized the offices of the president and other members of the administration and occupied them for days until local police forcibly ejected them. Over the next several years, hardly any major university was immune to some level of disruption. Small groups of especially dogmatic radicals—among them the "Weathermen," an offshoot of SDS—were responsible for a few cases of arson and bombing that destroyed campus buildings and claimed several lives.

Not many people ever accepted the radical political views that lay at the heart of the New Left. But many supported the position of SDS and other groups on particular issues, and above all on the Vietnam War. Between 1967 and 1969, student activists organized some of the largest political demonstrations in American history—in Washington, D.C., and around the country—to protest the war. They helped thrust the issue of Vietnam into the center of American politics.

Closely related to opposition to the war—and another issue that helped fuel the New Left—was opposition to the military draft. The gradual abolition of many traditional deferments—for graduate students, teachers, husbands, fathers, and others—swelled the ranks of those faced with conscription (and thus likely to oppose it). Draft card burnings became common features of antiwar rallies on college campuses. Many draft-age Americans simply refused induction, accepting what were occasionally long terms in jail as a result. Thousands of others fled to Canada, Sweden, and elsewhere (where they were joined by many deserters from the armed forces) to escape conscription. Not until 1977, when President Jimmy Carter issued a general pardon to draft resisters and a far more limited amnesty for deserters, did the Vietnam exiles begin to return to the country in substantial numbers.

The Counterculture

Closely related to the New Left was a new youth culture openly scornful of the values and conventions of middle-class society. The most visible characteristic of the counterculture, as it became known, was a change in life style. As if to display their contempt for conventional standards, young Americans flaunted long hair, shabby or flamboyant clothing, and a rebellious disdain for traditional speech and decorum. Central to the counterculture were drugs: marijuana smoking—which after 1966 became almost as common a youthful diversion as beer drinking had once been—and the use of other, more potent hallucinogens, such as LSD. There was also a new, more permissive view of sex.

The counterculture's iconoclasm and hedonism sometimes masked its philosophy, which offered a fundamental challenge to the American middle-class mainstream. Like the New Left, with which it in many ways overlapped, the counterculture challenged the structure of modern American society, attacking its banality, its hollowness, its artificiality, its isolation from nature. The most committed adherents of the counterculture—the hippies, who came to dominate the Haight-Ashbury neighborhood of San Francisco and other places, and the social dropouts, many of whom retreated to rural communes—rejected modern society altogether and attempted to find refuge in a simpler, more "natural" existence. But even those whose commitment to the counterculture was less dramatic shared a commitment to the idea of personal fulfillment through rejecting the inhibitions and conventions of middle-class culture. In a corrupt and alienating society, the new creed seemed to suggest, the first responsibility of the individual is cultivation of the self, the unleashing of one's own full potential for pleasure and fulfillment.

The effects of the counterculture reached out to the larger society and helped create a new set of social norms that many young people (and some adults) chose to imitate. Long hair and freakish clothing became the badge not only of hippies and radicals but of an entire generation. The use of marijuana, the freer attitudes toward sex, the iconoclastic (and often obscene) language—all spread far beyond the realm of the true devotees of the counterculture. And perhaps the most pervasive element of the new youth society was one that even the least radical members of the generation embraced: rock music. Rock's driving rhythms, its undisguised sensuality, its often harsh and angry tone—all made it an appropriate vehicle for expressing the themes of the social and political unrest of the late 1960s.

Virtually no Americans could avoid evidence of how rapidly the norms of their society were changing in the late 1960s. Those who attended movies saw a gradual shift away from the banal, conventional messages that had dominated films since the 1920s. Instead, they saw explorations of political issues, of new sexual mores, of violence, of social conflict. Television too began to turn (even if more slowly than the other media) to programming that reflected social and cultural conflict—as exemplified by the enormously popular *All in the Family*, whose protagonist, Archie Bunker, was a lower-middle-class bigot.

THE MOBILIZATION
OF MINORITIES

The growth of black protest, and of a significant white response to it, both preceded the political and cultural upheavals of the 1960s and helped to produce them. It also encouraged other minorities to assert themselves and demand redress of their grievances. For Indians, Hispanic Americans, gay men and women, and others, the late 1960s and 1970s were a time of growing self-expression and political activism.

Seeds of Indian Militancy

Few minorities had deeper or more justifiable grievances against the prevailing culture than American Indians—or Native Americans, as some began defiantly to call themselves in the 1960s. Indians were the least prosperous, least healthy, and least stable group in the nation. Average annual family income for Indians was $1,000 less than that for blacks. The Native American unemployment rate was ten times the national rate. Joblessness was particularly high on the reservations, where nearly half of all Indians lived. But even most Indians living in cities were victims of limited education and training and could find only menial jobs. Life expectancy among Indians was more than twenty years less than the national average. Suicides among Indian youths were a hundred times more frequent than among white youths. And while black Americans attracted the attention (for good or for ill) of many whites, Indians for many years remained largely ignored.

For much of the postwar era, and particularly after the resignation of John Collier as Commissioner of Indian Affairs in 1945, federal policy toward the tribes had been shaped by a determination to incorporate Indians into mainstream American society whether Indians wanted to assimilate or not. Two laws passed in 1953 established the basis of a new policy, which became known as "termination." Through termination, the federal government withdrew all official recognition of the tribes as legal entities, administratively separate from state governments, and made them subject to the same local jurisdictions as white residents. At the same time, the government encouraged Indians to assimilate into the white world and worked to funnel Native Americans into cities, where, presumably, they would adapt themselves to the white world and lose their cultural distinctiveness.

To some degree, the termination and assimilation policies achieved their objectives. The tribes grew weaker as legal and political entities. Many Native Americans adapted to life in the cities, at least to a degree. On the whole, however, the new policies were a disastrous failure. Indians themselves fought so bitterly against them that in 1958 the Eisenhower administration barred further "terminations" without the consent of the affected tribes. In the meantime, the struggle against termination had mobilized a new generation of Indian militants and had breathed life into the principal Native American organization, the National Congress of American Indians (NCAI), which had been created in 1944.

The Democratic administrations of the 1960s did not disavow the termination policy, but neither did they make any effort to revive it. Instead, they made modest efforts to restore at least some degree of tribal autonomy. The funneling of OEO money to tribal organizations through the Community Action program was one prominent example. In the meantime, the tribes themselves were beginning to fight for self-determination—partly in response to the black civil-rights movement and partly in response to other social and cultural changes (among them, the expanding mobility and rising educational levels of younger Indians, who were becoming more aware of the world around them and of their own anomalous place within it). The new militancy also benefited from the rapid increase in the Indian population, which was growing much faster than that of the rest of the nation (nearly doubling between 1950 and 1970 to a total of about 800,000).

The Indian Civil-Rights Movement

In 1961, more than 400 members of 67 tribes gathered in Chicago to discuss ways of bringing all Indians together in an effort to redress common wrongs. The manifesto they issued, the Declaration of Indian Purpose, stressed the "right to choose our own way of life" and the "responsibility of preserving our precious heritage."

The 1961 meeting was only one example of a growing Indian self-consciousness. The National Indian Youth Council, created in the aftermath of the 1961 Chicago meeting, promoted the idea of Indian nationalism and intertribal unity. In 1968, a group of young, militant Indians established the American Indian Movement (AIM), which drew its greatest support from those Indians who lived in urban areas but which soon established a significant presence on the reservations as well.

The new activism had some immediate political results. In 1968, Congress passed the Indian Civil Rights Act, which guaranteed reservation Indians many of the protections accorded other citizens by the Bill of Rights but which also recognized the legitimacy of tribal laws within the reservations. But leaders of AIM and other insurgent groups were not satisfied and turned increasingly to direct action. In 1968, Indian fishermen, citing old treaty rights, clashed with Washington state officials on the Columbia River and in Puget Sound. The following year, members of several tribes occupied the abandoned federal prison on Alcatraz Island in San Francisco Bay, claiming the site "by right of discovery."

In response to the growing pressure, the new Nixon administration appointed Louis Bruce, a Mohawk-Sioux, to the position of Commissioner of Indian Affairs in 1969; and in 1970, the president promised both increased tribal self-determination and an increase in federal aid. But the protests continued. In November 1972, nearly a thousand demonstrators, most of them Lakota (or Sioux) Indians, forcibly occupied the building of the Bureau of Indian Affairs in Washington for six days. A more celebrated protest occurred later that winter at Wounded Knee, South Dakota, the site of the 1890 massacre of Sioux by federal troops.

In the early 1970s, Wounded Knee was part of a large Sioux reservation, two-thirds of which had been leased to white ranchers for generations as an outgrowth of the Dawes Act. Conditions for the Indian residents were desperate, and passions grew quickly in 1972 in response to the murder of a Sioux by a group of whites, who were not, many Indians believed, adequately punished. In February 1973, members of AIM seized and occupied the town of Wounded Knee for two months, demanding radical changes in the administration of the reservation and insisting that the government honor its long-forgotten treaty obligations. A brief clash between the occupiers and federal forces left one Indian dead and another wounded. Shortly thereafter the siege came to an end.

More immediately effective than these militant protests were the victories that various tribes were achieving in the 1970s in the federal courts. In 1985, the United States Supreme Court, in *County of Oneida* v. *Oneida Indian Nation* supported Indian claims to 100,000 acres in upstate New York that the Oneida tribe claimed by virtue of treaty rights long forgotten by whites. In doing so, the Court raised the possibility that some longstanding grievances could be addressed through judicial action.

The Indian civil-rights movement, like other civil-rights movements of the same time, fell far short of winning full justice and equality for Native Americans. But it helped the tribes win a series of new legal rights and protections that, together, gave them a stronger position than they had enjoyed at any previous time in this century. It also helped many Indians gain a renewed awareness of and pride in their identity as Indians and as part of a distinct community within the larger United States.

Hispanic-American Activism

More numerous and more visible than Indians were Hispanic Americans (sometimes known as Latinos), the fastest-growing minority group in the United States. Large numbers of Mexican-Americans (or Chicanos) had entered the country during World War II in response to the wartime labor shortage, and many had remained in the cities of the Southwest and the Pacific coast. After the war, when the legal agreements that had allowed Mexican contract workers to enter the country expired, large numbers of immigrants continued to move to the United States illegally. In 1953, the government launched what it called Operation Wetback to deport the illegals, but the effort failed to stem the flow of new arrivals. By 1960, there were already substantial Chicano neighborhoods (or *barrios*) in American cities from El Paso to Detroit. The largest (with more than 500,000 people, according to census figures) was in Los Angeles, which by then had a bigger Mexican population than anyplace except Mexico City.

But the greatest expansion in the Hispanic population of the United States was yet to come. In 1960, the census reported slightly more than 3 million Hispanics living in the United States. By 1970, that number had grown to 9 million and by 1990 to 20 million. Hispanics constituted more than a third of all legal immigrants to the United States after 1960. Since there was also an uncounted but very large number of illegal immigrants in those years (estimates ranged from 7 million to 12 million), the real percentage of Hispanic immigrants was undoubtedly much larger.

Large numbers of Puerto Ricans (who were entitled to American citizenship by birth) migrated to Eastern urban areas, particularly New York, where they formed one of the poorest communities in the city. South Florida's substantial Cuban population began with a wave of middle-class refugees fleeing the Castro regime in the early 1960s. These first Cuban migrants quickly established themselves as a successful and highly assimilated part of Miami's middle class. In 1980, a second, much poorer wave of Cuban immigrants—the so-called Marielistas, named for the port from which they left Cuba—arrived in Florida when Castro temporarily relaxed exit restrictions. (This group included a large number of criminals, whom Castro had, in effect, expelled from the country.) This second wave was less welcomed by the government (and the existing Cuban community) and less easily assimilated. Later in the 1980s, large numbers of immigrants (both legal and illegal) began to arrive from Central and South America—from Guatemala, Nicaragua, El Salvador, Peru, and others. The most numerous Hispanic group, however, remained the Mexican-Americans, who were concentrated in the Southwest and California but who were also spreading throughout the nation's interior.

Many Hispanic Americans were affluent and successful people. But most newly arrived Chicanos and others were less well educated than either "Anglo" or black Americans and hence less well prepared for high-paying jobs. The fact that many spoke English poorly or not at all further limited their employment prospects. As a result, they found themselves concentrated in poorly paid service jobs.

Like blacks and Indians, many Hispanic Americans responded to the highly charged climate of the 1960s by strengthening their ethnic identification and by organizing for political and economic power. Affluent Hispanics in Miami filled influential positions in the professions and local government; in the Southwest, they elected Mexican-Americans to seats in Congress and to governorships. A Mexican-American political organization, La Raza Unida, exercised influence in southern California and elsewhere in the Southwest in the 1970s and beyond.

CÉSAR CHÁVEZ As the leader of the United Farm Workers, the first Chicano-dominated labor organization to attract national attention, Chávez became for a time the most visible spokesman for and symbol of the needs of Hispanic-Americans. He is shown here leading a demonstration outside the headquarters of the Safeway supermarket chain in San Diego, California, in 1973, protesting the arrest of other UFW members several days earlier.

One of the most visible efforts to organize Hispanics occurred in California, where an Arizona-born Mexican-American farm worker, César Chávez, created an effective union of itinerant farm workers. His United Farm Workers (UFW), a largely Hispanic organization, launched a prolonged strike in 1965 against growers to demand, first, recognition of the union and, second, increased wages and benefits. When employers resisted, Chávez enlisted the cooperation of college students, churches, and civil-rights groups (including CORE and SNCC) and organized a nationwide boycott, first of table grapes and then of lettuce. In 1968, Chávez campaigned openly for Robert Kennedy. Two years later, he won a substantial victory when the growers of half of California's table grapes signed contracts with his union.

For most Hispanics, however, the path to economic and political power was more difficult. Partly because of language barriers, partly because of ineffective organization, and partly because of discrimination, Mexican-Americans and others were slow to develop political influence in proportion to their numbers. In the meantime, Hispanics formed one of the poorest segments of the United States population.

Challenging the "Melting Pot" Ideal

The efforts of blacks, Hispanics, Indians, and others to forge a clearer group identity seemed to challenge a longstanding premise of American political thought—the idea of the "melting pot." Older, European immigrant groups liked to believe that they had advanced in American society by adopting the values and accepting the rules of the world to which they had moved and advancing within it on its own terms. The newly militant ethnic groups of the 1960s were less willing to accept the standards of the larger society and more likely to demand recognition of their own ethnic identity. African-Americans, Indians, and Hispanics all challenged the assimilationist idea and advocated instead a culturally pluralist society, in which racial and ethnic groups would preserve not only a sense of their own heritage (which older, more "assimilationist" ethnic groups did as well) but also their own social and cultural norms.

To a large degree, the advocates of cultural pluralism succeeded. Recognition of the special character of particular groups was embedded in federal law through a wide range of affirmative action programs, which extended not only to blacks, but to Indians, Hispanics, and others as well. Ethnic studies programs proliferated in schools and universities. Eventually, this impulse led to an even more assertive (and highly controversial) cultural movement that in the 1980s and 1990s became known as "multiculturalism," which challenged the "Eurocentric" basis of American education and culture and demanded that non-European civilizations be accorded equal attention.

Gay Liberation

The last important liberation movement to emerge in the 1960s, and the most unexpected, was the effort by homosexuals and lesbians to win political and economic rights and, more important, social acceptance. Homosexuality had been an unacknowledged reality throughout American history. Nonheterosexual men and women had long been forced either to suppress their sexual preferences, to exercise them surreptitiously, or to live within isolated and often persecuted communities. But by the late 1960s, the liberating impulses that had affected other groups helped mobilize gay men and women (as homosexuals and lesbians had come to term themselves) to fight for their own rights.

On June 27, 1969, police officers raided the Stonewall Inn, a gay nightclub in New York City's Greenwich Village, and began arresting patrons simply for frequenting the place. The raid was not unusual, but the response was. Gay onlookers taunted the police and then attacked them. Someone started a blaze in the Stonewall Inn itself, almost trapping the policemen inside. Rioting continued throughout Greenwich Village (the center of New York's gay community) through much of the night.

The "Stonewall Riot" marked the beginning of the gay liberation movement—one of the most controversial challenges to traditional values and assumptions of its time. New organizations—among them the Gay Liberation Front, founded in New York in 1969—sprang up around the country. Public discussion and media coverage of homosexuality, long subject to an unofficial taboo, quickly and dramatically increased. Gay activists were having some success in challenging the longstanding assumption that homosexuality was aberrant behavior and were arguing that no sexual preference was any more normal than another.

Most of all, however, the gay liberation movement transformed the outlook of gay men and women themselves. It helped them to "come out," to express their preferences openly and unapologetically, and to demand from society a recognition that gay relationships could be as significant and worthy of respect as heterosexual ones. Some gays advocated not only an acceptance of homosexuality as a valid and "normal" preference but a change in the larger society as well: a redefinition of personal identity to give much greater importance to erotic impulses. Those changes did not quickly occur. But by the early 1980s, the gay liberation movement had made remarkable strides. Even the ravages of the AIDS epidemic, which, in the beginning at least, affected the gay community more disastrously than it affected any other group, failed to halt the growth of gay liberation. In many ways, it strengthened it.

By the early 1990s, homosexuals and lesbians were achieving many of the same milestones that other oppressed minorities had attained in earlier decades. Openly gay politicians were winning election to public office. Universities were establishing gay and lesbian studies programs. And laws prohibiting discrimination on the basis of sexual preference were making slow, halting progress at the state and local level.

THE NEW FEMINISM

American women constituted 51 percent of the population in the 1960s. But during the 1960s and 1970s, many women began to identify with minority groups as they renewed demands for a liberation of their own. Sexual discrimination was so deeply embedded in the fabric of society that when feminists first began to denounce it, many men (and even many women) responded with bafflement and anger. By the 1970s, however, public awareness of the issue had increased greatly, and the role of women in American life had changed more dramatically than that of any other group in the nation.

The Rebirth

Feminism had been a weak and often embattled force in American life for more than forty years after the adoption of the woman suffrage amendment in 1920. A few determined women kept feminist political demands alive in the National Woman's Party and other organizations. Many more women expanded the acceptable bounds of female activity by entering new areas of the workplace or engaging in political activities. Nevertheless, through the 1950s and early 1960s, active feminism was often difficult to detect. Yet within a very few years, it evolved from an almost invisible remnant to one of the most powerful social movements in American history.

The 1963 publication of Betty Friedan's *The Feminine Mystique* is often cited as the first event of contemporary women's liberation. Friedan, who had been a writer for women's magazines in the 1950s, traveled around the country interviewing the women who had graduated with her from Smith College in 1947. Most of these women were living out the dream that postwar American society had created for them; they were affluent wives and mothers living in comfortable suburbs. And yet many of them were deeply frustrated and unhappy, with no outlets for their intelligence, talent, and education. By chronicling their unhappiness and frustration, Friedan's book had a powerful impact. But it did not so much cause the revival of feminism as help give voice to a movement that was already stirring.

By the time *The Feminine Mystique* appeared, John Kennedy had established the President's Commission on the Status of Women, which brought national attention to sexual discrimination and helped create important networks of feminist activists who would lobby for legislative redress. Also in 1963, the Kennedy administration helped win passage of the Equal Pay Act, which barred the pervasive practice of paying women less than men for equal work. A year later, Congress incorporated into the Civil Rights Act of 1964 an amendment—Title VII—that extended to women many of the same legal protections against discrimination that were being extended to blacks.

In 1966, Friedan joined with other feminists to create the National Organization for Women (NOW), which was to become the nation's largest and most influential feminist organization. NOW reflected the varying constituencies of the emerging feminist movement. It responded to the complaints of the women Friedan's book had examined—affluent suburbanites with no outlet for their interests—by demanding greater educational opportunities for women and denouncing the domestic ideal and the traditional concept of marriage. But the heart of the movement, at least in the beginning, was directed toward the needs of women in the workplace. NOW denounced the exclusion of women from professions, from politics, and from countless other areas of American life. By the end of the decade, its membership had expanded to 15,000.

Women's Liberation

By the late 1960s, new and more radical feminist demands were also attracting a large following, especially among younger, affluent, white, educated women. Many of them drew inspiration from the New Left and the counterculture. Some were involved in the civil-rights movement, others in the antiwar crusade. Many had found that even within those movements, they faced discrimination and exclusion and were subordinated to male leaders.

In its most radical form, the new feminism rejected the whole notion of marriage, family, and even heterosexual intercourse (a vehicle, some women claimed, of male domination). Not many women, not even many feminists, embraced such extremes. But by the early 1970s large numbers of women were coming to see themselves as an exploited group banding together against oppression and developing a culture of their own. The women's liberation movement inspired the creation of grass-roots organizations and activities through which women not only challenged sexism and discrimination but created communities of their own. In cities and towns across the country, feminists opened women's bookstores, bars, and coffee shops. They founded feminist newspapers and magazines. They created centers to assist victims of rape and abuse, women's health clinics (and, particularly after 1973, abortion clinics), and day-care centers.

Expanding Achievements

By the early 1970s, the public and private achievements of the women's movement were already substantial. In 1971, the government extended its affirmative action guidelines to include women—linking sexism with racism as an officially acknowledged social problem. Women were making rapid progress, in the meantime, in their efforts to move into the economic and political mainstream. The nation's major all-male educational institutions began to open their doors to women. (Princeton and Yale did so in 1969, and most other colleges and universities soon did the same.) Some women's colleges, in the meantime, began accepting male students.

Women were also becoming an important force in business and the professions. Nearly half of all married women held jobs by the mid-1970s, and almost nine-tenths of all women with college degrees worked. The two-career family, in which both the husband and the wife maintained active professional lives, was becoming a widely accepted norm; many women were postponing marriage or motherhood for the sake of their careers. There were also important symbolic changes, such as the refusal of many women to adopt their husbands' names when they married and the use of the term "Ms." in place of "Mrs." or "Miss" to denote the irrelevance of a woman's marital status in the professional world.

In politics, women began to compete effectively with men for both elected and appointive positions in the 1970s. By the mid-1980s, women were serving in both houses of Congress, on the Supreme Court, in numerous federal cabinet positions, as governors of several states, and in many other political positions. And in 1984, the Democratic party chose a woman, Representative Geraldine Ferraro of New York, as its vice presidential candidate. In academia, women were expanding their presence in traditional scholarly fields; they were also creating a field of their own—women's studies, which in the 1980s and early 1990s was the fastest-growing area of American scholarship. Women even joined what had previously been the most celebrated all-male fraternity in American culture: the space program. Sally Ride became the first woman astronaut to travel in space in 1983.

In 1972, Congress approved the Equal Rights Amendment (ERA) to the Constitution, which some feminists had been promoting since the 1920s, and sent it to the states. For a while ratification seemed almost certain. By the late 1970s, however, the momentum behind the amendment had died. The ERA was in trouble not because of indifference but because of a rising chorus of objections to it from people (including many antifeminist women) who feared that it would disrupt traditional social patterns. In 1982, the amendment finally died when the ten years allotted for ratification expired.

The Abortion Controversy

A vital element of American feminism since the 1920s has been the effort by women to win greater control of their own sexual and reproductive lives. In its least controversial form, this impulse helped produce an increasing awareness in the 1960s and 1970s of the problems of rape, sexual abuse, and wife beating. There continued to be some controversy over the dissemination of contraceptives and birth-control information; but that issue, at least, seemed to have lost much of the explosive character it had once possessed. A related issue, however, stimulated as much popular passion as any question of its time: abortion.

Abortion had once been legal in much of the United States, but by the beginning of the twentieth century it was banned by statute in most of the country and remained so into the 1960s (although many abortions continued to be performed quietly, and often dangerously, out of sight of the law). The women's movement created strong new pressures on behalf of the legalization of abortion. Several states had abandoned restrictions on abortion by the end of the 1960s. And in 1973, the Supreme Court's decision in *Roe* v. *Wade*, based on a new theory of a constitutional "right to privacy" first recognized by the Court only a few years earlier, invalidated all laws prohibiting abortion during the "first trimester"—the first three months of pregnancy. The issue, it seemed, was finally settled. But it soon became clear that it was not.

In many ways, feminism was much like other "liberation" movements of the 1960s and 1970s. But it differed from them in one fundamental respect: its success. The women's movement may not have fulfilled all its goals. But it achieved fundamental and permanent changes in the position of women in American life, and it promised to do much more.

NIXON, KISSINGER, AND THE WAR

Richard Nixon assumed office in 1969 committed not only to restoring stability at home but to creating a new and more stable order in the world. Central to Nixon's hopes for international stability was a resolution of the stalemate in Vietnam. Yet the new president felt no freer than his predecessor to abandon the American commitment there.

Vietnamization

Despite Nixon's own deep interest in international affairs, he brought with him into government a man who ultimately seemed to overshadow the president himself in the conduct of diplomacy: Henry Kissinger, a Harvard professor whom Nixon appointed as his special assistant for national security affairs. Kissinger quickly established dominance over the secretary of state, William Rogers, and the secretary of defense, Melvin Laird, who were both more experienced in public life. That was in part a result of Nixon's passion for concentrating decision making in the White House. But Kissinger's keen intelligence, his bureaucratic skills, and his success in handling the press were at least equally important. Together, Nixon and Kissinger set out to find an acceptable solution to the stalemate in Vietnam.

The new Vietnam policy moved along several fronts. One was an effort to limit domestic opposition to the war so as to permit the administration more political space in which to maneuver. Aware that the military draft was one of the most visible targets of dissent, the administration devised a new "lottery" system, through which only a limited group—those nineteen-year-olds with low lottery numbers—would be subject to conscription. Later, the president urged the creation of an all-volunteer army. By 1973, the Selective Service System was on its way to at least temporary extinction.

More important in stifling dissent, however, was a new policy: the "Vietnamization" of the war—that is, the training and equipping of the South Vietnamese military to assume the burden of combat in place of American forces. In the fall of 1969, Nixon announced the withdrawal of 60,000 American ground troops from Vietnam, the first reduction in United States troop strength since the beginning of the war. The withdrawals continued steadily for more than three years, so that by the fall of 1972 relatively few American soldiers remained in Indochina. From a peak of more than 540,000 in 1969, the number had dwindled to about 60,000.

Vietnamization did help quiet domestic opposition to the war for a time. It did nothing, however, to break the stalemate in the negotiations with the North Vietnamese in Paris. The new administration quickly decided that new military pressures would be necessary to do that.

Escalation

By the end of their first year in office, Nixon and Kissinger had decided that the most effective way to tip the military balance in America's favor was to destroy the bases in Cambodia from which the American military believed the North Vietnamese were launching many of their attacks. Very early in his presidency, Nixon ordered the air force to begin bombing Cambodian territory to destroy the enemy sanctuaries. He kept the raids secret from Congress and the public. In the spring of 1970, whether with American encouragement and support is not clear, conservative military leaders overthrew the neutral government of Cambodia and established a new, pro-American regime under General Lon Nol. Lon Nol quickly gave his approval to American incursions into his territory; and on April 30, Nixon went on television to announce that he was ordering American troops across the border into Cambodia to "clean out" the bases that the enemy had been using for its "increased military aggression."

Literally overnight, the Cambodian invasion restored the dwindling antiwar movement to vigorous life. The first days of May saw the most widespread and vocal antiwar demonstrations ever. A mood of crisis was already mounting when, on May 4, four college students were killed and nine others injured after members of the National Guard opened fire on antiwar demonstrators at Kent State University in Ohio. Ten days later, police killed two black students at Jackson State University in Mississippi during a demonstration there.

The clamor against the war spread into the government and the press. Congress angrily repealed the Gulf of Tonkin Resolution in December, stripping the president of what had long served as the legal basis for the war. Nixon ignored the action. Then, in June 1971, first the *New York Times* and later other newspapers began publishing excerpts from a secret study of the war prepared by the Defense Department during the Johnson administration. The so-called Pentagon Papers, leaked to the press by former Defense official Daniel Ellsberg, provided confirmation of what many had long believed: the government had been dishonest, both in reporting the military progress of the war and in explaining its own motives for American involvement. The administration went to court to suppress the documents, but the Supreme Court finally ruled that the press had the right to publish them.

Particularly troubling, both to the public and to the government itself, were signs of decay within the American military. Morale and discipline among American troops in Vietnam, who had been fighting a savage and inconclusive war for more than five years, was rapidly deteriorating. The

KENT STATE UNIVERSITY, MAY 4, 1970 A student lies dead at Kent State University, one of four who died after National Guardsmen opened fire on a group of protesters.

trial and conviction in 1971 of Lieutenant William Calley, who was charged with overseeing a massacre of more than 100 unarmed South Vietnamese civilians, attracted wide public attention to the dehumanizing impact of the war on those who fought it—and to the terrible consequences for the Vietnamese people of that dehumanization. Less publicized were other, more widespread problems among American troops in Vietnam: desertion, drug addiction, racial bias, refusal to obey orders, even the killing of unpopular officers by enlisted men.

The continuing carnage, the increasing savagery, and the social distress at home had largely destroyed public support for the war. By 1971, nearly two-thirds of those interviewed in public-opinion polls were urging American withdrawal from Vietnam. President Nixon, however, was determined to resist, and if possible destroy, his critics, convinced that a defeat in Vietnam would cause unacceptable damage to the nation's (and his own) credibility. The FBI, the CIA, the White House itself, and other federal agencies increased their efforts to discredit and harass antiwar and radical groups, often through illegal means.

In Indochina, meanwhile, the fighting raged on. In February 1971, the president ordered the air force to assist the South Vietnamese army in an invasion of Laos—a test, as he saw it, of his Vietnamization program. Within weeks, the South Vietnamese scrambled back across the border in defeat. American bombing in Vietnam and Cambodia increased, despite its apparent ineffectiveness. In March 1972, the North Vietnamese mounted their biggest offensive since 1968 (the so-called Easter Offensive). American and South Vietnamese forces managed to halt the communist advance, but it was clear that without American support the South Vietnamese would not have succeeded. At the same time, Nixon ordered American planes to bomb targets near Hanoi, the capital of North Vietnam, and Haiphong, its principal port, and called for the mining of seven North Vietnamese harbors (including Haiphong).

"Peace with Honor"

As the 1972 presidential election approached, the administration stepped up its effort to produce a breakthrough in negotiations with the North Vietnamese. In April 1972, the president dropped his longtime insistence on a removal of North Vietnamese troops from the south before any American withdrawal. Meanwhile, Henry Kissinger was meeting privately in Paris with the North Vietnamese foreign secretary, Le Duc Tho, to work out terms for a cease-fire. On October 26, only days before the presidential election, Kissinger announced that "peace is at hand."

Several weeks later (after the election), negotiations broke down once again. Although both the American and the North Vietnamese governments were ready to accept the Kissinger-Tho plan for a cease-fire, President Nguyen Van Thieu of South Vietnam balked, still insisting on a full withdrawal of North Vietnamese forces from the south. Kissinger tried to win additional concessions from the communists to meet Thieu's objections; but on December 16, talks broke off.

The next day, December 17, American B-52s began the heaviest and most destructive air raids of the entire war on Hanoi, Haiphong, and other North Vietnamese targets. Civilian casualties were high. And fifteen American B-52s were shot down by the North Vietnamese; in the entire war to that point, the United States had lost only one of the giant bombers. On December 30, Nixon terminated the "Christmas bombing." The United States and the North Vietnamese returned to the conference table. And on January 27, 1973, they signed an "agreement on ending the war and restoring peace in Vietnam." Nixon claimed that the Christmas bombing had forced the North Vietnamese to relent. At least equally important, however, was the enormous American pressure on Thieu to accept the cease-fire.

The terms of the Paris accords were little different from those Kissinger and Tho had accepted in principle a few months before. There would be an immediate cease-fire. The North Vietnamese would release several hundred American prisoners of war, whose fate had become an emotional issue of great importance within the United States. The Thieu regime would survive for the moment, but North Vietnamese forces already in the south would remain there. An undefined committee would work out a permanent settlement.

Defeat in Indochina

American forces were hardly out of Indochina before the Paris accords collapsed. In March 1975, finally, the North Vietnamese launched a full-scale offensive against the now greatly weakened forces of the south. Thieu appealed to Washington for assistance; the president (now Gerald Ford) appealed to Congress for additional funding; Congress refused. Late in April 1975, communist forces marched into Saigon, shortly after officials of the Thieu regime and the staff of the American embassy had fled the

THE FALL OF SAIGON The chaotic evacuation of Americans from Saigon in the spring of 1975, only hours before victorious North Vietnamese troops entered the city, was a humiliating spectacle. Desperate South Vietnamese soldiers and officials fought with American soldiers and diplomats for space on the few airplanes and helicopters available.

country in humiliating disarray. Communist forces quickly occupied the capital, renamed it Ho Chi Minh City, and began the process of reuniting Vietnam under the harsh rule of Hanoi. At about the same time, the Lon Nol regime in Cambodia fell to the murderous communists of the Khmer Rouge—whose brutal policies led to the death of more than a third of the country's people over the next several years.

Such were the dismal results of more than a decade of direct American military involvement in Vietnam. More than 1.2 million Vietnamese soldiers had died in combat, along with countless civilians throughout the region. A beautiful land had been ravaged, its agrarian economy left in ruins; even in the early 1990s, Vietnam remained one of the poorest and most politically oppressive nations in the world. The United States had paid a heavy price as well. The war had cost the nation almost $150 billion in direct costs and much more indirectly. It had resulted in the deaths of over 57,000 young Americans and the injury of 300,000 more. And the nation had suffered a blow to its confidence and self-esteem from which it would not soon recover.

NIXON, KISSINGER, AND THE WORLD

The continuing war in Vietnam provided a dismal backdrop to what Nixon considered his larger mission in world affairs: the construction of a new international order. The president had become convinced that the old assumptions of a "bipolar" world—in which the United States and the Soviet Union were the only truly great powers—were now obsolete. America must adapt to the new "multipolar" international structure, in which China, Japan, and Western Europe were becoming major, independent forces. Nixon and Kissinger believed it was possible to construct something like the "balance of power" that had permitted nineteenth-century Europe to enjoy nearly a century of relative stability. To do so, however, required a major change in several longstanding assumptions of American foreign policy.

The China Initiative and Détente

For more than twenty years, ever since the fall of Chiang Kai-shek in 1949, the United States had treated China, the second-largest nation on earth, as if it did not exist. Instead, America recognized the forlorn regime-in-exile on Taiwan as the legitimate government of mainland China. Nixon and Kissinger wanted to forge a new relationship with the Chinese communists—in part to strengthen them as a counterbalance to the Soviet Union. The Chinese, for their part, were eager to forestall the possibility of a Soviet-American alliance against China and to end China's own isolation from the international arena.

In July 1971, Nixon sent Henry Kissinger on a secret mission to Beijing. When Kissinger returned, the president made the startling announcement that he would visit China himself within the next few months. That fall, with American approval, the United Nations admitted the communist government of China and expelled the representatives of the Taiwan regime. Finally, in February 1972, Nixon paid a formal visit to China and, in a single stroke, erased much of the deep American animosity toward the Chinese communists. Nixon did not yet formally recognize the communist regime, but in 1972 the United States and China began low-level diplomatic relations.

The initiatives in China coincided with (and probably assisted) an effort by the Nixon administration to improve relations with the Soviet Union. In 1969, American and Soviet diplomats met in Helsinki, Finland, to begin talks on limiting nuclear weapons. In 1972, they produced the first Strategic

A M E R I C A N   V O I C E S

RICHARD NIXON

The China Trip, 1972

ON FEBRUARY 17, 1972, at 10:35 A.M. we left Andrews Air Force Base for Peking. . . . We stopped briefly in Shanghai . . . ; an hour and a half later we prepared to land in Peking. I looked out the window. It was winter, and the countryside was drab and gray. The small towns and villages looked like pictures I had seen of towns in the Middle Ages. . . .

Chou En-lai stood at the foot of the ramp, hatless in the cold. Even a heavy overcoat did not hide the thinness of his frail body. When we were about halfway down the steps, he began to clap. I paused for a moment and then returned the gesture, according to the Chinese custom.

I knew that Chou had been deeply insulted by Foster Dulles's refusal to shake hands with him at the Geneva Conference in 1954. When I reached the bottom step, therefore, I made a point of extending my hand as I walked toward him. When our hands met, one era ended and another began. . . .

I stood on Chou's left while the band played the anthems. "The Star-Spangled Banner" had never sounded so stirring to me as on that windswept runway in the heart of Communist China. . . .

Chou and I rode into the city in a curtained car. As we left the airport, he said, "Your handshake came over the vastest ocean in the world—twenty-five years of no communication." When we came into Tienamen Square at the center of Peking . . . I noticed that the streets were empty.

SOURCE: *RN: The Memoirs of Richard Nixon,* pp. 559–560. Copyright © 1978 by Richard Nixon. Reprinted by permission of Warner Books, Inc.

Arms Limitation Treaty (SALT I), which froze some nuclear missiles (ICBMs) of both sides at present levels. In May of that year, the president traveled to Moscow to sign the agreement. The next year, the Soviet premier, Leonid Brezhnev, visited Washington; and the two leaders pledged renewed efforts to speed the next phase of arms control negotiations.

The Problems of Multipolarity

The policies of rapprochement with communist China and détente with the Soviet Union reflected Nixon's and Kissinger's belief in the importance of stable relationships among the great powers. But great-power relationships could not alone ensure international stability, for the Third World remained the most volatile and dangerous source of international tension.

Central to the Nixon-Kissinger policy toward the Third World was the effort to maintain the status quo without involving the United States too deeply in local disputes. In 1969 and 1970, the president described what became known as the Nixon Doctrine, by which the United States would "participate in the defense and development of allies and friends" but would leave the "basic responsibility" for the future of those "friends" to the nation's themselves. In practice, the Nixon Doctrine meant a declining American interest in contributing to Third World development; a growing contempt for the United Nations, where underdeveloped nations were gaining influence through their sheer numbers; and increasing support to authoritarian regimes attempting to withstand radical challenges from within.

In 1970, for example, the CIA poured substantial funds into Chile to help support the established government against a communist challenge. When the Marxist candidate for president, Salvador Allende, came to power anyway through an honest election, the United States began funneling more money to opposition forces in Chile to help "destabilize" the new government. In 1973, a military junta seized power from Allende, who was subsequently murdered. The United States developed a friendly relationship with the new, repressive military government of General Augusto Pinochet.

In the Middle East, conditions were growing more volatile in the aftermath of the 1967 war, in which Israel had occupied substantial new territories and had increased the number of refugee Palestinians. These Arabs claimed the lands now controlled by Israel; dislodged from their homes, the refugees were a source of considerable instability in Jordan, Lebanon, and the other surrounding countries into which they moved.

In October 1973, on the Jewish high holy day of Yom Kippur, Egyptian and Syrian forces attacked Israel. For ten days, the Israelis struggled to recover from the surprise attack; finally, they launched an effective counter-offensive against Egyptian forces in the Sinai. At that point, the United States intervened, placing heavy pressure on Israel to accept a cease-fire rather than press its advantage.

The imposed settlement of the Yom Kippur War demonstrated the growing dependence of the United States and its allies on Arab oil. Permitting Israel to continue its drive into Egypt might have jeopardized the ability of the United States to purchase needed petroleum from the Arab states. A brief but painful embargo by the Arab governments on the sale of oil to America in 1973 provided an ominous warning of the costs of losing access to the region's resources. The lesson of the Yom Kippur War, therefore, was

DÉTENTE AT HIGH TIDE The visit of Soviet Premier Leonid Brezhnev to Washington in 1973 was a high-water mark in the search for détente between the two nations. Here, Brezhnev and Nixon share friendly words on the White House balcony.

that the United States could not ignore the interests of the Arab nations in its efforts on behalf of Israel.

A larger lesson of 1973 was that the nations of the Third World could no longer be expected to act as passive, cooperative "client states." And the United States could not depend on cheap, easy access to raw materials as it had in the past.

POLITICS AND ECONOMICS IN THE NIXON YEARS

For a time in the late 1960s, it had seemed to many Americans that the forces of chaos and radicalism were taking control of the nation. The domestic policy of the Nixon administration was, the president claimed, an attempt to restore balance: between the needs of the poor and the desires of the middle class, between the power of the federal government and the interests of local communities. In the end, however, economic and political crises sharply limited the administration's ability to fulfill its domestic goals.

Domestic Initiatives

Many of Nixon's domestic policies were a response to what he believed to be the demands of his constituency—conservative, middle-class people, whom he liked to call the "silent majority," who wanted to reduce federal "interference" in local affairs. He tried, unsuccessfully, to persuade Congress to pass legislation prohibiting school desegregation through the use of forced busing. He forbade the Department of Health, Education, and Welfare to cut off federal funds from school districts that had failed to comply with court orders to integrate. At the same time, he began to reduce or dismantle many of the social programs of the Great Society and the New Frontier. In 1973, he abolished the Office of Economic Opportunity, the centerpiece of the antipoverty program of the Johnson years.

Yet Nixon's domestic policies had progressive and creative elements as well. One of the administration's boldest efforts was an attempt to overhaul the nation's enormous welfare system. Nixon proposed replacing the existing system, which almost everyone agreed was cumbersome, expensive, and inefficient, with what he called the Family Assistance Plan (FAP). It would in effect have created a guaranteed annual income for all Americans: $1,600 in federal grants, which could be supplemented by outside earnings up to

$4,000. Even many liberals applauded the proposal as an important step toward expanding federal responsibility for the poor. Nixon, however, presented the plan as something that would reduce the supervisory functions of the federal government and transfer to welfare recipients themselves daily responsibility for their own lives. Although the FAP won approval in the House in 1970, concerted attacks by welfare recipients (who considered the benefits inadequate), members of the welfare bureaucracy (whose own influence stood to be sharply diminished by the bill), and conservatives (who opposed a guaranteed income on principle) helped kill it in the Senate.

From the Warren Court to the Nixon Court

Of all the liberal institutions that aroused the enmity of the "silent majority" in the 1950s and 1960s, none evoked more anger and bitterness than the Supreme Court. Not only did its rulings on racial matters disrupt traditional social patterns in both the North and the South, but its staunch defense of civil liberties directly contributed, in the eyes of many Americans, to the increase in crime, disorder, and moral decay. In *Engel* v. *Vitale* (1962), the Court ruled that prayers in public schools were unconstitutional, sparking outrage among religious fundamentalists and others. In *Roth* v. *United States* (1957), the Court had sharply limited the authority of local governments to curb pornography. In a series of other decisions, the Court greatly strengthened the civil rights of criminal defendants and, many Americans believed, greatly weakened the power of law enforcement officials to do their jobs. For example, in *Gideon* v. *Wainwright* (1963), the Court ruled that every felony defendant was entitled to a lawyer regardless of his or her ability to pay. In *Escobedo* v. *Illinois* (1964), it ruled that a defendant must be allowed access to a lawyer before questioning by police. In *Miranda* v. *Arizona* (1966), the Court confirmed the obligation of authorities to inform a criminal suspect of his or her rights. By 1968, the Warren Court had become the target of Americans of all kinds who felt the balance of power in the United States had shifted too far toward the poor and dispossessed at the expense of the middle class.

Nixon was determined to use his judicial appointments to give the Court a more conservative cast. His first opportunity came almost as soon as he entered office. When Chief Justice Earl Warren resigned early in 1969, Nixon replaced him with a federal appeals court judge of known conservative leanings, Warren Burger. A few months later, Associate Justice Abe Fortas resigned his seat after the disclosure of a series of alleged financial improprieties. To replace him, Nixon named Clement F. Haynsworth, a respected federal circuit court judge from South Carolina. But Haynsworth came under fire from Senate liberals, black organizations, and labor unions for his conservative record on civil rights and for what some claimed was a conflict of interest in several of the cases on which he had sat. The Senate rejected him. Nixon's next choice was G. Harrold Carswell, a judge of the Florida federal appeals court almost entirely lacking in distinction and widely considered unfit for the Supreme Court. The Senate rejected his nomination too.

Nixon angrily denounced the votes, calling them expressions of prejudice against the South. But he was careful thereafter to choose men of standing within the legal community to fill vacancies on the Supreme Court: Harry Blackmun, a moderate jurist from Minnesota; Lewis F. Powell, Jr., a respected judge from Virginia; and William Rehnquist, a member of the Nixon Justice Department. In the process, he transformed the court.

The new Court, however, fell short of what the president and many conservatives had expected. Rather than retreating from its commitment to social reform, the Court in many areas actually moved further toward it. In *Swann* v. *Charlotte-Mecklenburg Board of Education* (1971), it ruled in favor of the use of forced busing to achieve racial balance in schools. Not even the intense and occasionally violent opposition of local communities as diverse as Boston and Louisville, Kentucky, was able to weaken the judicial commitment to integration. In *Furman* v. *Georgia* (1972), the Court overturned existing capital punishment statutes and established strict new guidelines for such laws in the future. In *Roe* v. *Wade* (1973), it struck down laws forbidding abortions.

In other decisions, however, the Burger Court did demonstrate a more conservative temperament than the Warren Court had shown. Although the justices approved busing as a tool for achieving integration, they rejected, in *Milliken* v. *Bradley* (1974), a plan to transfer students across district lines (in this case, between Detroit and its suburbs) to achieve racial balance. While the Court upheld the principle of affirmative action in its celebrated 1978 decision in *Bakke* v. *Board of Regents of California*, it established restrictive new guidelines for such programs in the future. In *Stone* v. *Powell* (1976), the Court agreed to certain limits on the right of a defendant to appeal a state conviction to the federal judiciary.

The Election of 1972

However unsuccessful the Nixon administration may have been in achieving some of its specific goals, Nixon entered the presidential race in 1972 with a substantial reserve of strength. The events of that year improved his position immeasurably. His energetic reelection committee collected enormous sums of money to support the campaign. The president himself used the powers of incumbency, refraining from campaigning and concentrating on highly publicized international decisions and state visits. Agencies of the federal government dispensed funds and favors to strengthen Nixon's political standing in questionable areas.

Nixon was most fortunate in 1972, however, in his opposition. The return of George Wallace to the presidential fray caused some early concern, for Nixon's own reelection strategy rested on the same appeals to the troubled middle class that Wallace was expressing. But the possibility of another third-party campaign in the fall vanished in May, when a would-be assassin shot the Alabama governor during a rally at a Maryland shopping center. Paralyzed from the waist down, Wallace was unable to continue campaigning.

The Democrats, in the meantime, were making the greatest contribution to the Nixon cause by nominating for president a representative of their most liberal wing: Senator George S. McGovern of South Dakota. An outspoken critic of the war, a forceful advocate of advanced liberal positions on virtually every social and economic issue, McGovern seemed to embody those aspects of the turbulent 1960s that middle-class Americans were most eager to reject. McGovern profited greatly from party reforms (which he himself had helped to draft) that gave increased influence to women, blacks, and young people in the selection of the Democratic ticket. But those same reforms helped make the Democratic Convention of 1972 an unappealing spectacle to much of the public. The candidate then disillusioned even some of his own supporters by his indecisive reaction to revelations that his running mate, Senator Thomas Eagleton of Missouri, had undergone treatment for an emotional disturbance. Eagleton finally withdrew from the ticket. The remainder of the Democratic presidential campaign was an exercise in futility.

On election day, Nixon won reelection by one of the largest margins in history: 60.7 percent of the popular vote compared with 37.5 percent for the forlorn McGovern, an electoral margin of 520 to 17. The Democratic candidate had carried only Massachusetts and the District of Columbia. The new commitments that Nixon had so effectively expressed—to restraint in social reform, to decentralization of political power, to the defense of traditional values, and to a new balance in international relations—had clearly won the approval of the American people. But other problems, some beyond the president's control and some of his own making, were already lurking in the wings.

The Troubled Economy

Although it was political scandal that would ultimately destroy the Nixon presidency, the most important national crisis of the early 1970s was the decline of the American economy. For three decades, the American economy had been the envy of the world. It had produced as much as a third of the world's industrial goods and had dominated international trade. The American dollar had been the strongest currency in the world, and the American standard of living had risen steadily from its already substantial heights. Most Americans assumed that this remarkable prosperity was the normal condition of their society. In fact, however, it rested in part on several artificial conditions that were by the late 1960s rapidly disappearing: the absence of significant foreign competition and easy access to raw materials in the Third World.

The most disturbing economic problem of the 1970s was inflation, which had been creeping upward for several years when Richard Nixon took office and which soon began to soar. Its most visible cause was the major increase in federal deficit spending in the 1960s, when the Johnson administration tried to fund the war in Vietnam and its ambitious social programs without raising taxes. But there were other, equally important causes of the inflation and of the economic problems that lay behind it. No more did the United States have exclusive access to cheap raw materials around the globe; not only were other industrial nations now competing for increasingly scarce raw materials, but Third World suppliers of those materials were beginning to realize their value and demand higher prices for them.

The greatest immediate blow to the American economy was the increasing cost of energy. More than any nation on earth, the United States based its economy on the easy availability of cheap and plentiful fuels. No society was more dependent on the automobile; none was more wasteful in its use of oil and gas in its homes, schools, and factories. Domestic petroleum reserves were no longer sufficient to meet this demand, and the nation was growing increasingly dependent on imports from the Middle East and Africa.

For many years, the Organization of Petroleum Exporting Countries (OPEC) had operated as an informal bargaining unit for the sale of oil by Third World nations but had seldom managed to exercise any real strength. But in the early 1970s, OPEC began to assert itself, to use its oil both as an economic tool and as a political weapon. In 1973, in the midst of the Yom Kippur War, Arab members of OPEC announced that they would no longer ship petroleum to nations supporting Israel—that is, to the United States and its allies in Western Europe. At about the same time, the OPEC nations agreed to raise their prices 500 percent (from $3 to $15 a barrel). These twin shocks produced momentary economic chaos in the West. The United States suffered its first fuel shortage since World War II. And although the crisis eased a few months later, the price of energy continued to skyrocket both because of OPEC's new militant policies and because of the weakening competitive position of the dollar in world markets. No single factor did more to produce the soaring inflation of the 1970s.

The Nixon Response

Nixon's initial answer to these mounting economic problems was to reduce spending and raise taxes. But those policies produced both congressional and popular protest, and Nixon turned increasingly to an economic tool more readily available to him: control of the currency. Placing conservative economists at the head of the Federal Reserve Board, he ensured sharply higher interest rates and a contraction of the money supply. But the tight money policy did little to curb inflation. The cost of living rose a cumulative 15 percent during Nixon's first two and a half years in office. Economic growth, in the meantime, declined. The United States was encountering a new and puzzling dilemma: "stagflation," a combination of rising prices and general economic stagnation.

In the summer of 1971, Nixon imposed a ninety-day freeze on all wages and prices at their existing levels. Then, in November, he launched Phase II of his economic plan: mandatory guidelines for wage and price increases, to be administered by a federal agency. Inflation subsided temporarily, but the recession continued. Fearful that the recession would be more damaging than inflation in an election year, the administration reversed itself late in 1971: interest rates were allowed to drop sharply, and government spending increased—producing the largest budget deficit since World War II. The new tactics helped revive the economy in the short term, but inflation rose substantially—particularly after the administration abandoned the strict

Phase II controls and replaced them with a set of voluntary, and almost entirely ineffective, guidelines. In 1973, prices rose 9 percent; in 1974, after the Arab oil embargo and the OPEC price increases, they rose 12 percent—the highest rate since shortly after World War II. The value of the dollar continued to slide, and the nation's international trade continued to decline. The new energy crisis, in the meantime, was quickly becoming a national preoccupation. But while Nixon talked often about the need to achieve "energy independence," he offered few concrete proposals.

The erratic economic programs of the Nixon administration were a sign of a broader national confusion about the prospects for American prosperity. The Nixon pattern—of lurching from a tight money policy to curb inflation at one moment to a spending policy to cure recession at the next—repeated itself during the two administrations that followed. Nowhere was there any serious attempt to address the deeper problems that lay at the heart of the erosion of the American economy.

THE WATERGATE CRISIS

Although economic problems greatly concerned the American people in the 1970s, another stunning development almost entirely preoccupied the nation beginning early in 1973: the fall of Richard Nixon. The president's demise was a result in part of his own personality. Defensive, secretive, resentful of his critics, he brought to his office an element of mean-spiritedness that helped undermine even his most important accomplishments. But the larger explanation for the crisis lay in Nixon's view of American society and the world, and of his own role in both. The president believed the United States faced grave dangers from the radicals and dissidents who were challenging his policies. He came increasingly to consider any challenge to his policies a threat to "national security." By identifying his own political fortunes with those of the nation, Nixon was creating a climate in which he and those who served him could justify almost any tactics to stifle dissent and undermine opposition.

The Scandals

Nixon's approach to his office was in part a culmination of long-term changes in the presidency. Public expectations of the president had increased dramatically in the years since World War II; yet the constraints on the authority of the office had grown as well. In response, a succession of presidents had sought new methods for the exercise of power, often stretching the law, occasionally breaking it.

Nixon not only continued but greatly accelerated these trends. Facing a Democratic Congress hostile to his goals, he attempted to find ways to circumvent the legislature whenever possible. Saddled with a federal bureaucracy unresponsive to his wishes, he constructed a hierarchy of command in which virtually all executive power became concentrated in the White House. Operating within a rigid, even autocratic staff structure, the president became a solitary, brooding figure, whose contempt for his opponents and impatience with obstacles to his policies festered and grew. Unknown to all but a few intimates, he also became mired in a pattern of illegalities and abuses of power that late in 1972 began to break through to the surface.

Early on the morning of June 17, 1972, police arrested five men who had broken into the offices of the Democratic National Committee in the Watergate office building in Washington, D.C. Two others were seized a short time later and charged with supervising the break-in. When reporters for the *Washington Post* began researching the backgrounds of the culprits, they discovered that among those involved in the burglary were former employees of the Committee for the Re-Election of the President (CRP). One of them had worked in the White House itself. They had, moreover, been paid for the break-in from a secret fund of the reelection committee, a fund controlled by members of the White House staff.

Public interest in the disclosures grew slowly in the last months of 1972. Few Americans questioned the president's assurances that neither he nor his staff had any connection with what he called "this very bizarre incident." Early in 1973, however, the Watergate burglars went on trial; and under relentless prodding from federal judge John J. Sirica, one of the defendants, James W. McCord, agreed to cooperate both with the grand jury and with a special Senate investigating committee recently established under Senator Sam J. Ervin of North Carolina. McCord's testimony opened a floodgate of confessions, and for months a parade of White House and campaign officials exposed one illegality after another. Foremost among them was a member of the inner circle of the White House, John Dean, counsel to the president, who leveled allegations against Nixon himself.

Two different sets of scandals were emerging from the investigations. One was a general pattern of abuses of power involving both the White House and the Nixon campaign committee, which included, but was not limited to, the Watergate break-in. The other scandal, and the one that became the major focus of public attention for nearly two years, was the way in which the administration tried to manage the investigations of the Watergate break-in and other abuses—a pattern of behavior that became known as the "cover-up." There was never any conclusive evidence that the president had planned or approved the burglary in advance. But there was mounting evidence that he had been involved in illegal efforts to obstruct investigations of and withhold information about the episode. Testimony before the Ervin Committee provided evidence of the complicity of Dean, Attorney General John Mitchell, top White House assistants H. R. Haldeman and John Ehrlichman, and others. As interest in the case grew to something approaching a national obsession, the investigation focused increasingly on a single question: In the words of Senator Howard Baker of Tennessee, a member of the Ervin Committee, "What did the President know and when did he know it?"

Nixon accepted the departure of those members of his administration implicated in the scandals. But the president himself continued to insist on his own innocence. There the matter might have rested had it not been for the disclosure during the Senate hearings of a White House taping system that had recorded virtually every conversation in the president's office during the period in question. All those investigating the scandals sought access to the tapes; Nixon, pleading "executive privilege," refused to release them. A special prosecutor appointed by the president to handle the Watergate cases, Harvard law professor Archibald Cox, took Nixon to court in October 1973 in an effort to force him to relinquish the recordings. Nixon, now clearly growing desperate, fired Cox and suffered the humiliation of watching both Attorney General Elliot Richardson and his deputy resign in protest. This "Saturday night massacre" made the president's predicament infinitely worse. Not only did public pressure force him to appoint a new special prosecutor, Texas attorney Leon Jaworski, who proved just as determined as Cox to subpoena the tapes; but the episode precipitated an investigation by the House of Representatives into the possibility of impeachment.

The Fall of Richard Nixon

Nixon's situation deteriorated further in the following months. Late in 1973, Vice President Spiro Agnew became embroiled in a scandal of his own when evidence surfaced that he had accepted bribes and kickbacks while serving as governor of Maryland and even as vice president. In return for a

Justice Department agreement not to press the case, Agnew pleaded no contest to a lesser charge of income-tax evasion and resigned from the government. With the controversial Agnew no longer in line to succeed to the presidency, the prospect of removing Nixon from the White House became less worrisome to his opponents. The new vice president (the first appointed under the terms of the Twenty-fifth Amendment, which had been adopted in 1967) was House Minority Leader Gerald Ford, an amiable and popular Michigan congressman.

The impeachment investigation quickly gathered momentum. In April 1974, in an effort to head off further subpoenas of the tapes, the president released transcripts of a number of relevant conversations, claiming that they proved his innocence. Investigators and much of the public felt otherwise. Even these edited tapes seemed to suggest Nixon's complicity in the cover-up. In July, the crisis reached a climax. First the Supreme Court ruled unanimously, in *United States* v. *Richard M. Nixon*, that the president must relinquish the tapes to Special Prosecutor Jaworski. Days later, the House Judiciary Committee voted to recommend three articles of impeachment, charging that Nixon had, first, obstructed justice in the Watergate cover-up; second, misused federal agencies to violate the rights of citizens; and third, defied the authority of Congress by refusing to deliver tapes and other materials subpoenaed by the committee. Even without additional evidence, Nixon might well have been impeached by the full House and convicted by the Senate. Early in August, however, he provided at last the "smoking gun"—the concrete proof of his guilt—that his defenders had long contended was missing from the case against him. Among the tapes that the Supreme Court compelled Nixon to relinquish were several that offered apparently incontrovertible evidence of his involvement in the Watergate cover-up. Only three days after the burglary, the recordings disclosed, the president had ordered the FBI to stop investigating the break-in. Impeachment and conviction now seemed inevitable.

For several days, Nixon brooded in the White House, on the verge, some claimed, of a breakdown. Finally, on August 8, 1974, he announced his resignation—the first president in American history ever to do so. At noon the next day, while Nixon and his family were flying west to their home in California, Gerald Ford took the oath of office as president.

Many Americans expressed relief and exhilaration that, as the new president put it, "our long national nightmare is over." They were relieved to be rid of Richard Nixon, who had lost virtually all of the wide popularity that had won him his landslide reelection victory only two years before. And they were exhilarated that, as some boasted, "the system had worked." But the wave of good feeling could not obscure the deeper and more lasting damage of the Watergate crisis. In a society in which distrust of leaders and institutions of authority was already widespread, the fall of Richard Nixon seemed to confirm the most cynical assumptions about the character of American public life.

CHAPTER THIRTY-THREE

The Unfinished Nation

Politics and Diplomacy After Watergate ~ *The "Reagan Revolution"*
George Bush and the Post-Cold War World ~ *Modern Times*

T HE FRUSTRATIONS OF the 1970s—the defeat in Vietnam, the Watergate crisis, the decay of the American economy—inflicted damaging blows to the confident, optimistic nationalism that had characterized so much of the postwar era. At first, many Americans responded to these problems by announcing the arrival of an "age of limits," in which America would have to learn to live with increasingly constricted expectations. By the end of the decade, however, the contours of another response to the challenges had become visible in both American culture and American politics. It was a response that combined a conservative retreat from some of the heady visions of the 1960s with a reinforced commitment to the idea of economic growth, international power, and American exceptionalism. The election of Ronald Reagan to the presidency in 1980 seemed to mark a repudiation of the doubts and "defeatism" of the previous decade.

But the turbulence that had plagued America in the 1970s could not be so easily banished. By the beginning of the 1990s, the American economy was in the midst of a deep and many believed long-term crisis. The complexity and diversity that had always characterized American society, and the problems associated with them, were straining the nation's social and cultural fabric. And the international system, which had experienced a dismal stability for more than forty years, was in the throes of a genuinely revolutionary transformation. Even for a nation accustomed to rapid change, the events of the 1980s and 1990s seemed at times dizzying and disorienting. The result was an impassioned and at times divisive debate about both the nature of the American past and the prospects for the American future.

POLITICS AND DIPLOMACY AFTER WATERGATE

In the aftermath of Richard Nixon's ignominious departure from office, many wondered whether faith in the presidency, and in the government as a whole, could easily be restored. The administrations of the two presidents who succeeded Nixon did little to answer those questions.

The Ford Custodianship

Gerald Ford inherited the presidency under unenviable circumstances. He had to try to rebuild confidence in government after the Watergate scandals. And he had to try to restore prosperity in the face of domestic and international challenges to the American economy. He enjoyed some success in the first of these efforts but very little in the second.

The new president's effort to establish himself as a symbol of political integrity suffered a setback only a month after he took office, when he granted Richard Nixon "a full, free, and absolute pardon" for any crimes he may have committed during his presidency. Ford explained that he was attempting to spare the nation the ordeal of years of litigation and to spare Nixon himself any further suffering. But much of the public suspected a secret deal with the former president. The pardon caused a decline in Ford's popularity from which he never fully recovered. Nevertheless, most Americans considered Ford a decent man; his honesty and amiability did much to reduce the bitterness and acrimony of the Watergate years.

The Ford administration enjoyed less success in its effort to solve the problems of the American economy. In his attempts to curb inflation, the president rejected the idea of wage and price controls and called instead for largely ineffective voluntary efforts. After supporting high interest rates, opposing increased federal spending (through liberal use of his veto power), and resisting pressures for a tax reduction, Ford had to deal with a serious recession in 1974 and 1975. Central to the economic problems was the continuing energy crisis. In the aftermath of the Arab oil embargo of 1973, the OPEC cartel began to raise the price of oil—by 400 percent in 1974 alone. Even so, American dependence on OPEC supplies continued to grow—one of the principal reasons why inflation reached 11 percent in 1976.

At first it seemed that the foreign policy of the new administration would differ little from that of its predecessor. The new president retained

Henry Kissinger, whom Nixon had appointed secretary of state in 1973, and continued the general policies of the Nixon years. Late in 1974, Ford met with Leonid Brezhnev at Vladivostok in Siberia and signed an arms control accord that was to serve as the basis for SALT II, thus achieving a goal the Nixon administration had long sought. The following summer, after a European security conference in Helsinki, Finland, the Soviet Union and Western nations agreed to ratify the borders that had divided Europe since 1945; and the Soviets pledged to increase respect for human rights within their own country. In the Middle East, in the meantime, Henry Kissinger helped produce a new accord by which Israel agreed to return large portions of the occupied Sinai to Egypt; the two nations pledged not to resolve future differences by force. In China, finally, the death of Mao Zedong in 1976 brought to power a new, apparently more moderate government, eager to expand its ties with the United States.

Nevertheless, as the 1976 presidential election approached, Ford's policies were coming under attack from both the right and the left. In the Republican primary campaign, Ford faced a powerful challenge from former California governor Ronald Reagan, leader of the party's conservative wing, who spoke for many on the right who were unhappy with any conciliation of communists. The president only barely survived the assault to win his party's nomination. The Democrats, in the meantime, were gradually uniting behind a new and, before 1976, almost entirely unknown candidate: Jimmy Carter, a former governor of Georgia who organized a brilliant primary campaign and appealed to the general unhappiness with Washing-

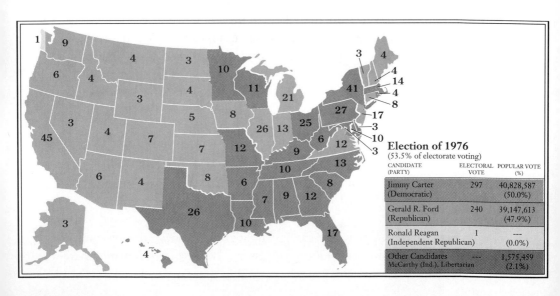

Election of 1976
(53.5% of electorate voting)

CANDIDATE (PARTY)	ELECTORAL VOTE	POPULAR VOTE (%)
Jimmy Carter (Democratic)	297	40,828,587 (50.0%)
Gerald R. Ford (Republican)	240	39,147,613 (47.9%)
Ronald Reagan (Independent Republican)	1	--- (0.0%)
Other Candidates McCarthy (Ind.), Libertarian	---	1,575,459 (2.1%)

ton by offering honesty, piety, and an outsider's skepticism of the federal government. And while Carter's mammoth lead dwindled to almost nothing by election day, unhappiness with the economy and a general disenchantment with Ford enabled the Democrat to hold on for a narrow victory. Carter emerged with 50 percent of the popular vote to Ford's 47.9 percent and 297 electoral votes to Ford's 240.

The Trials of Jimmy Carter

Jimmy Carter assumed the presidency at a moment when the nation faced problems of staggering complexity and difficulty. Perhaps no leader could have thrived in such inhospitable circumstances. But Carter seemed at times

JIMMY AND ROSALYNN CARTER, JANUARY 20, 1977
Jimmy Carter startled the crowds (and alarmed the Secret Service) on his Inauguration Day by walking down Pennsylvania Avenue from the Capitol to the White House after taking the oath of office. Not since Jefferson, whose effort to identify with the "common man" Carter hoped to emulate, had a president walked in his inaugural parade.

to make his predicament worse by a style of leadership that many considered self-righteous and inflexible. He left office in 1981 as one of the least popular presidents of the century.

Carter had campaigned for the presidency as an "outsider," representing Americans suspicious of entrenched bureaucracies and complacent public officials. He carried much of that suspiciousness with him to Washington. He surrounded himself in the White House with a group of close-knit associates from Georgia; and in the beginning, at least, he seemed deliberately to spurn assistance from more experienced political figures. Carter was among the most intelligent and quick-witted men ever to serve in the White House, but his critics charged that he provided no overall vision or direction to his government.

Carter devoted much of his time to the problems of energy and the economy. Entering office in the midst of a recession, he moved first to reduce unemployment by raising public spending and cutting federal taxes. Unemployment declined, but inflation soared. During Carter's last two years in office, prices rose at well over a 10-percent annual rate. Like Nixon and Ford before him, Carter responded with a combination of tight money and calls for voluntary restraint. He appointed first G. William Miller and then Paul Volcker, conservative economists, to head the Federal Reserve Board, thus ensuring a policy of high interest rates and reduced currency supplies. By 1980, interest rates had risen to the highest levels in American history; at times, they exceeded 20 percent.

The problem of energy also grew steadily more troublesome in the Carter years. In the summer of 1979, instability in the Middle East produced a second major fuel shortage in the United States. In the midst of the crisis, OPEC announced another major price increase, clouding the economic picture still further. Faced with increasing pressure to act (and with public-opinion polls showing his approval rating at a dismal 26 percent), Carter withdrew to Camp David, the presidential retreat in the Maryland mountains. Ten days later, he emerged to deliver a remarkable television address. It included a series of proposals for resolving the energy crisis. But it was most notable for Carter's bleak assessment of the national condition. Speaking with unusual fervor, he complained of a "crisis of confidence" that had struck "at the very heart and soul of our national will." The address became known as the "malaise" speech (although Carter himself had never used that word), and it helped fuel attacks that the president was trying to blame his own problems on the American people. Carter's sudden firing of several members of his cabinet a few days later deepened his political problems.

Human Rights and National Interests

Among Jimmy Carter's most frequent campaign promises was a pledge to build a new basis for American foreign policy, one in which the defense of "human rights" would replace the pursuit of "selfish interests." Carter spoke out sharply and often about violations of human rights in many countries (including, most prominently, the Soviet Union). Beyond that general commitment, the Carter administration focused on several more traditional concerns. Carter completed negotiations begun several years earlier on a pair of treaties to turn over control of the Panama Canal to the government of Panama. Domestic opposition to the treaties was intense, especially among conservatives who viewed the new arrangements as part of a general American retreat from international power. But the administration argued that relinquishing the canal was the best way to improve relations with Latin America and avoid violence in Panama. After an acrimonious debate, the Senate ratified the treaties by 68 to 32, only one vote more than the necessary two-thirds.

Less controversial, within the United States at least, was Carter's success in arranging a peace treaty between Egypt and Israel—the crowning accomplishment of his presidency. Middle East negotiations had seemed hopelessly stalled when a dramatic breakthrough occurred in November 1977. The Egyptian president, Anwar Sadat, accepted an invitation from Prime Minister Menachem Begin to visit Israel. In Tel Aviv, he announced that Egypt was now willing to accept the state of Israel as a legitimate political entity. But translating these good feelings into an actual peace treaty proved more difficult.

When talks between Israeli and Egyptian negotiators stalled, Carter invited Sadat and Begin to a summit conference at Camp David in September 1978, holding them there for two weeks while he and others helped mediate the disputes between them. On September 17, Carter escorted the two leaders into the White House to announce agreement on a framework for an Egyptian-Israeli peace treaty. Carter intervened again several months later, when talks stalled once more, and helped produce a compromise on the most sensitive issue between the two parties: the Palestinian refugee issue. On March 26, 1979, Begin and Sadat returned together to the White House to sign a formal peace treaty between their two nations.

In the meantime, Carter continued trying to improve relations with China and the Soviet Union and to complete a new arms agreement. He responded eagerly to the overtures of Deng Xiaoping, the new Chinese leader who was attempting to open his nation to the outside world. On

December 15, 1978, Washington and Beijing announced the resumption of formal diplomatic relations between the two nations. A few months later, Carter traveled to Vienna to meet with the aging and visibly ailing Brezhnev to finish drafting the new SALT II arms control agreement. The treaty set limits on the number of long-range missiles, bombers, and nuclear warheads on each side. Almost immediately, however, SALT II met with fierce conservative opposition in the United States. Central to the arguments was a fundamental distrust of the Soviet Union that nearly a decade of détente had failed to destroy. By the fall of 1979, with the Senate scheduled to begin debate over the treaty shortly, ratification was already in jeopardy. Events in the following months would provide a final blow, both to the treaty and to the larger framework of détente.

The Year of the Hostages

Ever since the early 1950s, the United States had provided political support and, more recently, massive military assistance to the government of the Shah of Iran, hoping to make his nation a bulwark against Soviet expansion in the Middle East. By 1979, however, the Shah was in deep trouble with his own people. Iranians resented the repressive, authoritarian tactics through which the Shah had maintained his autocratic rule. At the same time, Islamic clergy (and much of the fiercely religious populace) opposed his efforts to modernize and Westernize a fundamentalist society. The combination of resentments produced a powerful revolutionary movement. In January 1979, the Shah fled the country.

The United States made cautious efforts in the first months after the Shah's abdication to establish cordial relations with the succession of increasingly militant regimes that followed. By late 1979, however, revolutionary chaos in Iran was making any normal relationships impossible. What power there was resided with a zealous religious leader, the Ayatollah Ruhollah Khomeini, whose hatred of the West in general and the United States in particular was intense.

In late October 1979, the deposed Shah arrived in New York to be treated for cancer. Days later, on November 4, an armed mob invaded the American embassy in Teheran, seized the diplomats and military personnel inside, and demanded the return of the Shah to Iran in exchange for their freedom. Fifty-three Americans remained hostages in the embassy for over a year. Coming after years of what many Americans considered international humiliations and defeats, the hostage seizure released a deep well of anger and emotion.

Only weeks after the hostage seizure, on December 27, 1979, Soviet troops invaded Afghanistan, the mountainous nation lying between the Soviet Union and Iran. The Soviet Union had, in fact, been a power in Afghanistan for years, and the dominant force since April 1978, when a coup had established a Marxist government there with close ties to the Kremlin. But while some observers claimed that the Soviet invasion was a Russian attempt to secure the status quo, others—most notably the president—claimed that the invasion was a Russian "stepping stone to their possible control over much of the world's oil supplies." It was also the "gravest threat to world peace since World War II." Carter angrily imposed a series of economic sanctions on the Russians, canceled American participation in the 1980 summer Olympic Games in Moscow, and announced the withdrawal of SALT II from Senate consideration.

The Campaign of 1980

By the time of the crises in Iran and Afghanistan, Jimmy Carter was in desperate political trouble. His standing in popularity polls was lower than that of any president in history. Senator Edward Kennedy, younger brother of John and Robert Kennedy, was preparing to challenge him in the

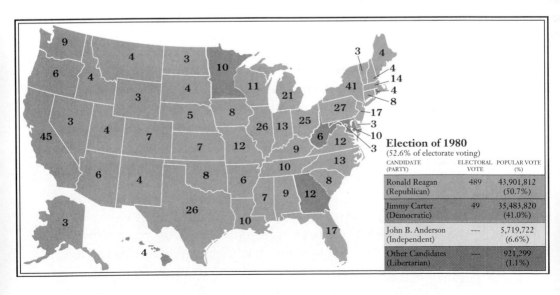

Election of 1980
(52.6% of electorate voting)

CANDIDATE (PARTY)	ELECTORAL VOTE	POPULAR VOTE (%)
Ronald Reagan (Republican)	489	43,901,812 (50.7%)
Jimmy Carter (Democratic)	49	35,483,820 (41.0%)
John B. Anderson (Independent)	----	5,719,722 (6.6%)
Other Candidates (Libertarian)	----	921,299 (1.1%)

primaries. For a short while, the seizure of the hostages and the stern American response to the Soviet invasion revived Carter's candidacy. But as the hostage crisis dragged on, public impatience grew. Kennedy won a series of victories over the president in the later primaries. Carter managed in the end to stave off Kennedy's challenge and win his party's nomination. But it was an unhappy convention that heard the president's listless call to arms, and Carter's campaign aroused little popular enthusiasm as he prepared to face a powerful challenge.

The Republican party, in the meantime, had rallied enthusiastically behind a man whom, not many years before, many Americans had considered a frightening reactionary. Ronald Reagan, a one-time film actor, a former California governor, and a poised and articulate campaigner, was a sharp critic of the size and expense of the federal government. More important, he championed a restoration of American "strength" and "pride" in the world. Although he refrained from discussing the issue of the hostages, Reagan clearly benefited from the continuing popular frustration at Carter's inability to resolve the crisis. In a larger sense, he benefited as well from the accumulated frustrations of more than a decade of domestic and international disappointments.

On election day 1980, the anniversary of the seizure of the hostages in Iran, Reagan swept to victory with 51 percent of the vote to 41 percent for Jimmy Carter and 7 percent for John Anderson—a moderate Republican congressman from Illinois who had mounted an independent campaign. Carter carried only five states and the District of Columbia, for a total of 49 electoral votes to Reagan's 489. The Republican party won control of the Senate for the first time since 1952; and although the Democrats retained a diminished majority in the House, the lower chamber too seemed firmly in the hands of conservatives.

On the day of Reagan's inauguration, the American hostages in Iran were released after their 444-day ordeal. Jimmy Carter, in the last hours of his presidency, had concluded months of negotiations by agreeing to release several billion dollars in Iranian assets that he had frozen in American banks shortly after the seizure of the embassy. The government of Iran, desperate for funds to support its floundering war against neighboring Iraq, ordered the hostages freed in return. Americans welcomed the hostages home with demonstrations of joy and patriotism not seen since the end of World War II. But while the celebration in 1945 had marked a great American triumph, the euphoria in 1981 marked something quite different—a troubled nation grasping for reassurance. Ronald Reagan set out to provide it.

REAGAN AT THE RANCH Ronald Reagan relaxes at his ranch in the mountains near Santa Barbara, California, demonstrating the informal geniality that accounted for much of his remarkable popularity.

THE "REAGAN REVOLUTION"

Ronald Reagan assumed the presidency in January 1981 promising a change in government more profound than any since the New Deal of fifty years before. His eight years in office produced a significant shift in public policy, but they brought nothing so fundamental as many of his supporters had hoped or his opponents had feared. There was, however, no ambiguity about his administration's purely political achievements. Ronald Reagan succeeded brilliantly in making his own engaging personality the central fact of American politics in the 1980s.

Reagan in the White House

Even many people who disagreed with the president's policies found themselves drawn to his attractive and carefully honed public image. Reagan was a master of television and a gifted public speaker. He was the oldest man ever to serve as president, but he seemed vigorous, resilient, even youthful.

When he was wounded in an assassination attempt in 1981, he joked with doctors on his way into surgery and appeared to bounce back from the ordeal with remarkable speed. Four years later, he seemed to rebound from cancer surgery with similar zest. He had few visible insecurities. Even when things went wrong, as they often did, the blame seemed seldom to attach to Reagan himself (inspiring some Democrats to begin referring to him as "the Teflon president").

Reagan was not much involved in the day-to-day affairs of running the government; he surrounded himself with tough, energetic administrators who insulated him from many of the pressures of the office and apparently relied on him largely for general guidance, not specific decisions. But Reagan did make active use of his office to generate support for his administration's programs, by appealing repeatedly to the public over television and by fusing his proposals with a highly nationalistic rhetoric.

"Supply-Side" Economics

Reagan's 1980 campaign for the presidency had promised, among other things, to restore the economy to health by a bold experiment that became known as "supply-side" economics or, to some, "Reaganomics." Supply-side economics operated from the assumption that the woes of the American economy were in large part a result of excessive taxation, which left inadequate capital available to investors to stimulate growth. The solution, therefore, was to reduce taxes, with particularly generous benefits to corporations and wealthy individuals, in order to encourage new investments. The result would be a general economic revival that would help everyone. Because a tax cut would reduce government revenues (at least at first), it would also be necessary to reduce government expenses. A cornerstone of the Reagan economic program, therefore, was a dramatic cut in the federal budget.

In its first months in office, accordingly, the new administration hastily assembled a legislative program based on the supply-side idea. It proposed $40 billion in budget cuts and managed to win congressional approval of almost all of them. In addition, the president proposed a bold, three-year rate reduction on both individual and corporate taxes. In the summer of 1981, Congress passed it too. Not since Lyndon Johnson had a president compiled so impressive a legislative record in his first months in office.

By early 1982, however, the nation had sunk into the most severe recession since the 1930s. The Reagan economic program was not directly to blame for the problems, but critics claimed that the administration's policies were doing nothing to improve the situation. In fact, however, the economy recovered more rapidly and impressively than almost anyone had expected. By the middle of 1983, unemployment (which had reached nearly 11 percent in 1982, the highest level in over forty years) had fallen to 8.2 percent. The gross national product had grown 3.6 percent, the largest increase since the mid-1970s. Inflation had fallen below 5 percent. The economy continued to grow, and both inflation and unemployment remained low (at least by the new and more pessimistic standards the nation seemed now to have accepted) through most of the decade.

The recovery was a result of many things. Years of tight money policies by the Federal Reserve Board had helped lower inflation. A worldwide "energy glut," the virtual collapse of the OPEC cartel, and the deregulation of natural gas production had produced at least a temporary end to the inflationary pressures of spiraling fuel costs. And staggering federal budget deficits were pumping billions of dollars into the flagging economy but also, many warned, threatening ultimately to destroy the recovery they were helping to create.

The Fiscal Crisis

By the mid-1980s, the growing fiscal crisis had become one of the central issues in American politics. Having entered office promising a balanced budget within four years, Reagan presided over record budget deficits and accumulated more debt in his eight years in office than the American government had accumulated in its entire previous history. Before the 1980s, the highest single-year budget deficit in American history had been $66 billion (in 1976). Throughout the 1980s, the annual budget deficit consistently exceeded $100 billion (and in 1986 peaked at $221 billion). The national debt rose from $907 billion in 1980 to nearly $3 trillion by 1990.

The enormous deficits had many causes, some of them stretching back over decades of American public policy decisions. In particular, the budget suffered from enormous increases in the costs of "entitlement" programs (especially Social Security and Medicare), a result of the aging of the population and dramatic increases in the cost of health care. But some of the causes of the deficit lay in the policies of the Reagan administration. The 1981 tax cuts, the largest in American history, sharply eroded the revenue base of the federal government and accounted for a large percentage of the deficit. The massive increase in military spending (a proposed $1.6 trillion over five years) on which the Reagan administration insisted added more to the federal budget than its cuts in domestic spending removed.

In the face of these deficits, the administration refused to consider raising income taxes (although it did agree to a major increase in the Social Security tax). It would not agree to reductions in military spending. It could not much reduce the costs of entitlement programs, and it could do nothing to reduce interest payments on the massive (and growing) debt. Its answer to the fiscal crisis, therefore, was further cuts in "discretionary" domestic spending, which included many programs aimed at the poorest (and politically weakest) Americans. There were reductions in funding for food stamps; a major cut in federal subsidies for low-income housing (which contributed to the radical increase in homelessness that by the late 1980s was plaguing virtually all American cities); strict new limitations on Medicare and Medicaid payments; reductions in student loans, school lunches, and other educational programs; and an end to many forms of federal assistance to the states and cities—which helped precipitate years of local fiscal crises as well.

By the end of Reagan's third year in office, funding for domestic programs had been cut nearly as far as the Congress (and, apparently, the public) was willing to tolerate. Congress responded with the Gramm-Rudman-Hollings Act, passed late in 1985, which mandated major deficit reductions over five years and provided for automatic budget cuts in all areas of government spending should the president and Congress fail to agree on an alternative solution. Under Gramm-Rudman-Hollings, the budget deficit did decline for several years from its 1983 high. But much of that decline was a result of a substantial surplus in the Social Security trust fund (which the sharply increased Social Security taxes had produced), not of any larger fiscal successes.

Reagan and the World

Reagan encountered a similar combination of triumphs and difficulties in international affairs. Determined to restore American pride and prestige in the world, he argued that the United States should once again become active and assertive in opposing communism and supporting friendly governments whatever their internal policies.

Relations with the Soviet Union, which had been steadily deteriorating in the last years of the Carter administration, grew still more chilly in the first years of the Reagan presidency. The president spoke harshly of the Soviet regime (which he once called the "evil empire"), accusing it of sponsoring world terrorism and declaring that any armaments negotiations must be "linked" to negotiations about Soviet behavior in other areas. Relations with the Russians deteriorated further after the government of Poland (under strong pressure from Moscow) imposed martial law on the country in the winter of 1981 to crush a growing challenge from an independent labor organization, Solidarity.

Although the president had long denounced the SALT II arms control treaty as unfavorable to the United States, he continued to honor its provisions. But the Reagan administration at first made little progress toward arms control in other areas, despite the growing political power of a popular antinuclear movement in both Europe and the United States. In fact, the president proposed the most ambitious new military program in many years: the Strategic Defense Initiative (SDI), widely known as "Star Wars" (after a popular science-fiction movie). Reagan claimed that SDI, through the use of lasers and satellites, could provide an effective shield against incoming missiles and thus make nuclear war obsolete. The Soviet Union claimed that the new program would elevate the arms race to new and more dangerous levels and insisted that any arms control agreement begin with an American abandonment of SDI.

At the same time, the Reagan administration began, rhetorically at least, to support opponents of communism anywhere in the world, whether or not the regimes they were challenging were directly allied to the Soviet Union. This policy became known as the Reagan Doctrine, and it meant, above all, a new American activism in the Third World. The most conspicuous examples of the new activism came in Latin America. In October 1983, the administration sent American soldiers and marines to the tiny Caribbean island of Grenada to oust an anti-American Marxist regime that was forging a relationship with the Soviet Union. In El Salvador, where first a repressive military regime and later a moderate civilian one were engaged in murderous struggles with left-wing revolutionaries (who were supported, according to the Reagan administration, by Cuba and the Soviet Union), the president provided increased military and economic assistance. In neighboring Nicaragua, a pro-American dictatorship had fallen to the revolutionary "Sandinistas" in 1979; the new government had grown increasingly anti-American (and increasingly Marxist) throughout the early 1980s. The administration gave both rhetorical and material support to the so-called contras, a guerrilla movement drawn from several antigovernment groups and fighting (without great success) to topple the Sandinista regime. Indeed, support of the contras became a mission of special importance to the president, and later the source of some of his greatest difficulties.

In other parts of the world, the administration's bellicose rhetoric seemed to hide an instinctive restraint. In June 1982, the Israeli army launched an invasion of Lebanon in an effort to drive guerrillas of the Palestinian Liberation Organization from the country. The United States supported the Israelis rhetorically but also worked to permit PLO forces to leave Lebanon peacefully. An American peacekeeping force entered Beirut to supervise the evacuation. American marines then remained in the city, apparently to protect the fragile Lebanese government, which was embroiled in a vicious civil war. Now identified with one faction in the struggle, Americans themselves became the targets; a 1983 terrorist bombing of a United States military barracks in Beirut left 241 marines dead. Rather than become more deeply involved in the Lebanese struggle, Reagan withdrew the American forces.

The tragedy in Lebanon was an example of the changing character of Third World struggles: an increasing reliance on terrorism by otherwise powerless groups to advance their political aims. A series of terrorist acts in the 1980s—attacks on airplanes, cruise ships, commercial and diplomatic posts; the seizing of American and other Western hostages—alarmed and frightened much of the Western world. The Reagan administration spoke bravely about its resolve to punish terrorism; and at one point in 1986, the president ordered American planes to bomb sites in Tripoli, the capital of Libya, whose controversial leader Muammar al-Qaddafi was widely believed to be a leading sponsor of terrorism. In general, however, terrorists remained difficult to identify or control.

The Election of 1984

Reagan approached the campaign of 1984 at the head of a united Republican party firmly committed to his candidacy. The Democrats, as had become their custom, followed a more fractious course. Former vice president Walter Mondale established an early and commanding lead in the race by soliciting support from a wide range of traditional Democratic interest groups. But for a time, he lost the initiative to a younger and apparently more dynamic candidate, Senator Gary Hart of Colorado, who presented himself as a leader of a "new generation" and the spokesman for vaguely defined "new ideas." The magnetic and controversial African-American leader, Jesse Jackson, also staged an impressive primary campaign that drew substantial minority support away from Mondale. But with the help of the AFL-CIO and other established groups, Mondale revived his campaign and managed to capture the nomination. He brought momentary excitement to the Democratic Convention in San Francisco that summer by selecting a woman, Representative Geraldine Ferraro of New York, to be his running mate and the first female candidate ever to appear on a major-party national ticket.

The Republican party, by contrast, rallied comfortably behind its revered leader, whose triumphant campaign that fall scarcely took note of his opponents. Reagan's victory in 1984 was decisive. He won approximately 59 percent of the vote, and he carried every state except Mondale's native Minnesota and the District of Columbia. But Reagan was much stronger than his party. Democrats gained a seat in the Senate and maintained only slightly reduced control of the House of Representatives.

The Reagan Scandals

For a time, Reagan's personal popularity deflected attention from a series of scandals that might well have destroyed another administration. Top officials in the Environmental Protection Agency resigned when it was disclosed that they were flouting the laws they had been appointed to enforce. Officials of the CIA and the Defense Department resigned after revelations of questionable stock transactions. Reagan's secretary of labor left office after being indicted for racketeering (although he was later acquitted). Edwin Meese, the White House counsel and later attorney general, finally resigned in 1988 after years of attacks for controversial financial arrangements that many believed had compromised his office.

Unnoticed at first were several larger scandals that surfaced only as Reagan was about to leave office. One involved misuse of funds by the Department of Housing and Urban Development, abuses so widespread that for a time the survival of the agency itself was in question. Another, more serious scandal involved the savings and loan industry. The Reagan administration and Congress had sharply reduced regulatory controls over the troubled savings and loans. Many responded by rapidly, often recklessly, and sometimes corruptly expanding. By the end of the decade, the industry was in chaos, and the government was forced to step in to prevent a complete collapse. Predictions of the eventual cost to the government of the savings and loan debacle ran as high as half a trillion dollars.

But the most damaging scandal of the Reagan years came to light in November 1986. After reports appeared in foreign newspapers, the White House conceded that it had sold weapons to the revolutionary government of Iran, apparently as part of a largely unsuccessful effort to secure the release of several Americans being held hostage by radical Islamic groups in the Middle East. Even more damaging was the administration's revelation that some of the money from the arms deal with Iran had been covertly and illegally funneled into a fund to aid the contras in Nicaragua.

In the months that followed, aggressive reporting and a highly publicized series of congressional hearings exposed a remarkable and previously unsuspected feature of the Reagan White House: the existence within it of something like a "secret government," unknown to the State Department, the Defense Department, even parts of the CIA, dedicated to advancing the administration's foreign policy aims through secret and at times illegal means. The principal figure in this covert world appeared at first to be an obscure marine lieutenant colonel assigned to the staff of the National Security Council, Oliver North. But gradually it became clear that North was acting in concert with other, more powerful figures in the administration. The Iran-contra scandal, as it became known, did serious damage to the Reagan presidency, and the investigations into the affair continued for years. In 1992, the special prosecutor handling the case won an indictment against former secretary of defense Caspar Weinberger.

There were other signs in the late 1980s that the glow of the "Reagan Revolution" was beginning to fade. In October 1987, the American stock market—whose spectacular success had been one of the most conspicuous features of the economic boom—experienced the greatest single-day decline in its history (stocks lost 22 percent of their value); and although stock prices gradually recovered over the next two years, the crash damaged the confidence that had fueled the financial markets. At about the same time, one of the most popular financial innovations of the 1980s, the "leveraged buyout," which had permitted a wave of corporate takeovers financed by huge loans, began to unravel. Some of the nation's largest corporations, unable to carry the enormous debt they had acquired in their takeover efforts, began to flounder or collapse.

The Election of 1988

The fraying of the Reagan administration helped the Democrats regain control of the United States Senate in 1986 and fueled hopes in the party for a presidential victory in 1988. Even so, several of the most popular figures in the Democratic party refused to run. And the early front runner, Senator Gary Hart of Colorado, withdrew from the race in May 1987 after embarrassing revelations of an extramarital relationship with a young model. That left the field to a group of lesser-known candidates and to Jesse Jackson, whose fervent support among African-Americans made him a major force in the party.

The man who emerged from the pack was relatively little known: Michael Dukakis, a three-term governor of Massachusetts who claimed to have helped produce a dramatic revival in the New England economy (a revival frequently described as "the Massachusetts miracle"). Dukakis was a dry, even dull campaigner. But Democrats remained optimistic about their prospects in 1988, largely because of the identity of their opponent, Vice President George Bush.

In nearly thirty years in public life—as a member of Congress from Texas, as ambassador to the United Nations and minister to China, as director of the CIA, head of the Republican National Committee, and finally vice president—Bush had identified himself clearly with no major issue and could take credit for no major accomplishments. He had been an ineffective campaigner in 1980, when he ran unsuccessfully for president, and had attracted derision for his performance in the 1984 campaign, when he was running for reelection as vice president. Capitalizing on his ties to the still-popular Reagan, Bush overcame challenges from other major figures in the party to win the Republican nomination, but he entered the last months of the campaign substantially behind Dukakis.

Beginning at the Republican Convention, however, Bush staged a remarkable turnaround by making his campaign a long, relentless attack on

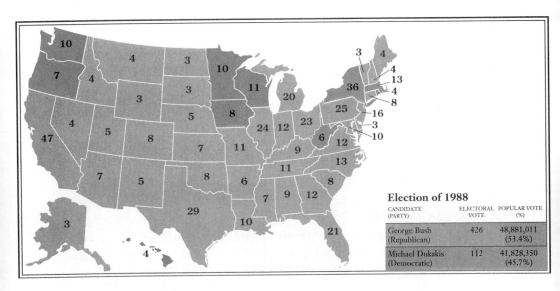

Election of 1988

CANDIDATE (PARTY)	ELECTORAL VOTE	POPULAR VOTE (%)
George Bush (Republican)	426	48,881,011 (53.4%)
Michael Dukakis (Democratic)	112	41,828,350 (45.7%)

Michael Dukakis, tying him to all the unpopular social and cultural stances Americans had come to identify with "liberals." Indeed, the Bush campaign was almost certainly the most negative, and many believed among the most discreditable, of the twentieth century. It was also, apparently, one of the most effective, although the listless, indecisive character of the Dukakis campaign contributed to the Republican cause as well. Having trailed Dukakis by a sizable margin as late as August, Bush won a substantial victory in November. He received 54 percent of the popular vote to Dukakis's 46, and he won 426 electoral votes to Dukakis's 111. But Bush carried few Republicans into office with him; the Democrats retained secure majorities in both houses of Congress.

GEORGE BUSH AND THE POST-COLD WAR WORLD

The Bush presidency was notable for a series of dramatic developments in international affairs and an almost complete absence of initiatives or ideas on domestic issues. For a time, Bush's apparent successes in foreign policy managed to obscure the absence of a domestic agenda. By 1992, however, with the nation in the second year of a serious recession, the president's once-overwhelming popularity had declined substantially.

The End of the Cold War

The broad popularity Bush enjoyed during his first three years in office was partly because of his subdued, unthreatening public image. But it was primarily because of the success of several international initiatives. Late in 1989, he dispatched American troops to Panama to overthrow the unpopular military leader Manuel Noriega. Noriega had worked for years as an informant for the CIA and United States drug agencies. But now he was himself under indictment in the United States for drug trafficking, and his contemptuous defiance of American pressures had embarrassed the government in Washington for two years. The Panama invasion—which installed an elected, pro-American, civilian government in Panama—was highly popular within the United States.

But Bush's early popularity also owed a great deal to a series of genuinely revolutionary transformations in the international order that made 1989 and 1990 one of the truly epochal moments in modern world history. There were many theories as to why the world changed so quickly and dramatically in those years. But the most frequent explanation centered on Mikhail Gorbachev, who succeeded to the leadership of the Soviet Union in 1985 and quickly became the most revolutionary figure in world politics in at least four decades. Benefiting from years of social and economic frustration in his country, Gorbachev transformed Soviet politics by launching two dramatic new policies. *Glasnost* (openness) introduced new levels of personal and political liberties to Soviet life. *Perestroika* (reform, or restructuring) attempted to revive the rigid and unproductive Soviet economy by introducing, among other things, such elements of capitalism as private ownership and the profit motive.

The forces Gorbachev unleashed changed Soviet life more quickly than he had imagined. Various Soviet republics began agitating for independence. Reformers demanded that Gorbachev move even faster to restructure the economy, as shortages in food and consumer goods grew severe. Gorbachev attempted through it all both to lead the reform forces he had helped unleash and, simultaneously, to placate conservative hard-liners who believed he was

CROSSING THE BERLIN WALL, NOVEMBER 9, 1989 Jubilant Germans swarm over the infamous Berlin Wall, which had divided the city since 1961, on the day the East German government opened the gates. A few months later, the wall was gone and Germany was on the way to reunification.

moving too fast. He insisted that he was still a communist and that he was only attempting to perfect the Soviet system.

One dramatic result of the Gorbachev reforms was the collapse of the Soviet empire, which occurred with startling speed in 1989. In the space of a few months, every nation in the so-called Soviet bloc in Central and Eastern Europe—Poland, Hungary, Czechoslovakia, Bulgaria, Romania, and East Germany—either overthrew its government or forced it to transform itself into an essentially noncommunist (and in some cases, actively anticommunist) regime. The Communist parties of Europe all but collapsed. And in every case, Gorbachev and the Soviet Union not only refused to oppose but actively encouraged the changes. Perhaps the most dramatic moment in the transformation of Europe came on November 9, 1989, when the government of East Germany began dismantling the notorious Berlin Wall, for nearly thirty years a symbol of the Cold War, and allowed free passage between the two Germanys. Within a year, German reunification—which only a few months earlier had seemed at best a distant dream—was a reality.

The challenges to communism were not successful everywhere. In May 1989, students in China began staging large demonstrations calling for greater democratization, which the post-Mao government had long been promising but had never delivered. But as the democracy movement grew, hard-line leaders seized control of the Chinese government and sent military forces to crush the uprising. The result was a massacre on June 3, 1989, in Tiananmen Square in Beijing. A still-unknown number of demonstrators, perhaps several thousand, died. The assault crushed the democracy movement, restored hard-liners to power, and inaugurated a period of harsh repression, to which the Bush administration reacted with seeming indifference.

But the events in China had no counterpart elsewhere in the communist world. And in 1991, communism began to collapse at the site of its birth: the Soviet Union itself. An unsuccessful coup by hard-line Soviet leaders on August 19 precipitated a dramatic unraveling of communist power. Within days, not only did the coup itself collapse in the face of resistance from the public and, more important, crucial elements within the military; not only did Mikhail Gorbachev return to power; but the forces of disunion that had been gathering strength for several years made a quantum leap forward. It soon became evident that the legitimacy of both the Communist party and the central Soviet government had been fatally injured. By the end of 1991, every republic in the Soviet Union had declared independence; Boris Yeltsin, the president of Russia, in effect outlawed the Communist party—barring it from owning property or playing any meaningful role in the life of the largest and most important republic in the Soviet Union; and the Soviet government, powerless to stop the fragmentation, had collapsed. On December 25, 1991, Mikhail Gorbachev resigned as president; and the U.S.S.R., nearly 75 years after its birth, ceased to exist.

In the face of these dramatic changes, American foreign policy, which for over four decades had remained securely tied to the premises of "containment," suddenly seemed obsolete. And while a new strategic doctrine to replace containment did not quickly emerge, the pattern of American international behavior began inevitably to change.

The Gorbachev regime had all but repudiated the arms race with the United States in the late 1980s and had been working energetically to produce arms control agreements well before Bush entered office. In 1988, the two superpowers signed a treaty eliminating American and Soviet intermediate-range nuclear forces from Europe. Over the next four years, the United States and the Soviet Union moved rapidly toward even more far-reaching arms reduction agreements, including major troop reductions in Europe and the dismantling of new categories of strategic weapons. At the same time, the nations of the former Soviet Union and the new, noncommunist governments in Central and Eastern Europe were appealing to the West for economic assistance through subsidies, loans, and investments; the United States, beset with its own fiscal and economic difficulties, was slow to respond.

The Gulf War

The events of 1989–1991 left the United States in the unanticipated position of being the only real "superpower" in the world. The Soviet Union and its successor nations were too embroiled in their own problems to play a major international role any longer. Germany and Japan, the emerging economic superpowers, had no significant military strength. China remained largely isolated from international affairs. The Bush administration, therefore, had to consider what to do with America's formidable political and military power in a world in which the major justification for that power—the Soviet threat—was now removed.

The events of 1990–1991 suggested two possible answers, both of which had some effect on policy. One was that the United States would reduce its military strength dramatically and concentrate its energies and resources on pressing domestic problems. And, indeed, there was considerable movement in that direction both in Congress and within the administration. The other was that America would continue to use its power actively, not to fight communism but to defend its economic interests. Once again, that drew the United States into the perilous politics of the Middle East.

On August 2, 1990, the armed forces of Iraq invaded and quickly overwhelmed their small, oil-rich neighbor, the emirate of Kuwait. Saddam Hussein, the militaristic leader of Iraq, soon announced that he was annexing Kuwait and set out to entrench his forces there. After some initial indecision, the Bush administration agreed to join with other nations to force Iraq out of Kuwait—through the pressure of economic sanctions if possible, through military force if necessary. Within a few weeks, Bush had persuaded virtually every important government in the world, including almost all the Arab and Islamic states, to join in a United Nations–sanctioned trade embargo of Iraq. That meant the Iraqis, whose economy was already weak, would be unable to sell any oil on world markets and would be unable to buy any products from abroad or generate hard currency with which to pay their massive debts.

At the same time, the United States and its allies (including the British, French, Egyptians, and Saudis) began deploying a massive military force along the border between Kuwait and Saudi Arabia. The force ultimately reached 690,000 troops (540,000 of them American) and assembled the largest and most sophisticated collection of military technology ever used in warfare.

By late 1990, the Bush administration was clearly losing patience with the sanctions and was preparing for war. On November 29, the United Nations, at the request of the United States, voted to authorize military action to expel Iraq from Kuwait if Iraq did not leave by January 15, 1991. On January 12, both houses of Congress voted to authorize the use of force against Iraq, although many Democrats opposed the resolution, arguing that sanctions should be given more time to work. And on January 16, American and allied air forces began a massive bombardment of Iraqi forces in Kuwait and of military and industrial installations in Iraq itself.

The allied bombing continued for six weeks, meeting only token resistance from the small Iraqi air force and ground defenses. On February 23, allied (primarily American) forces under the command of General Norman Schwarzkopf began a major ground offensive—not primarily against the heavily entrenched Iraqi forces along the Kuwait border, as expected, but into Iraq itself. The allied armies encountered almost no resistance and suffered only light casualties (141 fatalities). There were no reliable figures for the number of Iraqi casualties, but official estimates of deaths ranged as high as 100,000. On February 28, Iraq announced its acceptance of allied terms for a cease-fire, and the brief war came to an end.

The quick and relatively painless victory over Iraq was highly popular in the United States. But the longer range results of the Gulf War were more ambiguous. The tyrannical regime of Saddam Hussein survived, militarily weakened perhaps, but still capable of challenging the United States and its allies when they tried to enforce the terms of the 1991 ceasefire. By late 1992, there was considerable evidence that Iraq's efforts to construct nuclear weapons had not been as decisively thwarted by the allied bombing as the Bush administration had claimed at the time; the Baghdad government was, many believed, now accelerating its efforts to develop an atomic bomb. Kuwait, in the meantime, returned to the control of its prewar government, an undemocratic monarchy increasingly unpopular with its own people.

The Search for a Domestic Agenda

President Bush's popularity reached a record high in the immediate aftermath of the Gulf War. For a time, over 90 percent of those surveyed claimed to approve of the way he was handling his office—the highest approval rating in the history of polling. But as the nation's attention turned back to domestic issues, and as the recession that began late in 1990 persisted into 1992, the president's popularity declined with startling speed. That was in part because of the widespread perception that Bush was uninterested in domestic issues and had no ideas or plans for dealing with them.

The Bush administration faced several obstacles in promoting an effective domestic agenda. First, it inherited a staggering burden of debt and a federal deficit that had been out of control for nearly a decade. Any domestic agenda that required significant federal spending was, therefore, incompatible with the president's pledge to reduce the deficit and his 1988 campaign promise of "no new taxes." Second, President Bush faced a Democratic Congress, which was not, on the whole, disposed to cooperate with him. Third, the president was constantly concerned about the right wing of his own party and, in his eagerness to ingratiate himself with that group, took firm positions on divisive cultural issues such as abortion and affirmative action that further damaged his ability to work with Congress.

Despite this political stalemate, Congress and the White House managed on occasion to agree on significant measures. They cooperated in producing a plan to salvage the floundering savings and loan industry. In 1990, the president agreed to a significant tax increase as part of a multiyear "budget package" designed to reduce the deficit significantly—although in doing so, the president had to repudiate his most prominent 1988 campaign promise. In 1991, after almost two years of acrimonious debate, the president and Congress agreed on a civil-rights bill to combat job discrimination.

But the most serious domestic problem facing the Bush administration was one to which neither the president nor Congress had any answer. The recession that began in 1990 slowly increased its grip on the national economy in 1991 and receded only slightly in 1992. Because of the enormous level of debt that corporations (and individuals) had accumulated in the 1980s, the recession caused an unusual number of bankruptcies. It created a growing frustration among middle-class Americans and growing pressure on the government to address such problems as the rising cost of health care. And as the Bush administration responded to these problems with indecision and passivity, the president's popularity eroded.

The Election of 1992

Because the early maneuvering for the presidential election of 1992 occurred when President Bush's popularity remained high, many leading Democrats declined to run. Bill Clinton, the young, five-term governor of Arkansas, emerged early as the front-runner among the remaining candidates by virtue of a skillful campaign that emphasized broad economic issues over the racial and cultural questions that had so divided Democrats in the past. Clinton survived a bruising primary campaign and a series of damaging personal controversies to capture his party's nomination. George Bush withstood a primary challenge from the conservative journalist Pat Buchanan to become the Republican nominee again. In the meantime, Ross Perot, a blunt, forthright Texas billionaire, launched an independent presidential campaign by appealing to public unhappiness with the political system in general and the fiscal crisis in particular. He produced an astonishing popular response; at several moments in the spring, he led both Clinton and Bush in public opinion polls. In July, as he began to face hostile scrutiny in the press, he abruptly withdrew from the race. But early in October he re-entered and regained much of his earlier support.

After a campaign in which the economy and the president's unpopularity were the major issues, Bill Clinton won a decisive victory over Bush and Perot. He received 43 percent of the vote in the three-way race, to the president's 38 percent (the lowest percentage for an incumbent since Taft in 1912) and Perot's 19 percent (the best showing for a third-party or independent candidate since Theodore Roosevelt in 1912). Clinton won 370 electoral votes to Bush's 168; Perot won none. Democrats retained solid control of both houses of Congress. And a new administration prepared to face the mounting problems of a rapidly changing society.

MODERN TIMES

Much of the anxiety that beset American life beginning in the 1970s, and much of the conservative sentiment that emerged to dominate American politics in the 1980s and early 1990s, was a result of jarring public events that left many men and women shaken and uncertain. But much of it was a result as well of significant changes in the nature and behavior of American society.

The Graying of America

One of the most fundamental changes in American life in the postliberal era was the new profile of the American population. After decades of steady growth, the nation's birth rate began to decline in the 1970s and remained low through the 1980s and early 1990s. In 1970, there were 18.4 births for every 1,000 people in the population. By 1975, the rate had declined to 14.6, the lowest in the twentieth century. And despite a modest increase in the 1980s, the rate remained below 16 throughout the decade. The declining

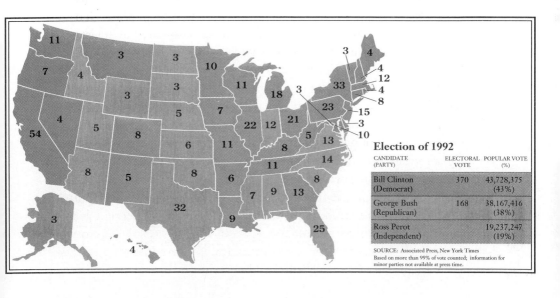

Election of 1992

CANDIDATE (PARTY)	ELECTORAL VOTE	POPULAR VOTE (%)
Bill Clinton (Democrat)	370	43,728,375 (43%)
George Bush (Republican)	168	38,167,416 (38%)
Ross Perot (Independent)		19,237,247 (19%)

SOURCE: Associated Press, New York Times
Based on more than 99% of vote counted; information for minor parties not available at press time.

birth rate and a significant increase in life expectancy produced a substantial increase in the proportion of elderly citizens. Over 12 percent of the population was more than sixty-five years old by 1990, as compared with 8 percent in 1970. That figure was projected to rise to over 20 percent by the end of the century. The median age in 1990 was 32.9 years, as compared with 28 in 1970. The aging of the population had important, if still not fully understood, implications. It was, for example, a cause of the increasing costliness of Social Security pensions. It meant rapidly increasing health costs, both for the federal Medicare system and for private hospitals and insurance companies.

Hispanics, Asians, and the New Immigration

Perhaps the most striking demographic change in America in the 1970s and 1980s, and the one likely to have the farthest-reaching consequences, was the enormous change in both the extent and the character of immigation. The nation's immigration quotas expanded significantly in those years (partly to accommodate refugees from Southeast Asia and other nations), allowing more newcomers to enter the United States legally than at any point since the beginning of the twentieth century. In the 1970s, more than 4 million legal immigrants entered the United States. In the 1980s, that number rose to more than 6 million. When the uncounted but very large numbers of illegal immigrants in those years are included, the wave of immigration in the twenty years after 1970 was the largest of the twentieth century.

Equally striking was the character of the new immigration. The Immigration Reform Act of 1965 (see p. 810) had eliminated quotas based on national origin; from then on, newcomers from regions other than Latin America were generally admitted on a first-come, first-served basis. In 1965, 90 percent of the immigrants to the United States came from Europe. Twenty years later, only 10 percent of the new arrivals were Europeans. The extent and character of the new immigration was causing a dramatic change in the composition of the American population. Already by the end of the 1980s, people of white European background constituted under 80 percent of the population (as opposed to 90 percent a half-century before). It seemed likely that by the middle of the twenty-first century, whites of European heritage would constitute less than 50 percent of the population.

Particularly important to the new immigration were two groups: Hispanics (or Latinos) and Asians. Both had been significant segments of the

A M E R I C A N   V O I C E S

A Vietnamese Immigrant Describes Her Life in America, 1984

HERE IN AMERICA, I just remain. I don't change my traditional ways. . . . My children have adapted to American customs in hair styles and dress. . . . The older women don't change much, and most of the older men don't change either.

Over here, for older people, we receive money from the government; if not, we would die of starvation because we are older and don't know what to do. In Vietnam, we have less fear of survival, but over here, I'm afraid that when I get older I'll have to go into a nursing home to stay there, because all of my children are working. . . . Old age here is scary. . . .

The difference is that over here children do not obey their parents; in Vietnam, they obeyed us more. Over here, whenever we say something, they like to argue about it. . . . Things we consider to be right they consider wrong. Like a wife they select whom we don't like. They argue with us, against it, saying that it's right for them and that they will take the responsibility for it. They claim it's their *right* and that we don't have the right to tell them what to do. It is just like we are strangers; they won't let us interfere. . . . Our children do not keep the old traditions. They live apart from one another.

SOURCE: Reprinted from *Hearts of Sorrow: Vietnamese-American Lives*, by James M. Freeman, with the permission of the publisher, Stanford University Press. © 1989 by the Board of Trustees of the Leland Stanford Junior University.

American population for many decades: Hispanics since the very beginning of the nation's history, Asians since the waves of Chinese and Japanese immigration in the nineteenth century. But both groups experienced enormous, indeed unprecedented, growth after 1965.

People from Latin America constituted more than a third of the total number of legal immigrants to the United States in every year after 1965—and a much larger proportion of the total number of illegal immigrants. In California and the Southwest, in particular, they became a major presence. There were also substantial Hispanic populations in Illinois, New York, and Florida. High birth rates among Hispanic communities already in the United States further increased their numbers. In the 1980 census, 6 percent of the population was listed as being of Hispanic origin. The 1990 census showed an increase to 9 percent.

In the 1980s and early 1990s, Asian immigrants arrived in even greater numbers than Hispanics. They constituted more than 40 percent of the total of legal newcomers. They came in particularly large numbers from Vietnam, Thailand, Cambodia, Laos, the Philippines, Korea, and India. By 1990, there were more than 7 million Asian-Americans in the United States, more than twice the number of ten years before. Like Hispanics, they were concentrated mainly in large cities and in the West.

Many of the new Asian immigrants were refugees, including Vietnamese driven from their homes in the aftermath of the disastrous war in which the United States had so long been involved. Large numbers of "boat people"—Vietnamese refugees who put to sea in crowded boats without any clear destination—ultimately found their way to the United States, usually after enduring terrible dangers and hardships. But many Asian immigrants were highly educated professionals seeking greater opportunities in the United States.

As with most new immigrant groups, Asian-Americans found adjustment to the very different culture of the United States difficult and disorienting. They also experienced resentment and discrimination. Whites feared Asian competition in economic activities that they had been accustomed to controlling. There were, for example, heated disputes between white and Vietnamese shrimpers on the Gulf Coast in Texas, Mississippi, and Louisiana. Some African-Americans resented the success of Asian merchants in black neighborhoods. In New York, for example, racial tensions led to a black boycott of some Korean grocery stores in African-American neighborhoods in 1990. Resentment of Asian-Americans may have been a result, in part, of their remarkable success. Indeed, some Asian groups (most notably Indians, Japanese, and Chinese) were by the 1980s earning larger average annual incomes than were whites. Chinese- and Japanese-Americans consistently ranked at or near the top of high-school and college classes in the 1980s. That was in part because Asian-American communities contained significant numbers of people who had been involved in business and the professions before coming to America and had arrived with a high degree of expertise. They also placed a high value on education.

Drug Abuse, AIDS, and Homelessness

The new immigrants of the 1980s and 1990s arrived in cities being ravaged by new and deadly epidemics. One was a dramatic increase in drug use, which by the end of the 1980s was penetrating nearly every community in the nation. The enormous demand for drugs, and particularly for "crack" cocaine, spawned what was in effect a multi-billion-dollar industry; and those reaping the enormous profits of the illegal trade fought strenuously and often savagely to protect their positions.

The Bush administration, and virtually all political figures, spoke heatedly about the need for a "war on drugs," but in the absence of significant funding for such programs, public efforts appeared to have little effect. There were signs at the end of the 1980s that drug use was in decline among middle-class people, but the epidemic showed no signs of abating in the poor urban neighborhoods, where it was doing the most severe damage.

The drug epidemic was directly related to another scourge of the cities in the 1980s: the epidemic spread of a new and lethal disease first documented in 1981 and soon named AIDS (acquired immune deficiency syndrome). AIDS is the product of the HIV virus, which is transmitted by the exchange of bodily fluids (blood or semen). The virus gradually destroys the body's immune system and makes its victims highly vulnerable to a number of diseases (particularly to various forms of cancer and pneumonia) to which they would otherwise have a natural resistance. Although those infected with the virus can live for many years without developing the disease, once they do become ill they are virtually certain to die from it. The first victims of AIDS (and in the early 1990s the group among whom cases remained the most numerous) were homosexual men. But by the late 1980s, as the gay community began to take preventive measures, the most rapid increase in the spread of the disease occurred among intravenous drug users, many of them heterosexuals, who spread the virus by sharing contaminated hypodermic needles. By the early 1990s, government agencies were estimating that between 1 and 1.5 million Americans were infected with the HIV virus. (Worldwide, the figure was approximately 10 million.) Nearly 200,000

Americans had actually contracted AIDS, and nearly 130,000 had died. Although by 1990 researchers had discovered several drugs that could delay or limit some effects of AIDS, neither a cure nor a vaccine seemed imminent.

The increasing scarcity of housing for low-income people contributed to another urban crisis of the 1980s and 1990s: homelessness. There had always been homeless men and women in most major cities; but their numbers were clearly increasing at an alarming rate in the face of rising housing costs, severe cutbacks in federal support for public housing, the closing of mental health institutions, reduced welfare assistance, the declining availability of unskilled jobs, and the increasing weakness of family structures. The phenomenon of tens of thousands of homeless people at large in the cities put pressure on municipal governments to provide shelter and assistance for the indigent; but in an age of fiscal stringency and greatly reduced federal aid, cities found it difficult to produce responses adequate to the dimensions of the crisis.

Nonwhites in the Postliberal Era

Nonwhites in America moved along several very different paths in the 1980s and early 1990s. On the one hand, there were increased opportunities for advancement available to those who were in a position to take advantage of them, a result in large part of the legal and political gains of the 1960s and 1970s. On the other hand, as the industrial economy declined and government services dwindled, there was a growing sense of helplessness and despair among the larger groups of nonwhites who continued to find themselves barred from upward mobility.

For the black middle class, which by the 1980s constituted nearly a third of the entire black population of America, the progress was striking. Economic disparities between black and white professionals did not vanish, but they diminished substantially. African-American families moved into affluent urban communities and suburbs—at times as neighbors of whites, often as residents of predominantly black suburban communities. The number of blacks attending college rose by 350 percent in the decade following the passage of the civil-rights acts (as opposed to the 150 percent increase among whites); by the early 1990s the percentage of black high-school graduates going on to college was nearly the same as that of white high-school graduates (although a far smaller proportion of blacks than whites managed to complete high school).

But the rise of a black middle class served also to accentuate the increasingly desperate plight of other African-Americans. This growing "underclass," as some called it, felt the impact of deindustrialization and urban decline with special force. In the early 1990s, more than one-third of all black families lived in poverty. (More than one-fourth of all the Hispanic families counted by the government likewise lived in poverty—as well as many more who remained uncounted.) At the same time, just under 11 percent of white families could be officially classified as poor.

The black family structure suffered from and contributed to the dislocations of urban poverty. There was a dramatic increase in the number of single-parent, female-headed black households. In the early 1990s, over half of all black children were born into single-parent families, as opposed to only 15 percent of white children. In 1960, only 20 percent of black children had lived in single-parent homes.

Nonwhites were victimized by many things in the changing social and economic climate of the 1980s. Among them was a growing impatience with affirmative action and other programs designed to advance their fortunes, as well as a growing reluctance among federal officials after 1980 to move aggressively to enforce affirmative action guidelines. Nonwhites also suffered from a steady decline in the number of unskilled jobs in the economy. They suffered from the deterioration of public education and other social services, which made it more difficult for them to find opportunities for advancement. And they suffered, in some cases, from a sense of futility and despair, born of years of entrapment in brutal urban ghettoes. By the early 1990s, several generations of nonwhites had grown to maturity living in destitute neighborhoods where welfare or crime (especially drug dealing) were the only means of support for some people. Residents of such neighborhoods also lived with the constant threat of gang violence and other mayhem; for young black males in the early 1990s, murder was the leading cause of death. They also lived with an increasing incidence of drug addiction and AIDs.

The frustration of the inner cities created a harsh new politics among some African-Americans—angry, confrontational, and intentionally abrasive. New black leaders emerged from the ghettoes who rejected the accommodationist rhetoric of the civil-rights movement and even the more militant rhetoric of Jesse Jackson. Instead, they argued that white society was incurably racist and insisted that African-Americans must fight for some form of autonomy. At one level, therefore, American society was becoming more successfully integrated than ever before as the white and black middle classes learned to live and work together reasonably harmoniously. At another level, however, the nation was experiencing a new kind of racial polarization, in which large numbers of African-Americans were living in virtual isolation from white society and coming to view it as fundamentally hostile.

The despair that had come to grip much of black America became graphically and tragically evident in the spring of 1992 in response to events in Los Angeles. In 1991, a group of white Los Angeles policemen had been videotaped savagely beating a black man, Rodney King, as they arrested him for a minor crime after an automobile chase. The tape precipitated the prosecution of the officers involved. In late April 1992, a white jury acquitted the policemen of virtually all charges—a decision that produced shock and disbelief among African-Americans (and many white Americans) through-out the nation. It also produced the worst urban violence of the twentieth century.

In south central Los Angeles, the predominantly African-American neighborhood where many of the poorest residents of the city lived, violence began the night of the verdict and continued for several days. By the time it subsided, more than 50 people were dead and hundreds of businesses and homes were gutted by fire. Smaller uprisings occurred in other cities at the same time. The Los Angeles riot drew attention once again to the failure of the United States to solve the problems of race and urban poverty. But in an age of slow economic growth, the prospects for a decisive public response seemed bleak.

The New Religion and the New Right

In the 1960s, many social critics had predicted the virtual extinction of religious influence in American life. But America in the 1970s experienced the beginning of a major religious revival, perhaps the most powerful since the second Great Awakening of the early nineteenth century. It continued in various forms into the 1990s.

The most important feature of this new awakening was the rise of evangelical Christianity. Evangelicals had been gathering strength for many years, and especially since the early 1950s, when fundamentalists such as Billy Graham and pentecostals such as Oral Roberts had begun to attract huge national (and international) followings—largely a result of their effec-tive use of television—for their energetic revivalism. By the 1980s, more than 70 million Americans (nearly a third of the nation) described them-selves as "born-again" Christians—men and women who had established a "direct personal relationship with Jesus." One of them had occupied the White House—Jimmy Carter, who during the 1976 campaign had talked proudly of his own "conversion experience" and who continued openly to proclaim his "born-again" Christian faith during his years in office. For Jimmy Carter, evangelical Christianity had formed the basis for his commitment to racial and economic justice and to world peace. To many others, however, the message of the new religion was very different—but no less political. In the 1980s, some Christian evangelicals became active on the political and cultural right.

The new political right, of which evangelical Christians were only a part, enjoyed rapid growth in the 1970s and early 1980s. The New Right displayed a remarkable organizing zeal—particularly in launching mass-mailing campaigns of staggering size and raising great sums of money to support conservative efforts. It also injected a series of moral and cultural issues into political debate, as the controversy in 1989 and 1990 over federal support for the arts suggested. Several provocative art exhibits—among them a collection of photographs by Robert Mapplethorpe, some of which contained graphic depictions of homosexual behavior—offended conservatives (as well as many others). The controversy over the content of the exhibits soon extended to a dispute over their funding. Both the artists and the museums displaying their work had received grants from the National Endowment for the Arts (NEA), which now came under attack from Senator Jesse Helms of North Carolina and other conservative leaders. For a time, the future of the NEA seemed in danger. Ultimately, Congress agreed to extend its life, but political pressures continued to bedevil the agency.

The power of the New Right in the early 1980s represented the culmination of many decades of steadily growing conservative sentiment, which had triumphed in 1980, when the right became a central force in propelling Ronald Reagan into the White House. But despite its conspicuous strength, the new conservatism was difficult to define. The most active groups within the New Right were not conservatives of traditional stripe—people associated with and supportive of the business community, defending the position of established economic and social elites. They were, rather, middle-class and lower-middle-class people, whose political demands centered more around social and cultural issues than economic ones, who seemed to exhibit not so much a staid conservatism as a right-wing populism.

By the beginning of the 1990s, the power of the New Right seemed to be in decline in some areas. A series of scandals discredited several leading evangelical ministers. Other factions of the New Right also began to experience hard times after the election of the centrist George Bush and during the recession of 1991–1992, when some working people began returning to a concern with traditional economic issues. Still, the right remained a significant force within the Republican party and a constant factor in the calculation of all those (among them President Bush) who hoped to secure a base within it. The surprising strength of the Louisiana politician David Duke, a former Nazi and Ku Klux Klan leader who received 39 percent of the vote in a 1991 gubernatorial race, suggested the tenacity of right-wing positions on race and religion.

Battles Against Feminism and Abortion

Among other things, the New Right continued to display impressive strength in launching an intense assault on feminism. Leaders of the New Right had campaigned successfully against the proposed Equal Rights Amendment to the Constitution. And they played a central role in the most

THE ABORTION BATTLE For many years, it was opponents of abortion who staged demonstrations each year in Washington. In the late 1980s, however, as the "right to life" movement made significant political and judicial gains, supporters of "choice" began staging large demonstrations of their own. This one, in March 1989, was part of a much larger march of 300,000 people organized by the National Organization for Women.

divisive issue of the late 1980s and early 1990s: the controversy over abortion rights. (See pp. 850–851.)

For those who favored allowing women to choose to terminate unwanted pregnancies, the Supreme Court's decision in *Roe* v. *Wade* (1973) had seemed to settle the question. By the 1980s, abortion was the most commonly performed surgical procedure in the country. But at the same time, opposition to abortion was creating a powerful grass-roots movement. The right-to-life movement, as it called itself, found its most fervent supporters among Catholics; and indeed, the Catholic church itself lent its institutional authority to the battle against legalized abortion. Religious doctrine also motivated the antiabortion stance of Mormons, fundamentalist Christians, and other groups. The opposition of other antiabortion activists had less to do with religion than with their commitment to traditional notions of family and gender relations. To them, abortion was a particularly offensive part of a much larger assault by feminists on the role of women as wives and mothers. It was also, many foes contended, a form of murder. Fetuses, they claimed, were human beings who had a "right to life" from the moment of conception.

Although the right-to-life movement was persistent in its demand for a reversal of *Roe* v. *Wade* or, barring that, a constitutional amendment banning abortion, it also attacked abortion in more limited ways, at its most vulnerable points. In the 1970s, Congress and many state legislatures began barring the use of public funds to pay for abortions, thus making them almost inaccessible for many poor women. The Reagan and Bush administrations imposed further restrictions on federal funding and even on the right of doctors in federally funded clinics to give patients any information on abortion.

The changing composition of the Supreme Court in the 1980s and 1990s (which saw six new conservative justices named by Presidents Reagan and Bush) renewed the right-to-life movement's hopes for a reversal of *Roe* v. *Wade*. In *Webster* v. *Reproductive Health Services* (1989), the Court upheld a Missouri law that prohibited any institution receiving state funds from performing abortions, whether or not those funds were used to finance the abortions. Hopes were high among anti-abortion forces that the Court would soon repudiate *Roe* v. *Wade* itself. To the surprise of people on both sides of the issue, however, the Court pulled back. In 1992, ruling (in *Planned Parenthood* v. *Casey*) on a Pennsylvania law that imposed still more restrictions on abortion, the Court upheld many of the restrictions but, in a precarious 5 to 4 decision, explicitly reaffirmed the validity of *Roe* v. *Wade* itself. Three justices appointed by Reagan and Bush voted with the majority.

The changing political and judicial climate of the late 1980s mobilized defenders of abortion as never before. They called themselves the "pro-choice" movement, because they were defending not so much abortion itself as every woman's right to choose whether and when to bear a child. It quickly became clear that the pro-choice movement was in many parts of the country at least as strong as, and in some areas much stronger than, the right-to-life movement.

The abortion controversy at times overshadowed other efforts by feminists to protect and expand the rights of women. But such efforts continued. Women's organizations and many individual women worked strenuously in the 1980s and 1990s to raise awareness of sexual harassment in the workplace, with considerable success. Colleges, universities, government agencies, and even many corporations established strict new standards of behavior for their employees in dealing with members of the opposite sex and created grievance procedures for those who believed they had been harassed.

Both the achievements and the limits of the feminists' progress on this issue were evident in the sensational controversy in 1991 over Judge Clarence Thomas, President Bush's nominee for a seat on the Supreme Court. Late in the confirmation proceedings, accusations of sexual harassment from a former employee of Thomas became public. Thomas's accuser, a law professor, testified before the Senate Judiciary Committee and, in doing so, dramatically polarized both the Senate and the nation. Feminists and others tended to believe the accusations and hailed the accuser for drawing national attention to the issue of harassment; but many Americans, apparently, did not believe her—or at least concluded that the alleged activities should not disqualify Thomas from serving on the Court. Thomas was ultimately confirmed by a narrow margin.

The Changing Left and the New Environmentalism

The New Left of the 1960s and early 1970s did not disappear after the end of the war in Vietnam, but it faded rapidly. Many of the students who had fought in its battles grew up, left school, and entered conventional careers. Some radical leaders, disillusioned by the unresponsiveness of American society to their demands, resignedly gave up the struggle and chose instead to work "within the system." Marxist critiques continued to flourish in academic circles, but to much of the public they came to appear dated and irrelevant—particularly as Marxist governments collapsed in disrepute beginning in 1989.

Yet a left of sorts did survive, giving evidence in the process of how greatly the nation's political climate had changed. Where 1960s activists had rallied to protest racism, poverty, and war, their counterparts in the 1980s and 1990s more often fought to stop the proliferation of nuclear weapons and power plants, save the wilderness, protect endangered species, limit reckless economic development, and otherwise protect the environment.

Public concerns about the environment had arisen intermittently since the beginning of the industrial era and had been growing in intensity ever since 1962, when the publication of Rachel Carson's *Silent Spring* aroused widespread public concern about the effect of insecticides on the natural world. Several highly visible environmental catastrophes in the 1960s and 1970s greatly increased that concern. Among them was a major oil spill off Santa Barbara, California, in 1969; the discovery of large deposits of improperly disposed toxic wastes in a residential community in upstate New York in 1978; and a frightening accident at the nuclear power plant at Three Mile Island, Pennsylvania, in 1979. These and other revelations of the extent to which human progress threatened the natural world helped produce a major popular movement.

In the spring of 1970, a nationwide "Earth Day" signaled the beginning of the environmental movement. It differed markedly from the "conservation" movements of earlier years. Modern environmentalists shared the concerns of such earlier figures as John Muir and Gifford Pinchot about preserving some areas of the wilderness and carefully managing the exploitation of resources. But the new activists went much further, basing their positions on the developing field of ecology, the study of the connections among all components of an environment. Toxic wastes, air and water pollution, the destruction of forests, the extinction of species: these were not separate, isolated problems. All elements of the earth's environment were intimately and delicately linked together, ecologists claimed. Damaging any one of those elements risked damaging all the others. Only by adopting a new social ethic, in which economic growth became less important than ecological health, could the human race hope to survive in a healthy world.

In the twenty years after the first Earth Day, environmental issues gained increasing attention and support. Although the federal government often displayed limited interest in the subject, environmentalists won a series of significant battles, mostly at the local level. They blocked the construction of roads, airports, and other projects (including American development of the supersonic transport airplane, or SST) that they claimed would be ecologically dangerous. By the end of the 1980s, the sense of urgency had grown, as scientists began warning that the release of certain industrial pollutants (most notably chlorofluorocarbons) into the atmosphere was depleting the ozone layer of the earth's atmosphere, which protects the globe from the sun's most dangerous rays. They warned, too, of the related danger of global warming, a rise in the earth's temperature as a result of emissions from the burning of fossil fuels (coal and oil).

The concern for the environment, the opposition to nuclear power, the resistance to economic development—all were reflections of a more fundamental characteristic of the post-Vietnam left. In a sharp break from the nation's long commitment to growth and progress, many dissidents argued that only by limiting growth and curbing traditional forms of progress could society hope to survive.

Some of these critics of the "idea of progress" expressed a gloomy resignation, urging a lowering of social expectations and predicting an inevitable deterioration in the quality of life. Other advocates of restraint believed that change did not require decline: human beings could live more

DOONESBURY Cartoonist Garry Trudeau created his celebrated comic strip in the 1960s while he was an undergraduate at Yale University. In this 1984 cartoon, Trudeau uses his title character, Mike Doonesbury, to illustrate the transformation of 1960s idealists into 1980s "yuppies."

comfortably and more happily if they learned to respect the limits imposed on them by their environment. But in either case, such arguments evoked strong opposition from conservatives and others, who ridiculed the no-growth ideology as an expression of defeatism and despair. Ronald Reagan, in particular, made an attack on the idea of "limits" central to his political success.

The Culture Wars

Few controversies attracted more attention in the late 1980s and early 1990s than the battle over what became known as "multiculturalism." Multiculturalism meant different things to different people, but at its core was an effort to legitimize the cultural pluralism of the rapidly diversifying American population. That meant acknowledging that "American culture," which had long been defined primarily by white males of European descent, also included other traditions: female, African-American, Indian, and increasingly in the late twentieth-century Hispanic and Asian. Although such demands were often controversial, especially when they became the basis of assaults on traditional academic curricula, much greater acrimony emerged out of efforts by some revisionists to portray traditional western culture as inherently racist and imperialistic. A prolonged, if somewhat muted, dispute over how to commemorate the 500th anniversary of Columbus's first voyage to the "New World" illustrated how sharply ideas of multiculturalism had changed the way Americans discussed their past. In 1892, the Columbian anniversary had been the occasion of boisterous national celebration—and a great world's fair in Chicago. In 1992, it produced agonizing debates over the impact of the European discovery on native peoples; and the only world's fair was in Spain.

Debates over multiculturalism and related issues helped produce an increasingly strained climate in academia and in the larger American intellectual world. People on the left complained that the ascendancy of conservative politics placed new and intolerable limits on freedom of expression, as the effort to restrict NEA grants to controversial artists suggests. Many on the right complained equally vigorously of a tyranny of "political correctness," by which feminists, cultural radicals, and others introduced a new form of intolerance to public discourse in the name of defending the rights of women and minorities.

The controversies surrounding multiculturalism and "political correctness" were illustrations of a painful change in the character of American society. Traditional patterns of authority faced challenges from women, minorities, and others. The liberal belief in tolerance and assimilation was fraying in the face of the growing cultural separatism of some ethnic and racial groups. Confidence in the nation's future was declining, and with it confidence in the capacity of American society to provide justice and opportunity to all its citizens.

The American Future

The American people had suffered many trials and disappointments since the heady days at the end of World War II, when an "American Century" seemed about to dawn, and since the mid-1950s, when the United States appeared poised for a prolonged era of domestic tranquillity, economic abundance, and international preeminence. By the early 1990s, America, like many other nations, was faced with the problems of a faltering industrial economy, an increasingly diverse and contentious population, and growing dangers to the environment that threatened the health of the entire world.

At the same time, however, the great changes in world affairs of the late 1980s and early 1990s seemed to vindicate one of the most important assumptions behind America's 200-year experiment in democracy: that the desire for personal freedom is a basic human impulse that even decades of repressive government cannot extinguish. The dramatically different world order that was emerging from the upheavals of the late twentieth century was filled with dangers. But the United States, despite its many problems, remained what it had long been: one of the stablest, wealthiest, and most resilient societies in modern history. At the dawn of a new era, the United States—whose example had done much to fuel the forces of change—faced the challenge of preserving and extending its own democracy in the face of major new perils and great new opportunities.

APPENDICES

CANADA

*Puget
Sound*
□ Seattle
Olympia ○
Spokane ○
WASHINGTON
MONTANA
Portland ○
Columbia River
Salem ○
Missouri *River*
Helena ☆
*Lake
Sakakawea*
● Minot
NORTH
DAKOTA
Eugene ○
OREGON
Yellowstone River
Bismarck ☆
Boise ○
IDAHO
Snake River
WYOMING
Pierre ☆
SOUTH
DAKOTA
Sioux Falls ○
*Great Salt
Lake*
Reno ○
Carson City ☆
Salt Lake
City ○
Cheyenne ☆
N. Platte River
NEBRASKA
Sacramento ○
Oakland ○
Stockton ○
Modesto ○
San Jose ○
San Francisco
NEVADA
UTAH
S. Platte River
Denver ○
Colorado
Springs ○
COLORADO
Platte River
Lincoln ○
KANSAS
Fresno ○
CALIFORNIA
Bakersfield ○
Las Vegas ○
Colorado River
Arkansas
Wichita ○
River
Pasadena
San
Bernardino
Santa Ana
Los Angeles
Long Beach
Santa Fe ☆
ARIZONA
Albuquerque ○
Amarillo ○
OKLAHOMA
Oklahoma
City ○
San Diego ●
Colorado River
Phoenix ○
NEW
MEXICO
Rio Grande
Lubbock ○
Red River
PACIFIC
OCEAN
Tucson ○
Dallas ●
Abilene ○
Fort Worth ○
Waco ○

□ El Paso

RUSSIA
*ARCTIC
OCEAN*
60°N
*Bering
Strait*
ALASKA
Yukon River
Austin ○
TEXAS
Bering Sea
Anchorage ○
CANADA
MEXICO
San Antonio □
Rio Grande
Laredo ○
Nueces
River
Corpus
Christi ○
ALEUTIAN ISLANDS
Juneau ○
Gulf of Alaska
Kauai PACIFIC OCEAN
Niihau *Oahu*
Honolulu ○ *Molokai* HAWAII
Lanai *Maui*
Kahoolawe
Brownsville ○
PACIFIC OCEAN
0 400 Miles
0 400 Kilometers
0 200 Miles
0 200 Kilometers
Hawaii

A-2

CANADA

Lake of the Woods

MINNESOTA

Lake Superior

MICHIGAN

Minneapolis ○ ○ St. Paul

Lake Huron

Lake Michigan

WISCONSIN
Milwaukee ○
Madison □

IOWA
Cedar Rapids ○
Des Moines ○

Grand Rapids ○ Lansing ○

Detroit ● Cleveland ○

Omaha ○

Illinois River
Mississippi River

Chicago ■
Gary ○ Toledo ○ Akron ○
Fort Wayne ○

OHIO

Columbus □

ILLINOIS
Peoria ○
Springfield □ Indianapolis □

Wabash River

INDIANA

Dayton ○
Cincinnati ○

Lake Ontario
Rochester ○

Lake Erie
Buffalo ○

NEW YORK
Albany ★

VERMONT Augusta ★
Montpelier ★ NEW HAMPSHIRE
Concord ★
Boston ◉
MASSACHUSETTS
○ Providence
Hartford ○ RHODE ISLAND
New Haven ○ CONNECTICUT

MAINE

St. Lawrence River

Hudson River
Connecticut R.

Newark □ ○ New York ■
NEW JERSEY
Trenton ★
Philadelphia ●

PENNSYLVANIA
Harrisburg ★
Pittsburgh ○

Kansas City ○ ○ Kansas City
Topeka ★ Jefferson City ★

Missouri River

St. Louis ○

MISSOURI

Ohio River *Tennessee R.*

Louisville ○ Frankfort ★
Lexington ○

KENTUCKY

Charleston ○
WEST VIRGINIA

VIRGINIA
Richmond ★

Baltimore □
Washington, D.C. ⊕ DELAWARE
Annapolis ★ Dover ★
MARYLAND

Potomac R.

Chesapeake Bay

Norfolk ○

ATLANTIC OCEAN

Tulsa ○

ARKANSAS
Little Rock ★

Arkansas River
Mississippi River
Yazoo River

Memphis ○

TENNESSEE
Nashville □
Chattanooga ○

Huntsville ○

Knoxville ○

Greensboro ○ ○ Raleigh ★
NORTH CAROLINA
Charlotte ○

Cape Hatteras

Shreveport ○

MISSISSIPPI
Jackson ○

ALABAMA
Birmingham ○
Montgomery ★
Columbus ○

Atlanta ★

Macon ○

GEORGIA

Columbia ★
SOUTH CAROLINA

Charleston ○

Cape Fear

Savannah ○

Sabine River

Beaumont ○
Houston ●

LOUISIANA
Baton Rouge ★
New Orleans ○

Mobile ○

Tallahassee ★

Jacksonville □

FLORIDA
Orlando ○

Cape Canaveral

Gulf of Mexico

St. Petersburg ○ Tampa ○

Lake Okeechobee

Hollywood ○ ○ Fort Lauderdale
Miami ○

The United States in 1990

⊛ National Capital

★ State Capitals

URBAN POPULATION CENTERS

■ Over 5,000,000

■ 3,000,000–5,000,000

● 1,000,000–3,000,000

□ 500,000–1,000,000

○ 100,000–500,000

• Less than 100,000 (selected)

0 ———— 300 Miles
0 ———— 400 Kilometers

A-3

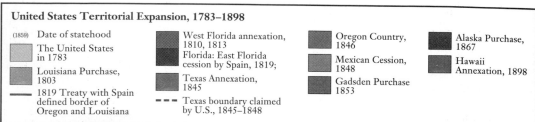

United States Territorial Expansion, 1783–1898

(1859) Date of statehood

The United States in 1783

Louisiana Purchase, 1803

1819 Treaty with Spain defined border of Oregon and Louisiana

West Florida annexation, 1810, 1813

Florida: East Florida cession by Spain, 1819;

Texas Annexation, 1845

- - - Texas boundary claimed by U.S., 1845–1848

Oregon Country, 1846

Mexican Cession, 1848

Gadsden Purchase 1853

Alaska Purchase, 1867

Hawaii Annexation, 1898

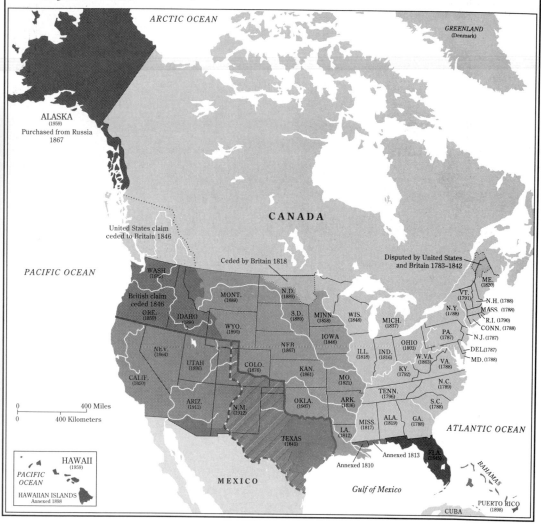

Documents and Tables

THE DECLARATION OF INDEPENDENCE

In Congress, July 4, 1776,

THE UNANIMOUS DECLARATION OF THE THIRTEEN UNITED STATES OF AMERICA

When, in the course of human events, it becomes necessary for one people to dissolve the political bands which have connected them with another, and to assume, among the powers of the earth, the separate and equal station to which the laws of nature and of nature's God entitle them, a decent respect to the opinions of mankind requires that they should declare the causes which impel them to the separation.

We hold these truths to be self-evident, that all men are created equal; that they are endowed by their Creator with certain unalienable rights; that among these, are life, liberty, and the pursuit of happiness. That, to secure these rights, governments are instituted among men, deriving their just powers from the consent of the governed; that, whenever any form of government becomes destructive of these ends, it is the right of the people to alter or to abolish it, and to institute a new government, laying its foundation on such principles, and organizing its powers in such form, as to them shall seem most likely to effect their safety and happiness. Prudence, indeed, will dictate that governments long established, should not be changed for light and transient causes; and, accordingly, all experience hath shown, that mankind are more disposed to suffer, while evils are sufferable, than to right themselves by abolishing the forms to which they are accustomed. But, when a long train of abuses and usurpations, pursuing invariably the same object, evinces a design to reduce them under absolute despotism, it is their right, it is their duty, to throw off such government and to provide new guards for their future security. Such has been the patient sufferance of these colonies, and such is now the necessity which constrains them to alter their former systems of government. The history of the present King of Great Britain is a history of repeated injuries and usurpations, all having, in direct object, the establishment of an absolute tyranny over these States. To prove this, let facts be submitted to a candid world:

He has refused his assent to laws the most wholesome and necessary for the public good.

He has forbidden his governors to pass laws of immediate and pressing importance, unless suspended in their operation till his assent should be obtained; and, when so suspended, he has utterly neglected to attend to them.

He has refused to pass other laws for the accommodation of large districts of people, unless those people would relinquish the right of representation in the legislature; a right inestimable to them, and formidable to tyrants only.

He has called together legislative bodies at places unusual, uncomfortable, and distant from the depository of their public records, for the sole purpose of fatiguing them into compliance with his measures.

He has dissolved representative houses repeatedly for opposing, with manly firmness, his invasions on the rights of the people.

He has refused, for a long time after such dissolutions, to cause others to be elected; whereby the legislative powers, incapable of annihilation, have returned to the people at large for their exercise; the state remaining, in the meantime, exposed to all the danger of invasion from without, and convulsions within.

He has endeavored to prevent the population of these States; for that purpose, obstructing the laws for naturalization of foreigners, refusing to pass others to encourage their migration hither, and raising the conditions of new appropriations of lands.

He has obstructed the administration of justice, by refusing his assent to laws for establishing judiciary powers.

He has made judges dependent on his will alone, for the tenure of their offices, and the amount and payment of their salaries.

He has erected a multitude of new offices, and sent hither swarms of officers to harass our people, and eat out their substance.

He has kept among us, in time of peace, standing armies, without the consent of our legislatures.

He has affected to render the military independent of, and superior to, the civil power.

He has combined, with others, to subject us to a jurisdiction foreign to our Constitution, and unacknowledged by our laws; giving his assent to their acts of pretended legislation:

For quartering large bodies of armed troops among us:

For protecting them by a mock trial, from punishment, for any murders which they should commit on the inhabitants of these States:

For cutting off our trade with all parts of the world:

For imposing taxes on us without our consent:

For depriving us, in many cases, of the benefit of trial by jury:

For transporting us beyond seas to be tried for pretended offences:

For abolishing the free system of English laws in a neighboring province, establishing therein an arbitrary government, and enlarging its boundaries, so as to render it at once an example and fit instrument for introducing the same absolute rule into these colonies:

For taking away our charters, abolishing our most valuable laws, and altering, fundamentally, the powers of our governments:

For suspending our own legislatures, and declaring themselves invested with power to legislate for us in all cases whatsoever.

He has abdicated government here, by declaring us out of his protection, and waging war against us.

He has plundered our seas, ravaged our coasts, burnt our towns, and destroyed the lives of our people.

He is, at this time, transporting large armies of foreign mercenaries to complete the works of death, desolation, and tyranny, already begun, with circumstances of cruelty and perfidy scarcely paralleled in the most barbarous ages, and totally unworthy the head of a civilized nation.

He has constrained our fellow citizens, taken captive on the high seas, to bear arms against their country, to become the executioners of their friends, and brethren, or to fall themselves by their hands.

He has excited domestic insurrections amongst us, and has endeavored to bring on the inhabitants of our frontiers, the merciless Indian savages, whose known rule of warfare is an undistinguished destruction of all ages, sexes, and conditions.

In every stage of these oppressions, we have petitioned for redress, in the most humble terms; our repeated petitions have been answered only by repeated injury. A prince, whose character is thus marked by every act which may define a tyrant, is unfit to be the ruler of a free people.

Nor have we been wanting in attention to our British brethren. We have warned them, from time to time, of attempts made by their legislature to extend an unwarrantable jurisdiction over us. We have reminded them of the circumstances of our emigration and settlement here. We have appealed to their native justice and magnanimity, and we have conjured them, by the ties of our common kindred, to disavow these usurpations, which would inevitably interrupt our connections and correspondence. They, too, have been deaf to the voice of justice and consanguinity. We must, therefore, acquiesce in the necessity which denounces our separation, and hold them as we hold the rest of mankind, enemies in war, in peace, friends.

We, therefore, the representatives of the United States of America, in general Congress assembled, appealing to the Supreme Judge of the world for the rectitude of our intentions, do, in the name, and by the authority of the good people of these colonies, solemnly publish and declare, that these united colonies are, and of right ought to be, free and independent states: that they are absolved from all allegiance to the British Crown, and that all political connection between them and the state of Great Britain is, and ought to be, totally dissolved; and that, as free and independent states, they have full power to levy war, conclude peace, contract alliances, establish commerce, and to do all other acts and things which independent states may of right do. And, for the support of this declaration, with a firm reliance on the protection of Divine Providence, we mutually pledge to each other our lives, our fortunes, and our sacred honor.

The foregoing Declaration was, by order of Congress, engrossed, and signed by the following members:

John Hancock

New Hampshire
Josiah Bartlett
William Whipple
Matthew Thornton

Massachusetts Bay
Samuel Adams
John Adams
Robert Treat Paine
Elbridge Gerry

Rhode Island
Stephen Hopkins
William Ellery

Connecticut
Roger Sherman
Samuel Huntington
William Williams
Oliver Wolcott

New York
William Floyd
Philip Livingston
Francis Lewis
Lewis Morris

New Jersey
Richard Stockton
John Witherspoon
Francis Hopkinson
John Hart
Abraham Clark

Pennsylvania
Robert Morris
Benjamin Rush
Benjamin Franklin
John Morton
George Clymer
James Smith
George Taylor
James Wilson
George Ross

Delaware
Caesar Rodney
George Read
Thomas M'Kean

Maryland
Samuel Chase
William Paca
Thomas Stone
Charles Carroll,
  of Carrollton

Virginia
George Wythe
Richard Henry Lee
Thomas Jefferson
Benjamin Harrison
Thomas Nelson, Jr.
Francis Lightfoot Lee
Carter Braxton

North Carolina
William Hooper
Joseph Hewes
John Penn

South Carolina
Edward Rutledge
Thomas Heyward, Jr.
Thomas Lynch, Jr.
Arthur Middleton

Georgia
Button Gwinnett
Lyman Hall
George Walton

Resolved, That copies of the Declaration be sent to the several assemblies, conventions, and committees, or councils of safety, and to the several commanding officers of the continental troops; that it be proclaimed in each of the United States, at the head of the army.

THE CONSTITUTION
OF THE UNITED STATES[1]

We the People of the United States, in Order to form a more perfect Union, establish Justice, insure domestic Tranquility, provide for the common defence, promote the general Welfare, and secure the Blessings of Liberty to ourselves and our Posterity, do ordain and establish this CONSTITUTION for the United States of America.

Article I

Section 1.
All legislative Powers herein granted shall be vested in a Congress of the United States, which shall consist of a Senate and House of Representatives.

Section 2.
The House of Representatives shall be composed of Members chosen every second Year by the People of the several States, and the Electors in each State shall have the Qualifications requisite for Electors of the most numerous Branch of the State Legislature.

No Person shall be a Representative who shall not have attained to the Age of twenty-five Years, and been seven Years a Citizen of the United States, and who shall not, when elected, be an Inhabitant of that State in which he shall be chosen.

[Representatives and direct Taxes[2] shall be apportioned among the several States which may be included within this Union, according to their respective Numbers, which shall be determined by adding to the whole Number of free Persons, including those bound to Service for a Term of Years, and excluding Indians not taxed, three fifths of all other Persons.][3] The actual Enumeration shall be made within three Years after the first Meeting of the Congress of the United States, and within every subsequent Term of ten Years, in such Manner as they shall by Law

---

[1] This version, which follows the original Constitution in capitalization and spelling, was published by the United States Department of the Interior, Office of Education, in 1935.
[2] Altered by the Sixteenth Amendment.
[3] Negated by the Fourteenth Amendment.

direct. The Number of Representatives shall not exceed one for every thirty Thousand, but each State shall have at Least one Representative; and until such enumeration shall be made, the State of New Hampshire shall be entitled to chuse three, Massachusetts eight, Rhode-Island and Providence Plantations one, Connecticut five, New York six, New Jersey four, Pennsylvania eight, Delaware one, Maryland six, Virginia ten, North Carolina five, South Carolina five, and Georgia three.

When vacancies happen in the Representation from any State, the Executive Authority thereof shall issue Writs of Election to fill such Vacancies.

The House of Representatives shall chuse their Speaker and other Officers; and shall have the sole Power of Impeachment.

Section 3.

The Senate of the United States shall be composed of two Senators from each State, chosen by the Legislature thereof, for six Years; and each Senator shall have one Vote.

Immediately after they shall be assembled in Consequence of the first Election, they shall be divided as equally as may be into three Classes. The Seats of the Senators of the first Class shall be vacated at the Expiration of the second Year, of the second Class at the Expiration of the fourth Year, and of the third Class at the Expiration of the sixth Year, so that one-third may be chosen every second Year; and if Vacancies happen by Resignation, or otherwise, during the Recess of the Legislature of any State, the Executive thereof may make temporary Appointments until the next Meeting of the Legislature, which shall then fill such Vacancies.

No Person shall be a Senator who shall not have attained to the Age of thirty Years, and been nine Years a Citizen of the United States, and who shall not, when elected, be an Inhabitant of that State for which he shall be chosen.

The Vice President of the United States shall be President of the Senate, but shall have no vote, unless they be equally divided.

The Senate shall chuse their other Officers, and also a President pro tempore, in the absence of the Vice President, or when he shall exercise the Office of President of the United States.

The Senate shall have the sole Power to try all Impeachments. When sitting for that purpose they shall be on Oath or Affirmation. When the President of the United States is tried, the Chief Justice shall preside: And no person shall be convicted without the Concurrence of two thirds of the Members present.

Judgment in Cases of Impeachment shall not extend further than to removal from Office, and disqualification to hold and enjoy any Office of honor, Trust, or Profit under the United States: but the Party convicted shall nevertheless be liable and subject to Indictment, Trial, Judgment, and Punishment, according to Law.

Section 4.

The Times, Places and Manner of holding Elections for Senators and Representatives, shall be prescribed in each State by the Legislature thereof; but the

Congress may at any time by Law make or alter such Regulations, except as to the Places of Chusing Senators.

The Congress shall assemble at least once in every Year, and such Meeting shall be on the first Monday in December, unless they shall by Law appoint a different Day.

Section 5.

Each House shall be the Judge of the Elections, Returns and Qualifications of its own Members, and a Majority of each shall constitute a Quorum to do Business; but a smaller number may adjourn from day to day, and may be authorized to compel the Attendance of absent Members, in such Manner, and under such Penalties, as each House may provide.

Each House may determine the Rules of its Proceedings, punish its Members for disorderly Behaviour, and, with the Concurrence of two thirds, expel a Member.

Each House shall keep a Journal of its Proceedings, and from time to time publish the same, excepting such Parts as may in their Judgment require Secrecy; and the Yeas and Nays of the Members of either House on any question shall, at the Desire of one fifth of those Present, be entered on the Journal.

Neither House, during the Session of Congress, shall, without the Consent of the other, adjourn for more than three days, nor to any other Place than that in which the two Houses shall be sitting.

Section 6.

The Senators and Representatives shall receive a Compensation for their Services, to be ascertained by Law, and paid out of the Treasury of the United States. They shall in all Cases, except Treason, Felony, and Breach of the Peace, be privileged from Arrest during their Attendance at the Session of their respective Houses, and in going to and returning from the same; and for any Speech or Debate in either House, they shall not be questioned in any other Place.

No Senator or Representative shall, during the Time for which he was elected, be appointed to any civil Office under the Authority of the United States, which shall have been created, or the Emoluments whereof shall have been increased, during such time; and no Person holding any Office under the United States shall be a Member of either House during his continuance in Office.

Section 7.

All Bills for raising Revenue shall originate in the House of Representatives; but the Senate may propose or concur with Amendments as on other bills.

Every Bill which shall have passed the House of Representatives and the Senate, shall, before it become a Law, be presented to the President of the United States; If he approve he shall sign it, but if not he shall return it, with his Objections, to that House in which it shall have originated, who shall enter the Objections at large on their Journal, and proceed to reconsider it. If after such Reconsideration two thirds of that House shall agree to pass the bill, it shall be sent, together with the objections, to the other House, by which it shall likewise be reconsidered, and if approved by two thirds of that House, it shall become a Law. But in all such Cases the Votes of both Houses shall be determined by Yeas and Nays, and the Names of the Persons voting for and against the Bill shall be entered on the Journal of each House respectively. If any Bill shall not be returned by the President within ten Days (Sundays excepted) after it shall have been presented to him, the Same shall be a Law, in like Manner as if he had signed it, unless the Congress by their Adjournment prevent its Return, in which Case it shall not be a Law.

Every Order, Resolution, or Vote to which the Concurrence of the Senate and House of Representatives may be necessary (except on a question of Adjournment) shall be presented to the President of the United States; and before the Same shall take Effect, shall be approved by him, or being disapproved by him, shall be repassed by two thirds of the Senate and House of Representatives, according to the Rules and Limitations prescribed in the Case of a Bill.

Section 8.

The Congress shall have Power To lay and collect Taxes, Duties, Imposts and Excises, to pay the Debts and provide for the common Defence and general Welfare of the United States; but all Duties, Imposts and Excises shall be uniform throughout the United States;

To borrow money on the credit of the United States;

To regulate Commerce with foreign Nations, and among the several States, and with the Indian Tribes;

To establish an uniform rule of Naturalization, and uniform Laws on the subject of Bankruptcies throughout the United States;

To coin Money, regulate the Value thereof, and of foreign Coin, and fix the Standard of Weights and Measures;

To provide for the Punishment of counterfeiting the Securities and current Coin of the United States;

To establish Post Offices and post Roads;

To promote the Progress of Science and useful Arts, by securing for limited Times to Authors and Inventors the exclusive Right to their respective Writings and Discoveries;

To constitute Tribunals inferior to the Supreme Court;

To define and punish Piracies and Felonies committed on the high Seas, and Offenses against the Law of Nations;

To declare War, grant Letters of Marque and Reprisal, and make Rules concerning Captures on Land and Water;

To raise and support Armies, but no Appropriation of Money to that Use shall be for a longer Term than two Years;

To provide and maintain a Navy;

To make Rules for the Government and Regulation of the land and naval forces;

To provide for calling forth the Militia to execute the Laws of the Union, suppress Insurrections and repel Invasions;

To provide for organizing, arming, and disciplining the Militia, and for governing such Part of them as may be employed in the Service of the United States, reserving to the States respectively, the Appointment of the Officers, and the Authority of training the Militia according to the discipline prescribed by Congress;

To exercise exclusive Legislation in all Cases whatsoever, over such District (not exceeding ten Miles square) as may, by Cession of particular States, and the acceptance of Congress, become the Seat of the Government of the United States, and to exercise like Authority over all Places purchased by the Consent of the Legislature of the State in which the Same shall be, for the Erection of Forts, Magazines, Arsenals, Dock-yards, and other needful Buildings;—And

To make all Laws which shall be necessary and proper for carrying into Execution the foregoing Powers, and all other Powers vested by this Constitution in the Government of the United States, or in any Department or Officer thereof.

Section 9.

The Migration or Importation of such Persons as any of the States now existing shall think proper to admit, shall not be prohibited by the Congress prior to the Year one thousand eight hundred and eight, but a tax or duty may be imposed on such Importation, not exceeding ten dollars for each Person.

The privilege of the Writ of Habeas Corpus shall not be suspended, unless when in Cases of Rebellion or Invasion the public Safety may require it.

No bill of Attainder or ex post facto Law shall be passed.

No capitation, or other direct, Tax shall be laid unless in Proportion to the Census or Enumeration herein before directed to be taken.

No Tax or Duty shall be laid on Articles exported from any State.

No Preference shall be given by any Regulation of Commerce or Revenue to the Ports of one State over those of another: nor shall Vessels bound to, or from, one State, be obliged to enter, clear, or pay Duties in another.

No Money shall be drawn from the Treasury, but in Consequence of Appropriations made by Law; and a regular Statement and Account of the Receipts and Expenditures of all public Money shall be published from time to time.

No Title of Nobility shall be granted by the United States: And no Person holding any Office of Profit or Trust under them, shall, without the Consent of the Congress, accept of any present, Emolument, Office, or Title, of any kind whatever, from any King, Prince, or foreign State.

Section 10.

No State shall enter into any Treaty, Alliance, or Confederation; grant Letters of Marque and Reprisal; coin Money; emit Bills of Credit; make any Thing but gold and silver Coin a Tender in Payment of Debts; pass any Bill of Attainder, ex post facto Law, or Law impairing the Obligation of Contracts, or grant any Title of Nobility.

No State shall, without the Consent of the Congress, lay any Imposts or Duties on Imports or Exports, except what may be absolutely necessary for executing its inspection Laws; and the net Produce of all Duties and Imposts, laid by any State on Imports or Exports, shall be for the use of the Treasury of the United States; and all such Laws shall be subject to the Revision and Control of the Congress.

No state shall, without the Consent of Congress, lay any duty of Tonnage, keep Troops, or Ships of War in time of Peace, enter into any Agreement or Compact with another State, or with a foreign Power, or engage in War, unless actually invaded, or in such imminent Danger as will not admit of delay.

Article II

Section 1.

The executive Power shall be vested in a President of the United States of America. He shall hold his Office during the Term of four years, and, together with the Vice President, chosen for the same Term, be elected, as follows:

Each State shall appoint, in such Manner as the Legislature thereof may direct, a Number of Electors, equal to the whole Number of Senators and Representatives to which the State may be entitled in the Congress: but no Senator or Representative, or Person holding an Office of Trust or Profit under the United States, shall be appointed an Elector.

[The Electors shall meet in their respective States, and vote by Ballot for two persons, of whom one at least shall not be an Inhabitant of the same State with themselves. And they shall make a List of all the Persons voted for, and of the Number of Votes for each; which List they shall sign and certify, and transmit sealed to the Seat of the Government of the United States, directed to the President of the Senate. The President of the Senate shall, in the Presence of the Senate and House of Representatives, open all the Certificates, and the Votes shall then be counted. The Person having the greatest Number of Votes shall be the President, if such Number be a Majority of the whole Number of Electors appointed; and if there be more than one who have such Majority, and have an equal Number of Votes, then the House of Representatives shall immediately chuse by Ballot one of them for President; and if no Person have a Majority, then from the five highest on the List the said House shall in like Manner chuse the President. But in chusing the President, the Votes shall be taken by States, the Representation from each State having one Vote; a quorum for this Purpose shall consist of a Member or Members from two-thirds of the States, and a Majority of all the States shall be necessary to a Choice. In every Case, after the Choice of the President, the Person having the greatest Number of Votes of the Electors shall be the Vice President. But if there should remain two or more who have equal votes, the Senate shall chuse from them by Ballot the Vice President.][4]

The Congress may determine the Time of chusing the Electors, and the Day

---

[4] Revised by the Twelfth Amendment

on which they shall give their Votes; which Day shall be the same throughout the United States.

No person except a natural-born Citizen, or a Citizen of the United States, at the time of the Adoption of this Constitution, shall be eligible to the Office of President; neither shall any Person be eligible to that Office who shall not have attained to the Age of thirty-five years, and been fourteen Years a Resident within the United States.

In Case of the Removal of the President from Office, or of his Death, Resignation, or Inability to discharge the Powers and Duties of the said Office, the same shall devolve on the Vice President, and the Congress may by Law provide for the Case of Removal, Death, Resignation, or Inability, both of the President and Vice President, declaring what Officer shall then act as President, and such Officer shall act accordingly, until the disability be removed, or a President shall be elected.

The President shall, at stated Times, receive for his Services a Compensation, which shall neither be increased nor diminished during the Period for which he shall have been elected, and he shall not receive within that Period any other Emolument from the United States, or any of them.

Before he enter on the execution of his Office, he shall take the following Oath or Affirmation:—"I do solemnly swear (or affirm) that I will faithfully execute the Office of President of the United States, and will, to the best of my Ability, preserve, protect, and defend the Constitution of the United States."

Section 2.

The President shall be Commander in Chief of the Army and Navy of the United States, and of the Militia of the several States, when called into the actual Service of the United States; he may require the Opinion, in writing, of the principal Officer in each of the executive Departments, upon any subject relating to the Duties of their respective Offices, and he shall have Power to Grant Reprieves and Pardons for Offenses against the United States, except in Cases of Impeachment.

He shall have Power, by and with the Advice and Consent of the Senate, to make Treaties, provided two-thirds of the Senators present concur; and he shall nominate, and by and with the Advice and Consent of the Senate, shall appoint Ambassadors, other public Ministers and Consuls, Judges of the supreme Court, and all other Officers of the United States, whose Appointments are not herein otherwise provided for, and which shall be established by Law: but the Congress may by Law vest the Appointment of such inferior Officers, as they think proper, in the President alone, in the Courts of Law, or in the Heads of Departments.

The President shall have Power to fill up all Vacancies that may happen during the Recess of the Senate, by granting Commissions which shall expire at the End of their next Session.

Section 3.

He shall from time to time give to the Congress Information of the State of the Union, and recommend to their Consideration such Measures as he shall judge necessary and expedient; he may, on extraordinary occasions, convene both Houses, or either of them, and in Case of Disagreement between them, with respect to the Time of Adjournment, he may adjourn them to such Time as he shall think proper; he shall receive Ambassadors and other public Ministers; he shall take care that the Laws be faithfully executed, and shall Commission all the Officers of the United States.

Section 4.

The President, Vice President and all civil Officers of the United States, shall be removed from Office on Impeachment for, and Conviction of, Treason, Bribery, or other high Crimes and Misdemeanors.

Article III

Section 1.

The judicial Power of the United States, shall be vested in one supreme Court, and in such inferior Courts as the Congress may from time to time ordain and establish. The Judges, both of the supreme and inferior Courts, shall hold their Offices during good Behaviour, and shall, at stated Times, receive for their Services, a Compensation, which shall not be diminished during their Continuance in Office.

Section 2.

The judicial Power shall extend to all Cases, in Law and Equity, arising under this Constitution, the Laws of the United States, and Treaties made, or which shall be made, under their Authority;—to all Cases affecting ambassadors, other public ministers and consuls;—to all cases of admiralty and maritime Jurisdiction;—to Controversies to which the United States shall be a Party;—to Controversies between two or more States;—between a State and Citizens of another State;[5]—between Citizens of different States—between Citizens of the same State claiming Lands under Grants of different States, and between a State, or the Citizens thereof, and foreign States, Citizens, or Subjects.

In all Cases affecting Ambassadors, other public Ministers and Consuls, and those in which a State shall be Party, the supreme Court shall have original Jurisdiction. In all the other Cases before mentioned, the supreme Court shall have appellate Jurisdiction, both as to Law and Fact, with such Exceptions, and under such Regulations as the Congress shall make.

The trial of all Crimes, except in Cases of Impeachment, shall be by Jury; and such Trial shall be held in the State where the said Crimes shall have been committed; but when not committed within any State, the Trial shall be at such Place or Places as the Congress may by Law have directed.

---

[5] Qualified by the Eleventh Amendment.

Section 3.

Treason against the United States, shall consist only in levying War against them, or in adhering to their Enemies, giving them Aid and Comfort. No Person shall be convicted of Treason unless on the Testimony of two Witnesses to the same overt Act, or on Confession in open Court.

The Congress shall have power to declare the Punishment of Treason, but no Attainder of Treason shall work Corruption of Blood, or Forfeiture except during the Life of the Person attained.

Article IV

Section 1.

Full Faith and Credit shall be given in each State to the public Acts, Records, and judicial Proceedings of every other State. And the Congress may by general Laws prescribe the Manner in which such Acts, Records and Proceedings shall be proved, and the Effect thereof.

Section 2.

The Citizens of each State shall be entitled to all Privileges and Immunities of Citizens in the several States.

A Person charged in any State with Treason, Felony, or other Crime, who shall flee from Justice, and be found in another State, shall on demand of the executive Authority of the State from which he fled, be delivered up, to be removed to the State having Jurisdiction of the crime.

No Person held to Service or Labour in one State, under the Laws thereof, escaping into another, shall, in Consequence of any Law or Regulation therein, be discharged from such Service or Labour, but shall be delivered up on Claim of the Party to whom such Service or Labour may be due.

Section 3.

New States may be admitted by the Congress into this Union; but no new State shall be formed or erected within the Jurisdiction of any other State; nor any State be formed by the Junction of two or more States, or parts of States, without the Consent of the Legislatures of the States concerned as well as of the Congress.

The Congress shall have Power to dispose of and make all needful Rules and Regulations respecting the Territory or other Property belonging to the United States; and nothing in this Constitution shall be so construed as to Prejudice any Claims of the United States, or of any particular State.

Section 4.

The United States shall guarantee to every State in this Union a Republican Form of Government, and shall protect each of them against Invasion; and on Application of the Legislature, or of the Executive (when the Legislature cannot be convened) against domestic Violence.

Article V

The Congress, whenever two-thirds of both Houses shall deem it necessary, shall propose Amendments to this Constitution, or, on the Application of the Legislatures of two-thirds of the several States, shall call a Convention for proposing Amendments, which, in either Case, shall be valid to all Intents and Purposes, as part of this Constitution, when ratified by the Legislatures of three-fourths of the several States, or by Conventions in three-fourths thereof, as the one or the other Mode of Ratification may be proposed by the Congress; Provided that no Amendment which may be made prior to the Year One thousand eight hundred and eight shall in any Manner affect the first and fourth Clauses in the Ninth Section of the first Article; and that no State, without its Consent, shall be deprived of its equal Suffrage in the Senate.

Article VI

All Debts contracted and Engagements entered into, before the Adoption of this Constitution, shall be as valid against the United States under this Constitution, as under the Confederation.

This Constitution, and the Laws of the United States which shall be made in Pursuance thereof; and all Treaties made, or which shall be made, under the Authority of the United States, shall be the supreme Law of the Land; and the Judges in every State shall be bound thereby, any Thing in the Constitution or Laws of any State to the Contrary notwithstanding.

The Senators and Representatives before mentioned, and the Members of the several State Legislatures, and all executive and judicial Officers, both of the United States and of the several States, shall be bound by Oath or Affirmation to support this Constitution; but no religious Tests shall ever be required as a qualification to any Office or public Trust under the United States.

Article VII

The Ratification of the Conventions of nine States shall be sufficient for the Establishment of this Constitution between the States so ratifying the same.

Done in Convention by the Unanimous Consent of the States present the Seventeenth Day of September in the Year of our Lord one thousand seven hundred and Eighty seven, and of the Independence of the United States of America the Twelfth. In Witness whereof We have hereunto subscribed our Names.[6]

George Washington
President and deputy and deputy from Virginia

New Hampshire
John Langdon
Nicholas Gilman

Massachusetts
Nathaniel Gorham
Rufus King

Connecticut
William Samuel
  Johnson
Roger Sherman

New York
Alexander Hamilton

New Jersey
William Livingston
David Brearley
William Paterson
Jonathan Dayton

Pennsylvania
Benjamin Franklin
Thomas Mifflin
Robert Morris
George Clymer
Thomas FitzSimons
Jared Ingersoll
James Wilson
Gouverneur Morris

Delaware
George Read
Gunning Bedford, Jr.
John Dickinson
Richard Bassett
Jacob Broom

Maryland
James McHenry
Daniel of
  St. Thomas Jenifer
Daniel Carroll

Virginia
John Blair
James Madison, Jr.

North Carolina
William Blount
Richard Dobbs
  Spaight
Hugh Williamson

South Carolina
John Rutledge
Charles Cotesworth
  Pinckney
Charles Pinckney
Pierce Butler

Georgia
William Few
Abraham Baldwin

Articles in Addition to, and Amendment of, the Constitution of the United States of America, Proposed by Congress, and Ratified by the Legislatures of the Several States, Pursuant to the Fifth Article of the Original Constitution.[7]

[Article I]

Congress shall make no law respecting an establishment of religion, or prohibiting the free exercise thereof; or abridging the freedom of speech, or of the press; or the right of the people peaceably to assemble, and to petition the Government for a redress of grievances.

---

[6] These are the full names of the signers, which in some cases are not the signatures on the document.
[7] This heading appears only in the joint resolution submitting the first ten amendments.

[Article II]

A well regulated Militia, being necessary to the security of a free State, the right of the people to keep and bear Arms shall not be infringed.

[Article III]

No Soldier shall, in time of peace, be quartered in any house, without the consent of the Owner, nor in time of war, but in a manner to be prescribed by law.

[Article IV]

The right of the people to be secure in their persons, houses, papers, and effects, against unreasonable searches and seizures, shall not be violated, and no Warrants shall issue, but upon probable cause, supported by Oath or affirmation, and particularly describing the place to be searched, and the persons or things to be seized.

[Article V]

No person shall be held to answer for a capital or otherwise infamous crime, unless on a presentment or indictment of a Grand Jury, except in cases arising in the land or naval forces, or in the Militia, when in actual service in time of War or public danger; nor shall any person be subject for the same offence to be twice put in jeopardy of life or limb; nor shall be compelled in any criminal case to be a witness against himself, nor be deprived of life, liberty, or property, without due process of law; nor shall private property be taken for public use, without just compensation.

[Article VI]

In all criminal prosecutions, the accused shall enjoy the right to a speedy and public trial, by an impartial jury of the State and district wherein the crime shall have been committed, which district shall have been previously ascertained by law, and to be informed of the nature and cause of the accusation; to be confronted with the witnesses against him; to have compulsory process for obtaining witnesses in his favour, and to have the Assistance of Counsel for his defense.

[Article VII]

In suits at common law, where the value in controversy shall exceed twenty dollars, the right of trial by jury shall be preserved, and no fact tried by a jury, shall be otherwise reexamined in any Court of the United States, than according to the rules of the common law.

[Article VIII]

Excessive bail shall not be required, nor excessive fines imposed, nor cruel and unusual punishments inflicted.

[Article IX]

The enumeration of the Constitution, of certain rights, shall not be construed to deny or disparage others retained by the people.

[Article X]

The powers not delegated to the United States by the Constitution, nor prohibited by it to the States, are reserved to the States respectively, or to the people.

[Amendments I–X, in force 1791.]

[Article XI][8]

The Judicial power of the United States shall not be construed to extend to any suit in law or equity, commenced or prosecuted against one of the United States by Citizens of another State, or by Citizens or Subjects of any Foreign State.

[Article XII][9]

The Electors shall meet in their respective States and vote by ballot for President and Vice-President, one of whom, at least, shall not be an inhabitant of the same State with themselves; they shall name in their ballots the person voted for as President, and in distinct ballots the person voted for as Vice-President, and they shall make distinct lists of all persons voted for as President, and of all persons voted for as Vice-President, and of the number of votes for each, which lists they shall sign and certify, and transmit sealed to the seat of the government of the United States, directed to the President of the Senate;—The President of the Senate shall, in the presence of the Senate and House of Representatives, open all the certificates and the votes shall then be counted;—The person having the greatest number of votes for President, shall be the President, if such number be a majority of the whole number of Electors appointed; and if no person have such majority, then from the persons having the highest numbers not exceeding three on the list of those voted for as President, the House of Representatives shall choose immediately, by ballot,

[8] Adopted in 1798.
[9] Adopted in 1804.

the President. But in choosing the President, the votes shall be taken by states, the representation from each state having one vote; a quorum for this purpose shall consist of a member or members from two-thirds of the states, and a majority of all the states shall be necessary to a choice. And if the House of Representatives shall not choose a President whenever the right of choice shall devolve upon them, before the fourth day of March next following, then the Vice-President shall act as President, as in the case of the death or other constitutional disability of the President.—The person having the greatest number of votes as Vice-President, shall be the Vice-President, if such number be a majority of the whole number of Electors appointed, and if no person have a majority, then from the two highest numbers on the list, the Senate shall choose the Vice-President; a quorum for the purpose shall consist of two-thirds of the whole number of Senators, and a majority of the whole number shall be necessary to a choice. But no person constitutionally ineligible to the office of President shall be eligible to that of Vice-President of the United States.

[Article XIII][10]

Section 1.
Neither slavery nor involuntary servitude, except as a punishment for crime whereof the party shall have been duly convicted, shall exist within the United States, or any place subject to their jurisdiction.

Section 2.
Congress shall have power to enforce this article by appropriate legislation.

[Article XIV][11]

Section 1.
All persons born or naturalized in the United States, and subject to the jurisdiction thereof, are citizens of the United States and of the State wherein they reside. No State shall make or enforce any law which shall abridge the privileges or immunities of citizens of the United States; nor shall any State deprive any person of life, liberty, or property, without due process of law; nor deny to any person within its jurisdiction the equal protection of the laws.

Section 2.
Representatives shall be apportioned among the several States according to their respective numbers, counting the whole number of persons in each State, excluding

[10] Adopted in 1865.
[11] Adopted in 1868.

Indians not taxed. But when the right to vote at any election for the choice of electors for President and Vice-President of the United States, Representatives in Congress, the Executive and Judicial officers of a State, or the members of the Legislature thereof, is denied to any of the male inhabitants of such State, being twenty-one years of age, and citizens of the United States, or in any way abridged, except for participation in rebellion, or other crime, the basis of representation therein shall be reduced in the proportion which the number of such male citizens shall bear to the whole number of male citizens twenty-one years of age in such State.

Section 3.

No person shall be a Senator or Representative in Congress, or elector of President and Vice-President, or hold any office, civil or military, under the United States, or under any State, who, having previously taken an oath, as a member of Congress, or as an officer of the United States, or as a member of any State legislature, or as an executive or judicial officer of any State, to support the Constitution of the United States, shall have engaged in insurrection or rebellion against the same, or given aid or comfort to the enemies thereof. But Congress may by a vote of two-thirds of each House, remove such disability.

Section 4.

The validity of the public debt of the United States, authorized by law, including debts incurred for payment of pensions and bounties for services in suppressing insurrection or rebellion, shall not be questioned. But neither the United States nor any State shall assume or pay any debts or obligation incurred in aid of insurrection or rebellion against the United States, or any claim for the loss or emancipation of any slave; but all such debts, obligations, and claims shall be held illegal and void.

Section 5.

The Congress shall have the power to enforce, by appropriate legislation, the provisions of this article.

[Article XV][12]

Section 1.

The right of citizens of the United States to vote shall not be denied or abridged by the United States or by any State on account of race, color, or previous condition of servitude—

Section 2.

The Congress shall have power to enforce this article by appropriate legislation.

12 Adopted in 1870.

[Article XVI][13]

The Congress shall have power to lay and collect taxes on incomes, from whatever source derived, without apportionment among the several States, and without regard to any census or enumeration.

[Article XVII][14]

The Senate of the United States shall be composed of two Senators from each State, elected by the people thereof, for six years; and each Senator shall have one vote. The electors in each State shall have the qualifications requisite for electors of the most numerous branch of the State legislatures.

When vacancies happen in the representation of any State in the Senate, the executive authority of such State shall issue writs of election to fill such vacancies: *Provided,* That the legislature of any State may empower the executive thereof to make temporary appointments until the people fill the vacancies by election as the legislature may direct.

This amendment shall not be so construed as to affect the election or term of any Senator chosen before it becomes valid as part of the Constitution.

[Article XVIII][15]

Section 1.
After one year from the ratification of this article the manufacture, sale, or transportation of intoxicating liquors within, the importation thereof into, or the exportation thereof from the United States and all territory subject to the jurisdiction thereof for beverage purposes is hereby prohibited.

Section 2.
The Congress and the several States shall have concurrent power to enforce this article by appropriate legislation.

Section 3.
This article shall be inoperative unless it shall have been ratified as an amendment to the Constitution by the legislatures of the several States, as provided in the Constitution, within seven years from the date of the submission hereof to the States by the Congress.

13 Adopted in 1913.
14 Adopted in 1913.
15 Adopted in 1918.

[Article XIX]¹⁶

The right of citizens of the United States to vote shall not be denied or abridged by the United States or by any State on account of sex.

Congress shall have power to enforce this article by appropriate legislation.

[Article XX]¹⁷

Section 1.

The terms of the President and Vice-President shall end at noon on the 20th day of January, and the terms of Senators and Representatives at noon on the 3d day of January, of the years in which such terms would have ended if this article had not been ratified; and the terms of their successors shall then begin.

Section 2.

The Congress shall assemble at least once in every year, and such meeting shall begin at noon on the 3d day of January, unless they shall by law appoint a different day.

Section 3.

If, at the time fixed for the beginning of the term of the President, the President elect shall have died, the Vice-President elect shall become President. If a President shall not have been chosen before the time fixed for the beginning of his term or if the President elect shall have failed to qualify, then the Vice-President elect shall act as President until a President shall have qualified; and the Congress may by law provide for the case wherein neither a President elect nor a Vice-President elect shall have qualified, declaring who shall then act as President, or the manner in which one who is to act shall be selected, and such person shall act accordingly until a President or Vice-President shall have qualified.

Section 4.

The Congress may by law provide for the case of the death of any of the persons from whom the House of Representatives may choose a President whenever the right of choice shall have devolved upon them, and for the case of the death of any of the persons from whom the Senate may choose a Vice-President whenever the right of choice shall have devolved upon them.

---

¹⁶ Adopted in 1920.
¹⁷ Adopted in 1933.

Section 5.
Sections 1 and 2 shall take effect on the 15th day of October following the ratification of this article.

Section 6.
This article shall be inoperative unless it shall have been ratified as an amendment to the Constitution by the legislatures of three-fourths of the several States within seven years from the date of its submission.

[Article XXI][18]

Section 1.
The eighteenth article of amendment to the Constitution of the United States is hereby repealed.

Section 2.
The transportation or importation into any State, Territory, or possession of the United States for delivery or use therein of intoxicating liquors, in violation of the laws thereof, is hereby prohibited.

Section 3.
This article shall be inoperative unless it shall have been ratified as an amendment to the Constitution by conventions in the several States, as provided in the Constitution, within seven years from the date of the submission hereof to the States by the Congress.

[Article XXII][19]

No person shall be elected to the office of the President more than twice, and no person who has held the office of President, or acted as President, for more than two years of a term to which some other person was elected President shall be elected to the office of the President more than once.

But this Article shall not apply to any person holding the office of President when this Article was proposed by the Congress, and shall not prevent any person who may be holding the office of President, or acting as President, during the term within which this Article becomes operative from holding the office of President or acting as President during the remainder of such term.

[18] Adopted in 1933.
[19] Adopted in 1961.

This article shall be inoperative unless it shall have been ratified as an amendment to the Constitution by the legislatures of three-fourths of the several states within seven years from the date of its submission to the states by the Congress.

[Article XXIII][20]

Section 1.
The District constituting the seat of Government of the United States shall appoint in such manner as the Congress may direct:

A number of electors of President and Vice-President equal to the whole number of Senators and Representatives in Congress to which the District would be entitled if it were a State, but in no event more than the least populous State; they shall be in addition to those appointed by the States, but they shall be considered, for the purposes of the election of President and Vice-President, to be electors appointed by a State; and they shall meet in the District and perform such duties as provided by the twelfth article of amendment.

Section 2.
The Congress shall have power to enforce this article by appropriate legislation.

[Article XXIV][21]

Section 1.
The right of citizens of the United States to vote in any primary or other election for President or Vice President, for electors for President or Vice President, or for Senator or Representative in Congress, shall not be denied or abridged by the United States or any state by reason of failure to pay any poll tax or other tax.

Section 2.
The Congress shall have the power to enforce this article by appropriate legislation.

[Article XXV][22]

Section 1.
In case of the removal of the President from office or of his death or resignation, the Vice President shall become President.

[20] Adopted in 1961.
[21] Adopted in 1964.
[22] Adopted in 1967.

Section 2.

Whenever there is a vacancy in the office of the Vice President, the President shall nominate a Vice President who shall take office upon confirmation by a majority vote of both Houses of Congress.

Section 3.

Whenever the President transmits to the President Pro Tempore of the Senate and the Speaker of the House of Representatives his written declaration that he is unable to discharge the powers and duties of his office, and until he transmits to them a written declaration to the contrary, such powers and duties shall be discharged by the Vice President as Acting President.

Section 4.

Whenever the Vice President and a majority of either the principal officers of the executive departments or of such other body as Congress may by law provide, transmit to the President Pro Tempore of the Senate and the Speaker of the House of Representatives their written declaration that the President is unable to discharge the powers and duties of his office, the Vice President shall immediately assume the powers and duties of the office as Acting President.

Thereafter, when the President transmits to the President Pro Tempore of the Senate and the Speaker of the House of Representatives his written declaration that no inability exists, he shall resume the powers and duties of his office unless the Vice President and a majority of either the principal officers of the executive departments or of such other body as Congress may by law provide, transmit within four days to the President Pro Tempore of the Senate and the Speaker of the House of Representatives their written declaration that the President is unable to discharge the powers and duties of his office. Thereupon Congress shall decide the issue, assembling within forty-eight hours for that purpose if not in session. If the Congress, within twenty-one days after receipt of the latter written declaration, or, if Congress is not in session, within twenty-one days after Congress is required to assemble, determines by two-thirds vote of both Houses that the President is unable to discharge the powers and duties of his office, the Vice President shall continue to discharge the same as Acting President; otherwise, the President shall resume the powers and duties of his office.

[Article XXVI][23]

Section 1.

The right of citizens of the United States, who are eighteen years of age or older, to vote shall not be denied or abridged by the United States or by any State on account of age.

Section 2.

The Congress shall have power to enforce this article by appropriate legislation.

[23] Adopted in 1971.

PRESIDENTIAL ELECTIONS

Year	Candidates	Parties	Popular Vote	Percentage of Popular Vote	Electoral Vote	Percentage of Voter Participation
1789	**GEORGE WASHINGTON (Va.)***				69	
	John Adams				34	
	Others				35	
1792	**GEORGE WASHINGTON (Va.)**				132	
	John Adams				77	
	George Clinton				50	
	Others				5	
1796	**JOHN ADAMS (Mass.)**	Federalist			71	
	Thomas Jefferson	Democratic-Republican			68	
	Thomas Pinckney	Federalist			59	
	Aaron Burr	Dem.-Rep.			30	
	Others				48	
1800	**THOMAS JEFFERSON (Va.)**	Dem.-Rep.			73	
	Aaron Burr	Dem.-Rep.			73	
	John Adams	Federalist			65	
	C. C. Pinckney	Federalist			64	
	John Jay	Federalist			1	
1804	**THOMAS JEFFERSON (Va.)**	Dem.-Rep.			162	
	C. C. Pinckney	Federalist			14	

Year	Candidate	Party	Popular Vote	%	Electoral Vote	
1808	**JAMES MADISON (Va.)**	Dem.-Rep.			122	
	C. C. Pinckney	Federalist			47	
	George Clinton	Dem.-Rep.			6	
1812	**JAMES MADISON (Va.)**	Dem.-Rep.			128	
	De Witt Clinton	Federalist			89	
1816	**JAMES MONROE (Va.)**	Dem.-Rep.			183	
	Rufus King	Federalist			34	
1820	**JAMES MONROE (Va.)**	Dem.-Rep.			231	
	John Quincy Adams	Dem.-Rep.			1	
1824	**JOHN Q. ADAMS (Mass.)**	Dem.-Rep.	108,740	30.5	84	26.9
	Andrew Jackson	Dem.-Rep.	153,544	43.1	99	
	William H. Crawford	Dem.-Rep.	46,618	13.1	41	
	Henry Clay	Dem.-Rep.	47,136	13.2	37	
1828	**ANDREW JACKSON (Tenn.)**	Democratic	647,286	56.0	178	57.6
	John Quincy Adams	National Republican	508,064	44.0	83	
1832	**ANDREW JACKSON (Tenn.)**	Democratic	687,502	55.0	219	55.4
	Henry Clay	National Republican	530,189	42.4	49	
	John Floyd	Independent			11	
	William Wirt	Anti-Mason	33,108	2.6	7	

* State of residence at time of election.

PRESIDENTIAL ELECTIONS (cont.)

Year	Candidates	Parties	Popular Vote	Percentage of Popular Vote	Electoral Vote	Percentage of Voter Participation
1836	**MARTIN VAN BUREN (N.Y.)**	Democratic	765,483	50.9	170	57.8
	W. H. Harrison	Whig			73	
	Hugh L. White	Whig	739,795	49.1	26	
	Daniel Webster	Whig			14	
	W. P. Mangum	Independent			11	
1840	**WILLIAM H. HARRISON (Ohio)**	Whig	1,274,624	53.1	234	80.2
	Martin Van Buren	Democratic	1,127,781	46.9	60	
	J. G. Birney	Liberty	7,069			
1844	**JAMES K. POLK (Tenn.)**	Democratic	1,338,464	49.6	170	78.9
	Henry Clay	Whig	1,300,097	48.1	105	
	J. G. Birney	Liberty	62,300	2.3	—	
1848	**ZACHARY TAYLOR (La.)**	Whig	1,360,967	47.4	163	72.7
	Lewis Cass	Democratic	1,222,342	42.5	127	
	Martin Van Buren	Free-Soil	291,263	10.1	—	
1852	**FRANKLIN PIERCE (N.H.)**	Democratic	1,601,117	50.9	254	69.6
	Winfield Scott	Whig	1,385,453	44.1	42	
	John P. Hale	Free-Soil	155,825	5.0		
1856	**JAMES BUCHANAN (Pa.)**	Democratic	1,832,955	45.3	174	78.9
	John C. Frémont	Republican	1,339,932	33.1	114	
	Millard Fillmore	American	871,731	21.6	8	
1860	**ABRAHAM LINCOLN (Ill.)**	Republican	1,865,593	39.8	180	81.2
	Stephen A. Douglas	Democratic	1,382,713	29.5	12	
	John C. Breckinridge	Democratic	848,356	18.1	72	
	John Bell	Union	592,906	12.6	39	

Year	Candidate	Party	Popular Vote	%	Electoral Vote	Turnout %
1864	ABRAHAM LINCOLN (Ill.)	Republican	2,213,655	55.0	212	73.8
	George B. McClellan	Democratic	1,805,237	45.0	21	
1868	ULYSSES S. GRANT (Ill.)	Republican	3,012,833	52.7	214	78.1
	Horatio Seymour	Democratic	2,703,249	47.3	80	
1872	ULYSSES S. GRANT (Ill.)	Republican	3,597,132	55.6	286	71.3
	Horace Greeley	Democratic; Liberal Republican	2,834,125	43.9	66	
1876	RUTHERFORD B. HAYES (Ohio)	Republican	4,036,298	48.0	185	81.8
	Samuel J. Tilden	Democratic	4,300,590	51.0	184	
1880	JAMES A. GARFIELD (Ohio)	Republican	4,454,416	48.5	214	79.4
	Winfield S. Hancock	Democratic	4,444,952	48.1	155	
1884	GROVER CLEVELAND (N.Y.)	Democratic	4,874,986	48.5	219	77.5
	James G. Blaine	Republican	4,851,981	48.2	182	
1888	BENJAMIN HARRISON (Ind.)	Republican	5,439,853	47.9	233	79.3
	Grover Cleveland	Democratic	5,540,309	48.6	168	
1892	GROVER CLEVELAND (N.Y.)	Democratic	5,556,918	46.1	277	74.7
	Benjamin Harrison	Republican	5,176,108	43.0	145	
	James B. Weaver	People's	1,041,028	8.5	22	
1896	WILLIAM McKINLEY (Ohio)	Republican	7,104,779	51.1	271	79.3
	William J. Bryan	Democratic-People's	6,502,925	47.7	176	
1900	WILLIAM McKINLEY (Ohio)	Republican	7,207,923	51.7	292	73.2
	William J. Bryan	Dem.-Populist	6,358,133	45.5	155	
1904	THEODORE ROOSEVELT (N.Y.)	Republican	7,623,486	57.9	336	65.2
	Alton B. Parker	Democratic	5,077,911	37.6	140	
	Eugene V. Debs	Socialist	402,283	3.0	—	

PRESIDENTIAL ELECTIONS *(cont.)*

Year	Candidates	Parties	Popular Vote	Percentage of Popular Vote	Electoral Vote	Percentage of Voter Participation
1908	**WILLIAM H. TAFT (Ohio)**	Republican	7,678,908	51.6	321	65.4
	William J. Bryan	Democratic	6,409,104	43.1	162	
	Eugene V. Debs	Socialist	420,793	2.8	—	
1912	**WOODROW WILSON (N.J.)**	Democratic	6,293,454	41.9	435	58.8
	Theodore Roosevelt	Progressive	4,119,538	27.4	88	
	William H. Taft	Republican	3,484,980	23.2	8	
	Eugene V. Debs	Socialist	900,672	6.0		
1916	**WOODROW WILSON (N.J.)**	Democratic	9,129,606	49.4	277	61.6
	Charles E. Hughes	Republican	8,538,221	46.2	254	
	A. L. Benson	Socialist	585,113	3.2	—	
1920	**WARREN G. HARDING (Ohio)**	Republican	16,152,200	60.4	404	49.2
	James M. Cox	Democratic	9,147,353	34.2	127	
	Eugene V. Debs	Socialist	919,799	3.4	—	
1924	**CALVIN COOLIDGE (Mass.)**	Republican	15,725,016	54.0	382	48.9
	John W. Davis	Democratic	8,386,503	28.8	136	
	Robert M. LaFollette	Progressive	4,822,856	16.6	13	
1928	**HERBERT HOOVER (Calif.)**	Republican	21,391,381	58.2	444	56.9
	Alfred E. Smith	Democratic	15,016,443	40.9	87	
	Norman Thomas	Socialist	267,835	0.7	—	
1932	**FRANKLIN D. ROOSEVELT (N.Y.)**	Democratic	22,821,857	57.4	472	56.9
	Herbert Hoover	Republican	15,761,841	39.7	59	
	Norman Thomas	Socialist	881,951	2.2	—	

Year	Candidates	Parties	Popular Vote	Electoral Vote	% of Popular Vote	% Voter Participation
1936	**FRANKLIN D. ROOSEVELT (N.Y.)**	Democratic	27,751,597	523	60.8	61.0
	Alfred M. Landon	Republican	16,679,583	8	36.5	
	William Lemke	Union	882,479	—	1.9	
1940	**FRANKLIN D. ROOSEVELT (N.Y.)**	Democratic	27,244,160	449	54.8	62.5
	Wendell L. Willkie	Republican	22,305,198	82	44.8	
1944	**FRANKLIN D. ROOSEVELT (N.Y.)**	Democratic	25,602,504	432	53.5	55.9
	Thomas E. Dewey	Republican	22,006,285	99	46.0	
1948	**HARRY S. TRUMAN (Mo.)**	Democratic	24,105,695	304	49.5	53.0
	Thomas E. Dewey	Republican	21,969,170	189	45.1	
	J. Strom Thurmond	State-Rights Democratic	1,169,021	38	2.4	
	Henry A. Wallace	Progressive	1,156,103	—	2.4	
1952	**DWIGHT D. EISENHOWER (N.Y.)**	Republican	33,936,252	442	55.1	63.3
	Adlai E. Stevenson	Democratic	27,314,992	89	44.4	
1956	**DWIGHT D. EISENHOWER (N.Y.)**	Republican	35,575,420	457	57.6	60.6
	Adlai E. Stevenson	Democratic	26,033,066	73	42.1	
	Other	—		1		
1960	**JOHN F. KENNEDY (Mass.)**	Democratic	34,227,096	303	49.9	62.8
	Richard M. Nixon	Republican	34,108,546	219	49.6	
	Other	—		15		
1964	**LYNDON B. JOHNSON (Tex.)**	Democratic	43,126,506	486	61.1	61.7
	Barry M. Goldwater	Republican	27,176,799	52	38.5	

PRESIDENTIAL ELECTIONS *(cont.)*

Year	Candidates	Parties	Popular Vote	Percentage of Popular Vote	Electoral Vote	Percentage of Voter Participation
1968	**RICHARD M. NIXON (N.Y.)**	Republican	31,770,237	43.4	301	60.6
	Hubert H. Humphrey	Democratic	31,270,533	42.7	191	
	George Wallace	American Independent	9,906,141	13.5	46	
1972	**RICHARD M. NIXON (N.Y.)**	Republican	47,169,911	60.7	520	55.2
	George S. McGovern	Democratic	29,170,383	37.5	17	
	Other	—			1	
1976	**JIMMY CARTER (Ga.)**	Democratic	40,828,587	50.0	297	53.5
	Gerald R. Ford	Republican	39,147,613	47.9	241	
	Other	—	1,575,459	2.1	—	
1980	**RONALD REAGAN (Calif.)**	Republican	43,901,812	50.7	489	52.6
	Jimmy Carter	Democratic	35,483,820	41.0	49	
	John B. Anderson	Independent	5,719,722	6.6	—	
	Ed Clark	Libertarian	921,188	1.1	—	
1984	**RONALD REAGAN (Calif.)**	Republican	54,455,075	59.0	525	53.3
	Walter Mondale	Democratic	37,577,185	41.0	13	
1988	**GEORGE BUSH (Texas)**	Republican	47,946,422	54.0	426	50.2
	Michael S. Dukakis	Democratic	41,016,429	46.0	112	
1992	**BILL CLINTON (Ark.)**	**Democratic**	43,728,375	43.0	370	55
	George Bush	Republican	38,167,416	38.0	168	
	Ross Perot	Independent	19,237,247	19.0	0	

POPULATION OF THE UNITED STATES,
1790–1990

Year	Population	Percent Increase	Population per Square Mile	Percent Urban/ Rural	Percent White/ Nonwhite	Median Age
1790	3,929,214		4.5	5.1/94.9	80.7/19.3	NA
1800	5,308,483	35.1	6.1	6.1/93.9	81.1/18.9	NA
1810	7,239,881	36.4	4.3	7.3/92.7	81.0/19.0	NA
1820	9,638,453	33.1	5.5	7.2/92.8	81.6/18.4	16.7
1830	12,866,020	33.5	7.4	8.8/91.2	81.9/18.1	17.2
1840	17,069,453	32.7	9.8	10.8/89.2	83.2/16.8	17.8
1850	23,191,876	35.9	7.9	15.3/84.7	84.3/15.7	18.9
1860	31,443,321	35.6	10.6	19.8/80.2	85.6/14.4	19.4
1870	39,818,449	26.6	13.4	25.7/74.3	86.2/13.8	20.2
1880	50,155,783	26.0	16.9	28.2/71.8	86.5/13.5	20.9
1890	62,947,714	25.5	21.2	35.1/64.9	87.5/12.5	22.0
1900	75,994,575	20.7	25.6	39.6/60.4	87.9/12.1	22.9
1910	91,972,266	21.0	31.0	45.6/54.4	88.9/11.1	24.1
1920	105,710,620	14.9	35.6	51.2/48.8	89.7/10.3	25.3
1930	122,775,046	16.1	41.2	56.1/43.9	89.8/10.2	26.4
1940	131,669,275	7.2	44.2	56.5/43.5	89.8/10.2	29.0
1950	150,697,361	14.5	50.7	64.0/36.0	89.5/10.5	30.2
1960	179,323,175	18.5	50.6	69.9/30.1	88.6/11.4	29.5
1970	203,302,031	13.4	57.4	73.5/26.5	87.6/12.4	28.0
1980	226,545,805	11.4	64.0	73.7/26.3	86.0/14.0	30.0
1990	248,709,873	9.9	70.3	77.5/22.5	80.3/19.7	32.9

NA = Not available.

EMPLOYMENT, 1870–1990

Year	Number of Workers (in millions)	Male/Female Employment Ratio	Percentage of Workers in Unions
1870	12.5	85/15	—
1880	17.4	85/15	—
1890	23.3	83/17	—
1900	29.1	82/18	3
1910	38.2	79/21	6
1920	41.6	79/21	12
1930	48.8	78/22	7
1940	53.0	76/24	27
1950	59.6	72/28	25
1960	69.9	68/32	26
1970	82.1	63/37	25
1980	108.5	58/42	23
1985	108.9	57/43	19
1988	114.9	55/45	17
1990	124.8	54/46	16

PRODUCTION, TRADE, AND FEDERAL SPENDING/DEBT, 1790–1990

Year	Gross National Product (GNP) (in billions $)	Balance of Trade (in millions $)	Federal Budget (in billions $)	Federal Surplus/Deficit (in billions $)	Federal Debt (in billions $)
1790	—	-3	.004	+0.00015	.076
1800	—	-20	.011	+0.0006	.083
1810	—	-18	.008	+0.0012	.053
1820	—	-4	.018	-0.0004	.091
1830	—	+3	.015	+0.100	.049
1840	—	+25	.024	-0.005	.004
1850	—	-26	.040	+0.004	.064
1860	—	-38	.063	-0.01	.065
1870	7.4	-11	.310	+0.10	2.4
1880	11.2	+92	.268	+0.07	2.1
1890	13.1	+87	.318	+0.09	1.2
1900	18.7	+569	.521	+0.05	1.2
1910	35.3	+273	.694	-0.02	1.1
1920	91.5	+2,880	6.357	+0.3	24.3
1930	90.7	+513	3.320	+0.7	16.3
1940	100.0	-3,403	9.6	-2.7	43.0
1950	286.5	+1,691	43.1	-2.2	257.4
1960	506.5	+4,556	92.2	+0.3	286.3
1970	992.7	+2,511	196.6	+2.8	371.0
1980	2,631.7	+24,088	579.6	-59.5	914.3
1990	5,465.1	-100,997.1	1,251.8	-220.3	3,223.3

Suggested Readings

CHAPTER 1 THE MEETING OF CULTURES

American Indians. Wilcomb E. Washburn, *The Indian in America* (1975); James H. Merrell, *The Indians' New World* (1989); Bruce G. Trigger, *Natives and Newcomers* (1985); Carl Sauer, *Sixteenth-Century North America* (1985); Francis Jennings, *The Invasion of America: Indians, Colonialism, and the Cant of Conquest* (1975); Neal Salisbury, *Manitou and Providence: Indians, Europeans, and the Making of New England* (1982); Nathan Wachtel, *The Vision of the Vanquished* (1977); Kenneth MacGowan and J. A. Hester, Jr., *Early Man in the New World* (1950); Harold E. Driver, *Indians of North America*, 2nd ed. (1970); Francisco Guerra, *The Pre-Columbian Mind* (1971); Gary B. Nash, *Red, White, and Black*, rev. ed. (1982); Alfred W. Crosby, Jr., *The Columbian Exchange: Biological and Cultural Consequences of 1492* (1972); Henry Warner Bowden, *American Indians and Christian Missions* (1982); James Axtell, *The European and the Indian: Essays in the Ethnohistory of Colonial North America* (1981) and *The Invasion Within: The Contest of Cultures in Colonial North America* (1983); R. F. Spencer, J. D. Jennings, et al., *The Native Americans* (1978); Christopher L. Miller, *Prophetic Worlds: Indians and Whites on the Columbia Plateau* (1985).

European Explorations and Spanish America. Samuel Eliot Morison, *Admiral of the Ocean Sea*, 2 vols. (1942), *The European Discovery of America: The Northern Voyages* (1971), and *The European Discovery of America: The Southern Voyages* (1974); J. H. Parry, *The Age of Reconnaissance* (1963); David B. Quinn, *North America from Earliest Discovery to First Settlements* (1977); Charles Gibson, *Spain in America* (1966); James Lockhart, *Spanish Peru, 1532–1560: A Colonial Society* (1968); James Lang, *Conquest and Commerce: Spain and England in the Americas* (1975); J. H. Elliott, *The Old World and the New, 1492–1650* (1970); William H. Prescott, *History of the Conquest of Mexico*, 3 vols. (1843).

England Looks West. W. H. McNeill, *The Rise of the West* (1963); J. H. Parry, *Europe and the New World, 1415–1715* (1949) and *The Age of Reconnaissance* (1963); Wallace Notestein, *The English People on the Eve of Colonization, 1603–1630* (1954); Peter Laslett, *The World We Have Lost* (1965); Carl Bridenbaugh, *Vexed and Troubled Englishmen, 1590–1642* (1968); Patrick Collinson, *The Elizabethan Puritan Movement* (1967); C. H. George and Katherine George, *The Protestant Mind of the English Reformation* (1961); Michael Walzer, *The Revolution of the Saints* (1965); Keith Thomas, *Religion and the Decline of Magic* (1971); David Quinn, *The Elizabethans and the Irish* (1966); Nicholas Canny, *The Elizabethan Conquest of Ireland* (1976) and *Kingdom and Colony: Ireland in the Atlantic World* (1988); Lawrence Stone, *The Crisis of the Aristocracy* (1965); Margaret Spufford, *Contrasting Communities* (1974); David Underdown, *Pride's Purge* (1985); Christopher Hill, *The Century of Revolution, 1603–1714* (1961).

First English Colonies. Keith Wrightson, *English Society, 1580–1680* (1982); David B. Quinn, *The Roanoke Voyages, 1584–1590*, 2 vols. (1955), *Raleigh and the British Empire* (1947), and *Set Fair for Roanoke* (1985); Karen Ordahl Kupperman, *Roanoke: The Abandoned Colony* (1984).

CHAPTER 2 THE ENGLISH "TRANSPLANTATIONS"

General Histories. Charles M. Andrews, *The Colonial Period in American History*, 4 vols. (1934–1938); Clarence L. Ver Steeg, *The Formative Years, 1607–1763* (1964); John E. Pomfret and F. M. Shumway, *Founding the American Colonies, 1583–1660* (1970).

Jamestown. Philip L. Barbour, ed., *The Complete Works of Captain John Smith*, 3 vols. (1986); Bradford Smith, *Captain John Smith* (1953); Philip L. Barbour, *The Three Worlds of Captain John Smith* (1964); Alden T. Vaughn, *American Genesis* (1975).

The Chesapeake. Darret B. and Anita H. Rutman, *A Place in Time* (1984); Allan Kulikoff, *Tobacco and Slaves* (1986); Fredrick F. Siegel, *The Roots of Southern Distinctiveness* (1987); Suzanne Lebsock, *A Share of Honour* (1984); Aubrey Land et al., *Law, Society, and Politics in Early Maryland* (1977); T. H. Breen, *Tobacco Culture* (1985); Wesley Frank Craven, *The Dissolution of the Virginia Company* (1932), *The Southern Colonies in the Seventeenth Century* (1949), and *White, Red, and Black: The Seventeenth Century Virginian* (1971); Edmund S. Morgan, *American Slavery, American Freedom* (1975); Richard L. Morton, *Colonial Virginia*, 2 vols. (1960); Wilcomb E. Washburn, *The Governor and the Rebel* (1958); David W. Jordon, *Foundations of Representative Government: Maryland, 1632–1715* (1987); David B. Quinn, ed., *Early Maryland in a Wider World* (1982); Gloria Main, *Tobacco Colony: Life in Early Maryland, 1650–1720* (1982); Lois G. Carr and David W. Jordan, *Maryland's Revolution of Government, 1689–1692* (1974); Thad Tate and David L. Ammerman, eds., *The Chesapeake in the Seventeenth Century* (1979).

Plymouth and Massachusetts Bay. William Bradford, *Of Plymouth Plantation* (1952); George Langdon, *Pilgrim Colony* (1966); John Demos, *A Little Commonwealth* (1970); William Cronon, *Changes in the Land: Indians, Colonists, and the Ecology of New England* (1983); Samuel Eliot Morison, *Builders of the Bay Colony* (1930); Darrett Rutman, *Winthrop's Boston* (1965); R. E. Wall, *Massachusetts Bay: The Crucial Decade, 1640–1650* (1972); Edmund S. Morgan, *The Puritan Dilemma: The Story of John Winthrop* (1962); Alden T. Vaughn, *New England Frontier: Puritans and Indians* (1965); Bernard Bailyn, *The New England Merchants in the Seventeenth Century* (1955); Harold Selesky, *War and Society in Colonial Connecticut* (1990).

New England Puritanism. Perry Miller, *The New England Mind: The Seventeenth Century* (1939), *The New England Mind: From Colony to Province* (1953), *Orthodoxy in Massachusetts* (1933), and *Errand into the Wilderness* (1956); Edmund S. Morgan, *Visible Saints* (1963), *The Puritan Family* (1966), and *Roger Williams: The Church and the State* (1967); Kenneth Silverman, *The Life and Times of Cotton Mather* (1984); Charles Hambrick-Stowe, *The Practice of Piety* (1982); Philip F. Gura, *A Glimpse of Sion's Glory* (1984); Harry S. Stout, *The New England Soul* (1986); Norman Pettit, *The Heart Prepared: Grace and Conversion in Puritan Spiritual Life* (1989); Sacvan Bercovitch, *The American Jeremiad* (1978) and *The Puritan Origins of the American Self* (1975); Andrew Delbanco, *The Puritan Ordeal* (1989); David Hall, *The Faithful Shepherd* (1972) and *Worlds of Wonder, Days of Judgment* (1989); Robert Middlekauff, *The Mathers* (1971); Larzer Ziff, *Puritanism in America* (1973); Kai Erikson, *Wayward Puritans* (1966); W. K. B. Stoever, *A Faire and Easy Way to Heaven* (1978); J. V. James, *Colonial Rhode Island* (1975); M. J. A. Jones,

Congregational Commonwealth: Connecticut, 1636–1662 (1968); Paul R. Lucas, *Valley of Discord* (1976).

The Restoration Colonies. Christopher Hill, *The World Turned Upside Down* (1972); H. T. Merrens, *Colonial North Carolina* (1964); M. E. Sirmans, *Colonial South Carolina* (1966); Clarence L. Ver Steeg, *Origins of a Southern Mosaic* (1975); Robert Weir, *Colonial South Carolina* (1983); Roger Ekirch, *Poor Carolina* (1981); Peter H. Wood, *Black Majority* (1974); Oliver A. Rink, *Holland on Hudson* (1986); Thomas J. Archdeacon, *New York City, 1664–1710* (1976); Michael Kammen, *Colonial New York* (1975); Thomas J. Condon, *New York Beginnings* (1968); Van Cleaf Bachman, *Peltries or Plantations* (1969); George L. Smith, *Religion and Trade in New Netherland* (1973); Patricia Bonomi, *A Factious People* (1971); Barry Levy, *Quakers and the American Family* (1988); Alan Tully, *William Penn's Legacy* (1977); Edwin B. Bronner, *William Penn's Holy Experiment* (1962); Mary Maples Dunn, *William Penn: Politics and Conscience* (1967); James T. Lemmon, *The Best Poor Man's Country* (1972); J. E. Pomfret, *The Province of East and West New Jersey, 1609–1702* (1956) and *The Province of East New Jersey* (1962); T. R. Reese, *Colonial Georgia: A Study in British Imperial Policy in the Eighteenth Century* (1963); K. Coleman, *Colonial Georgia* (1976).

The Development of Empire. Lawrence Gipson, *The British Empire Before the American Revolution*, 15 vols. (1936–1970); Stephen S. Webb, *The Governors-General* (1979) and *1676: The End of American Independence* (1984); Leonard Labaree, *Royal Government in America* (1964); Michael Kammen, *Empire and Interest* (1970); Thomas C. Barrow, *Trade and Empire* (1967); I. K. Steele, *The Politics of Colonial Policy* (1968); James Henretta, *Salutary Neglect* (1972); Michael Hall, *Edward Randolph and the American Colonies* (1960); Viola Barnes, *The Dominion of New England* (1923); Lawrence Harper, *The English Navigation Laws* (1939); David S. Lovejoy, *The Glorious Revolution in America* (1972); J. M. Sosin, *English America and the Revolution of 1688* (1982) and *English America and the Restoration Monarchy of Charles II* (1980).

CHAPTER 3 LIFE IN PROVINCIAL AMERICA

General Social Histories. James A. Henretta and Gregory Nobles, *The Evolution of American Society, 1700–1815*, rev. ed. (1987); Richard Hofstadter, *America at 1750: A Social Portrait* (1971); David Hackett Fischer, *Albion's Seed* (1989).

Population and Family. Robert V. Wells, *The Population of the British Colonies in America Before 1776* (1975); Philip Greven, *Four Generations* (1970) and *The Protestant Temperament: Patterns of Child-Rearing, Religious Experience, and the Self in Early America* (1977); John Putnam Demos, *Past, Present, and Personal: The Family and Life Course in American History* (1986); Helena Wall, *Fierce Communion: Family and Community in Early America* (1990); Edmund S. Morgan, *The Puritan Family* (1966); J. William Frost, *The Quaker Family in Colonial America* (1972); Christopher Jedrey, *The World of John Cleaveland: Family and Community in Eighteenth-Century New England* (1979); Joan M. Jensen, *Loosening the Bonds: Mid-Atlantic Farm Women, 1750–1850* (1986); Laura Thatcher Ulrich, *Good Wives: Image and Reality in the Lives of Women in Northern New England, 1650–1750* (1982); Roger Thompson, *Women in Stuart England and America*

(1974); Lyle Koehler, *A Search for Power: 'The Weaker Sex' in Seventeenth-Century New England* (1982); Daniel Blake Smith, *Inside the Great House: Planter Family Life in Eighteenth Century Chesapeake Society* (1980); Judith Walzer Leavitt, *Brought to Bed: Child Bearing in America, 1750–1950* (1986).

Immigration. Bernard Bailyn, *The Peopling of British North America: An Introduction* (1986) and *Voyagers to the West: A Passage in the Peopling of America on the Eve of the Revolution* (1986); Albert B. Faust, *The German Element in the United States,* 2 vols. (1909); Ian C. C. Graham, *Colonists from Scotland: Emigration to North America, 1707–1783* (1956); James G. Leyburn, *The Scotch-Irish: A Social History* (1962); Frederic Klees, *The Pennsylvania Dutch* (1950); R. J. Dickson, *Ulster Immigration to the United States* (1966); Marcus L. Hanson, *The Atlantic Migration, 1607–1860* (1940); James Kettner, *The Development of American Citizenship* (1978).

Society and Slavery in the Colonial South. Edmund S. Morgan, *American Slavery, American Freedom* (1975); Peter Wood, *Black Majority* (1974); Winthrop Jordan, *White over Black* (1968); David Brion Davis, *The Problem of Slavery in Western Culture* (1966); Mechal Sobel, *The World They Made Together: Black and White Values in Eighteenth-Century Virginia* (1987); David W. Galenson, *Traders, Planters, and Slaves: Market Behavior in Early English America* (1986); Rhys Isaac, *The Transformation of Virginia, 1740–1790* (1982); Jean E. Friedman, *The Enclosed Garden: Women and Community in the Evangelical South* (1985); Jack P. Greene, *Pursuits of Happiness* (1988); Allan Kulikoff, *Tobacco and Slaves* (1986); Philip D. Curtin, *The Atlantic Slave Trade* (1969); Daniel Littlefield, *Rice and Slaves: Ethnicity and the Slave Trade in Colonial South Carolina* (1981); David Eltis, *Economic Growth and the Ending of the Transatlantic Slave Trade* (1987); Jay Coughtry, *The Notorious Triangle: Rhode Island and the African Slave Trade, 1799–1807* (1981); Abbot E. Smith, *Colonists in Bondage* (1947); Gerald Mullin, *Flight and Rebellion* (1972); Eugene Genovese, *From Rebellion to Revolution* (1979); Gary B. Nash, *Red, White, and Black,* rev. ed. (1982); Charles Joyner, *Down by the Riverside: A South Carolina Slave Community* (1984); T. H. Breen and Stephen Innes, *'Myne Own Ground,' Race and Freedom on Virginia's Eastern Shore* (1980); T. H. Breen, *Tobacco Culture* (1985); Julia C. Spruill, *Women's Life and Work in the Southern Colonies* (1972); J. Leitch Wright, Jr., *Anglo-Spanish Rivalry in North America* (1971) and *The Only Land They Knew: The Tragic Story of the American Indians in the Old South* (1981).

Society and Town in Colonial New England. Kenneth Lockridge, *A New England Town* (1970); Michael Zuckerman, *Peaceable Kingdoms* (1970); Darrett Rutman, *Winthrop's Boston* (1965); Charles Grant, *Democracy in the Connecticut Frontier Town of Kent* (1961); Paul Boyer and Stephen Nissenbaum, *Salem Possessed* (1974); John Putnam Demos, *Entertaining Satan: Witchcraft and the Culture of Early New England* (1982); Carol Karlsen, *The Devil in the Shape of a Woman: Witchcraft in Colonial New England* (1987); E. M. Cook, Jr., *The Fathers of Towns* (1975); Sumner Chilton Powell, *Puritan Village* (1963); Steven Foster, *The Long Argument: English Puritanism and the Shaping of New England Culture, 1570–1700* (1991); Richard Bushman, *From Puritan to Yankee* (1967); Robert Gross, *The Minutemen and Their World* (1976).

The Colonial Economy. Alice Hanson Jones, *Wealth of a Nation to Be* (1980); Jackson Turner Main, *The Social Structure of Revolutionary America* (1965); Stuart Bruchey, *Roots* *of American Economic Growth, 1607–1861* (1965); John J. McCusker and Russell R. Menard, *The Economy of British America, 1607–1787* (1985); Carl Bridenbaugh, *Myths and Realities: Societies of the Colonial South* (1963); Paul G. E. Clemens, *The Atlantic Economy and Colonial Maryland's Eastern Shore: From Tobacco to Grain* (1980); Edmund S. Morgan, *Virginians at Home* (1952); Jacob M. Price, *France and the Chesapeake*, 2 vols. (1973), *The Tobacco Adventure to Russia* (1961), and *Capital and Credit in the British Overseas Trade: The View from the Chesapeake, 1700–1776* (1980); Harry R. Merrens, *Colonial North Carolina in the Eighteenth Century* (1964); Stephen Innes, *Labor in a New Land: Economy and Society in Seventeenth Century Springfield* (1983); Stephen Innes, ed., *Work and Labor in Early America* (1988); David W. Galenson, *White Servitude in Colonial America: An Economic Analysis* (1982); Sharon U. Salinger, *"To Serve Well and Faithfully": Labor and Indentured Servants in Pennsylvania, 1692–1800* (1987).

Cities and Commerce. Carl Bridenbaugh, *Cities in the Wilderness* (1938) and *Cities in Revolt* (1955); Gary B. Nash, *The Urban Crucible* (1979) and *Forging Freedom: The Formation of Philadelphia's Black Community, 1720–1840* (1988); G. B. Warden, *Boston, 1687–1776* (1970); Stephanie G. Wolf, *Urban Village* (1976); Stuart Bruchey, *The Colonial Merchant* (1966); J. F. Shepherd and G. M. Walton, *The Economic Rise of Early America* (1979); James B. Hedges, *The Browns of Providence Plantation*, vol. 1 (1952); Frederick B. Tolles, *Meeting House and Counting House: The Quaker Merchants of Colonial Philadelphia, 1682–1763* (1948); Thomas M. Doerflinger, *A Vigorous Spirit of Enterprise: Merchants and Economic Development in Revolutionary Philadelphia* (1986); Bernard Bailyn, *The New England Merchants in the Seventeenth Century* (1955); Marcus Rediker, *Between the Devil and the Deep Sea: Merchant Seamen, Pirates, and the Anglo-American Maritime World, 1700–1750* (1987); Arthur Jensen, *The Maritime Commerce of Colonial Philadelphia* (1963); Randolph S. Klein, *Portrait of an Early American Family* (1975).

Colonial Religion. For studies of Puritanism, see Suggested Readings for Chapter 2. Patricia U. Bonomi, *Under the Canopy of Heaven: Religion, Society, and Politics in Colonial America* (1986); Sidney Ahlstrom, *A Religious History of the American People* (1972); W. W. Sweet, *Religion in Colonial America* (1942); Carl Bridenbaugh, *Mitre and Sceptre: Transatlantic Faiths, Ideas, Personalities, and Politics, 1689–1775* (1962); Sidney Mead, *The Lively Experiment: The Shaping of Christianity in America* (1963); J. T. Ellis, *Catholics in America* (1965); J. R. Marcus, *Early American Jewry* (1951); Janet Whitman, *John Woolman, American Quaker* (1942); William C. McLoughlin, *New England Dissent, 1630–1833*, 2 vols. (1971); Marilyn Westerkamp, *Triumph of Laity* (1988); J. William Frost, *A Perfect Freedom: Religious Liberty in Pennsylvania* (1990); Edwin S. Gaustad, *The Great Awakening in New England* (1957); J. M. Bumsted and John E. Van de Wetering, *What Must I Do to Be Saved? The Great Awakening in Colonial America* (1976); Alan Heimert, *Religion and the American Mind* (1966); Perry Miller, *Jonathan Edwards* (1949); Ola Winslow, *Jonathan Edwards* (1940); Patricia Tracy, *Jonathan Edwards: Pastor* (1980); Conrad Wright, *The Beginnings of Unitarianism in America* (1955); J. W. Davidson, *The Logic of Millennial Thought* (1977).

Education. Lawrence A. Cremin, *American Education: The Colonial Experience, 1607–1783* (1970); Bernard Bailyn, *Education in the Forming of American Society* (1960); James Axtell, *The School upon a Hill: Education and Society in Colonial New England* (1974); Robert Middlekauff, *Ancients and Axioms* (1963); Samuel Eliot Morison, *The Founding of Harvard*

College (1935); Jurgen Herbst, *From Crisis to Crisis* (1982); Kenneth Lockridge, *Literacy in Colonial New England* (1974).

Culture and the Enlightenment. Jack Greene, *Pursuits of Happiness* (1988); Louis B. Wright, *The Cultural Life of the American Colonies* (1957); Daniel J. Boorstin, *The Americans: The Colonial Experience* (1958); Richard Beale Davis, *Intellectual Life in the Colonial South*, 2 vols. (1978); Henry May, *The Enlightenment in America* (1976); Howard Mumford Jones, *O Strange New World* (1964); Jean-Christophe Agnew, *Worlds Apart: The Market and the Theater in Anglo-American Thought, 1550–1750* (1986); Brook Hindle, *The Pursuit of Science in Revolutionary America* (1956); Carl Van Doren, *Benjamin Franklin* (1941); V. W. Crane, *Benjamin Franklin and a Rising People* (1954); H. Leventhal, *In the Shadow of Enlightenment* (1976).

Law and Politics. Bernard Bailyn, *The Origins of American Politics* (1968); Jack P. Greene, *The Quest for Power* (1963); J. R. Pole, *Political Representation in England and the Origins of the American Republic* (1966); Michael Kammen, *Spheres of Liberty: Changing Perceptions of Liberty in American Culture* (1986); Thomas Curry, *The First Freedoms: Church and State in America to the Passage of the First Amendment* (1986); Leonard W. Labaree, *Royal Government in America* (1930); Robert Zemsky, *Merchants, Farmers, and River Gods* (1971); Caroline Robbins, *The Eighteenth-Century Commonwealthman* (1959); J. G. A. Pocock, *The Machiavellian Moment* (1975); Robert Ferguson, *Law and Letters in American Culture* (1984); Marylynn Salmon, *Women and the Law of Property in Early America* (1986); Gerald W. Gawalt, *The Promise of Power: The Emergence of the Legal Profession in Massachusetts, 1760–1840* (1979); A. G. Roeber, *Faithful Magistrates and Republican Lawyers: Creators of Virginia Legal Culture, 1680–1810* (1981).

CHAPTER 4 THE EMPIRE UNDER STRAIN

General Histories. Robert Middlekauff, *The Glorious Cause: The American Revolution, 1763–1789* (1982); Edward Countryman, *The American Revolution* (1985); Alfred E. Young, Jr., ed., *The American Revolution* (1976); John C. Miller, *Origins of the American Revolution* (1957); Merrill Jensen, *The Founding of a Nation* (1968); Edmund S. Morgan, *The Birth of the Republic* (1956); J. R. Alden, *A History of the American Revolution* (1969); Charles M. Andrews, *The Colonial Background of the American Revolution* (1924, rev. 1931); Lawrence Henry Gipson, *The Coming of the Revolution, 1763–1775* (1954); Ian R. Christie and Benjamin W. Labaree, *Empire or Independence, 1760–1776* (1976); Ian R. Christie, *Crisis of Empire* (1966).

The British Imperial System. Lawrence Henry Gipson, *The British Empire Before the American Revolution*, 15 vols. (1936–1970); Robert C. Newbold, *The Albany Congress and Plan of Union of 1754* (1955); Richard Pares, *War and Trade in the West Indies, 1739–1763* (1936); Howard H. Peckham, *The Colonial Wars, 1689–1762* (1963); Alan Rogers, *Empire and Liberty* (1974); Lewis B. Namier, *England in the Age of the American Revolution*, rev. ed. (1961) and *The Structure of Politics at the Accession of George III*, rev. ed. (1961); John Brewer, *Party Ideology and Popular Politics at the Accession of George III* (1967); Bernard Donoughue, *British Politics and the American Revolution: The Path to War, 1773–1775* (1965); John Brooke, *King George III* (1972); Michael Kammen, *A Rope of Sand* (1968).

The French and the Indians.   Fred Anderson, *A People's Army: Massachusetts Soldiers and Society in the Seven Years War* (1984); Thomas P. Abernethy, *Western Lands and the American Revolution* (1937); J. M. Sosin, *Whitehall and the Wilderness* (1961); David H. Corkran, *The Cherokee Frontier* (1962); R. S. Cotterill, *The Southern Indians* (1954); Howard H. Peckham, *Pontiac and the Indian Uprising* (1947); William Pencak, *War, Politics, and Revolution in Provincial Massachusetts* (1981); Francis Jennings, *Empire of Fortune* (1988) and *The Ambiguous Iroquois Empire* (1984).

Merchants and the Empire.   Joseph Ernst, *Money and Politics in America, 1755–1775* (1973); Arthur M. Schlesinger, *The Colonial Merchants and the American Revolution* (1917); Oliver M. Dickinson, *The Navigation Acts and the American Revolution* (1951); Thomas Doerflinger, *A Vigorous Spirit of Enterprise: Merchants and Economic Development in Revolutionary Philadelphia* (1986).

American Resistance.   David Ammerman, *In the Common Cause* (1974); Hiller B. Zobel, *The Boston Massacre* (1970); Edmund S. Morgan and Helen M. Morgan, *The Stamp Act Crisis* (1953); Benjamin W. Labaree, *The Boston Tea Party* (1964); John Shy, *Toward Lexington* (1965); Pauline Maier, *From Resistance to Revolution* (1972); Dirk Hoerder, *Crowd Action in Revolutionary Massachusetts* (1977); Paul A. Gilje, *The Road to Mobocracy: Popular Disorder in New York City, 1763–1834* (1987).

Revolutionary Ideology.   Bernard Bailyn, *The Ideological Origins of the American Revolution* (1967); Ian R. Christie, *Wilkes, Wyvil, and Reform* (1962); George Rudé, *Wilkes and Liberty* (1962); Isaac Kramnick, *Bolingbroke and His Circle* (1968); Clinton Rossiter, *Seedtime of the Republic* (1953); Nathan Hatch, *The Sacred Cause of Liberty* (1977); Richard Merritt, *Symbols of American Community, 1735–1775* (1966); Gary B. Nash, *The Urban Crucible* (1979); Rhys Isaac, *The Transformation of Virginia, 1740–1790* (1982); David Brion Davis, *Revolutions: Reflections on American Equality and Foreign Liberations* (1990).

Revolutionary Politics.   Carl Becker, *The History of Political Parties in the Province of New York* (1909); Richard D. Brown, *Revolutionary Politics in Massachusetts* (1970); David Lovejoy, *Rhode Island Politics and the American Revolution* (1958); L. R. Gerlach, *Prologue to Independence* (1976); Theodore Thayer, *Pennsylvania Politics and the Growth of Democracy* (1953); Ronald Hoffman, *A Spirit of Dissension* (1973); R. E. Brown and B. K. Brown, *Virginia, 1705–1786* (1964); Charles S. Sydnor, *Gentlemen Freeholders* (1952).

CHAPTER 5 THE AMERICAN REVOLUTION

General Histories.   Robert Middlekauff, *The Glorious Cause: The American Revolution, 1763–1789* (1985); Edward Countryman, *The American Revolution* (1985); Alfred E. Young, Jr., ed., *The American Revolution* (1976); Merrill Jensen, *The Founding of a Nation, A History of the American Revolution, 1763–1789* (1968); Edmund S. Morgan, *The Birth of the Republic, 1763–1789* (1956); Michael Kammen, *A Season of Youth: The American Revolution and the Historical Imagination* (1978).

The Road to Independence.   Carl Becker, *The Declaration of Independence* (1922); Morton White, *The Philosophy of the American Revolution* (1978); Gary Wills, *Inventing*

America (1978); Eric Foner, *Tom Paine and Revolutionary America* (1976); David Hawke, *Paine* (1974); Peter Shaw, *The Character of John Adams* (1976) and *American Patriots and the Rituals of Revolution* (1981); John R. Howe, Jr., *The Changing Political Thought of John Adams* (1966); Edmund S. Morgan, *The Meaning of Independence* (1976).

The War. Willard Wallace, *Appeal to Arms* (1950); John R. Alden, *The American Revolution* (1964); Piers Mackesy, *The War for America* (1964); Don Higginbotham, *The American War for Independence* (1971) and *George Washington and the American Military Tradition* (1985); Howard H. Peckham, *The War for Independence* (1958); Christopher Ward, *The War of the Revolution*, 2 vols. (1952); John Shy, *A People Numerous and Armed* (1976); Charles Royster, *A Revolutionary People at War* (1979); G. W. Allen, *Naval History of the American Revolution*, 2 vols. (1913); Samuel Eliot Morison, *John Paul Jones* (1959); T. G. Frothingham, *Washington: Commander in Chief* (1930); Douglas Southall Freeman, *George Washington*, 7 vols. (1948–1957); James T. Flexner, *George Washington in the American Revolution* (1968); Charles Royster, *Light-Horse Harry Lee and the Legacy of the American Revolution* (1981); E. Wayne Carp, *To Starve the Army at Pleasure: Continental Army Administration and American Political Culture, 1775–1783* (1984).

Revolutionary Diplomacy. Samuel F. Bemis, *The Diplomacy of the American Revolution* (1935); Richard B. Morris, *The Peacemakers* (1965); Gerald Stourzh, *Benjamin Franklin and American Foreign Policy*, rev. ed. (1969); Jonathan R. Dull, *A Diplomatic History of the American Revolution* (1985); L. S. Kaplan, *Colonies into Nation: American Diplomacy, 1763–1801* (1972); Clarence L. Ver Steeg, *Robert Morris* (1954); E. J. Ferguson, *The Power of the Purse* (1961).

The Loyalists. Wallace Brown, *The King's Friends* (1965); Robert M. Calhoon, *The Loyalists in Revolutionary America* (1973); Mary Beth Norton, *The British Americans: The Loyalist Exiles in England 1774–1789* (1972); William H. Nelson, *The American Tory* (1962); Bernard Bailyn, *The Ordeal of Thomas Hutchinson* (1974); Paul H. Smith, *Loyalists and Redcoats* (1964); James W. St. G. Walker, *The Black Loyalists* (1976).

Women, Family, and the Revolution. Mary Beth Norton, *Liberty's Daughters* (1980); Linda K. Kerber, *Women of the Republic* (1980); Linda Grant DePauw, *Founding Mothers* (1975); Joan Jensen, *Loosening the Bonds: Mid-Atlantic Farm Women, 1750–1850* (1986); Joy Day Buel and Richard Buel, Jr., *The Way of Duty: A Woman and Her Family in Revolutionary America* (1984); Jay Fliegelman, *Prodigals and Pilgrims* (1982).

Indians and Blacks in the Revolution. James H. O'Donnell, III, *Southern Indians in the American Revolution* (1973); Barbara Graymont, *The Iroquois in the American Revolution* (1973); Isabel T. Kelsay, *Joseph Brant, 1743–1807* (1984); Anthony F. C. Wallace, *The Death and Rebirth of the Seneca* (1969); Benjamin Quarles, *The Negro in the American Revolution* (1961); Duncan McLeod, *Slavery, Race and the American Revolution* (1974); Ira Berlin and Ronald Hoffman, eds., *Slavery in the Revolutionary Era* (1982); David Brion Davis, *The Problem of Slavery in the Age of Revolution* (1975); Edmund S. Morgan, *American Slavery, American Freedom* (1975); Arthur Zilversmit, *The First Emancipation* (1967).

Social Effects. Gordon S. Wood, *The Radicalism of the American Revolution* (1992); J. F. Jameson, *The American Revolution Considered as a Social Movement* (1962); Staughton Lynd, *Class Conflict, Slavery and the United States Constitution* (1968); Merrill Jensen, *The American Revolution Within America* (1974); Richard McCormick, *Experiment in Independence* (1950); Jackson Turner Main, *The Social Structure of Revolutionary America* (1965); Jerome J. Nadlehaft, *The Disorders of War: The Revolution in South Carolina* (1981); Robert Gross, *The Minutemen and Their World* (1976); Charles G. Steffen, *The Mechanics of Baltimore: Workers and Politics in the Age of Revolution, 1763–1812* (1984); Edward Countryman, *A People in Revolution* (1981).

State Governments. Gordon S. Wood, *The Creation of the American Republic* (1969); Stephen E. Patterson, *Political Parties in Revolutionary Massachusetts* (1973); Irwin Polishook, *Rhode Island and the Union, 1774–1795* (1969); Willi Paul Adams, *The First American Constitutions* (1980); Jackson Turner Main, *Political Parties Before the Constitution* (1973), *The Sovereign States, 1775–1783* (1973), and *The Upper House in Revolutionary America, 1763–1788* (1967).

The Articles of Confederation. John Fiske, *The Critical Period of American History, 1783–1789* (1883); Jack N. Rakove, *The Beginnings of National Politics* (1979); Merrill Jensen, *The New Nation* (1950) and *The Articles of Confederation*, rev. ed. (1959); H. James Henderson, *Party Politics in the Continental Congress* (1974); Jack Eblen, *The First and Second United States Empires* (1968); David Szatmary, *Shays' Rebellion: The Making of an Agrarian Insurrection* (1980); Andrew R. L. Cayton, *The Frontier Republic: Ideology and Politics in the Ohio Country, 1780–1825* (1986); Steven Watts, *The Republic Reborn: War and the Making of Liberal America, 1790–1800* (1987).

CHAPTER 6 THE CONSTITUTION AND THE NEW REPUBLIC

The Constitution. Max Farrand, ed., *Records of the Federal Convention of 1787*, 4 vols. (1911–1937); Max Ferrand, *The Framing of the Constitution of the United States* (1913); Michael Kammen, *A Machine that Would Go of Itself: The Constitution in American Culture* (1986) and *Sovereignty and Liberty: Constitutional Discourse in American Culture* (1988); Charles A. Beard, *An Economic Interpretation of the Constitution of the United States* (1913); Forrest McDonald, *We the People: The Economic Origins of the Constitution* (1958), *E Pluribus Unum: The Formation of the American Republic, 1776–1790* (1965) and *Novus Ordo Seclorum: The Intellectual Origins of the Constitution* (1985); Robert E. Brown, *Charles Beard and the Constitution* (1956); Leonard Levy, *Constitutional Opinions: Aspects of the Bill of Rights* (1986) and *Original Intent and the Framers' Constitution* (1988); Thomas Curry, *The First Freedom: Church and State in America to the Passage of the First Amendment* (1986); William L. Miller, *The First Liberty: Religion and the American Republic* (1986); Richard B. Morris, *The Forging of the Union, 1781–1789* (1987); Clinton Rossiter, *1787: The Grand Convention* (1965); Christopher Collier and James Lincoln Collier, *Decision: Philadelphia: The Constitutional Convention of 1787* (1986); Douglas Adair, *Fame and the Founding Fathers* (1974); Jackson Turner Main, *The Anti-Federalists* (1961); Alpheus T. Mason, *The State Rights Debate* (1964); J. E. Cooke, ed., *The Federalist* (1961); Garry Wills, *Explaining America* (1981); Linda G. DePauw, *The Eleventh Pillar: New York State and* the Federal Constitution (1966); Gerald Stourzh, *Alexander Hamilton and the Idea of Republican Government* (1970); Robert A. Rutland, *The Ordeal of the Constitution* (1966); Michael Lienesch, *New Order of the Ages: Time, the Constitution, and the Making of Modern American Political Thought* (1988); Edmund S. Morgan, *Inventing the People: The Rise of Popular Sovereignty in England and America* (1988).

The Federalist Era. John C. Miller, *The Federalist Era, 1789–1801* (1960); Leonard D. White, *The Federalists* (1948); Forrest McDonald, *The Presidency of George Washington* (1974); Ralph Adams Brown, *The Presidency of John Adams* (1975); Stephen Kurtz, *The Presidency of John Adams* (1957); John R. Howe, *The Changing Political Thought of John Adams* (1966); Manning Dauer, *The Adams Federalists* (1953); Richard Kohn, *Eagle and Sword: The Federalists and the Creation of the Military Establishment in America, 1783–1802* (1975); Carl E. Prince, *The Federalists and the Origins of the U.S. Civil Service* (1978); Ralph Ketchum, *Presidents Above Party: The First American Presidency, 1789–1829* (1984); Leonard Levy, *Legacy of Suppression: Freedom of Speech and Press in Early American History,* rev. ed. (1985); James M. Smith, *Freedom's Fetters: The Alien and Sedition Laws and American Civil Liberties* (1956); Leland D. Baldwin, *The Whiskey Rebels* (1939); Thomas P. Slaughter, *The Whiskey Rebellion: Frontier Epilogue to the American Revolution* (1986); Irving Brant, *The Bill of Rights* (1965); John C. Miller, *Crisis in Freedom* (1951).

The Jeffersonian Republicans. Charles A. Beard, *The Economic Origins of the Jeffersonian Opposition* (1915); Joseph Charles, *The Origins of the American Party System* (1956); Noble Cunningham, *The Jeffersonian Republicans* (1957); Merrill D. Peterson, *Thomas Jefferson and the New Nation* (1970); Richard Hofstadter, *The Idea of a Party System* (1970); Norman K. Risjord, *Chesapeake Politics, 1781–1800* (1978); Alfred F. Young, *The Democratic-Republicans of New York* (1967); William N. Chambers, *Political Parties in a New Nation* (1963); Patricia Watlington, *The Partisan Spirit* (1972); John Zvesper, *Political Philosophy and Rhetoric: A Study of the Origins of American Party Politics* (1977); Richard W. Buel, Jr., *Securing the Revolution: Ideology in American Politics, 1789–1815* (1972); Joyce Appleby, *Capitalism and a New Social Order: The Republican Vision of the 1790s* (1984); Drew McCoy, *The Elusive Republic: Political Economy in Jeffersonian America* (1980) and *The Last of the Fathers: James Madison and the Republican Legacy* (1989).

Federalist Diplomacy. Felix Gilbert, *To the Farewell Address* (1961); Samuel F. Bemis, *Jay's Treaty* (1923) and *Pinckney's Treaty* (1926, rev. 1960); Alexander DeConde, *Entangling Alliance* (1958) and *The Quasi-War* (1966); Lawrence S. Kaplan, *Jefferson and France* (1967); Harry Ammon, *The Genêt Mission* (1973); Louis M. Sears, *George Washington and the French Revolution* (1960); Bradford Perkins, *The First Rapprochement: England and the United States* (1967); Charles Ritcheson, *Aftermath of Revolution: British Policy Toward the United States, 1783–1795* (1969); Paul A. Varg, *Foreign Policies of the Founding Fathers* (1963).

The Founders. Douglas Southall Freeman, *George Washington,* 7 vols. (1948–1957); Garry Wills, *Cincinnatus: George Washington and the Enlightenment* (1984); Barry Schwartz, *George Washington: The Making of a Symbol* (1987); Esmond Wright, *Franklin of Philadelphia* (1986); Dumas Malone, *Jefferson and His Time,* 6 vols. (1948–1981); Merrill Peterson, *Thomas Jefferson and the New Nation* (1970); Irving Brant, *James Madison* (1950); James T. Flexner, *George Washington,* 4 vols. (1965–1972); Page Smith, *John Adams*

(1962); John C. Miller, *Alexander Hamilton* (1959); Milton Lomask, *Aaron Burr*, 2 vols. (1979, 1982); Richard B. Morris, *Witnesses at the Creation: Hamilton, Madison, Jay, and the Constitution* (1985).

CHAPTER 7 THE JEFFERSONIAN ERA

General Histories. Henry Adams, *History of the United States During the Administration of Jefferson and Adams*, 9 vols., (1889–1891); Marcus Cunliffe, *The Nation Takes Shape, 1789–1832* (1959); Charles Mayfield, *The New Nation* (1981); Marshall Smelser, *The Democratic Republicans, 1801–1815* (1968).

Society and Culture. Joseph J. Ellis, *After the Revolution: Profiles of Early American Culture* (1979); Russel B. Nye, *The Cultural Life of the New Nation* (1960); Kenneth Silverman, *A Cultural History of the American Revolution* (1976); Lawrence A. Cremin, *American Education: The National Experience* (1981); Carl F. Kaestle, *The Evolution of an Urban School System* (1973); Harry Warfel, *Noah Webster, Schoolmaster to America* (1936); Priscilla F. Clement, *Welfare and the Poor in the Nineteenth-Century City* (1985); William W. Sweet, *Revivalism in America* (1944); William G. McLoughlin, *Revivals, Awakenings, and Reform* (1978); Sydney Ahlstrom, *A Religious History of the American People* (1972); Whitney R. Cross, *The Burned Over District* (1950); John Boles, *The Great Revival in the South* (1972); Cathy Davidson, *The Revolution and the Word* (1986); Terry D. Bilhartz, *Urban Religion and the Second Great Awakening* (1986); Jan Lewis, *The Pursuit of Happiness: Family and Values in Jefferson's Virginia* (1983); Richard Slotkin, *Regeneration Through Violence* (1973).

Economic Growth. Stuart Bruchey, *The Roots of American Economic Growth* (1965); Thomas C. Cochran, *Frontiers of Change: Early Industrialization in America* (1981); Douglas C. North, *The Economic Growth of the United States, 1780–1860* (1961); W. Elliot Brownlee, *Dynamics of Ascent* (1979); Nathan Rosenberg, *Technology and American Economic Growth* (1972); Merritt Roe Smith, *Harpers Ferry Armory and the New Technology* (1977); Anthony F. C. Wallace, *Rockdale* (1978); Arthur H. Cole, *The American Wool Manufacture*, 2 vols. (1926); Caroline F. Ware, *Early New England Cotton Manufacture* (1931); C. M. Green, *Eli Whitney and the Birth of American Technology* (1956); W. J. Rorabaugh, *The Craft Apprentice: From Franklin to the Machine Age in America* (1986); Barbara M. Tucker, *Samuel Slater and the Origins of the American Textile Industry, 1790–1860* (1984); George R. Taylor, *The Transportation Revolution* (1951); James Henretta and Gregory Nobles, *The Evolution of American Society, 1700–1815*, rev. ed. (1987).

Politics and Government. Morton Borden, *Parties and Politics in the Early Republic* (1967); Noble Cunningham, *The Jeffersonian Republicans in Power* (1963) and *The Process of Government Under Jefferson* (1978); Robert Dawidoff, *The Education of John Randolph* (1979); James S. Young, *The Washington Community* (1966); David Hackett Fischer, *The Revolution of American Conservatism* (1965); Linda Kerber, *Federalists in Dissent* (1970); James M. Banner, *To the Hartford Convention* (1967); Leonard White, *The Jeffersonians* (1951); Alexander Balinky, *Albert Gallatin: Fiscal Theories and Policy* (1958); Robert M. Johnstone, Jr., *Jefferson and the Presidency* (1978); Dumas Malone, *Jefferson the President:*

First Term (1970) and *Jefferson the President: Second Term* (1974); Richard Ellis, *The Jeffersonian Crisis* (1971); Leonard Baker, *John Marshall: A Life in Law* (1974).

Jeffersonian Thought. Adrienne Koch, *The Philosophy of Thomas Jefferson* (1943); Charles M. Wiltse, *The Jeffersonian Tradition in American Democracy* (1935); Merrill Peterson, *The Jeffersonian Image in the American Mind* (1960); Leonard W. Levy, *Jefferson and Civil Liberties: The Darker Side* (1963); Drew McCoy, *The Elusive Republic: Political Economy in Jeffersonian America* (1980) and *The Last of the Fathers: James Madison and the Republican Legacy* (1989).

Foreign Policy. Irving Brant, *James Madison: Secretary of State* (1953); Bradford Perkins, *Prologue to War: England and the United States, 1805–1812* (1961); Alexander DeConde, *The Affair of Louisiana* (1976); Arthur P. Whitaker, *The Mississippi Question* (1934); George Dangerfield, *Chancellor Robert R. Livingston of New York* (1960); Harry Ammon, *James Monroe and the Quest for National Identity* (1971); Bernard deVoto, *Course of Empire* (1952); Bernard deVoto, ed., *The Journals of Lewis and Clark* (1953); Nathan Schachner, *Aaron Burr* (1937); Thomas P. Abernethy, *The Burr Conspiracy* (1954); Milton Lomask, *Aaron Burr*, 2 vols. (1979, 1982).

Indians and the West. B. W. Sheehan, *Seeds of Extinction* (1973); Francis S. Philbrick, *The Rise of the New West* (1965); Ray Allen Billington and Martin Ridge, *Westward Expansion*, rev. ed. (1982); Richard White, *The Roots of Dependency* (1983); James P. Ronda, *Lewis and Clarke Among the Indians* (1984); Charles Wilkinson, *American Indians, Time, and the Law*, rev. ed. (1987); Francis P. Prucha, *American Indian Policy in the Formative Years* (1962); Reginald Horsman, *Expansion and American Indian Policy, 1783–1812* (1962) and *Matthew Elliott, British Indian Agent* (1964); R. David Edmunds, *The Shawnee Prophet* (1983) and *Tecumseh and the Quest for Indian Leadership* (1984).

CHAPTER 8 WAR AND EXPANSION

The War of 1812. J. C. A. Stagg, *Mr. Madison's War: Politics, Diplomacy, and Warfare in the Early American Republic, 1783–1830* (1983); Julius W. Pratt, *Expansionists of 1812* (1925); Reginald Horsman, *The Causes of the War of 1812* (1962) and *The War of 1812* (1969); Bradford Perkins, *Prologue to War: England and the United States, 1805–1812* (1961); A. L. Burt, *The United States, Great Britain, and British North America* (1940); Roger H. Brown, *The Republic in Peril: 1812* (1964); Harry L. Coles, *The War of 1812* (1965); F. F. Beirne, *The War of 1812* (1949); John Mahon, *The War of 1812* (1975); William Wood, *The War with the United States* (1915); Irving Brant, *James Madison: Commander-in-Chief* (1961); Robert V. Remini, *Andrew Jackson and the Course of American Empire* (1977); Alfred T. Mahan, *Sea Power in Its Relation to the War of 1812*, 2 vols. (1905); Samuel F. Bemis, *John Quincy Adams and the Foundations of American Foreign Policy* (1949); Bradford Perkins, *Castlereagh and Adams* (1964); R. David Edmunds, *The Shawnee Prophet* (1983) and *Tecumseh and the Quest for Indian Leadership* (1984).

Postwar Expansion. George Dangerfield, *The Awakening of American Nationalism* (1965) and *The Era of Good Feelings* (1952); Shaw Livermore, Jr., *The Twilight of Federalism*

(1962); Bray Hammond, *Banks and Politics in America from the Revolution to the Civil War* (1957); Murray N. Rothbard, *The Panic of 1819* (1962).

The West.   Francis S. Philbrick, *The Rise of the West, 1745–1830* (1965); Thomas P. Abernethy, *The South in the New Nation* (1961); Frederick Jackson Turner, *The Rise of the New West* (1906) and *The Frontier in American History* (1920); Ray Allen Billington, *The Far Western Frontier* (1965); Ray Allen Billington and Martin Ridge, *Westward Expansion*, rev. ed. (1982); John A. Hawgood, *America's Western Frontier* (1967); David J. Wishart, *The Fur Trade of the American West* (1979); Frederick Merk, *History of the Westward Movement* (1978); Dale Van Every, *The Final Challenge* (1964); Julie Roy Jeffrey, *Frontier Women: The Trans-Mississippi West* (1979); Glenda Riley, *The Female Frontier* (1988); Colin Calloway, *Crown and Calumet* (1987).

CHAPTER 9 A RESURGENCE OF NATIONALISM

The Economic Revolution.   See Suggested Readings for Chapter 7. W. Elliot Brownlee, *Dynamics of Ascent* (1974); Stuart Bruchey, *The Growth of the Modern American Economy* (1975); George R. Taylor, *The Transportation Revolution* (1951); Nathan Miller, *The Enterprise of a Free People* (1962); R. E. Shaw, *Erie Water West* (1966); Harry N. Scheiber, *Ohio Canal Era* (1969); Albert Fishlow, *American Railroads and the Transformation of the Ante-Bellum Economy* (1965); E. P. Douglas, *The Coming of Age of American Business* (1971); Thomas C. Cochran and William Miller, *The Age of Enterprise* (1942); Thomas C. Cochran, *Business in American Life* (1972); Richard D. Brown, *Modernization: The Transformation of American Life, 1600–1865* (1976); Diane Lindstrom, *Economic Development in the Philadelphia Region, 1810–1850* (1978); Merritt Roe Smith, *Harpers Ferry Armory and the New Technology* (1977); David J. Jeremy, *Transatlantic Industrial Revolution: The Diffusion of Textile Technologies Between Britain and America, 1780–1830* (1981); H. J. Habbakuk, *American and British Technology in the Nineteenth Century* (1962); Nathan Rosenberg, *Technology and American Economic Growth* (1972).

Factories and the Working Class.   Arthur H. Cole, *The American Wool Manufacture*, 2 vols. (1926); Caroline Ware, *The Early New England Cotton Manufacture* (1931); Barbara M. Tucker, *Samuel Slater and the Origins of the American Textile Industry, 1790–1860* (1985); Thomas Dublin, *Women at Work* (1979); Alan Dawley, *Class and Community: The Industrial Revolution in Lynn* (1976); Alice Kessler-Harris, *Out to Work: A History of Wage-Earning Women in the United States* (1982); Mary Blewett, *Men, Women, and Work* (1988); Christine Stansell, *City of Women: Sex and Class in New York, 1789–1860* (1986); Bruce Laurie, *Working People of Philadelphia* (1980); Susan E. Hirsch, *Roots of the American Working Class: The Industrialization of Crafts in Newark, 1800–1860* (1978); Steven J. Ross, *Workers on the Edge: Work, Leisure, and Politics in Industrializing Cincinnati, 1788–1890* (1985); Sean Wilentz, *Chants Democratic: New York City and the Rise of the American Working Class, 1788–1850* (1984).

Political Affairs.   George Dangerfield, *The Awakening of American Nationalism* (1965) and *The Era of Good Feelings* (1952); Glover Moore, *The Missouri Compromise* (1953); Paul C. Nagle, *One Nation Indivisible: The Union in American Thought, 1815–1828* (1965); Glyndon Van Deusen, *The Life of Henry Clay* (1937); Harry Ammon, *James Monroe: The*

Quest for National Identity (1971); Charles M. Wiltse, *John C. Calhoun: American Nationalist* (1944); Wesley Frank Craven, *The Legend of the Founding Fathers* (1956); Shaw Livermore, *The Twilight of Federalism* (1962); Samuel F. Bemis, *John Quincy Adams and the Union* (1956); Robert V. Remini, *The Election of Andrew Jackson* (1963); Norman K. Risjord, *The Old Republicans: Southern Conservatism in the Age of Jefferson* (1965).

The Courts. Albert J. Beveridge, *The Life of John Marshall*, 4 vols. (1916–1919); Leonard Baker, *John Marshall: A Life in Law* (1974); Francis N. Stites, *John Marshall: Defender of the Constitution* (1981); Richard E. Ellis, *The Jeffersonian Crisis: Courts and Politics in the Young Republic* (1971); R. Kent Newmyer, *The Supreme Court Under Marshall and Taney* (1968); Charles G. Haines, *The Role of the Supreme Court in American Government and Politics, 1789–1835* (1970); D. O. Dewey, *Marshall Versus Jefferson: The Political Background of* Marbury v. Madison (1970); Alexander M. Bickel, *Justice Joseph Story and the Rise of the Supreme Court* (1971); James McClellan, *Joseph Story and the American Constitution* (1971).

The Monroe Doctrine. Arthur P. Whitaker, *The United States and the Independence of Latin America* (1941); Dexter Perkins, *The Monroe Doctrine* (1927) and *Hands Off: A History of the Monroe Doctrine* (1941); Ernest R. May, *The Making of the Monroe Doctrine* (1975); Samuel F. Bemis, *John Quincy Adams and the Foundations of American Foreign Policy* (1940); Bradford Perkins, *Castlereagh and Adams: England and the United States, 1812–1823* (1964); Frank Thistlethwaite, *The Anglo-American Connection in the Early Nineteenth Century* (1959).

CHAPTER 10 JACKSONIAN AMERICA

General History. Glyndon Van Deusen, *The Jacksonian Era* (1959); John Mayfield, *The New Nation, 1800–1845* (1981); James C. Curtis, *Andrew Jackson and the Search for Vindication* (1976); Edward Pessen, *Jacksonian America*, rev. ed. (1979).

Democracy. Alexis de Tocqueville, *Democracy in America*, 2 vols. (1835); Moisie Ostrogorskii, *Democracy and the Organization of Political Parties*, 2 vols. (1902); Chilton Williamson, *American Suffrage from Property to Democracy, 1760–1860* (1960); Louis Hartz, *The Liberal Tradition in America* (1955); Michael Kammen, *Spheres of Liberty: Changing Perceptions of Liberty in American Culture* (1986); Marvin E. Gettleman, *The Dorr-Rebellion* (1973); Patrick T. Conley, *Democracy in Decline* (1977); Alexander Sexton, *The Rise and Fall of the Republic: Class Politics and Mass Culture in Nineteenth-Century America* (1990).

Jacksonian Society. Edward Pessen, *Riches, Class, and Power Before the Civil War* (1973); Douglas T. Miller, *Jacksonian Aristocracy* (1967); Sean Wilentz, *Chants Democratic: New York City and the Rise of the American Working Class, 1788–1850* (1984); Mary Ryan, *Cradle of the Middle Class: The Family in Oneida County, New York, 1790–1865* (1981); Christine Stansell, *City of Women: Sex and Class in New York, 1789–1860* (1986); Nancy Hewitt, *Women's Activism and Social Change: Rochester, New York, 1822–1872* (1984); Carroll Smith-Rosenberg, *Religion and the Rise of the City* (1971).

Jacksonian Politics. Arthur M. Schlesinger, Jr., *The Age of Jackson* (1945); Marvin Meyers, *The Jacksonian Persuasion* (1960); Richard Hofstadter, *The American Political Tradition* (1948); John William Ward, *Andrew Jackson: Symbol for an Age* (1955); Lee Benson, *The Concept of Jacksonian Democracy* (1961); Leonard White, *The Jacksonians: A Study in Administrative History* (1954); Richard B. Latner, *The Presidency of Andrew Jackson: White House Politics, 1829–1837* (1979); Richard B. McCormick, *The Second American Party System: Party Formation in the Jacksonian Era* (1966); Ronald P. Formisano, *The Birth of Mass Political Parties: Michigan, 1827–1861* (1971); Harry L. Watson, *Jacksonian Politics and Community Conflict: The Emergence of the Second Party System in Cumberland County, North Carolina* (1981); C. B. Swisher, *Roger B. Taney* (1936); Morton Horwitz, *The Transformation of American Law, 1780–1860* (1977).

Andrew Jackson. Robert V. Remini, *Andrew Jackson and the Course of American Empire: 1767–1821* (1977), *Andrew Jackson and the Course of American Freedom: 1822–1832* (1981), *Andrew Jackson and the Course of American Democracy* (1984), and *Andrew Jackson* (1966); Marquis James, *Andrew Jackson*, 2 vols. (1933–1937); James Parton, *Life of Andrew Jackson*, 3 vols. (1860).

Nullification. William V. Freehling, *Prelude to Civil War: The Nullification Controversy in South Carolina* (1966) and *The Road to Disunion: I: Secessionists at Bay, 1776–1854* (1990); Charles S. Sydnor, *The Development of Southern Sectionalism 1819–1848* (1948); Merrill D. Peterson, *Olive Branch and Sword: The Compromise of 1833* (1983).

Indian Policies. Ronald N. Satz, *American Indian Policy in the Jacksonian Era* (1975); Michael Rogin, *Fathers and Children: Andrew Jackson and the Destruction of American Indians* (1975); Grant Foreman, *Indian Removal: The Emigration of the Five Civilized Tribes* (1932) and *Indians and Pioneers: The Story of the American Southwest Before 1830* (1936); Arthur H. DeRosier, Jr., *The Removal of the Choctaw Indians* (1970); Theda Perdue, *Slavery and the Evolution of Cherokee Society, 1540–1866* (1979); Daniel F. Littlefield, Jr., *Africans and Seminoles: From Removal to Emancipation* (1976) and *Africans and Creeks: From the Colonial Period to the Civil War* (1979); Thurman Wilkins, *Cherokee Tragedy* (1970); Michael D. Green, *The Politics of Indian Removal: Cherokee Government and Society in Crisis* (1982); Richard White, *The Roots of Dependency* (1983); Angie Debo, *A History of the Indians of the United States* (1970), *The Road to Disappearance: A History of the Creek Indians* (1941), and *And Still the Waters Run: The Betrayal of the Five Civilized Tribes* (1973); Wilcomb E. Washburn, *The Indian in America* (1975); William Brandon, *The Last Americans* (1974); B. W. Sheehan, *Seeds of Extinction: Jeffersonian Philanthropy and the American Indian* (1973); Francis P. Prucha, *American Indian Policy in the Formative Years* (1962); Cecil Elby, *"That Disgraceful Affair"* (1973).

The Bank War. Robert V. Remini, *Andrew Jackson and the Bank War* (1967); Bray Hammond, *Banks and Politics in America from the Revolution to the Civil War* (1957); Peter Temin, *The Jacksonian Economy* (1969); J. M. McFaul, *The Politics of Jacksonian Finance* (1972); William G. Shade, *Banks or No Banks: The Money Issue in Western Politics, 1832–1865* (1972); J. A. Wilburn, *Biddle's Bank* (1967); T. P. Govan, *Nicholas Biddle; Nationalist and Public Banker* (1959); Reginald C. McGrane, *The Panic of 1837* (1924); J. R. Sharp, *The Jacksonians Versus the Banks* (1970).

Post-Jacksonian Politics. Robert V. Remini, *Martin Van Buren and the Making of the Democratic Party* (1959); James C. Curtis, *The Fox at Bay: Martin Van Buren and the Presidency* (1970); John Niven, *Martin Van Buren: The Romantic Age of American Politics* (1983); Paul Goodman, *Toward a Christian Republic: Anti-Masonry and the Great Transition in New England, 1826–1836* (1988); E. M. Carroll, *Origins of the Whig Party* (1925); Daniel Walker Howe, *The Political Culture of the American Whigs* (1979); Thomas Brown, *Politics and Statesmanship: Essays on the American Whig Party* (1985); Claude M. Fuess, *Daniel Webster*, 2 vols. (1930); Richard N. Current, *Daniel Webster and the Rise of National Conservatism* (1955); Irving Bartlett, *Daniel Webster* (1978); Norman D. Brown, *Daniel Webster and the Politics of Availability* (1969); Sydney Nathans, *Daniel Webster and Jacksonian Democracy* (1973); Robert Dalzell, *Daniel Webster and the Trial of American Nationalism* (1973); Maurice C. Baxter, *One and Inseparable: Daniel Webster and the Union* (1984); Clement Eaton, *Henry Clay and the Art of American Politics* (1957); George R. Poage, *Henry Clay and the Whig Party* (1936); Merrill D. Peterson, *The Great Triumvirate: Webster, Clay, and Calhoun* (1987); Thomas H. O'Connor, *Lords of the Loom: The Cotton Whigs and the Coming of the Civil War* (1968); William Preston Vaughn, *The Anti-Masonic Party in the United States, 1826–1843* (1983); Oscar D. Lambert, *Presidential Politics in the United States, 1841–1844* (1936); R. G. Gunderson, *The Log Cabin Campaign* (1957); Oliver P. Chitwood, *John Tyler: Champion of the Old South* (1939); Howard Jones, *To the Webster-Ashburton Treaty* (1977); A. B. Corey, *The Crisis of 1830–1842 in Canadian-American Relations* (1941); John B. Brebner, *North Atlantic Triangle* (1945).

CHAPTER 11 THE NORTH AND THE SOUTH: DIVERGING SOCIETIES

The Northern Economy. See Suggested Readings for Chapters 7 and 9. Thomas C. Cochran, *Frontiers of Change: Early Industrialization in America* (1981); David A. Hounshell, *From the American System to Mass Production, 1800–1932: The Development of Manufacturing Technology in the United States* (1985); Paul W. Gates, *The Farmer's Age* (1960); Peter Temin, *Iron and Steel in Nineteenth-Century America* (1964); Alfred D. Chandler, Jr., *The Visible Hand: The Managerial Revolution in American Business* (1977); James Norris, *R.G. Dun & Co., 1841–1900* (1978); Joseph E. Walker, *Hopewell: A Social and Economic History of an Ironmaking Community* (1966); Robert W. Fogel, *Railroads and American Economic Growth* (1964); Carter Goodrich, *Government Promotion of Canals and Railroads, 1800–1890* (1960); John F. Stover, *The Life and Decline of the American Railroad* (1970) and *Iron Road to the West: American Railroads in the 1850s* (1978); R. L. Thompson, *Wiring a Continent* (1947).

Immigration. John Bodnar, *The Transplanted: A History of Immigrants in America* (1985); Marcus Hansen, *The Immigrant in American History* (1940) and *The Atlantic Migration, 1607–1860* (1940); Maldwyn A. Jones, *American Immigration* (1960); Oscar Handlin, *The Uprooted* (1951, rev. 1973) and *Boston's Immigrants* (1941); Charlotte Erickson, *Invisible Immigrants* (1972); Philip Taylor, *The Distant Magnet* (1971); Robert Ernst, *Immigrant Life in New York City, 1825–1863* (1949); Kathleen N. Conzen, *Immigrant Milwaukee: 1836–1860* (1976); Carl Wittke, *We Who Built America*, rev. ed.

(1964), *Refugees of Revolution: The German Forty-Eighters in America* (1952), and *The Irish in America* (1956); Hasia Diner, *Erin's Daughters in America* (1983); Harold Runblom and Hans Norman, *From Sweden to America* (1976); Theodore C. Blegen, *Norwegian Migration to America*, 2 vols. (1931–1940); Stuart C. Miller, *The Unwelcome Immigrant* (1969); Rowland T. Berthoff, *British Immigrants in Industrial America, 1790–1950* (1953); Jay P. Dolan, *The Immigrant Church: New York's Irish and German Catholics* (1975); Ray Billington, *The Protestant Crusade, 1800–1860* (1938); I. M. Leonard and R. D. Parmet, *American Nativism, 1830–1860* (1971); T. J. Curran, *Xenophobia and Immigration* (1975); Allan Nevins, *The Ordeal of the Union*, 2 vols. (1947).

Northern Labor, Society, and Culture. Susan E. Hirsch, *Roots of the American Working Class: The Industrialization of Crafts in Newark, 1800–1860* (1978); W. J. Rorabaugh, *The Craft Apprentice: From Franklin to the Machine Age* (1986); Bruce Laurie, *Working People of Philadelphia* (1980); Norman Ware, *The Industrial Worker, 1840–1860* (1924); Henry Pelling, *American Labor* (1960); Hannah Josephson, *The Golden Threads* (1949); David Thelen, *Paths of Resistance: Tradition and Dignity in Industrializing Missouri* (1986); Mary Ryan, *Cradle of the Middle Class: The Family in Oneida County, New York, 1790–1865* (1981); Christine Stansell, *City of Women: Sex and Class in New York, 1789–1860* (1986); Carroll Smith-Rosenberg, *Disorderly Conduct: Visions of Gender in Victorian America* (1985); Alan Dawley, *Class and Community: The Industrial Revolution in Lynn* (1976); John Brooke, *The Heart of the Commonwealth: Society and Political Culture in Worcester County, Massachusetts, 1713–1861* (1990); Michael Frisch, *Town into City: Springfield, Massachusetts, and the Meaning of Community, 1840–1880* (1972); Elizabeth Blackmar, *Manhattan for Rent* (1989); Peter Knights, *The Plain People of Boston, 1830–1860* (1971); Christopher Clark, *The Roots of Rural Capitalism: Western Massachusetts, 1780–1860* (1990); Don Doyle, *The Social Order of a Frontier Community: Jacksonville, Illinois, 1825–1870* (1978); Stuart Blumin, *The Urban Threshold: Growth and Change in a Nineteenth-Century Community* (1976); Sam Bass Warner, Jr., *The Urban Wilderness* (1972); Richard C. Wade, *The Urban Frontier, 1790–1830* (1957); Raymond A. Mohl, *Poverty in New York, 1783–1825* (1971); Edward Pessen, *Riches, Classes, and Power Before the Civil War* (1973); Stephan Thernstrom, *Poverty and Progress* (1964); Frank Luther Mott, *American Journalism* (1950); Glyndon Van Deusen, *Horace Greeley* (1953).

The Southern Mind. W. J. Cash, *The Mind of the South* (1941); Avery Craven, *The Growth of Southern Nationalism* (1953); James Oakes, *Slavery and Freedom: An Interpretation of the Old South* (1990); John McCardell, *The Idea of a Southern Nation* (1979); Charles S. Sydnor, *The Development of Southern Sectionalism, 1819–1848* (1948); Clement Eaton, *Freedom of Thought in the Old South* (1940) and *The Growth of Southern Nationalism, 1848–1861* (1961); William R. Taylor, *Cavalier and Yankee: The Old South and American National Character* (1961); Rollin G. Osterweis, *Romanticism and Nationalism in the Old South* (1949); John Hope Franklin, *The Militant South* (1956); Drew Gilpin Faust, *A Sacred Circle: The Dilemma of the Intellectual in the Old South* (1977) and *James Henry Hammond and the Old South: A Design for Mastery* (1982); Bertram Wyatt-Brown, *Southern Honor: Ethics and Behavior in the Old South* (1982) and *Yankee Saints and Southern Sinners* (1985); Edward L. Ayers, *Vengeance and Justice* (1984); Donald G. Mathews, *Religion in the Old South* (1977); Ann C. Loveland, *Southern Evangelicals and the Social*

Order, 1800–1860 (1980); Frank Freidel, *Francis Lieber* (1947); Don Fehrenbacher, *Constitutions and Constitutionalism in the Slaveholding South* (1989).

The Plantation Economy. Gavin Wright, *The Political Economy of the Cotton South: Households, Markets, and Wealth in the Nineteenth Century* (1978); Lewis C. Gray, *History of Agriculture in the Southern United States to 1860*, 2 vols. (1933); Ulrich B. Phillips, *Life and Labor in the Old South* (1929); R. R. Russel, *Economic Aspects of Southern Sectionalism, 1840–1861* (1924); Frank L. Owsley, *Plain Folk of the Old South* (1949); Ralph A. Wooster, *Politicians, Planters, and Plain Folk* (1975); J. William Harris, *Plain Folk and Gentry in a Slave Society* (1985); Peter Kolchin, *Unfree Labor: American Slavery and Russian Serfdom* (1987).

The Planters. Robert Manson Myers, ed., *The Children of Pride* (1972); Mary D. Robertson, ed., *Lucy Breckinridge of Grove Hill* (1979); Carol Bleser, *The Hammonds of Redcliffe* (1981); Frances Ann Kemble, *Journal of a Residence on a Georgian Plantation in 1838–1839* (1863); Eugene Genovese, *The Political Economy of Slavery* (1965) and *The World the Slaveholders Made* (1969); James Oakes, *The Ruling Race: A History of American Slaveholders* (1982); Kenneth S. Greenberg, *Masters and Statesmen: The Political Culture of American Slavery* (1985).

Southern White Women. Anne Firor Scott, *The Southern Lady* (1970); Catherine Clinton, *The Plantation Mistress: Woman's World in the Old South* (1982); Mary Boykin Chesnut, *A Diary from Dixie* (1981, ed. by C. Vann Woodward); Suzanne Lebsock, *The Free Women of Petersburg: Status and Culture in a Southern Town* (1984); Jane Turner Censer, *North Carolina Planters and Their Children, 1800–1860* (1984); Elizabeth Fox-Genovese, *Within the Plantation Household* (1988).

Slavery. Kenneth Stampp, *The Peculiar Institution* (1955); Stanley Elkins, *Slavery* (1959); Herbert Aptheker, *American Negro Slave Revolts* (1943); Melville J. Herskovits, *The Myth of the Negro Past* (1941); John Blassingame, *The Slave Community* (1973); Eugene Genovese, *Roll, Jordan, Roll: The World the Slaves Made* (1974); Herbert Gutman, *The Black Family in Slavery and Freedom* (1976); Judith Chase, *Afro-American Art and Craft* (1971); Dena Epstein, *Sinful Tunes and Spirituals* (1977); Lawrence W. Levine, *Black Culture and Black Consciousness: Afro-American Folk Thought from Slavery to Freedom* (1977); Michael P. Johnson and James L. Roark, *Black Masters* (1984); G. P. Rawick, *From Sundown to Sunup: The Making of the Black Community* (1973); Leslie Howard Owens, *This Species of Property* (1976); Robert Fogel and Stanley Engerman, *Time on the Cross*, 2 vols. (1974); Herbert Gutman, *Slavery and the Numbers Game* (1975); P. A. David et al., *Reckoning with Slavery* (1976); Barbara Jean Fields, *Slavery and Freedom on the Middle Ground* (1985); Jacqueline Jones, *Labor of Love, Labor of Sorrow* (1985); Deborah G. White, *Ar'n't I a Woman?* (1985); Robert Starobin, *Industrial Slavery in the Old South* (1970); Richard C. Wade, *Slavery in the Cities* (1964); Stephen B. Oates, *The Fires of Jubilee* (1974); Robert Starobin, *Denmark Vesey* (1970); Carl Degler, *Neither Black nor White* (1971); Joel Williamson, *New People: Miscegenation and Mulattoes in the United States* (1980); Ira Berlin, *Slaves Without Masters* (1974); Leon Litwack, *North of Slavery* (1961); Orlando Patterson, *Slavery and Social Death: A Comparative Study* (1982); David Brion Davis, *Slavery and Human Progress* (1984).

CHAPTER 12 AN AGE OF REFORMS

Antebellum Literature. Vernon L. Parrington, *The Romantic Revolution in America, 1800–1860* (1927); F. O. Matthiessen, *American Renaissance* (1941); David Reynolds, *Beneath the American Renaissance: The Subversive Imagination in the Age of Emerson and Melville* (1988); Leo Marx, *The Machine and the Garden* (1964); Henry F. May, *The Enlightenment in America* (1976); Van Wyck Brooks, *The Flowering of New England, 1815–1865* (1936); Neil Harris, *Humbug: The Art of P. T. Barnum* (1973); Mary Kelley, *The Limits of Sisterhood* (1988).

Social Philosophies and Utopias. Ann Rose, *Transcendentalism as a Social Movement* (1981); P. F. Boller, Jr., *American Transcendentalism, 1830–1860: An Intellectual Inquiry* (1974); Gay Wilson Allen, *Waldo Emerson* (1981); Arthur M. Schlesinger, Jr., *Orestes A. Brownson: A Pilgrim's Progress* (1939); Henry Steele Commager, *Theodore Parker* (1936); Richard Lebeaux, *Young Man Thoreau* (1977); Perry Miller, *The Transcendentalists* (1950) and *The Life of the Mind in America: From the Revolution to the Civil War* (1966); Arthur Bestor, *Backwoods Utopias: The Sectarian and Owenite Phases of Communitarian Socialism in America, 1663–1829* (1950); M. L. Carden, *Oneida: Utopian Community to Modern Corporation* (1971); Raymond Muncy, *Sex and Marriage in Utopian Communities* (1973); Priscilla Brewer, *Shaker Communities and Shaker Lives* (1986); R. D. Thomas, *The Man Who Would Be Perfect: John Humphrey Noyes and the Utopian Impulse* (1977); Fawn Brodie, *No Man Knows My Name: The Life of Joseph Smith* (1945); Klaus J. Hansen, *Quest for Empire* (1967); Wallace Stegner, *The Gathering of Zion* (1964).

Antebellum Reforms. Alice Felt Tyler, *Freedom's Ferment* (1944); Ronald G. Walters, *American Reformers, 1815–1860* (1978); William G. McLoughlin, *Revivals, Awakenings and Reform* (1978); Whitney R. Cross, *The Burned-Over District* (1950); Paul Johnson, *A Shopkeeper's Millennium* (1978); Timothy L. Smith, *Revivalism and Social Reform in Mid-Nineteenth Century America* (1957); William W. Sweet, *Revivalism in America* (1949); Charles A. Johnson, *The Frontier Camp Meeting* (1955); C. C. Cole, Jr., *The Social Ideas of the Northern Evangelists, 1826–1860* (1954); W. J. Rorabaugh, *The Alcoholic Republic* (1979); Ian R. Tyrrell, *Sobering Up: From Temperance to Prohibition in Antebellum America, 1800–1860* (1979); David Rothman, *The Discovery of the Asylum* (1971); Estelle Freedman, *Their Sister's Keepers: Women's Prison Reform in America, 1830–1930* (1981).

Education. Michael Katz, *The Irony of Early School Reform* (1968); Lawrence A. Cremin, *American Education: The National Experience* (1980); Stanley K. Schultz, *The Culture Factory: Boston's Public Schools, 1789–1860* (1973); Paul Monroe, *The Founding of the American Public School System* (1949); Carl Bode, *The American Lyceum* (1956); Jonathan Messerli, *Horace Mann* (1972); Robert Trennert, *Alternatives to Extinction: Federal Indian Policy and the Beginning of the Reservation System* (1975).

Feminism. Barbara J. Berg, *The Remembered Gate: Origins of American Feminism. The Woman and the City* (1977); Ellen C. Du Bois, *Feminism and Suffrage: The Emergence of an Independent Woman's Movement in America, 1848–1860* (1978); Mary Ryan, *Women in Public: Between Banners and Ballots, 1825–1880* (1990); Nancy Cott, *The Bonds of Wom-*

anhood: *"Woman's Sphere" in New England, 1780–1835* (1977); Nancy A. Hewitt, *Women's Activism and Social Change: Rochester, New York, 1822–1872* (1988); Ann Douglas, *The Feminization of American Culture* (1977); Margaret H. Bacon, *Mothers of Feminism: The Story of Quaker Women in America* (1986); Jean Fagan Yellin, *Women and Sisters: The Antislavery Feminists in American Culture* (1989); Lois Banner, *Elizabeth Cady Stanton* (1980); Kathleen Barry, *Susan B. Anthony* (1988); Kathryn K. Sklar, *Catharine Beecher: A Study in American Domesticity* (1973); William L. O'Neill, *Everyone Was Brave: The Rise and Fall of Feminism in the United States* (1970); Eleanor Flexner, *Century of Struggle*, rev. ed. (1975); Barbara Leslie Epstein, *The Politics of Domesticity: Women, Evangelism, and Temperance in Nineteenth-Century America* (1981).

Antislavery and Abolitionism. Louis Filler, *The Crusade Against Slavery* (1960); Gerald Sorin, *Abolitionism* (1972); M. L. Dillon, *The Abolitionists* (1974); Blanche G. Hersh, *Slavery of Sex: Feminist Abolitionists in America* (1978); John McKivigan, *The War Against Proslavery Religion* (1984); Alan Kraut, ed., *Crusaders and Compromisers* (1983); J. B. Stewart, *Holy Warriors* (1976); Peter F. Walker, *Moral Choices: Memory, Desire, and Imagination in Nineteenth Century Abolition* (1978); Lawrence J. Friedman, *Gregarious Saints: Self and Community in American Abolitionism* (1982); Lewis Perry and Michael Fellman, eds., *Antislavery Reconsidered: New Perspectives on the Abolitionists* (1979); Aileen Kraditor, *Means and Ends in American Abolitionism: Garrison and His Critics on Strategy and Tactics, 1834–1850* (1967); G. H. Barnes, *The Antislavery Impulse* (1933); Gerda Lerner, *The Grimké Sisters of South Carolina: Rebels Against Slavery* (1967); John L. Thomas, *The Liberator* (1963); James Brewer Stewart, *Wendell Phillips* (1987); Bertram Wyatt-Brown, *Lewis Tappan and the Evangelical War Against Slavery* (1969); Robert Abzug, *Theodore Dwight Weld* (1980); Irving Bartlett, *Wendell Phillips* (1962); Betty Fladeland, *James Gillespie Birney* (1955); Martin Duberman, ed., *The Anti-Slavery Vanguard* (1965); Benjamin Quarles, *Black Abolitionists* (1969); William H. Pease and Jane H. Pease, *They Would Be Free* (1974); Arna Bontemps, *Free at Last: The Life of Frederick Douglass* (1971); William McFeely, *Frederick Douglass* (1991); Nathan Huggins, *Slave and Citizen* (1980); Leonard Richards, *Gentlemen of Property and Standing* (1970); George Fredrickson, *The Black Image in the White Mind: The Debate on Afro-American Character and Destiny, 1817–1914* (1971).

CHAPTER 13 THE IMPENDING CRISIS

Westward Expansion. Ray Allen Billington, *Westward Expansion*, rev. ed. (1974) and *The Far Western Frontier, 1830–1860* (1956); John D. Unruh, *The Plains Across: The Overland Emigrants and the Trans-Mississippi West, 1840–1860* (1979); John M. Faragher, *Women and Men on the Overland Trail* (1979); Frederick Merk, *History of the Westward Movement* (1978), *Manifest Destiny and Mission in American History* (1963), *Fruits of Propaganda in the Tyler Administration* (1971), *Slavery and the Annexation of Texas* (1972), *The Oregon Question* (1967), and *The Monroe Doctrine and American Expansionism, 1843–1849* (1966); Albert K. Weinberg, *Manifest Destiny* (1935); William H. Goetzmann, *Exploration and Empire* (1966); Henry Nash Smith, *Virgin Land* (1950); Norman A. Graebner, *Empire of the Pacific* (1955); E. C. Barker, *Mexico and Texas, 1821–1835* (1928); William C. Binkley, *The Texas Revolution* (1952); Francis Parkman, *The Oregon Trail* (1849); R. L. Duffus, *The Santa Fe Trail* (1930); R. G. Cleland, *From Wilderness to Empire:*

A History of California, 1542–1900 (1944); R. W. Paul, *California Gold* (1947); J. S. Holliday, *The World Rushed In* (1981); O. O. Winther, *The Great Northwest*, rev. ed. (1950).

Expansion and the Mexican War. David J. Weber, *The Mexican Frontier, 1821–1846: The American Southwest Under Mexico* (1982); Charles G. Sellers, *James K. Polk: Continentalist, 1843–1846* (1966); J. S. Reeves, *American Diplomacy Under Tyler and Polk* (1907); David M. Pletcher, *The Diplomacy of Annexation: Texas, Oregon, and the Mexican War* (1973); G. M. Brack, *Mexico Views Manifest Destiny, 1821–1846* (1975); K. Jack Bauer, *The Mexican-American War, 1846–1848* (1974); John H. Schroeder, *Mr. Polk's War: American Opposition and Dissent* (1973); Otis A. Singletary, *The Mexican War* (1960); S. V. Conner and O. B. Faulk, *North America Divided* (1971); Holman Hamilton, *Zachary Taylor, Soldier of the Republic* (1941); C. W. Elliott, *Winfield Scott* (1937); Samuel F. Bemis, ed., *American Secretaries of State*, vols. 5 and 6 (1928); Basil Rauch, *American Interest in Cuba, 1848–1855* (1948); Robert E. May, *The Southern Dream of a Caribbean Empire, 1854–1861* (1973); Robert W. Johnson, *To the Halls of Montezuma: The Mexican War in the American Imagination* (1985).

The Sectional Crisis: General Studies. Allan Nevins, *The Ordeal of the Union*, 2 vols. (1947) and *The Emergence of Lincoln*, 2 vols. (1950); Michael Holt, *The Political Crisis of the 1850s* (1978); Roy F. Nichols, *The Disruption of American Democracy* (1948); Avery Craven, *The Coming of the Civil War* (1942); David Potter, *The Impending Crisis, 1848–1861* (1976); William J. Cooper, *The South and the Politics of Slavery, 1828–1856* (1978) and *Liberty and Slavery* (1983); James G. Randall and David Donald, *The Civil War and Reconstruction*, rev. ed. (1969); Richard H. Sewell, *A House Divided: Sectionalism and the Civil War, 1848–1865* (1988); James M. McPherson, *Ordeal by Fire* (1981) and *Battle Cry of Freedom* (1988).

The Compromise of 1850. Holman Hamilton, *Prologue to Conflict: The Crisis and Compromise of 1850* (1964); Chaplain W. Morrison, *Democratic Politics and Sectionalism: The Wilmot Proviso Controversy* (1973); Kinley J. Bauer, *Cotton Versus Conscience: Massachusetts Whig Politics and Southern Expansion, 1843–1858* (1967); Robert W. Johannsen, *Stephen A. Douglas* (1973); Charles M. Wiltse, *John C. Calhoun: Sectionalist, 1840–1850* (1951); Holman Hamilton, *Zachary Taylor: Soldier in the White House* (1951); Richard N. Current, *Daniel Webster and the Rise of National Conservatism* (1955); Robert F. Dalzell, Jr., *Daniel Webster and the Trial of American Nationalism, 1843–1852* (1973).

Sectional Crises in the 1850s. Kenneth Stampp, *America in 1857: A Nation on the Brink* (1990); Gerald Wolff, *The Kansas-Nebraska Bill* (1977); James C. Malin, *The Nebraska Question* (1953); Paul W. Gates, *Fifty Million Acres: Conflict over Kansas Land Policy, 1854–1890* (1954); Stephen Oates, *To Purge This Land with Blood: A Biography of John Brown* (1970); R. O. Boyer, *The Legend of John Brown* (1973); Truman Nelson, *The Old Man: John Brown at Harpers Ferry* (1973); J. C. Furnas, *The Road to Harpers Ferry* (1959); Benjamin Quarles, *Allies for Freedom* (1974); Eric Foner, *Free Soil, Free Labor, Free Men* (1970) and *Politics and Ideology in the Age of the Civil War* (1980); William E. Gienapp, *The Origins of the Republican Party, 1852–1856* (1987); David Donald, *Charles Sumner and the Coming of the Civil War* (1960); Dale Baum, *The Civil War Party System: The Case of Massachusetts, 1848–1876* (1984); William Jenkins, *Pro-Slavery Thought in the*

Old South (1935); Harvey Wish, *George Fitzhugh: Propagandist of the Old South* (1943); Don E. Fehrenbacher, *The Dred Scott Case* (1978).

The Emergence of Lincoln. Richard N. Current, *The Lincoln Nobody Knows* (1958); David Donald, *Lincoln Reconsidered* (1956); Don E. Fehrenbacher, *Prelude to Greatness: Lincoln in the 1850's* (1962); George B. Forgie, *Patricide in the House Divided* (1979).

CHAPTER 14 THE CIVIL WAR

General Studies. James M. McPherson, *Battle Cry of Freedom* (1988) and *Ordeal by Fire*, rev. ed. (1985); James G. Randall and David Donald, *The Civil War and Reconstruction*, rev. ed. (1969); Allan Nevins, *The War for the Union*, 4 vols. (1959–1971); Shelby Foote, *The Civil War: A Narrative*, 3 vols. (1958–1974); Bruce Catton, *This Hallowed Ground* (1956); Philip Shaw Paludan, *"A People's Contest": The Union and the Civil War, 1861–1865* (1988).

The Secession Crisis. Ralph A. Wooster, *The Secession Conventions of the South* (1962); David Potter, *Lincoln and His Party in the Secession Crisis* (1942); William L. Barney, *The Road to Secession* (1972) and *The Secessionist Impulse: Alabama and Mississippi in 1860* (1974); Kenneth M. Stampp, *And the War Came* (1950); Richard N. Current, *Lincoln and the First Shot* (1963); Steven A. Channing, *Crisis of Fear* (1970); Michael P. Johnson, *Toward a Patriarchal Republic* (1977).

Lincoln. Benjamin Thomas, *Abraham Lincoln* (1952); Stephen B. Oates, *With Malice Toward None* (1979); James G. Randall, *Lincoln the President*, 4 vols. (1945–1955), the final volume with Richard N. Current; Carl Sandburg, *Abraham Lincoln*, 6 vols. (1929–1939); T. Harry Williams, *Lincoln and the Radicals* (1941) and *Lincoln and His Generals* (1952); William B. Hesseltine, *Lincoln and the War Governors* (1948); Robert V. Bruce, *Lincoln and the Tools of War* (1956); Harry J. Carman and Reinhard Luthin, *Lincoln and the Patronage* (1943); LaWanda Cox, *Lincoln and Black Freedom* (1981).

Politics and Society in the North. David Donald, *Charles Sumner and the Rights of Man* (1970); Benjamin P. Thomas and Harold M. Hyman, *Stanton* (1962); Glyndon Van Deusen, *William Henry Seward* (1967); Martin Duberman, *Charles Francis Adams* (1961); James G. Randall, *Constitutional Problems Under Lincoln* (1926); Robert P. Sharkey, *Money, Class, and Party* (1959); Wood Gray, *The Hidden Civil War* (1942); Frank Klement, *The Copperheads in the Middle West* (1960); Mark Neely, Jr., *The Fate of Liberty: Abraham Lincoln and Civil Liberties* (1990); George Fredrickson, *The Inner Civil War* (1965); Daniel Aaron, *The Unwritten War* (1973); Edmund Wilson, *Patriotic Gore* (1962); John P. Bugardt, ed., *Civil War Nurse* (1980); Susan M. Reverby, *Ordered to Care: The Dilemma of American Nursing, 1850–1945* (1987); Iver Bernstein, *The New York City Draft Riots* (1990); J. Matthew Gallman, *Mastering Wartime: A Social History of Philadelphia During the Civil War* (1990).

Blacks and Emancipation. Ira Berlin, Leslie Rowland, et al., eds., *Freedom: A Documentary History of Emancipation, 1861–1867*, Series II: *The Black Military Experience* (1982); Clarence L. Mohr, *On the Threshold of Freedom: Masters and Slaves in Civil War*

Georgia (1986); Benjamin Quarles, *Lincoln and the Negro* (1962) and *The Negro in the Civil War* (1953); James M. McPherson, *The Struggle for Equality* (1964) and *The Negro's Civil War* (1965); Peter Kolchin, *First Freedom* (1972); John W. Blassingame, *Black New Orleans* (1973); Dudley T. Cornish, *The Sable Arm* (1966).

The Confederacy. Emory Thomas, *The Confederate Nation* (1979) and *The Confederate State of Richmond* (1971); Clement Eaton, *A History of the Southern Confederacy* (1954); Charles P. Roland, *The Confederacy* (1960); E. Merton Coulter, *The Confederate States of America* (1950); Clement Eaton, *Jefferson Davis* (1978); Hudson Strode, *Jefferson Davis*, 3 vols. (1955–1964); Thomas B. Alexander and Richard E. Beringer, *The Anatomy of the Confederate Congress* (1972); W. Buck Yearns, *The Confederate Congress* (1960); Emory Thomas, *The Confederacy as a Revolutionary Experience* (1971); Drew Gilpin Faust, *The Creation of Confederate Nationalism* (1988); Frank L. Owsley, *State Rights in the Confederacy* (1952); Bell I. Wiley, *The Life of Johnny Reb* (1943) and *The Plain People of the Confederacy* (1943); Paul D. Escott, *After Secession* (1978), *Slavery Remembered* (1979), and *Many Excellent People* (1985); James L. Roark, *Masters Without Slaves* (1977); Georgia Lee Tatum, *Disloyalty in the Confederacy* (1934); Ella Lonn, *Desertion During the Civil War* (1928); C. Vann Woodward, ed., *Mary Chestnut's Civil War* (1982).

Diplomacy. David P. Crook, *Diplomacy During the American Civil War* (1975) and *The North, the South, and the Powers, 1861–1865* (1974); Frank L. Owsley and Harriet Owsley, *King Cotton Diplomacy*, rev. ed. (1959); Gordon H. Warren, *Fountain of Discontent: The Trent Affair and Freedom of the Seas* (1981); Stuart L. Bernath, *Squall Across the Atlantic: American Civil War Prize Cases and Diplomacy* (1970).

Military Histories. Douglas Southall Freeman, *Robert E. Lee*, 4 vols. (1934–1935); Thomas L. Connelly, *The Marble Man* (1977); John Carpenter, *Ulysses S. Grant* (1976); Williams McFeely, *Grant* (1981); Bruce Catton, *Mr. Lincoln's Army* (1951), *Glory Road* (1952), *A Stillness at Appomattox* (1954), *America Goes to War* (1958), *Banners at Shenandoah* (1956), and *Grant Moves South* (1960); Bell Wiley, *The Life of Billy Yank* (1952); Kenneth P. Williams, *Lincoln Finds a General*, 4 vols. (1949–1952); Richard S. West, Jr., *Mr. Lincoln's Navy* (1957); C. E. MacCartney, *Mr. Lincoln's Admirals* (1956); John Niven, *Gideon Welles, Lincoln's Secretary of the Navy* (1973); William N. Still, Jr., *Iron Afloat: The Story of the Confederate Armorclads* (1971) and *Confederate Shipbuilding* (1969); T. Harry Williams, *McClellan, Sherman, and Grant* (1962) and *P. G. T. Beauregard, Napoleon in Gray* (1955); Burke Davis, *Sherman's March* (1980); Thomas L. Livermore, *Numbers and Losses in the Civil War in America* (1957); Herman Hattaway and Archer Jones, *How the North Won* (1983); Archer Jones et al., *Why the South Lost the Civil War* (1986).

CHAPTER 15 RECONSTRUCTING THE NATION

General Studies. Eric Foner, *Reconstruction: America's Unfinished Revolution, 1863–1877* (1988); Kenneth Stampp, *The Era of Reconstruction* (1965); John Hope Franklin, *Reconstruction After the Civil War* (1961); William A. Dunning, *Reconstruction, Political and Economic, 1865–1877* (1907); W. E. B. Du Bois, *Black Reconstruction* (1935); E. Merton Coulter, *The South During Reconstruction* (1947); Rembert Patrick, *The Reconstruction of the Nation* (1967).

Early Reconstruction. Herman Belz, *Reconstructing the Union* (1969); William B. Hesseltine, *Lincoln's Plan of Reconstruction* (1960); Willie Lee Rose, *Rehearsal for Reconstruction: The Port Royal Experiment* (1964); Louis S. Gerteis, *From Contraband to Freedman* (1973); Richard H. Abbott, *The First Southern Strategy* (1986).

Congressional Reconstruction. William R. Brock, *An American Crisis* (1963); Howard K. Beale, *The Critical Year: A Study of Andrew Johnson and Reconstruction* (1930); Eric McKitrick, *Andrew Johnson and Reconstruction* (1960); Hans Trefousse, *Andrew Johnson* (1989); Michael Les Benedict, *A Compromise of Principle: Congressional Republicans and Reconstruction, 1863–1869* and *The Impeachment and Trial of Andrew Johnson* (1973); Hans L. Trefousse, *The Radical Republicans* (1963) and *The Impeachment of a President* (1975); David Donald, *The Politics of Reconstruction* (1965); La Wanda Cox and John H. Cox, *Politics, Principles, and Prejudice, 1865–1867* (1963); Richard N. Current, *Old Thad Stevens* (1942); Fawn Brodie, *Thaddeus Stevens* (1959); David Donald, *Charles Sumner and the Rights of Man* (1970); Harold Hyman, *A More Perfect Union* (1973); Stanley Kutler, *The Judicial Power and Reconstruction Politics* (1968); Mark W. Summers, *Railroads, Reconstruction, and the Gospel of Prosperity* (1984); Charles Fairman, *Reconstruction and Reunion* (1971); Herman Belz, *A New Birth of Freedom* (1976) and *Emancipation and Equal Rights* (1978); William Gillette, *The Right to Vote* (1965).

The South in Reconstruction. Dan T. Carter, *When the War Was Over: The Failure of Self-Reconstruction in the South, 1865–1867* (1985); Michael Perman, *Reunion Without Compromise* (1973) and *The Road to Redemption: Southern Politics, 1869–1879* (1984); Joel G. Taylor, *Louisiana Reconstructed* (1974); Vernon Wharton, *The Negro in Mississippi, 1865–1890* (1965); Peyton McCrary, *Abraham Lincoln and Reconstruction* (1978); Joel Williamson, *After Slavery: The Negro in South Carolina During Reconstruction* (1965); Thomas Holt, *Black over White* (1977); Roberta Alexander, *North Carolina Faces the Freedmen: Race Relations During Presidential Reconstruction, 1865–1867* (1985); C. Peter Ripley, *Slaves and Freedmen in Civil War Louisiana* (1976); Barbara Fields, *Slavery and Freedom on the Middle Ground* (1985); Michael Wayne, *The Reshaping of Plantation Society: The Natchez District* (1983); William Gillette, *Retreat from Reconstruction* (1980); James D. Anderson, *The Education of Blacks in the South* (1989); Roger Ransom and Richard Sutch, *One Kind of Freedom* (1977); Robert Higgs, *Competition and Coercion* (1977); Crandall A. Shifflett, *Patronage and Poverty in the Tobacco South: Louisa County, Virginia 1860–1900* (1982); Leon Litwack, *Been in the Storm So Long* (1979); Eric Foner, *Nothing but Freedom: Emancipation and Its Legacy* (1983); Peter Kolchin, *First Freedom* (1972); Allen Trelease, *White Terror* (1967); William S. McFeely, *Yankee Stepfather: General O. O. Howard and the Freedmen* (1968); George Bentley, *A History of the Freedmen's Bureau* (1955); Otto Olsen, *Carpetbagger's Crusade: Albion Winegar Tourgée* (1965); L. N. Powell, *New Masters: Northern Planters During the Civil War and Reconstruction* (1980); William Harris, *Day of the Carpetbagger* (1979); Elizabeth Jacoway, *Yankee Missionaries in the South* (1979); Richard N. Current, *Those Terrible Carpetbaggers* (1988); William C. Harris, *The Day of the Carpetbagger: Republican Reconstruction in Mississippi, 1867–1875* (1979); Sarah Wiggins, *The Scalawag in Alabama Politics, 1865–1881* (1977); Jacqueline Jones, *Soldiers of Light and Love* (1980) and *Labor of Love, Labor of Sorrow: Black Women, Work, and the Family from Slavery to the Present* (1985); James Sefton, *The United States Army and Reconstruction* (1967).

The Grant Administration. Williams McFeely, *Grant* (1981); Margaret S. Thompson, *The "Spider Web": Congress and Lobbying in the Age of Grant* (1985); Allan Nevins, *Hamilton Fish* (1936); William B. Hesseltine, *U. S. Grant, Politician* (1935); David Loth, *Public Plunder* (1938); John G. Sproat, *"The Best Men"* (1968); Ari Hoogenboom, *Outlawing the Spoils* (1961); Irwin Unger, *The Greenback Era* (1964); C. Vann Woodward, *Reunion and Reaction* (1951); K. I. Polakoff, *The Politics of Inertia* (1973); Edwin C. Rozwenc, ed., *Reconstruction in the South*, rev. ed. (1952).

CHAPTER 16 THE NEW SOUTH AND THE FAR WEST

The New South. C. Vann Woodward, *Origins of the New South* (1951), *The Burden of Southern History* (rev. 1968), *American Counterpoint* (1971), *Thinking Back* (1986), and *The Future of the Past* (1989); Jonathan Wiener, *Social Origins of the New South: Alabama, 1860–1885* (1978); Paul Buck, *The Road to Reunion* (1937); Paul Gaston, *The New South Creed* (1970); W. J. Cash, *The Mind of the South* (1941); Orville Vernon Burton, *In My Father's House* (1985); Orville Vernon Burton and Robert C. McMath, Jr., eds., *Toward a New South?* (1982); J. Morgan Kousser and James M. McPherson, eds., *Region, Race, and Reconstruction* (1982).

Southern Politics. C. Vann Woodward, *Reunion and Reaction* (1951) and *Tom Watson: Agrarian Rebel* (1938); Stanley P. Hirshson, *Farewell to the Bloody Shirt: Northern Republicans and the Southern Negro* (1962); Kenneth E. Davison, *The Presidency of Rutherford B. Hayes* (1972); Vincent P. DeSantis, *Republicans Face the Southern Question: The New Departure Years, 1877–1897* (1959); J. Morgan Kousser, *The Shaping of Southern Politics: Suffrage Restriction and the Establishment of the One-Party South, 1880–1910* (1974); Paul Lewinson, *Race, Class, and Party* (1932); V. O. Key, Jr., *Southern Politics and the Nation* (1949); Francis B. Simkins, *Pitchfork Ben Tillman* (1944); Joseph F. Wall, *Henry Watterson: Reconstructed Rebel* (1956); Sheldon Hackney, *Populism to Progressivism in Alabama* (1959); David Potter, *The South and the Concurrent Majority* (1972); Carl Degler, *The Other South: Southern Dissenters in the Nineteenth Century* (1974).

Race, Economics, and Social Structure. Gavin Wright, *Old South, New South* (1986); Melvin Greenhut and W. Tate Whitman, eds., *Essays in Southern Economic Development* (1964); Jacquelyn Dowd Hall et al., *Like a Family: The Making of a Southern Cotton Mill World* (1987); David Carlton, *Mill and Town in South Carolina, 1880–1920* (1982); Don Doyle, *New Men, New Cities, New South: Atlanta, Nashville, Charleston, Mobile, 1860–1910* (1990); Melton A. McLaurin, *Paternalism and Protest: Southern Cotton Mill Workers and Organized Labor* (1971); Altina L. Waller, *Feud: Hatfields, McCoys, and Social Changes: Appalachia, 1860–1900* (1988); Steven Hahn, *The Roots of Southern Populism: Yeoman Farmers and the Transformation of the Georgia Upcountry* (1983); Steven Hahn and Jonathan Prude, eds., *The Countryside in the Age of Capitalist Transformation* (1985); Roger Ransom and Richard Sutch, *One Kind of Freedom* (1977); C. Vann Woodward, *The Strange Career of Jim Crow* (rev. 1974); Howard Rabinowitz, *Race Relations in the Urban South, 1865–1890* (1978); Cynthia Neverdon-Morton, *Afro-American Women of the South and the Advancement of the Race, 1895–1925* (1989); James M. McPherson, *The Abolitionist*

Legacy: From Reconstruction to the NAACP (1975); Robert Higgs, *Competition and Coercion: Blacks in the American Economy, 1865–1914* (1977); Joel Williamson, *After Slavery* (1965), *The Crucible of Race: Black-White Relations in the American South Since Emancipation* (1985), and *A Rage for Order* (1986), an abridgment of *The Crucible of Race;* Neil McMillen, *Dark Journey: Black Mississippians in the Age of Jim Crow* (1989); Louis R. Harlan, *Booker T. Washington: The Making of a Black Leader, 1856–1901* (1972) and *Booker T. Washington: The Wizard of Tuskegee: 1901–1915* (1983); August Meier, *Negro Thought in America* (1963); Francis Broderick, *W. E. B. DuBois* (1959); Elliott M. Rudwick, *W. E. B. DuBois: Propagandist of Negro Protest* (rev. 1969).

The Far West.   Ray Allen Billington and Martin Ridge, *Westward Expansion*, rev. ed. (1982); Robert V. Hine, *The American West*, 2nd ed. (1984); Frederick Merk, *History of the Westward Movement* (1978); Richard White, *It's Your Misfortune and None of My Own: A New History of the American West* (1991); Patricia Limerick, *The Legacy of Conquest: The Unbroken Past of the American West* (1987); Richard Slotkin, *The Fatal Environment: The Myth of the Frontier in the Age of Industrialization* (1985); Rodman W. Paul and Richard W. Etulain, *The Frontier and the American West* (1977); Thomas D. Clark, *Frontier America* (rev. 1969); Howard R. Lamar, *The Far Southwest, 1846–1912* (1966); Henry Nash Smith, *Virgin Land* (1950); Frederick Jackson Turner, *The Frontier in American History* (1920); Ray A. Billington, *Frederick Jackson Turner* (1973).

Miners and Cattlemen.   Rodman W. Paul, *Mining Frontiers of the Far West, 1848–1880* (1963) and *The Far West and the Great Plains in Transition, 1859–1900* (1988); William S. Greever, *Bonanza West: Western Mining Rushes* (1963); Duane A. Smith, *Rocky Mountain Mining Camps* (1967); Lewis Atherton, *The Cattle Kings* (1961); Ernest E. Osgood, *The Day of the Cattleman* (1929); Edward E. Dale, *The Range Cattle Industry*, rev. ed. (1969); J. M. Skaggs, *The Cattle Trailing Industry* (1973); Robert K. Dykstra, *The Cattle Towns* (1968); Andy Adams, *The Log of a Cowboy* (1927); Joe B. Frantz and Julian Choate, *The American Cowboy: The Myth and the Reality* (1955); L. Steckmesser, *The Western Hero in History and Legend* (1965); Odie B. Faulk, *Tombstone: Myth and Reality* (1972); Earl Pomeroy, *The Pacific Slope* (1965); Gunther Barth, *Instant Cities* (1975).

Indians.   Wilcomb E. Washburn, *The Indian in America* (1975) and *Red Man's Land/White Man's Law* (1971); Ralph K. Andrist, *The Long Death: The Last Days of the Plains Indians* (1964); Francis P. Prucha, *American Indian Policy in Crisis* (1976) and *The Great White Father: The United States Government and the American Indians* (1984); William T. Hagan, *The Indian Rights Association: The Herbert Welsh Years, 1882–1904* (1985); Robert M. Utley, *Last Days of the Sioux Nation* (1963), *Frontiersmen in Blue: The United States Army and the Indian, 1848–1865* (1967), *Frontier Regulars: The United States Army and the Indian* (1973), and *The Indian Frontier of the American West, 1846–1890* (1984); Dee Brown, *Bury My Heart at Wounded Knee: An Indian History of the American West* (1970); Thomas W. Dunlay, *Wolves for the Blue Soldiers* (1982); Margaret Coel, *Chief Left Hand: Southern Arapaho* (1981); Loretta Fowler, *Arapahoe Politics, 1851–1978: Symbols in Crisis of Authority* (1982); John Powell, *People of the Sacred Mountain: A History of the Northern Cheyenne Chiefs and Warrior Societies, 1830–1879*, 2 vols. (1981); Angie Debo, *Geronimo* (1976); Mari Sandoz, *Crazy Horse* (1961); James C. Olson, *Red Cloud and the Sioux Problem* (1965); Donald J. Berthrong, *The Southern Cheyennes* (1963); Frederick E. Hoxie, *A Final Promise: The Campaign to Assimilate the*

Indians, 1880–1920 (1984); Robert Mardock, *Reformers and the American Indian* (1971); Robert F. Berkhofer, Jr., *The White Man's Indian* (1978); Richard White, *The Roots of Dependency* (1983).

Western Women. Julie Jeffrey, *Frontier Women: The Trans-Mississippi West, 1840–1880* (1979); Sandra L. Myres, *Westering Women and the Frontier Experience, 1880–1915* (1982); Polly Welts Kaufman, *Women Teachers on the Frontier* (1984); Joanna L. Stratton, *Pioneer Women: Voices from the Kansas Frontier* (1981); John Mack Faragher, *Women and Men on the Overland Trail* (1979); Glenda Riley, *Women and Indians on the Frontier, 1825–1915* (1984) and *The Female Frontier* (1988); Susan Armitage and Elizabeth Jameson, eds., *The Women's West* (1987); Ruth Moynihan, *Rebel for Rights: Abigail Scott Dunaway* (1983).

Western Agriculture. Walter Prescott Webb, *The Great Plains* (1931); Fred A. Shannon, *The Farmer's Last Frontier, 1860–1897* (1945); Gilbert C. Fite, *The Farmer's Frontier* (1966); Paul W. Gates, *History of Public Land Development* (1968); Everett Dick, *The Sod-House Frontier* (1937); Allan Bogue, *From Prairie to Corn Belt* (1963); John Mack Faragher, *Sugar Creek: Life on the Illinois Prairie* (1986). See also Suggested Readings for Chapter 19.

CHAPTER 17 INDUSTRIAL SUPREMACY

General Histories. John A. Garraty, *The New Commonwealth* (1968); Edward C. Kirkland, *Industry Comes of Age: Business, Labor, and Public Policy, 1860–1897* (1961); Samuel P. Hays, *The Response to Industrialism, 1885–1914* (1957); Ray Ginger, *The Age of Excess* (1963); Carl Degler, *The Age of the Economic Revolution* (1977); Daniel Boorstin, *The Americans: The Democratic Experience* (1973); Thomas C. Cochran and William Miller, *The Age of Enterprise* (1942); Robert Higgs, *The Transformation of the American Economy, 1865–1914* (1971); Robert Wiebe, *The Search for Order, 1877–1920* (1968).

Technology. Roger Burlingame, *Engines of Democracy: Inventions and Society in Mature America* (1940) and *Henry Ford* (1957); Lewis Mumford, *Technics and Civilization* (1934); George Daniels, *Science and Society in America* (1971); Nathan Rosenberg, *Technology and American Economic Growth* (1972); Elting E. Morison, *Men, Machines, and Modern Times* (1966); Judith McGaw, *Most Wonderful Machine: Mechanization and Social Change in Berkshire Paper Making, 1801–1885* (1988); Robert W. Bruce, *Bell* (1973); Frank E. Hill, *Ford* (1954); Allan Nevins, *Ford*, 3 vols. (1954–1962); Peter Temin, *Steel in Nineteenth Century America* (1964); Frederick A. White, *American Industrial Research Laboratories* (1961); Robert Conot, *A Streak of Luck* (1979); Richard N. Current, *The Typewriter and the Men Who Made It* (1954).

Railroads. George R. Taylor and I. D. Neu, *The American Railroad Network, 1861–1890* (1956); John F. Stover, *The Life and Decline of the American Railroad* (1970) and *The Railroads of the South, 1865–1900* (1955); Richard C. Overton, *Burlington West* (1941) and *Gulf to Rockies* (1953); Edward C. Kirkland, *Men, Cities, and Transportation*, 2 vols. (1948); Thomas C. Cochran, *Railroad Leaders* (1953); Edward G. Campbell, *The Reorganization of the American Railroad System* (1938); Gabriel Kolko, *Railroads and Regulation, 1877–*

1916 (1965); Lee Benson, *Merchants, Farmers, and Railroads* (1955); George H. Miller, *Railroads and the Granger Laws* (1971); Robert Fogel, *Railroads and American Economic Growth* (1964); Anthony F. C. Wallace, *St. Clair: A Nineteenth-Century Coal Town's Experience with a Disaster-Prone Industry* (1987).

The Corporation. Alfred D. Chandler, Jr., *Strategy and Structure: Chapters in the History of the American Industrial Enterprise* (1962), *Pierre S. DuPont and the Making of the Modern Corporation* (1971), *The Visible Hand: The Managerial Revolution in American Business* (1977), and *Scale and Scope: The Dynamics of Industrial Capitalism* (1990); Glenn Porter, *The Rise of Big Business* (1973); Glenn Porter and Harold C. Livesay, *Merchants and Manufacturers* (1971); Olivier Zunz, *Making America Corporate, 1870–1920* (1990); Norma R. Lamoreaux, *The Great Merger Movement in American Business, 1895–1904* (1985); Matthew Josephson, *The Robber Barons* (1934); Maury Klein, *The Life and Legend of Jay Gould* (1986); Harold C. Livesay, *Andrew Carnegie and the Rise of Big Business* (1975); Allan Nevins, *Study in Power: John D. Rockefeller*, 2 vols. (1953); David F. Hawkes, *John D.: The Founding Father of the Rockefellers* (1980); Joseph Wall, *Andrew Carnegie* (1970); Bernard Weisberger, *The Dream Maker* (1979).

Ideologies. Edward C. Kirkland, *Dream and Thought in the Business Community, 1860–1900* (1956); Sidney Fine, *Laissez Faire and the General Welfare State: A Study of Conflict in American Thought, 1865–1901* (1956); Irvin G. Wylie, *The Self-Made Man in America* (1954); Daniel T. Rodgers, *The Work Ethic in Industrial America, 1850–1920* (1978); David Thelen, *Paths of Resistance: Tradition and Dignity in Industrializing Missouri* (1986); Louis Galambos, *The Public Image of Big Business in America, 1880–1940* (1975); Richard Hofstadter, *Social Darwinism in American Thought*, rev. ed. (1955); Robert G. McCloskey, *American Conservatism in the Age of Enterprise* (1951); Samuel Chugerman, *Lester F. Ward: The American Aristotle* (1939); Arthur E. Morgan, *Edward Bellamy* (1944); Charles A. Baker, *Henry George* (1955); John L. Thomas, *Alternative America: Henry George, Edward Bellamy, Henry Demarest Lloyd, and the Adversary Tradition* (1983); T. J. Jackson Lears, *No Place of Grace: Antimodernism and the Transformation of American Culture, 1880–1920* (1981).

Labor. Melvyn Dubofsky, *Industrialism and the American Worker, 1865–1920* (1975); Henry Pelling, *American Labor* (1960); Herbert G. Gutman, *Work, Culture, and Society in Industrializing America* (1976); David Montgomery, *Beyond Equality* (1975), *Workers' Control in America: Studies in the History of Work, Technology, and Labor Struggles* (1979), and *The Fall of the House of Labor* (1987); Richard J. Oestreicher, *Solidarity and Fragmentation: Working People and Class Consciousness: Detroit, 1875–1900* (1986); Brian Greenberg, *Worker and Community: Response to Industrialization in a Nineteenth-Century American City, Albany, New York, 1850–1884* (1985); Daniel Nelson, *Managers and Workers: Origins of the New Factory System in the United States, 1880–1920* (1975); Stuart Kaufman, *Samuel Gompers and the Origins of the American Federation of Labor* (1978); Philip Taft, *The A.F. of L. in the Time of Gompers*, 2 vols. (1957–1959); Samuel Gompers, *Seventy Years of Life and Labor*, 2 vols. (1975); Stanley Buder, *Pullman* (1967); Henry David, *The Haymarket Affair* (1936); P. K. Edwards, *Strikes in the United States, 1881–1974* (1981); Sheldon Stromquist, *A Generation of Boomers: The Pattern of Railroad Labor Conflict in Nineteenth-Century America* (1987); Steven J. Ross, *Workers on the Edge: Work, Leisure,* *and Politics in Industrializing Cincinnati, 1788–1890* (1985); Roy Rosenzweig, *"Eight Hours for What We Will": Workers and Leisure in an Industrial City, 1870–1920* (1983); Alexander Keyssar, *Out of Work: The First Century of Unemployment in Massachusetts* (1986).

Women.   Susan E. Kennedy, *If All We Did Was to Weep at Home* (1979); Barbara Wertheimer, *We Were There: The Story of Working Women in America* (1977); Patricia Cooper, *Once a Cigar Maker: Men, Women, and Work Culture in American Cigar Factories, 1900–1919* (1987); Mary Blewett, *Men, Women, and Work Culture: Class, Gender, and Protest in the New England Shoe Industry* (1988); Tamara Hareven, *Family Time and Industrial Time: The Relationship Between the Family and Work in a New England Industrial Community* (1982); Alice Kessler-Harris, *Out to Work: A History of Wage-Earning Women in the United States* (1982); Susan Levine, *Labor's True Women: Carpet Weavers, Industrialization, and Labor Reform in the Gilded Age* (1984).

The Left.   J. H. M. Laslett, *Labor and the Left* (1970); Nick Salvatore, *Eugene V. Debs: Citizen and Socialist* (1982); Mari Jo Buhle, *Women and American Socialism, 1870–1920* (1981); Melvyn Dubofsky, *We Shall Be All: A History of the Industrial Workers of the World* (1969); Gerald N. Grob, *Workers and Utopia* (1961).

CHAPTER 18 THE AGE OF THE CITY

General Histories.   Howard Chudacoff, *The Evolution of American Urban Society*, rev. ed. (1981); Blake McKelvey, *The Urbanization of America* (1963); Constance M. Green, *The Rise of Urban America* (1965); Charles N. Glaab and Andrew T. Brown, *A History of Urban America* (1967); Arthur M. Schlesinger, *The Rise of the City, 1878–1898* (1933); Sam Bass Warner, Jr., *The Urban Wilderness* (1972) and *Streetcar Suburbs* (1962); Jon C. Teaford, *City and Suburb: The Political Fragmentation of Urban America* (1979) and *The Twentieth-Century American City: Problem, Promise, and Reality* (1986); Lewis Mumford, *The Culture of the Cities* (1938) and *The City in History* (1961).

Mobility and Race.   Stephan Thernstrom, *Poverty and Progress* (1964) and *The Other Bostonians* (1973); Michael Frisch, *Town into City* (1972); Richard Sennett, *Families Against the City* (1970); Clyde Griffen and Sally Griffen, *Natives and Newcomers* (1977); Howard Chudacoff, *Mobile Americans* (1972); Stephan Thernstrom and Richard Sennett, eds., *Nineteenth Century Cities* (1969); Gilbert Osofsky, *Harlem: The Making of a Ghetto* (1966); Allan H. Spear, *Black Chicago* (1967); Kenneth L. Kusmer, *A Ghetto Takes Shape* (1976); David M. Katzman, *Before the Ghetto* (1966); Olivier Zunz, *The Changing Face of Inequality: Urbanization, Industrial Development, and Immigrants in Detroit, 1880–1920* (1982).

Immigration.   John Bodnar, *The Transplanted: A History of Immigrants in America* (1985) and *Immigration and Industrialization* (1977); Oscar Handlin, *The Uprooted*, rev. ed. (1973); Thomas Kessner, *The Golden Door: Italian and Jewish Immigrant Mobility* (1977); Josef Barton, *Peasants and Strangers: Italians, Rumanians, and Slovaks in an American City* (1975); Virginia Yans-McLaughlin, *Family and Community: Italian Immigrants in Buffalo,*

1880–1930 (1977); Philip Taylor, *The Distant Magnet: European Emigration to the U.S.A.* (1971); Marcus Hansen, *The Immigrant in American History* (1940); Maldwyn A. Jones, *American Immigration* (1960); David Ward, *Cities and Immigrants* (1965); Barbara Solomon, *Ancestors and Immigrants* (1965); Elizabeth Ewen, *Immigrant Women in the Land of Dollars: Life and Culture on the Lower East Side, 1890–1925* (1985); Ewa Morawska, *For Bread and Butter: The Life-Worlds of East Central Europeans in Johnstown, Pennsylvania, 1890–1940* (1985); Jack Chen, *The Chinese of America* (1980); Francis L. K. Hsu, *The Challenge of the American Dream: The Chinese in the United States* (1971); Moses Rischin, *The Promised City: New York's Jews* (1962); Humbert S. Nelli, *The Italians of Chicago* (1970); John W. Briggs, *An Italian Passage* (1978); John B. Duff, *The Irish in the United States* (1971); Mario T. Garcia, *Desert Immigrants: The Mexicans of El Paso, 1880–1920* (1981); Matt S. Maier and Feliciano Rivera, *The Chicanos: A History of Mexican-Americans* (1972); Harry Kitano, *Japanese-Americans: The Evolution of a Subculture* (1969); Victor Greene, *For God and Country: The Rise of Polish and Lithuanian Ethnic Consciousness in America* (1975); Edward R. Kantowicz, *Polish-American Politics in Chicago* (1975); Nathan Glazer and Daniel P. Moynihan, *Beyond the Melting Pot* (1963); Leonard Dinnerstein and David Reimers, *Ethnic Americans: A History of Immigration and Assimilation* (1975); Milton M. Gordon, *Assimilation in American Life* (1964); Thomas Sowell, *Ethnic America* (1981); Robert D. Cross, *The Church and the City* (1967); John Higham, *Strangers in the Land* (1955) and *Send These to Me* (1975).

Urban Poverty and Reform.   Robert H. Bremner, *From the Depths* (1956); James T. Patterson, *America's Struggle Against Poverty* (1981); Thomas L. Philpott, *The Slum and the Ghetto* (1978); Jacob Riis, *How the Other Half Lives* (1890), *Children of the Poor* (1892), and *The Battle with the Slum* (1902); Allen F. Davis, *Spearheads for Reform* (1967); Marvin Lazerson, *Origins of the Urban School* (1971); Stephan F. Brumberg, *Going to America, Going to School* (1986); Selwyn K. Troen, *The Public and the Schools* (1975); David B. Tyack, *The One Best System: A History of American Urban Education* (1974); Barbara Gutmann Rosencrantz, *Public Health and the State* (1972); James H. Cassedy, *Charles V. Chapin and the Public Health Movement* (1962); James F. Richardson, *The New York Police* (1970).

Urban Politics.   John M. Allswang, *Bosses, Machines and Urban Voters* (1977); Alexander B. Callow, *The Tweed Ring* (1966); Seymour Mandelbaum, *Boss Tweed's New York* (1965); Lyle Dorsett, *The Pendergast Machine* (1968); Zane Miller, *Boss Cox's Cincinnati* (1968); John Sproat, *The Best Men* (1968).

Social Thought and Urban Culture.   Stuart Blumin, *The Emergence of the Middle Class: Social Experience in the American City, 1760–1900* (1989); Lawrence Levine, *Highbrow/Lowbrow: The Emergence of a Cultural Hierarchy in America* (1988); Morton White, *Social Thought in America* (1949); D. W. Marcell, *Progress and Pragmatism* (1974); Charles Forcey, *The Crossroads of Liberalism* (1961); Lawrence Cremin, *The Transformation of the School* (1961); Frank Luther Mott, *American Journalism*, rev. ed. (1962); Larzer Ziff, *The American 1890s: Life and Times of a Lost Generation* (1966); Jay Martin, *Harvests of Change* (1967); Susan Porter Benson, *Counter Cultures: Saleswomen, Managers, and Customers in American Department Stores, 1890–1940* (1986); Godfrey M. Lebhar, *Chain Stores in America* (1962); John F. Kasson, *Amusing the Million: Coney Island at the Turn of the*

Century (1978) and *Rudeness and Civility: Manners in Nineteenth-Century Urban America* (1990); Kathy Peiss, *Cheap Amusements: Working Women and Leisure in Turn-of-the-Century New York* (1986); Marc Carnes, *Secret Ritual and Manhood in Victorian America* (1989); Gunther Barth, *City People* (1980); Allen Guttmann, *A Whole New Ball Game: An Interpretation of American Sports* (1988); Donald R. Mrozek, *Sport and American Mentality, 1880–1910* (1983); Harvey Green, *Fit for America: Fitness, Sport, and American Society* (1986); John A. Lucas and Ronald Smith, *Saga of American Sport* (1978); Dale Somers, *The Rise of Sports in New Orleans* (1972); Eliot Gorn, *The Manly Art: Bare-Knuckle Prize Fighting in America* (1986); Lewis Mumford, *The Brown Decades* (1931); T. J. Jackson Lears, *No Place of Grace: Antimodernism and the Transformation of American Culture, 1880–1920* (1981); T. J. Jackson Lears and Richard Wightman Fox, eds., *The Culture of Consumption* (1983); Christopher Tunnard and H. H. Reed, *American Skyline* (1955).

CHAPTER 19 FROM STALEMATE TO CRISIS

General Histories. Nell Irvin Painter, *Standing at Armageddon: The United States, 1877–1919* (1987); R. Hal Williams, *Years of Decision: American Politics in the 1890s* (1978); John H. Dobson, *Politics in the Gilded Age* (1972); John A. Garraty, *The New Commonwealth* (1969); Harold U. Faulkner, *Politics, Reform, and Expansion* (1959); Samuel P. Hays, *The Response to Industrialism, 1885–1914* (1957); Robert Wiebe, *The Search for Order, 1877–1920* (1967); Sean Denis Cashman, *America and the Gilded Age* (1984); Alan Trachtenberg, *The Intercorporation of America: Culture and Society in the Gilded Age* (1982).

Politics, Reform, and the States. Morton Keller, *Affairs of State* (1977); Stephen Skowronek, *Building a New American State: The Expansion of National Administrative Capacities, 1877–1920* (1982); Martin J. Sklar, *The Corporate Reconstruction of American Capitalism, 1890–1916* (1988); Matthew Josephson, *The Politicos* (1963); David J. Rothman, *Politics and Power: The United States Senate, 1869–1901* (1966); Robert D. Marcus, *Grand Old Party* (1971); H. Wayne Morgan, *From Hayes to McKinley* (1969); Leonard D. White, *The Republican Era* (1958); Ari Hoogenboom, *Outlawing the Spoils* (1961) and *The Presidency of Rutherford B. Hayes* (1988); Walter T. K. Nugent, *Money and American Society* (1968); Allen Weinstein, *Prelude to Populism* (1970); Irwin Unger, *The Greenback Era* (1964); John Sproat, *"The Best Men"* (1968); Geoffrey Blodgett, *The Gentle Reformers* (1966); James Bryce, *The American Commonwealth*, 2 vols. (1888); Paul Kleppner, *The Cross of Culture: A Social Analysis of Midwestern Politics, 1850–1900* (1970) and *The Third Electoral System, 1853–1892* (1979); Richard Jensen, *The Winning of the Midwest: Social and Political Conflict, 1888–1896* (1971); Ruth Bourdin, *Women and Temperance: The Quest for Power and Liberty, 1873–1900* (1980); Michael E. McGerr, *The Decline of Popular Politics* (1986).

Party Leaders. Harry Barnard, *Rutherford B. Hayes and His America* (1954); Kenneth Davison, *The Presidency of Rutherford B. Hayes* (1972); Allan Peskin, *Garfield* (1978); Margaret Leech and Harry J. Brown, *The Garfield Orbit* (1978); Thomas C. Reeves, *Gentleman Boss: The Life of Chester Alan Arthur* (1975); David Jordan, *Roscoe Conkling of New York* (1971); Allan Nevins, *Grover Cleveland: A Study in Courage* (1933); Horace Samuel Merrill, *Bourbon Leader: Grover Cleveland and the Democractic Party* (1957); Harry

J. Sievers, *Benjamin Harrison*, 3 vols. (1952–1968); H. Wayne Morgan, *William McKinley and His America* (1963); Lewis L. Gould, *The Presidency of William McKinley* (1981); Margaret Leech, *In the Days of McKinley* (1959); Herbert Croly, *Marcus Alonzo Hanna* (1912); Nick Salvatore, *Eugene V. Debs: Citizen and Socialist* (1982).

The Depression. Samuel McSeveney, *The Politics of Depression* (1972); Donald McMurray, *Coxey's Army* (1929); Carlos A. Schwantes, *Coxey's Army* (1955); Ray Ginger, *The Bending Cross* (1949); Almot Lindsey, *The Pullman Strike* (1942); Ray Ginger, *Altgeld's America* (1958).

Populism. John D. Hicks, *The Populist Revolt* (1931); Lawrence Goodwyn, *Democratic Promise* (1976) and *The Populist Moment* (1978), an abridgement of *Democratic Promise;* Norman Pollack, *The Populist Response to Industrial America* (1962) and *The Just Polity: Populism, Law, and Human Welfare* (1987); Allan Weinstein, *Prelude to Populism: Origins of the Silver Issue* (1970); Richard Hofstadter, *The Age of Reform* (1954); Sheldon Hackney, *Populism to Progressivism in Alabama* (1969); C. Vann Woodward, *Origins of the New South* (1972); Steven Hahn, *The Roots of Southern Populism* (1983); Robert McMath, *Populist Vanguard* (1975); Bruce Palmer, *Man over Money* (1980); Walter T. K. Nugent, *The Tolerant Populists* (1960); Theodore Saloutos, *Farmer Movements in the South, 1865–1933* (1960); Fred Shannon, *The Farmer's Last Frontier* (1945); Peter Argersinger, *Populism and Politics: William Alfred Peffer and the People's Party* (1974); Barton C. Shaw, *The Wool-Hat Boys: Georgia's Populist Party* (1984); Theodore R. Mitchell, *Political Education in the Southern Farmers Alliance, 1887–1900* (1987); C. Vann Woodward, *Tom Watson, Agrarian Rebel* (1938); Francis B. Simkins, *Pitchfork Ben Tillman* (1944).

The Election of 1896. Paul Glad, *McKinley, Bryan, and the People* (1964) and *The Trumpet Soundeth* (1960); Stanley Jones, *The Presidential Election of 1896* (1964); J. Rogers Hollingsworth, *The Whirligig of Politics: The Democracy of Cleveland and Bryan* (1963); Paolo Coletta, *William Jennings Bryan: Political Evangelist* (1964).

CHAPTER 20 THE IMPERIAL REPUBLIC

General Histories. Charles S. Campbell, *The Transformation of American Foreign Relations, 1865–1900* (1976); Robert L. Beisner, *From the Old Diplomacy to the New, 1865–1900* (1975); Julius W. Pratt, *Expansionists of 1898* (1936); Albert K. Weinberg, *Manifest Destiny: A Study in Nationalist Expansion in American History* (1935); Walter LeFeber, *The New Empire* (1963); William Appleman Williams, *The Tragedy of American Diplomacy*, rev. ed. (1972); Ernest May, *Imperial Democracy* (1961) and *American Imperialism: A Speculative Essay* (1968); David F. Healy, *U.S. Expansionism: Imperialist Urge in the 1890s* (1970); John Dobson, *America's Ascent: The United States Becomes a Great Power, 1880–1914* (1978); H. Wayne Morgan, *America's Road to Empire* (1965); J. A. S. Grenville and George Berkeley Young, *Politics, Strategy and American Diplomacy: Studies in Foreign Policy, 1873–1917* (1966); Milton Plesur, *America's Outward Thrust: Approaches to Foreign Affairs, 1865–1890* (1971); David M. Pletcher, *The Awkward Years: American Foreign Relations under Garfield and Arthur* (1962).

The Spanish-American War. David F. Trask, *The War with Spain in 1898* (1981); Frank Freidel, *The Splendid Little War* (1958); Joyce Milton, *The Yellow Journalists* (1989); Walter Millis, *The Martial Spirit* (1931); Louis A. Perez, Jr., *Cuba Between Empires, 1868–1902* (1983); Philip S. Foner, *The Spanish-Cuban-American War and the Birth of American Imperialism*, 2 vols. (1972); Graham A. Cosmas, *An Army for Empire: The United States Army in the Spanish-American War* (1971); Richard S. West, Jr., *Admirals of the American Empire* (1948); Richard Challener, *Admirals, Generals, and American Foreign Policy, 1889–1914* (1973); Willard B. Gatewood, Jr., *Black Americans and the White Man's Burden, 1898–1903* (1975) and *"Smoked Yankees": Letters from Negro Soldiers, 1898–1902* (1971); Edmund Morris, *The Rise of Theodore Roosevelt* (1979); Gerald F. Linderman, *The Mirror of War: American Society and the Spanish-American War* (1974).

Imperialism and Anti-Imperialism. Robert L. Beisner, *Twelve Against Empire* (1968); E. Berkeley Tompkins, *Anti-Imperialism in the United States, 1890–1920: The Great Debate* (1970); Thomas J. Osborne, *"Empire Can Wait": American Opposition to Hawaiian Annexation, 1893–1898* (1981); Kendrick A. Clements, *William Jennings Bryan* (1983); Frederick Merk, *Manifest Destiny and Mission in American History* (1963); Julius W. Pratt, *America's Colonial Empire* (1950); James H. Hitchman, *Leonard Wood and Cuban Independence, 1898–1902* (1971).

The Pacific Empire. Peter Stanley, *A Nation in the Making: The Philippines and the United States* (1974); Paul M. Kennedy, *The Samoan Tangle* (1974); Glenn May, *Social Engineering in the Philippines* (1980); Merze Tate, *The United States and the Hawaiian Kingdom* (1965); Richard E. Welch, Jr., *Response to Imperialism: The United States and the Philippine-American War, 1899–1902* (1979); Leon Wolff, *Little Brown Brother* (1961); Stuart Creighton Miller, *"Benevolent Assimilation": The American Conquest of the Philippines, 1899–1903* (1982); John Morgan Gates, *Schoolbooks and Krags: The United States Army in the Philippines, 1898–1902* (1971); Daniel B. Schirmer, *Republic or Empire? American Resistance to the Philippine War* (1972); Stanley Karnow, *In Our Image: America's Empire in the Philippines* (1989).

America and Asia. James C. Thomsen, Jr., Peter W. Stanley, and John Curtis Perry, *Sentimental Imperialists: The American Experience in East Asia* (1981); Marilyn B. Young, *The Rhetoric of Empire* (1968); Warren Cohen, *America's Response to China*, rev. ed. (1980); Akira Iriye, *Across the Pacific* (1967) and *Pacific Estrangement: Japanese and American Expansion* (1972); Robert McClellan, *The Heathen Chinese: A Study of American Attitudes Toward China* (1971); Jane Junter, *The Gospel of Gentility: American Women Missionaries in Turn-of-the-Century China* (1984); Charles Neu, *The Troubled Encounter* (1975); Paul Varg, *The Making of a Myth: The United States and China, 1897–1912* (1968) and *Missionaries, Chinese, and Diplomats* (1958); Patricia Hill, *The World Their Household: The American Women's Foreign Mission Movement and Cultural Transformation* (1985).

CHAPTER 21 THE RISE OF PROGRESSIVISM

Progressivism: Overviews. Richard Hofstadter, *The Age of Reform: From Bryan to FDR* (1955); Robert Wiebe, *The Search for Order, 1877–1920* (1967); Gabriel Kolko, *The*

Triumph of Conservatism (1963); James Weinstein, *The Corporate Ideal in the Liberal State, 1900–1918* (1969); Arthur Link and Richard L. McCormick, *Progressivism* (1983); John Whiteclay Chambers, *The Tyranny of Change* (1980); Nell Irvin Painter, *Standing at Armageddon: The United States, 1877–1919* (1987).

The Muckrakers. Harold S. Wilson, *McClure's Magazine and the Muckrakers* (1970); C. C. Regier, *The Era of the Muckrakers* (1932); David Chambers, *The Social and Political Ideas of the Muckrakers* (1964); Justin Kaplan, *Lincoln Steffens* (1974); Leon Harris, *Upton Sinclair* (1975); Louis Filler, *The Muckrakers*, rev. ed. (1980).

Progressive Thought. Arthur Ekirch, *Progressivism in America* (1974); Morton White, *Social Thought in America* (1949); D. W. Marcell, *Progress and Pragmatism: James, Dewey, Beard and the American Idea of Progress* (1974); Charles Forcey, *The Crossroads of Liberalism: Croly, Weyl, Lippmann* (1961); Richard Abrams, *The Burdens of Progress* (1978); Sudhir Kakar, *Frederick Taylor* (1970); David W. Noble, ed., *The Progressive Mind*, rev. ed. (1981); Carl Degler, *In Search of Human Nature: The Decline and Revival of Darwinism in American Social Thought* (1991).

Social Work and the Social Gospel. Allen F. Davis, *Spearheads of Reform: The Social Settlements and the Progressive Movement, 1890–1914* (1968) and *American Heroine: The Life and Legend of Jane Addams* (1973); Roy Lubove, *The Progressives and the Slums: Tenement House Reform in New York City* (1962); Jane Addams, *Twenty Years at Hull House* (1910); C. H. Hopkins, *The Rise of the Social Gospel in American Protestantism* (1940); Henry May, *Protestant Churches and Industrial America* (1949); William R. Hutchinson, *The Modernist Impulse in American Protestantism* (1982); Robert M. Cruden, *Ministers of Reform: The Progressives' Achievement in American Civilization, 1889–1920* (1982); Paul Boyer, *Urban Masses and Moral Order, 1820–1920* (1978); Timothy Miller, *Following in His Steps: A Biography of Charles M. Sheldon* (1987).

Education and the Professions. Burton Bledstein, *The Culture of Professionalism* (1976); Thomas L. Haskell, *The Emergence of Professional Social Science* (1977); Paul Starr, *The Social Transformation of American Medicine* (1982); Regina Markell Morantz-Sanchez, *Sympathy and Science: Women Physicians in American Medicine* (1985); Kenneth M. Ludmerer, *Learning to Heal: The Development of American Medical Education* (1985); David Tyack and Elizabeth Hansot, *Managers of Virtue: Public School Leadership in America, 1820–1980* (1982); Lawrence Veysey, *The Emergence of the American University* (1970); Barbara Miller Solomon, *In the Company of Educated Women: A History of Women in Higher Education in America* (1985); Ellen Fitzpatrick, *Endless Crusade: Women Social Scientists and Progressive Reform* (1990); Barbara Harris, *Beyond Her Sphere: Women and the Professions in American History* (1978).

Municipal Reform. Zane Miller, *Boss Cox's Cincinnati* (1968); John D. Buenker, *Urban Liberalism and Progressive Reform* (1973); James B. Crooks, *Politics and Progress: The Rise of Urban Progressivism in Baltimore* (1968); Melvin G. Holli, *Reform in Detroit* (1969); J. Joseph Huthmacher, *Senator Robert F. Wagner and the Rise of Urban Liberalism* (1971); Oscar Handlin, *Al Smith and His America* (1958); Michael Kazin, *Barons of Labor: The San Francisco Building Trades and Union Power in the Progressive Era* (1981).

Women, Reform, and Suffrage. Eleanor Flexner, *Century of Struggle* (1959); Nancy Cott, *The Grounding of Modern Feminism* (1987); Karen Blair, *The Clubwoman as Feminist* (1980); Anne F. Scott, *Making the Invisible Woman Visible* (1984); Nancy Shrom Dye, *As Equal as Sisters: Feminism, the Labor Movement, and the Women's Trade Union League of New York* (1981); Sheila M. Rothman, *Woman's Proper Place* (1978); Ellen C. Lagemann, *A Generation of Women: Education in the Lives of Progressive Reformers* (1979); Rosalind Rosenberg, *Beyond Separate Spheres: Intellectual Roots of Modern Feminism* (1982); Jacquelyn Dowd Hall, *The Revolt Against Chivalry* (1979); Elaine Tyler May, *Great Expectations: Marriage and Divorce in Post-Victorian America* (1980); Mari Jo Buhle, *Women and American Socialism* (1983); Aileen S. Kraditor, *Ideas of the Woman Suffrage Movement* (1965); Alan P. Grimes, *The Puritan Ethic and Woman Suffrage* (1967); David Morgan, *Suffragists and Democrats: The Politics of Woman Suffrage in America* (1972); Ellen C. DuBois, *Feminism and Suffrage: The Emergence of an Independent Women's Movement in America, 1848–1869* (1978); Ruth Rosen, *The Lost Sisterhood: Prostitutes in America, 1900–1918* (1982); William O'Neill, *Divorce in the Progressive Era* (1967) and *Everyone Was Brave: The Rise and Fall of Feminism in America* (1969); David M. Kennedy, *Birth Control in America: The Career of Margaret Sanger* (1970); Linda Gordon, *Woman's Body, Woman's Right: A Social History of Birth Control* (1976); Elyce J. Rotella, *From Home to Office: U.S. Women and Work, 1870–1930* (1981).

Racial Issues. Louis Harlan, *Booker T. Washington: The Making of a Black Leader* (1972) and *Booker T. Washington: The Wizard of Tuskegee, 1901–1915* (1983); Elliott Rudwick, *W. E. B. Du Bois* (1969); August Meier, *Negro Thought in America, 1880–1915* (1963); Donald Spivey, *Schooling for the New Slavery: Black Industrial Education* (1978); Charles F. Kellogg, *NAACP* (1970); James M. McPherson, *The Abolitionist Legacy: From Reconstruction to the NAACP* (1975); George Fredrickson, *The Black Image in the White Mind* (1968); Joel Williamson, *The Crucible of Race: Black-White Relations in the American South Since Emancipation* (1985); John Dittmer, *Black Georgia in the Progressive Era, 1900–1920* (1977); Paula Giddings, *When and Where I Enter: The Impact of Black Women on Race and Sex in America* (1984); Cynthia Neverdon-Morton, *Afro-American Women of the South and the Advancement of the Race, 1885–1925* (1989).

State-Level Reform. George E. Mowry, *California Progressives* (1951); David P. Thelen, *The New Citizenship: Origins of Progressivism in Wisconsin* (1972), *Robert M. La Follette and the Insurgent Spirit* (1976), and *Paths of Resistance: Tradition and Dignity in Industrializing Missouri* (1986); Sheldon Hackney, *Populism to Progressivism in Alabama* (1969); Robert S. Maxwell, *La Follette and the Rise of Progressivism in Wisconsin* (1944); Russel B. Nye, *Midwestern Progressive Politics* (1951); Richard M. Abrams, *Conservatism in a Progressive Era: Massachusetts* (1964); Robert F. Wesser, *Charles Evans Hughes: Politics and Reform in New York State, 1905–1910* (1967); Irwin Yellowitz, *Labor and the Progressive Movement in New York State* (1965); Richard L. McCormick, *From Realignment to Reform: Political Change in New York State, 1893–1910* (1981); Dewey Grantham, *Southern Progressivism: The Reconciliation of Progress and Tradition* (1983); C. Vann Woodward, *Origins of the New South* (1951).

National Issues. Ruth Bourdin, *Women and Temperance: The Quest for Power and Liberty, 1873–1900* (1980); James T. Timberlake, *Prohibition and the Progressive Movement*

(1963); Joseph Gusfield, *Symbolic Crusade: Status Politics and the Temperance Movement* (1963); John Higham, *Strangers in the Land* (1955); James Weinstein, *The Decline of Socialism in America* (1967); Robert Wiebe, *Businessmen and Reform* (1962); Sidney Fine, *Laissez Faire and the General Welfare State* (1956); Melvyn Dubofsky, *We Shall Be All* (1969); Michael E. McGerr, *The Decline of Popular Politics: The American North, 1865–1928* (1986).

CHAPTER 22 THE BATTLE FOR NATIONAL REFORM

General Histories. George E. Mowry, *The Era of Theodore Roosevelt* (1958); Arthur Link, *Woodrow Wilson and the Progressive Era, 1910–1917* (1954); John Milton Cooper, Jr., *The Warrior and the Priest: Woodrow Wilson and Theodore Roosevelt* (1983). See also Suggested Readings for Chapter 21.

Theodore Roosevelt. Edmund Morris, *The Rise of Theodore Roosevelt* (1979); Henry F. Pringle, *Theodore Roosevelt* (1931); William H. Harbaugh, *Power and Responsibility* (1961), published in paperback as *The Life and Times of Theodore Roosevelt*; John Morton Blum, *The Republican Roosevelt* (1954); G. Wallace Chessman, *Theodore Roosevelt and the Politics of Power* (1969); John A. Garraty, *The Life of George W. Perkins* (1960); Horace S. Merrill and Marion G. Merrill, *The Republican High Command* (1971).

William Howard Taft. Henry F. Pringle, *The Life and Times of William Howard Taft*, 2 vols. (1939); Paolo E. Coletta, *The Presidency of Taft* (1973); Donald E. Anderson, *William Howard Taft* (1973); James L. Penick, *Progressive Politics and Conservation: The Ballinger-Pinchot Affair* (1968); Harold T. Pinkett, *Gifford Pinchot: Private and Public Forester* (1970); George Mowry, *Theodore Roosevelt and the Progressive Movement* (1946); Norman Wilensky, *Conservatives in the Progressive Era: The Taft Republicans of 1912* (1965).

Woodrow Wilson. Arthur S. Link, *Woodrow Wilson*, 5 vols. (1947–1965); John Morton Blum, *Woodrow Wilson and the Politics of Morality* (1956); Alexander George and Juliette George, *Woodrow Wilson and Colonel House* (1956); Edwin A. Weinstein, *Woodrow Wilson: A Medical and Psychological Biography* (1981); John Morton Blum, *Joseph Tumulty and the Wilson Era* (1951); L. J. Holt, *Congressional Insurgents and the Party System, 1909–1916* (1967).

National Issues. Samuel P. Hays, *The Gospel of Efficiency: The Progressive Conservation Movement, 1890–1920* (1962); Elmo P. Richardson, *The Politics of Conservation* (1962); O. E. Anderson, *The Health of a Nation* (1958); Craig West, *Banking Reform and the Federal Reserve, 1863–1923* (1977).

Roosevelt's Foreign Policy. Howard K. Beale, *Theodore Roosevelt and the Rise of America to World Power* (1956); Richard Challener, *Admirals, Generals, and American Foreign Policy, 1898–1914* (1973); David H. Burton, *Theodore Roosevelt: Confident Imperialist* (1969); Julius W. Pratt, *Challenge and Rejection: The United States and World Leadership, 1900–1921* (1967); Richard Leopold, *Elihu Root and the Conservative Tradition*

(1954); Akira Iriye, *Pacific Estrangement: Japanese and American Expansion, 1897–1911* (1972); Charles E. Neu, *An Uncertain Friendship: Roosevelt and Japan, 1906–1909* (1967); Charles Vevier, *United States and China* (1955).

America and the Caribbean. Dana G. Munro, *Intervention and Dollar Diplomacy in the Caribbean, 1900–1921* (1964); Louis A. Perez, Jr., *Cuba Under the Platt Amendment* (1988); Dwight C. Miner, *Fight for the Panama Route* (1966); Walter LaFeber, *The Panama Canal* (1978); David McCullough, *The Path Between the Seas* (1977); Walter Scholes and Marie Scholes, *The Foreign Policies of the Taft Administration* (1970).

Wilson's Foreign Policy. Arthur Link, *Wilson the Diplomatist* (1957) and *Woodrow Wilson: Revolution, War, and Peace* (1979); Robert Freeman Smith, *The United States and Revolutionary Nationalism in Mexico, 1916–1932* (1972); Kenneth Grieb, *The United States and Huerta* (1969); Robert Quirk, *An Affair of Honor: Woodrow Wilson and the Occupation of Veracruz* (1962) and *The Mexican Revolution, 1914–1915* (1960); David Healy, *Gunboat Diplomacy in the Wilson Era: The U.S. Navy in Haiti, 1915–1916* (1976); Dana Munro, *Intervention and Dollar Diplomacy in the Caribbean, 1900–1914* (1964).

CHAPTER 23 AMERICA AND THE GREAT WAR

The Road to War. Ernest R. May, *The World War and American Isolation* (1959); Patrick Devlin, *Too Proud to Fight: Woodrow Wilson's Neutrality* (1974); Jeffrey J. Sanford, *Wilsonian Maritime Diplomacy* (1978); Manfred Jonas, *The United States and Germany* (1984); John Milton Cooper, Jr., *The Vanity of Power: American Isolation and the First World War* (1969); Ross Gregory, *The Origins of American Intervention in the First World War* (1971); Daniel Smith, *Robert Lansing and American Neutrality* (1958); C. Roland Marchand, *The American Peace Movement and Social Reform* (1973); Thomas A. Bailey and Paul B. Ryan, *The Lusitania Disaster* (1975); Barbara Tuchman, *The Zimmerman Telegram* (1958).

Military Histories. Edward M. Coffman, *The War to End All Wars* (1969); Harvey A. De Weerd, *President Wilson Fights His War* (1968); A. E. Barbeau and Florette Henri, *The Unknown Soldiers: Black American Troops in World War I* (1974); J. Garry Clifford, *The Citizen Soldiers* (1972); Russell Weigley, *The American Way of War* (1973); Frank Freidel, *Over There* (1964); David Trask, *The United States in the Supreme War Council* (1961); John Whiteclay Chambers, *To Raise an Army* (1987); Donald Smythe, *Pershing* (1986).

Wartime Diplomacy. Arno Mayer, *Political Origins of the New Diplomacy* (1959); George F. Kennan, *Russia Leaves the War* (1956) and *Russia and the West Under Lenin and Stalin* (1961); W. B. Fowler, *British-American Relations, 1917–1918* (1969); Carl Parrini, *Heir to Empire: United States Economic Diplomacy, 1916–1923* (1969).

Domestic Impact. David M. Kennedy, *Over Here* (1980); Neil A. Wynn, *From Progressivism to Prosperity: World War I and American Society* (1986); Jordan Schwarz, *The Speculator* (1981); Robert D. Cuff, *The War Industries Board: Business-Government Relations During World War I* (1973); Valerie Jean Conner, *The National War Labor Board*

(1983); George Nash, *The Life of Herbert Hoover: The Humanitarian, 1914–1917* (1990); Daniel Beaver, *Newton D. Baker and the American War Effort, 1917–1919* (1966); Seward Livermore, *Politics Is Adjourned* (1966); Charles Gilbert, *American Financing of World War I* (1970); George T. Blakey, *Historians on the Homefront* (1970); J. R. Mock and Cedric Larson, *Words That Won the War* (1939); Stephen Vaughn, *Holding Fast the Inner Lines: Democracy, Nationalism, and the Committee on Public Information* (1979); Richard Polenberg, *Fighting Faiths: The Abrams Case, the Supreme Court, and Free Speech* (1987); Zechariah Chaffee, Jr., *Free Speech in the United States* (1941); William Preston, Jr., *Aliens and Dissenters: Federal Suppression of Radicals, 1903–1933* (1963); H. C. Peterson and Gilbert Fite, *Opponents of War, 1917–1918* (1957); Harry N. Scheiber, *The Wilson Administration and Civil Liberties, 1917–1921* (1960); Donald Johnson, *The Challenge to America's Freedoms* (1963); John Higham, *Strangers in the Land* (1955); Frederick C. Luebke, *Bonds of Loyalty* (1974); Alfred W. Crosby, Jr., *Epidemic and Peace, 1918* (1976); Allan M. Brandt, *No Magic Bullet: A Social History of Venereal Disease in the United States* (1985); Maurine W. Greenwald, *Women, War, and Work* (1980); Barbara J. Steinson, *American Women's Activism in World War I* (1982); Carol S. Gruber, *Mars and Minerva* (1975); Charles Chatfield, *For Peace and Justice: Pacifism in America, 1914–1941* (1971); Sondra Herman, *Eleven Against War* (1969); Charles DeBenedettis, *Origins of the Modern Peace Movement* (1978); Otis L. Graham, Jr., *The Great Campaigns* (1971); Ellis W. Hawley, *The Great War and the Search for a Modern Order* (1979).

Wilson and the Peace. Arthur S. Link, *Wilson the Diplomatist* (1957); N. Gordon Levin, Jr., *Woodrow Wilson and World Politics* (1968); Lloyd Ambrosius, *Woodrow Wilson and the American Diplomatic Tradition* (1987); Arthur Walworth, *Wilson and the Peacemakers* (1986); Robert H. Ferrell, *Woodrow Wilson and World War I* (1985); Arno Mayer, *Wilson vs. Lenin* (1959) and *Politics and Diplomacy of Peacemaking* (1965); Peter Filene, *Americans and the Soviet Experiment* (1967); Christopher Lasch, *The American Liberals and the Russian Revolution* (1962); Lloyd C. Gardner, *Safe for Democracy: The Anglo-American Response to Revolution, 1913–1923* (1984); Inga Floto, *Colonel House at Paris* (1980); John A. Garraty, *Henry Cabot Lodge* (1953); Ralph Stone, *The Irreconcilables* (1970); Warren F. Kuehl, *Seeking World Order* (1969); Denna Fleming, *The United States and the League of Nations* (1932); Arthur Link, *Woodrow Wilson: War, Revolution, and Peace* (1979); Gene Smith, *When the Cheering Stopped* (1964); George Kennan, *Decision to Intervene* (1958); John L. Gaddis, *Russia, the Soviet Union, and the United States* (1978); William C. Widenor, *Henry Cabot Lodge and the Search for an American Foreign Policy* (1980); Robert E. Osgood, *Ideals and Self-Interest in American Foreign Relations* (1953).

Postwar America. Burl Noggle, *Into the Twenties* (1974); Stanley Coben, *A. Mitchell Palmer* (1963); Robert K. Murray, *The Red Scare* (1955); Roberta Strauss Feuerlicht, *Justice Crucified: The Story of Sacco and Vanzetti* (1977); David Brody, *Steelworkers in America* (1960) and *Labor in Crisis* (1965); Francis Russell, *A City in Terror* (1975); Robert L. Friedheim, *The Seattle General Strike* (1965); James Grossman, *Land of Hope: Chicago, Black Southerners, and the Great Migration* (1989); William M. Tuttle, Jr., *Race Riot: Chicago in the Red Summer of 1919* (1970); Elliott Rudwick, *Race Riot at East St. Louis* (1964); Robert V. Haynes, *A Night of Violence: The Houston Riot of 1917* (1976); Kenneth Kusmer, *A Ghetto Takes Shape* (1976); Alan Spear, *Black Chicago* (1967); David Cronon, *Black Moses* (1955); Amy J. Garvey, *Garvey and Garveyism* (1963); Judith Stein, *The World of Marcus Garvey* (1986); Theodore Vincent, *Black Power and the Garvey Movement* (1971);

Wesley M. Bagby, Jr., *The Road to Normalcy* (1962); Stuart I. Rochester, *American Liberal Disillusionment in the Wake of World War I* (1977).

CHAPTER 24 THE NEW ERA

General Studies. William Leuchtenburg, *The Perils of Prosperity* (1958); John D. Hicks, *Republican Ascendancy* (1960); Arthur M. Schlesinger, Jr., *The Crisis of the Old Order* (1957); Ellis Hawley, *The Great War and the Search for a Modern Order* (1979); Donald R. McCoy, *Coming of Age* (1973); John Braeman, ed., *Change and Continuity in Twentieth Century America: The 1920s* (1968); Frederick Lewis Allen, *Only Yesterday* (1931); Isabel Leighton, ed., *The Aspirin Age* (1949); George Soule, *Prosperity Decade* (1947).

Labor, Agriculture, and Economic Growth. Alfred Chandler, *Strategy and Structure* (1962); Louis Galambos, *Competition and Cooperation* (1966); Louis Galambos and Joseph Pratt, *The Rise of the Corporate Commonwealth: U.S. Business and Public Policy in the Twentieth Century* (1988); Irving Bernstein, *The Lean Years: A History of the American Worker, 1920–1933* (1960); David Brody, *Steelworkers in America* (1960) and *Workers in Industrial America* (1980); Lizabeth Cohen, *Making a New Deal: Industrial Workers in Chicago, 1919–1939* (1990); Gerald Zahavi, *Workers, Managers, and Welfare Capitalism: The Shoe Workers and Tanners of Endicott Johnson, 1890–1950* (1988); Peter Gottlieb, *Making Their Own Way: Southern Blacks' Migration to Pittsburgh, 1916–1930* (1987); Robert Zieger, *Republicans and Labor* (1969); Leslie Woodcock, *Wage-Earning Women* (1979); Gilbert Fite, *George Peek and the Fight for Farm Parity* (1954); Theodore Saloutos and John D. Hicks, *Twentieth Century Populism* (1951).

The New Culture. Daniel Boorstin, *The Americans: The Democratic Experience* (1973); Ed Cray, *Chrome Colossus* (1980); James J. Flink, *The Car Culture* (1975) and *The Automobile Age* (1988); Bernard A. Weisberger, *The Dream Maker* (1979); Lary May, *Screening Out the Past* (1980); Robert Sklar, *Movie-Made America* (1975); Sumiko Higashi, *Virgins, Vamps, and Flappers: The American Silent Movie Heroine* (1978); Susan J. Douglas, *Inventing American Broadcasting* (1987); Erik Barnouw, *A Tower of Babel*, vol. 1 (1966); Philip T. Rosen, *The Modern Stentors: Radio Broadcasting and the Federal Government, 1920–1933* (1980); Robert Creamer, *Babe* (1974); Kenneth S. Davis, *The Hero: Charles A. Lindbergh* (1959); Randy Roberts, *Jack Dempsey, The Manassa Mauler* (1979); Robert Lynd and Helen Lynd, *Middletown* (1929); Stanley Coben, *Rebellion Against Victorianism* (1991); Paul Carter, *Another Part of the Twenties* (1977); Kathy Peiss, *Cheap Amusements* (1986); Stewart Ewen, *Captains of Consciousness* (1976); Roland Marchand, *Advertising the American Dream* (1985); Stephen Fox, *The Mirror Makers: A History of American Advertising and Its Creators* (1984); Daniel Horowitz, *The Morality of Spending: Attitudes Toward the Consumer Society in America, 1875–1940* (1985); Ronald Edsforth, *Class Conflict and Cultural Consensus: The Making of a Mass Consumer Society: Flint, Michigan* (1987).

Women and Family. Nancy Cott, *The Grounding of American Feminism* (1987); Alice Kessler-Harris, *Out to Work: A History of Wage-Earning Women in America* (1982); Sheila Rothman, *Woman's Proper Place* (1978); William Chafe, *The American Woman* (1972); Linda Gordon, *Woman's Body, Woman's Right* (1976); J. Stanley Lemons, *The Woman Citizen: Social Feminism in the 1920s* (1973); Winifred Wandersee, *Women's Work and*

Family Values, 1920–1940 (1981); Susan Strasser, *Never Done: A History of American Housework* (1982); Ruth Schwarz Cowan, *More Work for Mother* (1983); Phyllis Palmer, *Domesticity and Dirt* (1989); Lois Scharf, *To Work and to Wed* (1980); Paula Fass, *The Damned and Beautiful* (1977); Helen Lefkowitz Horowitz, *Campus Life: Undergraduate Cultures from the End of the Eighteenth Century to the Present* (1987); Susan Porter Benson, *Counter Cultures* (1986); Lois Banner, *American Beauty* (1983); John D'Emilio and Estelle B. Friedman, *Intimate Matters: A History of Sexuality in America* (1988); W. Andrew Achenbaum, *Shades of Gray: Old Age, American Values, and Federal Policies Since 1920* (1983); Howard P. Chudacoff, *How Old Are You? Age in American Culture* (1989); David H. Fischer, *Growing Old in America* (1977).

Intellectuals. Roderick Nash, *The Nervous Generation: American Thought, 1917–1930* (1969); Robert Crunden, *From Self to Society: Transition in American Thought, 1919–1941* (1972); Malcolm Cowley, *Exiles Return* (1934); Edmund Wilson, *The Twenties* (1975); Frederick J. Hoffman, *The Twenties* (1949); Houston Baker, Jr., *Modernism and the Harlem Renaissance* (1987); Nathan I. Huggins, *Harlem Renaissance* (1971); David L. Lewis, *When Harlem Was in Vogue* (1981); Kenneth M. Wheeler and Virginia L. Lussier, eds., *Women and the Arts and the 1920s in Paris and New York* (1982); John Stewart, *The Burden of Time* (1965); Paul Conkin, *The Southern Agrarians* (1988); Cleanth Brooks, *William Faulkner: The Yoknapatawpha Country* (1963).

Cultural Conflict. Norman Clark, *Deliver Us from Evil* (1976); Joseph Gusfeld, *Symbolic Crusade* (1963); Andrew Sinclair, *The Era of Excess* (1962); Herbert Asbury, *The Great Illusion* (1950); John Higham, *Strangers in the Land* (1963); David Chalmers, *Hooded Americanism* (1965); Kenneth Jackson, *The Ku Klux Klan in the City* (1965); Ray Ginger, *Six Days or Forever?* (1958); Norman Furniss, *The Fundamentalist Controversy* (1954); William G. McLoughlin, *Modern Revivalism* (1959); George M. Marsden, *Fundamentalism and American Culture* (1980); Lawrence Levine, *Defender of the Faith, William Jennings Bryan: The Last Decade, 1915–1925* (1965).

Politics and Government. Robert K. Murray, *The Politics of Normalcy* (1973) and *The Harding Era* (1969); Eugene Trani and David Wilson, *The Presidency of Warren G. Harding* (1977); Burl Noggle, *Teapot Dome* (1962); James N. Giglio, *H. M. Daugherty and the Politics of Expediency* (1978); Francis Russell, *The Shadow of Blooming Grove* (1968); Andrew Sinclair, *The Available Man* (1965); Donald McCoy, *Calvin Coolidge* (1967); William Allen White, *A Puritan in Babylon* (1940); James Gilbert, *Designing the Industrial State* (1972); John Hoff Wilson, *Herbert Hoover: Forgotten Progressive* (1975); David Burner, *Herbert Hoover* (1979); Robert F. Himmelberg, *The Origins of the National Recovery Administration: Business, Government, and the Trade Association Issue, 1921–1933* (1976); Ellis Hawley, *Herbert Hoover as Secretary of Commerce: Studies in New Era Thought and Practice* (1974); LeRoy Ashby, *Spearless Leader* (1972); Richard Lowitt, *George W. Norris*, vol. 2 (1971); David P. Thelen, *Robert M. La Follette and the Insurgent Spirit* (1978); George B. Tindall, *The Emergence of the New South* (1967); Christine Bolt, *American Indian Policy and American Reform* (1987); William Harbaugh, *Lawyer's Lawyer* (1973); David Burner, *The Politics of Provincialism* (1967); Alan Lichtman, *Prejudice and the Old Politics* (1979); Kristi Andersen, *The Creation of a Democratic Majority, 1928–1936* (1979); Oscar Handlin, *Al Smith and His America* (1958); Paula Elder, *Governor Alfred E. Smith: The Politician as Reformer* (1983); Elisabeth Israels Perry, *Belle Moskowitz: Feminine Politics* *and the Exercise of Power in the Age of Alfred E. Smith* (1987); Frank Freidel, *Franklin D. Roosevelt: The Ordeal* (1954) and *Franklin D. Roosevelt: The Triumph* (1956).

CHAPTER 25 THE GREAT DEPRESSION

The Coming of the Depression. Michael Bernstein, *The Great Depression: Delayed Recovery and Economic Change in America, 1929–1939* (1987); Robert Sobel, *The Great Bull Market* (1968); John Kenneth Galbraith, *The Great Crash* (1954); Milton Friedman and Anna Schwartz, *The Great Contraction* (1965) or Chapter 7 of *A Monetary History of the United States* (1963); Peter Temin, *Did Monetary Forces Cause the Great Depression?* (1976); Broadus Mitchell, *Depression Decade* (1947); Lester V. Chandler, *America's Greatest Depression* (1970); Charles Kindelberger, *The World in Depression* (1973); Susan E. Kennedy, *The Banking Crisis of 1933* (1973).

The Impact of the Depression. Irving Bernstein, *The Lean Years* (1960); Arthur M. Schlesinger, Jr., *The Crisis of the Old Order* (1957); Robert S. McElvaine, ed., *Down and Out in the Great Depression: Letters from the Forgotten Man* (1983); Studs Terkel, *Hard Times* (1970); Federal Writers' Project, *These Are Our Lives* (1939); Tom Terrill and Jerrold Hirsch, *Such as Us* (1978); Ann Banks, *First-Person America* (1980); Janet Poppendieck, *Breadlines Knee-Deep in Wheat: Food Assistance in the Great Depression* (1986); Donald Worster, *Dust Bowl* (1979); Walter Stein, *California and the Dust Bowl Migration* (1973); James N. Gregory, *American Exodus: The Dust Bowl Migration and Okie Culture in California* (1989); William Mullins, *The Depression and the Urban West Coast, 1929–1933* (1991).

Depression Culture and Society. Robert Lynd and Helen Merrell Lynd, *Middletown in Transition* (1935); Frederick Lewis Allen, *Since Yesterday* (1940); Richard Pells, *Radical Visions and American Dreams: Culture and Social Thought in the Depression Years* (1973); Warren Susman, *Culture as History* (1984); Richard Krickus, *Pursuing the American Dream* (1976); Gilman Ostrander, *American Civilization in the First Machine Age* (1970); Andrew Bergman, *We're in the Money: Depression America and Its Films* (1971); Alice Goldfarb Marquis, *Hopes and Ashes: The Birth of Modern Times, 1929–1939* (1986); David P. Peeler, *Hope Among Us Yet: Social Criticism and Social Thought in the Depression Years* (1987). See Suggested Readings for Chapter 26 for literature on blacks, Hispanics, Indians, and labor during the Depression.

Women and the Depression. Julia K. Blackwelder, *Women of the Depression: Caste and Culture in San Antonio, 1919–1939* (1984); William Chafe, *The American Woman* (1972); Lois Scharf, *To Work and to Wed: Female Employment, Feminism, and the Great Depression* (1980); Joan Jensen and Lois Scharf, eds., *Decades of Discontent: The Women's Movement, 1920–1940* (1983); Susan Ware, *Holding Their Own: American Women in the 1930s* (1982); Jeane Westin, *Making Do: How Women Survived the '30s* (1976).

The Hoover Presidency. Albert Romasco, *The Poverty of Abundance* (1965); Joan Hoff Wilson, *Herbert Hoover* (1975); David Burner, *Herbert Hoover* (1978); Harris Warren, *Herbert Hoover and the Great Depression* (1959); Jordan Schwarz, *The Interregnum of Despair* (1970); Herbert Hoover, *The Great Depression* (1952); James S. Olsen, *Herbert*

Hoover and the Reconstruction Finance Corporation (1977) and *Saving Capitalism: The Reconstruction Finance Corporation and the New Deal, 1933–1940* (1988); Martin Fausold and George Mazuzun, eds., *The Hoover Presidency* (1974); Martin Fausold, *The Presidency of Herbert C. Hoover* (1985); William J. Barber, *From New Era to New Deal: Herbert Hoover, The Economists, and American Economic Policy, 1921–1933* (1985).

Politics and Protest. John Shover, *Cornbelt Rebellion* (1965); Roger Daniels, *The Bonus March* (1971); David Beito, *Taxpayers in Revolt* (1989); Donald Lisio, *The President and Protest* (1974); Harvey Klehr, *The Heyday of American Communism: The Depression Decade* (1984); Mark Naison, *Communists in Harlem During the Depression* (1983); Robin D. G. Kelley, *Hammer and Hoe: Alabama Communists During the Great Depression* (1990); Arthur M. Schlesinger, Jr., *The Crisis of the Old Order* (1957); David Burner, *The Politics of Provincialism* (1967); Thomas Kessner, *Fiorello H. LaGuardia and the Making of Modern New York* (1989); Frank Freidel, *The Triumph* (1956) and *Launching the New Deal* (1973); Eliot Rosen, *Hoover, Roosevelt, and the Brains Trust* (1977); Rexford G. Tugwell, *The Brains Trust* (1968).

CHAPTER 26 THE NEW DEAL

General and Biographical Studies. William E. Leuchtenburg, *Franklin D. Roosevelt and the New Deal* (1963) and *In the Shadow of FDR* (1983); Robert S. McElvaine, *The Great Depression* (1984); Anthony J. Badger, *The New Deal* (1989); Arthur M. Schlesinger, Jr., *The Age of Roosevelt*, 3 vols. (1957–1960); Paul Conkin, *The New Deal* (1967); Edgar Robinson, *The Roosevelt Leadership* (1955); James MacGregor Burns, *Roosevelt: The Lion and the Fox* (1956); Gerald Nash, *The Great Depression and World War II* (1979); Frank Freidel, *Franklin D. Roosevelt*, 4 vols. (1952–1973) and *Franklin D. Roosevelt: A Rendezvous with Destiny* (1990); Geoffrey Ward, *Before the Trumpet: Young Franklin Roosevelt, 1882–1905* (1985) and *A First-Class Temperament: The Emergence of Franklin Roosevelt* (1989); Kenneth Davis, *FDR: The Beckoning of Destiny* (1972), *FDR: The New York Years: 1928–1933* (1985) and *FDR: The New Deal Years, 1933–1937* (1986); Joseph P. Lash, *Eleanor and Franklin* (1971); J. H. Wilson and Marjorie Lightman, eds., *Without Precedent: The Life and Career of Eleanor Roosevelt* (1984); Steve Fraser and Gary Gerstle, eds., *The Rise and Fall of New Deal Liberalism* (1988); Harvard Sitkoff, ed., *Fifty Years Later: The New Deal Evaluated* (1985); John Braeman et al., eds., *The New Deal*, 2 vols. (1975); Katie Louchheim, *The Making of the New Deal* (1983); Peter Fearon, *War, Prosperity, and Depression* (1987).

New Deal Politics and Programs. Frank Freidel, *Launching the New Deal* (1973); Raymond Moley and Eliot Rosen, *The First New Deal* (1966); Herbert Feis, *Characters in Crisis* (1966); Otis Graham, *Encore for Reform* (1967); Ellis Hawley, *The New Deal and the Problem of Monopoly* (1966); Donald Brand, *Corporatism and the Rule of Law* (1988); Bernard Bellush, *The Failure of the NRA* (1975); Sidney Fine, *The Automobile Under the Blue Eagle* (1963); Peter H. Irons, *The New Deal Lawyers* (1982); Susan Ware, *Beyond Suffrage* (1981) and *Partner and I: Molly Dewson, Feminism, and New Deal Politics* (1987); Thomas K. McCraw, *TVA and the Power Fight* (1970); Michael Parrish, *Securities Regulation and the New Deal* (1970); Ralph F. De Bedts, *The New Deal's SEC* (1964); Mark Leff, *The Limits of Symbolic Reform: The New Deal and Taxation, 1933–1939* (1984); Albert

U. Romasco, *The Politics of Recovery: Roosevelt's New Deal* (1983); Searle Charles, *Minister of Relief* (1963); George McJimsey, *Harry Hopkins: Ally of the Poor and Defender of Democracy* (1987); John Salmond, *The Civilian Conservation Corps* (1967); Bonnie Fox Schwartz, *The Civil Works Administration, 1933–1934* (1984); James T. Patterson, *America's Struggle Against Poverty, 1900–1980* (1981); Mimi Abramowitz, *Regulating the Lives of Women* (1988); William R. Brock, *Welfare, Democracy, and the New Deal* (1987).

Agriculture. David Hamilton, *From New Day to New Deal: American Farm Policy from Hoover to Roosevelt, 1928–1933* (1991); Van L. Perkins, *Crisis in Agriculture* (1969); Richard S. Kirkendall, *Social Scientists and Farm Politics in the Age of Roosevelt* (1966); Christina Campbell, *The Farm Bureaus* (1962); Gilbert Fite, *George M. Peek and the Fight for Farm Parity* (1954); David Conrad, *The Forgotten Farmers* (1965); Paul Mertz, *The New Deal and Southern Rural Poverty* (1978); Lowell K. Dyson, *Red Harvest: The Communist Party and American Farmers* (1982); Bruce Shulman, *From Cotton Belt to Sunbelt* (1991).

Depression Dissidents. Arthur M. Schlesinger, Jr., *The Politics of Upheaval* (1960); George Wolfskill, *Revolt of the Conservatives* (1962); Donald Grubbs, *Cry from the Cotton* (1971); Donald McCoy, *Angry Voices* (1958); R. Alan Lawson, *The Failure of Independent Liberalism* (1971); Alan Brinkley, *Voices of Protest: Huey Long, Father Coughlin, and the Great Depression* (1982); David H. Bennett, *Demagogues in the Depression* (1969); Leo Ribuffo, *The Old Christian Right: The Protestant Far Right from the Great Depression to the Cold War* (1983); Glen Jeansonne, *Gerald L. K. Smith: Minister of Hate* (1988); Abraham Holzman, *The Townsend Movement* (1963); Charles J. Tull, *Father Coughlin and the New Deal* (1965); T. Harry Williams, *Huey Long* (1969).

The "Second New Deal." J. Joseph Huthmacher, *Senator Robert Wagner and the Rise of Urban Liberalism* (1968); W. D. Rowley, *M. L. Wilson and the Campaign for Domestic Allotment* (1970); Sidney Baldwin, *Poverty and Politics: The Farm Security Administration* (1968); Roy Lubove, *The Struggle for Social Security* (1968); Paul Conkin, *Tomorrow a New World* (1971); Jane deHart Matthews, *The Federal Theater* (1967); Jerre Mangione, *The Dream and the Deal* (1972); William F. McDonald, *Federal Relief Administration and the Arts* (1968).

The Late New Deal. James T. Patterson, *Congressional Conservatism and the New Deal* (1967); Frank Freidel, *FDR and the South* (1965); George Wolfskill and John Hudson, *All But the People* (1969); Leonard Baker, *Back to Back* (1967); Richard Polenberg, *Reorganizing Roosevelt's Government* (1966); Barry Karl, *Executive Reorganization and Reform in the New Deal* (1963); James T. Patterson, *The New Deal and the States* (1969); Charles Trout, *Boston: The Great Depression and the New Deal* (1977); Herbert Stein, *The Fiscal Revolution in America* (1969); Dean May, *From New Deal to New Economics* (1981); Theodore Rosenof, *Patterns of Political Economy in America* (1983).

Blacks, Hispanics, Indians. Harvard Sitkoff, *A New Deal for Blacks* (1978); Nancy Weiss, *Farewell to the Party of Lincoln: Black Politics in the Age of FDR* (1983) and *The National Urban League* (1974); John B. Kirby, *Black Americans in the Roosevelt Era* (1980); Raymond Wolters, *Negroes and the Great Depression* (1970); Ralph Bunche, *The Political Status of the Negro in the Age of FDR* (1973); John Dollard, *Caste and Class in a Southern*

Town, 3rd ed. (1957); Dan T. Carter, *Scottsboro* (1969); Robert L. Zangrando, *The NAACP Crusade Against Lynching* (1980); Abraham Hoffman, *Unwanted Mexican Americans in the Great Depression* (1974); Francisco E. Balerman, *In Defense of La Raza* (1982); Rodolfo Acuña, *Occupied America*, rev. ed. (1981); Carey McWilliams, *Factories in the Field* (1939); Sarah Deutsch, *No Separate Refuge: Culture, Class, and Gender on the Anglo-Hispanic Frontier in the American Southwest, 1880–1940* (1987); Donald L. Parman, *The Navajos and the New Deal* (1976); Laurence M. Hauptman, *The Iroquois and the New Deal* (1981); Laurence C. Kelly, *The Assault on Assimilation: John Collier and the Origins of Indian Policy Reform* (1983); Vine DeLoria, Jr., *The Nations Within* (1984); Clifford Lytle, *American Indians, American Justice* (1983); Kenneth R. Philp, *John Collier's Crusade for Indian Reform, 1920–1954* (1977); Graham D. Taylor, *The New Deal and American Indian Tribalism* (1980).

Labor. Irving Bernstein, *Turbulent Years* (1970) and *A Caring Society: The New Deal, the Worker, and the Great Depression* (1985); Gary Gerstle, *Working-Class Americanism: The Politics of Labor in a Textile City, 1914–1960* (1989); Bruce Nelson, *Workers on the Waterfront: Seamen, Longshoremen, and Unionism in the 1930s* (1988); Joshua Freeman, *In Transit: The Transport Workers Union in New York City, 1933–1966* (1989); Lizabeth Cohen, *Making a New Deal: Industrial Workers in Chicago, 1919–1939* (1990); Melvyn Dubofsky and Warren Van Tine, *John L. Lewis* (1977); Daniel Nelson, *American Rubber Workers and Organized Labor, 1900–1941* (1988); Robert H. Zieger, *John L. Lewis: Labor Leader* (1988) and *American Workers, American Unions, 1920–1985* (1986); Christopher L. Tomlins, *The State and the Unions* (1985); George G. Suggs, Jr., *Union Busting in the Tristate: The Oklahoma, Kansas, and Missouri Metal Workers Strike of 1935* (1986); John W. Hevener, *Which Side Are You On? The Harlan County Coal Miners, 1931–1939* (1978); David Brody, *Workers in Industrial America* (1980); Jerold Auerbach, *Labor and Liberty* (1966); Sidney Fine, *Sit-Down* (1969); Bert Cochran, *Labor and Communism* (1977); Peter Friedlander, *The Emergence of a UAW Local* (1975); John Barnard, *Walter Reuther and the Rise of the Auto Workers* (1983); Ronald W. Schatz, *The Electrical Workers* (1983); David Milton, *The Politics of U.S. Labor: From the Great Depression to the New Deal* (1980); August Meier and Elliott Rudwick, *Black Detroit and the Rise of the UAW* (1979).

CHAPTER 27 THE GLOBAL CRISIS, 1921–1941

The 1920s. L. Ethan Ellis, *Republican Foreign Policy, 1921–1933* (1968); Merlo J. Pusey, *Charles Evans Hughes*, 2 vols. (1963); Joan Hoff Wilson, *American Business and Foreign Policy, 1920–1933* (1968) and *Ideology and Economics* (1974); William Appleman Williams, *The Tragedy of American Diplomacy* (1962); Frank Costigliola, *Awkward Dominion: American Political, Economic, and Cultural Relations with Europe, 1919–1933* (1984); Akira Iriye, *After Imperialism* (1965); Warren Cohen, *America's Response to China* (1971) and *Empire Without Tears* (1987); Roger Dingman, *Power in the Pacific* (1976); Thomas Buckley, *The United States and the Washington Conference* (1970); Robert H. Ferrell, *Peace in Their Time* (1952); Joseph Tulchin, *The Aftermath of War* (1971); William Kamman, *A Search for Stability* (1968); Michael J. Hogan, *Informal Entente: The Private Structure of Cooperation in Anglo-American Economic Diplomacy, 1918–1928* (1977); Melvyn P. Leffler, *The Elusive Quest* (1979).

The Hoover Years. Robert H. Ferrell, *American Diplomacy in the Great Depression* (1970); Elting Morison, *Turmoil and Tradition* (1960); Alexander DeConde, *Hoover's Latin American Policy* (1951); Raymond O'Connor, *Perilous Equilibrium* (1962); Armin Rappaport, *Stimson and Japan* (1963).

New Deal Diplomacy. Robert Dallek, *Franklin D. Roosevelt and American Foreign Policy, 1932–1945* (1979); Lloyd Gardner, *Economic Aspects of New Deal Diplomacy* (1964); Frank Freidel, *Launching the New Deal* (1973); Beatrice Farnsworth, *William C. Bullitt and the Soviet Union* (1967); Robert Browder, *The Origins of Soviet-American Diplomacy* (1953); Peter Filene, *Americans and the Soviet Experiment, 1917–1933* (1967); Edward E. Bennett, *Recognition of Russia* (1970); Walter LaFeber, *Inevitable Revolutions* (1983); Bruce J. Calder, *The Impact of Intervention* (1984); Lorenzo Meyer, *Mexico and the United States in the Oil Controversy* (1977); Bryce Wood, *The Making of the Good Neighbor Policy* (1961); Irwin F. Gellman, *Good Neighbor Diplomacy: United States Policies in Latin America, 1933–1945* (1979); David Green, *The Containment of Latin America* (1971); Dorothy Borg, *The United States and the Far Eastern Crisis of 1933–1938* (1964).

Isolationism and Pacifism. Selig Adler, *The Uncertain Giant* (1966) and *The Isolationist Impulse* (1957); Robert Divine, *The Reluctant Belligerent* (1965); William Langer and S. Everett Gleason, *The Challenge to Isolation* (1952) and *The Undeclared War* (1953); Manfred Jonas, *Isolationism in America* (1966); Wayne S. Cole, *America First* (1953), *Senator Gerald P. Nye and American Foreign Relations* (1962), *Charles A. Lindbergh and the Battle Against American Intervention in World War II* (1974), and *Roosevelt and the Isolationists, 1932–1945* (1983); Warren I. Cohen, *The American Revisionists* (1967); Thomas C. Kennedy, *Charles A. Beard and American Foreign Policy* (1975); Richard Lowitt, *George W. Norris*, 3 vols. (1963–1978); John K. Nelson, *The Peace Prophets* (1967); Lawrence Wittner, *Rebels Against War* (1984); Charles Chatfield, *For Peace and Justice: Pacifism in America, 1914–1941* (1971); Charles DeBenedetti, *Origins of the Modern American Peace Movement, 1915–1929* (1978) and *The Peace Reform in American History* (1980).

The Coming of World War II. Arnold Offner, *The Origins of the Second World War* (1975); Bernard F. Donahoe, *Private Plans and Public Dangers* (1965); Garry Clifford and Samuel R. Spencer, Jr., *The First Peacetime Draft* (1986); Waldo H. Heinrichs, Jr., *Threshold of War* (1988); Manfred Jonas, *The United States and Germany* (1984); James Leutze, *Bargaining for Supremacy* (1977); Michael S. Sherry, *The Rise of American Airpower* (1987); Joseph Lash, *Roosevelt and Churchill* (1976); Warren Kimball, *The Most Unsordid Act: Lend-Lease, 1939–1941* (1970); David Reynolds, *The Creation of the Anglo-American Alliance, 1937–1941* (1982); David F. Schmitz, *The United States and Fascist Italy, 1922–1944* (1988); Roger Dingman, *Power in the Pacific* (1976); Akira Iriye, *Across the Pacific* (1967), *After Imperialism: The Search for a New Order in the Far East, 1921–1933* (1965), and *The Origins of the Second World War in Asia and the Pacific* (1987); Hebert Feis, *The Road to Pearl Harbor* (1950); Jonathan Utley, *Going to War with Japan* (1985); James MacGregor Burns, *Roosevelt: The Soldier of Freedom* (1970); Roberta Wohlstetter, *Pearl Harbor: Warning and Decision* (1962); Gordon Prange, *At Dawn We Slept* (1981) and *Pearl Harbor* (1986); Martin V. Melosi, *The Shadow of Pearl Harbor* (1977).

CHAPTER 28 AMERICA IN A WORLD AT WAR

War and American Society. John Morton Blum, *V Was for Victory* (1976); Richard Polenberg, *War and Society* (1972); Mark J. Harris et al., *The Homefront* (1984); Alan Clive, *State of War: Michigan in World War II* (1979); Gerald D. Nash, *The American West Transformed: The Impact of the Second World War* (1985); Richard R. Lingeman, *Don't You Know There's a War On?* (1970); Studs Terkel, *"The Good War": An Oral History of World War II* (1984).

War Mobilization and Wartime Politics. Donald Nelson, *Arsenal of Democracy* (1946); Bruce Catton, *War Lords of Washington* (1946); David Brinkley, *Washington Goes to War* (1987); Eliot Janeway, *Struggle for Survival* (1951); Joel Seidman, *American Labor from Defense to Reconversion* (1953); Nelson Lichtenstein, *Labor's War at Home* (1982); Howell John Harris, *The Right to Manage* (1982); Leslie R. Groves, *Now It Can Be Told* (1962); Oscar E. Anderson, Jr., *The New World* (1962); Chester Bowles, *Promises to Keep* (1971); Lester V. Chandler, *Inflation in the United States, 1940–1948* (1951); Richard Steele, *Propaganda in an Open Society* (1985); Patrick S. Washburn, *A Question of Sedition: The Federal Government's Investigation of the Black Press During World War II* (1986); Alan Winkler, *The Politics of Propaganda* (1978); Philip Knightley, *The First Casualty* (1975); James MacGregor Burns, *Roosevelt: The Soldier of Freedom* (1970); Godfrey Hodgson, *The Colonel: The Life and Wars of Henry Stimson* (1990); Ellsworth Barnard, *Wendell Willkie* (1966); Maurice Isserman, *Which Side Were You On? The American Communist Party During World War II* (1982).

The War and Race. Louis Ruchames, *Race, Jobs, and Politics* (1953); Neil Wynn, *The Afro-American and the Second World War* (1976); Herbert Garfinkel, *When Negroes March* (1959); Richard M. Dalfiume, *Desegregation of the U.S. Armed Forces* (1969); Domenic J. Capeci, Jr., *The Harlem Riot of 1943* (1977) and *Race Relations in Wartime Detroit* (1987); Philip McGuire, ed., *Taps for a Jim Crow Army: Letters from Black Soldiers in World War II* (1982); August Meier and Elliott Rudwick, *CORE* (1973); Mauricio Mazon, *The Zoot-Suit Riots* (1984); Roger Daniels, *The Politics of Prejudice* (1962) and *Concentration Camps, USA* (1971); Audrie Girdner and Anne Loftis, *The Great Betrayal* (1969); Bill Hosokawa, *Nisei* (1969); Peter Irons, *Justice at War* (1983); Thomas James, *Exiles Within: The Schooling of Japanese-Americans, 1942–1945* (1987).

Women and the War. Ruth Milkman, *Gender at Work: The Dynamics of Job Segregation by Sex During World War II* (1987); Susan M. Reverby, *Ordered to Care: The Dilemma of American Nursing, 1850–1945* (1987); Karen Anderson, *Wartime Women: Sex Roles, Family Relations, and the Status of Women During World War II* (1981); D'Ann Campbell, *Women at War with America* (1984); Sherna B. Gluck, *Rosie the Riveter Revisited* (1987); Maureen Honey, *Creating Rosie the Riveter: Class, Gender, and Propaganda During World War II* (1984); Margaret R. Higgonet et al., *Behind the Lines: Gender and the Two World Wars* (1987); Susan Hartmann, *The Homefront and Beyond: American Women in the 1940s* (1982); Leila Rupp, *Mobilizing Women for War* (1978).

Wartime Military and Diplomatic Experiences. James MacGregor Burns, *Roosevelt: The Soldier of Freedom* (1970); Robert Divine, *Roosevelt and World War II* (1969) and *Second*

Chance (1967); Albert Russell Buchanan, *The United States and World War II*, 2 vols. (1962); Fletcher Pratt, *War for the World* (1951); Margaret Hoyle, *A World in Flames* (1970); Kenneth Greenfield, *American Strategy in World War II* (1963); Samuel Eliot Morison, *Strategy and Compromise* (1958), *History of United States Naval Operations in World War II*, 14 vols. (1947–1960), and *The Two Ocean War* (1963); Winston S. Churchill, *The Second World War*, 6 vols. (1948–1953); Chester Wilmot, *The Struggle for Europe* (1952); Charles B. McDonald, *The Mighty Endeavor* (1969); Stephen Ambrose, *The Supreme Commander* (1970) and *Eisenhower: Soldier, General of the Army, President-Elect* (1983); Michael Howard, *The Mediterranean Strategy in World War II* (1968); Dwight D. Eisenhower, *Crusade in Europe* (1948); Forrest Pogue, *George C. Marshall*, 2 vols. (1963–1966); D. Clayton James, *A Time for Giants: Politics of the American High Command in World War II* (1987); Max Hastings, *Overlord: D-Day and the Battle for Normandy* (1984); Russel F. Weigley, *The American Way of War* (1973); Cornelius Ryan, *The Last Battle* (1966); John Toland, *The Last Hundred Days* (1966); Ronald Schaffer, *Wings of Judgment: American Bombing in World War II* (1985); David S. Wyman, *The Abandonment of the Jews: America and the Holocaust, 1941–1945* (1984); Warren Kimball, *The Juggler: Franklin Roosevelt as Wartime Statesman* (1991); Gaddis Smith, *American Diplomacy During the Second World War* (1964); E. J. Kind and W. M. Whitehill, *Fleet Admiral King* (1952); Barbara Tuchman, *Stilwell and the American Experience in China* (1971); John W. Dower, *War Without Mercy: Race and Power in the Pacific War* (1986); John Toland, *The Rising Sun* (1970); Ronald Spector, *Eagle Against the Sun: The American War with Japan* (1985); William Manchester, *American Caesar* (1979).

Atomic Warfare. Martin Sherwin, *A World Destroyed* (1975); Gar Alperovitz, *Atomic Diplomacy* (1965); Robert Jungk, *Brighter Than a Thousand Suns* (1958); Nuel Davis, *Lawrence and Oppenheimer* (1969); Gregg Herken, *The Winning Weapon* (1980); W. S. Schoenberger, *Decision of Destiny* (1969); Robert Donovan, *Conflict and Crisis* (1977); John Hersey, *Hiroshima* (1946); Herbert Feis, *The Atomic Bomb and the End of World War II* (1966); Richard Rhodes, *The Making of the Atomic Bomb* (1987); Leon V. Sigal, *Fighting to a Finish* (1988).

CHAPTER 29 AMERICA AND THE COLD WAR

Origins of the Cold War. Walter LaFeber, *America, Russia, and the Cold War, 1945–1967* (1967, rev. 1980); Stephen Ambrose, *Rise to Globalism*, 5th ed. (1988); Bernard Weisberger, *Cold War, Cold Peace* (1984); Adam Ulam, *The Rivals: America and Russia Since World War II* (1971); John Lewis Gaddis, *Strategies of Containment* (1982), *The United States and the Origins of the Cold War, 1941–1947* (1972), and *The Long Peace* (1987); John L. Snell, *Illusion and Necessity* (1967); Gaddis Smith, *American Diplomacy During the Second World War* (1965) and *Dean Acheson* (1972); Herbert Feis, *Churchill, Roosevelt, and Stalin* (1957); William Taubman, *Stalin's American Policy* (1982); William McNeill, *America, Britain and Russia* (1953); Diane Clemens, *Yalta* (1970); Herbert Feis, *Between War and Peace: The Potsdam Conference* (1960); Athan G. Theoharis, *The Yalta Myths* (1970); W. L. Neumann, *After Victory* (1969); George C. Herring, Jr., *Aid to Russia* (1973); Daniel Yergin, *Shattered Peace* (1977); Thomas G. Paterson, *Soviet–American Confrontation* (1974), *On Every Front: The Making of the Cold War* (1979), and *Meeting the Communist*

Threat (1988); Gregg Herken, *The Winning Weapon* (1980); Martin Sherwin, *A World Destroyed* (1975); Gar Alperovitz, *Atomic Diplomacy: Hiroshima and Potsdam*, rev. ed. (1985); Robert A. Pollard, *Economic Security and the Origins of the Cold War* (1985).

Truman's Foreign Policy. Robert Donovan, *Conflict and Crisis* (1977); Lloyd Gardner, *Architects of Illusion* (1970); Joyce Kolko and Gabriel Kolko, *The Limits of Power* (1970); George F. Kennan, *American Diplomacy, 1900–1950* (1952) and *Memoirs, 1925–1950* (1967); David Mayer, *George Kennan and the Dilemmas of U.S. Foreign Policy* (1988); Anders Stephanson, *Kennan and the Art of Foreign Policy* (1989); Dean Acheson, *Present at the Creation* (1970); Fraser J. Harbutt, *The Iron Curtain: Churchill, America, and the Origins of the Cold War* (1986); Thomas Schwartz, *America's Germany: John J. McCloy and the Federal Republic of Germany* (1991); Richard J. Barnet, *The Alliance* (1983); Laurence Kaplan, *The United States and NATO* (1984); Hadley Arkes, *Bureaucracy, the Marshall Plan and National Interest* (1973); Michael Hogan, *The Marshall Plan* (1987); Imanuel Wexler, *The Marshall Plan Revisited* (1983); Akira Iriye, *The Cold War in Asia* (1974); Robert M. Blum, *Drawing the Line: The Origin of the American Containment Policy in East Asia* (1982); John King Fairbank, *The United States and China*, rev. ed. (1971); Edwin O. Reischauer, *The United States and Japan*, rev. ed. (1965); Warren I. Cohen, *America's Response to China*, rev. ed. (1980); Michael Schaller, *The U.S. Crusade in China* (1979), *Communists* (1971), and *The American Occupation of Japan: The Origins of the Cold War in Asia* (1985); Lisle Rose, *Roots of Tragedy* (1976); Gary May, *China Scapegoat* (1979); Christopher Thorne, *Allies of a Kind* (1978); Bruce R. Koniholm, *The Origins of the Cold War in the Middle East* (1980); William R. Louis, *The British Empire in the Middle East* (1984); Michael B. Stoff, *Oil, War, and American Security* (1980).

Truman's Domestic Policies. Alonzo Hamby, *Beyond the New Deal* (1973); Robert Donovan, *Conflict and Crisis* (1977) and *Tumultuous Years* (1982); Richard L. Miller, *Truman: The Rise to Power* (1986); Roy Jenkins, *Truman* (1986); William E. Pemberton, *Harry S. Truman* (1989); Barton J. Bernstein, ed., *Politics and Policies of the Truman Administration* (1970); Andrew J. Dunar, *The Truman Scandals and the Politics of Morality* (1984); Robert H. Ferrell, *Harry S. Truman and the Modern American Presidency* (1983); Donald R. McCoy, *The Presidency of Harry S. Truman* (1984); Susan Hartmann, *Truman and the 80th Congress* (1971); Stephen K. Bailey, *Congress Makes a Law* (1950); Gary Reichard, *Politics as Usual* (1988); Richard O. Davies, *Housing Reform During the Truman Administration* (1966); R. Alton Lee, *Truman and the Steel Seizure Case* (1977); Allen J. Matusow, *Farm Policies and Politics in the Truman Years* (1967); Arthur F. McClure, *The Truman Administration and the Problems of Postwar Labor* (1969); R. Alton Lee, *Truman and Taft-Hartley* (1967); Christopher L. Tomlins, *The State and the Unions* (1985); William Berman, *The Politics of Civil Rights in the Truman Administration* (1970); Donald McCoy and Richard Ruetten, *Quest and Response* (1973); Richard M. Dalfiume, *Desegregation of the U.S. Armed Forces* (1969); Maeva Marcus, *Truman and the Steel Seizure* (1977); William O'Neill, *American High* (1986); John P. Diggins, *The Proud Decades* (1988).

Cold War Politics. James T. Patterson, *Mr. Republican* (1972); Irwin Ross, *The Loneliest Campaign* (1968); Norman Markowitz, *The Rise and Fall of the People's Century* (1973); Maurice Isserman, *If I Had a Hammer . . .: The Death of the Old Left and the Birth of the New Left* (1987); Allen Yarnell, *Democrats and Progressives* (1974); Steven M. Gillon,

Politics and Vision: The ADA and American Liberalism, 1947–1985 (1987); Richard Norton Smith, *Thomas E. Dewey and His Times* (1982); Richard Pells, *The Liberal Mind in a Conservative Age: American Intellectuals in the 1940s and 1950s* (1985).

The Korean War. Bruce Cumings, *The Origins of the Korean War* (1980) and Cummings, ed., *Child of Conflict: The Korean–American Relationship, 1943–1953* (1983); Glenn D. Paige, *The Korean Decision* (1968); Joseph C. Goulden, *Korea: The Untold Story of the War* (1982); John Spanier, *The Truman–MacArthur Controversy* (1959); Allen Whiting, *China Crosses the Yalu* (1960); Carl Berger, *The Korean Knot* (1957); Ronald Caridi, *The Korean War and American Politics* (1969); Robert Leckie, *Conflict* (1962); Robert R. Simmons, *The Strained Alliance* (1975); Charles W. Dobbs, *The Unwanted Symbol* (1981).

Countersubversion. David Caute, *The Great Fear* (1978); Edward Shils, *The Torment of Secrecy* (1956); Allen Weinstein, *Perjury* (1978); Ronald Radosh and Joyce Milton, *The Rosenberg File* (1983); Walter and Miriam Schneer, *Invitation to an Inquest,* rev. ed. (1983); Richard Freeland, *The Truman Doctrine and the Origins of McCarthyism* (1971); Athan Theoharis, *Seeds of Repression* (1971); Alan Harper, *The Politics of Loyalty* (1969); Michael R. Belknap, *Cold War Political Justice: The Smith Act, the Communist Party, and American Civil Liberties* (1977); Stanley Kutler, *The American Inquisition* (1982); Larry Ceplair and Steven Englund, *The Inquisition in Hollywood* (1983); Mary Sperling McAuliffe, *Crisis on the Left* (1978); Harvey Levenstein, *Communism, Anticommunism, and the CIO* (1981); Thomas C. Reeves, *The Life and Times of Joe McCarthy* (1982); David Oshinsky, *A Conspiracy So Immense* (1983); Michael Paul Rogin, *The Intellectuals and McCarthy* (1967); Robert Griffith, *The Politics of Fear* (1970); Richard Fried, *Men Against McCarthy* (1976) and *Nightmare in Red* (1990); Richard Rovere, *Senator Joe McCarthy* (1959); Victor Navasky, *Naming Names* (1980); William O'Neill, *A Better World* (1983); Joseph Starobin, *American Communism in Crisis* (1972).

CHAPTER 30 THE AFFLUENT SOCIETY

General Studies. William Leuchtenburg, *A Troubled Feast* (1979); Carl Degler, *Affluence and Anxiety* (1968); John Brooks, *The Great Leap* (1966); Godfrey Hodgson, *America in Our Time* (1976); William Chafe, *The Unfinished Journey* (1986); Eric Goldman, *The Crucial Decade and After* (1960); John P. Diggins, *The Proud Decades* (1989); Douglas T. Miller and Marion Novak, *The Fifties* (1977); William O'Neill, *American High* (1986).

The Postwar Economy. John K. Galbraith, *The Affluent Society* (1958) and *The New Industrial State (1967); Loren J. Okroi, Galbraith, Harrington, Heilbroner* (1986); C. Wright Mills, *The Power Elite* (1956); Harold G. Vatter, *The U.S. Economy in the 1950s* (1963); Robert Heilbroner, *The Limits of American Capitalism* (1965); Joel Seidman, *American Labor from Defense to Reconversion* (1953); John Hutchinson, *The Imperfect Union* (1970).

Culture and Society. William Graebner, *The Age of Doubt: American Thought and Culture in the 1940's* (1991); Paul Carter, *Another Part of the Fifties* (1983); Marty Jezer, *The Dark Ages: Life in the U.S. 1945–1960* (1982); George Lipsitz, *Class and Culture in*

Cold War America (1981); Douglas T. Miller and Marion Novak, *The Fifties* (1977); Herbert Gans, *The Levittowners* (1967); Kenneth Jackson, *The Crabgrass Frontier* (1985); Ruth Cowan, *More Work for Mother: The Irony of Household Technology* (1983); Elaine Tyler May, *Homeward Bound: American Families in the Cold War* (1988); Eugenia Kaledin, *Mothers and More: American Women in the 1950s* (1984); Edward J. Epstein, *News from Nowhere* (1973); David Halberstam, *The Powers That Be* (1979); Tom Wolfe, *The Right Stuff* (1979); Walter A. McDougall, . . . *the Heavens and the Earth: A Political History of the Space Age* (1985); R. L. Rosholt, *An Administrative History of NASA* (1966); Walter Sullivan, ed., *America's Race for the Moon* (1962); Barbara B. Clowse, *Brainpower for the Cold War: The Sputnik Crisis and the National Defense Education Act of 1958* (1981); Paul Boyer, *By the Bomb's Early Light* (1986); David Riesman, *The Lonely Crowd* (1950); William Whyte, *The Organization Man* (1956); C. Wright Mills, *White Collar* (1956); Bruce Cook, *The Beat Generation* (1971); John Tytell, *Naked Angels* (1976); Ann Charters, *Kerouac* (1973); Dennis McNally, *Desolate Angel* (1979); Arthur M. Schlesinger, Jr., *The Vital Center* (1949); Daniel Bell, *The End of Ideology* (1960); Howard Brick, *Daniel Bell and the Decline of Intellectual Radicalism* (1986); Richard H. Pells, *The Liberal Mind in a Conservative Age* (1985); David Potter, *People of Plenty* (1954); Richard Hofstader, *The Age of Reform* (1954); Mary Sperling McAuliffe, *Crisis on the Left* (1978); Daniel Bell, ed., *The Radical Right* (1963).

The Eisenhower Presidency.   Stephen Ambrose, *Eisenhower the President* (1984); Piers Brendon, *Ike* (1986); Robert F. Burk, *Dwight D. Eisenhower* (1986); Fred Greenstein, *The Hidden-Hand Presidency* (1982); Charles C. Alexander, *Holding the Line* (1975); Herbert S. Parmet, *Eisenhower and the American Crusades* (1972); Peter Lyon, *Eisenhower: Portrait of a Hero* (1974); Dwight D. Eisenhower, *The White House Years*, 2 vols. (1963–1965); Emmet John Hughes, *The Ordeal of Power* (1963); Sherman Adams, *Firsthand Report* (1961); Richard Nixon, *Six Crises* (1962); Nicol C. Rae, *The Decline and Fall of the Liberal Republicans* (1989); Gary Reichard, *The Reaffirmation of Republicanism* (1975); David W. Reinhard, *The Republican Right Since 1945* (1983); Mark H. Rose, *Interstate: Express Highway Politics, 1941–1956* (1979).

Foreign Policy.   Robert Divine, *Eisenhower and the Cold War* (1981); Townsend Hoopes, *The Devil and John Foster Dulles* (1973); Louis Gerson, *John Foster Dulles* (1967); Stephen Ambrose, *Ike's Spies* (1981); Cecil Currey, *Edward Lansdale: The Unquiet American* (1988); Michael Beschloss, *MAYDAY* (1986); Chester Cooper, *Lost Crusade* (1970); Frances Fitzgerald, *Fire in the Lake* (1972); John T. McAlister, Jr., *Vietnam: The Origins of Revolution* (1969); George Herring, *America's Longest War* (1979); Chester Cooper, *The Lion's Last Roar* (1978); Hugh Thomas, *Suez* (1967); Mira Wilkins, *The Maturing of Multinational Enterprise* (1974); Kermit Roosevelt, *Counter-coup* (1980); Burton Kaufman, *The Oil Cartel Case* (1978); Richard Immerman, *The CIA in Guatemala* (1982); Walter LaFeber, *Inevitable Revolutions* (1983); Stephen G. Rabe, *Eisenhower and Latin America* (1988); Robert A. Divine, *Foreign Policy and U.S. Presidential Elections*, 2 vols. (1974) and *Blowing in the Wind: The Nuclear Test Ban Debate, 1954–1960* (1978); Blanche W. Cooke, *The Declassified Eisenhower* (1981); Richard A. Melanson and David A. Mayers, eds., *Reevaluating Eisenhower* (1986); Burton I. Kaufman, *Trade and Aid* (1982); Howard Ball, *Justice Downwind: America's Nuclear Testing Program in the 1950s* (1986); Gregg Herken, *Counsels of War* (1985); Richard G. Hewlett and Jack M. Hall,

Atoms for Peace and War, 1953–1961 (1989); Richard Smoke, *National Security and the Nuclear Dilemma* (1988).

Legal and Constitutional Issues. Philip Stern, *The Oppenheimer Case* (1969); Michael Straight, *Trial by Television* (1954); Paul Murphy, *The Constitution in Crisis Times* (1972); Alexander Bickel, *Politics and the Warren Court* (1965) and *The Supreme Court and the Idea of Progress* (1970); Philip Kurland, *Politics, the Constitution, and the Warren Court* (1970); John Weaver, *Earl Warren* (1967).

Civil Rights. Richard Kluger, *Simple Justice* (1975); Stephen J. Whitfield, *A Death in the Delta: The Story of Emmett Till* (1988); Anthony Lewis, *Portrait of a Decade* (1964); Martin Luther King, Jr., *Stride Toward Freedom* (1958); William Chafe, *Civilities and Civil Rights* (1980); Harvard Sitkoff, *The Struggle for Black Equality, 1954–1980* (1981); John W. Anderson, *Eisenhower, Brownell, and the Congress* (1964); Robert F. Burk, *The Eisenhower Administration and Black Civil Rights* (1984); Numan V. Bartley, *The Rise of Massive Resistance* (1969); Elizabeth Huckaby, *Crisis at Central High* (1980); David Garrow, ed., *The Montgomery Bus Boycott and the Women Who Started It: A Memoir of Jo Ann Gibson Robinson* (1987); Robert J. Norrell, *Reaping the Whirlwind: The Civil Rights Movement in Tuskegee* (1985); Howell Raines, *My Soul Is Rested* (1977).

CHAPTER 31 THE ORDEAL OF LIBERALISM

General Studies. Godfrey Hodgson, *America in Our Time* (1976); Charles R. Morris, *A Time of Passion* (1984); Allen J. Matusow, *The Unraveling of America* (1984); Theodore H. White, *America in Search of Itself* (1982); William Chafe, *The Unfinished Journey* (1986).

Kennedy and Johnson. Theodore H. White, *The Making of the President, 1960* (1961); Arthur M. Schlesinger, Jr., *A Thousand Days* (1965); Theodore Sorensen, *Kennedy* (1965); Richard N. Goodwin, *Remembering America* (1988); Herbert Parmet, *Jack* (1980) and *JFK* (1983); Henry Fairlie, *The Kennedy Promise* (1973); David Burner, *John F. Kennedy and a New Generation* (1988); Lewis Paper, *The Promise and the Performance* (1975); Bruce Miroff, *Pragmatic Illusions* (1976); Garry Wills, *The Kennedy Imprisonment* (1982); Thomas Brown, *JFK: The History of an Image* (1988); *The Report of the Warren Commission* (1964); William Manchester, *The Death of a President* (1967); Anthony Summers, *Conspiracy* (1980); Edward J. Epstein, *Inquest* (1966) and *Legend* (1978); Henry Hurt, *Reasonable Doubt* (1985); Doris Kearns, *Lyndon Johnson and the American Dream* (1976); Eric Goldman, *The Tragedy of Lyndon Johnson* (1968); Ronnie Dugger, *The Politician* (1982); Robert Caro, *The Years of Lyndon Johnson: The Path to Power* (1982) and *Means of Ascent* (1990); Lyndon B. Johnson, *Vantage Point* (1971); George Reedy, *The Twilight of the Presidency* (1970); Jim Heath, *Decade of Disillusionment* (1975); Vaughn D. Bornet, *The Presidency of Lyndon B. Johnson* (1983); Paul K. Conkin, *Big Daddy from the Pedernales* (1986).

Domestic Policies. Tom Wicker, *JFK and LBJ* (1968); Jim Heath, *John F. Kennedy and the Business Community* (1969); Victor Navasky, *Kennedy Justice* (1971); James

Sundquist, *Politics and Policy* (1968); Sar Levitan, *The Great Society's Poor Law* (1969); Sar Levitan and Robert Taggart, *The Promise of Greatness* (1976); Daniel Knapp and Kenneth Polk, *Scouting the War on Poverty* (1971); Robert H. Haveman, ed., *A Decade of Federal Antipoverty Programs* (1977); Greg J. Duncan, *Years of Poverty, Years of Plenty* (1984); Charles Murray, *Losing Ground* (1984); Frances Fox Piven and Richard Cloward, *Regulating the Poor* (1971); Nicholas Lemann, *The Promised Land: The Great Black Migration and How It Changed America* (1991); Hugh Davis Graham, *Uncertain Trumpet* (1984); Allen J. Matusow, *The Unraveling of America: A History of Liberalism in the 1960s* (1984); James T. Patterson, *America's Struggle Against Poverty, 1900–1980* (1981); Henry J. Aaron, *Politics and the Professors* (1978); John E. Schwarz, *America's Hidden Success* (1983).

Race Relations. David Lewis, *King* (1970); Carl Brauer, *John F. Kennedy and the Second Reconstruction* (1977); Martin Luther King, Jr., *Why We Can't Wait* (1964); David Garrow, *Protest at Selma* (1978), *The FBI and Martin Luther King* (1981), and *Bearing the Cross* (1986); Taylor Branch, *Parting the Waters* (1988); William Chafe, *Civilities and Civil Rights* (1980); Hugh Davis Graham, *The Civil Rights Era* (1990); Nancy Weiss, *Whitney M. Young, Jr., and the Struggle for Civil Rights* (1989); Steven Lawson, *Black Ballots: Voting Rights in the South, 1966–1969* (1976); Abigail Thernstrom, *Whose Votes Count? Affirmative Action and Minority Voting Rights* (1987); Harris Wofford, *Of Kennedys and Kings* (1980); Stephen Oates, *Let the Trumpet Sound* (1982); Doug McAdam, *Freedom Summer* (1988); Stokely Carmichael and Charles Hamilton, *Black Power* (1967); Alex Haley, *The Autobiography of Malcolm X* (1966); Benjamin Muse, *The American Negro Revolution* (1969); Eugene Wolfenstein, *The Victims of Democracy: Malcolm X and the Black Revolution* (1981); Robert Fogelson, *Violence as Protest* (1971); Joe R. Feagin and Harlan Hahn, *Ghetto Revolts* (1973); *Report of the National Advisory Commission on Civil Disorders* (1968); Paul Burstein, *Discrimination, Jobs, and Politics* (1985).

Foreign Policy. Richard Walton, *Cold War and Counterrevolution* (1972); Louise Fitzsimmons, *The Kennedy Doctrine* (1972); Roger Hilsman, *To Move a Nation* (1965); Philip Geyelin, *Lyndon B. Johnson and the World* (1966); Richard Barnet, *Intervention and Revolution* (1968); Haynes Johnson, *The Bay of Pigs* (1964); Peter Wyden, *Bay of Pigs* (1969); Trumbull Higgins, *The Perfect Failure: Kennedy, Eisenhower, and the CIA at the Bay of Pigs* (1987); Elie Abel, *The Missile Crisis* (1966); Graham Allison, *Essence of Decision* (1971); Robert Kennedy, *Thirteen Days* (1969); Herbert Dinerstein, *The Making of a Missile Crisis* (1976); Dan Kurzman, *Santo Domingo* (1966); Jerome Slater, *Intervention and Negotiation* (1970); Richard D. Mahoney, *JFK: Ordeal in Africa* (1983); Warren Cohen, *Dean Rusk* (1980); Gerald T. Rice, *The Bold Experiment: JFK's Peace Corps* (1985).

Vietnam. George C. Herring, *America's Longest War*, rev. ed. (1986); Stanley Karnow, *Vietnam* (1983); R. B. Smith, *An International History of the Vietnam War: The Kennedy Strategy* (1985); *The Pentagon Papers*, Senator Gravel edition (1975); David Halberstam, *The Best and the Brightest* (1972); Neil Sheehan, *A Bright Shining Lie* (1988); Guenter Lewy, *America in Vietnam* (1978); John Galloway, *The Gulf of Tonkin Resolution* (1970); Alexander Kendrick, *The Wound Within* (1974); Norman Podhoretz, *Why We Were in Vietnam* (1982); Leslie Gelb and Richard Betts, *The Irony of Vietnam: The System Worked* (1979); Larry Berman, *Planning a Tragedy* (1982) and *Lyndon Johnson's War* (1989); George McT. Kahin, *Intervention* (1986); Gabriel Kolko, *The Anatomy of a War* (1985);

Wallace J. Thies, *When Governments Collide* (1980); Michael Herr, *Dispatches* (1977); Lawrence Baskir and William Strauss, *Chance and Circumstance* (1978); Gloria Emerson, *Winners and Losers* (1976); Mark Baker, *Nam* (1982); Al Santoli, *Everything We Had* (1981); Wallace Terry, *Bloods* (1984); William Broyles, Jr., *Brothers in Arms: A Journey from War to Peace* (1986); Thomas Powers, *Vietnam: The War at Home* (1973); Irwin Unger, *The Movement* (1974); Peter Braestrup, *Big Story* (1977, abridged ed. 1978); Don Oberdorfer, *Tet* (1971); Bruce C. Palmer, Jr., *The 25-Year War* (1984); Col. Harry Summers, *On Strategy* (1981); Thomas C. Thayer, *War Without Fronts* (1985); Robert W. Komer, *Bureaucracy at War* (1986); Ronald Spector, *Advice and Support* (1983).

1968. David Caute, *The Year of the Barricades* (1988); Lewis Chester, Godfrey Hodgson, and Lewis Page, *American Melodrama* (1969); David Farber, *Chicago '68* (1988); Charles Kaiser, *1968 in America* (1988); Godfrey Hodgson, *America in Our Time* (1976); Arthur M. Schlesinger, Jr., *Robert Kennedy and His Times* (1978); Norman Mailer, *Miami and the Siege of Chicago* (1968); Ben Stavis, *We Were the Campaign* (1969); Marshall Frady, *Wallace*, rev. ed (1976); Theodore White, *The Making of the President, 1968* (1969).

CHAPTER 32 THE CRISIS OF AUTHORITY

General Studies.   William O'Neill, *Coming Apart* (1971); Ronald Berman, *America in the Sixties* (1968); Allen J. Matusow, *The Unraveling of America* (1984); Peter N. Carroll, *It Seemed Like Nothing Happened* (1982).

The New Left and the Counterculture.   James Miller, *"Democracy in the Streets"*: *From Port Huron to the Siege of Chicago* (1987); Maurice Isserman, *If I Had a Hammer . . .: The Death of the Old Left and the Birth of the New Left* (1987); Milton Viorst, *Fire in the Streets* (1979); Todd Gitlin, *The Whole World Is Watching* (1981) and *The Sixties: Years of Hope, Days of Rage* (1987); Irwin Unger, *The Movement* (1974); Lawrence Lader, *Power on the Left* (1979); Kirkpatrick Sale, *SDS* (1973); Sara Evans, *Personal Politics* (1979); W. J. Rorabaugh, *Berkeley at War* (1989); Peter Clecak, *Radical Paradoxes* (1973); Kenneth Keniston, *Young Radicals* (1968); Lewis Feuer, *The Conflict of Generations* (1969); Paul Goodman, *Growing Up Absurd* (1960); Theodore Roszak, *The Making of a Counter Culture* (1969); Charles Reich, *The Greening of America* (1970); Ronald Berman, *America in the Sixties* (1968); Joan Didion, *Slouching Towards Bethlehem* (1967) and *The White Album* (1979); John Diggins, *The American Left in the Twentieth Century* (1973); Richard Flacks, *Youth and Social Change* (1971); Morris Dickstein, *Gates of Eden* (1977); Jon Wiener, *Come Together: John Lennon in His Time* (1984).

Indians and Hispanics.   Larry W. Burt, *Tribalism in Crisis: Federal Indian Policy, 1953–1961* (1982); Charles F. Wilkinson, *American Indians, Time, and the Law*, rev. ed. (1987); Wilcomb Washburn, *Red Man's Land/White Man's Land* (1971); Vine Deloria, Jr., *Behind the Trail of Broken Treaties* (1974) and *Custer Died for Your Sins* (1969); D'Arcy McNickle, *Native American Tribalism* (1973); Stan Steiner, *The New Indians* (1968); Peter Iverson, *The Navajo Nation* (1981); Rodolfo Acuña, *Occupied America*, 2nd ed. (1981); Julian Samora, *Los Mojados* (1971); Oscar Lewis, *La Vida* (1969); Matt Meier and Feliciano Rivera, *The Chicanos* (1972); Ronald Taylor, *Chávez and the Farm Workers* (1975).

Feminism. Susan M. Hartmann, *From Margin to Mainstream: Women and American Politics Since 1960* (1989); Cynthia Harrison, *On Account of Sex* (1990); Winifred Wandersee, *On the Move: American Women in the 1970s* (1988); William Chafe, *The American Woman* (1972); Sheila Rothman, *Woman's Proper Place* (1978); Jo Freeman, *The Politics of Women's Liberation* (1975); Gayle Yates, *What Women Want* (1975); Betty Friedan, *The Feminine Mystique* (1963); Carol Gilligan, *In a Different Voice* (1982); Alice Kessler-Harris, *Out to Work: A History of Wage-Earning Women in the United States* (1982); Donald Matthews and Jane Sherson De Hart, *Sex, Gender, and the Politics of ERA* (1990); Robin Morgan, ed., *Sisterhood Is Powerful* (1970); Ethel Klein, *Gender Politics* (1984); Kristin Luker, *Abortion and the Politics of Motherhood* (1984); Rosalind Petchesky, *Abortion and Women's Choice* (1984); Marian Faux, *Roe v. Wade* (1988); Nancy Cott, *The Grounding of Modern Feminism* (1987).

Nixon and the World. Franz Schurman, *The Foreign Policies of Richard Nixon* (1987); Richard Stevenson, *The Rise and Fall of Détente* (1985); Robert S. Litwak, *Détente and the Nixon Doctrine: American Foreign Policy and the Pursuit of Stability* (1984); Henry A. Kissinger, *White House Years* (1979) and *Years of Upheaval* (1982); Gareth Porter, *A Peace Denied* (1975); William Shawcross, *Sideshow: Nixon, Kissinger, and the Destruction of Cambodia* (1978); Roger Morris, *Uncertain Greatness* (1977); Seyom Brown, *The Crisis of Power* (1979); David Landau, *Kissinger: The Uses of Power* (1972); Marvin Kalb and Bernard Kalb, *Kissinger* (1974); Seymour Hersh, *The Price of Power* (1983); Tad Szulc, *The Illusion of Peace* (1978); Roger Hilsman, *The Crouching Future* (1975); Harland Moulton, *From Superiority to Parity* (1973); John Newhouse, *Cold Dawn* (1973); John Stockwell, *In Search of Enemies* (1977); Thomas Powers, *The Man Who Kept the Secrets* (1979); Michael Oksenberg and Robert Oxnam, eds., *Dragon and Eagle* (1978); William Quandt, *Decade of Decision* (1977); Robert Stookey, *America and the Arab States* (1975).

Nixon's Domestic Policies. Herbert Parmet, *Richard Nixon and His America* (1989); Stephen Ambrose, *Nixon: The Triumph of a Politician, 1962–1972* (1989); William Safire, *Before the Fall* (1975); Raymond Price, *With Nixon* (1977); Daniel P. Moynihan, *The Politics of a Guaranteed Income* (1973); Vincent Burke and Vee Burke, *Nixon's Good Deed* (1974); R. L. Miller, *The New Economics of Richard Nixon* (1972); R. P. Nathan et al., *Monitoring Revenue Sharing* (1975); John Ehrlichman, *Witness to Power* (1982); Bob Woodward and Scott Armstrong, *The Brethren* (1980); Theodore H. White, *The Making of the President, 1972* (1973); Richard Barnet, *The Lean Years* (1980); Joan Edelman Spero, *The Politics of International Economic Relations* (1977); J. C. Hurewitz, ed., *Oil, the Arab–Israeli Dispute, and the Industrial World* (1976).

Nixon and Watergate. Garry Wills, *Nixon Agonistes* (1970); Fawn Brodie, *Richard Nixon* (1981); Bruce Mazlish, *In Search of Nixon* (1972); Jonathan Schell, *The Time of Illusion* (1975); Stanley J. Kutler, *The Wars of Watergate* (1990); Richard M. Nixon, *RN: The Memoirs of Richard Nixon* (1978); Theodore H. White, *Breach of Faith* (1975); Anthony Lukas, *Nightmare* (1976); Bob Woodward and Carl Bernstein, *All the President's Men* (1974) and *The Final Days* (1976); John Dean, *Blind Ambition* (1976); Richard Cohen and Jules Witcover, *A Heartbeat Away* (1974); Arthur M. Schlesinger, Jr., *The Imperial Presidency* (1973).

CHAPTER 33 THE UNFINISHED NATION

The Ford Presidency. Gerald Ter Horst, *Gerald Ford* (1975); Robert T. Hartmann, *Palace Politics* (1980); Richard Reeves, *A Ford Not a Lincoln* (1976); Gerald Ford, *A Time to Heal* (1979); James L. Sundquist, *The Decline and Resurgence of Congress* (1981); A. James Reichley, *Conservatives in an Age of Change: The Nixon and Ford Administrations* (1981); Edward and Frederick Schapsmeier, *Gerald R. Ford's Date with Destiny: A Political Biography* (1989).

The Carter Presidency. Jimmy Carter, *Why Not the Best?* (1975) and *Keeping Faith* (1982); Rosalynn Carter, *First Lady from Plains* (1984); Erwin Hargrove, *Jimmy Carter as President* (1989); Jules Witcover, *Marathon* (1977); James Wooten, *Dasher* (1978); Clark Mollenhoff, *The President Who Failed* (1980); Jack Bass and Walter Devries, *The Transformation of Southern Politics* (1976); Hamilton Jordan, *Crisis* (1982); Haynes Johnson, *In the Absence of Power* (1980); Steven Gillon, *The Democrats' Dilemma: Walter F. Mondale and the Liberal Legacy* (1992); Charles O. Jones, *The Trusteeship Presidency* (1988); Zbigniew Brzezinski, *Power and Principle* (1983); Cyrus Vance, *Hard Choices* (1983); Gaddis Smith, *Morality, Reason, and Power* (1986); James Bill, *The Eagle and the Lion* (1988); Walter LaFeber, *Panama Canal* (1978); A. Glenn Mower, Jr., *Human Rights and American Foreign Policy* (1987); William B. Quandt, *Camp David* (1986).

The New Right. Peter Steinfels, *The Neo-Conservatives* (1979); Sidney Blumenthal, *The Rise of the Counter-Establishment* (1986); Burton Yale Pines, *Back to Basics* (1982); David W. Reinhard, *The Republican Right Since 1945* (1983); John K. White, *The New Politics of Old Values* (1988).

The Reagan Presidency. Theodore H. White, *America in Search of Itself* (1982); William Boyarsky, *The Rise of Ronald Reagan* (1968); Anne Edwards, *Early Reagan* (1987); Garry Wills, *Reagan's America* (1987); Hedrick Smith et al., *Reagan: The Man, the President* (1980); Hedrick Smith, *The Power Game* (1988); Lou Cannon, *Reagan* (1982); Robert Dallek, *Ronald Reagan: The Politics of Symbolism* (1984); Ronnie Dugger, *On Reagan* (1983); Richard Reeves, *The Reagan Detour* (1985); Laurence I. Barrett, *Gambling with History* (1984); Rowland Evans and Robert Novak, *The Reagan Revolution* (1981); Fred I. Greenstein, ed., *The Reagan Presidency* (1983); John L. Palmer and Isabel V. Sawhill, eds., *The Reagan Experiment* (1982); Joan Claybrook, *Retreat from Safety* (1984); Jonathan Lash, *A Season of Spoils* (1984); Jane Mayer and Doyle McManus, *Landslide: The Unmaking of the President, 1984–1988* (1988); George Gilder, *Wealth and Poverty* (1981); Frank Ackerman, *Reaganomics* (1982); Thomas Byrne Edsall, *The New Politics of Inequality* (1984); Sidney Weintraub and Marvin Goodstein, eds., *Reaganomics in the Stagflation Economy* (1983); Michael J. Piore and Charles F. Sabel, *The Second Industrial Divide* (1984); David Stockman, *The Triumph of Politics* (1986); William Greider, *The Education of David Stockman and Other Americans* (1982); Donald T. Regan, *For the Record* (1988); Nancy Reagan, *My Turn* (1989).

Reagan and the World. Alexander Haig, *Caveat: Realism, Reagan and Foreign Policy* (1984); Strobe Talbott, *Deadly Gambits* (1984) and *The Master of the Game: Paul Nitze and the Nuclear Peace* (1988); Walter LaFeber, *Inevitable Revolutions*, rev. ed. (1984);

Raymond Bonner, *Weakness and Deceit: U.S. Policy and El Salvador* (1984); Tom Buckley, *Violent Neighbors* (1984); Robert O. Pastor, *Condemned to Repetition: The United States and Nicaragua* (1987); Bob Woodward, *Veil: The Secret Wars of the CIA* (1987); Seweryn Bialer and Michael Mandelbaum, eds., *Gorbachev's Russia and American Foreign Policy* (1988); John Newhouse, *War and Peace in the Nuclear Age* (1989).

Politics After Reagan. Thomas Ferguson and Joel Rogers, *Right Turn* (1986); Adolph L. Reed, Jr., *The Jesse Jackson Phenomenon* (1986).

Postliberal Society and Culture. Peter N. Carroll, *It Seemed Like Nothing Happened* (1982); Peter Clecak, *America's Quest for the Ideal Self* (1983); Jim Hougan, *Decadence: Radical Nostalgia, Narcissism, and Decline in the Seventies* (1975); Christopher Lasch, *The Culture of Narcissism* (1978); Edwin Schur, *The Awareness Trap* (1976); Kirkpatrick Sale, *Power Shift* (1975); John Woodridge, *The Evangelicals* (1975); Marshall Frady, *Billy Graham* (1979); Jonathan Schell, *The Fate of the Earth* (1982); Randy Shilts, *And the Band Played On: Politics, People, and the AIDS Epidemic* (1987); John Langone, *AIDS: The Facts* (1988); Frank Levy, *Dollars and Dreams: The Changing American Income Distribution* (1987); Studs Terkel, *The Great Divide* (1988).

Gender and Family. Andrea Dworkin, *Right-Wing Women* (1983); Barbara Ehrenreich, *The Hearts of Men: American Dreams and the Flight from Commitment* (1983); Susan M. Bianchi, *American Women in Transition* (1987); Elizabeth Fox-Genovese, *Feminism Without Illusions: A Critique of Individualism* (1991); Mary Francis Berry, *Why ERA Failed* (1986); Jane Mansbridge, *Why We Lost the ERA* (1986); Kristin Luker, *Abortion and the Politics of Motherhood* (1984); Rosalind Pechesky, *Abortion and Woman's Choice* (1984); Winifred D. Wandersee, *On the Move: American Women in the 1970s* (1988); Jonathan Kozol, *Rachel and Her Children: Homeless Families in America* (1988); Ruth Sidel, *Women and Children Last* (1986); Harrell R. Rodgers, Jr., *Poor Women, Poor Families* (1986); Hilda Scott, *Working Your Way to the Bottom: The Feminization of Poverty* (1985).

Nonwhites in the 1970s and 1980s. Derrick Bell, *And We Are Not Saved: The Elusive Quest for Racial Justice* (1987); Douglas Glasgow, *The Black Underclass* (1980); Leslie W. Dunbar, ed., *Minority Report* (1984); Marian Wright Edelman, *Families in Peril* (1987); William Julius Wilson, *The Truly Disadvantaged* (1987); Frank D. Bean and Marta Tienda, *The Hispanic Population of the United States* (1987); James D. Cockcroft, *Outlaws in the Promised Land: Mexican Immigrant Workers and America's Future* (1986); David M. Reimers, *Still the Golden Door* (1985); John Crewden, *The Tarnished Door* (1983); Stan Steiner, *The New Indians* (1968); Vine Deloria, Jr., *American Indian Policy in the Twentieth Century* (1985).

Illustration Credits

Page(s): **2** The Thomas Gilcrease Institute. **10** Apostolic Library, Vatican City. **23, 26, 41** New York Public Library. **62** National Maritime Museum, Greenwich, England. **67** American Heritage. **75** Essex Institute, Salem, MA. **80** American Antiquarian Society. **91** Bettmann Archive. **102** The Metropolitan Museum of Art. **110** John Carter Brown Library, Brown University. **116** Brown University Library. **142** Bettmann Archive. **156** Library of Congress. **163** The Metropolitan Museum of Art, Gift of Edgar William and Bernice Chrysler Garbisch, 1963. **165** Bettmann Archive. **168** New York Public Library. **176** Lithograph by Kennedy and Lucas, after A. Rider. The New York Historical Society. **180** Rhode Island Historical Society. **183** Thomas Jefferson Memorial Foundation. **203** New Orleans Museum of Art. **207** The Metropolitan Museum of Art, Purchase, Joseph Pulitzer Bequest, 1942 (42.138). **210** Maryland Historical Society. **214** Bettman Archive. **218** Susan Merritt, American, 1826–1879, Picnic Scene, watercolor and collage on paper, c. 1853, 66 x 91.4 cm, Gift of Elizabeth R. Vaughan, 1950.1846 ©1992 Art Institute of Chicago. All Rights Reserved. **220** New York Public Library. **224** Museum of the City of New York. **228** Culver. **232** Boston Athenaeum. **244** Library of Congress. **248** Yale University Art Gallery. **254** Woolaroc Museum, Bartlesville, Oklahoma. **264** Bettmann Archive. **275, 278** Library of Congress. **293** New York Historical Society. **297** Sophia Smith Collection, Smith College. **307** Rare Book Division, The New York Public Library, Astor Lenox and Tilden Foundations. **312, 320** Library of Congress. **323** New York Historical Society. **329** Bettmann Archive. **336** Library of Congress. **357** The Granger Collection. **360** Library of Congress. **373** Bettmann Archive. **376** Cook Collection, Valentine Museum. **379, 382, 403, 406** Library of Congress. **414** Culver. **417** Bettmann Archive. **440** Library of Congress. **444** Henry Ford Museum. **454** Smithsonian Institution, National Anthropological Archives, Bureau of American Ethnology Collection. **456** Union Pacific Railroad Museum Collection. **468** Culver. **475** Bettmann Archive. **478** International Museum of Photography at George Eastman House. **483** Carnegie Library, Pittsburgh. **494** International Museum of Photography at George Eastman House. **500** New York Historical Society. **503** Culver. **510** Wellesley College Archives. **515** Library of Congress. **522, 527** Culver. **531** Smithsonian Institution. **543** The Granger Collection. **547** Theodore Roosevelt Association. **550** Culver. **554** Bettmann Archive. **558** Culver. **564** Bettmann Archive. **570** State Historical Society of Wisconsin. **575, 585** Culver. **590** Brown Brothers. **601** Smithsonian Institution. **605** Bettmann Archive. **613** UPI/Bettmann Newsphotos. **615** National Archives. **623** Bettmann Archive. **626** Culver. **632** International Museum of Photography at George Eastman House. **644** Culver. **650** Bettmann Archive. **657** Culver. **658** Bettmann Archive. **669** UPI/Bettmann Newsphotos. **674** ©1933, 1961 Peter Arno, Franklin D. Roosevelt Library. **677** AP/Wide World. **685** UPI/Bettmann Newsphotos. **688** Culver. **693** AP/Wide World. **701** UPI/Bettmann Newsphotos. **710** Culver. **716** Brown Brothers. **721** U.S. Navy Photo. **732** Culver. **737** National Archives. **741** U.S. Coast Guard/National Archives. **745** Brown Brothers. **758** Federal

Index

Note: Pages followed by the letter "m" refer to maps.

About the Author

ALAN BRINKLEY is professor of American history at Columbia University. Educated at Princeton and Harvard, he has served on the faculties of the Massachusetts Institute of Technology, Harvard University, the City University of New York Graduate School, and Princeton University. He is the author of *Voices of Protest: Huey Long, Father Coughlin, and the New Deal,* which won the 1983 National Book Award for History; coauthor of *American History: A Survey;* and the writer of many articles, essays, and reviews in both scholarly and nonscholarly periodicals.

A Note on the Type

The text of this book is a digitized version of Janson, a typeface long thought to have been made by the Dutchman Anton Janson, who was a practicing type founder in Leipzig during the years 1668–1687. However, it has been conclusively demonstrated that this family of type is actually the work of Nicholas Kis (1650–1702), a Hungarian, who most probably learned his trade from the master Dutch type founder Dirk Voskens. Janson is an excellent example of the influential and sturdy Dutch types that prevailed in England up to the time William Caslon developed his own incomparable designs from them.